Encyclopedia
of the
American Constitution

Original 1986 Editorial Board

Encyclopedia
of the
American Constitution

SECOND EDITION

Edited by
LEONARD W. LEVY
and
KENNETH L. KARST

ADAM WINKLER, Associate Editor for the Second Edition

DENNIS J. MAHONEY, Assistant Editor for the First Edition
JOHN G. WEST, JR., Assistant Editor for Supplement I

MACMILLAN REFERENCE USA
An imprint of the Gale Group
New York

Macmillan Library Reference USA
1633 Broadway
New York, NY 10019

Printed in the United States of America

Printing Number
10 9 8 7 6 5 4 3 2

Library of Congress Cataloging-in-Publication Data
Encyclopedia of the American Constitution / edited by Leonard W. Levy and Kenneth L. Karst.—2nd ed. / Adam Winkler, associate editor for the second edition.
    p. cm.
   Includes bibliographical references and indexes.
   ISBN 0-02-864880-3 (hard cover : alk. paper)
     1. Constitutional law—United States—Encyclopedias.   I. Levy, Leonard Williams, 1923–   II. Karst, Kenneth L.   III. Winkler, Adam.
   KF4548 .E53   2000
   342.73—dc21   00-029203

This paper meets the requirements of ANSI-NISO Z39.48-1992 (Permanence of Paper).

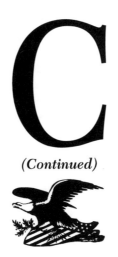

(Continued)

CLAIMS COURT

The Claims Court hears actions for money damages against the United States, except for tort claims. The court thus hears claims for contract damages, tax refunds, and JUST COMPENSATION for property taken. With the consent of all parties to an action against the government under the FEDERAL TORT CLAIMS ACT, the court can substitute for a court of appeals and review the decision of a federal district court.

Under the doctrine of SOVEREIGN IMMUNITY, the United States cannot be sued without its consent. At first, persons with claims against the government had to ask Congress for relief under private acts. This practice became burdensome, and in 1855 Congress established the Court of Claims to hear nontort money claims against the United States, and report its recommendations to Congress. Much of the congressional burden remained; thus, in 1863, Congress empowered the court to give judgments against the government. In 1866 the process became fully "judicial" when Congress repealed a provision delaying payment of such a judgment until the Treasury estimated an appropriation.

The Court of Claims retained the nonjudicial function of giving ADVISORY OPINIONS on questions referred to it by the houses of Congress and heads of executive departments. However, its judges from the beginning had life tenure during GOOD BEHAVIOR. In 1933 the question arose whether the Court of Claims was a CONSTITUTIONAL COURT. Congress, responding to the economic depression, reduced the salaries of federal employees, except for judges protected by Article III against salary reductions. In *Williams v. United States* (1933), the Supreme Court, taking the preposterous position that claims against the government fell outside the JUDICIAL POWER OF THE UNITED STATES, held that the Court of Claims was a LEGISLATIVE COURT whose judges' salaries could constitutionally be reduced.

In 1953 Congress declared explicitly that the Court of Claims was established under Article III. In *Glidden v. Zdanok* (1962) the Supreme Court accepted this characterization on the basis of two separate (and incompatible) theories, pieced together to make a majority for the result. Two Justices relied on the 1953 Act; three others would have overruled *Williams* and held that the court had been a constitutional court since 1866 when Congress allowed its judgments to be paid without executive revision, and its business became almost completely "judicial." (The same decision confirmed that the COURT OF CUSTOMS AND PATENT APPEALS was a constitutional court.) The Court of Claims transferred new congressional reference cases to its chief commissioner, and Congress ratified this practice. The court's business became wholly "judicial."

In the FEDERAL COURTS IMPROVEMENT ACT (1982) Congress reorganized a number of specialized federal courts. The Court of Claims disappeared, and its functions were reallocated. The commissioners of that court became judges of a new legislative court, the United States Claims Court. They serve for fifteen-year terms. The Article III judges of the Court of Claims became judges of a new constitutional court, the UNITED STATES COURT OF APPEALS FOR THE FEDERAL CIRCUIT. That court hears appeals from a number of specialized courts, including the Claims Court.

The availability of a suit for damages in the Claims Court serves to underpin the constitutionality of some governmental action that might otherwise raise serious constitutional problems. Some regulations, for example, are arguable TAKINGS OF PROPERTY; if the regulated party can recover compensation in the Claims Court, however, the constitutional issue dissolves (*Blanchette v. Connecticut General Insurance Corps.*, 1974).

KENNETH L. KARST
(1986)

Bibliography

SYMPOSIUM 1983 The Federal Courts Improvement Act. *Cleveland State Law Review* 32:1–116.

CLARK, CHARLES E.
(1889–1963)

Charles Edward Clark, the son of a Connecticut farmer and a graduate of Yale College, achieved distinction as a legal educator and a federal judge. In 1919 he began teaching at Yale Law School, where he had earned his law degree, and became its dean in 1929. Within the year he had modernized the curriculum, stressing interdisciplinary studies. Originally a Republican, Clark became a New Dealer and in 1937 was the only law school dean to testify in favor of President FRANKLIN D. ROOSEVELT's court reorganization plan. In 1939 Roosevelt appointed him to the UNITED STATES COURT OF APPEALS, Second Circuit. As a federal judge for twenty-five years he tended to be a liberal activist even though his opinions on the rights of the criminally accused strongly supported prosecutorial positions. But Clark's opinions favored trade unions, CIVIL RIGHTS, and government regulation of the economy. As a FIRST AMENDMENT absolutist, he eloquently and ardently championed views that Justices HUGO L. BLACK and WILLIAM O. DOUGLAS of the Supreme Court later endorsed.

LEONARD W. LEVY
(1986)

Bibliography

SCHICK, MARVIN 1970 *Learned Hand's Court*. Baltimore: Johns Hopkins University Press.

CLARK, TOM C.
(1899–1977)

Tom Campbell Clark, Associate Justice of the Supreme Court and ATTORNEY GENERAL of the United States, was born September 23, 1899, in Dallas, Texas. He was educated at the University of Texas at Austin, receiving his B.A. in 1921 and his LL.B. in 1922. Admitted to the Texas Bar in 1922, he joined his family's firm in Dallas.

Clark began his twelve-year career with the Department of Justice in 1937 as a special assistant to the attorney general. He held a number of posts in the department,

capped by his 1945 appointment as attorney general by President HARRY S. TRUMAN. With this promotion, Clark became the first person to become attorney general by working himself up from the lower ranks of the department.

Four years later, President Truman appointed Clark Associate Justice of the Supreme Court; he took his oath of office on August 24, 1949. His tenure on the bench spanned eighteen years, and he served on both the VINSON COURT and WARREN COURT. He retired from the Court on June 12, 1967, to avoid the appearance of a conflict of interests when his son, Ramsey Clark, was appointed attorney general by President LYNDON B. JOHNSON. Clark, however, continued to sit as a judge in the various courts of appeal, and to be a vigorous and vocal advocate of judicial reform until his death on June 13, 1977.

On the Supreme Court, Clark built a reputation as a pragmatic jurist. Early on, he voted regularly with Chief Justice FRED M. VINSON and the other Truman appointees. In time, however, he began to assert his independence. In YOUNGSTOWN SHEET AND TUBE COMPANY V. SAWYER (1952), the steel seizure case, Clark voted against Vinson and Truman, concurring in the Court's decision holding unconstitutional Truman's order for governmental seizure of the nation's steel mills.

While Clark was generally viewed as politically conservative, he was relatively nonideological, and his views changed throughout his tenure, especially during the years of the Warren Court (1953–1969). He was a nationalist, a liberal on racial matters, and, in general, a conservative on issues of CRIMINAL PROCEDURE and CIVIL LIBERTIES.

Clark's most significant opinions in the area of FEDERALISM are his landmark opinion on STATE REGULATION OF COMMERCE in DEAN MILK COMPANY V. MADISON (1951), and his dissent in *Williams v. Georgia* (1955), which provided the classic definition of "independent and ADEQUATE STATE GROUNDS" that insulate state court decisions from the Supreme Court. In the racial area, speaking for the Court in BURTON V. WILMINGTON PARKING AUTHORITY (1961), he rejected as unlawful STATE ACTION racial discrimination by private persons who had leased public property. In addition, he wrote for the Court in HEART OF ATLANTA MOTEL, INC., V. UNITED STATES, (1964) where, in a case involving both national power and racial justice, a unanimous Court upheld the PUBLIC ACCOMMODATIONS provisions of the CIVIL RIGHTS ACT OF 1964.

In the areas of criminal procedure and civil liberties Clark was less consistent. Although he may be best known for his controversial opinion in MAPP V. OHIO (1961), declaring that illegally seized evidence must be excluded from a state criminal prosecution, this opinion was atypical. More often, especially in his later years on the bench, he disagreed with the liberalization of criminal procedure wrought by the Warren Court. For instance, he dissented strongly—indeed almost violently—in MIRANDA V. ARIZONA (1966).

Similarly, Clark's record on civil liberties, though generally conservative, was not completely consistent. Probably Clark was most consistent as to those issues arising out of anticommunist and LOYALTY-SECURITY PROGRAMS. As attorney general, he had been instrumental in setting up some of these programs, and as a Justice he continued to support government efforts to suppress what he regarded as the communist conspiracy. Thus, he dissented in WATKINS V. UNITED STATES (1957) and joined the majority in BARENBLATT V. UNITED STATES (1959). In addition, he was the sole dissenter in *Greene v. McElroy* (1959), a decision which badly damaged the loyalty-security program for employees of private companies.

On the other hand, Clark was generally less sympathetic to efforts by the states to cope with what he regarded as a national problem. Thus, he wrote for a unanimous Court in WIEMAN V. UPDEGRAFF (1952), which held unconstitutional an Oklahoma LOYALTY OATH statute requiring state employees to swear that they were not members of organizations designated by the attorney general as subversive or a "Communist front." Clark emphasized that under the Oklahoma law an individual could be guilty of perjury even though he did not know the character of the organization that he had innocently joined. And he joined the majority in PENNSYLVANIA V. NELSON (1956), which invalidated state SEDITION laws on the ground that Congress had preempted the field.

In other areas of civil liberties, Justice Clark tended more often to vote in favor of asserted constitution rights. Thus, in the area of church-state relations, he wrote the opinion in ABINGTON TOWNSHIP SCHOOL DISTRICT V. SCHEMPP (1963), which held unconstitutional a Pennsylvania statute that required that each school day start with the reading of at least ten verses from the Bible. Similarly, he voted with the majority in a series of cases that drastically narrowed court-martial jurisdiction over civilians, the most significant of which was *Kinsella v. Singleton* (1960).

JOHN KAPLAN
(1986)

Bibliography

KIRKENDALL, RICHARD 1969 Tom C. Clark. In Leon Friedman and Fred L. Israel, eds., *The Justices of the United States Supreme Court, 1789–1969.* New York: Chelsea House.

CLARK DISTILLING CO. v. WESTERN MARYLAND RAILWAY CO.
242 U.S. 311 (1917)

With Justices OLIVER WENDELL HOLMES and WILLIS VAN DEVANTER dissenting without opinion, the Court upheld the WEBB-KENYON ACT. Chief Justice EDWARD D. WHITE, for the majority, rejected the assertion that the act constituted an unconstitutional legislative DELEGATION OF POWER to the states. No delegation occurred because Congress provided for uniform regulation throughout the states.

DAVID GORDON
(1986)

CLARKE, JOHN H.
(1857–1945)

With the exception of OLIVER WENDELL HOLMES and LOUIS D. BRANDEIS, John H. Clarke was the most consistently progressive member of the Supreme Court during the final years of EDWARD D. WHITE's chief justiceship and the early tenure of WILLIAM HOWARD TAFT. A prosperous newspaper publisher and attorney who defended many midwestern railroads, Clarke belonged to the moderate wing of the Democratic Party in Ohio which defended the gold standard in 1896 and looked skeptically upon reform programs. WOODROW WILSON appointed Clarke to the federal district court in 1914 and two years later elevated him to the Supreme Court to fill the vacancy left by Wilson's presidential rival, CHARLES EVANS HUGHES.

Intellectually, Clarke could not fill Hughes's shoes, but he surprised many critics by his voting record in cases involving CORPORATIONS and labor. Despite his earlier representation of big business, Clarke became a strong judicial supporter of the antitrust laws. He dissented in the two leading cases of the period, *United States v. United Shoe Machinery Company* (1918) and *United States v. United States Steel Corporation* (1920), when the WHITE COURT spurned the government's efforts to convict these industrial giants for monopolistic behavior.

In 1920, however, Clarke won a majority to his side when the Justices ordered the dissolution of a major railroad monopoly in *United States v. Lehigh Valley Railroad*, and found the Reading Railroad guilty of restraint of trade in the anthracite coal industry. Over a powerful dissent by Holmes, Clarke also wrote for the Court that upheld indictments for open price agreements in the hardwood lumber industry.

Clarke rejected the dominant judicial ideology of FREEDOM OF CONTRACT, which had been used to stifle legislative reforms to benefit labor. He endorsed Oregon's ten-hour law for all industrial workers in BUNTING V. OREGON (1917), approved of the federal ADAMSON ACT which mandated an eight-hour day for railroad workers in WILSON V. NEW (1917), and refused to endorse the INJUNCTION at issue in the YELLOW DOG CONTRACT case of HITCHMAN COAL & COKE CO. V. MITCHELL (1917). He voted as well to sustain the constitutionality of the KEATING-OWEN CHILD LABOR ACT in HAMMER V. DAGENHART (1918), refused to sanction the prosecution of labor unions under the antitrust laws in UNITED MINE WORKERS V. CORONADO COAL CO. (1922), and upheld a union's right to conduct a SECONDARY BOYCOTT in the notorious case of DUPLEX PRINTING CO. V. DEERING (1921).

Despite his progressive record with respect to ECONOMIC REGULATION and the rights of labor, Clarke will probably always be remembered as the Justice who wrote for the majority in the case of ABRAMS V. UNITED STATES (1919), which sustained the conviction of pro-Bolshevik pamphleteers under the wartime ESPIONAGE ACT and SEDITION ACT. Clarke's opinion provoked Holmes's famous and biting dissent. Arguing that "men must be held to have intended and to be accountable for the effects which their acts were likely to produce," Clarke transformed Holmes's CLEAR AND PRESENT DANGER test into something approximating the BAD TENDENCY TEST that came to dominate the Court's FIRST AMENDMENT jurisprudence for several decades.

MICHAEL E. PARRISH
(1986)

Bibliography

WARNER, HOYT L.   1959   *Life of Mr. Justice Clarke.* Cleveland, Ohio: Western Reserve University Press.

CLASS ACTION

The class action is a procedural device aggregating the claims or defenses of similarly situated individuals so that they may be tried in a single lawsuit. In recent decades the class action has frequently served as the vehicle by which various groups have asserted constitutional claims. For example, all the minority-race school children in various districts have sued (through their parents) to rectify alleged RACIAL DISCRIMINATION on the part of school authorities; or, to illustrate a nonconstitutional claim, the buyers of home freezers have sued as a group claiming that the dealer had made fraudulent misrepresentations. In both examples the members of the class could have sued separately. The class action pulled these potential individual actions into a single lawsuit making litigation feasible for the members of the class (by permitting a single lawyer to try all their claims together). For the party opposing the class the suit has the advantage of providing a single adjudication of all similar claims and the disadvantage, especially marked in suits for money damages, that the entire potential liability to a large group turns on a single suit.

The class action depends on representation, and that concept draws the Constitution into the picture. In the class action most class members are represented by an active litigant whose success or failure binds the class members. Opinions interpreting the DUE PROCESS clauses of the Constitution (in the Fifth and FOURTEENTH AMENDMENTS) suggest that normally one may not be bound by the results of litigation to which one is not a party. Yet the class action purports to do just that—to bind the absentee class members to the results of a suit in which they played no active role.

The Supreme Court and the drafters of state and federal class action rules have supplied two solutions to this apparent tension. The Supreme Court's answer came in *Hansberry v. Lee* (1940), in which the justices indicated that class actions could bind absentee class members if the active litigants *adequately represented* the class. If not, the Court reasoned, binding the absentees would deprive them of due process of law.

Adequate representation has two aspects, competence and congruence of interests. All would agree that adequate representation implies some absolute level of competence and diligence on the part of the class representative and attorney. Though few cases have specifically discussed the question, it seems virtually a matter of definition that an adequate representative must pursue the cause with some minimum level of professional skill.

The second aspect of adequate representation presents a more difficult problem, forcing us to decide whether such representation requires the class members to have *agreed* that the action is in their interests, or whether it is possible to define such interests abstractly, without specific consent. Such an abstract definition relies on common intuitions about what would benefit persons in the class's circumstances. In *Hansberry* the Court did not need to decide between these definitions of interest because the attempted class representation failed on either count. Subsequent cases and procedural rules have not clearly resolved the question.

Contemporary procedural rules require that a judge presiding over a class action suit consider initially whether the action is in the class's interest, abstractly considered; that much seems constitutionally required. Beyond that, some rules also require that the absentee members receive individual notice permitting them to exclude themselves from the litigation.

Founded on the constitutional proposition that some form of representation will suffice to bind members of a class, the class suit has come to play an important role in twentieth-century American litigation.

STEPHEN C. YEAZELL
(1986)

(SEE ALSO: *Groups and the Constitution.*)

Bibliography

KALVEN, HARRY, JR. and ROSENFIELD, MAURICE   1941   The Contemporary Function of the Class Suit. *University of Chicago Law Review* 8:684–721.

WRIGHT, CHARLES A. and MILLER, ARTHUR 1972 *Federal Practice and Procedure*, Vols. 7 & 7a. St. Paul, Minn.: West Publishing Co.

YEAZELL, STEPHEN C. 1980 From Group Litigation to Class Action; Part II: Interest, Class and Representation. *UCLA Law Review* 28:1067–1121.

CLASSIC, UNITED STATES v.
313 U.S. 299 (1941)

This became a TEST CASE used by the United States Attorney in Louisiana and the newly created CIVIL RIGHTS DIVISION of the Department of Justice to ascertain the federal government's power to protect VOTING RIGHTS in PRIMARY ELECTIONS. Louisiana election commissioners charged with willfully altering and falsely counting congressional primary election ballots were indicted under what are now sections 241 and 242 of Title 18, United States Code. To analyze the INDICTMENT under section 241, the Supreme Court had to determine whether the right to have one's ballot counted in a state primary election was a right or a privilege secured by the Constitution. Relying in part on Article I, section 2, of the Constitution, the Court held, 4–3, that the right to choose a congressman was "established and guaranteed" by the Constitution and hence secured by it. The Court then reaffirmed earlier holdings that Congress could protect federally secured voting rights against individual as well as STATE ACTION and squarely held that those rights included participation in state primary elections for members of Congress, thus overruling *Newberry v. United States* (1921).

In articulating those rights "secured by the Constitution" within the meaning of section 241, *Classic* forms a link between early interpretations of the phrase, as in EX PARTE YARBROUGH (1884), and later consideration of it, as in UNITED STATES V. GUEST (1966) and GRIFFIN V. BRECKENRIDGE (1971), the latter case decided under the civil counterpart to section 241, section 1985(3) of Title 42, United States Code. *Classic* also constitutes an important link in the chain of precedents specifically pertaining to federal power over elections. Later cases from the 1940s include SMITH V. ALLWRIGHT (1944) and *United States v. Saylor* (1944).

Because the *Classic* indictment also charged a violation of section 242, which requires action "under COLOR OF LAW." the case provides an early modern holding on the question whether action in violation of state law can be action under color of law. With virtually no discussion of the issue, the Court held such action to be under color of law, a holding later used to support similar holdings in *Screws v. United States* (1945) and MONROE V. PAPE (1961).

Dissenters in *Screws* and *Monroe* would object to reliance on *Classic* because of its abbreviated consideration of the issue.

THEODORE EISENBERG
(1986)

CLAY, HENRY
(1777–1852)

Henry Clay, distinguished politician and legislator, was a product of the Jeffersonian Republicanism that took possession of the Trans-Appalachian West, fought a second war against Great Britain, and was nationalized in the process. Born in Hanover County, Virginia, young Clay clerked for Chancellor GEORGE WYTHE and read law in Richmond before emigrating to Kentucky in his twentieth year. Settling in the rising metropolis of Lexington, Clay was promptly admitted to the bar, and by virtue of extraordinary natural talent, aided by the fortune of marriage into a prominent mercantile family, he soon became a leading member of the Bluegrass lawyer-aristocracy.

The chaos of land titles in Kentucky—a legacy of the state's Virginia origins—made it a paradise for lawyers. Clay mastered this abstruse branch of jurisprudence but earned his reputation as a trial lawyer in capital cases, in which he was said never to have lost a client. He rode the circuit of the county courts, acquiring a character for high spirits and camaraderie; he practiced before the court of appeals and also before the United States district court at Frankfort. When he first went to Congress in 1806, Clay was admitted to the bar of the Supreme Court. Occasionally in years to come he argued important constitutional cases before the court. He was chief counsel for the defendant in OSBORN V. BANK OF THE UNITED STATES (1824), for instance, in which the Court struck down a prohibitive state tax on branches of the bank. At about the same time he conducted Kentucky's defense of its Occupying Claimants Law, enacted years earlier in order to settle thousands of disputed land titles. Here Clay was unsuccessful, as the Court, in GREEN V. BIDDLE (1823), found the Kentucky law in violation of the CONTRACT CLAUSE. Justice JOSEPH STORY remarked after hearing Clay in this case that, if he chose, Clay might achieve "great eminence" at the bar. This interesting judgment would never be tested, however, for Clay sought eminence in politics rather than law.

Clay entered politics in 1798 as a Jeffersonian Republican protesting the ALIEN AND SEDITION ACTS and seeking liberal reform of the state constitution. Elected to the legislature in 1803, he became chief spokesman and protector of the Lexington-centered "court party." He was also very popular, rising rapidly to the speakership of the lower house. In 1806 he was sent to the United States Senate to complete three months of an unexpired term; this experience was repeated, upon the resignation of another incumbent, in 1810. Clay distinguished himself as a bold patriot and orator, as an advocate of federal INTERNAL IMPROVEMENTS and encouragement of domestic manufactures, both of great interest to Kentucky, and as the leading opponent of recharter of the national bank on strict Jeffersonian grounds. He then sought and won election to the Twelfth Congress. Upon its meeting in November 1811, he achieved recognition as chief of the "war hawks" who, though a small minority, took command of the House and elected Clay speaker. Whether or not the war hawks caused, in some significant degree, the War of 1812 is a matter in dispute among historians; but there is no doubt that they brought fresh westerly winds of nationalism into Congress and that Clay, as speaker, mobilized congressional action behind the JAMES MADISON administration's prosecution of the war. Clay transformed this constitutional office, the speakership, from that of an impartial moderator into one of political leadership. Five times he would be reelected speaker, always virtually without opposition; and when he finally retired from the House there was no one to fill his shoes.

After the Peace of Ghent, which he had helped negotiate as an American commissioner, Clay supported President Madison's national Republican platform with its broad constitutional principles. This support required an about-face on the constitutionality of a national bank. Clay candidly chalked up his error to experience, saying that the financial exigencies of the war had shown the necessity of a national bank; he now agreed with Madison on the need for a central institution to secure a stable and uniform currency. Henceforth, certainly, Clay's principal significance with respect to the Constitution lay in the affirmation of congressional powers.

The protective tariff was the core of the maturing national system of political economy that Clay named "the AMERICAN SYSTEM." The country ought not any longer, he argued, look abroad for wealth, but should turn inward to the development of its own resources. Manufactures would rise and flourish behind the tariff wall, consuming the growing surplus of American agriculture; and a balanced, sectionally based but mutually supportive, economy of agriculture, commerce, and manufactures would be the result. Because the system premised a positive role for the national government in economic development, it carried immense implications for the Constitution. When the protective tariff was first attacked on constitutional grounds in 1824, Clay rejected the narrow view that limited the TAXING POWER to raising revenue and continued the liberal interpretation of the COMMERCE CLAUSE that began with Jefferson's embargo. The infrastructure of the "home market" would be provided by a national system of INTERNAL IMPROVEMENTS. Madison, in his surprising veto of

the Bonus Bill in 1817, interposed the constitutional objection that neither the funding nor the building of roads and canals was among the enumerated powers. When Madison's successor, JAMES MONROE, persisted in this view, Clay mounted a campaign to overturn it. He appealed to the Jeffersonian precedent of the National (Cumberland) Road; he appealed to the WAR POWERS (transportation as an element of national defense), to the power of Congress to establish post roads, and, above all, to the commerce power. To the old fears of a runaway Constitution Clay opposed his trust in democratic elections and the balance of interests to keep order. Monroe finally conceded the unlimited power of Congress to appropriate money for internal improvements, though not to build or operate them. Clay protested that the concession was of greater scope than the principle he had advocated. But he took satisfaction in the result, most immediately in the General Survey Act of 1824.

Clay's coalition with JOHN QUINCY ADAMS in 1825, in which he secured the New Englander's election to the presidency and accepted appointment as his secretary of state, contributed to a growing sectional and partisan opposition to the American System and the constitutional doctrines that supported it. South Carolina's NULLIFICATION of the protective tariff in 1832 provoked a crisis that Clay, now in the Senate, helped to resolve with his Compromise Tariff Act. Under it protective duties would be gradually lifted until in 1842 they would be levied for revenue only. Without surrendering any constitutional principle, Clay nevertheless seemed to surrender the policy of protectionism. Some politicians said he courted southern votes in his quest for the presidency. As the National Republican candidate against President ANDREW JACKSON in the recent election, he had been badly defeated, winning nothing in the South, and he may have seen in this crisis an opportunity for a useful change of political direction. But Clay insisted he acted, first, to save the Union from the disaster of nullification, which was compounded by Jackson's threatened vengeance, and second, to save what he could of the American System. A high protective tariff could no longer be sustained in any event. The national debt was about to be paid off; the treasury faced an embarrassing surplus unless the revenue was drastically reduced. Clay sought to offset the impact of the surplus on the tariff by diverting the soaring revenue of public land sales to the states. Although Congress passed Clay's Distribution Bill in 1833, Jackson vetoed it.

This veto, with many others, above all JACKSON'S VETO OF THE BANK BILL, fueled Clay's assault on the alleged executive usurpations and monarchical designs of the President. The senator proposed to curtail the powers of the presidency. The abuse of the veto power should be corrected by a constitutional amendment allowing override by a majority of both houses. The despotic potential of the office, which Jackson was the first to disclose, should be curbed further by an amendment limiting the president to a single term, perhaps of six years. Clay also rejected the 1789 precedent on the REMOVAL POWER, arguing that the power of removal in the President effectively negated the Senate's agency in appointment. Removal, like appointment, should be a joint responsibility. The Whig Party, under Clay's leadership, consistently advocated these measures. None was ever enacted. Clay continued the campaign even after the Whigs came to power in 1841, assailing President John Tyler as he had earlier assailed Jackson.

Although Clay usually supported national authority in the debates of his time, he became increasingly cautious and protective of the Constitution under the threats posed, first, by reckless Jacksonian Democracy, and second, by the combination of abolitionism in the North and aggressive slavocracy in the South. He accepted the "federal consensus" on slavery: it was a matter entirely within the JURISDICTION of the states. Nevertheless, he raised no bar to the use of federal funds to advance gradual emancipation and colonization by the states, indeed advocated it in certain contexts. In the controversy over the right of petition for abolition of slavery in the DISTRICT OF COLUMBIA, he held that a gag was not only indefensible in principle but impolitic in practice, because it would make libertarian martyrs of the abolitionists. Clay opposed the ANNEXATION OF TEXAS, believing that the expansion of slavery it entailed must seriously disrupt the Union. When he seemed to equivocate on the issue in the election of 1844—his third run for the presidency—he lost enough northern votes to ensure his defeat. Returning to the Senate in 1849, he proposed a comprehensive plan for settlement of critical issues between North and South. It eventually became the COMPROMISE OF 1850. Here, as in all of his constructive legislative endeavors, Clay evaded spurious questions of constitutional law and sought resolution on the level of policy in that "spirit of compromise" which, he said, lay at the foundation of the American republic. From his earlier part in effecting the MISSOURI COMPROMISE (1820–1821) and the Compromise of 1833, he had earned the title of The Great Pacificator. The Compromise of 1850 added a third jewel to the crown.

Henry Clay was the most popular American statesman of his generation and one of the most respected. He helped to shape the course of constitutional development during forty years, not as a lawyer, judge, or theorist, but as a practical politician and legislator in national affairs.

MERRILL D. PETERSON
(1986)

Bibliography

COLTON, CALVIN, ed. (1856) 1904 *The Works of Henry Clay.* 10 Vols. New York: G. P. Putnam's.

HOPKINS, JAMES F. and HARGREAVES, MARY W. M., eds. 1959–1981 *The Papers of Henry Clay.* Vols. 1–6. Lexington: University of Kentucky Press.

SEAGER, ROBERT II; WINSLOW, RICHARD E., III; and HAY, MELBA PORTER, eds. 1982–1984 *Papers of Henry Clay.* Vols. 7–8. Lexington: University of Kentucky Press.

VAN DEUSEN, GLYNDON G. 1937 *The Life of Henry Clay.* Boston: Houghton, Mifflin.

CLAYTON ACT
38 Stat. 730 (1914)

Mistakenly hailed by Samuel Gompers as labor's MAGNA CARTA, the Clayton Act represented a new generation's attempt to deal with trusts. Acclaimed for its specificity, the new act in reality contained crucial ambiguities as vague as the SHERMAN ANTITRUST ACT it was intended to supplement. WOODROW WILSON'S ANTITRUST policy included both the FEDERAL TRADE COMMISSION ACT and the Clayton Act; in his view the latter would leave the Sherman Act intact while specifying conduct henceforth prohibited. Framed by Representative Henry Clayton, chairman of the House Judiciary Committee, the antitrust bill pleased no one: labor objected to the absence of an explicit guarantee of immunity for unions, many congressmen found the list of restraints of trade incomplete, and agrarian radicals believed that the bill betrayed Democratic pledges. In the face of this opposition, Wilson abandoned the Clayton bill in Congress. The HOUSE, unhappy over the vagueness of the Sherman Act and wishing to leave businessmen no loopholes, sought as specific a bill as possible. The SENATE objected, but a compromise was reached naming only a few, particularly pernicious, practices which were declared unlawful "where the effect may be to substantially lessen competition or tend to create monopoly"—hardly a model of certainty. Four provisions of the Clayton Act contain this operative phrase. Section 7 prohibited the acquisition of stock by one corporation of another or mergers, but, by neglecting to forbid acquisitions of assets as well as stock, it provided a loophole not plugged until 1950. The act also placed strict limitations on interlocking directorates (section 8), and outlawed price discrimination (section 2) and exclusive dealing and tying contracts (section 3). The Federal Trade Commission would enforce these provisions by procedures paralleling those in the FTC Act. In addition, the act rendered individual officers personally liable for corporate violations, permitted private individuals to secure INJUNCTIONS and to file treble damage suits, and allowed final judgments in government suits to be considered *prima facie* EVIDENCE in private cases.

Of two labor provisions, section 6, which declared that labor was "not a commodity or article of commerce" and that antitrust laws could not be used to forbid legitimate organizing activities, conceded nothing new. Section 20 prohibited the issuance of injunctions in labor cases unless "necessary to prevent irreparable injury to property." Together with a further clause which declared that peaceful strikes and boycotts were not in violation of federal antitrust laws, this section represented the only victory labor gained in this act.

DAVID GORDON
(1986)

(SEE ALSO: *Labor and the Constitution.*)

Bibliography

NEALE, A. D. and GOYDER, D. G.   1980   *The Antitrust Laws of the United States of America*, 3rd ed. Cambridge: At the University Press.

CLEAN AIR ACT

See: Environmental Regulation and the Constitution

CLEAR AND PRESENT DANGER

The clear and present danger rule, announced in SCHENCK V. UNITED STATES (1919), was the earliest FREEDOM OF SPEECH doctrine of the Supreme Court. Affirming Schenck's conviction, Justice OLIVER WENDELL HOLMES concluded that a speaker might be punished only when "the words are used in such circumstances and are of such a nature as to create a clear and present danger that they will bring about the substantive evils that Congress has a right to prevent." Holmes was drawing on his own earlier Massachusetts Supreme Judicial Court opinion on the law of attempts. There he had insisted that the state might punish attempted arson only when the preparations had gone so far that no time was left for the prospective arsonist to change his mind, so that the crime would have been committed but for the intervention of the state. In the free speech context, Holmes and Justice LOUIS D. BRANDEIS assimilated this idea to the MARKETPLACE OF IDEAS rationale, arguing that the best corrective of dangerous speech was more speech rather than criminal punishment; government should intervene only when the speech would do an immediate harm before there was time for other speech to come into play.

In the context of *Schenck*, the danger rule made particular sense; the federal statute under which the defendant was prosecuted made the *act* of espionage a crime, not the speech itself. The danger rule in effect required that before speech might be punished under a statute that forbade action, a close nexus between the speech and the action be shown. The concentration of the rule on the intent of the speaker and the circumstances surrounding the speech also seem most relevant in those contexts in which speech is being punished as if it constituted an attempt at a criminal act. Opponents of the danger rule have often insisted that Holmes initially intended it not as a general FIRST AMENDMENT test but only for cases in which a statute proscribing action was applied to a speaker.

In *Schenck*, Holmes wrote for the Court. The most extended statement of the danger rule came some months later in ABRAMS V. UNITED STATES (1919), but by then it was to be found in a Holmes dissent, joined by Brandeis. In GITLOW V. NEW YORK (1925) the Court used the BAD TENDENCY TEST which openly rejected the imminence or immediacy element of the danger rule—again over dissents by Holmes and Brandeis. Brandeis kept the danger rule alive in a concurrence in WHITNEY V. CALIFORNIA (1927) in which he added to the immediacy requirement that the threatened evil be serious. The danger of minor property damage, for example, would not justify suppression of speech.

In the 1930s and 1940s the Court was confronted with a series of cases involving parades and street corner speakers in which the justification offered for suppressing speech was not concern for the ultimate security of the state but the desire to maintain peaceful, quiet, and orderly streets and parks free of disturbance. Behind the proffered justifications usually lurked a desire to muzzle unpopular speakers while leaving other speakers free. In this context the clear and present danger rule was well designed to protect unpopular speakers from discrimination. It required the community to prove that the particular speaker whom it had punished or denied a license did in fact constitute an immediate threat to peace and good order. In such cases as HERNDON V. LOWRY (1937) (subversion), THORNHILL V. ALABAMA (1941) (labor PICKETING), BRIDGES V. CALIFORNIA (1941) (contempt of court), WEST VIRGINIA BOARD OF EDUCATION V. BARNETTE (1943) (compulsory flag salute), and *Taylor v. Mississippi* (1943) (state sedition law), the clear and present danger rule became the majority constitutional test governing a wide range of circumstances, not only for statutes punishing conduct but also those regulating speech itself.

Even while enjoying majority status the rule came under attack from two directions. The "absolutists" led by ALEXANDER MEIKLEJOHN criticized the rule for allowing too broad an exception to First Amendment protections. The rule made the protection of speech dependent on judicial findings whether clear and present danger existed; judges had notoriously broad discretion in making findings of fact, as FEINER V. NEW YORK (1951) and TERMINIELLO V. CHICAGO (1949) illustrated. When applied to radical or subversive speech, the danger test seemed to say that ineffectual speech would be tolerated but that speech might be stifled just when it showed promise of persuading substantial numbers of listeners. On the other hand, those favoring judicial self-restraint, led by Justice FELIX FRANKFURTER, argued that the rule was too rigid in its protection of speech and ought to be replaced by a BALANCING TEST that weighed the interests in speech against various state interests and did so without rendering the immediacy of the threat to state interests decisive.

Later commentators have also argued that the distinction between speech and conduct on which the danger rule ultimately rests is not viable, pointing to picketing and such SYMBOLIC SPEECH as FLAG DESECRATION which intermingle speech and action. The danger rule also engenders logically unresolvable HOSTILE AUDIENCE problems. If Holmes's formula had demanded a showing of the specific intent of the speaker to bring about violence or of specific INCITEMENT to crime in the content of the speech, it might have afforded greater protection to some speakers. The independent weight the danger formula gives to surrounding circumstances may permit the stifling of speakers because of the real or imagined act or threats of others. Yet focusing exclusively upon intent or upon the presence of the language of incitement may lead to the punishment of speakers whose fervently revolutionary utterances in reality have little or no chance of bringing about any violent action at all.

In DENNIS V. UNITED STATES (1951) the clear and *present* danger test was converted overtly into a clear and *probable* danger test and covertly into a balancing test. As its origin in the law of attempts reminds us, the cutting edge of Holmes's test had been the imminence or immediacy requirement. Speech might be punished only if so closely brigaded in time and space with criminal action that no intervening factor might abort the substantive evil. The probable danger test held that if the anticipated evil were serious enough the imminence requirement might be greatly relaxed. In practice this evisceration of the danger test left the Court free to balance the interests to be protected against the degree of infringement on speech, as the proponents of judicial self-restraint argued the Court had always done anyway under the danger standard.

Since *Dennis* the Court has consistently avoided the precise language of the clear and present danger test and with few exceptions commentators announced its demise. In BRANDENBURG V. OHIO (1969), however, the Court announced that "constitutional guarantees of free speech . . . do not permit a State to forbid . . . advocacy of the use of force or of law violation except where such advocacy is directed to inciting or producing imminent lawless action and is likely to incite or produce such action." The text and footnotes surrounding this pronouncement, its careful avoidance of the literal clear and present danger formula itself, plus the separate opinions of several of the Justices

indicate that *Brandenburg* did not seek to revive Holmes's danger rule per se. Such earlier proponents of the rule as HUGO L. BLACK and WILLIAM O. DOUGLAS, feeling that it had been too corrupted by its *Dennis* conversion to retain any power to protect speech, had moved to the position of Meiklejohnian absolutism and its rejection of the danger standard. On the other hand, those Justices wishing to preserve low levels of protection for subversive speech and the high levels of judicial self-restraint toward legislative efforts to curb such speech that had been established in *Dennis* and YATES V. UNITED STATES (1957), shied away from the danger test because they knew that, in its Holmesian formulation, it was antithetical to the results that had been achieved in those cases. Apparently, then, Holmes's formula was avoided in *Brandenburg* because some of the participants in the PER CURIAM opinion thought the danger rule protected speech too little and others thought it protected speech too much.

Yet *Brandenburg* did revive the imminence requirement that was the cutting edge of the danger test, and it did so in the context of subversive speech and of OVERRULING *Whitney v. California*, in which the Brandeis and Holmes clear and present danger "concurrence" was in reality a dissent. Even when the danger test was exiled by the Supreme Court it continued to appear in state and lower federal court decisions and in popular discourse. Although the distinction between speech and action—like all distinctions the law seeks to impose—is neither entirely logical nor entirely uncontradicted by real life experience, clear and present danger reasoning survives because most decision makers do believe that the core of the First Amendment is that people may be punished for what they do, not for what they say. Yet even from this basic rule that speech alone must not be punished, we are compelled to make an exception when speech becomes part of the criminal act itself or a direct incitement to the act. Even the most absolute defenders of free speech would not shy from punishing the speaker who shouts at a mob, "I've got the rope and the dynamite. Let's go down to the jail, blow open the cell and lynch the bastard." However imperfectly, the Holmesian formula captures this insight about where the general rule of free speech ends and the exception of punishment begins. It is for this reason that the danger rule keeps reappearing in one form or another even after its reported demise.

The danger rule is most comforting when the speech at issue is an open, particular attack by an individual on some small segment of government or society, such as a street corner speech denouncing the mayor or urging an end to abortion clinics. In such instances the general government and legal system clearly retain the strength to intervene successfully should the danger of a substantive evil actually become clear and present. The emasculation of the danger test came in quite a different context, that of covert speech by an organized group constituting a general attack on the political and legal system as a whole. Unlike the situation in particularized attacks, where the reservoir of systemic power to contain the anticipated danger remains intact, should subversive speech actually create a clear and present danger of revolution the system as a whole might not have the capacity to contain the danger. It is one thing to wait until the arsonist has struck the match and quite another to wait until the revolution is ready to attack the police stations. For this reason the Court in *Dennis* reverted to the *Gitlow*-style reasoning that the government need not wait until the revolutionaries had perfected their campaign of conversion, recruitment, and organization. *Dennis* and *Yates* carve out a Communist party exception to the immediacy requirement of the clear and present danger rule. They say that where the speech is that of a subversive organization, the government need not prove a present danger of revolution but only that the organization intends to bring about the revolution as speedily as circumstances permit. Thus the government is permitted to intervene early enough so that its own strength is still intact and that of the revolutionaries still small. When in defense of the danger rule Holmes argued that time had overthrown many fighting faiths, he did so with a supreme confidence that it was the American, democratic, fighting faith that time favored and that subversive movements would eventually peter out in America's liberal climate. It was a failure of that faith in the face of the communist menace that led to the emasculation of the danger rule during the Cold War of the 1950s. With hindsight we can see that Holmes's confidence remained justified, and that communist subversion could not have created even a probable, let alone a present danger. Nonetheless American self-confidence has eroded sufficiently that the Supreme Court remains careful not to reestablish the full force of the danger rule lest it handicap the political and legal system in dealing with those who organize to destroy it.

MARTIN SHAPIRO
(1986)

(SEE ALSO: *Judicial Activism and Judicial Restraint.*)

Bibliography

ANTIEAU, CHESTER JAMES 1950 "Clear and Present Danger"— Its Meaning and Significance. *Notre Dame Lawyer* 1950:3–45.

—— 1950 The Rule of Clear and Present Danger: Scope of Its Applicability. *Michigan Law Review* 48:811–840.

MENDELSON, WALLACE 1952 Clear and Present Danger— From Schenck to Dennis. *Columbia Law Review* 52:313–333.

—— 1953 The Degradation of the Clear and Present Danger Rule. *Journal of Politics* 15:349–355.

—— 1961 Clear and Present Danger—Another Decade. *Texas Law Review* 39:449–456.

STRONG, FRANK 1969 Fifty Years of "Clear and Present Danger": From Schenck to Brandenburg—And Beyond. *Supreme Court Review* 1969:427–480.

CLEBURNE (CITY OF) v. CLEBURNE LIVING CENTER, INC.
473 U.S. 432 (1985)

Cleburne v. Cleburne Living Center, Inc. (1985) is one of a handful of cases in which the Supreme Court invalidated a law while applying RATIONAL BASIS review, a traditionally deferential standard of judicial scrutiny that usually results in upholding the challenged law. In *Cleburne*, the Justices applied what commentators have called "rational basis with bite" to overturn a city ZONING ordinance that prevented the operation of a group home for the mentally disabled within the city.

Under the rational basis test, challengers must show that the law in question has no legitimate purpose or, assuming a legitimate purpose, that the means adopted by the law bear no reasonable relationship to the achievement of that end. The City of Cleburne argued that its zoning ordinance served the legitimate purpose of preserving property values and protecting the disabled from harassment by nearby school children. According to Justice BYRON R. WHITE, writing for a 6–3 majority, the city's justifications rested on nothing more than "negative attitudes" or "fear" of the mentally disabled. The indulgence of arbitrary prejudice, the Court held, was not a legitimate government purpose.

Some supporters of *Cleburne* hoped that the decision would mark the beginning of heightened judicial scrutiny of laws discriminating against the mentally disabled, much in the way the Court's use of rational basis with bite in SEX DISCRIMINATION cases in the early 1970s previewed the application of more stringent "intermediate scrutiny" to gender classifications. The REHNQUIST COURT dashed such hopes in *Heller v. Doe* (1993), where it returned to the more deferential version of the rational basis test in upholding an involuntary commitment law that discriminated between mentally retarded and mentally ill individuals.

The few other cases in which the Court has applied the rational basis test yet nevertheless invalidated the challenged law include *United States Department of Agriculture v. Moreno* (1973), PLYER V. DOE (1982), *Zobel v. Williams* (1982), *Metropolitan Life Insurance Co. v. Ward* (1985), *Allegheny Pittsburgh Coal Co. v. County Commis-*

sion (1989), and ROMER V. EVANS (1996). The growing number of rational basis with bite cases reveals that, despite the Court's insistence that there are but three STANDARDS OF REVIEW under the EQUAL PROTECTION clause—STRICT SCRUTINY, intermediate scrutiny, and rational basis—in practice the Justices apply a spectrum of different standards depending on the context of the particular controversy.

ADAM WINKLER
(2000)

CLERKS

Each Justice of the Supreme Court employs two or more law clerks. (In recent years, typically each Justice, other than the CHIEF JUSTICE, has employed four clerks.) Most of the clerks are not long-term career employees, but honor law school graduates who have previously served for a year as clerk to a lower federal judge. Typically, the term of service for these noncareer clerks is one year.

The practice of employing recent law school graduates as short-term clerks began with Justice HORACE GRAY. Gray employed a highly ranked Harvard Law School graduate each year at his own expense while serving on the Massachusetts Supreme Judicial Court. He continued to do so when appointed to the United States Supreme Court in 1882. Congress assumed the cost of Justices' law clerks in 1886, but only Gray and his sucessor, OLIVER WENDELL HOLMES, continued the pattern of employing recent law school graduates. The widespread use of the Holmes-Gray practice began in 1919, when Congress authorized each Justice to employ both a "law clerk" and a "stenographic clerk." The use of young law school graduates as judges' law clerks for one- or two-year periods is now the prevailing pattern in most lower federal courts. A clerkship position with a Supreme Court Justice is prestigious, and former clerks have become prominent in the legal profession, government, the judiciary and academe. Three Justices had themselves served as law clerks to Supreme Court Justices (BYRON R. WHITE, WILLIAM H. REHNQUIST, and JOHN PAUL STEVENS).

The employment of noncareer clerks has been defended as exposing the Justices to fresh ideas and the new theories current in their clerks' law schools. Concern that clerks have too large a role in decisions has been expressed, but this is exaggerated, given the clerks' brief tenure and what is known of the Court's decision process. A distinct concern is that with employment of more clerks, they increasingly play an inappropriately large part in the drafting of opinions. That concern is not so easily rebutted, since each Justice has used clerks' services in a distinct fashion, and there is insufficient reliable public information of the roles played by the Court's current clerks. Court opinions, however, have become longer, more elaborate in their arguments, and studded with citations. The opinions of several Justices appear to be written in a uniform law review style, suggesting that staff plays a large part in their drafting.

WILLIAM COHEN
(1986)

Bibliography

OAKLEY, JOHN B. and THOMPSON, ROBERT S. 1980 *Law Clerks and the Judicial Process.* Berkeley: University of California Press.

CLEVELAND, GROVER
(1837–1908)

The first Democratic President since JAMES BUCHANAN, Grover Cleveland supported civil service reform and tariff reduction. Cleveland devoted much of his two terms (1884–1888, 1892–1896) to eliminating corruption, inefficiency, and the exploitation of government for private benefit. Generally STATES' RIGHTS and probusiness in viewpoint, he insisted that the federal government function within constrained constitutional limits. As the first executive in decades willing to fight Congress, he frequently used the VETO POWER. A 6–3 Supreme Court sustained Cleveland's view of presidential removal power in *McAllister v. United States* (1891). (See APPOINTING AND REMOVAL POWER.)

Cleveland played almost no part in passage of the INTERSTATE COMMERCE ACT. He had no public reaction to the unpopular decision in POLLOCK V. FARMERS' LOAN & TRUST COMPANY (1895), voiding the income tax, for he believed criticism of the Court unseemly.

Cleveland was the second President with an opportunity to enforce the SHERMAN ANTITRUST ACT, but he expressed serious doubts about the act's effectiveness. Cleveland promised action "to the extent that [trusts] can be reached and restrained by Federal power," although he contended that state action provided the proper remedy. What antitrust successes his administration won (such as UNITED STATES V. TRANS-MISSOURI FREIGHT ASSOCIATION, 1897, and *United States v. Addyston Pipe & Steel Corp.,* 1899) belong to his second attorney general, Judson Harmon. Cleveland's last annual message even contains an exculpatory announcement about the "thus far . . . ineffective" act.

Cleveland and his first attorney general, RICHARD OLNEY, helped secure a federal INJUNCTION against the Pullman strike in 1894. Over the Illinois governor's objections, Cleveland sent 2,000 troops to Chicago to protect the mails and insure the free flow of INTERSTATE COMMERCE, purposes specifically approved by the Court in IN RE DEBS (1895). The troops broke the strike, killing twelve workers; this incident gave rise to the epithet "government by injunction."

Cleveland appointed four men to the Court—L. Q. C. LAMAR, MELVILLE FULLER, EDWARD WHITE, and RUFUS PECKHAM—but he was also the first President to suffer the embarrassment of having two successive appointments rejected by the SENATE.

DAVID GORDON
(1986)

Bibliography

MERRILL, HORACE   1957   *Bourbon Leader: Grover Cleveland.* Boston: Little, Brown.

CLEVELAND BOARD OF EDUCATION v. LAFLEUR
414 U.S. 632 (1974)

The Cleveland school board required a pregnant school teacher to take maternity leave, without pay, for five months before the expected birth of her child. A Virginia county school board imposed a similar four-month leave requirement. The Supreme Court, 7–2, held these rules unconstitutional. Justice POTTER STEWART, for the majority, invoked the IRREBUTTABLE PRESUMPTIONS doctrine. The school boards, by assuming the unfitness of pregnant teachers during the mandatory leave periods, had denied teachers individualized hearings on the question of their fitness, in violation of the guarantee of PROCEDURAL DUE PROCESS. Justice WILLIAM O. DOUGLAS concurred in the result, without opinion. Justice LEWIS F. POWELL rejected the irrebuttable presumptions ground as an EQUAL PROTECTION argument in disguise, but concluded that the boards' rules lacked rationality and denied equal protection. Justice WILLIAM H. REHNQUIST, for the dissenters, aptly characterized the irrebuttable presumptions doctrine as "in the last analysis nothing less than an attack upon the very notion of lawmaking itself."

KENNETH L. KARST
(1986)

CLIFFORD, NATHAN
(1803–1881)

Nathan Clifford came to the Supreme Court in 1858 after an active political career. He served in the Maine legislature in the 1830s and in the House of Representatives in the early 1840s. He was JAMES K. POLK's attorney general, and during his term he represented (in a private capacity)

the rebellious Dorr faction before the Supreme Court in LUTHER V. BORDEN (1849). Clifford's most significant political achievement came in 1848 when Polk dispatched him to persuade Mexico to accept the TREATY OF GUADALUPE HIDALGO as amended by Congress. A decade later, President JAMES BUCHANAN selected him to succeed Justice BENJAMIN R. CURTIS. At a time when the Court was perceived in many quarters as an instrument of southern and Democratic party interests, the choice of a Northerner with southern principles was viewed as blatant partisanship. After a lengthy confirmation battle, the SENATE narrowly approved him.

Clifford, a "doughface" in politics, regarded himself as a Jeffersonian "strict constructionist" in constitutional matters. He resolutely opposed the centralization of governmental power during the 1860s and early 1870s. But in ABLEMAN V. BOOTH (1859) he voted to affirm federal judicial supremacy. During the war, Clifford generally supported the government. He wrote opinions upholding the seizure of slave-trading ships; he joined his colleagues in declining to decide any constitutional questions involving the legal tender laws; and he supported the Court's refusal to consider the martial law issues in EX PARTE VALLANDIGHAM (1864). In the PRIZE CASES (1863), however, Clifford joined the dissenters who questioned the legality of President ABRAHAM LINCOLN's blockade of southern ports.

Following the war, Clifford consistently opposed Republican RECONSTRUCTION policy. He joined the majority opinion in EX PARTE MILLIGAN (1866), which struck down trials by military commissions where the civil courts were functioning; he supported the majority in the TEST OATH CASES (1867); he agreed with the majority's narrow construction of the FOURTEENTH AMENDMENT in the SLAUGHTERHOUSE CASES (1873); and in separate opinions in several VOTING RIGHTS cases, including UNITED STATES V. REESE (1876) and UNITED STATES V. CRUIKSHANK (1876), he went beyond the majority opinions to condemn federal interference with state elections. Finally, he joined the Court's majority that overturned the legal tender laws in *Hepburn v. Griswold* (1870), but when that decision was reversed a year later in *Knox v. Lee* (1871), he dissented in a strict construction of Congress's power to regulate currency. (See LEGAL TENDER CASES.)

In HALL V. DECUIR (1878) Clifford wrote for the Court, nullifying a Louisiana law prohibiting segregation of steamboat passengers. "Governed by the laws of Congress," he wrote, "it is clear that a steamer carrying passengers may have separate cabins and dining saloons for white persons and persons of color, for the plain reason that the laws of Congress contain nothing to prohibit such an arrangement." In short, the absence of federal policy negated state policy—a strange position for an old STATES' RIGHTS Democrat.

Clifford generally supported state regulatory policies.

His concurrence in *Slaughterhouse* signified his unwillingness to embrace a nationalizing interpretation of the Fourteenth Amendment; likewise, it reflected Clifford's traditionalist views of the STATE POLICE POWER. In *Munn v. Illinois* (1877), for example, he joined the majority to sustain Illinois's regulation of grain elevators. (See GRANGER CASES.) Clifford's most articulate statements on state powers came in his dissent in LOAN ASSOCIATION V. TOPEKA (1875). Rejecting the majority's invalidation of a state bonding authorization, Clifford struck at the Court's invocation of natural law doctrine and notions of judicial superintendence. Contending that state legislative power was "practically absolute," subject only to specific state and federal constitutional prohibitions, Clifford protested against JUDICIAL REVIEW that went beyond such limitations in tones reminiscent of older Jeffersonian doctrine: such power, he said, "would be to make the courts sovereign over both the constitution and the people, and convert the government into a judicial despotism."

Clifford dissented ninety-one times during his tenure, an extraordinarily high figure for the time. To some extent, it reflected his isolation and his archaic views. Throughout his judicial career, he consistently was perceived as a partisan Democrat. He served as president of the Electoral Commission to resolve the disputed election of 1876, and most accounts generally credit him with fairness in his conduct of the meetings. Nevertheless, the political purpose of his appointment in 1858 shadowed his work. He did not disappoint his benefactors; yet it was a career best characterized as dull and mediocre.

STANLEY I. KUTLER
(1986)

Bibliography

CLIFFORD, PHILIP Q. 1922 *Nathan Clifford, Democrat.* New York: Putnam's.

FAIRMAN, CHARLES 1939 *Mr. Justice Miller and the Supreme Court, 1862–1890.* Cambridge, Mass.: Harvard University Press.

CLINTON, WILLIAM JEFFERSON
(1946–   )

The forty-second President of the United States, William J. Clinton, was the first popularly elected President to be impeached by the U.S. HOUSE OF REPRESENTATIVES. While he will be best known for the events that precipitated his IMPEACHMENT (the purposeful misrepresentation of his affair with a White House intern), Clinton also played a critical role in redefining the Democratic Party. In particular, rather than seek to transform the nation through government initiatives, Clinton presided over a downsizing of the federal government, especially the reach and prestige of the presidency. By scaling down expectations of what the White House can accomplish and by blurring, if not obliterating, the line separating the personal from the public, Clinton will be long remembered. This legacy permeates the Clinton presidency, including the ways in which Clinton helped shape constitutional values.

Born on August 19, 1946, Clinton was raised in Hope and then Hot Springs, Arkansas. After graduating from high school in 1964, Clinton attended Georgetown University, Oxford University (as a Rhodes Scholar), and, starting in 1970, Yale Law School. Following law school, he returned to Arkansas. After a year teaching at the University of Arkansas, Clinton, in 1974, became the Democratic nominee for Arkansas's Third Congressional District. After losing a close election, Clinton turned his attention to state politics. In 1976, he was elected Attorney General of Arkansas. In 1978, at the age of 32, he was elected governor of Arkansas. Although failing to win reelection in 1980, Clinton was reelected in 1982 and served as governor from 1982 until his 1993 presidential inauguration.

In October 1991, Clinton announced his candidacy for President. During his campaign, Clinton was plagued by charges of marital infidelity and dishonesty. In response to questions about whether he had smoked marijuana, for example, Clinton at first claimed that he did not violate any law and—after admitting that he had smoked marijuana while in England—later argued that he did not inhale. Clinton likewise claimed that he did not act improperly when, after learning that he would not be drafted to serve in the VIETNAM WAR, he reneged on a commitment to join the National Guard. Nevertheless, Clinton persevered, earning his "comeback kid" reputation. Blaming presidential incumbent GEORGE H. W. BUSH for the high unemployment rate and other economic problems, Clinton successfully convinced voters that he would stimulate the economy, recommit the presidency to domestic issues, and reduce the size of government. Clinton's election, moreover, signaled that voters cared most about the ability to govern, not moral leadership.

Thanks to, among other things, a much-improved economy, Clinton secured the 1996 Democratic Party nomination without opposition. In the November 1996 elections, he defeated Republican Robert Dole and Reform Party candidate Ross Perot. In so doing, Clinton became the first Democratic President to be reelected since FRANKLIN D. ROOSEVELT.

Political expediency, not visionary leadership, was the hallmark of the Clinton presidency. Rather than expend political capital on controversial Supreme Court nominees, for example, Clinton embraced easily confirmable pragmatic liberals RUTH BADER GINSBURG and STEPHEN G. BREYER. Likewise, rather than defend the unconventional views of his nominee to the U.S. Department of Justice

CIVIL RIGHTS DIVISION, Lani Gunier, Clinton withdrew the nomination. In the end, although sometimes reminding the nation that he is especially concerned with constitutional matters because he "used to teach constitutional law," Clinton was quite willing to place other agenda items ahead of the advancement of some vision of what the Constitution means. One of these agenda items, the use of the APPOINTING POWER "to give you an administration that looks and feels like America," proved especially important in the nomination of judges and high-ranking officials at the Justice Department.

By downplaying the role of ideology in his constitutional policymaking, the Clinton administration often took a situational approach to constitutional matters. This brand of PRAGMATISM ruled the day on questions of CIVIL RIGHTS and CIVIL LIBERTIES. On gay rights, for example, Clinton promised gay and lesbian leaders that he would "stand with you in the struggle for equality for all Americans." But that promise was only partially fulfilled. While lifting most restrictions on federal civilian employment and supporting LEGISLATION to extend some EMPLOYMENT DISCRIMINATION protections to SEXUAL ORIENTATION discrimination, the Clinton administration neither lifted the ban on gays in the military nor participated in the Supreme Court litigation, ROMER V. EVANS (1996), challenging Colorado's exclusion of sexual orientation discrimination from state and local ANTIDISCRIMINATION LEGISLATION. Clinton, moreover, signed the Defense of Marriage Act, legislation condemning SAME-SEX MARRIAGE. For Clinton, the moral imperative of full equality for gays and lesbians gave way to the political costs of siding too often with gay rights interests.

On AFFIRMATIVE ACTION, political pragmatism likewise dominated administration policymaking. At first, the President sounded a cautionary note, launching a government-wide review of affirmative action by saying that "[w]e shouldn't be defending things that we cannot defend." Concern that Jesse Jackson would run for President in 1996, however, prompted a recalibration of administration policymaking. In an effort to shore up its minority base and neutralize Jackson, the Clinton administration embraced affirmative action. In particular, responding to a 1995 Supreme Court decision, ADARAND CONSTRUCTORS, INC. V. PEÑA, that called into doubt many federal affirmative action programs, Clinton reaffirmed the principle of affirmative action by declaring that the "job of ending discrimination is not done." More significant, by narrowly interpreting the Court's 1995 decision, the Clinton administration kept in place nearly all federal affirmative action programs.

Through his defense of affirmative action and his occasional support of gay rights, Clinton distanced himself from his Republican predecessors, Bush and RONALD REAGAN. Clinton's constitutional politics also varied from his predecessors' on ABORTION rights. Two days after his inauguration, Clinton dismantled the pro-life regulatory initiatives of the Reagan and Bush administrations. Clinton, moreover, vetoed legislation outlawing partial-birth abortions. Unlike his Republican predecessors, however, Clinton neither made hard-hitting bully pulpit speeches on abortion rights nor formulated a pro-choice legislative agenda. Apparently, with the Court's having reaffirmed a woman's right to terminate her pregnancy in PLANNED PARENTHOOD V. CASEY (1992), Clinton saw little political gain in staking out a hard-line position on abortion.

Where the White House did stake out hard-line positions were on legal issues affecting PRESIDENTIAL POWERS, especially WAR POWERS, EXECUTIVE IMMUNITY, and EXECUTIVE PRIVILEGE. On war powers, Clinton invoked military force on a number of occasions without seeking congressional support or approval. He sent cruise missiles into Afghanistan, ordered air strikes in Iraq, Bosnia, and Kosovo, conducted military operations in Somalia, and threatened to invade Haiti. In each case, he pointed to his inherent constitutional power to "command" the military. Indeed, by striking deals with both the North Atlantic Treaty Organization (NATO) and the UNITED NATIONS, Clinton relied more on the sanction of these multinational organizations than on the support of Congress.

On presidential immunity, the Clinton administration unsuccessfully argued before the Court that sitting Presidents were immune from civil lawsuits. In an earlier decision, the Court had concluded that a President was entitled to absolute immunity from civil lawsuits based on his officials duties. In defending a sexual harassment lawsuit filed against the President, CLINTON V. JONES (1997), the administration sought to extend this principle to lawsuits based on unofficial actions before he became President.

On executive privilege, the Clinton administration sought to expand the scope of presidential privileges in the face of both congressional and Office of Independent Counsel investigations of the President. Among other things, the administration claimed that the attorney–client privilege extends to government attorneys working in the White House Counsel's office, that U.S. Secret Service agents could refuse to appear as witnesses in a criminal proceeding concerning presidential activities, and that presidential claims of executive privilege extend to private matters, including communications with White House aides about civil lawsuits filed against the President and criminal investigations. These administration claims were rejected by lower federal courts. In a related case, however, the Supreme Court rejected Office of Independent Counsel efforts to subpoena the notes of meetings between a White House attorney (who had committed suicide) and his private counsel.

This melding of personal and public was also a prominent feature of impeachment proceedings against Clinton. Defenders of the President argued that the proceedings concerned personal sins (inappropriate sexual relations with a White House intern). Critics of the President claimed that the President turned these personal sins into public wrongs—lies and misrepresentations before a federal court judge and a federal GRAND JURY as well as the obstruction of justice. With most members of Congress voting along party lines, a majority of the House voted to impeach Clinton while the U.S. SENATE did not come close to the two-thirds vote necessary to remove him from office. Most senators, however, did condemn the President for his lies, obfuscation, and philandery.

NEAL DEVINS
(2000)

(SEE ALSO: *Articles of Impeachment of William J. Clinton.*)

CLINTON v. JONES
520 U.S. 681 (1997)

Clinton v. Jones is one of the Supreme Court's most important decisions on PRESIDENTIAL IMMUNITY. The case involved the issue of whether a sitting President was immune to civil actions based on his conduct before he took office. Whereas the Court had held 5–4 in NIXON V. FITZGERALD (1982) that a President was entitled to absolute immunity from civil lawsuits arising from the discharge of his official duties, a unanimous Court held in *Clinton v. Jones* that a President is not entitled to immunity from lawsuits based on his unofficial actions.

The plaintiff in *Clinton v. Jones*, Paula Corbin Jones, alleged that President WILLIAM J. CLINTON sexually harassed her while he was governor of Arkansas in 1991. Although Clinton denied any wrongdoing, his lawyers argued the lawsuit should be delayed until Clinton left office because burdening a President with litigation would allow judges or legal proceedings to interfere unduly with the performance of his official duties. In an opinion for eight Justices, Justice JOHN PAUL STEVENS explained this kind of burden would never impair the "Executive's ability to perform its constitutionally mandated functions." The Court maintained that denying the President's immunity claim would not produce horrible consequences. It noted that all prior civil suits based on pre-presidential conduct— brought against THEODORE ROOSEVELT, HARRY S. TRUMAN, and JOHN F. KENNEDY—had been quickly dismissed or settled.

The Court explained that two principles supported its conclusion. The first, employed in YOUNGSTOWN SHEET & TUBE CO. V. SAWYER (1952) and MARBURY V. MADISON (1803), was "that when the President takes official action, the Court has the authority to determine whether he has acted within the law." The second principle, applied in UNITED STATES V. NIXON (1973) and *United States v. Burr* (1807), was that "the President is subject to judicial process in appropriate circumstances." Indeed, sitting Presidents, including JAMES MONROE, RICHARD M. NIXON, and even Clinton himself, "have responded to court orders to provide testimony and other information with sufficient frequency that such interactions between the Judicial and Executive Branches" have become commonplace.

The Court remarked that a trial court could accommodate a President's scheduling needs, but refused to recognize a constitutional immunity that required such accommodations. In a separate concurrence, Justice STEPHEN G. BREYER recognized a constitutional principle "that forbids a federal Judge . . . to interfere with the President's discharge of his public duties." Breyer explained this principle would apply once a President had shown "a conflict between judicial proceedings and public duties."

After completing discovery in *Clinton v. Jones*, District Judge Susan Webber Wright dismissed the lawsuit for failing to state a legally cognizable cause of action. Her ruling did not, however, end the President's legal troubles. Before the lawsuit's dismissal, Kenneth Starr, the INDEPENDENT COUNSEL who had been investigating charges of possible misconduct by Clinton regarding a failed land-deal while he was governor of Arkansas, was tipped off that the President and a former White House intern, Monica Lewinsky, might each have lied under oath in *Clinton v. Jones* about the nature of their relationship. Lewinsky had filed an affidavit in the case denying that she had ever had a sexual relationship with the President, while Clinton testified in a deposition on January 17, 1998, that he had never had a sexual relationship with the intern nor ever been alone with her. Subsequent to the dismissal of Jones's lawsuit, the Independent Counsel granted Lewinsky limited immunity to testify about the President's efforts to obstruct the Jones lawyers' and Independent Counsel's lawful attempts to learn about the real nature of her relationship with the President. In an appearance before a federal GRAND JURY on August 18, 1998, Clinton acknowledged an "inappropriate relationship" with Lewinsky but defended the truthfulness of his prior testimony and actions to conceal his relationship with Lewinsky.

Shortly after the President's grand jury appearance, Starr referred to the U.S. HOUSE OF REPRESENTATIVES materials that he claimed indicated that the President had committed eleven possible impeachable offenses in trying to conceal his relationship with Lewinsky from Jones's lawyers and Starr's office. The referral sparked an IMPEACHMENT inquiry against the President. In the midst of the House's proceedings, the President settled Paula Jones's lawsuit then pending on appeal before the U.S. Court of

Appeals for the Eighth Circuit. Nevertheless, the House impeached the President for perjury and obstruction of justice. On February 12, 1999, the U.S. SENATE acquitted the President on both charges.

Within a month of the President's acquittal, Wright cited him for CONTEMPT based on his untruthful testimony in his deposition. In the contempt citation, Wright concluded that "the President's deposition testimony regarding whether he had ever been alone with Ms. Lewinsky was intentionally false, and his statements regarding whether he had ever engaged in sexual relations with Ms. Lewinsky likewise were intentionally false." Consequently, Wright fined the President for the reasonable expenses incurred by the plaintiff's attorneys because of his testimony and by the judge in attending to the deposition. She also referred the matter "to the Arkansas Supreme Court's Committee on Professional Conduct for review and any disciplinary action it deems appropriate."

Clinton v. Jones and its fallout have engendered criticism of every institution with which the case has come into contact. For many scholars, the fact that the lawsuit and its fallout paralyzed the national government for over a year flatly contradicts the Supreme Court's assumption in *Clinton v. Jones* that a civil lawsuit based on a President's activities before taking office could proceed without substantially interfering with a President's ability to do his job. Many other scholars, prosecutors, and members of Congress have abandoned support for the Independent Counsel Act; they claim Starr's relentless investigation of the President for nearly six years, including Starr's controversial investigation of matters relating to *Clinton v. Jones* (a case many believe was politically motivated), demonstrates the dangerous and uncontrollable lengths to which a politically unaccountable prosecutor will go to vindicate his charge.

A vocal minority defends *Clinton v. Jones* by placing primary responsibility on the President for the case's fallout. They suggest he could have avoided impeachment and contempt by being more candid in his deposition and grand jury testimony. Moreover, the President's acquittal ironically tracks the logic of the Court's decision in *Clinton v. Jones*. After all, the Court indicated that it would not have allowed the lawsuit against Clinton to proceed had it involved anything that implicated his official duties. Many senators voted against—and much of the public consistently opposed—the President's removal because his misconduct lacked a sufficiently public dimension or nexus to his official duties.

Consequently, the questions remain in what other fora and when a sitting President may be held accountable for unimpeachable misconduct. The suggestion in *Clinton v. Jones* that one such forum is a civil proceeding generates more concerns than it allays, because it plainly allows, as the fallout from the case demonstrates, a plaintiff or judge to interfere, perhaps substantially, with a President's performance of his duties. Indeed, *Clinton v. Jones* exacerbates these concerns further, for it leaves unaddressed whether a President before being impeached may be criminally prosecuted or imprisoned. Regardless of the legitimacy of these concerns, *Clinton v. Jones* clarified that in the future a President's only options in the face of burdensome litigation will not be constitutional immunity but rather a congressional act creating immunity or a sympathetic exercise of a trial judge's scheduling discretion.

MICHAEL J. GERHARDT
(2000)

CLOSED SHOP

A workplace is a closed shop if, by virtue of a labor contract, only the members of a particular union may be hired. After passage of the TAFT-HARTLEY ACT (1947), the closed shop was replaced by the "union shop" wherein one must join the union after being hired.

DENNIS J. MAHONEY
(1986)

CLOTURE

Cloture terminates debate in a legislative body. The rules of the SENATE encourage extended debates and, by taking advantage of those rules, sectional or ideological cliques can prevent action on bills they oppose. Only after rules reforms in the early 1960s made cloture easier did Congress pass effective CIVIL RIGHTS ACTS.

DENNIS J. MAHONEY
(1986)

CLYMER, GEORGE
(1739–1813)

George Clymer, who represented Pennsylvania at the CONSTITUTIONAL CONVENTION OF 1787, was a signer of both the DECLARATION OF INDEPENDENCE and the Constitution. Clymer did not speak often, but he was a member of the committees on state debts and the slave trade.

DENNIS J. MAHONEY
(1986)

COCHRAN v. LOUISIANA
281 U.S. 370 (1930)

Louisiana provided books to all public and private school children. The private school support was challenged on

FOURTEENTH AMENDMENT grounds as a use of public money for private purposes. Chief Justice CHARLES EVANS HUGHES held that the state's purpose was public.

Cochran is sometimes cited as an accommodationist precedent, but it was not decided under the establishment clause, which was not considered to apply to the states at that time.

RICHARD E. MORGAN
(1986)

CODISPOTI v. PENNSYLVANIA
418 U.S. 506 (1974)

A 5–4 Court here extended its decision in DUNCAN V. LOUISIANA (1968) to persons receiving serious punishment for criminal contempt. Following their trial, two defendants were cited for contempt and given several consecutive sentences for contempt of court. *Bloom v. Illinois* (1968) served as the basis for Justice BYRON R. WHITE's opinion that the defendants were entitled to a TRIAL BY JURY. Even though no single sentence exceeded six months, the consecutive sentences could not be separated; they all stemmed from one trial conducted as a single proceeding by one judge.

DAVID GORDON
(1986)

COEFFICIENT CLAUSE

See: Necessary and Proper Clause

COERCED CONFESSION

See: Police Interrogation and Confessions

COERCED SPEECH

See: Compelled Speech

COERCIVE ACTS

See: Constitutional History Before 1776; First Continental Congress, Declarations and Resolves of

COHEN, MORRIS R.
(1880–1947)

Morris Raphael Cohen came to the United States from Russia in 1892. After receiving his doctorate from Harvard in 1906, Cohen taught philosophy at the City College of New York from 1912 until 1938, when he retired to devote the rest of his life to writing.

A disciple of Justice OLIVER WENDELL HOLMES, Cohen rejected the conventional belief that judges decide cases by mechanical application of independently existing legal rules; he argued that the process of judicial lawmaking should be guided by the scientific method, a thorough understanding of the social consequences of judicial decisions, and a hierarchical set of social values. Believing natural law to be the measure of justice and advocating the philosophical analysis of legal systems, Cohen attacked such proponents of LEGAL REALISM as JEROME FRANK and THURMAN ARNOLD for their refusal to recognize any external standard by which positive law could be criticized. Cohen's legal writings are collected in *Law and the Social Order* (1933) and *Reason and Law* (1950).

RICHARD B. BERNSTEIN
(1986)

Bibliography

HOLLINGER, DAVID A. 1975 *Morris R. Cohen and the Scientific Ideal.* Cambridge, Mass.: M.I.T. Press.

COHEN v. CALIFORNIA
403 U.S. (1971)

Cohen was convicted of disturbing the peace. He wore a jacket bearing the words "Fuck the draft" while walking down a courthouse corridor. In overturning the conviction, a 5–4 Supreme Court held that the FIGHTING WORDS exception to FIRST AMENDMENT protection did not apply where "no individual . . . likely to be present could reasonably have regarded the words . . . as a direct personal insult," and there was no showing that anyone who saw Cohen was in fact violently aroused or that . . . [he] . . . intended such a result." Both majority and dissenters suggested that the failure to show that violence was imminent as the result of the words was fatal to the state's case. The Court thus made clear that words, in the abstract, cannot be read out of the First Amendment; the "fighting words" doctrine depends on the context in which words are uttered.

The state's assertion of other justifications for punishing Cohen were similarly rejected: the jacket's message was not OBSCENITY, because it was not erotic; the privacy interests of offended passers-by were insubstantial in this public place, and anyone offended might look away; there was no CAPTIVE AUDIENCE.

Cohen's chief doctrinal importance lies in its rejection of the notion that speech can constitutionally be prohibited by the state because it is offensive. Because offensiveness is an "inherently boundless" category, any such prohibition would suffer from the vice of VAGUENESS. And the First Amendment protects not only the cool expression of ideas but also "otherwise inexpressible emotions."

MARTIN SHAPIRO
(1986)

COHEN v. COWLES MEDIA CO.
501 U.S. 663 (1991)

Late in the 1983 Minnesota gubernatorial campaign, Dan Cohen, an active Republican, offered to provide politically sensitive documents to a *Minneapolis Star and Tribune* reporter. Cohen insisted his name not be mentioned, and the reporter promised confidentiality. Senior editors decided, however, to publish the documents and to cite Cohen as the source.

When the story appeared, Cohen was fired. He sued the newspaper for damages on the basis of the broken promise. A jury returned a verdict in Cohen's favor, but the Minnesota Supreme Court held that such an award would violate the FREEDOM OF THE PRESS. The U.S. Supreme Court reversed the state court. A 5–4 majority, speaking through Justice BYRON R. WHITE, relied on a "line of decisions holding that generally applicable laws do not offend the First Amendment simply because their enforcement against the press has incidental effects on its ability to gather and report the news."

Four Justices dissented, in an opinion by Justice DAVID H. SOUTER, arguing that a state's interest in granting damages for a broken promise is "insufficient to outweigh the interest in unfettered publication of the information revealed in this case." Justice HARRY A. BLACKMUN also wrote a separate DISSENTING OPINION, analogizing the case to HUSTLER MAGAZINE AND LARRY FLYNT V. JERRY FALWELL (1988).

ROBERT M. O'NEIL
(2000)

(SEE ALSO: *Journalistic Practices, Tort Liability, and the Freedom of the Press.*)

COHENS v. VIRGINIA
6 Wheat. 265 (1821)

In the rancorous aftermath of MCCULLOCH V. MARYLAND (1819), several states, led by Virginia and Ohio, denounced and defied the Supreme Court. State officers of Ohio entered the vaults of a branch of the Bank of the United States and forcibly collected over $100,000 in state taxes. (See OSBORN V. BANK OF THE UNITED STATES.) Virginia's legislature resolved that the Constitution be amended to create "a tribunal for the decision of all questions, in which the powers and authorities of the general government and those of the States, where they are in conflict, shall be decided." Widespread and vitriolic attacks on the Court, its doctrine of IMPLIED POWERS, and section 25 of the JUDICIARY ACT OF 1789 showed that MARTIN V. HUNTER'S LESSEE (1816) and *McCulloch* were not enough to settle the matters involved, especially as to the JURISDICTION of the Court over state acts and decisions in conflict with the supreme law of the land as construed by the Court. Accordingly a case appears to have been contrived to create for Chief Justice JOHN MARSHALL an opportunity to reply officially to his critics and to reassert both national supremacy and the supreme appellate powers of his Court.

Two brothers surnamed Cohen sold lottery tickets in Norfolk, Virginia, contrary to a state act prohibiting their sale for a lottery not authorized by Virginia. The Cohens sold tickets for a lottery authorized by an act of Congress to benefit the capital city. In Norfolk the borough court found the defendants guilty and fined them $100. By Virginia law, no appeal could be had to a higher state court. The Cohens, prosperous Baltimore merchants who could easily afford the paltry fine, claimed the protection of the act of Congress and removed the case on WRIT OF ERROR from the local court to the highest court of the land; moreover they employed the greatest lawyer in the nation, William Pinckney, whose usual fee was $2,000 a case, and another distinguished advocate, David B. Ogden, who commanded a fee of $1,000. More was at stake than appeared. "The very title of the case," said the Richmond *Enquirer*, "is enough to stir one's blood"—a reference to the galling fact that the sovereign state of Virginia was being hauled before the Supreme Court of the United States by private individuals in seeming violation of the ELEVENTH AMENDMENT. The state governor was so alarmed that he notified the legislature, and its committee, referring to the states as "sovereign and independent nations," declared that the state judiciaries were as independent of the federal courts as the state legislatures were of Congress, the twenty-fifth section of the 1789 notwithstanding. The legislature, having adopted solemn resolutions of protest and repudiating federal JUDICIAL REVIEW, instructed counsel representing Virginia to argue one point alone: that the Supreme Court had no jurisdiction in the case. Counsel, relying on the Eleventh Amendment to argue that a state cannot be sued without its consent, also contended that not a word in the Constitution "goes to set up the federal judiciary above the state judiciary."

Marshall, for a unanimous Court dominated by Republicans, conceded that the main "subject was fully discussed and exhausted in the case of *Martin v. Hunter*," but that did not stop him from writing a fifty-five-page treatise which concluded that under section 25 the Court had jurisdiction in the case. Marshall said little that was new, but he said it with a majestic eloquence and a forcefulness that surpassed JOSEPH STORY's, and the fact that the Chief Justice was the author of the Court's nationalist exposition, addressed to STATES RIGHTS' advocates throughout the country, added weight and provocation to his utterances. He was sublimely rhapsodic about the Constitution and the Union it created, sarcastic and disparaging in restating Virginia's position. Boldly he piled inference upon inference, overwhelming every particle of disagreement in the course of his triumphs of logic and excursions into the historical record of state infidelity. And he had a sense of the melodramatic that Story lacked, as when Marshall began his opinion by saying that the question of jurisdiction "may be truly said vitally to affect the Union." The defendant in error—Virginia—did not care whether the Constitution and laws of the United States had been violated by the judgment of guilt that the Cohens sought to have reviewed. Admitting such violation, Virginia contended that the United States had no corrective. Virginia, Marshall continued, maintained that the nation possessed no department capable of restraining, peaceably and by authority of law, attempts against the legitimate powers of the nation. "They maintain," he added, "that the constitution of the United States has provided no tribunal for the final construction of itself, or of the laws or treaties of the nation; but that this power may be exercised in the last resort by the courts of every state of the Union." Virginia even maintained that the supreme law of the land "may receive as many constructions as there are states. . . ." Marshall confronted and conquered every objection.

Quickly turning to Article III, Marshall observed that it authorizes Congress to confer federal jurisdiction in two classes of cases, the first depending on the character of the case and the second on the character of the parties. The first class includes "all" cases involving the Constitution and federal laws and treaties, "whoever may be the parties," and the second includes all cases to which states are parties. By ratifying the Constitution the states consented to judicial review in both classes of cases, thereby making possible the preservation of the Union. That Union is supreme in all cases where it is empowered to act, as Article VI, the SUPREMACY CLAUSE, insures by making the Constitution and federal law the supreme law of the land. The Court must decide every case coming within its constitutional jurisdiction to prevent the supreme law of the land from being prostrated "at the feet of every state in the Union" or being vetoed by any member of the Union. Collisions between the United States and the states will doubtless occur, but, said Marshall, "a constitution is framed for ages to come, and is designed to approach immortality as nearly as human institutions can approach it." To prevail, the government of the Union derived from the Constitution the means of self-preservation. The federal courts existed to secure the execution of the laws of the Union. History proved, Marshall declared, that the states and their tribunals could not be trusted with a power to defeat by law the legitimate measures of the Union. Thus the Supreme Court can take APPELLATE JURISDICTION even in a case between a state and one of its own citizens who relied on the Constitution or federal law. Otherwise Article III would be mere surplusage, as would Article VI. For the Court to decline the jurisdiction authorized by Article III and commanded by Congress would be "treason to the Constitution."

Although Marshall's rhetoric certainly addressed itself, grandiosely, to the question of jurisdiction, his critics regarded all that he had declared thus far as OBITER DICTA, for he had not yet faced the Eleventh Amendment, which Virginia thought concluded the case on its behalf. Upon finally reaching the Eleventh Amendment question, Marshall twisted a little history and chopped a little logic. The amendment, he said, was adopted not to preserve state dignity or sovereignty but to prevent creditors from initiating suits against states that would raid their treasuries. The amendment did not, therefore, apply to suits commenced by states and appealed by writ of error to the Supreme Court for the sole purpose of inquiring whether the judgment of a state tribunal violated the Constitution or federal law.

The argument that the state and federal judiciaries were entirely independent of each other considered the Supreme Court as "foreign" to state judiciaries. In a grand peroration, Marshall made his Court the apex of a single judicial system that comprehended the state judiciaries to the extent that they shared a concurrent jurisdiction over cases arising under the supreme law of the land. For most important purposes, Marshall declared, the United States was "a single nation," and for all those purposes, its government is supreme; state constitutions and laws to the contrary are "absolutely void." The states "are members of one great empire—for some purposes sovereign, for some purposes subordinate." The role of the federal judiciary, Marshall concluded, was to void state judgments that might contravene the supreme law; the alternative would be "a hydra in government."

Having sustained the jurisdiction of the Court, Marshall offered a sop to Virginia: whether the congressional lottery act intended to operate outside the DISTRICT OF COLUMBIA, he suggested, depended on the words of that act. The case was then reargued on its merits, and Marshall, again for a unanimous Court, quickly sustained the Cohens' conviction: Congress had not intended to permit the sale of lottery tickets in states where such a sale was illegal.

Virginia "won" its case, just as Madison had in *Marbury*

v. Madison (1803), but no one was fooled this time either. The governor of Virginia in a special message to his legislature spoke of the state's "humiliation" in having failed to vindicate its sovereign rights. A legislative committee proposed amendments to the Constitution that would cripple not only the JUDICIAL POWER OF THE UNITED STATES but also (reacting to *McCulloch*) the powers of Congress in passing laws not "absolutely" necessary and proper for carrying out its ENUMERATED POWERS. In the United States Senate, enemies of the Court proposed constitutional amendments that would vest in the Senate appellate jurisdiction in cases where the laws of a state were impugned and in all cases involving the federal Constitution, laws, or treaties. Intermittently for several years senators introduced a variety of amendments to curb the Court or revoke section 25, but those who shared a common cause did not share a common remedy, though GREEN V. BIDDLE (1823) and OSBORN V. BANK OF THE UNITED STATES (1824) inflamed their cause.

In Virginia, where the newspapers published Marshall's long opinion to the accompaniment of scathing denunciations, SPENCER ROANE and JOHN TAYLOR returned to a long battle that had begun with the *Martin* case and expanded in the wake of *McCulloch*. Roane, as "Algernon Sydney," published five articles on the theme that *Cohens* "negatives the idea that the American states have a real existence, or are to be considered, in any sense, as sovereign and independent states." He excoriated federal judicial review, implied powers, and the subordination of the states, by judicial construction, to "one great consolidated government" that destroyed the equilibrium of the Constitution, leaving that compact of the states nonexistent except in name. Taylor's new book, *Tyranny Unmasked* (1822), continued the themes of his *Construction Construed* (1820), where he argued that the "federal is not a national government: it is a league of nations. By this league, a limited power only over persons and property was given to the representatives of the united nations." The "tyranny" unmasked by the second book turned out to be nationalist programs, such as the protective tariff, and nationalist powers, including the power of the Supreme Court over the states.

THOMAS JEFFERSON read Roane and Taylor, egged them on, and congratulated them for their orthodox repudiation of the Court's "heresies." To Justice WILLIAM JOHNSON, who had joined Marshall's opinion, Jefferson wrote that Roane's articles "appeared to me to pulverize every word which had been delivered by Judge Marshall, of the extrajudicial part of his opinion," and to Jefferson "all was extrajudicial"—and he was not wholly wrong—except the second *Cohens* opinion on the merits. Jefferson also wrote that the doctrine that courts are the final arbiters of all constitutional questions was "dangerous" and "would

place us under the despotism of an oligarchy." Recommending the works of Roane and Taylor to a friend, Jefferson militantly declared that if Congress did not shield the states from the dangers originating with the Court, "the states must shield themselves, and meet the invader foot to foot." To Senator NATHANIEL MACON of Virginia, Jefferson wrote that the Supreme Court was "the germ of dissolution of our federal government" and "an irresponsible body," working, he said, "like gravity, by day and night, gaining a little today and a little tomorrow, and advancing its noiseless step, like a thief over the fields of jurisdiction, until all shall be usurped from the States, the government of all becoming a consolidated one."

JAMES MADISON deplored some of the Court's tactics, especially its mingling of judgments with "comments and reasoning of a scope beyond them," often at the expense of the states; but Madison told Roane flatly that the judicial power of the United States "over cases arising under the Constitution, must be admitted to be a vital part of the System." He thought Marshall wrong on the Eleventh Amendment and extreme on implied powers, but, he wrote to Roane, on the question "whether the federal or the State decisions ought to prevail, the sounder policy would yield to the claims of the former," or else "the Constitution of the U.S. might become different in every State."

The public reaction to *Cohens* depressed Marshall, because, as he wrote to Story, the opinion of the Court "has been assaulted with a degree of virulence transcending what has appeared on any former occasion." Roane's "Algernon Sydney" letters, Marshall feared, might be believed true by the public, and Roane would be hailed as "the champion of state rights, instead of being what he really is, the champion of dismemberment." Marshall saw "a deep design to convert our government into a mere league of States. . . . The attack upon the Judiciary is in fact an attack upon the Union." The whole attack originated, he believed, with Jefferson, "the grand Lama of the mountains." An effort would be made, predicted Marshall, accurately, "to repeal the 25th section of the Judiciary Act." Doubtless the personal attacks on him proved painful. A bit of anonymous doggerel, which circulated in Virginia after *Cohens*, illuminates public feeling.

> Old Johnny Marshall what's got in ye
> To side with Cohens against Virginny.
> To call in Court his "Old Dominion."
> To insult her with your foul opinion!
> I'll tell you that it will not do
> To call old Spencer in review.
> He knows the law as well as you.
> And once for all, it will not do.
> Alas! Alas! that you should be
> So much against State Sovereignty!

You've thrown the whole state in a terror,
By this infernal "Writ of Error."

The reaction to *Cohens* proves, in part, that the Court's prose was overbroad, but Marshall was reading the Constitution in the only way that would make the federal system operate effectively under one supreme law.

LEONARD W. LEVY
(1986)

Bibliography

BEVERIDGE, ALBERT J. 1916–1919 *The Life of John Marshall,* 4 vols. Vol. IV: 340–375. Boston: Houghton-Mifflin.

HAINS, CHARLES GROVE 1944 *The Role of the Supreme Court in American Government and Politics, 1789–1835.* Pages 427–461. Berkeley: University of California Press.

KONEFSKY, SAMUEL J. 1964 *John Marshall and Alexander Hamilton.* Pages 93–111. New York: Macmillan.

COKE, EDWARD
(1552–1634)

Edward Coke (pronounced Cook) was an English lawyer, judge, and parliamentarian who influenced the development of English and American constitutional law by promoting the supremacy of the COMMON LAW in relation to parliamentary powers and the royal prerogative.

After studying at Trinity College, Cambridge, Coke entered the Inner Temple and was called to the Bar in 1578. His career was outstanding from the start. He was elected to Parliament in 1589 and in 1593 he became Speaker of the House of Commons. Appointed attorney-general in 1594, he prosecuted several notable TREASON cases, including that of Sir Walter Raleigh in 1603.

In 1600, Coke began publication of his *Reports.* Eleven volumes had been published by 1615; two additional volumes appeared after his death. These were not collections of appellate opinions; rather, they consisted of case notes made by Coke, legal history, and general criticism. Coke had mastered the precedents, and he brought symmetry to scattered authority. Thereafter, *The Reports*, as they were usually called, were the authoritative common law precedents in England and colonial America.

Coke was appointed Chief Justice of the Court of Common Pleas in 1606, serving until 1613, when he was appointed Chief Justice of the Court of King's Bench. His judicial career was terminated in 1616 when King James I removed him from office. During these years Coke began enunciating ideas concerning the supremacy of the common law, foreshadowing modern concepts of government under law.

Coke's judicial pronouncement most influential on the American doctrine of JUDICIAL REVIEW came in BONHAM'S CASE (1610). The College of Physicians had fined and imprisoned Dr. Bonham for practicing medicine without a license. The court held that because the College would share in the fine, the charter and parliamentary act conferring this authority were contrary to the common law principle that no man can be a judge in his own case. Coke stated: "And it appears in our books, that in many cases, the common law will control acts of parliament, and sometimes adjudge them to be utterly void: for when an act of parliament is against common right and reason, or repugnant, or impossible to be performed, the common law will control it, and adjudge such act to be void. . . ." Coke believed that the common law contained a body of fundamental, although not unchangeable, principles to be ascertained and enunciated by judges through the "artificial reason" of the law. In *Bonham's Case* he seemed to be reasoning that parliamentary acts must be interpreted consistently with those principles. Whatever Coke's precise meaning, however, the statement foreshadowed the American DOCTRINE of judicial review; it was influential in the developing concept of the supremacy of law as interpreted and applied by the judiciary.

Another incident of Coke's judicial career that contributed to the modern idea of government under law came in 1608 during a confrontation with James I. The king had claimed authority to withdraw cases from the courts and decide them himself. In a dramatic Sunday morning meeting convened by the king and attended by all the judges and bishops, Coke maintained that there was no such royal authority. He asserted, quoting Bracton, that the king was not under man "but under God and law," one of the earliest and most quoted expressions of this concept.

Coke returned to Parliament in 1620 and in the final phase of his career made two major contributions to constitutional government and English and American law.

Drawing on the provision in MAGNA CARTA that "no free man shall be taken [or] imprisoned . . . except by the . . . law of the land," he launched the concept of "due process of law." Coke asserted that this provision referred to the established processes of the common law. He expressed this view in the parliamentary debates leading to the PETITION OF RIGHT in 1628, raising Magna Carta to new heights with statements such as "Magna Carta is such a fellow that he will have no sovereign." Coke's arguments presaged the later American concept of a written constitution superior to other law. He also linked Magna Carta with HABEAS CORPUS, although there was little historical support for the connection. He believed that there must be a remedy for imprisonment contrary to common law process and the remedy was to be had through the writ of habeas corpus.

Coke's other major contribution in his last years was the writing of his *Institutes.* This four-part work, published in 1641, became a basic text in the education of lawyers in England and America. In America, where law books were few, the *Institutes* were the standard work before the publication of WILLIAM BLACKSTONE's *Commentaries* in 1767. As noted by the Supreme Court in one of its several twentieth-century references to Coke (KLOPFER V. NORTH CAROLINA, 1967): "Coke's Institutes were read in the American Colonies by virtually every student of the law. Indeed, THOMAS JEFFERSON wrote that at the time he studied law (1762–1767), *Coke Lyttleton* was the universal elementary book of law students. And to JOHN RUTLEDGE of South Carolina, the Institutes seemed to be almost the foundation of our law." Because few lawyers in England and America had either the inclination or the resources to go behind Coke's *Institutes* and his *Reports*, these works, despite historical inaccuracies revealed by later scholarship, became the authoritative legal source on both sides of the Atlantic.

Coke represents a transition from medieval to modern law. He lived in the dawn of the modern constitutional era, when the British colonization of North America was beginning. As the colonists later sought authority to support their arguments that royal power was limited by law, they found it in Coke. Since the American Revolution, Coke has been regarded as an early authority for the proposition that all government is under law and that it is ultimately for the courts to interpret the law.

DANIEL J. MEADOR
(1986)

Bibliography

BOUDIN, LOUIS B. 1929 Lord Coke and the American Doctrine of Judicial Power. *New York University Law Review* 6:223–246.

BOWEN, CATHERINE D. 1957 *The Lion and the Throne: The Life and Times of Sir Edward Coke.* Boston: Little, Brown.

MULLETT, CHARLES F. 1932 Coke and the American Revolution. *Economica* 12:457–471.

COKER v. GEORGIA
433 U.S. 584 (1977)

Ehrlich Coker, an escaped felon, was convicted of rape with aggravating circumstances and sentenced to die. The Supreme Court, in a 7–2 decision, overturned the sentence. Justice BYRON R. WHITE, in a PLURALITY OPINION, argued that CAPITAL PUNISHMENT is "grossly disproportionate and excessive punishment for the crime of rape," and therefore unconstitutional under the Eighth Amendment, binding on the states through the FOURTEENTH AMENDMENT. Justice LEWIS F. POWELL's concurring opinion was applicable to the facts of this case only, while Justice WILLIAM J. BRENNAN and THURGOOD MARSHALL would have held the death penalty unconstitutional in any case whatsoever. Chief Justice WARREN E. BURGER and Justice WILLIAM H. REHNQUIST dissented, arguing that Coker's sentence was within the reserved power of the State.

DENNIS J. MAHONEY
(1986)

COLEGROVE v. GREEN
328 U.S. 549 (1946)

Colegrove v. Green and BAKER V. CARR (which all but overruled *Colegrove* in 1962) bracket the passage of the ONE PERSON, ONE VOTE movement from failure to success. Migration had drastically enlarged urban electoral districts and reduced rural ones in most states, but legislators and voters were slow to reapportion, and reapportionists turned to courts for relief. But courts were wary of tampering with legislators' seats.

The Supreme Court dismissed Colegrove's suit to enjoin Illinois congressional elections in "malapportioned" districts. The Justices gave two reasons: the case wanted EQUITY to make an INJUNCTION appropriate, and it presented a POLITICAL QUESTION reserved for decision of the elected branches both by constitutional mandate and by lack of judicially appropriate standards of judgment. "Courts," said Justice FELIX FRANKFURTER, "ought not to enter this political thicket." Three Justices dissented, arguing that the case did not lack equity, that the question was not political, and that constitutional mandate and standards could be found in Article I, section 2, and the EQUAL PROTECTION clause of the FOURTEENTH AMENDMENT—a debatable assertion little argued in either *Colegrove* or *Baker*. Justice WILEY RUTLEDGE, the tiebreaker, thought the question nonpolitical but joined in the vote for dismissal for want of equity.

Though the Court dismissed all REAPPORTIONMENT cases for sixteen years, citing *Colegrove*, Rutledge's discretionary rationale left room for the debate between Justices WILLIAM J. BRENNAN and Frankfurter in *Baker*, and for the intervention that led to the reapportionment revolution. The applicability of the equal protection clause to reapportionment was not seriously debated until REYNOLDS V. SIMS (1964) and OREGON V. MITCHELL (1970). Justices HUGO L. BLACK and JOHN MARSHALL HARLAN debated the applicability of Article I, section 2, in WESBERRY V. SANDERS (1964), which finally overruled *Colegrove*.

WARD E. Y. ELLIOTT
(1986)

Bibliography

AUERBACH, CARL A. 1964 The Reapportionment Cases: One Person, One Vote—One Vote, One Value." *Supreme Court Review* 1964:1–87.

COLEMAN v. MILLER
307 U.S. 433 (1939)

The lieutenant governor of Kansas had broken a tie vote in the Kansas senate to endorse a CHILD LABOR AMENDMENT, which Kansas had previously rejected. The losing senators, opponents of the amendment, challenged the vote because the lieutenant governor was not a part of the state "legislature" within the meaning of Article V and because the previous rejection of the amendment, plus the lapse of thirteen years, had cost the amendment its "vitality."

Over objections from dissenting Justices PIERCE BUTLER and JAMES C. MCREYNOLDS that the lapse of time issue had not been briefed or argued, Chief Justice CHARLES EVANS HUGHES declined to hear the challenge, citing the ratification of the FOURTEENTH AMENDMENT and arguing that efficacy of ratification—both as to lapse of time and as to the prior rejection—was a POLITICAL QUESTION, requiring "appraisal of a great variety of relevant conditions, political, social, and economic," not "within the appropriate range of EVIDENCE receivable in a court." Dominant considerations in political questions, he noted, are the "appropriateness of final action" by the elected branch and the "lack of satisfactory criteria for judicial determination."

Justice HUGO L. BLACK, writing for four concurring Justices, thought that Hughes had not sufficiently emphasized Congress's "exclusive power to control submission of constitutional amendments." An evenly divided Court expressed no opinion as to whether counting the lieutenant governor as part of the legislature was a political question.

WARD E. Y. ELLIOTT
(1986)

Bibliography

SCHARPF, FRITZ W. 1966 Judicial Review and the Political Question: A Functional Analysis. *Yale Law Journal* 75:517–597.

COLGATE v. HARVEY
296 U.S. 404 (1935)

This case is a historical curiosity. Vermont taxed the income from money loaned out of state but exempted from taxation any income from money loaned in the state at not more than five percent interest. The Supreme Court, in an opinion by Justice GEORGE SUTHERLAND, held the act unconstitutional as a violation of the EQUAL PROTECTION and PRIVILEGES AND IMMUNITIES clauses of the FOURTEENTH AMENDMENT. Justices HARLAN F. STONE, LOUIS D. BRANDEIS, and BENJAMIN N. CARDOZO, in dissent, found difficulty in perceiving a privilege of national CITIZENSHIP which the state had violated, especially because the Court had decided forty-four cases since 1868 in which state acts had been attacked as violating the privileges and immunities clause and until this case had held none of them unconstitutional. MADDEN V. KENTUCKY (1940) overruled *Colgate*.

LEONARD W. LEVY
(1986)

COLLATERAL ATTACK

As a general proposition a litigant gets one chance to present his case to a trial court; if he is dissatisfied with the result, he may APPEAL. What he cannot do, however, is to attack it "collaterally," starting the lawsuit all over again at the bottom, not so much asserting error in the first proceeding as ignoring it or trying to have the second trial court undo its results. This COMMON LAW doctrine forbidding collateral attack exists independently of the Constitution, which makes no direct mention of it. But the Constitution is frequently incomprehensible without some reference to its common law background. In this instance the document at three points implicates the doctrine of collateral attack. One section, the FULL FAITH AND CREDIT clause, seems to forbid collateral attack in civil cases (except where DUE PROCESS may require otherwise); the HABEAS CORPUS clause, by contrast, seems to require it in at least some criminal cases.

What constitutes collateral attack is itself often a difficult question; different JURISDICTIONS attach different significance to their judgments. As a general proposition, though, the full faith and credit clause requires that State A give the JUDGMENTS of State B the same effect State B would; to that extent the clause prohibits collateral attack in the interstate context. (A federal statute imposes the same requirements on federal courts.) The due process clause, however, limits the full faith and credit clause; if the courts of the state rendering the first judgment lacked jurisdiction over the defendant, the full faith and credit clause does not bar collateral attack. Due process requires that a defendant be able collaterally to attack a judgment rendered by a court that lacked authority over him. The due process clause, however, requires a court to permit collateral attack only when the party using it has not previously litigated the issue of jurisdiction; if he has, that question, like all others, is closed. Moreover, one who engages in litigation without raising the question of jurisdiction is generally treated as if he had done so and lost; the justification for such treatment is that the litigant had an opportunity to do so: due process does not require giving a second chance to one who has actually engaged in a lawsuit. The operation of this proposition leaves open to collateral attack only those judgments entered without any participation by the defendant—default judgments.

Collateral attack is thus available but is rather tightly circumscribed in civil cases; those held in detention on criminal charges have a somewhat wider scope of collateral attack available to them. The habeas clause requires federal courts (and arguably also those of the states) to entertain challenges to detention. Interpreting the federal statutes implementing the clause, federal courts have permitted those in custody to complain of various basic constitutional defects in the trials leading to their conviction; courts in some circumstances have permitted such collateral attack even though the asserted constitutional defect could have been raised in a direct appeal. To that extent present habeas practice, like the due process clause, requires courts to permit collateral attack. Unlike the due process clause, however, the habeas statute has been interpreted to permit litigants in some circumstances to raise again issues already litigated in the criminal trial.

At one level, then, the Constitution appears to issue contradictory commands: recognize judgments as conclusive—except when they are not. At another level the contradiction disappears, for both commands flow from the same impulse: under normal conditions only direct attack by appeal is permissible, but when the basic prerequisites of proper adjudication are absent (the basis of judicial authority or the incidents of a fair criminal trial), the normal rules must give way.

STEPHEN C. YEAZELL
(1986)

Bibliography

AMERICAN LAW INSTITUTE 1971 *Restatement of the Law 2d, Conflicts of Laws.* St. Paul, Minn.: American Law Institute Publishers.

EISENBERG, THEODORE 1981 *Civil Rights Legislation.* Charlottesville, Va.: Michie Co.

NOTE 1957 The Value of the Distinction between Direct and Collateral Attacks on Judgments. *Yale Law Journal* 66:526–544.

COLLECTIVE BARGAINING

Collective bargaining is the process of negotiation between employers and LABOR unions to establish the wages, hours, and working conditions of employees. Collective bargaining has been regulated by the federal government since passage of the WAGNER (NATIONAL LABOR RELATIONS) ACT (1935) and the TAFT-HARTLEY ACT (1947).

DENNIS J. MAHONEY
(1986)

COLLECTOR v. DAY
11 Wallace 113 (1871)

In MCCULLOCH V. MARYLAND (1819) the Supreme Court had held unconstitutional a state tax on an instrumentality of the national government, and in *Dobbins v. Commissioners* (1842) the Court had forbidden a state to tax the salary of a federal officer. The Court had reasoned that a sovereign government must be immune from the taxes of another government to preserve its independence. Here the Court applied that doctrine reciprocally, holding that the United States had no constitutional power to tax the salary of a state judge. In GRAVES V. NEW YORK EX REL. O'KEEFE (1939) the Court overruled both *Dobbins* and *Collector*, vitiating the DOCTRINE of reciprocal tax immunities.

LEONARD W. LEVY
(1986)

(SEE ALSO: *Intergovernmental Immunity.*)

COLLINS v. CITY OF HARKER HEIGHTS
503 U.S. 115 (1992)

Larry Collins, a city employee, died of asphyxia after entering a manhole to unstop a sewer line. His widow sued under SECTION 1983, TITLE 42, UNITED STATES CODE, alleging that municipalities must train and warn their employees about known workplace hazards. She claimed that the city's inadequate training, warning, and supplying of safety equipment violated the FOURTEENTH AMENDMENT guarantee of DUE PROCESS OF LAW. The Supreme Court, in a unanimous opinion by Justice JOHN PAUL STEVENS, rejected the claim. The Court viewed the claim as being analogous "to a fairly typical state-law tort claim" based on a breach of duty of care. It distinguished cases involving due process claims by those deprived of their liberty, such as prisoners. The holding extended a line of cases, beginning with PAUL V. DAVIS (1976), in which the Court has refused to find constitutional violations for what it regards as merely tortious misbehavior.

THEODORE EISENBERG
(2000)

COLLUSIVE SUIT

Article III of the Constitution limits the federal courts to the decision of CASES OR CONTROVERSIES. One component of that limitation bars adjudication of the merits of a claim absent a real dispute between parties who have conflicting interests. If nominally opposing parties manufacture a lawsuit to secure a judicial ruling, if one party controls or finances both sides of a case, or if both parties in fact desire the same ruling, the suit will be dismissed as collusive. The issues in a case need not be contested, so long as the parties' ultimate interests in the litigation are opposed. Hence, a default judgment can be entered, or a guilty plea accepted. Nor are all TEST CASES forbidden as collusive—only those where the contestants seek the same outcome. Of course, other JUSTICIABILITY barriers may prevent adjudication.

Like the ban on ADVISORY OPINIONS, the rule banning collusive suits saves judicial resources for disputes that need resolution, helps assure that federal courts act only on the basis of the information needed for sound decision making, and, in constitutional cases, prevents premature judicial intervention in the political process. The rule also may block efforts by supposed adversaries (but actual allies) to procure a ruling detrimental to opponents who are not represented in the collusive action.

JONATHAN D. VARAT
(1986)

COLONIAL CHARTERS

Perhaps no other American constitutional topic has been subject to such changing and contrary interpretations as has that of colonial charters. For example, GEORGE BANCROFT, who in 1834 had written that the Massachusetts charter of 1629 "established a CORPORATION, like other corporations within the realm," wrote in 1883 that the charter "constituted a body politic by the name of the Governor and Company of the Massachusetts Bay." Bancroft's apparent inconsistency is less contradiction than part of a constitutional controversy. Even during the colonial period constitutional experts disagreed about the legal nature of charters.

A few North American colonies (Plymouth, New Haven) had no charters. Most did, however, and the earliest charters were of two types. The first (Virginia, Massachusetts Bay), modeled on trading company charters granted to merchants, stressed commerce and settlement. The second (Maryland, Maine, Carolina) was based on the palatinate bishopric of Durham County, England. Later, a third type of charter was issued: "royal" charters for colonies in which the governor and other designated officers were appointed by the Crown. Containing more provisions directing government functions, royal charters generally defined a colony's relations with the mother country, not its internal constitution. No matter the type, charters were statements of privileges, not organic acts of government; they conferred immunities from prosecution and did not define structures of governance. Colonial charters, therefore, did not contribute significantly to constitutional law or history except when Americans claimed immunity from parliamentary authority.

American legal theory held that charters were contracts by which the king promised to protect and defend his American subjects in exchange for the subjects' allegiance. A better theory was that charters were evidence of a contract between the English crown and the first settlers of America. By either theory charters were not CONSTITUTIONS but one of the sources of constitutional rights along with the ancient English constitution, the current British constitution, the original contract, the second original contract, COMMON LAW, custom, and, to a minor degree, natural law. The first charter of Virginia stated a principle, repeated in later Virginia charters and in the charters of several other colonies, that the colonists "shall have and enjoy all Liberties, Franchises, and Immunities . . . to all Intents and Purposes as if they had been abiding and born within this our Realm of England. . . ." Americans of the Revolutionary period read such provisions as supporting their constitutional arguments against Britain. The legal theory subscribed to on the imperial side of the controversy held that charters created corporations not unlike municipal and commercial corporations in the mother country. As JOSEPH GALLOWAY declared, the colonies were only "corporations, or subordinate bodies politic, vested with *legislative* powers, to regulate their own internal police, under certain regulations and restrictions, and no more." A more extreme imperial theory held that charters were irrelevant; that the powers and limitations of colonial government came not from charters but from the instructions that British ministers issued to colonial governors. This theory, which American legislatures repudiated, contributed to the coming of the Revolution.

The American theory that charters were inviolable contracts confirming inalienable rights was premised on Old Whig constitutional definitions of LIMITED GOVERNMENT which still enjoyed some support in Britain during the second half of the eighteenth century and found expression in arguments that Parliament lacked constitutional authority to revoke or amend charters. This argument had little support in Britain, where all charters were viewed as revocable. In fact, a majority of colonies had their charters revoked and regranted at various times by the British government. Indeed, no single action so provoked the AMERICAN REVOLUTION as the Massachusetts Government Act asserting the authority of Parliament to amend colonial charters by unilateral decision.

When the Revolution commenced there were only two proprietary charters (Pennsylvania, Maryland) and two corporate charters (Connecticut, Rhode Island). Remaining colonies had royal charters, except Quebec and Georgia, which were governed by instructions. When Americans began to draft organic acts, they came more and more to think of charters as constitutions. To resist the Massachusetts Government Act, which revoked the charter of 1691, colonial leaders gave consideration to "resuming" the original charter of 1629 granted by Charles I. Connecticut and Rhode Island retained their charters as state constitutions, Connecticut until 1818 and Rhode Island until 1843.

JOHN PHILLIP REID
(1986)

Bibliography

REID, JOHN PHILLIP 1976 In the First Line of Defense: The Colonial Charters, the Stamp Act Debate and the Coming of the American Revolution. *New York University Law Review* 51:177–215.

COLORADO v. CONNELLY
479 U.S. 157 (1986)

Narrowly seen, this case deals with true confessions by mentally deranged people, but it resulted in the major holding that the Fifth Amendment's right against compulsory self-incrimination operates only when the coercion is linked to government. A confession that is involuntary in the sense that it is not the product of a rational intellect or free will may, nevertheless, be introduced in EVIDENCE because no government agent misbehaved or was responsible for the involuntary character of the confession. In this case, the murderer confessed in obedience to God's voice. He received his MIRANDA rights, waived them, and insisted on confessing. The court, in a 7–2 decision, found no violation of DUE PROCESS OF LAW and no involuntary self-incrimination. The dissenters believed that the Court was wrong to think that the only involuntary confessions are those obtained by government misconduct. Justice JOHN PAUL STEVENS, concurring with the decision, sensibly acknowledged that the confession in this case was involuntary but not of such a character that it had to be excluded from evidence.

LEONARD W. LEVY
(1992)

(SEE ALSO: *Police Interrogation and Confessions; Right Against Self-Incrimination.*)

COLOR OF LAW

Some CIVIL RIGHTS statutes proscribe only behavior "under color of" state law, and this requirement has played an important role in the development of FEDERAL PROTECTION OF CIVIL RIGHTS. Ironically, civil rights statutes have been interpreted in a manner that strips the color of law requirement of most of its contemporary significance. Judicial interpretation usually equates the color of law requirement with STATE ACTION. Because in most contexts in which the color of law requirement appears state action also is required, there is no obvious independent role for the color of law requirement.

The phrase "under color of . . . law" appears in the nation's first civil rights act, the CIVIL RIGHTS ACT OF 1866. There it seemed to limit the act's coverage to actions taken pursuant to—under color of—the post-CIVIL WAR southern BLACK CODES. Subsequent revisions of the 1866 act and civil rights statutes modeled after it retained the concept as a way of limiting their coverage. It currently appears in section 242 of the federal criminal code, SECTION 1983, TITLE 42, UNITED STATES CODE, and section 1343(3) of the judicial code, the jurisdictional counterpart to section 1983.

In deciding what constitutes action under color of law, two extreme readings have been rejected. One view, advocated in dissenting opinions by Justices OWEN ROBERTS, FELIX FRANKFURTER, and ROBERT H. JACKSON in SCREWS V. UNITED STATES (1945) and by Justice Frankfurter in MONROE V. PAPE (1961), deems behavior to be under color of state law only when it is authorized by state law. In this view, any action by state officials in violation of state law cannot be under color of law. Where, as in *Screws*, a law officer murders his prisoner, in clear violation of state law, the officer's act would not be regarded as being under color of law and, therefore, would not be subject to civil or criminal penalties under federal statutes containing the requirement. This view of the color of law requirement would limit the significance of modern civil rights statutes, for much official behavior that civil rights litigants allege to violate the Constitution or federal law also violates state law. This view, however, would make the color of law requirement meaningful in the context of the times during which the requirement first appeared. During the post-Civil War era, much of the most disturbing official behavior, particularly behavior aimed at recently freed blacks, was authorized by state law.

The expansive extreme view of color of law arises not in interpreting the phrase itself but in interpreting it in conjunction with a series of nouns that accompany it. Section 1983, for example, refers to action "under color of any statute, ordinance, regulation, custom or usage." In *Adickes v. S. H. Kress & Co.* (1970), Justices WILLIAM J.

BRENNAN and WILLIAM O. DOUGLAS interpreted "color of custom" to include virtually all segregative activity in the South, public or private, because the activity sprang from widespread custom. The majority in *Adickes* interpreted color of custom to include only action that constituted state action. Color of custom thus encompasses private behavior only to the extent that private persons act sufficiently in concert with public officials to render their action state action. This interpretation, combined with rejection in *Screws* and *Monroe* of the view limiting color of law to action authorized by law, leaves the color of law concept with little independent meaning. In general, action is under color of law if and only if the action satisfies the state action requirement.

There are, however, two areas in which it is useful to differentiate between state action and action under color of law. First, some constitutional rights, such as the THIRTEENTH AMENDMENT right not to be enslaved, are protected against both governmental and private infringement. A private person who caused the deprivation of such a right would be liable under statutes containing the "color of law" requirement even though his action was not state action. In these rare cases, action that is under color of law but that is not state action would lead to federal civil rights liability. Second, where a constitutional right, such as the right to DUE PROCESS, can be violated only by the government, private behavior authorized by statute may be action under color of law but, for want of state action, it may not subject the actor to civil rights liability. For example, when, pursuant to state statutes, creditors repossessed property without judicial proceedings, the Court in FLAGG BROS., INC. V. BROOKS (1978) held that the action taken was under color of law but that it was not state action.

In the pre-Civil War era, Congress employed the color of law requirement in a fashion related to its later use in civil rights statutes. States upset with expanding federal power and the behavior of federal officials would go so far as to initiate in state court criminal or civil proceedings against federal officers. Fearful of a biased forum, Congress, in a series of provisions commencing in 1815, provided federal officials with a right to remove these proceedings to federal court. (See REMOVAL OF CASES.) But Congress limited the power of removal to instances when the state proceedings were attributable to action by the officers under color of their office or of federal law. In this sense, as the Court noted in *Tennessee v. Davis* (1880), the color of law requirement clearly meant only action authorized by law, a point emphasized by the dissenters in *Screws*.

Nevertheless, it may be consistent with the purposes of both the removal and civil rights provisions to interpret color of law as limited to action authorized by law only in the case of the removal statute. If one views Congress in each case as desiring to protect only lawful behavior, it makes sense to interpret color of law in the removal statute to require action authorized by law and to interpret color of law in civil rights statutes to encompass official action, whether or not authorized by law. Use of the broad civil rights interpretation of color of law would immunize from state process action by federal officers not authorized by federal law. And in the context of civil rights statutes, adhering to the interpretation given the removal provision would immunize from federal remedies action by state officers not authorized by state law. The different interpretations serve a common function, subjecting a wrongdoer to liability.

THEODORE EISENBERG
(1986)

Bibliography

EISENBERG, THEODORE 1982 Section 1983: Doctrinal Foundations and an Empirical Study. *Cornell Law Review* 67:507–510.

COLUMBIA BROADCASTING SYSTEM, INC. v. DEMOCRATIC NATIONAL COMMITTEE
412 U.S. 94 (1973)

The Supreme Court here considered a FIRST AMENDMENT challenge to a broadcaster's refusal to accept editorial advertisements except during political campaigns. Some Justices maintained that the broadcaster's action did not amount to governmental action, but the Court did not reach the question. Even assuming STATE ACTION, it held that the First Amendment permitted broadcasters to discriminate between commercial and political advertisements. Broadcasters, the Court observed, were obligated by the FAIRNESS DOCTRINE to cover political issues, and their choice to cover such issues outside of commercials protected CAPTIVE AUDIENCES and avoided a threat that the wealthy would dominate broadcast decisions about political issues.

STEVEN SHIFFRIN
(1986)

COLUMBIA BROADCASTING SYSTEM, INC. v. FEDERAL COMMUNICATIONS COMMISSION
453 U.S. 367 (1981)

A 1971 amendment to the COMMUNICATIONS ACT OF 1934 permits the Federal Communications Commission (FCC) to revoke a broadcaster's license for failure to allow reasonable access to a candidate for federal office. The Supreme Court here interpreted this provision to create a right of access for an individual candidate. Further, reaffirming the much criticized precedent of RED LION BROADCASTING CO. V. FCC (1969), the Court sustained the law, as so interpreted, against a FIRST AMENDMENT challenge. The dissenters argued that the statute created no right of access.

KENNETH L. KARST
(1986)

COLUMBUS BOARD OF EDUCATION v. PENICK
443 U.S. 449 (1979)

DAYTON BOARD OF EDUCATION v. BRINKMAN
433 U.S. 406 (1977); 443 U.S. 526 (1979)

These cases demonstrated the artificiality of the DE FACTO/DE JURE distinction in school DESEGREGATION litigation. Both cases arose in cities in Ohio, where racially segregated schools had not been prescribed by law since 1888. In both, however, blacks charged another form of de jure segregation: intentional acts by school boards aimed at promoting SEGREGATION.

When the *Dayton* case first reached the Supreme Court, a related doctrinal development was still a fresh memory. WASHINGTON V. DAVIS (1976) had held that RACIAL DISCRIMINATION was not to be inferred from the fact that governmental action had a racially disproportionate impact; rather the test was whether such an impact was intended by the legislative body or other officials whose conduct was challenged. (See LEGISLATION.) *Dayton I* in 1977 applied this reasoning to school segregation, emphasizing that a constitutional violation was to be found only in cases of established segregative intent. The Court remanded the case for more specific findings on the question of intent, and said that any remedy must be tailored to the scope of the segregation caused by any specific constitutional violations.

Many observers took *Dayton I* to portend the undermining of KEYES V. SCHOOL DISTRICT NO. 1 (1973). In *Keyes* the Court had held that, once a significant degree of de jure segregation was established, systemwide desegregation remedies (including SCHOOL BUSING) were appropriate unless the school board showed that any remaining racially separate schools were the product of something other than the board's segregative intent. When the case returned to the Supreme Court two years later, these predictions were confounded.

Dayton II came to the Court along with the *Columbus* case, and they were decided together. *Columbus*, decided by a 7–2 vote, provided the main opinions. Writing for a majority of five, Justice BYRON R. WHITE applied the *Keyes* presumptions approach so vigorously that the dissenters remarked that the de facto/de jure distinction had been drained of most of its meaning. None of the Justices disputed the finding that in 1954–1955, when BROWN V. BOARD OF EDUCATION was decided, the Columbus school board had deliberately drawn boundary lines and selected school sites to maintain racial segregation in a number of schools. What divided the Court was the question of inferences to be drawn from these undisputed facts.

Justice White reasoned that this de jure segregation placed the school board under an affirmative duty to dismantle its dual system. Its actions since 1954, however, had aggravated rather than reduced segregation; the foreseeability of those results helped prove the board's segregative intent. A districtwide busing remedy was thus appropriate under *Keyes*. Justice WILLIAM H. REHNQUIST, dissenting, pointed out the tension between this decision and *Dayton I*. Here there was no showing of a causal relationship between pre-1954 acts of intentional segregation and current racial imbalance in the schools. Thus present-day de facto segregation was enough to generate districtwide remedies, so long as some significant pre-1954 acts of deliberate segregation could be shown.

It will be a rare big-city school district in which such acts cannot be found—with a consequent presumption of current de jure segregation. A school board cannot overcome this presumption merely by relying on a neighborhood school policy and showing that the city's residences are racially separated. This analysis obviously blurs the de facto/de jure distinction.

Dayton II made clear that a school board's segregative purpose was secondary to its effectiveness in performing its affirmative duty to terminate a dual system—and that effectiveness was to be measured in the present-day facts of racial separation and integration. Justice White again wrote for the majority, but now there were four dissenters. Justice POTTER STEWART, the Court's one Ohioan, concurred in Columbus but dissented in *Dayton II*, deferring in each case to the district court's determination as to a continuing constitutional violation. In *Dayton II*, the district court had found pre-1954 acts of deliberate segregation, but had found no causal connection between those acts and present racial separation in the schools. That separation, the district judge concluded, resulted not from any segregative purpose on the part of the school board but from residential segregation. Justice Stewart would have accepted that judgment, but the majority, following the *Columbus* line of reasoning, held that the board had not fulfilled its affirmative duty to dismantle the dual system that had existed in 1954. Chief Justice WARREN E. BURGER joined Justice Stewart in both cases; Justice Rehnquist dissented in *Dayton II* chiefly on the basis of his *Columbus* dissent.

Justice LEWIS F. POWELL joined Justice Rehnquist's dissents, and also wrote an opinion dissenting in both cases. Justice Powell had argued in *Keyes* for abandoning the de factode jure distinction, and he did not defend that distinction here. Rather he repeated his skepticism that court orders could ever end racial imbalance in large urban school districts and his opposition to massive busing as a desegregation remedy. Justice Powell, a former school board president, argued that, twenty-five years after *Brown*, the federal courts should be limiting rather than expanding their control of public school operations.

KENNETH L. KARST
(1986)

Bibliography

KITCH, EDMUND W. 1979 The Return of Color-Consciousness to the Constitution: Weber, Dayton, and Columbus. *Supreme Court Review* 1979:1–15.

COMITY, JUDICIAL

Comity is the deference paid by the institutions of one government to the acts of another government—not out of compulsion, but in the interest of cooperation, reciprocity, and the stability that grows out of the satisfaction of mutual expectations. When the courts of one nation give effect to foreign laws and the orders of foreign courts, that deference is called judicial comity. (See ACT OF STATE DOCTRINE.)

The states of the United States are, for many purposes, separate sovereignties. A state court, in deciding a case, starts from the assumption that it will apply its own state law. When it applies the law of another state, normally it does so as a matter of comity. (See CHOICE OF LAW.) Because comity is not so much a rule as an attitude of accommodation, state courts generally feel free to refuse to apply a law that violates their own state's public policy. In *Nevada v. Hall* (1979) California courts upheld a million-dollar verdict against the State of Nevada in an automobile injury case, rejecting Nevada's claim of SOVEREIGN IMMUNITY; the Supreme Court affirmed, saying that the Constitution left to California's courts the degree of comity they should afford to Nevada law.

A state court's enforcement of the valid judgment of a court of another state is not merely a matter of comity but is required by the FULL FAITH AND CREDIT CLAUSE. Similarly, the SUPREMACY CLAUSE binds state courts to enforce valid federal laws and regulations, along with the valid judgments of federal courts.

Notions of comity have recently taken on increased significance in the federal courts themselves. A federal court may, under some circumstances, stay its proceedings because another action between the same parties is pending in a state court. The Supreme Court in *Fair Assessment of Real Estate Association v. McNary* (1981) discovered in the Tax Injunction Act (1937) a general principle of comity forbidding federal courts not only to enjoin the collection of state taxes but also to award DAMAGES in state tax cases. And comity has been a major consideration in the development of the "equitable restraint" doctrine of YOUNGER V. HARRIS (1971), which generally forbids a federal court to grant an INJUNCTION against the continuation of a pending state criminal prosecution.

KENNETH L. KARST
(1986)

(SEE ALSO: *Abstention Doctrine.*)

COMITY CLAUSE

See: Full Faith and Credit

COMMAGER, HENRY STEELE
(1902–1998)

Henry Steele Commager was one of America's most widely read and influential historians. His two dozen books and scores of articles reflect his keen interest in CONSTITUTIONAL HISTORY as well as an elegant and vivid style. He earned his degrees from the University of Chicago and taught for over sixty years at New York University, Columbia, and Amherst. He also held endowed chairs at Oxford and Cambridge and was a visiting professor at universities on four continents. His first book, *The Growth of the American Republic* (1930) with Samuel E. Morison, has been a standard text for over six decades, and his *Documents in American History*, often updated since its original publication in 1934, dominates its field. *Theodore Parker* (1936) is a riveting study of a transcendentalist reformer. *Majority Rule and Minority Rights* (1943) is a critique of JUDICIAL REVIEW based on Commager's devotion to majoritarianism and respect for dissent. *Civil Liberties Under Attack* (1951) and *Freedom, Loyalty, and Dissent* (1954) blasts MCCARTHYISM and defends constitutional freedoms.

Commager co-edited the *New American Nation* series in over forty volumes and co-authored *The Encyclopedia of American History* (1953). His *Search for a Usable Past*

(1967) is historiographical, and *Freedom and Order* (1966) is an incisive commentary of contemporary America. *The American Mind* (1960) is an interpretation of American thought and culture as influenced by constitutionalism, PRAGMATISM, evolution, and economics. *Empire of Reason* (1977) stresses the ways America fulfilled Enlightenment ideas by institutionalizing them, as in CONSTITUTIONAL CONVENTIONS, FEDERALISM, and BILLS OF RIGHTS. Commager concerned himself with describing the American national character as a product of history, which he regarded as a branch of *belle lettres*. His books reveal the influence of Emersonians as well as pragmatists such as William James, Lester Frank Ward, and John Dewey, whom he depicted as exponents of Americanism. His work also reflects his liberalism and acceptance of government as an agency of popular welfare.

LEONARD W. LEVY
(2000)

COMMANDER-IN-CHIEF

In every state, the command of the armed forces is the ultimate component of executive power. Article II of the Constitution, adapting British practice, designates the President commander-in-chief both of the nation's armed forces and of the state militia when it is called into national service. Article IV, guaranteeing each state a REPUBLICAN FORM OF GOVERNMENT, somewhat qualifies that authority. It provides that the national force be used to suppress domestic violence only on application of the state legislature or of the governor when the state legislature cannot be convened.

With regard to domestic (and republican) tranquillity, it became apparent soon after 1789 that the deference of Article IV to STATES' RIGHTS did not permit the national government fully to protect the peace of the United States. Although state governments dealt with most episodes of domestic disorder—and still do—some of those episodes had a national dimension. As early as 1792, Congress declared that "it shall be lawful for the President" to use national troops or call forth the militia whenever he deems such action necessary to protect the functioning of the government or the enforcement of its laws. President GEORGE WASHINGTON leading more than 12,000 national guardsmen to suppress the WHISKEY REBELLION of 1793 is the classic symbol of an independent national power to enforce what the President, echoing Jean-Jacques Rousseau, called "the general will." This power has been invoked regularly, most notably during and after the CIVIL WAR, but also in major strikes affecting the national economy (IN RE DEBS, 1895) and in the enforcement of judicial decisions ordering racial DESEGREGATION during the 1950s and 1960s. President WILLIAM HOWARD TAFT used the national force to protect Asian ALIENS threatened by a local mob, relying on his duty as President to carry out the international responsibility of the United States for the safety of aliens.

The formula of the 1792 statute, like that used in later statutes, straddles an unresolved controversy between the President and Congress. Congress insists that its power to pass laws NECESSARY AND PROPER to implement the President's authority as commander-in-chief includes the right to restrict the President's capacity to act. All Presidents, on the other hand, while recognizing the necessity for legislation in many situations, claim that statutes cannot subtract from their constitutional duty and power to preserve the Constitution and enforce the laws. Although the pattern of usage is by no means uniform, Presidents generally conform to statutes that purport to reinforce and structure the President's use of the armed forces in domestic disorders, at least as a matter of courtesy, unless "sudden and unexpected civil disturbances, disasters, or calamities," in the language of Army regulations, leave no alternative. Some Presidents have even paid lip service to the POSSE COMITATUS ACT (1878), a dubious relic of the end of Reconstruction. That act prohibits the use of the Army in suppressing domestic turbulence unless "expressly" authorized. Presidents have evaded this restriction by employing marines for the purpose.

Modern statutes usually retain the ancient requirement of a public proclamation before force is used to restore order, although Presidents sometimes ignore the tradition. The use of force by the President (or by a governor) in dealing with civil disorder does not alone justify suspending the writ of HABEAS CORPUS. According to the DOCTRINE of EX PARTE MILLIGAN (1807) and other cases, the writ can not be suspended so long as the courts remain capable of carrying out their duties normally.

The use of force as an instrument of diplomacy, or of war and other extended hostilities, does not involve issues of dual SOVEREIGNTY but has presented significant constitutional conflicts both between Congress and the President, and between individuals and the state. (See WAR, FOREIGN AFFAIRS, AND THE CONSTITUTION.) The President's power as commander-in-chief under such circumstances goes far beyond the conduct of military operations. As the Supreme Court declared in *Little v. Barreme* (1804), it is also the President's prerogative to deploy troops and weapons at home and abroad in times of peace and war, and to use them when no valid law forbids him to do so. The purposes for which the President may use the armed forces in carrying on the intercourse of the United States with foreign nations are infinite and unpredictable. They include diplomatic ceremony and demonstrations of power; the employment of force in self-defense in order to deter, anticipate, or defeat armed attack against the interests of the United States, or any other act in violation of international law that would justify the use of force in time of peace; and the prosecution of hostilities after a congressional DECLARATION OF WAR. In actual hostilities, it is the President's sole responsibility to negotiate truces, armistices, and cease-fires; to direct the negotiation of peace treaties or other international arrangements terminating a condition of war; and to govern foreign territory occupied in the course of hostilities until peace is restored.

These powers are extensive. The use, threat, or hint of force is a frequent element of diplomacy. Military occupations lasted for years during and after the Civil War, the Philippine campaign, a number of Caribbean episodes, WORLD WAR I, and WORLD WAR II. The Cold War has required the apparently permanent deployment abroad of American armed forces on a large scale; novel legal arrangements have developed to organize these activities. Although the broad political and prudential discretion of both the President and Congress is taken fully into account by the courts in reviewing such exercises of the commander-in-chief's authority, constitutional limits have nonetheless emerged.

In recent years Congress has effectively employed its appropriation power to qualify the President's discretion as commander-in-chief in conducting military or intelligence operations that are not "public and notorious" general wars under international law. While such contests between the power of the purse and the power of the sword are largely political, they raise the principle of the SEPARATION OF POWERS applied in IMMIGRATION AND NATURALIZATION SERVICE V. CHADHA (1983). The judicial response to these contests can be expected further to clarify a particularly murky part of the boundary between the President and Congress.

EUGENE V. ROSTOW
(1986)

Bibliography

BISHOP, JOSEPH W., JR.   1974   *Justice under Fire.* New York: Charter House.
CORWIN, EDWARD S.   (1940) 1957   *The President: Office and Powers 1787–1957.* New York: New York University Press.
WILCOX, FRANCIS   1971   *Congress, the Executive, and Foreign Policy.* New York: Harper & Row.

COMMENTATORS ON THE CONSTITUTION

The first important analysis of the Constitution appeared during the ratification contests of 1787 and 1788. ALEXANDER HAMILTON and JAMES MADISON, who had participated in the CONSTITUTIONAL CONVENTION, collaborated with JOHN JAY on THE FEDERALIST (1788), a series of essays defending the proposed new plan of government. Appealing to the rationalistic temper of the eighteenth century, they justified the creation of a strong central government on logical and philosophical grounds, and developed a model of CONSTITUTIONALISM that relied upon structural CHECKS AND BALANCES to promote harmony within the system. Ultimate SOVEREIGNTY, they argued, inhered in the American people; the Constitution, as an instrument of the popular will, defined and limited the powers of both the national government and the states. *The Federalist* provided valuable insights into the thinking of the Founding Fathers and established the guidelines for further constitutional commentary down to the CIVIL WAR.

Between 1789 and 1860 two major groups of commentators emerged in response to recurring political crises and sectional tensions. Legally trained publicists from New England and the middle states espoused a national will theory of government to justify the expansion of federal power, while southern lawyers and statesmen formed a state compact school of constitutional interpretation that championed decentralization and state sovereignty. Each group approached constitutional issues in a formal and mechanistic way, and relied upon close textual analysis to support its position.

The nationalists argued that the American people, acting in a collective national capacity, had divided sovereign power between the nation and the states and established the Constitution as the supreme LAW OF THE LAND. Under the resulting federal system, the states retained control of their internal affairs but were subordinate to the general government in all important national concerns, including taxation, INTERSTATE COMMERCE, and FOREIGN AFFAIRS. The Constitution, moreover, created a permanent union, whose basic features could be changed only by resort to a prescribed AMENDING PROCESS. Although several nationalists conceded that the Constitution had originated in a compact of the people of the several states, they insisted that such a compact, once executed, was inviolate, and could not be modified thereafter by the parties. Such was the message of NATHANIEL CHIPMAN's *Sketches of the Principles of Government* (1793) and William Alexander Duer's *Lectures on Constitutional Jurisprudence* (1843).

Other advocates of national supremacy rejected contractual assumptions altogether, and moved toward an organic theory of the Union. Nathan Dane, in *A General Abridgment and Digest of American Law* (1829), contended that the states had never been truly sovereign, because they owed their independence from British rule to the actions of the CONTINENTAL CONGRESS, a national body that represented the American people. The people, not the states, had ratified the Constitution through the exercise of majority will; therefore, any state efforts to nullify federal law or to withdraw from the Union amounted to illegal and revolutionary acts. JAMES KENT's *Commentaries on American Law* (1826–1830) and Timothy Walker's *Introduction to American Law* (1837) further noted that the Constitution provided for the peaceful resolution of federal-state disputes through the Supreme Court's power of JUDICIAL REVIEW.

In attacking the compact model of constitutionalism, these commentators stressed the noncontractual language of the PREAMBLE and the SUPREMACY CLAUSE. A similar preoccupation with formal textual analysis characterized JOSEPH STORY's *Commentaries on the Constitution of the United States* (1833), the most influential and authoritative statement of the nationalist position. Story, an associate Justice of the Supreme Court, interpreted the Constitution on a line-by-line basis, in light of the nationalistic jurisprudence of JOHN MARSHALL. Like Marshall, he insisted that the powers of the federal government had to be construed broadly, as the Framers had intended. On both theoretical and pragmatic grounds, Story defended the power of the Supreme Court to strike down unconstitutional state laws. Yet he also emphasized the limits of national authority, noting that the states retained control over matters of internal police that affected the daily lives of their citizens. Although Congress alone could regulate interstate commerce, for example, state legislatures might pass health and safety measures that indirectly affected such commerce. By focusing upon questions of terminology and classification, Story sought to demonstrate the stability of the federal system and to place the Constitution above partisan politics.

Nationalist historians described the formation of the Union in similarly legalistic and reverential terms. GEORGE TICKNOR CURTIS's *History of the Origin, Formation, and Adoption of the Constitution of the United States* (1854–1858), the first work to deal exclusively with a constitutional topic, quoted at length from the journals of the Continental Congress and other public records, but largely ignored surrounding political and economic circumstances. For Curtis and other romantic nationalists, the Founding Fathers were disinterested and divinely inspired patriots, who enjoyed the full confidence and support of the American people. Only RICHARD HILDRETH's *History of the United States of America* (1849–1852) presented a contrary view. Hildreth stressed the importance of conflicting economic groups in the new nation and pointed out that the Constitution had been ratified by conventions representing only a minority of American voters.

Although state compact theorists shared the prevailing belief in a fixed and beneficent Constitution, they deplored what they perceived as the aggrandizing tendencies of the national government. St. George Tucker's "View of the Constitution of the United States," appended to his edition of WILLIAM BLACKSTONE's *Commentaries* (1803), established the basic premises of the southern constitutional argument. The states and their respective citizens, Tucker contended, had entered into a compact—the Constitution—and had delegated some of their sovereign powers to the resulting federal government for specific and limited purposes. Because the Union remained subordinate to its creators, the states, and depended upon their cooperation for its continued existence, all positive grants of national power had to be construed strictly. If the federal government overstepped its constitutional powers, Tucker suggested that individuals might look to the state or federal courts for redress, while violations of STATES' RIGHTS would be answered by appropriate action from the state legislatures.

Later commentators refined Tucker's ideas and fashioned new remedies for the protection of state rights. The Philadelphia lawyer WILLIAM RAWLE introduced the possibility of peaceable SECESSION through the action of state CONSTITUTIONAL CONVENTIONS in *A View of the Constitution of the United States* (1825). Rawle's reasoning was hypothetical: because the people of each state had agreed to form a permanent union of representative republics, they could withdraw from their compact only by adopting a new state constitution based upon nonrepublican principles. A more realistic assessment of the nature and consequences of secession appeared in HENRY ST. GEORGE TUCKER's *Lectures on Constitutional Law* (1843). In Tucker's view, secession provided the only mode of resistance available to a state after a controversial federal law had been upheld by the judiciary. Secession was a revolutionary measure, however, because the Constitution had established the courts as the permanent umpires of federal-state relations.

Advocates of NULLIFICATION proposed a more extreme version of the state sovereignty argument, whose origins went back to JOHN TAYLOR of Caroline's *Construction Construed; and Constitutions Vindicated* (1820) and *New Views of the Constitution of the United States* (1823). Unlike the southern moderates, Taylor insisted that sovereignty was indivisible and inhered exclusively in the states. Each "state nation" thus retained the power to construe the terms of the federal compact for itself, and to interpose its authority at any time to protect its citizens against the consolidating tendencies of the federal government. Whenever a federal law violated the Constitution, asserted Abel Parker Upshur in *A Brief Inquiry into the Nature and Character of Our Federal Government* (1840), a state might summon its citizens to a special convention and declare the act null and void within its borders.

As the influence of the slaveholding South continued to decline in national politics, some commentators sought to preserve the Union by adding still more checks and balances to the constitutional structure. In *A Disquisition on Government* and *A Discourse on the Constitution and Government of the United States* (1851), JOHN C. CALHOUN called for amendments that would establish a dual executive and base REPRESENTATION upon broad interest groups, any one of which might block the enactment of undesirable congressional legislation. ALEXANDER H. STEPHENS' *A Constitutional View of the Late War Between the States* (1868–1870) and JEFFERSON DAVIS's *The Rise and Fall of the Confederate Government* (1881) confirmed the mechanistic cast of southern constitutional thought, as they summed up the case for secession in its final form. With the defeat of the Confederacy, the secessionist option ceased to exist, and later commentators treated the issue as a historical footnote. During the 1950s conservative Southerners tried unsuccessfully to circumvent federal CIVIL RIGHTS policy by reviving the idea of INTERPOSITION in such works as William Old's *The Segregation Issue: Suggestions Regarding the Maintenance of State Autonomy* (1955).

For Civil War Unionists the exercise of sweeping WAR POWERS by the President and Congress provoked vigorous constitutional debate. Conservative publicists, committed to a restrictive view of federal power, insisted that no departure from prewar constitutional norms was permissible, despite the wartime emergency. Former Supreme Court Justice BENJAMIN R. CURTIS charged in *Executive Power* (1862) that President ABRAHAM LINCOLN had acted illegally in authorizing the military to arrest and imprison suspected disloyal civilians in areas removed from a war zone. Joel Parker's *The War Powers of Congress, and of the President* (1863) denounced the EMANCIPATION PROCLAMATION and related CONFISCATION ACTS for impairing property rights and revolutionizing federal-state relations.

A rival group of Lincolnian pragmatists defended the actions of federal authorities by appealing to an organic theory of constitutional development. Evolving national values and practices had shaped the Constitution far more than abstract legal rules, asserted FRANCIS LIEBER in *What Is Our Constitution—League, Pact, or Government?* (1861). The Founding Fathers had not anticipated the problem of secession; therefore, the Lincoln administration might, in conformity with natural law principles, take whatever measures it deemed necessary to preserve the nation. Sidney George Fisher's *The Trial of the Constitution* (1862) discovered new sources of federal power in the doctrine of popular sovereignty and other unwritten democratic dogmas. Charging that adherence to the checks and balances of the formal Constitution had immobilized the government in practice, Fisher urged Congress to create a new constitutional tradition by transforming itself into an American parliament immediately responsive to the popular will. William Whiting, solicitor of the War Department, contended that existent constitutional provisions authorized the federal government to pursue almost any wartime policy it chose. In *The War Powers of the President and the Legislative Powers of Congress in Relation to Rebellion, Treason, and Slavery* (1862), Whiting looked to the GENERAL WELFARE CLAUSE and other statements of broad national purpose to legitimize controversial Union measures.

The leading commentators of the late nineteenth century carried forward an organic view of the Constitution, but linked it to a laissez-faire ideology that sharply restrained the exercise of governmental power at all levels. Influenced by the conservative Darwinism of Herbert Spencer and William Graham Sumner, these economic libertarians feared legislative innovation and called upon the judiciary to preserve the fundamental economic rights of the individual against arbitrary state action. In *A Treatise on the Constitutional Limitations Which Rest upon the Legislative Power of the States of the American Union* (1868), THOMAS MCINTYRE COOLEY argued that a libertarian tradition stretching back to MAGNA CARTA protected private property from harmful regulation, even in the absence of specific constitutional guarantees. By appealing to these historic liberties, Cooley sought to broaden the scope of the DUE PROCESS clause, transforming it into a substantive restraint upon economic legislation. JOHN FORREST DILLON's *A Treatise on Municipal Corporations* (1872) discovered implied limits to the taxing power. Taxes could only be levied for a PUBLIC PURPOSE, Dillon maintained, and could not benefit one social class at the expense of another. CHRISTOPHER G. TIEDEMAN took an equally restrictive view of state and federal POLICE POWER in *A Treatise on the Limitations of Police Power in the United States* (1886), condemning usury laws and efforts to control wages and prices.

In the area of civil rights, commentators opposed "paternalistic" legislation and insisted that the Civil War had not destroyed the traditional division of power between the nation and the states. Amendments must conform to the general principles underlying the Constitution, asserted John Norton Pomeroy in *An Introduction to the Constitutional Law of the United States* (1868); and these principles included FEDERALISM, as defined by the Founding Fathers. Despite the broad language of the FOURTEENTH AMENDMENT, therefore, Congress lacked power to remedy most civil rights violations, which remained subject to state control. JOHN RANDOLPH TUCKER's *The Constitution of the United States* (1899) warned that federal attacks on customary racial practices in the South would undermine local institutions and create a dangerous centralization of power in the national government. The racist assumptions shared by most libertarians surfaced clearly in John Ordronaux's *Constitutional Legislation in the United States* (1891). Noting that national progress depended upon "race instincts," Ordronaux suggested that blacks, Orientals, and other non-Aryans were unfit for the full responsibilities of democratic CITIZENSHIP.

Constitutional historians of the late nineteenth century used a Darwinian model of struggle and survival to explain the rise of the American nation. HERMANN VON HOLST, the first scholar to make systematic use of the records of congressional debates, combined antislavery moralism with a laissez-faire attitude toward northern business in his ponderous *Constitutional and Political History of the United States* (1876–1892). Equally moralistic and libertarian was JAMES SCHOULER's *History of the United States under the Constitution* (1880–1913). In the growth of republican institutions and the triumph of Union arms Schouler discerned the unfolding of a divine plan. From a Social Darwinist perspective, William A. Dunning's *The Constitution of the United States in Civil War and Reconstruction, 1860–1867* (1885) and JOHN W. BURGESS' *Reconstruction and the Constitution, 1866–1876* (1902) criticized federal policymakers for enfranchising blacks at the expense of their Anglo-Saxon superiors.

In its mature form libertarian theory created a twilight zone on the borders of the federal system, within which neither the national government not the states could act. While the TENTH AMENDMENT prevented Congress from regulating local economic activities, state legislatures found their police powers circumscribed by the restrictive principles defined by Cooley and his associates. These extraconstitutional restraints also limited the federal government when it sought to exercise its express powers over taxation and commerce. Twentieth-century economic and racial conservatives have continued to defend the libertarian viewpoint and to protest the expansion of federal regulatory power. In *Neither Purse Nor Sword* (1936), James M. Beck and Merle Thorpe condemned early New Deal legislation for violating property rights and invading the reserved powers of the states. Charles J. Bloch's *States' Rights—The Law of the Land* (1958), written in the aftermath of the *Brown* decision, charged that the VINSON COURT and WARREN COURT had subverted the meaning of the Fourteenth Amendment in civil rights cases, and called upon Congress to revitalize the Tenth Amendment, "the cornerstone of the Republic."

As the excesses of a period of industrial growth threatened the welfare of workers and consumers, however, other commentators condemned the laissez-faire model of constitutionalism as archaic and unsuited to the needs of a modern democracy. Impressed by the empiricism of the emerging social sciences, these democratic instrumentalists approached constitutional questions from a pragmatic and reformist perspective. Although they did not deny the existence of fundamental principles, they argued that these principles needed to be adapted to changing environmental conditions. Through intelligent social planning, they maintained, federal and state lawmakers might control an expanding economy in accordance with the popular will.

Mechanistic eighteenth-century concepts, such as SEPARATION OF POWERS, impaired the efficiency of modern government, charged WOODROW WILSON in *Congressional Government* (1885) and *Constitutional Government in the United States* (1908). Constitutional grants of power to the national government established only "general lines of definition," he added, and should be broadly construed by the courts in response to developing societal needs. In a similar vein, WESTEL W. WILLOUGHBY's *The Constitutional Law of the United States* (1910) and FRANK J. GOODNOW's *Social Reform and the Constitution* (1911) criticized judges for obstructing progressive reforms through their continued adherence to laissez-faire idealism.

The advent of the welfare state in the 1930s magnified disagreements between libertarians and instrumentalists, and provoked a major confrontation between President FRANKLIN D. ROOSEVELT and the Supreme Court. EDWARD S. CORWIN, the most influential constitutional commentator of the time, applauded the programs of the early NEW DEAL for establishing a new COOPERATIVE FEDERALISM. In *The Twilight of the Supreme Court* (1934), Corwin urged the Justices to uphold legislative policymaking in economic matters, and pointed to the nationalistic decisions of John Marshall as appropriate precedents. When judicial intransigence persisted, according to Attorney General ROBERT H. JACKSON in *The Struggle for Judicial Supremacy* (1941), the administration adopted a court-packing plan as the only apparent means of restoring the full constitutional powers of the national government. Although the plan failed, a majority of Justices began to redefine congressional power in more liberal terms. Corwin welcomed the Court's belated acceptance of sweeping federal regulation in *Constitutional Revolution, Ltd.* (1941), and correctly predicted that the Justices would thereafter focus their review power on protection of CIVIL LIBERTIES and the rights of minorities.

Instrumentalist historians tended to seek the causes of constitutional change in underlying social and economic developments. CHARLES A. BEARD's pathbreaking study, *An Economic Interpretation of the Constitution of the United States* (1913), encouraged Progressive reformers by demythologizing the work of the Philadelphia Convention. Using previously neglected Treasury and census records, Beard presented the Founding Fathers as a conspiratorial elite who had devised an undemocratic Constitution to protect their property from the attacks of popular legislative majorities. In *American Constitutional Development*

(1943) CARL BRENT SWISHER drew upon other nontraditional sources to explain, and justify, the emergence of the positive state. With comparable erudition WILLIAM W. CROSSKEY's *Politics and the Constitution in the History of the United States* (1953) used linguistic analysis to demonstrate the legitimacy of New Deal regulatory measures. After an exhaustive inquiry into the eighteenth-century meaning of "commerce" and other key words, Crosskey concluded that the Framers had intended to create a unitary, centralized system in which "the American people could, through Congress, deal with any subject they wished, on a simple, straightforward, nation-wide basis."

Although the instrumentalists emphasized the need to adapt the Constitution to changing socioeconomic conditions, they remained committed to the RULE OF LAW and acknowledged the binding force of constitutional norms. This moderate position failed to satisfy a small group of radical empiricists, who argued that written codes were meaningless in themselves and merely served to rationalize the political decisions of legislators and judges. "The language of the Constitution is immaterial since it represents current myths and folklore rather than rules," asserted THURMAN W. ARNOLD in *The Folklore of Capitalism* (1937). "Out of it are spun the contradictory ideals of governmental morality." Howard L. McBain's *The Living Constitution: A Consideration of the Realities and Legends of Our Fundamental Law* (1927) similarly contended that law had no life of its own, but depended for its substance on the unpredictable actions of men. Because the American people believed the fiction of a government of law, they had grown politically apathetic, charged J. ALLEN SMITH in *The Growth and Decadence of Constitutional Government* (1930). Although constitutionalism had been designed to limit arbitrary power, he noted, it protected an irresponsible governing elite from popular scrutiny and control.

The empiricists were more successful in diagnosing ills than in prescribing remedies. Because they stressed the determining influence of ideology and personality upon decision making, they could find no satisfactory way to limit the discretionary power of public officials. The scope of administrative discretion must necessarily broaden as society grows more complex, contended William B. Munro in *The Invisible Government* (1928). He welcomed the trend, which promised to give government agencies greater flexibility in dealing with contemporary problems. Yet unrestrained power might also encourage irresponsible behavior, such as judges so often displayed in reviewing legislative measures. Both LOUIS B. BOUDIN's *Government by Judiciary* (1932) and Fred Rodell's *Nine Men: A Political History of the Supreme Court of the United States from 1790 to 1955* (1955) reduced jurisprudence to politics, and charged that judges wrote their conservative policy preferences into law under the guise of legal principles. The only remedy they could suggest, however, was the appointment to the bench of liberals who would promote the public welfare in a more enlightened, albeit equally subjective, fashion.

During the past quarter-century commentators, preeminently ALEXANDER M. BICKEL, have continued to debate the nature and scope of JUDICIAL REVIEW, in the context of the Supreme Court's enlarged role as guardian of individual and minority rights. The timely aspects of such recent studies attest to the constructive role that commentators have historically played in the shaping of American constitutional law. Responsive to changing trends in social and political thought, they have often helped to redefine and clarify the terms of constitutional discourse. As Corwin once quipped, "If judges make law, so do commentators."

MAXWELL BLOOMFIELD
(1986)

Bibliography

BAUER, ELIZABETH K. 1952 *Commentaries on the Constitution, 1790–1860.* New York: Columbia University Press.

BELZ, HERMAN 1971 The Realist Critique of Constitutionalism in the Era of Reform. *American Journal of Legal History* 15: 288–306.

HYMAN, HAROLD M. 1973 *A More Perfect Union: The Impact of the Civil War and Reconstruction on the Constitution.* New York: Knopf.

KONEFSKY, ALFRED S. 1981 Men of Great and Little Faith: Generations of Constitutional Scholars. *Buffalo Law Review* 30:365–384.

LARSEN, CHARLES E. 1959 Nationalism and States' Rights in Commentaries on the Constitution after the Civil War. *American Journal of Legal History* 3:360–369.

MURPHY, PAUL L. 1963 Time to Reclaim: The Current Challenge of American Constitutional History. *American Historical Review* 69:64–79.

NEWTON, ROBERT E. 1965 Edward S. Corwin and American Constitutional Law. *Journal of Public Law* 14:198–212.

COMMERCE CLAUSE

The commerce clause is the small part of the Constitution that provides that "The Congress shall have power . . . to regulate commerce with foreign nations, and among the several states, and with the Indian tribes."

The phrase relating to the Indians was derived from the provision in the 1781 ARTICLES OF CONFEDERATION which gave the federal congress "the sole and exclusive right and power of . . . regulating the trade and managing all affairs with the Indians." Despite the elimination of the sweeping second phrase, there never has been any question that the Indian part of the commerce clause (plus the

TREATY and WAR POWERS) gave Congress power over all relations with the Indians, and no more need be said about it.

Nor has there been much question as to the scope of the federal power to regulate foreign commerce. Combined with the tax and WAR POWERS and the provisions prohibiting the states from entering treaties and agreements with foreign powers and from imposing duties on imports and exports, this power clearly gave the federal government complete authority over relations with foreign nations.

The short clause relating to "commerce among the several states," however, has become one of the most significant provisions in the Constitution. It has been in large part responsible for the development of the United States as a single integrated economic unit, with no impediments to the movement of goods or people at state lines.

The draftsmen of the commerce clause could not have envisaged the eventual magnitude of the national commercial structure or the breadth of the CONSTITUTIONAL INTERPRETATION which that structure would produce. Nevertheless the need for a national power over commerce led to the calling of the CONSTITUTIONAL CONVENTION OF 1787, and the seed for the growth of the power was planted in the early years.

In 1786 the Virginia General Assembly, and then a commission representing five states meeting at Annapolis, called for the appointment of commissioners to consider "the trade of the United States" and "how far a uniform system in their commercial regulation may be necessary to their common interest and their permanent harmony." The Congress created under the Articles of Confederation thereupon approved the calling of a convention to meet in Philadelphia in May 1787 for the purpose of revising the Articles and reporting its recommendations to the Congress and the States.

The Convention, after considerable debate, adopted a resolution generally describing the powers to be given the National Legislature, in the form proposed by the Virginia delegation led by GEORGE WASHINGTON, Governor EDMUND RANDOLPH, and JAMES MADISON. It was resolved that "the national legislature ought ... to legislate in all cases for the general interests of the Union, and also in those to which the states are separately incompetent, or in which the harmony of the United States may be interrupted by the exercise of individual legislation." This and other resolutions were sent to a drafting committee, which reported out the commerce clause and other powers to be conferred on Congress in substantially the form finally adopted.

Although the needs of commerce had been principally responsible for the calling of the Convention, the clause was accepted with hardly any debate. The same was true

in the state ratifying conventions. All reflected the view that in general the new Constitution gave the federal government power over matters of national but not of local concern.

The same view was expressed in the first commerce clause case in 1824 (GIBBONS V. OGDEN), written for a unanimous Supreme Court by Chief Justice JOHN MARSHALL, who had been a member of the Virginia ratifying convention. The Court declared that the commerce power did not extend to commerce that is completely internal, and "which does not extend to or affect other states." It "may very properly be restricted to that commerce which concerns more states than one. . . . The genius and character of the whole government seems to be, that its action is to be applied to all the concerns of the nation, and to these internal concerns which affect the States generally."

Of course, neither in 1787 nor in 1824 did those who wrote or ratified or interpreted the Constitution contemplate the tremendous and close-knit economic structure that exists today and the accompanying inability of the states, or of any agency but the nation, to meet the governmental problems that structure presents. Indeed, in the 1820s and into the 1850s many persons regarded even the construction of the principal highways within each state as purely internal matters not subject to federal power, as appeared from President JAMES MONROE's veto on constitutional grounds of an appropriation to construct what is now Interstate 70 from Maryland to the Western states. Although the MARSHALL COURT would not have agreed, some of the more STATES' RIGHTS-minded Supreme Court Justices of the 1840s and 1850s did.

In general, during the century from 1787 to 1887, the only national commercial problems concerned foreign trade and navigation and the removal of state-imposed barriers to interstate trade. Affirmative federal regulation applied almost entirely to matters of navigation on the oceans, lakes, and rivers. An early statute required vessels engaged in coastal traffic to obtain federal licenses. Reasonably enough, none of these were challenged as falling outside the commerce power.

All of the commerce clause cases during the first 100 years, and a great many of them thereafter, were concerned with the negative effect of the clause upon state legislation—even though the clause did not mention the states. The Constitution merely said that Congress should have the power to regulate commerce. Other clauses imposed specific prohibitions upon the states, but the commerce clause did not. On the other hand, it was well known during the early period that the principal evil at which the commerce clause was directed was state restrictions upon the free flow of commerce.

The issue first came before the Supreme Court in *Gibbons v. Ogden* (1824). New York had granted Robert Fulton and ROBERT LIVINGSTON the exclusive right for thirty years to operate vessels propelled by steam in New York waters, thereby excluding steamboats coming from neighboring states. New Jersey, Connecticut, and Ohio had promptly passed retaliatory legislation forbidding the New York monopoly from operating in their waters. The case presented an example (though unforeseeable in 1787) of the type of interstate commercial rivalry which the commerce clause had been designed to prevent.

A unanimous Supreme Court held that Congress's commerce power extended to all commercial intercourse among the states, rejecting arguments that it did not apply to navigation and passenger traffic. The Court, speaking through Marshall, further concluded that Congress had exercised its power in the Coastal Licensing Act, that Gibbons's vessels were operating in compliance with that statute, and that New York's attempt to prohibit them from operating in New York waters was inconsistent with the federal statute and therefore unconstitutional under the SUPREMACY CLAUSE of the Constitution. The Court did not find it necessary to decide whether the power of Congress to regulate interstate commerce was exclusive or whether the states had CONCURRENT POWER in the absence of a conflicting federal law, although Marshall seemed to favor the former view. But Marshall recognized that, although the states had no power to regulate interstate or FOREIGN COMMERCE as such, they could exercise their preexisting powers to enact laws on such subjects as health, quarantine, turnpikes and ferries, and other internal commerce, even though that might overlap the subjects that Congress could reach under the commerce clause. Thus, as a practical matter, the Court recognized that the states had concurrent powers over many aspects of commerce, or of internal matters that might affect external commerce.

After ROGER B. TANEY became Chief Justice in 1835, a number of the Justices, including Taney, took the flat position that only state laws inconsistent with acts of Congress were preempted, and that the commerce clause itself had no preemptive effect. But in none of the cases could a majority of the Court agree on any theory.

This unhappy and unhealthy state of the law was formally resolved in 1852, when, speaking through newly appointed Justice BENJAMIN R. CURTIS, the Court sustained a Pennsylvania law governing the use of pilots in the port of Philadelphia in COOLEY V. BOARD OF WARDENS OF PHILADELPHIA (1852). Six Justices agreed that whatever subjects of this power are in their nature national, or admit only of one uniform system, or plan of regulation, may justly be said to be of such a nature as to require exclusive legislation by Congress. Where there was no need for regulation on a national scale, only state laws inconsistent with federal would fall.

The Court still cites the *Cooley* principle with approval,

although the *Cooley* formula has been largely superseded by an interest-balancing approach to STATE REGULATION OF COMMERCE. (See SELECTIVE EXCLUSIVENESS; STATE POLICE POWER; STATE TAXATION OF COMMERCE.) But in a number of cases during the years following *Cooley*, the Court adopted a more simplistic approach. If the subject of the state regulation was interstate commerce, only Congress could regulate it; if it was not, only the states could. In these cases the Court held—or at least said—that the United States could not tax or regulate manufacturing or PRODUCTION because they were beyond the scope of the federal commerce power, a pronouncement that later caused substantial difficulty but was not explicitly disavowed until *Commonwealth Edison Co. v. Montana* (1981).

During the twenty years after the CIVIL WAR, the Court held that states could not directly tax or regulate interstate commerce, but that they could, for example, fix railroad rates between points in the same state. (See GRANGER CASES.) When, however, Illinois attempted to apply its prohibition against charging more for a shorter rail haul than a longer one to freight between Illinois cities and New York, the Court, applying the *Cooley* formula, held in WABASH, ST. LOUIS & PACIFIC RAILWAY V. ILLINOIS (1886) that the state had no such power. The opinion made it clear that interstate rates, even for the part of a journey within a state, were not subject to state regulation. Such transportation was "of that national character" that can be "only appropriately" regulated by Congress rather than by the individual states.

Because leaving shippers subject to unregulated rail rates was unthinkable at that time, Congress reacted in 1887 by adopting the INTERSTATE COMMERCE ACT, the first affirmative federal regulation of land transportation.

Three years later, in response to a similar public reaction against uncontrolled monopolies, Congress enacted the SHERMAN ANTITRUST ACT, which prohibited combinations that restrained or monopolized interstate and foreign trade or commerce. The Court easily upheld the applicability of the statute to interstate railroads, but, amazingly, by a vote of 8–1, held the act inapplicable to the Sugar Trust which combined all the sugar refiners in the United States. UNITED STATES V. E. C. KNIGHT CO. (1895) held that such a combination concerned only manufacture and production, and not "commerce," as the act (and, presumably, the Constitution) used the word. This ruling left the country remediless against national monopolies of manufacturers. Since interstate manufacturers are of course engaged in interstate trade—selling, buying, and shipping—as well as manufacture, this was a strange decision. It was soon devitalized, though not expressly OVERRULED, in SWIFT & COMPANY V. UNITED STATES (1905), STANDARD OIL COMPANY V. UNITED STATES (1911), and UNITED STATES V.

AMERICAN TOBACCO COMPANY (1911), which similarly involved combinations of manufacturers.

In a number of cases the Court upheld congressional regulation of interstate transportation for noncommercial reasons. Federal statutes forbidding the interstate sale of lottery tickets, the interstate transportation of women for immoral purposes, stolen motor vehicles, diseased cattle which might range across state lines, misbranded food and drugs, and firearms were all held valid, usually without much question. The effect was to establish that the commerce clause applied to things or persons moving across state lines, whether or not they had anything to do with trade or commerce in the usual sense. (See NATIONAL POLICE POWER.) This conclusion was consistent with Marshall's original definition of commerce as intercourse in *Gibbons v. Ogden*.

The Court's narrow approach to the commerce power in the early twentieth century was demonstrated by its invalidation in 1908 of a law creating a WORKER'S COMPENSATION system for all railroad employees, because it included those doing intrastate shop and clerical work, and a law prohibiting railroads from discharging employees because of membership in a labor organization. (See EMPLOYERS' LIABILITY CASES; ADAIR V. UNITED STATES.) In HAMMER V. DAGENHART (1918) the Court even held that Congress could not prohibit the interstate transportation of child-made goods because the prohibition's purpose was to prevent child labor in manufacturing plants within the states.

Decisions other than the monopoly cases during the same period recognized that the congressional commerce power could apply to intrastate transactions that had an effect upon or relation to interstate commerce. Although strikes blocking interstate shipments from manufacturing plants were found to affect interstate commerce only indirectly, the result was different when an intent to restrain interstate commerce was found, or when a SECONDARY BOYCOTT extended to other states. (See LOEWE V. LAWLOR.) Intrastate trains were held subject to federal safety regulations because of the danger to interstate trains on the same tracks. Intrastate freight rates were held subject to federal control when a competitive relationship to interstate rates or a general effect on all rail rates could be shown. (See SHREVEPORT DOCTRINE.) In 1930 the Court sustained the application of the Railway Labor Act to clerks performing intrastate work so as to protect the right to COLLECTIVE BARGAINING and thereby avert strikes disrupting interstate commerce, contrary to the *Adair* decision in 1908.

Perhaps of greatest significance were cases sustaining federal regulation of the stockyards and the Chicago Board of Trade which, even though located in a single city, were found to control interstate prices for agricultural products. (See STAFFORD V. WALLACE.) The Court was not disturbed by the fact that the sales of grain futures which had such an effect were often completely local, since most of them were not followed by any shipments of physical products.

Thus by 1930 there were lines of cases saying that the federal power did not extend to business activity occurring in a single state, and other cases holding the contrary where some kinds of relationship to interstate commerce were shown.

The Great Depression running from 1929 through the 1930s brought the nation its severest economic crisis. Inaction during HERBERT HOOVER's administration proved ineffective and left thirteen million persons unemployed, prices and wages dropping in a self-perpetuating spiral, and banks, railroads, and many other businesses insolvent. The amount of revenue freight carried by railroad, a fair measure of the quantity of interstate commerce, had fallen by fifty-one percent. The public expected FRANKLIN D. ROOSEVELT, who took office in March 1933, to do something about the Depression. Although no one was sure what would work—and no one is yet quite sure what, if anything, did work—the President and Congress tried. Obviously the economy could not be restored by states acting separately. Only measures taken on a national scale could possibly be effective.

To stop the downward spiral in wages and prices, and to increase employment by limiting the number of hours a person could work, MAXIMUM HOURS AND MINIMUM WAGES were prescribed for industry generally, not merely for employees in interstate commerce. Collective bargaining was made mandatory, and protected against employer interference. The object was to increase national employment, national purchasing power, and the demand for and consumption of all products, which would benefit employers, employees, and the flow of commodities in interstate commerce. All this was originally sought to be accomplished by the NATIONAL INDUSTRIAL RECOVERY ACT (NIRA), which authorized every industry to prepare a code of competition designed to accomplish the above purposes; the code would become effective and enforceable when approved by the President.

The same statute and the AGRICULTURAL ADJUSTMENT ACT OF 1933 (AAA) attempted to cope with the overproduction of petroleum and agricultural products, which had forced prices down to absurd levels, such as five cents per barrel of crude oil and thirty-seven cents per bushel of wheat. The petroleum code under the NIRA and programs adopted under the AAA provided for the fixing of production quotas for oil producers and farmers.

The two lines of authorities summarized above supported opposing arguments as to the constitutionality of these measures under the commerce clause. For Congress to prescribe wages, hours, and production quotas for factories, farms, and oil wells undoubtedly would regulate intrastate activities, which prior opinions had frequently said were regulable only by the states.

On the other hand, the reasoning of opinions sustaining federal regulation of intrastate features of railroading and the intrastate marketing practices of stockyards and grain exchanges also supported the use of the commerce power to regulate intrastate acts that had an effect upon interstate commerce. The same was true of many of the antitrust cases referred to above. None of the relationships previously found insufficient to support federal regulation had involved general economic effects that halved the flow of interstate trade. But Congress had never sought to regulate the main body of manufacturing, mining, and agricultural production.

In the mid-1930s the Supreme Court included four Justices—WILLIS VAN DEVANTER, JAMES MCREYNOLDS, GEORGE SUTHERLAND, and PIERCE BUTLER—who looked askance at any enlargement of the scope of governmental power over business and who steadily voted against extension of the congressional commerce power, and also voted to invalidate both federal and state regulation under the due process clauses. Chief Justice CHARLES EVANS HUGHES and Justice OWEN J. ROBERTS sometimes voted with these four, while Justices LOUIS D. BRANDEIS, HARLAN FISKE STONE, and BENJAMIN N. CARDOZO usually voted to sustain the legislative judgments as to how to deal with economic problems.

In a series of cases in 1935 and 1936, passing upon the validity of the NIRA, the AAA, and the Guffey Snyder (BITUMINOUS COAL CONSERVATION) ACT regulating the bituminous coal industry, Hughes and Roberts joined the conservative four to hold these acts unconstitutional.

The government had hoped and planned to test the constitutionality of the NIRA in a case involving the nationally integrated petroleum industry, PANAMA REFINING CO. V. RYAN (January 1935). But the Court found it unnecessary to decide the commerce issue in the *Panama* case. Instead, that question came before the Court in SCHECHTER POULTRY CORP. V. UNITED STATES (May 1935), in which the defendant had violated the provisions of the Live Poultry Code with respect to wages and hours and marketing practices of seemingly little consequence. The poultry slaughtered and sold by the defendant had come to New York City from other states, but there was nothing in the record to show that this interstate movement was greatly affected by the practices in question.

The only persuasive argument supporting the constitutionality of the Poultry Code was that the depressed state of the entire economy and of interstate commerce in general could be remedied only by increasing national purchasing power, and that prescribing minimum wages and maximum hours for all employees, whether or not in interstate industries, was a reasonable method of accomplishing that purpose. None of the Justices was willing to go that far. Indeed, the opinion of Chief Justice Hughes for the Court and the concurring opinion of Justice Cardozo emphasized as a principal defect in the argument that it would extend federal power to all business, interstate or intrastate. The fact that little would be left to exclusive state control, rather than the magnitude of the effect on interstate commerce from a national perspective, was treated as decisive. On the same day, in RAILROAD RETIREMENT BOARD V. ALTON, an act establishing a retirement program for railroad employees was held, by a vote of 5–4, not to be within the federal commerce power.

In theory, the *Schechter* decision left open the power of Congress to regulate production in major interstate industries such as petroleum or coal. But that opening, if it existed, seemed to be closed by two decisions in 1936. Because of the foreseeable risks from reliance on the commerce power, Congress had utilized the taxing power to "persuade" farmers to limit the production of crops in order to halt the collapse of farm prices. In UNITED STATES V. BUTLER (1936), over Justice Stone's vigorous dissent, six Justices, speaking through Justice Roberts and including Chief Justice Hughes, thought it unnecessary to determine whether this legislative scheme came within the ENUMERATED POWERS of Congress. The majority avoided this inquiry by concluding that the law intruded upon the area of production reserved to the states by the TENTH AMENDMENT, which reserves to the states or the people "the powers not delegated to the United States." The Court invoked the same theory a few months later in CARTER V. CARTER COAL COMPANY (1936) to invalidate the Guffey Act's regulation of wages, hours, and collective bargaining in the coal industry. Although the evidence submitted in a long trial proved indisputably the obvious fact that coal strikes could and did halt substantially all interstate commerce moving by rail, as most commerce then did, five Justices, speaking through Justice Sutherland, found decisive not the magnitude of an effect on interstate commerce but whether the effect was immediate, without an intervening causal factor. Even Chief Justice Hughes concurred to this extent, although not in other parts of the majority opinion. Only Justices Brandeis, Stone, and Cardozo challenged the reasoning of the majority.

The *Butler* and *Carter* cases made it plain—or so it seemed—that the Constitution as construed by the Court completely barred the federal government from endeavoring to resolve the national economic problems which called for control of intrastate transactions at the production or manufacturing stage. As an economic matter, individual states were unable to set standards for their own industries that were in competition with producers in other states. The result was that in the United States no government could take action deemed necessary to deal with such matters no matter how crippling their effect upon the national economy might be.

In early 1937 the same type of collective bargaining regulation which the *Carter* case had stricken for the coal industry was on its way to the Supreme Court in the first cases under the WAGNER (NATIONAL LABOR RELATIONS) ACT of 1935. That statute by its terms applied to unfair labor practices that burdened or obstructed interstate commerce or tended to lead to a labor dispute that had such an effect. The courts of appeals, following the *Carter* case, had held that the act could not constitutionally reach a steel manufacturing company, a trailer manufacturer, and a small clothing manufacturer.

Three days before the arguments in these cases in the Supreme Court were to commence, President Roosevelt, who had recently been reelected by a tremendous majority, announced a plan to add up to six new Justices to the Supreme Court, one for each Justice over seventy years of age, purportedly for the purpose of providing younger judges who could enable the Court to keep up with its workload. The Court and many others vigorously opposed the plan. Two months later, in the WAGNER ACT CASES (1937), Chief Justice Hughes and Justice Roberts joined Justices Brandeis, Stone, and Cardozo to sustain the applicability of the National Labor Relations Act to the three manufacturers. The evidence as to the effect of their labor disputes upon interstate commerce was obviously much weaker than that presented in the *Carter* case as to the entire bituminous coal industry. Within the next few months, Justices Van Devanter and Sutherland retired, to be succeeded by Senator HUGO L. BLACK and Solicitor General STANLEY F. REED, and the court-packing plan gradually withered away, even though for a long time President Roosevelt refused to abandon it. No one can be certain whether the plan influenced the Chief Justice and Justice Roberts, but many persons thought the facts spoke for themselves.

Chief Justice Hughes's opinion for the Court in *National Labor Relations Board v. Jones & Laughlin Steel Corp.* (1937) flatly declared that practices in productive industry could have a sufficient effect upon interstate commerce to justify federal regulation under the commerce clause. The test was to be "practical," based on "actual experience." The reasoning of the *Carter* and *Butler* cases was repudiated, although the majority opinion did not say so.

In 1938 a revised AGRICULTURAL ADJUSTMENT ACT and a new FAIR LABOR STANDARDS ACT were enacted. Under the former, the secretary of agriculture, after obtaining the necessary approval of two-thirds of the tobacco growers in a referendum, prescribed marketing quotas determining the maximum quantity of tobacco each grower could sell. Although the practical effect was to limit what would be produced, the object was to stabilize prices by keeping an excessive supply off the market. In *Mulford v. Smith* (1939), the Court, speaking through Justice Roberts, found that because interstate and intrastate sales of tobacco were commingled at the auction warehouses where tobacco was sold, Congress clearly had power to limit the amount marketed by each farmer. HAMMER V. DAGENHART, UNITED STATES V. BUTLER, and the Tenth Amendment were mentioned only in the dissenting opinion of Justice McReynolds and Butler.

The Fair Labor Standards Act of 1938 in substance reenacted the minimum wage and maximum hour provision of the NIRA for employees engaged in interstate commerce or the production of goods for such commerce, and also forbade the shipment in interstate commerce of goods produced under the proscribed labor conditions. The minimum wage then prescribed was twenty-five cents per hour. The prevailing wage in the lumber industry in the South ranged from ten cents to twenty-seven and a half cents per hour, which made it difficult for employers paying more than the lowest amount to compete. A case involving a Georgia sawmill (UNITED STATES V. DARBY LUMBER COMPANY) came to the Supreme Court late in 1940, and was decided in early 1941 after Justice Butler had died and Justice McReynolds had retired. By that time Justices FELIX FRANKFURTER and WILLIAM O. DOUGLAS had replaced Cardozo and Brandeis, and Justice FRANK MURPHY had succeeded Butler.

The Supreme Court, speaking unanimously through Justice Stone, upheld the statute. The Court held that Congress had the power to exclude from interstate commerce goods that were not produced in accordance with prescribed standards, and to prescribe minimum wages and maximum hours for employees producing goods which would move in interstate commerce. Overruling HAMMER V. DAGENHART, the Court declared that the power of Congress to determine what restrictions should be imposed upon interstate commerce did not exclude regulations whose object was to control aspects of industrial production. The Court invoked the interpretation of the NECESSARY AND PROPER CLAUSE in MCCULLOCH V. MARYLAND (1819): the commerce power extended not merely to the regulation of interstate commerce but also "to those activities intrastate which so affect interstate commerce or the exercise of the power of Congress over it as to make regulation of them appropriate means to the attainment of a legitimate end, the exercise of the granted power of Congress to regulate interstate commerce." The emphasis was not on direct or indirect effects, a judge-made concept not tied to constitutional language, or even to the substantiality of an effect. The Court found it sufficient that the establishment of federal minimum labor standards was a reasonable means of suppressing interstate competition based on substandard labor conditions. In KIRSCHBAUM V. WALLING (1942) the Court broadly construed the commerce clause to make the Fair Labor Standards Act apply to service and maintenance employees who were not directly engaged in the production of goods for commerce but in the performance of services ancillary to such production.

A year and a half after *Darby*, in WICKARD V. FILBURN (1942), a unanimous Court, speaking through Justice ROBERT H. JACKSON, upheld marketing quotas under the amended Agricultural Adjustment Act, even though they limited the amount of wheat allowed to be consumed on the farm as well as the amount sold. The object was to reduce the supply of wheat in order to increase the price—and the total supply of wheat, including the twenty percent of the crop consumed on the farm for feed or seed, not only was in at least potential competition with wheat in commerce but had a substantial influence on prices and market conditions for the wheat crop throughout the nation. Reviewing the prior law, and explicitly noting the cases that were being disapproved—*E. C. Knight, Employers' Liability, Hammer v. Dagenhart, Railroad Retirement Board, Schechter*, and *Carter*—Justice Jackson's opinion laid to rest the prior controlling effect attributed to nomenclature such as "production" and "indirect," as distinct from the actual economic effect of an activity upon interstate commerce. Even if an "activity be local" and not itself commerce, "it may still, whatever its nature, be reached by Congress if it exerts a substantial economic effect on interstate commerce." The proper point of reference was "what was necessary and proper to the exercise by Congress of the granted power." The Court further declared, as it had in *Darby*, that the magnitude of the contribution of each individual to the EFFECT ON COMMERCE was not the criterion but the total contribution of persons similarly situated, which meant that the insignificant effect of the amount consumed on any particular farm was not decisive.

In 1944 and 1946, in cases holding that Congress could regulate the insurance industry and public utility holding companies (UNITED STATES V. SOUTH-EASTERN UNDERWRITERS ASSOCIATION, 1944; *North American Co. v. Securities and Exchange Commisssion*, 1946), the Court broadly summarized the teachings of its prior cases beginning with the words of Chief Justice Marshall in *Gibbons v. Ogden*:

> Commerce is interstate . . . when it "concerns more States than one." . . . The power granted is the power to legislate concerning transactions which, reaching across State boundaries, affect the people of more states than one;—to govern affairs which the individual states, with their limited territorial jurisdictions, are not fully capable of

governing. This federal power to determine the rules of intercourse across state lines was essential to weld a loose confederacy into a single, indivisible Nation; its continued existence is equally essential to the welfare of that Nation.

Since these decisions there has been no doubt that Congress possesses full power to regulate all aspects of the integrated national economy. The few commerce clause cases of importance since that time concerned the use of the commerce power for noncommercial purposes: to combat racial SEGREGATION, crime, and environmental problems.

In *Katzenbach v. McClung* (1964) the Court sustained the provisions of the CIVIL RIGHTS ACT OF 1964 prohibiting RACIAL DISCRIMINATION by restaurants serving interstate travelers or obtaining a substantial portion of their food from outside the state, both because discrimination had a highly restrictive effect upon interstate travel by Negroes and because it reduced the amount of food moving in interstate commerce (which seems quite doubtful). (See also HEART OF ATLANTA MOTEL V. UNITED STATES.)

PEREZ V. UNITED STATES (1971) upheld the application of the federal loanshark statute to purely intrastate extortion on the ground that Congress had rationally found that organized crime was interstate in character, obtaining a substantial part of its income from loansharking which to a substantial extent was carried on in interstate and foreign commerce or through instrumentalities of such commerce. Unmentioned rationales might have been the difficulty of proving that loansharking in a particular case had an interstate connection and the belief that it was necessary to prohibit all loansharking as an appropriate means of prohibiting those acts that did affect interstate commerce.

In *Hodel v. Virginia Surface Mining and Reclamation Association* (1981) the Court unanimously upheld federal regulation of surface or strip coal mining operations, rejecting the contention that this was merely a regulation of land use not committed to the federal government. There had been legislative findings that surface coal mining causes water pollution and flooding of navigable streams and that it harms productive farm land and hardwood forests in many parts of the country. The Court found, following *Darby*, that this was a means of preventing destructive interstate competition favoring the producers with the lowest mining and reclamation standards, that Congress can regulate the conditions under which goods shipped in interstate commerce are produced when that in itself affects interstate commerce, and that the commerce power permits federal regulation of activities causing air or water pollution, or other environmental hazards that may have effects in more than one state.

The more recent decisions, which in some respects

went far beyond the classical statements as to the modern scope of the commerce power in *Darby* and *Wickard v. Filburn,* were expected and accepted with little comment or concern. The country now appears to recognize that the national government should have and does have power under the commerce clause to deal with problems that do not limit themselves to individual states—as Chief Justice Marshall had declared in 1824, though doubtless with no idea of how far that principle would eventually be carried.

The enlargement of the commerce power since 1789 is attributable not to the predilections of judges but to such inventions as steamboats, railroads, motor vehicles, airplanes, the telegraph, telephone, radio, and television. When the nation was young, composed mainly of farms and small towns, there was little interstate trade, except by water or near state lines. Now persons and goods can cross the continent in less time than a traveler in 1789 would have taken to reach a town thirty miles away. Business and the economy have adjusted to these changes. Somewhat more slowly than the people and Congress, the Supreme Court has recognized that an integrated national economy is predominantly interstate or related to interstate commerce, and must be subject to governmental control on a national basis.

The expansion of the concept of interstate commerce and of the subjects which Congress can regulate under the commerce power was not accompanied by a contraction of the powers of the states. Only those state laws that discriminate against or unduly burden interstate commerce are forbidden.

ROBERT L. STERN
(1986)

(SEE ALSO: *Dormant Commerce Clause.*)

Bibliography

CORWIN, EDWARD S. 1959 *The Commerce Power versus States Rights.* Princeton, N.J.: Princeton University Press.

FRANKFURTER, FELIX 1937 *The Commerce Clause under Marshall, Taney and Waite.* Chapel Hill: University of North Carolina Press.

GAVIT, BERNARD C. 1932 *Commerce Clause of the United States Constitution.* Bloomington, Ind.: Principia Press.

STERN, ROBERT L. 1934 That Commerce Which Concerns More States Than One. *Harvard Law Review* 47:1335–1366.

—— 1946 The Commerce Clause and the National Economy, 1933–1946. *Harvard Law Review* 59:645–693, 883–947.

—— 1951 The Problems of Yesteryear—Commerce and Due Process. *Vanderbilt Law Review* 4:446–468.

—— 1955 The 1955 Ross Prize Essay: The Scope of the Phrase "Interstate Commerce." *American Bar Association Journal* 41:823–826, 871–874.

—— 1973 The Commerce Clause Revisited—The Federalization of Interstate Crime. *Arizona Law Review* 15:271–285.

COMMERCE COURT

In 1910 Congress established the Commerce Court, with the JURISDICTION, formerly held by the district courts and courts of appeals, to review decisions of the Interstate Commerce Commission (ICC). Although the ICC acquiesced in the establishment of the new court, acceptance soon turned to opposition. The Commerce Court reversed the ICC's decisions in a number of important cases, and congressional Democrats saw the court as a threat to the program of railroad regulation. Two 1912 bills to abolish the court were vetoed by President WILLIAM HOWARD TAFT. In 1913, a third abolition bill received President WOODROW WILSON's blessing.

The creation of specialized federal courts is often proposed but not often enacted. The short, unhappy life of the Commerce Court is regularly offered as a cautionary tale.

KENNETH L. KARST
(1986)

Bibliography

DIX, GEORGE E. 1964 The Death of the Commerce Court: A Study in Institutional Weakness. *American Journal of Legal History* 8:238–260.

COMMERCIAL SPEECH

Until 1976 "commercial speech"—a vague category encompassing advertisements, invitations to deal, credit or financial reports, prospectuses, and the like—was subject to broad regulatory authority, with little or no protection from the FIRST AMENDMENT. The early decisions, epitomized by *Valentine v. Chrestensen* (1942), followed the then characteristic judicial approach of defining certain subject-matter categories of expression as wholly outside the scope of First Amendment protection. Under this TWO-LEVEL THEORY, a "definitional" mode of First Amendment adjudication, commercial speech was considered to be, along with OBSCENITY, and LIBEL, outside First Amendment protection.

When facing combinations of unprotected commercial speech and protected political speech in subsequent cases, the Court made First Amendment protection turn on the primary purpose of the advertisement. Thus, in MURDOCK V. PENNSYLVANIA (1943), the Court struck down an ordinance requiring solicitors of orders for goods to get a license and pay a fee as it applied to Jehovah's Witnesses who sold religious pamphlets while seeking religious converts. On the other hand, in *Bread v. Alexandria* (1951) the Court held that a door-to-door salesman of national magazine subscriptions was subject to a town ordinance barring such sales techniques, because his primary purpose was to sell magazines rather than to disseminate ideas.

The "primary purpose" test unraveled in NEW YORK TIMES V. SULLIVAN (1964), more prominently known for another rejection of the definitional approaches in its holding that defamation is not beyond First Amendment protection. In *Sullivan*, the *New York Times* had printed an allegedly defamatory advertisement soliciting funds for civil rights workers. Although the advertisement's primary purpose was, arguably, to raise money, the Court held that it was protected by the First Amendment because it "communicated information, expressed opinion, recited grievances, protested claimed abuses, and sought financial support on behalf of a movement whose existence and objectives are matters of the highest public interest and concern."

Recent decisions have gone well beyond *Sullivan* and moved advertising and other commercial speech—political or not—within the protection of the First Amendment. In the leading case, VIRGINIA PHARMACY BOARD V. VIRGINIA CITIZENS CONSUMER COUNCIL (1976), the Court struck down a state ban on prescription drug price advertising. The Court rejected the state's "highly paternalistic approach," preferring a system in which "people will perceive their own best interests if only they are well enough informed, and that the best means to that end is to open the channels of communication rather than to close them." The Court cautioned, however, that because untruthful speech has never been protected for its own sake government may take effective action against false and misleading advertisements. And it indicated a greater scope for regulating false or misleading commercial speech than is permitted in relation to false political statements, such as defamations of public officials, because advertising is more easily verifiable and is less likely to be "chilled" by regulation because it is a commercial necessity.

Virginia Pharmacy Board fixed the principle that advertising may be controlled when it is false, misleading, or takes undue advantage of its audience; but the case left open the issue whether whole categories of commercial speech deemed inherently misleading or difficult to police can be suppressed. This issue divided the Supreme Court with respect to lawyers' advertising, when a narrow majority extended First Amendment protection to price advertising of routine legal services, rejecting the dissenters' claim that the complex and variegated nature of legal services gave lawyers' advertising a high potential for deception and impeded effective regulation of particular deceptions. However, the Court held that "ambulance chasing"—in-person solicitation of accident victims for pecuniary gain—could be barred entirely because of its potential for deception and overbearing.

Where regulation of commercial expression is not directed at potential deception but intended to advance other interests such as aesthetics or conservation, the Supreme Court has followed a relatively permissive approach to state regulatory interests, while becoming hopelessly fragmented about the First Amendment principles that ought to govern. Thus, in *Metromedia, Inc. v. San Diego* (1981) a shifting majority coalition of Justices made clear that commercial billboards could be entirely banned in a city for aesthetic or traffic safety reasons. Recent decisions, following CENTRAL HUDSON GAS V. PUBLIC SERVICE COMMISSION (1980), have fashioned a four-part test to appraise the validity of restrictions on commercial speech. Protection will not be extended to commercial speech that is, on the whole, misleading or that encourages unlawful activity. Even protected commercial speech may be regulated if the state has a substantial interest, if the regulation directly advances that interest, and if the regulation is no broader than necessary to effectuate the state's interest. The elastic properties of this four-part test in actual application have generated considerable disarray within the Supreme Court.

The commercial speech decisions of the BURGER COURT have made clear that freedom of expression principles extend beyond political and religious expression, protecting not only the MARKETPLACE OF IDEAS but expression in the marketplace itself. Second, in affirming relatively broad regulatory power over commercial speech, even though it is deemed to be protected by the First Amendment, the Court has reinforced the notion that the First Amendment extends different levels of protection to different types of speech. The commercial speech decisions thus lend support to Justice ROBERT H. JACKSON'S OBITER DICTUM in KOVACS V. COOPER (1949) that under the First Amendment each type and medium of expression "is a law unto itself."

BENNO C. SCHMIDT, JR.
(1986)

Bibliography

JACKSON, THOMAS H. and JEFFRIES, J. C., JR. 1979 Commercial Speech: Economic Due Process and the First Amendment. *Virginia Law Review* 65:1–41.

WEINBERG, JONATHON 1982 Constitutional Protection of Commercial Speech. *Columbia Law Review* 82:720–750.

COMMERCIAL SPEECH
(Update 1)

For most of this century commercial speech was regarded as outside the scope of the FIRST AMENDMENT. Indeed, the Supreme Court so held in 1942. But in 1976 the Supreme Court reversed course in the case of VIRGINIA STATE BOARD OF PHARMACY V. VIRGINIA CITIZENS' CONSUMER COUNCIL. There the Court held that Virginia had violated the First Amendment by prohibiting pharmacists from advertising prices of prescription drugs. The Court was unpersuaded that the state's fear that product advertising would lower the "professional" character of the practice of pharmacy outweighed the First Amendment interest in open competition of information and ideas, even about products of commerce.

In 1980 in CENTRAL HUDSON GAS ELECTRIC CORPORATION V. PUBLIC SERVICE COMMISSION, the Court announced a four-part test for deciding when commercial speech is entitled to First Amendment protection. To determine whether commercial speech is protected, the Court held, it must be found that the speech concerns a lawful activity and is not misleading, that "the regulation directly advances the governmental interest asserted," and that the regulation "is not more extensive than is necessary to serve that interest." Applying that standard to the case before it, the Court invalidated a Public Service Commission regulation that prohibited electrical utilities from engaging in promotional advertising. While the Court acknowledged that the commission's purpose was legitimate (namely, to conserve energy), the commission's case failed in the Court's view because there was no showing that this legitimate purpose could not be achieved by regulation less intrusive on First Amendment interests.

In recent years the Supreme Court has seemed to retreat from the *Central Hudson* trend of extending broader First Amendment rights when it comes to protection of commercial speech. In a major decision in 1986 in POSADAS DE PUERTO RICO ASSOCIATES V. TOURISM COMPANY, the Court upheld a Puerto Rican government regulation that forbade casino advertising directed at Puerto Rican residents; advertising aimed at tourists, on the other hand, was permitted. Though casino gambling was legal in Puerto Rico, and though the advertising prohibited was neither misleading nor fraudulent, the Court held that the government's interest in avoiding the debilitating effects of gambling on the internal culture of Puerto Rico was "substantial," that the restriction "directly advanced" that goal, and that the legislature could reasonably conclude that residents would "be induced by widespread advertising to engage in such potentially harmful conduct." The Court refused to require Puerto Rico to use means other than

an advertising prohibition to achieve its goal of discouraging gambling by residents. The Court reasoned that, because casino gambling could be prohibited entirely, that power "includes the lesser power to ban advertising of casino gambling."

The *Posadas* case seems a step backward from the direction taken in *Virginia Pharmacy* and *Central Hudson* for two reasons. First, it appears to signal that the Court will not demand that governments demonstrate the inadequacy of nonspeech restrictive measures in controlling supposedly harmful effects of commercial speech. While *Central Hudson* required the state to "demonstrat[e] that its interest in conservation cannot be protected adequately by more limited regulation," *Posadas* was satisfied by the assumption that the legislature "could" conclude, as it "apparently did," that alternative remedies were insufficient. The Court explicitly articulated this limitation in the *Central Hudson* formula in BOARD OF TRUSTEES OF STATE UNIVERSITY OF NEW YORK V. FOX (1989).

Second, the Court's reasoning in *Posadas* that the state's potential power to forbid gambling includes the power to regulate the speech itself even when gambling is not prohibited raises serious questions about the continuing strength of earlier decisions protective of commercial speech. In *Virginia Pharmacy*, for example, although prescription drugs presumably could have been banned by Virginia, that fact did not stop the Court from holding that a ban on advertising for such drugs was unconstitutional.

The most that can be said at the present time about the commercial speech doctrine is that it is not yet on a consistent track, although some level of First Amendment protection for commercial speech is now firmly established.

LEE C. BOLLINGER
(1992)

COMMERCIAL SPEECH
(Update 2)

Since 1976, the Supreme Court has reviewed FIRST AMENDMENT challenges to regulations affecting "commercial speech" under a standard of intermediate scrutiny. To meet that standard, established in CENTRAL HUDSON GAS AND ELECTRIC CORP. V. PUBLIC SERVICE COMMISSION (1980), a law dictating or restricting the manner, extent, or content of commercial matter must be a law for which a substantial showing can be furnished of actual (rather than merely speculative) need, and of adequate justification in light of the kind and extent of regulation or restriction it enacts.

Protecting consumers from false or misleading information in commercial representations is a typical interest of sufficiently substantial weight to count heavily in this area, as the opinions of the Court readily admit. Regulations requiring various disclosures such as a product's actual price, ingredients, and full effects (including its effects on the environment, insofar as these, too, may be regarded as important for the consumer to understand) generally tend to be sustained in the courts. The commercial speaker may be constrained to make far more elaborate disclosures in his representations than he might wish to do, or than others not subject to the *Central Hudson* test (for example, candidates for public office) can be compelled to declare. He may likewise be held far more strictly responsible for the accuracy of his affirmative representations in what he presents in his publicity for his product or services, consistent with *Central Hudson*. Subject to meeting the other requirements of the *Central Hudson* test, regulations competently drawn to serve these objectives tend not to be intrusively second-guessed in the courts. It is left quite substantially to the discretion of legislative bodies and to specialized regulatory agencies (such as the Food and Drug Administration and the Federal Trade Commission), moreover, to determine the particular boundary lines—of how much disclosure or in what detail, and of what kind of affirmative claims may or may not be asserted, and on the strength of what measure of empirical support—such as the regulatory agency may require.

In contrast, a restriction severely limiting the time, place, or manner of advertising a particular product or service, not to protect the public from anything identifiably either false or misleading in such commercial material, but rather to protect a competitor's market (whether of the same good or a rival product) is far less likely to be sustained in the courts under the *Central Hudson* test. It may fail at the first step. For insulating certain producers or products from losing market hegemony or market share to competing goods, of whatever importance it may be asserted to have in the minds of legislators, is generally not regarded by the Court as a suitable justification for biasing the manner and extent to which the public receives equally accurate information respecting those respective products, such as each may be.

To be sure, insofar as the legislature may decide to favor certain producers over others (such as dairy farmers producing butter over producers of equally nutritious, lower-cost nondairy substitutes), it may do so with little First Amendment hindrance, virtually as it may choose to do by other means, for example, by imposing a higher tax on the legislatively disfavored product or by providing some kind of price support for the favored product as it may see fit to do. Still, the Court has suggested, it may not by the same gesture attempt to manipulate consumer response by the different technique of biasing what the public may merely learn about each product by denying an equal freedom of (truthful, accurate) commercial communication. Proceeding in this information-biasing way, in the view of the Court, is generally foreclosed by the First Amendment itself. While some critics have wondered over the point, the distinction for the Court is quite clear. The legislature may "fix the fight" between product rivals to a very considerable extent, even by tying one boxer's legs or arms (as imposing a nearly prohibitive tax upon his product may do), but yet may not do so by putting a gag in one fighter's mouth, stopping his breath.

The First Amendment is quintessentially concerned with gags on speech. When gags are used, the burden of justification on government under *Central Hudson* tends at once to rise, even as it sharply does as in the more ordinary instance of political or social advocacy speech. A compelling justification must be provided, and insulating preferred producers of preferred products from having to contend with comparative claims, no less accurate or truthful than their own, is unlikely to suffice.

As an additional consideration pursuant to the *Central Hudson* test, even more conventional regulations (including those discussed earlier respecting what must be disclosed in commercial material in order to make the advertisement permissible), must in each instance have a reasonably close fit to the problem to which they are allegedly addressed. This general requirement of "close fit," in turn, has two matching elements or bookends. On the one side, the law enacted to meet an alleged need must meet it in substantial (not insubstantial) fashion, that is, in a fashion likely to make a real and significant difference rather than very little difference at all. On the other side, the restriction or regulation must not extend further than can be fairly defended in terms of the need it is alleged to be appropriate to meet.

In this latter respect, current commercial speech DOCTRINE has picked up protection from what has been elsewhere described as the First Amendment legislative vice of OVERBREADTH, albeit not yet with all of the consequences that that doctrine has meant in its aplication to laws affecting political, rather than commercial, speech. Specifically, a law on its face prohibiting a greater range of political utterance than the First Amendment will tolerate a legislature to prohibit may risk the fate of being held unconstitutional on its face, solely on that account. It may be impugned even at the behest of one with respect to whom there is no question that his conduct was not merely well within the coverage of the statute, but was conduct itself not protected by the First Amendment. Even so, he is nonetheless able to escape any sanction for his conduct by having the statute declared "void on its face," fatally tainted by its "overbreadth" per se.

Here, however, there is this significant difference. An equivalently "overly broad" restriction on commercial speech may not be as easily impugned—and probably cannot by a party whose conduct it clearly fits, and as to whom there is no First Amendment problem in its application to him. Rather, insofar as the commercial speech restriction may go too far, it may await a person with better STANDING to be heard on that complaint. So, in this respect, the extent to which commercial speech may claim First Amendment protection remains significantly short of that accorded political or social advocacy speech.

Even so, overall the now-revised *Central Hudson* test has somewhat more First Amendment "bite" than some of its earlier applications by the Court implied. Moreover, this is especially true as it bears on LEGISLATION or regulations that seek to suppress commercial information, rather than to assure its accuracy and completeness, or rather than merely to channel it in various ways. Thus, even as some of the preceding review has already suggested, recent decisions of the Court strongly suggest that where the regulation is one that reflects a desire more to keep the public "underinformed" of certain goods or services than merely to insure it is not deceived or misled, the burden on the state to sustain its commercial speech restrictions may be stepped up to a significant degree. Indeed, suppression of advertisements for products or services a legislature may not wish the public to have brought to their attention ranks hardly better with several members of the current Court than suppression of advertisements for candidates, ballot issues, or for particular books or films a legislature would as readily suppress and keep from public attention, were it free to do so (which it is not). Thus, while legislature authority to channel commercial speech is doubtless greater than its power to direct or channel political speech, yet it is very far from being absolute.

And, in this respect, the Court's suggestion in POSADAS DE PUERTO RICO ASSOCIATES V. TOURISM COMPANY (1986), that a legislature may totally forbid any advertising by any business it would otherwise have the power to forbid to exist or compete at all, is no longer valid. Not only has a majority of the Court now squarely held against that proposition (rather, any restriction must meet the *Central Hudson* test at a minimum), but Chief Justice WILLIAM H. REHNQUIST, who first offered it as an alternative holding in *Posadas*, has also now laid it aside. (See *44 Liquormart, Inc. v. Rhode Island*, 1996; *Greater New Orleans Broadcasting Ass'n v. United States*, 1999.) Commercial speech has thus achieved a strengthened intermediate level of First Amendment protection more robust than before its assimilation began, a mere quarter of a century ago, in *Virginia State Board of Pharmacy v. Virginia Citizens Counsumer Council* (1976).

WILLIAM W. VAN ALSTYNE
(2000)

COMMITTEE FOR PUBLIC EDUCATION AND RELIGIOUS LIBERTY v. NYQUIST
413 U.S. 752 (1973)
SLOAN v. LEMON
413 U.S. 825 (1973)

These cases, said Justice LEWIS F. POWELL in his opinion for a 6–3 SUPREME COURT, "involve an intertwining of societal and constitutional issues of the greatest importance." After LEMON V. KURTZMAN (1971), New York State sought to aid private sectarian schools and the parents of children in them by various financial plans purporting to maintain the SEPARATION OF CHURCH AND STATE. Avowing concern for the health and safety of the children, the state provided direct financial grants to "qualifying" schools for maintenance costs. But as Justice Powell observed, "virtually all" were Roman Catholic schools, and the grants had the inevitable effect of subsidizing religious education, thus abridging the FIRST AMENDMENT's prohibition against an ESTABLISHMENT OF RELIGION. New York, as well as Pennsylvania, also provided for the reimbursement of tuition paid by parents who sent their children to nonpublic sectarian schools; New York also had an optional tax relief plan. The Court found that the reimbursement plans constituted grants whose effect was the same as grants made directly to the institutions, thereby advancing religion. The tax benefit plan had the same unconstitutional result, because the deduction, like the grant, involved an expense to the state for the purpose of religious education. The Court distinguished outright tax exemptions of church property for reasons given in WALZ V. TAX COMMISSION (1970). By distinguishing *Nyquist* in MUELLER V. ALLEN (1983), the Court sustained the constitutionality of a tax benefit plan that aided the parents of children in nonpublic sectarian schools.

LEONARD W. LEVY
(1986)

COMMITTEE FOR PUBLIC EDUCATION AND RELIGIOUS LIBERTY v. REGAN
444 U.S. 646 (1980)

A New York statute directed the reimbursement to nonpublic schools of costs incurred by them in complying with certain state-mandated requirements, including the administration of standardized tests. The participation of church-related schools in this program was challenged as an unconstitutional ESTABLISHMENT OF RELIGION, but the Supreme Court rejected the challenge.

Justice BYRON R. WHITE, writing for a narrowly divided Court, noted that a previous New York law authorizing reimbursement for test services performed by nonpublic schools had been found unconstitutional in *Levitt v. Committee* (1973). However, the new statute, unlike its predecessor, provided for state audit of school financial records to insure that public monies were used only for secular purposes.

Justice HARRY BLACKMUN, with whom Justices WILLIAM J. BRENNAN and THURGOOD MARSHALL joined, dissented. Blackmun stressed that New York's program involved direct payments by the state to a school engaged in a religious enterprise. Justice JOHN PAUL STEVENS also filed a brief dissent.

Committee v. Regan is another illustration of the blurred nature of the line the Court has attempted to draw between permissible and impermissible state support to church-related schools.

RICHARD E. MORGAN
(1986)

COMMON LAW
(Anglo-American)

The common law is a system of principles and rules grounded in universal custom or natural law and developed, articulated, and applied by courts in a process designed for the resolution of individual controversies. In this general sense, the common law is the historic basis of all Anglo-American legal systems. It is also an important element in the origin and plan of the United States Constitution.

Though sometimes characterized as "unwritten" in reference to their ultimate source, the principles and rules of the Anglo-American common law are in fact found in thousands of volumes of written judicial opinions reporting the grounds of decision in countless individual cases adjudicated over the course of centuries. The process that produced this body of law has three important aspects. First, common law principles and rules derive their legitimacy from the adversary process of litigation. They are valid only if they are HOLDINGS, that is, propositions necessary to the resolution of actual controversies. Second, the common law is applied through a characteristic reasoning process that compares the facts of the present case to the facts of earlier cases. The holdings of those earlier cases are PRECEDENTS, which must be followed unless their facts can be distinguished or unless they can be overruled because their grounds are deemed unsound in light of changing social conditions or policy. In the latter situation, or if no existing precedent is applicable, a new rule may be fashioned from the logic of related rules or underlying

principle. Third, the common law is a process in the procedural sense. Litigation is governed by rules designed to shape issues of fact and law so that a case may be fairly and efficiently presented to and decided by the jury, the traditional mode of trial.

The principles and rules of the common law grow and change within this threefold process at the initiative of parties to litigation as they bring forward issues falling outside, or challenging, existing precedents. The common law may also be changed by legislative enactment, but in Anglo-American countries legislation is relied on chiefly to supplement or revise or codify the common law in specific situations.

The Anglo-American common law evolved from decisions of the three great English courts of King's Bench, Common Pleas, and Exchequer, which were firmly established by the end of the thirteenth century. These courts, though created under the royal prerogative, became effectively independent by virtue of their ancient origins and the prestige and life tenure of their judges.

By the time of the AMERICAN REVOLUTION, two strands were apparent in the English common law. The private law, which developed in actions between subjects, included complex DOCTRINES of property, contract, and tort appropriate to a sophisticated landed and commercial society. The public law, product of actions in which the king was a litigant, consisted of rules defining and limiting his political and fiscal prerogatives, defining criminal conduct as a reflection of his role as peacekeeper, and establishing a series of procedural rights accorded to the criminally accused. In the largely unwritten English constitution, Parliament as supreme sovereign had power to alter or abolish even the most fundamental common law rules, but by convention basic governmental institutions and individual rights were ordinarily beyond legislative change.

The English common law had by 1776 been received in the American colonies. The full array of English law books was the source of common law principles and rules, and the courts followed the common law process. Though the colonists argued otherwise, the English view was that colonial reception of the common law was a matter of grace, not right. In legal theory, the colonies, as the king's dominions, were directly governed by the prerogative, free of common law constraints. Colonial governmental powers were expressly granted and defined by charter or statute. King and Parliament, when England's interests demanded, would set aside rights guaranteed by the common law. As the DECLARATION OF INDEPENDENCE shows, the Revolution was in part fought to rectify violations of charter grants of legislative and judicial power and invasions of individual rights such as TRIAL BY JURY and freedom from unreasonable SEARCH AND SEIZURE.

In reaction to the prerevolutionary experience, the people of the United States asserted SOVEREIGNTY through the federal and state constitutions, under which the executive, legislative, and judiciary were separate branches subject to the written FUNDAMENTAL LAW. The constitutions, however, were adopted against a common law backdrop. The states had expressly received the common law, assuming that their courts would develop it through application of the common law process. The federal Constitution contained no express reception provision, but it did authorize Congress to establish federal courts with JURISDICTION over cases arising under federal law and between citizens of diverse citizenship. Once the federal courts were established, important and difficult questions arose concerning their power to develop a FEDERAL COMMON LAW.

The result of two centuries of learned disputation is that today there is little federal common law. The Supreme Court in ERIE RAILROAD V. TOMPKINS (1938) settled the most enduring controversy by holding that in diversity-of-citizenship cases federal courts must apply the common law as though they were courts of the states where they sit, overruling Justice JOSEPH STORY's famous contrary decision in SWIFT V. TYSON (1842). Earlier the Court had concluded, as DUE PROCESS might have required, that there was no FEDERAL COMMON LAW OF CRIMES, even where federal interests were involved. In civil matters affecting federal interests the Court has held that there is no general federal common law, but the federal courts may articulate common law rules to supplement a comprehensive federal statutory scheme or implement an EXCLUSIVE JURISDICTION. These results are consistent with the basic premise of FEDERALISM that the national government is one of limited powers and other powers are reserved to the states, or to the people.

While the federal Constitution did not adopt the common law as a general rule of decision, many of its specific provisions were of common law origin. In its delineation of the SEPARATION OF POWERS, the Constitution incorporated common law limitations upon the prerogative and Parliament which had been honored in England and disregarded in the colonies. The BILL OF RIGHTS, adopted in part because of doubts about the existence and efficacy of a federal common law, codified specific common law procedural rights accorded the criminally accused. It also incorporated common law protections of more fundamental interests, including that basic guarantee of reason and fairness in governmental action, the right to due process of law.

Most important, the common law process has enabled the federal judiciary to attain its intended position in the constitutional plan. Chief Justice JOHN MARSHALL's opinion in MARBURY V. MADISON (1803), asserting judicial power to review legislation and declare it unconstitutional, was founded on the common law obligation of courts to apply all the relevant law, including the Constitution, in deciding cases. A declaration of unconstitutionality in one case is effective in other similar situations because of the force of precedent. In refining *Marbury*'s principle, the Supreme Court more recently has developed the doctrine of JUSTICIABILITY, designed to establish in constitutional cases the existence of a truly adversary CASE OR CONTROVERSY, to which decision of a constitutional issue is necessary. Together, these rules, by proclaiming that the federal courts are confined to the traditional common law judicial role, provide both legitimacy and effectiveness to court enforcement of the Constitution's limits upon the powers of the other branches and the states.

L. KINVIN WROTH
(1986)

Bibliography

GOEBEL, JULIUS, JR. 1971 *Antecedents and Beginnings to 1801.* Volume 1 of *The Oliver Wendell Holmes Devise History of the Supreme Court of the United States.* New York: Macmillan.

LLEWELLYN, KARL N. 1960 *The Common Law Tradition: Deciding Appeals.* Boston: Little, Brown.

PLUCKNETT, THEODORE F. T. (1929) 1956 *A Concise History of the Common Law.* Boston: Little, Brown.

TRIBE, LAURENCE H. 1978 *American Constitutional Law.* Mineola, N.Y.: Foundation Press.

COMMON LAW, CONSTITUTIONAL

See: Constitutional Common Law

COMMON LAW, FEDERAL CIVIL

See: Federal Common Law, Civil

COMMON LAW, FEDERAL CRIMINAL

See: Federal Common Law of Crimes

COMMONWEALTH v. ALGER

See: State Police Power

COMMONWEALTH v. AVES
18 Pickering (Mass.) 193 (1836)

This became the nation's leading case on sojourner slaves. It posed an unprecedented question: can a slave brought temporarily into a free state be restrained of liberty and be removed from the state on the master's return? Chief Justice LEMUEL SHAW rejected the contention that COMITY between the states compelled recognition of the laws of the master's domicile. SLAVERY, Shaw replied, was so odious that only positive local law recognized it. (See SOMERSET'S CASE.) In Massachusetts slavery was unconstitutional. Any nonfugitive slave entering Massachusetts became free because no local law warranted restraint and local laws could prevent involuntary removal.

LEONARD W. LEVY
(1986)

COMMONWEALTH v. CATON
4 Call's (Va.) Reports (1782)

Decided by the highest court of Virginia in 1782, this case is a disputed precedent for the legitimacy of JUDICIAL REVIEW. The state constitution of 1776, which did not empower courts to void enactments in conflict with the constitution, authorized the governor to grant pardons except in impeachment cases. A statute on TREASON deprived the governor of his PARDONING POWER and vested it in the general assembly. Caton, having been sentenced to death for treason, claimed a pardon granted by the lower house, though the upper house refused to concur. The court had only to rule that the pardon was not valid.

Call's unreliable report of the case, a reconstruction made in 1827, indicates that the court considered the constitutionality of the statute on treason and that seven of the eight judges were of the opinion that the court had the power to declare an act of the legislature unconstitutional, though the court unanimously held the act constitutional. In fact, only one of the eight judges ruled the act unconstitutional, one held that it had no power to so rule, and another, GEORGE WYTHE, declared that the court had the power but need not exercise it in this case; he decided that the pardon had no force of law because it was not in conformity with the disputed act, which he found constitutional. A majority of the court, including Chief Justice EDMUND PENDLETON and Chancellor JOHN BLAIR, declined to decide the question whether they had the power to declare an act unconstitutional. Writing to JAMES MADISON a week later, Pendleton reported, "The great Constitutional question . . . was determined . . . by 6 Judges against two, that the Treason Act was not at variance with the Constitution but a proper exercise of the Power reserved to the Legislature by the latter. . . ." Both houses subsequently granted the pardon. The legitimacy of the case as a precedent for judicial review is doubtful.

LEONARD W. LEVY
(1986)

COMMONWEALTH v. JENNISON
(Massachusetts, 1783, Unreported)

In 1781 Quock Walker, a Massachusetts slave, left his master, Nathaniel Jennison, to work as a hired laborer for Seth and John Caldwell. Jennison went to the Caldwell farm, seized Walker, beat him severely, and brought him home where he was locked up.

Three legal cases resulted from this event. In *Walker v. Jennison* (1781) Walker sued his former master for assault and battery. A jury ruled Walker was a free man and awarded him fifty pounds in damages. Jennison then successfully sued the Caldwells for twenty-five pounds for enticing away his "slave property." This decision was overturned by a jury in *Caldwell v. Jennison* (1781). Here attorney LEVI LINCOLN paraphrased arguments from SOMERSET V. STEWART (1772) in a stirring speech against slavery. In 1783 Jennison was convicted under a criminal INDICTMENT for assault and battery against Walker (*Commonwealth v. Jennison*). Chief Justice WILLIAM CUSHING charged the jury that the Massachusetts Constitution of 1780 abolished slavery by declaring "All men are born free and equal. . . ." Although some blacks were held as slaves after these cases, the litigation, known collectively as the "Quock Walker Cases," was instrumental in ending the peculiar institution in Massachusetts.

PAUL FINKELMAN
(1986)

Bibliography

FINKELMAN, PAUL 1981 *An Imperfect Union: Slavery, Federalism, and Comity.* Chapel Hill: University of North Carolina Press.

COMMONWEALTH v. SACCO AND VANZETTI
(Massachusetts, 1921)

On August 23, 1927, the Commonwealth of Massachusetts electrocuted two Italian immigrants, Nicola Sacco and Bartolomeo Vanzetti, for the crimes of armed robbery and murder. The executions stirred angry protest in the United States and throughout the world by millions of people who believed that the two men had been denied a fair trial because of their ethnic background and political opinions.

Sacco and Vanzetti, ALIENS and anarchists who had fled to Mexico to avoid the draft during WORLD WAR I, were arrested in 1920 and quickly brought to trial in Dedham, Massachusetts, for the murder of a paymaster and a guard during the robbery of a shoe factory. The trial took place at the end of the postwar Red Scare in a political atmosphere charged with hysteria against foreigners and radicals. Although the ballistics evidence was inconclusive and many witnesses, most of them Italian, placed the two men elsewhere at the time of the robbery, the jury returned guilty verdicts after listening to patriotic harangues from the chief prosecutor, Frederick Katzmann, and the trial judge, Webster Bradley Thayer.

During his cross-examination of the two defendants, Katzmann constantly emphasized their unorthodox political views and their flight to Mexico during the war. Thayer tolerated a broad range of political questions, mocked the two men's anarchism, and urged the members of the jury to act as "true soldiers . . . in the spirit of supreme American loyalty."

A diverse coalition of Bay State aristocrats, law professors such as FELIX FRANKFURTER, Italian radicals, and New York intellectuals attempted to secure a new trial for the condemned men during the next seven years. They marshaled an impressive amount of evidence pointing to Thayer's prejudice, the doubts of key prosecution witnesses, and the possibility that the crime had been committed by a gang of professional outlaws. The Massachusetts Supreme Judicial Court, however, relying on principles of trial court discretion that made it virtually impossible to challenge any of Thayer's rulings, spurned these appeals and refused to disturb either the verdict or the death sentences. A similar conclusion was reached by a special commission appointed by Governor Alvan T. Fuller and headed by Harvard University president A. Lawrence Lowell.

Last-minute efforts to secure a stay of execution from federal judges, including Supreme Court Justices OLIVER WENDELL HOLMES and LOUIS D. BRANDEIS, also proved unavailing. Attorneys for Sacco and Vanzetti argued that because of Thayer's hostility their clients had been denied a FAIR TRIAL guaranteed by the DUE PROCESS clause of the FOURTEENTH AMENDMENT. But with the exception of MOORE V. DEMPSEY (1923), where a state murder trial had been intimidated by a mob, the Supreme Court had shown great reluctance to intervene in local criminal proceedings. "I cannot think that prejudice on the part of a presiding judge however strong would deprive the Court of jurisdiction," wrote Holmes, "and in my opinion nothing short of a want of legal power to decide the case authorizes me to interfere. . . ." Whether Sacco and Vanzetti received a fair trial is questionable; however, Francis Russell has shown how illusory is the old contention that they were wholly innocent.

MICHAEL E. PARRISH
(1986)

Bibliography
JOUGHN, G. LOUIS and MORGAN, EDMUND M. 1948 *The Legacy of Sacco and Vanzetti*. New York: Harcourt, Brace.
RUSSELL, FRANCIS 1962 *Tragedy in Dedham: The Story of the Sacco-Vanzetti Case*. New York: Harper & Row.

COMMONWEALTH STATUS

Commonwealths are TERRITORIES in free association with the United States, enjoying virtual autonomy in internal affairs but subject to the United States in foreign and defense matters. Citizens of commonwealths are citizens of the United States: they pay federal taxes and may move freely to, from, and within the United States. Public officials are elected by the people of the commonwealths and neither the officials nor their acts require approval by the President or Congress. Constitutional limitations on state legislation are applicable to commonwealth legislation; and APPEAL lies from the highest court of a commonwealth to the Supreme Court of the United States. When Congress established commonwealth status for the Philippines in 1934 it intended an interim state en route to independence, but commonwealth status has become a practically permanent condition for PUERTO RICO and the Northern Marianas.

The basis of the commonwealth relationship is a "covenant" between the American people and the people of the territory. Since Congress's authority to ratify the covenant derives from its plenary power over territories (Article IV, section 3, clause 2), most legal authorities maintain that Congress could repeal the covenant and impose direct rule. But any attempt to do so would constitute a grievous breach of faith and would excite overwhelming domestic and international political opposition.

DENNIS J. MAHONEY
(1986)

COMMUNICATIONS ACT
48 Stat. 1064 (1934)

The Communications Act of 1934, enacted under Congress's COMMERCE POWER, provides the statutory basis for federal regulation of BROADCASTING and electronic communication. The act describes the electromagnetic spectrum as a national resource and permits private parties to use portions of it only as trustees in the public interest. To administer its provisions the act established the seven-member Federal Communications Commission (FCC), authorizing it to make regulations with the force of law and to issue licenses to broadcasters that may be granted, renewed, or revoked in accordance with "public interest, convenience, and necessity." Under the authority of the act the FCC has promulgated the FAIRNESS DOCTRINE, requiring broadcasters to provide equal time for replies to controversial messages, as well as regulations to prohibit the broadcasting of OBSCENITY.

The act was based on both technological and ideological considerations. The assumption that broadcasting channels are extremely limited has been disproved by improvements in technology; however, the ideological bias in favor of public ownership and regulation has not yet been overcome. Because of the Supreme Court's deference to Congress's findings of LEGISLATIVE FACT regarding the scarcity of broadcasting channels, as embodied in the Communications Act, in the face of the manifest reality that such channels are far more numerous than, for example, presses capable of producing a major metropolitan newspaper or an encyclopedia, the protection afforded broadcasters' FREEDOM OF SPEECH and FREEDOM OF THE PRESS is significantly reduced.

DENNIS J. MAHONEY
(1986)

COMMUNICATIONS AND COMMUNITY

The essence of community—indeed, its sine qua non—is communications. In terms of constitutionalism, the question arises as to the role of government intervention in the structure of BROADCASTING and other forms of communication to foster or reshape communities. The Federal Communications Commission (FCC) in the United States has, for example, encouraged minority ownership of broadcast channels or, more directly, minority-related programming, as a means (in part) of strengthening certain notions of community. In Europe, the Television Without Frontiers Directive imposed European quotas on national broadcasters to help frame a European information space. In some highly restricted societies that consider control of imagery essential to a notion of community—such as Iran and Iraq—government intervention to affect the pictures and words that swirl into the minds of its citizens is an important art form.

"Community" has informed much of American broadcast policy. It is reflected in the original allocation patterns of radio frequencies. In 1927, and then again in 1934, Congress determined that each local community should have a radio station—that allocations should be designed not to favor a regional or national market, but one that has local roots. This pattern of allocation of licenses based on cities and towns, rather than vast regions, was the chief characteristic of the 1954 Table of Allocations for television frequencies, and it is that pattern that is the imprint of broadcasting in the United States today. In a famous FCC publication, the 1947 Blue Book, the Commission stressed the importance of the broadcaster as a "mouth-

piece" for the community, and local management and ownership were big advantages in contested applications for licenses.

One haunting question, always, was whether this emphasis on community was a sham—merely a way for congressional representatives to deliver wealth to individuals within their districts—with the inevitable rise of national impersonal networks and the transfer of licenses to impersonal chains or groups. Artifacts of community included, for example, a requirement that station management go through a formal ascertainment process, asking local leaders what issues were important to the community, with the assumption that this survey would yield coverage in news. But ascertainment was mechanical, and, often, there was no enforcement mechanism to ensure that community needs were met.

A combination of cynicism about the values and practice of localism, recognition of vast changes in ownership, and constitutional doubts about federal requirements (or even pressure) toward localism led in the 1980s to the abandonment of most of the regulatory architecture underlying the allocation of stations to communities. There is no more ascertainment requirement, no more integration of ownership and management, and even no requirement of local news and public affairs. In TURNER BROADCASTING SYSTEM V. FCC (1994), the Supreme Court implied that requiring local coverage (or, in this case, preferring over-the-air channels for mandatory coverage on cable), might not be "content neutral" and, therefore, might mean that legislation would have to surmount the very high STRICT SCRUTINY hurdle to be constitutional.

The Court's growing hostility to AFFIRMATIVE ACTION programs imposed by government also led to the withering away of the minority preference program, with its implications for the use of broadcasting to enhance the place of African Americans, Hispanics, and others within the United States community. In METRO BROADCASTING, INC. V. FCC (1990), the Court narrowly affirmed a minority preference in contested license applications, but the reasoning was wan, and the constitutional support for intervention to assist in community-building of this sort was moving in the wrong direction. *Metro Broadcasting* was undermined in ADARAND CONSTRUCTION, INC. V. PEÑA (1995).

Cable television, too, saw a playing, at the edges, with the use of communications to build community. Tied to the idea that cities had control of the streets and the physical space for wires, cable television became franchised, almost universally, at the local level. As a result, applicants for valuable licenses boasted how adoption of their systems would mean more community-building in the franchise area. Operators guaranteed local studios, channel space for local government and local schools, and public access channels. These became known as PEG (Public Access, Educational and Governmental) commitments. Congress, in the 1984 Cable Act, while precluding much local control over program content, continued to permit franchises to contain these PEG requirements. The constitutionality of these requirements has never been fully tested.

These three outcroppings—the architecture of the original allocation of radio and television licenses, an extensive effort to expand minority broadcasting, and the existence of PEG channels—are examples of a fundamental understanding that the nature of community is a function of the organization of communications. But these three outcroppings also indicate the complexity of government ordering of broadcasting and the press to achieve what are deemed to be positive results.

MONROE E. PRICE
(2000)

(SEE ALSO: *Communications and Democracy; First Amendment; Freedom of Speech; Freedom of the Press; "Must Carry" Laws.*)

COMMUNICATIONS AND DEMOCRACY

The infrastructure of communications is an indicator of the participatory quality of a democratic society. Ideally, the media in a democratic society help create a public sphere in which a critical nongovernmental voice is formed; they perform a checking function against government abuses; and they inform the public, helping to shape a citizenry capable of assuming the duties of making the intelligent decisions necessary for sound choices.

Underlying this idea of the role of communications in reinforcing democracy are a group of assumptions about law and the role of law. In the United States, the role of government is somewhat circumscribed in its capacity to energize or structure media so as to achieve these goals. Government can impose obligations on broadcasters to provide candidates better access to the airwaves or prohibit overcharging for political advertising. Yet, in terms of foreign policy, the United States has sought to shape media in transition societies, such as in the former Soviet Union, on the grounds that a better media structure will lead to a more stable democracy.

Part of this effort involves indicating to parliaments in other societies what elements of law are important to create an enabling environment for a democratic media. These elements almost always include constitutional provisions. A FIRST AMENDMENT model is usually preferred, but many societies opt for a version of the European Convention for the Protection of Human Rights and Fundamental Freedoms. The United States's view is generally that there should not be an elaborate media law; but often in these transition societies a comprehensive press and BROADCASTING law, which includes a statement of positive contributions that should be obtained in terms of information and its relationship to democratic processes, is enacted.

But such an enabling environment also includes defamation and LIBEL laws, preferably with exemptions for a broad range of criticisms of public officials. Omnipresent are licensing provisions for electronic media, but the general pattern—reflected in American practice—is that the press should not be licensed. Many societies provide special rights, privileges, and responsibilities for accredited journalists, while others accord no special status to journalists. These differences, and how they are implemented, can have a substantial impact on the contribution of a media law to an appropriate enabling environment.

More complicated are rules concerning breaches of NATIONAL SECURITY, HATE SPEECH, or spreading propaganda. The United States internal constitutional position is that such laws are generally incompatible with an enabling environment for a media contribution to a democratic society. European models of media regulation often embed such restrictions in the very definition of constitutionally regulable speech. In some societies, including the United States, there is a concern that media too prone to indecent, violent, and pornographic imagery rob the civil space of democratic discussion. This has led to efforts—usually vague, vain, and clumsily enforced—to regulate elements of such speech. In the new technologies, filtering devices are increasingly urged as noninterventionist means to regulate access to speech that the user (or the society) may deem harmful.

The area of speech directly related to the political process remains an area of legislative concern worldwide in terms of adjusting the democratic impact of media organization. In *Arkansas Educational Television Commission v. Forbes* (1998), the Supreme Court concluded that public broadcasters, at least those licensed to state entities, have an obligation, if they hold public debates, to include all candidates, except those who are excluded not because of their viewpoint, but because of poor public performance or other reasonable but narrow bases.

The formal laws themselves are not sufficient to provide an enabling environment for the role of communications in a democratic society. There is also the question of the RULE OF LAW and the institutional infrastructure in which the law exists. The existence of a JUDICIAL SYSTEM or of REGULATORY AGENCIES that have traditions of fairness and independence are essential aspects of a rule of law that protects a free and democratic media sector.

A third strategic area involves the social and political setting in which the modules of law are introduced and the infrastructure is found. How communications function as an aspect of democratic values involves such background elements as the structure of political governance. In some transition societies in the late 1990s, such as Bosnia and Herzegovina, the existence of a monopoly political party controlling the media meant that law alone could not yield democratic values. Forms of media ownership also influence the democratic character of the media. Many societies, including the United States, have foreign investment restrictions on the electronic media to secure indigenous control over the mechanisms of self-governance. Ownership alone does not reveal whether a medium of communication contributes to the growth of democratic values. Patterns of access are also highly relevant to whether the media serve forums for wide-ranging public debates.

MONROE E. PRICE
(2000)

Bibliography

FISS, OWEN M.   1996   *The Irony of Free Speech.* Cambridge, Mass.: Harvard University Press.

SHIFFRIN, STEVEN H.   1990   *The First Amendment, Democracy, and Romance.* Cambridge, Mass.: Harvard University Press.

SUNSTEIN, CASS R.   1993   *Democracy and the Problem of Free Speech.* New York: Free Press.

COMMUNICATIONS DECENCY ACT
110 Stat. 56 (1996)

The INTERNET has revolutionized the world of communications in an unprecedented fashion. Growing at an exponential rate, the Internet has become a new and unique global marketplace of images, ideas, and information. But the Internet's ease of access and wealth of available material have also raised problems, most notably access to certain kinds of information—particularly words and images of a sexual nature—either by unsuspecting adults or by children. Because of that concern, Congress passed the Communications Decency Act of 1996. That law was part of the much larger Telecommunications Act of 1996, an unusually important legislative enactment designed to encourage the rapid deployment of new telecommunications technologies and to promote competition in the local telephone service market, the multichannel video market, and the market for over-the-air BROADCASTING. In contrast to the rest of the Telecommunications Act, the communications decency provisions were not given careful or extensive consideration by the Congress.

The Communications Decency Act contained two controversial features: the "indecent" communication provision and the "patently offensive" display provision.

The first part of the law prohibited the knowing transmission of "obscene or indecent" messages to any recipient under 18 years of age, by making it a crime when any person "by means of a telecommunications device knowingly . . . makes, creates, or solicits, and . . . initiates the transmission of, any comment, request, suggestion, proposal, image, or other communication which is obscene or indecent, knowing that the recipient of the communication is under 18 years of age. . . ." and regardless of who initiated the communication. The law also made it a crime to permit one's communication facility to be used for such activity.

The other provision of the law prohibited the knowing sending or displaying of "patently offensive" messages in a manner that is available to a person under 18 years of age. This portion of the law focused on the use of any "interactive computer service" (or "chatroom") to display any written or visual communication that, "in context, depicts or describes, in terms patently offensive as measured by contemporary community standards, sexual or excretory activities or organs. . . ." Any person who controlled such facilities was criminally liable as well. The act nowhere defined or explained the meaning of the key terms "indecent" or "patently offensive" display beyond the text just set forth.

Although the act also provided certain defenses against criminal responsibility for individuals or organizations who take "appropriate measures" to restrict access by minors, the nature of those measures was unclear (most would be extremely expensive), and violation of the act carried significant criminal penalties. The act effectively meant that all who published covered information to people under 18 years of age did so at their peril.

Because of the very real CHILLING EFFECT on FREEDOM OF SPEECH on the Internet, the act was challenged on FIRST AMENDMENT grounds the moment it went into effect. In a 1997 ruling, *American Civil Liberties Union v. Reno*, the Supreme Court declared the act to be unconstitutional. The Court concluded that the proper goal of protecting children could not be pursued through means that so broadly stifled the speech of adults on this vital new medium of communication.

JOEL M. GORA
(2000)

Bibliography

LARUE, JANET M.   1996   The Communications Decency Act of 1996: Sensible Not Censorship. *St. John's Journal of Legal Commentary* 11:721–726.

LESSIG, LAWRENCE J.   1996   Reading the Constitution in Cyberspace. *Emory Law Journal* 45:886–910.

COMMUNIST CONTROL ACT
68 Stat. 775 (1954)

This measure marked the culmination of the United States government's program to prevent subversion from within during the loyalty-security years. Conservative senators, eager to facilitate removal of communists from positions of union leadership, and Senator HUBERT H. HUMPHREY, tired of hearing liberals smeared as "soft on communism," pushed the measure through Congress with large majorities in each chamber. Clearly tied to the 1954 elections, the act outlawed the Communist party as an instrumentality conspiring to overthrow the United States government. The bill as initially drafted made party membership a crime. Responding to criticism of the DWIGHT D. EISENHOWER administration that the membership clause would make the provisions of the 1950 INTERNAL SECURITY ACT unconstitutional, because compulsory registration would violate the RIGHT AGAINST SELF-INCRIMINATION, the bill's sponsors removed its membership clause. However, Congress deprived the Communist party of all "rights, privileges, and immunities attendant upon legal bodies created under the jurisdiction of the laws of the United States or any political subdivision thereof." The act added a new category of groups required to register—"communist-infiltrated" organizations. These, like communist and "front" organizations, although outlawed, were expected to register with the SUBVERSIVE ACTIVITIES CONTROL BOARD.

The measure, virtually inoperative from the beginning, raised grave constitutional questions under the FIRST AMENDMENT, the Fifth Amendment, and the ban against BILLS OF ATTAINDER. The Justice Department ignored it and pushed no general test of its provisions in the court. The act summarized well the official policy toward the Communist party at the time—to keep it legal enough for successful prosecution of its illegalities.

PAUL L. MURPHY
(1986)

Bibliography

AUERBACH, CARL   1956   The Communist Control Act of 1954. *University of Chicago Law Review* 23:173–220.

COMMUNIST PARTY

See: Subversive Activity

COMMUNIST PARTY OF THE UNITED STATES v. SUBVERSIVE ACTIVITIES CONTROL BOARD
367 U.S. 1 (1961)

The Supreme Court upheld application to the Communist party of provisions of the Subversive Activities Control Act requiring "any organization . . . substantially controlled by the foreign government . . . controlling the world Communist movement" to register with the Board, providing lists of officers and members. The Court postponed considering self-incrimination objections, held that where an individual might escape regulation merely by ceasing to engage in the regulated activity no BILL OF ATTAINDER existed, and deferred to the congressional balance between national security and the FREEDOM OF ASSOCIATION arguing that any inhibition on communists' associational freedom caused by exposure was incidental to regulation of their activities on behalf of foreign governments.

MARTIN SHAPIRO
(1986)

(SEE ALSO: *Subversive Activities Control Board.*)

COMMUNISTS

See: Extremist Speech

COMMUNITARIANISM

Communitarianism is a political philosophy that emphasizes the good society's need for strong bonds of community, civic virtue, solidarities of CITIZENSHIP, and public deliberation about moral issues. It generally offers its vision as an alternative to contemporary LIBERALISM, criticizing liberals for overly emphasizing doctrines of individual autonomy at the expense of nurturing the social allegiances that give depth and substance to an individual's identity. Communitarians hark back to the traditional republican political theory which crucially taught that democratic freedom is accomplished not so much by leaving persons alone as by fostering the virtue it takes to govern according to the common good rather than self-interest.

As a matter of CONSTITUTIONAL INTERPRETATION, communitarians object to prevailing legal trends that insist government must be neutral as among the competing views and values of citizens. For instance, in FIRST AMENDMENT cases, the DOCTRINE of content neutrality means that government cannot regulate speech merely because it judges the subject matter of the speech to be unimportant, unworthy, or imminently dangerous. But communitarians argue that the lofty purposes of the First Amendment are trivialized when the public interest in FREEDOM OF SPEECH about commerce or sex is equated with the public interest in free speech about politics. For communitarians, freedom of speech is basic precisely because open, democratic government is impossible without it. The same heightened public importance is absent when courts analyze COMMERCIAL SPEECH or sexual speech and courts go too far, argue communitarians, when they read the First Amendment as if its purpose were to protect the individual's personal interest in self-expression. To interpret the First Amendment as if the Framers were neutral as between the importance in a democracy of free speech about politics and free speech about the price of commercial products is to trivialize free speech and to misread the Constitution as exalting protection of individual self-expression into a sovereign, absolute value.

Many communitarians also object to interpreting the FOURTEENTH AMENDMENT DUE PROCESS clause as granting implicit constitutional status to a RIGHT OF PRIVACY, as the Supreme Court did in ROE V. WADE (1973) and subsequent cases protecting a woman's right to choose ABORTION. The same purported right of privacy is at stake in cases involving state regulation of SEXUAL ORIENTATION and assisted suicide (or the RIGHT TO DIE). The problem communitarians have with the privacy cases is not necessarily with the results reached but with the legal reasoning that insists constitutional analysis must bracket or put aside any substantive moral discussion of the public good at stake when individuals make private choices. In regard to abortion in particular, communitarians thus would prefer to reframe the issue along lines suggested by Justice RUTH BADER GINSBURG, who has argued that abortion regulations should be analyzed in reference to legal principles prohibiting SEX DISCRIMINATION as a violation of democracy's commitment to equal respect for all persons.

Communitarians also distinguish between two senses of citizenship implicit in the Constitution. One is the liberal view of citizens as individuals who enjoy the protection of legal rights against the state. The other is a stronger, republican vision of citizens who enjoy the legal status of participating in democratic self-governance and the rights and responsibilities of public service. This participatory notion of citizenship stands behind the constitutional status of TRIAL BY JURY of Article III and the Sixth Amendment's stipulation that criminal juries must be chosen from the district within a state where the crime occurred. The battle to amend the Constitution to protect the so-called jury of the "vicinage" or community affected by the crime, communitarians point out, was waged along civic republican lines and shows a continuing commitment among many in the Founding era to preserve opportunities for local communities, through the jury system, to participate in shaping governing principles of law. Likewise, the SECOND AMENDMENT embodies a philosophy of localism insofar as it protects state militias and the right to bear arms in them against the dangers of a single, standing national army. Historically, communitarians have also defended the constitutionality of the military draft (as in the SELECTIVE SERVICE ACTS) by stressing the Framers' commitment to the civic duty and public service obligations of democratic citizens.

When it comes to issues involving the state and religion, communitarians more readily accept the liberal view that RELIGIOUS LIBERTY should be the same everywhere in the United States, protected by federal courts against local, majoritarian preferences. For instance, communitarians' view of open and egalitarian communities premised on participatory opportunities for all leads them to accept the leading Supreme Court cases prohibiting public SCHOOL PRAYERS, which rest on the principle that public schools best educate children to be democratic citizens when they teach children both to respect RELIGIOUS DIVERSITY and to share civic ties despite those religious divisions.

Finally, communitarians balk at the increasing judicialization of politics, a process whereby resolution of core issues about justice and liberty is removed from the power of the people and entrusted to unelected federal judges. The result is dimunition of democracy and the disempowerment of citizens and their representatives. Communitarians concede that individual rights sometimes trump majority power in our constitutional government and that courts therefore need to enforce constitutional guarantees even against the contrary will of political majorities. But communitarians believe that a better balance can be struck between the rights-based liberalism that controls constitutional interpretation currently and the older, civic republican ideals of the Framers, ideals that stressed public duty as well as private rights and that praised participation in self-governing communities, rather than the protection of individual against community, as the key to political liberty.

JEFFREY ABRAMSON
(2000)

Bibliography

ABRAMSON, JEFFREY 1994 *We, the Jury: The Jury System and the Ideal of Democracy.* New York: Basic Books.

ETZIONI, AMITAI, ed. 1995 *New Communitarian Thinking: Persons, Virtues, Institutions, and Communities.* Charlottesville: University Press of Virginia.

———, ed. 1998 *The Essential Communitarian Reader.* Lanham, Md.: Rowman and Littlefeld.

GLENDON, MARY ANN 1991 *Rights Talk: The Impoverishment of Political Discourse.* New York: Free Press.

SANDEL, MICHAEL J. 1996 *Democracy's Discontent: America in*

Search of a Public Philosophy. Cambridge, Mass.: Harvard University Press.

SMITH, ROGERS M. 1997 *Civic Ideals: Conflicting Visions of Citizenship in U.S. History.* New Haven, Conn.: Yale University Press.

SUNSTEIN, CASS R. 1999 *One Case at a Time: Judicial Minimalism and the Supreme Court.* Cambridge, Mass.: Harvard University Press.

TAM, HENRY BENEDICT 1998 *Communitarianism: A New Agenda for Politics and Citizenship.* New York: New York University Press.

TUSHNET, MARK V. 1999 *Taking the Constitution Away from the Courts.* Princeton, N.J.: Princeton University Press.

COMPACT THEORY

See: Social Compact Theory; Theories of the Union

COMPANION CASE

Cases decided by the Supreme Court on the same day are called companion cases when they involve the same issues or issues that are closely related. Sometimes a single OPINION is used to explain two or more companion cases, and sometimes separate opinions are written. Occasionally a Justice writing for the Court will select the strongest of a group of companion cases for explanation in a full opinion, leaving the weaker cases to be discussed only briefly, with heavy reliance on the conclusions in the full opinion.

KENNETH L. KARST
(1986)

COMPARABLE WORTH

The term "comparable worth" refers to the claim that workers in predominantly female occupations should be compensated at rates similar to those paid to workers in predominantly male occupations, when the labor involved in both is comparable in value to the employer. The claim assumes (1) that significant sex segregation exists in American employment; (2) that, as a result, women are disadvantaged economically; and (3) that job classifications that are different can nonetheless be compared by analyzing their component skill, effort, responsibility, working conditions, and training requirements.

The first assumption is not controversial. More than half of the jobs that fall under the most commonly used occupational designations are over eighty percent male- or female-dominated. At least part of the second claim is likewise firmly established. On average, women earn only sixty percent of what men do, and the higher the percentage of women in a particular job category, the lower the average wage tends to be.

One of the controversies over comparable worth centers on how much of the male-female wage disparity can be explained by "nondiscriminatory" factors, such as length of time in continuous employment, trade-offs between work and family responsibility, and personal choice. Although these factors may themselves be products of prior SEX DISCRIMINATION, they can nevertheless be distinguished from the employer's own current intentional discrimination, reliance on sex stereotypes, or use of wage-setting devices that do not measure job requirements or performance. Proponents of comparable-worth claims argue that the latter factors produce a significant part of the general wage disparity, so that the disparity is properly challenged as discriminatory under laws guaranteeing equal employment opportunity. Opponents who agree that there is a relationship between employers' undervaluation of certain kinds of work and the fact that such work is predominantly done by women, nonetheless reject comparable-worth claims as a useful strategy for improving the economic condition of women. They prefer strategies that would move large numbers of women into fields in which men are currently overrepresented.

Controversy also surrounds the questions of which jobs are comparable and how to measure comparability. Courts generally accept statistical analysis in claims of EMPLOYMENT DISCRIMINATION, but do not always agree on the validity, appropriateness, or evidentiary weight of particular statistical analyses. Neither do they agree on whether and how comparable-worth claims should fit within the framework of employment discrimination claims created by Title VII of the CIVIL RIGHTS ACT OF 1964, the Equal Pay Act of 1964, or the EQUAL PROTECTION clause of the FOURTEENTH AMENDMENT to the Constitution. *County of Washington v. Gunther* (1981), the only Supreme Court opinion to mention comparable worth, expressly declined to address the issue, although it did hold that intentional sex discrimination in wages could be challenged under Title VII, despite differences in male and female job classifications.

Most comparable worth litigation is brought against public employers, who generally employ large numbers of people in a wide variety of job classifications. Although public employers are subject to both Title VII and constitutional prohibitions on discrimination, equal protection claims are generally not raised by plaintiffs seeking comparable-worth decrees. As PERSONNEL ADMINISTRATOR OF MASSACHUSETTS V. FEENEY (1979) illustrates, an employment practice does not violate the Constitution unless its discriminatory impact has been intentionally created. Employers are more likely to set wages on the basis of prevailing market rates for certain job classifications or even on unconscious stereotypes about the relative worth of female-dominated occupations than on an intentional desire to undercompensate women simply because they are women.

Even in the statutory arena, much uncertainty remains. For example, it is unclear whether the availability of statutory "disparate impact" claims against other types of alleged employment discrimination extends to sex-based wage discrimination. Some courts have asserted that wage-setting practices are too subjective, too multifaceted, or both, to be effectively tested by the disparate impact model of discrimination. Others have simply stated that an employer's reliance on the market in setting wages is not the kind of practice to which the model should apply. The Supreme Court has spoken only obliquely on these issues.

Given uncertainty whether equal pay for work of comparable worth is required by existing federal law, advocates of comparable worth have not confined their efforts to the courtroom. Pay equity, including comparable worth, has to date been more successfully achieved through collective bargaining, state legislation, and local ordinances than through litigation.

CHRISTINE A. LITTLETON
(1992)

(SEE ALSO: *Feminist Theory*.)

Bibliography

BLUMROSEN, RUTH G.   1980   Wage Discrimination, Job Segregation and Women Workers. *Women's Rights Law Reporter* 6:19–57.

DOWD, NANCY E.   1986   The Metamorphosis of Comparable Worth. *Suffolk University Law Review* 20:833–865.

FELDSTEIN, HYDEE R.   1981   Sex-based Wage Discrimination Claims. *Columbia Law Review* 81:1333–1347.

NOTE [LITTLETON, CHRISTINE]   1981   Toward a Redefinition of Sexual Equality. *Harvard Law Review* 95:487–508.

COMPELLED SPEECH

The FIRST AMENDMENT mandate that "Congress shall make no law ... abridging the freedom of speech" implies a stricture against compelling or coercing persons to engage in speech they do not wish to make—either because they disagree with the speech or because they wish to remain silent. Substantially the same considerations that drive the prohibition against abridgement of FREEDOM OF SPEECH—whether derived from the notion of the speaker's autonomy or from the listener's entitlement or the societal value of undistorted public discourse—drive the strictures against coercion of speech. The speech protected by the First Amendment may consist of utterances or other forms of expressive conduct by a person or the publication or transmission of expression of others, not all of which are equally protected as speech. Protected speech may also consist of the contribution of funds or furnishing of facilities to be used by the recipients, inter alia, for expressive conduct (i.e., the contribution may be assimilated to speech of the contributor).

Government mandates to utter or publish particular expressions or kinds of expression produce coerced speech, but the coercion's unconstitutionality appears to turn in large part on the content of the expression. High- value speech (such as a LOYALTY OATH or support for an expressive association) may not be coerced, but low-value or low-cost or content-neutral speech (such as disclosure of relevant facts in the sale of goods or securities) may be coerced. Government award, or threat of denial of benefits (like licensing, tax relief, subsidy, employment, or admission to the bar) conditioned on expression by the recipient may also unconstitutionally compel expression, apparently without regard to the magnitude of the benefits. The decisions of the Supreme Court appear to rest on the quality of the compelled expression's expected inhibiting effect on other high-value expression or association, and to vary with the content of the compelled expression.

Another framework for analyzing the problem of compelled speech entails connecting one person's compelled contribution of funds or facilities or opportunities to speak with another person's expression, so as to impute to the former the latter's expression. Justification for the assimilation is not self-evident, and the circumstances under which such contribution is, or should be, equated with speech of the contributor are difficult to state. The problem is most acute if an institution whose essential function is expression claims that it is being coerced to speak because the government directs it to admit unwanted expression or speakers to its own expressive voice (as in the case of the sponsor of a parade), or to give access to its facilities for expression (as the print or electronic media) to persons whose expressions it does not wish to be associated with or to enable. For some expressive organizations, like a parade's sponsor or a political or ideological group, the special value of aggregating funds or voices for the purpose of expression may be sacrificed if the effect of such required admission is to dilute or alter the expression they wish to utter. For others, like the print or broadcast media, the effect of the requirement may be less costly. This may explain why compelling the parade sponsors to include an unwanted participant's speech is held to be unconstitutional, but compelling inclusion in the media sometimes is unconstitutional (as when allowing others' expression may have an inhibiting effect on the medium's expression) and sometimes is constitutionally permitted; particularly in the case of a BROADCASTING medium that originates and exists more as a carrier than a voice, in a framework of expressly government- granted power. The question of compelling such speech in cyberspace remains to be examined.

The special value of purposefully aggregated voice is not sacrificed if the institution's essential function is not expression and the government should require it either to convey expression that it does not wish to convey, as in the case of SHOPPING CENTER owners who are forbidden by state law from excluding leafleters; or public utility CORPORATIONS that send out communications or bills and are required by the state to let other speakers insert related public messages in the unfilled envelope space; or organizations such as the Chamber of Commerce or Rotary Club who want to exclude from membership persons with potentially contrary voices but are forbidden to do so by state CIVIL RIGHTS laws. Those persons or institutions can vent their expression by other means without materially diminishing achievement of their essential nonexpressive functions. As the different outcomes in the shopping mall case, where the state's regulation was upheld, and the envelope case, where it was denied, suggest, the closeness with which the contribution mechanism publicly associates the forced contributor with the making or content of the expression may determine whether the speech is unconstitutionally coerced. The Chamber of Commerce, the Rotary Club, and the parade cases illustrate the difficulty in formulating criteria for separating "essentially" expressive from "essentially" nonexpressive institutions.

A variation of the problem derives from a nonexpressive institution requiring persons to pay dues and then using the dues to fund expression that those persons do not want to express or to be expressed. For the institution's expression to be considered unconstitutionally compelled speech by the contributor, the institutional power to require the contribution must be sufficiently attributable to special government (legislative) empowerment of the institution to acquire membership or funding for its nonexpressive function, as in the case of an integrated bar association that can exclude nonmembers from the practice of law, or a union empowered to enforce a union shop or agency shop agreement that can exclude from employment those who decline to join or contribute. In contrast, the contribution (i.e., speech) does not appear to be viewed by the courts as unconstitutionally compelled if it is required by the "private" power of a voluntary bar association or possibly a local medical society to acquire membership—even though each has the power to deny access to vital earning facilities or privileges to persons who decline to pay dues that will fund the association's speech. The Supreme Court offers few clues as to what separates government-driven private compulsion from "purely" private compulsion in a society in which any institution's coercive power derives from the entire structure of government support embodied in the allocation of rights and duties by law. Moreover, the Court has not explained why, or by what criteria, the group's speech should be imputed to the contributor at the cost of pro tanto abridging the speech of the group and its other members, as when state universities impose extracurricular activities fees, some of which go to student groups supporting policies that some contributors wish not to support. Nor has it squarely addressed the problem of the extent of government power to protect an individual member's freedom from compelled expression by abridging the expression of a "private" nonexpressive institution, like a business corporation, funded by contributions that are not freely given for expression.

In any event, not all institutional expression that can be imputed to a coerced contributor is protected, or equally protected, speech—as the distinctions between the kinds of speech permitted and prohibited by compelled funding in the union shop and integrated bar cases indicate. The point was made, perhaps more sharply, in *Glickman v. Wileman Brothers and Elliott Inc.* (1997), which involved expression by a trade association (generic advertising of the virtues of an industry's product) that was an integral component of a comprehensive government-sponsored economic program for the industry, under which industry members were required to make payment to the association. The Court ruled that the member's contributions to the association's advertising were not to be characterized as compelled speech by the member. But it is not entirely clear whether the opinion deemed the complainant's contribution to be insufficiently tied to the particular expression to impute it to the contributor; or, alternatively, deemed the tie to be close enough to make the expression coerced but deemed the expression not to be protected speech. Similarly, it is unclear from this opinion how a court should measure and balance either the sufficiency of the tie between contribution and expression or the extent to which the particular expression is entitled to be considered protected speech.

A pervasive problem, for which the Court's opinions give no clues, implicates the extent to which the constitutional limits on government coercion of speech are, or should be, less rigorous than the constitutional limits on government prohibition of speech—for example, to what extent, and by what criteria, government prohibition of political expenditures or of solicitation of favorable treatment from officeholders should be more critically scrutinized (and less tolerated) by courts than government compelling disclosure in such matters.

VICTOR BRUDNEY
(2000)

(SEE ALSO: *Hurley v. Irish-American Gay, Lesbian, and Bisexual Group of Boston; PruneYard Shopping Center v. Robins.*)

COMPELLING STATE INTEREST

When the Supreme Court concludes that STRICT SCRUTINY is the appropriate STANDARD OF REVIEW, it often expresses its searching examination of the justification of legislation in a formula: the law is invalid unless it is necessary to achieve a "compelling state interest." The inquiry thus touches not only legislative means but also legislative purposes.

Even the permissive RATIONAL BASIS standard of review demands that legislative ends be legitimate. To say that a governmental purpose must be one of compelling importance is plainly to demand more. How much more, however, is something the Court has been unable to say. What we do know is that, once "strict scrutiny" is invoked, only rarely does a law escape invalidation.

Any judicial examination of the importance of a governmental objective implies that a court is weighing interests, engaging in a kind of cost-benefit analysis as a prelude to deciding on the constitutionality of legislation. Yet one would be mistaken to assume that the inquiry follows such a neat, linear, two-stage progression. Given the close correlation between employing the "strict scrutiny" standard and invalidating laws, the very word "scrutiny" may be misleading. A court that has embarked on a search for compelling state interests very likely knows how it intends to decide.

In many a case a court does find a legislative purpose of compelling importance. That is not the end of the "strict scrutiny" inquiry; there remains the question whether the law is necessary to achieve that end. If, for example, there is another way the legislature might have accomplished its purpose, without imposing so great a burden on the constitutionally protected interest in liberty or equality, the availability of that LEAST RESTRICTIVE MEANS negates the necessity for the legislature's choice. The meaning of "strict scrutiny" is that even a compelling state interest must be pursued by means that give constitutional values their maximum protection.

The phrase "compelling state interest" originated in Justice FELIX FRANKFURTER's concurring opinion in *Sweezy v. New Hampshire* (1957), a case involving the privacy of political association: "For a citizen to be made to forego even a part of so basic a liberty as his political autonomy, the subordinating interest of the State must be compelling." The Supreme Court uses some variation on this formula not only in FIRST AMENDMENT cases but also in cases calling for "strict scrutiny" under the EQUAL PROTECTION clause or under the revived forms of SUBSTANTIVE DUE PROCESS. The formula, in short, is much used and little explained. The Court is unable to define "compelling state interest" but knows when it does not see it.

KENNETH L. KARST
(1986)

Bibliography

TRIBE, LAURENCE H. 1978 *American Constitutional Law.* Pages 1000–1002. Mineola, N.Y.: Foundation Press.

COMPETITIVE FEDERALISM

This is a term often used in analysis of constitutional DOCTRINE or working governmental practice. Competitive federalism is closely related to DUAL FEDERALISM, and in contrast with COOPERATIVE FEDERALISM stresses the conflict between the national government and the states.

HARRY N. SCHEIBER
(1986)

COMPROMISE OF 1850

The Compromise of 1850 comprised a related series of statutes enacted by Congress in an attempt to settle sectional disputes related to SLAVERY that had flared since 1846, with the outbreak of the Mexican War and the introduction of the WILMOT PROVISO. After California's 1849 demand for admission as a free state and the concurrent appearance of southern disunionist sentiment, what had begun as a contest over the constitutional status of SLAVERY IN THE TERRITORIES absorbed other issues related to the security of slavery in the extant states and expanded into a crisis of the Union.

From proposals submitted by President Zachary Taylor and Senator HENRY CLAY, Senator STEPHEN A. DOUGLAS marshaled measures through Congress that admitted California as a free state; established the Texas-New Mexico boundary and compensated Texas and holders of Texas securities for territory claimed by Texas but awarded to New Mexico; abolished the slave trade in the DISTRICT OF COLUMBIA (but Congress rejected a proposal to abolish slavery itself there); amended the Fugitive Slave Act of 1793 by the drastic new measure known as the Fugitive Slave Act of 1850; and created Utah and New Mexico Territories. (See FUGITIVE SLAVERY.)

Both major parties hailed the Compromise as a final settlement of all problems relating to slavery. Southern disunion sentiment abated, while the Free Soil coalition, which had made a respectable beginning in the 1848 election, began to disintegrate. FRANKLIN PIERCE was elected President in 1852 on a platform extolling the finality of the Compromise and condemning any further agitation of the slavery issue.

But the territorial and fugitive-slave measures only extended and inflamed the slavery controversy. The New Mexico and Utah acts were couched in ambiguous language that left the status of slavery in those two immense territories unsettled, though Congress did decisively reject the Free Soil solution embodied in the Wilmot Proviso of 1846. The acts also contained sections providing for APPEAL of slavery controversies from the TERRITORIAL COURTS directly to the United States Supreme Court, an effort to resolve a politically insoluble problem by non-political means.

The Fugitive Slave Act of 1850 was a harsh and provocative measure that virtually legitimated the kidnapping of free blacks. It thrust the federal presence into northern communities in obtrusive ways by potentially forcing any adult northern male to serve on slave-catching posses, by creating new pseudo-judicial officers encouraged by the fee structure to issue certificates of rendition, and by authorizing use of federal military force to enforce the act. It was therefore widely unpopular in the northern states. Subsequent recaptures, renditions, and rescues provided numerous real-life counterparts to the fictional drama of *Uncle Tom's Cabin*.

The finality supposedly achieved by the Compromise of 1850 was shattered by the controversy over the KANSAS-NEBRASKA ACT of 1854. But as ALEXANDER STEPHENS noted back in 1850, "the present adjustment may be made, but the great question of the permanence of slavery in the Southern states will be far from being settled thereby."

WILLIAM M. WIECEK
(1986)

Bibliography

POTTER, DAVID M.   1976   *The Impending Crisis, 1848–1861.* New York: Harper & Row.

COMPROMISE OF 1877

Four of the sectional compromises in nineteenth-century America were efforts to settle quarrels by mutual concessions and forestall danger of violence. Three of the four efforts were temporarily successful, and only the fourth, that of 1861, broke down in failure. For the next sixteen years, during the CIVIL WAR and RECONSTRUCTION, differences were resolved by resort to force. The Compromise of 1877 differed from the earlier ones in several ways, one of them being that its main purpose was to foreclose rather than to forestall resort to armed force. Since the Republican party was committed to force when necessary to protect freedmen's rights under the constitutional amendments and CIVIL RIGHTS acts of the Reconstruction period, any repudiation of such commitments had to be negotiated discreetly.

Under President ANDREW JOHNSON and President ULYSSES S. GRANT, the government had been backing away from enforcement of freedmen's rights almost from the start. In part the result of white resistance in the South, this retreat from Reconstruction was also a consequence of the prevalence of white-supremacy sentiment in the North. In the elections of 1874, regarded by some as a referendum on Reconstruction, the Republican House majority of 110 was replaced by a Democratic majority of sixty. And in the ensuing presidential election of 1876 the Democratic candidate, Samuel J. Tilden, won a majority of the popular votes and was conceded 184 of the 185 electoral votes required for election. He also claimed all the nineteen contested votes of South Carolina, Florida, and Louisiana, the only southern states remaining under Republican control. But so did his Republican opponent, Rutherford B. Hayes, who also claimed the election. The impasse was solved by an agreement between the two political parties (not the sections) to create a bipartisan electoral commission of fifteen to count the votes. An unanticipated last minute change of one member of the commission gave the Republicans a majority of one, and by that majority they counted all contested votes for Hayes. That eliminated Tilden, but to seat Hayes required formal action of the House. The Democratic majority, enraged over what they regarded as a "conspiracy" to rob them of their victory, talked wildly of resistance and started a filibuster.

Foreseeing the victory of Hayes, southern Democrats sought to salvage whatever they could out of defeat. Their prime objective was "home rule," which meant not only withdrawal of troops that sustained Republican rule in South Carolina and Louisiana but also a firm Republican commitment to abandon use of force in the future for defending rights of freedmen, carpetbaggers, and scalawags. This amounted to the virtual nullification of the FOURTEENTH and FIFTEENTH AMENDMENTS and the CIVIL RIGHTS ACT. In return southern conservatives promised to help confirm Hayes's election, and many Democrats of the old Whig persuasion promised to cooperate with the new administration, but not to defect to the Republican party unless it abandoned "radicalism."

With control of the army and the submission of enough northern Democrats, Republicans could have seated Hayes anyway. But the southerners exploited Republican fears of resistance and skillfully played what they later admitted was "a bluff game." An old Whig himself, Hayes fell in with the idea of reconstituting his party in the South under conservative white leaders in place of carpetbaggers. He not only pledged "home rule" but promised to appoint a conservative southern Democrat to his cabinet and sweetened his appeal to that constituency by publicly pledging generous support to bills for subsidizing " INTERNAL IMPROVEMENTS of a national character" in the South. Hayes's election was confirmed only two days before he took office.

As in earlier sectional compromises, not all the terms of that of 1877 were fulfilled, but the main ones were.

Hayes appointed a southern Democrat his postmaster general, chief dispenser of patronage, and placed many other white conservatives in southern offices. Bills for federal subsidies to internal improvements met with more success than ever before. The troops sustaining Republican rule in the two states were removed and Democrats immediately took over. In the CIVIL RIGHTS CASES (1883) the Supreme Court erected the STATE ACTION barrier, severely limiting the reach of the Fourteenth Amendment. The Court's opinion was written by Justice JOSEPH P. BRADLEY, who had been a member of the 1877 electoral commission. More important than all this was the pledge against resort to force to protect black rights. That commitment held firm for eighty years, until the military intervention at Little Rock, Arkansas, in 1957. This set a record for durability among sectional compromises.

C. VANN WOODWARD
(1986)

Bibliography

GILLETTE, WILLIAM   1980   *Retreat from Reconstruction, 1869–1879.* Baton Rouge: Louisiana State University Press.

POLAKOFF, KEITH J.   1973   *The Politics of Inertia: The Election of 1876 and the End of Reconstruction.* Baton Rouge: Louisiana State University Press.

WOODWARD, C. VANN   1966   *Reunion and Reaction: The Compromise of 1877 and the End of Reconstruction.* Boston: Little, Brown.

COMPULSORY PROCESS, RIGHT TO

The first state to adopt a constitution following the Declaration of Independence (New Jersey, 1776) guaranteed all criminal defendants the same "privileges of witnesses" as their prosecutors. Fifteen years later, in enumerating the constitutional rights of accused persons, the framers of the federal BILL OF RIGHTS bifurcated what New Jersey called the "privileges of witnesses" into two distinct but related rights: the Sixth Amendment right of the accused "to be confronted with the witnesses against him," and his companion Sixth Amendment right to "compulsory process for obtaining witnesses in his favor." The distinction between witnesses "against" the accused and witnesses "in his favor" turns on which of the parties—the prosecution or the defense—offers the witness's statements in evidence as a formal part of its case. The CONFRONTATION clause establishes the government's obligations regarding the production and examination of witnesses whose statements the prosecution puts into evidence either in its case in chief or in rebuttal. The compulsory process clause establishes the government's obligations regarding the production and examination of witnesses whose statements the defendant seeks to put into evidence in his respective case.

The constitutional questions of compulsory process are twofold: What is "compulsory process?" Who are the "witnesses in his favor" for whom a defendant is entitled to compulsory process? The first is the easier of the two questions to answer. "Compulsory process" is a term of art used to denominate the state's coercive devices for locating, producing, and compelling evidence from witnesses. A common example is the SUBPOENA *ad testificandum,* a judicial order to a person to appear and testify as a witness, or suffer penalty of CONTEMPT for failing to do so. The right of compulsory process, in turn, is the right of a defendant to invoke such coercive devices at the state's disposal to obtain evidence in his defense. The right of compulsory process is therefore no guarantee that defendants will succeed in locating, producing, or compelling witnesses to testify in their favor; it does not entitle defendants to the testimony of witnesses who have died or otherwise become unavailable to testify through no fault of the state. Rather, it assures defendants that the state will make reasonable, good-faith efforts to produce such requested witnesses as are available to testify at trial. It gives a defendant access to the same range of official devices for producing available evidence on his behalf as the prosecution enjoys for producing available evidence on its behalf.

The more significant question for a defendant is: Who are the witnesses for whom a defendant is entitled to compulsory process? What law defines "witnesses in his favor"? Early commentators argued that a defendant might claim compulsory process only with respect to witnesses whose testimony had already been determined to be admissible, according to the governing rules of evidence in the respective jurisdiction. The Supreme Court in its seminal 1967 decision in *Washington v. Texas* rejected that narrow interpretation of "witnesses in his favor." The defendant had been tried in state court for a homicide that he asserted his accomplice alone had committed. The accomplice, who had already been convicted of committing the murder, had appeared at the defendant's trial and offered to testify that he, the accomplice, had acted alone in committing the homicide. The trial court, invoking a state rule of evidence disqualifying accomplices from testifying for one another in criminal cases, refused to allow the accomplice to testify in Washington's favor, and Washington was convicted. The Supreme Court held, first, that the compulsory process clause of the Sixth Amendment, like other clauses of the Sixth Amendment, had become applicable to the states through the DUE PROCESS clause of the FOURTEENTH AMENDMENT. Second, and more significantly, the Court held that the meaning of "witnesses in [a defendant's] favor" was to be determined not by state or federal evidentiary standards of admissibility but by independent constitutional standards of admissibility. The compulsory process clause, it said, directly defines the "witnesses" the defendant is entitled to call to the witness stand. The state in *Washington* violated the defendant's right of compulsory process by "arbitrarily" preventing him from eliciting evidence from a person "who was physically and mentally capable of testifying to events that he had personally observed, and whose testimony would have been relevant and material to the defense."

Having determined that the compulsory process clause operates to render exculpatory evidence independently admissible on a defendant's behalf, the Court found *Washington* to be an easy case; the accomplice's proffered testimony was highly probative of the defendant's innocence, and the state's reasons for excluding it were highly attenuated. The Court has since invoked the authority of *Washington* to prohibit a trial judge from silencing a defense witness by threatening him with prosecution for perjury; to prohibit a state from invoking state HEARSAY RULES to exclude highly probative hearsay evidence in a defendant's favor; and to prohibit a trial judge from instructing a jury that defense witnesses are less worthy of belief than prosecution witnesses. Lower courts have invoked the compulsory process clause to compel the government to disclose the identity of informers; to compel defense witnesses to testify over claims of EVIDENTIARY PRIVILEGES; and to compel the prosecution to grant use IMMUNITY to defense witnesses asserting the RIGHT AGAINST SELF-INCRIMINATION. Although the Supreme Court in *Washington* did not define the outer limits of the compulsory process clause, it subsequently emphasized in *Chambers v. Mississippi* (1973) that "few rights are more fundamental than the right of an accused to present witnesses in his defense."

The companion clause to compulsory process, the confrontation clause, is the more widely known and the more often litigated of the Sixth Amendment witness clauses. The issues of confrontation can be grouped into two questions: What does the right "to be confronted" with witnesses mean? Who are the "witnesses against him" whom a defendant is entitled to confront? The answer to the first question has become relatively clear in recent years. Some commentators, including JOHN HENRY WIGMORE, once argued that the right to be "confronted" with witnesses meant no more than the right of a defendant to be brought face to face with the state's witnesses and to cross-examine them in accord with the ordinary (nonconstitutional) rules of evidence. The Supreme Court in 1974 rejected that position in *Davis v. Alaska*. Davis was convicted in a state court on the basis of testimony for the prosecution by a

juvenile delinquent. On cross-examination, the witness refused to answer impeaching questions relating to his current delinquency status, invoking a state-law privilege for the confidentiality of juvenile court records. The Supreme Court held that the right to be confronted with prosecution witnesses creates an independent right in defendants, overriding state rules of evidence to the contrary, to elicit probative evidence from the state's witnesses by cross-examining them for exculpatory evidence they may possess. The Court has yet to decide how far the right to examine prosecution witnesses extends in circumstances other than those presented in *Davis*. The parallel right of compulsory process suggests, however, that the confrontation clause entitles a defendant to elicit by cross-examination from prosecution witnesses the same range of probative evidence that the compulsory process clause entitles him to elicit by direct examination from defense witnesses. Both witness clauses serve the same purpose—to enable an accused to defend himself by examining witnesses for probative evidence in his defense.

The more difficult, and still uncertain, question of confrontation is the meaning of "witnesses against him." A defendant certainly has a right to face and cross-examine whichever witnesses the prosecution actually produces in court. The question is whether the confrontation clause also defines the "witnesses" whom the prosecution must call to the witness stand. Does the confrontation clause specify which witnesses the prosecution must produce in person? Or does it merely entitle a defendant to confront whichever witnesses the prosecution in its discretion chooses to produce? These questions arise most frequently in connection with hearsay, that is, evidence whose probative value rests on the perception, memory, narration, or sincerity of a "hearsay declarant," someone not present in court—and thus not subject to cross-examination. Most jurisdictions address the hearsay problem by treating hearsay as presumptively inadmissible, subject to numerous exceptions for particular kinds of hearsay that are admissible either because of their reliability or for other reasons. The Sixth Amendment potentially comes into play whenever the prosecution invokes such an exception to introduce hearsay evidence against the accused. The confrontation question is whether the hearsay declarant is a "witness against" the defendant, within the meaning of the Sixth Amendment, who must be produced for cross-examination under oath and in the presence of the jury.

The Supreme Court held in *Bruton v. United States* (1968) that a prosecutor must produce in person a declarant whose out-of-court statements are being offered against an accused, not to prove him guilty but to spare the state the administrative burden of conducting separate trials. The more difficult question is what other declarants are "witnesses" against an accused for constitutional purposes.

Some authorities have argued that hearsay declarants are always witnesses against the accused for Sixth Amendment purposes and, hence, must always be produced in person as a predicate for using their out-of-court statements against an accused, even if they are no longer available to appear or testify in person. Other authorities argue that hearsay declarants are never witnesses against the accused for Sixth Amendment purposes. The Supreme Court appears to have adopted a middle position. *Ohio v. Roberts* (1980) arguably held that although the state has a Sixth Amendment obligation to produce in person available hearsay declarants whom it can reasonably assume the defendant would wish to examine in person at the time their out-of-court statements are introduced into evidence, the state has no Sixth Amendment obligation to produce hearsay declarants who have become unavailable through no fault of the state. The state remains constitutionally free to use the hearsay statements of these declarants, provided that the statements possess sufficient "indicia of reliability" to afford the trier of fact "a satisfactory basis" for evaluating their truth—such as statements that fall within "firmly rooted hearsay exceptions." Significantly, the state's burden of production under the confrontation clause thus parallels its burdens under the compulsory process clause. Both clauses require the state to make reasonable, good-faith efforts to produce in person witnesses the defendant wishes to examine for evidence in his defense. Yet neither clause requires the state to produce witnesses whom a defendant is not reasonably expected to wish to examine for evidence in his defense, or witnesses who have died, disappeared, or otherwise become unavailable through no fault of the state.

Although the confrontation clause does not require the state to produce declarants who are unavailable to testify in person or whom a defendant is not reasonably expected to wish to examine in person, other constitutional provisions do regulate the state's use of their hearsay statements. *Manson v. Brathwaite* (1977) held that the due process clauses of the Fifth and Fourteenth Amendments require the state to ensure that every item of evidence it uses against an accused, presumably including hearsay evidence, possesses sufficient "features of reliability" to be rationally evaluated by the jury for its truth. The compulsory process clause, in turn, requires states to assist the defendant in producing every available witness, including available hearsay declarants, whose presence the defendant requests and who appears to possess probative evidence in his favor. It follows, therefore, that although the state has no obligation under the confrontation clause to produce hearsay declarants who are unavailable to testify in person, it has a residual due process obligation to ensure that their hearsay statements possess sufficient "indicia of reliability" to support a conviction of the accused. Although the state has no obligation under the confrontation clause to produce as prosecution witnesses available declarants whom it does not reasonably believe the defendant would wish to examine in person at the time their out-of-court statements are introduced into evidence, it has a residual obligation under the compulsory process clause to assist him in producing such declarants whenever the defendant indicates that he wishes to call and examine them as witnesses in his defense.

PETER WESTEN
(1986)

Bibliography

WELLBORN III, OLIN GUY   1982   The Definition of Hearsay in the Federal Rules of Evidence. *Texas Law Review* 61:49–93.

WESTEN, PETER   1974   The Compulsory Process Clause. *Michigan Law Review* 73:73–184.

——— 1978   Confrontation and Compulsory Process: A Unified Theory of Evidence for Criminal Cases. *Harvard Law Review* 91:567–628.

——— 1979   The Future of Confrontation. *Michigan Law Review* 77:1185–1217.

COMPUTERS

The rapid advance of computer technology has drastically expanded our ability to store, analyze, and disseminate information. This development has implications for three areas of constitutional doctrine: the RIGHT OF PRIVACY, PROCEDURAL DUE PROCESS OF LAW, and the FREEDOM OF SPEECH and FREEDOM OF THE PRESS.

Because the field is so new, the Supreme Court has not yet had many opportunities to confront these issues. An account of the Court's JURISPRUDENCE so far reveals that it is only slowly beginning to recognize in computer technology a danger different in kind from that presented by information technologies supplanted. Thus, in LAIRD V. TATUM (1972), the earliest of the Court's computer cases, the question presented was whether the Constitution limits the government's right to store publicly available information in computerized form. One of the complaints in *Laird* was that the storage of such information in army-intelligence data banks for undefined subsequent use had a CHILLING EFFECT on the expression of those targeted for observation. In finding that the effect was so speculative that the controversy was not ripe for adjudication, the Court in effect held that government storage of personal information in a computer does not in itself give rise to a constitutionally based complaint.

WHALEN V. ROE (1977) was the first opinion expressly addressing the right of privacy in a computer context. A New York law required centralized computer storage of the names and addresses of persons prescribed certain drugs. The Court acknowledged "the threat to privacy implicit in the accumulation of vast amounts of personal information in computerized data banks." In a CONCURRING OPINION, Justice WILLIAM J. BRENNAN noted that the potential for abuse of computerized information might necessitate "some curb on such technology." Nonetheless, the Court analyzed the law under the same BALANCING TEST used in other cases involving government invasions of privacy, balancing the state's interest in collecting drug-use information against the interest in privacy, and upheld the statute. Although the Court emphasized the stringent security measures taken to prevent unnecessary or unauthorized access to New York's computer files, lower courts have given *Whalen* a narrow reading and placed few constitutional restrictions on government use of computerized data banks. These lower courts have given greater weight to the earlier decision in PAUL V. DAVIS (1976), where the Court had held that alleged LIBEL and public disclosure of arrest records by government officials did not amount to a deprivation of "liberty."

Although the Court seems headed toward a narrow conception of privacy of computerized records as protected by the Constitution, it has embraced a broader view in statutory contexts. In *Department of Justice v. Reporters' Committee for Freedom of the Press* (1989), for example, the Court upheld a privacy interest against a request by CBS News under the FREEDOM OF INFORMATION ACT for disclosure of "rap sheets." Here, the Court noted that "there is a vast difference between public records that might be found after a diligent search of courthouse files, county archives, and local police stations throughout the country and a computerized summary located in a single clearinghouse of information."

A second important set of privacy questions raised by governmental use of computers is the extent to which computers may be used as an aid or substitute for other decision-making processes. This is a question not merely of the use of stored information but also the use of sophisticated programs that make possible new modes of analysis. One example is computerized matching, now a widespread practice at both the federal and state levels. These powerful programs can, for instance, help determine the eligibility of recipients of governmental benefits by matching lists of the individuals receiving such benefits with other governmental records (such as tax returns, employment files, and automobile licenses), with publicly available information, or with privately supplied informa-

tion. Although some statutes and regulations limit these computerized matching programs, most courts have failed to perceive the practices as raising constitutional concerns. Some, however, have suggested that computerized matching is the kind of search that should require a SEARCH WARRANT.

The more important issue posed by computerized matching is what action is to be taken on a "hit" (that is, a match between records). What, for example, happens when an individual on a list of recipients of unemployment benefits also turns up on a file of federal employees? This is a question of procedural due process, and once again, the analysis applied so far has not differed from situations in which computers are not used. Similar questions arise in the criminal context, where computerized records may be used to determine whether a person has outstanding arrest warrants or is driving a stolen vehicle.

A closely related question is whether sophisticated computerized analysis techniques may be utilized to develop profiles of certain kinds of individuals that are then used to identify specific people as the focus of governmental law enforcement and investigation. Thus, the government has, in part through computerized analysis of cases, developed certain statistically based profiles of typical drug smugglers. Those who meet the profile are targeted for intense examination, sometimes involving other computerized techniques. In *United States v. Sokolow* (1989) the Court analogized drug-courier profiles to the "hunches" on which police officers typically operate. It then required the same showing of reasonable suspicion required in other instances in which persons are stopped for questioning. Although the Court did not see in the "empirical documentation" of the profile any greater basis for suspecting persons meeting the profile, it also did not find in the profiling technique any cause for heightened constitutional scrutiny.

A final area in which computers figure directly in constitutional analysis is the freedom of speech and freedom of the press. In this area, the question is the extent to which computerized forms of communication are protected by the FIRST AMENDMENT. Is, for example, a computerized bulletin board protected against libel judgments to the same extent as a newspaper under the standard of NEW YORK TIMES V. SULLIVAN (1964)? Can the government subject computers to greater restrictions than other forms of communication? In *Marshfield Family Skateland, Inc. v. Town of Marshfield* (1983), the Supreme Court dismissed a challenge to an ordinance banning video games on the ground it failed to present a substantial federal question, but has not otherwise addressed the issue. Lower court cases have thus far largely involved criminal prosecution, for example, for using computers in gambling. Although these decisions held that the computer programs were unprotected speech, the computers were so integral to the commission of the crime that these cases are not necessarily indicative of the extent to which courts will find that computers raise unique constitutional questions.

ROCHELLE C. DREYFUS
DAVID W. LEEBRON
(1992)

(SEE ALSO: *Science, Technology, and the Constitution.*)

Bibliography

FREEDMAN, WARREN 1987 *The Right of Privacy in the Computer Age.* New York: Quorum Books.
PRIVACY PROTECTION STUDY COMMISSION 1977 *Personal Privacy in an Information Society.* Washington, D.C.: U.S. Government Printing Office.
SHATTUCK, JOHN 1984 In the Shadow of 1984: National Identification Systems, Computer Matching, and Privacy in the United States. *Hastings Law Journal* 35:991–1005.
U.S. DEPARTMENT OF HEALTH, EDUCATION AND WELFARE 1973 *Records, Computers and the Rights of Citizens* (Report of the Secretary's Advisory Committee on Automated Personal Data Systems). Washington, D.C.: U.S. Government Printing Office.
WESTIN, ALAN F. 1972 *Databanks in a Free Society: Computers, Record-Keeping and Privacy.* New York: Quadrangle Books.

CONCORD TOWN MEETING RESOLUTIONS
(October 21, 1776)

The people of Concord, Massachusetts, at a town meeting in 1776, were the first to recommend a CONSTITUTIONAL CONVENTION as the only proper body to frame a CONSTITUTION. Earlier that year the provisional legislature of Massachusetts had requested permission from the people of the state to draw up a constitution. The legislature had recommended that the free males of voting age assemble in all the towns to determine that issue and also to decide whether the constitution should be made public for the towns to consider before the legislature ratified it. Nine towns objected to the recommended procedure on the grounds that a legislature was not competent for the purpose. Among the nine, Concord best described the procedure that should be followed.

Concord's resolutions declared that the legislature was not competent for three reasons: a constitution is intended to secure the people in their rights against the government; the body that forms a constitution has the power to alter it; a constitution alterable by the legislature is "no security at all" against the government's encroachment on the rights of the people. Accordingly, Concord resolved, a convention representing the towns should be chosen by all the free male voters. The sole task of the convention should be to frame the constitution. Having completed its task, the convention should publish the proposed constitution "for the Inspection and Remarks" of the people. One week later the town of Attleboro, endorsing the Concord principle of a convention, recommended that the constitution be ratified by the people of the towns rather than by the legislature.

The legislature, ignoring the dissident towns, framed a constitution but submitted it for ratification. The people overwhelmingly rejected it. In 1780 the people ratified a state constitution that was framed by a constitutional convention, the first in the history of the world to be so framed. Concord had designed an institution of government that conformed with the SOCIAL COMPACT theory of forming a FUNDAMENTAL LAW.

LEONARD W. LEVY
(1986)

CONCURRENT JURISDICTION

The Constitution does not require Congress to create lower federal courts. The Framers assumed that state courts would be competent to hear the cases included in Article III's definition of the JUDICIAL POWER OF THE UNITED STATES. When Congress does choose to confer some of the federal judicial power on lower federal courts, state courts normally retain their JURISDICTION as well. This simultaneous or concurrent jurisdiction of state and federal courts normally exists unless Congress enacts a law stating that the federal power shall be exclusive. Only in unusual circumstances, as when state jurisdiction would gravely disrupt a federal program, has the Supreme Court required an explicit grant of congressional authority for concurrent state jurisdiction to exist. Indeed, in the limited instance of DIVERSITY JURISDICTION, the Framers intended concurrent jurisdiction to be mandatory, so that Congress could not divest state courts of judicial power they possessed before adoption of the Constitution.

Concurrent jurisdiction allows plaintiffs initial choice of a forum more sympathetic to their claims. In many circumstances, however, a defendant may supplant that choice by exercising a right under federal law to remove the case from state to federal court. (See REMOVAL OF CASES.)

State courts need not always agree to exercise their concurrent jurisdiction. If a state court declines to hear a federal claim for nondiscriminatory reasons tied to the sound management of the state judicial system, the Supreme Court will respect that decision.

When concurrent jurisdiction exists, state and federal courts may be asked to adjudicate the same rights or claims between parties at the same time. Ordinarily neither the federal nor the state court is required to stay its proceeding in such situations. However, the federal courts do possess a limited statutory power to enjoin pending state proceedings, and a state or federal court that is the first to obtain custody of property that is the subject of the dispute may enjoin the other.

CAROLE E. GOLDBERG-AMBROSE
(1986)

Bibliography

CURRIE, DAVID 1981 *Federal Jurisdiction in a Nutshell*, 2nd ed. St. Paul, Minn.: West Publishing Co.

CONCURRENT POWERS

In THE FEDERALIST, JAMES MADISON, wrote that in fashioning the federal relationship "the convention must have been compelled to sacrifice theoretical propriety to the force of extraneous circumstances." These sacrifices which produced a "compound republic, partaking both of the national and federal character" were "rendered indispensable" by what Madison termed "the peculiarity of our political situation." An important feature of the compound republic is the idea of concurrent powers.

Concurrent powers are those exercised independently in the same field of legislation by both federal and state governments, as in the case of the power to tax or to make BANKRUPTCY laws. As ALEXANDER HAMILTON explained in *The Federalist* #32, "the State governments would clearly retain all the rights of SOVEREIGNTY which they before had, and which were not, by that act, *exclusively* delegated to the United States." Hamilton goes on to explain that this "alienation" would exist in three cases only: where there is in express terms an exclusive delegation of authority to the federal government, as in the case of the seat of government; where authority is granted in one place to the federal government and prohibited to the states in another, as in the case of IMPOSTS; and where a power is granted to the federal government "to which a similar authority in the States would be absolutely and totally *contradictory* and *repugnant,* as in the case of prescribing naturalization rules." This last, Hamilton notes, would not comprehend the exercise of concurrent powers which "might be productive of occasional interferences in the *policy* of any branch of administration, but would not imply any direct contradiction or repugnancy in point of constitutional authority." The only explicit mention of concurrent power in the Constitution occurred in the ill-fated EIGHTEENTH AMENDMENT which provided that "the Congress and the several States shall have concurrent power to enforce this article."

The story of concurrent power in modern American constitutional history has largely been the story of federal PREEMPTION. The concurrent authority of the states is always subordinate to the superior authority of the federal government and generally can be exercised by the states only where the federal government has not occupied the field, or where Congress has given the states permission to exercise concurrent powers. Thus in MCCULLOCH V. MARYLAND (1819), Maryland's concurrent power of taxation had to give way when the state sought to tax a federal instrumentality, because such a tax was utterly repugnant to federal supremacy.

In the years since *McCulloch* the Supreme Court has devised an intricate system for determining when a federal exercise of power has implicitly or explicitly worked to diminish or extinguish the concurrent powers of the states. The federal government's steady expansion of power over the years has, of course, placed more restrictions on concurrent action by the states as, in more and more areas, the federal government has occupied the whole field of legislation.

The Court's decision in *Pacific and Electric Company v. Energy Resources Commission* (1983) provides a useful summary of the factors that determine whether federal preemption may be said to have taken place: whether Congress is acting within constitutional limits and explicitly states its intention to preempt state authority; whether the scheme of federal regulation is so pervasive as to make reasonable the inference that Congress intended for the state to be excluded from concurrent regulation; whether, even though the regulation of Congress is not pervasive, the operation of concurrent powers on the part of the state would actually conflict with federal law; and whether, in the absence of pervasive legislation, state law stands as an obstacle to the accomplishment of the full purposes and objectives of Congress. It is not difficult to see that most of the states' concurrent powers today exist at the forbearance of the federal legislature. This result was not entirely anticipated by the Framers of the Constitution; but it was the inevitable consequence of the centripetal forces embodied in the national features of the compound republic.

EDWARD J. ERLER
(1986)

Bibliography

DODD, WALTER F. 1963 Concurrent Powers. In Edwin R. Seligman, ed., *Encyclopedia of the Social Sciences*, Vol. 4:173–174. New York: Macmillan.

STORY, JOSEPH 1833 *Commentaries on the Constitution of the United States*, Vol. 1:407–433. Boston: Hilliard, Gray & Co.

CONCURRENT RESOLUTION

Concurrent resolutions adopted by the Congress, unlike JOINT RESOLUTIONS, do not require the president's signature and do not ordinarily have the force of law. Concurrent resolutions may be used to express the "sense of Congress" or to regulate the internal affairs of Congress (such as expenditure of funds for congressional housekeeping).

Since 1939, concurrent resolutions have been the normal means of expressing the LEGISLATIVE VETO when by law that limit on PRESIDENTIAL ORDINANCE-MAKING POWER requires action by both houses. Recent examples of this requirement are found in the WAR POWERS ACT (1973) and the CONGRESSIONAL BUDGET AND IMPOUNDMENT CONTROL ACT (1974).

DENNIS J. MAHONEY
(1986)

CONCURRING OPINION

When a member of a multi-judge court agrees with the DECISION reached by the majority but disagrees with the reasoning of the OPINION OF THE COURT or wishes to add his own remarks, he will customarily file a concurring opinion. The concurring opinion usually proposes an alternative way of reaching the same result. Once relatively rare, separate concurrences have become, in the late twentieth century, a normal part of the workings of the Supreme Court of the United States.

A concurring opinion may diverge from the majority opinion only slightly or only on technical points, or it may propose an entirely different line of argument. One example of the latter sort is found in ROCHIN V. CALIFORNIA (1952) in which the concurring opinions staked out a much bolder course of constitutional interpretation than the majority was willing to follow. In a constitutional system in which great issues of public policy are decided in controversies between private litigants, the principles of law enunciated in the opinions are usually of far greater importance than the decision with respect to the parties to the case. Sometimes dissenting Justices are closer to the majority on principles than are concurring Justices.

In the most important cases, several Justices may write separate opinions, even though there is substantial agreement on the grounds for deciding the case. DRED SCOTT V. SANDFORD (1857) and the CAPITAL PUNISHMENT CASES (1972) are examples of cases in which every Justice filed a separate concurring or DISSENTING OPINION.

Scholars generally agree that separate concurrences often diminish the authority of the court's decision and reduce the degree of certainty of the law. Some critics have suggested elimination of concurring opinions, especially when they are filed by Justices who also subscribe to the MAJORITY OPINION. But concurring opinions, no less than dissenting opinions, provide alternative courses for future constitutional development.

DENNIS J. MAHONEY
(1986)

CONDITIONAL SPENDING

The United States Constitution allocates legislative authority between a federal Congress and state governments. Congress may legislate or regulate only pursuant to specific powers expressly delegated in the Constitution; excepting IMPLIED POWERS, all powers not delegated to the national government are retained by the state governments. The power to spend money for the common defense or the GENERAL WELFARE, however, is a power separate from, and in addition to, all of Congress's other ENUMERATED POWERS. Thus, Congress may spend federal funds for any purpose that can be thought to contribute to the general welfare, even though none of Congress's enumerated powers encompasses the subject of the expenditure. Congress may not impose regulatory requirements, however, even though admittedly in the interest of the common defense and general welfare, unless the area regulated is one over which regulatory control is delegated to Congress.

The power to spend carries with it the power to attach certain conditions to the expenditure. Those conditions in effect specify how federal grants will be used. For example, if Congress grants the states funds to build highways, Congress has the concomitant power to specify where the highways should run or how they should be built. This power to impose conditions permits Congress to ensure that its money is actually spent as Congress intends.

The conditional spending problem is presented when Congress seeks to purchase, not the usual goods and services, but compliance with a legislative objective that normally would be pursued by a simple regulation backed by a regulatory penalty such as a fine. When Congress uses its spending power to offer a financial inducement—a reward—for conduct that it could not directly require or regulate under any of its other enumerated powers, the core constitutional conception of specifically delegated powers is threatened. The problem posed by conditional spending is the extent to which federally induced state reliance on federal moneys gives Congress effective regulatory authority over the states beyond the powers delegated to Congress in the Constitution.

The question is of central importance to the basic constitutional scheme of FEDERALISM. Over the course of the last several decades, the federal tax burden on individuals has increased substantially, making it increasingly difficult as a political matter for state legislatures to raise state taxes. At the same time that the federal tax burden has deterred states from raising their own revenue, national grant programs for general welfare purposes, such as highways, education, and health, have induced states to rely increasingly on national funds to finance state services. Substantial state reliance on the distribution of money raised by national taxation is now a fact of political life in the federal system. This financial dependence of the states on Congress's beneficence invites Congress to extract concessions from the states, to require the states to accept "conditions" in return for the revenues now under Congress's control. If there are no constitutional limitations on the conditions Congress can attach to federal grants, Congress may extract tax revenue from the citizens of the several states, pursuant to the taxing power, and then return that revenue to the states, under the spending power, on the condition that the states impose on themselves or their citizens some regulation that Congress constitutionally could not have imposed under its other enumerated powers.

There are two competing views on the constitutionality of conditions attached by Congress to federal grants. The first view holds that offering a government benefit as a reward for compliance with some congressional objective is in effect identical to regulatory coercion by imposition of a fine to obtain the same end. Under this view, if achievement of an end is beyond Congress's delegated regulatory powers, it also should be constitutionally invalid when pursued through a conditional spending scheme. The second view is that the use of the spending power to offer a reward for compliance with some congressional objective is distinguishable from regulatory coercion in the form of a fine for noncompliance because the latter removes the freedom of choice while the former does not. According to this view, a state or individual confronted with the offer of a conditional grant may refuse the reward and persist in noncompliance, while one confronting a regulatory fine has no freedom of choice. Moreover, a fine takes money but a spending scheme awards it; refusing takes no money. Under this view, then, direct congressional regulation is confined to the enumerated powers, but Congress's purchase of compliance through a scheme of conditional spending is not similarly restrained.

Early spending power cases asserted that there is no conceptual difference between withholding a benefit and imposing a fine to achieve a regulatory end, and applied this principle to protect STATES' RIGHTS. UNITED STATES V. BUTLER (1936) involved a challenge to the AGRICULTURAL ADJUSTMENT ACT OF 1933 (AAA). Under the act, processors of agricultural goods were taxed and the proceeds from the tax were used to pay farmers to allow their land to lie fallow. The purpose of the scheme was to stabilize farm prices by reducing the supply of farm goods in the market. Respondents challenged the scheme as beyond the scope of Congress's delegated powers, primarily the INTERSTATE COMMERCE power, because the act sought to regulate the purely local activity of agricultural production. The United States did not attempt to defend the scheme as a valid commerce regulation, but argued it could be sustained as a valid exercise of Congress's authority to spend "for the general welfare."

The Court disagreed in *Butler,* holding that the scheme was invalid precisely because Congress used its spending power to achieve a regulatory effect on agriculture, otherwise outside the scope of its delegated powers and subject only to state control. The Court expressly endorsed the Hamiltonian view that although Congress had limited powers, the spending power is not limited to the subjects of the enumerated powers; but the Court said the scheme was not a simple exercise of Congress's power to spend. It was "at best . . . a scheme for purchasing with federal funds submission to federal regulation of a subject reserved to the states." The Court distinguished between a conditional appropriation where the condition specifies how the money is to be spent, which is valid, and a conditional appropriation where the goal of the condition is regulation: "There is an obvious difference between a statute stating the conditions upon which moneys shall be expended and one effective only upon assumption of a contractual obligation to submit to a regulation which otherwise could be enforced. . . . If in lieu of compulsory regulation of subjects within the states' reserved JURISDICTION, which is prohibited, the Congress could invoke the taxing and spending power as a means to accomplish the same end, clause 1 of Section 8 of article 1 would become the instrument for total subversion of the governmental powers reserved to the individual states."

By modern standards *Butler* was decided wrongly. *Butler's* real error, however, was not in holding that spending legislation could not be used to accomplish regulatory ends outside Congress's delegated powers; rather, it was in adopting a narrow interpretation of Congress's power under the COMMERCE CLAUSE that disallowed price-support legislation. Such a result would not hold up today. But in *Butler* the Court's perception that the AAA was regulation, not spending, seems unassailable.

The conceptual foundation of *Butler*—that a reward for compliance is regulation, not spending—has been carried forward and expanded by the modern Court in some CIVIL LIBERTIES cases, FIRST AMENDMENT cases in particular. In those cases, the Court has recognized that offering a governmental benefit on the condition that the individual refrain from engaging in protected activities is the economic and constitutional equivalent of imposing a fine for the violation of a regulation prohibiting the activity. For example, the Court has held that if government offers a financial reward in return for the recipient's agreement to forgo a practice commanded by her religion, the conditional grant presents the same RELIGIOUS LIBERTY problem that would be presented by a fine for engaging in the religious practice. Either presents the same governmental interference with the individual's constitutionally protected liberty. In either case, the individual may choose to continue the protected activity and suffer the economic loss or forgo the protected activity and avoid the economic loss. In individual liberties cases this proposition is known as the doctrine of UNCONSTITUTIONAL CONDITIONS and is often identified with the Court's decision in SHERBERT V. VERNER (1963).

In its most recent encounter with conditional spending, the Supreme Court appears to have abandoned the conceptual foundation of *Butler* and ignored its currency in the individual liberties area. In *South Dakota v. Dole* (1987) the Court confronted a challenge to the national minimum drinking age (NMDA) amendment to the National Surface Transportation Act. The act authorizes federal grants to the states for the construction of national highways. The NMDA instructed the secretary of transportation to withhold up to ten percent of a state's federal highway funds if that state fails to enact a minimum drinking age of twenty-one within the next year. Thus, by attaching a condition to a grant, Congress sought to impose a uniform national minimum drinking age. In *Dole* the Court assumed for purposes of the case that Congress, after the TWENTY-FIRST AMENDMENT, could not have enacted a regulation requiring each state to adopt such a minimum drinking age for the state. Nor, the Court assumed arguendo, could Congress constitutionally have enacted a simple regulation directly prohibiting the purchase or consumption of alcohol by persons under twenty-one years of age. Thus, the only issue left for the *Dole* Court to resolve was whether the MNDA was constitutional as a condition accompanying a grant of federal funds to the states, even assuming that Congress could not regulate drinking ages directly under any of its delegated legislative powers.

The *Dole* Court observed that "Congress has acted indirectly under its spending power to encourage uniformity in the States' drinking ages." Thus, the legislation was held to be "within constitutional bounds even if Congress may not regulate drinking ages directly." In essence, the Court held that although Congress lacks regulatory authority to achieve a legislative end directly, Congress may "purchase" state compliance through the use of conditions attached to spending grants. The basis of the Court's holding is that there is a difference between coercing compliance (an exercise of regulatory power) and buying compliance (an exercise of the spending power). The *Dole* holding is in tension with other Supreme Court PRECEDENTS, notably *Butler* and the individual liberties cases, which recognize that conditional spending can be the conceptual and economic equivalent of direct regulation. In effect, the Court in *Dole*, voting 7–2, reverted to the notion that compliance with a condition attached to a benefit is "voluntary" as long as the potential recipient can choose to forgo the benefit in order to avoid compliance with the condition.

The Supreme Court's decision in *Dole* appears to invite the complete abrogation of all limits on delegated federal LEGISLATIVE POWER through the simple device of burdensome taxes accompanied by "financial incentives" to comply with any federal legislative objective that is outside the range of concerns constitutionally delegated to Congress. Chief Justice WILLIAM H. REHNQUIST's opinion in *Dole*, however, suggested some limitations on the breadth of the Court's holding.

First, said the Chief Justice, Congress may "induce" or "tempt" voluntary compliance, but may not "coerce" compliance. The difficulty with the coercion-inducement test as a limit on congressional action is that it simply restates the distinction—discredited in some modern individual liberties cases—between achieving an end by regulation and achieving an end by withholding a benefit. The question of "how much benefit" simply is beside the point, for as *Sherbert v. Verner* concluded, any benefit withheld is tantamount to a fine in that amount. One who is subject to the threat of a regulatory fine may choose to violate the regulation and pay the fine because the amount of the fine is modest. But that "freedom" of choice does not eliminate constitutional objections to the substance of the regulation.

The facts of the *Dole* case suggest that Chief Justice Rehnquist was relying upon a distinction Congress would not even credit. Congress's very purpose in enacting the NMDA would have been undercut seriously if not every state had complied; it is clear that Congress had no intention of offering a choice, but threatened to withhold a benefit to obtain regulatory compliance.

Second, in a footnote Rehnquist suggested a constitutional requirement that any condition attached to a federal grant bear some relationship to that grant. In applying this suggestion to the facts of *Dole*, however, the Chief Justice simply noted that the condition related to the national problem of teenage drunk driving. Teenage drunk driving may well be a problem national in scope, but the condition did not in any way specify the characteristics of the highways that the conditioned funds were intended to purchase. Requiring only that the condition relate to a national problem rather than specify characteristics of the particular goods and services to be purchased by the grant seems tantamount to a statement that Congress can regulate perceived national problems through the spending power. Of course, Congress may with greater legitimacy reach many of the same subjects by the exercise of its wide-ranging commerce powers.

THOMAS R. McCOY
BARRY FRIEDMAN
(1992)

(SEE ALSO: *Federal Grants-in-Aid; Taxing and Spending Powers.*)

Bibliography

McCOY, THOMAS R. and FRIEDMAN, BARRY 1988 Conditional Spending: Federalism's Trojan Horse. *Supreme Court Review* 1988:85–127.

MIZERK, DONALD J. 1987 The Coercion Test and Conditional Federal Grants to the States. *Vanderbilt Law Review* 40: 1159–1195.

ROSENTHAL, ALBERT J. 1987 Conditional Federal Spending and the Constitution. *Stanford Law Review* 39:1103–1164.

SULLIVAN, KATHLEEN 1989 Unconstitutional Conditions. *Harvard Law Review* 102:1413–1506.

CONFEDERATE CONSTITUTION

The Constitution of the Confederate States of America, adopted in 1861, closely followed, and was in a sense a commentary upon, the Constitution of the United States. The most important points of divergence were: provision for the heads of executive departments to sit and speak in the Congress, a single six-year term for the President, a line-item VETO POWER over appropriations, explicit provision for presidential power to remove appointed officials, and the requirement of a two-thirds vote in each house to admit new states.

The Confederate Constitution prohibited laws impairing the right of property in slaves; but it also prohibited the foreign slave trade (except with the United States). Other innovations included a ban on federal expenditures for INTERNAL IMPROVEMENTS and provision for state duties on sea-going vessels, to be used for improvement of harbors and navigable waters. The AMENDING PROCESS provided for a convention of the states to be summoned by Congress upon the demand of state conventions; Congress did not have the power to propose amendments itself.

The provisions of the BILL OF RIGHTS of the United States Constitution were written into the body of the Confederate Constitution, as were those of the ELEVENTH and TWELFTH AMENDMENTS.

DENNIS J. MAHONEY
(1986)

Bibliography

COULTER, E. MERTON 1950 *The Confederate States of America, 1861–1865.* Baton Rouge: Louisiana State University Press.

CONFERENCE

When the Justices of the Supreme Court refer to themselves in the aggregate as "the Conference"—as distinguished from "the Court"—they are alluding to their deliberative functions in reaching decisions. The Conference considers, discusses, even negotiates; the Court acts.

The name comes from the Justices' practice of meeting to discuss cases and vote on their disposition. Two kinds of questions are considered at these Conferences: whether the Court should review a case, and how to decide a case under review. Just before the beginning of each term, the Conference considers a great many applications for review. (See APPEAL; CERTIORARI, WRIT OF; APPELLATE JURISDICTION; ORIGINAL JURISDICTION.) During the term, in weeks when ORAL ARGUMENTS are scheduled, the Conference generally meets regularly to consider the cases argued within the preceding few days.

The Conference is limited to the nine Justices. Clerks and secretaries do not attend, and if messages are passed into the room, tradition calls for the junior Justice to be doorkeeper. By another tradition, each Justice shakes hands with all the other Justices before the Conference begins. The CHIEF JUSTICE presides.

The Chief Justice calls a case for discussion, and normally speaks first. The other Justices speak in turn, according to their seniority. (Interruptions are not unknown.) The custom has been for Justices to vote in inverse order of seniority, the Chief Justice voting last. Recent reports, however, suggest flexibility in this practice; when the Justices' positions are already obvious, a formal vote may be unnecessary. The vote at the Conference meeting is not final. Once draft opinions and memoranda "to the Conference" have begun to circulate, votes may change, and even the Court's decision may change.

KENNETH L. KARST
(1986)

(SEE ALSO: *Concurring Opinion; Dissenting Opinion; Opinion of the Court.*)

Bibliography

HUGHES, CHARLES EVANS 1928 *The Supreme Court of the United States: Its Foundation, Methods and Achievements: An Interpretation.* New York: Columbia University Press.

WOODWARD, BOB and ARMSTRONG, SCOTT 1979 *The Brethren: Inside the Supreme Court.* New York: Simon & Schuster.

CONFESSIONS

See: Police Interrogation and Confessions

CONFIRMATIO CARTARUM
1297

Within two centuries after its adoption MAGNA CARTA was reconfirmed forty-four times. The reconfirmation of 1297 is significant because it was the first made after representatives of the commons were admitted to Parliament; because it embodied the inchoate principle that TAXATION WITHOUT REPRESENTATION is unlawful; and because it regarded Magna Carta as FUNDAMENTAL LAW. By one section the king agreed to exact certain taxes only "by the common assent of the realm...." Another section declared that any act by the king's judges or ministers contrary to the great charter "shall be undone, and holden for nought." WILLIAM PENN ordered the charter and its reconfirmation of 1297 reprinted in the colonies for the first time in 1687. JOHN ADAMS, THOMAS JEFFERSON, and other lawyers of the era of the American Revolution were familiar with the principles of the statute of 1297, and in MARBURY V. MADISON (1803) the Supreme Court declared that any act contrary to the fundamental law of the written constitution is void.

LEONARD W. LEVY
(1986)

Bibliography

PERRY, RICHARD L., ed. 1959 *Sources of Our Liberties*. Pages 23–31. New York: American Bar Foundation.

CONFIRMATION PROCESS

The Constitution vests in the President the power to appoint, with the ADVICE AND CONSENT of the U.S. SENATE, "Ambassadors, other public Ministers and Consuls, Judges of the Supreme Court, and all other officers of the United States whose Appointments are not herein otherwise provided for." The Framers, however, were mindful that the lifetime appointment of judges to a coequal branch might demand different procedures and considerations from the appointment of officers serving limited terms in the executive branch and, as a result, throughout a good deal of the CONSTITUTIONAL CONVENTION OF 1787 the method of appointing judges was considered separately from the process of choosing executive officers. Particularly in the case of judicial appointments, achieving agreement among the delegates required a delicate balance to be struck between competing interests at the convention. Smaller states, for example, tended to favor greater senatorial control while representatives from the larger states sought enhanced executive authority through presidential appointment. Complicating the cleavage between small and large was the fundamental issue of where the center of power would be in the new national government; fearful of monarchy, some at the convention sought legislative dominance while others, extolling the virtue of efficiency, called for executive supremacy. Throughout the summer of 1787, the procedures for the appointment of judges and officers of the United States were the subject of spirited debate. The eventual compromise of presidential appointment joined with the advice and consent of the Senate only emerged from the Committee on Postponed Matters in the waning days of the convention. The product of a rather hasty trade-off among sharply held divergent views, the language and history of the APPOINTMENTS CLAUSE leave indefinite the precise nature of the role of the Senate in the appointment and confirmation process. The net result is that, although the phrase "advice and consent" has roots deep in British history, in the American context its interpretation has been shaped by the reality of contemporary politics rather than history or constitutional construction.

ALEXANDER HAMILTON, for example, in THE FEDERALIST, advocated limiting the role of the Senate in the confirmation process to guarding against presidential appointment of "unfit characters." Whatever the constitutional merits of this position, Hamilton's preference quickly proved to be politically unworkable. By the early nineteenth century, the development of a full-fledged party system made the confirmation process, particularly in the case of federal judges, a contentious and often highly partisan affair. During this era senators were selected by state legislatures, and the typical senator was a state party leader sent to the Senate with the task of funneling federal PATRONAGE back to the local party organization. Federal judgeships quickly became part of the patronage package and the successful confirmation of these judges, regardless of individual merit, routinely hinged almost exclusively on the approval of home-state senators. The only indication of Senate deference to presidential prerogative was in the confirmation of cabinet-level appointments. Generally speaking, this was an era of congressional dominance and the Senate had the political autonomy to challenge a wide array of presidential appointments on a variety of partisan and ideological grounds.

During the initial decades of the twentieth century, a series of Progressive-era reforms—including the development of the direct primary, the introduction of nonpartisan local elections, and the passage of the SEVENTEENTH AMENDMENT providing for the direct election of senators—produced weakened party control and organization in the Senate. By the time of the NEW DEAL, the center of influence and power at the national level had shifted from the legislative to the executive branch. The Senate began a period of relative quietude in which widely accepted norms of behavior worked to check the power and independence of individual senators and enhanced the authority and prestige of a few key Senate leaders. At mid-century, the Senate was a conservative, hierarchical, closed institution in which individual senators were content to concentrate on committee assignments and legislative work. Few senators sought media attention and there was little incentive for the average senator to challenge leadership decisions. In such an environment the confirmation process was a highly predictable, low-key, frequently invisible exercise in which a President, having secured the consent of a few key Senate leaders to any nomination, could be reasonably confident of success. Presidential APPOINTMENT OF SUPREME COURT JUSTICES provided a ready example; from the turn of the century to 1968 the Senate confirmed all but one nominee to the Court.

The modern era of the Senate confirmation process begins in the late 1960s with the protracted hearings in the SENATE JUDICIARY COMMITTEE over the nomination of THURGOOD MARSHALL to the Supreme Court and the full Senate's failure to confirm ABE FORTAS as CHIEF JUSTICE in 1968. It is a process that is frequently nasty, brutish, and not particularly short. It is, in fact, a thoroughly democratic process, resembling at times a modern electoral campaign in which powerful interests employ sophisticated media techniques to mobilize public support or opposition. Senate proceedings, both in committee and on the floor, are often contentious and protracted, with the ultimate outcome being anything but predictable. One explanation for this development is the transformation of the modern Senate from an inner-directed, stable, hierarchical institution to a more fluid body populated by senators who are motivated to seek power and influence through national media exposure, unhampered by constraining norms. Contested, highly visible confirmation proceedings suit the public style of contemporary senators. With Senate leadership exercising few, if any, controls over the behavior of the members, the President is forced to negotiate with one hundred independent contractors in order to find the votes to secure confirmation. In the case of judicial appointments, this task is made even more formidable because the JUDICIAL ACTIVISM of the modern era has been marked by a willingness on the part of the federal courts to expand the range of litigants permitted access to the federal courts and to subject a wide sweep of public and private disputes to judicial intervention. This expansion of JUDICIAL POWER has made the question of who sits on the federal bench a matter of grave concern to diverse and powerful interests and makes a contentious confirmation process even more likely.

In the final analysis, a more contentious confirmation process simply reflects a general trend in modern American politics. Institutional combat through mechanisms such as congressional investigations, INDEPENDENT COUNSELS, criminal prosecutions, and media revelations increasingly have come to supplant elections as the means by which opposing political forces vie for influence, power, and control. Confirmation proceedings provide a ready opportunity for political groups to embarrass opposing interests, to impede policy implementation, and to weaken the executive branch by denying the President an expeditious route to filling important posts. As long as elections in the United States fail to define who will and who will not exercise political control, contentious confirmation proceedings for both executive and judicial appointments are ever more likely to be the rule rather than the exception.

MARK SILVERSTEIN
(2000)

(SEE ALSO: *Bork Nomination; Clarence Thomas.*)

Bibliography

ABRAHAM, HENRY J.   1992   *Justices and Presidents: A Political History of Appointments to the Supreme Court,* 3rd ed. New York: Oxford University Press.

GINSBERG, BENJAMIN and SHEFTER, MARTIN   1998   *Politics by Other Means,* 2nd ed. New York: W. W. Norton & Co.

SILVERSTEIN, MARK   1994   *Judicious Choices: The New Politics of Supreme Court Confirmations.* New York: W. W. Norton & Co.

TWENTIETH CENTURY FUND   1996   *Obstacle Course: The Report of the Twentieth Century Fund Force on the Presidential Appointment Process.* New York: Twentieth Century Fund.

CONFISCATION ACTS
12 Stat. 319 (1861)
12 Stat. 589 (1862)

Congress enacted the Confiscation Acts "to insure the speedy termination of the present rebellion." Both statutes liberated the slaves of certain rebels and authorized the confiscation of other types of property by judicial procedures based on admiralty and revenue models. Both statutes were compromise measures, influenced by the progressive goal of emancipation of slaves and by a respect for the rights of private property.

The Supreme Court upheld the constitutionality of the acts in the 6–3 decision of *Miller v. United States* (1871), finding congressional authority in the WAR POWERS clauses of Article I. The majority shrugged off Fifth and Sixth Amendment objections on the grounds that the statutes were not ordinary punitive legislation but rather were extraordinary war measures.

The acts were indifferently and arbitrarily enforced, producing a total of less than $130,000 net to the Treasury. Property of Confederates was also virtually confiscated in proceedings for nonpayment of the wartime direct tax, under the Captured and Abandoned Property Act of 1863, and through President ABRAHAM LINCOLN's contraband emancipation policies.

WILLIAM M. WIECEK
(1986)

Bibliography

RANDALL, JAMES G. 1951 *Constitutional Problems under Lincoln.* Urbana: University of Illinois Press.

CONFRONTATION, RIGHT OF

The confrontation clause of the Sixth Amendment, which guarantees an accused person the right "to be confronted with the witnesses against him," is one of the two clauses in the BILL OF RIGHTS that explicitly address the right of criminal defendants to elicit evidence in their defense from witnesses at trial. The other clause is its Sixth Amendment companion, the COMPULSORY PROCESS clause, which guarantees the accused the right to "compulsory process for obtaining witnesses in his favor." Together these two clauses provide constitutional foundations for the right of accused persons to defend themselves through the production and examination of witnesses at trial.

PETER WESTEN
(1986)

(SEE ALSO: *Hearsay Rule.*)

CONFRONTATION, RIGHT OF
(Update)

The Supreme Court has explained that the accused's Sixth Amendment right "to be confronted with the witnesses against him" has the primary function of furthering the trial's truth-determining process. But recent cases reveal conflicts over the best way to ascertain truth and competing visions of a trial's shape. Cases involving children especially have posed the question whether a dramatic and adversarial trial, with the accusing witness and accused as protagonist and antagonist, tends to produce the most accurate results. They have also posed the question of the extent to which values other than truth-seeking—such as protecting a witness from the trauma of trial—can supervene the confrontation right.

Taking its cue from Shakespeare's *Richard II*—"Then call them to our presence; face to face and frowning brow to brow, ourselves will hear the accuser and the accused freely speak" (1.1.15–17)—the Court in COY V. IOWA (1988)

held that the core of the right, manifest in the Sixth Amendment's text, involves physical face-to-face confrontation between witness and accused. Keeping the dramatis personae together on the trial's stage contributes not only to honest testimony but to maintaining our dramatic sense of what a trial is: "There is something deep in human nature that regards face-to-face confrontation between accused and accuser as "essential to a fair trial." Accordingly, *Coy* held unconstitutional a statute allowing in all such cases a screen to obstruct a sexually abused minor witness's view of the accused.

MARYLAND V. CRAIG (1990) answered affirmatively the question *Coy* reserved: whether a court may employ such a device if it first makes an individualized finding that an important state interest justifies its use in a particular case. But *Craig* did not clarify whether protecting a witness from serious distress or trauma can justify a device that does not also aid truth-seeking by enabling a child, whom distress would otherwise render substantially unavailable, to testify. The device, upheld in *Craig*, altered the nature of the trial by mixing the media of stage and television: in the courtroom, the defendant, judge, and jury watched, via closed-circuit television, real-time pictures of the child testifying in another room in the presence of the prosecutor and defense counsel. In contrast to *Coy*, the *Craig* decision described face-to-face confrontation only as a preference and emphasized that the confrontation clause's interest in reliability can be furthered sufficiently by a witness's testifying under oath and being cross-examined while observed by the trier of fact. In addition, *Kentucky v. Stincer* (1987) determined that the accused may be excluded from a routine witness-competency hearing of a sexually abused minor, because his right to confrontation regarding the witness's substantive testimony remains intact.

Other opinions focus entirely on cross-examination as the core of the confrontation right. While emphasizing that a judge has wide latitude to impose reasonable limits on cross-examination to avoid harassment, prejudice, confusion, trauma, repetition, and the like, recent cases, such as *Delaware v. Van Arsdall* (1986) and *Olden v. Kentucky* (1988), hold that, save for HARMLESS ERROR, a trial judge cannot exclude all inquiry into traditionally relevant subject areas, such as bias and other credibility matters. For example, *Davis v. Alaska* (1974) holds that a court cannot restrict cross-examination about a witness's juvenile court record, despite a statute protecting the record's confidentiality. With respect to the adversarial manner of cross-examination, lower courts do not readily restrict the cross-examination of children to a gentle inquiry using age-appropriate language and concepts, despite claims that traditional cross-examination on counsel's terms is not conducive to a child's truth-telling.

The Court is divided on whether the cross-examination right is exclusively a procedural trial right that guarantees only an opportunity to cross-examine or whether it is also a right that can enhance effective cross-examination by affording PRETRIAL DISCLOSURE, and DISCOVERY. The EYE-WITNESS IDENTIFICATION rules established by UNITED STATES V. WADE (1967) exemplify this latter approach. The former is found in *Pennsylvania v. Ritchie* (1987), in which a trial court refused to give defense counsel access to a child welfare office's investigatory file of a sexual abuse case, pursuant to a statute establishing its confidentiality. Because defense counsel had the opportunity to examine the accusing daughter at trial, a plurality found no confrontation clause violation. The Court did require the trial judge to conduct a review of the file in camera to determine whether the accused's due process rights required disclosure. The view that the confrontation clause assures an opportunity to cross-examine but not effective cross-examination led the Court, in *United States v. Owens* (1988) and *Delaware v. Fensterer* (1985), to uphold the admission of a testifying witness's out-of-court statements, even though he had lost all memory concerning the statements other than the fact that he had previously made them.

Finally, the Supreme Court continues to address the admission of HEARSAY and of codefendant statements. *Ohio v. Roberts* (1980), involving the admission of the prior testimony of an unavailable witness, indicated that the confrontation clause imposes a strong preference for in-court statements, which requires the state to make a good-faith effort to produce the declarant in court, and a requirement that the admission of an out-of-court statement be based on indicia of reliability, established either by its coming "within a firmly rooted hearsay exception" or by a showing of "particularized guarantees of trustworthiness." But in *Bourjaily v. United States* (1987) and *United States v. Inadi* (1986), the Court interpreted the two *Roberts* requirements as applying primarily to the admission of prior testimony. *Bourjaily* limited the *Roberts* indicia of reliability requirement by admitting coconspirator statements under an agency theory without regard to their reliability. *Inadi* permitted the prosecutor to introduce out-of-court statements of a coconspirator without making much effort to produce him. It distinguished prior testimony in *Roberts* from these coconspirator statements, in that the latter, precisely because they were made during the conspiracy, may be more probative than a declarant's subsequent postconspiracy in-court statements. This view—that a trial can best achieve truth through the consideration of statements made in a natural setting rather than through the artifice of a dramatic and adversarial replaying at trial—finds support in some lower court decisions admitting children's out-of-court statements made near the time of their abuse or in the context of a trusted relationship. However, by reemphasizing the *Roberts* requirements, the Supreme Court, in *Idaho v. Wright* (1990), rejected the admission, under a residual hearsay exception, of a sexual abuse accusation made by an unavailable three-year-old in response to the allegedly suggestive questions of an examining pediatrician. With little consideration of the growing psychological evidence on the subject, the Court emphasized that to be admissible the out-of-court statement must have been made under circumstances evidencing such trustworthiness that, subsequently at trial, "adversarial testing would add little to its reliability."

With respect to codefendant confessions, in *Cruz v. New York* (1987), *Richardson v. Marsh* (1987), *Lee v. Illinois* (1986), and *Tennessee v. Street* (1985), the Court reaffirmed (if only narrowly) and refined *Bruton v. United States* (1968) by prohibiting the limited admission against a nontestifying codefendant of that portion of his confession that directly implicates the defendant but is not admissible against him.

In noncriminal cases, the DUE PROCESS clause can afford some sort of confrontation right to enhance the truth-determining process. IN RE GAULT (1967) held that a minor who risks loss of liberty in a state juvenile institution enjoys a right of confrontation, including sworn testimony subject to cross-examination. Lower courts have similarly guaranteed such a right in civil commitment proceedings for those suffering from MENTAL ILLNESS, even though these proceedings in practice are not particularly adversarial and rely heavily on out-of-court statements not strictly within traditional hearsay exceptions. The scope of confrontation rights in proceedings involving the custody of children, as in civil child abuse cases, is currently disputed in doctrine and in practice. The Supreme Court recognized the right to confront and cross-examine adverse witnesses in administrative hearings prior to the termination of WELFARE BENEFITS in GOLDBERG V. KELLY (1970) and prior to a prisoner's transfer to a mental hospital in *Vitek v. Jones* (1980). But the Court has permitted decision making without confrontation, based on a written record or on hearing the affected individual's side of the story, in other cases, such as a prison disciplinary proceeding in *Wolff v. McDonnell* (1974) and a PUBLIC EMPLOYEE predischarge review that precedes a fuller post-deprivation hearing in *Cleveland Board of Education v. Loudermill* (1985).

ROBERT D. GOLDSTEIN
(1992)

Bibliography

GRAHAM, MICHAEL H. 1988 The Confrontation Clause, the Hearsay Rule, and Child Sexual Abuse Prosecutions: The

State of the Relationship. *Minnesota Law Review* 72:523–601.

HADDAD, JAMES B. 1990 The Future of Confrontation Clause Developments: What Will Emerge When the Supreme Court Synthesizes the Diverse Lines of Confrontation Decisions. *Journal of Criminal Law and Criminology* 81:77–98.

JONAKAIT, RANDOLPH N. 1988 Restoring the Confrontation Clause to the Sixth Amendment. *UCLA Law Review* 35:557–622.

CONGRESS AND FOREIGN POLICY

Congress has three principal functions. As a forum for debate, it is a vital instrument for creating and crystallizing public opinion, the source of all legitimate governmental power and policy in a democratic society. Through the investigatory power of its committees, it is the grand inquest of the nation, watching society and government with an eye for new and emerging problems. And it has the sole power of legislation on certain subjects, qualified only by the President's veto. All three aspects of Congress's work are important to its activities in the field of FOREIGN AFFAIRS. This article, however, will concentrate on Congress's role in legislation and its attempt to become a major participant in administration, the only area of its foreign policy agenda currently generating serious constitutional problems.

The Constitution divides the task of making and carrying out foreign policy in accordance with the rule that except where the Constitution provides otherwise, Congress is vested with the legislative part of American foreign policy and the President with the executive portion. Articles I and II mention certain subjects that illustrate the distinction between "legislative" and "executive" functions, and Article I, section 6, paragraph 2, provides that "no person holding any office under the United States shall be member of either House during his continuance in office." In a sentence focused on safeguards against corruption of the governmental process by either Congress or the President, paragraph 2 reveals the clear expectation that the new American constitutional order was not to be a cabinet government, but that Congress and the executive were to be separated institutionally as well as by function. During the period of drafting the Constitution, the presidency was deliberately made unitary rather than plural. And much was said and written about an executive capable of "energy, secrecy, and dispatch," as contrasted with a deliberative legislature not directly involved in the execution of the laws.

Drawing a line between the legislative and executive spheres has been conspicuously difficult in the area of foreign policy, however. One reason why this should be so is that foreign policy includes much more than the passage of statutes and the negotiation of international agreements and their subsequent execution. Much foreign policy is necessarily made in the ordinary course of diplomacy. And from the beginnings under the Constitution of 1787, the President has been recognized as the sole agent of the nation in its dealings with other states. He alone receives ambassadors and, from time to time, declares them unacceptable and sends them away. The power to recognize nations and to withhold recognition was accepted early as entirely presidential. The President is the chief diplomat of the nation; he smiles and frowns, speaks or remains silent, warns, praises, protests, and negotiates.

Even when diplomacy results in treaties that require approval by the Senate before ratification or in EXECUTIVE AGREEMENTS, which the President may or may not submit for a congressional vote, the process of making foreign policy is more heavily influenced by the President than is the passage of most statutes, which make policy in advance of action. The President can shape the circumstances in which issues of foreign policy come before Congress more often and more effectively than he can in dealing with issues of domestic policy. On the other hand, the negotiating process has its own constitutional pitfalls. If the Senate has to consent to the ratification of a major treaty or if Congress must pass enabling legislation in support of a treaty or executive agreement, members of Congress may be surly and uncooperative if they have not somehow participated in the negotiations themselves within or even beyond the limits of Article I, section 6, of the Constitution. Since the failure of the Versailles Treaty in 1919, every President has sought to anticipate the problem through briefings, consultations, or even membership or observer status for senators on negotiating delegations. If, on the other hand, members of Congress are suitably consulted about the instructions given to the negotiators and the ultimate bargain falls short of the goals specified in the instructions, pitfalls of another kind appear. The relation of Congress and the President in the making and ratification of treaties and executive agreements has therefore been a major political and constitutional irritant at least since 1795, when JAY'S TREATY was barely ratified.

ALEXANDER HAMILTON took the view that the executive, legislative, and judicial powers were to be distinguished by their "nature." The EXECUTIVE POWER, he said, is all governmental power that is neither judicial nor legislative in character. From this somewhat circular eighteenth-century axiom, Hamilton, THOMAS JEFFERSON, and JOHN MARSHALL drew a conclusion that has been of critical importance to CONSTITUTIONAL INTERPRETATION ever since. Where a power is executive in character, Hamilton wrote, it is deemed to be presidential unless that conclusion is excluded by the constitutional text. In such cases, presidential supremacy is the rule and congressional authority

control of a congressional cabinet in the exercise of his responsibilities for intelligence and is actively considering applying that model to the process of making "presidential" decisions about the use of force and foreign policy more generally. If that possibility should materialize, the presidency the nation has known since 1789, the presidency of ABRAHAM LINCOLN and Franklin D. Roosevelt, would be no more.

The Persian Gulf crisis of 1990–1991, however, demonstrated once again the functional necessity for the historic powers of the President. The abject failure of Congress to manage that episode should do much to restore the constitutional balance.

EUGENE V. ROSTOW
(1992)

(SEE ALSO: *Advice and Consent; Congressional War Powers; Foreign Affairs; Senate and Foreign Policy; Treaty Power.*)

Bibliography

CRABB, CECIL V., JR. and HOLT, PAT 1989 *Invitation to Struggle: Congress, the President, and Foreign Policy,* 3rd ed. Washington, D.C.: Congressional Quarterly Press.

FISHER, LOUIS 1985 *Constitutional Conflicts Between Congress and the President.* Princeton, N.J.: Princeton University Press.

———1988 *Constitutional Dialogues.* Princeton, N.J.: Princeton University Press.

FRANCK, THOMAS M. and WEISBAND, EDWARD 1979 *Foreign Policy by Congress.* New York: Oxford University Press.

ROSTOW, EUGENE V. 1989 *President, Prime Minister, or Constitutional Monarch?* Washington, D.C.: National Defense University Press.

WILSON, WOODROW (1885) 1967 *Congressional Government.* Cleveland, Ohio: Meridan Books.

CONGRESS AND THE SUPREME COURT

The delegates to the CONSTITUTIONAL CONVENTION OF 1787 confronted two fundamental problems in their quest to correct the political defects of the ARTICLES OF CONFEDERATION. First, they needed to bolster the powers of government at the national level so as to transform the "league of friendship" created by the Articles into a government with all the coercive powers requisite to government. Second, the Framers sought to create energetic but limited powers that would enable the new national government to govern, but in ways safe to the rights of the people. As JAMES MADISON put it in THE FEDERALIST #51, the task was to "enable the government to control the governed, but in the next place oblige it to control itself."

Their successful solution to this political problem was to separate the powers of government. Because the primary source of trouble in a popular form of government would be the legislative branch, the object was to bolster the coordinate executive and judicial branches, to offer "some more adequate defence. . . . for the more feeble, against the more powerful members of the government." The arrangement of checked and balanced institutions would at once avoid "a tyrannical concentration of all the powers of government in the same hands" while rendering the administration of the national government more efficient.

When the Framers examined the existing federal system under the Articles to determine precisely what it was that rendered it "altogether unfit for the administration of the affairs of the Union," the want of an independent judiciary "crown[ed] the defects of the confederation." As ALEXANDER HAMILTON put it in *The Federalist* #22, "Laws are a dead letter without courts to expound and define their true meaning and operation." Thus the improved science of politics offered by the friends of the Constitution prominently included provision for "the institution of courts composed of judges, holding their offices during good behavior."

But to some Anti-Federalist critics of the Federalist-backed Constitution, the judiciary was too independent and too powerful. To the New York ANTI-FEDERALIST "Brutus," the proposed judiciary possessed such independence as to allow the courts to "mould the government into almost any shape they please." The "Federal Farmer" was equally critical: his fellow citizens were "more in danger of sowing the seeds of arbitrary government in this department than in any other." With such unanticipated criticism, the Federalists were forced to defend the judicial power more elaborately than had been done in the early pages of *The Federalist*.

So compelling were the Anti-Federalist arguments that Hamilton saw fit to explain and defend the proposed judicial power in no fewer than six separate essays (#78–83) in *The Federalist*. His task was to show how an independent judiciary was not only *not* a threat to safe popular government but was absolutely essential to it. In making his now famous argument in *The Federalist* #78 that the judiciary would be that branch of the new government "least dangerous to the political rights of the Constitution," Hamilton made the case that the courts were "designed to be an intermediate body between the people and the legislature, in order, among other things, to keep the latter within the limits assigned to their authority." By exercising neither force nor will but merely judgment, the courts would prove to be the "bulwarks of a limited constitution." Such an institution, Hamilton argued, politically independent yet constitutionally rooted, was essential to resist the overwhelming power of the majority of the community. Only with such a constitutional defense could the rights of individuals and of minor parties be protected against majority tyranny; only an independent judiciary could allow the powers of the national government to be sufficiently enhanced, while simultaneously checking the unhealthy impulses of majority rule that had characterized politics at the state level under the Articles.

To counter the Anti-Federalist complaint that the courts would be imperiously independent, Hamilton reminded them that the courts would not be simply free-wheeling sources of arbitrary judgments and decrees. The Constitution, in giving Congress the power to regulate the APPELLATE JURISDICTION of the Supreme Court "with such exceptions, and under such regulations, as the Congress shall make," hedged against too expansive a conception of judicial power. "To avoid an arbitrary discretion in the courts," Hamilton noted, "it is indispensable that they should be bound down by strict rules and precedents, which serve to define and point out their duty in every particular case that comes before them." Thus the stage was set for a history of political confrontation between the Congress and the Court.

The tension between Congress and the Court has been a constant part of American politics at least since CHISHOLM V. GEORGIA (1793) led to the ELEVENTH AMENDMENT. Each generation has seen dramatic Supreme Court rulings that have prompted political cries to curb the courts. JOHN MARSHALL's now celebrated opinions in MARBURY V. MADISON (1803) and MCCULLOCH V. MARYLAND (1819), for example, caused him a good bit of political grief when he wrote them; the decision in DRED SCOTT V. SANDFORD (1857) soon came to be viewed as a judicially "self-inflicted wound" that weakened the Court and exacerbated the conflict that descended into civil war; and more recently, protests against the rulings in BROWN V. BOARD OF EDUCATION (1954) and ROE V. WADE (1973) have caused not only political demands for retaliation against the Court but social conflict and even violence as well. But through it all the Court has weathered the hostility with its independence intact.

Only once were the critics successful in persuading Congress to act against the Court, and the Court validated that move. In EX PARTE MCCARDLE (1869) the Court confirmed Congress's power to withdraw a portion of the Court's appellate jurisdiction. Fearing that the Court would use William McCardle's petition for a writ of HABEAS CORPUS under the HABEAS CORPUS ACT OF 1867 as a vehicle for invalidating the Reconstruction Acts *in toto*, the Congress repealed that portion of the act under which McCardle had brought his action—and after the Court had heard arguments in the case. The Court upheld the con-

stitutionality of Congress's action in repealing this particular part of the Court's JURISDICTION. The extent of Congress's power to withdraw the Court's appellate jurisdiction remains a matter of constitutional controversy.

The constitutional relationship between Congress and the Court is one thing; their political relationship is another matter. Although there are often loud cries for reaction against the Court, the critics usually lack sufficient force to achieve political retribution. The reason is most often explained as a matter of political prudence. The courts by their decisions frequently irritate a portion of the community—but usually only a portion. For most decisions will satisfy certain public constituencies that are as vociferous as the critics. Even the most errant exercises of judicial decision making are rarely sufficient to undermine the public respect for the idea of an independent judiciary.

The reason for this is simple enough: an independent judiciary makes good political sense. To make the judiciary too much dependent upon "popularity" as that popularity may be reflected in Congress would be to lower the constitutional barriers to congressional power, barriers generally agreeable to most people most of the time. The arguments of Hamilton in *The Federalist* still carry considerable weight.

Thus in the constitutional design of separating the powers of government through the device of "partial agency"—mingling the powers enough to give each branch some control over the others—is to be found the inevitable gulf between legitimate power and prudent restraint. For Congress to be persuaded to restrict judicial power, the case must first be made that such restrictions are both necessary and proper.

Despite the dangers of legislative power, it was still considered by the Framers to be the cardinal principle of POPULAR SOVEREIGNTY. Basic to this principle is the belief that it is legitimate for the people through the instrumentality of law to adjust, check, or enhance certain institutions of the government. This belief embraces the power of the legislature to exert some control over the structure and administration of the executive and judicial branches.

The qualified power of the legislature to tamper with the judiciary is not so grave a danger to the balance of the Constitution as some see it. For even when a judicial decision runs counter to particular—and perhaps pervasive—political interests, the institutional arrangements of the Constitution are such as to slow down the popular outrage and give the people time for "more cool and sedate reflection." And given the distance between the people and LEGISLATION afforded by such devices as REPRESENTATION (with its multiplicity of interests), BICAMERALISM, and the executive VETO POWER, an immediate legislative backlash to judicial behavior is unlikely. Experience demonstrates that any backlash at all is likely to be "weak and ineffectual." But if the negative response is not merely transient and is widely and deeply felt, then the Constitution wisely provides well-defined mechanisms for a deliberate political reaction to what the people hold to be intolerable judicial excesses.

But ultimately the history of court-curbing efforts in America, from the failed IMPEACHMENT of Justice SAMUEL CHASE to the Court-packing plan of FRANKLIN D. ROOSEVELT, teaches one basic lesson: the American political system generally operates to the advantage of the judiciary. Presidential court-packing is ineffective as a means of exerting political influence, and impeachment is too difficult to use as an everyday check against unpopular decisions. Not since John Marshall saw fit pseudonymously to defend his opinion in *McCulloch v. Maryland* (1819) in the public press has any Justice or judge felt obliged to respond to public outrage over a decision.

Political responses to perceived excesses of judicial power tend to take one of two forms: either a policy response against a particular decision or an institutional response against the structure and powers of the courts. In either event, the response may be either partisan or principled. Usually a policy response will take the form of a proposed constitutional amendment or statute designed to overrule a decision. An institutional response will generally seek to make jurisdictional exceptions, to create special courts with specific jurisdiction, or to make adjustments regarding the personnel, administration, or procedures of the judicial branch. Whatever the response, court-curbing is difficult. Although a majority of one of the houses of Congress may object to particular cases of "judicial impertinence," as one congressman viewed Justice DAVID DAVIS's controversial opinion in EX PARTE MILLIGAN (1866), a variety of objections will issue in different views of what should be done.

On the whole, there has consistently been a consensus that tampering with judicial independence is a serious matter and that rash reprisals against the Court as an institution may upset the constitutional balance. Underlying the occasional outbursts of angry public sentiment against the court is that "moral force" of the community of which ALEXIS DE TOCQUEVILLE wrote. On the whole, the American people continue to view the judiciary as the "boast of the Constitution."

For any political attempt to adjust or limit the judicial power to be successful it is necessary that it be—and be perceived to be—a principled rather than a merely partisan response. Only then will the issue of JUDICIAL ACTIVISM be met on a ground high enough to transcend the more common—and generally fruitless—debates over judicial liberalism and conservatism. The deepest issue is not whether a particular decision or even a particular court is too liberal for some and too conservative for others; the point is whether the courts are exercising their powers capably and legitimately. Keeping the courts constitutionally legitimate and institutionally capable benefits both the liberal and the conservative elements in American politics.

The system the Framers devised is so structured that the branch the Framers thought "least dangerous" is not so malleable in the hands of Congress as to be powerless. Yet the threat of congressional restriction of the Court remains, a threat that probably helps to keep an otherwise largely unfettered institution within constitutional bounds.

GARY L. McDOWELL
(1986)

Bibliography

BERGER, RAOUL   1969   *Congress versus the Supreme Court.* Cambridge, Mass.: Harvard University Press.

BRECKENRIDGE, A. C.   1971   *Congress Against the Court.* Lincoln: University of Nebraska Press.

MORGAN, DONALD L.   1967   *Congress and the Constitution.* Cambridge, Mass.: Harvard University Press.

MURPHY, WALTER F.   1962   *Congress and the Courts.* Chicago: University of Chicago Press.

CONGRESSIONAL BUDGET AND IMPOUNDMENT CONTROL ACT
88 Stat. 297 (1974)

President RICHARD M. NIXON's IMPOUNDMENT of billions of dollars appropriated by Congress for purposes which he did not approve amounted to the assertion of virtually uncontrollable power to block any federal program involving monetary expenditures. Nixon used impoundment as a weapon to alter legislative policy rather than to control the total level of government spending.

Congress, in the 1974 act, strengthened its own budgeting process, establishing new budget committees in each house and creating the Congressional Budget Office to give Congress assistance comparable to that given the President by the OFFICE OF MANAGEMENT AND BUDGET. The act required the President to recommend to Congress, in a special message, any proposal to impound funds. Thereafter, either house might veto the impoundment proposal by resolution, thereby forcing release of the funds. If the President refused to comply, the Comptroller General was authorized to seek a court order requiring the President to spend the money. The constitutionality of the LEGISLA-

TIVE VETO was thrown into doubt by the IMMIGRATION AND NATURALIZATION SERVICE V. CHADHA (1983).

PAUL L. MURPHY
(1986)

(SEE ALSO: *Budget Process; Constitutional History, 1961–1977.*)

CONGRESSIONAL GOVERNMENT

In creating the Constitution, the Framers created a functional SEPARATION OF POWERS, with separate institutions exercising the legislative, executive, and judicial powers. The Constitution also creates a system of CHECKS AND BALANCES, however, with each of the three branches participating in the functions of the others to some degree. In creating this system, the Framers did not specify exactly how much power the various branches were to have relative to one another. As a consequence, the precise balance of power has been left to subsequent historical development.

The late nineteenth century was a period of legislative dominance of the federal government. In 1885, a young WOODROW WILSON described the workings of the constitutional system as "congressional government." The label has stuck as a description of the federal government from roughly 1867 to the turn of the century. This system did not arise by accident. It was a product of the political and constitutional struggles of the CIVIL WAR. The victorious REPUBLICAN PARTY was largely composed of former Whigs, who had originally organized in the 1830s in opposition to the strong presidency of ANDREW JACKSON, or "King Andy." Their preference for congressional leadership, however, was delayed by the exigencies of civil war, which required giving extraordinary powers to the Republican President ABRAHAM LINCOLN. Lincoln's death and disagreements with his successor, ANDREW JOHNSON, led Congress to take legislative control of RECONSTRUCTION. For the first time, Congress overrode a significant presidential veto. Soon, Congress routinely overrode Johnson's vetoes, before eventually attempting to remove him from office through an IMPEACHMENT in 1867 for his resistance to congressional policy.

After the Johnson impeachment (and despite his acquittal), Presidents were on the political defensive and Congress effectively dictated national policy. Executive appointments were a crucial source of political power in the nineteenth century, as well as an important policy decision. In sharp contrast to the modern deference to presidential nominations, the postbellum U.S. SENATE aggressively used its confirmation powers to force Presidents to select officials who were friendly to Congress. At the same time, civil service reforms removed a potential tool for rewarding party loyalists from congressional party leaders, but it also took away a political weapon that earlier Presidents had used to win control of the POLITICAL PARTIES and exert pressure on legislators. The presidential APPOINTING AND REMOVAL POWER was carefully curtailed during this period.

Congress also dominated policymaking. In this period, federal policy was overwhelming made through legislation, which in turn was effectively made by congressional committees. The limitations on presidential appointments prevented the President from developing a system of advisors with whom to develop independent policy recommendations. Even when Presidents urged policies, their proposals carried little weight in what was seen as an exclusively legislative prerogative. The British observer James Bryce found that presidential messages had less effect than "an article in a prominent party newspaper," and their suggestions were "neglected." Congress also restricted presidential discretion in carrying out federal policy. The "EXECUTIVE POWER" was to be narrowly understood, requiring the implementation of the legislative will without any independent policy choice on the part of the President. When the federal government began to take on new regulatory burdens late in the century, Congress chose to create independent commissions or deal directly with executive departments rather than delegate additional powers to the President. A bureaucratic "fourth branch" was seen as preferable to a strengthened presidency.

Congressional government affected the stature as well as the power of the president. Presidential candidates during the period were creatures of the congressionally based political parties. Nominees were not intended to be threatening to existing congressional interests, and as a consequence, the late-nineteenth-century presidency attracted "small men," who came to office with little national reputation and gained no additional stature while in office. Presidents were merely caretakers, and their public appearances were few and largely ceremonial.

Congressional government arose through a combination of the scheme of government created by the separation of powers and the political interpretation of those constitutional powers. Congress had important tools that it was willing to use, such as the power to confirm or reject presidential appointments. And the political actors of the time generally agreed on a theory of government that emphasized the "popular branch" to the exclusion of executive power. Presidents spent the late nineteenth century gradually attempting to regain the influence that they had lost after the war, but congressional government was not overturned until America's emergence as a world power at the turn of the century and the rise of aggressive Presidents willing to challenge inherited political practices and constitutional understandings.

KEITH E. WHITTINGTON
(2000)

Bibliography

BINKLEY, WILFRED E. 1962 *President and Congress*, 3rd rev. ed. New York: Vintage.

BRYCE, JAMES 1941 *The American Commonwealth*, 3rd rev. ed. New York: Macmillan.

WILSON, WOODROW 1885 *Congressional Government: A Study in American Politics*. Boston, Mass.: Houghton, Mifflin.

CONGRESSIONAL INVESTIGATIONS

See: Legislative Investigation

CONGRESSIONAL MEMBERSHIP

Congress under the ARTICLES OF CONFEDERATION was a unicameral body representing thirteen states. But delegates to the CONSTITUTIONAL CONVENTION, influenced by the example of the British Parliament and almost all of the states, agreed rather early to the principle of a two-house legislature. Members of the HOUSE OF REPRESENTATIVES were to be popularly elected, with each state's members proportionate to population. But membership in the SENATE and selection of senators caused intense controversy.

The large states wanted the Senate also to represent population, but the smaller states were adamantly opposed. They forced a compromise under which every state would have two senators, elected by the state legislatures for six-year terms. This solution gave effect to the federal principle, the Senate representing the states and the House providing popular representation. However, legislative election of senators ultimately proved unacceptable. During the nineteenth century the elections were often marked by scandals and deadlocks, and a rising progressive temper in the country led to adoption of the SEVENTEENTH AMENDMENT in 1913 providing for direct popular election of senators.

The size of the House was initially set by Article I at sixty-five, to be revised thereafter on the basis of decennial censuses. As the population grew and more states were admitted to the Union, Congress increased the number of seats until it reached 435 after the 1910 census. Congress then concluded that further enlargement would make the House unwieldy, and by statute in 1929 fixed 435 as the permanent size of the House.

After each census the 435 House seats are apportioned among the states according to a statutory formula. It is then the responsibility of each state legislature to draw the lines for congressional districts. There was initially no legal obligation to assure equality of population among districts. Particularly in the early twentieth century rural-dominated state legislatures refused to revise district lines to provide equitable representation for growing urban areas. Judicial relief failed when the Supreme Court in COLEGROVE V. GREEN (1946) ruled that drawing the boundary lines of congressional districts was a POLITICAL QUESTION for decision by the state legislatures and Congress, not the courts. This HOLDING was implicitly overruled by the Court in BAKER V. CARR (1962), and in WESBERRY V. SANDERS (1964) the Court made equality of population in congressional districts a constitutional requirement.

The drawing of congressional district lines typically generates bitter legislative controversy as the majority party endeavors to protect its dominance by gerrymandering and incumbents of both parties seek to safeguard their own districts. In numerous states since 1964 legislative deadlocks have required the courts to intervene and draw the district lines.

Members of the House have two-year terms. Proposals for extending the term to four years have been made because of the increased costs of campaigning, longer sessions of Congress, and more complex legislative problems. In the Senate, the fact that only one-third of the seats fall vacant every two years gives it the status of a "continuing body," in contrast to the House which must reconstitute itself and elect its officers every two years.

The presiding officer of the House is its Speaker, chosen by the majority party from among its members. The Speaker has a vote and may on rare occasions participate in debate. The Senate's presiding officer is the vice-president; when serving in this capacity his title is President of the Senate. He has no vote except in case of a tie. The Constitution authorizes the Senate to choose a president *pro tempore* to preside in the absence of the vice-president. The president *pro tempore* is typically the senior member of the majority party.

Article I requires that a senator be thirty years of age, nine years a citizen of the United States, and an inhabitant of the state from which elected. A representative need be only twenty-five years of age and a citizen for seven years. By custom a representative should reside in the district from which elected. Members of Congress are disqualified for appointment to executive office, a provision that prevents the development of anything approaching a parliamentary system. To accept an executive post, a member of Congress must resign.

Each house is authorized to "be the judge of the elections, returns and qualifications of its own members" (Article I, section 5). The "qualifications," it has been established by POWELL V. MCCORMACK (1969), are only the age, residence, and CITIZENSHIP requirements stated in the Constitution. However, on several occasions both houses have in effect enforced additional qualifications by refusing to seat duly elected members who met the constitutional qualifications. In 1900 the House refused to seat a Utah polygamist; similar action was taken in 1919 against a Wisconsin socialist who had been convicted under the ESPIONAGE ACT for opposing American participation in WORLD WAR I. The most prominent black member of Congress, Adam Clayton Powell, was denied his seat in 1967. There was a judgment of criminal contempt outstanding against him, and his conduct as a committee chairman had been irregular. The Supreme Court ruled, however, that he possessed the constitutional qualifications and so could not be denied his seat. Members of Congress cannot be impeached, but they are subject to vote of censure by their chamber, and to expulsion by two-thirds vote. The Court indicated that the House might have expelled Powell for his alleged conduct. Vacancies in the Senate can be filled by the state governor, but in the House only by special election.

Members of Congress have immunity from arrest during legislative sessions except for cases of " FELONY, and breach of the peace" (Article I, section 6). They are guaranteed FREEDOM OF SPEECH by the provision that "for any speech or debate in either house, they shall not be questioned in any other place." (See SPEECH OR DEBATE CLAUSE.) The purpose is to prevent intimidation of legislators by the executive or threat of prosecution for libel or slander. They can be held accountable for statements or actions in their legislative capacity only by their own colleagues. This immunity covers not only speeches in Congress but also written reports, resolutions offered, the act of voting, and all other things generally done in a legislative session. However, immunity does not extend to press releases, newsletters, or telephone calls to executive agencies, the Supreme Court held in HUTCHINSON V. PROXMIRE (1979). Also, taking a bribe to influence legislation is not a "legislative act," according to BREWSTER V. UNITED STATES (1972).

C. HERMAN PRITCHETT
(1986)

Bibliography

DAVIDSON, ROGER H. and OLESZEK, WALTER J. 1985 *Congress and Its Members*, 2nd ed. Washington, D.C.: Congressional Quarterly.

CONGRESSIONAL PRIVILEGES AND IMMUNITIES

The Constitution specifically protects members of Congress against interference with their deliberative function. The special privileges and immunities attendant on CONGRESSIONAL MEMBERSHIP are contained in the first clause of Article I, section 6, of the Constitution. The Framers of the Constitution, familiar with the devices used by the British king against members of Parliament and by royal governors against members of the provincial legislatures, sought to insulate the members of the federal legislature against pressures that might preclude independence of judgment.

The PRIVILEGE FROM ARREST, other than for FELONY, or BREACH OF THE PEACE, has been known in Anglo-American constitutional history since the advent of parliaments; WILLIAM BLACKSTONE cited an ancient Gothic law as evidence of the privilege's immemorial origins. The English Parliament claimed freedom of debate, that is, immunity from prosecution or civil lawsuit resulting from utterances in Parliament, at least from the thirteenth century; that immunity was finally established in the English BILL OF RIGHTS (1689). In America, privilege from arrest during legislative sessions was first granted in Virginia in 1623, and freedom of debate was first recognized in the FUNDAMENTAL ORDERS OF CONNECTICUT (1639).

The ARTICLES OF CONFEDERATION extended both the privilege from arrest and the freedom of debate to members of Congress, in words transcribed almost verbatim from the English Bill of Rights: "Freedom of speech and debate in Congress shall not be impeached or questioned in any court, or place out of Congress, and the members of Congress shall be protected in their persons from arrests and imprisonments, during the time of their going to and from, and attendance on Congress, except for treason, felony, or breach of the peace." At the CONSTITUTIONAL CONVENTION, these congressional privileges and immunities first appeared in the report of the Committee of Detail; they were agreed to without debate and without dissent. The Committee of Style gave final form to the wording of the clause.

The privilege from arrest, limited as it is to arrest for debt, no longer has any practical application. The immunity from having to answer in court, or in any other place out of Congress, for congressional SPEECH OR DEBATE is now primarily a shield against civil actions by private parties rather than against an executive jealous of his prerogative. That shield has been expanded to protect the whole legislative process, but not, as one senator learned to his chagrin in HUTCHINSON V. PROXMIRE (1979), to every public utterance of a member of Congress concerning a public issue.

DENNNIS J. MAHONEY
(1986)

Bibliography

WORMSER, MICHAEL D., ed. 1982 *Guide to Congress*, 3rd ed. Pages 850–855. Washington, D.C.: Congressional Quarterly.

CONGRESSIONAL STANDING

Members of Congress occasionally sue in federal court to challenge the constitutionality of executive or legislative action. Although such interbranch litigation is commonplace in some European constitutional systems, the Supreme Court has ruled that members of Congress usually are not the proper people to prosecute these cases. They lack STANDING to sue.

The leading case in this area is *Raines v. Byrd* (1997). Members of Congress challenged the constitutionality of LEGISLATION giving the President a LINE-ITEM VETO. They claimed that the line-item veto injured them by diminishing the legal and practical effect of their votes on appropriations bills. The Court held that the plaintiffs lacked standing to sue because the legislation injured them only in their institutional, rather than personal, capacities. If the legislation had reduced their salaries or forced them from office, they would have had standing. The Court distinguished the line-item veto case from POWELL V. MCCORMACK (1969), where the Court upheld Adam Clayton Powell's standing to sue the U.S. HOUSE OF REPRESENTATIVES for wrongful expulsion. Powell had been singled out for expulsion, which caused him personalized injury. The line-item veto injured all members of Congress indiscriminately, and only in an official sense.

The Court's approach to congressional standing is broadly consistent with its general policies governing the occasions on which federal courts may adjudicate constitutional challenges to legislation or other government action. Through the standing, MOOTNESS, and RIPENESS doctrines, the Court has usually barred plaintiffs from federal court unless they hold concrete personal stakes in the controversy. People who sue because government action threatens their personal liberty or PROPERTY are generally permitted to maintain actions in federal court. People who sue because they are ideologically opposed to the government action in question are usually turned away from federal court. Put another way, the Court grants federal court adjudication to selfishly interested plaintiffs but withholds it from altruistic ones. One of the Court's official explanations for this seeming paradox is that self-interested litigants will bring out the best arguments in favor of their positions. Self-appointed guardians of the public good might lack the litigating initiative so crucial to sharp adversarial presentation.

Another thread running through standing doctrine, especially congressional standing, is the notion that the federal courts must carefully husband their political capital. Members of the public may chafe when they see unelected federal judges undoing the handiwork of the majoritarian branches of government. By restricting constitutional challenges to "proper" plaintiffs, the Court sharply limits the occasions upon which federal courts can exercise JUDICIAL REVIEW. This idea has particular application in the context of congressional standing, where allowing members of Congress to challenge the constitutionality of legislation or executive action would appear to put the courts smack in the middle of the political battlefield. In these situations, the standing doctrine is thought to preserve the judiciary's credibility with the public.

EVAN TSEN LEE
(2000)

Bibliography

McGOWAN, CARL 1981 Congressmen in Court: The New Plaintiffs. *Georgia Law Review* 15:241–267.

CONGRESSIONAL VETO

See: Legislative Veto

CONGRESSIONAL WAR POWERS

The Constitution assigns the power to declare war solely to the Congress, one of the wisest of the many CHECKS AND BALANCES built into the American political system. Throughout American history, however, Presidents have committed acts of war without congressional authorization. The question of where to assign the power to initiate and conduct war was thoroughly debated during the framing of the Constitution. The outcome of that debate was a document that clearly did not give the President unlimited WAR POWERS but in fact separated the power to conduct war from the power to initiate war.

The Constitution grants Congress the power to issue a DECLARATION OF WAR and to "grant letters of Marque and reprisal." There is no question that the ORIGINAL INTENT of the Framers of the Constitution was to vest in the Congress the complete power to decide on war or peace, with the sole exception that the President could respond to sudden attack on the United States without congressional authorization. During the CONSTITUTIONAL CONVENTION OF 1787, the debates centered on an original draft of the war power providing that "the legislature of the United States shall have the power . . . to make war." One member of the convention, CHARLES PINCKNEY, opposed giving this power to Congress, claiming that its proceedings would be too slow; PIERCE BUTLER said that he was "voting for vesting the power in the President, who will have all the requisite qualities, and will not make war but when the Nation will support it." Butler's motion received no second, however.

JAMES MADISON and ELBRIDGE GERRY, meanwhile, were not satisfied with the original wording, that the legislature be given the power to make war. They moved to substitute "declare" for "make," "leaving to the Executive the power to repel sudden attacks." The meaning of this motion, which eventually was carried by a vote of seven states to two, was clear. The power to initiate war was left to Congress, with the reservation from Congress to the President to repel a sudden attack on the United States. As THOMAS JEFFERSON explained in 1789, "We have already given . . . one effectual check to the dog of war by transferring the power of letting him loose, from the executive to the legislative body, from those who are to spend to those who are to pay."

Acts of war, acts of reprisal, and acts of self-defense—all have been taken by past Presidents, but seldom without a rationalization of the legal implications of their actions that reflected recognition of the necessity of congressional authorization of all presidential acts of war except self-defense. At a time of national crisis, notably during the CIVIL WAR, the President has acted illegally and depended on Congress to ratify his action after the fact. In the latter half of the twentieth century, however, a major change in the concept of the war power began to be propounded. Beginning with the KOREAN WAR and the VIETNAM WAR, some presidents, congressmen, and publicists claimed for the executive the power to initiate war without the consent of Congress.

Covert war, as we have come to know it, grew out of the United States' experiences in WORLD WAR II . Two factors have combined to encourage covert action and covert war. First, nuclear weapons—forces of utter destruction—have deterred more overt and massive forms of violence. Second, the intensity of the ideological and geopolitical struggle between the United States and the Soviet Union nevertheless assured that violence, albeit covert, would continue. Shortly after World War II, in January 1946, President HARRY S. TRUMAN issued a directive establishing the Central Intelligence Group, the precursor of the Central Intelligence Agency. Previously, no non-military covert operations group had existed in the United States during peacetime. Later intelligence groups would build on this meager institutional foundation, often without questioning either the appropriateness of its methods or the basic assumptions behind its organization.

The Constitution commits the entire power to decide for war or peace to Congress, not the President, with the exception noted above—in the event of sudden attack. No action of covert war is likely to fit within that narrow exception. The COMMANDER-IN-CHIEF clause gives that President no additional power to commit forces of the United Stater to war or acts of war when the nation is at peace. Only Congress is empowered to change this condition.

The Constitution's grant to Congress of the power to grant "letters of Marque and reprisal" covers most of what we think of as covert war. Originally a letter of marque merely authorized crossing into a foreign state to obtain redress for wrongs inflicted by a foreigner, and a letter of reprisal permitted the use of force to secure compensation for an unlawful taking of property or goods within the territorial jurisdiction of the sovereign. When combined, a letter of marque and reprisal permitted a particular person to seize property or even foreign citizens who refused to redress injuries they caused. By the eighteenth century, letters of marque had evolved into means of legitimating acts of war against other sovereign states by private parties. Likewise, reprisals developed into public acts of war against another state or citizens of another state in retaliation for an injury for which the state is held responsible. Under international law a reprisal is legal only if the acts are responsive and proportional to previous hostile acts of another state and the reprisal is first preceded by unsuccessful attempts at a peaceful resolution.

The war clause in its completeness, then, grants to Congress all power to decide on war, including both public and private or covert war, declared or undeclared. The Constitution grants no power to the President to wage private war against states with whom the nation is at peace by hiring modern mercenaries, pirates, or privateers without the express authorization of Congress. Nor does the President or the National Security Council have the authority to privatize the conduct of American foreign policy in the sale of arms or transfer of money. Absent a direct attack on the United States, a decision to go to war is constitutional only when it is publicly arrived at by congressional debate.

EDWIN B. FIRMAGE
(1992)

(SEE ALSO: *Congress and Foreign Policy; Executive Power; Executive Prerogative; Foreign Affairs; Presidential War Powers; Senate and Foreign Policy; War, Foreign Affairs, and the Constitution.*)

Bibliography

LOBEL, JULES 1986 Covert War and Congressional Authority: Hidden War and Forgotten Power. *University of Pennsylvania Law Review* 134:1035–1110.

PRADOS, JOHN 1986 Presidents' Secret Wars: Cia and Pentagon Covert Operations Since World War II. New York: William Morrow.

WORMUTH, FRANCIS D. and FIRMAGE, EDWIN B. 1989 *To Chain the Dog of War: The Power of Congress in History and Law,* 2nd ed. Urbana: University of Illinois Press.

CONKLING, ROSCOE
(1829–1888)

A New York attorney, congressman (1859–1863, 1865–1867), and senator (1867–1881), Roscoe Conkling in 1861 initiated legislation creating the Joint Committee on the Conduct of the War. In 1865, as a member of the JOINT COMMITTEE ON RECONSTRUCTION, Conkling supported CIVIL RIGHTS for blacks. In 1867 he sponsored military reconstruction legislation. Conkling and other supporters of the bill argued that the South was still in the "grasp of war" and only a military occupation and RECONSTRUCTION would insure protection of the freedmen. After Reconstruction Conkling continued to support civil rights and helped Frederick Douglass become the first black Recorder of Deeds in Washington, D.C. Douglass placed Conkling alongside ULYSSES S. GRANT, CHARLES SUMNER, and BENJAMIN F. BUTLER as a protector of freedmen. In 1880 Conkling led a movement to renominate Grant because of disagreements with President RUTHERFORD B. HAYES over Reconstruction and PATRONAGE. In 1881 Conkling resigned his Senate seat to protest JAMES A. GARFIELD's appointments in New York State. As the undisputed leader of the New York Republican party, Conkling thought he, and not the President, should dispense patronage in the Empire State. Earlier he had opposed Hayes's attempts to remove federal officeholders in New York and had defended CHESTER A. ARTHUR from corruption charges. In 1873 Conkling declined Grant's offer of the Chief Justiceship of the United States; in 1882 the Senate confirmed him for an Associate Justiceship, but he declined to serve.

PAUL FINKELMAN
(1986)

Bibliography

JORDON, DAVID M. 1971 *Roscoe Conkling of New York: Voice in the Senate.* Ithaca, N.Y.: Cornell University Press.

CONNALLY, THOMAS T.
(1877–1963)

A conservative Texas Democrat and internationalist, Tom Connally, as he officially called himself, served twelve years in the HOUSE OF REPRESENTATIVES and twenty-four in the SENATE. When he retired from politics in 1953, he said he was most proud of his leadership against FRANKLIN D. ROOSEVELT's COURT-PACKING plan of 1937 and in favor of the creation of the United Nations. Connally's main achievements were in the field of FOREIGN AFFAIRS, from managing the Lend Lease Act to confirmation of the NORTH ATLANTIC TREATY. He was cool toward much of the NEW DEAL, except when it benefited Texas cattle, oil, and cotton interests. The Supreme Court struck down the Connally "Hot Oil" Act in PANAMA REFINING CO. V. RYAN (1935), but he secured a revised measure that constitutionally prohibited the shipment in INTERSTATE COMMERCE of oil produced in excess of government quotas. He opposed every CIVIL RIGHTS measure that came before the SENATE and joined every southern FILIBUSTER, preventing the enactment of antilynching and anti-POLL TAX bills. Connally was one of the last of colorful, powerful, demagogic, and grandiloquent southern politicians who affected a drawl, string-tie, frock coat, and flowing hair.

LEONARD W. LEVY
(1986)

Bibliography

CONNALLY, TOM and STEINBERG, ALFRED 1954 *My Name Is Tom Connally.* New York: Crowell.

CONNECTICUT COMPROMISE

See: Great Compromise

CONQUERED PROVINCES THEORY

"Conquered provinces" was one of a half dozen constitutional theories concerning the relationship of the seceded states and the Union. Representative THADDEUS STEVENS (Republican, Pennsylvania), the principal exponent of conquered provinces, argued that SECESSION had been de jure as well as de facto effective, and destroyed the normal constitutional status of the seceded states. Union victory required that they be governed under the principles of international law, which would have authorized essentially unlimited congressional latitude in setting RECONSTRUCTION policy. Congressional legislation for the ex-states had to be based on the premise that "the foundation of their institutions, both political, municipal, and social, must be broken up and relaid." This was to be accomplished through extensive confiscation of Confederates' properties and the abolition of slavery. The state constitutions would have to be rewritten and submitted to Congress, which would then readmit each "province" as a new state.

Other principal theories of Reconstruction were: territorialization, popular among some Republicans since 1861, which would have treated the seceded states as territories; STATE SUICIDE, expounded by CHARLES SUMNER since 1862; state indestructibility, the basis of varying southern and presidential views, and being the central assumption of ABRAHAM LINCOLN's programs; Richard Henry Dana's "Grasp of War" theory of 1865, which would have sanctioned congressional policy under the WAR POWERS; and forfeited rights, a theory propounded by Rep. Samuel

Shellabarger (Republican, Ohio), which ultimately came as close as any to being the constitutional basis of congressional Republican Reconstruction.

Stevens's conquered provinces theory was logically consistent with Republican objectives, and Lincoln's policies concerning the wartime Reconstruction of Louisiana, Arkansas, and Tennessee resembled parts of Stevens's program. But because the idea of conquered provinces was widely considered unconstitutional and draconian, it was never adopted as the basis of Republican policy.

WILLIAM M. WIECEK
(1986)

Bibliography

MCKITRICK, ERIC L. 1960 *Andrew Johnson and Reconstruction.* Chicago: University of Chicago Press.

CONSCIENTIOUS OBJECTION

A conscientious objector is a person who is opposed in conscience to engaging in socially required behavior. Since the genuine objector will not be easily forced into acts he abhors and since compelling people to violate their own moral scruples is usually undesirable in a liberal society, those who formulate legal rules face the question whether conscientious objectors should be excused from legal requirements imposed on others. The issue is most striking in relation to compulsory military service: should those whose consciences forbid killing be conscripted for combat? Historically, conscientious objection has been considered mainly in that context, and the clash has been understood as between secular obligation and the sense of religious duty felt by members of pacifist sects. The Constitution says nothing directly about conscientious objection, and for most of the country's existence Congress was thought to have a free hand in deciding whether to afford any exemption and how to define the class of persons who would benefit. By now, it is evident that the religion clauses of the FIRST AMENDMENT impose significant constraints on how Congress may draw lines between those who receive an exemption from military service and those who do not. The Supreme Court has never accepted the argument that Congress is constitutionally required to establish an exemption from military service, but it has indicated that the Constitution does entitle some individuals to exemption from certain other sorts of compulsory laws.

The principle that society should excuse conscientious objectors from military service was widely recognized in the colonies and states prior to adoption of the Constitution. JAMES MADISON's original proposal for the BILL OF RIGHTS included a clause that "no person religiously scrupulous of bearing arms shall be compelled to render military service in person," but that clause was dropped, partly because conscription was considered a state function. The 1864 Draft Act and the SELECTIVE SERVICE ACT of 1917 both contained exemptions limited to members of religious denominations whose creeds forbade participation in war. The 1917 act excused objectors only from combatant service, but the War Department permitted some of those also opposed to noncombatant military service to be released for civilian service.

The 1940 Selective Service Act set the basic terms of exemption from the system of compulsory military service that operated during WORLD WAR II, the KOREAN WAR, and the VIETNAM WAR, and during the intervening periods of uneasy peace. A person was eligible "who, by reason of religious training and belief, [was] conscientiously opposed to participation in war in any form." Someone opposed even to noncombatant service could perform alternate civilian service. In response to a court of appeals decision interpreting "religious training and belief" very broadly, Congress in 1948 said that religious belief meant belief "in relation to a Supreme Being involving duties superior to those arising from any human relation. . . ." What Congress had attempted to do was relatively clear. It wanted to excuse only persons opposed to participation in all wars, not those opposed to particular wars, and it wanted to excuse only those whose opposition derived from religious belief in a rather traditional sense. The important Supreme Court cases have dealt with these lines of distinction.

By dint of strained interpretation of the statute, the Court has avoided a clear decision whether Congress could limit the exemption to traditional religious believers. First, in UNITED STATES V. SEEGER (1965), a large majority said that an applicant who spoke of a "religious faith in a purely ethical creed" was entitled to the exemption because his belief occupied a place in his life parallel to that of a belief in God for the more orthodox. Then, in *Welsh v. United States* (1970), four Justices held that someone who laid no claim to being religious at all qualified because his ethical beliefs occupied a place in his life parallel to that of religious beliefs for others. Four other Justices acknowledged that Congress had explicitly meant to exclude such applicants. Justice JOHN MARSHALL HARLAN urged that an attempt to distinguish religious objectors from equally sincere nonreligious ones constituted a forbidden ESTABLISHMENT OF RELIGION; the three other Justices thought that Congress could favor religious objectors in order to promote the free exercise of religion. Because the plurality's view of the statute was so implausible, most observers have supposed that its members probably agreed with Justice Harlan about the ultimate constitutional issue, but this particular tension between "no establishment" and "free exercise" concepts has not yet been decisively resolved.

In *Gillette v. United States* (1971), a decision covering both religious and nonreligious objectors to the Vietnam War, the Court upheld Congress's determination not to exempt those opposed to participation in particular wars. Against the claim that the distinction between "general" and "selective" objectors was impermissible, the Court responded that the distinction was supported by the public interest in a fairly administered system, given the difficulty officials would have dealing consistently with the variety of objections to particular wars. The Court also rejected the claim that the selective objector's entitlement to free exercise of his religion created a constitutionally grounded right to avoid military service.

In other limited areas, the Court has taken the step of acknowledging a free exercise right to be exempt from a generally imposed obligation. Those religiously opposed to jury duty cannot be compelled to serve, and adherents of traditional religious groups that provide an alternative way of life for members cannot be required to send children to school beyond the eighth grade. (See WISCONSIN V. YODER.) Nor can a person be deprived of unemployment benefits when an unwillingness to work on Saturday is religiously based, though receptivity to jobs including Saturday work is a usual condition of eligibility. (See SHERBERT V. VERNER.) What these cases suggest is that if no powerful secular reason can be advanced for demanding uniform compliance, the Constitution may require that persons with substantial religious objections be excused. To this degree the Constitution itself requires special treatment for conscientious objectors. Beyond that, its recognition of religious liberty and of governmental impartiality toward religions provides a source of values for legislative choice and constrains the classifications legislatures may make.

KENT GREENAWALT
(1986)

Bibliography

FINN, JAMES, ed. 1968 *A Conflict of Loyalties.* New York: Pegasus.

GREENAWALT, KENT 1972 All or Nothing At All. *Supreme Court Review* 1971: 31–94.

SIBLEY, MULFORD QUICKERT and JACOB, PHILIP E. 1952 *Conscription of Conscience: The American State and the Conscientious Objector, 1940–1947.* Ithaca, N.Y.: Cornell University Press.

CONSCRIPTION

The power of the federal government to conscript may derive either from its power to raise armies or, more debatably, from its broadly interpreted power to regulate commerce. It is restricted by the THIRTEENTH AMENDMENT's prohibition of involuntary servitude or, conceivably, by the Fifth Amendment's guarantee of liberty. The manner in which conscription is conducted must comport with a familiar range of constitutional protections, notably those that guarantee EQUAL PROTECTION and RELIGIOUS LIBERTY.

Though the nation has employed systems of military conscription during the CIVIL WAR, WORLD WAR I, WORLD WAR II, and for all but twelve months between 1945 and 1972, the interplay of these different constitutional considerations has been remarkably underdeveloped. Two hundred years after the Constitution was written, at least two fundamental questions about conscription remain unresolved. What is the power of Congress (or the states) to conscript for civilian purposes? How, if at all, is a conscription system obliged to take account of CONSCIENTIOUS OBJECTION?

The ambiguity surrounding these questions derives in part from the fact that although the constitutionality of military conscription is well settled, the issue has not been settled well. In SELECTIVE DRAFT LAW CASES (1917) the Supreme Court reviewed the World War I military conscription statute and declared that it was "unable to conceive" how the performance of the "supreme and noble duty" of military service in time of war "can be said to be the imposition of involuntary servitude." Therefore, in its view, this contention was "precluded by its mere statement."

This terse comment establishes no conceptual basis for the analysis of later questions. Unfortunately, also, history is not a particularly helpful guide. The intention of the Framers is not clear. At the time of the Constitution, it was accepted that state militias could conscript soldiers, but the central government could not do so. At the same time, the Constitution gave the Congress the power to "raise armies" and it was widely recognized that it could not tenably rely on volunteers. On the basis of this evidence some scholars have argued that to conclude that conscription (as opposed to enlistment) was a power given to Congress is logical, and others have called this conclusion absurd.

Legislative history and judicial PRECEDENT in this first century of the Republic are similarly uninformative. When the Supreme Court decided the *Selective Draft Law Cases* it had only two precedents for a military draft: first, Secretary of War JAMES MONROE's proposal for conscription during the War of 1812, a proposal still under compromise deliberation by Congress when peace arrived; and, second, the Civil War Enrollment Act, the constitutionality of which had been ruled on only by a sharply divided and perplexed Supreme Court of Pennsylvania.

The most significant judicial precedent, *Butler v. Perry* (1916), had been decided only a year before by the Supreme Court itself. Here the Court rejected a Thirteenth Amendment challenge to a Florida statute requiring adult men to work one week a year on public roads: "from colonial days to the present time, conscripted labor has been much relied on for the construction and maintenance of public roads," and the Thirteenth Amendment "certainly was not intended to interdict enforcement of those duties which individuals owe to the state."

No subsequent Supreme Court decision limits this sweeping view of the power to conscript. To the contrary, the Court held in *United States v. Macintosh* (1931) that the right of conscientious objection is only statutory and in ROSTKER V. GOLDBERG (1981) that the government can compel an all-male military registration in the face of equal protection contentions founded on a theory of SEX DISCRIMINATION.

Notwithstanding these decisions, it seems likely that a major constitutional issue would arise if the power to conscript were asserted more aggressively. Such an issue might arise if, for example, participation were coerced in a system of civilian national service or if the statutory right of conscientious objection were abolished. In that event, the question thus far begged—what "duties . . . individuals owe to the state"—would have to be, for the first time, seriously addressed.

RICHARD DANZIG
IRA NERKEN
(1986)

Bibliography

ANDERSON, MARTIN and BLOOM, VALERIE 1976 *Conscription: A Select and Annotated Bibliography.* Stanford, Calif.: Hoover Institution Press.

FRIEDMAN, LEON 1969 Conscription and the Constitution: The Original Understanding. *Michigan Law Review* 67:1493–1552.

MALBIN, MICHAEL J. 1972 Conscription, the Constitution, and the Framers: An Historial Analysis. *Fordham Law Review* 40: 805–826.

CONSCRIPTION ACT

See: Selective Service Acts

CONSENT DECREE

In a civil suit in EQUITY, such as a suit for an INJUNCTION or a DECLARATORY JUDGMENT, the court's order is called a decree. By negotiation, the plaintiff and the defendant may agree to ask the court to enter a decree that they have drafted. If the court approves, its order is called a consent decree. Federal courts frequently enter consent degrees

in actions to enforce regulatory laws in fields such as ANTITRUST, EMPLOYMENT DISCRIMINATION, and ENVIRONMENTAL REGULATION.

KENNETH L. KARST
(1986)

(SEE ALSO: *Plea Bargaining.*)

CONSENT SEARCH

When an individual consents to a search, he effectively waives his rights under the FOURTH AMENDMENT and makes it unnecessary for the police to obtain a SEARCH WARRANT. In determining the validity of such a consent, the trial court must determine whether the consent was voluntary. The consent of a person illegally held is not considered voluntary. However, an explicit warning about one's constitutional rights, which MIRANDA V. ARIZONA (1966) made mandatory for custodial interrogation, is not a condition for effective consent to a search, under the decision in SCHNECKLOTH V. BUSTAMONTE (1973).

Consent must obviously be obtained from a person entitled to grant it. Not ownership of the premises but the right to occupy and use them to the exclusion of others is the decisive criterion. Thus, the consent of a landlord to search premises let to others is worthless. The consenting party controls the terms of the consent: it may be as broad or as narrow as he wishes to make it, allowing a search of an entire dwelling or merely of one small item.

For a consent by another person to be valid as against a defendant, it must be shown that the consenting party possessed common authority in the place or things searched. Anyone with joint access or control of the premises may consent to a search.

JACOB W. LANDYNSKI
(1986)

Bibliography

LAFAVE, WAYNE R. 1978 *Search and Seizure: A Treatise on the Fourth Amendment.* Vol. 2:610–774. St. Paul, Minn.: West Publishing Co.

CONSERVATISM

Conservatives would agree with Robert Bork's understanding of the role of the Supreme Court under the Constitution and with its implicit understanding of the Constitution itself. Bork concluded a 1984 lecture at the American Enterprise Institute in Washington with the following words:

In a constitutional democracy the moral content of the law must be given by the morality of the framer or the legislator, never by the morality of the judge. The sole task of the latter—and it is a task quite large enough for anyone's wisdom, skill, and virtue—is to translate the framer's or the legislator's morality into a rule to govern unforeseen circumstances. That abstinence from giving his own desires free play, that continuing and self-conscious renunciation of power, that is the morality of the jurist.

Bork's is not, of course, the popular view of the judge's role, a fact made manifest by the reaction to his nomination for a seat on the Supreme Court. Some 1,925 law professors—surely a good proportion of the total—publicly opposed his appointment and took the trouble of communicating their opposition to the SENATE JUDICIARY COMMITTEE. Bork, they said in one way or another, was out of the "mainstream," as surely as he was and is. Whereas Bork would appeal to the Framers' morality, mainstream lawyers, arguing that the Framers represented "a world that is dead and gone," tend to prefer their own; some of them go so far so to accuse the Framers of being morally indifferent, a view popularized by Ronald Dworkin, one of Bork's principal opponents. Dworkin sees the Constitution as in need of moral principles and would supply that need. What is required, he says, is a "fusion of constitutional law and moral theory, a connection that, incredibly, has yet to take place."

Conservatives would protest that a Constitution that secures the rights of man—the *equal* rights of man—to the end of "securing the blessings of liberty" is not lacking in moral principle. Still, had he chosen to do so, Dworkin could have found in the mill of the founding documents an abundance of the grist he wants to grind. There is, for example, JAMES MADISON's famous statement in THE FEDERALIST #10 to the effect that the first object of government is the protection of different and unequal faculties of acquiring property. Protecting the equal rights of unequally endowed men can only lead to what Madison said it would lead to, and has in fact led to, namely, different degrees and kinds of property. In short, liberty leads to inequality, not of Madisonian rights but of wealth, position, and rank.

Unlike mainstream (or liberal) lawyers, conservatives are willing to live with this dispensation, and not only because they object to the means used by the mainstream lawyers to change it. The history of Title VII of the CIVIL RIGHTS ACT OF 1964 provides an example of those means. That piece of legislation was enacted by Congress to put an end to EMPLOYMENT DISCRIMINATION against blacks and women. But the Supreme Court, over the objections of conservative Justices, including Chief Justice WILLIAM REHNQUIST and Justice ANTONIN SCALIA, has converted it into a statute permitting, and in effect compelling, discrimination favoring blacks and women. Concurring in a case dealing with gender discrimination, a somewhat shamefaced Justice SANDRA DAY O'CONNOR indicated how this was accomplished: "As Justice Scalia illuminates with excruciating clarity, [Title VII] has been interpreted . . . to permit what its language read literally would prohibit." When necessary to further their political agendas, mainstream lawyers, on and off the bench, favor appeals to the "spirit," instead of the written text, of statutes and to what they contend is the "unwritten," instead of the written, Constitution.

No case better illustrates this practice than the 1965 BIRTH CONTROL case GRISWOLD V. CONNECTICUT, and none has given rise to so much criticism from conservatives (and even from a few liberals) as the most prominent of the cases it spawned, ROE V. WADE, the 1973 ABORTION decision. To strike down the Connecticut statute forbidding the use of contraceptives—a statute that for practical reasons could not be enforced and for political reasons could not be repealed—the Court found a right to privacy not in a specific constitutional provision but in "penumbras, formed by emanations" from the FIRST AMENDMENT, THIRD AMENDMENT, FOURTH AMENDMENT, FIFTH AMENDMENT, NINTH AMENDMENT, and ultimately the FOURTEENTH AMENDMENT. To strike down the abortion laws of all fifty states, the Court again invoked this right to privacy, now locating it in the "liberty" protected by the Fourteenth Amendment.

The principal proponent of this kind of constitutional construction, and the chief target of conservative criticism, was Justice WILLIAM J. BRENNAN, and nothing better illustrates his understanding of JUDICIAL POWER than a draft opinion he wrote during the Court's consideration of FRONTIERO V. RICHARDSON (1973), a case decided when the so-called EQUAL RIGHTS AMENDMENT was awaiting ratification by the states. Frontiero was a female air force officer who was denied certain dependents' benefits—benefits that would automatically have been granted with respect to the wife of a male officer—because she failed to prove that her husband was dependent on her for more than one half of his support. The issue on which the Court was divided was whether sex, like race, should be treated as a suspect, and therefore less readily justified, classification. Brennan, we are told, circulated an opinion declaring classification by sex virtually impermissible. "He knew that [this] would have the effect of enacting the equal rights amendment [but he] was accustomed to having the Court out front, leading any civil rights movement" (Bob Woodward and Scott Armstrong, *The Brethren*, p. 254). The authors of this account conclude by quoting Brennan as being of the opinion that there "was no reason to wait several years for the states to ratify the amendment"—no reason other than the fact, which Brennan knew to be a fact, that the Constitution *as then written* would not support the decision he wanted the Court to render.

Conservatives call this JUDICIAL ACTIVISM, or government by the judiciary. It is not for the judiciary—the least responsible and, conservatives could charge, frequently the most irresponsible branch of government—to make the laws or amend the Constitution (or "bring it up to date"). Those powers belong, in the one case, to the Congress and, in the other, to the people in their sovereign capacity. Judges, they say, quoting *The Federalist* #78, are supposed to be "faithful guardians of the Constitution," not evangels of new modes and orders: "Until the people have, by some solemn and authoritative act, annulled or changed the established form, it is binding upon themselves collectively, as well as individually." As conservatives see it, one issue dividing them from mainstream (or liberal) lawyers is that of legitimacy: The legitimacy of judge-made law and, ultimately, the legitimacy of the Constitution itself. If, as James Madison put it, the judges are not guided by the sense of the people who ratified the Constitution, "there can be no security for a consistent and stable, more than for a *faithful* exercise of its powers." The legitimacy of government depends on adherence to the written text, the text the people ratified.

The classic statement of these (conservative) propositions can be found in JOHN MARSHALL's opinion for the Court in MARBURY V. MADISON (1803): The "whole American fabric has been erected" on the principle that government derives from, and is dependent on, the will of the people. "The original and supreme will organizes the government, and assigns to different departments their respective powers."

Statements of this sort abound in the literature of the founding period. "In a government which is emphatically stiled [*sic*] a government of laws, the least possible range ought to be left for the discretion of the judges." "If the constitution is to be expounded, not by its written text, but by the opinions of the rulers for the time being, whose opinions are to prevail, the first or the last? [And if the last] what certainty can there be in those powers [which it assigns and limits]?" Both certainty and legitimacy would be put in jeopardy by rules of constitutional construction that, in effect, permit the judges to do as they will. "Would [the Constitution] not become, instead of a supreme law for ourselves and our posterity, a mere oracle of the powers of the rulers of the day, to which implicit homage is to be paid, and speaking at different times the most opposite commands, and in the most ambiguous voices?"

Connected to this issue of legitimacy is the cause of constitutional government itself. As conservatives see it, inequality of wealth, rank, and position is the price we pay for liberty, and it was to secure the blessings of liberty that the Constitution was ordained and established. In Madison's words in *The Federalist* #10, the Constitution serves to secure liberty by providing "a republican remedy for the diseases most incident to republican government," egalitarian diseases manifested in "a rage for paper money, for an abolition of debts, for an equal division of property, or for any other improper or wicked project." The remedy was to be found in the limits embodied "in the extent and proper structure of the Union"—in a word, in the Constitution. And as Marshall said in *Marbury*, The Constitution is written in order that "those limits not be mistaken or forgotten." THOMAS JEFFERSON made the same point when he said that "the possession of a written constitution [was America's] peculiar security."

What conservatives want to conserve is this *liberal* Constitution, which, as they see it, is endangered by persons styling themselves liberals today. First, there are academic lawyers who treat the Constitution not as *law*—in Marshall's words, "a superior paramount law, unchangeable by ordinary means"—but as a mere "epiphenomenon," which is to say, as merely one of the factors (and, typically, not a controlling factor) entering into judicial decisions. As one of them puts it, rather than carry any precise meaning that judges are bound by oath to recognize and obey, the most important constitutional provisions "do *not* rule out any answer a majority of the Court is likely to want to give." The social, historical, and economic conditions take precedence over the Constitution's written text, and they may dictate any outcome. "There is nothing that is unsayable in the language of the Constitution," writes another.

Second, there is Justice Brennan, who writes that "the genius of the Constitution rests not in any static meaning it might have had in a world that is dead and gone, but in the adaptability of its great principles to cope with current problems and current needs."

Third are historians who, in the course of ridiculing the conservatives' appeal for a jurisprudence of ORIGINAL INTENT, insist that "our Constitution is no more important to the longevity and workability of our government than MAGNA CARTA is to the longevity and workability of the British government. Our Constitution is as unwritten as theirs."

Finally, there are journalists who say that "the mere idea of original intent is an absurdity . . . [that] those men in Philadelphia could not have possibly had an "original intent."

As these statements indicate, the conservative effort to preserve that liberal Constitution will gain little support in the liberal community. Unlike the Framers, today's liberals prefer equality to liberty, an equality of status to an equality of rights, a development foreseen by ALEXIS DE TOCQUEVILLE. Democratic peoples have a natural taste for liberty, he wrote, but their passion for equality is "invincible" and "irresistible," and anyone who tries to stand up against it "will be overthrown and destroyed by it."

In addition, conservatives have to contend with developments in the realm of political thought that, it is said, deprive the Constitution of its philosophical foundations. The Constitution put constraints on the popular will, but, according to Professor Sanford Levinson, those constraints have been deprived of whatever moral authority they might once have had. Constitutional arguments have been rendered meaningless. Indeed, the very idea of CONSTITUTIONALISM is dead: "The death of "constitutionalism' may be the central event of our time," Levinson writes, "just as the death of God was that of the past century (and for much the same reason)." If, as he claims, this view of our situation is "shared by most major law schools," conservatives are engaged in an almost hopeless enterprise. Care of the Constitution was put in the hands of the judges, but the judges are trained in those "major law schools."

Admittedly, and quite apart from the influence of this legal and political thought, governing within the limit imposed by a STRICT CONSTRUCTION of the Constitution has never been an easy matter. FEDERALISM is one of its prominent features, and conservatives, today if not in the past, would preserve it in its integrity. They would do so for political, as well as for constitutional, reasons. Like Tocqueville, they appreciate the political importance of what he called "mores," those "habits of the heart" that characterize a people and, in our case, he argued, made free goverment possible. Conservatives would attribute the Constitution's "longevity and workability" not to its flexibility but, at least in part, to the laws of the states where these mores, or morals and manners, are fostered and protected. Directly or indirectly (by supporting the private institutions whose business it is to provide it), these laws are intended to promote the sort of civic or moral education required of citizens in a democracy. Many of them—such as laws dealing with FLAG DESECRATION, OBSCENITY, indecency, illegitimacy, school prayer, and religious instruction and institutions, the list of which is not endless but is long—have been declared unconstitutional under the Fourteenth Amendment INCORPORATION DOCTRINE. These laws have been declared unconstitutional, conservatives insist, in the absence of any evidence that the framers of the Fourteenth Amendment intended it— originally intended it—to be used for that purpose.

There is, however, an abundance of evidence that the Fourteenth and other post-CIVIL WAR amendments were intended to affect the federal structure of the Constitution in material respects. The same freedom that allowed the states to be concerned about the moral character of their citizens also allowed them to decide who among their residents were to be citizens and, therefore, who among them were to enjoy the CIVIL RIGHTS and the PRIVILEGES AND IMMUNITIES of citizens. Thus, and without any question, those amendments were intended to deprive states of this power; they would do so by providing what Madison in 1787 criticized the original Constitution for its failure to provide, namely, "a constitutional negative on the laws of the States [in order to] secure individuals agst. encroachments on their rights."

The consequence—if only in our own time—has been a tremendous growth of national power at the expense of the states, and especially national judicial power. Conservatives cannot (and, in most cases, do not) complain when this power has been used to put an end to RACIAL DISCRIMINATION; as amended, the Constitution not only authorized this but required it. Given what proved to be almost a century of congressional inaction, they would also agree with the Supreme Court's decision in BROWN V. BOARD OF EDUCATION (1954,1955), the public school desegregation case. Read literally (or construed strictly), the words of the equal protection clause do not lend themselves to the use to which they were put in that case, but—to paraphrase what was said by conservative Chief Justice CHARLES EVANS HUGHES on an earlier occasion—while emergencies may not create power, they do furnish the occasions when it may properly be exercised. On such occasions, the conservative rule of "strict construction" must give way to necessity.

Conservatives concede, as they must, that necessity is the mother of invention; where they differ from mainstream liberals, to cite still another aphorism, is in their refusal to make a virtue of necessity. They cannot say, because it would be foolish to say, that the times must be kept in tune with the Constitution; but because our freedom and prosperity depend upon it, they do say, and say emphatically, that the times, *to the extent possible*, should be kept in tune with the Constitution.

WALTER BERNS
(1992)

(SEE ALSO: *Bork Nomination; Critical Legal Studies; Liberalism; Political Philosophy of the Constitution; Suspect Classification; Unwritten Constitution.*)

Bibliography

BORK, ROBERT H.   1990   *The Tempting of America: The Political Seduction of the Law.* New York: Free Press.
GOLDWIN, ROBERT A. and ART KAUFMAN, eds.   1987   *How Does the Constitution Protect Religious Freedom?* Washington: American Enterprise Institute.
LERNER, RALPH   1987   *The Thinking Revolutionary: Principle*

and Practice in the New Republic. Ithaca, N.Y.: Cornell University Press.

McDowell, Gary L. 1988 *Curbing the Courts: The Constitution and the Limits of Judicial Power.* Baton Rouge: Louisiana State University Press.

Pangle, Thomas L. 1988 *The Spirit of Modern Republicanism: The Moral Vision of the American Founding and the Philosophy of Locke.* Chicago: University of Chicago Press.

Rabkin, Jeremy 1989 *Judicial Compulsions: How Public Law Distorts Public Policy.* New York: Basic Books.

CONSPIRACY

See: Criminal Conspiracy

CONSPIRACY LAW

The crime of conspiracy is charged regularly in state and federal courts throughout the United States. This crime consists in an agreement by two or more individuals to commit an additional crime. The conspiracy charge is widely used in a number of different areas, particularly with respect to white-collar crimes and narcotics offenses. The prosecution views the crime of conspiracy as advantageous because it allows, in a single trial, for the prosecution of all conspirators wherever they are located, and it allows the government to prosecute the case in any city in which any act in furtherance of the agreement took place. In addition, statements made by any conspirator are allowed to be used against all other conspirators, and each conspirator can be found criminally responsible for other conspirators' crimes found to be in furtherance of the agreement.

Three major constitutional questions have arisen in conspiracy trials in the United States. The first deals with the DOUBLE JEOPARDY clause of the Fifth Amendment, which provides in part, "nor shall any person be subject for the same offense to be twice put in jeopardy of life or limb." Most judges have concluded that the purpose of the double jeopardy clause was to ensure that a person could not be charged more than once for the same offense in the same jurisdiction. Individuals who are prosecuted for the conspiracy offense contend that if they are also charged with the crime that was the subject of the agreement (for example, bank robbery), their double jeopardy rights have been violated. The courts have consistently rejected this claim, however, holding that conspiracy (the agreement to commit bank robbery) and the crime (the actual bank robbery) are separate offenses. Hence, the defendant can receive separate punishment for each without the double jeopardy clause being violated.

Defendants also contend that being charged with conspiracies in two different courts violates their double jeopardy rights. For instance, conspiracy to rob a bank may be a violation of both state and federal law. It is a violation of state law because robbing any institution within the state is a crime. It is a violation of federal law because the bank may be a federally insured institution. Under the principle of "dual sovereignties" the Supreme Court has concluded that separate prosecutions and separate penalties for a federal conspiracy and a state conspiracy do not violate the double jeopardy clause, because such prosecutions are not multiple trials for the same offense by the same jurisdiction.

An additional constitutional issue is raised when defendants are charged with conspiring not to commit a crime but to commit acts that are "injurious to the public health or morals." These cases usually involve situations in which a particular form of behavior, such as charging usurious interest rates, is not itself criminal, but the defendant is charged with *conspiring* to commit that act. The Supreme Court in *Musser v. Utah* (1948) cast considerable doubt on the constitutionality of these prosecutions. The chief argument here is that such conspiracy prosecutions violate the DUE PROCESS clause of both the Fifth Amendment and FOURTEENTH AMENDMENT because the phrase "acts injurious to the public health or morals" is so vague as to give insufficient guidance to citizens. As a consequence of the *Musser* decision, few prosecutions have been based upon this rather open-ended charge; instead, the government typically contends that the defendants have conspired to commit a particular crime and that crime is then set forth in some detail.

The third constitutional issue is perhaps the most famous and controversial, involving free speech implications under the FIRST AMENDMENT. The problem surfaces when the defendants are charged with agreeing to advocate activities challenging the government. In such situations, the question is whether the agreement can be viewed as purely criminal behavior or whether, under the First Amendment, the behavior is protected speech. The most important Supreme Court case in the area is YATES V. UNITED STATES (1956). There the defendants were mid-level officials of the Communist party charged with conspiring to advocate the overthrow of the government of the United States by force and violence. In construing the Smith Act, the Court concluded that the prosecution, to succeed, must show an agreement to engage in unlawful action and a specific intent by each conspirator to engage in that action. If, however, the charge against the defendants were based upon their agreement to advocate the abstract principle of forcible overthrow of the government, that agreement would not violate the statute, even if such advocacy promoted violent activity.

PAUL MARCUS
(1992)

Bibliography

COOK, JOSEPH and MARCUS, PAUL 1991 *Criminal Procedure*, 3rd ed. New York: Matthew Bender.

MARCUS, PAUL 1991 *The Prosecution and Defense of Criminal Conspiracy Cases*. New York: Matthew Bender.

CONSTITUTION

At the time of the Stamp Act controversy, a British lord told BENJAMIN FRANKLIN that Americans had wrong ideas about the British constitution. British and American ideas did differ radically. The American Revolution repudiated the British understanding of the constitution; in a sense, the triumph in America of a novel concept of "constitution" *was* the "revolution." The British, who were vague about their unwritten constitution, meant by it their system of government, the COMMON LAW, royal proclamations, major legislation such as MAGNA CARTA and the BILL OF RIGHTS, and various usages and customs of government animating the aggregation of laws, institutions, rights, and practices that had evolved over centuries. Statute, however, was the supreme part of the British constitution. After the Glorious Revolution of 1688–1689, Parliament dominated the constitutional system and by ordinary legislation could and did alter it. Sir WILLIAM BLACKSTONE summed up parliamentary supremacy when he declared in his *Commentaries* (1766), "What Parliament doth, no power on earth can undo."

The principle that Parliament had unlimited power was at the crux of the controversy leading to the American Revolution. The American assertion that government is limited undergirded the American concept of a constitution as a FUNDAMENTAL LAW that imposes regularized restraints upon power and reserves rights to the people. The American concept emerged slowly through the course of the colonial period, yet its nub was present almost from the beginning, especially in New England where covenant theology, SOCIAL COMPACT THEORY, and HIGHER LAW theory blended together. THOMAS HOOKER in 1638 preached that the foundation of authority lay in the people who might choose their governors and "set bounds and limitations on their powers." A century later Jared Elliot of Massachusetts preached that a "legal government" exists when the sovereign power "puts itself under restraints and lays itself under limitations. This is what we call a legal, limited, and well constituted government." Some liberal theologians viewed God himself as a constitutional monarch, limited in power because he had limited himself to the terms of his covenant with mankind. Moreover God ruled a constitutional universe based on immutable natural laws that also bound him. Jonathan Mayhew preached in Boston that no one has a right to exercise a wanton SOVEREIGNTY over the property, lives, and consciences of the people—"such a sovereignty as some inconsiderately ascribe to the supreme governor of the world." Mayhew explained that "God himself does not govern in an absolute, arbitrary, and despotic manner. The power of this almighty king is limited by law; not indeed, by acts of Parliament, but by the eternal laws of truth, wisdom, and equity. . . ."

Political theory and law as well as religion taught that government was limited; so did history. But the Americans took their views on such matters from a highly selective and romanticized image of seventeenth-century England, which they perpetuated in America even as England changed. Seventeenth-century England was the England of the great struggle for constitutional liberty by the common law courts and Puritan parliaments against despotic Stuart kings. Seventeenth-century England was the England of EDWARD COKE, JOHN LILBURNE, and JOHN LOCKE. It was an England in which religion, law, and politics converged with theory and experience to produce limited monarchy and, ironically, parliamentary supremacy. To Americans, however, Parliament had bound itself by reaffirming Magna Carta and passing the HABEAS CORPUS ACT, the Bill of Rights, and the TOLERATION ACT, among others. Locke had taught the social contract theory; advocated that taxation without representation or consent is tyranny; written that "government is not free to do as it pleases," and referred to the "bounds" which "the law of God and Nature have set to the legislative power of every commonwealth, in all forms of government."

Such ideas withered but did not die in eighteenth-century England. CATO'S LETTERS popularized Locke on both sides of the Atlantic; Henry St. John (Viscount Bolingbroke) believed that Parliament could not annul the constitution; Charles Viner's *General Abridgment of Law and Equity* endorsed Coke's views in Dr. BONHAM'S CASE (1610); and even as Parliament debated the Declaratory Act (1766), which asserted parliamentary power to legislate for America "in all cases whatsoever," CHARLES PRATT (Lord Camden) declared such a power "absolutely illegal, contrary to the fundamental laws of . . . this constitution. . . ." Richard Price and Granville Sharpe were two of the many English radicals who shared the American view of the British constitution.

TAXATION WITHOUT REPRESENTATION provoked Americans to clarify their views. JAMES OTIS, arguing against the tax on sugar, relied on *Dr. Bonham's Case* and contended that legislative authority did not extend to the "fundamentals of the constitution," which he believed to be fixed. THOMAS HUTCHINSON, a leading supporter of Parliament, summed up the American constitutional reaction to the stamp tax duties by writing, "The prevailing reason at this time is, that the Act of Parliament is against Magna Charta and the NATURAL RIGHTS of Englishmen, and therefore according to Lord Coke, null and void." The TOWNSHEND ACT duties led to American declarations that the supreme legislature in any free state derives its power from the constitution, which limits government. JOHN DICKINSON, in an essay reprinted throughout the colonies, wrote that a free people are not those subject to a reasonable exercise of government power but those "who live under a government so constitutionally checked and controlled, that proper provision is made against its being otherwise exercised." J. J. Zubly of Georgia was another of many who argued that no government, not even Parliament, could make laws against the constitution any more than it could alter the constitution. An anonymous pamphleteer rhapsodized in 1775 about the "glorious constitution worthy to be engraved in capitals of gold, on pillars of marble; to be perpetuated through all time, a barrier, to circumscribe and bound the restless ambition of aspiring monarchs, and the palladium of civil liberty. . . ." TOM PAINE actually argued that Great Britain had no constitution, because Parliament claimed to exercise any power it pleased. To Paine a constitution could not be an act of the government but of "people constituting government. . . . A constitution is a thing antecedent to a government; a government is only the creature of the constitution."

Thus, by "constitution," Americans meant a supreme law creating the government, limiting it, unalterable by it, and above it. When they said that an act of government was unconstitutional, they meant that the government had acted lawlessly because it lacked the authority to perform that act. Accordingly the act was not law; it was null and void, and it could be disobeyed. By contrast when the British spoke of a statute being unconstitutional, they meant only that it was impolitic, unwise, unjust, or inexpedient, but not that it was beyond the power of the government to enact. They did not mean that Parliament was limited in its powers and had exceeded them.

The American view of "constitution" was imperfectly understood even by many leaders of the revolutionary movement as late as 1776. The proof is that when the states framed their first constitutions, the task was left to legislatures, although some received explicit authorization from the voters. THOMAS JEFFERSON worried because Virginia had not differentiated fundamental from ordinary law. Not until Massachusetts framed its constitution of 1780 by devising a CONSTITUTIONAL CONVENTION did the American theory match practice. When the CONSTITUTIONAL CONVENTION OF 1787 met in Philadelphia, the American meaning of a constitution was fixed and consistent.

LEONARD W. LEVY
(1986)

Bibliography

ADAMS, RANDOLPH G. (1922) 1958 *Political Ideas of the American Revolution.* 3rd ed. New York: Barnes & Noble.

BAILYN, BERNARD 1967 *Ideological Origins of the American Revolution.* Cambridge, Mass.: Harvard University Press.

BALDWIN, ALICE M. (1928) 1958 *The New England Clergy and the American Revolution.* New York: Frederick Ungar.

McLAUGHLIN, ANDREW C. 1932 *The Foundations of American Constitutionalism.* New York: New York University Press.

MULLETT, CHARLES F. 1933 *Fundamental Law and the American Revolution.* New York: Columbia University Press.

CONSTITUTIONAL ARGUMENT

See: History in Constitutional Argumentation

CONSTITUTIONAL COMMON LAW

"Constitutional common law" refers to a theory about the lawmaking competence of the federal courts. The theory postulates that much of what passes as constitutional adjudication is best understood as a judicially fashioned COMMON LAW authorized and inspired, but not compelled, by the constitutional text and structure. Unlike the "true" constitutional law exemplified by MARBURY V. MADISON (1803), constitutional common law is ultimately amenable to control and revision by Congress. The theory originated in an effort to explain how the Supreme Court could legitimately insist upon application of the EXCLUSIONARY RULE in state criminal proceedings, once the Court had recast the exclusionary rule as simply a judicially fashioned remedy designed to deter future unlawful police conduct rather than as part and parcel of a criminal defendant's underlying constitutional rights or a necessary remedy for the violation thereof. On this view of the exclusionary rule, why does the state court have a constitutional obligation to do more than provide an "adequate" remedy for the underlying constitutional violation, such as an action for DAMAGES? The source of the Supreme Court's authority to insist that the state courts follow any rule not required by the constitution or authorized by some federal statute is not evident. ERIE RAILROAD V. TOMPKINS (1938) makes plain that the federal courts have no power to create a general FEDERAL COMMON LAW. This limitation exists not simply because of Congress's express statutory command, applicable to civil cases in the federal district courts, but because of the perception that there is no general federal judicial power to displace state law. To the contrary, the courts must point to some authoritative source—a statute, a treaty, a constitutional provision—as explicitly or implicitly authorizing judicial creation of substantive federal law. That federal statutes can constitute such authority has long been clear, and the result has been in many areas judicial creation of a federal common law designed to implement federal statutory policies. There is no a priori reason to suppose that the Constitution itself should differ from statutes in providing a basis for the generation of an interstitial federal common law. Not surprisingly, therefore, a significant body of federal common law has been developed on the basis of constitutional provisions. For example, the Supreme Court has developed bodies of federal substantive law on the basis of the constitutional (and statutory) grants of jurisdiction to hear cases in ADMIRALTY, as well as cases involving disputes among the states or implicating FOREIGN AFFAIRS. Because the Court's decisions are ultimately reversible by Congress, its decisions holding statutes to be invalid burdens upon INTERSTATE COMMERCE are also best understood as federal common law created by the Court on the authority of the COMMERCE CLAUSE.

In the foregoing examples, constitutional common law has been created to govern situations where state interests are subordinated to interests of special concern to the national government, and thus come within the reach of the plenary national legislative power. They are FEDERALISM cases, in that the federal common law implements and fills out the authority that has been committed to the national government by the constitutional text and structure. Thus, the principle of these cases arguably is limited to the generation of federal constitutional common law in support of national legislative competence. These "federalism" cases do not by themselves establish that the Court may fashion a common law based solely upon constitutional provisions framed as *limitations* on governmental power in order to vindicate CIVIL LIBERTIES, such as those protected by the FIRST AMENDMENT and FOURTH AMENDMENT. Such a judicial rule-making authority—which seeks to create federal rules in areas of primary *state* concern—intersects with federalism concerns in ways that sets these cases apart from the federalism cases. Moreover, at the national level judicial creation of common law implicates SEPARATION OF POWERS considerations. Nonetheless, the Court's constitutionally based common law decisions in areas of plenary national legislative authority at least invite inquiry whether the specific constitutional guarantees of individual liberty might also authorize the creation of a substructure of judicially fashioned rules to carry out the purposes and policies of those guarantees. Several COMMENTATORS have, directly or indirectly, argued for acceptance of judicial power to fashion such a subconstitutional law of civil liberties. They argue that recognition of such a power is the most satisfactory way to rationalize a large and steadily growing body of judicial decision, not only in the criminal procedure area but also with many of the Court's administrative DUE PROCESS cases, while at the same time recognizing a coordinate and controlling authority in Congress. There has, however, been no significant judicial consideration of this theory apart from the decision in *Turpin v. Mailet* (2d Cir., *en banc,* 1978–1979).

Whatever its perceived advantages, a theory that posits a competence in the courts to fashion a constitutionally inspired constitutional common law of civil liberties must deal adequately with a series of objections: that development of such a body of law is inconsistent with the original intent of the Framers; that the line between true constitutional interpretation and constitutional common law is too indeterminate to be useful; and that the existence of such judicial power is inconsistent with the autonomy of the executive department in enforcing law as well as the rightful independence of the states in the federal system. The theory of constitutional common law bears a family resemblance to the views of those commentators who hold that the Court may legitimately engage in "noninterpretive" review—that is, the Court may properly impose values on the political branches not fairly inferrable from the constitutional text or the structure it creates—but who insist that Congress may control those decisions by regulating the JURISDICTION of the Supreme Court. Other differences aside, the constitutional common law view would permit Congress to overrule the noninterpretive decisions directly, bypassing the awkward theoretical and political problems associated with congressional attempts to manipulate jurisdiction for substantive ends.

HENRY P. MONAGHAN
(1986)

Bibliography

MONAGHAN, HENRY P. 1975 The Supreme Court, 1974 Term—Foreword: Constitutional Common Law. *Harvard Law Review* 89:1–45.

SCHROCK, THOMAS S. and WELSH, ROBERT C. 1978 Reconsidering the Constitutional Common Law. *Harvard Law Review* 91:1117–1176.

CONSTITUTIONAL CONVENTION

Constitutional conventions, like the written constitutions that they produce, are among the American contributions to government. A constitutional convention became the means that a free people used to put into practice the SOCIAL COMPACT THEORY by devising their FUNDAMENTAL LAW. Such a convention is a representative body acting for the sovereign people to whom it is responsible. Its sole commission is to frame a CONSTITUTION; it does not pass laws, perform acts of administration, or govern in any way. It submits its work for popular ratification and adjourns. Such a convention first came into being during the AMERICAN REVOLUTION. The institutionalizing of constitutional principles during wartime was the constructive achievement of the Revolution. The Revolution's enduring heroics are to be found in constitution-making. As JAMES

MADISON exultantly declared, "Nothing has excited more admiration in the world than the manner in which free governments have been established in America; for it was the first instance, from the creation of the world . . . that free inhabitants have been seen deliberating on a form of government and selecting such of their citizens as possessed their confidence, to determine upon and give effect to it."

Within a century of 1776 nearly two hundred state constitutional conventions had been held in the United States. The institution is so familiar that we forget how novel it was even in 1787. At the CONSTITUTIONAL CONVENTION, which framed this nation's constitution, OLIVER ELLSWORTH declared that since the framing of the ARTICLES OF CONFEDERATION (1781), "a new sett [sic] of ideas seemed to have crept in. . . . Conventions of the people, or with power derived expressly from the people, were not then thought of. The Legislatures were considered as competent."

Credit for understanding that legislatures were not competent for that task belongs to JOHN LILBURNE, the English Leveller leader, who probably originated the idea of a constitutional convention. In his *Legall Fundamentall Liberties* (1649), he proposed that specially elected representatives should frame an Agreement of the People, or constitution, "which Agreement ought to be above Law; and therefore [set] bounds, limits, and extent of the people's Legislative Deputies in Parliament." Similarly, Sir Henry Vane, once governor of Massachusetts, proposed, in his *Healing Question* (1656), that a "convention" be chosen by the free consent of the people, "not properly to exercise the legislative power" but only to agree on "fundamentall constitutions" expressing the will of the people "in their highest state of soveraignty. . . ." The idea, which never made headway in England, was reexpressed in a pamphlet by Obadiah Hulme in 1771, recommending that a constitution should "be formed by a convention of delegates of the people, appointed for the express purpose," and that the constitution should never be "altered in any respect by any power besides the power which first framed [it]." Hulme's work was reprinted in Philadelphia in 1776 immediately before the framing of the PENNSYLVANIA CONSTITUTION by a specially elected convention. That convention, however, in accordance with prevailing ideas, simultaneously exercised the powers of government and after promulgating its constitution remained in session as the state legislature. Until 1780 American legislatures wrote constitutions.

The theory underlying a constitutional convention, but not the actual idea of having one, was first proposed in America by the town meeting of Pittsfield, Massachusetts, on May 29, 1776. Massachusetts then had a provisional revolutionary extralegal government. Pittsfield asked, "What Compact has been formed as the foundation of Government in this province?" The collapse of British power over the colonies had thrown the people, "the foundation of power," into "a state of Nature." The first step to restore civil government on a permanent basis was "the formation of a fundamental Constitution as the Basis ground work of Legislation." The existing legislature, Pittsfield contended, although representative, could not make the constitution because, "They being but servants of the people cannot be greater than their Masters, must be responsible to them." A constitution is "above the whole Legislature," so that the "legislature cannot certainly make it. . . ." Pittsfield understood the difference between fundamental and ordinary law, yet inconsistently concluded that the legislature should frame the constitution on condition that it be submitted to the people for ratification.

Pittsfield was merely inconsistent, but the Continental Congress was bewildered. The provisional government of Massachusetts, requesting advice from Congress on how to institute government, said that it would accept a constitution proposed by Congress. That was in May 1775. Many years later, when his memory was not to be trusted, JOHN ADAMS recalled in his autobiography that congressmen went around asking each other, "How can the people institute government?" As late as May 1776, Congress, still lacking an answer, merely recommended that colonies without adequate governments should choose representatives to suppress royal authority and exercise power under popular authority. By then the temporary legislatures of New Hampshire and South Carolina, without popular authorization, had already framed and promulgated constitutions as if enacting statutory law, and continued to operate as legislatures. Adams, however, credited himself with knowing how to "realize [make real] the theories of the wisest writers," who had urged that sovereignty resides in the people and that government is made by contract. "This could be done," he explained, "only by conventions of representatives chosen by the people in the several colonies. . . ." How, congressmen asked him, can we know whether the people will submit to the new constitutions, and he recalled having replied, if there is doubt, "the convention may send out their project of a constitution, to the people in their several towns, counties, or districts, and the people may make the acceptance of it their own act." Congress did not follow his advice, he wrote, because of his "new, strange, and terrible doctrines."

Adams had described a procedure followed only in Massachusetts, and only after the legislature had asked the people of the towns for permission to frame a constitution and submit it for popular ratification. Several towns, led by Concord (see CONCORD TOWN MEETING RESOLUTIONS) protested that the legislature was not a competent body for the task, because a constitution had been overwhelmingly rejected in 1778. Concord had demanded a constitutional convention. In 1779 the legislature asked the towns to vote on the question whether a state constitution should be framed by a specially elected convention. The towns, voting by universal manhood suffrage, overwhelmingly approved. In late 1779 the delegates to the first constitutional convention in world history met in Cambridge and framed the MASSACHUSETTS CONSTITUTION of 1780, which the voters ratified after an intense public debate. With pride Thomas Dawes declared in an oration, "The people of Massachusetts have reduced to practice the wonderful theory. A numerous people have convened in a state of nature, and, like our ideas of the patriarchs, have authorized a few fathers of the land to draw up for them a glorious covenant." New Hampshire copied the procedure when revising its constitution in 1784, and it rapidly became standard procedure. Within a few years American constitutional theory had progressed from the belief that legislatures were competent to compose and announce constitutions, to the belief that a convention acting for the sovereign people is the only proper instrument for the task and that the sovereign must have the final word. A constitution, then, in American theory, is the supreme fundamental law that creates the legislature, authorizes its powers, and limits the exercise of its powers. The legislature is subordinate to the Constitution and cannot alter it.

LEONARD W. LEVY
(1986)

Bibliography

ADAMS, WILLI PAUL 1980 *The First American Constitutions: Republican Ideology and the Making of the State Constitutions in the Revolutionary Era.* Chapel Hill: University of North Carolina Press.

DODD, WALTER F. 1910 *The Revision and Amendment of State Constitutions.* Baltimore: Johns Hopkins University Press.

JAMESON, JOHN ALEXANDER 1887 *A Treatise on Constitutional Conventions.* 4th ed. Chicago: Callahan & Co.

McLAUGHLIN, ANDREW C. 1932 *The Foundations of American Constitutionalism.* New York: New York University Press.

WOOD, GORDON S. 1969 *The Creation of the American Republic, 1776–1787.* Chapel Hill: University of North Carolina Press.

CONSTITUTIONAL CONVENTION, RECORDS OF

The records of the CONSTITUTIONAL CONVENTION OF 1787 are not so full as scholars and jurists would like them to be. A verbatim account of the proceedings does not exist and, absent modern technology, could not have been produced. Stenographers in Philadelphia covered the state ratifying convention, which met in the fall of 1787; but the Federal Convention met in secrecy and, even if the local stenographers had been admitted, the rudimentary state of their craft and assorted personal shortcomings would have made a satisfactory result unlikely.

We must rely for information about the Convention on a journal kept by its secretary, William Jackson, and on notes kept by various delegates. Some of the notes, especially those made by JAMES MADISON, are extensive; others are fragmentary. Taken together, the existing records give us a satisfactory narrative of events at the Convention—although details of the drafting of many key provisions are sparse, leaving the ORIGINAL INTENT of the Framers enigmatic. It is also true that the documentation becomes poorer toward the end of the Convention. The delegates, tired and eager to go home, recorded less than they did earlier, and what they recorded was sketchier. This is unfortunate, because the last weeks of the Convention saw many important compromises and changes about which, in the absence of adequate records, we know far too little.

The story of how Madison created his notes is familiar: "I chose a seat in front of the presiding member, with the other members, on my right and left hand. In this favorable position for hearing all that passed I noted in terms legible and in abbreviations and marks intelligible to myself what was read from the Chair or spoken by the members; and losing not a moment unnecessarily between the adjournment and reassembling of the Convention I was enabled to write out my daily notes during the session or within a few finishing days after its close." Conscientiously completed at considerable physical cost—Madison later confessed that the task "almost killed" him—these notes are the principal source of information about the convention. That Madison kept his notes in his possession until his death caused one suspicious scholar, WILLIAM W. CROSSKEY, to charge that during his life he had tampered with them—"forged" them, in fact—to make them consistent with political actions he had taken after 1787, an accusation since proven to be without foundation. The one considerable problem with Madison's notes is that they contain only a small proportion of each day's debates. They should not be used with the assumption that they are comprehensive.

The source next in importance to Madison's notes is the Convention records kept by New York delegate ROBERT YATES. They were published in 1821 under the title *Secret Proceedings and Debates of the Convention Assembled at Philadelphia in the Year 1787* by an anonymous editor, who turned out to be Citizen Edmond Genêt, the incendiary ambassador of revolutionary France to the United States in 1793. When Madison first saw the published version of Yates's notes, he warned against their "extreme incorrectness"—and with good reason, for it has been discovered that Genêt was guilty of the sin Crosskey laid at Madison's door: tampering with the manuscript version of Yates's notes, deleting some parts and changing others. The *Secret Proceedings* must therefore be used with extreme caution.

Several other delegates left notes, records, and scraps of paper that shed varying amounts of light on what occurred at Philadelphia, among which the notes of RUFUS KING and JOHN DICKINSON are the fullest. ALEXANDER HAMILTON, JAMES MCHENRY, WILLIAM PIERCE, PIERCE BUTLER, WILLIAM PATERSON, CHARLES PINCKNEY, and JAMES WILSON left more fragmentary materials. OLIVER ELLSWORTH and LUTHER MARTIN said a good deal about the workings of the Convention in polemics generated by the campaign for the RATIFICATION OF THE CONSTITUTION during 1787–1788. Their accounts should be consulted, but their partisanship obviously dictates that their statements be used with caution.

The remaining source of information about the Convention is the official journal published in 1819 at the direction of Congress and edited by then Secretary of State JOHN QUINCY ADAMS. Although Adams complained that the manuscript record left by Convention Secretary William Jackson was "very loosely and imperfectly kept," he was able to make perfect sense of it, with the result that the journal that issued from his editorship is a reliable, if barebones, narrative of the daily business of the Convention.

Scholars are aware that several delegates kept manuscript notes of Convention proccedings that have not been found. It is possible that in the future our understanding of Convention proceedings will be enriched, if not fundamentally changed, by the discovery of yet another set of Convention notes.

JAMES HUTSON
(1992)

Bibliography

FARRAND, MAX, ed.   1987   *The Records of the Federal Convention of 1787*, rev. ed., 4 vols. New Haven, Conn.: Yale University Press.
HUTSON, JAMES H.   1986   The Creation of the Constitution: The Integrity of the Documentary Record. *Texas Law Review* 65: 1–39.

CONSTITUTIONAL CONVENTION OF 1787

Over the last two centuries, the work of the Constitutional Convention and the motives of the Founding Fathers have been analyzed under a number of different ideological auspices. To one generation of historians, the hand of God

was moving in the assembly; under a later dispensation, the dialectic replaced the Deity: "relationships of production" moved into the niche previously reserved for Love of Country. Thus, in counterpoint to the Zeitgeist, the Framers have undergone miraculous metamorphoses: at one time acclaimed as liberals and bold social engineers, today they appear in the guise of sound Burkean conservatives.

The "Fathers" have thus been admitted to our best circles; the revolutionary generation that confiscated all Tory property in reach and populated New Brunswick with outlaws has been converted into devotees of "consensus" and "prescriptive rights." Indeed, there is one fundamental truth about the Founding Fathers that every generation of Zeitgeisters has done its best to obscure: they were first and foremost superb democratic politicians. They were political men—not metaphysicians, disembodied conservatives, or agents of history—and, as recent research into the nature of American politics in the 1780s confirms, they were required to work within a democratic framework. The Philadelphia Convention was not a council of Platonic guardians working within a manipulative, predemocratic framework; it was a nationalist reform caucus which had to operate with great delicacy and skill in a political cosmos full of enemies to achieve the one definitive goal—popular approbation.

Perhaps the time has come, to borrow WALTON HAMILTON's fine phrase, to promote the Framers from immortality to mortality, to give them credit for their magnificent demonstration of the art of democratic politics: they made history and they did it within the limits of consensus. What they did was hammer out a pragmatic compromise that would both bolster the "national interest" and be acceptable to the people. What inspiration they got came from collective experience as politicians in a democratic society. As JOHN DICKINSON put it to his fellow delegates on August 13, "Experience must be our guide. Reason may mislead us."

When the Constitutionalists went forth to subvert the ARTICLES OF CONFEDERATION, they employed the mechanisms of political legitimacy. Although the roadblocks confronting them were formidable, they were also endowed with certain political talents. From 1786 to 1790 the Constitutionalists used those talents against bumbling, erratic behavior by the opponents of reform. Effectively, the Constitutionalists had to induce the states, by democratic techniques, to cripple themselves. To be specific, if New York should refuse to join the new Union, the project was doomed; yet before New York was safely in, the reluctant state legislature had to take the following steps: agree to send delegates to the Convention and maintain them there; set up the special ratifying convention; and accept that convention's decision that New York should ratify the

Constitution. The same legal hurdles existed in every state.

The group that undertook this struggle was an interesting amalgam of a few dedicated nationalists and self-interested spokesmen of various parochial bailiwicks. Georgians, for example, wanted a strong central authority to provide military protection against the Creek Confederacy; Jerseymen and Connecticuters wanted to escape from economic bondage to New York; Virginians sought a system recognizing that great state's "rightful" place in the councils of the Republic. These states' dominant political figures therefore cooperated in the call for the Convention. In other states, the cause of national reform was taken up by the "outs" who added the "national interest" to their weapons systems; in Pennsylvania, for instance, JAMES WILSON's group fighting to revise the state Constitution of 1776 came out four-square behind the Constitutionalists.

To say this is not to suggest that the Constitution was founded on base motives but to recognize that in politics there are no immaculate conceptions. It is not surprising that a number of diversified private interests promoted the nationalist public interest. However motivated, these men did demonstrate a willingness to compromise in behalf of an ideal that took shape before their eyes and under their ministrations.

What distinguished the leaders of the Constitutionalist caucus from their enemies was a "continental" approach to political, economic, and military issues. Their institutional base of operations was the Continental Congress (thirty-nine of the fifty-five designated delegates to the Convention had served in Congress), hardly a locale that inspired respect for the state governments. One can surmise that membership in the Congress had helped establish a continental frame of reference, particularly with respect to external affairs. The average state legislator was probably about as concerned with foreign policy then as he is today, but congressmen were constantly forced to take the broad view of American prestige, and to listen to the reports of Secretary JOHN JAY and their envoys in Europe. A "continental" ideology thus developed, demanding invigoration of our domestic institutions to assure our rightful place in the international arena. Indeed, an argument with the force of GEORGE WASHINGTON as its incarnation urged that our very survival in the Hobbesian jungle of world politics depended upon a reordering and strengthening of our national SOVEREIGNTY.

MERRILL JENSEN seems quite sound in his view that to most Americans, engaged as they were in self-sustaining agriculture, the "Critical Period" was not particularly critical. The great achievement of the Constitutionalists was their ultimate success in convincing the elected representatives of a majority of the white male population that change was imperative. A small group of political leaders with a continental vision and essentially a consciousness of the United States' international impotence, was the core of the movement. To their standard rallied other leaders' parallel ambitions. Their great assets were active support from George Washington, whose prestige was enormous; the energy and talent of their leadership; a communications "network" far superior to the opposition's; the preemptive skill which made "their" issue The Issue and kept the locally oriented opposition on the defensive; and the new and compelling credo of American nationalism.

Despite great institutional handicaps, the Constitutionalists in the mid-1780s got the jump on the local oppositions with the demand for a Convention. Their opponents were caught in an old political trap: they were not being asked to approve any specific reform but only to endorse a meeting to discuss and recommend needed reforms. If they took a hard line, they were put in the position of denying the need for any changes. Moreover, because the states would have the final say on any proposals that might emerge from the Convention, the Constitutionalists could go to the people with a persuasive argument for "fair play."

Perhaps because of their poor intelligence system, perhaps because of overconfidence generated by the failure of all previous efforts to alter the Articles, the opposition awoke too late. Not only did the Constitutionalists manage to get every state but Rhode Island to appoint delegates to Philadelphia but they also dominated the delegations. The fact that the delegates to Philadelphia were appointed by state governments, not elected by the people, has been advanced as evidence of the "undemocratic" character of the gathering, but this argument is specious. The existing central government under the Articles was considered a creature of the states—not as a consequence of elitism or fear of the mob but as a logical extension of STATES' RIGHTS doctrine. The national government was not supposed to end-run the state legislatures and make direct contact with the people.

With delegations named, the focus shifted to Philadelphia. While waiting for a quorum to assemble, JAMES MADISON drafted the so-called VIRGINIA PLAN. This was a political masterstroke: once business got underway, this plan provided the framework of discussion. Instead of arguing interminably over the agenda, the delegates took the Virginia Plan as their point of departure, including its major premise: a new start on a Constitution rather than piecemeal amendment. This proposal was not necessarily revolutionary—a new Constitution might have been formulated as "amendments" to the Articles of Confederation—but the provision that amendments take effect after approval by nine states was thoroughly subversive. The Articles required unanimous state approval for any amendment.

Standard treatments of the Convention divide the delegates into "nationalists" and "states' righters" with various shadings, but these latter-day characterizations obfuscate more than they clarify. The Convention was remarkably homogeneous in ideology. ROBERT YATES and JOHN LANSING, Clinton's two chaperones for ALEXANDER HAMILTON, left in disgust on July 10. LUTHER MARTIN left in a huff on September 4; others went home for personal reasons. But the hard core of delegates accepted a grinding regimen throughout a Philadelphia summer precisely because they shared the Constitutionalist goal.

Basic differences of opinion emerged, of course, but these were not ideological; they were structural. If the so-called states' rights group had not accepted the fundamental purposes of the Convention, they could simply have pulled out and aborted the whole enterprise. Instead of bolting, they returned day after day to argue and to compromise. An index of this basic homogeneity was the initial agreement on secrecy: these professional politicians wanted to retain the freedom of maneuver that would be possible only if they were not forced to take public stands during preliminary negotiations. There was no legal means of binding the tongues of the delegates: at any stage a delegate with basic objections to the emerging project could have denounced the convention. Yet the delegates generally observed the injunction; Madison did not even inform THOMAS JEFFERSON in Paris of the course of the deliberations. Secrecy is uncharacteristic of any assembly marked by ideological polarization. During the Convention the *New York Daily Advertiser* called the secrecy "a happy omen, as it demonstrates that the spirit of party on any great and essential point cannot have arisen to any height."

Some key Framers must have been disappointed. Commentators on the Constitution who have read THE FEDERALIST but not Madison's record of the actual debates (secret until after his death in 1836), have credited the Fathers with a sublime invention called "Federalism." Yet the Constitution's final balance between the states and the nation must have dissatisfied Madison, whose Virginia Plan envisioned a unitary national government effectively freed from and dominant over the states. Hamilton's unitary views are too well known to need elucidation.

Under the Virginia Plan the general government was freed from state control in a truly radical fashion, and the scope of its authority was breathtaking. The national legislature was to be empowered to disallow the acts of state legislatures, and the central government would be vested, in addition to the powers of the nation under the Articles

of Confederation, with plenary authority "wherever . . . the separate States are incompetent or in which the harmony of the United States may be interrupted by the exercise of individual legislation." Finally, the national Congress was to be given the power to use military force on recalcitrant states.

The Convention was not scandalized by this militant program for a strong autonomous central government. Some delegates were startled, some leery of so comprehensive a reform, but nobody set off any fireworks and nobody walked out. Moreover, within two weeks the general principles of the Virginia Plan had received substantial endorsement. The temper of the gathering can be deduced from its unanimous approval, on May 31, of a resolution giving Congress authority to disallow state legislation "contravening in its opinion the Articles of Union."

Perhaps the Virginia Plan was the delegates' ideological Utopia, but as discussions became more specific many of them had second thoughts. They were practical politicians in a democratic society, and they would have to take home an acceptable package and defend it—and their own political futures—against predictable attack. June 14 saw the breaking point between dream and reality. Apparently realizing that under the Virginia Plan, Massachusetts, Virginia, and Pennsylvania could virtually dominate the national government, the delegates from the small states demanded time for a consideration of alternatives. John Dickinson reproached Madison: "You see the consequences of pushing things too far. Some of the members from the small States wish for two branches in the General Legislature and are friends to a good National Government; but we would sooner submit to a foreign power than . . . be deprived of an equality of suffrage in both branches of the Legislature, and thereby be thrown under the domination of the large States."

Now the process of accommodation was put into action smoothly—and wisely, given the character and strength of the doubters. Madison had the votes, but mechanical majoritarianism could easily have destroyed the objectives of the majority: the Constitutionalists sought a qualitative as well as a quantitative consensus, a political imperative to attain ratification.

According to the standard script, the "states' rights" group now united behind the NEW JERSEY PLAN, which has been characteristically portrayed as no more than a minor modification of the Articles of Confederation. The New Jersey Plan did put the states back into the institutional picture, but to do so was a recognition of political reality rather than an affirmation of states' rights.

Paterson, the leading spokesman for the project, said as much: "I came here not to speak my own sentiments, but the sentiments of those who sent me. Our object is not such a Government as may be best in itself, but such a one as our Constituents have authorized us to prepare, and as they will approve." This is Madison's version; in Yates's transcription, a crucial sentence follows: "I believe that a little practical virtue is to be preferred to the finest theoretical principles, which cannot be carried into effect."

The advocates of the New Jersey Plan concentrated their fire on what they held to be the political liabilities of the Virginia Plan—which were matters of institutional structure—rather than on the proposed scope of national authority. Indeed, the SUPREMACY CLAUSE of the Constitution first saw the light of day in Paterson's Sixth Resolution; for Paterson, under either the Virginia or the New Jersey system the general government would "act on individuals and not on states." From the states' rights viewpoint, this was heresy.

Paterson thus reopened the agenda of the Convention, but within a distinctly nationalist framework. Paterson favored a strong central government but opposed putting the big states in the saddle. As evidence for this there is an intriguing proposal among Paterson's preliminary drafts of the New Jersey Plan:

> Whereas it is necessary in Order to form the People of the U.S. of America in to a Nation, that the States should be consolidated, . . . it is therefore resolved, that all the Lands contained within the Limits of each state individually, and of the U.S. generally be considered as constituting one Body or Mass, and be divided into thirteen or more integral parts.
>
> Resolved, That such Divisions or integral Parts shall be styled Districts.

He may have gotten the idea from his New Jersey colleague Judge DAVID BREARLEY, who on June 9 had commented that the only remedy to the dilemma over representation was "that a map of the U.S. be spread out, that all the existing boundaries be erased, and that a new partition of the whole be made into 13 equal parts." According to Yates, Brearley added at this point, "then a government on the present [Virginia Plan] system will be just."

Thus, the delegates from the small states announced that they were unprepared to be offered up as sacrificial victims to a "national interest" that reflected Virginia's parochial ambition. Caustic CHARLES PINCKNEY was not far off when he remarked sardonically that "the whole conflict comes to this: Give New Jersey an equal vote, and she will dismiss her scruples, and concur in the National system." What he rather unfairly did not add was that the Jersey delegates were not free agents who could adhere to their private convictions; they had to stake their reputations and political careers on the reforms approved by the Convention—in New Jersey, not Virginia.

Paterson spoke on Saturday, and the weekend must have seen a good deal of consultation, argument, and caucusing. One delegate prepared a full-length address: on Monday Alexander Hamilton, previously mute, rose and delivered a six-hour oration. It was a remarkably apolitical speech; the gist of his position was that both the Virginia and New Jersey Plans were inadequately centralist, and he detailed a reform program reminiscent of the Protectorate under the Cromwellian *Instrument of Government* of 1653. He wanted, to take a striking phrase from a letter to George Washington, a "strong well mounted government."

From all accounts this was a compelling speech, but it had little practical effect; the Convention adjourned, admired Hamilton's rhetoric, and returned to business. Hamilton, never a patient man, stayed another ten days and then left in disgust for New York. Although he returned to Philadelphia sporadically and attended the last two weeks of the Convention, Hamilton played no part in the laborious task of hammering out the Constitution. His day came later when he led the New York Constitutionalists into the savage imbroglio over ratification—an arena in which his unmatched talent for political infighting surely won the day.

On June 19 James Madison led off with a long, carefully reasoned speech analyzing the New Jersey Plan; although intellectually vigorous in his criticisms, Madison was quite conciliatory in mood: "The great difficulty lies in the affair of REPRESENTATION; and if this could be adjusted, all others would be surmountable." When he finished, a vote was taken on whether to continue with the Virginia Plan as the nucleus for a new constitution: seven states voted yes; New York, New Jersey, and Delaware voted No; and Maryland was divided.

Paterson, it seems, lost decisively; yet in a fundamental sense he and his allies had achieved their purpose: from that day onward, it could never be forgotten that the state governments loomed ominously in the background. Moreover, nobody bolted the convention. Paterson and his colleagues set to work to modify the Virginia Plan, particularly with respect to representation in the national legislature. They won an immediate rhetorical bonus; when OLIVER ELLSWORTH of Connecticut moved that the word "national" be expunged from the Third Virginia Resolution ("Resolved that a *national* Government ought to be established consisting of a *supreme* Legislative, Executive and Judiciary"), Randolph agreed and the motion passed unanimously. The process of compromise had begun.

For two weeks the delegates circled around the problem of legislative representation. The Connecticut delegation appears to have evolved a possible compromise early in the debates, but the Virginians, particularly Madison, fought obdurately against providing for equal representation of states in the second chamber. There was enough acrimony for BENJAMIN FRANKLIN to propose institution of a daily prayer, but on July 2, the ice began to break when the majority against equality of representation was converted into a dead tie. The Convention was ripe for a solution and the South Carolinians proposed a committee. Madison and James Wilson wanted none of it, but with only Pennsylvania dissenting, a working party was established to cope with the problem of representation.

The members of this committee, one from each state, were elected by the delegates. Although the Virginia Plan had held majority support up to that date, neither Madison nor Randolph was selected. This was not to be a "fighting" committee; the members could be described as "second-level political entrepreneurs."

There is a common rumor that the Framers divided their time between philosophical discussions of government and reading the classics in political theory. In fact, concerns were highly practical; they spent little time canvassing abstractions. A number of them had some acquaintance with the history of political theory, and it was a poor rhetorician indeed who could not cite JOHN LOCKE, Montesquieu, or James Harrington in support of a desired goal. Yet up to this point no one had expounded a defense of states' rights or the SEPARATION OF POWERS on anything resembling a theoretical basis. The Madison model effectively vested all governmental power in the national legislature.

Because the critical fight was over representation of the states, once the GREAT COMPROMISE was adopted on July 17 the Convention was over the hump. Madison, James Wilson, and GOUVERNEUR MORRIS fought the compromise all the way in a last-ditch effort to get a unitary state with parliamentary supremacy. But their allies deserted them and after their defeat they demonstrated a willingness to swallow their objections and get on with the business. Moreover, once the compromise had carried (by five states to four, with one state divided), its advocates threw themselves into the job of strengthening the general government's substantive powers. Madison demonstrated his devotion to the art of politics when he later prepared essays for *The Federalist* in contradiction to the basic convictions he expressed in the Convention.

Two ticklish issues illustrate the later process of accommodation. The first was the institutional position of the executive. Madison argued for a chief magistrate chosen by the national legislature, and on May 29 this proposal had been adopted with a provision for a seven-year nonrenewable term. In late July this was reopened; groups now opposed election by the legislature. One felt that the states should have a hand in the process; another small but influential circle urged direct election by the people.

There were a number of proposals: election by the people, by state governors, by electors chosen by state legislatures, by the national legislature. There was some resemblance to three-dimensional chess in the dispute because of the presence of two other variables: length of tenure and eligibility for reelection. Finally the thorny problem was consigned to a committee for resolution.

The Brearley Committee on Postponed Matters was a superb aggregation of talent and its compromise on the Executive was a masterpiece of creativity. Everybody present knew that under any system devised, George Washington would be the first President; thus they were dealing in the future tense. To a body of working politicians the merits of the Brearley proposal were obvious: everyone could argue to his constituents that he had really won the day. First, the state legislatures had the right to determine the mode of selection of the electors; second, the small states were guaranteed a minimum of three votes in the ELECTORAL COLLEGE while the big states got acceptance of the principle of proportional power; third, if the state legislatures agreed (as six did in the first presidential election), the people could be involved directly in the choice of electors; and finally, if no candidate received a majority in the College, the decision passed to the House of Representatives with each state having one vote.

This compromise was almost too good to be true, and the Framers snapped it up with little debate or controversy. Thus the Electoral College was neither an exercise in applied Platonism nor an experiment in indirect government based on elitist distrust of the masses. It was merely an improvisation which was subsequently, in *The Federalist* #68, endowed with high theoretical content.

The second issue on which some substantial bargaining took place was SLAVERY. The morality of slavery was, by design, not an issue; but in its other concrete aspects, slavery influenced the arguments over taxation, commerce, and representation. The THREE-FIFTHS RULE—that three-fifths of the slaves would be counted both for representation and for purposes of DIRECT TAXATION—had allayed some northern fears about southern overrepresentation, but doubts remained. Southerners, on the other hand, were afraid that congressional control over commerce would lead to the exclusion of slaves or to their prohibitive taxation as imports. Moreover, the Southerners were disturbed over "navigation acts" (tariffs), or special legislation providing, for example, that exports be carried only in American ships. They depended upon exports, and so urged inclusion of a proviso that navigation and commercial laws require a two-thirds vote in Congress.

These problems came to a head in late August and, as usual, were handed to a committee in the hope that, in Gouverneur Morris's words, "these things may form a bargain among the Northern and Southern states." The Committee reported its measures of reconciliation on August 25, and on August 29 the package was wrapped up and delivered. What occurred can best be described in George Mason's dour version. Mason anticipated JOHN C. CALHOUN in his conviction that permitting navigation acts to pass by majority vote would put the South in economic bondage to the North. Mainly on this ground, he refused to sign the Constitution. Mason said:

> The Constitution as agreed to till a fortnight before the Convention rose was such a one as he would have set his hand and heart to. . . . Until that time the 3 New England States were constantly with us in all questions . . . so that it was these three States with the 5 Southern ones against Pennsylvania, Jersey and Delaware. With respect to the importation of slaves, [decision making] was left to Congress. This disturbed the two Southernmost States who knew that Congress would immediately suppress the importation of slaves. Those two States therefore struck up a bargain with the three New England States. If they would join to admit slaves for some years, the two Southernmost States would join in changing the clause which required the 2/3 of the Legislature in any vote [on navigation acts]. It was done.

On the floor of the Convention there was a love-feast. When Charles Pinckney of South Carolina attempted to overturn the committee's decision, by insisting that the South needed protection from the imperialism of the northern states, General CHARLES COTEWORTH PINCKNEY arose to spread oil on the waters:

> It was in the true interest of the S[outhern] States to have no regulation of commerce; but considering the loss brought on the commerce of the Eastern States by the Revolution, their liberal conduct towards the views of South Carolina [on the regulation of the slave trade] and the interests the weak South. States had in being united with the strong Eastern states, he thought it proper that no fetters should be imposed on the power of making commercial regulations; and that his constituents, though prejudiced against Eastern States, would be reconciled to this liberality. He had himself prejudices against the Eastern States before he came here, but would acknowledge that he had found them as liberal and candid as any men whatever.

Drawing on their vast collective political experience, employing every weapon in the politician's arsenal, looking constantly over their shoulders at their constituents, the delegates put together a Constitution. It was a makeshift affair; some sticky issues they ducked entirely; others they mastered with that ancient instrument of political sagacity, studied ambiguity, and some they just overlooked. In this last category probably fell the matter of the power of the federal courts to determine the constitutionality of acts of Congress. When the judicial article was formulated, deliberations were still at the stage where the legislature was endowed with broad authority which by its own terms was scarcely amenable to JUDICIAL REVIEW. In essence, courts could hardly determine when "the separate States are incompetent or . . . the harmony of the United States may be interrupted"; the national legislature, as critics pointed out, was free to define its own jurisdiction. Later the definition of legislative authority was changed into the form we know, a series of stipulated powers, but the delegates never seriously reexamined the jurisdiction of the judiciary under this new limited formulation. All arguments on the intention of the Framers in this matter are thus deductive and *a posteriori*.

The Framers were busy and distinguished men, anxious to get back to their families, their positions, and their constituents, not members of the French Academy devoting a lifetime to a dictionary. They were trying to do an important job, and do it in such a fashion that their handiwork would be acceptable to diverse constituencies. No one was rhapsodic about the final document, but it was a beginning, a move in the right direction, and one they had reason to believe the people would endorse. In addition, because they had modified the impossible amendment provisions of the Articles of Confederation to one demanding approval by only three-quarters of the states, they seemed confident that gaps in the fabric which experience would reveal could be rewoven without undue difficulty.

So, with a neat phrase introduced by Benjamin Franklin that made their decision sound unanimous and an inspired benediction by the Old Doctor urging doubters to question their own infallibility, the delegates accepted the Constitution. Curiously, Edmund Randolph, who had played so vital a role throughout, refused to sign as did his fellow Virginian George Mason and ELBRIDGE GERRY of Massachusetts. Presumably, Randolph wanted to check the temper of the Virginia populace before he risked his reputation, and perhaps his job, in a fight with PATRICK HENRY. Events lend some justification to this speculation: after much temporizing and use of the conditional tense, Randolph endorsed ratification in Virginia and ended up getting the best of both worlds.

Madison, despite his reservations about the Constitution, was the campaign manager for ratification. His first task was to get the Congress in New York to light its own funeral pyre by approving the "amendments" to the Articles and sending them on to the state legislatures. Above all, momentum had to be maintained. The anti-Constitutionalists, now thoroughly alarmed and no novices in politics, realized that their best tactic was attrition rather than direct opposition. Thus they settled on a position expressing qualified approval but calling for a second Convention to remedy various defects (the one with the most demagogic appeal was the lack of a BILL OF RIGHTS). Madison knew that to accede to this demand would be equivalent to losing the battle, nor would he agree to conditional approval (despite wavering even by Hamilton). This was an all-or-nothing proposition: national salvation or national impotence, with no intermediate position possible. Unable to get congressional approval, he settled for second best: a unanimous resolution of Congress transmitting the Constitution to the states for whatever action they saw fit to take. The opponents then moved from New York and the Congress, where they had attempted to attach amendments and conditions, to the states for the final battle.

At first, the campaign for RATIFICATION went beautifully: within eight months after the delegates set their names to the document, eight states had ratified. Theoretically, a ratification by one more state convention would set the new government in motion, but in fact until Virginia and New York acceded to the new Union, the latter was a fiction. New Hampshire was the next to ratify; "Rogues' Island" was involved in its characteristic political convulsions; North Carolina's convention did not meet until July and then postponed a final decision. Finally in New York and Virginia, the Constitutionalists outmaneuvered their opponents, forced them into impossible political positions, and won both states narrowly.

Victory for the Constitution meant simultaneous victory for the Constitutionalists; the anti-Constitutionalists either capitulated or vanished into limbo—soon Patrick Henry would be offered a seat on the Supreme Court and Luther Martin would be known as the Federalist "bulldog." And, irony of ironies, Alexander Hamilton and James Madison would shortly accumulate a reputation as the formulators of what is often alleged to be our political theory, the concept of "federalism." Arguments would soon appear over what the Framers "really meant"; although these disputes have assumed the proportions of a big scholarly business in the last century, they began almost before the ink on the Constitution was dry. One of the best early ones featured Hamilton versus Madison on the scope of presidential power.

The Constitution, then, was not an apotheosis of "constitutionalism," a triumph of architectonic genius; it was a patchwork sewn together under the pressure of time and events by a group of extremely talented democratic politicians. They refused to attempt the establishment of a strong, centralized sovereign on the principle of legislative supremacy for the excellent reason that the people would not accept it. They risked their political fortunes by opposing the established doctrines of state sovereignty because they were convinced that the existing system was leading to national impotence and, probably, to foreign domination. For two years, they worked to get a convention established. For over three months, in what must have

seemed to the faithful participants an endless process of give-and-take, they reasoned, cajoled, threatened, and bargained amongst themselves. The results were a Constitution which the voters, by democratic processes, did accept, and a new and far better national government.

JOHN P. ROCHE
(1986)

Bibliography

BROWN, ROBERT E. 1956 *Charles Beard and the Constitution.* Princeton, N.J.: Princeton University Press.
DINKIN, ROBERT J. 1977 *Voting in Provincial America.* Westport, Conn.: Greenwood Press.
ELKINS, STANLEY and MCKITRICK, ERIC 1961 The Founding Fathers: Young Men of the Revolution. *Political Science Quarterly* 76:181–203.
FARRAND, MAX, ed. 1937 *Records of the Federal Convention of 1787.* New Haven, Conn.: Yale University Press.
KENYON, CECILIA M. 1955 Men of Little Faith: The Anti-Federalists on the Nature of Representative Government. *William and Mary Quarterly,* 3rd series, 12: McDonald, Forrest T. 1958 *We the People.* Chicago: University of Chicago Press.
ROCHE, JOHN P. 1961 The Founding Fathers: A Reform Caucus in Action. *American Political Science Review* 55:799–816.
ROSSITER, CLINTON 1966 *1787: The Grand Convention.* New York: Macmillan.
WARREN, CHARLES (1928) 1937 *The Making of the Constitution.* Boston: Little, Brown.

CONSTITUTIONAL COURT

Article III vests the federal judicial power in the Supreme Court and in any lower courts that Congress may create. The judiciary so constituted was intended by the Framers to be an independent branch of the government. The judges of courts established under Article III were thus guaranteed life tenure "during GOOD BEHAVIOR" and protected against the reduction of their salaries while they held office. The federal courts so constituted are called "constitutional courts." They are to be distinguished from LEGISLATIVE COURTS, whose judges do not have comparable constitutional guarantees of independence.

Constitutional courts, sometimes called "Article III courts," are limited in the business they can be assigned. They may be given JURISDICTION only over CASES AND CONTROVERSIES falling within the JUDICIAL POWER OF THE UNITED STATES. For example, Congress could not constitutionally confer jurisdiction on a constitutional court to give ADVISORY OPINIONS, or to decide a case that fell outside Article III's list of cases and controversies included within the judicial power. That list divides into two categories of cases: those in which jurisdiction depends on the issues at stake (for example, FEDERAL QUESTION JURISDICTION) and those in which jurisdiction depends on the parties to the case (for example, DIVERSITY JURISDICTION.)

Congress can, of course, create bodies other than constitutional courts and assign them the function of deciding cases—even cases falling within the judicial power, within limits that remain unclear even after NORTHERN PIPELINE CONSTRUCTION CO. V. MARATHON PIPE LINE CO. (1982). Such a legislative court is not confined by Article III's specification of the limits of the federal judicial power, any more than an administrative agency would be so confined. However, a legislative court's decisions on matters outside the limits of Article III cannot constitutionally be reviewed by the Supreme Court or any other constitutional court.

KENNETH L. KARST
(1986)

Bibliography

WRIGHT, CHARLES ALAN 1983 *The Law of Federal Courts*, 4th ed. Pages 39–52. St. Paul, Minn.: West Publishing Co.

CONSTITUTIONAL DUALISM

The phrases "dualist Constitution" and "dualist democracy" were coined by Yale Law School Professor Bruce Ackerman. "Dualism" lies at the heart of his influential *We, The People*, a three-volume reinterpretation of the history and meaning of American Constitutional democracy, and probably the single most important and controversial work in constitutional theory of the 1990s. "Dualism," on Ackerman's account, is the United States' distinctive contribution to democratic theory and practice. It refers to a "two-track" scheme of lawmaking and rests on a two-tiered conception of ordinary citizens' involvement in national politics.

The notion of "private citizenship" aims to combine private freedom and public liberty in a fashion that is normatively attractive and historically faithful. Thus, "private citizenship" strikes a realistic—and, Ackerman claims, distinctly American—balance between full-time devotion to the common good and relentless pursuit of self-interest. It describes a world in which citizens are free, for the most part and most of the time, to pursue their own interests, sacrificing private lives to a modest extent by voting and keeping abreast of important events. On rare occasions, however, issues arise that demand more active involvement. In such moments, Americans must assume the full mantle of a self-governing citizenry. By rising to these "constitutional moments," however, they succeed in governing themselves without losing themselves—in the fashion of more single-minded theories of participatory democracy or civic republicanism—to government.

Ackerman's "two-track" theory of lawmaking runs along the same dual lines. Our constitutional tradition contemplates two types of politics: normal politics and "higher lawmaking" or "constitutional politics." Normal politics is the business of politicians, as private citizens pursue their largely private lives. Then the rare occasion for constitutional politics emerges. Crises and conflicts put on the national agenda fundamental choices about national identity and the role of government. Spurred by prophetic political leaders, the people awake from their civic slumber, mobilize, and participate in extended popular deliberation, debate, and decisionmaking. Framed by the intricate clash of competing leaders, POLTICAL PARTIES, and institutions, including rival branches of the national government, this process of constitutional questions: who belongs to the national political community, what are the rights of CITIZENSHIP, and what are the powers and duties of government.

The higher lawmaking process produced the Constitution and the major changes in it—the RECONSTRUCTION amendments and the "amendment analogues" embodied in the great NEW DEAL cases, UNITED STATES V. DERBY LUMBER COMPANY (1941) and WICKARD V. FILBURN (1942). Thus, on Ackerman's account, there have been but three "constitutional moments"—the Founding, Reconstruction, and the New Deal—each ushering in a new constitutional regime. What legitimated change in each instance was not observance of the formal rules of the constitutional AMENDING PROCESS; in each case, those rules were flaunted. Rather, it was the participation of an engaged citizenry, for this ensured that the constitutional changes wrought by these moments represented the considered wishes of the people.

From this, Ackerman derives a dualist theory of JUDICIAL REVIEW. When the people return to their private pursuits, and normal politics resumes, the constitutional courts have a mandate to protect the result of the people's higher lawmaking from future ordinary politicians and normal politics—that is, a "preservationist function." Striking down the products of normal politics when these trench on the fruits of higher lawmaking cannot fairly be called countermajoritarian or anti-democratic.

In some key respects, there is nothing new about dualism. ALEXANDER HAMILTON, in FEDERALIST No. 78, famously justified judicial review in preservationist terms. The Constitution was an act of the sovereign people; the constitutional court voiding LEGISLATION as incompatible with the Constitution would be enforcing the people's will over and against errant representatives. What is new, then, is Ackerman's candid account of how major constitutional changes on the part of "We, the People" flouted the prescribed rules for amendment, combined with his claim to redeem the lawfulness of these great changes by dint of his discovery of an elaborate and evolving pattern of higher lawmaking norms, a common law of higher lawmaking, that has governed constitutional transformations outside Article V.

Critics have cast doubt on whether Ackerman's common law of higher lawmaking is a serviceable tool for courts to determine the bona fides of alleged non-Article V amendments and on what kind of guidance, if any, courts, lawmakers, or citizens, finding themselves in the thick of constitutional politics, can derive from Ackerman's ex post rules of recognition. However, many critics left unpersuaded by Ackerman's effort to derive a formal grammar of higher lawmaking have acknowledged that Ackerman has brought into brilliantly detailed focus a genuine tradition of constitutional politics. He has shown how the parties to New Deal and Reconstruction controversies clashed as much over constitutional process as substance. Politicians and reform movements not only addressed the electorate on constitutive questions of national identity and popular government in ways 1990s Americans have almost forgotten; they also fought over the rules of engagement and the processes of change and resistance to change in self-conscious and sophisticated constitutional terms. To this extent, Ackerman succeeds in vindicating the constitutional creativity of ordinary citizens continuing into the twentieth century.

Having reminded us that American politics sometimes has proceeded upon a "higher" and more citizenry-engaging track than the "ordinary," however, Ackerman has been met by another brand of critics who suggest that U.S. history has been punctuated by many more moments of constitutive change than three. The elections and presidencies of THOMAS JEFFERSON and ANDREW JACKSON, the defeat of POPULISM and emergence of Jim Crow in the 1890s, the rise of U.S. imperialism at the turn of the twentieth century, the PROGRESSIVE era, and the CIVIL RIGHTS MOVEMENT of the mid-twentieth century all have been put forward as candidates. Ackerman's own most recent writings note that movements for fundamental reform—attended by popular mobilization around constitutive issues of national identity, POPULAR SOVEREIGNTY, and the powers and duties of government—brought forth new parties, pivotal elections, major institutional changes, and doctrinal innovations in each generation of the nineteenth century. Thus, Ackerman himself now seems to agree that even if his original three moments involved more sweeping changes, the differences between them and these others are not so great as to warrant the simple division of American historical time into three long periods of "normal politics" and three bursts of "constitutional politics." Not all these other (perhaps partial) constitutional moments fit tidily into the Whiggish, progressive arc of Ackerman's scheme; some were moments of reactionary, not liberal, reforms. Not all of them followed Ackerman's legitimating rules; some were more or less democratic but

others involved a great measure of force and fraud. Taken together, these criticisms do not undo the dualist scheme so much as complicate and enrich it, suggesting a more complex narrative of constitutional development—more constantly changing, more tenaciously remaining the same, more constrained by the institutional inheritances of conflicts whose resolutions merit little legitimacy even by Ackerman's forgiving lights, and arrayed into many overlapping periods of ordinary and constitutional politics and lawmaking.

By bringing politics and popular political action into focus in the realm of constitutional theory, Ackerman's dualism has forever changed the legal academy's reigning narrative of constitutional development. Whether it will affect how courts interpret the Constitution remains an open question.

WILLIAM E. FORBATH
(2000)

(SEE ALSO: *Amendment Process (Outside Aritcle V); Constitutional Theory.*)

Bibliography

ACKERMAN, BRUCE A. 1991 *We the People: Foundations.* Cambridge, Mass:. Harvard University Press.
———— 1998 *We the People: Transformations.* Cambridge, Mass:. Harvard University Press.

CONSTITUTIONAL FICTIONS

The leading modern American discussion of legal fictions remains Lon Fuller's articles first published in 1930–1931. Fuller argued that legal fictions promote function, form, and sometimes fairness. It has become increasingly clear, however, that legal fictions no longer serve merely as an "awkward patch" on the fabric of law, as Fuller put it. Fuller considered legal fictions a necessary evil for systematic thinking about law. He viewed legal fictions as akin to working assumptions in physics: they provide a kind of scaffolding, but are not intended to give essential support nor to deceive. After their useful function ends, legal fictions should and could be readily removed.

Fuller defined a legal fiction as "either (1) a statement propounded with a complete or partial consciousness of its falsity, or (2) a false statement recognized as having utility." In today's postrealist world, however, there is a widespread sense that legal fictions are not some small awkward patch, but rather virtually all of law's seamless cloth. This transforms the problem of defining and explaining legal fictions. The very pervasiveness of legal fictions helps to camouflage them. We may generally ignore a phenomenon that permeates our LEGAL CULTURE.

Fuller's taxonomy of legal fictions illuminated Henry Maine's earlier assertion that legal fictions "satisfy the desire for improvement, which is not quite wanting, at the same time that they do not offend the superstitious disrelish for change which is always present." To Maine, legal fictions were "invaluable expedients for overcoming the rigidity of law," but they were also "the greatest of obstacles to symmetrical classification." Fuller advanced beyond Maine's complacent legal anthropology, but he still somewhat desperately sought symmetry. Today we tend to regard all law as a gyrating classification system full of overlaps, gaps, and incommensurate variations. In Grant Gilmore's words, "The process by which a society accommodates to change without abandoning its fundamental structure is what we mean by law."

Precisely because legal fictions are not static, they may grow to influence or even control how we think or refuse to think about basic matters. The fiction that a corporation is a person warranting certain constitutional protections, for example, obviously has spread like kudzu since the Supreme Court first propounded this notion in dicta in *Santa Clara County v. Southern Pacific Railroad* (1886). We employ legal fictions to preserve a notion of continuity with the past, yet legal fictions help short-circuit attempts to comprehend the complexity behind the assumptions a legal fiction conveys. Like sunlight, legal fictions affect the directions of growth.

There is a basic irony in our commitment to perserving the RULE OF LAW alongside our reverence for pragmatic immediate solutions to pluralistic problems. Nevertheless, few Americans have ever gone as far in condemning legal fictions as did Jeremy Bentham. Bentham claimed that "n English law, fiction is a syphilis, which runs in every vein, and carries into every part of the system the principle of rotteness." If fictions are to justice "[e]xactly as swindling is to trade," as Bentham put it, Americans tend to exalt trade so much that we tolerate and even celebrate the trader, the flimflam man, and the innovative judge.

In constitutional law, legal fictions are at least as pervasive as in what is still nostalgically called private law. Obviously, a great judge in a constitutional case has to do more than look up the answer in the constitutional text. But what it is we want a good or great postrealist judge to do remains intensely controversial.

The paradoxical way in which Americans revere but fail to heed closely constitutional law suggests that it may be impossible to separate basic constitutional fictions from constitutional governance. Yet political history in the United States has been dominated by an ongoing, multifaceted debate about proper interpretation of the Constitution. Controversies about specific instances of JUDICIAL REVIEW and proposals for constitutional change ebb and flow, but debate about what is true to the Constitution never disappears.

Americans generally display remarkable respect for an old ambiguous text despite—perhaps because of—widespread uncertainty about what it contains. Yet the Constitution and its most important amendments surely were not ratified by a majority of Americans. Moreover, whoever "we the people" may have excluded or included, it is clear that the American people have not actually endorsed the centuries of judicial gloss on the Constitution that provides much basic constitutional law. Nevertheless, sacerdotalizing of the Constitution amounts to a civic religion. General acquiescence in the interpretations of the text by unelected judges thus provides a central constitutional fiction that ironically also has proved to be a notably sturdy foundation. It is important to distinguish this crucial, general trapeze act involving the assumption of societal consent from the more specific uses of fictions in constitutional law.

As early as the 1830s ALEXIS DE TOCQUEVILLE declared: "The government of the Union rests almost entirely on legal fictions. The union is an ideal nation which exists, so to say, only in men's minds and whose extent and limits can only be discerned by understanding." Tocqueville made his point about the central role of legal fictions in American governance, ironically, just as constitutional debate about the abolition of SLAVERY began to spiral toward the CIVIL WAR. That example of the terrible cost of fundamental disagreements about the meaning of the Constitution helps explain why most Americans most of the time are willing to accept the central constitutional fiction that judicial interpretations of the Constitution somehow can settle even the most controversial questions.

An important initial question is whether the American model of judicial review, promulgated most famously by Chief Justice JOHN MARSHALL in MARBURY V. MADISON (1803), may not itself be a fiction of elemental proportions. Marshall insisted that to deserve the "high appellation" of "a government of laws and not of men," the American system required the power of federal judges to declare legislative acts unconstitutional, but this was hardly necessary to decide the case before the Court and lacked explicit support in the constitutional text. Additional fictions that have played particularly important roles in our constitutional history range from markedly inconsistent judicial declarations enforcing FEDERALISM to decisions granting FOURTEENTH AMENDMENT protection to CORPORATIONS. Among the most important recent examples are decisions applying most but not all of the BILL OF RIGHTS to the states, on the theory that their protections were incorporated through the DUE PROCESS clause of the Fourteenth Amendment, and decisions making EQUAL PROTECTION doctrine applicable to the federal government through a theory of "reverse incorporation" premised on the Fifth Amendment.

Less obvious but equally important constitutional fictions limit or ignore the constitutional text. For example, the SLAUGHTERHOUSE CASES (1873) rendered the privileges or immunities clause of the Fourteenth Amendment essentially redundant. Also, there has been long-standing reluctance to give the NINTH AMENDMENT any content at all. Constitutional fictions thus may restrain as well as enlarge judicial authority.

Particularly flagrant constitutional fictions have produced a smattering of serious scholarly and political criticism, but most Americans apparently continue to revere the Supreme Court and to accept its interpretations even when not pleased by the results in specific cases. For example, there were withering attacks on the Court's aggressive use of what many saw as fictional limitations on progressive legislation in the 1920s and 1930s, but the failure of President FRANKLIN D. ROOSEVELT's COURT-PACKING PLAN suggested that Americans, even when outraged at specific results and dubious about their bases, nevertheless were more willing to accept judicially created fictions than to tinker with the institution of judicial review.

As James Russell Lowell stated in 1888, "After our Constitution got fairly into working order it really seemed as if we had invented a machine that would go of itself, and this begot a faith in our luck which even the civil war itself but momentarily disturbed." But Lowell sardonically continued, "I admire the splendid complacency of my countrymen, and find something exhilarating and inspiring in it. . . . And this confidence in our luck with the absorption in material interests, generated by unparalleled opportunity, has in some respects made us neglectful of our political duties."

It might be thought that legal fictions ought to play a diminished role in constitutional law, in contrast to their prevalence in COMMON LAW. For instance, constitutional law does not lack a text, whereas the common law, in Frederick Pollock's words, "professes . . . to develop and apply principles that have never been committed to any authentic form of words." Despite the best efforts of interpretivists, originalists, and self-proclaimed strict constructionists, however, constitutional law as we know it—and as it has been from the start—demonstrates clearly that even our written "authentic form of words" requires additional criteria for everyday construction and interpretation. In fact, we seem to grow ever more doubtful about what sources we should consult, to say nothing of what might be thought authoritative.

We lack any rule of recognition to distinguish constitutional truth from constitutional fiction. Moreover, our constitutional history clearly reveals that some sections of the authentic text have been relegated to limbo through nonoriginalist hierarchical principles, whereas other sections have acquired so many levels of added meaning that it is now hard to discern any original shape beneath the layers of barnacles added over the years.

The constitutional text is manipulable, but that need not mean it is infinitely manipulable. Federal judges have declared themselves less bound by STARE DECISIS in the constitutional realm than they are in other domains, but they tend to remain concerned with the past and with their won places in history. Yet these same judges use legal fictions to purge the past of its blemishes and discontinuities.

There seems to be a kind of ideological frontier thesis in constitutional law. Justices who start anew and never actually look back are applauded. Because they usually can find PRECEDENTS readily and tend not to consider contexts, these judges reinforce a tendency to turn our backs on past unpleasantness. Fundamental assumptions in constitutional doctrine posit an America full of openings: we may all escape the sins of the past; we all enjoy a fair and equal start in the race of life.

Equality among citizens, for example, is virtually always assumed, whether actual or not. This formal ideal of equality generally provides a complete defense against those who seek remedies for past discrimination unless they can demonstrate that the defendants actually violated the plaintiffs' equality; thus, the victim must place the defendant at the scene of past crimes. This fiction was essential a century ago in the CIVIL RIGHTS CASES (1883) and PLESSY V. FERGUSON (1896); a similar fiction was crucial when the Court vigorously enforced its version of FREEDOM OF CONTRACT before the NEW DEAL; and its formal fictional counterpart seems prevalent in RACIAL DISCRIMINATION cases today.

In constitutional law we are devoted to the artificial doctrinal categories and analytic tests that judges create. This remains so even if we are subliminally aware, as Justice OLIVER WENDELL HOLMES noted, that a particular doctrine may be "little more than a fiction intended to beautify what is disagreeable to the sufferers." Judicial reliance on binary tests to foster pseudocertainty is not new, of course, as anyone who recalls the twilight zone of DUAL FEDERALISM must acknowledge. In constitutional cases today, however, judges seem to rely even more frequently on multipart formulas to convey that "delusive exactness" Holmes decried—and sometimes practiced.

Legal fictions are quite different from literary fictions. As ROBERT COVER pointed out, potential violence lurks beneath the fictions created by judges, whereas the nexus between real force and even the most powerful literary fiction is attenuated. Additionally, the author of literary fiction enjoys more freedom than the creator of legal fiction. The poet, even the novelist, usually tries to operate on multiple levels and even dreams of reaching a broad and varied audience. Writers of literary fiction also tend to acknowledge and even to use the possibility of complicity between the teller of the tale and the recipient of it, so that shared understanding is a core concern. By contrast, legal fiction employs a specialized shorthand; many creators and users of legal fiction intend their work product to be confined to, or even ignored by, only a narrow audience of professionals.

Americans find it easy to read prepossessions into the Constitution. We resemble religious sects who are able to find diverse creeds in the same Bible. A century ago, CHRISTOPHER G. TIEDEMAN, a leading conservative treatise writer, admiringly noted that "when public opinion . . . requires the written words to be ignored the court justly obeys the will of the popular mandate, at the same time keeping up a show of obedience to the written word by a skillful use of legal fictions." Today heated political and social controversies often revolve around whether the Constitution resolves, or is even relevant to, the debate over ABORTION or AFFIRMATIVE ACTION, for example. Many people will consider whatever answers the Supreme Court hands down to be constitutional fictions at best. Yet, as the historian CHARLES BEARD put it in 1930, "Humanity and ideas, as well as things, are facts." Constitutional fictions tend to grow into fundamental facts of life in a culture that reveres law.

AVIAM SOIFER
(1992)

(SEE ALSO: *Constitution as Civil Religion; Constitutional Interpretation; Incorporation Doctrine; Legal Realism.*)

Bibliography

FULLER, LON   1967   *Legal Fictions.* Palo Alto, Calif.: Stanford.
KAMMEN, MICHAEL   1986   *A Machine That Would Go of Itself.* New York: Knopf.
SOIFER, AVIAM   1986   Reviewing Legal Fictions. *Georgia Law Review* 20:871.

CONSTITUTIONAL HISTORY BEFORE 1776

The opening words of the United States Constitution, "We the People," startled some of the old revolutionaries of 1776. PATRICK HENRY, after expressing the highest veneration for the men who wrote the words, demanded "What right had they to say, *We the People*. . . . Who authorized them to speak the language of *We, the People,* instead of *We, the States?*" It was a good question and, as Henry

knew, not really answerable. No one had authorized the members of the CONSTITUTIONAL CONVENTION to speak for the people of the United States. They had been chosen by the legislatures of thirteen sovereign states and were authorized only to act for the governments of those states in redefining the relationships among them. Instead, they had dared not only to act for "the people of the United States" but also to proclaim what they did as "the supreme law of the land," supreme apparently over the actions of the existing state governments and supreme also over the government that the Constitution itself would create for the United States. Because those governments similarly professed to speak and act for the people, how could the Constitution claim supremacy over them and claim it successfully from that day to this, however contested in politics, litigation, and civil war? The answer lies less in logic than in the centuries of political experience before 1787 in which Englishmen and Americans worked out a political faith that gave to "the people" a presumptive capacity to constitute governments.

The idea that government originates in a donation by the people is at least as old as classical Greece. Government requires some sort of justification, and a donation of power by the governed or by those about to be governed was an obvious way of providing it. But such a donation has seldom if ever been recorded as historical fact, because it is virtually impossible for any substantial collection of people to act as a body, either in conveying powers of government or in prescribing the mode of their exercise. The donation has to be assumed, presumed, supposed, imagined—and yet be plausible enough to be acceptable to the supposed donors.

In the Anglo-American world two institutions have lent credibility to the presumption. The first to emerge was the presence in government of representatives chosen by a substantial portion of the people. With the powers of government thus shared, it became plausible to think of the representatives and the government as acting for the people and deriving powers from them. But as these popular representatives assumed a dominant position in the government, it was all too easy for them to escape from the control of those who chose them and to claim unlimited power in the name of the almighty people. A second device was necessary to differentiate the inherent sovereign powers of the people from the limited powers assigned to their deputed agents or representatives. The device was found in written CONSTITUTIONS embodying the people's supposed donation of power in specific provisions to limit and define the government.

Such written constitutions were a comparatively late development; the United States Constitution was one of the first. They came into existence not simply out of the need to specify the terms of the putative donation of power by the people but also out of earlier attempts by representatives or spokesmen of the people to set limits to governments claiming almighty authority from a different source. Although the idea of a popular donation was an ancient way of justifying government, it was not the only way. Indeed, since the fall of Rome God had been the favored source of authority: earthly rulers, whether in church or state, claimed His commission, though the act in which He granted it remained as shadowy as any donation by the people. Up to the seventeenth century, the persons who spoke for the people spoke as subjects, but they spoke as subjects of God as well as of God's lieutenants. While showing a proper reverence for divinely ordained authority, they expected those commissioned by God to rule in a godlike manner, that is, to abide by the natural laws (discernible in God's government of the world) that were supposed to guide human conduct and give force to the specific "positive" laws of nations derived from them. Even without claiming powers of government, those who spoke for the people might thus set limits to the powers of government through "fundamental" laws that were thought to express the will of God more reliably than rulers who claimed His commission. The link is obvious between such FUNDAMENTAL LAWS and written constitutions that expressed the people's will more reliably than their elected representatives could. The one grew out of the other.

Written constitutions were a deliberate invention, designed to overcome the deficiencies of representative government, but representative government itself was the unintended outcome of efforts by kings to secure and extend their own power. The story begins with the creation of the English House of Commons in the thirteenth century, when the English government centered in a hereditary king who claimed God-given authority but had slender means for asserting it. The king, always in need of funds, summoned two representatives from each county and from selected boroughs (incorporated towns) to come to his court for the purpose of consenting to taxes. He required the counties and boroughs in choosing representatives, by some unspecified electoral process, to give them full powers of attorney, so that no one could later object to what they agreed to. Although only a small part of the adult population shared in the choice of representatives, the House of Commons came to be regarded as having power of attorney for the whole body of the king's subjects; every man, woman, and child in the country was held to be legally present within its walls.

The assembly of representatives, thus created and identified with the whole people, gradually acquired an institutional existence, along with the House of Lords, as one branch of the king's Parliament. As representatives, the members remained subjects of the king, empowered by other subjects to act for them. But from the beginning they were somewhat more than subjects: in addition to granting the property of other subjects in taxes, they could petition the king for laws that would direct the actions of government. From petitioning for laws they moved to making them: by the sixteenth century English laws were enacted "by authority" of Parliament. Theoretically that authority still came from God through the king, and Parliament continued to be an instrument by which English monarchs consolidated and extended their government, never more so than in the sixteenth century. But in sharing their authority with Parliament the kings shared it, by implication, with the people. By the time the first American colonies were founded in the early seventeenth century, the king's instrument had become a potential rival to his authority, and the people had become a potential alternative to God as the immediate source of authority.

The potential became actual in the 1640s when Parliament, discontented with Charles I's ecclesiastical, military, and fiscal policies, made war on the king and itself assumed all powers of government. The Parliamentarians justified their actions as agents of the people; and at this point the presumption of a popular origin of government made its appearance in England in full force. The idea, which had been overshadowed for so long by royal claims to a divine commission, had been growing for a century. The Protestant Reformation had produced a contest between Roman Catholics and Protestants for control of the various national governments of Europe. In that contest each side had placed on the people of a country the responsibility for its government's compliance with the will of God. The people, it was now asserted, were entrusted by God with creating proper governments and with setting limits on them to insure protection of true religion. When the limits were breached, the people must revoke the powers of rulers who had betrayed their trust. For Roman Catholics, Protestant rulers fitted the definition, and vice versa.

When Englishmen, mostly Protestant, challenged their king, who leaned toward Catholicism, these ideas were ready at hand for their justification, and the House of Commons had long been recognized as the representative of the people. The House, the members now claimed, to all intents and purposes *was* the people, and the powers of the people were supreme. Both the king and the House of Lords, lacking these powers, were superfluous. In 1649 the Commons killed the king, abolished the House of Lords, and made England a republic.

By assuming such sweeping powers the members of the House of Commons invited anyone who felt aggrieved by their conduct of government not only to question their claim to represent the people but also to draw a distinction between the powers of the people themselves and of the persons they might choose, by whatever means, to represent them.

The first critics of the Commons to draw such a distinction were, not surprisingly, the adherents of the king, who challenged the Commons in the public press as well as on the field of battle. The House of Commons, the royalists pointed out, had been elected by only a small fraction of the people, and even that fraction had empowered it only to consent to positive laws and taxes, not to alter the government. Parliament, the royalists insisted, must not be confused with the people themselves. Even if it were granted that the people might create a government and set limits on it in fundamental laws, the House of Commons was only one part of the government thus created and could not itself change the government by eliminating the king or the Lords.

More radical critics, especially the misnamed Levellers, called not only for a reform of Parliament to make it more truly representative but also for a written "Agreement of the People" in which the people, acting apart from Parliament, would reorganize the government, reserving certain powers to themselves and setting limits to Parliament just as Parliament had formerly set limits to the king. Although the Levellers were unsuccessful, other political leaders also recognized the need to elevate supposed acts of the people, in creating a government and establishing its fundamental laws, above acts of the government itself. They also recognized that even a government derived from popular choice needed a SEPARATION OF POWERS among legislative, executive, and judicial branches, not merely for convenience of administration but in order to prevent government from escaping popular control.

Although the English in these years generated the ideas that have guided modern republican government, they were unable to bring their own government into full conformity with those ideas. By the 1650s they found that they had replaced a monarch, whose powers were limited, first with a House of Commons that claimed unlimited powers and refused to hold new elections, and then with a protector, Oliver Cromwell, whose powers knew only the limits of his ability to command a conquering army. In 1660 most Englishmen were happy to see the old balance restored with the return of a hereditary king and an old-style but potent Parliament to keep him in line. In 1688 that Parliament again removed a king who seemed to be getting out of control. This time, instead of trying to eliminate monarchy, they replaced one king with another who promised to be more tractable than his predecessor. William III at the outset of his reign accepted a parliamentary declaration of rights, spelling out the fundamental laws that limited his authority.

JOHN LOCKE, in the classic defense of this "Glorious Revolution," refined the distinction made earlier by the Levellers between the people and their representatives. Locke posited a SOCIAL COMPACT in which a collection of hitherto unconnected individuals in a "state of nature" came together to form a society. Only after doing so did they enter into a second compact in which they created a government and submitted to it. This second compact or constitution could be broken—the government could be altered or replaced—without destroying the first compact and throwing the people back into a state of nature. Society, in other words, came before government; and the people, once bound into a society by a social compact, could act without government and apart from government in order to constitute or change a government.

Locke could point to no historical occurrence that quite fitted his pattern. Even the Glorious Revolution was not, strictly speaking, an example of popular constituent action; rather, one branch of an existing government had replaced another branch. And the Declaration of Rights, although binding on the king, was no more than an act of Parliament that another Parliament might repeal. Moreover, the authority of the king remained substantial, and he was capable of extending his influence over Parliament by appointing members to lucrative government offices.

Locke's description of the origin of government nevertheless furnished a theoretical basis for viewing the entire British government as the creation of the people it governed. That view was expressed most vociferously in the eighteenth century by the so-called commonwealthmen, who repeated the call for reforms to make Parliament more representative of the whole people and to reduce the king's influence on its members. But it was not only commonwealthmen who accepted Locke's formulation. By the middle of the eighteenth century the doctrine of the divine right of kings was virtually dead in England, replaced by the sovereignty of the people, who were now accepted as the immediate source of all authority whether in king, lords, or commons.

In England's American colonies the idea that government originates in the people had been familiar from the outset, nourished not only by developments in England but also by the special conditions inherent in colonization. Those conditions were politically and constitutionally complex. The colonies were founded by private individuals or corporations under charters granted by the king, in which Parliament had no part. In the typical colony the king initially conveyed powers of government to the founders, who generally remained in England and directed the enterprise through agents. As time went on, the king took the powers of government in most colonies to himself, acting through appointed governors. But whether the immediate source of governmental authority in a colony rested in the king or in royally authorized corporations or individual proprietors, it proved impossible to govern colonists at 3,000 miles' distance without current information about changing local conditions. That kind of information could best be obtained through a representative assembly of the settlers, empowered to levy taxes and make laws. As a result, in each of England's colonies, within a short time of the founding, the actual settlers gained a share in the choice of their governors comparable to that which Englishmen at home enjoyed through their Parliament.

England's first permanent colony in America, Virginia, was the first to exhibit the phenomenon. The Virginia Company of London, which founded the colony in 1607 and was authorized to govern it in 1609, did so for ten years without participation of the actual settlers. The results were disastrous, and in 1618 the company instructed its agents to call a representative assembly. The assembly met in 1619, the first in the present area of the United States. When the king dissolved the Virginia Company and resumed governmental authority over the colony in 1624, he declined to continue the assembly, but the governors he appointed found it necessary to do so on their own initiative until 1639, when the king recognized the need and made the Virginia House of Burgesses an official part of the government.

In most other colonies representatives were authorized from the beginning or came into existence spontaneously when colonists found themselves beyond the reach of existing governments. The Pilgrims who landed at Plymouth in 1620 provided for their own government by the MAY-FLOWER COMPACT, with a representative assembly at its center. The initial governments of Rhode Island and Connecticut began in much the same way. In these Puritan colonies religious principle worked together with pragmatic necessity to emphasize the popular basis of government. Puritans believed that government, though ordained by God, must originate in a compact (or covenant) between rulers and people, in which rulers promised to abide by and enforce God's laws, while the people in return promised obedience. Even in Massachusetts, where from the beginning the government rested officially on a charter from the king, Governor John Winthrop took pains to explain that he regarded emigration to Massachusetts as a tacit consent to such a covenant on the part of everyone who came. The emigrants themselves seem to have agreed; and because the king's charter did not spell out the laws of God that must limit a proper government, the representative assembly of the colony in 1641 adopted the MASSACHUSETTS BODY OF LIBERTIES, which did so.

The model for the colonial representative assemblies was the House of Commons of England; but from the beginning the colonial assemblies were more representative than the House of Commons, in that a much larger proportion of the people shared in choosing them. In England REPRESENTATION was apportioned in a bizarre fashion among the towns and boroughs, with nearly empty villages sending members while many populous towns sent none. In the colonies, although the extension of representation did not everywhere keep up with the spread of population westward, the imbalance never approached that in England, where virtually no adjustments to shifts of population were made after the sixteenth century and none at all between 1675 and the nineteenth century. And while in England a variety of property qualifications and local regulations excluded the great majority of adult males from voting, in the colonies, because of the abundance of land and its widespread ownership, similar restrictions excluded only a minority of adult males.

In addition to its broader popular base, representation in the colonies retained more of its original popular function than did the English counterpart. Representatives in both England and the colonies were initially identified more with a particular group of subjects than with their rulers. As representatives assumed a larger and larger role in government, they necessarily came to consider themselves as acting more in an authoritative capacity over the whole people and less as the designated defenders of their immediate constituents. This conception grew more rapidly in England, as the power of the king declined and that of Parliament increased, than it did in the colonies, where representatives continued to champion the interests of their constituents against unpopular directives from England. The divergence in the American conception of representation was to play a key role both in the colonies' quarrel with England and in the problems faced by the independent Americans in creating their own governments.

By 1763, when France surrendered its North American possessions, Great Britain stood at the head of the world's greatest empire. But the place of the American colonists in that empire remained constitutionally uncertain. Officially their governments still derived authority not from popular donation but directly or indirectly from the king. In two colonies, Rhode Island and Connecticut, the king had conveyed power to the free male inhabitants to choose their own governor, governor's council, and legislative assembly. In two more the king had conveyed governmental power to a single family, the Penns in Pennsylvania and the Calverts in Maryland, who exercised their authority by appointing the governor and his council. In the rest of the colonies the king appointed the governor and (except in Massachusetts) his council, which in all colonies except Pennsylvania doubled as the upper house of the legislature. Thus in every colony except Rhode Island, Connecticut, and Massachusetts, a representative assembly made laws and levied taxes, but neither the governor nor the members of the upper house of the legislature owed their positions even indirectly to popular choice.

It might have been argued that the king himself owed his authority to some sort of popular consent, however tacitly expressed, but it would have been hard to say whether the people who gave that consent included those living in the colonies. It would have been harder still to say what relationship the colonists had to the king's Parliament. In England the king's subordination to Parliament had become increasingly clear. It was Parliament that recognized the restoration of Charles II in 1660; it was Parliament that, in effect, deposed James II in 1688; it was Parliament that placed George I on the throne in 1714 and established the succession of the House of Hanover. Insofar as England's kings ruled Great Britain after 1714 they ruled through Parliament. But they continued to rule the colonies through royal governors and councils, and Parliament still had no hand officially in the choice of royal governors and councils or in the formulation of instructions to them.

Because each colony had its own little parliament, its representative assembly, the people of each colony could have considered themselves as a separate kingdom and a separate people, separate not only from the people who chose the representative assemblies of the other colonies but separate also from the people of Great Britain who chose the British Parliament. If any colonist thought that way—and probably few did before the 1760s or 1770s—he would have had to consider a complicating fact: the British Parliament did on occasion legislate for the colonies and the colonies submitted to that legislation, most notably to the Navigation Acts of 1660 and 1663, which limited the trade of the colonies for the benefit of English merchants. Did this submission mean that the people of the colonies, who elected no representatives to Parliament, were subordinate to, as well as separate from, the people of Great Britain?

In one sense the answer had to be yes: if the king was subordinate to Parliament and the colonists were subordinate to the king, that would seem to make the colonists subordinate to Parliament and thus to the people who elected Parliament. But since Parliament had so seldom legislated for the colonies, it could be argued that the colonists' subordination to it was restricted to those areas where it had in fact legislated for them, that is, in matters that concerned their trade. In other areas, they would be subordinate to Parliament only through the king, and the subordination of the colonial representative assemblies to the king was by no means unlimited. Through the taxing power the colonial assemblies had achieved, over the years, a leverage in the operation of their respective governments comparable to that which had raised Parliament above the king in Great Britain. To be sure, they had not arrived at so clear a position of superiority over their royal governors as Parliament enjoyed over the king. For example, while Queen Anne was the last monarch to veto an act of Parliament, royal governors regularly vetoed acts of colonial assemblies; and even an act accepted by the king's governor could still be vetoed by the king himself. The assemblies nevertheless enjoyed considerable power; by refusing to authorize taxation or to appropriate funds, they could thwart royal directives that they considered injurious to the interests or rights of their constituents. And in some ways they enjoyed a greater independence of royal influence than did Parliament. Because there were few sinecures or places of profit in colonial governments within the appointment of the king or his governors, it was difficult for a governor to build a following in an assembly through patronage.

Despite its constitutional and political ambiguities the British imperial system worked. It continued to work until the power of Parliament collided with the power of the colonial assemblies, thus requiring a resolution of the uncertainties in their relationship. The collision occurred when Parliament, facing a doubled national debt after the Seven Years War, passed the Revenue Act of 1764 (usually called the Sugar Act), levying duties on colonial imports, and the Stamp Act of 1765, levying direct taxes on legal documents and other items used in the colonies. In these acts, probably without intending to, Parliament threatened to destroy the bargaining power through which the colonial assemblies had balanced the authority of the king and his governors. If Parliament could tax the colonists directly, it might free the king's governors from dependence on the assemblies for funds and ultimately render the assemblies powerless.

In pamphlets and newspaper articles the colonists denounced the new measures. The assemblies, both separately and in a STAMP ACT CONGRESS, to which nine colonies sent delegates, spelled out in resolutions and petitions what they considered to be fundamental constitutional rights that Parliament had violated. In doing so the assemblies were obliged to define their constitutional relationship to Parliament with a precision never before required.

Parliament, it must be remembered, had been regarded for centuries as the bulwark of English liberties. It was the representative body of the English people, and through it the English had tamed their king as no other Europeans had. To question its supremacy might well seem to be a reactionary retreat toward absolute monarchy by divine right. The colonists were therefore hesitant to deny all subordination to Parliament. Yet, if they were to enjoy the same rights that other British subjects enjoyed in Great Britain, they must reserve to their own assemblies at the very least the power to tax. They acknowledged, therefore, the authority of Parliament to legislate for the whole empire as it had hitherto done in regulating colonial trade, but they drew a distinction between the power to legislate and the power to tax.

The colonists associated legislation with the sovereign

power of a state, and they wanted to consider themselves as remaining in some still undefined way under the sovereign power of the British government. But taxation had from the time of England's first Parliaments been a function of representatives, authorized by those who sent them to give a part of their property to the king in taxes. Taxation, the colonial assemblies affirmed, was not a part of the governing 1869 or legislative power, but an action taken in behalf of the king's subjects. This distinction could be seen, they pointed out, in the form given to Parliamentary acts of taxation: such acts originated in the House of Commons and were phrased as the gift of the commons to the king.

Now the difference between American and British conceptions of representation began to appear. The colonists did not think of the English House of Commons as representing them, for no county or town or borough in the colonies sent members. The British government had never suggested that they might, and the colonists themselves rejected the possibility as impracticable. Given their conception of the representative's subservient relation to his constituents, it would have been impossible, they felt, to maintain adequate control over representatives at 3,000 miles' distance. Thus the colonists had not authorized and could not authorize any representative in Parliament to give their property in taxes. When Parliament taxed them, therefore, it deprived them of a fundamental right of Englishmen, sacred since before the colonies were founded. For a Parliament in which the colonists were not represented to tax them was equivalent to the king's taxing Englishmen in England without the consent of the House of Commons. The colonists called in vain on English courts to nullify this violation of fundamental law.

In answering the colonial objections, British spokesmen did not claim that the colonists could be taxed without the consent of their representatives. Thomas Whately, speaking for the ministry that sponsored the taxes, went even further than the colonists by denying that any legislation affecting British subjects anywhere could be passed without consent of their representatives. But he went on to affirm what to the colonists was an absurdity, that the colonists were represented in the House of Commons. Although they did not choose members, they were *virtually* represented by every member chosen in Britain, each of whom was entrusted with the interests not merely of the few persons who chose him but of all British subjects. The colonists were represented in the same way as Englishmen in towns that sent no members, in the same way also as English women and children.

However plausible this reasoning may have been to Englishmen, to the colonists it was sheer sophistry. They made plain in resolutions of their assemblies, as for example in Pennsylvania, "That the only legal Representatives of the Inhabitants of this Province are the Persons they annually elect to serve as Members of Assembly." Pamphlets and newspapers were even more scathing in rejecting the pretensions of Parliament to represent Americans. In Massachusetts JAMES OTIS asked, "Will any man's calling himself my agent, representative, or trustee make him so in fact?" On that basis the House of Commons could equally pretend "that they were the true and proper representatives of all the common people upon the globe." (See TAXATION WITHOUT REPRESENTATION.)

In reaction to the objections of the colonists and of the English merchants who traded with them, Parliament in 1766 repealed the Stamp Act and revised the Sugar Act. But at the same time it passed a Declaratory Act, affirming its right to legislate for the colonies "in all cases whatsoever." The framers of the act deliberately omitted specific mention of the power to tax, but in the following year Parliament again exercised that presumed power in the TOWNSHEND ACTS, levying more customs duties on colonial imports. The colonists again mounted protests, but they were still reluctant to deny all Parliamentary authority over them and clung to their distinction between legislation and taxation, which the great William Pitt himself had supported (unsuccessfully) in Parliamentary debate. Parliament, they said, could regulate their trade, even by imposing customs duties, but must not use the pretext of trade regulation for the purpose of raising revenue.

Once again the colonial protests, backed by boycotts, secured repeal of most of the offending taxes, but once again Parliament reaffirmed the principle of its unlimited power, not in a declaration, but by retaining a token tax on tea. The colonists, relieved of any serious burden, were left to ponder the implications of their position. In one sense Parliament was treating them as part of a single people, over all of whom, whether in England or elsewhere, Parliament reigned supreme. In rejecting the notion that they were, or even could be, represented in Parliament, the colonists implied that they were a separate people or peoples.

A reluctance to face this implication had prompted their continued recognition of some sort of authority in Parliament. If Parliament in the past had secured the rights of Englishmen, was it not dangerous (as Whately had indeed said it was) to rely instead on the powers of their own little assemblies? If they were a separate people, or peoples, not subject to Parliament, would they not be foregoing the rights of Englishmen, the very rights they were so vigorously claiming? Could they expect their own assemblies to be as effective defenders of those rights as the mighty British Parliament?

As the quarrel over taxation progressed, with the Boston Tea Party of 1773 and Parliament's punitive Coercive Act of 1774 against Massachusetts, more and more Americans overcame the doubts raised by such questions. The Coercive Acts regulated trade with a vengeance by interdicting Boston's trade, and the acts also altered the government of Massachusetts as defined by its royal charter (ending the provincial election of the governor's council), thereby showing once and for all that guarantees given by the king could not stand before the supremacy claimed by Parliament. In the treatment of Massachusetts the other colonies read what was in store for them, and the various colonial assemblies sent delegates to the FIRST CONTINENTAL CONGRESS in 1774 in order to concert their response.

As in the earlier Stamp Act Congress, the delegates had to determine what they considered to be the limits of Parliament's authority. This time, abandoning their distinction between legislation and taxation (which Parliament had never recognized), they denied that Parliament had or had ever had constitutional authority over them. As a last conciliatory gesture, they expressed a willingness voluntarily to submit to bona fide regulations of trade, but made clear that Parliament had no constitutional right to make such regulations. Following the lead given in tracts by JOHN ADAMS, JAMES WILSON, and THOMAS JEFFERSON, they elevated their separate representative assemblies to a constitutional position within their respective jurisdictions equal to that of Parliament in Great Britain. The only remaining link connecting them with the mother country was their allegiance to the same king, who must be seen as the king of Virginia, Massachusetts, and so on, as well as of England, Scotland, Wales, and Ireland. (Ireland, it was noted, also had its separate Parliament.) Over his peoples beyond the seas the king exercised his powers through separate but equal governments, each with its own governor, council, and representative assembly.

The king did not, of course, rule by divine right. In the colonies as in England he derived his authority from the people themselves, that is, from the separate consent or constituent act of each of the peoples of his empire. John Adams of Massachusetts, perceiving the need to identify such an act, pointed to the Glorious Revolution of 1688 as an event in which each of the king's peoples participated separately. "It ought to be remembered," he said, "that there was a revolution here, as well as in England, and that we as well as the people of England, made an original, express contract with King William." That contract, as Adams and other colonists now saw it, limited royal power in the same way it was limited in England and guaranteed in each colony the exclusive legislative and taxing authority of the representative assembly.

Although the First Continental Congress gave a terminal clarity to the colonists' views of their constitutional position in the empire, it looked forward uncertainly toward a new relationship among the colonies themselves. The membership of the Congress reflected the uncertainty. Some of the members had been chosen by regularly constituted assemblies; others had been sent by extralegal conventions or committees; and a few were self-appointed. What authority, if any, the members had was not clear. Given the view of representation that had guided colonial reaction to Parliamentary taxation, no one was ready to claim for Congress the powers denied to Parliament. Though delegates from every colony except Georgia were present, they had not been chosen by direct popular elections and therefore were not, by their own definition, representatives. At best, as one of them put it, they were "representatives of representatives."

Yet they had not come together simply for discussion. Boston was under military occupation and Massachusetts was under military government. Regular royal government throughout the colonies was fast approaching dissolution. It was time for action, and the Congress took action. Without pausing to determine by what authority, it adopted an ASSOCIATION forbidding not only exports to and imports from Great Britain but also the consumption of British goods. And it called for the creation of committees in every county, city, and town to enforce these restrictions.

In the misnamed Association (membership in which was scarcely voluntary) the Congress took the first steps toward creating a national government separate from that of the (not yet independent) states. If the members believed, as presumably they did, that the authority of government derives from the people, they implied, perhaps without quite realizing what they were doing, that there existed a single American people, distinct not only from the people of Great Britain but also from the peoples of the several colonies and capable of conveying a political authority distinct from that either of Great Britain or of the several colonies.

The implication would not become explicit until the Constitution of 1787, but the Second Continental Congress, which assembled in May 1775, looked even more like the government of a single people than had the First. Fighting had already broken out in April between British troops and Massachusetts militiamen, and Congress at once took charge of the war and began the enlistment of a Continental Army. It sent envoys to France to seek foreign assistance. It opened American commerce to foreign nations. It advised the peoples of the several colonies to suppress all royal authority within their borders. And finally, after more than a year of warfare, it declared the independence of the United States.

Despite the boldness of these actions, the DECLARATION OF INDEPENDENCE itself betrayed the ambiguities that Americans felt about their own identity. It unequivocally put an end to royal authority (parliamentary authority had already been rejected) and consequently to all remaining connection with the people of Great Britain. But it was not quite clear whether the independence thus affirmed was of one people, or of several, or of both one and several.

While the preamble spoke of "one people" separating from another, the final affirmation was in the plural, declaring that "these United Colonies are, and of Right ought to be Free and Independent States." Yet in stating what constituted free and independent statehood, the Declaration specified only "power to levy war, conclude peace, contract alliances, establish commerce." These were all things, with the possible exception of the last, that had been done or would be done by the Congress.

But if the Congress sometimes acted like the government of a single free and independent state, the members still did not recognize the implication that they represented a single free and independent people. They did not consider their Declaration of Independence complete until it had been ratified by each of the separate states whose freedom and independence it declared. And when they tried to define their own authority, they found it difficult to reach agreement. ARTICLES OF CONFEDERATION, first drafted in 1776, were not ratified by the several states until 1781. The Articles entrusted Congress with the powers it was already exercising but declined to derive those powers from a single American people. The old local committees of the Association of 1774, tied directly to Congress, were now a thing of the past, and the enactments of Congress became mere recommendations, to be carried out by the various states as they saw fit.

Even before the Declaration of Independence, in response to the recommendation of the Congress, the states had begun to create governments resting solely on the purported will of the people within their existing borders. In every state a provisional government appeared, usually in the form of a provincial congress resembling the old colonial representative assembly. In most of the states, beginning with Virginia in June 1776, these provincial congresses drew up and adopted, without further reference to the people, constitutions defining the structure of their governments and stating limitations on governmental powers in bills of rights. In every case the constitution was thought or proclaimed to be in some way an act of the people who were to be governed under it, and therefore different from and superior to acts of representatives in a legislative assembly. But often the provincial congress that drafted a state constitution continued to act as the legislative body provided in it. Although a constitution might affirm its own superiority to ordinary legislation, the fact that it was created by legislative act rendered doubtful its immunity to alteration by the body that created it.

A similar doubt surrounded the principle, also enunciated in most of the constitutions, that (as in Virginia) "The legislative, executive, and judiciary departments shall be separate and distinct, so that neither exercise the powers properly belonging to the other." The several provincial congresses that drafted the constitutions inherited the aggressiveness of the colonial assemblies against executive and, to a lesser degree, judicial powers, which had hitherto rested in an overseas authority beyond their reach. In spite of the assertion of the separation of powers, and in spite of the fact that executives and judges would now derive authority solely from the people they governed, the state constitutions generally gave the lion's share of power in government to the representative assemblies.

The result was to bring out the shortcomings of the view of representation that had directed the colonists in their resistance to British taxation. For a decade the colonists had insisted that a representative must act only for the particular group of persons who chose him. They occasionally recognized but minimized his responsibility, as part of the governing body, to act for the whole people who were to be governed by the laws he helped to pass. Now the representative assemblies were suddenly presented with virtually the entire powers of government, which they shared only with a weak executive and judiciary and with a Continental Congress whose powers remained uncertain, despite Articles of Confederation that gave it large responsibilities without the means to perform them. Undeterred by any larger view of their functions, too many of the state assemblymen made a virtue of partiality to their particular constituents and ignored the long-range needs not only of their own state but of the United States.

The solution lay ahead in 1787. By 1776 the inherited ingredients of the settlement then adopted were in place. A rudimentary distinction between the constituent actions of a putative people and the actions of their government had been recognized, though not effectively implemented, in the state governments. All government officers were now selected directly or indirectly by popular choice, with their powers limited, at least nominally, by a reservation to the people of powers not specifically conveyed. And a national center of authority, not quite a government but nevertheless acting like a government, was in operation in the Continental Congress.

What was needed—and with every passing year after 1776 the need became more apparent—was a way to relieve popular government from the grip of short-sighted representative assemblies. Two political inventions filled the need. The first was the constitutional convention, an assembly without legislative powers, entrusted solely with the drafting of a constitution for submission to popular ratification, a constitution that could plausibly be seen as the embodiment of the popular will superior to the ordinary acts of representative assemblies. Massachusetts provided this invention in 1779, in the convention that drafted the state's first constitution. (See MASSACHUSETTS CONSTITUTION.)

The first invention made way for the second, which was

supplied by JAMES MADISON and his colleagues at Philadelphia in 1787. They invented the American people. It was, to be sure, an invention waiting to be made. It had been prefigured in the assumptions behind the Continental Association and the Declaration of Independence. But it reached fulfillment only in the making of the Constitution. By means of a national constitutional convention the men at Philadelphia built a national government that presumed and thus helped to create an American people, distinct from and superior to the peoples of the states.

The idea of popular SOVEREIGNTY was, as we have seen, an old one, but only occasionally had it dictated the formation of popular governments, governments in which all the officers owed their positions directly or indirectly to popular election. Though the idea surfaced powerfully in the England of the 1640s and 1650s, it eventuated there in a restored monarchy, and it won only partial recognition in England's Revolution of 1688. In the AMERICAN REVOLUTION it had seemingly found full expression in thirteen separate state governments, but by 1787 the actions of those governments threatened once again to discredit the whole idea. The signal achievement of the constitutional convention was expressed in the opening words of the document it produced: "We the People of the United States." The United States Constitution rescued popular sovereignty by extending it. It inaugurated both a new government and a new people.

EDMUND S. MORGAN
(1986)

Bibliography

ADAMS, WILLI PAUL 1980 *The First American Constitutions.* Chapel Hill: University of North Carolina Press.

BAILYN, BERNARD 1967 *The Ideological Origins of the American Revolution.* Cambridge, Mass.: Harvard University Press.

—— 1968 *The Origins of American Politics.* New York: Knopf.

FIGGIS, JOHN NEVILLE 1914 *The Divine Right of Kings.* Cambridge: At the University Press.

GREENE, JACK P. 1963 *The Quest for Power.* Chapel Hill: University of North Carolina Press.

KANTOROWICZ, ERNST H. 1957 *The King's Two Bodies.* Princeton: N.J.: Princeton University Press.

LABAREE, LEONARD W. 1930 *Royal Government in America.* New Haven, Conn.: Yale University Press.

MCILWAIN, CHARLES H. 1923 *The American Revolution.* New York: Macmillan.

MORGAN, EDMUND S. and MORGAN, HELEN M. 1953 *The Stamp Act Crisis.* Chapel Hill: University of North Carolina Press.

POCOCK, JOHN G. A. 1957 *The Ancient Constitution and the Feudal Law.* Cambridge: At the University Press.

RUSSELL, CONRAD 1979 *Parliaments and English Politics 1621–1629.* Oxford: Clarendon Press.

SCHUYLER, ROBERT L. 1929 *Parliament and the British Empire.* New York: Columbia University Press.

SKINNER, QUENTIN 1978 *The Foundations of Modern Political Thought.* Cambridge: At the University Press.

TUCKER, ROBERT W. and HENRICKSON, DAVID C. 1982 *The Fall of the First British Empire.* Baltimore: Johns Hopkins University Press.

CONSTITUTIONAL HISTORY, 1776–1789

On July 4, 1776, King George III wrote in his diary, "Nothing of importance this day." When the news of the DECLARATION OF INDEPENDENCE reached him, he still could not know how wrong he had been. The political philosophy of SOCIAL COMPACT, NATURAL RIGHTS, and LIMITED GOVERNMENT that generated the Declaration of Independence also spurred the most important, creative, and dynamic constitutional achievements in history; the Declaration itself was merely the beginning. Within a mere thirteen years Americans invented or first institutionalized a bill of rights against all branches of government, the written CONSTITUTION, the JUDICIAL REVIEW, and a solution to the colonial problem (admitting TERRITORIES to the Union as states fully equal to the original thirteen). RELIGIOUS LIBERTY, the SEPARATION OF CHURCH AND STATE, political parties, SEPARATION OF POWERS, an acceptance of the principle of equality, and the conscious creation of a new nation were also among American institutional "firsts," although not all these initially appeared between 1776 and 1789. In that brief span of time, Americans created what are today the oldest major republic, political democracy, state constitution, and national constitution. These unparalleled American achievements derived not from originality in speculative theory but from the constructive application of old ideas, which Americans took so seriously that they constitutionally based their institutions of government on them.

From thirteen separate colonies the Second Continental Congress "brought forth a new nation," as ABRAHAM LINCOLN said. In May 1776, Congress urged all the colonies to suppress royal authority and adopt permanent governments. On that advice and in the midst of a war the colonies began to frame the world's first written constitutions. When Congress triggered the drafting of those constitutions, Virginia instructed its delegates to Congress to propose that Congress should declare "the United Colonies free and independent states." Neither Virginia nor Congress advocated state sovereignty. Congress's advice implied the erection of state governments with sovereign powers over domestic matters or "internal police."

On June 7, 1776, Congressman RICHARD HENRY LEE of Virginia introduced the resolution as instructed, and Congress appointed two committees, one to frame the document that became the Declaration of Independence and the other to frame a plan of confederation—a constitution for a continental government. When Lincoln declared, "The Union is older than the States, and in fact created them as States," he meant that the Union (Congress) antedated the states. The Declaration of Independence, which stated that the colonies had become states, asserted the authority of the "United States of America, in General Congress, Assembled."

The "spirit of '76" tended to be strongly nationalistic. The members of Congress represented the states, of course, and acted on their instructions, but they acted for the new nation, and the form of government they thought proper in 1776 was a centralized one. As a matter of fact BENJAMIN FRANKLIN had proposed such a government on July 21, 1775, when he presented to Congress " ARTICLES OF CONFEDERATION and perpetual Union." Franklin urged a congressional government with an executive committee that would manage "general continental Business and Interests," conduct diplomacy, and administer finances. His plan empowered Congress to determine war and peace, exchange ambassadors, make foreign alliances, settle all disputes between the colonies, plant new colonies, and, in a sweeping omnibus clause, make laws for "the General Welfare" concerning matters on which individual colonies "cannot be competent," such as "our general Commerce," "general Currency," the establishment of a post office, and governance of "our Common Forces." Costs were to be paid from a common treasury supplied by each colony in proportion to its male inhabitants, but each colony would raise its share by taxing its inhabitants. Franklin provided for an easy amendment process: Congress recommended amendments that would become part of the Articles when approved by a majority of colonial assemblies. Franklin's plan of union seemed much too radical in July 1775, when independence was a year away and reconciliation with Britain on American terms was the object of the war. Congress simply tabled the Franklin plan.

As the war continued into 1776, nationalist sentiment strengthened. THOMAS PAINE's *Common Sense* called for American independence and "a Continental form of Government." Nationalism and centralism were twin causes. JOHN LANGDON of New Hampshire favored independence and "an American Constitution" that provided for appeals from every colony to a national congress "in everything of moment relative to governmental matters." Proposals for a centralized union became common by the spring of 1776, and these proposals, as the following representative samples suggest, tended to show democratic impulses. Nationalism and mitigated democracy, not nationalism and conservatism, were related. A New York newspaper urged the popular election of a national congress with a "superintending power" over the individual colonies as to "all

commercial and Continental affairs," leaving to each colony control over its "internal policy." A populistic plan in a Connecticut newspaper recommended that the congress be empowered to govern "all matters of general concernment" and "every other thing proper and necessary" for the benefit of the whole, allowing the individual colonies only that which fell "within the territorial jurisdiction of a particular assembly." The "Spartacus" essays, which newspapers in New York, Philadelphia, and Portsmouth printed, left the state "cantons" their own legislatures but united all in a national congress with powers similar to those enumerated by Franklin, including a paramount power to "interfere" with a colony's "provincial affairs" whenever required by "the good of the continent." "Essex" reminded his readers that "the strength and happiness of America must be Continental, not Provincial, and that whatever appears to be for the good of the whole, must be submitted to by every Part." He advocated dividing the colonies into many smaller equal parts that would have equal representation in a powerful national congress chosen directly by the people, including taxpaying widows. Carter Braxton, a conservative Virginian, favored aristocratic controls over a congress that could not "interfere with the internal police or domestic concerns of any Colony. . . ."

Given the prevalence of such views in the first half of 1776, a representative committee of the Continental Congress probably mirrored public opinion when it framed a nationalist plan for confederation. On July 12, one month after the appointment of a thirteen-member committee (one from each state) to write a draft, JOHN DICKINSON of Pennsylvania, the committee chairman, presented to Congress a plan that borrowed heavily from Franklin's. The Committee of the Whole of Congress debated the Dickinson draft and adopted it on August 20 with few changes. Only one was significant. Dickinson had proposed that Congress be empowered to fix the western boundaries of states claiming territory to the Pacific coast and to form new states in the west. The Committee of the Whole, bending to the wishes of eight states with extensive western claims, omitted that provision from its revision of the Dickinson draft. That omission became a stumbling block.

On August 20 the Committee of the Whole reported the revised plan of union to Congress. The plan was similar to Franklin's, except that Congress had no power over "general commerce." But Congress, acting for the United States, was clearly paramount to the individual states. They were not even referred to as "states." Collectively they were "the United States of America"; otherwise they were styled "colonies" or "colony," terms not compatible with sovereignty, to which no reference was made. Indeed, the draft merely reserved to each colony "sole and exclusive Regulation and Government of its internal police, in all matters that shall not interfere with the Articles of this Confederation." That crucial provision, Article III, making even "internal police" subordinate to congressional powers, highlighted the nationalist character of the proposed confederation.

The array of congressional powers included exclusive authority over war and peace, land and naval forces, treaties and alliances, prize cases, crimes on the high seas and navigable rivers, all disputes between states, coining money, borrowing on national credit, Indian affairs, post offices, weights and measures, and "the Defence and Welfare" of the United States. Congress also had power to appoint a Council of State and civil officers "necessary for managing the general Affairs of the United States." The Council of State, consisting of one member from each of the thirteen, was empowered to administer the United States government and execute its measures. Notwithstanding this embryonic executive branch, the government of the United States was congressional in character, consisting of a single house whose members were to be elected annually by the legislatures of the colonies. Each colony cast one vote, making each politically equal in Congress. On all important matters, the approval of nine colonies was required to pass legislation. Amendments to the Articles needed the unanimous approval of the legislatures of the various colonies, a provision that later proved to be crippling.

The Articles reported by the Committee of the Whole provoked dissension. States without western land claims opposed the omission of the provision in the Dickinson draft that gave Congress control over western lands. Large states opposed the principle of one vote for each state, preferring instead proportionate representation with each delegate voting. Sharp differences also emerged concerning the rule by which each state was to pay its quota to defray common expenses. Finally some congressmen feared the centralizing nature of the new government. Edward Rutledge of South Carolina did not like "the Idea of destroying all Provincial Distinctions and making every thing of the most minute kind bend to what they call the good of the whole. . . ." Rutledge resolved "to vest the Congress with no more Power than what is absolutely necessary." JAMES WILSON of Pennsylvania could declare that Congress represented "all the individuals of the states" rather than the states, but ROGER SHERMAN of Connecticut answered, "We are representatives of states, not individuals." That attitude would undo the nationalist "spirit of '76."

Because of disagreements and the urgency of prosecuting the war, Congress was unable to settle on a plan of union in 1776. By the spring of 1777 the nationalist momentum was spent. By then most of the states had adopted constitutions and had legitimate governments. Previously,

provisional governments of local "congresses," "conventions," and committees had controlled the states and looked to the Continental Congress for leadership and approval. But the creation of legitimate state governments reinvigorated old provincial loyalties. Local politicians, whose careers were provincially oriented, feared a strong central government as a rival institution. Loyalists no longer participated in politics, local or national, depleting support for central control. By late April of 1777, when state sovereignty triumphed, only seventeen of the forty-eight congressmen who had been members of the Committee of the Whole that adopted the Dickinson draft remained in Congress. Most of the new congressmen opposed centralized government.

James Wilson, who was a congressman in 1776 and 1777, recalled what happened when he addressed the Constitutional Convention on June 8, 1787:

> Among the first sentiments expressed in the first Congs. one was that Virga. is no more. That Massts. is no more, that Pa. is no more c. We are now one nation of brethren. We must bury all local interests and distinctions. This language continued for some time. The tables at length began to turn. No sooner were the State Govts. formed than their jealousy & ambition began to display themselves. Each endeavored to cut a slice from the common loaf, to add to its own morsel, till at length the confederation became frittered down to the impotent condition in which it now stands. Review the progress of the articles of Confederation thro' Congress & compare the first and last draught of it [Farrand, ed., *Records*, I, 166–67].

The turning point occurred in late April 1777 when Thomas Burke of North Carolina turned his formidable localist opinions against the report of the Committee of the Whole. Its Article III, in his words, "expressed only a reservation [to the states] of the power of regulating the internal police, and consequently resigned every other power [to Congress]." Congress, he declared, sought even to interfere with the states' internal police and make its own powers "unlimited." Burke accordingly moved the following substitute for Article III, which became Article II of the Articles as finally adopted: "Each State retains its sovereignty, freedom and independence, and every power, jurisdiction and right, which is not by this confederation expressly delegated to the United States in Congress assembled." Burke's motion carried by the votes of eleven states, vitiating the powers of the national government recommended by the Committee of the Whole.

In the autumn of 1777 a Congress dominated by state-sovereignty advocates completed the plan of confederation. Those who favored proportionate representation in Congress with every member entitled to vote lost badly to those who favored voting by states with each state having one vote. Thereafter the populous wealthy states had no stake in supporting a strong national government that could be controlled by the votes of lesser states. The power of Congress to negotiate commercial treaties effectively died when Congress agreed that under the Articles no treaty should violate the power of the states to impose tariff duties or prohibit imports and exports. The power of Congress to settle all disputes between states became merely a power to make recommendations. The permanent executive branch became a temporary committee with no powers except as delegated by the votes of nine states, the number required to adopt any major measure. Congress also agreed that it should not have power to fix the western boundaries of states claiming lands to the Pacific.

After the nationalist spurt of 1776 proved insufficient to produce the Articles, the states made the Confederation feckless. Even as colonies the states had been particularistic, jealous, and uncooperative. Centrifugal forces originating in diversity—of economics, geography, religion, class structure, and race—produced sectional, provincial, and local loyalties that could not be overcome during a war against the centralized powers claimed by Parliament. The controversy with Britain had produced passions and principles that made the Franklin and Dickinson drafts unviable. Not even these nationalist drafts empowered Congress to tax, although the principle of no TAXATION WITHOUT REPRESENTATION had become irrelevant as to Congress. Similarly, Congress as late as 1774 had "cheerfully" acknowledged Parliament's legitimate "regulation of our external commerce," but in 1776 Congress denied that Parliament had any authority over America, and by 1777 Americans were unwilling to grant their own central legislature powers they preferred their provincial assemblies to wield. Above all, most states refused to repose their trust in any central authority that a few large states might dominate, absent a constitutionally based principle of state equality.

Unanimous consent for amendments to the Articles proved to be too high a price to pay for acknowledging the "sovereignty" of each state, although that acknowledgment made Maryland capable of winning for the United States the creation of a national domain held in common for the benefit of all. Maryland also won the promise that new states would be admitted to the union on a principle of state equality. That prevented the development of a colonial problem from Atlantic to Pacific, and the NORTHWEST ORDINANCE OF 1787 was the Confederation's finest and most enduring achievement.

The Constitution of 1787 was unthinkable in 1776, impossible in 1781 or at any time before it was framed. The Articles were an indispensable transitional stage in the development of the Constitution. Not even the Constitution would have been ratified if its Framers had submitted it

for approval to the state legislatures that kept Congress paralyzed in the 1780s. Congress, representing the United States, authorized the creation of the states and ended up, as it had begun, as their creature. It possessed expressly delegated powers with no means of enforcing them. That Congress lacked commerce and tax powers was a serious deficiency, but not nearly so crippling as its lack of sanctions and the failure of the states to abide by the Articles. Congress simply could not make anyone, except soldiers, do anything. It acted on the states, not on people. Only a national government that could execute its laws independently of the states could have survived.

The states flouted their constitutional obligations. The Articles obliged the states to "abide by the determinations of the United States, in Congress assembled," but there was no way to force the states to comply. The states were not sovereign, except as to their internal police and tax powers; rather, they behaved unconstitutionally. No foreign nation recognized the states as sovereign, because Congress possessed the external attributes of sovereignty especially as to FOREIGN AFFAIRS and WAR POWERS.

One of the extraordinary achievements of the Articles was the creation of a rudimentary federal system. It failed because its central government did not operate directly on individuals within its sphere of authority. The Confederation had no independent executive and judicial branches, because the need for them scarcely existed when Congress addressed its acts mainly to the states. The framers of the Articles distributed the powers of government with remarkable acumen, committing to Congress about all that belonged to a central government except, of course, taxation and commercial regulation, the two powers that Americans of the Revolutionary War believed to be part of state sovereignty. Even ALEXANDER HAMILTON, who in 1780 advocated that Congress should have "complete sovereignty," excepted "raising money by internal taxes."

Congress could requisition money from the states, but they did not pay their quotas. In 1781 Congress requisitioned $8,000,000 for the next year, but the states paid less than half a million. While the Articles lasted, the cumulative amount paid by all the states hardly exceeded what was required to pay the interest on the public debt for just one year.

Nationalists vainly sought to make the Articles more effective by both interpretation and amendment. Madison devised a theory of IMPLIED POWERS by which he squeezed out of the Articles congressional authority to use force if necessary against states that failed to fulfill their obligations. Congress refused to attempt coercion just as it refused to recommend an amendment authorizing its use. Congress did, however, charter a bank to control currency, but the opposition to the exercise of a power not expressly delegated remained so intense that the bank had to be rechartered by a state. Congress vainly sought unanimous state consent for various amendments that would empower it to raise money from customs duties and to regulate commerce, foreign and domestic. In 1781 every state but Rhode Island approved an amendment empowering Congress to impose a five percent duty on all foreign imports; never again did an amendment to the Articles come so close to adoption. Only four states ratified an amendment authorizing a congressional embargo against the vessels of any nation with whom the United States had no treaty of commerce. Congress simply had no power to negotiate commercial treaties with nations such as Britain that discriminated against American shipping. Nor had Congress the power to prevent states from violating treaties with foreign nations. In 1786 JOHN JAY, Congress's secretary of foreign affairs, declared that not a day had passed since ratification of the 1783 treaty of peace without its violation by at least one state. Some states also discriminated against the trade of others. Madison likened New Jersey, caught between the ports of Philadelphia and New York, "to a cask tapped at both ends." More important, Congress failed even to recommend needed amendments. As early as 1784 Congress was so divided it defeated an amendment that would enable it to regulate commerce, foreign and domestic, and to levy duties on imports and exports. Often Congress could not function for lack of a quorum. The requisite number of states was present for only three days between October 1785 and April 1786. In 1786 Congress was unable to agree on any amendments for submission to the states.

The political condition of the United States during the 1780s stagnated partly because of the constitutional impotence of Congress and the unconstitutional conduct of the states. The controversy with Britain had taught that liberty and localism were congruent. The 1780s taught that excessive localism was incompatible with nationhood. The Confederation was a necessary point of midpassage. It bequeathed to the United States the fundamentals of a federal system, a national domain, and a solution to the colonial problem. Moreover the Articles contained several provisions that were antecedents of their counterparts in the Constitution of 1787: a free speech clause for congressmen and LEGISLATIVE IMMUNITY, a PRIVILEGES AND IMMUNITIES clause, a clause on the extradition of FUGITIVES FROM JUSTICE, a FULL FAITH AND CREDIT clause, and a clause validating United States debts. The Confederation also started an effective government bureaucracy when the Congress in 1781 created secretaries for foreign affairs, war, marine, and finance—precursors of an executive branch. When the new departments of that branch began to function in 1789, a corps of experienced administrators, trained under the Articles, staffed them. The courts established by Congress to decide prize and admiralty cases

as well as boundary disputes foreshadowed a national judiciary. Except for enactment of the great Northwest Ordinance, however, the Congress of the Confederation was moribund by 1787. It had successfully prosecuted the war, made foreign alliances, established the national credit, framed the first constitution of the United States, negotiated a favorable treaty of peace, and created a national domain. Congress's accomplishments were monumental, especially during wartime, yet in the end it failed.

By contrast, state government flourished. Excepting Rhode Island and Connecticut, all the states adopted written constitutions during the war, eight in 1776. Madison exultantly wrote, "Nothing has excited more admiration in the world than the manner in which free governments have been established in America, for it was the first instance, from the creation of the world that free inhabitants have been seen deliberating on a form of government, and selection of such of their citizens as possessed their confidence to determine upon and give effect to it."

The VIRGINIA CONSTITUTION OF 1776, the first permanent state constitution, began with a Declaration of Rights adopted three weeks before the Declaration of Independence. No previous bill of rights had restrained all branches of government. Virginia's reflected the widespread belief that Americans had been thrown back into a state of nature from which they emerged by framing a social compact for their governance, reserving to themselves certain inherent or natural rights, including life, liberty, the enjoyment of property, and the pursuit of happiness. Virginia's declaration explicitly declared that as all power derived from the people, for whose benefit government existed, the people could reform or abolish government when it failed them. On the basis of this philosophy Virginia framed a constitution providing for a bicameral legislature, a governor, and a judicial system. The legislature elected a governor, who held office for one year, had no veto power, and was encumbered by an executive council. The legislature chose many important officials, including judges.

Some states followed the more democratic model of the PENNSYLVANIA CONSTITUTION OF 1776, others the ultraconservative one of Maryland, but all state constitutions prior to the MASSACHUSETTS CONSTITUTION OF 1780 were framed by legislatures, which in some states called themselves "conventions" or assemblies. Massachusetts deserves credit for having originated a new institution of government, a specially elected constitutional convention whose sole function was to frame the constitution and submit it for popular ratification. That procedure became the standard. Massachusetts's constitution, which is still operative, became the model American state constitution. The democratic procedure for making it fit the emerging theory that the sovereign people should be the source of the con-

eral welfare of the United States is not concerned." His motion to protect the "internal police" of the states brought no debaters to his side and was summarily defeated; only Maryland supported Connecticut. Immediately after, another small-state delegate, GUNNING BEDFORD of Delaware, shocked even EDMUND RANDOLPH of Virginia, who had presented the Virginia Plan, by a motion to extend the powers of Congress by vesting authority "to legislate in all cases for the general interest of the Union." Randolph observed, "This is a formidable idea indeed. It involves the power of violating all the laws and constitution of the States, of intermeddling with their police." Yet the motion passed.

On July 26 the Convention adjourned until August 6 to allow a Committee on Detail to frame a "constitution conformable to the Resolutions passed by the Convention." Generously construing its charge, the committee acted as a miniature convention and introduced a number of significant changes. One was the explicit enumeration of the powers of Congress to replace the vague, omnibus provisions adopted previously by the Convention. Although enumerated, these powers were liberally expressed and formidable in their array. The committee made specific the spirit and intent of the Convention. Significantly the first enumerated power was that of taxation and the second that of regulating commerce among the states and with foreign nations: the two principal powers that had been withheld from Congress by the Articles. When the Convention voted on the provision that Congress "shall have the power to lay and collect taxes, duties, imposts and excises," the states were unanimous and only one delegate, Elbridge Gerry, was opposed. When the Convention next turned to the commerce power there was no discussion and even Gerry voted affirmatively.

Notwithstanding its enumeration of the legislative powers, all of which the Convention accepted, the Committee on Detail added an omnibus clause that has served as an ever expanding source of national authority: "And to make all laws that shall be necessary and proper for carrying into execution the foregoing powers." The Convention agreed to that clause without a single dissenting vote by any state or delegate. The history of the great supremacy clause, Article Six, shows a similar consensus. Without debate the Convention adopted the supremacy clause, and not a single state or delegate voted nay. Finally, Article One, section 10, imposing restrictions on the economic powers of the states with respect to paper money, ex post facto laws, bills of credit, and contracts also reflected a consensus in the Convention. In sum, consensus, rather than compromise, was the most significant feature of the Convention, outweighing in importance the various compromises that occupied most of the time of the delegates.

But why was there such a consensus? The obvious an-

swer (apart from the fact that opponents either stayed away or walked out) is the best: experience had proved that the nationalist constitutional position was right. If the United States was to survive and flourish, a strong national government had to be established. The Framers of the Constitution were accountable to public opinion; the Convention was a representative body. That its members were prosperous, well-educated political leaders made them no less representative than Congress. The state legislatures, which elected the members of the Convention, were the most unlikely instruments for thwarting the popular will. The Framers, far from being able to do as they pleased, were not free to promulgate the Constitution. Although they adroitly arranged for its ratification by nine state ratifying conventions rather than by all state legislatures, they could not present a plan that the people of the states would not tolerate. They could not control the membership of those state ratifying conventions. They could not even be sure that the existing Congress would submit the Constitution to the states for ratification, let alone for ratification by state conventions that had to be specially elected. If the Framers got too far astray from public opinion, their work would have been wasted. The consensus in the Convention coincided with an emerging consensus in the country that recaptured the nationalist spirit of '76. That the Union had to be strengthened was an almost universal American belief.

For its time the Constitution was a remarkably democratic document framed by democratic methods. Some historians have contended that the Convention's scrapping of the Articles and the ratification process were revolutionary acts which if performed by a Napoleon would be pronounced a coup d'état. But the procedure of the Articles for constitutional amendment was not democratic, because it allowed Rhode Island, with one-sixtieth of the nation's population, to exercise a veto power. The Convention sent its Constitution to the lawfully existing government, the Congress of the Confederation, for submission to the states, and Congress, which could have censured the Convention for exceeding its authority, freely complied—and thereby exceeded its own authority under the Articles! A coup d'état ordinarily lacks the deliberation and consent that marked the making of the Constitution and is characterized by a military element that was wholly lacking in 1787. A Convention elected by the state legislatures and consisting of many of the foremost leaders of their time deliberated for almost four months. Its members included many opponents of the finished scheme. The nation knew the Convention was considering changes in the government. The proposed Constitution was made public, and voters in every state were asked to choose delegates to vote for or against it after open debate. The use of state ratifying conventions fit the theory that a

stitution and authorize its framing by a constitutional convention, rather than the legislature to which the constitution is paramount. Massachusetts was also the first state to give more than lip service to the principle of separation of powers. Everywhere else, excepting perhaps New York, unbalanced government and legislative supremacy prevailed. Massachusetts established the precedent for a strong, popularly elected executive with a veto power; elsewhere the governor tended to be a ceremonial head who depended for his existence on the legislature.

The first state constitutions and related legislation introduced significant reforms. Most states expanded VOTING RIGHTS by reducing property qualifications, and a few, including Vermont (an independent state from 1777 to 1791), experimented with universal manhood suffrage. Many state constitutions provided for fairer apportionment of REPRESENTATION in the legislature. Every southern state either abolished its ESTABLISHMENT OF RELIGION or took major steps to achieve separation of church and state. Northern states either abolished SLAVERY or provided for its gradual ending. Criminal codes were made more humane. The confiscation of Loyalist estates and of crown lands, and the opening of a national domain westward to the Mississippi, led to a democratization of landholding, as did the abolition of feudal relics such as the law of primogeniture and entail. The pace of democratic change varied from state to state, and in some states it was nearly imperceptible, but the Revolution without doubt occasioned constitutional and political developments that had long been dammed up under the colonial system.

The theory that a constitution is supreme law encouraged the development of judicial review. Written constitutions with bills of rights and the emerging principle of separation of powers contributed to the same end. Before the Revolution appellate judges tended to be dependents of the executive branch; the Revolution promoted judicial independence. Most state constitutions provided for judicial tenure during good behavior rather than for a fixed term or the pleasure of the appointing power. Inevitably when Americans believed that a legislature had exceeded its authority they argued that it had acted unconstitutionally, and they turned to courts to enforce the supreme law as law. The dominant view, however, was that a court holding a statute unconstitutional insulted the sovereignty of the legislature, as the reactions to HOLMES V. WALTON (1780) and TREVETT V. WEEDEN (1786) showed. COMMONWEALTH V. CATON (1782) was probably the first case in which a state judge declared that a court had power to hold a statute unconstitutional, though the court in that case sustained the act before it. In RUTGERS V. WADDINGTON (1784) Alexander Hamilton as counsel argued that a state act violating a treaty was unconstitutional, but the court declared that the judicial power advocated by counsel was

"subversive of all government." Counsel in *Trevett* also contended that the court should void a state act. Arguments of counsel do not create precedents but can reveal the emergence of a new idea. Any American would have agreed that an act against a constitution was void; although few would have agreed that courts have the final power to decide matters of constitutionality, that idea was spreading. The TEN POUND ACT CASES (1786) were the first in which an American court held a state enactment void, and that New Hampshire precedent was succeeded by a similar decision in the North Carolina case of BAYARD V. SINGLETON (1787). The principle of MARBURY V. MADISON (1803) thus originated at a state level before the framing of the federal Constitution.

The Constitution originated in the drive for a strong national government that preceded the framing of the Articles of Confederation. The "critical period" of 1781–1787 intensified that drive, but it began well before the defects of the Articles expanded the ranks of the nationalists. The weaknesses of the United States in international affairs, its inability to enforce the peace treaty, its financial crisis, its helplessness during SHAYS' REBELLION, and its general incapacity to govern resulted in many proposals—in Congress, in the press, and even in some states—for national powers to negotiate commercial treaties, regulate the nation's commerce, and check state policies that adversely affected creditor interests and impeded economic growth. Five states met at the Annapolis Convention in 1786, ostensibly to discuss a "uniform system" of regulating commerce, but those who masterminded the meeting had a much larger agenda in mind—as Madison put it, a "plenipotentiary Convention for amending the Confederation."

Hamilton had called for a "convention of all the states" as early as 1780, before the Articles were ratified, to form a government worthy of the nation. Even men who defended state sovereignty conceded the necessity of a convention by 1787. William Grayson admitted that "the present Confederation is utterly inefficient and that if it remains much longer in its present State of imbecility we shall be one of the most contemptible Nations on the face of the earth. . . ." LUTHER MARTIN admitted that Congress was "weak, contemptibly weak," and Richard Henry Lee believed that no government "short of force, will answer." "Do you not think," he asked GEORGE MASON, "that it ought to be declared . . . that any State act of legislation that shall contravene, or oppose, the authorized acts of Congress, or interfere with the expressed rights of that body, shall be *ipso facto* void, and of no force whatsoever?" Many leaders, like THOMAS JEFFERSON, advocated executive and judicial branches for the national government with "an appeal from state judicatures to a federal court in all cases where the act of Confederation controlled the question. . . ."

with appropriate powers. But in many there was also a conspicuous strain of negativism, reflecting disillusionment with state government and a determination to curb extravagance, corruption, and favoritism. Notably, the framers often placed new restrictions on legislative authority, particularly with reference to public finance, banks, and corporations. These subjects were political issues, of course, but then every CONSTITUTIONAL CONVENTION became to some extent a party battle. As a rule, Democrats were more hostile than their opponents to corporate enterprise and government promotion of it. Attitudes varied according to local circumstances, however, and much depended upon which party in the state had the upper hand at the time. The states of the Old Northwest, where prodigal internal improvement policies in the 1830s had proved disastrous, were especially emphatic in their restraint of legislative power. Their new constitutions approved in the years 1848–1851 forbade state investment in private enterprise and put strict limits on public indebtedness. They also restricted banking in various ways, such as ordering double liability for stockholders, prohibiting the suspension of specie payments, and requiring that any general banking act must be submitted to a popular REFERENDUM.

State constitutional change occurred in many ways and resulted from the work of many hands, including those of voters, convention delegates, legislators, governors, and judges. Appellate courts particularly often shaped or reshaped the fundamental law in the course of performing their routine duties, although JUDICIAL REVIEW of state legislation by state courts was a fairly rare occurrence until after the Civil War. Despite all the constitutional activity, innovation was by no means the dominant mode in the antebellum period. States borrowed much from one another, and old forms were sometimes retained well beyond the limits of their appropriateness. Vermont in 1860 still had its quaint Council of Revision, elected every seven years to examine the condition of the constitution and propose amendments. North Carolina had not yet given its governor a veto power, and in South Carolina, the legislature continued to choose the state's presidential electors. Yet the new problems of the age did encourage some experimentation. For example, certain states had begun to develop the quasi-judicial regulatory commission as an extra branch of government, and framers of the Kansas constitution in 1859 introduced the item veto, a device that most states would eventually adopt.

Although federal and state constitutional development proceeded in more or less separate grooves, the fundamental constitutional problem of the age was the relation between the nation and its constituent parts. The problem had been present and intermittently urgent since the birth of the republic, but after 1846 it became associated much more than ever before with the interrelated issues of slavery and expansion and with the dynamics of party politics.

In the federal system established by the Constitution, the national government and the state governments were each supreme within their respective spheres. This principle of DUAL FEDERALISM, even though it accorded rather well with the actual structure and distribution of governmental power in antebellum America, was by no means universally accepted as a true design of the Republic. Nationalists like Webster and Lincoln asserted the primacy of the nation, the sovereignty of its people, and the perpetuity of the Union. Sectionalists like Calhoun and Davis lodged sovereignty with the states, insisted upon strict construction of federal authority, and viewed the Union as a compact that could be abrogated. Logical consistency was not a characteristic of the intersectional debate, however. Both proslavery and antislavery forces invoked federal power and appealed to states' rights whenever either strategy suited their purposes. With regard to the recovery of fugitive slaves, for instance, Southerners demanded expansion and vigorous use of national authority, while the resistance to that authority of some northern state officials amounted to a revival of nullification. (See UNION, THEORIES OF THE.)

Most Americans agreed that slavery was a state institution, but from that premise they drew conflicting inferences. In the radical antislavery view of SALMON P. CHASE, the institution had no standing beyond the bounds of slave-state JURISDICTION, and the federal government had no constitutional power to establish it, protect it, or even acknowledge its legal existence. In short, slavery was local and freedom national. (See ABOLITIONIST CONSTITUTIONAL THEORY.) According to Calhoun, however, the federal government, as the mere agent of the states, was constitutionally obligated to give slavery as much protection as it gave any other kind of property recognized by state law. Only the sovereign power of a state could restrict or abolish the institution. In short, slavery was national and antislavery the local exception.

The practice of the United States government over the years ran closer to Calhoun's theory than to Chase's. All three branches recognized property rights in slaves and extended aid of some kind to their masters. Congress went beyond the requirements of the Constitution in making the recovery of fugitive slaves a federal business, and under congressional rule the national capital became a slave state in miniature, complete with a slave code, whipping posts, and a thriving slave trade. The image of the nation consistently presented in diplomatic relations was that of a slaveholding republic. With a persistence amounting to dedication, the Department of State sought compensation for owners of slaves escaping to foreign soil, and repeatedly it tried to secure Canadian cooperation in the return of fugitives. In the *Dred Scott* decision, Chief Justice ROGER B. TANEY laid down the one-sided rule that the federal government had no power over slavery except "the power coupled with the duty of guarding and protecting the owner in his rights."

To be sure, national authority was also used for antislavery purposes. In outlawing the foreign slave trade, Congress plainly acted within the letter and intent of the Constitution. In prohibiting slavery throughout much of the Western territory, however, the lawmakers probably drew as much sanction from the example of the NORTHWEST ORDINANCE as from the somewhat ambiguous passage in Article IV, section 3, that seemed to be relevant— namely, "The Congress shall have Power to dispose of and make all needful Rules and Regulations respecting the Territory or other Property belonging to the United States." By 1840, such prohibition had been enacted in six territorial organic acts, as well as in the Missouri Compromise. Furthermore, Chief Justice JOHN MARSHALL in AMERICAN INSURANCE COMPANY V. CANTER (1828) had given the territory clause a broad construction. In legislating for the TERRITORIES, he declared, "Congress exercises the combined powers of the general and of a State government." Since the authority of a state government to establish or abolish slavery was generally acknowledged, Marshall's words seemed to confirm Congress in possession of the same authority within the territories.

The constitutionality of legislation excluding slavery from federal territory did not become a major issue in American public life until after introduction of the WILMOT PROVISO in 1846. Although the question had arisen at times during the Missouri controversy of 1819–1820, the famous 36°30' restriction had been approved without extensive discussion and with the support of a majority of southern congressmen. The subject had arisen again during the 1830s, but only as a secondary and academic consideration in the debate over abolitionist attacks upon slavery in the District of Columbia. As a practical matter, the Missouri Compromise had presumably disposed of the problem by reviving and extending a policy of having two different policies, one on each side of a dividing line. North of that line (first the Ohio River and then 36°30'), slavery was prohibited; south of the line, slavery was permitted if desired by the white inhabitants.

In the summer of 1846, with Texas annexed and admitted to statehood, with title to Oregon secured by treaty, and with the war against Mexico under way, the United States found itself engaged in territorial expansion on a grand scale. Texas entered the Union as a slaveholding state, and Oregon was generally understood to be free soil, but what about New Mexico and California, if they should be acquired by conquest? To many Americans, including President Polk, the obvious answer seemed to be extending the Missouri Compromise line to the Pacific Ocean. But the issue arose at a time when sectional antagonism had been inflamed by a decade of quarreling over abolitionist petitions, the GAG RULE, and the Texas question. Furthermore, whereas the 36°30' line had meant partial abolition in a region previously open to slavery, extension of the line through New Mexico and California would have meant a partial rescinding of the abolition already achieved there by Mexican law. So David Wilmot's proposal to forbid slavery in any territory that might be acquired from Mexico won the overwhelming approval of northern congressmen when it was introduced in the House of Representatives on August 8, 1846. Southerners were even more united and emphatic in their opposition; for the Proviso would have completed the exclusion of slaveholders from all the newly acquired land in the Far West. Such injustice, they warned, could not fail to end in disunion.

The Proviso principle of "no more slave territory" quickly became the premier issue in American politics and remained so for almost fifteen years. Virtually the raison d'être of the Free Soil and Republican parties, the principle was rejected by Congress in 1850 and again in 1854, deprived of its legitimacy by the Supreme Court in 1857, and supported by less than forty percent of the electorate in the presidential contest of 1860. Yet forty percent proved sufficient to put a Republican in the White House and thereby precipitate SECESSION. During those years of intermittent sectional crisis from 1846 to 1861, the Southerners and northern conservatives who controlled government policy sought desperately and sometimes discordantly for a workable alternative to the Proviso. One thing that complicated their task was the growing tendency of all elements in the controversy to constitutionalize their arguments.

Southerners especially felt the need for constitutional sanction, partly because of their vulnerability as a minority section but also in order to offset the moral advantage of the antislavery forces. It was not enough to denounce the Proviso as unfair; they must also prove it to be unconstitutional despite the string of contrary precedents running back to the venerated Northwest Ordinance. One way of doing so was to invoke the Fifth Amendment, arguing that any congressional ban on slavery in the territories amounted to deprivation of property without DUE PROCESS OF LAW. But this argument, though used from time to time and incorporated rather vaguely in Taney's *Dred Scott* opinion, did not become a significant part of anti-Proviso strategy. For one thing, the Fifth Amendment had another cutting edge, antislavery in its effect. Free Soilers and Republicans could and did maintain that slavery was illegal in federal territory because it amounted to deprivation of *liberty* without due process of law.

More in keeping with the strict constructionism generally favored by Southerners was the principle of "nonintervention," that is, congressional nonaction with respect to slavery in the territories. Actually, nonintervention had been government policy in part of the West ever since 1790, always with the effect of establishing slavery. But in earlier years the policy had been given little theoretical underpinning. Then, after the introduction of the Wilmot Proviso, there were strenuous efforts to convert nonintervention into a constitutional imperative. The emerging argument ignored Marshall's opinion in *American Insurance Company v. Canter* and held that the territory clause of the Constitution referred only to disposal of public land. In providing government for a territory, Congress could do nothing more than what was absolutely necessary to prepare the territory for statehood. That did not include either the prohibition or the establishment of slavery. Thus nonintervention became a doctrine of federal incapacity. It left open, however, the question of what authority prevailed in the absence of congressional power. One answer, associated with Calhoun, was that property rights in slavery were silently legitimized in every territory by the direct force of the Constitution. Another answer, associated with Lewis Cass and Douglas, was that nonintervention meant leaving the question of slavery to be decided by the local territorial population. The latter theory, given the name POPULAR SOVEREIGNTY, had the advantage of seeming to be in tune with the spirit of Jacksonian democracy.

Thus, by 1848, when American acquisition of New Mexico and California was confirmed in the TREATY OF GUADALUPE HIDALGO, four distinct solutions to the problem of slavery in the territories had emerged. At one political extreme was the free soil doctrine requiring enactment of the Wilmot Proviso. At the other extreme was the Calhoun property rights doctrine legitimizing slavery in all federal territory by direct force of the Constitution. Between them were two formulas of compromise: extension of the 3630 line and the principle of popular sovereignty. Presumably the choice rested with Congress, but the constitutionalizing of the argument opened up another possibility—that of leaving the status of slavery in the territories to judicial determination. Legislation facilitating referral of the question to the Supreme Court was proposed in 1848 and incorporated in the historic set of compromise measures enacted two years later. The COMPROMISE OF 1850 admitted California as a free state, but for the rest of the Mexican Cession it adopted the principle of nonintervention. The effect was to reject the 3630 and Proviso solutions while leaving the field still open to popular sovereignty, the property rights doctrine, and judicial disposition.

Although neither of the major parties took a formal stand on the territorial question in the elections of 1848 and 1852, it was the Democrats who became closely associated with the principle of nonintervention. Cass, their presidential nominee in 1848, declared that Congress lacked the power to prohibit slavery in the territories and that the territorial inhabitants should be left free to regulate their internal concerns in their own way. This seemed to endorse popular sovereignty as the appropriate corollary to nonintervention, but for about a decade the Democratic party managed to invest both terms with enough ambiguity to accommodate both its northern and southern wings. More specifically, Southerners found that they could assimilate popular sovereignty to their own purposes by viewing it as the right of a territorial population to accept or reject slavery *at the time of admission to statehood.* That would presumably leave the Calhoun doctrine operative during the territorial period. At the same time, northern Democrats like Douglas went on believing that popular sovereignty meant the right of a territorial legislature to make all decisions regarding slavery, within the limits of the Constitution. The Whigs failed to achieve any such convenient doctrinal ambiguity, and that failure may have contributed to the disintegration of their party.

In 1854, a heavily Democratic Congress organized the territories of Kansas and Nebraska, repealing the antislavery restriction of the Missouri Compromise and substituting the principle of nonintervention. "The true intent and meaning of this act," the measure declared, "[is] not to legislate slavery into any Territory or State, nor to exclude it therefrom, but to leave the people thereof perfectly free to form and regulate their domestic institutions in their own way, subject only to the Constitution of the United States." This passage, since it could be interpreted to mean either the northern or the southern brand of popular sovereignty, preserved the ambiguity so necessary for Democratic unity. But of course the Kansas-Nebraska Act, by removing a famous barrier to slavery, provoked a storm of anger throughout the free states and set off a political revolution.

The crisis of the late 1850s was in one respect a confrontation between the emerging Republican party and the increasingly united South—that is, between the Wilmot Proviso and the principles of Calhoun. Yet it was also a struggle within the Democratic party over the meaning of nonintervention and popular sovereignty. The *Dred Scott* decision in March 1857 cleared the air and intensified the crisis. In ruling that Congress had no power to prohibit slavery in the territories, the Supreme Court officially constitutionalized the principle of nonintervention and virtually rendered illegal the main purpose of the Republican party. But Chief Justice Taney went further and disqualified the northern Democratic version of popular sovereignty. If Congress had no such power over slavery, he declared, then neither did a territorial legislature. Douglas responded with his FREEPORT DOCTRINE, insisting that a territorial government, by unfriendly legislation, could effectively exclude slavery, no matter what the Court might decide to the contrary. Southern Democrats, in turn, demanded federal protection of slavery in the territories, and on that issue the party split at its national convention in 1860.

By 1860 it had become apparent that slavery was not taking root in Kansas or in any other western territory. Yet when secession began after Lincoln's election, the efforts at reconciliation concentrated on the familiar territorial problem. The centerpiece of the abortive Crittenden compromise was an amendment reviving and extending the 3630 line, so recently outlawed by the Supreme Court. This continued fascination with an essentially empty issue was not so foolish as it now may seem; for the territorial question had obviously taken on enormous symbolic meaning. Because of the almost universal agreement that slavery in the states was untouchable by the federal government, the territories had come to be the limited battleground of a fierce and fundamental struggle. Thus the sectional conflict of the 1850s, whatever its origins and whatever its substance, was decisively shaped by constitutional considerations.

DON E. FEHRENBACHER
(1986)

Bibliography

BESTOR, ARTHUR 1961 State Sovereignty and Slavery: A Reinterpretation of Proslavery Constitutional Doctrine, 1846–1860 Illinois State Historical Society Journal 54:117–80.

DEALEY, JAMES QUAYLE 1915 Growth of American State Constitutions. Boston: Ginn & Co.

FEHRENBACHER, DON E. 1978 The Dred Scott Case: Its Significance in American Law and Politics. New York: Oxford University Press.

PARKINSON, GEORGE PHILLIP, JR. 1972 "Antebellum State Constitution-Making: Retention, Circumvention, Revision." Ph.D. dissertation, University of Wisconsin.

POTTER, DAVID M. 1976 The Impending Crisis, 1848–1861. Completed and edited by Don E. Fehrenbacher. New York: Harper & Row.

WHITE, LEONARD D. 1954 The Jacksonians: A Study in Administrative History, 1829–1861. New York: Macmillan.

CONSTITUTIONAL HISTORY, 1861–1865

If expediency and ideology ordinarily conflict with the constitutionalist desire for procedural regularity and limitations on government, in time of war they pose a fundamental challenge to CONSTITUTIONALISM and the RULE OF LAW. The first fact to be observed about the constitutional history of the CIVIL WAR, therefore, is that the federal Constitution, as in the prewar period, served as both a symbol and a source of governmental legitimacy and as a normative standard for the conduct of politics. Because the rule of the Constitution continued without interruption, it is easy to overlook the pressures that the war generated to institute a regime based exclusively on necessity and the public safety. To be sure, considerations of public safety entered into wartime constitutionalism, and there were those who believed passionately that the Union government in the years 1861 to 1865 did indeed cast aside the Constitution and resort to arbitrary rule. Yet, considered from either a comparative or a strictly American perspective, this judgment is untenable. The record abundantly demonstrates the persistence of constitutional controversy in Congress, in the executive branch, in the courts, and in the forum of public opinion—evidence that the nation's organic law was taken seriously in time of war, even if it was not applied in the same manner as in time of peace. Indeed, a constitutionalizing impulse may be said to have manifested itself in the business of warfare itself. General Order No. 100 for the government of Union armies in the field, promulgated by President ABRAHAM LINCOLN in 1863, was an attempt to limit the destructiveness of modern war that had resulted from developments in weaponry and from the emergence of other aspects of total war.

The most important constitutional question resolved by the events of the war concerned the nature of the Union. (See THEORIES OF THE UNION.) The Framers of the Constitution had created a mixed regime that in some respects resembled a confederation of autonomous states and in others a centralized unitary government. Its distinguishing feature—the chief characteristic of American FEDERALISM—was the division of SOVEREIGNTY between the federal government and the state governments. In constitutional law several decisions of the Supreme Court under Chief Justice JOHN MARSHALL had confirmed this dual-sovereignty system; yet periodically it was questioned by political groups who insisted that the Union was simply a league of sovereign states, and that the federal government possessed no sovereignty whatsoever except as the agent of the states. From 1846 to 1860 defenders of slavery asserted this state-sovereignty theory of the Union; although they never secured a congressional majority for the theory, they did force northern Democrats to adopt positions that virtually abandoned any claim to federal sovereignty in matters concerning slavery. The SECESSION policy of President JAMES BUCHANAN, which regarded secession as illegal but nonetheless tolerated the existence of the newly forming Confederate States of America, signified the constitutional and political bankruptcy of Democratic DUAL FEDERALISM and the practical repudiation of federal sovereignty.

The constitutional results of the Civil War must be measured against the effective triumph of proslavery state sovereignty which permitted the disintegration of the Union in 1860–1861. Northern victory in the war established federal sovereignty in political fact and in public policy, and by the same token repudiated the state-sovereignty theory of the Union. From the standpoint of constitutional law, this result vindicated the divided-sovereignty concept of federalism asserted in the early national period. From the standpoint of federal-state relations in the field of public policy, the war produced a significant centralizing trend, evident principally in military recruitment and organization, internal security, the regulation of personal liberty and CIVIL RIGHTS, and the determination of national economic policy.

The changes in federalism produced by the war have usually been described—sometimes in almost apocalyptic terms—as the destruction of STATES' RIGHTS and the old federal Union and their replacement by a centralized sovereign nation. In fact, however, the changes in federal-state relations that occurred between 1861 and 1865 did not seriously erode or alter the decentralized constitutional system and political culture of the United States. The centralizing of policy was based on military need rather than the appeal of a new unitary constitutional model, and it was of limited scope and duration. In no comprehensive way did the federal government become supreme over the states, nor were states' rights obliterated either in law or in policy. The theoretical structure of American federalism, as explicated by John Marshall, persisted, the actual distribution of power between the states and the federal government, the result of policy struggles on questions raised by the war, was different.

Perhaps the best way to describe the change in federalism that occurred during the Civil War is to say that after a long period of disinclination to use the constitutional powers assigned to it, the federal government began to act like an authentic sovereign state. Foremost among its achievements was the raising of armies and the providing and maintaining of a navy for the defense of the nation.

At the start of the war the decision to resist secession was made by the federal government, but the task of raising a military force fell largely upon the states. The regular United States Army, at approximately 16,000 men, was inadequate for the government's military needs, and federal authorities were as yet unprepared to call for United States volunteers. To meet the emergency it was necessary to rely on the militia, a form of military organization that, while subject to national service, was chiefly a state institution. Accordingly President Lincoln on April 15, 1861, acting under the Militia Act of 1795, issued a call to the

state governors to provide 75,000 militia for three months of national service. By August 1861, in pursuance of additional presidential requests, the War Department had enrolled almost 500,000 men for three years' duty. Yet, although carried out under federal authority, the actual recruiting of troops and to a considerable extent their preparation for combat were done by the state governors, acting as a kind of war ministry for the nation.

This arrangement did not last long. Within a year declining popular enthusiasm and the utility of centralized administrative management severely impeded state recruiting efforts and led to greater federal control. Eventually national CONSCRIPTION was adopted. Congress took a half-way step toward this policy in the Militia Act of July 1862, authorizing the President, in calling the militia into national service, to make all necessary rules and regulations for doing so where state laws were defective or inadequate. Under this statute a draft was planned by the War Department, to be enforced by provost marshals nominated by state governors and appointed by the department. Political resistance in the states prevented implementation of this plan. At length, in the Enrollment Act of March 1863, Congress instituted an exclusively national system of conscription. Directed at male citizens ages twenty to forty-five and foreigners who declared their intention to become citizens, the draft law omitted all reference to the state militia. Conscription was to be enforced by federal provost marshals under a Provost Marshal General, operating under an administrative structure organized according to congressional districts. The Civil War draft, which permitted substitutes and money commutation, aroused widespread and often violent opposition and was directly responsible for inducting only six percent of the total Union military force. Nevertheless, it proved to be a decisive constitutional precedent on which the federal government relied in meeting its manpower needs in the wars of the twentieth century. (See SELECTIVE SERVICE ACTS.)

Closely related to the raising of armies was the task of maintaining internal security on the home front against the treasonable and disloyal acts of persons interfering with the war effort. In this sphere too the Union government exercised previously unused powers, asserting an unwonted sovereignty in local affairs that challenged the states' exclusive power to regulate civil and political liberty.

The law against TREASON, the elements of which had been defined in the Constitution, was the most formidable instrument for protecting national security outside the theater of war. Yet in its various manifestations—the Treason Act of 1790 requiring the death penalty and the Seditious Conspiracies Act of 1861 and the treason provisions of the CONFISCATION ACT of 1862 imposing less severe penalties—it was inapplicable in the South as long as federal courts could not operate there. It was also unsuited to the task of containing the less than treasonable activities of Confederate sympathizers and opponents of the war in the North. Loyalty oaths were a second internal security measure. The third, and by far the most important, component of Union internal security policy was military detention of persons suspected of disloyal activities, suspension of the writ of HABEAS CORPUS, and the imposition of martial law.

In April 1861 and on several occasions thereafter, President Lincoln authorized military commanders in specific areas to arrest and deny the writ of habeas corpus to persons engaging in or suspected of disloyal practices, such as interfering with troop movements or discouraging enlistments. In September 1862 the President issued a general proclamation that such persons were liable to trial by military commission or court-martial. Initially the State Department supervised civilian arrests made by secret service agents, federal marshals, and military officers. In February 1862 the War Department assumed responsibility for this practice and created a commission to examine the causes of arrests and provide for the release of persons deemed to be political prisoners. Congress further shaped internal security policy in the HABEAS CORPUS ACT of March 1863, requiring the secretaries of war and state to provide lists of prisoners to federal courts for GRAND JURY consideration. If no indictment for violation of federal law should be forthcoming, a prisoner was to be released upon taking an oath of allegiance.

The Union government arrested approximately 18,000 civilians, almost all of whom were released after brief detention for precautionary rather than punitive purposes. The policy was extremely controversial, however, for what Unionists might consider a precaution to prevent interference with the war effort could easily be regarded by others as punishment for political dissent. Evaluation of internal security policy depended upon conflicting interpretations of CIVIL LIBERTIES guarantees under the Constitution, and differing perceptions of what critics and opponents of the government were in reality doing. As with conscription, however, there was no denying that internal security measures had a significant impact on federal-state relations.

In carrying out this policy the federal government for the first time intervened significantly in local regulation of civil and political liberty. Not only did the federal government make arbitrary or irregular arrests but it also temporarily suspended the publication of many newspapers. Not surprisingly, considering the traditional exclusivity of state power over civil liberty and the partisan context in which the internal security question was debated, the states resisted this extension of federal authority. In sev-

eral states persons adversely affected by internal security measures, or by enforcement of federal laws and orders concerning conscription, trade restrictions, internal revenue, or emancipation, initiated litigation charging federal officers with violations of state law, such as false arrest, unlawful seizure, kidnaping, assault, and battery. Under prewar federalism no general recourse was available to national officials involved as defendants in state litigation of this sort. Congress remedied this defect, however, in the Habeas Corpus Act of 1863.

The 1863 act provided that orders issued by the President or under his authority should be a defense in all courts against any civil or criminal prosecution for any search, seizure, arrest, or imprisonment undertaken in pursuance of such an order. The law further authorized the removal of litigation against national officers from state to federal courts, and it imposed a two-year limit on the initiation of such litigation. On only two previous occasions, in 1815 and 1833 in response to state interference with customs collection, had Congress given protection for federal officers acting under authority of a specific statute by permitting removal of litigation from state to federal courts. The Habeas Corpus Act of 1863, by contrast, protected actions taken under any federal law or EXECUTIVE ORDER. Critics argued that the law gave immunity rather than indemnity, denied citizens judicial remedies for wrongs done by the government, and usurped state power. The logic of even a circumscribed national sovereignty demanded some means of protection against state JURISDICTION, however, and during reconstruction Congress extended the removal remedy and the federal judiciary upheld its constitutionality. The wartime action marked an important extension of federal jurisdiction that made the national government, at least in time of national security crisis, more able to compete with the states in the regulation of civil liberty.

The most novel and in the long run probably the most important exercise of federal sovereignty during the Civil War led directly to the abolition of slavery and the protection of personal liberty and civil rights by the national government. No constitutional rule was more firmly established than that which prohibited federal interference with slavery in the states that recognized it. The outbreak of hostilities did not abrogate this rule, but it did create the possibility that, under the war power, the federal government might emancipate slaves for military purposes. After prohibiting slavery where it could under its peacetime constitutional authority (in the DISTRICT OF COLUMBIA and in the TERRITORIES), Congress struck at slavery in the Confederacy itself. In the Confiscation Act of 1862, it declared "forever free" slaves belonging to persons in rebellion, those who were captured, or who came within Union army lines. Executive interference with slavery went considerably farther. After trying unsuccessfully in 1862 to persuade loyal slaveholding states to accept a federally sponsored plan for gradual, compensated emancipation to be carried out by the states themselves, Lincoln undertook military emancipation. In the EMANCIPATION PROCLAMATION of January 1, 1863, he declared the freedom of all slaves in states still in rebellion and pledged executive-branch protection of freedmen's personal liberty.

Federal power over personal liberty was further made manifest in the work of local police regulation undertaken by Union armies as they advanced into southern territory. All persons in occupied areas were affected by the rule of federal military commanders, and none more so than freed or escaped slaves. From the first incursions of national force in May 1861, War and Treasury Department officials protected blacks' personal liberty, provided for their most pressing welfare needs in refugee camps, and assisted their assimilation into free society by organizing their labor on abandoned plantations and by recruiting them into the army. In March 1865 Congress placed emancipation-related federal police regulation on a more secure footing by creating the Bureau of Refugees, Freedmen, and Abandoned Lands. Authorized to control all subjects relating to refugees and freedmen for a period of one year after the end of the war, the FREEDMEN'S BUREAU throughout 1865 established courts to protect freedmen's personal liberty and civil rights, in the process superseding the states in their most traditional and jealously guarded governmental function.

Federal emancipation measures, based on the war power, did not accomplish the permanent abolition of slavery as it was recognized in state laws and constitutions. To accomplish this momentous change, and the invasion of state power that it signified, amendment of the Constitution was necessary. Accordingly, Congress in January 1865 approved for submission to the states a constitutional amendment prohibiting slavery or involuntary servitude, except as a punishment for crime, in the United States or any place subject to its jurisdiction. Section 2 of the amendment gave Congress authority to enforce the prohibition by appropriate legislation.

Controversy surrounded this terse, seemingly straightforward, yet rather delphic pronouncement, which became part of the Constitution in December 1865. Though it appeared to be a legitimate exercise of the amending power under Article V, Democrats argued that the THIRTEENTH AMENDMENT was a wrongful use of that power because it invaded state jurisdiction over local affairs, undermining the sovereign power to fix the status of all persons within a state's borders and thus destroying the unspoken premise on which the Constitution and the government had been erected in 1787. The Republican fram-

ers of the amendment for their part were uncertain about the scope and effect of the guarantee of personal liberty that they would write into the nation's organic law. At the least, the amendment prohibited chattel slavery, or property in people; many of its supporters believed it also secured the full range of civil rights appurtenant to personal liberty that distinguished a free republican society. No determination of this question was required in order to send the amendment to the states, however, and when a year later the precise scope of the guarantees provided and congressional enforcement power became issues in reconstruction, more detailed and specific measures, such as the CIVIL RIGHTS ACT OF 1866 and the FOURTEENTH AMENDMENT, were deemed necessary. Constitutionally speaking, the Thirteenth Amendment played a minor role in reconstruction.

The federal government further exercised sovereignty characteristic of a nation-state in the sphere of economic policy. This development raised few questions of constitutional propriety; the instruments for accomplishing it lay ready to hand in the ALEXANDER HAMILTON-John Marshall doctrines of BROAD CONSTRUCTION and IMPLIED POWERS. These doctrines had fallen into desuetude in the Jacksonian era, when mercantilist-minded state governments effectively determined economic policy. The exodus of Southerners from the national government in 1861 altered the political balance, however, and Republicans in control of the wartime Congress seized the opportunity to adopt centralizing economic legislation. They raised the tariff for protective purposes, authorized construction of a transcontinental railway, facilitated settlement on the public domain (HOMESTEAD ACT), provided federal aid to higher education (MORRILL ACT), established a uniform currency asserted federal control over the nation's banking institutions, and taxed the American people in innovative ways (income tax, DIRECT TAX). These measures laid the foundation for increasing federal ECONOMIC REGULATION in the late nineteenth and early twentieth centuries. Yet they did not make the determination of economic policy an exclusively national function. In this field, as in civil rights, the federal government's acquisition of a distinct and substantial share of sovereignty diminished, but by no means obliterated, state power.

As the federal government gained power relative to the states during the war, so within the SEPARATION OF POWERS structure of the national government the executive expanded its authority relative to the other branches. Lincoln was the instrument of this constitutional change. Unlike his predecessor Buchanan, Lincoln was willing to acknowledge the necessity of an inflexible defense of the Union during the secession crisis, and after the bombardment of Fort Sumter he acted swiftly and unhesitatingly to commit the nation to arms.

To raise a fighting force Lincoln called the state militia into national service, ordered—without authority from Congress—a 40,000-man increase in the regular army and navy, requested 42,000 volunteers, and proclaimed a blockade of ports in the seceded states. He also instituted the main elements of the internal security program previously described, closed the postal service to treasonable correspondence, directed that $2,000,000 be paid out of the federal treasury, and pledged the credit of the United States for $250,000,000. Lincoln did all this without congressional authority, but not without regard for Congress. Ordering the militia into national service, he called Congress into session to meet in mid-summer. Directing the enlargement of the army and navy, he said he would submit these actions to Congress. He did so, and Congress voted approval of the President's military orders, "as if they had been done under the previous express authority and direction of the Congress." Thereafter Lincoln was ever mindful of the lawmaking branch, and in some respects deferential to it. Yet in war-related matters he continued to take unilateral actions. Thus he proclaimed martial law, suspended habeas corpus, suppressed newspaper publication, issued orders for the conduct of armies in the field, ordered slave emancipation, and directed the political reorganization of occupied southern states.

How could these extraordinary actions be rationalized under the nation's organic law? The question aroused bitter controversy at the time, giving rise to charges of dictatorship which continued to find echo in scholarly debate. No more penetrating analysis of the problem has ever been offered than that presented by Lincoln himself.

In his message to Congress of July 4, 1861, Lincoln said his actions were required by "public necessity" and "popular demand." Referring to suspension of the writ of habeas corpus, he stated that if he violated "some single law," his doing so was justified on the ground that it would save the government." "[A]re all the laws, *but one*, to go unexecuted, and the government itself go to pieces, lest that one be violated?" he asked. On another occasion Lincoln posed the question whether it was possible to lose the nation and yet preserve the Constitution. "By general law life and limb must be protected," he reasoned, "yet often a limb must be amputated to save a life; but a life is never wisely given to save a limb." This appears to mean that the Constitution might be set aside, as a limb is amputated, to save the life of the nation. The inference can be drawn that emergency action, while expedient, is unconstitutional.

What is required to understand the lawfulness of the emergency measures in question, however, is not legalistic analysis of the constitutional text but rather consideration of the fundamental relationship between the nation and the Constitution. Lincoln's principal argument was that the steps taken to defend the government were constitutional because the Constitution implicitly sanctioned its own preservation. The Constitution in this view was not a mere appendage of the living nation or a derivative expression or reflection of national life, as a legal code might be considered to be. Coeval and in an ultimate political sense coterminous with it, the Constitution *was* the nation. This conception is present in Lincoln's statement of April 1864 that "measures, otherwise unconstitutional, might become lawful, by becoming indispensable to the preservation of the constitution, through the preservation of the nation." "Is there," he asked in his message of July 1861, "in all republics, this inherent and fatal weakness? Must a government, of necessity, be too *strong* for the liberties of its own people, or too *weak* to maintain its own existence?" Not that Lincoln conceded to his critics at the level of positivistic, text-based constitutional argument. Concerning habeas corpus suspension, for example, he tenaciously insisted that as the Constitution did not specify who might exercise this power, he was justified in doing so when Congress was not in session. Congress, in fact, subsequently ratified Lincoln's suspension of habeas corpus. Although his argument conformed to the requirements of American constitutional politics, his principal justification of emergency actions was that they were necessary to preserve the substance of political liberty, which was the end both of the Constitution and the Union.

It is sometimes said that Lincoln established in American public law the principle of constitutional dictatorship. Yet at no time did Lincoln exercise unlimited power. The notion of constitutional dictatorship also obscures the fact that although Lincoln applied military power on a far wider scale than previous Presidents, in doing so he merely accelerated a tendency toward expansion of the executive's defensive war-making capability. In 1827 the Supreme Court, in MARTIN V. MOTT, had upheld the President's power under the Militia Act of 1795 to call out the militia (and by extension the army and navy) in the event of actual or imminent invasion. President JAMES K. POLK had used this defensive war-making power to commit the nation to war against Mexico, and Presidents Millard Fillmore and Franklin Pierce had employed military force in circumstances that could have led to wars with foreign states. In his exercise of executive power Lincoln merely widened a trail blazed by his predecessors.

Yet in minor matters unrelated to the war, emancipation, and reconstruction, Lincoln was a passive President. Although as party leader he made effective use of his patronage powers, he did little to influence congressional legislation aside from formal suggestions in annual messages. Moreover he exercised the veto sparingly, gave broad latitude to his department heads, and made little use of the cabinet for policymaking purposes. Lincoln's respect for legislative independence complemented and encouraged another important nineteenth-century constitutional trend—the strengthening of congressional power.

To an extent that is difficult to appreciate in the late twentieth century, nineteenth-century government was preeminently legislative in nature. Lawmakers shaped public policy, resolved constitutional controversies through debate and legislation, controlled the TAXING AND SPENDING process, and exercised significant influence over administration. The years between the presidencies of THOMAS JEFFERSON and ANDREW JACKSON had been a period of legislative assertiveness, and although the struggle over slavery had brought Congress to near-paralysis, still the political foundation existed for wartime exertions of power that anticipated the era of congressional government during and after reconstruction.

Although Congress approved Lincoln's emergency measures in 1861, its action by no means signified general deference to executive power. On the contrary, reciting constitutional provisions that gave Congress power to declare war and regulate the military establishment, members made vigorous claim to exercise the WAR POWER. Accordingly, they raised men and supplies for the war, attempted through the Joint Committee on the Conduct of the War to influence military strategy, modified internal security policy, and enacted laws authorizing confiscation, emancipation, and reconstruction. The need for party unity notwithstanding, the Republican majority in Congress insisted on civilian control over the military, monitored executive department administration, and, in an unusual maneuver in December 1862, even tried to force a change in the cabinet. Tighter internal organization and operational procedures made Congress more powerful as well as more efficient during the war. The speaker of the House, for example, assumed greater control over committee memberships and the flow of legislative business; the party caucus became a more frequent determinant of legislative behavior; and standing committees and their chairmen enjoyed enhanced prestige and influence, gradually superseding select committees as the key agencies for accomplishing legislative tasks. Exercising power conferred by statute in 1857 to punish recalcitrant or uncooperative witnesses, Congress used its investigative authority to extend its governmental grasp.

In the 1930s and 1940s, Civil War historiography regarded conflict between a radical-dominated Congress and the soberly conservative Lincoln administration as the central political struggle of the war. Recent research has shown, however, that disagreement between the Democratic and Republican parties was more significant in shaping the course of political and constitutional events than was the radical versus moderate tension within the Republican party. Conflict occurred between the executive and legislative branches, as much as a result of institutional rivalry inherent in the structure of separated powers as of programmatic differences. Congressional-presidential relations were not notably more strained than they have been in other American wars. Although Lincoln demonstrated the potentially vast power inherent in the presidency, his wartime actions did not measurably extend the executive office beyond the sphere of crisis government. He evinced no tendency toward the so-called stewardship conception of the presidency advanced by THEODORE ROOSEVELT in the early twentieth century. The power of Congress waxed, its wartime achievements in policymaking and internal organization providing a solid basis for a subsequent era of congressional government.

A significant portion of American constitutional history from 1861 to 1865 occurred south of the Potomac, where were manifested many of the same problems and tendencies that appeared in the wartime experience of the United States government. The CONFEDERATE CONSTITUTION, modeled closely on that of the United States, revealed the most bitterly contested issues that had led to the war. It recognized and protected the right of slave property; proclaimed state sovereignty as the basis of the Confederacy; omitted the GENERAL WELFARE clause and the TAXING AND SPENDING POWER contained in the United States Constitution; stated that all federal power was expressly delegated; and prohibited a protective tariff and INTERNAL IMPROVEMENTS appropriations. Yet the right of secession was not recognized, evidence that the Confederacy was intended to be a permanent government.

Confederate constitutional history was marked by war-induced centralization and conflicts between federal and state authority. The Confederate government conscripted soldiers; suspended the writ of habeas corpus and declared martial law; confiscated enemy property and seized for temporary use the property of its own citizens; taxed heavily and imposed tight controls on commerce and industry; and owned and operated munitions, mining, and clothing factories. These actions and policies aroused strong opposition as expressed in the rhetoric of states' rights and through the institutions of state government. Some governors refused to place their troops under the Confederacy's authority and challenged conscription and internal security measures. Many state judges granted writs of habeas corpus that interfered with military recruitment. Lack of effective leverage over the states seriously hampered the Confederate war effort.

The most significant difference between Union and Confederate constitutionalism centered on POLITICAL PARTIES. Driven by the desire to create national unity, Southerners eschewed political party organization as unnecessary and harmful. When political differences arose, they had to find resolution in the conflict-inducing methods of the system of states' rights. In the North, by contrast, political parties continued to compete, with beneficial results. Political disagreements between the government and its Democratic critics were kept within manageable bounds by the concept of a loyal opposition, while among members of the governing party differences were directed into policy alternatives. Moreover, party organization encouraged federal-state cooperation in the implementation of controversial measures like conscription, thus helping to minimize the centrifugal effects of federal organization. Indeed, the persistence of organized party competition, even in the critical year of 1864 when military success was uncertain and the Democratic party campaigned on a platform demanding a cessation of hostilities, was perhaps the most revealing fact in Civil War constitutional history. It showed that despite important changes in federal-state relations and reliance on techniques of emergency government, the American commitment to constitutionalism was firm, even amidst events that tested it most severely.

HERMAN BELZ
(1986)

Bibliography

BELZ, HERMAN 1978 *Emancipation and Equal Rights: Politics and Constitutionalism in the Civil War Era.* New York: Norton.

CURRY, LEONARD P. 1968 *Blueprint for Modern America: Nonmilitary Legislation of the First Civil War Congress.* Nashville, Tenn.: Vanderbilt University Press.

FEHRENBACHER, DON E. 1979 Lincoln and the Constitution. In Cullom Davis, ed., *The Public and Private Lincoln: Contemporary Perspectives.* Carbondale: University of Southern Illinois Press.

HYMAN, HAROLD M. 1973 *A More Perfect Union: The Impact of the Civil War and Reconstruction on the Constitution.* New York: Knopf.

McKITRICK, ERIC 1967 Party Politics and the Union and Confederate War Efforts. In Walter Dean Burnham and William N. Chambers, eds., *The American Party System: Stages of Political Development.* New York: Free Press.

McLAUGHLIN, ANDREW C. 1936 Lincoln, the Constitution, and Democracy. *International Journal of Ethics* 47:1–24.

RANDALL, JAMES G. (1926) 1951 *Constitutional Problems under Lincoln,* rev. ed. Urbana: University of Illinois Press.

WEIGLEY, RUSSELL F. 1967 *A History of the United States Army.* New York: Macmillan.

CONSTITUTIONAL HISTORY, 1865–1877

The great political and constitutional issue of the period 1865–1877 was the RECONSTRUCTION of the Union after the CIVIL WAR. Reconstruction presented several closely re-

lated issues. There were issues involving the nature of the federal system. One of these arose even before the war ended: what was the constitutional relationship to the Union of the states that had attempted to secede? Another arose after the southern states were restored to normal relations: what powers did the national government retain to protect the rights of its citizens? There was the problem of defining the constitutional status of black Americans—a problem that finally forced Americans to define American CITIZENSHIP and the rights incident to it. Also, because the President and Congress disagreed on these issues, Reconstruction brought about a crisis in legislative-executive relations that culminated in the only impeachment of an American President. Finally, the Reconstruction controversy had a powerful effect upon Americans' conception of the proper role of government, laying the groundwork for the development of laissez-faire constitutionalism.

These issues would be adjusted in the context of the established party system. During the war, the Republican party worked diligently and fairly successfully to broaden its support. Renaming their organization the Union party, Republican leaders accepted as colleagues men who had been influential Democrats until the outbreak of war. In 1864 the party nominated Tennessee's Democratic former governor and senator, ANDREW JOHNSON, to the vice-presidency. Despite this, the Union party, which would revive the name Republican after the war, was the heir to the governmental activism of the old Federalist and Whig parties. Likewise Republicans inherited nationalist theories of the federal system. (See UNION, THEORIES OF THE.), The war confirmed and extended their distrust of STATES' RIGHTS doctrines; yet many Republicans would resist going too far in the direction of "consolidation" of the Union at the expense of traditional areas of state jurisdiction. On the other hand, the majority of Democrats had remained loyal to their party and its heritage of states' rights and small government. Naturally, the Reconstruction issue, which involved both questions, found the two parties ranged against one another.

Northerners faced a paradox when they considered the status of the Confederate states at war's end. They had denied that a state could leave the Union, but few wanted the same governments that had attempted secession to return as if nothing had happened. Only so-called Peace Democrats argued that the Union should be restored through negotiations between the Confederate state governments and the national government. Somehow, Republicans and War Democrats insisted, the national government must have power to secure some changes in the South and in the federal system before final restoration. As the war progressed, and especially in 1865 and 1866, when they were forced to grapple with the problem, Republicans propounded a variety of constitutional justifications for such power. Unlike Democrats, who insisted that state government had existed before the Union and independent of it, Republicans insisted that states could exist only in the Union and by virtue of their connection with it. Thus, by trying to secede, the southern states had committed STATE SUICIDE, in the graphic language of Senator CHARLES SUMNER; or, as other Republicans put it, they had "forfeited their rights." Given this view, there were several ways to justify national power over Southerners. Many Republicans argued that if Southerners now lacked state governments, Congress must restore them under the clause of the Constitution requiring the national government to guarantee a REPUBLICAN FORM OF GOVERNMENT to each state. Moreover, in the 1849 case of LUTHER V. BORDEN the Supreme Court, citing this clause, had seemed to concede to the "political branches" of the government the power to recognize whether a state government was legitimate in case of doubt. The Court had held that the admission of state representatives to Congress was conclusive. With state governments defunct, Republicans argued, the Court's holding meant that the political branches of the national government would have final say about what government would be recognized as restored to the Union and when that recognition would take place. Implicit in this power was the authority to determine what sort of government would be acceptable.

But when some Republicans insisted that the GUARANTEE CLAUSE entitled the national government to require changes it believed necessary for states to be considered republican, most of their colleagues rebelled. Such an interpretation would give the national government power to modify "unrepublican" political and civil laws in states that had never left the Union.

Other Republicans found a safer source of power over states that had forfeited their rights: the national government had recovered control over the territory and citizens of the South through exercise of its WAR POWERS, which had overridded the peacetime provision of the Constitution that guaranteed citizens' and states' rights. The government could continue to hold Southerners in this "grasp of war" until they agreed to meet the government's conditions for the restoration of peace. On this theory, national power would be temporary, providing no precedent for intruding in states that had not been in rebellion.

Finally, other Republicans—those who wanted the most radical changes in southern society—argued that, having broken away from national authority de facto, the southern states were conquered provinces no different from any other newly acquired territory. Thus Southerners were subject to the direct control of the national government, which ought to provide ordinary territorial governments through which they could govern themselves under the revisory power of Congress. In this way the national

government would retain authority to legislate directly for the South until new states were created there—establishing a public school system, for example, or confiscating the great landed estates and distributing them among the people as small farms. But this theory also seemed too radical for most Northerners, and most Republicans endorsed the more limited "grasp-of-war" doctrine.

Congress was adjourned in April and May 1865, as Lincoln was assassinated and the war ended. Lincoln's successor, the former Democrat Johnson, accepted the key elements of the WADE-DAVIS BILL developed during the war, but he followed Lincoln's policy of carrying it out under presidential authority, rather than calling Congress back into session to enact Reconstruction legislation. Johnson called for white, male voters in each southern state to elect a state constitutional convention as soon as fifty percent of them had taken a loyalty oath that would entitle them to AMNESTY. Thus blacks would have to depend on governments elected by whites for protection of life and property. The conventions were required to pronounce their states' SECESSION ordinances null and void, repudiate debts incurred by their Confederate state governments, and abolish slavery. Finally, the southern states would have to ratify the proposed THIRTEENTH AMENDMENT, which abolished slavery throughout the land. Then the conventions could organize elections to ratify the new constitutions, elect state officials, and elect congressmen. By December 1865, as Congress reconvened, this process had been completed in most of the southern states and would soon be completed in the remainder.

At first Johnson was vague about his constitutional theory of Reconstruction, but as congressional opposition developed his supporters articulated a position that left little power to Congress. Secession had merely "suspended" the operation of legal governments in the South, they insisted. As COMMANDER-IN-CHIEF of the armed forces, the President had the duty under the government's war powers to reanimate state governments. War powers were inherently presidential, Johnson insisted. He had exercised them in such a way as to preserve the traditional federal system. Congress could do no more than exercise its constitutional power to "judge of the elections, returns and qualifications of its own members" by deciding whether individual congressmen-elect were disqualified by their roles in the war; it could not deny REPRESENTATION to whole states. Gaining the support of northern Democrats for this states'-rights-oriented policy, Johnson set the stage for a bitter struggle over the relative powers of the branches of the national government.

A majority of congressmen might have acquiesced in the President's position had they been confident that loyalists would control the southern state governments or that the rights of the newly freed slaves would be respected there. However, it soon became apparent that the states were controlled by former rebels and that the rights of the freedmen would be severely circumscribed. Compounding the problem, the ex-Confederate-dominated South would increase its congressional representation now that slavery was abolished; the constitutional provision counting only three-fifths of the slave population would no longer apply. All this persuaded congressional Republicans to refuse immediate admission of southern state representatives to Congress and to seek a compromise with the President.

There were two thrusts to the congressional policy: protection of freedmen's rights and a new system of apportionment of representation in Congress. Most congressional leaders believed that the Thirteenth Amendment automatically conferred citizenship upon the freedmen when it abolished slavery. Moreover, the amendment's second section authorized Congress to pass legislation appropriate to enforce abolition. Republicans acted upon this understanding by passing a new FREEDMEN'S BUREAU bill, augmenting one passed during the war, and proposing the bill that became the CIVIL RIGHTS ACT OF 1866. The first, a temporary measure justified under the war powers, authorized an Army bureau to supervise the transition from slave to free labor, protecting the rights and interests of the freedmen in the process. The second was designed to secure permanent protection for the freedmen in their basic rights. Few Republicans thought that Americans would accept so drastic a change in the federal system as to give Congress instead of the states the job of protecting people in their ordinary rights. Therefore they adopted the idea of leaving that job to the states but requiring them to treat all groups equally. At the same time, Republicans intended to require equality only in the protection of *basic* rights of citizenship. This goal forced them to define just what those rights were. So the Civil Rights Act declared all persons born in the United States, except Indians who did not pay taxes, to be citizens of the United States; it granted all citizens, regardless of race, the same basic rights as white citizens. What were these basic rights of citizenship? "To make and enforce contracts; to sue, be parties, and give evidence; to inherit, purchase, lease, sell, hold, and convey real and personal property; and to full and equal benefit of all laws and proceedings for the security of persons and property" and to "be subject to like punishment, pains, and penalties." To secure these rights without centralizing power of ordinary legislation in Washington, the bill permitted citizens to remove legal cases from state to federal court jurisdiction in any state that did not end discrimination. (See CIVIL RIGHTS REMOVAL.) The idea was to force states to abolish RACIAL DISCRIMINATION in their own laws in order to preserve their jurisdictions. As its author explained, the act would "have no operation in any State where the laws are equal, where

all persons have the same civil rights without regard to color or race."

At the same time Republicans prepared a fourteenth amendment to define citizenship and its rights; to change the way seats in Congress were apportioned, so as to reflect the number of voters rather than gross population; to disqualify leading Confederates from holding political office; and to guarantee payment of the United States debt while repudiating the Confederate debt. Congress was to have power to enforce this amendment, too, by "appropriate" legislation.

Republicans expected Johnson to endorse these measures, which after all did not attempt to replace the governments he had instituted in the South, and they expected Southerners to signify their acceptance of these "terms of peace" by ratifying the new amendment. However, Johnson insisted that the Republican program would revolutionize the federal system. He vetoed the legislation and urged Southerners to reject the proposed amendment. At the same time he attacked the Republicans bitterly. Republicans responded by passing the Civil Rights Act over Johnson's veto, enacting the new Freedman's Bureau Act, and sending the FOURTEENTH AMENDMENT to the states for RATIFICATION. To the voters, they stressed the moderation of their proposals, and Johnson's supporters were badly beaten in the congressional elections of 1866. Nonetheless, Southerners followed Johnson's advice and refused to ratify the amendment.

This refusal angered and frightened Republican congressmen. If the conflict drifted into stalemate, northern voters might tire of it and blame the Republicans for not completing restoration. Outraged at southern recalcitrance and Johnson's "betrayal," the Republicans passed new Reconstruction laws over his veto early in 1867. Designating Johnson's southern governments as temporary only, the Republicans instructed Southerners to begin the process anew. This time many leading Confederates would be disfranchised while the freedmen were permitted to vote. New state conventions would have to be elected to write new constitutions banning racial discrimination in civil and political rights. The voters would have to ratify these constitutions, and then newly elected state officials would have to ratify the Fourteenth Amendment. In 1869 the Republican Congress proposed to the states the FIFTEENTH AMENDMENT, banning racial discrimination in voting; southern states that had not yet finished the process of being readmitted would be required to ratify this amendment, too. In some ways the new program was a relief to Republicans. They expected that once southern blacks could vote, their state governments would have to provide them with the protection of the laws, thus rendering unnecessary the exercise of national power and preserving the old balance of the federal system.

Until the southern states complied with the new Reconstruction laws, they were to be under the control of the Army, subject to martial law and, if necessary, military courts. Southerners insisted that this whole program was unconstitutional, and they tried to persuade the Supreme Court to declare it so. In 1867 and 1868 representatives of Johnson's state governments asked the Supreme Court to enjoin Johnson and his secretary of war, respectively, from enforcing the MILITARY RECONSTRUCTION ACTS. They hoped for success, because the majority of the Justices were suspected of opposing the Republican program. In earlier cases, including EX PARTE MILLIGAN (1866), a narrow majority had held that military courts could not operate upon civilians where civil courts were functioning, and in the TEST OATH CASES the Court had ruled unconstitutional laws requiring persons to swear oaths of past loyalty in order to follow certain professions. However, even Johnson would not sustain an effort to secure Court intervention in so plainly a political issue, and the Court dismissed both suits. (See MISSISSIPPI V. JOHNSON.)

Southerners tried again in EX PARTE MCCARDLE (1869), where a Southerner convicted of murder in a military court asked for a write of HABEAS CORPUS, citing the Supreme Court's Milligan decision. At least some Reconstruction laws might be jeopardized if the Court endorsed this argument, and Republicans responded by repealing the law under which McCardle had brought his suit. The Court grudgingly acquiesced in the repeal but virtually invited a new application for the writ under another law.

These developments produced ambivalent feelings about the courts among Republicans. Before the war the judiciary had tended to sustain laws protecting slavery and discrimination against black Americans. During the war Chief Justice ROGER B. TANEY had seemed to obstruct the military effort, and the Court's course since the war had hardly been reassuring. Fearing judicial interference, several leading Republicans proposed narrowing the Court's jurisdiction and requiring a two-thirds majority of Justices to rule a congressional law unconstitutional, or denying that power altogether. On the other hand, the judiciary was the only national institution besides the military capable of enforcing the new laws protecting the rights of American citizens. Not only did Congress refrain from passing the court-limitation bills but it also expanded judicial authority by making the national judiciary the forum in which citizens and even businesses were to secure justice if their rights were denied in the states. Indeed, even as Republicans worried whether the Court would impair Reconstruction, in their roles as circuit court judges the Justices were upholding the power of the national government to protect rights under the Thirteenth and Fourteenth Amendments. Altogether, the Reconstruction era witnessed a great expansion of the jurisdiction and activity of the federal courts.

While the southern attack on the Reconstruction laws failed in the Supreme Court, Johnson was able to use against the laws the fact that they employed the military in their enforcement. As COMMANDER-IN-CHIEF of the armed forces, Johnson sought to limit the authority of military commanders and to give command of occupying forces to officers sympathetic to his position. When Secretary of War EDWIN M. STANTON resisted these efforts, Johnson suspended him from office and appointed the popular General ULYSSES S. GRANT in his place. By late 1867 Johnson's obstruction was so successful that Reconstruction was grinding to a halt, with white Southerners ready to prevent ratification of their new, egalitarian constitutions.

Many Republicans denied that the President had the constitutional right to obstruct legislation in this way, and they urged the House of Representatives to impeach him. However, most Republicans were frightened of taking so radical a step, and many insisted that IMPEACHMENT lay only for indictable crimes. Despite his obstructionism, Johnson had not clearly broken any law, and they would not support impeachment until he did. Therefore in December 1867 the first impeachment resolution failed.

However, in February 1868 Johnson did finally seem to break a law. As noted, Johnson had earlier suspended Secretary of War Stanton. He had done this while the Senate was adjourned, conforming to the TENURE OF OFFICE ACT, passed in 1867, which made all removals of government officers temporary until the Senate confirmed a successor, or, in certain circumstances, voted to accept the President's reasons for removal. In Stanton's case, the Senate in 1867 refused to concur in the removal, and Stanton returned to office. Now Johnson defied the Senate and the law, ordering Stanton's permanent removal. The House impeached him immediately, and from March through May the Senate established rules of procedure, heard arguments and testimony, and deliberated.

Although many questions were raised during Johnson's trial in the Senate, the decision finally turned for most senators on whether they believed Stanton was in reality covered by the Tenure of Office Act. Despite Johnson's initial compliance with the act, his lawyers persuaded just enough Republican senators that the act did not cover Stanton, and Johnson was acquitted. But the price for acquittal was Johnson's promise to end his obstruction of the Reconstruction laws. With that interference ended, most southern states adopted new state constitutions, and in nearly all those states Republicans took control of the governments.

The new southern constitutions and Republican governments were among the most progressive in the nation.

Elected mainly by black voters, southern Republican leaders thought they could secure enough white support to guarantee continued victory by using government power to promote prosperity and provide services. Thus they emulated northern Republican policies, using state taxes and credit to subsidize railroads and canals, to develop natural resources, and to control flooding along the Mississippi River. They created the first centralized state public school systems and opened state hospitals and asylums. At the same time southern Republicans were committed to improving the conditions of former slaves, both on principle and to keep the support of their largest constituency. They passed laws to provide them with the same state services that whites received, put blacks in important positions, banned discrimination in many businesses, shaped labor laws to protect workers' interests, and appointed local judges who would be sympathetic to blacks in disputes with whites.

All these activities required the states to spend and borrow far more money than they had before the war. Because it was primarily whites who owned enough property to pay taxes, the Republican policies redistributed wealth, something not acceptable to nineteenth-century Americans. Bitterly, white Southerners charged that "ignorant," "brutal" voters were being duped by venal politicians with promises of "class legislation." Southern whites denied that such governments were really democratic. Unable to defeat Republicans at the polls in most states, they turned to violence and fraud. From 1868 through 1872, midnight riders, known by such names as the Ku Klux Klan, terrorized local Republican leaders. After 1872 the violence became more organized and more closely linked to anti-Republican political organizations.

A few southern Republican governors were at first able to suppress the violence. But by 1870 they were appealing to the national government for help, thus causing serious problems for national Republican leaders. Republicans had hoped that enfranchising the freedmen would protect them without a massive expansion of national power. Moreover, everyone believed that legislation must be based on the Fourteenth and Fifteenth Amendments, ignoring the earlier view that the Thirteenth Amendment gave power to protect citizens' basic rights. But the language of the two later amendments only protected rights against STATE ACTION, and Republicans had a difficult time justifying laws protecting blacks and white Republicans from attacks by private individuals. Nonetheless, in 1871 Republicans passed such laws and also authorized President Grant to take drastic action to crush violence, including suspension of the writ of habeas corpus. They insisted that the Fourteenth Amendment required states to protect their residents; failure to do so would amount to state denial of EQUAL PROTECTION.

At first this response seemed successful, and violence abated. However, it soon flared anew. In many southern states Republicans claimed that Democratic violence and intimidation should nullify apparent Democratic majorities in elections, and they refused to count Democratic votes from areas where violence was most intense. In return Democrats organized armed militia to press their claims. In state after state Republicans had to appeal for national troops to protect them against such opponents. Where it was difficult to afford protection, the Democratic militias—often called "White Leagues"—drove Republican officials from office.

It became ever more difficult for national Republicans to respond. More and more Northerners feared that continued national intervention in the South was undermining the federal system. At the same time the Supreme Court manifested its concern to preserve a balance between state and national authority. In *Texas v. White* (1869) the Justices emphasized the importance of states in the Union, and in *Collector v. Day* (1871) they seemed to endorse the doctrine of DUAL FEDERALISM, by denying the national government's power to tax the incomes of officers of the "sovereign" states. In the SLAUGHTERHOUSE CASES (1873) the Court, in an implicitly dual federalist opinion, ruled that national and state citizenships were distinct. The Fourteenth Amendment protected only a limited number of rights inherent in national citizenship; those rights usually identified as basic remained the sole province of the states. This decision severely curtailed national power to protect black Southerners and southern Republicans from violence. In UNITED STATES V. CRUIKSHANK (1876) the Court held invalid indictments against white conspirators who had massacred blacks, in part on the grounds that the Fourteenth Amendment was aimed only at state action and could not justify prosecution of private individuals.

At the same time a growing number of Northerners were coming to share Southerners' concern about "class legislation." To these Northerners, calls for a protective tariff, for artificial inflation of the currency, for repudiation of state-guaranteed railroad bonds, for regulation of railroad rates, and for government imposition of an eight-hour work day all indicated a growing clamor for "class legislation" in the North. City political organizations, which taxed urban property holders to provide services to the less wealthy, seemed to be engaging in the same kind of "plunder" that southern whites alleged against their Republican governments. Many Northerners began to argue that the state and national constitutions required judges to overturn class legislation. They had some initial successes. The Supreme Court ruled part of the Legal Tender Act unconstitutional, only to overrule itself a year later (see LEGAL TENDER CASES), and state courts ruled that business and railroad promotion laws exceeded legislative power. However, the courts generally declined the invitation to write the doctrine of "laissez faire" into the Constitution. The majority in the *Slaughterhouse Cases* rejected the argument, and the Court sustained broad state regulatory power over businesses AFFECTED WITH A PUBLIC INTEREST—railroads, grain warehouses, and others that were left undefined. (See GRANGER CASES.)

Nonetheless, the conviction was growing that the sort of wealth-redistributing policies followed by southern Republicans was fundamentally wrong and so was fear that such ideas might spread north. More and more Northerners agreed with southern whites that southern proponents of such policies were "carpetbaggers" and "scalawags." By 1875 President Grant was refusing to help his beleaguered political allies; all but three southern states had returned to Democratic control, often through force and intimidation; and white Southerners were planning similarly violent campaigns to "redeem" the last three in 1876. Their effort to do so led to one of the greatest political and constitutional crises in American history.

In the presidential election of 1876 the violence and fraud endemic in the South threatened to engulf the nation. In the three remaining Republican states in the South—South Carolina, Louisiana, and Florida—Democrats engaged in campaigns of violence and intimidation. Republican officials threw out votes from districts they claimed Democrats had carried by force. Democrats once again charged fraud and armed to confront Republicans; southern Republicans once again appealed to the national government for protection. However, this time the outcome of the presidential election itself turned upon who had carried these three states. Without them, Democrat Samuel J. Tilden was one electoral vote short of victory. Republican RUTHERFORD B. HAYES needed the electoral votes of all three to win.

As the time drew near to count the electoral vote and declare a winner, two sets of electoral votes were sent to Congress from each of the contested states—the Republican votes certified by appropriate state agencies, and Democratic competitors. The Constitution requires electoral votes to be counted by the president of the Senate (normally the vice-president of the United States) in the presence of both houses of Congress. Republicans insisted that, absent a specific congressional resolution governing the subject, the Republican president pro tempore of the Senate would have the power to decide which set of votes were the correct ones to count (the vice-president having died in office). Controlling the Senate, Republicans prepared to block any contrary resolution that might come from the Democratic House. Democrats, on the other hand, insisted that if the two houses of Congress could not agree upon which set of votes was legitimate, neither could be counted. Then no candidate would have a majority, and according to the Constitution the House would name the winner.

With no clear precedent, and with the Supreme Court not yet accepted as the usual arbiter of such constitutional disputes, it seemed that the conflict might be resolved by force. Republican President Grant controlled the Army; if he recognized a President counted in by the Republicans, a competitor named by the House would have a hard time pressing his claim. To counter this Republican program, Democrats threatened forcible resistance.

As Americans demanded a peaceful end to the crisis, the two sides were forced to compromise. Congress passed a resolution turning all disputed electoral votes over to an Electoral Commission of ten congressmen and five Supreme Court Justices for decision. The commission decision would stand in each case unless *both* houses voted to disagree to it—an early example of a LEGISLATIVE VETO.

To the Democrats' dismay, the three Republican Supreme Court Justices joined the five Republican congressmen on the commission to decide every disputed vote in favor of the Republican candidate. In each case the majority accepted the votes certified by the agency authorized by state law. Republicans insisted the commission had no power "to go behind" these returns.

Furious, Democrats charged that this was a partisan decision. Many of them urged Democratic congressmen to prevent the completion of the count by filibustering, saying that the House could name the President if the count were not completed by the constitutional deadline of March 3. But most Democrats felt that Americans would not support such a radical course after Democrats had agreed to the compromise. To strengthen these moderates, Hayes promised not to help southern Republicans against rival claimants for state offices. As a result Hayes was declared President just within the deadline. When he honored his commitment to the Democrats, the last southern Republican governments collapsed, even though the Republicans had claimed state victories based on the same election returns that elected Hayes. (See COMPROMISE OF 1877.)

The collapse of Reconstruction was related directly to the development of constitutional commitments that would dominate the last quarter of the nineteenth century. It marked a renewal of a state-centered federalism that would characterize succeeding years. Furthermore, it was a direct result of the growing fear of "class legislation" that would lead to the acceptance of "laissez-faire constitutionalism" in the 1890s.

MICHAEL LES BENEDICT
(1986)

Bibliography

BENEDICT, MICHAEL LES 1975 *A Compromise of Principle: Congressional Republicans and Reconstruction, 1863–1869.* New York: W. W. Norton.

FAIRMAN, CHARLES 1971 *Reconstruction and Reunion, 1864–*

88—*Part One*, Volume 6 of *The History of the Supreme Court of the United States*. New York: Macmillan.

GILLETTE, WILLIAM 1979 *Retreat from Reconstruction, 1869–1879*. Baton Rouge: Louisiana State University Press.

HYMAN, HAROLD M. 1973 *A More Perfect Union: The Impact of the Civil War and Reconstruction upon the Constitution*. New York: Knopf.

MCKITRICK, ERIC L. 1960 *Andrew Johnson and Reconstruction*. Chicago: University of Chicago Press.

STAMPP, KENNETH M. 1965 *The Era of Reconstruction, 1865–1877*. New York: Knopf.

CONSTITUTIONAL HISTORY, 1877–1901

American public life during the CIVIL WAR–RECONSTRUCTION years was dominated by clashes over constitutional issues of the most basic sort: race and CITIZENSHIP; FEDERALISM, STATES' RIGHTS, and the Union; the power of the President, Congress, and the courts; and the bounds of military and civil authority. This was a time when the interpretation of the Constitution held center stage in American public life. The resolution of fundamental issues was sought in Congress and the courts, in party politics and elections, ultimately through force of arms. Merely to list the milestones of the period—the great debate over SLAVERY IN THE TERRITORIES; *Dred Scott v. Sandford* (1857); SECESSION and CIVIL WAR; the Thirteenth, Fourteenth, and FIFTEENTH AMENDMENTS; the CIVIL RIGHTS, Reconstruction, and Enforcement Acts; and the IMPEACHMENT OF ANDREW JOHNSON—is to make the point that during the years from 1850 to 1877 the Constitution provided the context in which Americans expressed, and fought over, their most fundamental social beliefs.

How different was the period that followed! The structure of government—the relationship of the states and territories to the Union; the powers of Congress, the courts, and the President; the role of the POLITICAL PARTIES—often was a matter of political but rarely of constitutional concern. Nor were the major economic and social issues of the time confronted primarily in constitutional terms. It is revealing that no amendment to the Constitution was adopted between 1870 and 1913.

This does not mean, though, that constitutional issues had no place in American public policy between 1877 and 1900. Rather, what happened was that a sea change was taking place in American life, and the issues generated by this change took time to assume a full-fledged constitutional guise. Just as the basic constitutional issues of states' rights and slavery did not fully emerge until the 1850s, so too the constitutional issues generated by the rise of an urban-industrial society did not come into their own until after 1900, in many respects not until the 1930s.

Where should we look, in the late nineteenth century, for the seeds of the great twentieth-century effort to adapt the Constitution to the realities of an urban-industrial society? The primary structural concern of the time was over the role of the judiciary, and here was a foreshadowing of the conflict between the administrative state and the representative state that would assume such great importance after 1900. Second, economic issues—in particular, those involving the regulation of large enterprises—were a fruitful area of contention in the late nineteenth century. And finally, questions of citizenship and race—partly a legacy of the Civil War-Reconstruction years but also a product of the social strains generated by an industrializing society—continued to engage the attention of the public and of policymakers.

Frank Goodnow in his *Comparative Administrative Law* (1893) observed that while constitutional issues set the terms of debate over the character of American government before the Civil War, administrative issues took center stage afterward. Certainly it seemed that, as much as anything could, the war had settled the question of the relationship of the states to the Union. Nor did the desuetude of the post-Reconstruction Presidency, the dominance of Congress, or the still-nascent administrative state generate much in the way of constitutional debate.

Late nineteenth-century Presidents were caught up in party politics and patronage and did relatively little to formulate and conduct public policy. But America's evolution into a powerful industrial nation began to leave its mark. RUTHERFORD B. HAYES and GROVER CLEVELAND used federal troops to restore order during the railroad strikes of 1877 and 1894. The federal bureaucracy, though small, was growing; and something like a professional civil service took form, in part under the aegis of the Civil Service Commission established by the PENDLETON ACT of 1883. Tariff and fiscal policy came to be more closely identified with presidential leadership. But in constitutional terms the chief executive at the end of the century was little changed from what he had been in 1877.

Congress, however, became a considerably more powerful and effective branch of government during this period. WOODROW WILSON in 1885 called "Congressional Government" the "predominant and controlling force, the centre and source of all motive and of all regulative power." This enhanced authority came from the fact that state and local party leaders served as senators and representatives; from congressional control over budgetary and fiscal policy; and from the increasing regularity and stability of congressional leadership and procedure.

Perhaps the most striking change in the balance of governmental powers during the late nineteenth century was the rise of JUDICIAL ACTIVISM. The Supreme Court found only two federal laws unconstitutional between 1790 and

1864, but it voided federal acts in seven cases between 1868 and 1877 and in eleven cases between 1878 and 1899. The Court voided state acts in thirty-eight cases before 1865, in thirty-five cases between 1865 and 1873, and in ninety-one cases between 1874 and 1899. A debate as old as the Constitution heated up once again in the 1890s: what were the proper limits of JUDICIAL REVIEW?

The belief was then widespread—and has been gospel since—that the late nineteenth-century courts declared open season on laws threatening corporate interests. The *American Law Review* observed in 1894 that "it has come to be the fashion . . . for courts to overturn acts of the State legislatures upon mere economical theories and upon mere casuistical grounds." Federal and state courts found in the DUE PROCESS and EQUAL PROTECTION clauses of the Fourteenth Amendment and in the doctrine of FREEDOM OF CONTRACT grounds for voiding laws that regulated working conditions or taxed CORPORATIONS. This judicial conservatism culminated in an unholy trinity of Supreme Court decisions in the mid-1890s: IN RE DEBS (1895), which sustained a federal INJUNCTION against striking railroad workers; UNITED STATES V. E. C. KNIGHT COMPANY (1895), which severely limited the scope of the SHERMAN ANTITRUST ACT; and POLLOCK V. FARMERS' LOAN AND TRUST (1895), which struck down the 1894 federal income tax law. Arnold Paul has called these decisions "related aspects of a massive judicial entry into the socioeconomic scene, . . . a conservative oriented revolution."

But the extent of the courts' antilabor and antiregulatory decision making has been exaggerated; and its purpose has been distorted. A review in 1897 of 1,639 state labor laws enacted during the previous twenty years found that 114 of them—only seven percent—were held unconstitutional. The STATE POLICE POWER to regulate working conditions was widely accepted legal doctrine: in ninety-three percent of 243 Fourteenth Amendment challenges before 1901 the Supreme Court upheld the state laws. By the late 1890s the influential New York and Massachusetts courts looked favorably on laws affecting the conditions of labor, as did the Supreme Court in HOLDEN V. HARDY (1898).

Nor did judicial policy rest only on a tender concern for the rights of property. The desire to foster a national economy was evident in many federal court decisions. And many Justices shared the widespread public sense that American society was being wrenched beyond recognition by industrialism and its consequences. Justice STEPHEN J. FIELD and jurist THOMAS M. COOLEY were as ill at ease with large corporate power as they were with legislative activism. The influential judge and treatise writer JOHN F. DILLON, who called all attempts "to pillage and destroy" private property "as baneful as they are illegal," insisted "with equal earnestness upon the proposition that such

property is under many important duties toward the State and society, which the owners generally fail to appreciate."

By far the most important applications of the Constitution to issues of public policy during the late nineteenth century involved large corporate enterprise, that increasingly conspicuous and troubling presence on the American scene. Railroads led the way both in the scale of their corporate organization and in the consequent public, regulatory, and judicial response.

The roads were great beneficiaries of private and state loans before the Civil War. In the years after 1865, they received substantial federal and state land grants, and loans and subsidies from counties and townships. There were 35,000 miles of track in 1865; 93,000 in 1880. But by the mid-1870s railroads were staggering beneath the weight of their expansion. Fierce competition in the East and Midwest forced down rates and earnings. The overcapitalized lines, with high fixed costs, suffered also from the price deflation of the time. Bankruptcies and reorganizations, rate discrimination, and price-fixing pools were among the consequences. All had the effect of feeding popular anti-railroad sentiment.

That great Civil War venture in mixed enterprise, the Union Pacific Railroad, was a prolific breeder of controversy. Political and constitutional difficulties sprang up around the federal government's role in the capitalization and direction of the road. Congressmen bitterly assailed the Union Pacific's inability (or disinclination) to meet its financial obligations to the government. But not until the SINKING FUND CASES (1879) did the Supreme Court sustain the right of Congress to require this and other transcontinental lines to repay their debts. The Credit Mobilier scandal of 1872, in which stock in the construction company that built the Union Pacific was distributed to a number of influential politicians, epitomized the difficulty of fitting a semipublic enterprise into the American system of government. The Pacific Railroad Commission finally concluded: "The sovereign should not be mated with the subject."

Railroad land grants were no less a source of contention. The House unanimously resolved in 1870 that "the policy of granting subsidies in public lands to railroads and other corporations ought to be discontinued." Once again, the very principle of such aid came under attack: "These grants . . . have been made on the theory that government is an organized benevolence, and not merely a compact for the negative function of repelling a public enemy or repressing disorders."

The consequences of state and local railroad aid also were distressing, and were equally productive of doubts as to whether such aid was part of the proper role of government. The Supreme Court heard more than 350 bonding cases between 1870 and 1896. While the courts felt constrained to enforce most of those obligations, they made clear their displeasure with government subsidization. John F. Dillon condemned subsidies as "a coercive contribution in favor of private railway corporations" which violated "the general spirit of the Constitution as to the sacredness of private property." Thomas M. Cooley objected to railroad subsidies on similar grounds, arguing that "a large portion of the most urgent needs of society are relegated exclusively to the law of demand and supply." In LOAN ASSOCIATION V. TOPEKA (1875) the Supreme Court used this argument to block direct government subsidization of private enterprise.

During the years from 1880 to 1900, public, political, and (inevitably) judicial attention shifted from subsidization to regulation of the economy. The prevailing economic thought of the time, the weakness of government supervision, and the power of private interests worked against an effective system of ECONOMIC REGULATION. But inevitably the strains and conflicts attending the rise of an industrial economy produced demands on the state to intervene.

Journalist E. L. Godkin observed in 1873: "The locomotive is coming in contact with the framework of our institution. In this country of simple government, the most powerful centralizing force which civilization has yet produced must, within the next score years, assume its relation to that political machinery which is to control and regulate it." Nor surprisingly the railroads, the biggest of America's national enterprises, were the first to come under federal regulation.

During the 1870s, state railroad policy had moved from subsidy to containment. The 1870 Illinois constitution required the legislature to "pass laws establishing maximum rates of charges for the transportation of passengers and freight." That body in 1871 set maximum freight and grain elevator rates, forbade price discrimination, and created a railroad commission with supervisory and enforcement powers. Similar laws were adopted in Minnesota, Wisconsin, and Iowa. Because Grange members often were prominent advocates of rate regulation, these acts came to be known as the Granger laws.

The Supreme Court in *Munn v. Illinois* (1877), the first of the GRANGER CASES, upheld the regulatory power of the legislatures and opened up yet another path to regulation by resurrecting the old COMMON LAW doctrine that when private property was AFFECTED WITH A PUBLIC INTEREST it was subject to public accountability and control. But at the same time the Court conceded that "under some circumstances" legislation might be held to violate the Fourteenth Amendment: a portent of the conservative jurisprudence of later years.

Whatever constitutional authority might adhere to state regulation, its effectiveness was severely limited by compliant state railroad commissions, the political and legal influence of the roads, and above all the national character of the enterprise. From the mid-1880s on, federal courts increasingly struck down state railroad tax and rate laws that in their view interfered with the flow of INTERSTATE COMMERCE. The implicit policy decision was that ratemaking should be in the hands of the railroads—and be subject to the review of federal courts, not state courts and legislatures. One observer thought that "long tables of railway statistics, with the accompanying analyses, look strangely out of place in a volume of United States Reports": testimony to the fact that the courts of necessity were taking on a quasi-administrative role.

The scale and complexity of the interests affected by the railroads, the competitive problems of the lines themselves, the limited effectiveness of state regulation, and the growing intervention of the federal courts all fed a movement for national railroad regulation culminating in the INTERSTATE COMMERCE ACT of 1887. That act defined and laid down penalties for rate discrimination, and created an Interstate Commerce Commission (ICC) with the power to investigate and prosecute violators. Its primary purpose was negative: to block pooling and other cartel practices, not to secure a stable railroad rate structure. What the ICC gained thereby in constitutionality it lost in administrative effectiveness. Its early performance showed how difficult it was—given the power of private interests, popular distrust of government, and constitutional limits on the exercise of public power—to establish a bureaucratic mode of regulation. Instead, the ICC adopted what was in fact the only functioning American mode of economic supervision, that of the judiciary. Cooley, the judge and treatise writer who became the ICC's first chairman, announced: "The Commissioners realize that they are a new court, . . . and that they are to lay the foundations of a new body of American law."

During the first ten years of its existence the ICC handed down rulings on more than 800 rate controversies. But the Commission's impact was limited by the size, complexity, and competitiveness of the railroad business and by its lack of supervisory power. Demands rose in the 1890s for government ownership and operation of the lines, or at least for more rigorous supervision by a national Department of Transportation. But, as Cooley observed, these proposals were beyond the range of the late nineteenth-century American polity: "The perpetuity of free institutions in this country requires that the political machine called the United States Government be kept from being overloaded beyond its strength. The more cumbrous it is the greater is the power of intrigue and corruption under it."

The regulation of large enterprise in general posed the same problems, and produced the same response, as did that of the railroads. Mid-nineteenth-century general incorporation acts, and the competition among states to attract corporation charters, guaranteed that the terms of incorporation would remain easy, the regulation of company affairs loose and permissive. In theory the internal affairs of corporations were the business of the states; in practice, the states exercised little control.

But as in the case of the railroads, the growth of business corporations into national enterprises created a demand for federal regulation. Once again, judicial interpretation fostered the growth of a national economy. State and federal courts strengthened the legal status of foreign (out-of-state) corporations, in effect reversing the severe constraints imposed on them by PAUL V. VIRGINIA (1869). In *Barron v. Burnside* (1887) the Supreme Court for the first time held that state regulation of foreign corporations could be of doubtful constitutionality. By the turn of the century the "liberal theory" of foreign corporations was the prevailing one.

Even more dramatic was the courts' use of the Fourteenth Amendment to protect corporate rights and privileges. During the 1870s, said Howard Jay Graham, "the rule that corporations were *not* to be regarded as constitutional " PERSONS' theoretically was the LAW OF THE LAND." But this rule was more theory than fact, and during the late nineteenth century the judiciary explicitly brought corporations under the protection afforded to persons by the due process and equal protection clauses of the Amendment.

The rise of large enterprise in the late nineteenth century took forms that roused public concern and ultimately evoked a legislative and judicial response. The urge to override the limitations of state chartering led to the invention of the corporate trust and then the holding company. Although only about ten trusts were created during the 1880s, the word in the generic sense of a "huge, irrepressible, indeterminate" corporation came to be the object of great public concern. By 1890 several states had ANTITRUST laws, and six state supreme courts had held that trust agreements were against public policy or were illegal as monopolies or conspiracies in RESTRAINT OF TRADE. And public pressure grew for a federal antitrust law, as it had for railroad regulation.

The SHERMAN ANTITRUST ACT of 1890, passed overwhelmingly by Congress, relied on the legislature's power under the COMMERCE CLAUSE to outlaw "every contract, combination in the form of trust or otherwise, or conspiracy, in restraint of trade or commerce." The breadth of the law's formulation, and its dependence on the courts rather than on an administrative agency to define its provisions, testified to the still underdeveloped state of federal regulation. But in other ways the statute was sophisticated. By relying on the old common law concept

of the illegality of conspiracies in restraint of trade, the drafters minimized the risk of having the law declared unconstitutional. And the Sherman Act was widely understood to be aimed at great combinations, not to fix an unrealistic standard of small-unit competition on the economy.

Even so, enforcement was full of difficulty. The Department of Justice in the 1890s lacked the manpower, the money, and the inclination to prosecute vigorously. The courts, too, severely limited the utility of the act. They held that a firm could come to dominate a sector of the economy without doing anything illegal, and they developed distinctions between reasonable and unreasonable restraint of trade, between legitimate business practices and "illegal commercial piracy." And in its Sugar Trust decision of 1895 (*United States v. E. C. Knight Company*) the Supreme Court dealt the law a heavy blow, holding that the Sherman Act applied only to "commerce" and not to manufacturing, and that the activities of the American Sugar Refining Company lay outside the act's coverage even though that firm controlled over ninety percent of the nation's sugar refining capacity.

The *American Law Review* called this decision "the most deplorable one that has been rendered in favor of incorporated power and greed . . . since the Dartmouth College case." In fact, the Court did take a narrow and mechanical view of interstate commerce. On that premise, its decision reflected a long-held distinction between state regulation of manufacturing and federal responsibility for interstate commerce. When private parties brought suit against trade and price cartels (particularly by those prime instances of enterprises in interstate commerce, the railroads), the Supreme Court was not reluctant to find that they violated the Sherman Act.

By the turn of the century it was apparent that the problem of corporate regulation was "rapidly assuming phases which seem beyond the scope of courts of justice." The rise of corporate capitalism, and the question of what to do about it, called as much for political-administrative a will and wisdom as for legal-constitutional power and propriety.

The primary legal and, ultimately, constitutional justification for late nineteenth-century state regulation was the police power: the obligation of the states to protect the health, morals, safety, and welfare of their citizens. Many thought that the potential of that power was great indeed. The president of the American Bar Association estimated in 1897 that more than ninety percent of state legislation rested on the police power. CHRISTOPHER TIEDEMAN's *Limitations of the Police Power in the United States* (1886) was an elaborate attempt to find constitutional grounds for containing what he took to be a widely applied principle of government intervention. OLIVER WENDELL

HOLMES caustically said of the police power: "We suppose the phrase was invented to cover certain acts of the legislature which are seen to be unconstitutional, but which are believed to be necessary."

The police power had its greatest appeal when public health and morals appeared to be at stake. A case in point was regulation of the liquor business. The Supreme Court upheld the right of the states to forbid the manufacture and sale of alcohol, and refused to accept the due process clause of the Fourteenth Amendment as a defense against state liquor legislation. (See INALIENABLE POLICE POWER.) Still more dramatic was judicial acceptance of extensive regulation—indeed, the near-crippling—of the oleomargarine industry. By 1886, twenty-two states either heavily taxed that product or required unattractive packaging or labeling. An 1886 federal law—"protection run mad," said an outraged critic—required that the product be called "oleo" (rather than "butterine" or other enticing names), and subjected it to a high license and manufacturing tax. The Supreme Court in *Powell v. Pennsylvania* (1888) upheld a similar Pennsylvania statute on the basis of the state's police power to protect public health.

The insufficiency of the state police power as a basis of state economic regulation became more and more apparent as the century neared its end. Corporate interests effectively espoused a laissez-faire, SUBSTANTIVE DUE PROCESS constitutionalism. More fundamentally, courts recognized the growing imbalance between state supervision and an economy that was becoming national in scope.

By 1899 the Supreme Court had held twenty-nine state laws unconstitutional because they conflicted with the commerce clause of the Constitution. In LEISY V. HARDIN (1890) the Court voided an Iowa law blocking the entry of liquor into the state, holding that the movement of an original package was protected by the national commerce power, so long as Congress had not authorized the state regulation. Responding to this invitation, Congress quickly passed the Wilson Act, which made liquor subject to state law regardless of where it was packaged. The Court validated the law on the grounds that "the common interest did not require entire freedom in the traffic in ardent spirits." But without similar congressional authorization, it continued to apply the original package doctrine against state laws restricting the entry of oleomargarine and cigarettes. And in CHAMPION V. AMES (1903) the Court upheld a statute forbidding the interstate transportation of lottery tickets, thus opening the prospect of NATIONAL POLICE POWER.

The constraints that limited the application of government authority to economic problems were at least as evident in the realm of social policy. During the period of the Civil War and Reconstruction, citizenship and race had been issues of prime importance not only in constitutional law but in politics and legislation as well. In the twentieth century these and other social concerns—education, crime, poverty, social mores, CIVIL LIBERTIES—would draw comparable attention from the public, Congress, and the courts. But such was not the case during the years between 1871 and 1900. With American society in transit from its small-unit agrarian past to its large-unit urban, industrial future, the political or constitutional standing of individual or social rights was largely ignored.

These years saw relatively little redefinition—in either constitutional law or legislative action—of the status of women, Orientals, blacks, or AMERICAN INDIANS. Legal barriers to female equality occasionally fell, but by legislation, not constitutional adjudication. Opposition to women's suffrage remained strong. Between 1870 and 1910 suffrage advocates conducted 480 campaigns in thirty-three states to get the issue on the ballot. Seventeen state REFERENDA (all but three west of the Mississippi) were held; only two were successful, in Colorado in 1893 and in Idaho in 1896.

The position of Orientals and blacks in society worsened. Organized labor agitated for the exclusion of Chinese immigrants, and anti-Chinese riots in the West testified to the intensity of public feeling. An 1882 federal law banned Chinese immigration for ten years. Supplementary acts in 1884 and 1888 tightened the exclusion law and imposed restrictions on Chinese already in the country. The Supreme Court in 1887 refused to apply the Civil Rights and Enforcement Acts of the Reconstruction period to Chinese, and in 1889 the Court upheld the restriction of Chinese immigration.

In 1892 Congress overwhelmingly renewed Chinese exclusion for another decade; it also required the registration of every resident Chinese laborer, with affidavits by one or more whites that the registrant had entered the country legally. The Supreme Court upheld this law in 1893. These policies had palpable consequences. About 100,000 lawful Chinese immigrants were in the United States in 1880; there were about 85,000 in 1900. In 1902 Chinese immigration was suspended indefinitely.

An even more pervasive white public opinion supported—or at least remained unconcerned about—discrimination against blacks. Late nineteenth-century northern courts generally upheld state laws that forbade discrimination in theaters, restaurants, and other public places, as a proper exercise of the police power. (The degree to which those laws were enforced is another matter.) But on similar grounds the courts accepted the growing number of SEGREGATION statutes. State laws separating the races in public transportation and accommodation, forbidding racial intermarriage, limiting access to the vote, and segregating schools met with no judicial obstacle.

In this sense the Supreme Court's acceptance of a

Louisiana railroad segregation law in PLESSY V. FERGUSON (1896) represented the approval of an already widely established public policy, not the promulgation of new constitutional doctrine. When in 1903 the Court refused to agree that the Fifteenth Amendment might be used against Alabama officials who kept blacks from voting, Holmes suggested that relief "from a great political wrong" must come from "the legislative and political department of the government of the United States." At the same time the Court's invention of the STATE ACTION limitation on congressional power encouraged Congress to refrain from remedying private RACIAL DISCRIMINATION. (See CIVIL RIGHTS CASES.)

On the face of things, Indian public policy in the late nineteenth century had a different goal: it sought not to foster but to reduce separatism. Indian Commissioner Thomas J. Morgan declared in 1891: "The end at which we aim is that the American Indians shall become as speedily as possible Indian Americans; that the savage shall become a citizen." But majority sentiment still regarded even nontribal Indians as inferior, and the Supreme Court went along. In *Elk v. Wilkins* (1884)—coterminous with the CIVIL RIGHTS CASES that invalidated the CIVIL RIGHTS ACT OF 1875—the Court held that Indians were not citizens within the understanding of the Fourteenth Amendment.

At the end of the century the acquisition of noncontiguous territory with substantial populations (Hawaii, the Philippines, Puerto Rico) raised old problems of statehood and citizenship in new forms. The Supreme Court in the INSULAR CASES (1901) limited the degree to which the Constitution applied to these peoples, much as the Court had been inclined to do with regard to Orientals, blacks, and Indians.

In most of the areas of social policy—education, crime, FIRST AMENDMENT freedoms—that in the twentieth century became important battlegrounds of public policy and constitutional law, there was little or no late nineteenth-century constitutional controversy. Only two such issues—prohibition and religion—raised substantial questions of constitutionality. New Hampshire Senator Henry W. Blair first proposed a national prohibition amendment to the Constitution in 1876, and a proposal to this effect was before Congress continuously until its adoption in 1918. State and local restrictions on the distribution and sale of liquor increased, and in general the courts sustained them against Fourteenth Amendment attacks, as proper applications of the police power.

The place of RELIGION IN THE PUBLIC SCHOOLS led to much political and legal conflict. State courts frequently dealt with the thorny issue of school Bible reading. Most states allowed this practice without exegesis, and the courts approved so long as attendance or participation was voluntary. The Iowa Supreme Court upheld a law that forbade the exclusion of Bible reading from the schools. But the Wisconsin court denied the constitutionality of such reading: "The connection of church and state corrupts religion, and makes the state despotic."

Protestant-Roman Catholic hostility underlay much of the conflict over school Bible reading, as it did the issue of state aid to parochial schools. Maine Republican James G. Blaine sought a constitutional amendment forbidding aid in the 1870s (see BLAINE AMENDMENT), and by 1900 twenty-three states had banned public grants to parochial schools. But the interrelationship of religion and education did not come before the Supreme Court until well into the twentieth century.

FELIX FRANKFURTER once told of a distinguished professor of property law who was called on to teach a course in constitutional law. Dutifully he did so. But he soon abandoned the effort, on the ground that the subject was "not law at all but politics." At no time in American history did this pronouncement seem more justified than in the period from 1877 to 1901. Except for the regulation of large enterprise, Americans debated the problems of a developing industrial society more in political than in constitutional terms. After 1900 the fit—or lack of fit—between those problems and the American constitutional system would be faced more directly.

MORTON KELLER
(1986)

Bibliography

BETH, LOREN P. 1971 *The Development of the American Constitution 1877–1917.* New York: Harper & Row.

GRAHAM, HOWARD J. 1968 *Everyman's Constitution: Historical Essays on the Fourteenth Amendment, The "Conspiracy Theory," and American Constitutionalism.* Chaps. 10–13. Madison, Wisc.: State Historical Society.

KELLER, MORTON 1977 *Affairs of State: Public Life in Late Nineteenth Century America.* Cambridge, Mass.: Harvard University Press.

PAUL, ARNOLD M. 1960 *Conservative Crisis and the Rule of Law.* Ithaca, N.Y.: Cornell University Press.

SKOWRONEK, STEPHEN 1982 *Building a New American State: The Expansion of National Administrative Capacities 1877–1920.* Cambridge: At the University Press.

CONSTITUTIONAL HISTORY, 1901–1921

American public life profoundly changed during the early twentieth century. The policy agenda during the Progressive era stands in dramatic contrast, both quantitatively and qualitatively, to its nineteenth-century predecessors. A substantial body of state and national legislation sought to subject large corporations and public utilities to far greater regulation than had been the case before. A comparable surge of enactments dealt with social issues ranging from the hours and working conditions of women and children to housing, the quality of food and drugs, the conservation of land, and the control of drinking and prostitution.

More than at any time since the CIVIL WAR and RECONSTRUCTION, Americans paid substantial attention to the structure of their government. The pace of lawmaking that dealt with politics and government quickened, stimulated by the dual motives (not always complementary) of expanding popular democracy and of bringing greater honesty and efficiency to the workings of the American state. A burst of innovation led to the creation of direct PRIMARY ELECTIONS, the INITIATIVE and REFERENDUM, and new registration and voting laws, as well as to the direct election of senators and to women's suffrage. A flood of discussion and a lesser flow of administrative, judicial, and legislative action sought to increase the effectiveness of the executive branch and the BUREAUCRACY, to improve the workings of Congress and the functioning of the courts, and to modernize the relationship between federal and state authorities and the governance of the nation's cities.

American involvement in WORLD WAR I was the capstone to the Progressive era. Federal involvement in the American economy and society reached new heights; and in both technique and spirit wartime governance drew heavily on the immediate prewar experience.

THEODORE ROOSEVELT, WILLIAM HOWARD TAFT, and WOODROW WILSON were far more activist than their predecessors both in leadership styles and in domestic and foreign policy. But perhaps the most dramatic result of the quickened pace of government and the new policy agenda was the adoption between 1913 and 1920 of four constitutional amendments, providing for a federal income tax, the direct election of senators, PROHIBITION, and women's suffrage. Only at the beginning of the Republic and during the Reconstruction era had constitutional revision occurred on so large a scale.

Insofar as there was a common denominator to the public policy of the Progressive era, it lay in the belief that the time had come to deal with some of the more chaotic and unjust aspects of a mature industrial society; to bring public policy (and the nation's political and governing institutions) into closer accord with new social and economic realities. This impulse cannot be simply explained away by the once fashionable label of "reform," or the now fashionable label of "social control." A quest for social justice coexisted in complex ways with a search for order. Some Progressives wanted society (and the polity) to be more efficient: more honest and economical, less wasteful and corrupt. Others sought policies that would make society safer: more secure from the threats of big business and corrupt political machines, or from the vagaries of competition and the business cycle, or from radicals, immigrants, or blacks. Still others wanted society to be fairer: more humane and less inequitable.

This was not solely an American development. H. G. Wells observed in 1906 that "the essential question for America, as for Europe, is the rescue of her land, her public service, and the whole of her great economic process from the anarchic and irresponsible control of private owners . . . and the organization of her social life upon the broad, clear, humane conceptions of modern science."

Could it be said that a substantially changed constitutional order was one consequence of American Progressivism? Did the complex structure of ECONOMIC REGULATION embodied in the Interstate Commerce Commission, enforcement of the SHERMAN ACT, the Federal Trade Commission, railroad regulation, and a host of other economic measures fundamentally alter the relationship of the state to the economy? Did the interventionism embodied in the growing body of social legislation, accumulating restrictions on IMMIGRATION, the CIVIL LIBERTIES onslaught of the war years, and the passage of national prohibition fundamentally alter the relationship of government to American society and the individual rights of its citizens? Did the sequence of interventionist foreign policy actions, delimited at one end by the acquisition of overseas colonies after the Spanish American War of 1898, and at the other by American intervention in World War I, fundamentally alter the place of FOREIGN AFFAIRS in the American political order?

In sum, did the early twentieth-century outburst of legislation, executive leadership, new agencies, and new government functions lead to what has been called "a qualitatively different kind of state"? Did a corporate-bureaucratic system of government supplant the nineteenth-century American "state of courts and parties"? JOHN W. BURGESS held in 1923 that the past generation had seen the transformation of American constitutional law from a stress on the protection of individual liberty to the imposition of "autocratic" governmental power over property, persons, and thought.

The distinctive American style of government that took form during the first century of the nation's history rested on the balance and SEPARATION OF POWERS among the executive, legislative, and judicial branches; on a FEDERALISM that rendered (through the POLICE POWER) to the states the things that were social; and on a conception of individual rights that, for all its abuses and distortions (the sacrifice of southern blacks to the not-so-tender mercies of southern whites; the use of the DUE PROCESS clause of the FOURTEENTH AMENDMENT to spare CORPORATIONS the indignity of state regulation and taxation), arguably gave nineteenth-century Americans more individual freedom from the interposition of the state than any other people in the world. To what degree was that constitutional order changed between 1901 and 1921?

Of course there can be no definitive answer: the glass of change inevitably will remain partially filled for some, partially empty for others. But an obscure chapter in the constitutional history of the United States may come into clearer focus if we abandon the traditional historiographical emphasis on Progressive "reform" in favor of an examination of the major instrumentalities of government: Congress, the presidency, the bureaucracy, and the mechanisms governing federal-state relations.

Congress was the branch of government that underwent the most overt and formal alteration during the early twentieth century. Two major changes, the popular election of senators through the passage of the SEVENTEENTH AMENDMENT, and the reduction of the powers of the speaker of the House of Representatives, came about in these years. These changes were products of the widespread view that Congress, like the parties, was under the control of corrupt, machine-bound politicos and sinister business interests.

Six times between 1893 and 1911 the House approved a direct election amendment. Finally, spurred by an arrangement whereby progressive Republicans agreed to drop the cause of black voting in the South in return for southern Democratic support, the Senate accepted the change. The Southerners assured that control of the time, place, and manner of holding senatorial elections would remain the province of each state.

A 1911 law sought also to assure that congressional districts would be compact, contiguous, and of roughly equal populations. But enforcement was so difficult, and the courts were so loath to intervene, that it had little effect. And although the direct election of senators gradually reversed the tendency (at least until recent times) for the Senate to become a "millionaires's club," it cannot be said that that body's role in the governmental process was substantially different in the 1920s from what it had been before 1900.

The controversy over the House speaker's authority was more intense. Joseph G. Cannon, the speaker from 1901 to 1911, appointed and was himself one of the five-member Committee on Rules, thus controlling assignments to the key committees of the House, which he populated with like-thinking conservatives. His power to expedite the work of an unwieldy legislature had been a late-nineteenth-century reform, designed to keep a boss-ridden legislature from working its will. Now it appeared to a majority of congressmen as an obstacle to the more programmatic demands of Progressive government. In 1910–1911 a coalition of Democrats and insurgent Republicans deprived Cannon of his power to serve on and appoint the Rules Committee, to choose standing committees, and to recognize members on the floor.

The seniority system came into general use as a more equitable means of choosing committee chairmen—a "reform" of the sort that Finley Peter Dunne's Mr. Dooley presumably had in mind when he commented on the Progressive predilection for structural change: "I wisht I was a German, and believed in machinery." But by the 1920s the House was as much under the control of the majority party leadership as it had ever been. During most of the decade, the Republican speaker, rules committee chairman, and floor leader ran the GOP Steering Committee and, hence, Congress. Surely Cannon would have nodded approval of floor leader John G. Tilson's estimate of his role in the 69th Congress (1929): "It will probably be said with truth that the most important work I have done during the session has been in the direction of preventing the passage of bad or unnecessary laws."

Much of the constitutional controversy of the early twentieth century focused on the character of the presidency—and of the Presidents. The Spanish American War and the governance of territories afterward gave WILLIAM MCKINLEY's administration some of the attributes of the modern presidency, and led to concern over "The Growing Power of the President." But it was the chief executives of the Progressive years who gave a dramatically new shape to the office.

Theodore Roosevelt's executive vigor, his flamboyant efforts to turn the presidency into a "bully pulpit," his concern with issues such as the relations between capital and labor, the trusts, and conservation, and his assertiveness in foreign policy gave his presidency a cast of radicalism. Critics often spoke of him—more so than of any president since ABRAHAM LINCOLN—as having stretched the Constitution to its limits and beyond. Roosevelt himself thought that the power of the presidency enabled him "to do anything that the needs of the nation demanded. . . . Under this interpretation of executive power, I did and caused to be done many things not previously done. . . . I did not usurp power, but I did greatly broaden the use of executive power." But Roosevelt's innate conservatism, the traditionalist goals that informed most of his actions, and his political skill meant that few of his initiatives ran into constitutional difficulties. The most serious congressional objections on constitutional grounds came in the debate over the HEPBURN ACT expanding the power of the Interstate Commerce Commission (ICC); and Roosevelt adroitly compromised by leaving untouched the courts' power to review the ICC's decisions.

A contemporary said that the difference between Roosevelt and his successor, William Howard Taft, was that when a desirable course of action was proposed to Roosevelt he asked if the law forbade it; if not, then it should be done. Taft, on the other hand, tended to ask if the law allowed it; if not, then Congress must be asked. Taft brought a judicial temperament and experience (and almost no elective experience) to his office. He was thus a more self-conscious advocate of a limited presidency, and celebrator of the supremacy of law and of constitutional limitations, than any of his Republican predecessors.

Yet these views did not prevent his administration from adopting a more vigorous antitrust policy than that of Roosevelt. And Taft advocated innovations such as the establishment of a COMMERCE COURT to review ICC decisions and the institution of a federal BUDGET drawn up by the executive branch. The realities of early-twentieth-century American public life weighed more heavily than the niceties of constitutional theory.

Woodrow Wilson as a scholar of American government had long been critical of the traditional relationship between President and Congress. He often praised the British system of ministerial responsibility; his ideal President resembled the British Prime Minister. But as chief executive Wilson more closely followed Roosevelt's conception of the presidency as a bully pulpit (though perhaps with less bullying and more pulpit-pounding). And even more than Roosevelt he took the lead in formulating and seeing to the passage of legislation, a course symbolized by his breaking a tradition that dated from the time of THOMAS JEFFERSON by personally proposing legislation in a message to Congress.

The scope and coherence of Wilson's legislation was far greater than that of his predecessors. But it is worth noting that of the numerous major bills passed in his administration, including the Federal Reserve Act, the FEDERAL TRADE COMMISSION ACT, the CLAYTON ANTITRUST ACT, the WEBB-KENYON ACT, the ESPIONAGE ACT, and the SEDITION ACT, only the KEATING-OWEN CHILD LABOR ACT was struck down by the Supreme Court.

With the entry of the United States into World War I, Wilson assumed presidential leadership of a sort that had not been seen since the time of Lincoln and the Civil War. The mobilization of American agriculture, industry, military manpower, and public opinion led to federal intervention into private activity on a massive scale. The creation of agencies such as the War Industries Board, the Food, Fuel, and Railroad Administrations, the War Finance Corporation, the National War Labor Board, and the Committee on Public Information, and statutes such as the SELECTIVE SERVICE ACT, the ESPIONAGE ACT, the Webb-Pomerene Act (which allowed exporters to organize cartels), and the Overman Act (which greatly expanded the President's power over federal bureaus and agencies) amounted to an unprecedented increase of federal power and its concentration under the President.

Did these circumstances in fact add up to a basic change in the constitutional character of the presidency? Certainly the administrations of WARREN G. HARDING and CALVIN COOLIDGE did not suggest so: they would have been comfortable with the most ardent (and least efficacious) practitioners of the limited presidency of the nineteenth century. Nor did HERBERT HOOVER, whose ambitions resembled those of his Progressive predecessors, exercise effective executive leadership on a bold new scale. And when FRANKLIN D. ROOSEVELT came into office in the trough of the Depression in 1933, he found it necessary to rest his call for a "temporary departure from [the] normal balance" of "executive and legislative authority" on the need for a "broad executive power to wage a war against the emergency as great as the power that would be given me if we were in fact invaded by a foreign foe."

For all the pressures of early-twentieth-century social, economic, and cultural change, the executive branch's constitutional position altered little if at all. After 1921, as before 1900, the powers of the presidency depended not upon alterations in Article II of the Constitution, or upon what the Supreme Court made of that article, but on the political skills of the incumbent and on the course of events: war and peace, prosperity and depression, the growth and alteration of government itself.

The argument that the character of American government underwent major change during the early twentieth century rests on the rise of an administrative state. Certainly one distinguishing characteristic of this period was the proliferation of administrative courts, boards, and commissions, with an attendant expansion of the powers, rules, and regulations of the public administration sector of the American state.

The ideal of expert administrators functioning through (or above) restraints such as party politics, federalism, or the balance of powers had a strong appeal to the Progressive generation. Abbot Lawrence Lowell warned: "If democracy is to be conducted with the efficiency needed in a complex modern society it must overcome its prejudice against permanent expert officials as undemocratic."

The courts had performed a number of essentially administrative and regulatory duties during the nineteenth century. Now, as economic and social problems became more complex and technical, so grew routinized and prescribed administrative processes, in which rule replaced discretion in public law. State laws and constitutions became ever more detailed and codelike; state regulatory agencies multiplied and gained substantially in independence. Federal laws increasingly left to administrative officers the "power to make supplementary law through rules and regulations."

The American involvement in World War I led to an exponential growth of administrative agencies and their power. The War Industries Board and its allied commissions had control over the American economy of a sort only dreamed of in Theodore Roosevelt's New Nationalism. Under the wartime ESPIONAGE ACT, the Post Office Department, the Department of Justice, and the Committee on Public Information wielded powers of suppression and persuasion over American thought and opinion that had no analogue in the nation's past.

Just where administrative law and its accompanying instrumentalities stood in the constitutional system was a matter of continuing concern. Woodrow Wilson observed in his pioneering 1887 essay "The Study of Administration" that "the field of administration is a field of business. It is removed from the hurry and strife of politics; it at most points stands apart even from the debatable ground of constitutional study." But administration was political in its relationship to law, to policy, and to interest group pressures; and it had an intimate relationship to—indeed, was very much a part of—the constitutional system of American government. In many ways the history of American public administration between 1900 and 1921 was a painful instruction in those home truths.

Administrative law of a sort had been part of the American constitutional system since the nineteenth century. Pensions, customs, internal revenue, land grants, and patents were administered by governmental agencies subject to little or no JUDICIAL REVIEW. There was continuing resistance to the idea that public administration had a distinct place in the constitutional order. Bruce Wyman, in one of the earliest systematic discussions of administrative law, set the subject in the context of Anglo-American COMMON LAW rather than constitutional law, holding that the central issue was whether public administration was subject to the same rules of law as governed the relations of citizens with one another.

Adolph Berle took another tack, arguing that administrative law was in fact the application of the will of the state by all three branches, for modern conditions made the traditional differentiation of functions impossible. Administrative law's constitutionality, he implied, rested on the proposition that all of the branches of government were essentially instruments for the expression of the popular will. Thus administrative law was "not a supplement to constitutional law. It is a redivision of the various bodies of law which previously had been grouped under the head of constitutional law."

The courts created evasive categories—"quasi-legislative," "quasi-judicial"—which enabled them to accept administrative powers without addressing the question of whether or not these threatened the separation of powers. By 1914 it appeared that "the exercise of certain discretionary power by administrative officers formally considered legislative is now held unobjectionable."

The growth of the federal bureaucracy, its increasing adherence to its own norms and standards, the fact that it was more and more under the civil service rather than political patronage—all of this has been taken to herald the arrival on the American scene of an autonomous administrative state. But the continuing subservience of government and public policy to the dictates of party politics, the competing governmental units of Congress and the courts, and underlying it all the persisting individualism, hostility to the state, and diversity of American life and thought, meant that the administrative expansion of the early twentieth century did not go on unchecked.

During the war, and immediately after, a number of intellectuals put forward schemes of postwar domestic economic and social reconstruction; they thought that the wartime infrastructure of governmental control and direction might be turned to more basic postwar problems. It soon became apparent, however, that both ideology and politics were working in another direction. Wilson himself told Congress in December 1918: "Our people . . . do not want to be coached and led. . . . [f]rom no quarter have I seen any general scheme of "reconstruction' which . . . we could force our spirited businessmen and self conscious laborers to accept with due pliancy and obedience."

Similar forces worked to constrain the outward reach of postwar foreign policy embodied in the League of Nations. Both courts and legislatures after the mid-1920s began to turn from the radical-bashing of the Espionage Acts and the 1919–1920 Red Scare to begin the erection of the broad definition of FIRST AMENDMENT freedoms that would come to prevail in the modern American definition of civil liberties. A 1918 survey of American ADMINISTRATIVE LAW (probably by the young HAROLD LASKI, surely no enemy of the active state) warned that "with the great increase of state activity . . . there never was a time "when the value of the BILL OF RIGHTS" will have been so manifest."

As in so many other areas of American government, surface changes did not necessarily alter underlying continuities. Congressmen and party leaders may no longer have had the patronage power that once had been theirs. Yet Congress as an institution, and congressmen as party politicians, remained intensely sensitive to the political implications of administrative appointments, activities, and, perhaps most of all, budgets.

Attempts by the Presidents of the time to extend the control of the executive branch over the bureaucracy frequently ran afoul of congressional opposition. By 1921 it was an arguable point—as, indeed, it always had been—whether the bureaucracy was more subject to the direction of the President or to the will of Congress. One thing was certain: the autonomy of the bureaucracy—from Congress, from the parties, from politics—was not markedly greater than it had been a generation before.

True, administrative law as a field of theoretical concern and practical application would continue to develop. The New Deal did not spring fully armed from the brow of Franklin Roosevelt, but was built on a solid foundation of national and state precedents. From an international (and a later American) perspective, the New Deal's experiments did not seem especially bold and revolutionary. But the scale and passion of the charges of a broached constitutionalism raised by the New Deal's opponents in the 1930s suggests just how limited was the pre-1933 acceptance of an American administrative state.

One more aspect of the evolution (or non-evolution) of the American Constitution during the early twentieth century demands attention. That is the hoary principle of federalism: the distribution of functions between the state and federal governments.

In theory the Civil War and the postwar amendments had settled the nagging early-nineteenth-century question as to the degree to which the states were independent governmental entities. Relatively little attention was paid to the question of federalism during the late nineteenth century, in large part because the issues that most engaged the national government—tariff and currency policy, foreign relations, Indian affairs—were of marginal concern to the states. But as the full force of industrialism and urbanism began to change public policy in the early twentieth century, the relative roles of the federal and state governments once again became a matter of constitutional importance. The police power over health, safety, morals, and (from the late nineteenth century on) welfare, was the major legal basis for state social and economic legislation. For the most part the court accepted this; as ZECHARIAH CHAFEE, JR. observed in 1920, "The health, comfort, and general welfare of the citizens are in charge of the state governments, not of the United States."

But of the 194 Supreme Court decisions that invalidated state laws between 1899 and 1921, 102 were explained on the ground that the laws violated the distribution of powers embodied in the principle of federalism. By the 1920s and the early 1930s there was much talk of a judicial DUAL FEDERALISM that had created a "twilight zone" in which neither state nor federal power applied. And the attempt of the New Deal to create a new level of national intervention in the realms of economic regulation and social welfare led to one of the great constitutional controversies in American history. Once again, it would appear that the policy changes of the 1900–1921 period were not accompanied by a significant alteration of the constitutional order.

MORTON KELLER
(1986)

Bibliography

BERLE, A. A., JR. 1916–1917 The Expansion of American Administrative Law. *Harvard Law Review* 30:430–448.

BETH, LOREN 1971 *The Development of the American Constitution 1877–1917.* New York: Harper & Row.

BLUM, JOHN M. 1954 *The Republican Roosevelt.* Cambridge, Mass.: Harvard University Press.

BERGESS, JOHN W. 1923 *Recent Changes in American Constitutional Theory.* New York: Columbia University Press.

HASBROUCH, PAUL D. 1927 *Party Government in the House of Representatives.* New York.

LOWELL, A. LAWRENCE 1913 Expert Administrators in Popular Government. *American Political Science Review* 7:45–62.

NOTE 1915 Delegation of Legislative Power to Administrative Officials. *Harvard Law Review* 28:95–97.

—— 1918 The Growth of Administrative Law in America. *Harvard Law Review* 31:644–646.

SKOWRONEK, STEPHEN 1982 *Building a New American State: The Expansion of National Administrative Capacities, 1877–1920.* Cambridge: At the University Press.

WYMAN, BRUCE 1903 *The Principles of Administrative Law Governing the Relations of Public Officers.* St. Paul, Minn.: Keefe-Davidson Co.

CONSTITUTIONAL HISTORY, 1921–1933

If reverence for the federal Constitution had diminished in the Progressive era, it was revitalized in the 1920s, as the Constitution again became a symbol of national unity and patriotism. Organizations such as the American Bar Association and the National Security League launched national campaigns of patriotism, circulating leaflets and pamphlets by the hundreds of thousands, encouraging Constitution worship, promoting an annual Constitution Day, and working for state laws to require Constitution instruction in the public schools. Forty-three states passed laws mandating the study of the the Constitution; often such laws required loyalty oaths for teachers. Such laws were intended to affirm one hundred percent Americanism from every public school instructor.

The Constitution which was so apotheosized, however, was one geared primarily to the service of property interests. This meant, on the one hand, the protection of business from government regulation and from assault by radical and liberal critics; and, on the other, active intervention of courts and the executive branch to see that constitutional ways were found to insure that the free use of one's property be protected by positive government policies, both formal and informal. Thus, while constitutional changes did occur during the decade and new emphases were developed, these modulations were contained within the dominant ideological construct of free enterprise and individual property rights—rights, it was argued, that had been secured for all time by the sacred document and its amendments.

The most influential constitutionalist of the 1920s was

Chief Justice WILLIAM HOWARD TAFT. Taft set the tone for national political leadership. He was fully committed to the protection of a social order explained and justified by the tenets of JOHN LOCKE, Adam Smith, the Manchester Economists, WILLIAM BLACKSTONE, THOMAS COOLEY, and Herbert Spencer. Espousing a social ethic that stressed selfreliance, individual initiative and responsibility, and the survival of the fittest, Taft emphasized the virtually uninhibited privilege of private property and rationalized the growth of corporate collectivism in terms of individual liberty and private enterprise. For Taft it was time to move away from Progressive expansivism and restore the country to its traditional constitutional bases through a legal system that rested primarily upon judicial defense of a static Constitution and an immutable natural law.

In specific constitutional terms, these goals required restrictive, although selectively restrictive, interpretations of the federal government's taxing and commerce power; an emphasis upon the TENTH AMENDMENT as an instrument for precluding federal intrusion into the reserved powers of the states; and a limitation on the states themselves, through an interpretation of the FOURTEENTH AMENDMENT that emphasized SUBSTANTIVE DUE PROCESS and FREEDOM OF CONTRACT. These constitutional constructs would protect property against restrictive state laws but leave the states free through their police power to legislate against private activities that might threaten that property.

Operating from these assumptions, the Supreme Court majority in this period was activist in its hostility to legislative enactments that threatened or constrained the rights or privileges of the "haves" of society. Thus, between 1921 and 1933, that body ruled unconstitutional fourteen acts of Congress, 148 state laws placing governmental restraints on one or another form of business activity, and twelve city ordinances. Conversely, its majority had no trouble sustaining federal measures that aided business and sanctioning numerous state laws and city ordinances that abridged the CIVIL LIBERTIES of labor, radicals, too outspoken pacifists, and other critics of the capitalist system. In 1925, Taft took the further step of lobbying through Congress a new JUDICIARY ACT, granting the Supreme Court almost unlimited discretion to decide for itself what cases it would hear. (See CERTIORARI, WRIT OF.) Henceforth the Court could choose to take no more cases than it could handle expediently and could restrict adjudication to matters of more general interest. The result was an upgrading of the importance of the cases that the body did agree to hear and a commensurate enhancement of the Court's own prestige and power. Such a looming judicial presence dampened the enthusiasm of activist legislators, state and national, for pushing social reform legislation and made progressive members of REGULATORY COMMISSIONS cautious about exercising their frequently limited authority. Hence bodies such as the Interstate Commerce Commission and the Federal Trade Commission remained largely passive during the period, except when their business-oriented majorities sought to act solicitiously toward those being regulated.

The three presidential administrations of the period, while sharing a common constitutional philosophy, differed in concrete legislative and policy accomplishments. WARREN G. HARDING had begun his presidency with an ambitious legislative docket. His proposals included a National BUDGET AND ACCOUNTING ACT (previously vetoed by WOODROW WILSON), a new farm credit law, the creation of a system of national highways, the enactment of a Maternity Bill, the immediate development and effective regulation of aviation and radio, the passing of an antilynching law, and the creation of a Department of Public Welfare. A surprised Congress was confused over priorities and wound up passing little legislation. The PACKERS AND STOCKYARDS ACT of 1921 made it unlawful for packers to manipulate prices, create monopolies, and award favors to any person or locality. The regulation of stockyards provided for nondiscriminatory services, reasonable rates, open schedules, and fair charges. The measure, which was constitutionally based on a broad interpretation of the COMMERCE CLAUSE, gave the secretary of agriculture authority to entertain complaints, hold hearings, and issue CEASE AND DESIST ORDERS. The bill was a significant part of the agrarian legislation of the early 1920s, and its validation by the Supreme Court in STAFFORD V. WALLACE (1922) provided a constitutional basis for later New Deal legislation. The 1921 Congress also passed the Fess-Kenyon Act, appropriating money for disabled veteran rehabilitation, and the SHEPPARD-TOWNER MATERNITY ACT, subsidizing state infant and maternity welfare activities. Aside from the bill setting up a Budget Bureau in the Treasury Department with a director appointed by the President, little else was forthcoming. By the end of 1921 the *New York Times* observed: "It is evident, and it is clearly admitted in Washington, that the public is not counting any longer upon sound and constructive legislation from Congress." Indeed, Congress supported only occasional further legislation through the decade. One effect of such congressional inaction, along with the increasingly desultory Harding leadership and the even more quiescent CALVIN COOLIDGE presidency, was to direct the attention of reformers to the AMENDING PROCESS.

The immediate post-WORLD WAR I years had seen the ratification of the EIGHTEENTH AMENDMENT (prohibition) and the NINETEENTH AMENDMENT (woman suffrage). In the 1920s certain fallout from both occurred. Prohibition was unpopular from the start. In fact, noncompliance became such a problem that by the late 1920s President HERBERT HOOVER appointed a special commission, headed by former Attorney General GEORGE WICKERSHAM to "investigate problems of the enforcement of prohibition under the 18th Amendment." As the report of the commission stated, "the public was irritated at a constitutional "don't' in a matter where the people saw no moral question." More specifically, the commission pointed to enforcement problems, emphasizing the lack of an American tradition of concerned action between independent government instrumentalities. This, it felt, was now being painfully demonstrated by the Eighteenth Amendment's policy of state enforcement of federal laws, with responsibility too often falling between the two stools and enforcement occurring not at all. Not surprisingly, during the twelve years that the Eighteenth Amendment was in force, more than 130 amendments affecting the Eighteenth in some manner were introduced. Most of these amendments provided for outright repeal; others weakened the amendment in varying degrees. When FRANKLIN D. ROOSEVELT opposed prohibition in 1932, he attracted wide support. The TWENTY-FIRST AMENDMENT repealing the Eighteenth was ratified in December 1933, although prohibition's legal residue took some years to settle. (This measure came only nine months after passage of the relatively uncontroversial TWENTIETH AMENDMENT, eliminating the "lame duck" session of Congress and changing the time for the inauguration of presidents from March to January).

The momentum that carried woman suffrage to a successful amendment continued to some degree into the early 1920s. Some feminist leaders continued to push for improved working conditions for women, for minimum wage laws, and for laws bettering the legal status of women in marriage and DIVORCE. In 1922, Congress passed the Cable Act, providing that a married woman would thereafter retain and determine her own citizenship and make her own application for naturalization after lawful admission for permanent residence, which the Act reduced to three years. Supporters of the political emancipation of women, especially the National Women's Party, got the EQUAL RIGHTS AMENDMENT (ERA) introduced in Congress in 1923 and worked for its adoption by lobbying and exerting political pressure in the early years of the decade. At that time the ERA was opposed by most of the large women's organizations, by trade unions, and by the Women's Bureau primarily because it was seen as a threat to labor-protective legislation. Opponents contended that the ERA would deprive most working women and the poor of hard-won economic gains and would mainly benefit middle and upper class women. Thus the measure floundered at the time, not to be revived until toward the end of WORLD WAR II. The same period saw all native-born American Indians granted full citizenship through the Curtis Act of 1924. The measure, however, did not automatically entitle them to vote, and some states still disfranchised Indians as "persons under guardianship." In 1925 Congress passed the Federal Corrupt Practices Act, extending federal regulation of political corruption to the choice of presidential electors.

A CHILD LABOR AMENDMENT fared only slightly better. With the Supreme Court striking down federal child labor laws as unconstitutional under both the commerce and the taxing powers, advocates of children's rights turned to the amending process and Congress adopted a proposed Child Labor Amendment in June 1924. Opposed by manufacturers' associations and certain religious groups, the measure, by 1930, had secured ratification in only five states. More than three-fourths had rejected it, with the greatest hostility coming from the south and from agricultural regions, where child labor was seen as essential to family economic stability. The measure was eventually superseded by the FAIR LABOR STANDARDS ACT of 1938. By that time the evils of child exploitation were no longer felt to be beyond the constitutional reach of federal legislative power.

Other amendments were proposed: providing minimum wages for women; establishing uniform national marriage and divorce laws; giving the president an item veto in appropriation bills; abolishing congressional immunity for speeches and debates in either house; providing representation for the DISTRICT OF COLUMBIA; changing the amending process itself; providing for the election of judges; providing for the independence of the Philippine Islands; prohibiting sectarian legislation; defining the right of states to regulate employment of ALIENS; requiring teachers to take an oath of allegiance; preventing governmental competition with private enterprise; conferring upon the House of Representatives coordinate power for the ratification of treaties; limiting the wealth of individual citizens; providing for legislation by INITIATIVE; extending the civil service merit system; regulating industry; and prohibiting loans to any except allies. Varying support for all reflected, to a greater or lesser degree, public discontent with aspects of the political-constitutional system of the time. A segment of this discontent crystallized in the La Follette Progressive Party's 1924 platform, which even proposed the RECALL of judges, much to the alarm and ire of Chief Justice Taft. Such straws in the wind did not, however, portend a successful assault upon property-oriented constitutional interpretation. That assault would await the depths of the Depression.

The middle to later years of the decade saw continued congressional hostility to government interference in economic and personal activities, but no reluctance to use power when the result supported President Coolidge's aphorism that "the business of America is business." Antilynching legislation failed during the decade; northern conservatives joined white southerners in deploring it as an assault upon STATES' RIGHTS and individual freedom. In 1927, Congress enacted the McNary-Haugen Farm Bill, an elaborate measure calling for federal support for agricultural prices. The measure countered the prevailing temper of constitutional conservatism, for it extended national regulatory authority over agricultural PRODUCTION and thus not only invaded a sphere of authority traditionally reserved to the states but also interfered extensively with private property rights. President Coolidge vetoed the measure, denouncing it as "economically and constitutionally unsound." When Congress persisted, he vetoed a second McNary-Haugen Bill the following year on the same grounds.

Somewhat similar antistatist sentiments emerged when, in 1925, newly appointed Attorney General HARLAN FISKE STONE took the Bureau of Investigation out of politics and terminated its pursuit of radicals. "There is always the possibility," Stone stated in taking the action, "that a secret police may become a menace to free government and free institutions because it carries with it the possibility of abuses of power which are not always quickly apprehended or understood. The Bureau . . . is not concerned with political or other opinions of individuals. It is concerned with their conduct, and then only with such conduct as is forbidden by the laws of the United States." Store's action was popular with all but some patriotic and right-wing groups for whom radical, or even unorthodox, ideas were a threat which the government did have a responsibility actively to check.

On the other hand, Congress met little opposition when it enacted a broad, restrictive IMMIGRATION ACT in 1924 imposing stringent quotas on entry to the United States, heavily biased against southern and eastern European and Asiatic peoples. Such action was consonant with the strong tendency of the courts in the period to define the rights of aliens narrowly, with an eye to keeping such people in their proper place, particularly as easily exploitable members of the work force.

To the extent that an alternative constitutional tradition existed or was developed in the 1920s, its impact was not fully felt until Depression days. There were undertones of protest, however, coming from disparate sources. Justice LOUIS D. BRANDEIS, in his dissent in *Gilbert v. Minnesota* (1920), a decision sustaining a sedition conviction for criticism of the government's wartime policies, had stated: "I cannot believe that liberty guaranteed by the Fourteenth Amendment includes only liberty to acquire and to enjoy property." Others quickly picked up on the contradiction in this double standard, particularly when the same "liberty" was not then deemed applicable to FREEDOM OF THE PRESS, and FREEDOM OF ASSEMBLY. The AMERICAN CIVIL LIBERTIES UNION (ACLU), a product of the war, itself an opponent of strong government intervention in people's personal lives, worked through the decade to strengthen the power of labor and working people. The ACLU operated on the assumption that BILL OF RIGHTS freedoms flowed from economic power and that artificial impediments to the achievement of that power had to be removed. The National Association for the Advancement of Colored People was active in the decade in behalf of the constitutional rights of minorities, although its successes in producing constitutional change were decidedly limited. Similarly, organized labor saw itself as a beleaguered "minority" throughout the decade, attributing its position partly to conservation constitutionalism. Samuel Gompers stated shortly before his death: "The Courts have abolished the Constitution as far as the rights and interest of the working people are concerned."

The impact of such criticism ultimately was not so great as that from popularly elected constitutional liberals and an influential segment of the legal community. Senators William E. Borah and GEORGE NORRIS openly opposed the appointment of CHARLES EVANS HUGHES to the Chief Justiceship, arguing that there was a need for judges who would stop treating the Fourteenth Amendment only as a protection of property and recognize it as a guarantee of individual liberty. Although this opposition failed, partly because of Hughes's constitutional record and the public image of him as more progressive than reactionary, the Senate did block the subsequent nomination of John J. Parker, a prominent North Carolina Republican, to the Supreme Court in 1930; opponents particularly emphasized his racist and antilabor record. Both actions constituted unignorable Depression calls for constitutional liberalization, echoed increasingly by liberal lawyers, particularly in the law schools, many of which has been influenced by the LEGAL REALISM movement of the times. Such criticism combined with growing disillusionment with the business establishment and cynicism about a Supreme Court that could be aggressively activist in the protection of property rights and a paragon of self-restraint when it came to protecting human rights. Pressure for altered uses of government power mounted fairly early in Depression days.

Herbert Hoover was undoubtedly the most competent of the 1920s Presidents. A successful mining engineer and government bureaucrat, he had served effectively as wartime food administrator under Woodrow Wilson and as secretary of commerce in the Harding and Coolidge administrations. Hoover was eager to overhaul the executive branch of the government and reorganize it in ways that would achieve greater efficiency and greater economies in government. Saddled quickly with the worst depression in American history, Hoover was pressed to launch a large-scale national attack on the depression through federal governmental action. Such action had to fit his constitutional views, which were decidedly Taftian. For Hoover, "unless the enterprise system operated free from popular controls, constitutional freedoms would die." "Under the Constitution it was impossible to attempt the solution of certain modern social problems by legislation." "Constitutional change must be brought about only by the straightforward methods provided by the Constitution itself." Such a commitment to laissez faire economics and constitutional conservatism precluded sweeping federal actions and permitted only such remedial legislation as the AGRICULTURAL MARKETING ACT of 1929, designed to assist in the more effective marketing of agricultural commodities. Congress created the Reconstruction Finance Corporation in 1932 to rescue commercial, industrial, and financial institutions through direct government loans. Both measures so limited the scope of permissible federal activity that neither proved adequate to the challenge of providing successful depression relief.

A more specific example of Hoover's constitutionalism involved congressional enactment of the Muscle Shoals Bill of 1931. In 1918 President Wilson had authorized, as a war-time measure, the construction of government plants at Muscle Shoals on the Tennessee River for the manufacture of nitrates and of dams to generate electric power. After the war the disposition of these plants and dams produced bitter national controversy. Conservatives insisted that they be turned over to private enterprise. Congress twice enacted measures providing for government ownership and operation for the production and distribution of power and the manufacture of fertilizers. In vetoing the second of these bills (Coolidge had vetoed the first in 1928), Hoover reiterated his belief that government ownership and operation was an approach to socialism designed to break down the initiative and enterprise of the American people. He argued that such a measure was an unconstitutional federal entrance into the field of powers reserved to the states and as such deprived the people of local communities of their liberty.

A growing number of congressmen and senators, however, were convinced that such constitutional negativism was no longer useful. In 1932, Congress passed and sent to a reluctant President the NORRIS-LAGUARDIA ACT, probably the most important measure of the period. Ever since the 1890s, labor had protested against business's turn to the courts for INJUNCTIONS to prohibit its legitimate activities. Congress's only response was a Railway Labor Act, in 1926, giving railway labor the right to bargain collectively through its own representatives. By the late 1920s, a national campaign against the labor INJUNCTION was launched with liberal congressional leaders joined by groups as disparate as the ACLU, the Federal Council of Churches, and the American Federation of Labor, all protesting the unfairness and unconstitutionality of enjoining

labor's legitimate use of speech, press, and assembly. The Great Depression intensified this discontent. The Norris-LaGuardia Act made YELLOW DOG CONTRACTS unenforceable in federal courts; forbade the issuance of injunctions against a number of hitherto outlawed union practices; and guaranteed jury trials in criminal prosecutions based on violations of injunctions. The act thus removed the machinery for a variety of informal antilabor devices.

Hoover's response was to seek assurance from his attorney general, William Mitchell, that the more rigorous terms of the measure could be successfully bypassed. Having gained such assurance, he signed the bill, leaving Senator Norris to remark, bitterly, that the President dared not veto but did everything he could to weaken its effect. Yet the measure was generally popular, as was its symbolism, which presaged a more active role for the federal government in the achievement of social justice.

Such response was not lost on Franklin D. Roosevelt. During the presidential campaign of 1932, he called for a new, more liberal view of the Constitution and a BROAD CONSTRUCTION of congressional legislative power as a way of solving the nation's difficult problems. His overwhelming election victory seemed to assure that the minority liberal constitutional arguments of the 1920s would become majority ones when the NEW DEAL program was enacted.

PAUL L. MURPHY
(1986)

Bibliography

HICKS, JOHN D. 1960 *Republican Ascendancy, 1921–1933.* New York: Harper & Row.

LEUCHTENBURG, WILLIAM E. 1958 *The Perils of Prosperity, 1914–1932.* Chicago: University of Chicago Press.

MURPHY, PAUL L. 1972 *The Constitution in Crisis Times, 1918–1969.* New York: Harper & Row.

—— 1972 *The Meaning of Freedom of Speech: First Amendment Freedoms from Wilson to F.D.R.* Westport, Conn.: Greenwood Press.

CONSTITUTIONAL HISTORY, 1933–1945

With the exception of the CIVIL WAR–RECONSTRUCTION era and the turbulent decade of the 1960s, no period in our history generated more profound changes in the constitutional system than the years of the Great Depression and WORLD WAR II. Although the tenure of a Chief Justice of the United States often marks the boundary of a particular constitutional epoch, in this period it was a single President, FRANKLIN D. ROOSEVELT, whose personality and policies dominated the nation's political landscape, first as the leader of a domestic "war" against economic chaos, and, finally, as the architect of victory over the Axis powers. "Most of us in the Army have a hard time remembering any President but Franklin D. Roosevelt," remarked one soldier at the time of Roosevelt's death in April 1945. "He was the COMMANDER-IN-CHIEF, not only of the armed forces, but of our generation."

Roosevelt, described by Justice OLIVER WENDELL HOLMES as having a "second-rate intellect, but a first-rate temperament," was a charming, politically astute country squire from Hyde Park, New York. Crippled by polio at thirty-nine, elected President a decade later, he presided over five momentous revolutions in American life. The first, arising from his confrontation with the Supreme Court, has been aptly termed the "constitutional revolution" of 1937. The Court abandoned its long campaign, dating from the 1880s, to shape the content of the nation's economic policy by means of the judicial veto. The second revolution elevated the presidency, already revitalized by THEODORE ROOSEVELT and WOODROW WILSON in the Progressive era, to the pinnacle of leadership within the American political system. FDR did not invent the "imperial presidency," but his mastery of the radio, his legislative skills, and his twelve-year tenure went far toward institutionalizing it, despite several notable setbacks at the hands of Congress and the Court.

The third revolution, symbolized by the expansion of FEDERAL GRANT-IN-AID programs, the SOCIAL SECURITY ACT of 1935, and the efforts by the Department of Justice to protect CIVIL RIGHTS under the old Reconstruction-era statutes, significantly transformed American FEDERALISM by making the national government the chief custodian of economic security and social justice for all citizens. The fourth, marked by the revitalization of old independent REGULATORY COMMISSIONS such as the Interstate Commerce Commission, saw the final denouement of laissez-faire capitalism and the birth of state capitalism, managed by a bureaucratic elite drawn from the legal profession, the academic world, and private business. And the fifth revolution, characterized by the unionization of mass-production industries, the growing influence of urban-labor representatives in the Congress, and Roosevelt's successful effort to attract support from ethnic minorities, brought a major realignment in voting blocs and party strength that lasted three decades.

The triumph of Roosevelt and the Democratic party in the 1932 elections represented both the outcome of short-term political forces and the culmination of voting realignments that began much earlier. The inability of the HERBERT HOOVER administration to stop the slide into economic depression after the stock market crash of 1929 represented the most obvious and immediate source of Roosevelt's appeal. More significantly, his victory ended an era of Republican domination in national politics that began with WILLIAM MCKINLEY in 1896, and it ushered in a Democratic reign that lasted well into the 1980s. From McKinley to Hoover, the Republicans controlled the White House, except for Wilson's two terms (1913–1921), a Democratic interlude that rested mostly upon divisions in Republican ranks.

The Republicans also controlled both houses of Congress for twenty-eight of the thirty-six years between McKinley and Franklin Roosevelt, elected a majority of the nation's governors and state legislators outside the South, and even enjoyed great popularity in big cities among trade unionists, middle class professionals, and many ethnic-religious minorities. On a platform of high tariffs, sound money, low taxes, and rising prosperity, the GOP built a formidable national coalition.

The Republican coalition developed signs of collapse during the Warren G. Harding-Calvin Coolidge-Herbert Hoover years as economic distress increased among farmers and industrial workers despite the vaunted prosperity of the Republican New Era. In 1924, running as an independent on the Progressive party ticket, the aging Senator Robert LaFollette garnered a healthy share of votes from both urban workers and staple-crop farmers, who protested with their ballots against the economic conservatism of Coolidge and his Democratic rival, John W. Davis, a prosperous Wall Street lawyer. Hoover easily defeated New York governor Alfred E. Smith in 1928, but Smith—Irish, Roman Catholic, opposed to prohibition, and urban to the core—detached millions of ethnic, working class voters from the Republican party. Three years of economic distress which also alienated farmers, businessmen, and the once-affluent middle classes, completed the realignment process and assured Roosevelt victory in 1932.

From 1932 until his death, Roosevelt forged his own national coalition. Anchored in the lily-white South and the big cities where the Democratic party had been powerful since the days of ANDREW JACKSON and MARTIN VAN BUREN, Roosevelt welded together a collection of social, ethnic, regional, and religious minorities into a new political majority. In peace and war, the NEW DEAL gave power, status, and recognition to those who had been outsiders in American society before the Great Depression—Irishmen, Jews, Slavs, white Southerners, and blacks.

Within this broad, diverse "Roosevelt coalition," the power and influence of organized labor and the urban wing of the Democratic party grew impressively, especially after the elections of 1934 and 1936 and the passage of the WAGNER (NATIONAL LABOR RELATIONS) ACT in 1935. Roosevelt's nomination in 1932 had been made possible by the support of key southern leaders. The success of the New Deal after 1934 and Roosevelt's electoral victories in 1940 and 1944, however, rested upon the political acumen and money provided by big labor through the political action committees of the Congress of Industrial Organizations. Roosevelt built well. His coalition ran both houses of Congress in every year but eight during the next half century. It elected HARRY S. TRUMAN in 1948, JOHN F. KENNEDY in 1960, LYNDON B. JOHNSON in 1964, and JIMMY CARTER in 1976.

Neither of the two amendments to the Constitution ratified during this period owed their inspiration directly to Roosevelt or the New Deal, although the TWENTIETH AMENDMENT, eliminating the lame-duck session of Congress, had been pushed by leading progressives for over a decade, and the TWENTY-FIRST AMENDMENT, repealing national PROHIBITION of liquor, had been endorsed by the Democratic party in its 1932 platform. Both amendments were proposed in 1932, the first time since 1789 that a single Congress had sent to the states for RATIFICATION more than one amendment. Congress also specified an unusual ratification procedure for the Twenty-First Amendment, requiring the states to convene special ratifying conventions instead of submitting the measure to their legislatures. Proponents of prohibition repeal feared that the legislatures, most of them malapportioned in favor of rural constituencies, would not be sympathetic to ratification.

Supporters of the Twentieth Amendment, led by the venerable progressive senator from Nebraska, GEORGE NORRIS, argued that the existing short session of Congress which met from December until March was a barrier to effective majoritarian democracy. By an accident of history, Congresses elected in November of even-numbered years did not meet in regular session until December of the odd-numbered year. Norris's amendment, first passed by the Senate in 1923, proposed to correct this situation by moving forward to January 3 from December the date on which sessions of Congress began and shifting back to January 3 and 20 from March 4 the date on which the terms of office began for members of Congress, and the President and Vice-President, respectively. A newly elected Congress, reflecting the fresh mandate of the people, would meet two months after an election rather than thirteen months later.

The Senate passed the Norris plan five times after 1923, but it failed to advance in the Republican-dominated House of Representatives, where the Speaker, Nicholas Longworth, opposed it. Longworth wished to keep the lame-duck session as a check upon the turbulent masses and he also objected to a provision in the Norris amendment that allowed Congress to determine the date of its own adjournment each year. Such flexibility, he believed, would only encourage more lawmaking by Congress, a prospect that he and other conservatives viewed with great distaste. The 1930 elections returned Democratic majorities to both houses of Congress, who quickly passed the Twentieth Amendment and sent it on to the states where it was ratified three years later.

American temperance organizations struggled for more than a century to achieve their goal with the adoption of the EIGHTEENTH AMENDMENT in 1919. It took the "wet" forces little more than a decade to bring the brewery, the distillery, and the saloon back to American life through ratification of the Twenty-First Amendment nine months after Roosevelt took office. Like the resurgence of the Democratic party, the repeal of national prohibition reflected a fundamental shift in political forces. The Congress that passed the Eighteenth Amendment during WORLD WAR I was overwhelmingly rural, with House seats apportioned on the basis of the 1910 census, the last to record a majority for the countryside rather than the cities. The 72nd Congress, on the other hand, reflected the reapportionment of the House in 1929, where twenty-one states (mostly from the rural South and West) lost representation and eleven states (mostly in Eastern metropolitan areas) increased their share of seats.

In addition to providing urban-ethnic voters with a measure of symbolic revenge for the inconvenience of a "dry" decade, the repeal of prohibition had wide appeal in a nation reeling from economic depression and plagued by criminal violence. Sponsors argued that repeal would boost employment, raise tax revenues, and permit law enforcement personnel to concentrate upon the apprehension of major criminals such as John Dillinger. With equal vehemence, defenders of the "dry" faith claimed that repeal had been hatched by millionaires and rich corporations, eager to shift their tax burdens onto poor consumers of alcohol, and that Satan would conquer America. Thirty-six states, more concerned for the nation's fiscal problems than for the wiles of Satan, ratified the repeal amendment by December 1933.

The legislative program of the New Deal had a more direct impact upon the fate of the old CHILD LABOR AMENDMENT, which had passed Congress in 1924 but had failed to secure ratification by three-fourths of the states. As late as 1937, only twenty-eight state legislatures had ratified the proposal which would have authorized Congress to regulate or prohibit the labor of persons under eighteen years of age. Fifteen states, mostly in the South and border regions, had rejected it; five had failed to act. The amendment became moot, however, when Congress in 1938 passed the FAIR LABOR STANDARDS ACT, which contained a similar restriction, and when the Supreme Court upheld its constitutionality in UNITED STATES V. DARBY LUMBER COMPANY (1941).

As usual, formal constitutional revision on the state level during these years was more extensive and diverse than for the federal government, although only three states (New York, Missouri, and Georgia) entirely rewrote their constitutions. At one extreme were states such as Tennessee and Illinois, where constitutional innovation remained minimal. The fundamental law of Tennessee had not been amended since 1870, while the Illinois Constitution of 1890 had been revised only twice since that date. On the other hand, voters in Louisiana were asked to adopt twenty-eight constitutional amendments in 1938, nineteen in 1940, ten in 1942, and nineteen in 1944, creating an organic law that filled nearly 300 pages with 200,000 words. California ran a distant second. By the end of World War II, its constitution of 1879 had been amended 250 times and totaled close to 50,000 words.

Unlike the United States Constitution with its broad, sweeping language, most state charters in this period included detailed declarations of public policies; the amendment process often served as a surrogate for statutory changes. In 1944, for instance, 100 proposed amendments were put before the voters in thirty different states. In California, Arizona, Oregon, and Washington the electorates defeated amendments to enact old-age pension schemes. Arkansas and Florida adopted right-to-work amendments that banned union shops, while California spurned a similar amendment. In the same year voters in other states were asked to pass upon amendments dealing with the location of airports, POLL TAXES, dog racing, and preferential civil service hiring for veterans.

Because of the era's economic crisis, which combined high unemployment, business failures, and falling tax revenues, all of the states confronted similar constitutional crises, because their organic laws usually limited state indebtedness. Escalating relief burdens placed a severe strain upon the states' fiscal resources, especially before the New Deal picked up a larger share of these costs after 1935. Legislatures and governors often found paths around these obstacles through constitutional experimentation: amendment, REFERENDUM, and judicial interpretation.

The age of Roosevelt, marked by class conflict and intense political controversy over both the economy and FOREIGN AFFAIRS, spawned many durable myths about the presidency, the growth of federal authority, and the relationship between government and the private sector. Roosevelt's critics, who hated the New Deal and distrusted his diplomacy, accused him of erecting a Presidential dictatorship. The New Deal and the mobilization of the war economy, it has been argued, also transformed the federal union as well as business-government relationships by subjecting local government and business corporations to the despotism of Washington bureaucrats. There is some truth in these generalizations but also considerable exaggeration.

Few political leaders in our history could match Roosevelt's oratorical gifts, his skill at dispensing patronage, and his deft manipulation of subordinates, the press, Congress, and opponents. But Roosevelt also experienced a number of profound setbacks between 1933 and 1939 that limited presidential power even during the unparalleled economic crisis of the Great Depression. It was World War II that shifted the balance decisively in his favor, but even during those turbulent years he usually functioned within boundaries set by Congress and public opinion.

Under the New Deal, the years of presidential preeminence in the shaping of domestic policy were remarkably fertile but brief. During the so-called Hundred Days, from Roosevelt's inauguration to early June 1933, Congress rubber-stamped dozens of White House proposals, including new banking laws, the first federal securities statute, a complete overhaul of the nation's monetary system, legislation creating the Tennessee Valley Authority, as well as laws setting up the controversial National Recovery Administration and the New Deal's basic farm program. Acting under the dubious authority of the World War I Trading with the Enemy Act, Roosevelt banned gold exports and all foreign exchange transactions until Congress approved of the administration's monetary plans that nullified gold clauses in private and public contracts and devalued the dollar by almost twenty-five percent. Equating the Depression with war, Roosevelt asked for and received from Congress the resources appropriate for a military commander battling a foreign invader.

The 1934 elections gave the President even larger majorities in Congress. This mandate encouraged a second burst of New Deal reforms in 1935. Again responding to presidential initiatives, Congress adopted a series of pathbreaking laws, including the Social Security Act, the Wagner National Labor Relations Act, a $4.8 billion relief and public works measure, and a significant revision of the federal tax code that closed many loopholes and levied new surcharges on the very rich. Despite the judicial mutilation of key administration measures in 1935–1936, executive power probably stood at its peacetime zenith after Roosevelt's crushing reelection victory in 1936.

Even during these years of strong presidential leadership, Roosevelt's claims to authority did not go unchallenged. The federal courts remained a bastion of conservative Republicanism. Federal judges had issued hundreds of INJUNCTIONS against New Deal programs by early 1935, when the Supreme Court began to invalidate many of the laws of the Hundred Days, including the NATIONAL INDUSTRIAL RECOVERY ACT (NIRA) and the AGRICULTURAL ADJUSTMENT ACT. The most serious rebuff to the President came in the *Schechter* case, where the Justices invalidated the NIRA on the ground of improper DELEGATION OF POWER to the executive, and HUMPHREY'S EXEC-

UTOR V. UNITED STATES (1935), where they curbed the President's power to remove members of independent regulatory commissions.

These judicial affronts to presidential authority became a war during FDR's second term, beginning with his ill-devised scheme to "pack" the Supreme Court with additional Justices. His proposed "Judicial Reform Act of 1937" inspired criticism both from conservatives and from many of the President's liberal friends in the Congress as well. This bitter legislative struggle divided the New Deal coalition, squandered much of the political capital that Roosevelt had accumulated during the previous four years, and gave rise to cries of "dictatorship," "tyranny," and "fascism." When the dust settled, the Court-packing plan had been defeated by Chief Justice CHARLES EVANS HUGHES and opponents in the Congress, but the Supreme Court never again seriously challenged the New Deal.

The economic recession of 1937–1938 and Roosevelt's attempt to restructure the executive branch dealt new blows to presidential leadership and prestige. Having taken credit for the economic upturn in 1935–1936, the President had to absorb the blame for the "Roosevelt recession," which had been triggered in part by his own desire to cut federal expenditures and balance the budget. Congress also scuttled his plans to reorganize the executive branch which rested upon the recommendations of a blue-ribbon committee on administrative management. The original bill called for an enlargement of the White House staff, creation of the Executive Office of the President to include the Bureau of the Budget, and a consolidation of existing bureaus, agencies, and commissions into twelve superdepartments under the President's control. The independent regulatory commissions such as the Federal Trade Commission, the Interstate Commerce Commission, and the Securities Exchange Commission would have been regrouped under the authority of these executive departments.

Congressional opponents denounced the plan as another presidential power grab. Working in tandem with rebellious bureaucrats who hoped to protect their own fiefdoms from the White House, they easily defeated the most controversial features of the plan. Roosevelt got his Bureau of the Budget and a larger staff, but little more. His political fortunes hit rock bottom in the 1938 elections, when several conservative Democratic senators won reelection despite Roosevelt's effort to purge them during bitter primary campaigns. Confronted by an emerging conservative congressional coalition of southern Democrats and midwestern Republicans, Roosevelt had lost the initiative on domestic policy by the time German troops marched into Austria and Czechoslovakia.

The growth of presidential power, checked at the end of the 1930s, received new impetus after 1938 from the coming of World War II. Although the Supreme Court had reaffirmed in the broadest possible terms the President's constitutional authority over foreign policy in UNITED STATES V. CURTISS-WRIGHT EXPORT CORPORATION (1936), the actual limits of that authority remained to be tested. Sometimes alone and sometimes with congressional support, between 1939 and 1945 Roosevelt enlarged presidential power to an extent unknown even during World War I and the early New Deal.

Facing substantial isolationist sentiment both in Congress and among the public, Roosevelt initially attempted to counter Germany and Japan by means of EXECUTIVE AGREEMENTS and EXECUTIVE ORDERS that rested exclusively upon his claims to inherent presidential authority to conduct foreign relations and command the armed forces. He applied economic sanctions against Japan, terminating a 1911 commercial treaty, banning sales of scrap iron and steel, and freezing all Japanese financial assets in the United States. He ordered naval patrols of the western Atlantic—virtually assuring hostilities with German U-boats—and he ordered the military occupation of Iceland, with attendant naval convoys to protect ships supplying the occupation troops. In brief, Roosevelt waged an economic war in Asia and shooting war in the Atlantic without the consent of Congress.

The most extraordinary assertion of presidential power before Pearl Harbor was the destroyer-bases executive agreement in September 1940, by which Roosevelt transferred fifty over-age American destroyers to the British government in return for leases on seven naval bases in the Caribbean. This transaction, through which the President gave away a substantial portion of the United States Navy, rested upon a generous interpretation of an old nineteenth-century statute which permitted the President to dispose of worn-out ships. Most observers have believed that this action subverted the intention of Congress and violated a 1917 law specifically prohibiting the President in any foreign war "to send out of the jurisdiction of the United States any vessel built, armed, or equipped as a vessel of war." Attorney General ROBERT H. JACKSON, who advised Roosevelt on the legality of the transfer, dismissed this statute on the grounds that it applied only to ships built with the specific intention of giving them to a nation at war.

After the Japanese attack on Pearl Harbor Congress rapidly augmented presidential control over both military policy and the domestic economy. By means of the renewal of Lend-Lease, the Second WAR POWERS ACT, the EMERGENCY PRICE CONTROL ACT, the War Labor Dispute Act, and other laws, Congress gave the President the discretion, among other things, to allocate $50 billion of war supplies to America's allies, to reorganize all executive departments and agencies at will, to fix rents and prices throughout the land, and to seize industrial plants closed by strikes. In 1935, invalidating the NIRA, the Supreme Court had scolded Congress for vesting unbridled authority in the President to regulate the economy. Ten years later, as World War II drew to a close, executive discretion over the nation's economic structure far transcended that of the NIRA years.

A substantial enlargement of presidential discretion was essential for effective prosecution of World War II, but the growth of executive power carried with it threats to CIVIL LIBERTIES and unfathomable dangers to the survival of the human race. The Congress that permitted the President to restructure the executive branch also approved of the administration's plans to remove Japanese Americans from the West Coast. (See JAPANESE AMERICAN CASES.) The Congress that permitted the President to ration sugar and gasoline also gave the Commander-in-Chief a blank check for research, development, and potential use of nuclear weapons. This was truly, in Justice BENJAMIN N. CARDOZO's memorable phrase, "delegation run riot."

The expansion of federal responsibility for economic management and social services paralleled the growth of presidential power between 1933 and 1945. In a series of cases beginning with the WAGNER ACT CASES (1937) and ending with WICKARD V. FILBURN (1942), the Supreme Court laid to rest the antiquated notions of DUAL FEDERALISM, which had postulated the existence of rigid constitutional boundaries separating appropriate federal activities from those reserved exclusively to the states. In the wake of these decisions and those upholding the Social Security Act, there seemed to be no constitutional limitation upon the authority of Congress to regulate INTERSTATE COMMERCE and to tax and spend on behalf of the GENERAL WELFARE, even where these federal efforts intruded deeply into areas of social and economic life traditionally left to local government. Practice often preceded formal doctrinal legitimation. In 1934, for instance, the Bureau of Biological Survey in the Department of Commerce eradicated over seven million disease-carrying rodents in three states with a $8.7 million grant from the Civil Works Administration. Although this project produced no constitutional objection, a more sweeping federal intrusion into the domain of local health authorities is hard to imagine.

The most far-reaching instrument of expanding federal policymaking became the myriad programs of FEDERAL GRANTS-IN-AID which provided federal money for specific activities to be administered by state officials under federal guidelines. As early as 1862, the MORRILL ACT had conveyed federal lands to the states on condition that they be used for the construction and support of colleges and universities. In the Weeks Act of 1911, Congress had extended this principle to include cash grants to the states

for fighting forest fires in the watersheds of navigable streams. Similar grant-in-aid programs flourished during the Wilson administration for vocational education, highways, and agricultural extension work, but budget-conscious Republican administrations had put a cap on new programs during the 1920s.

In their efforts to fight the depression, both the Hoover and Roosevelt administrations increasingly used the grant-in-aid technique. The Emergency Relief and Construction Act of 1932, approved reluctantly by Hoover, offered over $600 million in federal loans to the states for work-relief projects. The Roosevelt administration substituted grants for loans in the relief programs of the New Deal. By 1940, in addition to these vast relief activities and the continuation of old programs from the Progressive era, the New Deal had undertaken grant-in-aid programs for employment services and unemployment compensation, old age assistance, child welfare services, and maternity care. Social Security, the largest New Deal grant-in-aid program, assisted the blind, the disabled, and the unemployed through combined federal-state efforts.

The growth of federal grant-in-aid programs during the New Deal years rested upon the realization that many social and economic problems required national attention and that only the federal government commanded the fiscal resources to deal with them. Between 1932 and the end of World War II, the federal government's share of total taxes collected rose from twenty-four percent to nearly seventy-four percent. At the same time, grant-in-aid programs avoided the growth of an even larger federal bureaucracy and left many important administrative decisions in the hands of state and local officials.

In addition to grant-in-aid programs, state and local elites played a major role in the implementation of other New Deal efforts as well, a pattern of political decision making that refuted simplistic ideas about rampant centralization of power in federal bureaucrats. The heart of the New Deal's farm program, the domestic allotment system, vested important decisions in county committees composed of farmers and extension-service personnel chosen by local authorities. Under the Taylor Grazing Act, local livestock ranchers determined the extent of grazing rights on the vast public lands in the western states. And the most coercive federal program in this period, the SELECTIVE SERVICE ACT of 1940, left life-and-death decisions about the drafting of millions of American citizens in the hands of local draft boards appointed by state governors. Without the active participation of state and local officials, the wartime rationing programs for gasoline, sugar, coffee, and butter would have broken down for lack of enforcement.

When New Deal reformers ignored the interests and sensibilities of local elites, they provoked instant political protest and retaliation. Roosevelt quickly dismantled the innovative Civil Works Administration in 1934 because it drew intense criticism from governors, county supervisors, and mayors who objected to the complete nationalization of its extensive work-relief efforts. The subsequent Works Projects Administration program gave a larger share of decision making to local officials, who systematically used the machinery to punish political enemies and to discriminate against racial minorities, especially in the South. When idealistic young lawyers in the Agricultural Adjustment Administration attempted to protect sharecroppers and tenants from wholesale eviction under the farm program, they stirred up a revolt by commercial farmers, who forced their removal from the agency. Much of the opposition from southern Democrats to the New Deal after 1935 grew out of their anger at the Department of Justice for attempting to protect blacks from local violence under the old Reconstruction-era civil rights laws. The New Deal nourished a new brand of COOPERATIVE FEDERALISM in many areas of American life, but it was not a federalism without conflict and tensions, especially when national reformers challenged entrenched local customs and power relationships.

While encouraging the growth of big labor and ministering to the needs of the elderly and the poor, the New Deal also provided substantial benefits to American capitalists. Business opposition to Roosevelt was intense, but it was narrowly based in labor-intensive corporations in textiles, automobiles, and steel which had the most to lose from collective bargaining. The New Deal found many business allies among firms in the growing service industries of banking, insurance, and stock brokerage where government regulations promised to reduce cutthroat competition and to weed out marginal operators. Because of its aggressive policies to expand American exports and investment opportunities abroad, the New Deal also drew support from high-technology firms and from the large oil companies who were eager to penetrate the British monopoly in the Middle East.

Sophisticated businessmen discovered that they could live comfortably in a world of government regulation. The "socialistic" Tennessee Valley Authority lowered the profits of a few utility companies, but cheap electric power for the rural South translated into larger consumer markets for the manufacturers of generators, refrigerators, and other appliances. In addition to restoring public confidence in the stock exchanges and the securities industry, the Securities and Exchange Commission promoted self-regulation among over-the-counter dealers. Motor trucking firms received a helping hand from the Interstate Commerce Commission in reducing rate wars, and the major airlines looked to the Civil Aeronautics Board to protect them from the competitive rigors of the marketplace. When "Dr. Win-the-War" replaced "Dr. New Deal" after 1942, businessmen began to play key roles as well in the wartime agencies that regulated production, manpower, and the allocation of raw materials. The New Deal thus laid the foundations of both the welfare state and the permanent warfare state.

MICHAEL E. PARRISH
(1986)

Bibliography

CAREY, JANE PERRY 1865 The Rise of a New Federalism: Federal-State Cooperation in the United States. New York: Russell & Russell.

HAWLEY, ELLIS P. 1965 The New Deal and the Problem of Monopoly. Princeton, N.J.: Princeton University Press.

LEUCHTENBURG, WILLIAM E. 1963 Franklin D. Roosevelt and the New Deal. New York: Harper & Row.

PATTERSON, JAMES T. 1969 The New Deal and the States: Federalism in Transition. Princeton, N.J.: Princeton University Press.

POLENBERG, RICHARD 1972 War and Society: The United States 1941–1945. Philadelphia: Lippincott.

SCHLESINGER, ARTHUR M., JR. 1957, 1959, 1960 The Age of Roosevelt, 3 vols. Boston: Houghton Mifflin.

CONSTITUTIONAL HISTORY, 1945–1961

Reconversion to a peacetime society required reestablishing balance among the branches of the government and a careful reassessment of the role of each. The same process occasioned a reexamination of the relations between government and private power. These immediate problems of reconstruction were joined by the emergence of a "cold war" with the Communist bloc of nations. Americans defined that struggle as one against totalitarian rule—the antithesis of constitutional democracy.

The wartime period had seen massive government regulation of the economy and the personal lives of citizens. Congress had authorized governmental reorganization in 1941, reenacting a WORLD WAR I measure giving the President almost unlimited power to reorganize federal agencies directing the nation's resources in wartime. (See WAR POWERS ACT.) At the end of WORLD WAR II, Congress created a bipartisan Commission on Organization of the Executive Branch of the government headed by ex-President HERBERT HOOVER. It recommended reforms designed to reduce administrative disorder and bureaucracy. Congress in 1947 proposed the TWENTY-SECOND AMENDMENT (ratified in 1951) limiting presidential service to two terms.

Although many congressional conservatives hoped to roll back various New Deal programs, few were prepared to return the nation's economy to the unregulated control of private business leaders. Depression lessons had been painful. The FULL EMPLOYMENT ACT of 1946 declared that it was the government's task to take all steps necessary to maximize employment, production, and purchasing power. And while certain conservative congressmen were disturbed by the economic management this measure obviously necessitated, few opposed its goal of securing national economic stability. The Housing and Rent Act of 1947, continuing the wartime Price Control Act, raised an important question: does the WAR POWER continue after the shooting has ceased? The Supreme Court, in WOODS V. MILLER (1948), answered affirmatively as to legislation responding to wartime dislocations.

The issue of restraints on organized labor dissolved presidential-congressional harmony. President HARRY S. TRUMAN in 1946 vetoed the TAFT-HARTLEY ACT, an amendment to the 1935 WAGNER ACT, the nation's principal labor law. Taft-Hartley sought to eliminate an alleged prolabor bias by arming management with new rights and imposing limitations on long-established trade union practices. Truman called the act "completely contrary to the national policy of economic freedom," and "a threat to the successful working of our democratic society." But Congress passed it over his veto, and thirty states also enacted antilabor statutes, including RIGHT-TO-WORK LAWS and antipicketing measures. The LANDRUM-GRIFFIN ACT of 1959 sought to combat growing charges of union scandal, extortion, and deprivation of members' rights by imposing more direct federal authority over internal union procedures.

Executive-legislative cooperation resulted in passage of the Cellar-Kefauver Act of 1950, authorizing more rigid enforcement of the antitrust laws against corporate mergers. Two years later, following a Supreme Court ruling striking at "fair trade" laws, Congress passed the McGuire Act exempting state-approved fair trading from the federal antitrust laws. Seen as a consumer protection law, the measure was politically acceptable at the time.

In the FOREIGN AFFAIRS area, Congress and the President clashed. Truman had inherited a presidency whose prerogatives in foreign policy had been greatly expanded. Committed to the realization of Roosevelt's postwar programs, Truman backed American participation in the new United Nations. Such action entailed expanding presidential prerogatives at the expense of congressional power. American participation meant applying military sanctions against an aggressor state at the discretion of the United States delegate to the Security Council, who was under the control of the President. By the United Nations Participation Act of 1945 Congress recognized that the President could not commit the United States to participation in United Nations military sanctions without congressional consent, but it acknowledged implicitly that Congress's warmaking power was conditioned by the necessity of international security action. Similarly, when the United States joined the NORTH ATLANTIC TREATY Organization in 1950, it pledged automatic intervention if any member suffered armed attack. The question was raised whether such a commitment upset the traditional balance between the executive and legislative branches in questions of war and peace.

With the invasion of South Korea by Communist forces, presidential discretion rather than congressional action provided a dramatic answer. Truman, on June 25, 1950, without asking for a formal DECLARATION OF WAR or consulting Congress, ordered United States POLICE ACTION in the area. This order brought charges from Senator ROBERT A. TAFT that Truman had "usurped power and violated the Constitution and the laws of the United States." In the "great debate" that followed, Truman's actions and presidential war power generally were condoned, but not without a strong attempt, led by Senator John Bricker, to curb the treaty-making power of the President by constitutional amendment. One form of the unsuccessful BRICKER AMENDMENT would have declared: "A provision of a treaty or other international agreement which conflicts with this Constitution shall not be of any force or effect."

The Supreme Court ultimately eased the minds of Bricker's supporters. The circumstances were constitutionally significant. As new treaties of alliance grew in the late 1940s and early 1950s, American military and civilian personnel spanned the globe. Questions grew regarding the legal status of American citizens living abroad. Did the Constitution follow the flag? In REID V. COVERT (1957) the Court held that an EXECUTIVE AGREEMENT was subject to the limits of the Constitution, and thus could not confer on Congress power to authorize trial by COURT-MARTIAL of a civilian dependent of a serviceman stationed overseas. "We must not," wrote Justice HUGO L. BLACK, "break faith with this nation's tradition of keeping military power subservient to civilian authority."

Earlier, Congress had enacted a NATIONAL SECURITY ACT, creating the National Security Council and reorganizing the means by which war powers were exercised. The measure constricted the President's foreign policy prerogatives by requiring him to consult Congress before taking certain actions. In practice, however, it did not constrain willful Presidents. The ATOMIC ENERGY ACT of 1946 sought to insure civilian control over atomic energy production and precluded dissemination of technical information to other nations. By the 1950s, however, President Eisenhower sought and obtained an amendment, as the basis for an international cooperation program, to develop peaceful applications of nuclear energy. Nuclear power was apparently to become an important bargaining chip in the international arena.

One incident growing out of the KOREAN WAR revealed public feelings regarding the swelling authority of the executive and the proper nature of constitutional government. During the war, the President felt that constitutional history was on his side, given earlier validated presidential interventions in national emergency crises. He authorized his secretary of commerce to seize and operate struck steel mills, thereby insuring production of vital defense materials. His executive order was not based on statutory authority, but only on the ground that a threatened strike of the nation's steelworkers created a national emergency. When the steel companies sought an INJUNCTION against the government, federal spokesmen argued that the seizure was based upon Article II of the Constitution, and "whatever inherent, implied, or residual powers may flow therefrom." The President's actions drew sharp criticism, especially his refusal to use the Taft-Hartley Act provisions hated by his labor constituency. Before the Supreme Court, government counsel stressed expanded presidential prerogative during national emergencies, but the Supreme Court drew a line between public regulation and governmental operation of private business. In one of its most celebrated postwar constitutional decisions, the Court, speaking through Justice Black, rejected claims for presidential EMERGENCY POWERS and INHERENT POWERS in domestic affairs. Truman promptly announced compliance with the ruling, and the public reacted favorably to JUDICIAL ACTIVISM in curtailing excessive federal power. (See STEEL SEIZURE CONTROVERSY; YOUNGSTOWN SHEET & TUBE V. SAWYER.)

Constitutional development in the Truman years had been heavily influenced by considerations of national security at home and abroad, some serious, some specious, and all heavily political. Republican and conservative southern Democratic opponents of the New Deal had begun in 1938 to "red-bait" the Roosevelt administration by associating its personnel with un-Americanism or by representing the government's extension of powers as socialistic or communistic. Wartime investigations of federal employees and postwar revelations of inadequate security procedures intensified conservative demands for a housecleaning of the executive branch. Capitalizing on this issue during the 1946 congressional elections, the Republicans secured control of both houses of Congress, insuring that the subsequent Congress would investigate the loyalty of federal employees. During this period, the HOUSE COMMITTEE ON UN-AMERICAN ACTIVITIES (HCUA) was given permanent committee status, and between 1947 and 1948 Congress instituted thirty-five committee investigations of federal personnel and policies.

Lacking Roosevelt's political capital, and alarmed by leaks of classified information, Truman moved quickly to take control of the loyalty issue. In November 1946 he appointed a special presidential commission to investigate the problem, and in 1947 he formally instituted, by EXECUTIVE ORDER 983 . . . permanent federal employee LOYALTY-SECURITY PROGRAM. To disarm congressional opposition further, Truman appointed conservatives to the loyalty program's major administrative positions. Under this program, negative information from any source was the potential basis for a security dismissal or the denial of government service. An ATTORNEY GENERAL'S LIST of subversive organizations was drawn up, with membership a basis for dismissal. The only guideline the order provided was that a designated organization must be "totalitarian, Fascist, Communist, or subversive," or one adopting a policy "approving the commission of acts of force or violence to deny to others their constitutional rights."

Civil libertarians attacked the program on constitutional grounds, charging that it presumed employees to be subversive and subject to dismissal unless they could prove themselves innocent. Critics of the program also charged that it lacked procedural protections, a charge raised chronically against HCUA. However, the administration moved with regard for justice and fair play during its loyalty probes, and by early 1951 the Civil Service Commission had cleared more than three million federal employees; the Federal Bureau of Investigation had made 14,000 investigations of doubtful cases; over 2,000 employees had resigned, although in very few cases because of the investigation; and 212 persons had been dismissed because of reasonable doubts of their loyalty. In 1948 the executive branch also sought to demonstrate concern for national security by obtaining indictments of the eleven national leaders of the Communist party under the Smith Act. A long and bombastic trial followed, ending in convictions for conspiracy to advocate overthrow of the government by force and violence. (See DENNIS V. UNITED STATES.)

Conservative critics claimed that the Truman administration's loyalty efforts were window dressing to divert attention from more serious problems. The sensational Alger Hiss-Whittaker Chambers hearings and the resultant conviction of Hiss, a former New Deal official, for perjury in connection with disclosures of secret security information, catalyzed Congress into launching its own loyalty program. The MUNDT-NIXON BILL, seeking to force communists out into the open by requiring them to register with the Justice Department, was caught in 1948 election year politics and failed passage; but by 1950, following the reelection of Truman, the INTERNAL SECURITY

ACT, a similar measure, was passed resoundingly over the President's veto. The act went beyond the Truman loyalty program for government employees. It attempted to extend loyalty probes into nongovernmental areas of American life and generally assumed a need to shift the authority for security matters to congressional leadership. Civil libertarians challenged the measure as violative particularly of FIRST AMENDMENT guarantees. But in the Korean War period, with burgeoning security apprehensions fed aggressively by Senator JOSEPH R. MCCARTHY of Wisconsin, the possibility of launching a successful test case of even the act's most extreme provisions promised little success. Instead, Senator Patrick A. McCarran of Nevada, one of the measure's principal champions, persuaded Congress in 1952 to pass, over another Truman veto, a revised immigration law. The act contained provisions to prevent the admission of possible subversives, and it authorized DEPORTATION of immigrants with communist affiliations even after they had become citizens.

The expanded activities of congressional committees in LEGISLATIVE INVESTIGATIONS of loyalty and security raised important constitutional questions about committee prerogatives and behavior. While practice varied, some of the more flamboyant committees, such as HCUA, Senator McCarthy's Committee on Governmental Operations, or McCarran's Senate Internal Security Committee with large, aggressive, and ruthless staffs, pried into federal activities and even investigated subversion in the movie and entertainment industries, various private organizations, the academic community, and the churches. Committee actions alarmed civil libertarians, because of growing disregard for the type of procedural guarantees and safeguards of individual liberty normally afforded any citizen in a court of law. The committees browbeat witnesses, denied a RIGHT TO COUNSEL, and afforded no opportunity to examine charges, which were often irresponsible and from dubious sources. Opportunity to cross-examine witnesses was denied. Individuals' past affiliations and activities were used as evidence of guilt, and they were expected to prove themselves innocent to an obviously biased congressional "jury." As a result many witnesses invoked the Fifth Amendment, refusing to testify on the grounds that any statement made might tend to incriminate them. This led to charges that such citizens were "Fifth Amendment Communists." Congress in 1954 passed a FEDERAL IMMUNITY ACT to force testimony in return for promises of immunity from prosecution. (See IMMUNITY GRANT.) Generally the courts, including the Supreme Court, were cautious about thwarting government measures, deciding cases on the narrowest of grounds and proscribing only the most overt abuses.

Postwar demands for greater constitutional protections for minorities within American society expanded CIVIL RIGHTS. Many Americans believed that the United States should extend first class CITIZENSHIP to all. The struggle with the Communist world for the minds of Third World people added urgency. Early in 1946, President Truman established a Committee on Civil Rights affirming that "the preservation of civil rights, guaranteed by the Constitution, is essential to domestic tranquillity, national security, the general welfare, and the continued existence of our free institutions." In 1947 the committee proposed extension of an approach initiated by Attorney General FRANK MURPHY in the late 1930s, stressing that the federal government should be a shield in protecting citizens against those who would endanger their rights, and a sword to cut away state laws violating those rights. The report called for strengthening the CIVIL RIGHTS DIVISION of the Justice Department, using the Federal Bureau of Investigation in cases involving violations of civil rights, enacting antilynching and anti-POLL TAX laws, and establishing a permanent Fair Employment Practices Commission. However, with Southerners dominating many key congressional committees, prospects were dim for any program extending full civil rights to black Americans.

Truman determined to make the effort. In early 1948 he sent Congress a message calling for prompt implementation of the commission's report. A southern revolt in the Congress culminated in the secession of members from the Democratic Party. These "Dixiecrats" ran their own presidential candidate, J. Strom Thurmond, on a STATES' RIGHTS platform calling for "segregation of the races" and denouncing national action in behalf of civil rights as a "totalitarian concept, which threatens the integrity of the states and the basic rights of their citizens." Although Truman won the election, in the civil rights area he had available only executive remedies. These he utilized, strengthening the Civil Rights Division and encouraging the Justice Department to assist private parties in civil rights cases. He also ordered that segregation be ended in federal employment and that the armed services be fully integrated. (See EXECUTIVE ORDERS 9980 AND 9981.) These developments encouraged civil rights activists to look to the courts for constitutional action in behalf of minority rights. Truman's Supreme Court appointees, however, were consistently conservative and espoused a narrow view of the judicial power. Only a few cautious rulings proscribed some forms of RACIAL DISCRIMINATION. (See SHELLEY V. KRAEMER; SWEATT V. PAINTER.)

Although DWIGHT D. EISENHOWER shared many of Truman's views regarding the President's vital and dominant leadership role in foreign policy, he conceived the domestic presidency in a different light. No social crusader, Eisenhower also had no desire to undo major programs of the New and Fair Deals. Rather he saw the presidency as a mediating agency, harmonizing the functioning of the team, and ratifying decisions and policies carefully prepared by responsible subordinates or by congressional leadership. Thus during Eisenhower's eight years in office Congress reasserted considerable domestic initiative, and when the President acted he usually complemented congressional desires.

During the 1952 campaign, Republicans made much of the "Communists in government" issue. Eisenhower realized that loyalty-security actions had to be taken to satisfy a nervous public. In 1953, he established a new executive loyalty program that expanded the criteria of the earlier Truman program. Discharge from federal service was now based on a simple finding that the individual's employment "may not be clearly consistent with the interests of national security." Several thousand "security risks" were dismissed. HCUA, cheering from the sidelines, then attempted to subpoena former President Truman to explain his security inadequacies. Truman responded with a polite letter giving the committee a lecture on SEPARATION OF POWERS and the independence of the executive.

Critics of the program focused on the absence of PROCEDURAL DUE PROCESS, the prevalence of GUILT BY ASSOCIATION, and the use of "faceless informers" as sources of damaging accusations. As long as Senator McCarthy was riding high such allegations remained just that. Tired of being smeared as "soft on Communists," frustrated liberal Democrats pushed through Congress a COMMUNIST CONTROL ACT in 1954, outlawing the party and initially seeking to make party membership a crime. The act proved virtually unenforceable. With the Senate censure and eventual demise of Senator McCarthy and the growing lack of enthusiasm of the Eisenhower administration for fueling the loyalty hysteria, security issues drifted into the background. By the late 1950s respectable bodies such as the New York City Bar Association and the League of Women Voters called for more precise standards for the federal government's loyalty-security program. With the Supreme Court also questioning aspects of that program's constitutional insensitivity, the President in early 1960 established a new industrial security program with vastly improved procedural safeguards. It included FAIR HEARINGS, the right of CONFRONTATION, and the right to examine all charges under ordinary circumstances. The same spirit came to prevail in the operation of other security programs.

The Eisenhower administration showed concern for state prerogatives and the need for balancing them against the rights of the individual. The federal government's growth in size and power since the late 1930s had been paralleled in state governments. During this period the states collected more money, spent more, employed more people, and engaged in more activities than ever before. When the expenditure and employment were assisted by FEDERAL GRANTS-IN-AID, lack of state compliance with federal standards meant potential loss of federal revenues. But states acted enthusiastically on their own in areas ranging from education and social services to a struggle with the federal government over control of natural resources. In 1947 the Supreme Court ruled that the United States had dominion over the soil under the marginal sea adjoining California. That state had maintained it was entitled, by virture of the "equal footing" clause in the act admitting it to the Union, to the rights enjoyed by the original states and that those states owned such offshore areas. The Court concluded that such ownership had not been established at the time of the Constitution, and the interests of SOVEREIGNTY favored national dominion. But following the victorious Eisenhower campaign of 1952, in which the Republicans had courted the West and the South with promises of offshore riches, Congress passed the Submerged Lands Act of 1953, vesting in the states the ownership of lands beneath the marginal sea adjacent to the respective states. The Supreme Court subsequently denied leave to file complaints challenging the statute's constitutionality.

At another level, states and municipalities became so concerned in the 1950s with employees' loyalty that they enacted restrictive security measures. These included prohibiting the employment of Communist party members, LOYALTY OATHS as a condition of employment for teachers, service personnel, and candidates for public office, and measures authorizing state prosecution for SEDITION against the United States. State bar associations in turn moved to exclude from admission candidates who were allegedly former Communist party members or who refused to answer questions regarding former suspect affiliations. When the Supreme Court struck at such state sedition laws (PENNSYLVANIA V. NELSON, 1956) and bar restraints (SCHWARE V. NEW MEXICO BOARD OF BAR EXAMINERS, 1958; KONIGSBERG V. CALIFORNIA STATE BAR, 1957) its actions were denounced by the Conference of Chief Justices of the States as "the high-water mark . . . in denying to a state the power to keep order in its own house." Bills were introduced in Congress to deny the Court APPELLATE JURISDICTION in cases of this kind.

In this atmosphere, national leaders were hesitant to push for early implementation of the Supreme Court's DESEGREGATION mandate, and preferred to interpret the command "with ALL DELIBERATE SPEED" by emphasizing deliberation. A pattern of "massive resistance" emerged in the southern states, constituting a crazy quilt of INTERPOSITION proclamations, pupil-assignment or placement laws, freedom-of-choice laws, TUITION GRANT plans, and state statutes prescribing discipline of teachers for violation of state policies on the school segregation question. Meanwhile, federal authorities sat on their hands until after the 1956 election. Then they took cautious steps to bring the federal government more directly into the civil rights area. Eisenhower's attorney general proposed a federal statute to authorize an investigation of rights violations, particularly VOTING RIGHTS. The CIVIL RIGHT ACT OF 1957 passed after Southerners had so amended it as to make it virtually toothless. When Eisenhower signed the act into law early in September, he could have used a much stronger bill. One week earlier Governor Orville Faubus of Arkansas, an acknowledged segregationist, had ordered state troops into Little Rock to prevent implementation of a federal court order approving the admission of a handful of black students into that city's Central High School. Confronted with military defiance of federal authority, Eisenhower had no choice but to respond. He reluctantly dispatched several companies of the United States Army to Little Rock, under a provision of the United States Code, which authorized the suppression of insurrection and unlawful combinations that hindered the execution of either state or federal law. (See POSSE COMITATUS ACT.) He also nationalized and thus neutralized the Arkansas National Guard. Black children attended school for a year under military protection and Arkansas's massive resistance was held at bay by bayonets.

After the Little Rock case was decided by the Supreme Court in COOPER V. AARON (1958), which sustained the school desegregation order, Congress also acted. The CIVIL RIGHTS ACT OF 1960 made it a federal crime for a person to obstruct or interfere with a federal court order, or to attempt to do so by threats of force. Other provisions expanded federal remedies for enforcing voting rights. The measure, for which the Republicans claimed credit in their 1960 platform, put Congress and the executive branch on record as committed to push ahead with rights enforcement.

For minority groups without the political constituency of blacks, little positive action was forthcoming. Women's rights in this period was a subliminal theme at best. Women's work in World War II had gone a long way toward shattering the stereotype of the helpless, weaker sex in need of protective legislation. Some leaders in Congress moved toward proposal of the EQUAL RIGHTS AMENDMENT as a vote of thanks to women for their magnificent wartime performance. Both parties endorsed the measure at war's end, and Harry Truman spoke publicly in its support. But Eleanor Roosevelt, with the support of organized labor, insisted that protective legislation was more valuable for working women than the establishment of an abstract principle of legal rights. Despite two attempts in the Senate to pass a bill proposing the amendment in the late 1940s, and a third in 1953 with a rider specifying that no protective legislation was to be affected, the measure was not seriously revived in this period.

The rights of American Indians suffered even more. In 1953, the Eisenhower administration set out on a policy of "termination," supporting a program designed to reduce the federal government's involvement in Indian affairs and to "free" Indians from federal supervision. Specifically, termination sought to end the existing supportive federal-tribal relationship and transfer almost all responsibilities and powers from the federal government to the states. The effects on "terminated" tribes was disastrous; many tribal members were soon on public assistance rolls. Indians detested the law embodying this policy, seeing it as an instrument for tribal extinction. They expended their energies to defeat it, and finally achieved victory in 1968. The Indian Civil Rights Act of that year encouraged Indian self-determination with continuing government assistance and services.

The judicial branch in the period from 1945 to 1961 changed from a cautious and accommodating agency, under Chief Justice FRED M. VINSON, to an active, aggressive, and controversial storm-center under Chief Justice EARL WARREN. Just as WILLIAM HOWARD TAFT had made the Supreme Court the principal instrument for the determination of constitutionality in the 1920s, Earl Warren, who assumed the chief justiceship 1953, came to play a similar role in the late 1950s. Often backlash resulted, but in Warren's case, from conservatives and not liberals. Statistically, the WARREN COURT's record was not so activist as that of the 1920s. Four acts of Congress, eighty-five state acts, and sixteen ordinances were ruled unconstitutional from 1945 through 1960, with the Justices overruling twenty-two prior decisions. But the activist image was strong because the Court entered explosive areas of sensitive public policy.

The Court's unanimous decision in BROWN V. BOARD OF EDUCATION (1954) had shocked southern states-righters into defensive and retaliatory actions. The Court's consistent pushing ahead in the civil rights area sustained and intensified this antipathy. But Warren, supported by a liberal majority, was not prepared to stop. In the loyalty-security area, the Court limited the more sweeping provisions of the Smith Act, the Internal Security Act of 1950, and state loyalty measures. The rights of individuals and their protection from the abuses of government seemed to come first to the Justices' minds. The Court struck at departures from fair procedure by congressional committees. In *Jencks v. United States* (1957) it ruled that a defendant in a criminal case should have access to prior recorded statements of witnesses against him. Congress promptly sought to limit that ruling by the passage of the JENCKS ACT. By the late 1950s, the Justices began the process of critically examining state anti-OBSCENITY and censorship laws. In Congress there was talk of the need to curtail the Court's authority through legislation limiting its appellate jurisdiction. National action by right-wing groups quickly emerged to bolster such a movement, contributing to a broad public dialogue on the Court's proper function.

Defenders and critics of the Warren Court's liberal activism debated the proper role of the Constitution in the American polity. Champions of liberal judicial activism defended the legitimacy of judicial activity to shape constitutional law in accordance with democratic values. Supporters of judicial restraint advocated deference to popularly elected legislatures with courts confined to a narrowly circumscribed role. To conservative constitutionalists, the rule of law meant more than the imposition by a liberal Court of its own ethical imperatives, with little concern for orthodox doctrinal consistency.

There were no winners in this debate. But it proved apropos to the developments of the 1950s and to the institutional interrelationships of those years.

PAUL L. MURPHY
(1986)

Bibliography

MURPHY, PAUL L. 1969 *The Constitution in Crisis Times, 1918–1969.* New York: Harper & Row.
MURPHY, WALTER F. 1962 *Congress and the Court.* Chicago: University of Chicago Press.
PRITCHETT, C. HERMAN 1954 *Civil Liberties and the Vinson Court.* Chicago: University of Chicago Press.

CONSTITUTIONAL HISTORY, 1961–1977

An examination of nonjudicial constitutional development from the administration of President JOHN F. KENNEDY to that of President GERALD R. FORD reveals at the outset an unusual amount of constitutional change through the process of constitutional amendment. Indeed, counting the adoption of the BILL OF RIGHTS in 1791 as only one episode of constitutional change via the AMENDMENT PROCESS, the period from 1961 to 1977 was characterized by an exceptionally high level of constitutional amending activity, with four amendments adopted during the period. In contrast, again counting the adoption of the Bill of Rights as one amendment episode, there were thirteen constitutional amendments adopted between 1789 and 1961.

Three of the constitutional amendments adopted during the 1961–1977 period were clear reflections of the expansion of egalitarianism that found expression in other fields in the policies of REAPPORTIONMENT, and the enlargement of the protection of CIVIL RIGHTS. The TWENTY-THIRD AMENDMENT, adopted on March 19, 1961, extended the right to vote in presidential elections to the residents of the DISTRICT OF COLUMBIA although restricting the District to the number of electoral votes allotted to the least populous state. The TWENTY-FOURTH AMENDMENT, ratified on January 23, 1964, outlawed the imposition of POLL TAXES in presidential and congressional elections and therefore removed a form of WEALTH DISCRIMINATION in federal elections. The addition of this amendment to the Constitution was subsequently rendered superfluous by the Supreme Court's holding in HARPER V. VIRGINIA BOARD OF ELECTIONS (1966) that poll taxes were a form of INVIDIOUS DISCRIMINATION prohibited by the Constitution. Further extension of VOTING RIGHTS occurred with the adoption of the TWENTY-SIXTH AMENDMENT on June 30, 1971, which extended the right to vote in both federal and state elections to eighteen-year-old citizens. The Twenty-Sixth Amendment was necessitated by the Supreme Court's holding in OREGON V. MITCHELL (1974) that Congress lacked the constitutional power to legislate the eighteen-year-old vote in state and local elections.

In contrast with the Twenty-Third, Twenty-Fourth, and Twenty-Sixth Amendments, the Twenty-Fifth Amendment, relating to PRESIDENTIAL SUCCESSION and disability and adopted in 1967, was the result of years of debate with regard to the problems that might arise if an incumbent president were temporarily or permanently disabled. Serious consideration of such an amendment to the Constitution was prompted by the illnesses afflicting President DWIGHT D. EISENHOWER during his term of office, and additional impetus for constitutional change in this area was created by the assassination of President Kennedy in 1963.

Under the provisions of the Twenty-Fifth Amendment, the President may declare his own disability to perform the duties of the office by informing the president pro tempore of the SENATE and the speaker of the HOUSE OF REPRESENTATIVES in writing of his own disability. Alternatively, the President's disability may be declared in writing to the same congressional officers by the vice-president and a majority of the Cabinet. In either instance, the vice-president assumes the duties of the presidency as acting President. A period of presidential disability may be ended either by the President's informing the congressional officers in writing of the termination of his disability, or if there is disagreement between the President and the vice-president and a majority of the Cabinet on the issue of the President's disability, the Congress may resolve the dispute. A two-thirds majority of both houses of Congress, however, is required to declare the President disabled; otherwise, the President resumes the duties of his office.

Although the disability provisions of the Twenty-Fifth Amendment have not been applied, Section 2 of the amendment had an important impact on the succession to the presidency during the administration of President RICHARD M. NIXON. Section 2 provides that whenever a vacancy in the office of vice-president occurs, the President shall appoint a new vice-president with the approval of a majority of both houses of Congress. These provisions of the Twenty-Fifth Amendment came into play when Vice-President Spiro T. Agnew resigned his office in 1973 under the threat of prosecution for income tax evasion. Pursuant to Section 2, President Nixon appointed Congressman Gerald R. Ford of Michigan as Agnew's successor, and the Congress confirmed Ford as vice-president. Subsequently, President Nixon resigned his office on August 9, 1974, when his IMPEACHMENT for his involvement in the WATERGATE affair and other abuses of office seemed imminent, and Vice-President Ford succeeded Nixon in the office of President. Under the provisions of the Twenty-Fifth Amendment, Ford thus became the first appointed vice-president as well as the first unelected vice-president to assume the office of the presidency.

The Watergate affair that led to President Nixon's resignation involved not only charges of bugging the Democratic National Committee headquarters, and the obstruction by the executive of the subsequent investigation of that incident, but also more generalized abuses of power by the executive. In addition to the issue of the scope of EXECUTIVE PRIVILEGE, which was ultimately resolved by the Supreme Court adversely to the President's claims in UNITED STATES V. NIXON (1974), the Watergate affair raised major constitutional issues concerning the nature of the impeachment process, as the impeachment of a President was seriously considered by the Congress for the first time since the impeachment of President ANDREW JOHNSON in 1868. Because the Constitution provides that governmental officers including the President may be removed from office on impeachment for TREASON, bribery, or other high crimes and MISDEMEANORS, the consideration of the impeachment of President Nixon by the Congress involved the determination of what constituted an impeachable offense, an issue that had also been at the heart of the debate over the Johnson impeachment.

In the deliberations of the Judiciary Committee of the House of Representatives regarding ARTICLES OF IMPEACHMENT against President Nixon, the President's supporters argued that the President could be impeached only within the meaning of the Constitution for an indictable criminal offense. The President's opponents, on the other hand, contended that articles of impeachment could embrace political offenses, such as the abuse of power by the President, which were not indictable under the criminal law. The latter position ultimately prevailed among a majority

of the Judiciary Committee when the committee adopted three articles of impeachment against President Nixon that contained charges that were essentially political, abuse of power offenses which were not indictable.

Article one of the articles of impeachment charged the President with obstruction of justice and with violating his oath of office requiring him to see to it that the laws were faithfully executed, but the second and third articles charged him with violating the constitutional rights of citizens, impairing the administration of justice, misusing executive agencies, and ignoring the SUBPOENAS of the Judiciary Committee through which it had sought EVIDENCE related to its impeachment inquiry. Although these charges included some indictable offenses, in adopting the articles the majority of the committee obviously construed the words "high crimes and misdemeanors" to include offenses that did not involve indictable crimes. In reaching this conclusion, the committee majority took a position that conformed with the view of the nature of the impeachment process that the House of Representatives had adopted in the Johnson impeachment proceedings in 1868.

Whether this broad view of the nature of impeachable offenses would have been sustained by a majority of the House of Representatives or the required two-thirds majority in the Senate remained an unanswered question because of President Nixon's resignation in August 1974. The Supreme Court rejected the President's claim of executive privilege and ordered the disclosure of the White House tape recordings relevant to the trial of those indicted in the Watergate affair. On the tapes thus released there appeared conversations clearly indicating President Nixon's participation in a conspiracy to obstruct justice, an indictable offense. In light of almost certain impeachment by the House of Representatives and likely conviction in the Senate, President Nixon resigned. With the impeachment process thus aborted, the answer to what properly could be considered an impeachable offense was left unresolved, as it had been in the proceedings against President Johnson over a hundred years earlier.

The Watergate affair and the abuses of presidential power associated with it, along with the involvement of the United States in the Vietnam War, had a profound impact upon the principal nonjudicial constitutional issue during the 1961–1977 period—the issue of the proper relation between the powers of the executive branch of the government and the powers of the Congress. Beginning at least as early as the administrations of FRANKLIN D. ROOSEVELT in the 1930s and 1940s, the presidency had increasingly become the dominant political institution at the national level, and Roosevelt's successors refined and added to the assertions of PRESIDENTIAL POWER that had characterized his administrations. By the late 1960s and early 1970s, therefore, the "Imperial Presidency" had become the focus of considerable attention and constitutional controversy, and a reassertion of congressional power against the aggrandizement of presidential power had clearly begun.

This reassertion of congressional power was to a great extent a reaction to the expansion of the powers of the presidency to new extremes during the administration of President Nixon. Although previous presidents had asserted the power to impound and to refuse to expend funds appropriated by Congress in limited areas, President Nixon asserted a much broadened IMPOUNDMENT power as a presidential prerogative. Instead of the relatively isolated instances of presidential refusals to spend congressionally appropriated monies that had occurred previously, during the 1970s the Nixon administration impounded billions of dollars in congressional appropriations and effectively asserted a presidential power to enforce only those congressionally authorized programs that received the president's approval.

The involvement of the United States in the war in VIETNAM and Southeast Asia contributed to further controversy regarding the scope of presidential power to commit the armed forces to foreign military conflicts in the absence of a DECLARATION OF WAR by the Congress. The involvement of the United States in Vietnam had begun under President Kennedy with the dispatch of military advisers to the South Vietnamese armed forces, but under Presidents LYNDON B. JOHNSON and Nixon the American military presence in Southeast Asia grew to hundreds of thousands of troops. The failure of the American military efforts in Southeast Asia and the high cost of those efforts in lives and resources bolstered the arguments of critics that the power of the President to commit the United States to foreign military conflicts must be reined in.

Because of the impoundment policy of the Nixon administration and the presidential war in Southeast Asia, a reassertion of congressional power occurred in the field of domestic as well as FOREIGN AFFAIRS. The congressional response to the impoundment controversy was the enactment of the CONGRESSIONAL BUDGET AND IMPOUNDMENT CONTROL ACT OF 1974. This legislation provided that if the President resolved to eliminate the expenditure of funds appropriated by Congress, he was required to inform both houses of Congress of: the amounts involved; the agencies and programs affected; and the fiscal, budgetary, and economic effects of, and the reasons for, the proposed impoundment of funds. Both houses of Congress, the act provided, must approve the impoundment within forty-five days. If the President proposed instead to defer the spending of congressionally authorized appropriations, the act provided that he must similarly inform Congress of his intention to defer expenditures, and within forty-

five days either house of Congress could require the expenditure of the funds by passing a resolution disapproving the President's proposed action. If the President refused to abide by congressional disapproval of impoundments, the act further authorized the Comptroller General to initiate legal action in the federal courts to force compliance with the will of the Congress.

In addition to addressing the problem of presidential impoundments, the Congressional Budget and Impoundment Control Act was directed at strengthening the powers of Congress over the budgetary process. To replace the practice of enacting appropriations without regard to the total amount that should be appropriated in a given fiscal year, the act provided that the Congress should agree upon a BUDGET resolution at the outset of the appropriations process, setting the total amount of money to be appropriated during the fiscal year. The amount so specified would then govern the actions of Congress in considering individual appropriations bills.

Finally, the act created a new agency, the Congressional Budget Office, and authorized that agency to advise Congress regarding revenue estimates, the likely amount of deficits or revenue surpluses and other economic data important to the budgetary process. Congress thus created a congressional agency, beyond the control of the executive, which would be an independent source of economic and budgetary information in competition with the executive branch's Treasury Department and Office of Management and Budget.

This reassertion of congressional power over domestic policy was matched in the field of foreign policy by the WAR POWERS RESOLUTION of November 7, 1973, passed over the veto of President Nixon. In the War Powers Resolution, Congress sought to deal with the problem of presidential wars such as the military involvement of the United States in Southeast Asia. Congress therefore not only imposed restrictions upon the power of the President to commit the country's armed forces in foreign conflicts but also sought to define the war-making powers of both the President and the Congress.

With regard to the war-making power of the President, the War Powers Resolution declared that the President could introduce United States armed forces into hostilities, or into a situation in which imminent involvement in hostilities was clearly indicated by the circumstances, only pursuant to a declaration of war, or under specific statutory authorization, or in response to a national emergency created by an attack upon the United States, its territories or possessions, or its armed forces. The language of the resolution thus clearly repudiated the argument, frequently asserted in the past, that the President was constitutionally authorized to take whatever action deemed necessary to protect the national interest. The impact of the resolution as an authoritative congressional interpretation of the President's constitutional war-making power was diluted, however, by the decision of Congress to include the interpretation of the President's war-making power in the "Purpose and Policy" section of the act, with the result that it did not purport to have legally binding effect.

The parts of the War Powers Resolution that did purport to be legally binding required the President to consult with Congress in every possible instance before committing the armed forces in hostilities or hostile situations. If the armed forces are introduced by the President into hostilities or hostile situations in the absence of a declared war, the resolution provided, the President must report the situation in writing to the presiding officers of the Congress within forty-eight hours and continue to report every six months thereafter. The resolution further required that in the absence of a declared war, the introduction of the armed forces must be terminated within sixty days, or ninety days if the military situation makes their safe withdrawal impossible within sixty days. Finally, in the absence of a declared war or congressional authorization, the President must withdraw the armed forces from hostilities occurring outside the territory of the United States if Congress directs him to do so by CONCURRENT RESOLUTION, which is not subject to the President's veto power.

Although the War Powers Resolution was plainly an attempt by Congress to reassert its authority over presidential war-making and over the conduct of foreign affairs generally, its impact upon presidential power did not appear to have been so great as its supporters hoped or it critics feared at the time of its passage. During the administration of President Ford, American armed forces were introduced into hostile situations during the evacuation of Vietnam as well as during the recapture of the American merchantman *Mayaguez* and its crew from Cambodia. President Ford nevertheless did not feel bound in these actions by the terms of the War Powers Resolution but rather made plain his conviction that he was acting under his constitutional powers as COMMANDER-IN-CHIEF and as chief executive. The War Powers Resolution was thus subjected to early challenge as an authoritative construction of the President's war-making power. Given the ability of Presidents to marshal public support for their actions in foreign affairs, particularly in times of crisis, it was clear that the act could not be considered the last word regarding the relative power of Congress and the President in the field of foreign policy and war-making.

Just as the War Powers Resolution and the Congressional Budget and Impoundment Control Act symbolized the reassertion of congressional power in relation to the executive, both also embodied the device which Congress increasingly used in reasserting power over executive policymaking—the LEGISLATIVE VETO. The legislative veto first emerged as a congressional device for controlling the executive during the 1930s when Congress reserved the right to veto presidential proposals to reorganize the executive branch, but by the 1970s the legislative veto in various forms had proliferated and had been embodied in almost two hundred statutes enacted by Congress. The increased use of the legislative veto reflected Congress's dissatisfaction with its relationship with the executive and a desire to reassert policymaking power that had been eroded during the previous decades of heightened executive power.

Congress employed the legislative veto to disapprove proposed presidential actions, to disapprove rules and regulations proposed by the executive branch or administrative agencies, and to order the termination of presidential actions. The device took several forms, with some statutes requiring a resolution of approval or disapproval by only one house of Congress, others requiring both houses to act through a concurrent resolution, and still others conferring upon congressional committees the power to exercise the legislative veto.

Despite its increased use by Congress, the legislative veto was frequently opposed by the executive branch since its introduction in the 1930s on the grounds that the practice violates the Constitution. The executive and other critics of the legislative veto argued that the practice violated the principle of SEPARATION OF POWERS, ignored the principle of bicameralism in the exercise of legislative power, and allowed Congress to avoid the President's veto power which is normally applicable to legislation passed by Congress.

The constitutional principle of separation of powers, critics of the legislative veto noted, permits Congress to shape national policy by passing statutes, but, properly construed, does not permit Congress to interfere in the enforcement or administration of policy—a power properly belonging to the executive branch. The legislative veto, it was argued, thus violated a fundamental constitutional principle, especially insofar as it was used to allow Congress to veto rules and regulations proposed by executive or administrative agencies under DELEGATIONS OF POWER from the Congress.

Opponents also argued that the Constitution contemplates that Congress's policy-making role ordinarily requires the passage of statutes by both houses of Congress with the presentation of the statutes to the President for his approval or disapproval. By allowing the approval or disapproval of national policy through single house resolutions, JOINT RESOLUTIONS, or decisions of congressional committees, it was argued, the legislative veto ignored the bicameral legislative process contemplated by the Constitution and in addition permitted congressional policymaking through mechanisms not subject to the President's veto power, as the Constitution also contemplated.

Congress, on the other hand, clearly viewed the legislative veto as a useful weapon in exercising oversight over the executive and the bureaucracy, both of which were recipients of massive delegations of legislative power since the 1930s. Striking at another source of the imperial presidency, Congress thus embodied the legislative veto in the National Emergencies Act of 1976, which terminated national emergencies declared by the President in 1933, 1950, 1970, and 1971, and required the President to inform the Congress of the existence of national emergencies and the powers the executive intends to use in managing the emergency. Such emergencies, the act provided, could be terminated at any time by Congress via a concurrent resolution. (See EMERGENCY POWERS.)

Despite the long-standing controversy regarding the constitutional legitimacy of the legislative veto, the Supreme Court did not pass upon the validity of the device until 1983. In IMMIGRATION AND NATURALIZATION SERVICE V. CHADHA (1983), however, the Court declared the legislative veto invalid on the ground that it violated the constitutional principles requiring legislative enactments to be passed by both houses of Congress and to be subject to the veto powers of the President.

Just as the period from the administration of President Kennedy to that of President Ford witnessed significant readjustments of presidential-congressional relations, dramatic changes also occurred during the period in the nature of the political party system and the electoral process. Perhaps the most significant development was the decline in the power and influence of the major political parties. The decline in the percentage of the public who identified with the Republican and Democratic parties that began in the 1950s continued during the 1960s and 1970s. In 1952 twenty-two percent of the voters indicated a strong identification with the Democratic party, while thirteen percent indicated such an identification with the Republican party. By 1976, these percentages had declined to fifteen and nine percent, respectively, while the number of voters identifying themselves as independents had risen significantly.

This decline in voter identification with the two major political parties was accompanied by a decline in the importance of the national conventions of the two parties in the selection of presidential candidates. In 1960, only sixteen states selected their delegations to the national party conventions through presidential primaries, but by 1976 thirty states used the primary system for the selection of national party convention delegates, with the result that almost three-quarters of the Democratic national convention delegates and well over sixty percent of the Republican delegates were selected through the presidential primary process. Nominations of presidential candidates were consequently no longer the products of negotiations among party leaders at the national conventions; rather the national conventions merely ratified the selection of a presidential candidate as determined in the presidential primaries. And this decline in the significance of the national conventions was furthered, in the Democratic party, by the adoption of rules during the 1970s diminishing the power of party leaders and requiring proportional representation of women, minority groups, and other constituent groups within the party.

The decline of power of the political parties was furthered by the adoption of federal CAMPAIGN FINANCING laws in 1971, 1974, and 1976 which limited the amounts that could be contributed to election campaigns by individuals and groups and provided for federal financing of presidential elections. The result was a further diminution of the importance of traditional party organizations to presidential candidates, who increasingly relied upon personal campaign organizations both to win nomination and to conduct their national election campaigns. In a governmental system based upon the separation of powers, the decline of the party system, which traditionally had served to bridge the gap between the executive and legislative branches, could only have profound effects upon the capacity of Presidents to lead as well as upon the formation of national policy.

The period between 1961 and 1977 witnessed an acceleration of a long-term trend toward the centralization of power in the national government, although by the end of the period a significant reaction to this trend had become apparent. Two primary factors contributed to this centralizing trend: increased subsidization by the national government of programs at the state and local levels, and the assumption of responsibility by the national government over vast areas that had traditionally been left to state and local governments.

When John F. Kennedy was elected in 1960, for example, FEDERAL GRANTS-IN-AID to state and local governments stood at just over seven billion dollars and accounted for approximately fifteen percent of the total expenditures of state and local governments. By 1976, these federal grants-in-aid had mushroomed to almost sixty billion dollars and constituted almost twenty-five percent of total state and local expenditures.

Not only did state and local governments become increasingly dependent financially upon federal largess during this period but the character of federal grant-in-aid programs was also significantly altered. Before the 1960s, federal aid was primarily directed at subsidizing programs identified by state and local governments, but during the

1960s the identification of program needs increasingly shifted to the national government, with federal funds allocated according to national priorities. In addition, many federal grants, especially during President Johnson's War on Poverty program, were distributed at the local community level, by-passing state governors and officials who had traditionally had a voice in the administration of federal grants. As a result of the ensuing outcry from state and local officials, during the late 1960s and 1970s the federal government resorted to the device of block grants to state and local governments, grants involving fewer nationally imposed restrictions on their use and thus allowing the exercise of greater discretionary power by state and local officials. In 1972, Congress also adopted the State and Local Fiscal Assistance Act, which embraced the principle of federal revenue sharing with state and local governments. Despite the greater flexibility allowed state and local decision makers under REVENUE SHARING and block grants, the financial dependence of state and local governments on the national government in 1976 was eight times what it had been in 1960.

During the same period, the federal government's power was significantly expanded through congressional passage of a host of new statutes that expanded the regulatory role of the federal government in numerous new fields. Civil rights, the environment, occupational safety, consumer protection, and many other fields for the first time were subjected to extensive federal regulation. Since almost all of the new regulatory statutes involved extensive delegation of legislative power by Congress to the bureaucracy, the new expansion of federal regulatory authority involved a massive increase in administrative rules and regulations, as the bureaucracy exercised the legislative powers that had been delegated to it.

This increased intrusion of the federal government into the lives and affairs of the public ultimately produced a backlash of hostility toward the federal bureaucracy. John F. Kennedy had campaigned for the presidency in 1960 with the promise to get the country moving again, a promise suggesting an activist role for the national government. Because of the backlash against the expansion of the regulatory role of the federal government, however, presidential candidates in 1976 found that attacks on the federal bureaucracy and the national government as a whole hit a responsive chord with the public and proved to be popular campaign rhetoric.

This unpopularity of the bureaucracy, however, was only one symptom of the American public's shaken confidence in its major political institutions that had become manifest by the mid-1970s. Between 1961 and 1976, one President had been assassinated, one had resigned in disgrace, the long and costly war in Vietnam had concluded in disaster, and the Watergate affair had revealed the betrayal of the public trust at the highest levels of the government as well as abuses of power with sinister implications for the liberties of the American people. Such traumatic events not only undermined public confidence in political institutions but also profoundly affected the course of constitutional development. The office of the presidency, which since the 1930s had evolved into the dominant political institution at the national level, was consequently diminished considerably by 1976 in both power and prestige. Although a resurgence of congressional power had occurred in the 1970s, there was little evidence that Congress was institutionally capable of assuming the role of national leadership previously performed by the presidency, and effective national leadership had been made even more difficult by the decline of the political party system.

The most basic problem confronting the American polity by 1976 was nevertheless the problem of the loss of public confidence in governmental institutions. And the restoration of that confidence was the most profoundly difficult and fundamentally important task American public leadership faced as this period of constitutional development came to a close.

RICHARD C. CORTNER
(1986)

Bibliography

ALEXANDER, HERBERT 1976 *Financing Politics: Money, Elections and Political Reform.* Washington, D.C.: Congressional Quarterly.

DRY, MURRAY 1981 The Congressional Veto and the Constitutional Separation of Powers. In Bessette, Joseph M. and Tulis, Jeffry, *The Presidency in the Constitutional Order.* Baton Rouge: Louisiana State University Press.

JACOB, HERBERT and VINES, KENNETH N., eds. 1976 *Politics in the American States: A Comparative Analysis*, 3rd ed. Boston: Little, Brown.

KEECH, WILLIAM R. and MATTHEWS, DONALD R. 1977 *The Party's Choice.* Washington, D.C.: Brookings Institution.

KURLAND, PHILIP B. 1977 *Watergate and the Constitution.* Chicago: University of Chicago Press.

SCHLESINGER, ARTHUR M., JR. 1973 *The Imperial Presidency.* Boston: Houghton Mifflin.

SCIGLIANO, ROBERT 1981 The War Powers Resolution and the War Powers. In Bessette, Joseph M. and Tulis, Jeffry, *The Presidency in the Constitutional Order.* Baton Rouge: Louisiana State University Press.

SUNDQUIST, LEONARD D. 1981 *The Decline and Resurgence of Congress.* Washington, D.C.: Brookings Institution.

CONSTITUTIONAL HISTORY, 1977–1985

As America moved from commemorating the bicentennial of the DECLARATION OF INDEPENDENCE to commemorating the bicentennial of the Constitution, the political order was in apparent disarray. Constitutional history is, primarily, an account of changes in the distribution of power and authority within a regime. At least since 1933, political power in the American regime had shifted toward the federal government, and, within the federal government, toward the executive branch. Commentators referred to an "imperial presidency"; and yet no one since DWIGHT D. EISENHOWER had held the presidential office for two full terms. JOHN F. KENNEDY had been assassinated; LYNDON B. JOHNSON had abandoned the quest for reelection; RICHARD M. NIXON had been forced to resign; GERALD R. FORD, the appointed vice-president who succeeded Nixon, lost his bid for election in his own right. JIMMY CARTER, who defeated Ford, was to prove unable to carry the burden of the presidency, and so to be crushed in his bid for reelection by the landslide that elected RONALD REAGAN.

The national consensus about what the government should be and should do, at bottom a consensus about the meaning of the Constitution, was breaking down. No longer did national majorities automatically form behind the notions of positive government, of redistribution of wealth and incomes, or of solving anything identified as a "national problem" by creating a new administrative agency within the federal BUREAUCRACY. There were indications that a new consensus was forming, but it was not yet fully formed. Less clearly than in the past—say, in 1800, 1832, 1860, or 1932—was the new consensus readily identified with the program of a particular POLITICAL PARTY, although the revitalization of the Republican party gave it the better claim to such identification.

Constitutional history can be understood either broadly or narrowly. In the broad sense, the constitution is the arrangement of offices and the distribution of powers in a country, it is how the country governs itself. In a narrow sense, the Constitution is a document in which the framework for self-government is spelled out. The process of constitutional change in the United States most often involves redistribution of power without constitutional amendment.

Formal amendment of the Constitution is a rare event. Only thirty-two amendments have ever been proposed by Congress, and two of those were pending as 1977 began; by 1985 both had died for want of RATIFICATION. The EQUAL RIGHTS AMENDMENT (ERA), ostensibly a guarantee that women and men would be treated equally under the law, but potentially a blank check for expansion of federal and judicial power, had been proposed in 1972. The DISTRICT OF COLUMBIA REPRESENTATION AMENDMENT, which would have made the national capital the equivalent of a STATE for most purposes, had been proposed in 1978. Even as those proposals failed to obtain the necessary votes in state legislatures, there was popular demand for more amendments: to mandate a balanced federal BUDGET; to proscribe SCHOOL BUSING as a remedy for de facto school segregation; to permit prayer in public schools; and to overturn the Supreme Court's proclamation of a constitutional right to abortion.

Amendments to accomplish each of these objectives were introduced in Congress, and the ERA was reintroduced, but none was proposed to the states. Indeed, only one amendment received a two-thirds vote in either house of Congress: the balanced budget amendment passed the Senate, but died when the House of Representatives failed to act on it. In the case of the balanced budget amendment, there were petitions from thirty-three states (one less than constitutionally required) calling for a convention to frame the proposal. Although there was much speculation among politicians, academicians, and pundits about how such a convention might work and whether it could be restricted in its scope, the failure of a thirty-fourth state to act made the speculation at least temporarily moot.

For three decades, constitutional innovation had been centered on the judicial branch. Between 1977 and 1985, however, constitutional development centered on the contest between Congress and the executive branch for predominance. The most important constitutional decision of the Supreme Court during the period, IMMIGRATION AND NATURALIZATION SERVICE V. CHADHA (1983), passed on a phase of that contest.

The only uniquely American constitutional doctrine is that of the SEPARATION OF POWERS attended by CHECKS AND BALANCES. The embodiment of that doctrine in the Constitution set up a constant rivalry for preeminence between the political branches and an intense jealousy of powers and prerogatives. Beginning in the FRANKLIN D. ROOSEVELT era, the President—or the institutionalized presidency—seemed to acquire ever more power within the political system, and appeared to have acquired a permanent position of dominance. But the VIETNAM WAR and the WATERGATE crisis led to a resurgence of Congress, represented especially in the War Powers Resolution of 1973 and the CONGRESSIONAL BUDGET AND IMPOUNDMENT CONTROL ACT of 1974.

The seizure of the American embassy in Iran by Islamic revolutionary guards in 1979 set the stage for reassessment of the constitutional status of the WAR POWERS. President Carter in April 1980 ordered the armed forces to attempt a rescue of the American citizens held hostage in Tehran. The secrecy necessarily surrounding such an attempt precluded the "consultations" mandated by the War Powers Resolution. When, through the coincidence of bad planning and bad weather, the operation proved a costly failure, congressional critics were quick to denounce Carter for his defiance of the law—some going so far as to call for his IMPEACHMENT. The hostages subsequently were released as the result of an EXECUTIVE AGREEMENT by which Carter canceled the claims of some Americans against the revolutionary government of Iran and caused other claims to be submitted to an international tribunal rather than to American courts. This settlement of the hostage crisis appeared to some observers to exceed the scope of presidential power, but it was upheld by the Supreme Court in DAMES & MOORE V. REGAN (1981).

The War Powers Resolution continued to bedevil presidential conduct of FOREIGN AFFAIRS during the Reagan administration; but the real character of that controversial resolution was revealed by the contrast between two incidents involving American military forces. In 1981 President Reagan, at the request of all of the governments of the region, and in conjunction with two foreign allies, detailed a battalion of marines to Beirut, Lebanon, as part of an international peacekeeping force. The operation was not of the sort explicitly covered by the War Powers Resolution, and Reagan, although he communicated with members of Congress, did not take steps to comply with the consultation or reporting requirements of the resolution. Congress, however, unilaterally acted to approve the President's course of action rather than precipitate a confrontation over either the applicability of the resolution or its constitutionality. Several months after a suicide bomber killed more than 200 marines, the President withdrew the rest of the marines from Lebanon, conceding a major foreign policy failure; but Congress, because it had acted affirmatively to approve the operation, was in no position to condemn the President for that failure.

Subsequently, in 1984, the President authorized a military operation to rescue American citizens trapped in the small Carribean nation of Grenada and to liberate that country from a Cuban-sponsored communist dictatorship. Such an operation was precisely within the terms of the War Powers Resolution, but it was planned and executed in secrecy and, again, the President complied with neither the consultation nor the reporting requirements of the resolution. However, because the operation was perceived as a success, most members of Congress refrained from complaining about the breach of the War Powers Resolution.

As the War Powers Resolution represented the resurgence of Congress in the foreign policy arena, the Congressional Budget Act was designed to reassert congressional control over government spending priorities. The federal budgetary process had been introduced in the 1920s to replace the chaotic amalgam of uncoordinated appropriations by which Congress had theretofore allocated federal revenues. But the executive budget, while coordinating expenditures and subjecting them to a common annual plan, remained detached from the appropriations process; hence disputes arose between the branches, especially when the aggregate of appropriations exceeded the executive's estimate of revenues. The deferral and cancellation of appropriated expenditures—called IMPOUNDMENT—became especially controversial when President Nixon was accused of using them for political, rather than economic, reasons.

The 1974 act purported to solve the problem by making budget planning a congressional function and by linking budgeting and appropriations in a single process. But, because the internal structure of Congress is not conducive to unified decision making and because the executive branch has not conceded that the detailed planning of expenditures is properly a legislative activity, the revised budget process has not been successful. The national government commonly operates for most of the year on the basis of resolutions authorizing continued spending at some percentage increase over the previous year's spending plus numerous special appropriations.

Between 1977 and 1985, as, to a lesser degree, between WORLD WAR II and 1977, one of the great tests of constitutional government in America was the fiscal crisis resulting from persistent excesses of governmental expenditures over governmental revenues. Under constant political pressure to maintain or increase expenditure levels, but facing the unpopularity of increases in taxation (combined with the economic difficulty that increased tax rates may, by diminishing the tax base, actually result in lower revenues), Congress has resorted to borrowing to finance chronic deficits. At the end of 1985, Congress enacted, and President Reagan signed, a law providing for automatic reductions of appropriations when projected deficits reached specified levels. However, the ink was hardly dry before that measure (the GRAMM-RUDMAN-HOLLINGS ACT) was challenged as unconstitutional, even by some members of Congress and some representatives of the administration.

State legislatures, commonly required by their state constitutions to balance their own annual budgets, have petitioned Congress for a convention to propose a balanced budget amendment to the federal constitution. How even a constitutional mandate could be enforced to make Congress do what it seems unable to do, that is, to make difficult choices about public affairs, remains unclear. Meanwhile, the Congressional Budget Act exists to frustrate any attempt of the executive branch to supply the decision making.

Yet another device by which Congress attempted to reassert itself in the contest for dominance under a constitution that separates powers was the LEGISLATIVE VETO. Long before 1977, the DELEGATION OF POWER to the executive branch and to various INDEPENDENT REGULATORY AGENCIES was so great that the published volumes of federal regulations exceeded in number by many times the volumes of federal statutes. In statutes delegating legislative power to administrative bodies, Congress began to include provisions allowing Congress, or one house of Congress, to deprive agency actions of effect by simple resolution. In June 1983 the Supreme Court, in IMMIGRATION AND NATURALIZATION SERVICE V. CHADHA, held that the legislative veto, in some or all of its forms, was unconstitutional. The effect of the *Chadha* decision on legislative veto provisions that differed significantly from that in the Immigration and Nationality Act remained unclear for some time after the decision, and Congress continued to enact new legislative veto provisions after the decision. The real winner in that struggle for power, however, was not the President, but the bureaucracy.

Congress also asserted itself in more traditional ways, especially by exploiting the constitutional requirement that certain presidential actions have the Senate's ADVICE AND CONSENT. One category of such action is treaty making. President Carter suffered embarrassment over the PANAMA CANAL TREATIES and defeat on the second Strategic Arms Limitation Treaty. The Panama Canal debate was the first extended debate on a major treaty since that on the Treaty of Versailles in 1919. The treaty was signed in September 1977 but the Senate did not consent to its ratification until the spring of 1978. The vote was 68–32 (only one affirmative vote more than required) and the Senate attached a "reservation" to the treaty, asserting that the United States could intervene militarily if the canal should ever be closed; the reservation nearly caused Panama to rescind its ratification of the treaty. President Carter signed the strategic arms treaty in July 1979 at a summit meeting with President Leonid Brezhnev of the Soviet Union. Although trumpeted as a major foreign policy achievement, the treaty was delayed in Senate hearings and finally shelved in 1980 after the Soviet Union invaded Afghanistan.

President Carter vigorously asserted the presidential treaty power when, after recognizing the People's Republic of China in Beijing as the lawful government of all of China he unilaterally abrogated the long-standing mutual defense treaty between the United States and the Republic of China on Taiwan. An affronted Congress immediately provided for a United States Institute to represent American interests in the Republic of China while delaying for over a year Carter's request that trade preferences be granted to the mainland regime. Congress was unable to salvage the mutual defense treaty, however; and the Supreme Court held in GOLDWATER V. CARTER (1979) that members of Congress lacked STANDING to challenge the President's action in court.

The other category of action requiring Senate approval is appointments. The Senate, although nominally controlled by the President's own party, frequently used confirmation hearings and votes to express disapproval of certain Reagan administration policies, especially the administration's reluctance to impose and enforce AFFIRMATIVE ACTION requirements. The Senate delayed for over a year appointment of Edwin Meese to be ATTORNEY GENERAL, and rejected outright the promotion of William Bradford Reynolds to be associate attorney general. Although Reagan's nomination of SANDRA DAY O'CONNOR to the Supreme Court (the only nomination to the Court between 1977 and 1985) was approved rapidly and without serious controversy, several other judicial appointments were delayed or rejected.

Another signal characteristic of American constitutionalism is FEDERALISM. From the mid-1930s on, the balance of power between the national government and the states has been shifting steadily in favor of the national government. President Reagan came to office pledging a reversal of that trend. However, his proposal for a "new federalism," in which governmental functions assumed by the national government would be relinquished to the states, was coolly received not only by Congress but also by state politicians, who feared that their responsibilities would increase even as their revenues continued to decrease. Somewhat more successful was Reagan's proposal to replace the myriad of categorical FEDERAL GRANTS IN-AID, by which the national government partially funded certain mandated programs and set the standards by which the programs were to be run, with block grants.

Congress, however, has increasingly imposed conditions and restrictions on the use of block grant funds; so even the limited victory may prove hollow. Although conservatives like President Reagan frequently express a principled aversion to the use of conditional grants of money as a means to coerce the states into acceding to federal goals and programs, they have not been so averse in practice. Examples of new uses of the TAXING AND SPENDING POWER to accomplish legislative goals not strictly within Congress's ENUMERATED POWERS include: a requirement that hospitals receiving federal funds perform certain lifesaving measures on behalf of handicapped newborn children; a requirement that states, as a condition of receiving highway building funds, enact certain provisions to counter drunken driving; and a requirement that schools, as a condition of receiving federal aid, permit religious groups to meet in their facilities on the same basis as do other extracurricular organizations.

Whether the election of 1980 wrought an enduring change in the constitution of American government remains an open question. Although President Reagan decisively defeated former Vice-President Walter F. Mondale in 1984, the House of Representatives remained under the control of Carter's and Mondale's party. And the

Senate, even with a Republican majority, did not prove to be so committed as the President to reduction of the role of the federal government in American society. Nevertheless, Reagan had considerable success in achieving the deregulation of some kinds of businesses and in returning to private enterprise some activities that had come under the ownership and management of the federal government. On the other hand, the heralded "new federalism" did not cause a resurgence in the relative importance of the state governments, and federal control continued to be maintained through the use of conditions attached to grants-in-aid. At the bicentennial of the Constitution, it is still too early to say whether Reagan effected, as he said he would, "another American revolution."

DENNIS J. MAHONEY
(1986)

Bibliography

CARTER, JIMMY 1984 *Keeping the Faith.* New York: Bantam.

FISHER, LOUIS 1984 *Congressional Conflicts between Congress and the President.* Princeton, N.J.: Princeton University Press.

GINSBERG, BENJAMIN 1987 *Reconstituting American Politics.* New York: Oxford University Press.

HOWITT, ARNOLD M. 1984 *Managing Federalism.* Washington: Congressional Quarterly.

SCHRAMM, PETER W. and MAHONEY, DENNIS J., eds. 1986 *The 1984 Election and the Future of American Politics.* Durham, N.C.: Carolina Academic Press.

CONSTITUTIONAL HISTORY, 1980–1989

The major constitutional development of the 1980s was the confirmation of divided government as a legitimate alternative to presidential party government as a model for constitutional administration. In the elections of 1980 and 1984 the people chose a Republican President while returning a Democratic majority to the HOUSE OF REPRESENTATIVES. In 1986 the Democratic party regained control of the Senate, which it retained in 1988 as the REPUBLICAN PARTY again won the presidency. This type of split-ticket voting was a relatively new phenomenon in modern American politics. From 1889 to 1953, no President on his inauguration faced a Congress one house of which was controlled by the opposition party. The contemporary period of divided government began in 1969 when the Republican RICHARD M. NIXON was elected President and the Democrats controlled Congress. After the resignation of Nixon in 1974, the Democrats briefly revived presidential party government with the election of JIMMY CARTER in 1976. Their inability to govern effectively despite having power over both political branches prepared the way for the Republican capture of the White House in 1980.

Throughout the 1980s, assessments of divided government tended to be uncertain because such government contradicted what had come to be accepted since the NEW DEAL as the constitutional norm, namely, presidential government under a dominant party after a critical or realigning election. In fact, there were indications in Nixon's two election victories of a disintegration of the New Deal liberal coalition and an expectation of a political realignment that would enable the presidential party system to continue. The problem with this analysis was that while twentieth-century presidential government was historically liberal, many students of politics believed it was also inherently or in its nature liberal. Many observers were therefore reluctant to conclude that divided government could represent the deliberate choice of the electorate or that it could be a satisfactory approach to running the Constitution, despite the fact that it brought the constitutional principle of the SEPARATION OF POWERS more directly to bear on the conduct of government.

Part of the difficulty observers had in recognizing the legitimacy of divided government was attributable to the political popularity of RONALD REAGAN. Despite having twice been elected governor of California, Reagan was an improbable candidate for President. This improbability owed less to his being a former Hollywood actor than to his advocacy of NATURAL RIGHTS individualism, LIMITED GOVERNMENT, and middle class social values that had come to be identified in the dominant political culture as the essence of right-wing reactionism. Labeled an "ideological" candidate by the national media, he ran on a platform that proposed to reverse the tide of centralized BUREAUCRACY, restore equal opportunity for individuals, stimulate economic growth through deregulation and market incentives, and rebuild national defense. Reagan's assertion of these policies made the election of 1980 the most significant since 1932. In effect, it was a REFERENDUM on the regulatory WELFARE STATE, broadly conceived in the light of the liberal reforms of the 1960s and 1970s. When President Reagan won reelection in 1984, and Vice-President GEORGE BUSH won election as President in 1988, in a significant sense the era of welfare state liberalism was over, a fact difficult to deny. Divided government was the constitutional expression of this political change.

In one sense, the source or cause of divided government was the Constitution. The FUNDAMENTAL LAW organizes government into three coordinate branches and, in the words of THE FEDERALIST #51, guards against a concentration of the several powers in the same department by "giving to those who administer each department the necessary constitutional means and personal motives to resist the encroachments of the others." Moreover, the Constitution permits voters to make a free political choice, including that of ticket splitting (which some critics of divided government have proposed to restrict by a constitutional amendment). Furthermore, the Constitution does not establish POLITICAL PARTIES in the structure of government, but allows them to exist as voluntary associations regulated by state and federal law. A contributing factor to divided government was the decline of partisan loyalty in the electorate, caused in part by antiparty reform measures, such as CAMPAIGN FINANCE laws. With the decline of party, political choice was based in part on the political values, principles, and governmental duties and functions associated with the executive and legislative branches or their leading officials. The separation of powers, one of the basic concepts of limited government, was thus the organizing principle of divided government.

A second apparent cause of divided government was uncertainty or ambivalence in the electorate about the basic direction of public policy. In electing Republican chief executives, the people approved of policies aimed at economic expansion, control of inflation, tax reform, limitations on government spending, and strengthened national defense. In voting Democratic control of Congress, the people expressed a desire to maintain the social welfare and regulatory programs that constituted the achievement of modern liberalism. These included ENTITLEMENT programs and legally conferred benefits for individuals and groups in every social class. Although politically contradictory, these policy alternatives might be seen as reflecting complementary dimensions of the public philosophy underlying American CONSTITUTIONALISM: individualism, based on natural rights principles that limit government power, and the public interest, based on community consensus that requires government regulation.

Nevertheless, in a relative historical sense, by contrast with the period of presidential party government which it succeeded, the public philosophy of divided government represented a partial attempt to restore an older conception of limited government. This was the idea that federal power was limited to specific ends or objects in accordance with the federal principle of divided SOVEREIGNTY. Reagan administration proposals for a new FEDERALISM that would return certain policy matters to the states expressed this outlook. Underlying these proposals was the more basic idea of restoring a sense of discipline and limitation in the conduct of government, seen in attempts to limit government spending, reduce the federal deficit, and revive the concept of a balanced BUDGET.

The political expression of this conservative idea was a state-based movement for a CONSTITUTIONAL CONVENTION to limit federal spending and achieve a balanced budget. By the mid-1980s this movement had begun to produce political effects in Washington. The Republican-controlled Senate and executive branch supported a BALANCED-BUDGET CONSTITUTIONAL AMENDMENT. The Democratic party switched from supporting deficit spending to arguing for deficit reduction as a reaction against Reagan administration defense spending in a year (1985) when the deficit reached $200 billion. With the executive and legislature each blaming the other for the deficits, the situation was ripe for a bipartisan solution. The result was the Balanced Budget and Emergency Deficit Control Act of 1985.

Known as the GRAMM-RUDMAN-HOLLINGS ACT, the law required the federal budget deficit to be reduced by stages until it was eliminated in 1991. It contained a triggering mechanism by which automatic across-the-board spending cuts were mandated if deficits exceeded specified levels at certain target dates. Finding it difficult to meet the reduction requirements, Congress put some spending items "off budget" so that they would not be counted in the reckoning of the deficit problem. In 1987 it revised the law to postpone the balanced budget date to 1993. Although the Washington political establishment generally disliked the law, it had the effect of reducing the deficit and slowing the rate of increase in government spending. Despite sharp differences over spending priorities, limitation of spending had become a bipartisan objective or requirement, replacing the presumption of indefinite government expansion based on taxing and spending that marked the 1960s and 1970s. In this sense, divided government signaled the kind of change in the policy agenda associated with a political realignment.

Although compromise could be said to be the logic of government under the separation of powers, as seen in the disposition of such major issues as the budget deficit, tax reform, and control of immigration, ideological conflict was the predominant political effect of divided government. The struggle between the executive and legislature for control of the administrative state, a continuing theme in twentieth-century CONSTITUTIONAL HISTORY, was exacerbated by the ideological polarization of the 1980s.

Powerful governing instruments were available for carrying on the struggle for policymaking and administrative control. Having forced President Nixon to resign through application of the IMPEACHMENT power, Congress curbed EXECUTIVE POWER by passing laws respecting presidential actions in regard to WAR POWERS, intelligence activities, and budgetary matters. In 1978, Congress took the major step of creating the office of special prosecutor outside the executive branch to investigate wrongdoing in high-level executive offices. By vigorous use of the LEGISLATIVE VETO and the appropriations and oversight powers, Congress in the 1980s challenged the president not only in domestic policy but also in FOREIGN AFFAIRS.

Although the executive was weaker than in the era of

presidential party government, this branch also experienced a restoration of authority under divided government. Despite legislative measures aimed at limiting the executive, the principal elements of presidential power from the pre-WATERGATE period remained intact. The White House staff of 600 and the Executive Office of the President staff of 5,000 employees were powerful institutions that functioned as a policymaking structure parallel to the regular executive departments. Perhaps the main element in the power of the chief executive was the fact that political responsibility for government continued to fall primarily upon the president. On the whole, despite severe second-term problems in the IRAN-CONTRA AFFAIR, President Reagan was reasonably successful in meeting that responsibility. Possessing aptitude suitable for a plebiscitary type of presidency, he used the media effectively to communicate directly with the electorate and shape public opinion in support of administration policies.

Although President Reagan's political appeal rested in part on his opposition to big government, he responded to the constitutional imperative of the modern administrative state by expanding executive authority to achieve the policy ends of his administration. In 1981 he issued Executive Order 12291, giving the OFFICE OF MANAGEMENT AND BUDGET (OMB) authority to require executive agencies to submit cost-benefit analyses. Focused on budgetary impact, the order was intended as a check on the regulatory process, aimed at eliminating waste and inefficiency. In 1985, President Reagan issued a more far-reaching directive, Executive Order 12498, intended to coordinate and establish White House control over bureaucratic policymaking. This order required executive agencies to submit proposed regulations to OMB for substantive approval to ensure that they were consistent with overall White House policy.

The Reagan EXECUTIVE ORDERS resisted an inherent tendency in Congress toward micromanagement of the executive branch, a tendency encouraged by the politics of divided government. Reaction to the directives revealed the ambiguous constitutional status of ADMINISTRATIVE AGENCIES subject to the control of both the President and Congress. Functionally the executive departments and independent REGULATORY AGENCIES are in the executive branch, for they are concerned with enforcing and administering laws. The President can order administrative officers to carry out policies within their statutory discretion, and if they fail to follow his direction, he should be able to remove them, on the theory that the Constitution intends law enforcement to be managed by the chief executive. Adminstrative departments and agencies owe their existence, however, to Congress. By its lawmaking power, it creates the units of the administrative state, defining the purpose and powers of each department or agency and

the terms and conditions of holding office. From this point of view, the executive departments and regulatory agencies are accountable to Congress and may exercise rulemaking discretion only within their statutory mandates.

Claiming discretionary rulemaking authority exercised by previous administrations, Reagan officials frequently acted to withdraw, revoke, or alter agency rules. When they did so, they were sometimes charged, by congressional committees and by private INTEREST GROUPS that opposed the changes, with violating their statutory authority. In the period of divided government, rulemaking under the delegation of LEGISLATIVE POWER to the executive, usually considered a basic feature of the modern administrative state, was thus subject to attack as lawless executive conduct.

Despite serious deregulatory efforts, the structure of the regulatory welfare state changed very little in the 1980s. Few agencies were eliminated, and given the balance of political forces and congressional defense of the status quo, it was difficult to effect major policy changes. On the government-expansion side, the Veterans Administration was elevated to cabinet rank. The main difference between this period and the 1970s was that the regulatory state functioned in a more accommodating and less antagonistic spirit in relation to regulated groups and associations. Corporations opposed the wholesale dismantling of regulatory structures that the "Reagan revolution" at first seemed to threaten, because it would reopen costly political and legal battles. What corporations wanted was greater flexibility in government—business relations and greater reliance on economic analysis in regulatory policy. After initially strong deregulatory efforts met stiff resistance in the subgovernments of the administrative constitution, the Reagan administration moderated its regulatory policy accordingly.

In seeking to preserve the regulatory welfare state, the Democratic congressional establishment evinced tendencies toward legislative supremacy inherent in the doctrine of the separation of powers and the theory of POPULAR SOVEREIGNTY. As in the past, the appropriations power, regarded as the quintessential legislative power, was the most effective instrument for asserting the congressional will.

The CONGRESSIONAL BUDGET AND IMPOUNDMENT CONTROL ACT of 1974 made Congress an equal participant in budget planning. The act created the Congressional Budget Office to compete with the OMB, and it solved the problem of presidential IMPOUNDMENT OF FUNDS by placing tight restrictions on presidential nonspending (called deferrals and rescissions). At the same time, the act succeeded in one of its implicit purposes, to facilitate congressional spending, which increased significantly in the 1970s and 1980s. Under divided government, the cooperation envisioned in the budget act between the executive and legislature was elusive, and by 1985 it was widely believed that the BUDGET PROCESS was not working satisfactorily, for reasons that implicated both branches. The Gramm-Rudman-Hollings Act did not improve the process.

Failing to reach agreement on the series of executive department appropriations bills required by the law, Congress from 1986 to 1988 enacted each year a single measure, the omnibus continuing resolution, to fund the entire federal government. The continuing resolution previously had been a technical expedient used to keep an agency in operation when action on an appropriations bill was not complete by the end of the congressional session. It now was transformed into a comprehensive budget act. Concealed within the continuing resolutions were many substantive policy decisions, unknown to anyone but their subcommittee sponsors, that were enacted into law without public scrutiny and debate. The continuing resolution for 1988, for example, appropriated $605 billion, was 1,057 pages long, and was accompanied by a 1,194-page conference report. President Reagan, with only one day to consider the bill, was virtually forced to sign it if he did not want to shut down the government for lack of funds. In effect, Congress deprived the President of his VETO POWER.

Another constitutional innovation of Congress was the creation of commissions outside the government to decide public policy matters. For example, Congress established the National Economic Commission; the Commission on Executive, Legislative, and Judicial Salaries; and the Commission on Sentencing Guidelines to deal with politically controversial subjects. These were but a few of 596 federal commissions created in 1988 by Congress, 117 of which were determined by the General Accounting Office to be concerned with substantive policy questions. A contemporary manifestation of the progressive belief that government could be purified by separating politics from administration, government by commission added a new wrinkle by proposing to separate politics from legislation. It was an acknowledgment that the legislative process itself, where interests are properly expressed, was so immobilized by faction and ideology that Congress was prepared to abdicate its constitutional responsibility for lawmaking.

If the policy environment was not conducive to legislation, Congress could influence administrative policymaking through the legislative veto. In the era of presidential party government the legislative veto was used mainly to effect executive reorganization plans and strengthen presidential policymaking. In the aftermath of Watergate, Congress used the veto extensively to supervise regulatory policymaking, including it in more than 200 statutes. The Supreme Court declared the legislative veto unconstitutional in the case of IMMIGRATION AND NATURALIZATION SERVICE V. CHADHA. Nevertheless, Congress continued to employ devices that were the functional equivalent of the legislative veto. For example, it required agencies to get the approval of appropriations committees before taking an action and used committee reports and notification requirement to supervise bureaucratic policymaking.

The most significant congressional constitutional innovation in the period of divided government was the creation of a major executive office, the INDEPENDENT COUNSEL, outside the executive branch. The independent counsel is a SPECIAL PROSECUTOR whose duty is to investigate allegations of criminality by high-level officials in the executive branch. After the Watergate affair, bills were introduced into Congress to provide for the prosecution of executive branch wrongdoing by an officer not subject to the political influence or legal control of the President. The premise on which these proposals rested was that an inherent conflict of interest prevented the President and the Justice Department from conducting an unbiased investigation of malfeasance in the executive branch. Publicly the proponents of the special prosecutor defended it as an "auxiliary precaution" under the theory of separation of powers and CHECKS AND BALANCES for controlling the government, especially the executive power. The Carter administration supported this legislation, and the office of special prosecutor—renamed independent counsel in 1983—was included in the Ethics in Government Act of 1978.

The independent counsel act assumes that the executive branch is peculiarly prone to illegal activity and conflict of interest. Its provisions apply to the President, vice-president, cabinet officers, senior White House staff, and sundry directors of agencies constituting a class of about seventy officials. The law provides that upon receiving information about a possible criminal violation by a covered official, the ATTORNEY GENERAL shall conduct an inquiry to decide whether an investigation by an independent counsel is needed. Restrictions on the attorney general make further investigation almost necessary for dealing with allegations of wrongdoing. The judiciary committee of either house is also authorized to request the appointment of a special prosecutor. At the request of the attorney general, a panel of judges from the District of Columbia Circuit Court (called the Special Division) appoints an independent counsel, whose jurisdiction is defined by the Special Division and who can be removed by the attorney general only for cause.

Although the act purports to separate the independent counsel from the legislative branch, the effect of the law is to create a major executive office outside the executive branch. It provides a means by which Congress can do things that for political reasons it might not wish to do through the use of constitutional powers otherwise available to it, such as impeachment. Investigation and INDICTMENT through the independent counsel process can be seen as a substitute for impeachment. Despite the appointment of the counsel by the attorney general and the appearance of administrative independence, the independent counsel is in effect an agent of Congress, for congressional committee investigations are the primary source of information on which the appointment process is based. Furthermore, when an executive official is targeted for investigation, the independent counsel is under political pressure to find a violation. The counsel searches for a crime to pin on the executive official, rather than looking for the person to fit the crime, as traditional law enforcement does.

In *Morrison v. Olson* (1988) the Supreme Court upheld the constitutionality of the independent counsel act. In earlier decisions, such as *Chadha,* NORTHERN PIPELINE CO. V. MARATHON PIPE LINE CO. (1981), and BOWSHER V. SYNAR (1986), the Court had struck down acts of Congress as violations of the separation of powers. Its acceptance of the independent counsel was therefore a major victory for Congress. The independent counsel's functions appeared to be a "purely executive power" that under the Court's previous separation of powers decisions required placing the officer under the full removal power of the President. The Court dropped this line of analysis, however, concluding simply that the removal provisions of the act and other limits on the President's ability to control the discretion of the independent counsel did not interfere with the President's exercise of his constitutional duty to execute the laws. *Morrison v. Olson* in effect invited Congress to create additional special prosecutors to enforce laws that are judged to be too important to leave to the discretionary litigation policy of politically appointed officers in the executive branch.

Although the office of independent counsel was created ostensibly to assure impartial investigation of executive branch improprieties, it encouraged lawmakers to pursue policy disagreements with the executive branch in a partisan manner, to the point of criminalizing them. The Iran-Contra affair illustrated this tendency. It also epitomized the conflicts of divided government carried into the sphere of foreign policy. In this pivotal event, the President relied on executive discretion in foreign affairs, congressional committees investigated executive officials in the accusatorial manner established in the McCarthy era, and independent counsel obtained indictments leading to criminal trials that obviated impeachment proceedings.

The Iran-Contra affair initially involved the secret sale of arms to Iran, with which the United States had been in a state of undeclared war since 1979. The sale was a for-eign policy maneuver intended to secure the release of American hostages held by Arab terrorists. This covert action arguably violated the requirement of the NATIONAL SECURITY ACT that the President, in conducting such an operation, make a factual "finding" and notify Congress. The Reagan administration used the profits from the Iranian arms sale to aid the Contras in Nicaragua seeking to overthrow the left-wing Sandinista government. The foreign policy question here was whether the United States should support the rebels. Congress cast the dispute in legal terms, which was made easier by a series of riders it had attached to defense appropriations acts from 1982 to 1986. These riders, known as the BOLAND AMENDMENTS, prohibited any funds from being spent by any agency of the United States involved in "intelligence activities," for the purpose of supporting the military overthrow of the Nicaraguan government.

Fundamental constitutional issues concerning the powers of President and Congress in foreign policy were hung on the peg of narrow statutory questions concerning the meaning of the Boland amendments. Yet as products of legislative compromise and executive-legislative accommodation in the (unacknowledged) spirit of divided government, the riders were deliberately vague and ambiguous. A key question was whether the National Security Council (NSC) was an "intelligence activity" in the sense intended by the legislation. The riders did not expressly identify it as such, although they did so identify other agencies. A further question, assuming that NSC was covered, was whether its activities conformed to the permissible scope of intelligence activities assisting the Contras that the Boland amendments approved. Neither the Iran-Contra hearings nor subsequent judicial trials of NSC officials satisfactorily resolved these questions.

If basic constitutional questions could not be reached, answers to narrow legal questions were also elusive because of the basic ambiguity in congressional foreign policy. Sometimes Congress voted for military and humanitarian aid to the Contras; at other times it barred using military equipment to overthrow the Nicaraguan government. Congress desired to challenge the President's control of foreign policy, but was afraid of critical public reaction if it did so too clearly or extremely. Therefore, it resorted to imprecise statutory language that did not unequivocally block the executive branch from carrying out its pro-Contra policy. For his part, President Reagan did not veto the Boland amendments, either because he viewed them as a compromise that permitted the administration to pursue its policy or because he feared impeachment.

The latter was a reasonable fear, for when information about the Iranian arms sale was revealed in 1986 a Watergate-type impeachment mood gripped many lawmakers and critics of the executive branch. The office of independent counsel, however, in conjunction with the traditional legislative power of investigation, was available as a less politically risky alternative. In November 1986, President Reagan promptly agreed to a congressional request to seek the appointment of an independent counsel to investigate the Iran-Contra affair. NSC officers Lt. Col. Oliver North, Admiral John Poindexter, and Robert McFarlane were the most prominent targets of the investigation, which resulted in at least six criminal convictions.

The trial of Oliver North illustrated the process by which constitutional controversy over the conduct of foreign policy was reduced to minor criminal convictions. North was a principal figure in the administration's policy who was called to testify in 1987 before the House and Senate select committees investigating the Iran-Contra matter. He was given a grant of criminal-use IMMUNITY, which meant that his testimony—televised to the nation in dramatically staged hearings—could not be used against him in any criminal prosecution that might result from the independent counsel's investigation. North's testimony was subsequently used against him, however, in a supposedly nonevidentiary way that arguably violated North's Fifth Amendment RIGHT AGAINST SELF-INCRIMINATION as interpreted by the Supreme Court in KASTIGAR V. UNITED STATES (1972). North was indicted on a dozen counts. He was not charged with violating the Boland amendments, and he was acquitted on the most serious charges, such as defrauding the government by diverting funds to the Contras. North was convicted on three charges: accepting an illegal gratuity, falsifying and destroying government documents, and obstructing Congress.

The precise purpose of Congress in the Iran-Contra affair was a matter of some dispute. In policy terms, the Democratic leadership opposed aiding the rebels, yet it pursued this policy ambiguously and inconsistently. More clear was the constitutional purpose of Congress—to assert the power of the legislative branch in foreign affairs. Historical practice and constitutional law recognized a broad sphere of executive power and discretion in this area. Congress therefore required cogent arguments against the administration's policy to overcome the presumption that tended to favor executive authority in the making of foreign policy, especially in the twentieth century. To bring foreign policy in a detailed operational sense under the RULE OF LAW, as the Boland amendments purported to do, asserted a congressional claim of authority to rival that of the President. Criminalizing the foreign policy disagreement through the use of independent counsel prosecutions was a suitable means of discrediting executive authority. An administration that conducted foreign policy by illegal or lawless means could not be con-

sidered constitutionally legitimate. This was the point that criminal convictions in the Iran-Contra affair were intended to make.

Criminal conviction was an effective policymaking tool because it could be justified by the traditional republican goal of imposing the rule of law on executive power, which is always the potential source of tyranny, according to the antiexecutive strain in American political thought. Although the Iran-Contra defendants were not tried for violating the Boland amendments, members of Congress did not hesitate to make accusations and to conclude that officials of the executive branch broke the laws enacted by Congress to prevent the United States from getting involved in a war in Latin America. Senators and representatives could make these accusations, confident that under the separation of powers doctrine their possession of the lawmaking power makes them superior to the executive branch and establishes a presumption that the will of Congress is tantamount to the rule of law.

Even if the Boland amendments are considered constitutional, it is questionable whether the lawmaking power can be effectively employed in making foreign policy. The reason is that in foreign affairs U.S. officials are required to deal with the representatives of other countries, who are not subject to the authority and rules of action that constitute U.S. law. The rule of law as propounded by legislative enactments under the separation of powers is further questionable because the purpose of foreign policy is to protect the public safety and national security. Prudence, wisdom, and discretion in the exercise of power are required to achieve this end, rather than the general and prospective rules of action that characterize the rule of law. The statesmanship on which the successful conduct of foreign policy depends has usually been thought more likely to result from the actions of the chief executive, who can be held politically accountable, than from the deliberations of hundreds of lawmakers in Congress.

In the 1980s, tendencies toward legislative assertiveness clashed with an executive authority that had significantly recovered from the power deflation and loss of respect suffered during the eras of the VIETNAM WAR and Watergate. President Reagan was in many respects a nonpolitical chief executive, uninterested in the details of partisan maneuvering and administrative management, who in spite of himself refurbished the presidential office. That he successfully served two terms and employed military force in foreign affairs without interference from Congress under the War Powers Resolution was evidence of executive branch revitalization.

Divided government contradicted the theory of presidential party government. Yet it was not, as some observers argued, a historical and procedural accident. On the contrary, divided government resulted from a reconsideration of the public philosophy of interest-group liberalism and the constitutional theory of the regulatory welfare state. It was a partial repudiation of the twentieth-century tendency toward governmental activism and centralized sovereignty. Divided government was a confirmation of the relevance and utility of the separation of powers principle, one of the basic concepts of limited government.

HERMAN BELZ
(1992)

(SEE ALSO: *Bork Nomination; Civil Liberties; Civil Rights; Congress and Foreign Policy; Congressional War Powers; Conservatism; Constitutional Reform; Criminal Justice System; Economy; Establishment Clause; First Amendment; Freedom of Speech; Freedom of the Press; Line-Item Veto; Procedural Due Process of Law, Civil; Procedural Due Process of Law, Criminal; Racketeer Influenced and Corrupt Organizations Act; Religious Fundamentalism; Religious Liberty.*)

Bibliography

CARTER, STEPHEN L. 1988 The Independent Counsel Mess. *Harvard Law Review* 102:105–141.

EASTLAND, TERRY 1989 *Ethics, Politics, and the Independent Counsel: Executive Power, Executive Vice, 1789–1989.* Washington, D.C.: National Legal Center for Public Interest.

HARRIS, RICHARD A. and MILKIS, SIDNEY M., eds. 1989 *Remaking American Politics.* Boulder, Colo.: Westview Press.

HELCO, HUGH 1986 General Welfare and Two American Political Traditions. *Political Science Quarterly* 101:179–196.

JONES, GORDON S. and MARINI, JOHN A., eds. 1988 *The Imperial Congress: Congress in the Separation of Powers.* New York: Pharos Books.

LOWI, THEODORE J. 1985 *The Personal President: Power Invested, Promise Unfulfilled.* Ithaca, N.Y.: Cornell University Press.

MANSFIELD, HARVEY C., JR. 1985 Pride Versus Interest in American Conservatism Today. *Government and Opposition* 20: 194–205.

SHAPIRO, MARTIN 1985 The Constitution and the Bureaucracy. *This Constitution* 9:11–16.

SUNDQUIST, JAMES L. 1989 Needed: A Political Theory for the New Era of Coalition Government in the United States. *Political Science Quarterly* 103:613–636.

WILDAVSKY, AARON 1980 *How to Limit Government Spending.* Berkeley: University of California Press.

CONSTITUTIONAL HISTORY, 1989–1999

During the years from 1989 to 1999, the Supreme Court fashioned a number of novel DOCTRINES for AFFIRMATIVE ACTION, FEDERALISM, RELIGIOUS LIBERTY, the RIGHT OF PRIVACY, and PRESIDENTIAL POWERS. Pressured by public criticism and challenges from Congress, the Court modified and in some cases OVERRULED earlier holdings. Nominations by Presidents GEORGE H. W. BUSH and WILLIAM J. CLINTON helped push the Court toward the center.

Policies for affirmative action bounced around because none of the branches provided consistent principles. Although language in some of the CIVIL RIGHTS ACTS of Congress appeared to announce a race-neutral policy, other statutes endorsed preferential treatment. In FULLILOVE V. KLUTZNICK (1980), the Court upheld a congressional statute that set aside a certain percentage of public works funds for "minority business enterprises." When the states and cities tried to adopt similar set-asides, the Court in RICHMOND (CITY OF) V. J. A. CROSON CO. (1989) struck them down. A year later, in METRO BROADCASTING, INC. V. FCC (1990), the Court again upheld affirmative action at the congressional level, this time a program that offered advantages to minorities in deciding licenses and ownership of radio and television BROADCAST stations.

The Court revisited these holdings in ADARAND CONSTRUCTORS, INC. V. PEÑA (1995), which required federal race-based policies to satisfy the same standard—STRICT SCRUTINY—applied to state and local programs. Such programs must serve a COMPELLING STATE INTEREST and be narrowly tailored to address identifiable past RACIAL DISCRIMINATION. Federal courts, Congress, and federal ADMINISTRATIVE AGENCIES must now reassess affirmative action programs in light of this heightened standard.

Following *Adarand*, Clinton summarized his administration's review of federal affirmative action programs. Acknowledging some problems, he concluded: "We should reaffirm the principle of affirmative action and fix the practices. We should have a simple slogan: Mend it, but don't end it." He directed agencies to eliminate affirmative action programs if they (1) create a quota, (2) create preferences for unqualified individuals, (3) create reverse discrimination, or (4) continue even after its equal opportunity purposes have been achieved. A moratorium was placed on some set-aside programs.

Affirmative action programs came under attack in a number of states, including California, Texas, and Michigan. Californians voted in support of a ballot INITIATIVE to end bilingual education—allowing immigrant students to receive one year of English immersion before moving into regular classes unless their parents obtain a waiver—and another initiative outlawing affirmative action in public hiring, contracting, and education.

The Court continues to struggle with federalism. Its attempt in NATIONAL LEAGUE OF CITIES V. USERY (1976) to distinguish between national and state powers proved so confusing and incapable of application that the Court rejected its handiwork nine years later, in GARCÍA V. SAN

ANTONIO METROPOLITAN TRANSIT AUTHORITY (1985). At that point, it appeared that the protection of federalism would depend largely on the political process operating within Congress.

However, several decisions in the 1990s seemed to revive state power. In GREGORY V. ASHCROFT (1991), the Court held that Missouri's constitution, which provided a mandatory retirement age of 70 for most state judges, did not violate the AGE DISCRIMINATION ACT (ADEA). Although the Court referred to the TENTH AMENDMENT and the GUARANTEE CLAUSE, the decision rested largely on STATUTORY INTERPRETATION, leaving the door open for Congress to rewrite the ADEA if it wanted to cover state judges.

A year later, the Court again cited the Tenth Amendment when it invalidated part of a 1985 congressional statute designed to force states to find disposal sites for low-level radioactive WASTE. The 6–3 decision in NEW YORK V. UNITED STATES (1992) ruled that the statutory provision, forcing states to take possession of the waste if they failed to discover other solutions, was an invalid effort by Congress to commandeer the states' legislative processes and thus inconsistent with the Tenth Amendment. The Court explained that states are not "mere political subdivisions" of the United States, nor are state governments regional offices or administrative agencies of the federal government. In terms of public policy, the decision had modest impact. Rather than try to draft new LEGISLATION to satisfy the Court, Congress decided to rely on the existing compacts that states had created to dispose of the waste.

On a similar ground, the Court in *Printz v. United States* (1997) struck down, by a 5–4 vote, a key portion of a 1993 GUN CONTROL law. That statute required state and local law enforcement officers to conduct background checks on prospective handgun purchasers. The Court said that Congress may not "command" state officers to administer a federal regulatory program. The decision is not expected to have a substantial effect on governmental policy. Most states already require background checks.

Great fanfare was given to UNITED STATES V. LÓPEZ (1995), the Court's decision striking down a congressional statute that banned guns within 1,000 feet of schools. Some commentators regarded the ruling as highly significant, but it may have been a case where Congress simply failed to present adequate findings to show an INTERSTATE COMMERCE link with guns on school playgrounds. Within two weeks of the decision, Clinton submitted legislation to Congress to amend the earlier statute by requiring the federal government to prove that the firearm has "moved in or the possession of such firearm otherwise affects interstate or foreign commerce." Congress enacted the legislation in 1996, finding that crime at the local level "is exacerbated by the interstate movement of drugs, guns, and criminal gangs," that the occurrence of violent crime in school zones has resulted in a decline in the quality of education, and that it has the power under the interstate COMMERCE CLAUSE to enact the legislation.

Also in 1995, federalism was at issue in the TERM LIMITS case decided by the Court, *U.S. Term Limits, Inc. v. Thornton.* A number of states had adopted constitutional amendments or other measures to place term limits on legislators not only in state legislatures but in Congress as well. Arkansas, for example, amended its constitution to limit members of Congress to three terms in the U.S. HOUSE OF REPRESENTATIVES and to two terms in the U.S. SENATE. The Court held that the Arkansas constitution violated the U.S. Constitution by adding to the qualifications established for members of Congress. The fifth vote in this 5–4 decision was supplied by Justice ANTHONY M. KENNEDY, who invoked principles of federalism by charging that Arkansas had invaded "the sphere of federal sovereignty."

Federalism became entwined with religious freedom in a case that arose in Oregon. Two members of the Native American Church had been fired by a private organization because they ingested peyote, a hallucinogenic drug. They took the drug as part of a religious sacrament. Their application for unemployment compensation was denied by Oregon under a state law that disqualifies employees who are fired for work-related "misconduct." Remaining drug-free was a condition of their employment.

Divided 6 to 3, the Court in EMPLOYMENT DIVISION, DEPARTMENT OF HUMAN RESOURCES OF OREGON V. SMITH (1990) held that the free exercise clause permits a state to prohibit sacramental peyote use and to deny unemployment benefits to persons fired for such use. State law may prohibit the possession and use of a drug even if it incidentally prohibits a religious practice. The Court distinguished this case from other unemployment-benefit cases by noting that the religious conduct in those cases was not prohibited by law. Oregon law made it a criminal offense to possess or use peyote.

Oregon remained free to make an exemption for the use of peyote by members of the Native American Church. Twenty-three states had statutory or judicially crafted exemptions for the religious use of peyote. One year after *Smith*, the Oregon legislature enacted a bill that protects the sacramental use of peyote by the Native American Church.

A number of religious groups urged Congress to pass legislation that would grant greater religious freedom than that recognized by the Court. The purpose was to reinstate the previous standard (compelling state interest) for testing federal, state, and local laws burdening religion. Proponents of the bill believed that the Court's ruling threatened a number of religious practices, including the use of ceremonial wine, the practice of kosher slaughter, and the Hmong (Laotian) religious objection to autopsy.

In 1993, Congress enacted the RELIGIOUS FREEDOM RESTORATION ACT (RFRA), which provided that government may substantially burden a person's religious exercise only if it demonstrates a compelling interest and uses the least restrictive means of furthering that interest. The statute therefore restored the compelling interest test that the Court had adopted in 1963 and 1972. In 1994, Congress passed legislation to legalize the use of peyote by Native Americans for ceremonial purposes.

In *Boerne v. Flores* (1997), the Court ruled that Congress, in passing the RFRA, had exceeded the scope of its enforcement power under the FOURTEENTH AMENDMENT, SECTION 5. Parts of the Court's decision were superficial, unpersuasive, and internally inconsistent, inviting continued challenges and legislative activity. Although the Court strongly hinted that it has the last and final word in deciding the meaning of the Constitution, in fact it left the door wide open for future congressional action. In 1998, new legislation (called "Son of RFRA") was introduced to rely more on congressional SPENDING POWER and commerce power. Also in 1998, the U.S. Court of Appeals for the Eighth Circuit held that RFRA was constitutional as applied to the federal government.

In 1999, the Court handed down a series of rulings that once again protected the independence of the states. In *Alden v. Maine; Florida Prepaid Postsecondary Education Expense Board v. College Savings Bank, U.S.;* and *College Savings Bank v. Florida Prepaid Postsecondary Education Expense Board,* the Court declared that Congress cannot subject states to suits in their own courts for violating federal rights unless they first give their consent. The Court also invalidated efforts by Congress to abrogate state immunity from suit for violations of intellectual property rights.

Privacy issues led to a number of important Court rulings. ROE V. WADE (1973), establishing a woman's right to ABORTION, was under steady attack from both conservatives and liberals as a prime example of judicial overreaching. As medical knowledge advanced, the Court's attempt to rely on the viability of a fetus was undermined by technology. Appointments to the Court by Presidents RONALD REAGAN and Bush further helped to erode *Roe.* In WEBSTER V. REPRODUCTIVE HEALTH SERVICES (1989), the Court retreated somewhat from *Roe* and continued that process three years later, in PLANNED PARENTHOOD V. CASEY (1992), jettisoning *Roe's* trimester framework while affirming the "core meaning" of *Roe* by preserving the right to abortion.

The Court's bitter experience with *Roe* may have convinced it to announce in two 1997 rulings that there was no RIGHT TO DIE with the assistance of a physician. Under

heavy criticism from the public, the Court had learned that it had to carve out a more modest role for itself while recognizing a larger function for elected branches and the states.

On May 6, 1994, Paula Corbin Jones filed suit in federal court against President Clinton and Danny Ferguson, an Arkansas state trooper, for actions that occurred in 1991 at a hotel in Little Rock, Arkansas. She alleged that Clinton, as governor of Arkansas, violated her constitutional rights to EQUAL PROTECTION and DUE PROCESS by sexually harassing and assaulting her. Clinton, claiming immunity from civil suit, filed a motion to dismiss the complaint without prejudice to its refiling after his presidency.

The Constitution does not provide an express immunity for the President. Nevertheless, federal courts have developed a doctrine of IMMUNITY OF OFFICIALS for official acts. Paula Jones was raising a different issue: Is the President entitled to immunity from civil liability for unofficial acts committed in his personal capacity? A district court ruled that the President did not have absolute immunity from civil causes of action that arise prior to assuming office. However, the judge held that the trial could be delayed until after Clinton left the presidency, but allowed the discovery and deposition process to go forward, including deposing the President.

The Eighth Circuit upheld the decision that Clinton was not entitled to immunity from civil liability for his unofficial acts, but reversed the district court by holding that the trial could proceed while he was in office. A unanimous Supreme Court, in CLINTON V. JONES (1997), affirmed the appellate court. If properly managed by the trial court, "it appears to us highly unlikely to occupy any substantial amount of petitioner's [Clinton's] time."

Clinton was deposed and the case was dismissed in 1998. After Paula Jones appealed to the Eighth Circuit, Clinton agreed to settle the case by offering her $850,000. However, his responses to questions about his relationship with former White House aide Monica Lewinsky led to new charges that he had committed perjury, suborned the perjury of witnesses, and obstructed justice. INDEPENDENT COUNSEL Kenneth Starr investigated these charges and concluded, in a report to the House of Representatives, that Clinton may have committed impeachable offenses. The House impeached Clinton on two articles (perjury and obstruction of justice), but the Senate voted 45 to 55 on the first article and 50 to 50 on the second, both votes being well short of the two-thirds required for removal from office.

Starr's investigation led to several constitutional claims by the White House. Presidential aides insisted that they could not be compelled to testify at a GRAND JURY. First Lady Hillary Clinton believed that her discussions with a government attorney were privileged. The U.S. Secret Service argued that the agents responsible for protecting the President should not be forced to testify about matters of Clinton's conduct. On all those matters Starr won at every level, including appeals by the administration to the Supreme Court.

As part of the "Contract With America," Republicans supported an item veto—often referred to as a LINE-ITEM VETO—for the President. Enacted in 1996, the Line Item Veto Act supplemented the rescission authority given to the President by the Impoundment Control Act of 1974. Instead of requiring the President to obtain the support of both Houses of Congress within a specified number of days, as set forth in the 1974 legislation, the Line Item Veto Act put the burden on Congress—during a thirty-day review period—to disapprove presidential rescission proposals. Any bill or joint resolution of disapproval would be subject to a presidential veto, ultimately requiring a two-thirds majority in each chamber for an override.

The Line Item Veto Act provided for expedited JUDICIAL REVIEW to test the constitutionality of the statute. Senator Robert C. Byrd and several colleagues filed suit to challenge this transfer of authority to the President. The Court in *Raines v. Byrd* (1997) held that the legislators did not have sufficient personal stake in the dispute, and did not allege a sufficiently concrete injury, to establish STANDING to bring the case. The next year, however, the Court in *Clinton v. New York* (1998) held that the private parties challenging the statute had standing and that the statute was unconstitutional because it violated the procedure that requires that all bills be presented to the President for his signature or veto. Writing for the majority, Justice JOHN PAUL STEVENS argued that there was no constitutional authorization for the President to amend or repeal a statute.

LOUIS FISHER
(2000)

Bibliography

BAKER, LYNN A. 1995 Conditional Federal Spending After *López*. *Columbia Law Review* 95:1911–1989.

DEVINS, NEAL 1996 *Shaping Constitutional Values: Elected Government, the Supreme Court, and the Abortion Debate.* Baltimore, Md.: Johns Hopkins University Press.

FISHER, LOUIS 1999 *American Constitutional Law*, 3rd ed. Durham, N.C.: Carolina Academic Press.

GARROW, DAVID J. 1994 *Liberty and Sexuality: The Right to Privacy and the Making of Roe v. Wade.* New York: Macmillan.

LESSIG, LAWRENCE 1995 Translating Federalism: *United States v. López. Supreme Court Review* 1995:125–215.

McCONNELL, MICHAEL W. 1997 Institutions and Interpretation: A Critique of *City of Boerne v. Flores. Harvard Law Review* 111:153–195.

STRAUSS, DAVID A. 1993 Abortion, Toleration, and Moral Certainty. *Supreme Court Review* 1993:1–28.

CONSTITUTIONAL INTERPRETATION

"Constitutional interpretation" comprehends the methods or strategies available to people attempting to resolve disputes about the meaning or application of the Constitution. The possible sources for interpretation include the text of the Constitution, its "original history," including the general social and political context in which it was adopted as well as the events immediately surrounding its adoption, the governmental structures created and recognized by the Constitution, the "ongoing history" of interpretations of the Constitution, and the social, political, and moral values of the interpreter's society or some subgroup of the society. The term "originalist" refers to interpretation concerned with the first three of these sources.

The extraordinary current interest in constitutional interpretation is partly the result of controversy over the SUPREME COURT's expansive readings of the FOURTEENTH AMENDMENT; it also parallels developments in literary theory and more generally the humanities. Received notions about the intrinsic meaning of words or texts, access to an author's intentions, and the very notion of "validity" in interpretation have been forcefully attacked and vehemently defended by philosophers, literary theorists, social scientists, and historians of knowledge. Legal writers have imported scholarship from these disciplines into their own, and some humanists have become interested in legal interpretation.

Issues of interpretive methodology have always been politically charged—certainly so in constitutional law. JOHN MARSHALL's foundational decisions asserting the power of the central government were met by claims that he had willfully misconstrued the document. In our own time, modernist interpretive theories tend to be invoked by proponents of JUDICIAL ACTIVISM, and more conventional views by its opponents. The controversy within the humanities and the social sciences is itself deeply political, for the modernist assertion that truth or validity is socially constructed and hence contingent is often perceived as destabilizing or delegitimating.

The Constitution is a political document; it serves political ends; its interpretations are political acts. Any theory of constitutional interpretation therefore presupposes a normative theory of the Constitution itself—a theory, for example, about the constraints that the words and intentions of the adopters should impose on those who apply or interpret the Constitution. As Ronald Dworkin observed, "Some parts of any constitutional theory must be independent of the intentions or beliefs or indeed the acts of the people the theory designates as Framers. Some part must stand on its own political or moral theory; otherwise the theory would be wholly circular."

The eclectic practices of interpreters and the continuing debate over the appropriate methods or strategies of constitutional interpretation suggest that we have no unitary, received theory of the Constitution. The American tradition of constitutional interpretation accords considerable authority to the language of the Constitution, its adopters' purposes, and the implications of the structures created and recognized by the Constitution. But our tradition also accords authority to precedents and the judicial exegesis of social values and practices, even when these diverge from plausible readings of the text and original understandings.

Any theory of constitutional interpretation must start from the fact that we have a written Constitution. Why is the written Constitution treated as binding? Because, as Chief Justice Marshall asserted in MARBURY V. MADISON (1803), it is law—the supreme law of the land—and because since 1789 public institutions and the citizenry have treated it as an authoritative legal document. It is no exaggeration to say that the written Constitution lies at the core of the American "civil religion."

Doubtless, the most frequently invoked canon of textual interpretation is the "plain meaning rule." Marshall wrote in STURGES V. CROWNINSHIELD (1819):

> [A]lthough the spirit of an instrument, especially of a constitution, is to be respected not less than its letter, yet the spirit is to be collected chiefly from its words. . . . [I]f, in any case, the plain meaning of a provision, not contradicted by any other provision in the same instrument, is to be disregarded, because we believe the framers of that instrument could not intend what they say, it must be one in which the absurdity and injustice of applying the provision to the case, would be so monstrous that all mankind would, without hesitation, unite in rejecting the application.

Marshall did not equate "plain" meaning with "literal" meaning, but rather (as Justice OLIVER WENDELL HOLMES later put it) the meaning that it would have for "a normal speaker of English" under the circumstances in which it was used. The distinction is nicely illustrated by Chief Justice Marshall's opinion in MCCULLOCH V. MARYLAND (1819), decided the same year as *Sturges*. Maryland had argued that the NECESSARY AND PROPER clause of Article I authorized Congress only to enact legislation "indispensable" to executing the ENUMERATED POWERS. Marshall responded with the observation that the word "necessary," as used "in the common affairs of the world, or in approved authors, . . . frequently imports no more than that

one thing is convenient, or useful, or essential to another." He continued:

> Such is the character of human language, that no word conveys to the mind, in all situations, one single definite idea; and nothing is more common than to use words in a figurative sense. Almost all compositions contain words, which, taken in their rigorous sense, would convey a meaning different from that which is obviously intended. It is essential to just construction that many words which import something excessive, should be understood in a more mitigated sense—in that sense which common usage justifies. . . . This word, then, like others, is used in various senses; and in its construction, the subject, the context, the intention of the person using them, are all to be taken into view.

To read a provision without regard to its context and likely purposes will yield either unresolvable indeterminacies or plain nonsense. An interpreter could not, for example, decide whether the FIRST AMENDMENT's " FREEDOM OF SPEECH" encompassed singing, flag-waving, and criminal solicitation; or whether the "writings" protected by the COPYRIGHT clause included photographs, sculptures, performances, television broadcasts, and computer programs. She would not know whether the provision in Article II that "No person except a natural born Citizen . . . shall be eligible to the Office of President" disqualified persons born abroad or those born by Caesarian section. We can identify interpretations as compelling, plausible, or beyond the pale only because we think we understand the concerns that underlie the provisions.

One's understanding of a provision, including the concerns that underlie it, depends partly on the ideological or political presuppositions one brings to the interpretive enterprise. Marshall could so readily label Maryland's construction of the word "necessary" as excessive because of his antecedent conception of a "constitution" as essentially different from a legal code—as a document "intended to endure for ages to come"—and because of his beliefs about the structure of FEDERALISM implicit in the United States Constitution. A judge starting from different premises might have found Maryland's construction more plausible.

A meaning thus is "plain" when it follows from the interpreter's presuppositions and when these presuppositions are shared within the society or at least within the relevant "community of interpretation"—for example, the legal profession. Kenneth Abraham has remarked, "The plain is plain because it is constantly recurring in similar contexts and there is general agreement about the meaning of language that may be applied to it. In short, meaning is a function of agreement. . . ."

When a provision is interpreted roughly contemporaneously with its adoption, an interpreter unconsciously places it in the social and linguistic context of her society. Over the course of several centuries, however, even a relatively stable nation will undergo changes—in social and economic relations, in technology, and ultimately in values—to an extent that a later interpreter cannot readily assume that she has direct access to the contexts in which a constitutional provision was adopted. This poses both a normative and a methodological question for the modern interpreter: should she attempt to read provisions in their original social and linguistic contexts, or in a modern context, or in some way that mediates between the two? And, to the extent that the original contexts are relevant, how can she ascertain them?

Original history includes "legislative history"—the debates and proceedings in the conventions and legislatures that proposed and adopted constitutional provisions—and the broader social, economic, and political contexts surrounding their adoption. Although it is widely acknowledged that original history should play a role in constitutional interpretation, there is little agreement over the aims and methods of historical inquiry. The controversy centers on the level of generality on which an interpreter should try to apprehend the adopters' intentions. On the highest or broadest level, an interpreter poses the questions: "What was the general problem to which this provision was responsive and how did the provision respond to it?" On the most specific level, she inquires: "How would the adopters have resolved the particular issue that we are now considering?"

The first or "general" question elicits answers such as: "The purpose of the COMMERCE CLAUSE was to permit Congress to regulate commerce that affects more than one state, or to regulate where the states are separately incompetent to regulate." Or: "The purpose of the EQUAL PROTECTION clause was to prohibit invidious discrimination." These characterizations do not purport to describe the scope of a provision precisely. On the contrary, they are avowedly vague or open-ended: the claim is not that the equal protection clause forbids every conceivable invidious discrimination (it may or may not) but that it is generally concerned with preventing invidious discriminations.

The general question is an indispensable component of any textual interpretation. The interpreter seeks a "purpose" that she can plausibly attribute to everyone who voted for the provision, and which, indeed, must have been understood as their purpose even by those who opposed its adoption. The question is often couched in objective-sounding terms: it seeks the "purpose of the provision" rather than the "intent of the framers." And its answer is typically sought in the text read in the social and linguistic context in which it was adopted. As Marshall wrote in *McCulloch*, "the spirit of an instrument . . . is to be collected chiefly from its words." If the status of the written Constitution as "law" demands textual interpretation, it also entails this general inquiry, without which textual interpretation cannot proceed.

The second inquiry, which can be called "intentionalist," seeks very specific answers, such as: "Did the adopters of the Fourteenth Amendment intend to prohibit school SEGREGATION?" or "Did they intend to prohibit 'reverse' discrimination?" One rationale for this focus was asserted by Justice GEORGE H. SUTHERLAND, dissenting in HOME BUILDING & LOAN ASSOCIATION v. BLAISDELL (1934): "[T]he whole aim of construction, as applied to a provision of the Constitution, is . . . to ascertain and give effect to the intent of its framers and the people who adopted it." Another rationale is that recourse to the adopters' intentions constrains the interpreter's discretion and hence the imposition of her own values. Some methodological problems are presented by any interpretive strategy that seeks to specify the adopters' intentions.

The procedures by which the *text* of a proposed constitutional provision is adopted are usually straightforward and clear: a text becomes a law if it is adopted by the constitutionally prescribed procedures and receives the requisite number of votes. For example, an amendment proposed in Congress becomes a part of the Constitution when it is approved by two-thirds of the members of each House and ratified by the legislatures in three-fourths of the states, or by conventions in three-fourths of the states, as Congress may prescribe.

How does an *intention* acquire the status of law? Some interpreters assume, without discussion, that by ratifying the framers' language, the thousands of people whose votes are necessary to adopt a constitutional provision either manifest their intent to adopt, or are somehow bound by, the intentions of certain of the drafters or framers— even if those intentions are not evident from the text itself. This view is not supported by anything in the Constitution, however, or by eighteenth- or nineteenth-century legal theory or practice.

If one analogizes the adoption of "an intention" concerning the text of the Constitution to the adoption of a text, an intention would become binding only when it was held by the number and combination of adopters prescribed by Article V. This poses no particular difficulty for an interpreter who wishes to understand the general aims or purposes of a provision. Statements by framers, proponents, and opponents, together with the social and political background against which the provision was adopted, often indicate a shared understanding. But these sources cannot usually answer specific questions about the adopters' intentions. The intentionalist interpreter thus often engages in a degree of speculation that undermines the very rationale for the enterprise.

The adopters of a provision may intend that it prohibit or permit some activity, or that it *not* prohibit or permit the activity; or they may have no intentions at all regarding the matter. An intentionalist interpreter must often infer the adopters' intentions from opaque sources, and must try to describe their intentions with respect to situations that they probably never thought about.

The effort to determine the adopters' intentions is further complicated by the problem of identifying the intended specificity of a provision. This problem is nicely illustrated by an example of Ronald Dworkin's. Consider the possible intentions of those who adopted the CRUEL AND UNUSUAL PUNISHMENT clause of the Eighth Amendment. They might have intended the language to serve only as a shorthand for the Stuart tortures which were their exemplary applications of the clause. Somewhat more broadly, they might have intended the clause to be understood to incorporate the principle of *ejusdem generis*—to include their exemplary applications and other punishments that they found, or would have found, equally repugnant.

More broadly yet, they might have intended to delegate to future decision makers the authority to apply the clause in light of the general principles underlying it. To use Dworkin's terms, they might have intended future interpreters to develop their own "conceptions" of cruel and unusual punishment within the framework of the adopters' general "concept" of the clause. If so, then the fact that they viewed a certain punishment as tolerable does not imply that they intended the clause "not to prohibit" such punishments. Like parents who instill values in their children both by articulating and applying a moral principle, the adopters may have accepted the eventuality that the principle would be applied in ways that diverged from their own particular views.

Whether or not such a motivation seems likely with respect to applications of the clause in the adopters' contemporary society, it may be more plausible with respect to applications by future interpreters, whose understandings of the clause would be affected by changing knowledge, values, and forms of society. On the other hand, the adopters may have thought of themselves as more virtuous or less corruptible than unknown future generations, and for that reason may have intended this and other clauses to be construed narrowly.

How can an interpreter determine the breadth of construction intended by the adopters of any particular provision? Primarily, if not exclusively, from the language of the provision itself. Justice FELIX FRANKFURTER wrote in *National Mutual Insurance Company v. Tidewater Transfer Company* (1949):

> The precision which characterizes [the jurisdictional provisions] . . . of Article III is in striking contrast to the im-

precision of so many other provisions of the Constitution dealing with other very vital aspects of government. This was not due to chance or ineptitude on the part of the Framers. The differences in subject-matter account for the drastic difference in treatment. Great concepts like "Commerce among the several states," "due process of law," "liberty," "property," were purposely left to gather meaning from experience. For they relate to the whole domain of social and economic fact, and the statesmen who founded this nation knew too well that only a stagnant society remains unchanged. But when the Constitution in turn gives strict definition of power or specific limitations upon it we cannot extend the definition or remove the translation. Precisely because "it is a *constitution* we are expounding," *M'Culloch v. Maryland,* we ought not to take liberties with it.

Charles Curtis put the point more generally: "Words in legal documents are simply delegations to others of authority to give them meaning by applying them to particular things or occasions. . . . And the more imprecise the words are, the greater is the delegation, simply because then they can be applied or not to more particulars. This is the only important feature of words in legal draftsmanship or interpretation."

This observation seems correct. Yet it is worth noting that the relative precision of a word or clause itself depends both on context and on interpretive conventions, and is often uncertain and contestable. For example, in UNITED STATES V. LOVETT (1946) Justice Frankfurter characterized the BILL OF ATTAINDER clause as among the Constitution's very "specific provisions." Yet he construed that clause to apply to punishments besides death, ignoring the technical eighteenth-century distinction between a bill of attainder, which imposed the death penalty, and a bill of "pains and penalties," which imposed lesser penalties.

The effort to characterize clauses as relatively open or closed confronts a different sort of historical problem as well. The history of interpretation of written constitutions was not extensive in 1787. Marshall's assertion that it is the nature of a constitution "that only its great outlines should be marked" (*McCulloch*) drew more on theory than on practice. But Marshall and his successors practiced this theory. Whatever assumptions the adopters of the original Constitution might have made about the scope of their delegations of authority, the RECONSTRUCTION amendments were adopted in the context of decades of "latitudinarian" constitutional interpretation. What bearing should this context have on the interpretation of provisions adopted since the original Constitution?

The intentionalist interpreter's initial task is to situate the provision and documents bearing on it in their original linguistic and social contexts. She can draw on the accumulated knowledge of American social, political, and intellectual history. Ultimately, however, constitutional interpretation is subject to the same limitations that attend all historical inquiry. Quentin Skinner has described the most pervasive of these:

> [I]t will never in fact be possible simply to study what any given classic writer has *sai*. . . . without bringing to bear some of one's own expectations about what he must have been saying. . . . [T]hese models and preconceptions in terms of which we unavoidably organize and adjust our perceptions and thoughts will themselves tend to act as determinants of what we think or perceive. We must classify in order to understand, and we can only classify the unfamiliar in terms of the familiar. The perpetual danger, in our attempts to enlarge our historical understanding, is thus that our expectations about what someone must be saying or doing will themselves determine that we understand the agent to be doing something which he would not—or even could not—himself have accepted as an account of what he *was* doing.

Trying to understand how the adopters intended a provision to apply in their own time and place is, in essence, doing history. But the intentionalist interpreter must take the further step of translating the adopters' intentions into the present. She must decide how the commerce power applies to modes of transportation, communication, and economic relations not imagined—perhaps not imaginable—by the adopters; how the cruel and unusual punishment clause applies to the death penalty in a society that likely apprehends death differently from a society in which death was both more commonplace and more firmly integrated into a religious cosmology. The Court invoked difficulties of this sort when it concluded that the history surrounding the adoption of the Fourteenth Amendment was "inconclusive" with respect to the constitutionality of school DESEGREGATION almost a century later. Noting the vastly different roles of public education in the mid-nineteenth and mid-twentieth centuries, Chief Justice EARL WARREN wrote in BROWN V. BOARD OF EDUCATION (1954): "[W]e cannot turn back the clock to 1868 when the Amendment was adopted. . . . We must consider public education in the light of its full development and its present place in American life throughout the Nation. Only in this way can it be determined if segregation in public schools deprives these plaintiffs of the equal protection of the laws." In sum, even the historian who attempts to meet and understand the adopters on their own ground is engaging in a creative enterprise. To project the adopters into a world they could not have envisioned borders on fantasy.

In an important lecture given in 1968, entitled "Structure and Relationship in Constitutional Law," Professor Charles L. Black, Jr., described a mode of constitutional interpretation based on "inference from the structure and relationships created by the constitution in all its parts or in some principal part." Professor Black observed that in *McCulloch v. Maryland*, "Marshall does not place principal reliance on the [necessary and proper] clause as a ground of decision. . . . [Before] he reaches it he has already decided, on the basis of far more general implications, that Congress possesses the power, not expressly named, of establishing a bank and chartering corporations: . . . [h]e addresses himself to the necessary and proper clause only in response to counsel's arguing its *restrictive* force." Indeed, the second part of *McCulloch*, which held that the Constitution prohibited Maryland from levying a tax on the national bank, rested exclusively on inferences from the structure of the federal system and not at all on the text of the Constitution. Similarly, *Crandall v. Nevada* (1868) was not premised on the PRIVILEGES AND IMMUNITIES clause of either Article IV or the Fourteenth Amendment. Rather, the Court inferred a right of personal mobility among the states from the structure of the federal system: "[The citizen] has the right to come to the seat of government to assert any claim he may have upon that government, or to transact any business he may have with it . . . and this right is in its nature independent of the will of any State over whose soil he must pass to exercise it."

Citing examples like these, Professor Black argued that interpreters too often have engaged in "Humpty-Dumpty textual manipulation" rather than relying "on the sort of political inference which not only underlies the textual manipulation but is, in a well constructed opinion, usually invoked to support the interpretation of the cryptic text."

Institutional relationships are abstractions from the text and the purposes of provisions—themselves read on a high level of abstraction. The implications of the structures of government are usually vague, often even ambiguous. Thus, while structural inference is an important method of interpretation, it shares the limitations intrinsic to other interpretive strategies. It seldom yields unequivocal answers to the specific questions that arise in the course of constitutional debates.

For the most part, the Supreme Court—the institution that most systematically and authoritatively interprets and articulates the meaning of the Constitution—has construed the language, original history, and structure of the Constitution on a high level of abstraction. It has treated most provisions in the spirit suggested by Chief Justice Marshall in *McCulloch v. Maryland*. This view of the Constitution is partly a political choice, based on the desire to accommodate a venerated and difficult-to-amend historical monument with changing circumstances, attitudes, and needs. But it is no less a consequence of the nature of language and history, which necessarily leave much of the meaning of the Constitution to be determined by its subsequent applications.

Constitutional disputes typically arise against the background of earlier decisions on similar subjects. A complete theory of constitutional interpretation therefore must deal with the role of precedent. Interpreting a judicial precedent is different from interpreting the constitutional provision itself. A precedent consists of a JUDGMENT based on a particular set of facts together with the court's various explanations for the judgment. The precedent must be read, not only in terms of its own social context, but against the background of the precedents it invokes or ignores. Lon Fuller wrote:

> In the common law it is not too much to say that the judges are always ready to look behind the words of a precedent to what the previous court was trying to say, or to what it would have said if it could have foreseen the nature of the cases that were later to arise, or if its perception of the relevant factors in the case before it had been more acute. There is, then, a real sense in which the written words of the reported decisions are merely the gateway to something lying behind them that may be called, without any excess of poetic license, "unwritten law."

The American doctrine of STARE DECISIS accords presumptive but not indefeasible authority to precedent. Courts sometimes have overruled earlier decisions to return to what is said to be the original understanding of a provision. They have also overruled precedents that seem inconsistent with contemporary norms. For example, in HARPER V. VIRGINIA STATE BOARD OF ELECTIONS (1966), the Supreme Court overruled a twenty-year-old precedent to invalidate, under the equal protection clause, a state law conditioning the right to vote in state election on payment of an annual POLL TAX of $1.50. After surveying intervening decisions protecting political participation and other interests, Justice WILLIAM O. DOUGLAS concluded: "In determining what lines are unconstitutionally discriminatory, we have never been confined to historic notions of equality, any more than we have restricted due process to a fixed catalogue of what was at a given time deemed to be the limits of fundamental rights. . . . Notions of what constitutes equal treatment for purposes of the Equal Protection clause *do* change."

The process of constitutional adjudication thus has a dynamic of its own. It creates an independent force which, as a DOCTRINE evolves, may compete with the text and original history as well as with older precedents. Whether or not, as Justice JOHN MARSHALL HARLAN argued in dissent, *Harper* was inconsistent with the original understanding of the Fourteenth Amendment, the decision would have been inconceivable without the intervening expansion of doctrine beyond applications contemplated by the adopters of the Fourteenth Amendment.

Disagreements about the propriety of this evolutionary process are rooted in differing theories of constitutional law. To a strict intentionalist like Raoul Berger, the process appears to be simply the accretion of errors, which should be corrected to the extent possible. Others hold that the process properly accommodates the Constitution to changing needs and values. As Justice Holmes wrote in MISSOURI V. HOLLAND (1920):

> [W]hen we are dealing with words that are also a constituent act, like the Constitution of the United States, we must realize that they have called into life a being the development of which could not have been foreseen completely by the most gifted of its begetters. It was enough for them to realize or to hope that they had created an organism; it has taken a century and cost their successors much sweat and blood to prove that they created a nation. The case before us must be considered in the light of our entire experience and not merely in that of what was said a hundred years ago. . . . We must consider what this country has become in deciding what the Amendment has reserved.

Chief Justice CHARLES EVANS HUGHES's opinion in *Home Building & Loan* stands as the Court's most explicit assertion of the independent force of precedents and of the changing values they reflect. The Court upheld a law, enacted during the Depression, which postponed a mortgagor's right to foreclose against a defaulting mortgagee. In dissent, Justice Sutherland argued that the CONTRACT CLAUSE, which had been adopted in response to state debtor-relief legislation enacted during the depression following the Revolutionary War, was intended to prohibit precisely this sort of law. Given his intentionalist premise this disposed of the case. Hughes did not dispute Sutherland's account of the original history. Rather, he reviewed the precedents interpreting the contract clause to conclude:

> It is manifest . . . that there has been a growing appreciation of public needs and of the necessity of finding ground for a rational compromise between individual rights and public welfare. The settlement and consequent contraction of the public domain, the pressure of a constantly increasing density of population, the interrelation of the activities of our people, and the complexity of our economic interests, have inevitably led to an increased use of the organization of society in order to protect the very bases of individual opportunity. . . . [T]he question is no longer merely that of one party to a contract as against another, but of the use of reasonable means to safeguard the economic structure upon which the good of all depends.

The views articulated by Holmes, Hughes, and Douglas reflect the Court's actual practice in adjudication under the BILL OF RIGHTS, the Fourteenth Amendment, and other provisions deemed relatively open-textured. The process bears more resemblance to COMMON LAW adjudication than to textual exegesis.

In an influential essay, Thomas Grey observed that the American constitutional tradition included practices of nonoriginalist adjudication purportedly based on principles of natural rights or FUNDAMENTAL LAW, or on widely shared and deeply held values not readily inferred from the text of the written Constitution. Several of the Supreme Court's contemporary decisions involving procreation and the family have invoked this tradition, and have given rise to a heated controversy over the legitimacy of adjudication based on "fundamental values."

Originalist and nonoriginalist adjudication are not nearly so distinct as many of the disputants assume. Constitutional provisions differ enormously in their closed- or open-texturedness. Indeed, a provision's texture is not merely a feature of its language or its original history, but of the particular situation in which it is applied. One's approach to a text is determined by tradition and by social outlooks that can change over time. Depending on one's political philosophy, one may bemoan this inevitability, or embrace it. For better or for worse, however, Terrance Sandalow described an important feature of our constitutional tradition when he remarked that "[t]he Constitution has . . . not only been read in light of contemporary circumstances and values; it has been read *so that* the circumstances and values of the present generation might be given expression in constitutional law."

Most disputes about constitutional interpretation and fundamental values concern interpretation in particular institutional contexts. Today's disputes center on the judicial power to review and strike down the acts of legislatures and agencies and are motivated by what ALEXANDER M. BICKEL dubbed the "counter-majoritarian difficulty" of JUDICIAL REVIEW. Urgings of "judicial restraint" or of a more expansive approach to constitutional adjudication tend to reflect differing opinions of the role of the judiciary in a democratic polity and, more crudely, differing views about the substantive outcomes that these strategies yield. The question, say, whether Congress, the Supreme Court, or the states themselves should take primary responsibility for elaborating the equal protection clause is essentially political and cannot be resolved by abstract principles of interpretation. But this observation also cautions against taking interpretive positions based on particular institutional concerns and generalizing them beyond the situations that motivated them.

Constitutional interpretation is as much a process of creation as one of discovery. If this view is commonplace among postrealist academics, it is not often articulated by judges and it probably conflicts with the view of many citizens that constitutional interpretation should reflect the will of the adopters of the Constitution rather than its interpreters.

So-called STRICT CONSTRUCTION is an unsatisfactory response to these concerns. First, the most frequently litigated provisions do not lend themselves to "strict" or unambiguous or literal interpretation. (What are the strict meanings of the privileges or immunities, due process, and equal protection clauses?) Second, attempts to confine provisions to their very narrowest meanings typically produce results so ludicrous that even self-styled strict constructionists unconsciously abandon them in favor of less literal readings of texts and broader conceptualizations of the adopters' intentions. (No interpreter would hold that the First Amendment does not protect posters or songs because they are not "speech," or that the commerce clause does not apply to telecommunications because the adopters could not have foreseen this mode of commerce.) An interpreter must inevitably choose among different levels of abstraction in reading a provision—a choice that cannot itself be guided by any rules. Third, the two modes of strict interpretation—literalism and strict intentionalism—far from being synergistic strategies of interpretation, are often antagonistic. (Although the adopters of the First Amendment surely did not intend to protect obscene speech, the language they adopted does not exclude it.) A strict originalist theory of interpretation must opt either for literalism or for intentionalism, or must have some extraconstitutional principle for mediating between the two.

To reject these strategies is not to shed constraints. The text and history surrounding the adoption of a provision originate a line of doctrine, set its course, and continue to impose limitations. Some interpretations are more plausible than others; some are beyond the pale. And the criteria of plausibility are not merely subjective. Rather, they are intersubjective, constituted by others who are engaged in the same enterprise. Beyond the problem of subjectivity, however, the demographic characteristics of the legal interpretive community gives rise to an equally serious concern: the judiciary and the bar more generally have tended to be white, male, Anglo-Saxon, and well-to-do, and one might well wonder whether their interpretations do not embody parochial views or class interests. The concerns cannot be met by the choice of interpretive strategies, however, but only by addressing the composition and structure of the institutions whose interpretations have the force of law.

PAUL BREST
(1986)

(SEE ALSO: *Interpretivism; Noninterpretivism.*)

Bibliography

ABRAHAM, KENNETH   1981   Three Fallacies of Interpretation: A Comment on Precedent and Judicial Decision. *Arizona Law Review* 23:771–783.

BERGER, RAOUL   1977   *Government by Judiciary: The Transfor-*

mation of the Fourteenth Amendment. Cambridge, Mass.: Harvard University Press.

BLACK, CHARLES L., JR. 1969 *Structure and Relationship in Constitutional Law.* Baton Rouge: Louisiana State University Press.

CURTIS, CHARLES 1950 A Better Theory of Legal Interpretation. *Vanderbilt Law Review* 3:407–437.

DWORKIN, RONALD 1981 The Forum of Principle. *New York Law Review* 56:469–518.

ELY, JOHN HART 1980 *Democracy and Distrust.* Cambridge, Mass.: Harvard University Press.

FULLER, LON 1968 *Anatomy of Law.* New York: Praeger.

GREY, THOMAS 1975 Do We Have an Unwritten Constitution? *Stanford Law Review* 27:703–718.

HOLMES, OLIVER W. 1899 The Theory of Interpretation. *Harvard Law Review* 12:417.

MONAGHAN, HENRY 1981 Our Perfect Constitution. *New York University Law Review* 56:353–376.

SANDALOW, TERRANCE 1981 Constitutional Interpretation. *Michigan Law Review* 79:1033–1072.

SKINNER, QUENTIN 1969 Meaning and Understanding in the History of Ideas. *History & Theory* 8:3–53.

SYMPOSIUM 1985 Constitutional Interpretation. *University of Southern California Law Review* 58:551–725.

SYMPOSIUM ON LAW AND LITERATURE 1982 *Texas Law Review* 60:373–586.

TEN BROEK, JACOBUS 1938–1939 Admissibility and Use by the Supreme Court of Extrinsic Aids in Constitutional Construction. *California Law Review* 26:287–308, 437–454, 664–681; 27:157–181, 399–421.

CONSTITUTIONALISM

Constitutionalism is a term not altogether congenial to American lawyers. It seems to share the characteristics of other "isms": it is neither clearly prescriptive nor clearly descriptive; its contours are difficult to discern; its historical roots are diverse and uncertain. Legal realist WALTON H. HAMILTON, who wrote on the subject for the *Encyclopedia of the Social Sciences,* began his article in an ironic vein: "Constitutionalism is the name given to the trust which men repose in the power of words engrossed on parchment to keep a government in order."

Historians, on the other hand, employ the concept with some confidence in its meaning. American historians tend to use it as a shorthand reference to the constitutional thought of the founding period. European historians have a somewhat harder time. Given a largely UNWRITTEN CONSTITUTION and the SOVEREIGNTY of Parliament, what does it mean to refer to British constitutionalism? What is the significance of Dicey's distinction between the "conventions of the constitution" and the "law of the constitution"? How meaningful is the distinction? As Dicey noted: "Whatever may be the advantages of a so-called unwritten constitution, its existence imposes special difficulties on teachers bound to expound its provisions." French authors

view constitutionalism as an important element of the French Revolution, but run into difficulties as they contemplate the fact that, since the constitution of 1791, France has had fifteen of them—and by no means all democratic. German historians tend to restrict the use of the term *Konstitutionalismus* to the Central European constitutional monarchies of the nineteenth century, though German-language equivalents for constitutionalism (*Verfassungsstaat, Verfassungsbegriff*) are frequently encountered in the literature. The German constitutionalist trauma is, of course, the ease with which the Weimar constitution, in its time viewed as one of the most progressive in the world, could be brought to collapse at the hands of determined enemies who then managed to organize arbitrariness in the form of law.

Constitutionalism has both descriptive and prescriptive connotations. Used descriptively, it refers chiefly to the historical struggle for constitutional recognition of the people's right to "consent" and certain other rights, freedoms, and privileges. This struggle extends roughly from the seventeenth century to the present day. Its beginnings coincide with the "enlightenment" of the seventeenth and eighteenth centuries. Used prescriptively, especially in the United States, its meaning incorporates those features of government seen as the essential elements of the American Constitution. Thus F. A. Hayek called constitutionalism the American contribution to the RULE OF LAW.

Constitutionalism obviously presupposes the concept of a CONSTITUTION. A Swiss authority of some influence in the American revolution, EMERICH DE VATTEL, in his famous 1758 treatise, *The Law of Nations or the Principles of Natural Law,* provided a definition: "The FUNDAMENTAL LAW which determines the manner in which the public authority is to be exercised is what forms the *constitution of the State.* In it can be seen the organization by means of which the Nation acts as a political body; how and by whom the people are to be governed; and what are the rights and duties of those who govern. This constitution is nothing else at bottom than the establishment of the system, according to which a Nation proposed to work in common to obtain the advantages for which a political society is formed."

This rather neutral definition has to be read against the background of Vattel's theory of natural law. Vattel recognized the right of the majority to reform its government and, most important, excluded fundamental laws from the reach of legislators, "unless they are expressly empowered by the nation to change them." Moreover, Vattel believed that the ends of civil society were "to procure for its citizens the necessities, the comforts, and the pleasures of life, and in general their happiness; to secure to each the peaceful enjoyment of his property and a sure means of obtaining justice; and finally to defend the whole body against all external violence."

Later in the eighteenth century strong prescriptive elements became part of the very definition of a constitution. Two examples are equally famous. On October 21, 1776, the town of Concord, Massachusetts, resolved "that a Constitution in its Proper Idea intends a System of Principles Established to Secure the Subject in the Possession and enjoyment of their Rights and Privileges, against any Encroachment of the Governing Part." (See CONCORD RESOLUTION.) Article 16 of the French Declaration of the Rights of Man of 1789 put it even more bluntly: "A society in which the guarantee of rights is not assured nor the SEPARATION OF POWERS provided for, has no constitution."

Although it would be impractical to make such substantive features a necessary part of one's definition of a written or unwritten constitution, a proper understanding of constitutionalism as a historical phenomenon depends on them. Constitutionalism does not refer simply to having a constitution but to having a particular kind of constitution, however difficult it may be to specify its content. This assertion holds true even in the case of the interplay of old forces (monarchies and estates) with new forces (the middle class in particular) which characterized the emergence of constitutional monarchies in Central Europe during the nineteenth century. Seen from a constitutionalist perspective, many of the German constitutional monarchies were influenced by concepts that had much in common with constitutionalist thought. The most important of these concepts was the *Rechtsstaat*: a state based on "reason" and a strict regulation of government by law.

The concepts of a constitution and of fundamental laws have not had a constant meaning over time. Since the eighteenth century (though not before), it has become customary to translate Aristotle's word *politeia* as "constitution": "A constitution is the arrangement of the offices in a *polis*, but especially of the highest office." This definition precedes Aristotle's differentiation among six forms of government—those for the common good (monarchy, aristocracy, and "polity") and their perversions, which serve individual interests (tyranny, oligarchy, and democracy). Aristotle thus introduced substantive, not merely formal, criteria into his teachings about constitutional arrangements.

Cicero is usually credited with first giving the Latin term *constitutio* something like its modern meaning. About a mixed form of government, he said in *De Re Publica:* "This constitution has a great measure of equability without which men can hardly remain free for any length of time." Indeed, Roman law was characterized by constitutional notions. The constitution of the Roman republic, putting other substantive arrangements aside, was marked by the power of the plebs to pass on laws which bound the entire Roman people. While this republican prerogative of the plebs was later replaced by Senate law-making and eventually by the emperor's legislative monopoly, its status is perhaps best illustrated by Augustus's repeated refusal, on "constitutional" grounds, to accept extraordinary powers to renew law and morals. Though this Augustan reticence may have been a triumph of form over substance, "triumphs" of this kind have frequently illustrated how constitutional notions have become deeply entrenched.

In subsequent Roman usage the term *constitutio* came to identify imperial legislation that preempted all other law. The understanding of *constitutio* as signifying important legislation was retained during the Middle Ages in the Holy Roman Empire, in the church, and throughout Europe. A well-known English example is the Constitution of Clarendon issued by Henry II in 1164.

In England, the modern use of constitution as referring to the nature, government, and fundamental laws of a state dates from the early seventeenth century. In the House of Commons, in 1610, James Whitelock argued that the imposition of taxes by James I was "against the natural frame and constitution of the policy of this kingdom, which is ius publicum regni, and so subverteth the fundamental law of the realm and induceth a new form of State and government."

In Europe, perception that some laws were more fundamental than others were well established before the eighteenth century. MAGNA CARTA (1215), the PETITION OF RIGHT (1628), and the HABEAS CORPUS ACT (1679) are the best known English illustrations of this point. In addition, by their coronation oaths English kings obliged themselves "to hold and keep the laws and righteous customs which the community of [the] realm shall have chosen." Even if the law could not reach the king, the king was viewed as under the law (and, of course, under God). The bounds of the king's discretion were defined by the ancient laws and customs of England or, put differently, the COMMON LAW. By the seventeenth century, EDWARD COKE was even prepared to claim that acts of Parliament were subject to review under the common law (and natural law).

Though the status of French kings was considerably more mysterious and legal constraints on them were far fewer than in England, they too were viewed as subject to fundamental laws. The French Protestant political theorists of the sixteenth century expressed far-reaching views on the matter. François Hotman subtitled the XXVth chapter of the third edition of his *Francogallia* (1586): "The king of France does not have unlimited domain in his kingdom but is circumscribed by settled and specific law."

Beginning in the seventeenth century, the struggle over the limits of power, the ends of government, and the limits of obedience was frequently expressed in terms of social contract theory. Johannes Althusius, Hugo Grotius, JOHN

LOCKE, and Jean-Jacques Rousseau all influenced the civil struggles of their age. Although the differences among these writers are profound, all of them stipulate a SOCIAL COMPACT as the foundation for the constitutional arrangements of the state. While such a contract is not necessarily based on an assumption of popular sovereignty, a social contract without the assumed or actual consent of "the people" or their representatives is unthinkable. Once this notion spread widely, it was difficult to maintain the divine right of kings, and it became almost irresistible to relocate sovereignty in the people—Thomas Hobbes notwithstanding.

One must not confuse the concept of a social contract with that of a constitution. For the "contractarians," constitutions follow from the social contract; they are not identical with it. Although the social contract is mostly a logical stipulation, at times the contract seems real enough, embodying or justifying specific constitutional arrangements. The Glorious Revolution in England, the American Revolution, the French Revolution—all appealed to the social contract.

The Glorious Revolution, like the English Civil War before it, was seen in contractarian terms. The Convention Parliament of 1689 resolved that James II "having endeavored to subvert the constitution of the kingdom by breaking the original contract between king and people . . . has abdicated the government and the throne is hereby vacant." The Declaration of Rights of 1689 was part of Parliament's contract with William and Mary and, later that year, was incorporated into the act of Parliament known as the BILL OF RIGHTS. After reciting Parliament's grievances against the absolutist tendencies of James II, the Bill of Rights prohibited the suspension of the laws by regal authority; provided for the election and privileges of Parliament (including a prohibition of prerogative taxation); and dealt with the right to petition, excessive bail, and the jury system.

Although this catalogue of constitutional concerns is modest by contemporary standards, the Bill of Rights, in conjunction with other British traditions and the "mixed government" confirmed by the Glorious Revolution, led MONTESQUIEU to celebrate England as the one nation in the world "that has for the direct end of its constitution political liberty." Montesquieu concluded his chapter on "The Constitution of England" in *The Spirit of the Laws* with the wry comment that it was not his task to examine whether the English actually enjoyed this liberty. "Sufficient it is for my purpose to observe, that it is established by their laws; and I inquire no further." When Montesquieu's book was published in 1748, some questions about constitutional liberty in England might indeed have been examined. For instance, the right to vote was extremely restricted and even that small electorate was not consulted

when, by the Septennial Act of 1716, Parliament extended its own duration by another four years. For the American colonists who fought more against the British Parliament than against their monarch, this example of the "sovereignty of Parliament" marked the limit of British constitutionalism. As JAMES MADISON wrote in THE FEDERALIST #53, citing the Septennial Act: "Where no constitution paramount to the government, either existed or could be obtained, no constitutional security similar to that established in the United States, was to be attempted."

American constitutionalism during the colonial and revolutionary periods included the notions of a constitution as superior to legislation and the notion of a written constitution. As concerns the "writing" of constitutions, Gerald Stourzh has remarked, for the period after 1776, that Americans clearly differentiated "between the functions of constitution-*making* (with an additional differentiation between drafting and ratifying functions), of *amending* constitutions, and of *legislating* within the framework of the constitution."

One formal element in the American colonies was bound to have a profound impact on American constitutionalism, especially its choice of written constitutions as the means for anchoring the organization of their governments and the protection of their rights and privileges. COLONIAL CHARTERS, fundamental orders, and other written documents were used in the establishment of the colonies. These contracts between rulers and ruled provided for the government of the colonies, secured property rights, and even extended the guaranteed liberties and privileges of the English constitution. The 1629 CHARTER OF MASSACHUSETTS BAY is an important early example.

Pennsylvania, however, provides the most vivid illustration of the essential features and conundrums of American constitutionalism. In England, in 1682, a "frame of government of the province of Pensilvania" was agreed to by the Governor, WILLIAM PENN, and "divers freemen" of the province. It was a revision of an earlier plan drawn up by Penn which he had called "Fundamental Constitutions of Pennsylvania." The frame of government was replaced by a new frame as early as 1683. Its place was taken in 1701 by the Pennsylvania Charter of Privileges, granted by Penn during his second visit to the province and formally approved by the General Assembly. (See PENNSYLVANIA COLONIAL CHARTERS.) Though the focus here is on the Charter of Privileges, William Penn's preface to the Frame of Government deserves quotation: "*Any government is free to the people under it* (whatever be the frame) *where the laws rule, and the people are a party to those laws*, and more than this is tyranny, oligarchy, or confusion." Having invoked the notions of government of laws and popular consent, Penn went on, however, to warn against excessive optimism about the RULE OF LAW: "Governments, like clocks, go from the motion men give them; and as governments are made and moved by men, so by them they are ruined too." It is difficult to imagine a better reflection on the challenges faced by the American constitution makers of the eighteenth century.

The Pennsylvania Charter of Privileges of 1701 was a remarkable constitutional document. First of all, the charter itself was adopted in a constitutional manner, according to the provisions for amending the Frame of Government. Second, it began, not with the organization of government, but with an issue of fundamental rights: it guaranteed the freedom of conscience and made all Christians eligible for public office. Third, the charter provided for a unicameral representative assembly to be elected annually by the freemen with the right to initiate LEGISLATION and with all parliamentary powers and privileges "according to the Rights of the free-born Subjects of *England,* and as is usual in any of the King's Plantations in *America.*" Fourth, far ahead of its time, it gave to all "criminals" "the same Privileges of Witness and Council as their Prosecutors." Fifth, it guaranteed the "ordinary Course of Justice" in all disputes concerning property. Sixth, the proprietor committed himself and his heirs not to breach the liberties of the charter; anything done to the contrary should "be held of no Force or Effect." Seventh, the liberties, privileges, and benefits granted by the charter were to be enjoyed, "any Law made and passed by this General Assembly, to the Contrary hereof, notwithstanding." Eighth, the charter could be amended only by a vote of "*Six* Parts of *Seven*" of the Assembly and the consent of the governor. Ninth, the guarantee of liberty of conscience was placed even beyond the power of constitutional amendment "because the Happiness of Mankind depends so much upon the Enjoying of Liberty of their Consciences."

This colonial charter, granted by a feudal landowner, embodies the most significant elements of American constitutionalism as it emerged in the course of the century—the concept of consent and the concept of a written constitution sharply differentiated from ordinary legislation and with provisions for its amendment and a bill of rights, however rudimentary. Indeed, by placing the liberty of conscience beyond the amending power it posed the ultimate conundrum of constitutionalism—the possibility of unconstitutional constitutional amendments.

The concept of consent had direct consequences for questioning the powers of Parliament over America and for the American understanding of REPRESENTATION. In terms of constitutionalism, the most important part of the long list of grievances against George III with which the DECLARATION OF INDEPENDENCE began (following the model of the Declaration of Rights of 1689) was the passage which stated that the king had "combined with others to subject us to a JURISDICTION foreign to our constitutions, and unacknowledged by our laws; giving his assent to their acts of pretended legislation." The nation began with an assertion of the right to consent.

In the decades of constitution-making following independence the main organizational task of American constitutionalism was to spell out in detail the implications of popular sovereignty for the structure of government. What, for instance, should follow from the famous formulation in the VIRGINIA DECLARATION OF RIGHTS, of June 12, 1776, "that all power is vested in, and consequently derived from, the people; the magistrates are their trustees and servants, and at all times amenable to them"? Four subjects were of overriding importance: the franchise; the separation of powers; the amending process; and the protection of individual rights.

Political status in the colonies had mostly depended on property ownership, and the Revolution had not done away with these requirements. The federal CONSTITUTIONAL CONVENTION OF 1787 could not agree on who should have the right to vote. Sovereignty of the people did not mean all the people. But who should have the right to vote was discussed frequently and with great seriousness. The voters of the Massachusetts town of Northampton, for instance, concluded in 1780 that restricting the franchise for the Massachusetts house to freeholders and other men of property was inconsistent with the concepts and principles of native equality and freedom, the social compact, personal equality, and no TAXATION WITHOUT REPRESENTATION. Their objections pertained only to elections to the house; indeed, they were based on the notion that in a bicameral legislature one chamber should represent property, the other persons. A few more decades had to elapse before property and taxpaying qualifications disappeared. The franchise was expanded in all Western societies in the course of the nineteenth century. The earliest and most inclusive expansion, however, came in the United States—although even here the vote was withheld from women, AMERICAN INDIANS, slaves, and, as a rule, free blacks.

The colonists widely believed that their governments were "mixed" in accord with the British model. A London compendium from 1755 said of the colonial governments: "By the governor, representing the King, the colonies are monarchical; by a Council they are aristocratical; by a house of representatives, or delegates from the people, they are democratical." While this was more an "ideal type" than an accurate description of the constitutional facts, the post-Revolution problem for those who had grown up within the tradition of mixed or balanced government was how to institute it under radically changed conditions. The question was not really whether to have balanced government, though some advocates of "simple" government existed.

The separation of powers doctrine, as put forward most influentially by Montesquieu, sought to limit power by separating factions and, to some extent, associating them with the executive and legislative functions of government. To Montesquieu the separation of powers was a necessary if not a sufficient condition of liberty. By 1776 the American constitutional problem had become not the separation of "powers" but the distribution of power flowing from a single source—the people.

Though the Americans continued to view the separation of powers as necessary to liberty and therefore indispensable to constitutionalism, they faced a formidable challenge in attempting to implement the concept. The towns of Essex County, Massachusetts, wrote "the Essex Result," a veritable dissertation on the subject in voicing their objections to the proposed Massachusetts constitution of 1778, which they considered insufficiently mindful of the separation of powers. They propounded the principle "that the legislative, judicial, and executive powers are to be lodged in different hands, that each branch is to be independent, and further, to be so balanced, and be able to exert such checks upon the others, as will preserve it from dependence on, or an union with them."

Practical problems were inevitable. The different powers of government do not imply clearly differentiated functions; they will necessarily be closely intertwined—especially if one adds the notion, urged in the Essex Result, of CHECKS AND BALANCES. In the major state constitutions enacted in 1776 and immediately after, the legislative branch usually dominated, but the constitutions distinguished conceptually between legislative, executive, and judicial functions. They made members of one branch ineligible to serve in the others, and they gave some measure of autonomy to the judiciary. However, with respect to such crucial features as the structure and election of the executive and the power of appointments, they differed radically one from the other.

As successful revolutionaries, the Americans faced a difficult political task. They needed to justify the power of the people to change their government and at the same time to assure the stability of the new order based on popular sovereignty. If, as a practical matter, consent meant consent by a majority, was that majority not also at liberty to change the states' new constitutions? If not, why not? Vattel had struggled valiantly to develop a satisfactory framework for thinking about constitutional change, though without much success. His argument in *The Law of Nations* that the legislative power could not amend the constitution is hardly a model of tight reasoning. Concluding his essay, Vattel observed: "However, in discussing changes in a constitution, we are here speaking only of the right; the expediency of such changes belongs to the field of politics. We content ourselves with the general remark

that it is a delicate operation and one full of danger to make great changes in the State; and since frequent changes are hurtful in themselves, a Nation ought to be very circumspect in this matter and never be inclined to make innovations, except for the most urgent reasons or from necessity."

In America, THOMAS JEFFERSON was the foremost theorist of constitutional change. He believed that each generation has "a right to choose for itself the form of government it believes most promotive of its happiness. . . ." The same man who provided us with this theory of constitutional change wanted to be remembered in his epitaph for the VIRGINIA STATUTE OF RELIGIOUS LIBERTY (1786), which ended with a proviso that sought to secure the statute forever: we "do declare, that the rights hereby asserted are of the NATURAL RIGHTS of mankind, and that if any act shall be hereafter passed to repeal the present or to narrow its operation, such act will be an infringement of natural right."

In a way, the matter was simple. Jefferson and many of his fellow citizens were for change, stability, and inalienable rights all at the same time. These disparate aims were somewhat reconciled in practice by having the constitutions provide for their own amendment and for bills of rights. This course had important practical implications: it legitimized the concept of constitutional change and thus dramatically reduced the need for revolutions; and it advised the majority that it had no power to regulate at will the structure of government or basic rights of individuals. Enlightened America was anything but unanimous on the status of specific rights. Not every state constitution had a bill of rights; those that did almost always included the liberty of conscience, FREEDOM OF PRESS, trial by jury, and protection of property. Some of the rights, as Penn and Jefferson suggested, were considered so fundamental that their amendment would conflict with the very nature of constitutional government.

The CONSTITUTIONAL CONVENTION OF 1787 and the main features of the federal constitution, after a decade of state constitutions, further defined American constitutionalism. The Constitution precariously provided for a mode of RATIFICATION hardly in accord with the ARTICLES OF CONFEDERATION. Among the ironies of history is the fact that the Constitutional Convention's preference for the convention method of ratification (rather than ratification by all state legislatures as required by the Articles) resulted in attaching to the Constitution, in 1791, a BILL OF RIGHTS, which the Framers of Philadelphia had considered unnecessary.

The most important aspect of the Constitution was its implementation of the goal "to form a more perfect Union." Carl J. Friedrich characterized the claim that FEDERALISM is an American invention a defensible overstatement. The Constitution's effort to delineate clearly the powers of the federal government as against those of the states is remarkable indeed. Its main accomplishment was not to get bogged down by the metaphysics of sovereignty and to enable the federal government to legislate and tax in a manner binding the people directly, without using the states as intermediaries. This structure of "dual sovereignty" assured the viability of the federal government and, at least well into the twentieth century, the viability of the states. It underwent one substantial modification. When the "perpetual" nature of the Union was challenged over the issue of SLAVERY, constitutional amendments were enacted at the end of the Civil War for the primary purpose of securing equal rights to recently emancipated black citizens. These amendments eventually legitimized a great expansion of federal influence on the law of the states in the interest of greater equality for blacks and other minorities.

The constitutional organization of the federal government is delineated by the organization of the constitutional text. The PREAMBLE speaks of the people of the United States as ordaining and establishing the Constitution. The first (and presumably most important) article deals with the election and LEGISLATIVE POWERS OF CONGRESS. Article II vests the executive power in a President. Article III concerns the JUDICIAL POWER and its jurisdiction. Although this organization seems to provide us with a rather pure example of the separation of powers, the Constitution combines elements of separate and independent powers (such as an independent judiciary or a President not dependent on Congress for his term of office) with a thorough mixing of powers, best summarized by the concept of checks and balances.

Superficially, the legislative and executive branches seem to be assigned separate functions: lawmaking and law executing. The judicial branch, through dispute-settling, performs one part of the executive function under special conditions and special procedures. In reality, however, both the executive and the judiciary engage in lawmaking through interpretation and rule-making. The executive intrudes into the legislative function by exercising the VETO POWER. Congress, on the other hand, performs executive functions through legislative oversight, appropriations decisions, and confirming appointments. One might better forgo the Framers' own characterization of the system as one of separation of powers. American constitutionalism indulged itself in heaping checks upon checks so that the love of power of officials occupying the various branches of government could be harnessed.

On one of the most important of these checks and the most distinctly American contribution to constitutionalist doctrine, the Constitution of 1787 was silent. Nowhere does the constitutional text grant the power of JUDICIAL REVIEW of legislation. On the basis of the debates in the Constitutional Convention one can make a strong case that some of the most influential Framers thought that judicial review was implied, but this is not the same as saying that the Constitution implies it. How then did the American judiciary end up as the guardian of the Constitution?

There had been instances of courts exercising the power of judicial review as well as public debate of the issue in the new states. The case for judicial review was based on a peculiarly American amalgam of various strands of constitutionalism. First, there was the notion of a constitution as fundamental law. If Lord Coke could claim the common law as a basis for reviewing acts of Parliament, how much more plausible the claim that judges were bound to obey a fundamental charter viewed as supreme law. Second, if the constitutions derived their authority from the sovereignty of the people, and if legislators and other government officials were simply the people's trustees and servants, it was no great leap to reason that judges had to obey the will of the whole people as expressed in the constitution. Third, the special procedures for constitutional amendment typically denied the legislatures the power to amend by ordinary legislation, which suggested that attempts of that kind should go unenforced. Fourth, those constitutions containing bills of rights reenforced the notion of a constitution as superior law with the aim of protecting the rights of individuals against tyrannical majorities. Fifth, in the case of the federal constitution there was the added need to assure its status as supreme law throughout the Union. The arguments for and practice of judicial review of state legislation served to consolidate the understanding of the American Constitution as the supreme law of the land to which all government actors were subject.

Chief Justice JOHN MARSHALL in MARBURY V. MADISON (1803) to the contrary notwithstanding, the issue of judicial review was an intricate one. No simple constitutionalist syllogism could be constructed that invariably led one to conclude that judges had the power of judicial review. The amalgam, however, proved powerful under the conditions prevailing in the United States. When the Supreme Court went ahead and in effect appointed itself and the other judges guardians of the Constitution (in the case of the Supreme Court, eventually to become the preeminent guardian), the people, by and large, acquiesced.

The American institution of judicial review has influenced developments abroad. Various forms of constitutional review exist in Austria, Germany, India, Italy, Japan, and, now, even France—to name the most important. While their historical roots are many and their institutional characteristics diverse, the American model was highly visible when they came into being. One of the most instructive contemporary instances is that of the Court of Justice of the European Community. Starting with the need of assuring the uniformity of Community law throughout the member nations, the Court of Justice has transformed the treaties underlying the European Community (especially the Treaty of Rome) into the constitution of the community. These are radical developments. The constitutionalization of the Treaty of Rome has led to the introduction of judicial review, or what one might more appropriately call Community review, even into countries that have not previously recognized the power of their courts to pass on the constitutionality of legislation.

As constitutionalism does not refer to having a constitution but to structural and substantive limitations on government, it would be a gargantuan task to determine its incidence in a world full of written constitutions, of which many do not mean what they say, while others do not accomplish what they mean. The need to distinguish between form and substance would necessitate impossibly vast empirical assessments. The distinction between form and substance would also make desirable a detailed examination of the legal situation in countries, such as Great Britain, that meet most substantive requirements of constitutionalism without a written constitution, an entrenched bill of rights, or the power of judicial review.

Constitutionalism matured in the context of the liberal democracies with their emphasis on civil and political rights and their attempts clearly to define the public and the private sphere. The rights guaranteed, with the exception of certain rights to participate in the exercise of governmental power, were rights of the citizen against infringement by government of his own sphere, or "defensive" rights (German constitutional law has coined the term *Abwehrrechte* for this category). The eighteenth- and nineteenth-century constitutions do not contain social rights aimed at guaranteeing citizens a fair measure of well-being. A notable aspect of the Weimar constitution was its effort to formulate rights that would guarantee everyone a worthwhile existence. As the concept of CITIZENSHIP expanded from the formal equality of sharing legal capacities to the substantive equality of sharing goods, the contemporary welfare state became clearly committed to some undefined (and probably undefinable) minimum of such substantive equality. The predominant means for accomplishing such goals has been legislation rather than constitutionalization. Certain legislation of this kind has been viewed by some as in actual conflict with the constitutionalist scheme. This alleged conflict has, in turn, led to substantial efforts in the United States and other countries to reinterpret the liberal constitutions as not only permitting but demanding government intervention on behalf of the underprivileged.

In conjunction with these difficulties, but by no means restricted to them, American constitutional scholarship engages in periodic debates about methods of CONSTITUTIONAL INTERPRETATION. Much of the discussion reinvents the interpretive wheels of earlier generations. Its main focus is the degree of fidelity which may be owed the words of the Constitution and the intentions of its Framers. Some contemporary writing argues that the Constitution can incorporate contemporary value preferences of a highly subjective kind. The tension is between the need to expound an essentially unaltered eighteenth-century Constitution in a manner consistent with "the progress of the human mind," on the one hand, and the danger of dissolving the Constitution in the process. The dispute is further complicated by endless varieties of highly refined theories concerning the proper scope of judicial review.

Over its two hundred years the American Constitution has been assigned the role of a national ideology. It has performed this role for a people that has grown from a few million to almost 250 million citizens of very diverse background. While the historical disinclination to amend the Constitution by means other than judicial review may help account for its durability, it has also subjected the Constitution to considerable strain. As the secular equivalent of the Bible, as Walton Hamilton observed, "it became the great storehouse of verbal conflict, and rival truths were derived by the same inexorable logic from the same infallible source." More often than not, Americans invoke constitutional principles in order to understand and resolve conflicts. This fact attests to the extraordinary vitality of American constitutionalism. It may also endanger its viability. Too frequent crossings of the line between "constitution as ideology" and "ideology as constitution" will blur the line. The American concept of the legitimacy of government is closely tied to the Constitution. Its limitless manipulation may endanger the very legitimacy that has been the great accomplishment of American constitutionalism.

GERHARD CASPER
(1986)

Bibliography

ADAMS, WILLI PAUL 1980 *The First American Constitutions.* Chapel Hill: University of North Carolina Press.
BAILYN, BERNARD 1967 *The Ideological Origins of the American Revolution.* Cambridge, Mass.: Belknap Press.
COOKE, JACOB E., ed. 1961 *The Federalist.* Middletown, Conn.: Wesleyan University Press.
DICEY, A. V. (1885) 1959 *Introduction to the Study of the Law of the Constitution.* London: Macmillan.
FRANKLIN, JULIAN H., ed. 1969 *Constitutionalism and Resistance in the Sixteenth Century.* Indianapolis: Bobbs-Merrill.
FRIEDRICH, CARL J. 1941 *Constitutional Government and Democracy.* Boston: Little, Brown.
——— 1967 *The Impact of American Constitutionalism Abroad.* Boston: Boston University Press.

HAMILTON, WALTON H. 1931 Constitutionalism. Pages 255–258 in Edwin R. A. Seligman et al. (eds.), *Encyclopedia of the Social Sciences*. New York: Macmillan.

MAITLAND, F. W. 1926 *The Constitutional History of England*. Cambridge: At the University Press.

McILWAIN, CHARLES HOWARD (1940) 1947 *Constitutionalism: Ancient and Modern*. Ithaca, N.Y.: Cornell University Press.

PENNOCK, J. RONALD and CHAPMAN, JOHN W., eds. 1979 *Constitutionalism*. New York: New York University Press.

PERRY, RICHARD L., ed. 1972 *Sources of Our Liberties*. New York: New York University Press.

STOURZH, GERALD 1977 The American Revolution, Modern Constitutionalism, and the Protection of Human Rights. Pages 162–176 in Kenneth Thompson et al. (eds.), *Truth and Tragedy: A Tribute to Hans J. Morgenthau*. Washington, D.C.: New Republic Book Co.

WOOD, GORDON S. 1969 *The Creation of the American Republic 1776–1787*. New York: Norton.

WORMUTH, FRANCIS D. 1949 *The Origins of Modern Constitutionalism*. New York: Harper.

CONSTITUTIONALISM AND THE AMERICAN FOUNDING

Between 1776 and 1789 the American people constituted themselves a nation by creating republican governments in the thirteen former English colonies and then, in the CONSTITUTIONAL CONVENTION OF 1787, by transforming the Union of confederated states into a genuine law-giving government. The novelty of this achievement was epitomized in the seal of the new nation, which, by incorporating the phrase "Novus Ordo Seclorum," announced "a new order of the ages." Yet in founding political societies Americans pursued a goal that had occupied Western man since antiquity: the establishment of government power capable of maintaining the stability and order necessary to realize the purposes of community, yet so defined and structured as to prevent tyranny. This age-old quest for the forms, procedures, and institutional arrangements most suitable for limiting power and implementing a community's conception of political right and justice, we know as CONSTITUTIONALISM.

Constitutionalism takes as its purpose resolution of the conflict that characterizes political life and makes government necessary, through procedures and institutions that seek to limit government and create spheres of individual and community freedom. Based on the paradoxical idea that the power to make law and to rule can be at once sovereign and effective, yet also defined, reasonable, and responsible, constitutionalism contains an inherent tension that sets it against utopianism and anarchism, which deny the reality of power, and against absolutism and totalitarianism, which tolerate no limitations on power. Nevertheless, although constitutionalists can in retrospect be

seen as sharing common assumptions, differences among them have sometimes led to irreconcilable conflict. One such division occurred in the eighteenth century when the American people separated from the English and adopted a new type of constitutional theory and practice for the conduct of their political life.

Perhaps the most obvious feature of American constitutionalism was its apparent dependence upon legally binding written instruments prescribing the organization of government and fixing primary principles and rules to guide its operation. Texts had of course long been used in law, government, and politics, and the English constitution comprised written elements. Americans' resort to documentary, positive law techniques of government was so much more systematic and complete than any previous undertaking, however, as to amount to constitutional innovation. Following the American example, peoples everywhere in the modern world have adopted the practice of forming governments by writing constitutions. But Americans in the founding era did more than invent a new approach to the old problem of limited government. Their constitution-making was informed with a new purpose— the liberal purpose of protecting the NATURAL RIGHTS of individuals. American charters of FUNDAMENTAL LAW were not simply ordinances of government; they were also constitutions of liberty. The meaning of liberty, especially the relation between the individual and the community that was central to any practical definition of it, was a deeply controversial issue that divided Americans in state and national constitution-making. The adoption of the federal Constitution in 1787, however, marked a decisive shift toward protection of individuals in the pursuit of their interests, and away from enforcement of community consensus aimed at making citizens virtuous and moral as the central purpose of constitutional government in America.

American constitutionalism is thus concerned with organizational and procedural matters, on the one hand, and with substantive questions of political purpose, on the other. Most constitutional politics in the United States deals with the former concern, as groups and individuals assert or deny the existence of proper governmental power or challenge methods used to employ it. Nevertheless, constitutionalism is ultimately normative and purposive. Every state may be said to have a constitution, in the sense of an institutional structure and established procedures for conducting political affairs. But not every state is a constitutional state. In the Western political tradition constitutional government exists where certain forms and procedures limit the exercise of power. American constitutionalism goes farther by pursuing not only the negative goal of preventing tyranny but also the positive end of promoting individual liberty, both in the passive sense of protection against government power and in the active sense of participation in the decisions of the political community. Viewed in this light, American constitutionalism raises basic questions of political purpose that connect it with the mainstream of Western political philosophy.

In the history of constitutionalism the great problem has not been to create power but to define and limit it. The Western constitutional tradition has employed two methods toward this end. The first is the theory and practice of arranging the internal structure of government so that power is distributed and balanced. A second method of constitutionalism has been to subject government to legal limitations, or the RULE OF LAW.

English constitutionalism in the period of American colonization comprised both strands of the constitutional tradition. The common law courts in the early seventeenth century insisted on the superiority of law to the royal prerogative. Sir EDWARD COKE gave famous expression to the idea of a higher law controlling government in asserting that "sovereign power' is no parliamentary word. . . . MAGNA CARTA is such a fellow, that he will have no sovereign." Coke also said that "when an act of Parliament is against common right and reason, or repugnant, or impossible to be performed, the common law will control it and adjudge such act to be void." Parliament itself, however, subsequently claimed supremacy in lawmaking, and vindication of its authority in the Glorious Revolution of 1688 effectively precluded development of the rule of law into a politically relevant form of HIGHER LAW constitutionalism. An internally balanced institutional structure, expressed in the revised and revitalized theory of mixed government in the eighteenth century, became the principal model of constitutional government in England.

Essentially descriptive in its connotation, the English constitution was the structure of institutions, laws, conventions, and practices through which political issues were brought to resolution and carried out in acts of government. Yet the constitution was also prescriptive or normative, or at least it was supposed to be. More specifically, as Montesquieu, WILLIAM BLACKSTONE, and other eighteenth-century writers affirmed, the end of the English constitution was civil and political liberty. From the standpoint of modern constitutionalism the legislative supremacy that contemporaries regarded as the foundation of English liberty was incompatible with effective restraints on governments. Nevertheless, Parliament was believed to be under a moral obligation to protect the rights and liberties of Englishmen, and the sanctions of natural law were still seen as effective restraints. Moreover, political accountability to public opinion through elections operated as a limitation on government. Englishmen thus continued to see their constitution as fixed and fundamental, notwithstanding legislative SOVEREIGNTY.

American constitutionalism began in the seventeenth century when English settlers founded political societies and institutions of government in North America. Two things stand out in this early constitutional experience. First, the formation of government was to a considerable extent based on written instruments. In corporate and proprietary colonies the founding documents were COLONIAL CHARTERS granted by the crown conferring enumerated powers on a particular person or group within a designated geographical area for specific purposes. Under these charters the colonists adopted further agreements, organic acts, ordinances, combinations, and frames of government giving more precise form to political institutions. In religiously motivated colonies government was more clearly the result of mutual pledging and association under civil-religious covenants. American colonists thus used constitutionlike instruments to create political community, define fundamental values and interests, specify basic rights, and organize governmental institutions.

The second outstanding fact in early American constitutional history was substantial community control over local affairs. To be sure, the colonies employed the forms and practices of English government and generally emulated the metropolitan political culture. Their institutions at the provincial and local level were patterned after English models, and the theory of mixed government and the balanced constitution was accepted as valid. Yet discordant tendencies pointed to a distinctive course of constitutional development. The fact that in most colonies the power of the governor depended on royal authority while the power of the assembly rested on a popular base, as well as frequent conflict of interest between them, made separation and division of power a political reality discrepant with the theory of mixed government. Furthermore, popularly elected assemblies responsive to growing constituencies and enjoying de facto local sovereignty under written charters introduced a republican element into American politics.

As English subjects, Americans believed they lived under a free and fixed English constitution. Long before the Revolution they expressed this view in the course of conflicts with imperial officials. Numerous writers asserted that the constitution was a SOCIAL COMPACT between the people and their rulers; that the legislature could not alter the fundamental laws from which government derived its form, powers, and very existence; that government must exercise power within limits prescribed by a compact with the people. Moreover, the compact chosen to organize and direct government, as a colonial sermon of 1768 put it, must coincide with "the moral fitness of things, by which alone the natural rights of mankind can be secured." Disputing the descriptive English constitution that included parliamentary sovereignty, Americans were coming to think of a constitution as normative rules limiting the exercise of power for the purpose of protecting the people's liberty, property, and happiness.

In declaring their independence from England, Americans in a sense reenacted the founding experience of the seventeenth century. They took what their history and political circumstances determined to be the logical step of writing constitutions to organize their political communities. Before issuing the DECLARATION OF INDEPENDENCE, Congress recommended that the colonies adopt governments that "in the opinion of representatives of the people, best conduce to the happiness and safety of their constituents in particular, and America in general." Although some argued that the people acting in convention should form the government, political exigencies and Whig political theory conferred legitimacy on legislatures which, in all but two instances, were responsible for writing or adopting the first state constitutions.

The most distinctive feature of the state constitutions, their documentary character, followed the decision to form new governments as a matter of course. Given the long tradition of founding documents in America, it seemed obvious that the purposes of political community and limitations on government could be better achieved by writing a constitution than by relying on an unstipulated, imprecise constitution like England's, which did not limit government and was not really a constitution after all. Although consisting in part of written documents, the English constitution was too subjective, ultimately existing in men's minds and premised on the idea that "thinking makes it so." Americans insisted that the principles and rules essential to organizing power and preserving liberty be separated from the government and objectively fixed in positive form. Old in the tendency it reflected, though new in its comprehensive application, American constitutionalism rested on the idea that "saying it makes it so," or at least the hope that putting something in writing so it can be authoritatively consulted makes it easier to achieve specified ends.

The state constitutions stood in a direct line of descent from colonial documents that created political communities and established institutions of government. One type of founding document (compact or covenant) signified mutual promise and consent by which individuals formed a political community and identified basic values, rights, and interests. A second type of document (ordinance or frame) specified governmental institutions. Half the state constitutions written between 1776 and 1789 were described as compacts and contained bills of rights that defined basic community values. In the other constitutions the design of government received principal attention. All the constitutions reflected tendencies of previous political development; none created institutions on a completely clean slate. This fact appeared more clearly in documents that were mainly concerned with establishing a framework of government. In these more modern documents, which anticipated the course of American constitutional development, community consensus yielded in importance to protection of individual rights as the main purpose of constitution-making.

Republicanism was the political philosophy of the AMERICAN REVOLUTION. Although lacking in precise meaning, the concept is most accurately defined as government resting on the consent of the people and directed by the public will expressed through representative institutions. In the perspective of Western political thought republican philosophy was formulated in the seventeenth century to defend liberty against absolutism. The state constitutions were republican insofar as they limited government by prescribing public decision-making procedures that prevented government officials from aggrandizing power for private benefit rather than for the public good. The constitutions were liberal also in confirming and extending the right of political participation that according to republican philosophy constituted true liberty for individuals. In many respects, however, state constitutionalism in the revolutionary era was a doctrine of community power and control that restricted individual rights in a way that would now be seen as illiberal.

Under the state constitutions the most important power in modern government—the power to make law and to compel obedience—was lodged in the legislature. Unimpeded by internal governmental checks under the extreme version of the SEPARATION OF POWERS that prevailed in the first phase of state making, and sustained by presumptive identity with POPULAR SOVEREIGNTY as the source of political authority after the rejection of monarchy, legislatures acted forcefully to promote public virtue and the common good. Requirements of public virtue frequently took the form of restrictions on individual liberty through sumptuary laws and statutes regulating the transfer and use of property. Bills of rights that were part of state constitutions had little effect on curbing legislative power because they were treated as hortatory rather than legally binding. In the name of popular sovereignty and patriotism, state legislatures fashioned a constitutionalism of unity and power in government.

The concentrated power of republican virtue acting through institutions of community control was a useful and perhaps necessary expedient in the wartime emergency. In the doctrines of state sovereignty and the POLICE POWER revolutionary republicanism entered into the American constitutional tradition, and has offered a compelling model of constitutional government throughout our history to reformers and radicals on both the left and the right. However, the actions of the state legislatures too plainly contradicted the constitutional meaning of the Revolution to become accepted as the principal or exclusive expression of American constitutionalism. That meaning was nowhere better stated than by the MASSACHUSETTS CIRCULAR LETTER of 1768, which declared: ". . . in all free States the Constitution is fixed; as the supreme Legislative derives its Power & Authority from the Constitution, it cannot overleap the Bounds of it, without destroying its own foundation." Yet this was precisely what was happening in the American republics.

The state constitutions may have been fundamental law in the sense of ordaining a framework of government, but they were not fundamental in the sense of controlling legislative power. In all but two states the constitution was written by the legislature and could be altered or abolished by that body. More than language of urging and admonition, contained in many of the constitutions, was needed to transform them into effective restraints on the actual exercise of power. Nor was the technique of internal institutional balance effectively employed to limit the state legislatures.

Attempts to restrict state legislative power in the 1780s broadened and reformed American constitutionalism. Writing and amending of constitutions by popularly elected conventions clarified the distinction between legislative law and fundamental law. Massachusetts in 1780 and New Hampshire in 1784 wrote their constitutions in conventions and required them to be ratified by the people in special elections. In theory this was the most effective way to make the constitution an antecedent higher law secure against legislative alteration. Further restriction of legislative power resulted from changes in the internal structure of government. Executive officers were given greater powers as CHECKS AND BALANCES—that is, a partial and limited sharing or mixing of functional powers among the departments—were introduced in some states as modification of the separation of powers. BICAMERALISM, a carry-over from colonial government, was recognized as a means of making legislative action more deliberate. And courts began to play a more prominent political role by treating constitutions as higher law in relation to legislative enactments.

So strong was the tradition of community self-government under legislative sovereignty, however, that it could not easily be dislodged as the main reliance of constitutionalism. Certainly little could be done to alter it by isolated efforts in the several states. Effective reform, if that was what was needed, could only come from an interstate collaboration working through the state system created by the colonies when they declared their independence. Heretofore peripheral to republican political development, the Union of the states in the Confederation became the focus of constitutional change.

The CONTINENTAL CONGRESS had been formed by the colonies in 1774 as a coordinating and advisory body to protect American interests and eventually to pursue the cause of national independence. Exigencies of war and common concerns among the states had given Congress political power, which it had exercised through informal rules and practices that were codified in the ARTICLES OF CONFEDERATION. Considered from a constitutional perspective as a limiting grant of power, the Articles were inadequate because, although they gave Congress ostensible power to do many things, they did not confer the lawmaking authority that is essential to government. Congress could at best make resolutions and recommendations, which in practice amounted to requests that the states could ignore. The Articles were unconstitutionlike in consequence of having been written by Congress and ratified by the states, rather than based in any direct way on popular authority. They were also unconstitutionlike with respect to institutional structure. Whether considered analogous to a legislative or executive body, Congress was the sole governmentlike organ, and only an evolving departmental system saved it from complete incompetence.

As an alliance or league of friendship, the Articles were a successful founding instrument. Yet in the form given it in the Articles, the confederation was incapable of addressing in a constructive manner the defects in American government revealed in the actions of the states. The confederation provided a field of political action, however, on which the reform of republican constitutionalism could take place. The practical impossibility of amending the Articles so as to strengthen Congress having been demonstrated, and the insecurity of liberty and property in the states apparently increasing, proponents of constitutional reform made a desperate move—the calling of a convention of the states at Philadelphia in May 1787—into an enduring achievement of statesmanship and constitutional invention.

Perhaps most significant, the Framers gave institutional expression to the idea that a constitution, in order to function as a limiting grant of power, must be higher as well as fundamental law. In addition to originating or organizing power, it must be maintained separate from and paramount to government. In a formal sense the Constitution as a founding document was superficially similar to the state constitutions. A preamble explained the reasons for the document, proclaimed the existence of a people and political community, defined specific purposes, and ordained a framework of government. In reality, however, the Framers departed from the model of the state constitutions. It was unnecessary to return to the fundamentals of the social compact and the purposes of republican government, as state constitution writers to varying degrees were inclined to do. The authors of the Constitution observed that they were not addressing the natural rights of man not yet gathered in society but natural rights modified by society and interwoven with the rights of the states. They knew that the nation whose existence they were recognizing was loosely related in its constituent parts and united by few principles and interests. It was far from the kind of cohesive, integrated community that the states by contrast seemed to be, and most unlike the nation-states of Europe. Hence the Framers briefly addressed in the PREAMBLE those few basic unifying purposes and values— liberty, justice, domestic peace, military defense, the general welfare—and gave virtually the entire document to stipulating the institutions and procedures of government. As fundamental law the Constitution thus was less a social compact for a coherent, like-minded community and more a contractlike specification of the powers, duties, rights, and responsibilities among the diverse polities and peoples that constituted the American Union.

Far more effectively than writers of earlier founding instruments, the Framers made the Constitution a paramount, controlling law. In a practical sense this was merely a question of law enforcement. Creating a real government to operate directly on individuals throughout a vast jurisdiction raised a new and potentially difficult compliance issue, but this received little attention at the Convention. It was the old compliance problem of the states that stood in the way of making the Constitution binding and effective. At first the delegates considered a congressional veto on state legislation to deal with this issue, but this was rejected as impracticable and was replaced by the SUPREMACY CLAUSE. This clause expressed the paramountcy of the federal Constitution over the states, and by inference, over national legislative law as well. Not explicitly stated, but implied in the judicial article, was the idea that the superior force of the Constitution depended on its application and interpretation by the courts.

The higher law character of the Constitution was further affirmed and institutionalized in the method of its drafting and in provisions for its ratification and amendment. Although delegates to the Philadelphia Convention were appointed by the state legislatures rather than elected by the people, the Constitution was a more genuine expression of the will of the people than were the Articles of Confederation, which were written by Congress. The Framers' apprehension about unlimited popular rule does not gainsay their commitment to the republican idea that government derives its just powers from the consent of the governed. Consistent with this commitment, institutions of direct popular consent that were still exceptional at the state level were incorporated into the national constitution. Ratification would be decided by conventions in the states, presumably popularly

elected. Amendment of the Constitution could occur through popular approval, in state legislatures or special conventions, of proposals recommended by Congress or by a convention to be called by Congress on the application of two-thirds of the state legislatures. The superiority of the Constitution to legislative law was enhanced by this provision for amendment, as an utterly fixed and inflexible political law would become irrelevant to the task of governing an expanding society. If the Constitution required change, however, the people would have to amend it. Thus were popular sovereignty and the higher law tradition incorporated into American constitutionalism.

To make the Constitution paramount law in operational fact, however, it was not enough to assert its supremacy and assume that the people's innate law-abidingness would give it effect. This was to rely on "paper barriers," concerning the efficacy of which there was much skepticism among the Framers. It was necessary also to structure the organs of government so that power would be internally checked and limited. Although the Framers' objective was to create coercive authority where none existed, they rejected concentrated sovereign power as a constitutional principle. Delegated, divided, reciprocally limiting power formed the motif of their institutional design.

Unlike the state constitutions, which organized the inherent plenary power of the community, the Constitution delegated specific powers to the general government. The contrast was most significant in the plan of the legislative department, to which the state constitutions assigned the LEGISLATIVE POWER and which the federal constitutions defined by the ENUMERATED POWERS. Stable and energetic government seeming to require a strong executive and independent judiciary, the Constitution made grants of power of a more general nature to these branches, which under the separation of powers were counterweights to the lawmaking department. The separation principle by itself, however, as the state experience showed, was not a sufficient limitation on legislative power. Accordingly, checks and balances, by which each branch was given a partial and limited agency in the others' power (for example, executive participation in legislation through the VETO POWER or legislative judging in the IMPEACHMENT process) built further restraints into the Constitution.

The structure of the Union, of course, presented the most urgent question of institutional arrangements affecting the constitutional reality of a supreme political law. A division of power was already evident in the plan of the Articles of Confederation; what was needed was to transform the Union's political authority into a genuine power to impose lawful requirements on its constituent parts. This was achieved by reconstituting the Confederation as a compound republic, based on both the people and the states. Once this was accomplished, the pertinent fact for the paramountcy of the Constitution was the division of sovereignty. By giving the central government power over objects of general concern and allowing the states to retain almost all of their authority over local matters, the Framers divided sovereignty, thereby effectively eliminating it from the constitutional order. Arguments were certain to arise about the nature and extent of the powers of the several governments in the American state system, but the effect of such controversy would be to focus attention on the Constitution as the authoritative source of answers to questions about the rights of constituent members.

The Constitution was both fundamental and higher law because it expressed the will of the people, the ultimate source of authority in America. But it would truly limit power only if it was superior to the people themselves as a political entity, as well as to the legislative law. At the time some theorists of popular sovereignty argued that the people could alter their government at will, exercising the right of peaceful revolution and disregarding legalities of form and procedure, even as the Framers did in drafting and securing RATIFICATION OF THE CONSTITUTION against the express requirements of the Articles of Confederation. However we view their action, the authors of the Constitution rejected the notion of unlimited popular sovereignty. They provided restraints on the people in the form of a limited number of offices, long terms of office, indirect elections, large electoral districts, and separated and balanced departments of government. Although these provisions have often been viewed as antidemocratic and in conflict with republican theory, they are more accurately seen as modifying the popular form of government adopted during the Revolution. The Framers' intent, as JAMES MADISON wrote in THE FEDERALIST #10, was to supply "a republican remedy for the diseases most incident to republican government." And it should not be forgotten that despite careful distribution and balancing of authority, Congress remained potentially the most powerful branch of the government, most responsive to the people and possessed of the lawmaking power.

Making the Constitution effective as a permanent higher law involved matters of form, procedure, and institutional structure. Yet as procedural issues carry substantive implications, and means sometimes become ends in themselves, it is also necessary to ask what a constitution is for. To prevent tyranny, the constitutionalist goal, is to create a space in which differences among people become manifest, in which politics can appear and questions of purpose arise. If running a constitution always reflects political concerns, making a constitution is all the more a form of political action that derives from or partakes of political philosophy.

Americans were emphatic in declaring liberty to be the purpose of their constitutions. Moreover, if the purpose of politics is to protect men's natural rights, then American constitutions were liberal in purpose. Yet the concept of liberty, universally embraced as a political good, can be defined in different ways. And while recognition of natural rights gave modern politics a new purpose, it is equally true that virtue and moral excellence did not disappear from political discourse. These considerations give rise to two conceptions of political freedom in the constitutionalism of the founding period. The first is the liberty of self-governing political communities that were thought to have an obligation to make men virtuous and on which individuals depended for their happiness and well-being. The second rests on the primacy of natural rights and generally asserts individual liberty over community consensus as the purpose of government.

Although these conceptions of liberty stand in theoretical opposition to each other, they coexisted in the revolutionary era. After protesting imperial policies in the language of English constitutional rights, Americans justified national independence by appealing to universal natural rights. Wartime exigencies required decisive political action, however, which was based on the right of local communities to control individuals for the sake of the common good. States interfered with the liberty and property of individuals by controlling markets, restricting personal consumption, awarding monopoly privileges, and limiting imports and exports. They also regulated the speech and press freedoms of persons suspected of disloyalty to the patriot cause. In many ways revolutionary republicanism subordinated the rights of individual citizens to those of the community, defining true liberty as the pursuit of public happiness through political action.

Reacting against state encroachments on liberty and property, the constitution makers of 1787 emphasized protection of individual rights rather than promotion of virtue and community consensus as the purpose of government. Rather than an unattainable ideal of public virtue in ordinary citizens, they appealed to enlightened self-interest as the social reality on which the Constitution would rest. The Framers recognized factional conflict as a limiting condition for creating a constitution, yet also as an opportunity for broadening and redefining republican government. Alongside the communitarian ideal, which remained strong in many states, they created a new constitutional model in the complex and powerful government of the extended republic, based partly on the people yet so structured and limited that individual liberty, property, and pursuit of personal interests would be substantially protected against local legislative interference. This is not to say that mere private enrichment at the expense of the community good or general welfare was the end of the Constitution. The concepts of virtue and the public interest remained integral to political thought and discourse. But virtue assumed a new meaning as the prudent and rational pursuit of private commercial activity. Instead of telling people how to live in accordance with a particular conception of political right or religious truth, the Framers would promote ends believed beneficial to all of society—peace, economic growth, and intellectual advancement—by accommodating social competition and upholding citizens' natural rights against invasion by the organized power of the community, whether local, state, or national.

The Founding Fathers often appear antidemocratic because they created a strong central government, removed from direct popular and local community control, which they expected to be managed by an aristocratic elite. Notwithstanding its foundation in popular sovereignty and protection of individual liberty and rights, the Constitution contradicted rule by local communities guided by republican civic virtue as the real meaning of the Revolution. Although the Revolution stood for government by consent, there is no sound reason for regarding revolutionary state making as the single true expression of the republican principle. Essential parts of that principle were that government should operate through laws to which all were subordinate, both citizens and government officials, and that legislative law should be controlled by the higher law of the constitution. This was the meaning of the rule of law in the United States, and its more complete realization in the Constitution of 1787 signified climax and fulfillment of the Revolution.

The Framers' purpose must also be considered in relation to the threat of national disintegration, either from internal discord or foreign encroachment. The weakness of Congress in discharging its responsibilities was surely an impediment to protecting American interests, and an embarrassment to patriotic men. Yet the problem in 1787 was not the threat of total rupture of the Union attended by actual warfare among the states; the problem was the character of American politics and government, or the nature and tendency of republican government. Republicanism was the defining idea of the nation, and without it America would no longer have existed. The country was growing in the 1780s as population expanded, economic development occurred, and westward settlement continued. Yet the state system of 1776 was incapable of adequately accommodating and guiding this development. The states were too strong for the good of republican principles, the Union not strong enough. By restructuring the state system, by reconstituting the Union on the basis of a republican constitution that crystallized tendencies in congressional-state relations in the 1780s, the Framers sought to reform American government to the end of securing the republican ideals of the Revolution.

A constitution must recognize and conform to a people's principal characteristics and nature. Considered from this point of view the achievement of the Founding Fathers is undeniable. They created a complex government of delegated and dispersed, yet articulated and balanced, powers based on the principle of consent. Confirmation of that principle was in turn required by the Constitution in the cooperation and concurrence among the branches of government that were necessary for the conduct of public business. Made for an open, acquisitive, individualistic, competitive, and pluralistic society, the Constitution ordered the diverse constituent elements of American politics. More than merely a neutral procedural instrument for registering the play of social forces, it was a statement of ends and means for maintaining the principles that defined Americans as a national people. The Framers made a liberal constitution for a liberal society.

The Constitution was not only formally ratified but also quickly accorded full political legitimacy. The state constitutions, although not merely pretextual or façade documents, were not invoked and applied in the actual conduct of government as the United States Constitution was. And the new federal instrument was more than accepted: it rapidly became an object of veneration. The Constitution took a deep and abiding hold on the American political mind because it reflected a sober regard for the propensities of ordinary human nature and the realities of republican society; created powerful institutions capable of attracting men of talent, ambition, and enlarged civic outlook; and introduced changes in the conduct of public affairs that most people saw as improvements and that caused them to form an interest in the government it created.

The Constitution stipulated institutions, rules, and procedures embodying and symbolizing the principles of republican liberty, national unity, and balance and limitation of power. It was a fixed, objective document that could be consulted and applied, not a formless assemblage of principles, statutes, and decisions carried about in men's minds and dependent on social internalization for its effect. Yet the Constitution's principles and provisions were general and ambiguous enough to allow varying interpretations. Liberty, union, and reciprocally limiting power meant different things to different people, as did the rules and institutional arrangements expressing and embodying them. At a superficial level this circumstance produced conflict, but at a deeper level the effect was unifying. For groups and individuals were encouraged to pursue political goals within the framework of rules and requirements established by the Constitution. Thus the document became permanent and binding. Only the most extreme groups (radical abolitionists and slaveholders in the nineteenth century, totalitarian parties in the twentieth) have repudiated the Constitution as a framework for political action.

The Constitution possessed force and effect because it was useful and relevant to political life. Responsive to the social environment, it had instrumental value. At the same time, repeated reference to the document as the source and symbol of legitimate authority confirmed its intrinsic value, apart from the practical results of specific controversies. People believed, in other words, that it was important to follow the Constitution for its own sake or for the common good, rather than for a particular political reason. The intrinsic value of the Constitution lay not only in the wisdom and reasonableness of its principles in relation to the nature of American society but also in the form those principles were given in a written instrument. The effect of the Constitution as binding political law has much to do with its textual character.

The Framers addressed this issue in discussing "parchment barriers." The state constitutions were evidence that written stipulations were no guarantee of performance, especially when it came to limiting legislative power. Madison in particular said that it was not enough to erect parchment barriers in the form of constitutional provisions stating that the legislative department must confine itself to lawmaking. It was further necessary to arrange the interior structure of government so the constituent parts would limit each other. Personal motives of ambition and interest, Madison reasoned, when linked with constitutional offices would lead men to resist encroachments from other departments. These were the "auxiliary precautions" (supplementing accountability to the people) that would oblige government to control itself. Madison was saying that pluralistic differences in opinion and interest are necessary to make the prescriptions of the text function effectively.

Nevertheless, American constitutionalism insists that the text of the fundamental law be given its due. Madison's auxiliary precautions are in fact rules written into the document. Although the written text may not be sufficient, it is necessary to achieve the purposes of constitutionalism, or so it has seemed most of the time to most Americans. In the Constitutional Convention RUFUS KING said that he was aware that an express guarantee of STATES' RIGHTS, which he favored, would be regarded as "a mere paper security." But "if fundamental articles of compact are not sufficient defence against physical power," King declared, "neither will there be any safety against it if there be no compact."

Reference to the constitutional text has been a fixed feature of American politics. Its significance and effect have been variously estimated. A long tradition of criticism holds that the document has failed to limit government, especially the federal government in relation to the states. Others argue that constant invoking of the Constitution has trivialized politics by translating policy debate into le-

galistic squabbles that discourage dealing with issues on their merits. Reformers seeking a more programmatic politics have lamented that the Constitution by fragmenting power prevents responsible party government. And still others contend that the Constitution has worked precisely as intended: to eliminate genuine political action and make citizens passive subjects interested in private economic pursuits rather than public happiness and civic virtue.

These criticisms misunderstand the nature of constitutional politics and hence the binding and configurative effect of the Constitution. If politics is concerned with the end or purpose of political community, the proper role of government, the relationship between the individual and society, then it is difficult to see how the Constitution can be said to have brought an end to politics or prevented political action. As an expression of modern liberalism, however, the Constitution did signify a change in the nature of politics. To elevate natural rights into constitutionally protected CIVIL RIGHTS, as the Framers did, was to discourage an older politics based on the pursuit of glory, honor, conquest, and political or religious truth, as well as a newer ideological politics born of modern revolution. The Framers' constitutionalism was a way of organizing political life that paradoxically placed certain principles, rules, and procedures beyond politics, according them the status of fundamental and paramount law. Premised on the idea that citizens could pursue private interests while preserving community, it was intended to limit the scope and intensity of politics, preventing a total absorption of society that would impose tyranny in the name of ruler, party, people, or community.

Starting in the 1790s and continuing with remarkable continuity to the present day, public policy advocates have charted courses of action with reference to the Constitution. Using constitutional language firmly embedded in political rhetoric, such as DUE PROCESS OF LAW, EQUAL PROTECTION OF THE LAW, separation of powers, and so forth, they invoke its principles and values to justify their goals, argue over the meaning of its requirements, and align themselves with its manifest tenor as explicated in constitutional law and legislation. Political leaders do this not because they are unwaveringly committed to a specific constitutional principle; in different circumstances they might advocate a different principle. The decisive fact is the high public status accorded the Constitution: policymakers and political actors know that the people take the Constitution seriously, regard it as supreme law, believe that it is powerful because it embodies sound principles of government and society's basic values, and, indeed, venerate it. Aware of this popular prejudice in favor of the Constitution, and seeking the approval of public opinion, political groups and individuals are constrained to act in conformity with its provisions. Thus the Constitution as binding political law shapes the form and content of policies and events.

The constraining effect of the Constitution might nevertheless be questioned, for it will appear obvious that while some requirements are unequivocally clear (for example, the minimum age of the President), many provisions are ambiguous and imprecise in meaning. Confronted with this fact, many scholars have concluded that there is no single, true meaning of the Constitution, but rather that there are several possible readings of it, none of which possesses exclusive legitimacy. Some contend there is no real Constitution against which arguments about it can be evaluated, only different assertions as to what the Constitution is at any given time, or as to what we want it to be. Expressed in the oft-cited statement that the Constitution is what the Supreme Court says it is, this view, carried to its logical conclusion, would mean that the American Constitution is a developing, evolving, growing thing that is changed by the actions of judges, lawmakers, and executive officers. In that case the Constitution ceases to be a fixed, prescriptive, paramount law.

Politically and historically realistic as this analysis appears, it has never been accepted as legitimate in constitutional theory or in the conduct of constitutional politics. From the standpoint of the people and their representatives, the Constitution, in both its procedural requirements and its essential principles, has a true, fixed, ascertainable meaning. This popular understanding has existed from the beginning of constitutional politics in the debate over ratification, and it will probably continue until the popular belief, that the Constitution as a document says what it means and means what it says, is eroded or superseded by a more sophisticated view of the character of texts and political language. There is still a strong tendency in public opinion to think that written constitutions, in THOMAS JEFFERSON's words, "furnish a text to which those who are watchful may again rally and recall the people: they fix too for the people principles for their political creed."

The importance of the constitutional text in American government has been raised anew in recent years in the controversy over original intent jurisprudence. Many legal scholars have expressed doubt about the wisdom and legitimacy of consulting the original intent of the Constitution or of its authors in settling constitutional disputes. The words of the text, it is argued, apart from anything that its authors may have written or said about its meaning, must be considered as expressing the original intent. And the text must be read and understood according to the accepted meaning of words in the interpreter's own time, place, and historical situation. Some dispose of original

intent more directly by asserting that constitutional interpretation need not be bound by the constitutional text, but may be based on fundamental social values and conceptions of justice and moral progress that judges are specially qualified to understand and apply. Either way, the Constitution is assured of its status as a "living document" adaptable to changing social conditions.

Although there may be sound reasons for disconnecting constitutional politics from original intent, from a historical standpoint it seems clear that neither the Framers nor the people over 200 years have taken so narrow a view of the meaning and relevance of original intent. The purpose of making a fixed, objective constitution was to decide the most important basic questions about politics and government once and for all—or until the people changed their mind and amended the document. The idea was to bind future generations in fundamental ways. This purpose would be defeated if those who later ran the Constitution were free to substitute their own definitions of its key terms. Yet the fact remains that constitutional principles and rules have been reinterpreted and redefined, in apparent contradiction of the Framers' intent, in decisions and statutes that have been accepted as politically legitimate. The Supreme Court has, in a sense, acted as a continuing constitutional convention.

Although the Founding Fathers intended the Constitution to be permanent and binding, the language of the document cannot realistically or reasonably, in a categorical sense, be frozen in its eighteenth-century meaning. It is the Constitution's essential purposes and its fundamental principles and procedures that were not intended to change. The question to be asked is whether fundamental principles and values—the values of individual liberty, national union, distributed and balanced power, the consent of the people—can be defined in an authoritative text and thereby realized in public law and policy to the satisfaction of the political community. American political history generally provides an affirmative answer to this question. But it is important to remember that an overriding imperative in American politics, law, and government has been to reconcile public policy with constitutional principles and rules as embodied in the text, and in accordance with the Framers' intentions. Moreover, original intent has not been viewed in a narrowly positivistic manner. The text was thought to have a definite and lasting meaning; and speeches, writings, and letters of the authors of the Constitution have always been thought pertinent to the task of elucidating its meaning. Whatever the practical effect of dismissal of the text and repudiation of original intent would be, such a step would alter the historic character of American constitutionalism.

Diverse in ethnic, religious, cultural, and social characteristics, Americans were united in 1776 by the political principles set forth in the Declaration of Independence. Inchoate though it was, the new nation was defined by these principles—liberty, equality, government by consent, the pursuit of happiness as an individual right—which in various ways were written into the state constitutions. By establishing a republican government for the nation, the Framers of the Constitution confirmed these principles, completing the Revolution and making it permanent. Since then American politics has derived from and been shaped by the Constitution, and has periodically been renewed by popular movements resulting in electoral realignments that have included a return to the first principles of the Founding as an essential element.

Understanding this attachment to the constitutional text has often been difficult for scholars and intellectuals, who tend to disparage it as "constitution worship." Perhaps reverence for the Constitution expresses not so much a naive literalism, however, as an awareness of the act of foundation as a source of authority. Considered in this perspective the constitutional text stands for the Founding, and the principles written into the document symbolically represent values evident in the actions of the Framers. The Founding required rational discussion, deliberation, compromise, and choice; consent, concurrence, and mutual pledging. These procedural values are embodied in constitutional provisions that require government under a fixed institutional structure and by deliberative processes that depend on compromise and concurrence, in accordance with substantive principles of natural rights, consent, and limited and balanced power.

HERMAN BELZ
(1986)

Bibliography

CORWIN, EDWARD S. 1955 The "Higher Law" Background of American Constitutional Law. Ithaca, N.Y.: Cornell University Press.

FRIEDRICH, CARL J. 1968 Constitutional Government and Democracy. Cambridge, Mass.: Harvard University Press.

GOUGH, J. W. 1955 Fundamental Law in English Constitutional History. Oxford: Oxford University Press.

LIENESCH, MICHAEL 1980 The Constitutional Tradition: History, Political Action, and Progress in American Political Thought. Journal of Politics 42:2–30.

LUTZ, DONALD 1980 From Covenant to Constitution in American Political History. Publius 10:101–133.

McILWAIN, CHARLES H. (1940) 1947 Constitutionalism: Ancient and Modern. Ithaca, N.Y.: Cornell University Press.

VILE, M. J. C. 1967 Constitutionalism and the Separation of Powers. New York: Oxford University Press.

WRIGHT, BENJAMIN F. 1958 Consensus and Continuity: 1776–1787. New York: Norton.

CONSTITUTIONAL REASON OF STATE

Reason of state is one of the illimitable silences of the Constitution. Derived directly from Niccolò Machiavelli and JOHN LOCKE (who called it the "prerogative"), it is "the doctrine that whatever is required to insure the survival of the state must be done by the individuals responsible for it, no matter how repugnant such an act may be to them in their private capacity as decent and moral men." Not labeled "reason of state" by the Supreme Court, the doctrine often travels under the banner of NATIONAL SECURITY or the "interests of society."

National survival is the ultimate value protected by the doctrine. But more is covered; it is used whenever an important interest of the state is jeopardized, as perceived by those who wield effective control over the state's apparatus (government). Wartime use is the most obvious, stated classically by ABRAHAM LINCOLN in 1861: "Is there in all republics this inherent and fatal weakness? Must a government of necessity be too *strong* for the liberties of its people, or too *weak* to maintain its own existence?" Other instances in which reason of state has been the validating principle include the treatment of American Indians, wars of conquest (such as the Mexican War), economic depressions, and the control of dissident groups. Justification for both the Korean and Vietnam "wars" rests on the doctrine. (See KOREAN WAR; VIETNAM WAR.)

The basic constitutional problem is to distinguish between the circumstances fit for republican (that is, democratic) rule and those suited for personal rule. With rare exceptions—the principal ones are the *Steel Seizure Case* (YOUNGSTOWN SHEET AND TUBE V. SAWYER, 1952) and UNITED STATES V. UNITED STATES DISTRICT COURT (1972)—the Supreme Court has deferred to the political branches of government. The President normally is the moving force, with Congress usually acquiescing in executive actions designed to meet perceived emergencies. The PRIZE CASES (1863) were the leading early judicial statement approving the doctrine. (See also JAPANESE AMERICAN CASES.)

To the extent that the doctrine of reason of state finds acceptance, the theory of LIMITED GOVERNMENT recedes. Government in the United States has always been relative to circumstances, precisely as strong as conditions necessitated. The Constitution, accordingly, has been updated by successive generations of Americans, often at least tacitly employing reason of state principles.

No criteria exist by which to determine whether reason of state has been validly invoked. The Supreme Court has thus far failed to define such synonymous terms as "national security" and "society." By employing a BALANCING TEST, the Justices rule for society—for the state—whenever the vital interests of the state are considered to be in danger. In so doing, the Court never divulges how it determines what the interests of society are or the weights to be given to them. Reason of state, therefore, often amounts to government by fiat, but with the legitimizing imprimatur of the Supreme Court.

The BILL OF RIGHTS was an effort to limit the application of reason of state. However, Supreme Court interpretations have converted many of those seemingly absolute commands into mere hortatory admonitions to act reasonably in the circumstances. For example, the FIRST AMENDMENT's presciption that "no law" should abridge freedom of speech or press has been interpreted into relative standards. Reason of state thus has been resurrected by the Supreme Court after the constitutional Framers tried to hem it in.

Every nation employs a variation of reason of state, whether or not it has a written constitution. France, for example, expressly provides for EMERGENCY POWERS in Article 16 of the constitution of the Fifth Republic. The United States has accomplished the same result without an express constitutional provision or even a stated constitutional principle.

If, as many assert, the United States has entered a period of great danger, one in which its constitutional institutions will be sorely tested, reason of state will doubtless often be invoked—probably tacitly—as emergencies and crises arise. The doctrine can and will be employed to justify presidential use of violence without congressional authorization, as Presidents have almost routinely done in the past. It is the ultimate basis for expansion of presidential powers in many directions.

The Constitution was written at a propitious time in history, a time when a coalescence of factors—geography, natural resources, freedom from external pressures, a small population, capital and cheap labor from Europe—provided a favorable milieu for the FUNDAMENTAL LAW and its structure of government to flourish. Today, Americans face polar opposites—a shrinking planet, dwindling resources, total immersion in FOREIGN AFFAIRS, a burgeoning population, a slowing of productivity and of economic growth. Crisis government, accordingly, is becoming the norm. More and more, government will call upon emergency powers—upon reason of state—in efforts to cope. The large meaning is that a new fundamental law is emerging, one that can be called the "Constitution of Control." It exists as another layer on the palimpsest that is the Constitution of 1787.

ARTHUR S. MILLER
(1986)

Bibliography

FRIEDRICH, CARL J. 1957 Constitutional Reason of State. Providence, R.I.: Brown University.
MILLER, ARTHUR SELWYN 1981 Democratic Dictatorship: The Emergent Constitution of Control. Westport, Conn.: Greenwood Press.
ROSSITER, CLINTON 1948 Constitutional Dictatorship: Crisis Government in the Modern Democracies. Princeton, N.J.: Princeton University Press.

CONSTITUTIONAL REFORM

Although any change in the Constitution can be labeled a reform, the broad term "constitutional reform" is usually reserved for proposed amendments that would alter in some fundamental way the structure of the government established by the nation's charter—that is, the organization of the legislative, executive, and judicial branches, the distribution of power among them, and their interrelationships.

Rarely have structural amendments to the Constitution been adopted. Of the twenty-six amendments ratified since 1787, only two have affected the form or character of the institutions as they were designed by the Framers. The SEVENTEENTH AMENDMENT, ratified in 1913, required United States senators to be chosen by popular election rather than by state legislatures. The TWENTY-SECOND AMENDMENT, approved in 1951, limits presidential tenure to two full terms. The other twenty-four amendments either have added substantive provisions (guaranteeing FREEDOM OF SPEECH and RELIGIOUS LIBERTY, abolishing SLAVERY, providing for WOMAN SUFFRAGE, and so on) or, while dealing with the governmental structure, have corrected flaws or made minor adaptations in the constitutional design without altering the nature or relationships of the institutions that compose the government.

The stability of the American constitutional structure contrasts sharply with the impermanence of governmental systems in many other countries, some of which have written, discarded, and rewritten entire constitutions during the period that the United States constitutional structure has remained virtually unchanged. The American experience undoubtedly reflects a general satisfaction with the governmental system, particularly with that system's original and distinctive feature—its SEPARATION OF POWERS and CHECKS AND BALANCES. It may also reflect the fact that the Constitution embodies probably the most difficult AMENDING PROCESS of any constitution in the world. In the normal process, an amendment must be approved by two-thirds of each house of Congress and then be ratified by the legislatures (or constitutional conventions) of three-fourths of the states. The requirement for such extraordinary majorities confers an effective VETO POWER on any sizable political bloc; an amendment must be favored by Republicans and Democrats alike, by both conservatives and liberals, by advocates of a strong presidency as well as defenders of Congress. Yet structural amendments redistribute power and hence create winners and losers among the political blocs. The potential losers can usually muster enough support, either in the Congress or in the state legislatures, to block action. (As an alternative to initiation by the Congress, amendments may be proposed by a CONSTITUTIONAL CONVENTION organized at the request of two-thirds of the state legislatures; but no such convention has ever been called. RATIFICATION by three-fourths of the states would still be required.)

During the 1980s, the objective of constitutional reform attracted authoritative and well-organized support, expressed through two organizations made up of persons with long experience in high office. One, which included former officials of every administration from DWIGHT D. EISENHOWER to RONALD REAGAN, was created in 1982 to advocate a single six-year term for the President—a proposal with a history of support going back to ANDREW JACKSON. Ineligibility for reelection, the group argued, would enable the President to rise above politics and put the national interest ahead of personal reelection concerns. But the proposal encountered the objections, among others, that if the President is ineligible for reelection, he becomes a "lame duck" and hence loses authority, and that six years would be too long for a President who turned out to be ineffective. The proposal failed to win widespread support, and the movement faded.

The second organization, established in 1981, was the Committee on the Constitutional System, consisting of former members of Congress, former high executive officials, academics, and other political observers. Identifying the principal structural problem as one of conflict and deadlock between the executive and legislative branches, the committee undertook a broad consideration of remedies. Rejecting the six-year term for the President, the group recommended instead that the term of members of the HOUSE OF REPRESENTATIVES be extended from two years to four (a proposal advanced in 1966 by President LYNDON B. JOHNSON) and the term of senators from six years to eight. All House members and half the senators would be chosen in each presidential election, thus eliminating the present midterm congressional contests. Proponents contend that a four-year time horizon for the whole government would enable it to make difficult decisions that it does not now make because the next election is always imminent; opponents respond that the midterm election is a necessary check to enable the voters to register approval or disapproval of their government.

The committee also endorsed an amendment to permit members of Congress to serve in the presidential CABINET and other executive branch positions (a variation of proposals that won considerable support in earlier decades to give cabinet members nonvoting seats in the Congress and to require cabinet members, or even the President, to appear before Congress to answer questions). And it proposed to ease the process for approving treaties, by reducing the present requirement for a two-thirds vote of the SENATE to either 60 percent of the Senate or a constitutional majority of both houses.

Finally, the committee recommended consideration of two more radical reforms. One would reduce the likelihood of divided government (that is, one party controlling the executive branch and the opposing party ruling one or both houses of Congress), which the committee identified as conducive to deadlock and inaction, by requiring voters to choose between party slates for President, vice-president, Senate, and House. The second would provide a means for reconstituting a government that had proved incapable of governing—because of deadlock between the branches, presidential incapacity, corruption, or any other reason—by means of a special election in which the presidency, vice-presidency, and congressional seats would be at stake. Such a procedure would correspond to those by which legislatures in parliamentary democracies are dissolved and new elections held. These proposals, too, attracted little popular support, and constitutional reform remained a subject only for academic debate.

JAMES L. SUNDQUIST
(1992)

Bibliography

ROBINSON, DONALD L. 1989 *A Government for the Third American Century.* Boulder, Colo.: Westview Press.
SUNDQUIST, JAMES L. 1986 *Constitutional Reform and Effective Government.* Washington, D.C.: Brookings Institution.

CONSTITUTIONAL REMEDIES

Constitutional remedies take different forms, including defenses to criminal prosecutions, postconviction HABEAS CORPUS actions, civil actions for DAMAGES, and declaratory and injunctive relief. Remedies for violations of constitutional rights, at first indistinguishable from more general legal remedies, became the focus of special congressional concern after the CIVIL WAR and are now a highly developed set of modern rules shaped by both Congress and the Supreme Court.

Until well into the twentieth century, misbehavior by state or federal officials was more likely to be viewed as tortious or otherwise merely unlawful rather than as unconstitutional. As in MARBURY V. MADISON (1803) and DRED SCOTT V. SANDFORD (1857), federal courts would refuse to enforce unconstitutional legislation, but the question of additional remedies for constitutional violations rarely arose. CRIMINAL PROCEDURE had not yet been federalized, and there were few constitutional rights that could give rise to distinctive remedies. Thus, early remedies against official misbehavior, such as the effort to vest jurisdiction in the Supreme Court to issue writs of MANDAMUS, invalidated in *Marbury*, were not thought of as distinct constitutional remedies. Even today, the liability for damages of the United States (but not United States officials) is governed largely by the FEDERAL TORT CLAIMS ACT, which does not by its terms distinguish between constitutional violations and other tortious conduct. It authorizes an action against the United States only if the challenged behavior also happens to violate state law. The conflating of constitutional violations and other legal wrongs limited and obscured constitutional remedies.

The Civil War led to the creation of new constitutional rights, and RECONSTRUCTION era CIVIL RIGHTS statutes demonstrated a new congressional belief in the need to give such rights special protection. Section 4 of the CIVIL RIGHTS ACT OF 1866, "with a view to affording reasonable protection to all persons in their constitutional rights of equality before the law," increased the number of federal judicial officers authorized to enforce the statutory protections of the act. The HABEAS CORPUS ACT OF 1867 established federal habeas corpus relief as a remedy in all cases "where any person may be restrained of his or her liberty in violation of the constitution," a provision that survives with little substantive change today. The Enforcement Act (the Civil Rights Act of 1870) imposed criminal penalties for the violation of constitutionally protected voting rights and for conspiracies to violate constitutional rights. The Ku Klux Klan Act (the Civil Rights Act of 1871)—part of which is now SECTION 1983, TITLE 42, U.S. CODE—created a civil action for every person deprived, under color of state law, of constitutional rights. Similar criminal prohibitions, largely ineffective, against violating constitutional rights continue in force in Sections 241 and 242, Title 18, U.S. Code.

These Reconstruction statutes, combined with increasing substantive constitutional protections, led to important judicially generated growth of constitutional remedies in both the criminal and civil areas. In the 1920s the Supreme Court began to treat the DUE PROCESS clause of the FOURTEENTH AMENDMENT as a limitation on state criminal procedure. The resulting constitutionalization of criminal procedure led to expanded direct review by the Supreme Court of the constitutionality of state court convictions and to greater use of federal habeas corpus to vindicate constitutional rights. The EXCLUSIONARY RULE for FOURTH AMENDMENT violations has been a particularly controversial remedy in the criminal sphere.

In the civil arena, the term "constitutional remedies" usually refers to damages actions and injunctive relief, each of which has had a distinct historical development. Injunctive relief for constitutional violations developed first. EX PARTE YOUNG (1908) established the availability, despite the ELEVENTH AMENDMENT and the doctrine of SOVEREIGN IMMUNITY, of injunctive relief against unconstitutional behavior by state officers. The remedial power to enjoin unconstitutional behavior figured prominently in the fight against SEGREGATION statutes.

As the use of the INJUNCTION to protect constitutional rights grew, different forms of injunctive relief emerged. Injunctions protecting constitutional rights may be subdivided into simple injunctions and structural, or institutional, injunctions. The simple injunction, ordering, for example, that the unconstitutional statute not be enforced, has remained relatively uncontroversial. The proper scope of broader injunctive relief has been debated since the 1960s, when federal courts found that recalcitrant state officials and legislatures did not comply with court orders to desegregate school systems and to improve conditions in prisons or mental institutions. Remedial orders in such INSTITUTIONAL LITIGATION involved courts in the details of running institutions. DESEGREGATION orders not promptly obeyed led to hard choices about obedience to the RULE OF LAW in the face of resistance to one particular remedy, court-ordered SCHOOL BUSING. Some observers raised questions about the legitimacy of judicial intervention in the operations of other public institutions and the capacity of courts as institutional managers. In a few cases, courts faced with years of noncompliance ordered local governments to finance constitutionally prescribed remedies, even going so far as to order increases in local taxes. In MISSOURI V. JENKINS (1990) the Court held that a federal district court may direct a local government to levy taxes to comply with desegregation requirements.

Damages were awarded against public officials in a few early twentieth-century decisions in cases brought under section 1983, and damages are one traditional remedy under the Fifth Amendment's TAKING OF PROPERTY clause. However, the modern right to recover damages against officials for constitutional violations is mainly traceable to MONROE V. PAPE (1961) and BIVENS V. SIX UNKNOWN NAMED AGENTS (1971). In *Monroe* the Court held that section 1983 authorized a damages action against police officers who violated the Fourth Amendment in an illegal arrest and search. Actions based on section 1983 have since grown to encompass most constitutional harms, and litigation under the section constitutes one of the largest segments of federal court civil dockets. The remedies available under section 1983 include compensatory damages, punitive damages (against individuals, but not governments), injunctive relief, and the award of attorneys' fees. The Eleventh Amendment severely limits monetary remedies for constitutional violations, but the Supreme Court made clear that a state may be required to pay the cost of prospective compliance with the Constitution, such as the cost of desegregating a school system.

Section 1983 authorizes actions only against state officials. In *Bivens* the Court allowed a damages action against federal officials for violating the Fourth Amendment. After *Bivens* the Court recognized IMPLIED CONSTITUTIONAL RIGHTS OF ACTION under the FIRST AMENDMENT, Fifth Amendment, and Eighth Amendment. In the 1980s, however, the Court began to rein in the *Bivens* remedy. In *Chappell v. Wallace* (1983) and *United States v. Stanley* (1987) the Court refused to recognize *Bivens* actions for enlisted military personnel who alleged that they had been injured by unconstitutional actions of their superiors and who had no cause of action against the United States. In *Bush v. Lucas* (1983) the Court refused to create a *Bivens* remedy for a violation of a civil service employee's First Amendment rights, because the violation arose "out of an employment relationship that is governed by comprehensive procedural and substantive provisions giving meaningful remedies against the United States." And in *Schweiker v. Chilicky* (1988) the Court held that the denial of SOCIAL SECURITY benefits in violation of due process did not give rise to a *Bivens* action against the wrongdoing officials.

Congress greatly influences constitutional remedies by expanding, contracting, and shaping them. The Fourteenth Amendment and other constitutional provisions authorize Congress to enact legislation, both remedial and substantive, to enforce constitutional rights. The Reconstruction statutes were enacted largely under this authority. Section 1983 and federal habeas corpus, both federal statutory remedies, are the two most frequently used constitutional remedies, aside from defenses to criminal prosecutions.

The limits of congressional power over constitutional remedies have not been fully tested. Congress has left in place the two most-used statutory protections and regularly rejects proposals to restrict federal court jurisdiction to hear particular classes of cases or to issue specific remedies. Congress did limit section 1983 by requiring, in the Civil Rights of Institutionalized Persons Act, that certain prisoners first exhaust state administrative remedies before bringing section 1983 actions. And, in refusing to extend *Bivens* actions, the Supreme Court, in *Bush v. Lucas* and *Schweiker v. Chilicky,* emphasized that comprehensive alternative congressional remedial schemes were already in place for protecting the constitutional rights asserted. Congress's refusal to enact jurisdictional limitations, together with the implausibility of repealing section 1983 or federal habeas corpus, suggests a deep national commitment to the ideal of remedying constitutional wrongs.

The modern growth of constitutional remedies may have modified that commitment in one important way. The increased availability of injunctive and damages relief taught that fully remedying each constitutional wrong comes at a cost, either in challenging the authority of governing officials or in increasing confrontations between the judicial and political branches of government or between federal courts and state officials. A full panoply of remedies to fix each constitutional wrong may have increased the Supreme Court's reluctance to acknowledge new constitutional rights. In PAUL V. DAVIS (1976), *Parratt v. Taylor* (1981), and subsequent cases involving both the due process clause and section 1983, the Court may have curtailed substantive constitutional protections in order to avoid triggering extensive remedial relief.

THEODORE EISENBERG
(1992)

Bibliography

EISENBERG, THEODORE 1982 Section 1983: Doctrinal Foundations and an Empirical Study. *Cornell Law Review* 67:482–556.

—— 1991 *Civil Rights Legislation,* 3rd ed. Charlottesville, Va.: Michie.

NAHMOD, SHELDON H. 1986 *Civil Rights and Civil Liberties Litigation,* 2nd ed. Colorado Springs, Colo.: Shepard's.

SCHWAB, STEWART J. and EISENBERG, THEODORE 1988 Explaining Constitutional Tort Litigation: The Influence of the Attorney Fees Statute and the Government as Defendant. *Cornell Law Review* 73:719–784.

CONSTITUTIONAL REMEDIES
(Update)

The 1990s began with MISSOURI V. JENKINS's (1990) 5–4 affirmation of federal JUDICIAL POWER to remedy constitutional violations. The case sustained federal court power to promote local tax increases to fund DESEGREGATION orders. Proposed constitutional amendments and LEGISLATION abrogating the decision failed to gain adequate support. And in *Crawford-El v. Britton* (1998), the Supreme Court, in a 5–4 decision, refused to require CIVIL RIGHTS plaintiffs to adduce clear and convincing evidence of improper motive, a heightened level of proof, to avoid dismissal of constitutional claims that depend on the defendant's motive.

Most developments in the 1990s, however, curtailed vindication of constitutional rights, especially for prisoners. The Federal Courts Improvement Act of 1996 amended SECTION 1983, TITLE 42, UNITED STATES CODE to limit actions alleging constitutional violations by state judges. It prohibits injunctive relief against judicial officers unless a DECLARATORY JUDGMENT has been violated or declaratory relief is unavailable. It thus limits the Court's allowance in *Pulliam v. Allen* (1984) of injunctive relief against judges. The same Act also limits attorney fee awards against judges to cases in which the judge's actions are "clearly in excess" of the judge's JURISDICTION, a standard that precludes fee awards in most cases.

The ANTITERRORISM AND EFFECTIVE DEATH PENALTY ACT OF 1996 capped years of efforts by conservatives to curtail federal HABEAS CORPUS. It limits the ability of prisoners to file repeat habeas petitions; imposes firmer deadlines for the filing of habeas petitions; and limits prison institutional reform litigation. The Prison Litigation Reform Act of 1996 echoes the same themes and further curtails the rights of prisoners to assert constitutional violations. It limits the circumstances under which courts may enter injunctions against unconstitutional prison conditions, including overcrowding and inadequate medical care. It also addresses the alleged problem of frivolous prisoner litigation by curtailing the authority of impoverished prisoners to file lawsuits without paying filing fees.

Ironically, data from the federal courts suggest that the aggressive statutory antiprisoner program was based in part on myth. No long-term increase in prisoner litigiousness is perceptible from the mid-1970s to the 1990s. Increases in prisoner filings can be explained by increases in the prison population, not by more filings per prisoner.

Court decisions also restricted the opportunities of prisoners to assert constitutional violations. *Wilson v. Seiter* (1991) held that prisoners claiming that prison conditions violate the Eighth Amendment's ban on CRUEL OR UNUSUAL PUNISHMENT must establish that prison officials had a culpable state of mind. But in *Farmer v. Brennan* (1994), the Court acknowledged that the Eighth Amendment requires prison officials to maintain minimally humane prison conditions. In *Heck v. Humphrey* (1994), the Court restricted the power of prisoners to challenge the constitutionality of their convictions under section 1983. A state prisoner has no cause of action under section 1983 unless the conviction is first invalidated by the grant of a writ of habeas corpus.

Actions against prosecutors are one area in which federal decisions did not curtail constitutional remedies. *Burns v. Reed* (1991), *Buckley v. Fitzsimmons* (1993), and *Kalina v. Fletcher* (1997) all tend to limit the absolute immunity of prisoners to acts directly related to the prosecution of cases, and to deny immunity for investigative or other prosecutorial activities.

THEODORE EISENBERG
(2000)

(SEE ALSO: *Immunity of Public Officials; Prisoners' Rights.*)

Bibliography

EISENBERG, THEODORE 1996 *Civil Rights Legislation*, 4th ed. Charlottesville, Virginia: Michie.

TUSHNET, MARK and YACKLE, LARRY 1997 Symbolic Statutes and Real Laws: The Pathologies of the Antiterrorism and Effective Death Penalty Act and the Prison Litigation Reform Act. *Duke Law Journal* 47:1–86.

CONSTITUTIONAL THEORY

The term "constitutional theory" refers to two aspects of constitutional law. First, it refers to general theories of the Constitution, which deal with the overall structure of the government, the relations among the branches, and the relation between the national and state governments. Second, it refers to theories of JUDICIAL REVIEW, which provide justifications for the occasions on which the courts, ruling on constitutional issues, will and will not displace the judgments of elected officials.

General theories of the Constitution consider the structure of the government as defined in the Constitution and, more important, as the institutions of the government have developed historically. The primary subjects of this sort of constitutional theory are the SEPARATION OF POWERS of the three branches of the national government, and FEDERALISM, or the division of authority between the national government and state governments. Constitutional theories of this sort attempt to explain how the institutional arrangements of the United States government promote the public interest by allowing the adoption of socially beneficial legislation that does not threaten FUNDAMENTAL RIGHTS.

Theories of the separation of powers fall into two basic groups. In one, the primary concern is the separateness of the branches of the national government. Within this version of constitutional theory, problems arise when one branch begins to assume duties historically performed by another branch. The LEGISLATIVE VETO, invalidated in IMMIGRATION AND NATURALIZATION SERVICE V. CHADHA (1983), offers an example. In the other version, the emphasis is on CHECKS AND BALANCES, and so the legislative veto is treated as a useful innovation to deal with problems of legislative control of executive actions in a government much larger than it was when created in 1789.

In general, checks and balances theories are more receptive to institutional innovations than separation of powers theories. Innovations tend to be seen as democratically chosen devices by which the executive and legislative branches respond to the demands for expansive substantive action generated by the political process; the public asks that the government expand its activity in the provision of social welfare or in international affairs, and the government responds first by acting to satisfy those demands and then, finding that either Congress or the President has grown too powerful, by developing new institutions like the legislative veto to check the branch that seems more threatening.

Yet, if checks and balances theories allow for institutional innovation and therefore for the adoption of policies that the public believes to be in its interest, they are less sensitive than separation of powers theories to the threats to fundamental freedoms that institutional innovations pose. If the original design of the Constitution carefully balanced the branches, as separation of powers theories suggest, then it is unlikely that current majorities will improve on that design.

Similar tensions pervade theories of federalism. At the outset, federalism appeared to be an important protection of democracy and social experimentation: state and local government, being closer to the people, could more readily be controlled by them than the more remote government in the national capital; and the variety of problems faced on the local level might elicit various responses, some of which would prove valuable enough to be adopted elsewhere while those that failed would do so only on a small scale. As the nation expanded, however, economic conditions appeared to require more coordinated responses than local governments could provide. As a result, federalism lost some of its value, to the point where on most issues the national government is free to act as national majorities wish, no matter how much some local governments and local majorities might object. The impairment of local democracy is apparent, yet alternative theories of federalism rely on notions of a sharp division of authority between state and nation that tend to seem quite artificial under modern circumstances.

These examples show how changes in both the scope of the national economy and the reach of the national government pose questions for general theories of the Constitution. Most dramatically, neither POLITICAL PARTIES nor ADMINISTRATIVE AGENCIES were contemplated by the designers of the Constitution, and yet any overall theory of the operation of the national government—a constitutional theory of the first sort—must somehow accommodate the importance of parties and BUREAUCRACIES.

General constitutional theory also deals with the role of the courts, though on a relatively high level of abstraction. Such theories agree that the courts exist to protect fundamental rights, but disagree primarily on the sources of those rights. One approach finds fundamental rights rooted in transcendental conceptions of rights, of the sort identified in classical theories of natural law. This approach often meets with skepticism about the existence of natural law. Another approach finds the fundamental rights enumerated in the text of the Constitution, but has

difficulty dealing with what have been called the "open-ended" provisions of the Constitution, such as the NINTH AMENDMENT and the PRIVILEGES AND IMMUNITIES clauses, which appear to refer to UNENUMERATED RIGHTS.

When general theories of the Constitution deal with the role of judicial review, they sometimes adopt varieties of the other basic type of constitutional theory, the concern of which is the justification of judicial review. Constitutional theories of this type must divide the universe of constitutional claims into those that the courts should uphold and those that they should reject. A powerful argument against a court's decision to exercise its power to invalidate legislation is that such a decision necessarily overturns the outcome of processes of majority rule that are themselves an important value in the American constitutional system. It should be noted, however, that the strength of the "countermajoritarian difficulty," as ALEXANDER M. BICKEL called it, can vary, depending on which government actor actually promulgated the rule in question—a city council, a state government, an administrative agency, Congress, or the President? Majoritarianism alone cannot answer the questions about judicial review. The constitutional system, though it values majority rule, does not take majority rule to be the sole value, as the Constitution's inclusion of limitations on the power of government demonstrates. If there is to be any judicial review, which seems required by the structure of the Constitution, on some occasions courts will displace the decisions of the majoritarian legislatures.

Most constitutional theories of the second type agree, however, that the courts should not simply substitute their determination of what is wise public policy for the legislature's. Not only do courts often lack the competence that legislatures have in developing information about social problems and possible methods of responding to those problems, but, more to the point, the countermajoritarian implications of such freewheeling exercises of the power of judicial review are, for most, unacceptable in the American constitutional system. Theories of this type therefore set themselves two tasks: they must specify when and why courts can invalidate legislation, and when and why they cannot.

Modern constitutional theories of this type fall into several basic groups, though many variants have been offered:

1. ORIGINALISM insists that the courts should invalidate legislation only when the legislation is inconsistent with provisions of the Constitution as those provisions were intended to be applied by their authors. This theory might significantly limit the power of courts if, as most of its proponents believe, the Framers of the Constitution did not intend to place substantial limits on government's powers. The theory is vulnerable on a number of grounds. For some provisions, the evidence is at least mixed, sometimes suggesting that the Framers did indeed intend to limit government power a great deal. Originalist theories,

because they seem to be primarily concerned about imposing limits on judicial discretion, have difficulty dealing with the kinds of ambiguities about intentions that historical inquiry almost invariably generates. The framers of the FOURTEENTH AMENDMENT, for example, were a coalition of Radical Republicans, who desired substantial changes in the overall operation of government with respect to individual rights, and more conservative Republicans, who wanted to preserve a substantial amount of state autonomy in that area. Whose intentions are to control in interpreting the amendment? In addition, technological change presents society with innovations that could not have been within the contemplation of the Framers, and social change sometimes means not only that contemporary values are different from those of the Framers of the Constitution but also that the meaning of practices with which they were familiar has changed so much that it is unclear why contemporary society ought to respond to those practices as the authors intended. WIRETAPPING, a practice that clearly has something to do with the values protected by the FOURTH AMENDMENT but which is significantly different from the practices the Framers actually contemplated, is an example of the first problem. The second problem is illustrated by the changed role of public schools between 1868, when the Framers of the Fourteenth Amendment foresaw little impact on SEGREGATION of public schools, and 1954, when the Supreme Court held that segregated public education is unconstitutional.

2. Natural law theories rely on substantive moral principles determined by philosophical reflection on the proper scope of government in relation to individual liberty, to specify the choices that are within the range of legislative discretion and those that violate individual rights. Contemporary versions of these theories are offered by conservative libertarians, who stress the importance of private property as a domain of liberty, and by liberal supporters of the WELFARE STATE, who stress the importance of nondiscrimination and the provision of the basic necessities of life for people to be able to lead morally acceptable lives. Natural law theories often face general skepticism about the existence of the kinds of rights on which they rely, and a more specific skepticism about the ability of judges as compared to legislators to identify whatever rights there might in fact be.

3. Precedent-oriented constitutional theories rely on past decisions by the courts to guide contemporary decisions. PRECEDENTS are taken to identify with sufficient clarity the kinds of choices that are to be left to legislatures. Using the ordinary techniques of legal reasoning, the courts can use precedents to determine constitutional questions that they have not faced before. Proponents of these theories argue that the techniques of legal reasoning are sufficiently constraining that courts will not be able to

do whatever their policy inclinations would suggest, but are also sufficiently loose that courts will be able to respond appropriately to innovations and social change. Precedent-oriented theories face a number of problems. Many critics find it difficult to give normative value to the decisions of prior courts simply because those decisions happen to have been made; for them, just because the courts at one time "got off the track" is no reason to continue on an erroneous course. Other critics are skeptical about these theories' claims regarding the degree to which precedent actually constrains judges. Influenced by the American legal realists, they argue that the accepted techniques of legal reasoning are so flexible that judges can choose policies they prefer and disguise those choices as dictated by, or at least consistent with, prior decisions.

4. Process-oriented theories attempt to minimize the countermajoritarian difficulty by pressing judicial review into the service of majority rule. They do so by identifying obstacles that make the government less than truly majoritarian. For theories of this sort, the democratic process is bound to malfunction when some people are excluded from the franchise, so that majoritarian legislatures can freely disregard their views. Similar problems arise when rights of expression are limited, so that supporters of certain positions are punished for advocating their adoption; majoritarian legislatures would not learn what these people actually prefer, and the outcome of the political process would therefore be distorted. Process-oriented theories have also dealt with questions of discrimination, which they typically treat as arising from situations in which, though there is no formal disfranchisement, prejudice leads legislators systematically to undervalue the true wishes of their constituencies taken as a whole, that is, including the victims of prejudice.

Critics of process-oriented theories point to limitations that the Constitution places on government that, though perhaps explicable in terms of preserving a majoritarian process, somehow seem devalued when treated solely in process terms; the THIRTEENTH AMENDMENT ban on SLAVERY is a notable example, as is the body of constitutional privacy law that the Supreme Court has developed. Other critics suggest that process-oriented theories, while purporting to serve majoritarian goals, actually subvert them, because the theories are loose enough to allow judges to identify so many obstacles in the processes of majority rule that they can use process-oriented theories to serve their own political goals. A libertarian process theory, for example, might rely on the economic theory of public choice to argue that the courts should be much more active in invalidating social and economic legislation because the beneficiaries of such laws tend to be concentrated INTEREST GROUPS that can readily organize and lobby for their interests, while the costs of the laws are borne by consumers and taxpayers who, because no individual has much at stake, are systematically underorganized in the political process. A social welfare process theory, in contrast, would argue that poor people are at a systematic disadvantage in the political process because they have insufficient income, compared to wealthier people, to devote to political activity; such a theory would suggest that the courts should invalidate restrictions on the provision of public assistance, and should uphold—and perhaps even require—limitations on contributions to political campaigns.

5. The final group of theories of judicial review focuses less on the limits that courts should face in deciding individual cases and more on the practical political limits the courts actually do face in exercising the power of judicial review. These theories stress that the courts are part of the general political process and can be constrained by the actions of the other branches. Some of these theories emphasize the formal limitations on judicial power built into the Constitution, such as Congress's ability to restrict the jurisdiction of the courts, its power to impeach judges, and the public's power to amend the Constitution. These formal limitations have rarely been invoked successfully where Congress or the public has simply disagreed with the results the judges have reached. Another mechanism built into the Constitution, the power to replace judges who resign or die in office with judges sympathetic to the political program of current political majorities, has been more effective in the long run. Replacement of judges in the ordinary way has often shifted the general tenor of the courts, though no one can guarantee that this mechanism will succeed in overturning any particular decision, such as the Supreme Court's ABORTION decision in 1973.

Other versions of this type of theory note that the courts have only infrequently succeeded in imposing their agenda on the public without having some substantial support in the political branches. In short, these theorists argue that the courts cannot get away with very much; the countermajoritarian difficulty, though real, has been exaggerated. Further, in this view, the courts have a limited amount of "political capital": they can invest their capital in decisions designed to enhance their reputation, either by invalidating unpopular laws that somehow have survived in the political process or by upholding popular laws, and thereby generate returns that they can use to preserve their public support when they invalidate genuinely popular statutes. These types of constitutional theory seem to pay attention to the realities of the operation of politics, but they are often too informal in their understanding of politics to be fully persuasive, and in any event, they fail to capture the important normative dimensions of most discussions of constitutional law.

MARK TUSHNET
(1992)

(SEE ALSO: *Conservatism; Constitutional Interpretation; Critical Legal Studies; Deconstructionism; Interpretivism; Jurisprudence and Constitutional Law; Law and Economics Theory; Legal Fictions; Liberal Constitutional Construction; Liberalism; Noninterpretivism; Political Philosophy of the Constitution.*)

Bibliography

BICKEL, ALEXANDER 1962 *The Least Dangerous Branch: The Supreme Court at the Bar of Politics.* Indianapolis, Ind.: Bobbs-Merrill.

ELY, JOHN HART 1980 *Democracy and Distrust.* Cambridge, Mass.: Harvard University Press.

TUSHNET, MARK 1988 *Red, White, and Blue: A Critical Analysis of Constitutional Law.* Cambridge, Mass.: Harvard University Press.

CONSTITUTIONAL THEORY
(Update)

Richard Posner, a leading academic-judge of the era, chose "Against Constitutional Theory" as the title of his 1997 James Madison Lecture on Constitutional Law at the New York University School of Law. Defining "constitutional theory" as "the effort to develop a generally accepted theory to guide the interpretation of the Constitution," he contrasts it with "inquiries of a social scientific character into the nature, provenance, and consequences of constitutionalism" and "commentary on specific cases and doctrines." He notes that "[c]onstitutional theorists are normativists; their theories are meant to influence the way judges decide difficult constitutional cases." What, then, is Posner's objection to constitutional theory? It is "that constitutional theory has no power to command agreement from people not already predisposed to accept the theorist's policy prescriptions." Although "constitutional theory" may often be "rhetorically powerful," it nonetheless "lacks the agreement-coercing power of the best natural and social science." At bottom, it is just not very helpful to the person grappling to make decisions as a judge or other official sworn to uphold the Constitution.

An immediate question is how "constitutional theory" as defined by Posner differs from "CONSTITUTIONAL INTERPRETATION", which is surely relevant to, and indeed constitutes, constitutional performance. In the initial *Encyclopedia of the American Constitution*, Paul Brest, writing on "constitutional interpretation," sketched a taxonomy of the legal arguments that have guided judges in giving content to the Constitution. Similarly, Philip Bobbitt in two books, *Constitutional Fate* and *Constitutional Interpretation*, has extensively elaborated what he terms the "modalities" of constitutional argument—text, history, structure, doctrine, prudence, and appeals to our constitutional "ethos." These modalities constitute the parts of speech, as it were, of the particular grammar of "constitutional law-talk," a proposition that Posner could scarcely deny.

One difference between the basically taxonomic approaches of Brest and Bobbitt and "theory," as described by Posner, may be the overtly normative thrust of the latter. To be sure, both Brest and Bobbitt are normativists to the extent that they would presumably declare "out of bounds," and thus illegitimate, modes of argument that defy standard notions of legal grammar, such as emphasizing the norms of revealed religion or, indeed, offering as a reason for a particular decision the probability that it would enhance the judge's prospects for relection, in many states, or promotion within the federal judiciary. Such moves would be as inappropriate as saying "I are going" or "Threw the ball Jack to I." Just as the latter would reveal the speaker as inept in English grammar, offering the ostensible "arguments" described above would illustrate the same degree of failure to grasp the structure of legal grammar. That being said, an important part of the Brest-Bobbitt project, and of other writers influenced by them, is to suggest that there does not exist a single royal road to "correct" constitutional interpretation, anymore than there is only one way correctly to convey a given idea. To that extent, the "modalities" are not agreement-forcing.

Instead, constitutional adjudicators may well find themselves tugged in different directions by the various modalities, with text leading in one direction, attention to history leading in another, and decided case law in yet a third. This means, among other things, that such modal analysts are unlikely to fall victim to Posner's jibe that constitutional theorists "cannot resist telling their readers which cases they think were decided consistently with or contrary to their theory," since they do not assign to one given approach a dominance that will necessarily resolve conflicts. It may be possible, of course, to condemn some particular ineptness in applying one of the modalities, such as purportedly history-based decisions that simply ignore relevant historial materials (see, e.g., DRED SCOTT V. SANDFORD (1857)) or a doctrinally oriented opinion that offers unusually tendentious readings of the cases relied on (see, e.g., EMPLOYMENT DIVISION, DEPARTMENT OF HUMAN RESOURCES OF OREGON V. SMITH (1990)). This, however, is very different from saying, as does Robert Bork, that ORIGINAL INTENT provides the only legitimate basis for constitutional judgment; or, as does John Hart Ely, in his enormously influential *Democracy and Distrust* (1980), that courts, though usually required to defer to decisions made by politically accountable branches of government, can nonetheless interpret the FOURTEENTH AMENDMENT as authorizing them to engage in "representation-reinforcement" of otherwise vulnerable minorities who are victimized by

prejudice but not, say, to protect the right of women (who constitute a majority of the population) to reproductive autonomy.

Law professors adopting a taxonomic approach are primarily concerned that their students are introduced to the array of argumentative possibilities and can use all of them effectively, as any given case might require. A professorial "theorist" as described by Posner would, on the other hand, be far more likely to spend time praising some decisions and condemning others by reference to their fit with the professor's favorite approach.

One must acknowledge that legal academics have always been in the habit of grading judicial handiwork. Most of the pre-judicial writings of FELIX FRANKFURTER, whether in the law reviews or in *The New Republic*, attempted to separate acceptable judicial wheat from the all too common chaff emanating from the "Old Court." No one referred to this as "constitutional theory," however. "Constitutional theory," as a self-conscious development within the legal academy, is almost certainly the consequence of the reinvigoration, following the apparent triumph in 1937 of Frankfurter and his devotees and the judicial retreats linked with that episode, of a significantly "activist" judiciary linked with BROWN V. BOARD OF EDUCATION (1954) and then many other cases identified with the WARREN COURT. *Brown* is central, though, because there Frankfurter joined Warren's opinion, and he and his devotees had to explain its propriety.

It is no coincidence, then, that the first major book clearly identified as a work in "constitutional theory," in Posner's sense, is ALEXANDER M. BICKEL *The Least Dangerous Branch* (1962). Bickel, a graduate of the Harvard Law School who clerked for Frankfurter (and who, as clerk, wrote a famous memorandum to Frankfurter, subsequently published in the *Harvard Law Review*, justifying the invalidation of school segregation), identified what he termed the "countermajoritarian difficulty"; that is, the purported anomaly of the politically nonaccountable Court invalidating legislation passed by majoritarian political institutions, and attempted to set out the (relatively uncommon) circumstances under which the Court would indeed be entitled to intervene. Many things might be said about Bickel's argument, including the fact that he did not talk about any of the other notable "countermajoritarian difficulties" in our political system, ranging from BICAMERALISM; the staggeringly antimajoritarian basis of political REPRESENTATION in the U.S. SENATE (reflected, to at least some extent, in the ELECTORAL COLLEGE); the presidential VETO POWER; and such accepted practices (far more pervasive, indeed, in our own time than even in the 1950s) as the use of the FILIBUSTER in the Senate to prevent a legislative majority from working its will. In any event, Bickel was willing to defend *Brown* (though not, later in the decade, such decisions as BAKER V. CARR (1962), where Frankfurter had dissented), and the combatants in the great theory wars— devoted to defending or attacking one or another normative view of the judiciary's role as presumptive "ultimate interpreter" of the Constitution (itself a highly tendentious term of the Court's creation)—were off and running.

Although important sallies continue to be delivered in these wars, the most important contemporary work in what might well be described as neotheory of the Constitution involves moving away from normative, methodologically driven inquiries of the type described above to broader, more historically grounded inquiries into the actual operation of the American constitutional order. Exemplary in this regard is Stephen M. Griffin's *American Constitutionalism: From Theory to Practice* (1996). Like Posner, Griffin rejects the obsessive emphasis on judicial review and concomitant attempts to construct a single master method that would at once resolve the "counter-majoritarian difficulty." Instead he asks to what extent is it truly plausible to view the Constitution, especially as interpreted by courts, as playing a significant role in channeling the great socioeconomic changes over the 200 years since its adoption. Griffin answers: Not much. As a descriptive practice, constitutional interpretation has changed to accommodate felt necessities of the times, as, indeed, OLIVER WENDELL HOLMES, JR., suggested so memorably in *The Common Law* (1881). To the extent that the Constitution can be assigned a significant role, the reason lies in basic structural features of the American order, including bicameralism, equal state membership in the Senate, or the dates established for inauguration of Presidents or the convening of Congress, provisions that have almost never been the subject of litigation, and so have lacked interest to legal academics for whom the agenda is set by the litigation practices of the Court. This interest in the implications of basic constitutional design has generated another important branch of contemporary constitutional neotheory, much influenced by so-called social choice or "positive political theory" within political science. These theorists assume that politics is carried on by rational individuals, where "rationality" is defined as the maximization of individual goals and sensitivity to the incentives generated by given institutional designs.

Perhaps the most crucial clause of the Constitution for Griffin and other practitioners of "neotheory" is Article V, which sets out an exceedingly difficult process of formal constitutional change. (Indeed, in Levinson (1995), political scientist Donald Lutz compared the U.S. Constitution to the constitutions of every state and of more than thirty other countries and determined that the U.S. Constitution has the highest "index of difficulty" in regard to formal amendment.) The consequence is that many of the most significant changes over the past 200 years have taken place outside of Article V. That is, there may be far more constitutional "amendments"—in the sense of changes in constitutional practice that cannot plausibly be derived from the original text or the formal amendments added to it—than the twenty-six (or twenty-seven, depending on one's acceptance of the purported TWENTY-SEVENTH AMENDMENT, proposed in 1789 and declared ratified only in 1992) set out as textual additions to the original 1787 Constitution. More to the point, to limit one's definition of "amendment" only to these textual additions is to adopt a basically atheoretical approach to the problem, explaining away, by stipulative definition, what is in fact the great mystery of American constitutionalism, which is how, adopting Chief Justice JOHN MARSHALL's language in MCCULLOCH V. MARYLAND (1819), the system has actually "adapted to the various *crises* of human affairs." These other "amendments" are unwritten, at least in the text of the Constitution itself (as against presidential statements, statutes, judicial opinions, and the like), but no analyst of American constitutionalism could possibly make sense of what has happened since 1789 without taking them into account.

Both Yale's Bruce Ackerman and Harvard's Laurence Tribe, among the most eminent of contemporary writers on the Constitution, agree, for example, that the TREATY clause of the 1787 Constitution is best read as covering such acts as the NORTH AMERICAN FREE TRADE AGREEMENT (NAFTA) or the General Agreement on Trades and Tariffs (GATT). Yet these extraordinarily important developments in international trade were "ratified" not by two-thirds of the Senate, as required by the clause, but, rather, by a majority of each house of Congress. For Tribe, this is enough to render unconstitutional both NAFTA and GATT. Ackerman, however, though agreeing with Tribe as to the meaning of the 1787 Constitution, and agreeing as well that no formal Article V amendment has changed the treaty clause, argues that a non-Article V amendment was affected by the response of the United States to the exigencies of WORLD WAR II and the de-facto ratification of these new procedures by the American electorate. Indeed, Ackerman makes similar, even more important, arguments in regard to the so-called RECONSTRUCTION amendments following the CIVIL WAR and then the NEW DEAL. He denies, for example, that the Fourteenth Amendment can be legitimately viewed as a simple Article V change of the Constitution. And, agreeing with conservatives that the New Deal violated the original Constitution and that, of course, no formal amendment changed Congress's powers to shape the national economy, Ackerman nonetheless argues that the New Deal represented what he calls a "constitutional moment" that legitimately transformed the operative Constitution. Tribe denounces such ideas a "free-form" theory unbefitting a disciplined legal analyst.

However unconventional Ackerman's approach may be, it responds to the fundamental reality identified by Griffin and others, the brute fact that the meanings ascribed to the Constitution have radically changed over time though there have been so few formal amendments. Those who resist "free-form" theory often either end up simply ignoring the most significant single episode in post-1787 CONSTITUTIONAL HISTORY, the process by which the Fourteenth Amendment became part of the Constitution, or, as with the New Deal, are forced to argue that the Old Court unaccountably failed to understand the Constitution and that the New Deal court simply "restored" the Constitution to its original meaning (or, at least, the meaning given it by Marshall in GIBBONS V. OGDEN (1824)). Or, as with GATT and NAFTA, Tribe, the author of the most significant treatise in constitutional law in the twentieth century, is forced to take a position that, in context, not only is reminscent of a disgruntled JOHN W. DAVIS railing against the New Deal, but also is one that would almost certainly be rejected by any Court to which it was presented, not least because of the political earthquake that would follow a declaration that, indeed, one-third plus one of a grotesquely malapportioned Senate is constitutionally entitled to reject such fundamental aspects of the modern globalized economy. This does not, of course, mean that Tribe is "wrong"; his arguments are well within the rules of acceptable legal grammar, just as were the arguments against the New Deal or, for that matter, the propriety of *Brown*. Nonetheless, there is an unbridgeable chasm between Tribean constitutional theory, at least in this instance, and the actual practices of American political institutions, including courts that offer often strained "interpretations" designed in effect to ratify the de-facto amendatory changes.

One should note that Ackerman's account of historical change, though significantly descriptive, also has a significant normative dimension. He wants to offer an account by which we can recognize "authorized" non-Article V amendments—that is, the results of "constitutional moments" and the particular kind of mobilized polity linked to such moments—and, concomitantly, reject other changes as illegitimate because they do not represent an authoritative, albeit unconventional, declaration by the sovereign "We the People." Whether "constitutional theory," even in its "neo" variety, can escape normativism is an important question. (Whether it should, even assuming it can, is, of course, another question.)

Another important aspect of Ackerman's work, reflected as well in Griffin's call for a new approach to constitutional analysis and a different conception of constitutional theory, is the emphasis on the crucial role of nonjudicial actors within the political system. The innovative actions of Presidents and legislatures, and of state governments, create new political realities to which courts must respond (even if the response, as in important areas of FOREIGN AFFAIRS, is to declare that these are POLITICAL QUESTIONS left to the discretion of political decisionmakers). Moreover, at least one strand of argument among contemporary constitutional theorists concerns the claims made by the Court for its own supremacy as a constitutional interpreter. Constitutional "protestants," who emphasize the legitimacy of multiple interpreters of the Constitution, contend with "catholics" who view the Court as indeed its "ultimate interpreter." Yet other theorists have begun emphasizing (and sometimes questioning) the difference between the interpretive freedom accorded the Supreme Court and the extraordinarily diminished freedom allowed the judges who serve in what the Constitution terms "inferior" courts, who are often expected to be almost literally unthinking satraps of their institutional superiors. If Supreme Court Justices swear loyalty to the Constitution, it appears that they expect their hierarchical inferiors to swear loyalty to themselves. Indeed, Posner, the Chief Judge of the Seventh Circuit Court of Appeals, wrote a famous article in *The New Republic* entitled "What am I, a Potted Plant?," taking issue with this notion.

The post-*Brown* fixation with "constitutional theory as the search for a definitive method of constitutional interpretation by judges on the Supreme Court" allowed its practitioners to avoid coming to terms with the actualities of the American polity, beginning with the fact that judges on the Court are only one, and not at all the most important, set of actors with responsibilities to think seriously about their constitutional duties. Even more to the point, knowledge of these actualities requires immersion in such disciplines as history, both American and comparative, and a number of the social sciences. Whether American legal academics are willing so to immerse themselves remains an open question.

SANFORD LEVINSON
(2000)

(SEE ALSO: *Amendment Process (Outside of Article V); Constitutional Dualism; Nonjudicial Interpretation of the Constitution; Originalism.*)

Bibliography

ACKERMAN, BRUCE   1991   *We the People: Foundations.* Cambridge, Mass.: Harvard University Press.
———   1998   *We the People: Transformations.* Cambridge, Mass.: Harvard University Press.
ACKERMAN, BRUCE and GOLOVE, DAVID   1995   Is NAFTA Constitutional? *Harvard Law Review* 108:799–929.
BOBBITT, PHILIP   1982   *Constitutional Fate.* New York: Oxford University Press.
———   1991   *Constitutional Interpretation.* Cambridge, Mass.: Basil Blackwell.

ESKRIDGE, WILLIAM and LEVINSON, SANFORD 1998 *Constitutional Stupidities, Constitutional Tragedies.* New York: New York University Press.

FRIEDMAN, BARRY 1998 The History of the Countermajoritarian Difficulty, Part One: The Road to Judicial Supremacy. *New York University Law Review* 73:333–433.

GRIFFIN, STEPHEN M. 1996 *American Constitutionalism: From Theory to Practice.* Princeton, N.J.: Princeton University Press.

LEVINSON, SANFORD, ed. 1995 *Responding to Imperfection: The Theory and Practice of Constitutional Amendment.* Princeton, N.J.: Princeton University Press.

POSNER, RICHARD 1998 Against Constitutional Theory. *New York University Law Review* 73:1–22.

SYMPOSIUM 1997 Fidelity in Constitutional Theory. *Fordham Law Review* 65:1247–1818.

TRIBE, LAURENCE H. 1995 Taking Text and Structure Seriously: Reflections on Free-Form Method in Constitutional Interpretation. *Harvard Law Review* 108:1221–1303.

CONSTITUTION AND CIVIC IDEALS

The renowned constitutional scholar ALEXANDER M. BICKEL believed that "the concept of citizenship plays only the most minimal role in the American constitutional scheme." The Constitution "bestowed rights on people and persons, not . . . some legal construct called citizen"— a state of affairs Bickel thought "idyllic."

Indeed, the unamended Constitution mentioned citizenship remarkably infrequently. Three times it made citizenship "of the United States" required for the elective federal offices (Article I, sections 1–2; Article II, section 1). It mentioned citizenship of a "State" four times in describing the JURISDICTION of the federal courts (Article III, section 2), and once in protecting citizens' PRIVILEGES AND IMMUNITIES by a principle of interstate equality (Article IV, section 2). Article I, section 8, also gave Congress the power to establish "an uniform Rule of naturalization." That was all. The Constitution did not define United States or state citizenship, explain their relationship, or specify their "Privileges and Immunities." Strikingly, it did not demand citizenship of voters, Supreme Court Justices, or even traitors (Article III, section 3).

Yet, despite its silences on citizenship, the Constitution embodied not one but several civic ideals, all of which presented a conception of the nature and meaning of membership in the Union that its Framers aimed to perfect. With deference to Bickel, the Constitution's reticence about these ideals traces only partly to an exaltation of universal personal rights over all particular political identities. In important ways the different civic ideals visible in the Constitution were in sharp tension with each other. The Constitution's silences also reflected the Framers' decisions not to confront, much less resolve, those difficulties. Subsequently, these initially postponed conflicts over rival civic ideals have shaped the nation's evolution profoundly. Over time, Americans have modified their original civic conceptions, and in the twentieth century many have supported a new ideal of American civic identity.

In framing the Constitution, American leaders drew on the classical republican tradition espoused by James Harrington and analyzed by Baron de MONTESQUIEU and from colonial and revolutionary struggles men like LUTHER MARTIN derived their beliefs that legitimate governments must be popularly controlled and that popular governance must be conducted preeminently in small republics. Hence, they favored FEDERALISM, opposed lodging any extensive power in the national government, and continued to believe in the primacy of state citizenship over national citizenship. From the Enlightenment LIBERALISM of JOHN LOCKE and, in most American readings, WILLIAM BLACKSTONE, others such as JAMES WILSON and JAMES MADISON derived their esteem for sacred personal rights, including rights of property and conscience (expressed in the CONTRACT CLAUSE limits on the states and the Article IV ban on RELIGIOUS TESTS for national office). Such men tended to favor national power and the primacy of Americans' more extended membership in their nation.

But beyond their liberalism and REPUBLICANISM, American leaders from GOUVERNEUR MORRIS to CHARLES PINCKNEY also expected that to be a full member of the American community, one would share in a special ethnocultural heritage clustered around Protestant Christianity, the white race, European or (preferably) American birth, and male predominance in most spheres. This version of "Americanism" led them to require all Presidents after the revolutionary generation to be "natural born" citizens (Article II, section 1); to countenance black chattel SLAVERY implicitly but recurrently (e.g., Article I, sections 2 and 9; Article IV, section 2; Article V); to distinguish tribal Indians from both Americans and foreigners twice (Article I, sections 2 and 8); and to accept tacitly the subordinate status of women. Such an Americanism was often bound up with Protestant visions of the new Union as a "redeemer nation," providentially selected to serve divine purposes. Christianity also pervaded the other early American civic conceptions, intertwining with republican espousals of public virtue as well as liberal precepts of human dignity that transcended temporal politics and nationalities.

None of these civic conceptions could gain exclusive sway in the Constitution; none could be wholly ignored. In some respects, the Framers invented a novel kind of national liberal republic that was a significant contribution to the development of modern regimes. But some fundamental conflicts were compromised or evaded precisely by leaving citizenship and the touchy relation between state and national political membership undefined: by avoiding, explicitly accepting, or opposing the illiberal institution of black chattel slavery; by not specifying civic privileges and immunities; and by refusing to establish a national religion while permitting state establishments to continue. Even the relationship of state authority to Congress's new power to naturalize citizens was left for later resolution.

Almost immediately, state-oriented republican anxieties about the Constitution's expansions of national power compelled Congress to propose the BILL OF RIGHTS, explicitly reserving powers to the states and protecting local institutions like MILITIA and juries, although several amendments, the FIRST AMENDMENT especially, also specified liberal protections of basic personal freedoms. Clashes between Jeffersonianism and Jacksonian STATES' RIGHTS republicanism and the FEDERALISTS' and Whigs' nationalist economic liberalism continued through the antebellum years, accompanied by growing conflicts pitting liberal and Christian advocates of expanded rights for blacks and other ethnic and religious minorities against Americanist defenses of Protestant white male supremacy. Finally, of course, issues of the primacy of state versus national citizenship and the status of blacks fueled the Union's great crisis in the 1860s. The CIVIL WAR amendments appeared to decide those disputes in favor of liberal nationalistic civic conceptions, but in the late nineteenth century both traditional republican views of federalism and Americanist views of racial and gender hierarchies were in many respects successfully reasserted.

Most Progressive Era reformers remained narrow Protestant Americanists, but Progressive intellectuals on the left, including John Dewey, Randolph Bourne, and Horace Kallen, began formulating a broader conception of American civic identity. They drew on republicanism's calls for democratic participation, liberalism's emphasis on equal human dignity, and Americanism's stress on the importance of constitutive social identities. But, relying on pragmatist philosophic foundations, these thinkers reformulated those conceptions into one that may be termed "democratic cultural pluralism." It represented American nationality as a democratically organized confederation of disparate ethnic, religious, and cultural groups, all entitled to equal respect in public institutions and policies; these groups would serve as the primary loci of most persons' social identities. Democratic pluralists saw national membership essentially as a means to advance the welfare of all such groups on a fair, neutral basis. The democratic cultural pluralist conception of American civic identity increasingly came to prevail in judicial constitutional doctrines and in American citizenship statutes after the NEW DEAL and especially during the Great Society years. The federal government repudiated racial SEGREGATION, ended ethnically exclusionary IMMIGRATION and naturalization policies, reduced legal discriminations against women, and promoted broader opportunities via bilingual and AFFIRMATIVE ACTION programs. In the 1970s and 1980s, criticisms of these measures mounted, with many contending that they promoted fragmentation and group selfishness instead of national unity. Thus, the great questions about American civic ideals that the Constitution did not answer still remain far from settled.

ROGERS M. SMITH
(1992)

(SEE ALSO: *Gender Rights; Jacksonianism; Jeffersonianism; Political Philosophy of the Constitution; Pragmatism; Progressive Constitutional Thought; Progressivism; Sex Discrimination; Whig Party.*)

Bibliography

KARST, KENNETH L. 1989 *Belonging to America: Equal Citizenship and the Constitution.* New Haven, Conn.: Yale University Press.

KETTNER, JAMES H. 1978 *The Development of American Citizenship, 1608–1870.* Chapel Hill: University of North Carolina Press.

CONSTITUTION AS ASPIRATION

What is the point of constitutional law? What fundamental purpose does it serve? And in what sense is the Constitution law? There are at least two possible types of response to these foundational questions; one quite familiar and one less so. The cluster of familiar responses might be called the "Constitution of constraints." On this view, the purpose of the Constitution is to constrain congressional and executive lawmaking at both the state and federal level. The Constitution imposes constraints, or boundaries, on what lawmakers might otherwise be inclined to do. The Constitution is a source of law, because the point of the enterprise, thus understood, is to impose limits, enforced judicially, on what popularly elected representatives or executives might enact, on behalf of the majority they purportedly represent. And limits, interpreted and enforced judicially, is precisely what we mean by "law."

It is this view of the Constitution that has inspired the outpouring of scholarship and judicial opinions concerned with the countermajoritarian difficulty, and it is this view of the Constitution that has defined the boundaries of most contemporary constitutional argument, at least as it pertains to the BILL OF RIGHTS. For while most constitutional theorists agree that the point of constitutional law is to impose legal constraints on lawmakers from what they might otherwise be inclined to do, they disagree fundamentally over the content of those constraints, and over what the legislative or executive evil is toward which the Constitution is aimed. Thus, liberal constitutionalists view the Constitution's core purpose as the protection of individual rights and liberties against LEGISLATION that serves the interests of majorities but runs roughshod over core individualistic values. Conservative constitutionalists view the Constitution's core purpose as the protection of institutions and traditions that might be endangered by a popular legislature's reckless leveling or egalitarian instincts, and proceduralists or process theorists view the Constitution's core purpose as the protection of the openness and fairness of the political process itself. Although these differences are profound, their common grounding is equally significant: they all concur in their understanding of the Constitution as a "Constitution of constraints," and more particularly of legal constraints to be enforced by the judiciary on behalf of interests, traditions, values, or rights that might otherwise be trammeled by an unconstrained majoritarian process.

As familiar and widely shared as this understanding might be, one can discern in our CONSTITUTIONAL HISTORY and even in our current debates an alternative conception of what the point of constitutionalism might be, and what sense we might make of its self-declared status as "law." On this alternative view, the point of the Constitution is to declare a set of moral and political aspirations for democratic self-governance, rather than a set of judicially enforced legal constraints upon it. These constitutional aspirations, one might argue, are intended to open up and then to guide, rather than constrain, political debate and legislative decisionmaking. They constitute a set of ideals for a DELIBERATIVE DEMOCRACY which the legislative and executive branches ought to aim for. They constitute law, but not in the adjudicative and judge- focused sense meant by the LEGAL REALISTS; rather, they constitute law in the sense often embraced by eighteenth-century natural lawyers: aspirations or ideals meant to guide the hand of the lawmaker. These ideals, or constitutional aspirations, are then realized not only or even primarily through judicial decisions that invalidate legislation, but rather through legislative or executive decisions that further them.

What those aspirations might be, of course, is open to question and a matter of controversy. But because constitutional aspirations, unlike constitutional constraints, are reflected in legislative or executive enactment rather than exclusively in judicial decisions, their content need not reflect the limiting practical and jurisprudential conventions of adjudicative enterprises. The meaning we ascribe to constitutional aspirations, or the content we find in them, or the interpretations on whose behalf we argue,

need not, for example, be subject to the limiting practical need to be reasonably subjected to judicial enforceability. Nor need the content ascribed to constitutional aspirations be subject to the jurisprudential or moral imperatives that constrain courts in all adjudicative lawmaking: that the decisions which give them meaning reflect the peculiarly judicial legal goals of horizontal equity, legal justice, and respect for past practice and PRECEDENT. Rather, our constitutional aspirations, and thus the interpretations we suggest for those constitutional phrases that might express them, should serve the quite different practical and moral conventions of legislative enterprises: Constitutional aspirations, understood as ideals governing lawmakers in a deliberative democracy, should, for example, encourage open and informed political democracy among all sectors of society, guide the legislature toward an appreciation and concern for the common good, direct it against favoritism, factionalism, or self-interest, forbid the creation or tolerance of castes, and point law toward the well-being of all.

If we attend to the aspirational content of our Constitution, different potential meanings of some of its key phrases emerge. For example, the FIRST AMENDMENT might be understood, aspirationally, as aimed at the invigoration of political debate and the protection of dissent, rather than as a constraint on all forms of legislation that in any way inhibits private expression. If so, then legislation that inhibits some private expression toward the end of opening up political debate—such as regulations limiting the amount of money spent in political campaigns—might be understood as fulfilling a constitutional aspiration rather than violating a constitutional constraint. The guarantee that no state shall deny an individual's liberty without DUE PROCESS OF LAW, found in the Fifth Amendment and the FOURTEENTH AMENDMENT, might also be understood as expressive of a constitutional aspiration: that each individual enjoy some measure of positive liberty—some measure of true self- governance—which no state may challenge and which Congress must aggressively protect, rather than a constraint on progressive legislation that interferes with private rights of contract or PROPERTY. In this perspective, a federal guarantee of minimal welfare or income sustenance might be understood as essential to this constitutional aspiration. The repeal of such a minimum might be viewed as violative of the aspiration.

To take a more extended example, the Fourteenth Amendment declares that no citizen shall be denied "EQUAL PROTECTION OF THE LAW," but it is silent on what that protection means. Over the last fifty years, the Supreme Court has produced a working and workable account: the equal protection clause, the Court now reasons, requires Congress to legislate in a way that is rational: legislative classifications must rationally track differences in the world that are relevant to some legitimate legislative end. Racial classifications, according to this standard understanding, are presumptively irrational: they do not reflect any legitimate and meaningful difference between citizens. Legislation that categorizes on the basis of race, therefore, violates the equal protection clause of the Fourteenth Amendment. More generally, any legislation, or any STATE ACTION, which fails this test of rationality is vulnerable to judicial invalidation. Thus, the constitutional guarantee of equal protection imposes a constraint of rationality on legislating majorities, who may otherwise legislate in whatever way and toward whatever end they see fit. Race, and to a lesser extent gender, are presumptively irrational bases for legislative categorization.

This interpretation of both the scope and the meaning of the equal protection clause follows directly—indeed inexorably—from the more basic understanding of the Constitution as one of constraints. First, scope: The equal protection clause, on this view, imposes a constraint of rationality on Congress, on state legislatures, and more broadly on state action. Where the legislating branch fails the test, the legislation is invalidated. Second, on content: The ideal of rationality imposed on Congress and on state legislatures by the Fourteenth Amendment echoes the ideal of horizontal equity or legal justice required of courts in all areas of lawmaking that "likes must be treated alike." The "equal protection" that emerges from the Fourteenth Amendment, when viewed as a part of the constitution as constraint, is an echo of the jurisprudential ideal of lawmaking required of courts. Likes must be treated alike, and claims of difference, and hence different treatment, carefully defended.

Viewed in this light, the paradigm moment of constitutional lawmaking under the Fourteenth Amendment is clearly BROWN V. BOARD OF EDUCATION (1954). The state legislature had legislated on the basis of race, thus failing the test of rationality. Racial differences between citizens, in this case school children, are not rationally relevant to any legitimate state interest. The Court properly invalidated the law. The Constitution thus acted as a constraint on errant legislation, and on the irrational legislature that produced it.

If, however, we view the Fourteenth Amendment's equal protection clause as expressive of a constitutional aspiration, quite different potential meanings emerge. Viewed as a moral and political guide to legislation, the clause might be read as urging upon the state and federal legislatures the task of providing equal protection, through proactive legislation, to groups that are, for whatever societal reason, in need of it. The constitutional mandate, then, is not a directive to courts to invalidate legislation based on impermissibly irrational categorical assumptions. Rather, the constitutional mandate is a directive to state legislatures to enact whatever law is necessary to equally protect citizens against whatever subordinating inequalities has rendered them in need of it—including, for example, the ravages of unchecked private violence, racism, or, arguably, societal neglect—and a grant of power to the federal Congress to take corrective action should the state legislatures fail. The role of the Court in this aspirational enterprise of equality is minimal, while the role of the state and federal legislatures is primary. The Fourteenth Amendment expresses an aspiration, and directs states and Congress to attempt to achieve it.

Both the scope and content of the equal protection clause, on this interpretation, are consistent with the fundamental commitments of the aspirational Constitution. First, on scope: The aim of the clause is to ensure that states and Congress respond to inequalities brought on by social privation or violence coupled with legislative or state neglect. The trigger for constitutionally inspired congressional action, in other words, is not a state's irrational legislation, but rather, private or societal inequality coupled with state inaction. Second, on content: The equal protection clause, on this view, requires of the states and Congress that they act so as to ensure that all people enjoy the equal protection of law. This echoes and instantiates quite general legislative aspirations: to legislate in a way that protects and furthers and enhances the general well-being of all, rather than in a way that furthers the particular interests of some.

Beyond the meaning of particular clauses, however, if we attend to our constitutional aspirations, rather than only heed constitutional constraints, a quite different history of that field of law and politics comes into focus. The history of the equal protection clause understood as a part of our "constitution of constraints" is a history of judicial decisions, reacting to and sometimes invalidating irrational legislative enactments. By contrast, the history of our constitutional aspiration to equal protection is a history of political struggles over the content of equality, periods of public quietude and unrest and eventual legislative enactments, sometimes followed and sometimes not by judicial response. It is a history of our politics, which are sometimes responsive to and sometimes inattentive to and even overtly hostile to constitutional guidance. The paradigm, ideal, climactic moments of this history are not *Brown,* or ROE V. WADE (1973), or ROMER V. EVANS (1996). Rather, the paradigm moments are the passage of the RECONSTRUCTION amendments themselves; the passage of the nineteenth- and twentieth- century CIVIL RIGHTS ACTS; the turn-of-the-century struggles over the constitutionality of progressive taxation and the LABOR MOVEMENT; the campaigns for WOMAN SUFFRAGE; and, in more recent times, the passage of the AMERICANS WITH DIS-

ABILITIES ACT; the VIOLENCE AGAINST WOMEN ACT; and, possibly, the passage, sometime in the next few decades, of a federal law forbidding private-sector discrimination on the basis of SEXUAL ORIENTATION. At each of these moments, Congress acted constitutionally, but in at least two senses, not just one. At each such moment, it acted in compliance with a constraint of rationality. More consequentially for our politics, at each such moment it acted in accordance with a constitutional aspiration: an aspiration to protect all citizens, and equally, against the damage done by societal privation and state neglect, to correct this damage with federal law, and thus to assure equal protection of the law. And at each such moment, Congress acted in harmony with a higher or natural legal obligation to legislate on behalf of the general good, the general will, or the general well-being—to legislate, in short, in the interest of all of the governed.

ROBIN WEST
(2000)

Bibliography

ACKERMAN, BRUCE 1991 *We the People: Foundations.* Cambridge, Mass.: Harvard University Press.
—— 1998 *We the People: Transformations.* Cambridge, Mass.: Harvard University Press.
AMAR, AKHIL 1990 40 Acres and a Mule: A Republican Theory of Minimal Entitlements. *Harvard Journal of Law and Public Policy* 13:37–43.
FISS, OWEN 1976 Groups and the Equal Protection Clause. *Philosophy and Public Affairs* 5:107–177.
HEYMAN, STEVEN 1991 The First Duty of Government: Protection, Liberty, and the Fourteenth Amendment. *Duke Law Journal* 41:507–571.
MICHELMAN, FRANK 1969 Foreword: On Protecting the Poor Through the Fourteenth Amendment. *Harvard Law Review* 83:7–59.
SUNSTEIN, CASS R. 1993 *Democracy and the Problem of Free Speech.* New York: Free Press.
—— 1993 *The Partial Constitution.* Cambridge, Mass.: Harvard University Press.
TRIBE, LAURENCE H. 1985 *Constitutional Choices.* Cambridge, Mass.: Harvard University Press.
TEN BROEK, JACOBUS 1965 *Equal Under Law.* New York: Collier Books.
WEST, ROBIN 1994 *Progressive Constitutionalism: Reconstructing the Fourteenth Amendment.* Durham, N.C.: Duke University Press.
WOOD, GORDON S. 1992 *The Radicalism of the American Revolution.* New York: Knopf.

CONSTITUTION AS CIVIL RELIGION

That there exist similarities between religious devotion and esteem for the Constitution of the United States is scarcely a new notion. JAMES MADISON wrote in 1792 that our fundamental charter should be the object of "more than common reverence for authority," treated indeed as "political scriptures" protected against "every attempt to add to or diminish them." Conversely, but in the same terms, Madison's great friend and colleague THOMAS JEFFERSON complained in 1816 about the propensity of Americans to "look at constitutions with sanctimonious reverence and deem them like the ark of covenant, too sacred to be touched." By 1885 the young scholar WOODROW WILSON could write in his classic *Congressional Government* of the "almost blind worship" directed at the Constitution's principles.

Perhaps the most important scholarly formulation of the role played by the Constitution within what later scholars would come to call the American civil religion was Max Lerner's 1937 article "Constitution and Court as Symbols." Influenced by Justice OLIVER WENDELL HOLMES, JR.'s famous assertion that "we live by symbols" and by the contemporary political-anthropological analysis of THURMAN ARNOLD, Lerner emphasized the "totem[ic]" aspect of the Constitution "as an instrument for controlling unknown forces in a hostile universe." It was no coincidence with Lerner that an American culture so influenced by Protestant Christianity would fix on the Constitution: "The very habits of mind begotten by an authoritarian Bible and a religion of submission to a higher power have been carried over to an authoritarian Constitution and a philosophy of submission to a higher law." The United States, whatever the prohibition of the FIRST AMENDMENT on an ESTABLISHMENT OF RELIGION, "ends by getting a state church after all, although in a secular form."

The very title of Lerner's article points to the dual aspect of this purported state church: there is not only an authoritative text but also an equally authoritative institution that can give privileged interpretations of that text. That institution, of course, is the Supreme Court. No less a skeptic than HENRY ADAMS confessed that "he still clung to the Supreme Court, much as a churchman clings to his bishops, because they are his only symbol of unity; his last rage of Right." Even the more scholarly Alpheus Mason suggested that the marble palace of the Supreme Court constituted our "Holy of Holies."

It is, then, easy enough to show that religious language and metaphors come readily to analysts of the Constitution. And it is also easy enough to agree with contemporary scholars like Robert Bellah that all societies, very much including our own, amass a variety of myths, symbols, narratives, and rituals that can be brought together under the rubric of "civil religion." But one may still wonder about such concepts, especially when applied quite specifically to suggest that an understanding of American CONSTITUTIONALISM is enhanced by placing it within the analogical context of religion. What, then, is genuinely learned by reference to Constitution "worship" or comparing the Supreme Court to the Vatican?

For almost all the persons mentioned and many others besides, the lesson has to do with the central role of the Constitution, as declared by the Court, in providing the basis of national unity. A striving for sources of unity is especially important in what Justice THURGOOD MARSHALL aptly described in *Gillette v. United States* (1971) as "a Nation of enormous heterogeneity in respect of political views, moral codes, and religious persuasions." The Constitution overcomes such heterogeneity by offering the individual membership in what one nineteenth-century analyst termed a "covenanting community." From this perspective, it is the Constitution that provides the political basis of the "unum" that overcomes the "pluribus" of American civil society.

One way of achieving this ostensible unity is by explicitly asking (or demanding) that the citizenry pledge commitment to it. The Constitution itself, in Article VI, even as it prohibits religious tests for public office, formally requires all public officials to take an oath recognizing the supremacy of the Constitution over alternate sources of political authority. Such oaths are scarcely meaningless. Thus, Justice WILLIAM J. BRENNAN, when asked if he had "ever had difficulty dealing with [his] own religious beliefs in terms of cases," responded by pointing to the oath he had taken upon appointment to the Court in 1956 as having "settled in my mind that I had an obligation under the Constitution which could not be influenced by any of my religious principles. . . . To the extent that [any duty of a Roman Catholic] conflicts with what I think the Constitution means or requires, then my religious beliefs have to give way."

Not only public officials must take oaths of allegiance to the Constitution: nationalized citizens since 1790 have been required to take an oath of allegiance not simply to the United States but to the Constitution. The United States has been rent by recurrent controversy over the propriety of loyalty oaths as a means both of achieving unity and of identifying those who, by their unwillingness to subscribe to such oaths, are insufficiently integrated into the civil faith.

Although analyzing the Constitution in terms of American civil religion is suggested here, the emphasis on the Constitution as the basis of unity has limits. No doubt there is some validity to this notion, but its adherents often overlook the extent to which shared belief in the abstract idea of the Constitution may often generate significant political conflict, including civil war. Just as the history of traditional religion is replete with actual, often extremely bitter, conflict even among persons purporting to share a common faith, so does the history of constitutional faith present a far more complex picture than the conventional focus on unity would suggest. The notion of the Constitution as the focus of attention in an American civil religion may have more ominous implications than are suggested by an analysis that sees only unity as the outcome of such attention.

Indeed, there are direct analogies between the cleavages observed within traditional religious communities and those seen within the American constitutional community. Two questions common to law and religion seem especially important. First, what constitutes the body of materials that counts as authoritative teachings for the community organized as a faith community? Within traditional religion, this question can take the form of debates about "canonical" texts, for example. But a recurrent struggle, seen vividly, in the history of Western Christianity, concerns the propriety of viewing as authoritative only the materials within a closed body of canonical texts. Counter to such a textual, or scriptural, understanding would be one emphasizing as well the authority of traditions derived from sources other than these canonical texts. From an early time the Catholic church invoked the propriety of its own teachings as a supplement to the teachings of the Bible. That propriety, of course, was specifically challenged by those Protestant reformers who took "Only the Scriptures" as their cry and rejected all nonscriptural teachings as totally without authority.

The second question common to law and religion centers on the need for an institutional structure that can authoritatively resolve disputes. Against the claims of the particular institutional authority of the Vatican, Protestants asserted a "priesthood of all believers" that could come to its own conclusions about the meaning of scripture. The more radical Protestant sects were often accused, not unfairly, of being anarchic in their implications. These are obviously oversimplified "ideal typical" evocations of Catholicism and Protestantism (which have their analogues within Judaism and Islam as well). Nonetheless, how might they help to illuminate the role played by the Constitution within the overall structure of American political culture?

What constitutes the Constitution? Is it composed only of the particular words of the canonical text associated with the outcome of the CONSTITUTIONAL CONVENTION OF 1787, as amended thereafter, or does it also include "unwritten" materials that are equally authoritative? Second, does there exist a particular institution whose interpretations of the Constitution (however defined) are treated as authoritative? Both of these questions allow divergent responses, each of them with their Protestant and Catholic analogues.

As to the first dimension, it is almost certainly true that

an important strain of American constitutionalism is Protestant inasmuch as it emphasizes, like Chief Justice JOHN MARSHALL in MARBURY V. MADISON (1803), a "reverence" for written constitutions, with the linked suggestion that the Constitution consists *only* of what is written down. Perhaps the most important twentieth-century judicial explicator of this strain was Justice HUGO L. BLACK, who began his book *A Constitutional Faith* (1968) by stating, "It is of paramount importance to me that our country has a written constitution." More recent adherents include former Attorney General Edwin Meese and ROBERT H. BORK, whose defeat for a seat on the Supreme Court can be explained in part by his antagonism to the legitimacy of any notion of an UNWRITTEN CONSTITUTION on which judges could draw equally with the written one.

The competing view, emphasizing a more Catholic, unwritten dimension to the Constitution, goes back at least as far as *Marbury*. Indeed, Justice SAMUEL CHASE made free reference to "certain vital principles in our free Republican government" that would "overrule an apparent and flagrant abuse of legislative power" even if not explicitly expressed. Many other Justices, including Chief Justice Marshall himself in FLETCHER V. PECK (1810), have expressed similar sentiments.

The most important modern Justice in this tradition is almost certainly JOHN MARSHALL HARLAN, who joined in an epic debate with Justice Black in the 1965 decision GRISWOLD V. CONNECTICUT, in which the Court invalidated a Connecticut birth control law on the grounds that it violated the RIGHT OF PRIVACY. Justice Black dissented. He could "find in the Constitution no language which either specifically or implicitly grants to all individuals a constitutional "right to privacy." Though he "like[d] my privacy as well as the next person," he refused to find it protected against state interference. For Black, evocation of an unwritten aspect of the Constitution threatened a return to the discredited jurisprudence of LOCHNER V. NEW YORK (1905) and its endorsement of a nontextual FREEDOM OF CONTRACT. Harlan, however, joined in striking down the Connecticut law and endorsed the necessity when interpreting DUE PROCESS OF LAW to look at "what history teaches are the traditions from [this country] developed as well as the traditions from which it broke. That tradition is a living thing." A central fault line of debate within the Supreme Court can thus be understood as pitting "Protestants," who emphasize a solely textual Constitution, against "Catholics," who look to unwritten tradition as well.

The second dimension of the Protestant-Catholic distinction—that concerning institutional authority—does not so much explain debate within the Supreme Court as it does the fundamental debate about the primacy of the Court as an expositor of the meaning of the Constitution.

The Court has several times in the modern era, most notably in the 1958 Little Rock school case COOPER V. AARON, interpreted *Marbury* to stand for the proposition that it is the "ultimate interpreter" of the Constitution. Justice Black, however Protestant his theory of the Constitution, was thoroughly Catholic in his embrace of the ultimate authority of the Supreme Court as constitutional interpreter.

Not surprisingly, it has usually been nonjudges who have proclaimed the merits of a more Protestant understanding of judicial authority. A classic account was given by President ANDREW JACKSON in his 1832 message (written by ROGER BROOKE TANEY) vetoing on constitutional grounds the renewal of the charter of the BANK OF THE UNITED STATES. He dismissed Marshall's opinion in MCCULLOCH V. MARYLAND (1819), which upheld the constitutionality of the bank, stating that the "authority" of the Supreme Court opinions was restricted only to "such influence as the force of their reasoning may deserve." ABRAHAM LINCOLN, when running against STEPHEN A. DOUGLAS for the Senate in 1858, took a similar stance in regard to the infamous DRED SCOTT V. SANDFORD decision of the previous year. More recently, former Attorney General Meese provoked significant controversy when he criticized JUDICIAL SUPREMACY and called for recognizing the primacy of the Constitution as against the decisions of the Supreme Court. Meese was castigated by many who not only defended the role of the Court as "ultimate interpreter" but also pronounced Meese's views as having dangerously anarchic tendencies.

To the extent that one accepts a reading of traditional religion as providing a base for disruption and fragmentation as well as unity, one should be prepared to accept the suggestion that the Constitution-oriented civil religion will have similar aspects and tendencies. In particular, the debates about the sources underlying legitimate decision making and about institutional authority to give privileged interpretations are likely to last at least as long as the schism between the Roman Catholic church and Protestant sects, however much the proponents of any given view would like to bring the debate to an end through surrender by the other side.

Finally, one should note that some critics have condemned the notion of civil religion not so much on empirical grounds—they often concede the existence of the phenomenon analyzed by Bellah, Lerner, and others—but rather on normative grounds. Embrace of the tenets of constitutional faith has been described by some of these critics as the equivalent of idolatry. They argue instead that constitutional faith, however important, must always be judged by the distinctly different claims of more traditional faith communities.

SANFORD LEVINSON
(1992)

(SEE ALSO: *Constitution and Civic Ideals; Political Philosophy of the Constitution.*)

Bibliography

BELLAH, ROBERT 1970 Civil Religion in America. Pages 168–189 in Bellah, ed., *Beyond Belief*. New York: Harper & Row.

GREY, THOMAS C. 1984 The Constitution as Scripture. *Stanford Law Review* 37:1–25.

KAMMER, MICHAEL 1986 *A Machine That Would Go of Itself: The Constitution in American Culture.* New York: Knopf.

LERNER, MAX 1937 Constitution and Court as Symbol. *Yale Law Journal* 42:1290–1319.

LEVINSON, SANFORD 1988 *Constitutional Faith.* Princeton, N.J.: Princeton University Press.

CONSTITUTION AS LITERATURE

Although presumably no one would say that the Constitution offers its readers an experience that cannot be distinguished from reading a poem or a novel, there is nonetheless a sense in which it is a kind of highly imaginative literature in its own right (indeed its nature as law requires that this be so), the reading of which may be informed by our experience of other literary forms. But to say this may be controversial, and the first step toward understanding how such a claim can be made may be to ask what it is we think characterizes imaginative literature in the first place.

It is common in our culture to marginalize "high literature," even while admiring it, and this mainly by thinking of it as offering nothing more than a refined pleasure, merely aesthetic in kind, and by assuming that it can therefore have nothing to do with practical affairs, with money or power. Those who think of themselves as literary people sometimes reciprocate with a marginalization of their own, speaking as if the merely practical offered nothing of interest to one who is devoted to what Wallace Stevens once called "the finer things of life." But this mutual marginalization impoverishes both sides, and the rest of us too, for it rests on a false dichotomy, between the aesthetic and the practical, which is like—and related to—those between fact and fiction, form and content, science and art.

For there is an important sense in which all literature is constitutive, great literature greatly so, of the resources of culture, which are simultaneously employed and remade in the creation of the text, and of what might be called the textual community as well. (By this I mean the relations that each text establishes between its author and its reader, and between those two and the others that it talks about.)

Beginning with the second point, we can say that every text, whether self-consciously literary or not, establishes what Aristotle called an ethos (or character) for its speaker and its reader and for those it speaks about as well; in addition, it establishes, or tries to establish, a relation among these various actors. In this sense every text is socially and ethically constitutive, a species of ethical and political action, and can be understood and judged as such. In fact, we make judgments of this sort all the time—although perhaps crudely so—for example whenever we find a politician's speech patronizing or a commercial advertisement manipulative or when we welcome frank correction at the hand of a friend.

The first point, that the text reconstitutes its culture, is perhaps more familiar, for we have long seen works of art as remaking the culture out of which they are made. This observation establishes a significant connection between the Constitution (and other legal texts) on the one hand and literary texts on the other; for in both, the material of the past is reworked in the present, and part of the art of each of these kinds of literature is the transformation, or reconstitution, of its resources.

To say this is to leave open, of course, the question how, and by what standards, such judgments of art and ethics are to be made. To pursue this question would be the work of a volume at least; let it suffice here to say these are judgments that expression of all sorts permits and that expression of a self-conscious kind—in the law and in fiction, as well as poetry and history—invites. Perhaps we can say in addition that through the reading of texts that address this question in interesting and important ways we may hope to develop our own capacities of analysis and judgment. For present purposes, the point is simply to suggest that once literature is seen as socially and culturally constitutive, the connection with the Constitution, and with the judicial literature elaborating it, may seem less strange than it otherwise might.

This line of thought began by rethinking what we mean by literature. We might wish to start from the other side, by thinking again about our ways of imagining law. In our culture the law is all too often seen simply as a set of rules or directives issuing from a sovereign to be obeyed or disobeyed by those subject to it. This is the understanding—crudely positivistic—that for many years dominated much of our theoretical thinking and much of our teaching as well; it still holds sway deeper in our minds than we may like to admit. In fact, as the history of the Constitution itself demonstrates with exemplary clarity, the meaning of legal directives is not self-evident or self-established, but requires the participation of readers who offer a variety of interpretations, often in competition with each other. In this sense the readers, as well as the writers, of our central legal texts are makers of the law, and any view of the law and the Constitution should reflect this fact.

Law is perhaps best thought of, then, not as a structure

of rules, but as a set of activities and practices through which people engage both with their language (and with the rest of their cultural inheritance) and with each other. One of its aims, deeply literary in character, is to give meaning to experience in language; this is the backward-looking role of law. When it looks forward, as it does above all in the Constitution (but also in contracts, statutes, loan agreements, and trust indentures), it seeks to establish through language a set of relations among various actors, each of whom is given by the legal text certain tasks, obligations, or opportunities that otherwise would not exist, but none of which can be perfectly defined in language. By its nature, then, the legal text gives rise to a set of rhetorical and literary activities through which alone it can work.

The point of such a line of thought is not to assert there is no difference between a judicial opinion, or a constitutional amendment, and a lyric poem—that would be silly—but that, by looking to the deeper structures of the activities in which we engage, we may see them as sharing certain concerns and do this in ways that improve our capacity to understand, to judge, and to perform them. We may perhaps free literature from the veil drawn over it by the claim that it is merely aesthetic and, at the same time, free law from its veil, made of the claims that it is purely practical, only about power, or simply a branch of one of the policy sciences.

The Constitution is constitutive in the two ways in which every text is: it recasts the material of its tradition into new forms, for good or ill; and it establishes a set of relations among the actors it addresses and defines. The first point is historical and quite familiar and usually takes the form of observing that the U.S. Constitution is not a wholly radical innovation, but built upon certain models—British and colonial—out of which it grew. To this fact indeed it owes much of its durability and, perhaps as well, much of its capacity to make what really was new (that is, dual sovereignty) both intelligible and real. The second point is really a suggested way of reading the Constitution: not as a document allocating something called "power" but as a rhetorical creation defining new places and occasions for talk, creating new speakers, and establishing conditions of guidance and restraint. All of these activities are imperfectly determinate and therefore call for the literary and rhetorical practices of reading and writing, interpretation and argument, that lie at the center of the law. Before the Constitution was adopted, none of its official actors existed; there was no President, no Senate, no Supreme Court. One of the effects of the text, as ratified, was to bring these actors into existence. But that is not the end of it; every act of these new actors depends for its validity upon a claim, implied or expressed, about the meaning of the Constitution itself, and every such claim

is in principle open to argument. This is not to say that the Constitution is incoherent, but that as a work of language it has much uncertainty built into it. In fact, it has the only kind of coherence that is open for human institutions to have.

This brings us to the most obvious, and best rehearsed, connection between literature and the law, especially constitutional law, namely, both of these fields work by the reading of texts, or by what it is now the fashion to call "interpretation." That word, however, is not without its dangers, for it may be taken to imply that an interpreter of a text reproduces in her own prose, in her "interpretation," a statement of what the original text means that is in some sense complete and exhaustive, which can indeed serve as an adequate substitute for it. But in neither literature nor the law can this be done; any "interpretation" is of necessity partial, in the sense that it is both incomplete and motivated by a set of understandings and desires that belong to the present reader (formed though these are in part from the materials of the past). The "interpretation" of an earlier text does not so much restate its meaning as elaborate possibilities of meaning that it has left open; the new text is the product of a new time, as well as the old.

Not solely the product of the present and of its partialities, both law and literature are grounded on the premise that the past speaks to us in texts that illumine and constrain though always incompletely so. Accordingly, there are similar interpretive vices in both fields; for example, the attempt to collapse the text, with all its difficulties and uncertainties, into some simplified statement of its "plain meaning," all too often in denial of the uncertainties that both kinds of texts necessarily have and with them the responsibilities for judgment that they generate. Or we may seek simplicity in another direction, defining the meaning of the text by reference to something outside it (for example, the biography of the writer or the "original intention" of the framer or legislator), usually without recognizing that what we think of ourselves as simply referring to is also, in part at least, our own creation—a text which itself requires interpretation. The result of both of these methods is the hidden arrogation of power to the so-called interpreters, who pretend to yield to an external authority, but actually exercise the power in question themselves. Or the vice may be of an opposite kind: to see so much complexity and indeterminacy in a text as to make its responsible reading hopeless and to say, therefore, that nothing can be clear but our own desires (if those) and that no respect needs to be paid (because none can) to the putatively authoritative texts of others. At its extreme, the tendency of this method is to destroy both law and culture.

In both kinds of work the process of reading requires

a toleration of ambiguity and uncertainty: a recognition of complexity, an acknowledgment that our own habits of mind condition both what we see in a text and what we feel about it, and a relinquishment of the hope of universal and absolute clarity. Yet it requires a recognition as well that the past can speak to the present, that culture can be transmitted and transformed, that it is possible, and worth doing, to look beyond ourselves to that which we have inherited from others. Here, in this uncertain struggle to discover and state meaning, to establish a connection with the texts of another, is the life of law and literature alike.

One feature of legal interpretation that is distinctive, or distinctively clear, and of special relevance to the Constitution is its idealizing character. The reading of legal texts inherently involves us in the expression of our ideals, and this in two ways. First, whenever we interpret the Constitution, or any other legal text, we necessarily imagine for it an author, with a certain imagined character and set of values, situated in a certain set of circumstances, and actuated by a certain set of motives or aims. For whatever our theory may pretend, the text cannot be read simply as an abstract order or as the decontextualized statement of an idea; it must be read as the work of a mind speaking to minds. Thus, in our every act of interpretation we define—indeed, we create—a mind behind the text. This is necessarily the expression of an ideal; although, of course, our sense of the past helps to shape it, and to call it an ideal is not to say that it is one that all people share. But we idealize the speakers of the law, or it is not law.

Second, the literature of the law is inherently idealizing in the way in which lawyers idealize their official audiences. We speak to a judge not as to the small-minded angry person we actually think him to be, but as his own version of the wisest and best judge in the world, as we imagine it. And the judge too speaks not to a world of greedy, selfish, and lazy people, as he may see us, but to an ideal audience, the best version of the public he can imagine. In both cases our acts of imagining are acts of idealization for which we are responsible; it is in this way the nature of law to make the ideal real.

JAMES BOYD WHITE
(1992)

(SEE ALSO: *Constitutional Interpretation*)

Bibliography
LEUBSDORF, JOHN 1987 Deconstructing the Constitution. *Stanford Law Review* 40:181–201.
VINING, JOSEPH 1986 *The Authoritative and The Authoritarian.* Chicago: University of Chicago Press.
WHITE, JAMES BOYD 1984 *When Words Lose Their Meaning: Constitutions and Reconstitutions of Language, Character, and Community.* Chapter 9. Chicago: University of Chicago Press.

CONTEMPT POWER, JUDICIAL

The Constitution nowhere mentions contempt of court. The courts' powers in this area flow instead from a COMMON LAW tradition of debated antiquity and legitimacy. Contempt power has, however, become entangled with the Constitution in two respects: first, courts have had to explain how they came to exercise a power that in some respects seems antithetical to constitutional values; second, the Constitution has been held to limit some aspects of the courts' exercise of contempt power.

Contempt is the disobedience of a court's order or interference with its processes. Most judicial decrees are not orders to do or refrain from doing some act. Contempt would not arise, for example, from the simple failure to pay a money judgment. Some judgments, however, directly order a party to perform or refrain from performing some act. A court might order a party to transfer land, to integrate a school system, to cease polluting a stream, to answer questions put by the other side, or to refrain from obstructive behavior in the courtroom.

Having disobeyed such an order, one might be charged with a crime (since many jurisdictions make such acts criminal) or with contempt. Either charge might result in a fine or jail sentence, but the accompanying process might differ. For some categories of contempt the contemnor may suffer punishment without many of the rights normally attaching to criminal trials: to be represented by counsel, to prepare for trial, to present testimony, to cross-examine witnesses, or to have a TRIAL BY JURY. The list is extreme and would not apply to all of the often confusing categories of contempt developed by the courts, but it illustrates the potentially drastic nature of the power.

Courts employ such "criminal" contempt sanctions to redress judicial dignity, but individual litigants may also use contempt sanctions to gain the benefit of court orders. A party seeking to compel obedience to an INJUNCTION entered at his request may ask a court for a "civil" contempt sanction. Such a sanction typically orders the contemnor to jail or to the payment of a progressively mounting fine until he "purges" himself of the contempt by obeying the injunction in question. Though an accused civil contemnor enjoys the rights of counsel, testimony, and cross-examination, his hearing has none of the protections accorded criminal defendants, for the courts have held that this is a "civil" rather than a "criminal" proceeding in spite of the risk of imprisonment. Nor is the duration of the imprisonment or the size of the fine subject to any limitation save the discretion of the judge and the contemnor's continuing ability to perform the act required of him.

Justifying the use of apparently criminal penalties without protections constitutionally accorded criminal defendants, the courts have relied on claims of history, necessity, and categorization. The claim of history has rested on the propositions that at the time the Constitution was framed courts had long exercised contempt powers and that the Framers did not intend to alter them. Those claims have been challenged but are still made. The claim of necessity still urges the need for orderly adjudicatory proceedings and enforceable orders. The argument rests on the hypothesis that, were the usual restrictions of the BILL OF RIGHTS to apply to contempt proceedings, the courts would be unable to function. The argument from categorization involves simply the assertion that because neither civil nor criminal contempts involve "crimes," the portions of the Bill of Rights applicable to crimes do not apply. In the case of imprisonment for civil contempt this argument is bolstered by the circumstance that the contemnor has the power at any time to obtain his release by complying with the order—a power not enjoyed by a convicted criminal.

Though the courts' exercise of contempt power has thus been remarkable for the absence of constitutional constraints, some limits do exist. First, state and federal legislatures have statutorily required greater protections that the Constitution mandates. Second, the Supreme Court has imposed some constitutional limits: in criminal contempts the judge must find the defendant guilty beyond a reasonable doubt; in "indirect" contempts (those not committed before a judge or involving judicial officers) the contemnor is, in addition, accorded the rights of counsel, testimony, and cross-examination. Even in cases of direct contempt the contemnor may have a trial by jury if the judge proposes to inflict a serious penalty. Yet even in enunciating these protections, the Court has steadfastly insisted that the judge has a wide power to impose sentence on the spot for contemptuous behavior in the courtroom.

Judicial use of contempt power involves a collision between two *desiderata:* that of having tribunals able to conduct their proceedings and enforce their orders; and that of having persons whose freedom stands in jeopardy enjoy the protections of the Bill of Rights. Thus far the courts have concluded that in many situations the first goal necessitates subordinating the second.

STEPHEN C. YEAZELL
(1986)

Bibliography

GOLDFARB, RONALD L. 1963 *The Contempt Power.* New York: Columbia University Press.

CONTEMPT POWER, JUDICIAL
(Update)

Contempt is an ancient process for punishing disrespect for, disruption of, or disobedience of a lawful order of the government. For centuries in England and the United States the process was essentially unregulated. Individual judges and legislative houses defined and punished contempt as they saw fit.

Arguably, little has changed. Federal contempt statutes are notoriously vague and do not limit the power to punish. Although contempt of Congress proceedings are not unheard of, most modern contempt proceedings (including contempt of Congress) involve the judiciary. Contempt is invoked to deal with conduct ranging from misbehavior in court, to refusals to supply information, to failures to make support payments, to disobedience of orders regulating protests at ABORTION clinics, and much else.

Contempt is nowhere mentioned in the Constitution, but repeated instances of serious abuse have led the Supreme Court to impose both substantive and procedural limits on the contempt power, relying on various provisions of the Constitution.

For example, judges long used contempt to punish those who criticized their decisions. The Court has in the last fifty years repeatedly held that such punishments abridge the FIRST AMENDMENT guarantee of FREEDOM OF SPEECH.

Another battle involved the right of accused contemnors to TRIAL BY JURY. Historically, there was no such right; however, the contempt power was frequently employed to deny jury trials for alleged conduct that constituted both crimes and violations of court orders. The Court, recognizing the judge's inherent conflict of interest in a proceeding to vindicate the dignity and authority of the court, OVERRULED centuries of PRECEDENT and held that the Sixth Amendment required a jury trial for serious contempt punishments.

Much in the law of contempt turns on the murky distinction between "civil" and "criminal" contempt. The distinction does not depend on whether the allegedly contumacious conduct constitutes a crime, but rather on the purpose of the contempt proceeding. If it is to punish a past act of contempt, the proceeding is said to be "criminal," and most of the constitutional protections afforded criminal defendants apply. If the purpose is to coerce compliance with an existing order—for example, by a cumulative fine or jail sentence until the contemnor obeys—or to compensate a party injured by the contumacious conduct, the proceeding is said to be "civil," and is governed by the more general standard of DUE PROCESS OF LAW. The civil/criminal distinction is difficult to apply, especially where on-going acts allegedly violate a judicial order, and thus all three purposes may be served by the same proceeding. This has led to much confusion over the procedural protections available to those accused of contempt.

Another distinction contributing to procedural confusion is between "direct" and "indirect" contempts. A "direct" contempt is an act of disrespect or disobedience personally observed by the judge. On the theory that no fact-finding process is necessary, "direct" contempts may be punished "summarily," that is, without a formal trial. "Indirect" contempts involve conduct outside the presence of the judge, requiring some form of trial to determine what occurred. Despite efforts by judges to expand the category of "direct" contempts, the Court has limited the summary contempt power as a matter of due process to acts committed in the judge's presence requiring immediate response to protect the court's ability to function.

The law of contempt thus presents many difficult issues. In addition to the procedurally confusing distinctions, there is still neither a generally accepted definition of contumacious behavior nor a framework for assessing the appropriate severity of sanctions. And there is the recurring problem posed by those who prove impervious to coercive contempt sanctions, some of whom endure years of incarceration rather than comply. The Court may tell us in the future how the Constitution applies to these and other questions.

EARL C. DUDLEY, JR.
(2000)

(SEE ALSO: *Clinton v. Jones.*)

Bibliography

BRAUTIGAM, RICHARD C. 1972 Constitutional Challenges to the Contempt Power. *Georgetown Law Journal* 60:1513–1536.

DOBBS, DAN B. 1971 Contempt of Court: A Survey. *Cornell Law Review* 56:183–284.

DUDLEY, EARL C., JR. 1993 Getting Beyond the Civil/Criminal Distinction: A New Approach to the Regulation of Indirect Contempts. *Virginia Law Review* 79:1025–1098.

FOX, SIR JOHN C. 1927 *The History of Contempt of Court.* Oxford, England: Clarendon Press.

GOLDFARB, RONALD 1963 *The Contempt Power.* New York: Columbia University Press.

KUHNS, RICHARD B. 1978 The Summary Contempt Power: A Critique and New Perspective. *Yale Law Journal* 88:39–123.

OSWALD, JAMES F. 1892 *Contempt of Court, Committal, and Attachment and Arrest Upon Civil Process in the Supreme Court of Judicature.* London, England: W. Clowes.

RAVESON, LOUIS S. 1990 A New Perspective on the Judicial Contempt Power: Recommendations for Reform. *Hastings Constitutional Law Quarterly* 18:1–65.

CONTEMPT POWER, LEGISLATIVE

See: Legislative Contempt Power

CONTINENTAL CONGRESS

On September 5, 1774, delegates from the colonies convened in Philadelphia in a "Continental" Congress, so called to differentiate it from local or provincial congresses. The FIRST CONTINENTAL CONGRESS adopted a Declaration and Resolves to protest British measures and promote American rights; it also adopted the ASSOCIATION. The Congress dissolved on October 24, 1774, having decided that the colonies should meet again if necessary on May 10, 1775. By that time, the colonies and Great Britain were at war. The Second Continental Congress adopted a Declaration of the Causes and Necessity of Taking Up Arms on July 6, 1775, and the DECLARATION OF INDEPENDENCE a year later. The Congress appointed GEORGE WASHINGTON as commander-in-chief of its armies, directed the war, managed FOREIGN AFFAIRS, and adopted a plan of union designated as the ARTICLES OF CONFEDERATION. After the thirteenth state ratified the Articles in 1781, the official governing body of the United States became known as "the Congress of the Confederation," but it was a continuation of the Continental Congress and was not reconstituted until 1789, when a Congress elected under the Constitution of the United States took office.

LEONARD W. LEVY
(1986)

Bibliography

BERNETT, EDMUND C. 1941 *The Continental Congress.* New York: Macmillan.

CONTRACEPTION

See: Birth Control; *Griswold v. Connecticut*; Reproductive Autonomy

CONTRACT CLAUSE

In a flashing aperçu Sir Henry Maine observed that "the movement of progressive societies has hitherto been a movement from Status to Contract." In feudal systems a person acquired a fixed, social status by birth, one's legal rights and duties being determined thereby for life. The decline of feudalism was a fading away of the status system in favor of personal rights and duties based largely on contractual relationships. Obligations imposed by ancestry gave way to obligations voluntarily undertaken. Generally thereafter a person's place in society depended upon success or failure in covenants with respect, for example, to wages, raw materials, farm and industrial goods, or artistic talent. In such a setting it is crucial that agreements be dependable—not merely to promote the individual's security and mobility but for the good of a society that relies for its sustenance upon a vast network of voluntary, contractual relationships. Thus Article I, section 10, of the Constitution, reflecting in part unfortunate experience under the ARTICLES OF CONFEDERATION, forbids *inter alia* state laws "impairing the OBLIGATION OF CONTRACTS." In THE FEDERALIST #44, JAMES MADISON, observed that such laws "are contrary to the first principles of the SOCIAL COMPACT and to every principle of sound legislation." In his view "the sober people of America" were "weary of fluctuating" legislative policy, and wanted reform that would "inspire a general prudence and industry, and give a regular course to the business of society."

Indeed the sanctity of contracts was deemed so vital to personal security that in fifty-five years following the Supreme Court's first contract clause decision (FLETCHER V. PECK, 1810), twenty-two states put such provisions in their own constitutions. With one exception each of them was included in the state's bill of rights. Prior to 1810 four states had already done this. All of them protected contracts generally (per *Fletcher*), not merely private contracts as in the NORTHWEST ORDIANCE. Plainly in JOHN MARSHALL's day and long thereafter his Court's broad view of the contract clause was widely accepted—along with FREEDOM OF RELIGION, and FAIR TRIALS—as one of those restrictions on government "which serve to protect the most valuable rights of the citizen."

Obviously those who thus equated property rights and civil liberty were—like the Founding Fathers and the MARSHALL COURT—disciples of JOHN LOCKE. He had taught that property and liberty go hand in hand; that neither thrives without the other; that to protect them both as indispensable to life itself is the reason for government. Generations later, in a radically changed economic setting, some Americans came to believe that property hampers liberty. Inevitably then (having forgotten Locke) they would misunderstand both the founders and our early judges—Lockians all. Thus the Progressive movement convinced itself and its heirs that the Marshall Court had erred in holding the contract clause applicable to state, that is, public, covenants and that in so holding the judges had revealed a pro-property bias. Both of these views—derived largely from *Fletcher* and *Dartmouth College v. Woodward* (1819)—seem erroneous. The first rests on the strange idea that unambiguous language of the Constitution means not what it plainly says, but rather something else, because of the supposed intent of its authors. (Of course authors' intent may be a proper key to the meaning of ambiguous terminology, but that is a very different matter.)

Had the CONSTITUTIONAL CONVENTION OF 1787 wanted the clause to cover only private agreements, that is, those between individuals, it need only have said so. The Continental Congress had done just that in the Northwest Ordinance: "... no law ought ever to be made, or to have force in the said territory, that shall in any manner whatever, interfere with or affect private contracts. . . ." Six weeks later, RUFUS KING moved to include its private contract approach in the Constitution. Following a brief discussion of possible ramifications of such a provision, it was dropped. A few days later, at the suggestion of the Committee of Style, the Constitutional Convention adopted the contract clause, which refers comprehensively to "contracts" without qualification. Nothing in our record of the proceedings explains the change of mind or the change of terminology. But this is certain: not a word there or in *The Federalist* even hints that the founders were concerned only with private covenants—that they thought a state should be free to violate its own agreements. ALEXANDER HAMILTON would later observe: "It is . . . impossible to reconcile the idea of a [state] promise which obliges, with a power to make a law which can vary the effect of it." Hamilton, of course, had been a member of the Constitutional Convention.

Long before John Marshall became a judge, Justice JAMES WILSON, in CHISHOLM V. GEORGIA (1793), had asked rhetorically: "What good purpose could this constitutional provision secure if a state might pass a law impairing the obligation of its own contracts, and be amendable, for such a violation of right, to no controlling judiciary power?" This from one who had been perhaps the second most important leader of the Constitutional Convention. Justice WILLIAM PATERSON, too, had been influential at the Convention. Years before *Fletcher* in a similar case, VAN HORNE'S LESSEE V. DORRANCE (1795), he had held that a state could not impair its own contractual obligations. So did the highest court of Massachusetts in *Derby v. Blake* (1799) and in *Wales v. Stetson* (1806). *Fletcher* was not without significant judicial precedent.

The argument that the contract clause does not mean what it says rests essentially on the proposition that the crucial contract problem in late eighteenth-century America was erosion of private contract obligations by debtors' relief legislation. No doubt this was a vexing and well-known difficulty. Yet surely it is no *ipso facto* basis for excluding related problems plainly covered by explicit constitutional language. State negligence with respect to state obligations was after all a matter of experience. Even if it were known that the Framers intended the written words to embrace only private contracts, judges could not properly adopt that view. For those who ratified can hardly be said to have ratified something other than the words of the document. To hold otherwise is to undermine the basic premise of a written constitution. As the Marshall Court put it in orthodox manner in *Dartmouth:* "This case being within the words of the Contract Clause, must be within its operation likewise, unless there be something in the literal construction so obviously absurd or mischievous, or repugnant to the general spirit of the instrument, as to justify those who expound the constitution in making it an exception. . . ." No such basis for an exception having been discovered, the Supreme Court ever since has found the contract clause applicable as written to contracts generally, whether public or private.

A related problem in *Fletcher* concerned the scope of the term "contract." The Georgia legislature had sold and granted to speculators millions of acres of public land. A subsequent legislature had repealed the grant on the ground that it had been obtained by bribery. Meanwhile part of the land had been conveyed to innocent third-party purchasers. The issue in *Fletcher* was whether the initial grant entailed obligations protected against impairment by the contract clause. The Court responded affirmatively. Of course, in modern usage a grant is not a contract, but that does not solve the problem. For it is quite clear that in the late eighteenth century the term "contract" had far broader connotations than it does today. As Dean ROSCOE POUND has explained:

> Contract was then used, and was used as late as Parsons on Contracts in 1853 to mean [what] might be called "legal transaction." . . . Not merely contract as we now understand it, but trust, will, conveyance, and grant of a franchise are included. . . . The writers on natural law considered that there was a natural legal duty not to derogate from one's grant. . . . This is the explanation of *Fletcher*, . . . and no doubt is what the [contract clause] meant to those who wrote it into the Constitution. ["The Charles River Bridge Case," *Massachusetts Law Quarterly* 27:19–20.]

In sum, in the context of the times a grant included an executory, contractual obligation of the grantor not to violate the terms of his grant.

On this and the public contract aspect of Marshall's opinions one finds no criticism or disagreement in a random selection of twelve legal treatises published before 1870, including THOMAS M. COOLEY's famous *Constitutional Limitations* (1868). Twelve years later, however, Cooley's *General Principles of Constitutional Law* (1880) took a somewhat critical stand. The change apparently reflected attacks upon the Marshall Court by C. M. Hill, R. Hutchinson, and J. M. Shirley writing separately in the *American Law Review* and the *Southern Law Review* from 1874 to 1879. In due course the Progressives would pick up these charges that the Marshall Court had erred, and they would add that "the great Chief Justice" was in fact "a stalwart . . . reactionary," a servant of property interests. It seems no coincidence that the Hill-Hutchinson-Shirley attacks germinated in an era (1865–1873) when nearly sixty percent of laws challenged under the contract clause were

held invalid—an all-time high. Many such cases of course "favored" business interests and thus tended to offend Progressives. The result was that John Marshall became for them a villain.

Fletcher, of course, upheld the property claims of innocent, third-party purchasers. The alternative would have been to sustain the property claims of the innocent people of Georgia. Either way the judges would be deciding in favor of some, and against other, property interests. Either way innocent people would suffer. One fails to see how *Fletcher* can be said to reveal a property bias. Was there, however, bias of another sort in deciding for the ultimate buyers rather than for the initial owners? Far from exceptional, the choice was informed by a long settled (and still prevailing) rule of Anglo-American EQUITY jurisprudence. Although a fraudulent purchaser takes a good title *at law*, it is subject to cancellation by a chancery decree. Thus in a clash between a cheating buyer and his innocent victim the latter prevails. But *Fletcher* involved a clash between the innocent victim and an equally innocent, subsequent purchaser for value. With the equities thus in balance and the social interest in security of transactions on the side of the purchaser in possession, the chancellor does not intervene (the victim's recourse being an action for damages against the fraudulent party). In short, Marshall and his Court read the contract clause in the light of a long familiar rule of equity.

In the *Dartmouth* case, a group of philanthropists had received a public charter to create a college in New Hampshire. Later the state tried to take over and govern the school contrary to the charter provisions. Marshall's Court, following *Fletcher*, held that the charter was a contract which the state was not free to violate. Viewed narrowly the case was won by the college trustees, but they had no beneficial interest in the college property. They won on behalf of the donor-philanthropists (presumably deceased) and generations of future students.

The Progressive response is that the *Dartmouth* decision was a crafty gambit purposefully designed for an ulterior purpose: protection of corporation charters from legislative interference. That it was highly successful is demonstrated, we are told, by the enormous growth of corporate enterprise thereafter. This is make-believe. Justice JOSEPH STORY in *Dartmouth* pointed out that no state need grant irrevocable or nonamendable charters— that the power to amend or revoke may be reserved. Damage resulting from failure to do so can hardly be held a fault of the judges. In fact reservation of power to alter corporate charters became widespread after *Dartmouth* and was not unknown before. (See RESERVED POLICE POWER.)

Fletcher and *Dartmouth* are not pro-property, but rather pro-transaction, cases. They mean that when judges find no clearly overriding public interest such as they found in GIBBONS V. OGDEN (1824) they will not disturb the contractual arrangements, that is, the *transactions*, by which women and men conduct their affairs—be they philanthropists (*Dartmouth*) or land speculators and farmers (*Fletcher*). As Marshall put it, "the intercourse between man and man would be very seriously obstructed, if this principle be overturned." Incidentally, by killing New York's restrictive steamboat law *Gibbons* too promoted transactional freedom.

An inclination toward unfettered private activity was deep in the temper of the times. Americans were on the make. They had escaped the old-world fetters: king, feudal aristocracy, and established church. They were the "new men." A vast geographical frontier invited initiative and ingenuity. The standard of living was low, but natural resources were plentiful. These conditions put a high premium on private, developmental effort. Such was the setting in which contract clauses found their way into bills of rights along with other basic protections then deemed indispensable to personal freedom and social well-being.

If the Marshall Court found that the Constitution forbade reneging on state obligations, it also recognized that public agreements raised special problems justifying a special rule of strict construction. In PROVIDENCE BANK V. BILLINGS (1830) Rhode Island had chartered the Providence Bank "in the usual form" with no reference of stipulation concerning taxation. Later, when the state enacted a bank tax, Providence Bank argued that a power (taxation) which might be used to destroy its charter was foreclosed by implication. The Court demurred: "as the whole community is interested in retaining [the power to tax] undiminished, that community has a right to insist that its abandonment ought not to be presumed, in a case in which the deliberate purpose to abandon it does not appear." Obviously the mere grant of a corporate charter for an ordinary banking operation could not rationally be held to imply an immunity from routine, nondiscriminatory taxation.

Marshall's Jacksonian successors under Chief Justice ROGER B. TANEY followed the established path with two modifications: a temporary enlargement of the rule of strict construction, and a decision that a state may not by covenant fetter its power of EMINENT DOMAIN. The former occurred in CHARLES RIVER BRIDGE CO. V. WARREN BRIDGE CO. (1837). Massachusetts had authorized private investors to build, operate, and maintain a public drawbridge in exchange for toll rights for a period of forty (later extended to seventy) years. Before that period expired the state authorized a competing, in effect toll-free, bridge only yards away from the original facility. Was the state free thus to jeopardize the revenue of the first bridge, or did the forty-year provision implicitly preclude such interference? It

must have been clear at the outset to all concerned that investors would not provide, maintain, and operate for forty years a public facility, if the state were free at any time to disrupt their only source of compensation. Surely in these circumstances the Marshall rule of strict construction was satisfied; the state's "deliberate purpose" to permit unimpeded toll collection for the period in question seems obvious.

The Taney Court did not repudiate—indeed it purported to follow—the *Providence Bank* rule of strict construction. In fact, it simply ignored the "deliberate purpose" aspect of that rule, and substituted an incompatible principle derived from English precedents: "nothing passes by implication in public grants." (Thus did Harvard College lose part of its endowment.) Justices Story and SMITH THOMPSON dissented on implied agreement grounds. Justice JOHN MCLEAN agreed with them on the merits, but thought the Court lacked JURISDICTION. In substance *Charles River* was a 4–3 decision—although five of the Justices had been appointed by President ANDREW JACKSON, the other two by his Jeffersonian predecessors.

The majority position—exalting form over substance— would have permitted construction of an adjacent, toll-free bridge immediately after construction of the first one. Yet surely no court would so decide. If this be true, the Taney rule against implied agreements must be untenable. The Court seems rarely to have used it, having returned long ago to the Marshall approach. See, for example, NORTHWESTERN FERTILIZING CO. V. HYDE PARK (1878): "Nothing is to be taken as conceded but what is given in unmistakable terms, *or by an implication equally clear*" (emphasis added). The major upshot of the Taney Court's stricter rule of construction was that those who covenanted with a state took care to secure elaborately explicit commitments.

Charles River Bridge exudes liberalism, stressing as it does the social interest in progress. Property rights, the Court proclaimed, must not impede developing technology. Old turnpike charters, for example, should be construed "strictly" lest they block new railroads. But no such clash of old and new was at issue before the Court. The real problem was that after some forty years the Massachusetts legislature had come to believe the tolls were no longer justified—the bridge having long since paid for itself. A severely split Court decided not the real, but a hypothetical, case—demonstrating once again that the framing of the issue largely determines the outcome of a controversy.

The other innovation of the Taney era came in *West River Bridge Co. v. Dix* (1848). Vermont had granted exclusive bridge rights. This did not prevent it from confiscating the grantees' bridge during the life of the grant—

subject of course to JUST COMPENSATION. The Court's rationale was that all contracts are subject to HIGHER LAW conditions. "Such a condition is the right of eminent domain." The indispensable power of taxation, however, is not such a "condition" and thus may be limited by state covenants, as the Court held in PIQUA BRANCH OF THE STATE BANK V. KNOOP (1854). Surely the distinction rests not on "higher law"—whatever that meant to the Court in the *Piqua* opinion—but upon the just compensation requirement in the one situation but not in the other, and the fact that there are many taxpayers and many ways to secure public revenue, but only one recourse when a specific piece of private property stands in the way of the public welfare.

The WAITE COURT followed a similar approach in generously defining the so-called STATE POLICE POWER. Thus a charter to operate a lottery does not bar enforcement of a later antilottery law. "All agree that the legislature can not bargain away the police power," the Court declared in STONE V. MISSISSIPPI (1880). Of course neither the state in question, nor any other, has ever undertaken to "bargain away" its POLICE POWER. The DOCTRINE as enunciated in *Stone* is at best a truism providing no standard for judgment. Had it been used in *Dartmouth*, the school would have lost its case and its independence. In fact, as Gerald Gunther has remarked, the *Stone* police power rule has been used mainly in cases "involving prohibitions of matters widely regarded as "evil": for example, lotteries and intoxicating beverages, in an era when "Court invalidations of state laws impairing corporate charter privileges reached its highest frequency." (See INALIENABLE POLICE POWER.)

The epidemic of railroad fever that began in the Midwest in the 1850s was a prolific source of contract clause litigation. Many towns, cities, counties, and states issued railroad-aid bonds at an overall face value exceeding half a billion dollars. The purpose was to induce railroad companies to build lines convenient to the various bond issuers. Some of the desired construction never materialized. Many, perhaps all, of the railroad companies were overcapitalized. Stock watering was common. Some public and company officials were less than honest. These developments produced widespread resentment which some communities may have used for selfish purposes. In any case, what Henry Adams called the "mortgaged generation" (1865–1895) tried in one form or another to evade or repudiate much of its bond obligation. These circumstances are reflected in the path-breaking case of GELPCKE V. DUBUQUE (1864). After several decisions upholding the authority of cities to issue railroad-aid bonds, the Iowa Supreme Court, reinterpreting state law, reversed itself. On review the nation's highest Court upheld the claims of the adversely affected bondholders. In doing so it inti-

mated that the state court's shift of position, retroactively altering the position of investors, was incompatible with contract clause principles. Popularly elected state judges apparently were more responsive to public sentiment than were appointed members of the federal Supreme Court. Ten years later *Pine Grove Township v. Talcott* (1874) brought the most extreme application of *Gelpcke* doctrine: to situations in which the state judiciary held bond issues invalid without overruling any prior decisions. The Supreme Court's rationale was that similar bond issues had been upheld in many other states before issuance of the bonds in question.

The contract clause intimations in *Gelpcke* and *Pine Grove* became an explicit basis of decision in *Douglass v. Pike* (1880). Much later the Court said that state court decisions did not produce contract obligations, and that neither *Gelpcke* nor its numerous offspring had in fact held otherwise. (*Tidal Oil Co. v. Flanagan*, 1924.)

Along with these bond cases another numerically important group involved the old problem of tax exemption. Without foregetting Marshall's *Providence Bank* rule of strict construction, the Court blocked a series of state efforts to annul pledges of corporate tax immunity.

After 1890 the contract clause as applied to state covenants gradually declined in favor or a more comprehensive, new device called SUBSTANTIVE (economic) DUE PROCESS—a gross perversion of the FOURTEENTH AMENDMENT. Years later, after the demise of that perversion, two cases suggested a possible renaissance of the contract clause. In UNITED STATES TRUST CO. V. NEW JERSEY (1977), the Court expounded a new principle of "particular" (more careful) scrutiny for cases involving public covenants "because the State's self-interest is at stake." New Jersey had issued transportation-system bonds pledging it would not substantially divert to other transportation needs the reserves and revenues securing them. Later it repealed this pledge. State courts upheld the repeal as a police power measure designed to promote additional transportation facilities. The Supreme Court reversed. No longer willing to defer to state determination of such issues, it ruled that judges must decide whether the contract impairment is "reasonable and necessary to serve an important public purpose." In this case it found that the state's needs could be served by less drastic means. In a bitter dissent Justices WILLIAM J. BRENNAN, BYRON R. WHITE, and THURGOOD MARSHALL insisted that for a century the "central principle" had been this: "unusual deference to [state and local] law-making authority." They could not accept a departure "from the virtually unbroken line of our cases" holding that "lawful" exercises of the police power are "paramount to private rights held under contract." The question remains, however, whether a particular exercise of power is lawful.

We turn now from public to private contract problems. No doubt the contract clause was inspired largely by debtor's relief laws, for example, measures authorizing postponed repayment of debts, installment payments, or payment in goods (often at a discount). In the Supreme Court's first encounter with this private contract problem it struck down a New York law discharging debts upon surrender of the debtor's property however inadequate to meet his obligations. Chief Justice Marshall's opinion for a unanimous Court in STURGES V. CROWNINSHIELD (1819) is noteworthy for two points: the "mere existence" of the national BANKRUPTCY POWER does not preclude state insolvency legislation; and, while a state may not impair contract obligations, it may alter the legal sanctions (remedies, such as imprisonment for debt) for enforcement of such obligations. Eight years later OGDEN V. SAUNDERS (1827) construed *Sturges* to prohibit only retrospective application of insolvency measures. Prospective application was deemed a different matter. The Court's rationale was that a debtor relief act in existence at the time of a contract became part of the contract; later enforcement thus would not constitute an impairment. On this basis, however, a retroactive insolvency law could also be upheld. After all, a state's power to adopt future insolvency measures may equally be deemed part of every contract. In his only recorded constitutional dissent "the great Chief Justice" along with Justices GABRIEL DUVALL and Story objected: the 4–3 majority had reduced a safeguard for contract rights to no more than a prohibition on "retrospectivity." Later, we shall see, even this restriction faded away.

Marshall's dissenting view in *Ogden* finds support in two separate votes in the Constitutional Convention. The contract clause of the Northwest Ordinance applied only to "private contracts . . . previously formed." In "copying" it, the Founders (as we have seen) dropped the limiting word "private." *They also dropped the limiting term "previously formed."* Later, on September 15, the Convention reaffirmed this position by rejecting George Mason's motion to insert the word "previous" after the words "obligation of" in the contract clause. Thus on two occasions the convention *rejected* the limitation that *Ogden v. Saunders* read into the Constitution.

The *Sturges* distinction between impairment of obligations and alteration of remedies threatened in later years to undermine the contract clause. Thus BRONSON V. KINZIE (1843), a leading Taney Court decision, taught that the allowable scope of remedial changes depends on their "reasonableness," provided "no substantial right" is impaired. As Justice BENJAMIN N. CARDOZO wrote with characteristic restraint in *Worthen Co. v. Kavanaugh* (1935), the dividing line "is at times obscure." The leading modern case, HOME BUILDING AND LOAN ASSOCIATION V. BLAISDELL (1934), upheld a Minnesota "mortgage moratorium"

law that extended the time of payment of mortgage loans, thus saving many homeowners, farmers, and businesses from foreclosure. The Court used the remedy and police power gambits to escape the *Sturges-Ogden* rule against retroactivity. The significance of the case is this: it is the culmination early in the Great Depression of a long, step-by-step process that replaced the absolute approach of the Constitution with a judicial balancing or "reasonableness" approach in private contract cases. Yet all agree these are the cases that above all else produced the unqualified language of the contract clause. Such absolutism does not mean that the founders were hard-hearted, preferring creditors to debtors. It means merely that, giving debtor-relief authority to Congress via the bankruptcy power, they opted for uniform, national treatment of the ubiquitous debtorcreditor tension.

Notwithstanding *Blaisdell* the "old Court" thereafter struck down several insolvency measures. One of them was LOUISVILLE JOINT STOCK LAND BANK V. RADFORD (1935). In effect it read the contract clause into the Fifth Amendment to invalidate a federal mortgage moratorium law (a matter of reverse INCORPORATION). Then with the advent of the Roosevelt Court in 1937 (until *United States Trust* in 1977) the contract clause all but vanished as a safeguard for contractual obligations—public or private. The only exceptions are *Indiana ex rel. Anderson v. Brand* (1938), protecting teacher tenure claims, and *Wood v. Lovett* (1941), protecting a tax-sale purchaser against repeal of a law that cured possible defects in his title. *Wood* is particularly interesting because it rests on the *Fletcher* principle that a state land grant entails an implied contractual obligation not to repudiate the grant in question. Then came ALLIED STRUCTURAL STEEL CO. V. SPANNAUS (1978). There an employer had adopted an employee pension agreement. The state tried to alter it by enlarging the employer's obligations retroactively. Finding the alternation too "severe" to be upheld, the Court observed: "If the Contract Clause is to retain any meaning at all . . . it must be understood to impose *some* limits upon the power of a State to abridge existing contractual relationships, even in the exercise of its otherwise legitimate police power." As in *United States Trust*, Justices Brennan, White, and Marshall dissented bitterly. Stressing again their view of minimal (or no) protection of economic interests vis-à-vis the police power, they added this: the contract clause at most prevents diminution, not enlargement, of contractual obligations.

All of these cases from *Fletcher* to *Spannaus* entail a common theme: the precept of reasonable expectations. To what extent, if any, is government free to disturb those formal pledges on which men and women acting in good faith have planned their lives? A healthy legal system accommodates changing social needs. When ours was a rich and vigorous, yet underdeveloped, nation with a low overall standard of living, our law encouraged capital formation, transactional freedom, and respect for contract obligations. The "design"—not always and everywhere fully perceived—was to encourage production in the interest of a more comfortable life for everyone. Given the propensity of successful institutions to press beyond the limits of their logic, such encouragement may take grotesque forms, for example, the judicial abuses called DUAL FEDERALISM and substantive due process. If eventually a "backward" nation becomes highly developed, emphasis seemingly shifts from economic rights to "personal rights," from production to welfare, as in the United States beginning in the 1930s. If such a shift results in overreaction, threatening the source of the "golden eggs," emphasis may focus again on production along with protection for property and contractual rights, as in *New Jersey Trust* and *Spannaus*.

WALLACE MENDELSON
(1986)

Bibliography

HALE, ROBERT L.   1944   The Supreme Court and the Contract Clause. *Harvard Law Review* 57:512–557, 621–674, 852–892.

HURST, WILLARD   1956   *Law and the Conditions of Freedom.* Madison: University of Wisconsin Press.

SCHWARTZ, BERNARD   1980   Old Wine in Old Bottles? The Renaissance of the Contract Clause. *Supreme Court Review* 1979:95–121.

WRIGHT, BENJAMIN F.   1938   *The Contract Clause of the Constitution.* Cambridge, Mass.: Harvard University Press.

CONTRACT THEORY

See: Social Compact Theory

CONTROLLED-SUBSTANCE ABUSE

Throughout the quarter-century from 1965 to 1990 the federal government waged a frustrating "war" against the growing problem of trafficking in, and abuse of, marijuana, heroin, cocaine, and other drugs. The government's war on drugs raises a number of issues of constitutional dimension: To what extent does the EQUAL PROTECTION clause permit differences in the regulation of various controlled substances? How specific must regulations be to conform to the requirements of the DUE PROCESS clause? To what extent is the use of controlled substances protected by a constitutional RIGHT OF PRIVACY or by RELIGIOUS LIBERTY? Does the FOURTH AMENDMENT prohibition of unreasonable SEARCH AND SEIZURE contain an exception for

seizure of illicit drugs? Does the prohibition of CRUEL AND UNUSUAL PUNISHMENT impose any limitations on the sanctions imposed on drug offenders?

The FOURTEENTH AMENDMENT guarantee of equal protection of the laws has been interpreted to require a RATIONAL BASIS for governmental classifications. A classification is "underinclusive" if it does not include all who are similarly situated and "overinclusive" if it includes those who do not rationally belong with the other members of a prohibited class. The earliest efforts to regulate the abuse of controlled substances raised substantial issues under the equal protection clause, because they failed to include many drugs and tended to apply the same punitive sanctions to all drugs, despite substantial differences in their dangerousness. In 1937, for example, the Marijuana Tax Act classified marijuana with narcotic drugs, imposing the same harsh penalties for possession of marijuana as for heroin or cocaine. For more than thirty years, the drug policy of the United States recognized no distinctions among drugs. The same strategy was used to control all drugs, and that strategy was simply to keep escalating the penalties. Only one exception was recognized, and that was alcohol. Alcohol was treated as though it were not a drug at all. Drug treatment programs racked it up as a success if they converted a drug addict into an alcoholic. Separate federal bureaucracies were created to deal with alcohol abuse and drug abuse so that no one would get the idea that America's ten million alcoholics were addicted to a drug.

In 1970 the federal Controlled Substances Act codified a comprehensive scheme for the classification of drugs on five different schedules, depending on their potential for abuse, risk of addiction, and legitimate medical use. Penalties for trafficking vary substantially, depending on the schedule on which a drug is placed. Since 1970, continuous legal challenges have been mounted against the classification of marijuana on Schedule I, along with heroin, LSD, and other drugs having no recognized medical use. Other drugs, such as PCP, have been moved from a lower schedule to a higher one as awareness of the potential for their abuse has increased.

The guarantee of due process of law contained in both the Fifth and Fourteenth Amendments has been interpreted to require adequate notice of a criminal prohibition, to ensure both that potential violators can comply with the law and that law enforcement officers are not given broad authority to discriminate in the enforcement of the laws. Laws not meeting this standard are struck down as unconstitutionally vague.

In two spheres drug laws have raised substantial problems of VAGUENESS. The first problem lies in the description of the prohibited drug itself. The development of "designer drugs" in clandestine laboratories has enabled new drugs to appear in the illicit market faster than laws can be amended to prohibit them. Congress responded in 1986 by prohibiting controlled-substances "analogues," which are defined as substances whose chemical structure is "substantially similar" to previously controlled substances. Legal challenges asserting that this language is unconstitutionally vague are currently pending.

Second, attempts to regulate the marketing of drug paraphernalia have run into vagueness challenges, because drug "paraphernalia" include common household objects, such as spoons and scales. In 1982 the Supreme Court upheld an ordinance regulating the sale of items "designed or marketed for use with illegal cannabis or drugs." The Court concluded that any problem of vagueness was cured by a requirement of proof of actual intent that the items be used for illegal purposes.

The constitutional guarantee of privacy has been interposed against many governmental efforts to regulate drug use, but the most significant battleground has been urine testing of employees to detect drug use. In 1989 the Supreme Court gave the green light to programs requiring DRUG TESTING of railway employees involved in train accidents and U.S. Customs Service employees applying for positions involving interdiction of drugs. The Court declared that the expectations of privacy are diminished for employees who participate in industries that are pervasively regulated or who are employed in drug enforcement efforts.

Whether drug use can ever be constitutionally protected as part of a religious exercise came before the Court in a 1990 case presenting a constitutional challenge to the discharge of Oregon employees who participated in a Native American Church ceremony that included the chewing of peyote buttons. In EMPLOYMENT DIVISION, DEPARTMENT OF HUMAN RESOURCES V. SMITH, the Court declared that a general criminal prohibition of the use of peyote could be enforced even when peyote was used as part of a legitimate, bona fide religious ceremony. The dissenting Justices argued that preference was being shown to some religions over others, noting that the alcohol used for sacramental wine in Catholic services was exempted from the PROHIBITION laws enacted in the 1920s.

The prohibition of UNREASONABLE SEARCHES and seizures in the Fourth Amendment has frequently been viewed as an obstacle by police charged with the enforcement of drug laws. The EXCLUSIONARY RULE, which requires the suppression of illegally seized evidence, may result in the dismissal of drug trafficking charges if the illicit drugs were seized without a valid SEARCH WARRANT. A study of New York City police revealed that immediately after the exclusionary rule was first announced in 1961, arrest reports in half of all cases related that the defendant "dropped the drugs on the ground upon seeing the police

officer." Any inquiry into the grounds for a search was thus avoided. During the prior year only fourteen percent of the reports claimed the defendant dropped the drugs. Obviously, the new rule did not cause an outbreak of "dropsy" in New York; it caused an outbreak of police perjury. Police were willing to lie to avoid application of the exclusionary rule to their searches.

Congress has frequently responded to the complaints of narcotics officers that the exclusionary rules make their jobs too tough. As part of President RICHARD M. NIXON's war on drugs, Congress enacted a NO-KNOCK ENTRY provision for drug cases in 1970, providing that search warrants for drugs could dispense with the normal requirement that police knock and announce themselves before entering the premises to be searched. Police argued that the exemption was necessary for drug cases because drugs are quickly destroyed if violators are warned of the police presence. What was forgotten was that police occasionally make mistakes. A series of "wrong-door" raids led to shootouts that left four innocent people dead, including one police officer. In 1974, Congress repealed the no-knock provision, restoring the requirement of a knock on the door even in drug cases.

During the 1980s the argument that search and seizure requirements should be relaxed in drug cases gained a receptive ear in the Supreme Court. In case after case, the Court carved out exceptions to the requirements of PROBABLE CAUSE and search warrants, citing the need for more pervasive police surveillance to prevent the smuggling of illicit drugs.

A common legislative response to the frustration of escalating drug use is simply to escalate the penalties for illegal possession or trafficking of drugs. Does the cruel and unusual punishment clause of the Eighth Amendment impose any limitation? In 1962 the Supreme Court struck down a California law that made it a criminal offense "to be addicted to the use of narcotics." The Court characterized addiction as an illness over which the victim had no control, and concluded it would be "cruel and unusual punishment" to imprison someone for simply being sick. Subsequent cases, however, have held that addiction offers no defense to someone arrested for such activities as possession of drugs or being intoxicated in public. The imposition of life prison sentences has been challenged as disproportionate to the seriousness of drug offenses, but the Supreme Court currently gives states a wide berth in setting the level of punishment for drug offenses.

In the early 1970s, New York's Governor Nelson Rockefeller successfully sponsored a law imposing mandatory life imprisonment for drug pushers. The law was hailed as the ultimate solution, one that would make drug selling such a serious offense that no one would want to take the risk. The total failure of that policy quickly became an embarrassment. Motorists began complaining that they could not drive down some streets in Harlem in broad daylight without being accosted at every corner by drug hustlers. The hustlers, of course, were addicts on the lowest rung of the distribution ladder. The threat of a mandatory prison sentence had little impact on them.

Today legislators are stymied. Although they have imposed a mandatory sentence of ten years to life and a fine of $100,000 for engaging in a drug enterprise, these penalties have no perceptible impact on the number of drug enterprises flourishing in America. A serious suggestion has been made that CAPITAL PUNISHMENT is the answer.

A potent weapon against drug traffickers has been found in the enactment of forfeiture laws. Under the Comprehensive Forfeiture Act of 1984, federal authorities can seize any property derived from the proceeds of a drug transaction or any property used to facilitate a drug offense. Houses, businesses, automobiles, airplanes, and boats have been forfeited to the government. In 1990 the Supreme Court ruled that money paid to criminal defense lawyers for representation in drug prosecutions could also be seized, without violating the Sixth Amendment RIGHT TO COUNSEL. Courts have split on the question of whether the Eighth Amendment prohibition of cruel and unusual punishment requires that a forefeiture be proportionate to the seriousness of the offense. In one case, forfeiture of a house worth $100,000 was upheld even though the property was used to grow less than $1,000 worth of marijuana plants.

As the war on drugs escalates, the tension between law enforcement techniques and traditional constitutional liberties will increase. In applying a BALANCING TEST, courts can be expected to give greater and greater weight to the need to suppress drug trafficking. One may hope that the casualties in the war on drugs will not include the Constitution itself.

GERALD F. UELMEN
(1992)

(SEE ALSO: *Crack Cocaine and Equal Protection; Drug Regulation.*)

Bibliography
KAPLAN, JOHN 1970 *Marijuana: The New Prohibition.* New York: Simon and Schuster.

NATIONAL COMMISSION ON MARIJUANA AND DRUG ABUSE 1973 *Drug Use in America: Problem in Perspective,* Second Report (March).

TREBACH, ARNOLD 1982 *The Heroin Solution.* New Haven, Conn.: Yale University Press.

UELMEN, GERALD F. and HADDOX, VICTOR G. 1990 *Drug Abuse and the Law.* New York: Clark Boardman.

WISOTSKY, STEVEN 1986 *Breaking the Impasse in the War on Drugs.* Westport, Conn.: Greenwood Press.

COOLEY, THOMAS M.
(1824–1898)

Thomas McIntyre Cooley was a distinguished law teacher, state judge, first chairman of the Interstate Commerce Commission, and author of the influential 1868 *Treatise on the Constitutional Limitations Which Rest upon the Legislative Power of the States of the American Union.* Born in western New York to a family with a Jeffersonian "bias," Cooley absorbed an anticorporate equal-rights ideology, fearful of "class legislation" that aided the few at the expense of many.

In 1843 Cooley went west to Michigan and combined activities in law, journalism, politics, and poetry. He helped organize the Free Soil Party in the state and in 1856 became a Republican. Narrowing his concerns to the law, he rapidly attained professional recognition. Appointed Compiler of the state's laws in 1857 and Reporter to the Supreme Court in 1858, he was selected in 1859 as a professor at the newly opened University of Michigan Law Department. In 1864 he was elected to the Michigan Supreme Court.

Cooley tempered his preoccupation with the law with historical and political values and naturally turned to constitutional questions. To Francis Thorpe's 1889 query on books for a constitutional law library he replied that "constitutional law is so inseparably connected with constitutional history and that is so vital a part of general history that I should not know where to draw the line."

Historical, COMMON LAW, and Jacksonian sensibilities were the presuppositions of Cooley's 1868 treatise, although his aim was merely to write "a convenient guidebook of elementary constitutional principles." The book was that; it had gone through six editions by 1890 and had a broader circulation, a greater sale, and more frequent citations than any other law book published in the second half of the nineteenth century.

The treatise was useful because no one prior to Cooley had systematically analyzed the cases and principles dealing with constitutional limitations on state legislative power. Chapters on constitutional protection to personal liberty, to liberty of speech, and to RELIGIOUS LIBERTY were supplemented with chapters on municipal government, EMINENT DOMAIN, taxation, and the POLICE POWER. Chapter Eleven, "Of the Protection to Property by the Law of the Land" attracted the most attention, for here Cooley discussed DUE PROCESS OF LAW and gave it a significant substantive definition. Cooley said that legislative restraints on property should be tested by "those principles of civil liberty and constitutional defense which have become established in our system of law, and not by any rules that pertain to forms of procedure only." His test of due process was historical: the "established principles" and "settled usages" of the common law protected property rights.

Cooley's definition of due process was used in the briefs of corporation lawyers who also distorted his comprehensive definition of the liberty protected by the FOURTEENTH AMENDMENT as embracing "all our liberties—personal, civil, and political" to a FREEDOM OF CONTRACT doctrine. Twentieth-century commentators have often accepted these briefs, misinterpreting Cooley as a zealous advocate of the judicial protection of property rights. To Cooley, however, due process did not necessarily mean judicial process nor did individual property rights mean corporate property rights. His views on judicial self-restraint were summarized in his treatise comment that judges "cannot run a race of opinions upon points of right, reason, or expediency with the law-making power." And Cooley repeated Justice LEMUEL SHAW's views on a strong police power.

When Cooley was writing his treatise he was lecturing students on "the struggle between corporations and the rights of the people," condemning the decision in DARTMOUTH COLLEGE v. WOODWARD (1819), issuing opinions criticizing special privileges for corporations, and using the principle of equal rights and the maxims of "no taxation except for a PUBLIC PURPOSE" and of "due process of law" to declare tax aid to railroad corporations unconstitutional.

Cooley anxiously observed the growth of corporate capitalism in post-CIVIL WAR America. Deploring the national sentiment "to become immediately rich and great," he worried over the conflict of labor and capital and felt "that *class legislation* has been making the rich richer and the poor poorer," adding that "property is never so much in danger of becoming master as when capital unjustly manipulates the legislation of the country." These remarks in an 1879 lecture at Johns Hopkins University have been overlooked, as has a similar warning in an 1884 article on "Labor and Capital Before the Law" that when constitutional protection to property especially benefits those who have possessions, "the Constitution itself may come to be regarded by considerable classes as an instrument whose office it is to protect the rich in the advantages they have secured over the poor, and one that should be hated for that reason."

In court decisions Cooley evidenced older Jeffersonian values, upholding free public education, the FREEDOM OF THE PRESS, the rights of local self-government, and the necessity for judicial self-restraint. But the changing America of the late nineteenth century diminished earlier Jeffersonian hopes. In a melancholic mood in 1883 he admitted that "the political philosophy of Burke never grows stale and is for all times and all people."

By the 1880s Cooley had a national reputation, earned by judicial duties and constant lecturing, editing, and writing, including editions of SIR WILLIAM BLACKSTONE and JOSEPH STORY and treatises on torts and taxation. Aspirations for a United States Supreme Court appointment were dashed in 1881 when railroad interests, Cooley thought, successfully lobbied for STANLEY MATTHEWS. But Cooley had given up on Republicans, and in 1886 wondered whether the Party "possesses any good reason for existence." He admired GROVER CLEVELAND and accepted his offer of the chairmanship of the Interstate Commerce Commission. Regulating the American railway system was a task beyond Cooley's declining powers, and the effort led to a breakdown that left him a semi-invalid after 1890.

An 1889 comment to the South Dakota Constitutional Convention reveals that Cooley had modified older beliefs in constitutional limitations to legislative power: "Even in the millennium people will be studying ways whereby—by means of corporate power—they can circumvent their neighbors. Don't do that to any such extent as to prevent the legislative power hereafter from meeting all the evils that may be within the reach of proper legislation."

ALAN R. JONES
(1986)

Bibliography

JONES, ALAN R. 1986 *The Constitutional Conservatism of Thomas McIntyre Cooley: A Study in the History of Ideas.* New York: Garland Publishing.

TWISS, BENJAMIN 1942 *Lawyers and the Constitution: How Laissez-Faire Came to the Constitution.* Princeton, N.J.: Princeton University Press.

COOLEY v. BOARD OF WARDENS OF PORT OF PHILADELPHIA
12 Howard 299 (1851)

The chaos in judicial interpretation that characterized the TANEY COURT'S COMMERCE CLAUSE cases was ended in *Cooley*, the most important decision on the subject between GIBBONS v. OGDEN (1824) and UNITED STATES v. E. C. KNIGHT CO. (1895). The Taney Court finally found a doctrinal formula that allowed a majority to coalesce around a single line of reasoning for the first time since the days of the MARSHALL COURT. That formula was the DOCTRINE of SELECTIVE EXCLUSIVENESS, announced for the majority by Justice BENJAMIN R. CURTIS. The doctrine was a compromise, combining aspects of the doctrines of CONCURRENT POWERS over commerce and EXCLUSIVE POWERS, but three Justices of the eight who participated rejected the compromise. Justices JOHN MCLEAN and JAMES M. WAYNE, whom Curtis privately called "high-toned Federalists," persisted in their nationalist view, expressed in dissent, that congressional powers over INTERSTATE and FOREIGN COMMERCE were always exclusive, while PETER V. DANIEL, an intransigent states-rightist, concurred in the majority's result on the ground that congressional power over commerce was never exclusive.

At issue in *Cooley* was the constitutionality of a Pennsylvania statute requiring ships of a certain size entering or leaving the port of Philadelphia to employ local pilots in local waters. Cooley, claiming that the state act unconstitutionally regulated foreign commerce, refused to pay the pilotage fee. The fact that the first Congress had provided that the states could enact pilotage laws did not alter Cooley's claim. Curtis for the Court acknowledged that if the grant of commerce powers to Congress had divested the states of a power to legislate, the act of Congress could not confer that power on the states. The problem was whether the power of Congress in this case was exclusive.

Commerce, Curtis declared, embraces a vast field of many different subjects. Some subjects imperatively demand a single uniform rule for the whole nation, while others, like pilotage, demand diverse local rules to cope with varying local situations. The power of Congress was therefore selectively exclusive. If the subject required a single uniform rule, the states could not regulate that subject even in the absence of congressional legislation. In such a case congressional powers would be exclusive. Such was the nationalist half of the doctrine. The other half, by which the Court sustained the state act, maintained that the states did possess concurrent powers over commerce if the subject required diversity of regulation. Thus Congress's power was exclusive or concurrent depending on the nature of the subject to be regulated. "It is the opinion of a majority of the court," Curtis declared, "that the mere grant to Congress of the power to regulate commerce, did not deprive the States of power to regulate pilots, and that although Congress has legislated on this subject, its legislation manifests an intention . . . to leave its regulation to the several States."

The Court's doctrine of selective exclusiveness gave it a point of departure for analyzing commerce clause issues. The doctrine, however, had to be interpreted. It did not even suggest how the Court could determine which subjects required national legislation, thus excluding state action, and which required diverse local regulations. The doctrine could be manipulated by Justices who employed nationalist doctrine to invalidate state enactments.

LEONARD W. LEVY
(1986)

Bibliography

SWISHER, CARL BRENT   1974   *History of the Supreme Court.* Vol. 5:404–407. New York: Macmillan.

COOLEY RULE

See: *Cooley v. Board of Wardens of Port of Philadelphia;* Selective Exclusiveness

COOLIDGE, CALVIN
(1872–1933)

John Calvin Coolidge, the thirtieth President of the United States, succeeded WARREN G. HARDING upon Harding's death in August 1923 and served until 1929. The heart of his legislative program was a series of tax reductions for individual taxpayers in all brackets, economy in government, and a balanced BUDGET.

The chief legislative controversy of the 1920s concerned the McNary-Haugen bills, which Coolidge vetoed in 1927 and 1928. These bills, proposed in response to a prolonged agricultural recession, would have authorized the federal government to buy and sell farm products in an effort to raise their prices. Coolidge opposed the bills as unworkable and as an unconstitutional expansion of the commerce power. The Congress, he argued, was limited to those powers granted to it or implied as incidental to the express powers. In language anticipating the opposition to the NEW DEAL, Coolidge cautioned against the dangers of bureaucracy. He also observed that the people of the United States could reallocate the constitutional powers of the federal government and the states by means of the AMENDING PROCESS. Coolidge supported national legislation to regulate child labor, but he believed that a constitutional amendment would be required first to grant such power to the federal government.

Coolidge's only appointment to the Supreme Court was of his Amherst College classmate, Attorney General HARLAN FISKE STONE.

THOMAS B. SILVER
(1986)

Bibliography

SILVER, THOMAS B.   1983   *Coolidge and the Historians.* Durham, N.C.: Carolina Academic Press.

COOLIDGE, UNITED STATES v.

See: Federal Common Law of Crimes

COOLIDGE v. NEW HAMPSHIRE
403 U.S. 443 (1971)

In *Coolidge v. New Hampshire,* police officers, acting pursuant to a SEARCH WARRANT issued by the state attorney general, seized and later searched an automobile parked in the driveway of a murder suspect's home. The Supreme Court ruled the warrant invalid because a prosecutor could not be regarded as a neutral and detached magistrate. The automobile seizure was too far removed in time and space from the suspect's arrest to be considered incident to that arrest, was not grounded in any EXIGENT CIRCUMSTANCES to qualify for an AUTOMOBILE SEARCH or PLAIN VIEW exception nor was the discovery of the automobile inadvertent. Later decisions have confined *Coolidge* to its facts, emphasizing the automobile's location on a private driveway and the fact that the automobile was not contraband, stolen, or itself dangerous.

STEVEN SHIFFRIN
(1986)

COOPER, THOMAS
(1759–1839)

Dr. Thomas Cooper, an English radical who settled in the United States in 1794, was an intellectual jack-of-all-trades, master of most, and the author of treatises on philosophy, law, religion, government, political economy, and various sciences. When he was a Jeffersonian editor, he was convicted of violating the SEDITION ACT OF 1798. His *Political Essays* and the report of his trial advocated a radically broad theory of FREEDOM OF THE PRESS. Later a Pennsylvania judge, he was removed from office and soured on liberalism, although his friend THOMAS JEFFERSON called him the "greatest man in America, in the powers of mind and in acquired information." When Cooper was president of what later became the University of South Carolina, he revised the state statutes and wrote *On the Constitution* (1826), which spoke for SLAVERY, state SOVEREIGNTY, and NULLIFICATION.

LEONARD W. LEVY
(1986)

COOPER v. AARON
358 U.S. 1 (1958)

For several years after its decision in BROWN V. BOARD OF EDUCATION (1954–1955), the Supreme Court gave little guidance or support to the lower courts charged with supervising the DESEGREGATION of the public schools. In this case, however, the Court was confronted with direct defiance of *Brown* by a state's highest officials, and it met that challenge head-on.

Even before the *Brown* remedial opinion in 1955, the school board of Little Rock, Arkansas, had approved a plan for gradual desegregation of the local schools, and the federal district court had upheld the plan. Just before the opening of the fall 1957 term, the state governor, Orval Faubus, ordered the state's National Guard to keep black children out of Little Rock's Central High School. The attorney general of the United States obtained an injunction against the governor's action, and the children entered the school. A hostile crowd gathered, and the children were removed by the police. President DWIGHT D. EISENHOWER was thus prodded into his first significant act supporting desegregation; he sent Army troops to Central High to protect the children, and eight black students attended the school for the full academic year.

In February 1958, the school board asked the district court, in *Cooper v. Aaron*, for a delay of two and one-half years in the implementation of its plan, and in June the court agreed, commenting on the "chaos, bedlam and turmoil" at Central High. In August the federal court of appeals reversed, calling for implementation of the plan on schedule. The Supreme Court, in an unusual move, accelerated the hearing to September 11, and the next day it issued a brief order affirming the decision of the court of appeals. Later the Court published its full opinion, signed by all nine Justices to emphasize their continued unanimous support of *Brown*.

The opinion dealt quickly with the uncomplicated merits of the case, saying that law and order were not to be achieved at the expense of the constitutional rights of black children. The Court then added a response to the assertion by the Arkansas governor and legislature that the state was not required to abide by *Brown*, because *Brown* itself was an unconstitutional assumption of judicial power.

The response scored two easy points first: the Constitution, under the SUPREMACY CLAUSE, is "the supreme Law of the Land," and MARBURY V. MADISON (1803) had held that it was the province of the judiciary to "say what the law is." The Court's next step, however, was not self-evident: *Marbury* meant that the federal courts are supreme in expounding the Constitution; thus *Brown* was the supreme law of the land, binding state officers. This view, which carried the assertion of judicial power further than *Marbury* had taken it, has been repeated by the Court several times since the *Cooper* decision.

Cooper's importance, however, was not so much doctrinal as political. It reaffirmed principle at a crucial time. The televised pictures of black children being escorted into school through a crowd of hostile whites galvanized northern opinion. The 1960 election brought to office a president committed to a strong civil rights program—although it took his death to enact that program into law.

KENNETH L. KARST
(1986)

(SEE ALSO: *Civil Rights Act of 1964.*)

COOPERATIVE FEDERALISM

The theory of cooperative federalism postulates that the relationship between the national government and the states is one in which: governmental functions typically are undertaken jointly by federal and state (including local) agencies, rather than exclusively by one or the other; a sharing of power characterizes an integrated system instead of an exclusive SOVEREIGNTY at either level of government; and power tends not to concentrate at either level, or in any one agency, because the fragmented and shared nature of responsibilities gives citizens and interest groups "access" to many centers of influence.

Cooperative federalism is a modern phenomenon. Its main features—sharing of policy responsibilities and financial resources, interdependence of administration, overlapping of functions—are associated mainly with the FEDERAL GRANT-IN-AID programs. Collaboration, grants-in-aid from the national government to the states, bypassing of the states through establishment of grant programs aiding local or special-district governments directly, and development of auditing procedures and conditional grant requirements all have characterized cooperative federalism in the period after 1933.

Numerous analysts who celebrate these developments as signifying that old-style FEDERALISM is "dead," displaced by "intergovernmental relations," argue that the tension, pretensions at autonomy, and the notion of separateness of responsibilities that characterized governance in the pre-New Deal periods of constitutional development no longer form part of the reality of the federal system. Some scholars argue that relative power distribution is no longer a relevant issue. Forgotten is the elementary notion that "sharing" does not necessarily mean equality. Characteristically, in the modern grant-in-aid programs, the national government has not only raised and distributed the revenues, it has also designed the programs and established the goals, quite apart from overseeing administration.

Fascination with the alleged "non-centralization of power," which is seen to result from cooperative federalism, also can obscure the evidence of the vast additions of discretionary power in the national executive branch since 1933. Presidents from both parties have contributed to the growth of the "Imperial Presidency," and the process of centralization of power that has gone forward in this century has been profoundly influenced by this development.

The decision in MASSACHUSETTS V. MELLON (1923) established the juridical foundation of modern grant-in-aid constitutional theory. The Court there dismissed the complaint of Massachusetts that state prerogatives were improperly invaded by conditional grant programs (in that instance, the maternity-aid program of national grants). The interpretation of the TENTH AMENDMENT as "but a tru-

ism," in UNITED STATES V. DARBY (1941), further advanced the constitutional basis for cooperative federalism in action. Subsequently the Court upheld the principle of making grants conditional, even in *Oklahoma v. United States Civil Service Commission* (1947), when the federal legislation required adherence to HATCH ACT restraints on political activity by state officials. A contrary note was sounded by the Court in NATIONAL LEAGUE OF CITIES V. USERY (1976), in which the Court asserted that "Congress may not exercise power in a fashion that impairs the states' integrity of their ability to function effectively in a federal system." Yet this assertion was made as the Court invalidated only a regulatory measure affecting hours and wages of local government employees, not a grant-in-aid or collaborative program. In GARCIA V. SAN ANTONIO TRANSIT AUTHORITY (1985) the Court overruled *Usery*, the majority declaring that case-by-case development since 1976 had failed to produce any principled basis for identifying "fundamental" elements of state sovereignty." The Court specifically cited the history of federal grants-in-aid as evidence that cooperative federalism and the political process gave adequate protection to the interests of the states.

HARRY N. SCHEIBER
(1986)

Bibliography

CORWIN, EDWARD 1941 *Constitutional Revolution, Ltd.* Claremont, Calif.: Claremont Colleges.

COPPAGE v. KANSAS
236 U.S. 1 (1915)

In *Adair v. United States* (1908), the Supreme Court had held that the section of the ERDMAN ACT that outlawed YELLOW DOG CONTRACTS was outside Congress's power to regulate INTERSTATE COMMERCE. Now, facing a question "not distinguishable in principle," a 6–3 Court struck down a Kansas statute banning yellow dog contracts. Justice MAHLON PITNEY for the majority, finding no reason to depart from *Adair*, reaffirmed the doctrine of FREEDOM OF CONTRACT. That "fundamental and vital" freedom fused rights of liberty and property so that any "arbitrary interference with that freedom of contract would impair those rights." Only a "legitimate" exercise of STATE POLICE POWER could limit it, and the majority could see no relation between the avowed purpose of the statute and the state's responsibility to protect the safety, morals, and health of its citizens. Indeed, "an interference with the normal exercise of personal liberty and property rights is the primary object of the statute." Concluding that it deprived employers and employees of the right to contract freely on their own terms, the majority voided the statute as a violation of SUB-

STANTIVE DUE PROCESS guaranteed by the FOURTEENTH AMENDMENT.

In a brief dissent, Justice OLIVER WENDELL HOLMES reiterated the position he had stated in LOCHNER V. NEW YORK (1905). He saw nothing in the Constitution forbidding the Kansas statute, and he declined to substitute the courts' judgment for the legislature's on this policy question. In a lengthier dissent joined by Justice CHARLES EVANS HUGHES, Justice WILLIAM R. DAY, who had voted with the majority in *Adair*, asserted that Kansas had enacted the statute to promote the general welfare, thereby validly limiting the freedom of contract.

DAVID GORDON
(1986)

COPYRIGHT

The Framers of the Constitution delegated to the national government authority to enact copyright laws. The copyright power, together with the PATENT power, is found in Article I, section 8, clause 8, which empowers Congress "to promote the progress of science and useful arts, by securing for limited times to authors and inventors the exclusive right to their respective writings and discoveries." Because there is no record of any debate on this clause at the CONSTITUTIONAL CONVENTION OF 1787, and mention of it in THE FEDERALIST is perfunctory, the meaning of the clause must be found in case law.

The phrase "to promote the progress of science" states what the Supreme Court, in *Mazer v. Stein* (1954), described as "the economic philosophy behind the clause," which is "the conviction that encouragement of individual effort by personal gain is the best way to advance public welfare through the talents of authors. . . ." Most courts, however, would deny that the introductory phrase permits the denial of copyright to any particular work on the ground that it does not contribute to such "progress." In fact, a United States Court of Appeals held in 1979 that obscene content does not invalidate copyright.

The words "by securing" came into contention in *Wheaton v. Peters* (1834), the first important copyright case decided by the Supreme Court, and a case involving two of the Court's own reporters. The plaintiff there argued that the federal copyright statute merely added additional remedies to a right that already existed at COMMON LAW. To bolster this position, he argued that the word "secure" meant to protect, insure, save, and ascertain, not to create. The Court rejected this contention, holding that the federal statute had created a new right, but that the author had not complied with the act's conditions.

Because the clause contains the words, "for limited times," a federal copyright statute that purported to grant copyright protection in perpetuity would clearly be unconstitutional. So too would a term that is nominally "limited" but is in fact the equivalent of perpetual protection (for example, a one thousand year term). The term currently provided for newly created works, the life of the author plus fifty years, conforms with the "limited times" requirement.

Only "authors" may be granted copyright in the first instance, although, once granted, copyright is transferable by an author to others. The term "authors" in the Constitution gives rise to the "originality" requirement in the law of copyright, which excludes from copyright protection material copied from others. An author is no less an author because others have anticipated his work, as long as he did not copy from such others. This Judge Frank contrasted with an "inventor" under the patent power, who must by definition produce something "novel," that is, not anticipated in the prior art. By reason of the phrase "exclusive right," it is clear that Congress has the power to grant to authors the "exclusive right" to exploit their works. But Congress is under no compulsion to exercise its full powers under the Constitution. If it may withhold copyright protection altogether from a given category of works, it may also grant something less than exclusive rights. The phrase "to their respective writings" means that only "writings" may be the subject of copyright. But the concept of a "writing" for copyright purposes has been liberally construed. The Court has held that photographic portraits and sound recordings constitute a "writing." Indeed, in *Goldstein v. California* (1973), the Court defined "writings" as "any physical rendering of the fruits of creative intellectual or aesthetic labor." A work that has not been physically fixed is ineligible for copyright protection.

In *Goldstein* the Court held that the copyright power is not exclusive, so that, subject to the SUPREMACY CLAUSE, the states retain concurrent power to enact copyright laws. Until adoption of the current Copyright Act in 1978 this reserved state power was significant, because most unpublished works were protected by so-called common law (or state law) copyright. However, under the current Copyright Act this area of state law has been largely preempted, so that most works, published or unpublished, are protected, if at all, under the federal act.

In recent years the courts have begun to question whether, and to what extent, the copyright laws are subject to the FREEDOM OF SPEECH and FREEDOM OF THE PRESS guarantees of the FIRST AMENDMENT. If the First Amendment were literally applied it would invalidate the Copyright Act, since the act clearly abridges the freedom of speech and press of those who would engage in copyright infringement by copying from others. Nothing in the First Amendment limits the freedom protected thereunder to speech that is original with the speaker. Nor does the fact that the Constitution also grants to Congress the power to enact copyright laws render the First Amendment inapplicable. The First Amendment and the remainder of the BILL OF RIGHTS limit only those powers that have otherwise been confided to the federal government. If it did not modify such powers, it would have no meaning at all. The conflict between these two socially useful, yet antithetical, interests is, of course, capable of resolution. The Ninth Circuit held in *Krofft v. McDonald's Corp.* (1977), and the Supreme Court implicitly agreed in *Zacchini v. Scripps-Howard Broadcasting Co.* (1977), that "ideas" lie in the domain of the First Amendment, so that copyright may not be claimed therein, but that the form of "expression" of ideas may be the subject of copyright, notwithstanding the First Amendment.

MELVILLE B. NIMMER
(1986)

(SEE ALSO: *Intellectual Property Law and the First Amendment.*)

Bibliography

NIMMER, MELVILLE B.   1978   *Copyright.* 4 Vols. Albany, N.Y.: Matthew Bender & Co.

COPYRIGHT AND THE FIRST AMENDMENT

See: Intellectual Property Law and the First Amendment

CORFIELD v. CORYELL
4 Wash. C.C. 371 (1823)
6 Fed. Case 546 (No. 3,230)

The importance of Justice BUSHROD WASHINGTON's circuit opinion derives from the fact that it contains the only exposition of Article IV, section 2, prior to the adoption of the FOURTEENTH AMENDMENT, that also uses the phrase PRIVILEGES AND IMMUNITIES. The clause in Article IV declares: "The Citizens of each state shall be entitled to all Privileges and Immunities of Citizens in the several states." *Corfield* arose because the plaintiff's vessel had been condemned under a state law forbidding nonresidents to take shell fish from state waters; in his TRESPASS action, the plaintiff relied upon the privileges and immunities clause. Washington declared, however, that the clause protected only the "fundamental" rights of CITIZENSHIP, such as the protection of government, the enjoyment of life, liberty, and property, the right to move about freely, the right to claim the benefit of the writ of HABEAS CORPUS, the right to sue, and the right to vote if qualified. This

category did not include the right to exploit the state's oyster beds.

LEONARD W. LEVY
(1986)

(SEE ALSO: *Slaughterhouse Cases.*)

CORNELIUS v. NAACP LEGAL DEFENSE AND EDUCATIONAL FUND, INC.
473 U.S. 788 (1985)

This decision demonstrated how cumbersome the Supreme Court's analysis of PUBLIC FORUM issues has become since its decision in PERRY EDUCATION ASSOCIATION V. PERRY LOCAL EDUCATORS' ASSOCIATION (1983).

A 1983 EXECUTIVE ORDER limited the Combined Federal Campaign (CFC), a charity drive among federal employees, to charities that provide direct health and welfare services, and expressly excluded legal defense and advocacy groups. Seven such groups sued in federal district court, challenging their exclusion as a violation of the FIRST AMENDMENT. That court agreed, and issued an INJUNCTION forbidding exclusion of the groups from CFC. The court of appeals affirmed, but the Supreme Court reversed, 4–3, in an opinion by Justice SANDRA DAY O'CONNOR.

The Court held that the government had not designated either the federal workplace or CFC in particular as a public forum, in the sense of the *Perry* opinion. Rather, each of these was a "nonpublic forum"—a government operation in which communications could be limited to those promoting the operation's mission. CFC's purpose was to provide a means for government employees to lessen the government's burden in meeting human health and welfare needs, by making their own contributions to those ends. It was not necessary, in excluding the plaintiffs from CFC, to show that their solicitations would be incompatible with the goals of CFC; the relevant standard was the reasonableness of the exclusion. The President could reasonably conclude that money raised for direct provision of food or shelter was more beneficial than money raised for litigation or advocacy on behalf of the needy. Furthermore, the government could properly avoid the appearance of political favoritism by excluding all such groups. Those organizations had alternative means for raising funds from government employees, including direct mail advertising and in-person solicitation outside the workplace.

The Court, recognizing that other groups not in the business of direct provision of health and welfare services had been allowed to participate in CFC, remanded the case for determination whether the government had excluded the plaintiff groups for the purpose of suppressing their particular viewpoints.

Justice HARRY A. BLACKMUN, joined by Justice WILLIAM J. BRENNAN, dissented, arguing that any governmental exclusion of a class of speakers from any forum must be justified by a showing that the would-be speakers' intended use of the forum was incompatible with the relevant governmental operation. Here no such incompatibility had been shown, he said. Justice JOHN PAUL STEVENS, also dissenting, expressed skepticism about the value of a DOCTRINE founded on a series of categories of forum. In this case, he said, the government's own arguments supported "the inference of bias" against the excluded groups.

KENNETH L. KARST
(1986)

CORONADO COAL COMPANY v. UNITED MINE WORKERS

See: *United Mine Workers v. Coronado Coal Company*

CORPORATE CITIZENSHIP

In American constitutional law, business CORPORATIONS are not endowed with rights of CITIZENSHIP. Corporations can neither vote nor claim protections afforded by the PRIVILEGES AND IMMUNITIES clauses of Article IV, section 2, and the FOURTEENTH AMENDMENT. However, the Supreme Court has consistently refused to say that citizenship is a precondition for the exercise of numerous other rights granted to "the people" or to "persons" in the BILL OF RIGHTS or the Fourteenth Amendment. Political rights normally thought to be essential attributes of citizenship in a democratic political community—rights of speech, association, assembly, press, and DUE PROCESS—extend to noncitizens and citizens alike. With the important exceptions of the rights to vote and to hold office, the constitutional status of citizenship does not bar a noncitizen from exercising political rights, or from otherwise participating in political activities. The fact that citizenship does not stand as a barrier to the enjoyment of many basic political rights has also afforded the Court the opportunity to extend rights of political participation to corporations. Indeed, in FIRST NATIONAL BANK OF BOSTON V. BELLOTTI (1978), the Court conferred FIRST AMENDMENT rights of speech upon business corporations. With this jurisprudential innovation, an ideological construct known as the "corporate citizen" acquired new meaning.

In early nineteenth-century American law, incorporation was a privilege that could be granted only by a special legislative act (a corporate charter) wherein the terms of

incorporation (e.g., purpose of the business, limitations on debt and capitalization) were stipulated. Anglo-American law endowed the legal entity of the corporation with a life of its own; as a fictitious individual distinct from the corporeal membership, the corporate entity could exist in perpetuity. Historically, the attribution of constitutional rights to the entity has contributed to the expansion of corporate autonomy. This has protected business corporations against dictation by the state while it has allowed for regulation of corporate power in the public interest. The metamorphosis of the corporate entity from a highly regulated creature of government to a constitutionally protected "individual" began in the early nineteenth century when American jurists vested the entity with rights and legal capacities that afforded protection against hostile state LEGISLATION. Legal reasoning also provided ideological support for the corporation in what can be termed the doctrine of "corporate individualism." Originally a defense of the corporation's constitutional rights of PROPERTY, as well as an imposition of responsibility and liability, corporate individualism gradually merged with the entrepreneurial ethos of competitive industrial capitalism to justify an expanding corporate autonomy.

The legal DOCTRINE of corporate individualism first acquired ideological significance outside the law in political argument that personified the corporation as an individual within the competitive marketplace. Beginning in the late 1830s, this mystification promoted the liberalization of state incorporation laws by undermining the widely held perception of the corporation as an instrument of special privilege and monopoly. By 1870, most states had passed statutes making incorporation a right available to all capitalists rather than a privilege granted only to a few. Moreover, the corporate individual achieved an enhanced legal status when the corporate entity became a "person" within the meaning of the Fourteenth Amendment in *Santa Clara County v. Southern Pacific Railroad* in 1886, an event that would facilitate the ascendancy of corporate power in industry and finance. By 1900, the business corporation had realized a significant measure of autonomy consistent with the protection afforded by property rights embodied in the Fourteenth Amendment's SUBSTANTIVE DUE PROCESS doctrine of FREEDOM OF CONTRACT.

In the last quarter of the nineteenth century, corporate leaders resorted to various means of regulating prices or combining capital in an effort to supplant competitive with cooperative methods of business. Widespread public opposition in the 1880s to the combination movement inspired Congress to pass the SHERMAN ANTITRUST ACT in 1890 to regulate monopolistic practices and unreasonable restraints of trade. However, in the absence of significant ANTITRUST enforcement in the mid-to-late 1890s, the combination movement gained momentum. Between 1898 and 1904, the first great merger wave of corporate capitalism transformed the very structure of the American economy. Far-reaching changes in the law of corporations greatly aided this development. Following New Jersey's lead in 1896, numerous state legislatures eliminated a host of traditional regulatory controls over their corporate creations and legalized mergers. During this same period, American jurists began to formulate the modern legal conception of the corporate entity as "real" or "natural." The "real entity theory"—by which corporations were understood as the natural and inevitable result of individuals seeking to operate efficently in the marketplace—further absorbed the personified corporate individual as it gradually supplanted the venerable "artificial entity theory" that viewed the corporation as a creature of government. This personified entity, therefore, both reflected and justified an accelerating progression toward corporate autonomy.

To many Americans during the Progressive era (1890–1916), *laissez-faire* ideology and its legal corollary, the doctrine of liberty of contract, seemed out of phase with economic and social realities. Having evolved from a legal protection of VESTED RIGHTS and the exclusive franchise into an ideological justification of the competitive marketplace, corporate individualism would undergo yet another ideological transfiguration in the era of the large corporation. Contrary to the precepts of *laissez-faire* liberalism, legal reasoning in the law of antitrust recognized not only that corporate power posed dangers to individual liberty and equality of opportunity, but that it also produced social and technological benefits when regulated in the public interest. In adopting the "RULE OF REASON in STANDARD OIL COMPANY V. UNITED STATES (1911), Justice EDWARD D. WHITE explained that freedom to contract is the rule, but restraints of trade in practicing this freedom must be reasonable, as judged in light of the standard of fair competition. Supreme Court decisions thereafter articulated a business ethic of fairness that imposed on the corporate individual a legal and moral obligation to obey the law. In this way, the idea of corporate social responsibility in antitrust law provided an enduring rationale that would influence the evolving concept of corporate citizenship in constitutional law.

During the twentieth century, Supreme Court decisions enhanced the legal standing of the corporate citizen as the business corporation acquired constitutional rights under the First, FOURTH, Fifth, Sixth, and SEVENTH AMENDMENTS. The debate over the political rights of the corporation was first joined on the Supreme Court in *Bellotti* in 1978. In AUSTIN V. MICHIGAN CHAMBER OF COMMERCE (1990), the *Bellotti* dissenters found themselves in the majority. *Austin* reformulates the issue of corporate political power debated in the Progressive era. It advances beyond the view that the threat posed by corporate power to democracy is rooted in corporate bribery and corruption of elected officials and asserts instead that the greater danger to electoral politics is the potential for large corporations to use their "immense aggregated wealth" to "distort" the political process. *Austin* invokes an ethic of fairness to define the rights of the corporate citizen with regard to candidate elections and thereby establishes a new standard of corporate social responsibility for the political MARKETPLACE OF IDEAS that is very similar, in principle, to that established by the rule of reason for the economic marketplace. However, in regulating corporate speech, the Supreme Court has conferred legitimacy on the corporate citizen which, as a member of the political community, can exercise its First and Fourteenth Amendment rights of political speech, press, petition, and association with minimal restrictions. With respect to the corporation's expanding constitutional freedoms, it is significant to note that Justice LEWIS F. POWELL, writing for a plurality in *Pacific Gas and Electric Company v. California Public Utilities Commission* (1986), did not distinguish negative First Amendment rights of corporations from those of real persons. In holding that a public utility cannot be compelled either to associate with disagreeable speech or to respond to others' views, Powell reasoned in effect that a business corporation possesses a mind or conscience. Thus corporate individualism and its ideological offspring, the corporate citizen, continue to justify and facilitate the widening scope of corporate power over economic, social, and political realms.

SCOTT R. BOWMAN
(2000)

(SEE ALSO: *Corporate Power, Free Speech, and Democracy; Dartmouth College v. Woodward; Progressive Constitutional Thought.*)

Bibliography

ARNOLD, THURMAN W. 1937 *The Folklore of Capitalism.* New Haven, Conn.: Yale University Press.

BOWMAN, SCOTT R. 1996 *The Modern Corporation and American Political Thought: Law, Power, and Ideology.* University Park: Pennsylvania State University Press.

BRUER, PATRICK J. 1992 Citizenship. Pages 145–147 in Kermit L. Hall, ed., *The Oxford Companion to the Supreme Court of the United States.* New York: Oxford University Press.

DODD, EDWIN MERRICK 1954 *American Business Corporations Until 1860.* Cambridge, Mass.: Harvard University Press.

HANDLIN, OSCAR and HANDLIN, MARY F. 1945 Origins of the American Business Corporation. *Journal of Economic History* 5:1–23.

HARTZ, LOUIS 1948 *Economic Policy and Democratic Thought: Pennsylvania, 1776–1860.* Chicago: Quadrangle Books.

HORWITZ, MORTON J. 1985 *Santa Clara* Revisited: The Development of Corporate Theory. *West Virginia Law Review* 88: 173–224.

HURST, JAMES WILLARD 1956 *Law and the Conditions of Freedom in the Nineteenth-Century United States.* Madison: University of Wisconsin Press.

MAYER, CARL J. 1990 Personalizing the Impersonal: Corporations and the Bill of Rights. *Hastings Law Journal* 41:577–667.

SKLAR, MARTIN J. 1988 *The Corporate Reconstruction of American Capitalism, 1890–1916: The Market, The Law, and Politics.* Cambridge, Eng.: Cambridge University Press.

CORPORATE FEDERALISM
(Historical Development)

Perhaps the most conspicuous aspect of the American federal system of government, aside from the continuing robustness of state government itself, is that CORPORATIONS in America are chartered overwhelmingly by the states and almost never by the national government. Despite the modern displacement and augmentation of state power by federal power in realms as diverse as criminal law and the regulation of morals, the power of states to create the corporations and other entities that conduct America's business affairs has steadfastly resisted federal encroachment. The United States is essentially alone among the commercialized industrial powers of the world in not allocating that power to the central governmental authority.

This allocation of power has long been controversial. Overwhelmingly, until the last quarter of the twentieth century, this allocation of governmental power has been regarded with hostility by those concerned with the parochialism of American state governments, with suspicion by historians explicating American political and institutional development, and with concern by economists committed to a planned economy. In these perspectives, the state power to charter corporations and control the existence of other business entities looked to be a "race to the bottom" in which states seeking the revenue provided by corporate chartering fees were the witting and unwitting pawns of businesses and those who controlled them. The states became pawns because corporations may freely do business in all states even though chartered by only one, and because they are also free to change their state of incorporation at will. Thus, businesses both covertly and overtly evaded or overcame regulations framed in the interest of shareholders and the larger public by pitting one state against another. Recently, however, scholars in economics and scholars in law influenced by them have posited a radical new interpretation of the allocation of the power to charter businesses. Congruent with the competitive principles of neoclassical economics, these scholars have reinterpreted the regime of state chartering as beneficial, not detrimental, both economically and politically. These scholars view the allocation of the power to charter businesses and its evolution not so much as evidence of the corruption of local politics, but as wealth- producing competition. This competitive process, these scholars suggest, is not necessarily corrupt but rather one that requires state governments to be attentive to the actual needs of successful businesses in a fluid and dynamic economy, balancing the necessary shareholder protection from incompetent and self-interested managers with managerial desire to obtain capital (from shareholders) cheaply, thus helping to maximize a business's production of wealth.

Proponents of each theory have propounded an admixture of history, economics, and political theory to make their claims. The story of FEDERALISM and the corporation thus has two components, one of which concerns the legal and economic nature of business entities and the other of which concerns the nature of the legal regime, constitutional, statutory, and COMMON LAW, relevant to the existence and status of those entities.

When the Constitution was adopted business was still largely a local phenomenon. Save for a handful of trading companies, few businesses reached beyond their local environment. The costs of communication and transportation, the uncertainties of the politics and the cultures of foreign environments, and the difficulties of controlling an organization over expanses of both time and space, made cosmopolitan enterprise expensive and problematic when possible, and more often impossible. Consequently, of necessity and habit, business enterprises were regarded as local.

At the time of the adoption of the Constitution, moreover, the corporation was not principally a business utility. Rather, it was a vehicle for the creation of entities more generally, such as municipal corporations and charitable corporations, as well as business corporations. Contemporary corporate law reflected that understanding. Each corporate entity, whether business or not, was a product of the energies of the local citizenry and the sanction of the sovereign body legislating the entity into existence. These creations came to be seen as products of the agreement of a sovereign body and a group of individuals who agreed to create a legal entity for certain purposes. Only occasionally were those purposes economic. Because business enterprise was local and severely limited in scale and scope, most businesses existed without being chartered by the sovereign.

In a federal constitutional system of DUAL SOVEREIGNTY, however, which sovereign had the power to create business entities quickly became controversial as the physical, temporal, and spatial boundaries for economic activity began very gradually to melt away. Entrepreneurial choice, however, was also legally limited.

States not only chartered corporations but also regulated them, usually through the charter itself. Entrepreneurs who sought the advantages of the corporate form, such as monopoly rights and limited liability (although there is today an important debate about whether these advantages, especially limited liability, were as prevalent or as advantageous as historians have long assumed), submitted to certain regulations as a condition of incorporation. Because state legislatures granted the charters—creation of subordinate legal entities being the prerogative of the sovereign, and SOVEREIGNTY residing ultimately in the legislature—corporations were legislative creations. Their creation thus occasioned, especially in times of antibusiness sentiment, stringent limits on corporate behavior and even outright denials of charters.

State legislative sovereignty was not, however, absolute. The courts, especially the Supreme Court, spent much effort, especially in the early nineteenth century, to create the preconditions for cosmopolitan, even national, businesses and to limit parochial control of those businesses by the states. In its early decisions it noted that corporations were creatures of common law as well as charter, thus claiming for itself a role in defining corporate existence. It laid this claim in DARTMOUTH COLLEGE V. WOODWARD (1816) by defining corporations as contracts between the sovereign and the individual corporators, and then using the CONTRACTS CLAUSE to prohibit states from changing the terms of such contracts after the charter was granted. It legimated congressional charters by validating the charter of the Bank of the United States in MCCULLOCH V. MARYLAND (1819) though Congress did not take advantage of this power often. The Court used its own power to create the presumption that a corporation might operate across state lines unless excluded from doing so, and then limited the terms on which a state might exclude. In these, and many other ways, the Court helped to create the legal regime that allowed corporations to reincorporate at will, and thus to take advantage of the economic and political conditions that made both the "race to the bottom" and the "climb to the top" plausible interpretations of the history of corporate federalism.

GREGORY A. MARK
(2000)

Bibliography

BUTLER, HENRY A. 1985 Nineteenth-Century Jurisdictional Competition in the Granting of Corporate Privileges. *Journal of Legal Studies* 14:129–166.
MARK, GREGORY A. 1998 The Court and the Corporation: Jurisprudence, Localism, and Federalism. *Supreme Court Review* 1997:403–437.

CORPORATE POWER, FREE SPEECH, AND DEMOCRACY

Although CORPORATIONS do not enjoy all constitutional rights enjoyed by individuals—for example, neither the RIGHT AGAINST SELF-INCRIMINATION under the Fifth Amendment nor the right against interstate discrimination under the PRIVILEGES AND IMMUNITIES clause of Article IV has been extended to corporate entities—they have been held to enjoy the right of FREEDOM OF SPEECH under the FIRST AMENDMENT. Numerous First Amendment claims have been litigated on behalf of media corporations invoking the FREEDOM OF THE PRESS as well as free speech. But the free speech clause has also been extended to nonmedia corporations. In FIRST NATIONAL BANK OF BOSTON V. BELLOTTI (1978), the Supreme Court invalidated a state law prohibiting any corporation from making contributions or expenditures for the purpose of influencing the vote on any state ballot INITIATIVE or REFERENDUM question other than one directly affecting its business. And in *Pacific Gas & Electric (PG&E) v. Public Utilities Commission* (1986), the Court invalidated a requirement that a utility corporation carry unwanted literature in its billing envelope. Each of these cases was decided over a vigorous DISSENTING OPINION objecting that speech rights should be limited to natural PERSONS, and that speech restrictions were a permissible condition upon government's grant of the considerable privileges of the corporate form.

Critics of corporate free-speech rights argue that corporations, which lack souls or personalities, cannot have any right comparable to that of individuals in self-expression. As Justice WILLIAM H. REHNQUIST wrote in dissent in *PG&E*, to ascribe "to such artificial entities an 'intellect' or 'mind' for freedom of conscience purposes is to confuse metaphor with reality." But the majority of the Court, in extending free-speech protection to corporations, has reasoned that the First Amendment protects values beyond speaker autonomy—specifically, the values of ensuring the free flow of information to the public and preventing the government from entrenching itself in power by distorting debate or suppressing dissident views. These systemic values, the Court has concluded, counsel against allowing government to regulate speech even when the speaker is a corporation.

A further reason for the Court's approach may well be the serious line-drawing problems that would attend any attempt to exclude corporations from free-speech protection. A tobacco manufacturer is a corporation, but so is a book publisher, a BROADCASTING company, a daily newspaper, and a nonprofit advocacy group. Excluding all corporations from the First Amendment would untenably exclude the speech of nonprofit advocacy organizations. But excluding only for-profit corporations would eliminate most newspapers, publishers, and broadcasters—an outcome incompatible with freedom of the press. Any attempt to exempt the institutional media would raise intractable problems of deciding who counts as a member. And although corporations do enjoy certain state-conferred advantages such as limited liability and tax benefits, government confers similar advantages on a range of other collective entities, from LABOR unions to POLITICAL PARTIES, that surely would not be disqualified from First Amendment protection on that account.

Still, critics object that corporate enjoyment of free-speech rights may itself distort or dampen debate and diversity in public discourse, so that corporate speech regulation will enhance rather than inhibit the freedom of speech. Such objections rest in part on the disproportionate market power of corporations, and the fear that freedom for corporate speakers will produce public debate dominated by those that are economically powerful. As Justice BYRON R. WHITE objected in dissent in *Bellotti*, corporations have acquired "vast amounts of money which may, if not regulated, dominate not only the economy but also the very heart of our democracy, the electoral process." A related but separate objection is that corporations will be able to use wealth aggregated for economic purposes to express political views without regard to whether they reflect the actual opinions of owners, customers, or employees.

The Court has acknowledged the second but not the first of these objections. It has maintained that regulations aimed at the content of speech may not be justified by the goal of equalizing relative speaking power—whether by inhibiting the speech of wealthy corporations or wealthy individuals. But in a narrowly divided 1990 decision, AUSTIN V. MICHIGAN CHAMBER OF COMMERCE, the Court held that for-profit corporations may be required to segregate their expenditures on behalf of political candidates from their corporate treasuries in order to deal with "the corrosive and distorting effects of immense aggregations of wealth that are accumulated with the help of the corporate form and that have little or no correlation to the public's support for the corporation's political ideas." Similar segregation requirements, the Court had previously held in *Federal Election Commission v. Massachusetts Citizens for Life* (1986), may not constitutionally be imposed on non-profit advocacy organizations, which present no similar danger of distortion. Thus, *Austin* stands as a shallow bow to the critics against a general backdrop of constitutional protection for corporate speech.

While the First Amendment has been held to bar most direct regulation of corporate speech through content-based laws, it also has been held to permit a wide range of content-neutral structural regulation of speech markets. For example, in TURNER BROADCASTING SYSTEM V. FEDERAL COMMUNICATIONS COMMISSION (1994, 1997), the Court held that Congress may require cable operators to carry broadcast programs they would otherwise drop in order to ensure competition in the video programming market and diversity in the broadcast choices available to households lacking cable television. Nor does current First Amendment law bar enforcement of general ANTITRUST LAW against media conglomerates found to have excessive market power. All that is required is that the goal of such structural regulation be economic rather than ideological, and that the regulation not be needlessly broad.

KATHLEEN M. SULLIVAN
(2000)

(SEE ALSO: *Corporate Citizenship; Electoral Process and the First Amendment.*)

Bibliography

BAKER, EDWIN C. 1995 Turner Broadcasting: Content-Based Regulation of Persons and Presses. *Supreme Court Review* 1994:57–128.

BEZANSON, RANDALL P. 1995 Institutional Speech. *Iowa Law Review* 80:735–824.

FISS, OWEN M. 1996 *Liberalism Divided: Freedom of Speech and the Many Uses of State Power.* Boulder, Colo.: Westview Press.

VARIOUS AUTHORS 1997 Speech and Power: Is First Amendment Absolutism Obsolete? *The Nation* 265:3:11–19.

CORPORATIONS AND THE CONSTITUTION

The United States is the organizational or the corporate society par excellence. Seen sociologically, numerous societal entities of a corporate nature exist. From the perspective of constitutional law, only the business corporation has the status of being a PERSON. Those enterprises are social organizations midway between the state and the individual, owing their existence to the latter's need for organization and the former's reluctance to supply it. They are part of the greatest silence of the Constitution—the nature and operation of the economy. Except for a few nebulous provisions in Article I, plus the OBLIGATION OF CONTRACTS clause and the property provisions of the Fifth Amendment, all is left to inference. Neither business corporations nor unions nor any other private organization (for example, universities, farmers' legions, veterans' leagues, and the like) are mentioned.

As a consequence, corporate organizations fit uneasily

into constitutional theory. As collectivities, they are the principal units of today's political pluralism. The giant corporations dominate the economy, both domestically and internationally. It was not always so. As late as 1800, only about 300 business corporations existed. Industrialization, coupled with massive governmental aid (pursuant to ALEXANDER HAMILTON's principles), so burgeoned corporate growth that during the 1850s more were formed than ever before. After the CIVIL WAR, the "trusts"—the forerunners of today's corporate giants—flowered.

The large corporations do not fit into democratic theory. Centers of economic and thus of political power, some are so mighty as to challenge the SOVEREIGNTY of the state. Constitutional decisions of the Supreme Court have formed a major part of the legal basis for that dominating position. DARTMOUTH COLLEGE V. WOODWARD (1819) set the tone. Chief Justice JOHN MARSHALL read the CONTRACT CLAUSE to nullify New Hampshire's attempt to alter Dartmouth's charter, originally granted by the English crown. In well-known language, Marshall called the corporation "an artificial being, invisible, intangible, and existing only in contemplation of law." He thus made it clear that corporations, although collectivities, were private entities, and by labeling them "artificial beings" he paved the way for the Court in 1886 to declare that corporations are PERSONS protected by the FOURTEENTH AMENDMENT. (Also in 1819, Marshall ruled that Congress had IMPLIED POWER to form corporations when "NECESSARY AND PROPER" to carry out its expressly granted powers. The decision, MCCULLOCH V. MARYLAND, is also noteworthy for its theory of BROAD CONSTRUCTION of the Constitution.)

As constitutional persons, corporations were able to invoke the DUE PROCESS clauses to fend off adverse regulations. By inventing the concept of SUBSTANTIVE (or economic) DUE PROCESS, the Supreme Court helped to defang the Granger, Populist, and nascent LABOR MOVEMENTS. FREEDOM OF CONTRACT was read into the Constitution; laissez-faire economics became constitutional DOCTRINE. By that one development the Court catapulted JUDICIAL REVIEW into a powerful instrument of governance.

LOCHNER V. NEW YORK (1905) is the best known economic due process decision. Over a famous dissent by Justice OLIVER WENDELL HOLMES, the Court invalidated a statute regulating the hours of workers in bakeries, because both the company's and the workers' freedoms to contract were improperly invaded. So many similar decisions were rendered that by 1924 John R. Commons called the Court "the first authoritative faculty of political economy in the world's history."

That practice was altered by the Great Depression: in 1937 the Court grudgingly conceded that economic policy was a province of federal legislation. The turning point came in WEST COAST HOTEL CORP. V. PARRISH (1937) and the

WAGNER ACT CASES (*National Labor Relations Board v. Jones & Laughlin Steel Corp.*, 1937). The latter decision in practical effect "constitutionalized" political pluralism. FERGUSON V. SKRUPA (1963) illustrates the modern, and doubtless permanent, attitude of the Court toward ECONOMIC REGULATION.

Noneconomic regulation is a different matter. In FIRST NATIONAL BANK OF BOSTON V. BELLOTTI (1978) the Court invalidated a Massachusetts statute prohibiting corporations from spending money to influence elections. Corporate managers now have an unabridgeable right not only to spend their personal funds to further their political views but to use the money of others (in legal theory, corporations are owned by the stockholders). Although fictional persons, corporations by judicial legislation are attaining many of the rights of natural persons.

Neither political theorists nor economists have produced a satisfactory theory of conscious economic cooperation and its effect on the constitutional order. The Supreme Court refuses to recognize the corporation for what it is—a private government that, save in label, differs little from public government. Americans are governed as much—perhaps more—by corporations as they are by the official organs of government. Corporations, moreover, have such an influence upon the governmental structure that a version of corporatism is in process of creation.

Corporations were originally considered to be arms of the state—divisions of society established to get some of the public's business done. Today, paradoxically, they are both associations of individuals and constitutional persons. As such, they challenge orthodox constitutional theory. Their governmental character could be acknowledged by the Supreme Court; but the Justices have usually refused to do so. However, SMITH V. ALLWRIGHT (1944) did apply constitutional norms to a corporate body (albeit not a chartered corporation)—the Democratic party; and in MARSH V. ALABAMA (1946) a business corporation operating a "company town" was subjected to the limits of the FIRST AMENDMENT.

The giant corporations have assets that overshadow those of most of the states (and, indeed, most nationstates). They have created a national economic system that makes a decentralized political order impractical. Traditional concepts of FEDERALISM have consequently had to give way to notions of nationalism. In recent decades, many corporations have become transnational and they are creating an international economic order. They thus challenge the political order of the nation-state much as their predecessors altered the original federal system.

Corporate bodies, whether business or otherwise, have become so socially significant that in one perspective they have replaced the individual (the natural person) as the basic unit of society. The modern corporation has created societies with structural foundations different from those of the past. Constitutional theory must therefore adapt itself to the corporation on three levels: federalism (in many respects corporations are in effect the most important units of local government); nationalism (where the transnational corporation challenges the sovereignty of the nation-state); and individualism (the natural person must become adapted to living in a hierarchic, bureaucratic society). To date, little scholarly activity has addressed any of these levels.

ARTHUR S. MILLER
(1986)

(SEE ALSO: *Corporate Citizenship; Corporate Federalism; Corporate Power, Free Speech, and Democracy; Multinational Corporations, Global Markets, and the Constitution.*)

Bibliography

COLEMAN, JAMES S. 1974 *Power and the Structure of Society.* New York: W. W. Norton.

COMMONS, JOHN R. 1924 *Legal Foundations of Capitalism.* Madison: University of Wisconsin Press.

MILLER, ARTHUR SELWYN 1976 *The Modern Corporate State: Private Governments and the Constitution.* Westport, Conn.: Greenwood Press.

CORRIGAN v. BUCKLEY
271 U.S. 323 (1926)

Reviewing a RESTRICTIVE COVENANT case from the DISTRICT OF COLUMBIA, the Supreme Court unanimously held that it presented no substantial constitutional question. The Court dismissed Fifth and FOURTEENTH AMENDMENT claims because they referred to government and state, not individual, actions. (Surprisingly, the Court failed to mention that the Fourteenth did not apply in the District.) Although these amendments provide for equal rights, they did not in any manner prohibit or invalidate contracts entered into by private individuals in respect to the control and disposition of their own property. The Court therefore dismissed the case for want of JURISDICTION.

DAVID GORDON
(1986)

(SEE ALSO: *Shelley v. Kraemer; State Action.*)

CORWIN, EDWARD S.
(1878–1963)

Edward S. Corwin, McCormick Professor of Jurisprudence at Princeton University, succeeded the nineteenth-century titans James Kent, Joseph Story, and THOMAS M.

COOLEY. Corwin's understanding of constitutional and political thought distinguished him from these lawyers and judges, who exemplified Edmund Burke's maxim that the study of law sharpens the mind by narrowing it. Matchless learning in government and history made him an eminent COMMENTATOR ON THE CONSTITUTION.

Corwin's *Liberty against Government* (1948) was a major defense of liberty as the fundamental American principle. *The Twilight of the Supreme Court* (1934) upheld the NEW DEAL with an idea of national power that left presidential and congressional power without statable limits. Corwin later more persuasively and moderately pondered the New Deal's extension of governmental power in relationship to the Founders' intention. In UNITED STATES V. DARBY (1941) Chief Justice HARLAN FISKE STONE had cited Chief Justice JOHN MARSHALL's definition of congressional power over INTERSTATE COMMERCE in GIBBONS V. OGDEN (1824) and Marshall's interpretation of NECESSARY AND PROPER in MCCULLOCH V. MARYLAND (1819). Corwin persuasively denied that Marshall would have consented to be "thus conscripted in the service of the New Deal": "Liberty, the spacious liberty of an expanding nation, not social equality, was the lodestar of his political philosophy." Corwin's bow to the "great Chief Justice" Marshall showed that Corwin, too, championed liberty.

Public law, said Corwin, is the "law that governs government itself"; political theory is the branch that explains the moral source of the law's authority. Corwin identified his topics and accomplishments in public law as the origins and development of the idea of liberty against government, "the most important theme of American constitutional legal history"; JUDICIAL REVIEW in historical perspective; DUAL FEDERALISM; and the Presidency.

The Constitution and What It Means Today (1920, 1958), his best known work, combined scholarship and simplicity. Popular education for Corwin kept the Constitution from becoming a "craft mystery," whether one of bench and bar or of behaviorism. Corwin's most important work was *The President: Office and Powers* (1957), which concluded that the autonomous and self-directing idea of the Presidency had triumphed. Decades before the WATERGATE crimes he prophetically challenged the excesses of presidential power with the idea of liberty against government. The most important condition of the people's moderation in liberty was religious instruction. Corwin's *Constitution of Powers in a Secular State* (1951) opposed Supreme Court decisions against religious instruction in the public schools, arguing that the American people understand democracy as a system of ethical principles "grounded in religion." Hence, religion in effect should habituate Americans to virtue; virtue should guide the use of liberty.

Corwin's preeminence arose in part from his emphasis

on fundamentals, restoration of natural law, explanations of doctrine, grasp of the perennial themes of American politics and history, and understanding of the enduring principles that prop the Constitution. In teaching future scholars, Corwin had, according to Alpheus T. Mason, the gift "of reaching within each person, of discovering something firm and worthwhile, of encouraging him to stand on it." As Corwin himself put it, "a noble emulation is the true source of excellence."

RICHARD LOSS
(1986)

Bibliography

LOSS, RICHARD 1977 Edward S. Corwin: The Constitution of the Dominant Presidency. *Presidential Studies Quarterly* 7: 53–65.
——, ed. 1981 Corwin on the Constitution, Volume I, The Foundations of American Constitutional and Political Thought, the Powers of Congress, and the President's Power of Removal. Ithaca, N.Y.: Cornell University Press.
STEVENS, RICHARD G. 1980 The Constitution and What It Meant to Corwin. *Political Science Reviewer* 10:1–53.

CORWIN AMENDMENT
(1861)

On 2 March 1861, in a futile attempt to prevent the secession of the slaveholding states, Congress proposed, and sent to the states for ratification, a constitutional amendment designed to protect SLAVERY in the states where it existed. The amendment, written by Representative Thomas Corwin of Ohio, would have prohibited any future constitutional amendment authorizing Congress to abolish or interfere with the "domestic institutions" of any state. Although the amendment went on specifically to include the institution of "persons held to service or labor," it is not clear what other domestic institutions, if any, might have been protected.

The Corwin Amendment was proposed after President-elect ABRAHAM LINCOLN rejected the CRITTENDEN compromise proposals, which would have permitted slavery in some federal territories. Its intended effect was that, although slavery would survive in the existing slave states, there would never be any new slave states admitted to the union, and slaveholders would be an ever diminishing minority. In any case, the Corwin Amendment was largely a symbolic gesture of conciliation, as six southern states had already seceded by the time it was proposed. The legislatures of only two states (Ohio and Maryland) voted to ratify the Corwin Amendment.

DENNIS J. MAHONEY
(1986)

Bibliography

HYMAN, HAROLD M. 1967 The Narrow Escape from the Compromise of 1860: Secession and the Constitution. Pages 149–166 in Harold M. Hyman and Leonard W. Levy, eds., *Freedom and Reform.* New York: Harper & Row.

COUNSEL, RIGHT TO BE REPRESENTED BY

See: Right to Counsel

COUNSELMAN v. HITCHCOCK
142 U.S. 547 (1892)

The first Supreme Court decision on immunity statutes, *Counselman* remained the leading case until it was distinguished away in KASTIGAR V. UNITED STATES (1972). Appellant refused to testify before a federal GRAND JURY on the ground that he might incriminate himself, though he had been granted USE IMMUNITY under an 1887 act of Congress guaranteeing that his evidence would not be used against him criminally, except in a prosecution for perjury. *Counselman* thus raised the question whether a grant of use immunity could supplant the Fifth Amendment right of a person not to be a witness against himself in a criminal case. The government contended that an investigation before a grand jury was not a criminal case, which could arise only after an INDICTMENT should be returned, but that in any instance, Counselman had received immunity in return for his testimony.

Justice SAMUEL BLATCHFORD for a unanimous Court declared that it is "impossible" that the clause of the Fifth Amendment could mean only what it says, for it is not limited to situations in which one is compelled to be a witness against himself in a "criminal case." The object of the clause is to insure that no person should be compelled as a witness "in any investigation" to testify to anything that might tend to show he had committed a crime. "The privilege is limited to criminal matters, but it is as broad as the mischief against which it seeks to guard," and therefore it applied to grand jury proceedings that might result in a prosecution. Clearly, said Blatchford, a statute cannot abridge a constitutional privilege nor replace one, "unless it is so broad as to have the same extent in scope and effect." The statute did not even do what it purported to do; it did not bar use of the compelled testimony, for its fruits could be used against the witness by searching out any leads, originating with his testimony, to other evidence that could convict him. No statute leaving the witness subject to prosecution after answering incriminating questions can have the effect of supplanting the constitutional provision. The 1887 act of Congress was unconstitutional because it was not a "full substitute" for that provision.

Thus the Court introduced the extraordinary doctrine that a statute could be a substitute for a provision of the Constitution, after having said that a statute could not "replace" such a provision. But the statute, to be constitutional, must serve "co-extensively" with the right it replaces. The Court laid down the standard for TRANSACTIONAL IMMUNITY: to be valid the statute "must afford absolute immunity against future prosecution for the offense to which the question relates."

LEONARD W. LEVY
(1986)

(SEE ALSO: *Right Against Self-Incrimination.*)

COUNTY OF ALLEGHENY v. AMERICAN CIVIL LIBERTIES UNION
492 U.S. 573 (1989)

Each year the County of Allegheny set up a variety of exhibits to commemorate the holiday season. Inside the county courthouse, a crèche was displayed on the grand staircase. Outside the courthouse stood a Christmas tree and a menorah, the latter a symbol of Hanukkah. The outside display was accompanied by a sign describing it as part of the city's salute to liberty. A splintered Supreme Court ruled that the crèche violated the ESTABLISHMENT CLAUSE, but the menorah did not.

Justice HARRY A. BLACKMUN delivered the opinion of the Court with respect to the crèche. He argued that the crèche violated the second prong of the LEMON TEST because it expressed a patently religious message, as indicated by an accompanying banner with the words "Gloria in Excelsis Deo!" ("Glory to God in the Highest!"). However, Blackmun argued that the menorah did not endorse religion because in context it was devoid of religious significance. The menorah and Christmas tree together merely symbolized the different facets of the "same winter-holiday season, which has attained a secular status in our society."

Justice SANDRA DAY O'CONNOR rejected Blackmun's reasoning with respect to the menorah, although she concurred in the Court's judgment. Unlike Blackmun, O'Connor readily acknowledged the religious meaning of the menorah, but argued that its display was permissible because in context it "conveyed a message of pluralism and freedom of belief" rather than endorsement. Justices WILLIAM J. BRENNAN, JOHN PAUL STEVENS, and THURGOOD MARSHALL disagreed. They contended that both the Christmas tree and the menorah were religious symbols and that their display effected a dual endorsement of Christianity and Judaism.

Four Justices on the Court—WILLIAM H. REHNQUIST, ANTONIN SCALIA, BYRON R. WHITE, and ANTHONY M. KENNEDY—took issue with the Court's ruling on the crèche. Writing for this group, Justice Kennedy argued that the guiding principle in establishment-clause cases should be government neutrality toward religion—but neutrality properly understood. Given the pervasive influence of the "modern administrative state," said Kennedy, complete government nonrecognition of religion would send "a clear message of disapproval." Hence, some government recognition of religion may actually further the goal of neutrality. As applied to this case, for the government to recognize only the secular aspects of a holiday with both secular and religious components would signal not neutrality but "callous indifference" toward the religious beliefs of a great many celebrants. Such hostility is not required by the Constitution according to Kennedy. As long as holiday displays do not directly or indirectly coerce people in the area of religion and the displays do not tend toward the establishment of a state religion, they should be constitutional. Under this standard, the crèche, the Christmas tree, and the menorah were all permissible.

JOHN G. WEST, JR.
(1992)

(SEE ALSO: *Establishment of Religion; Lynch v. Donnelly; Religious Liberty; Separation of Church and State.*)

COURT MARTIAL

See: Military Justice

COURT OF CLAIMS

See: Claims Court

COURT OF CUSTOMS AND PATENT APPEALS

The Court of Customs Appeals was established by Congress in 1909 to hear appeals from the Board of General Appraisers, a body that itself heard appeals from decisions by customs collectors. (In 1926 the Board became the United States Customs Court, and in 1980 that court was converted into the United States COURT OF INTERNATIONAL TRADE.) In 1929 Congress renamed the court and expanded its jurisdiction. The new Court of Customs and Patent Appeals (CCPA) heard, in addition, appeals from the Patent Office in both patent and trademark cases.

In 1958 Congress declared the CCPA to be a CONSTITUTIONAL COURT, created under Article III. In *Glidden Co. v. Zdanok* (1962) the Supreme Court held, 5–2, that the CCPA was, indeed, an Article III court, despite its statutory authorization to do some nonjudicial business. There was no opinion of the Court, and the theories supporting the decision were in conflict. Justice JOHN MARSHALL HARLAN, for three Justices, concluded that the CCPA had been an Article III court since 1930, when Congress had granted its members life tenure during good behavior. Justice TOM C. CLARK, for the other two majority Justices, said that the 1958 declaration of Congress had converted the CCPA into a constitutional court. Justice WILLIAM O. DOUGLAS, joined by Justice HUGO L. BLACK, dissented, arguing that the court remained a LEGISLATIVE COURT despite the congressional declaration. Thus, while a majority rejected each theory argued in support of the decision, the result was acceptance of the CCPA's Article III status.

In the FEDERAL COURTS IMPROVEMENT ACT (1982) Congress abolished the CCPA, transferring its JURISDICTION to a newly established UNITED STATES COURT OF APPEALS FOR THE FEDERAL CIRCUIT.

KENNETH L. KARST
(1986)

COURT OF INTERNATIONAL TRADE

In 1926 Congress converted the Board of General Appraisers, which had been hearing APPEALS from decisions of customs collectors, into the United States Customs Court. In 1956, Congress declared that the court was established under Article III. Because the court's business is strictly "judicial" and its members are appointed for life during good behavior, it is probably a CONSTITUTIONAL COURT on the same reasoning that was applied to the COURT OF CUSTOMS AND PATENT APPEALS (CCPA).

In 1980 Congress changed the Customs Court's name to the United States Court of International Trade and extended its JURISDICTION to include additional noncustoms matters relating to international trade. Its decisions, formerly reviewed by the CCPA, today are reviewed by the UNITED STATES COURT OF APPEALS FOR THE FEDERAL CIRCUIT.

KENNETH L. KARST
(1986)

COURT OF MILITARY APPEALS

In the Uniform Code of Military Justice, enacted in the aftermath of WORLD WAR II, Congress established the Court of Military Appeals (COMA). A civilian body, whose three judges serve for fifteen-year terms, COMA reviews questions of law arising in certain serious court-martial cases. COMA, which heard its first case in 1951, has never been part of the federal judiciary. The whole military justice system, COMA included, is part of the governance of the armed forces. Since 1983, however, many of COMA's decisions have been reviewable by the Supreme Court on petition for CERTIORARI. Whether or not such a review has taken place, a person in custody as a result of a court-martial decision can apply for HABEAS CORPUS in a federal district court. (See MILITARY JUSTICE.)

Like many another judicial or military institution, COMA has sought to expand its jurisdiction. It has developed a notion of its own "inherent powers," which it has used to nudge the military justice system toward increasing resemblance to the civilian system of criminal justice, notably by tightening the requirements of procedural fairness. Although some military officers have strongly criticized COMA's "constitutionalizing" innovations, most proposals for statutory restoration of the old order have died in congressional committees.

KENNETH L. KARST
(1986)

Bibliography

WILLIS, JOHN T. 1972 The Constitution, the United States Court of Military Appeals and the Future. *Military Law Review* 57:27–97.

——— 1972 The United States Court of Military Appeals: Its Origin, Operation and Future. *Military Law Review* 55:39–93.

COURT-PACKING PLANS

"Court packing" is an ambiguous phrase. It arises more frequently as an epithet in political disputation than as an analytical term in scholarly discourse. "Packing" connotes a deliberate effort by an executive, especially a President, to appoint one or more (usually more) judges to assure that decisions will accord with the ideological predisposition of that executive. *Webster's New International Dictionary* defines "pack" as "to . . . make up unfairly or fraudulently, to secure a certain result." Yet not everyone agrees on what is unfair, and it is not at all extraordinary for Presidents to take pains to ascertain that a prospective nominee is likely to behave in ways that will not be out of harmony with the ends of their administrations.

Furthermore, the word "packing" has been employed with respect to two different situations—when a President is filling vacancies that have arisen in the natural course of events, and when a President seeks legislation to increase the membership of courts to create additional opportunities for appointments that may shape the outcome of pending and future litigation.

Although political antagonists have taken advantage of the elasticity of the word to raise the charge of Court packing through much of our history, scholars have largely concentrated their attention on three particular episodes. The first of these events took place on the night of March 3, 1801, when in his final hours in office, President JOHN ADAMS sat up very late signing commissions of sixteen appointees to circuit judgeships and forty-two justices of the peace for the District of Columbia, including one William Marbury. All these offices had been created in the last three weeks of his term by an obliging Federalist Congress, and Adams, outraged by the victory of the Democratic Republicans in 1800 and fearful of its consequences for the nation, busied himself filling the posts with faithful partisans to serve as a restraint on his successor, THOMAS JEFFERSON. This melodrama of the "midnight judges" would subsequently lead to the landmark case of MARBURY V. MADISON (1803).

Historians long thought they had detected another instance of Court packing during RECONSTRUCTION. In 1870, at a time when the membership of the Court had been reduced, the Supreme Court, in *Hepburn v. Griswold*, struck down the Legal Tender Act of 1862 as applied to debts incurred before its enactment. The 4–3 vote strictly followed party lines. A year later, in *Knox v. Lee* and *Parker v. Davis*, the decision was reversed when the three dissenters in the earlier ruling were joined by two new appointees, both Republicans, of President ULYSSES S. GRANT. Their appointments followed the action of Congress restoring the Court to nine Justices. This sequence gave credibility to the allegation that the Court had been packed in order to save the Republican administration's monetary policy. In fact, however, scholars now agree that neither the augmentation of the size of the bench nor these appointments resulted from partisan or ideological motivations.

By far the most important Court-packing plan in American history emerged out of a conflict between the Supreme Court and the administration of FRANKLIN D. ROOSEVELT in the Great Depression. In 1935 and 1936, the Court again and again struck down NEW DEAL laws, including those creating the two foundation stones of Roosevelt's recovery program, the NATIONAL INDUSTRIAL RECOVERY ACT and the AGRICULTURAL ADJUSTMENT ACT OF 1935 (AAA). Most of these rulings came on split decisions, with OWEN J. ROBERTS joining the conservative "Four Horsemen"—PIERCE BUTLER, JAMES C. MCREYNOLDS, GEORGE SUTHERLAND, and WILLIS VAN DEVANTER—to form a five-man majority, sometimes augmented by the Chief Justice, CHARLES EVANS HUGHES.

The Roosevelt administration responded by exploring a number of possibilities for curbing the powers of the Supreme Court. As early as May 1935, Attorney General HOMER S. CUMMINGS directed one of his aides to look into how the Court's authority to pass on constitutional questions could be limited. Rumors had circulated from the beginning of the New Deal era that Court packing might someday be attempted, and at a cabinet meeting at the end of 1935, the President mentioned packing the Court as the first of a series of options. A cabinet official noted in his diary, however, that Roosevelt characterized it as "a distasteful idea." Still, Roosevelt more than once alluded to the episode in Great Britain earlier in the century when the threat of creating several hundred new peers had compelled the House of Lords to approve reform legislation.

Initially, critics of the judiciary assumed that redress could be achieved only by amending the Constitution, but the behavior of the Court in 1936 turned the thinking of the administration in new directions. When Justice HARLAN F. STONE, in a biting dissent in BUTLER V. UNITED STATES (1936), accused the majority in the 6–3 ruling invalidating the AAA processing tax of a "tortured construction of the Constitution," he fostered the idea that Congress need not alter the Constitution because properly interpreted it could accommodate most of the New Deal. Instead, Congress should concern itself with the composition of the Court.

The replacement of even one Justice could shift 5–4 decisions toward approval of FDR's policies without any modification of the Constitution. Yet, although this Court was the oldest ever, not a single vacancy developed in all of Roosevelt's first term. Increasingly, the administration looked for a solution that would eschew the tortuous process of constitutional amendment and instead, by the much simpler procedure of an act of Congress, overcome obstruction by elderly judges.

Shortly after winning reelection in November 1936, Roosevelt told Cummings that the time to act had come. Not only had the Court struck down fundamental New Deal laws in his first term, but in addition, it was expected to invalidate innovative legislation such as the National Labor Relations Act and the SOCIAL SECURITY ACT when it ruled on these statutes early in his second term. Moreover, although he had won an overwhelming endorsement from the people in a contest in which he had carried all but two of the states, he was constrained from taking advantage of this mandate because if he tried to put through measures such as a wages and hours law the Court was likely to wipe out those laws too. He saw little prospect that the Court might change its attitude; in the very last decision of the term, MOREHEAD V. NEW YORK EX REL. TIPALDO (1936), it had shocked the nation by striking down a New York State minimum wage law for women, thereby indicating that it did not merely oppose concentrated power in Washington, but was in the President's words, creating a "no-man's land" where no Government—State or Federal—can function." Under these circumstances, FDR was determined not to be like President JAMES BUCHANAN, who sat passively while his world collapsed about him.

During the month of December, Cummings put together the specific proposal that Roosevelt embraced. Cummings was influenced by the political scientist EDWARD S. CORWIN, who suggested linking an age limit of seventy years for Justices to the appointment of additional members of the bench, but he did not find the precise formula until he came upon a 1913 memorandum by James C. McReynolds, then attorney general, recommending that when a judge of the lower federal courts did not retire at seventy the President be required to appoint an additional judge. Cummings seized McReynolds's idea and applied it to the Supreme Court as well. He also worked out a rationale for the scheme by incorporating it in a package of proposals for relieving congestion in the federal judicial system. Roosevelt, for his part, savored the irony that the original notion had come from McReynolds, now the most hostile Justice on the Court.

Through all these months, the President had given little indication of what he was considering. After the adverse decision in SCHECHTER POULTRY CORPORATION V. UNITED STATES, he had said, "We have been relegated to the horse-and-buggy definition of interstate commerce," but so loud were objections to this remark that he made almost no public utterance about the Court for the next year and a half and did not raise the issue in the 1936 campaign. No cabinet officer save Cummings knew of the surprise he was about to spring, and he confided nothing to his congressional leaders until the very end.

On February 5, 1937, Roosevelt stunned the nation by sending to Congress a plan to reorganize the federal judiciary. He prefaced the proposal by claiming that aged and infirm judges and insufficient personnel had created overcrowded federal court dockets and by asserting that "a constant and systematic addition of younger blood will vitalize the courts." To achieve this goal, he recommended that when a federal judge who had served at least ten years waited more than six months after his seventieth birthday to resign or retire, a President might add a new judge to the bench. He could appoint as many as six new Justices to the Supreme Court and forty-four new judges to the lower federal tribunals.

The President's message elicited boisterous opposition. From the very first day, opponents characterized his scheme as "court packing" and accused Roosevelt of tampering with the judiciary. Within weeks, they had forced him to back away from his crowded dockets-old age rationale by demonstrating that the Supreme Court was abreast of his work. Especially effective was a letter from Chief Justice Hughes read by Senator BURTON K. WHEELER at the opening of hearings before the SENATE JUDICIARY COMMITTEE. An increase in the size of the Court, Hughes objected, would not promote efficiency, but would mean that "there would be more judges to hear, more judges to confer, more judges to discuss, more judges to be convinced and to decide."

Despite fervent and well-organized protests, commentators concluded that the legislation was likely to be approved because Roosevelt had such huge Democratic majorities in both houses of Congress. After the 1936 elections, the Republicans were reduced to only sixteen members in the Senate. In the House, the Democrats had a 4–1 advantage. Although there were some conspicuous defectors, such as Wheeler, it seemed unlikely that enough Democrats would break with a President who had just won such an emphatic popular verdict of approval to deny him the legislation he sought.

A series of unanticipated decisions by the Court, however, drastically altered this situation. On March 29, the Court, in a 5–4 ruling in WEST COAST HOTEL CO. V. PARRISH (1937), validated a minimum wage act of the state of Washington essentially the same as the New York law it had struck down the previous year. Two weeks later, in a cluster of 5–4 decisions, it upheld the constitutionality of the WAGNER (NATIONAL LABOR RELATIONS) ACT. In May, by 5–4 and 7–2, it validated the Social Security Act. The critical development in these votes was the switch of Justice Roberts, who for the first time since the spring of 1935, broke away from the Four Horsemen to uphold social legislation. Roberts's turnabout gave Roosevelt a 5–4 advantage, which swelled to a prospective 6–3 when, also in May, one of the Four Horsemen, Willis Van Devanter, announced that he was retiring. On that same day, the Senate Judiciary Committee voted, 10–8, to recommend against passage of the bill, and administration polls of the Senate found that as a consequence of these developments Roosevelt no longer had the votes. "A switch in time," it was said, "saved nine."

Roosevelt, however, persisted in trying to put through a modified Court-packing measure, and he almost succeeded. In June, he advanced a compromise raising the suggested retirement age from seventy to seventy-five years and permitting him only one appointment per calendar year. Although watered down, this new version preserved the principle of the original bill and would give him two new Justices by January 1, 1938 (one for the calendar year 1937 and one for 1938), as well as a third Justice for the Van Devanter vacancy. In July, when Court-packing legislation finally reached the Senate floor, the opposition found that Roosevelt had a majority for this new proposal if it could be brought to the floor. The President's advantage, however, rested on the influence of the domineering Senate Majority Leader, Joseph T. Robinson, but when shortly after the debate began, Robinson died, Roosevelt's expectation went down with him. On July 22, the Senate voted to inter the bill in committee.

Roosevelt had suffered a severe defeat, but he insisted that, although he had lost the battle, he had won the war. To the Van Devanter vacancy, he soon named HUGO L. BLACK, an ardent New Dealer and supporter of Court packing, and within two and a half years of his defeat, he was able to appoint a majority of the nine Justices. This "Roosevelt Court," as it was called, never again struck down a New Deal law. Indeed, it took so expansive a view of the commerce power and the spending power and so circumscribed the due process clause that scholars speak of the "Constitutional Revolution of 1937." Not once since then has the Court stuck down any significant law—federal or state—regulating business. The struggle over Court packing, however, cost Roosevelt dearly, for it solidified a bipartisan conservative coalition arrayed against further New Deal reforms.

Although no President since Roosevelt has advocated a Court packing statute, the charge of packing has been raised against three of his successors. When, in his final year in office, LYNDON B. JOHNSON sought to elevate Associate Justice ABE FORTAS to the Chief Justiceship, conservative Republicans charged him with a "midnight judge" kind of maneuver to deny his probable successor, RICHARD M. NIXON, the opportunity to make the selection, and after revelations about Fortas's comportment, the endeavor failed. So frank was Nixon in turn about stating his desire to reverse the doctrines of the WARREN COURT that he was accused of trying to pack the Supreme Court with conservative jurists when he made nominations such as those of Clement Haynsworth and G. Harrold Carswell. Both of these nominations were rejected, but Nixon won confirmation of four other choices, including WARREN E. BURGER as Chief Justice, although they were sometimes to disappoint him by their subsequent behavior. An even louder outcry arose over RONALD REAGAN's selections. His attempt to place Robert Bork on the Supreme Court was turned aside, but he secured approval of four other nominees, all regarded as sharing his conservative outlook. He had even greater success in the lower federal courts. His efforts were decried as, in the title of one book, *Packing the Courts: The Conservative Campaign to Rewrite the Constitution*, but neither Reagan nor Nixon had acted markedly differently from such twentieth-century predecessors as WILLIAM HOWARD TAFT, WARREN G. HARDING, and Franklin D. Roosevelt, although none of the others may have exhibited such sedulous ideological zeal.

WILLIAM E. LEUCHTENBURG
(1992)

Bibliography
ALSOP, JOSEPH and CATLEDGE, TURNER 1938 *The 168 Days.* Garden City, N.Y.: Doubleday, Doran.

LEUCHTENBURG, WILLIAM E. 1966 The Origins of Franklin D. Roosevelt's "Court Packing" Plan. In Philip B. Kurland, ed. *The Supreme Court Review: 1966.* Pages 347–400. Chicago: University of Chicago Press.
———— 1969 Franklin D. Roosevelt's Supreme Court "Packing" Plan. In Harold M. Hollingsworth and William F. Holmes, eds., *Essays on the New Deal.* Pages 69–115. Austin: University of Texas.

COURTS AND SOCIAL CHANGE, I

Since the mid-twentieth century, courts in the United States have been involved in many of the most important, difficult, and emotional issues of modern politics. From racial and gender equality to ABORTION to reform of CRIMINAL PROCEDURE, court decisions have ordered change on a broad scale on behalf of relatively powerless groups that have suffered from both past and present discrimination. Further, such litigation has often occurred, and appears to have been most successful, when the other branches of government have failed to act. Indeed, for many, part of what makes American democracy exceptional is that it includes the world's most powerful court system, protecting minorities and defending liberty, in the face of opposition from the democratically elected branches. But have courts contributed to social change?

Supreme Court decisions are not self-implementing. As ALEXANDER HAMILTON pointed out long ago, courts are particularly dependent on the actions of others. Hamilton argued in THE FEDERALIST #78, that the judiciary "has no influence over either the sword or the purse . . . and must ultimately depend upon the aid of the executive arm even for the efficacy of its judgments." Without the support of government, or of citizens, court decisions ordering social change are unlikely to affect or change people's lives in important ways.

Those seeking social change through litigation often must rely on the Constitution, and the set of beliefs that surround it. The problem they face is that the Constitution is not unbounded; certain rights are enshrined in it and others are not. For example, there are no constitutional rights to decent housing, adequate levels of welfare or health care, or clean air, while there are constitutional rights to minimal governmental interference in the use of one's PROPERTY. Lacking a strong constitutional foundation for their litigation, reformers often must push the courts to read the Constitution in an expansive or "liberal" way. This presents an additional obstacle to change due to judicial awareness of the need for predictability in the law and the politically exposed nature of judges whose decisions go beyond the positions of electorally accountable officials. Thus, the nature of rights in the U.S. legal system, embedded in the Constitution, and the institutional reticence of judges, may constrain the courts in producing social change by preventing them from hearing or responding positively to many claims.

The result of these factors—lack of constitutional rights, lack of power of implementation, lack of JUDICIAL INDEPENDENCE—is that courts are constrained from producing social change. Courts decisions can sometimes contribute to change, but only when there is broad political support for it. Consider, for example, one of the most famous Supreme Court decisions ordering social change on behalf of a relatively powerless group within society, BROWN V. BOARD OF EDUCATION (1954).

Given the praise accorded to the 1954 *Brown* decision and its holding that race-based SEGREGATION of public schools was unconstitutional, examining its actual effects produces quite a surprise. The surprise is that a decade after *Brown* little had changed for most African American students living in the eleven states of the old Confederacy that had required race-based school segregation by law. For example, in the 1963–1964 school year, barely one in one hundred (1.2 percent) of these African American children was in a nonsegregated school. That means that for nearly ninety-nine of every one-hundred African American children in the South a decade after *Brown*, the finding of a constitutional right changed nothing.

Change came to school systems in the South in the wake of congressional and executive branch action. Title VI of the CIVIL RIGHTS ACT OF 1964 required the cut-off of federal funds to programs receiving federal monies where RACIAL DISCRIMINATION was practiced and the 1965 Elementary & Secondary Education Act provided a great deal of federal money to generally poor Southern school districts. This combination of federal funding and Title VI gave the executive branch a tool to induce DESEGREGATION when it chose to do so. When the U.S. Department of Health, Education, and Welfare began to threaten fund cut-offs to school districts that refused to desegregate, dramatic change occurred. By the 1972–1973 school year, over 91 percent of African American school children in the eleven Southern states were in integrated schools, up from 1.2 percent in the 1963–1964 school year.

Brown shows that U.S. courts by themselves can almost never be effective producers of social change. At best, they can second the social reform acts of the other branches of government. Problems that are unsolvable in the political context can rarely be solved by courts. Turning to courts to produce social change substitutes the myth of America for its reality. It credits courts and judicial decisions with a power they do not have.

GERALD N. ROSENBERG
(2000)

Bibliography

DAHL, ROBERT A. 1957 Decision-Making in a Democracy: The Role of the Supreme Court as a National Policy-Maker. *Journal of Public Law* 6:279–295.

HAMILTON, ALEXANDER; MADISON, JAMES; and JAY, JOHN 1961 (1788) *The Federalist*. Clinton Rossiter, ed. New York: New American Library.

GALANTER, MARC 1974 Why the 'Haves' Come Out Ahead: Speculations on the Limits of Social Change. *Law & Society Review* 9:95–160.

HOROWITZ, DONALD L. 1977 *The Courts and Social Policy*. Washington, D.C.: Brookings Institution.

MCCLOSKEY, ROBERT G. 1994 *The American Supreme Court*, 2nd ed. Chicago: University of Chicago Press.

ROSENBERG, GERALD N. 1991 *The Hollow Hope: Can Courts Bring About Social Change?* Chicago: University of Chicago Press.

SCHEINGOLD, STUART A. 1974 *The Politics of Rights*. New Haven, Conn.: Yale University Press.

COURTS AND SOCIAL CHANGE, II

The apparent accomplishments of the WARREN COURT led liberals to believe that the Supreme Court could contribute substantially to social change. They saw BROWN V. BOARD OF EDUCATION (1954) as the precursor of the CIVIL RIGHTS movement of the 1960s, and the Court's CRIMINAL PROCEDURE decisions such as MIRANDA V. ARIZONA (1966) as the driving force behind substantial changes in police practices. Even after the retirement of Chief Justice EARL WARREN, ROE V. WADE (1973) suggested that the Court's decisions might lead to major changes in important social practices. The Court's decisions in the 1970s striking down statutes as SEX DISCRIMINATION similarly supported the view that the Court could be an important force for social change.

Overall, however, the BURGER COURT and the REHNQUIST COURT suggested to liberals that their enthusiasm for the courts might have been misplaced. The Burger Court initially invalidated CAPITAL PUNISHMENT, but then endorsed state efforts to reestablish it. The Court rejected an early challenge to state laws making homosexual sodomy illegal in BOWERS V. HARDWICK (1986). It also eroded important Warren Court PRECEDENTS, relieving school districts of further obligations to undo the effects of racial SEGREGATION, and refused to extend the Warren Court's criminal procedure holdings. By the 1990s, some liberal constitutional scholars thought, society's protection of the rights the Warren Court singled out was not significantly different from the situation that had existed in the early years of Warren's tenure.

These events led to a more subtle understanding of the Court's relation to social change. A long-standing view, going back to at least the early 1900s, is that the Court "follows the election returns": Court decisions simply ratify changes that have already taken place. A defender of this view would contend, for example, that major changes in the social role of women preceded the Court's gender discrimination decisions of the 1970s. The courts' withdrawal from the field of school desegregation occurred after changes in the political climate made SCHOOL BUSING and other desegregation remedies increasingly unpopular.

Political scientist Gerald Rosenberg mounted an important attack on the view that the courts could play a large part in inducing major social changes. Rosenberg pointed out that no significant amount of desegregation occurred in the deep South until the mid-1960s, a decade after *Brown,* and took place only when Congress enacted civil rights statutes that threatened recalcitrant districts with the loss of federal financial assistance. Then, observing that the Court's ABORTION decisions succeeded in making abortions more easily available, Rosenberg argued that the courts' ability to contribute to social change varied depending on the kind of change involved. The segregation cases showed that the courts could do little when success depended on the cooperation of other political actors. Abortion was different, in Rosenberg's view, because the Court's decisions created a market that could be satisfied by private parties without government support.

Rosenberg's critics believed that he failed adequately to take account of indirect effects of court decisions. They argued that *Brown* had important effects, which Rosenberg minimized, on the spirits of civil rights activists, encouraging them to continue their activities because they knew that the Court agreed with their vision of the Constitution.

This criticism suggests that the courts can affect social change along two dimensions. Rosenberg focused on immediate effects on actual practices, while his critics focused on longer-range effects accomplished by changing the understandings people have of what the Constitution requires. The critics' position is that courts change the way people think about the Constitution, and those changed views then lead people to support new policies. Contrary to this position are public opinion surveys showing that the courts have relatively small effects on public understandings, because the public either does not know of what the courts have done, or misinterprets the messages the courts have attempted to send.

In response, scholars who believe the courts do have important effects have directed attention away from immediate effects on social practices and on beliefs about the Constitution. They argue that the courts have produced a general American "rights-consciousness." For some, this makes Americans willing to sue to vindicate what they believe are their rights far more frequently than is appropriate, generating an "adversary culture" that makes it more difficult to resolve conflicts both large and small. For others, rights-consciousness endorses a highly individualist way of thinking about social problems, which makes it more difficult for Americans to develop group-oriented theories and strategies that might be more effective in vindicating the very rights at issue.

MARK TUSHNET
(2000)

Bibliography

GARROW, DAVID 1994 Hopelessly Hollow History: Revisionist Devaluing of *Brown v. Board of Education. Virginia Law Review* 80:151–160.
GLENDON, MARY ANN 1991 *Rights Talk: The Impoverishment of Political Discourse.* New York: Free Press.
ROSENBERG, GERALD 1991 *The Hollow Hope: Can Courts Bring About Social Change?* Chicago: University of Chicago Press.
TUSHNET, MARK 1984 An Essay on Rights. *Texas Law Review* 62:1363–1403.

COURTS OF APPEALS

See: United States Courts of Appeals

COVER, ROBERT M.
(1943–1986)

Born in Boston in 1943, Robert M. Cover earned his B.A. from Princeton University in 1965. In 1963 Cover had left Princeton to work for the Student Nonviolent Coordinating Committee (SNCC) in Georgia, where he was jailed and beaten. Although he became a superb scholar and an inspirational teacher and friend, Cover remained an engaged activist. He believed that "legal meaning is a challenging enrichment of social life, a potential restraint on arbitrary power and violence." He never separated himself or his work from that pursuit.

Cover received his LL.B. from Columbia Law School in 1968, at which time he immediately joined the Columbia faculty. He moved to Yale Law School in 1972 and was named the Chancellor Kent Professor of Law and Legal History in 1982.

Cover won the Ames Prize for *Justice Accused: Antislavery and the Judicial Process* (1975). This book probed the moral dilemma confronting northern judges opposed to slavery on moral grounds who nonetheless believed that the law of antebellum America required them to order fugitive slaves returned to their masters. In addition, Cover coauthored books on procedure and wrote numerous articles about how narrative, myth, and history "invite new worlds" by illuminating the tension between law and the normative worlds we construct.

Cover's pathbreaking work stressed that judicial language is unlike literary language because it involves actual violence, pain, and death. He explored new facets of jurisdiction, law and religion, civil rights, and civil liberties. If a dominant theme emerged in the radically interdisciplinary work of this "anarchist who love[d] law," it was exploration of how law might be a bridge toward the creation of new narratives and better actualities. To Cover, law should involve a conscious quest for a juster justice.

Cover died of a heart attack in 1986.

AVIAM SOIFER
(1992)

Bibliography

MEMORIAL ISSUE   1987   *Yale Law Journal* 96:1699–1984.

COX v. LOUISIANA
379 U.S. 536 (1965)
379 U.S. 559 (1965)

Some black students were jailed in a courthouse for PICKETING segregated lunch counters. About 2,000 other black students marched there and, in accordance with police instructions, lined a sidewalk 101 feet away. Whites gathered. Cox made a speech that elicited some grumbling from whites; the police ordered the demonstration broken up; the students were dispersed.

Justice ARTHUR GOLDBERG writing for the Supreme Court reversed Cox's BREACH OF THE PEACE conviction, finding that Cox's actions threatened no violence and that the police could have handled any threat from the whites. The Court also held the breach of peace statute unconstitutionally vague and overbroad as construed by the state supreme court to define breach as "to arouse from a state of repose . . . to disquiet."

In striking down Cox's conviction for obstruction of public passages because the statute's actual administration had vested discretion in city officials to forbid some parades and allow others, the Court emphasized that violation of nondiscriminatory traffic laws would not be protected by the FIRST AMENDMENT. The court reversed Cox's conviction for picketing near a courthouse because the police, by directing the demonstrators to a particular sidewalk, had led them to believe that it was not near the courthouse within the terms of the statute so that a subsequent conviction created a "sort of entrapment," in violation of DUE PROCESS. Nevertheless, in dictum it invoked the old doctrine that picketing was subject to reasonable regulation as "speech plus" and supported the authority

of a state legislature to forbid picketing near a courthouse because of its danger to the administration of justice.

Although *Cox* is often cited as a case establishing the concept of a PUBLIC FORUM, the Court went out of its way to say "We have no occasion . . . to consider the constitutionality of the . . . non-discriminatory application of a statute forbidding all access to streets and other public facilities for parades and meetings."

MARTIN SHAPIRO
(1986)

COX v. NEW HAMPSHIRE
312 U.S. 569 (1941)

In this seminal decision, Chief Justice CHARLES EVANS HUGHES, writing for a unanimous Supreme Court, synthesized a series of cases involving speeches, parades, and meetings in parks and on streets. He held that there was a "right of assembly . . . and . . . discussion of public questions immemorially associated with resort to public places," but that such a right was limited by the authority of local government to make reasonable regulations governing "the time, place and manner" of such speech, if the regulations did not involve "unfair discrimination" among speakers. The Court upheld a state law requiring parade licenses issued by local governments on the grounds that, as construed by the state supreme court, it authorized only such reasonable and nondiscriminatory regulations. *Cox* is one of the building blocks in the creation of the doctrine of the PUBLIC FORUM.

This case took on renewed importance in the context of the CIVIL RIGHTS demonstrations of the 1960s. The crucial problem under the *Cox* test is often whether a law purporting to be a neutral regulation of traffic and noise control is actually a façade behind which local authorities seek to deny a public forum to speakers whose speech they dislike.

MARTIN SHAPIRO
(1986)

COX BROADCASTING CORP. v. COHN
420 U.S. 469 (1975)

In *Cox Broadcasting Corp. v. Cohn* the Supreme Court held that broadcasting the name of a rape victim, derived from public court documents open to public inspection, could not constitutionally be made the basis for civil liability. The Court left open the questions whether liability could be imposed for a similar broadcast if the name had been obtained in an improper fashion, or if the name had not been directly derived from the public record, or if the name had not appeared in a public record open to public inspection, or if the public record were inaccurate.

STEVEN SHIFFRIN
(1986)

COY v. IOWA
487 U.S. 1012 (1988)

Coy was convicted of sexually assaulting two thirteen-year-old girls. During his trial, the girls gave testimony in front of a screen that blocked Coy from their sight. Coy claimed that use of the screen violated his right to CONFRONTATION guaranteed by the Fifth Amendment. The Supreme Court agreed, holding that face-to-face examination of witnesses testifying at trial is a fundamental guarantee of the confrontation clause.

Writing for the majority, Justice ANTONIN SCALIA argued that open accusations seem integral to the very idea of fairness; moreover, face-to-face confrontation serves the end of truth because it is more difficult for witnesses to lie (or lie convincingly) when they must do so to the face of the person their testimony will harm. Scalia argued that the Court's previously carved out exceptions to the confrontation clause were inapposite because they dealt with out-of-court statements and not testimony given during trial. Whether there may be exceptions to the confrontation clause even at trial, Scalia was unwilling to say. All he would acknowledge is that if such exceptions exist they must be "necessary to further an important public policy."

Justice SANDRA DAY O'CONNOR, in one of her characteristically narrow concurrences, claimed that nothing in the ruling should be construed as forbidding state efforts to protect child witnesses, and she listed several types of state action that she thought would not raise a "substantial Confrontation Clause problem." O'Connor also seized on the majority's concession that exceptions to the confrontation clause may exist when "necessary to further an important public policy." The key word, O'Connor pointed out, was "necessary," and this would likely be the focus of future litigation. It was; and in 1990, the Court took up the issue again in MARYLAND V. CRAIG.

JOHN G. WEST, JR.
(1992)

COYLE v. SMITH
221 U.S. 559 (1911)

This decision construed the guarantee of a REPUBLICAN FORM OF GOVERNMENT in a case involving a state's admission to the Union. The enabling act admitting Oklahoma spec-

ified the location of the state capital, a condition which the Oklahoma legislature soon violated. The Supreme Court struck down the limitation as outside the limits of Congress's power over admission.

DAVID GORDON
(1986)

CRACK COCAINE AND EQUAL PROTECTION

During the 1980s, the federal government and many states adopted particularly harsh sentences for possessing or trafficking in crack cocaine. This SENTENCING has become controversial because it is borne largely by African American defendants, and because penalties at both the federal and state level are much lower for possession or sale of powder cocaine, the form of cocaine with which defendants of other races tend to get caught. In federal court, for example, crack defendants since 1986 have received by statute the same sentences imposed upon defendants convicted of trafficking in one hundred times as much powder cocaine.

Crack and powder cocaine are different forms of the same drug. Indeed, crack cocaine is made from powder cocaine, and the conversion process is simple and inexpensive, so it tends to occur toward the end of the distribution chain. Unlike powder cocaine, though, crack cocaine can be smoked, which makes its psychotropic effects more intense and shorter lasting, and also makes it far more addictive. Crack also is easier than powder cocaine to handle in small quantities, and hence easier to sell to the poor.

Federal constitutional challenges to heightened sentences for crack cocaine trafficking have failed without exception. Because crack laws do not explicitly distinguish between defendants on the basis of race or any other SUSPECT CLASSIFICATION, courts have subjected the laws to "minimal scrutiny" under the EQUAL PROTECTION clause. Such scrutiny asks merely whether the lines the law draws have a RATIONAL BASIS. The crack laws have passed this test easily, because cocaine is demonstrably more dangerous when it comes in the form of crack. As a consequence, the federal courts of appeals have unanimously rejected equal protection challenges to the crack sentences. In contrast, the Minnesota Supreme Court struck down an enhanced state penalty for trafficking in crack cocaine, but only after concluding that the equal protection guarantee in Minnesota's state constitution was more demanding than its federal analogue.

Some commentators have applauded the federal decisions and criticized the Minnesota court, reasoning that because crack cocaine does particular damage in poor, black communities, heightened penalties for crack trafficking hurt black drug dealers but help blacks as a whole. But others have been less sanguine. Federal judges have repeatedly attacked the crack laws as draconian, and some scholars have suggested that conventional equal protection analysis takes no account of the most troubling features of the crack penalties: the extent of the difference between the treatment of crack and powder cocaine, the special need for fairness in meting out criminal sanctions, and the grounds for suspecting that the crack sentences might be less severe were they not imposed almost entirely upon black defendants. Thus, the resounding failure of constitutional challenges to the federal crack sentences may speak less to the merits of the sentences than to the inadequacies of equal protection DOCTRINE.

DAVID A. SKLANSKY
(2000)

(SEE ALSO: *Drug Regulation; Race and Criminal Justice.*)

Bibliography

KENNEDY, RANDALL   1997   *Race, Crime, and the Law.* New York: Random House.
SKLANSKY, DAVID A.   1995   Cocaine, Race, and Equal Protection. *Stanford Law Review* 47:1283–1322.

CRAIG v. BOREN
429 U.S. 190 (1976)

It is ironic that the leading modern decision setting the STANDARD OF REVIEW for claims of SEX DISCRIMINATION involved discrimination against men, concerning an interest of supreme triviality. Oklahoma allowed women to buy 3.2 percent beer upon reaching the age of eighteen; men, however, had to be twenty-one. A young male would-be buyer and a female beer seller challenged the law's validity. The young man became twenty-one before the Supreme Court's decision; his challenge was thus rejected for MOOTNESS. The Court held that the seller had STANDING to raise the young man's constitutional claims, and further held, 8–1, that the law denied EQUAL PROTECTION OF THE LAWS. Justice WILLIAM H. REHNQUIST dissented.

Speaking through Justice WILLIAM J. BRENNAN, the Court held that classifications based on gender were invalid unless they served "important governmental objectives" and were "substantially related to achievement of those objectives." This intermediate standard was a compromise between the two views of the majority in FRONTIERO V. RICHARDSON (1973) as to the level of judicial scrutiny of both legislative objectives and legislative means. Under the RATIONAL BASIS standard of review, the objective need be only legitimate, and the means (in equal protection lan-

guage, the classification) only rationally related to its achievement. At the opposite end of the continuum of standards of review, STRICT SCRUTINY demands a legislative objective that is a COMPELLING STATE INTEREST, and means that are necessary to achieving that objective. The *Craig* standard appears to have been deliberately designed to fall between these two levels of judicial scrutiny of legislation.

In the years since *Craig*, the Supreme Court has often invalidated classifications based on sex but typically has not challenged the importance of legislative objectives. Instead, the Court generally holds that a sex classification is not "substantially related" to a legislative goal. In *Craig* itself, the Court admitted that traffic safety, the state's objective, was important, but said maleness was an inappropriate "proxy for drinking and driving."

Justice JOHN PAUL STEVENS, concurring, doubted the utility of multitiered levels of judicial scrutiny in equal protection cases, and commented that men, as a class, have not suffered "pervasive discrimination." The classification was objectionable, however, because it was "based on the accident of birth," and perpetuated "a stereotyped attitude" of young men and women. Because the state's traffic safety justification failed, the law was invalid.

KENNETH L. KARST
(1986)

CRAIG v. MISSOURI
4 Peters 410 (1830)

Craig defined BILLS OF CREDIT, which no state may issue without violating Article I, section 10, of the Constitution. By a 4–3 vote the Supreme Court ruled that bills of credit mean any paper medium intended to circulate as money on the authority of a state, even if not designated as legal tender in payment of debts. Missouri, lacking currency, authorized state loan offices to issue loan certificates, on collateral, to private citizens, in amounts ranging from fifty cents to ten dollars; the certificates could be used for payment of taxes and official salaries. Chief Justice JOHN MARSHALL's opinion invalidating the state act, though constitutionally correct, ignored economic realities: many states desperately needed a circulating medium. Senator THOMAS H. BENTON, for Missouri, defending its certificate law before the Court, thunderingly defended state sovereignty. The disastrous consequences of *Craig* provoked denunciations of the court and yet another movement in Congress to repeal section 25 of the JUDICIARY ACT OF 1789, the grant of APPELLATE JURISDICTION under which the Court had reversed state court judgments and held state acts unconstitutional. The repeal movement failed, but a solid South ominously opposed the Court.

LEONARD W. LEVY
(1986)

(SEE ALSO: *Briscoe v. Bank of Commonwealth of Kentucky.*)

CRAMER v. UNITED STATES
325 U.S. 1 (1945)

On the night of June 12, 1942, several specially trained saboteurs were put ashore from a German submarine near Amagansett, New York, with orders to disperse throughout the United States and to sabotage the American war effort. Anthony Cramer, a naturalized American citizen of German background, befriended two of the saboteurs, met with them, and was suspected of assisting them in their mission. However, the only overt acts to which two witnesses could testify were two meetings between Cramer and one of the saboteurs, who was an old friend of Cramer's. The prosecution was unable to produce the testimony of two witnesses concerning what took place at the meetings or to establish that Cramer gave information, encouragement, shelter, or supplies to the saboteurs. Cramer was tried for and convicted of TREASON, and he appealed his conviction to the Supreme Court.

The *Cramer* case marked the first time that the Supreme Court passed on the meaning of the treason clause of Article III, section 2, of the Constitution. Justice ROBERT H. JACKSON, for a 5–4 Court, held that the overt acts testified to by two witnesses must be sufficient, in their setting, to sustain a finding that actual aid and comfort was given to an enemy of the United States. Although there was other EVIDENCE of Cramer's Nazi sympathies and of his assistance to the saboteur, the overt acts—the meetings—were not in themselves treasonable, and the conviction could not stand.

DENNIS J. MAHONEY
(1986)

(SEE ALSO: *Haupt v. United States; Quirin, Ex Parte.*)

Bibliography

BELKNAP, MICHAL R. 1980 The Supreme Court Goes to War: The Meaning and Implications of the Nazi Saboteur Case. *Military Law Review* 89:59–95.

CRANCH, WILLIAM
(1779–1855)

President JOHN ADAMS in March 1801 commissioned his nephew, William Cranch, assistant judge of the newly created Circuit Court for the DISTRICT OF COLUMBIA. President THOMAS JEFFERSON in 1806 surprised Cranch, a loyal Fed-

eralist, by elevating him to chief judge, a post he filled until his death, half a century later.

Cranch simultaneously undertook the unofficial position of reporter of the decisions of the Supreme Court of the United States. His nine volumes of reports, for which he derived compensation at public sale, covered the period from the August Term, 1801, to the February Term, 1815. The role of the law reporter in Cranch's time commanded professional respect and even glamour. These reports, which added luster to the judge's reputation, received favorable comment, even from Jeffersonian opponents.

Cranch's first major constitutional opinion, *United States v. Bollman et al.* (1807), stressed the independence and power of the federal judiciary, themes that pervaded his other major opinions. President Jefferson in early 1807 had sought a bench warrant for the arrest of Erik Bollman and Samuel Swartwout on charges of TREASON in the Burr Conspiracy. Cranch dissented from the decision by the court's other two judges to issue the warrant. He took exception to the English doctrine of constructive treason. He also rejected the proposition that an executive communication from the President, without either an oath or affirmation, established sufficient probability of treasonous activity.

Three decades later Cranch spoke for a unanimous court in upholding the power of the judiciary to intervene in executive affairs. *United States ex rel. Stokes v. Kendall* (1837) stemmed from an alleged debt due Stokes and others for services they claimed to have rendered to the Post Office. When Postmaster General Amos Kendall refused to pay, despite congressional direction to do so, Stokes sought a WRIT OF MANDAMUS. Although no circuit court had ever issued such a writ against the executive branch, Cranch held that his court could do so. He found that the judicial power could properly issue a writ to command performance of a purely ministerial function by the head of an executive department.

Cranch remained a thoroughgoing Federalist long after that party ceased to exist. His opinions powerfully affirmed the role of the federal judiciary. His most important legacy was the establishment of the Circuit Court and its successors in the District of Columbia as the major forums in which to adjudicate causes involving executive departments and agencies.

KERMIT L. HALL
(1986)

Bibliography

CARNEL, WILLIAM F. 1901 Life and Times of William Cranch, Judge of the District Circuit Court, 1801–1855. *Records of the Columbia Historical Society* 5:294–310.

CRAWFORD v. BOARD OF EDUCATION
458 U.S. 527 (1982)

WASHINGTON v. SEATTLE SCHOOL DISTRICT NO. 1
458 U.S. 457 (1982)

By statewide votes, both Washington and California sought to limit the use of SCHOOL BUSING for purposes of DESEGREGATION. A 1978 Washington INITIATIVE effectively prohibited school boards from assigning children to public schools outside their residential neighborhoods for purposes of racial integration. A 1979 amendment to the California Constitution prohibited state courts from ordering school busing unless busing would be available in a federal court as a remedy for a violation of the FOURTEENTH AMENDMENT. The Supreme Court sustained the California measure, 8–1, but held the Washington measure invalid, 5–4.

In the *Seattle* case, Justice HARRY A. BLACKMUN wrote for the majority. Following the precedent of HUNTER V. ERICKSON (1969), he concluded that the Washington law placed a special burden on racial minorities, using an issue's racial nature to define the local decision-making structure. For the dissenters, Justice LEWIS F. POWELL argued that the Washington law had not altered the political process at all, but had merely adopted a neighborhood school policy—something a local school board itself remained free to do, within the limits of the Fourteenth Amendment.

Justice Powell wrote for the Court in the *Crawford* case. The California courts had previously read the state constitution to forbid DE FACTO as well as DE JURE school SEGREGATION. There was, however, no "ratchet" principle in the Fourteenth Amendment; the state could constitutionally adopt federal EQUAL PROTECTION standards. The amendment, Powell said, was not adopted with a racially discriminatory purpose; it chiefly reflected a choice for the neighborhood school policy. Justice THURGOOD MARSHALL, dissenting, considered the two cases indistinguishable. Indeed, the opinions of Justice Powell in the two cases bear marked similarities; yet, if *Hunter* be taken as the critical precedent, the distinction is supportable. A line is none the worse for being thin.

KENNETH L. KARST

(1986)

CREATIONISM

Creationism is the belief that plants and animals were originally created by a supernatural being substantially as they now exist. Proponents of creationism today are primarily evangelical Christians who adopt a literal reading of the book of Genesis in the Bible. Several hundred creationists also hold advanced science degrees and claim that the best scientific evidence supports creationism; these creationists advocate what they call "scientific creationism."

Scientific creationism is far afield from prevailing scientific orthodoxy, and although most of its proponents are evangelicals, many evangelicals do not subscribe to it. Scientific creationism teaches that the earth is several thousand years old, rather than several billion, and that much of the fossil record was created in a worldwide deluge, rather than by the gradual accumulations of the ages. It harkens back to catastrophism of the type dominant in the scientific community before the theories of Charles Lyell and Charles Darwin gained acceptance. Scientific creationists claim that the fossil record supports the idea that when life first appeared it was already complicated and multifaceted; at the very least, they argue, the fossil record shows no support for the gradual progression of life forms taught by classical Darwinian theory. Much of the evidence cited by creation scientists comes from evolutionists, who continue to have marked disagreements with one another about the mechanism by which evolution occurs.

Creationism originally became a constitutional issue because creationists tried to keep evolution from being taught in the public schools, a policy the Supreme Court struck down as violative of the ESTABLISHMENT CLAUSE in EPPERSON V. ARKANSAS (1968). Creationism remains a constitutional issue, however, because creationists now seek to have scientific creationism taught in public schools. In fact, they have sought state laws that require the teaching of creationism side-by-side with evolution.

Opponents of these laws maintain that teaching creationism is tantamount to teaching religion and hence abridges the establishment clause; as evidence for their position, they point to the religious underpinnings of creationism and claim that few if any scientists hold creationist beliefs. Creationists respond that how they derived their theory is irrelevant; the sole question is whether or not it can be validated by scientific research. As for the dearth of scientists who are creationists, creation scientists point to their own doctorates in science from secular universities. Nevertheless, creationists readily admit that few scientists have adopted creationism, but claim that this is the result of prejudice on the part of evolutionists, marshaling evidence that graduate students and professors believing in creationism have been systematically discriminated against because of these beliefs. Creationists argue that laws requiring the teaching of scientific creationism alongside evolution are required to break the stranglehold of such prejudice.

In response to creationist concerns, Louisiana enacted

a law requiring the balanced treatment of the theories of "evolution science" and "creation science" in the public schools. The act defined the respective theories as "the scientific evidences for [creation or evolution] and inferences from those scientific evidences." The act did not mandate that either theory be taught in the schools; but it did demand that if one was taught the other must be taught. The act also required that neither evolution nor creation science be taught "as proven scientific fact."

The Supreme Court held 7–2 that the act failed the first part of the LEMON TEST because it did not have a valid secular purpose; hence, the statute was unconstitutional on its face under the establishment clause.

Writing for the majority, Justice WILLIAM J. BRENNAN rejected the act's explicitly stated secular purpose of "protecting ACADEMIC FREEDOM" because the statute did not in any way enhance the freedom of teachers to teach science. Brennan also rejected the contention that Louisiana wanted to ensure "fairness" by requiring that all the evidence regarding origins be taught, noting that the law unequally provided for the development of curriculum guides for creation science, but not evolution.

The core of Brennan's argument, however, was his determination that creation science embodies "religious doctrine" and that the "preeminent purpose of the Louisiana legislature was . . . to advance the religious viewpoint that a supernatural being created humankind." Brennan sought to show from the legislative record that legislators in fact supported the act because evolution contradicted their own religious beliefs. Hence, the motivations of the legislators, rather than the clear language of the act, was the decisive factor in invalidating the law.

Justice ANTONIN SCALIA, joined by Chief Justice WILLIAM H. REHNQUIST, filed a lengthy dissent attacking many of the central premises of the majority's opinion. Scalia maintained that the majority was able to dismiss the act's stated secular purpose only by misconstruing it. According to Scalia, the "academic freedom" the act sought to guarantee related not to the teachers, but to the students, whom the legislature wanted to be able to study various views of the origin and development of life. Furthermore, the act on its face treated evolution and creation science equally, and the few differences that did exist could be readily explained. For example, the state provided for the development of study guides for creation science, but not evolution because "of the unavailability of works on creation science suitable for classroom use . . . and the existence of ample materials on evolution."

Scalia saved his most cutting remarks for the majority's inquiry into the subjective motives of Louisiana's legislators. Scalia showed through copious citations that the majority had distorted legislators' intentions. But in Scalia's view, even had the majority correctly read the motives in this case, motives alone should not have invalidated the law. The act should have been struck down only if its objective language clearly violated the Constitution or if the primary effect of the law in practice was to advance religion impermissibly (a question not before the Court).

Edwards v. Aguillard raises questions both difficult and deep; it is not really analogous to cases dealing with school prayer or Bible reading because these practices are devotional exercises clearly designed to inculcate religious truth. In this case, however, the state officially disclaimed any intention to present creationism as "true." So even if creationism is inherently religious—as the Court determined—it is not necessarily the case that teaching about it promotes religion in violation of the establishment clause. As Justice LEWIS F. POWELL pointed out in his concurring opinion, the Court has often maintained that public schools have the right to teach objectively about religion. So to strike down the Louisiana law, the Court not only had to find creationism religious, but it had to maintain that the purpose of the law was to teach creationism as true. As a factual matter, however, this was by far the weakest link in the Court's logic.

Why then did the Court rule as it did? One can only speculate; but it would not be inappropriate to point out the obvious: creationism conjures up images of the Scopes trial and intolerant fundamentalists who are none too bright. In the battle between science and superstition, creationism has been accounted superstition, and one can readily understand why the Court would be reluctant to uphold a law that might appear to sanction creationism. Unfortunately, there are problems with excluding beliefs like creationism from the classroom entirely.

Evolution remains so controversial primarily because it is part of a much larger debate over the nature and meaning of life. The study of how life began almost inevitably raises questions of why: Why did life begin? Why are humans rational? Why is there order in the universe? Men and women have debated these questions for thousands of years, considering them to be some of the most important inquiries human beings can undertake. Yet these are the very sorts of questions that modern science cannot answer. All modern science can legitimately offer are tentative explanations about the physical process by which life developed after it first appeared; of its own accord, it can tell us nothing of the purpose or meaning of the development of life. Nor, in all probability, will it ever unravel the mystery of how life first arose from nonlife. The result is that if one relegates the discussion of the origin and development of life to science textbooks that discussion will be, at best, incredibly impoverished because modern science cannot legitimately provide answers to questions of meaning and purpose. At worst, the discussion will be disingenuous because attempts will be made to answer the questions of meaning in the guise of science. One does not need to know much of recent history to realize that science has been used quite often to justify a variety of philosophically laden schemes, from social darwinism to eugenics. The encroachment of science into the domains of philosophy and theology may be more subtle in the public schoolroom, but it occurs nevertheless. It can be seen in the 1959 biology text that declared that "nothing supernatural happened" when life first arose or in more recent texts that emphasize "chance" and "randomness" as the sole determinants of how life developed. Such statements advance philosophical and theological claims just as surely as creationism; yet these claims are allowed because they are made in the name of science. In such a situation, one can readily understand why some creationists have tried to distance their theory from its religious underpinnings; they know this is the only way their ideas will get a fair hearing.

It might be better if public schools—and the Court—recognized more forthrightly that both philosophy and theology have a place in the discussion of origins and that their inclusion in school curricula need not be equated with their advancement by the state. One can teach about various theories, after all, without advocating any of them.

JOHN G. WEST, JR.
(1992)

(SEE ALSO: *Religious Fundamentalism; Separation of Church and State.*)

Bibliography

BERGMAN, JERRY 1984 *The Criterion: Religious Discrimination in America.* Richfield, Minn.: Onesimus.

BIRD, WENDELL R. 1978 Freedom of Religion and Science Instruction in Public Schools. *Yale Law Journal* 87:515–570.

CURTIS, V. KAY 1988 Religion: Church and State Relations: Balanced Treatment of Theories of Origins—*Edwards v. Aguillard. Oklahoma Law Review* 41:740–758.

CRIMINAL CONSPIRACY

The modern crime of conspiracy punishes the act of agreement with another to do something unlawful, and the vagueness and breadth of its scope are the legacies of seventeenth-century English judges who invented its COMMON LAW progenitor. Constitutional DOCTRINE has not shaped the boundaries of this crime; it is, indeed, the other way around. Most paradoxically, the crime has served both as a tool for the suppression of FIRST AMENDMENT freedoms and as a weapon for the defense of rights to racial equality. Like all political issues, the definition of "unlawful" conspiracies fluctuates with the moral hemlines of history.

In the eighteenth century, the English crime came to encompass the agreement to do any "immoral" acts, even noncriminal ones. This became an element of American conspiracy law as well, and one of its early critics was Chief Justice LEMUEL SHAW of the Massachusetts Supreme Judicial Court. In *Commonwealth v. Hunt* (1842) Shaw put an end to conspiracy prosecutions of laborers who organized to seek such noncriminal goals as higher wages or a CLOSED SHOP. Criminal goals, of course, remained punishable, and trade union conspiracy prosecutions died out in the 1890s only because they were replaced by judicial resort to the labor INJUNCTION. Statutes prohibiting noncriminal conspiracies remained on the books, but their demise was hastened by state court decisions holding them void for VAGUENESS or violative of the EX POST FACTO clause.

Federal conspiracy prosecutions commenced in 1867 with the enactment of a Federal Criminal Code provision prohibiting conspiracies to defraud the United States. The rise of organized crime during Prohibition provided the impetus for the expansion of federal conspiracy offenses; the RACKETEER INFLUENCED AND CORRUPT ORGANIZATIONS ACT of 1970 is an exemplar of their sweeping scope. In 1925, Judge LEARNED HAND labeled conspiracy "the darling in the prosecutor's nursery," because of the progovernment features that mark conspiracy trials. HEARSAY statements of co-conspirators are admissible in evidence, and conspiratorial membership may be inferred solely from conduct showing a desire to further the conspiracy's goals. In *Pinkerton v. United States* (1946) the Court held conspirators liable for every crime committed by co-conspirators, including those of participants whose existence was unknown but foreseeable. The DOUBLE JEOPARDY clause does not bar separate, consecutive sentences for these offenses and the conspiracy itself. VENUE will lie anywhere an act is committed in furtherance of the conspiracy, often effectively nullifying the SIXTH AMENDMENT right to be tried where a crime is committed. Conspirators may be tried en masse, and fringe participants thus become tainted with the culpability of the ringleaders.

It is small wonder that in *Krulewitch v. United States* (1949) Justice ROBERT H. JACKSON declared that the "elastic, sprawling and pervasive" nature of the crime of conspiracy poses a "serious threat to fairness" in the administration of justice. Yet while many commentators call for limitations on the crime, DUE PROCESS arguments meet with recurrent failure in the courts. This amoeboid offense remains entrenched in state and federal law and in legislative proposals for criminal code reform.

Conspiracy was a potent weapon for the prosecution of political dissidents during WORLD WAR I, and these cases brought the Supreme Court to its first important encounter with the First Amendment's guarantees of FREEDOM OF

SPEECH and FREEDOM OF THE PRESS. The ESPIONAGE ACT of 1917 prohibited conspiracies to obstruct the draft or cause insubordination in the armed services, and in SCHENCK V. UNITED STATES (1919) and FROHWERK V. UNITED STATES (1919) a unanimous Court affirmed the conspiracy convictions of dissidents who had circulated antidraft publications. In *Schenck,* Justice OLIVER WENDELL HOLMES declared that only a CLEAR AND PRESENT DANGER of a conspiracy's success would justify conviction, but this formula was not an important limitation in these cases, where the danger was assumed. Justices Holmes and LOUIS D. BRANDEIS later argued for greater speech protections, but their pleas went unheeded for a generation. Conspiracy convictions of eleven national Communist party leaders were affirmed in DENNIS V. UNITED STATES (1951), even though the danger posed by their conspiracy to advocate the overthrow of the government was evidenced only by the party's structure and tenets. The doctrinal thaw came in 1957, with Justice JOHN MARSHALL HARLAN's opinion in YATES V. UNITED STATES portending the formula of BRANDENBURG V. OHIO (1969). *Brandenburg* allows prosecution for speech crimes—including conspiracy to advocate—only when advocacy of imminent, illegal action is likely to incite such action.

Brandenburg's weakness as a limit on conspiracy prosecutions is that it only guarantees defendants the benefit of appellate court scrutiny of jury verdicts. It provides no more than an indirect caution for legislative reliance on conspiracy statutes or prosecutorial decisions to seek indictments. Protection of speech interests rests ultimately in the court of public opinion, and the VIETNAM WAR era dissidents found an uncertain haven there. The "Chicago Seven" protesters at the 1968 Democratic National Convention were acquitted of conspiring to travel interstate with intent to incite a riot, but they were convicted of other INCITEMENT offenses. Benjamin Spock and William Sloane Coffin were convicted of conspiring to counsel draft evasion, based on their support of a DRAFT CARD BURNING rally in Boston. After appellate court reversals in *United States v. Dellinger* (1972) and *United States v. Spock* (1969), reprosecution was halted only because the government decided to give up trying. The CHILLING EFFECT of such prosecutions is irremediable, and judicial vindication of speech rights often becomes a matter of better late than never.

The concept of conspiracy can serve CIVIL LIBERTIES as aptly as it defeats them. After the CIVIL WAR, Congress prohibited conspiracies "to injure, oppress, threaten or intimidate" any citizen's free exercise of constitutional rights, and also provided a civil action for DAMAGES against conspirators. Narrow judicial construction of these rights defeated their enforcement in the era of UNITED STATES V. HARRIS (1883) and the CIVIL RIGHTS CASES (1883). But

Justice WILLIAM O. DOUGLAS's opinion in SCREWS V. UNITED STATES (1945) revived prosecutions of state officials, while UNITED STATES V. GUEST (1966) brought similar vindication against private individuals, and GRIFFIN V. BRECKENRIDGE (1971) opened the damage remedy door. Debate continues over the scope of rights protected by these remedies. But conspiracy's contribution toward curbing civil rights violators remains as notable as its role in rounding up racketeers.

CATHERINE HANCOCK
(1986)

Bibliography

FILVAROFF, DAVID B. 1972 Conspiracy and the First Amendment. *University of Pennsylvania Law Review* 121:189–253.

JOHNSON, PHILLIP E. 1973 The Unnecessary Crime of Conspiracy. *California Law Review* 61:1137–1188.

CRIMINAL JUSTICE ACT
78 Stat. 552 (1964)

By the Criminal Justice Act Congress provided that counsel must be furnished at public expense for INDIGENT defendants in federal criminal cases. The act requires each district court to formulate a plan for furnishing counsel, subject to supervision by the circuit judicial council and the Judicial Conference of the United States. The act provides that counsel shall be furnished from the defendant's first appearance before a court or magistrate through the APPEAL process, and authorizes reimbursement for such expenses as investigations and expert testimony.

DENNIS J. MAHONEY
(1986)

(SEE ALSO: *Right to Counsel.*)

CRIMINAL JUSTICE AND DUE PROCESS

The application to the CRIMINAL JUSTICE SYSTEM of the DUE PROCESS clauses of the Fifth Amendment and the FOURTEENTH AMENDMENT raises three principal issues. First, which of the provisions of the BILL OF RIGHTS relating to police practices and criminal trials are "incorporated" by the Fourteenth Amendment's due process clause so as to apply against the states as well as the federal government? Second, what doctrinal framework should be used to evaluate claims about PROCEDURAL DUE PROCESS in the criminal as opposed to civil context? Third, what doctrinal framework should be used to evaluate claims about substantive limits on police practices, or what has come to be known as SUBSTANTIVE DUE PROCESS?

The INCORPORATION question is a consequence of the Supreme Court's decision in the post–WORLD WAR II era to pursue a doctrinal strategy of "selective incorporation" by which it considered each individual provision of the Bill of Rights and determined whether that provision was so fundamental so as to apply against the states pursuant to the due process clause of the Fourteenth Amendment. Although the Court explicitly rejected Justice HUGO L. BLACK's theory of "total incorporation" (by which every provision of the Bill of Rights would be incorporated against the states), it accomplished much the same result through "selective incorporation," given that almost every provision of the Bill of Rights has been individually incorporated.

As for criminal justice, almost every provision of the Bill of Rights relating to police practices and the conduct of criminal trials has been incorporated against the states. The FOURTH AMENDMENT limit on unreasonable SEARCHES AND SEIZURES and its EXCLUSIONARY RULE have been incorporated, as have the Fifth Amendment RIGHT AGAINST SELF-INCRIMINATION and its MIRANDA RULES. In addition, the Fifth Amendment's DOUBLE JEOPARDY clause, the Eighth Amendment's CRUEL AND UNUSUAL PUNISHMENT clause, and almost every provision of the Sixth Amendment relating to criminal trials have all been incorporated.

Nonetheless, two important exceptions to this trend toward expansive incorporation are worth noting in the criminal justice context. First, the Fifth Amendment's GRAND JURY clause has never been incorporated. Although that clause has been interpreted to require that all federal FELONY cases be based on an INDICTMENT by a grand jury, the Court explicitly rejected such a requirement for state criminal proceedings in the nineteenth-century case HURTADO V. CALIFORNIA (1884), and it has never revisited the issue. Thus, states are constitutionally free to structure their charging mechanisms in other ways. A substantial number of states use grand juries for some cases, but some jurisdictions give prosecutors greater power to charge by information than would be constitutionally permissible in federal courts, and some jurisdictions use alternative (and perhaps more rigorous) methods to "check" prosecutorial charging decisions. Among those alternatives are judicially conducted preliminary hearings or judicial inquests, also known as "one-man grand juries." Second, although the Court incorporated the Sixth Amendment right to TRIAL BY JURY in nonpetty criminal cases in DUNCAN V. LOUISIANA (1968), it failed to incorporate that aspect of the jury right that requires JURY UNANIMITY in federal criminal trials. This peculiar result arose from the fragmentation of the Court in the 1970s. Four Justices (led by Justice BYRON R. WHITE) believed that the Sixth Amendment required neither federal nor state criminal juries to be unanimous; four other Justices (led by Justice WILLIAM O. DOUGLAS) believed that the Sixth Amendment required both federal and state criminal juries to be unanimous. Justice LEWIS F. POWELL, JR., provided the fifth, "swing" vote on the matter, declaring that the Sixth Amendment required jury unanimity in federal, but not in state, cases. Thus, both in grand jury practice and in the degree of unanimity required of criminal juries, states remain significantly freer than the federal government to pursue their own policies without running afoul of the Fourteenth Amendment's due process clause.

The second set of issues raised by the intersection of the due process clause and the criminal justice system—the requisites of procedural due process—have become murkier in recent years. On occasion in the last few decades, the Court has seemed to assume that the doctrinal framework for analyzing claims of inadequate procedures should be the same in the civil and criminal contexts. Thus, for example, in deciding whether indigent criminal defendants should be entitled to state-funded psychiatric assessments in CAPITAL PUNISHMENT trials, the Court applied the same BALANCING TEST that the Court had applied to claims regarding procedural due process in civil contexts. However, in a more recent case, *Medina v. California* (1992), the Court explicitly rejected this approach and held that the standard should be one more deferential to state interests: courts should uphold a challenged state procedure "unless it offends some principle of justice so rooted in the traditions and conscience of our people as to be ranked as fundamental." The Court reasoned that in light of the explicit provisions of the Bill of Rights relating to criminal procedure, expansive readings of the due process clause would give inadequate deference to considered legislative judgments. After *Medina*, it remains to be seen both how deferential the Court's standard will turn out to be, and how the Court will choose whether a particular procedural challenge should be considered under a specific provision of the Bill of Rights or under the more general due process clause.

The third principal issue—substantive due process—has likewise been addressed recently by the Court, and in a similar fashion that has both narrowed the scope of possible challenges and raised questions about the future. The Court has held, from the early part of this century, that the due process clause not only ensures fair procedures, as its text most obviously suggests; it also is the source of certain substantive limits on governmental power. In the criminal justice context, the Court has held that the due process clause renders unconstitutional some police practices and some treatment of pretrial detainees. The Court has assumed that the "deliberate indifference" of governmental actors to certain kinds of harms—for example, inattention to prisoners' medical needs—is enough to violate the due process clause. But in *County of Sacramento v. Lewis* (1998), a case involving a high-speed POLICE PURSUIT that resulted in death, the Court held that the "deliberate indifference" standard was too accommodating to plaintiffs in cases that involve on-the-spot police decisionmaking. In such a context, a court should decline to find a violation of due process unless the actions of the police were so egregious as to "shock the conscience." It remains to be seen which other contexts within the criminal justice system will be held to require the more deferential "shocks the conscience" standard. The narrowing of opportunities for substantive due process challenges within the criminal justice system reflects the growth of a more general skepticism on the Supreme Court for "substantive" regulation under the due process clause.

CAROL S. STEIKER
(2000)

CRIMINAL JUSTICE AND RACE

See: Race and Criminal Justice

CRIMINAL JUSTICE AND TECHNOLOGY

In 1928 Justice LOUIS D. BRANDEIS warned that "discovery and invention have made it possible for the government, by means far more effective than the rack, to obtain disclosure in court of what is whispered in the closet." And, he went on to ask, "can it be that the Constitution affords no protection against such invasion of individual security?" In OLMSTEAD V. UNITED STATES (1928) the Supreme Court responded yes to Brandeis's question: the Constitution "affords no protection."

Today the Court continues to give virtually the same answer. Thus, in *United States v. Knotts* (1983), Justice WILLIAM H. REHNQUIST wrote that "nothing in the FOURTH AMENDMENT prohibit[s] the police from augmenting the sensory facilities bestowed upon them at birth with such enhancement as science and technology afforded them in this case." That case involved a mobile tracking device, but the same attitude is reflected in many other cases and contexts. The Court has virtually abdicated any role in shaping a response to the threats to liberty and individual rights posed by the new technology, leaving the problem to the occasional efforts of the Congress and to the state legislatures and courts.

The *Olmstead* WIRETAPPING controversy set the pattern. There the Court construed the Fourth Amendment to deny any constitutional protection against devices that do not involve a physical trespass and the seizure of tangible documents. Nine years later, in NARDONE V. UNITED STATES (1937), the Court construed a federal statute codifying federal radio and telecommunications law to prohibit wiretapping, much to everyone's surprise. The limitations of this approach were reflected in the virtual failure of the statute to reduce wiretapping significantly and in the Court's understandable refusal in *Goldman v. United States* (1942) to apply the statute to the next significant technological development, a detectaphone placed against a wall that could overhear conversations in another room without physically trespassing.

Now, a half century later, Brandeis's warning is more timely than ever, for we have developed technologies that make these early devices seem primitive. These new technologies include tiny, almost invisible video and audio surveillance devices that can function at short or long distances and by night as well as day, such as a "miniawac," which can spot a car or a person from 30,000 feet in the air; electronic bracelets and anklets that signal a probation or parole officer if his or her charge goes more than a short distance from home; and chemical dust that can be used with ultraviolet detectors for tracking. Computer matching of records in different places can also provide vast amounts of information about a person. Many other techniques involving new biological and medical technology are also being developed.

The Court's resistance to imposing constitutional controls on the use of technological advances in the CRIMINAL JUSTICE SYSTEM stems in part from the law enforcement and constitutional contexts in which these issues arise. Almost always the question before the Court has been whether a convicted criminal is to go free because the enforcement authorities have used some technological device without meeting constitutional requirements. Only for a brief period in its history (1961–1967) has the Court not been reluctant to tolerate such an outcome.

The constitutional provision at issue in these cases is usually the Fourth Amendment, which imposes restrictions only on SEARCH AND SEIZURE. The Court's analytic approach has been to dichotomize surveillances into "searches" and "nonsearches," with the latter denied any Fourth Amendment protection at all; other constitutional provisions, such as the Fifth Amendment's ban on compelled self-incrimination, have been construed as inapplicable to the use of most technological devices. SCHMERBER V. CALIFORNIA (1966) illustrates that point.

This dichotomous approach, together with the Court's general reluctance to recognize the special impact of modern technology on individual liberty, was illustrated just a few years after it overruled *Olmstead* in KATZ V. UNITED STATES (1967). A sharply divided Court in UNITED STATES V.

WHITE (1971) refused to recognize a constitutionally protected right not to have one's conversation with another person secretly transmitted electronically by the latter to police listening some distance away. "Inescapably, one contemplating illegal activity must realize and risk that his companions may be reporting to the police," wrote Justice BYRON R. WHITE, and to him there was no significant difference "between probable informers on the one hand and probable informers with transmitters on the other." But as the dissenting Justice JOHN MARSHALL HARLAN wrote, "third-party bugging ... undermine[s] that confidence and sense of security that is characteristic of ... a free society. It goes beyond the ... ordinary type of "informer situation." The "assumption of risk" analysis used by the Court is circular, insisted Justice Harlan, for "the risks we assume are in large part reflections of laws that translate into rules [our] customs and values. ... The critical question, therefore, is whether ... we *should* impose on our citizens [such] risks ... without at least the protection of a warrant." Moreover, the Fourth Amendment is designed to protect all of us, not just people "contemplating illegal activities," and the Court's approach precluded constitutional protections when a confidential conversation turns out to be wholly innocent.

The *White* unconcern for differences in degree that become differences in kind has been reflected in virtually every constitutional case involving modern technology that the Court has faced. For example, seeking anonymity in a crowd and moving to out-of-the-way places are ways to preserve some privacy in a surveillance-pervaded crowded society. In *United States v. Knotts* the Court ruled that an electronic device, a "beeper," surreptitiously attached to a container that emitted electronic signals, enabling the police to trace the container wherever it went, did not call for constitutional protection; the Court reasoned that "visual surveillance from public places along [the] route" of the person with the container would have provided the same information. Only if the beeper enters a house with the container and continues to operate is there a privacy encroachment requiring a SEARCH WARRANT. The same reasoning can obviously apply to beepers secretly attached to people.

The Court has been equally indifferent to the threats to privacy and liberty posed by modern expansions of visual surveillance. Walls and distance—which we ordinarily use to protect privacy—are not very effective safeguards in today's world. Video surveillance can now be conducted from great distances and often with the capability of listening as well. So far, the Court has tended to ignore distance as a factor. In a series of three decisions in the late 1980s the Court consistently upheld surveillance from above enclosed areas, even when the surveillance was made possible only by the use of highly sophisticated equipment. In *Dow Chemical Co. v. United States* (1986), Dow had a 2,000-acre chemical factory, around which it maintained elaborate security that barred ground-level views; it also investigated any low-level flights. Any further protection against intrusion, such as a roof over the entire facility, would have been prohibitively expensive. An Environmental Protection Agency airplane took approximately seventy-five pictures of the plant from altitudes as high as 12,000 feet. The camera's precision was so great that the pictures could be enlarged over 240 times without significant loss of detail or resolution; it was possible to see pipes and wires as small as one-half inch in diameter. Finding the plant similar to an OPEN FIELD, a 5–4 majority of the Court denied constitutional protection against the surveillance.

In *Dow*, the Court suggested that more protection might be available to a private residence than to a large industrial complex. But in *California v. Ciraolo* (1986) the same 5–4 majority decided the same way when police flew a private plane 1,000 feet above Ciraolo's yard, which he tried to protect with a six-foot outer fence and a ten-foot inner fence; the police saw a marijuana plant in the yard on a small plot, which they photographed. Despite Ciraolo's precautions, Chief Justice WARREN E. BURGER concluded that even though Ciraolo had a REASONABLE EXPECTATION OF PRIVACY in his backyard, it was "unreasonable for [him] to expect that his marijuana plants were constitutionally protected from being observed with the naked eye from an altitude of 1,000 feet," because the observation occurred in public "navigable air space" and the members of the public could look down as they flew overhead. As Justice LEWIS F. POWELL observed in dissent, however, the likelihood of such an observation by a private person on a public or private plane is "virtually nonexistent."

The Court confirmed its indifference to the privacy of areas under surveillance a few years later in *Florida v. Riley* (1989), when it concluded that observations from a helicopter hovering 400 feet above a partially covered greenhouse in the defendant's backyard did not implicate the Fourth Amendment. The Court stressed that the helicopter was not violating the law, "did not interfere with respondent's normal use of the greenhouse," observed no "intimate details," and caused "no undue noise, no wind, dust or threat of injury." The Court did not explain why any of these should be determinative in deciding whether the greenhouse was entitled to be free from unrestricted surveillance.

An especially serious threat to individual liberty arises from the computer revolution. Seeking medical care, participating in public welfare programs, engaging in regulated activities, or even acting as consumers requires us to provide third parties vast amounts of personal information that previously we could have kept confidential. Data that were once either nonexistent or kept in a shoebox or file cabinet are now on someone else's computer disks. Moreover, those records that did exist were stored in public or private files usually scattered in a great many places, making it difficult to develop a full dossier on anyone. That difficulty is now a thing of the past. Computer matching pulls together masses of information in different files, information that can dog one throughout one's existence. As sociologist Gary Marx points out, "this can create a class of permanently stigmatized persons," making it impossible for people to overcome past mistakes and failures and to start a new life. Rehabilitation may be rendered impossible.

The Supreme Court has not dealt directly with computer matching, but has effectively denied constitutional protection to the privacy of a key element in that process: the records themselves. In *United States v. Miller* (1976) the Court refused to require police to meet Fourth Amendment requirements when they subpoenaed a bank's microfilm records of a suspect's checks, bank statements, deposit slips, and other bank transaction records. The Court found no "legitimate expectation of privacy in these records and documents because all contain only information voluntarily conveyed to the banks and exposed to their employees in the ordinary course of business. . . . The depositor takes the risk, in revealing his affairs to another, that the information will be conveyed by that person to the government." The result is that the enormous mass of information that we must "voluntarily convey" in order to live in a modern world is now without constitutional protection. This includes not only bank and medical records but even the telephone numbers we call, which are not conveyed to any one at all but simply recorded for billing purposes by usually inanimate equipment. In *Smith v. Maryland* (1979) the Court refused to require constitutional prerequisites for installation of a pen register that recorded the numbers of outgoing telephone calls. Justice HARRY A. BLACKMUN wrote that "the switching equipment that processed those numbers is merely the modern counterpart of the operator who, in an earlier day, personally completed calls for the subscriber." Wayne LaFave noted the "ominous proposition that modern technology cannot add to one's justified expectation of privacy, but can only detract from it."

Finally, the Court has extracted a principle from one of the oldest forms of "technology" that would render newer technology one of the greatest threats to privacy and other individual rights. In concluding in *United States v. Place* (1983) that use of a dog's sense of smell to detect drugs in a suitcase did not raise Fourth Amendment concerns, the Court said, "A 'canine sniff' by a well-trained narcotics detection dog . . . does not expose non-contraband items

that otherwise would remain hidden from public view . . . [and is] limited both in the manner in which the information is obtained and in the content of the information revealed." This approach would seem to be counter to the proposition that an intrusion cannot be validated by what it turns up. Moreover, if accuracy and unobtrusiveness are criteria, then what lies in store if, as Justice Brandeis feared, we do indeed develop ways that can unobtrusively detect the presence of incriminating materials by foolproof methods?

And why should techniques be limited to searching out tangible items; what of incriminating expressions or even thought revealed by new medical or chemical technology? At this point the Court might balk, but so far its CONSTITUTIONAL THEORY would impose few if any controls.

HERMAN SCHWARTZ
(1992)

Bibliography

FISHMAN, CLIFFORD S. 1985 Electronic Tracking Devices and the Fourth Amendment: *Knots, Karo* the Questions Still Unanswered. *Catholic University Law Review* 34:277–395.

LAFAVE, WAYNE 1987 *Search and Seizure.* St. Paul, Minn.: West Publishing Co.

MARX, GARY T. 1988 *Undercover Police Surveillance in America.* Berkeley: University of California Press.

OFFICE OF TECHNOLOGY ASSESSMENT 1985 *Federal Government Information Technology: Electronic Surveillance and Civil Liberties.* Washington, D.C.: U.S. Government Printing Office.

CRIMINAL JUSTICE SYSTEM

The BILL OF RIGHTS has sometimes been likened to a national code of CRIMINAL PROCEDURE. However, the Constitution regulates many important aspects of criminal justice that are not "procedural" in any sense; at the same time, it fails to regulate many other important aspects, both procedural and nonprocedural. Moreover, features of the criminal justice system that are subject to extensive constitutional limitations are not, in practice, so strictly regulated as is commonly believed. It is therefore appropriate to reflect on which important aspects of criminal justice are and are not governed by the Constitution, what factors explain these patterns, and what the future role of the Constitution should be in defining fundamental norms of criminal justice.

To evaluate the role of constitutional norms in criminal matters, it is necessary to analyze the entire criminal justice system. Each political entity in the United States (local, state, or federal) has such a system; it consists not only of the rules of EVIDENCE and procedure applicable in criminal matters, but also the major institutions of criminal justice (for example, the police, lawyers, judges, court and correctional officials), as well as the provisions of the criminal law (crimes, defenses, and penalties). This system can be envisioned as a process that begins with the definition of the criminal law and the institutions of justice; proceeds "chronologically" through increasingly selective stages of investigation, charging, adjudication, appellate review, and punishment; and ends with the continuing careers of convicted offenders, who all too often, begin the process all over again. Each of these stages of the process raises fundamental issues of justice and of individual-state relations that might be, but often are not, regulated by constitutional norms. At the same time, the enforcement of any such norm is limited by that norm's systemic context; specific rules are dependent on other rules, many of which are not subject to federal constitutional regulation. Thus, changes in specific constitutional norms are often canceled by compensating changes in other rules or practices in the same or different parts of the system.

The following is a list of the major issues at each stage of the above chronological flow model that are and are not subject to significant constitutional regulation:

1. The definition of crimes and penalties is largely unregulated by the Constitution, except for certain limitations imposed by the EX POST FACTO, BILL OF ATTAINDER, and EQUAL PROTECTION clauses, the FIRST AMENDMENT and Eighth Amendment, the RIGHT OF PRIVACY, and the VAGUENESS and fair notice doctrines. Almost all issues relating to the definition of defenses (e.g., self defense, intoxication, and insanity) are unregulated.

2. Except for the appointment and tenure of federal judges, the requirements of judicial neutrality in the issuance of warrants and at trial, and certain First Amendment limitations on the hiring and firing of public employees, the institutions of criminal justice are not regulated at all by the federal Constitution; many are also not closely governed by STATE CONSTITUTIONS. Important unregulated issues include selection and internal supervision of police, prosecutors, and correctional officials; selection and tenure of state judges; and training of police, prosecutors, judges, and defense attorneys.

3. The investigation of criminal charges is covered by highly detailed constitutional limitations as to SEARCH AND SEIZURE, POLICE INTERROGATION AND CONFESSIONS, the RIGHT TO COUNSEL, and BAIL. Important unregulated issues include police decisions to investigate or not investigate, to use informants and undercover police officers, and to charge some offenders and offenses, but not others; magistrate shopping; nighttime arrests and searches; searches when no one but police are present; use of arrest and pretrial detention in minor cases; prompt appearance in court; appellate review of pretrial detention; and nonbail release conditions.

4. Prosecutorial decisions to select offenders and charges, to later drop charges, and to engage in PLEA BARGAINING as to charges and the sentence, or both, have an enormous impact on case outcomes. However, except for very limited equal-protection and "vindictive prosecution" standards, these critical decisions are not regulated by the Constitution.

5. Other pretrial procedures covered by the Constitution include the GRAND JURY (in federal cases only), certain aspects of DISCOVERY, motions to exclude evidence, and SPEEDY TRIAL. However, the powers of the prosecution and the defense to obtain statements from potential witnesses (other than the defendant) before a trial are not regulated by the Constitution.

6. Extensive FAIR TRIAL rights are provided by the Constitution; examples are TRIAL BY JURY, right to counsel, CONFRONTATION with state witnesses, BURDEN OF PROOF, RIGHT AGAINST SELF-INCRIMINATION, and DOUBLE JEOPARDY. Important unregulated issues include the admissibility of the defendant's prior convictions or other misconduct, separation of guilt and sentencing evidence and findings, the necessity of written findings of guilt, multiple trials for the same offense in different states or in both state and federal systems, and most issues involving joinder of offenses and offenders in a single trial.

7. Many of the fair trial standards also apply to SENTENCING proceedings, but they apply more flexibly. The Constitution does not require formal findings or reasons for a particular sentence, nor does it limit guilty plea concessions. Except for the imposition of CAPITAL PUNISHMENT, sentencing decisions need not be structured by guidelines. The Eighth Amendment sets some limits on disproportionately severe prison terms and fines, and sentences are also limited by certain First Amendment, equal protection, and right of privacy rules, but most sentences are not constitutionally regulated either as to their form or severity.

8. The FREEDOM OF THE PRESS and fair trial principles govern media publicity and access to trials and certain pretrial proceedings.

9. Although HABEAS CORPUS rights are guaranteed, it is not clear whether the Constitution guarantees defendants any right to direct appeal in state cases. If an appellate system is provided, it must meet minimal equal protection and DUE PROCESS requirements, but the number of appellate levels, composition of courts, and nature of appealable issues are not regulated.

10. Victims have no rights under the Constitution—to be heard or to appeal, to be protected, or to receive compensation.

11. Compensation of citizens for unconstitutional search, arrest, pretrial detention, or imprisonment is available under federal CIVIL RIGHTS statutes, but is subject to

important limitations (for example, judicial immunity and police officer's defense of reasonable belief that arrest or search was lawful).

12. The Constitution guarantees very few PRISONERS' RIGHTS. Most fair trial rights do not apply to decisions such as prison discipline, transfers, parole, and revocation of probation.

To understand why the Constitution regulates criminal matters so selectively, it is necessary to consider not only the implications of FEDERALISM, but also the textual sources and historical development of federal constitutional norms. The constitutional texts applicable to criminal cases are mostly found in the Bill of Rights (1791) and the FOURTEENTH AMENDMENT (1868). Of these, only the latter applies directly to the states, and it did not provide much concrete guidance until the 1960s, when the WARREN COURT, with use of the INCORPORATION DOCTRINE, began to hold that certain Bill of Rights guarantees were implicit in the Fourteenth Amendment's due process clause. Because there were very few federal criminal cases until the twentieth century, there was little early case law interpreting Bill of Rights guarantees. Indeed, before the adoption of the EXCLUSIONARY RULE in federal cases in 1914, there was virtually no case law, because there was no criminal court remedy encouraging defendants to litigate constitutional claims.

The Supreme Court's application of the exclusionary rule to state criminal cases in 1961, along with its expansion of the availability of habeas corpus and right to counsel in 1963, set the stage for a veritable explosion of constitutional case law during the final years of the Warren Court. Nevertheless, this expansion was constrained by the texts of the Bill of Rights. These texts were written in response to specific perceived abuses of the late eighteenth century. Moreover, they were written at a time when crime tended to be local and relatively disorganized, and before the development of organized police forces and the emergence of the public prosecutor's monopoly over the bringing of cases to trial. Considering these dramatic changes in the nature of crime and criminal justice, the Bill of Rights remains remarkably relevant today, but it fails to address many fundamental issues of modern criminal justice. In the absence of specific provisions, the courts have had to create new rights either by broad analogy to specific rights, or by applying the more open-ended provisions of the due-process clauses of the Fifth and Fourteenth Amendments. However, both approaches weaken the legitimacy of such newly recognized rights and make them vulnerable to attack.

This inherent vulnerability of the Warren Court's jurisprudence, combined with the appointment of more conservative Justices by Presidents RICHARD M. NIXON and RONALD REAGAN, substantially slowed the expansion of

criminal-process safeguards during the 1970s; indeed, the Supreme Court began to cut back on the scope of substantive rights and the availability of exclusionary and habeas corpus remedies. Notions of federalism also provided justification for this conservative shift; many believed that the Warren Court had gone too far in imposing strict federal standards on state criminal justice systems faced with rapidly rising crime rates and inadequate resources. Also, the relatively late development of these standards in federal cases and their very recent application to state cases lent some support to the view that they were not truly fundamental, at least in state cases.

But the Supreme Court did not simply relax the standards in state cases. Because the majority of Justices still accepted the premise of the selective incorporation doctrine—that a uniform definition of each right should apply in state and federal criminal cases—the conservative decisions of the 1970s and 1980s resulted in the lowering of constitutional standards in federal cases as well. Congress responded with a few statutory safeguards, and the Supreme Court's own FEDERAL RULES OF CRIMINAL PROCEDURE continued to provide certain standards more restrictive than the Constitution requires. At the same time, many state courts responded by relying more and more on STATE CONSTITUTIONAL LAW to provide greater protections. In addition, state statutes, rules of procedure, and evidence codes continued to provide important safeguards in areas where constitutional law had retreated or had never been applied.

The degree of the Supreme Court's conservative shift since 1970 should not be overstated. Indeed, a closer analysis of the jurisprudence of the Warren Court reveals that it too had doubts about the wisdom of expanding and strictly enforcing constitutional standards in state and federal criminal cases. Six themes that cut across the spectrum of specific rights illustrate this ambivalence. Although these themes became much clearer in the 1970s and 1980s, they were already evident in the Warren Court era.

First, even the Warren Court recognized that some procedural rights are less important than others. The most important rights were those directly related to the integrity of the adversary system, particularly the right to counsel. Such rights, when violated, were more likely to receive retroactive application and to lead to automatic reversal of a conviction. At the other end of the spectrum, receiving the least protection, were FOURTH AMENDMENT rights. In theory, such rights involve fundamental issues of individual freedom from governmental oppression. In practice, however, they tend only to be asserted by defendants who, in light of illegally seized physical evidence, appear to be clearly guilty of criminal conduct. Thus, the Warren Court recognized several important limitations on these rights and related exclusionary remedies; for example, these rights received little if any retroactive application. Post-Warren Court decisions reflect this "hierarchy of rights" theme even more strongly.

Second, even the adversary-system rights given highest priority by the Warren Court were not applied with equal strictness at all stages of the criminal process. Except for police interrogations covered by MIRANDA V. ARIZONA (1966), the right to counsel was not applied before the filing of formal charges. Similarly, the Court did not show much interest in extending fair trial standards to critical decisions made by correctional authorities, such as disciplinary isolation and revocation of parole. Indeed, the Supreme Court (along with most lower courts) adopted a "hands off" approach toward the entire correctional process. Decisions after 1970 did recognize some rights for prisoners and extended counsel rights to some preindictment proceedings. It remains true, however, that constitutional fair trial guarantees apply primarily *at* trial; the criminal justice system is not, on the whole, really an "adversary" system.

Third, even some trial rights were not deemed applicable to all criminal cases: the Warren Court held that there is no right to a jury trial for "petty offenses" (maximum sentence not exceeding six months' imprisonment). The petty-offense limitation was later applied in different form to the right to counsel at trial. The rationale for this limitation, also widely followed in nonconstitutional procedural rules, is that more severe penalties require more exacting procedures of adjudication. During the pretrial investigative stage, however, the opposite rule applies: more serious offenses give the citizen fewer rights and the police greater power, for example, to make warrantless entries to arrest.

Fourth, the Warren Court's failure to condemn certain problematic features of American criminal justice implied that fundamental concepts, such as due process and equal protection, may mean different things in criminal cases than they do in other contexts. This view was later explicitly adopted by the Court in *Gerstein v. Pugh* (1975), holding that the Fourth Amendment defines (sometimes less strictly) "the 'process that due' for seizures of person or property in criminal cases." The Warren Court never questioned the traditional use of money bail to condition pretrial release, even though such use often constitutes blatant WEALTH DISCRIMINATION. The Court held that the right to vote could not be lost by inability to pay a POLL TAX,, yet it allowed the right of physical liberty before conviction to be lost by inability to post bail. Similarly, the Warren Court never seriously questioned the dominant form of adjudication of criminal cases, that is, plea bargaining, which would seem to be either an UNCONSTITU-

TIONAL CONDITION on the exercise of rights or a case of coerced waiver of rights. It scarcely seems imaginable that the Warren Court would have tolerated in any other context an institutionalized practice whose main purpose is to discourage the exercise of constitutional rights.

Fifth, the Warren Court recognized that police and courts have a practical need for easily administered "bright-line" rules that disregard the specific circumstances of each case. Although most of the Warren Court's bright lines tended to be overly broad with respect to individual rights, some tilted more in the other direction, for example, the automatic right to conduct a limited SEARCH INCIDENT TO ARREST. Later Supreme Court decisions have struck the opposite balance: most, but not all, bright-line rules favor the police.

Finally, the Warren Court undercut many of its liberal, prodefendant rights by recognizing significant limitations on the scope of exclusionary remedies. Thus, defendants lack STANDING to object to even the most outrageous violations of another person's rights; they cannot object to the use of illegally seized evidence to contradict their own testimony on the witness stand; remote products ("fruits") of illegality remain admissible in the prosecution's case, and there is no criminal court remedy for an illegal arrest that does not produce any such evidentiary fruits; and the admission of clearly excludable evidence generally does not require reversal if the reviewing court concludes, in light of the untainted evidence, that admission was HARMLESS ERROR. These exceptions were greatly expanded (and became more numerous) in later Supreme Court decisions; meanwhile, field studies of the exclusionary rule confirmed what perhaps was true even under the Warren Court: exclusion of evidence is rare, occurring in less than one percent of cases, many of which still result in conviction.

Why are fundamental constitutional rights so weakly enforced, even by liberal judges? In addition to the important reasons of history and federalism, noted earlier, there are a number of factors peculiar to the criminal process. First, enforcement of rights usually costs money, and the criminal justice system is inherently underfunded: crime often increases much faster than prisons can be built; legislatures enact moralistic and "get tough" laws, but not the tax increases necessary to pay for their enforcement; and criminal laws are rarely repealed or reduced in severity because there are no votes for the elected official who is, or even appears to be, "soft" on crime or immorality. Second, in part as a result of the first problem, almost all cases are resolved by a guilty plea rather than by trial; defendants who plead guilty waive not only their trial rights, but frequently also their rights to contest the introduction of illegally obtained evidence.

Third, the remedies for constitutional violations create problems of their own. The exclusionary rule often requires courts to throw out reliable evidence; retrial after appellate reversal of conviction may be impossible because of lost evidence, witnesses, and testimony. Fourth, the actors purportedly regulated by constitutional norms retain substantial unregulated discretion—not only because of the need to limit caseloads to stay within resource limits, but also because the correctness of the actors' decisions often turns on case-specific factual determinations, such as voluntariness of consent or waiver, which does not permit close regulation by legal norms. In any case, such norms govern relatively few issues; officials deal with cases and defendants under many rules and at many stages of system processing, and each stage provides opportunities to undercut or evade the occasionally strict rule.

Finally, it must be admitted that Americans are deeply ambivalent about some of their most fundamental ideals of justice. Such ideals often make it more difficult to arrest and convict criminals; particularly in times of rapidly increasing crime rates, most citizens prefer to protect themselves and their property rather than criminals. Even where constitutional norms are designed to protect the innocent, they are necessarily most likely to be asserted by a guilty defendant. As noted earlier, this is almost always true in the Fourth Amendment area, but it is generally true throughout the system. The presumption of innocence itself is somewhat counterintuitive: most arrested persons and certainly most defendants brought to trial are guilty, or ought to be; if they were not, our criminal justice system would be grossly defective. Similarly, the right against compelled self-incrimination is contrary to the general duty to testify and the view that wrongdoers have a duty to admit their mistakes; the right to a vigorous defense is contrary to the view that wrongdoers should not be assisted in their efforts to conceal the truth and avoid punishment; and limits on deceptive police practices are contrary to the view that sometimes it is necessary to fight fire with fire. In light of these value conflicts, citizens—and sometimes even lawyers and judges—may lose sight of the importance of our most fundamental criminal-procedure safeguards.

What, then, can we conclude about the proper role of the Constitution in criminal matters? Despite the problems described, Americans certainly must not stop trying to improve the quality of criminal justice. Moreover, constitutional norms play a central role in these efforts—defining, as the Supreme Court said of the CRUEL AND UNUSUAL PUNISHMENT clause, "the evolving standards of decency which mark the progress of a maturing society." At the same time, constitutional norm setting has its limits. Only the most fundamental and lasting norms can be expressed in the constitutional text. Moreover, the case law articulating such norms must not get too far ahead of our ability and willingness to enforce these rules; otherwise, idealism and hope turn to hypocrisy and cynicism.

The Constitution is only one source of norms in criminal cases; other major sources are state constitutions, statutes, codes of criminal procedure and evidence, model law and procedural codes, administrative regulations, and the COMMON LAW,. Increasingly, Americans have begun to look to statements of international human rights; although the INFLUENCE OF THE AMERICAN CONSTITUTION ABROAD once made the United States a leader in this field, international norms have now progressed to the point where they sometimes set standards more strict than, or in areas not covered by, the American Constitution.

RICHARD S. FRASE
(1992)

Bibliography

AMERICAN BAR ASSOCIATION   1980   *ABA Standards for Criminal Justice*, 4 vols., 2nd ed. Boston: Little, Brown.

AMERICAN LAW INSTITUTE   1975   *A Model Code of Prearraignment Procedure*. Philadelphia: American Law Institute.

FRASE, RICHARD S.   1986   Criminal Procedure in a Conservative Age: A Time to Rediscover the Critical Nonconstitutional Issues. *Journal of Legal Education* 36:79–82.

FRIENDLY, HENRY J.   1965   The Bill of Rights as a Code of Criminal Procedure. *California Law Review* 53:929–956.

KAMISAR, YALE; LAFAVE, WAYNE; and ISRAEL, JEROLD H.   1990   *Modern Criminal Procedure: Cases, Comments, Questions*, 7th ed. St. Paul, Minn.: West Publishing Co.

LAFAVE, WAYNE R. and SCOTT, AUSTIN W., JR.   1986   *Criminal Law*, 2nd ed. St. Paul, Minn.: West Publishing Co.

ZIMRING, FRANKLIN E. and FRASE, RICHARD S.   1980   *The Criminal Justice System: Materials on the Administration and Reform of the Criminal Law*. Boston: Little, Brown.

CRIMINAL LAW

See: Federal Criminal Law

CRIMINAL PROCEDURE

"It was a great day for the human race," Charles E. Merriam wrote in *Systematic Politics* (1945), "when the idea dawned that every man is a human being, an end in himself, with a claim for the development of his own personality, and that human beings had a dignity and a worth, respect for which is the firm basis of human association." This idea is the predicate for that branch of American constitutional law which is concerned with criminal procedure, for this body of law is deliberately weighted in favor of persons accused of crime. This pronounced tilt of the law is based on the assumption that it is vitally necessary to protect the dignity inherent in all human beings, regardless of their station in society.

The commitment of the Constitution to protect in some emphatic way the rights of criminal defendants is reflected in the fact that such protection is a principal theme of the federal BILL OF RIGHTS. Similar protections appear in the bills of rights that form parts of all state CONSTITUTIONS. Even before the ratification of the Bill of Rights in 1791, however, the Constitution in its original form did not ignore the subject altogether. Thus, the privilege of the writ of HABEAS CORPUS was guaranteed, and both BILLS OF AT-TAINDER (legislative convictions for crime) and EX POST FACTO laws (laws making criminal acts that were innocent when done) were forbidden (Article I, sections 9 and 10). TRIAL BY JURY "for all crimes" was also guaranteed (Article III, section 2), and the offense of TREASON was defined with meticulous care to prevent abuse of a charge often made on flimsy grounds in moments of great political excitement (Article III, section 3).

The Bill of Rights filled in many more details by spelling out a long list of guarantees designed to protect criminal defendants: freedom from "unreasonable SEARCHES AND SEIZURES" (FOURTH AMENDMENT), INDICTMENT, by GRAND JURY, freedom from DOUBLE JEOPARDY, the RIGHT AGAINST SELF-INCRIMINATION, the right to DUE PROCESS OF LAW (Fifth Amendment), the right to a speedy and PUBLIC TRIAL by an impartial local jury, the right to notice of charges, the right to confront adverse witnesses (*i.e.*, cross-examination), the right to have the assistance of counsel (SIXTH AMENDMENT), and freedom from excessive BAIL and from the infliction of CRUEL AND UNUSUAL PUNISHMENT (Eighth Amendment). In addition, section 1 of the FOUR-TEENTH AMENDMENT, with its provision that no state shall "deprive any person of life, liberty, or property, without due process of law," eventually opened the door to considerable supervision of criminal justice in the states by the federal courts.

This commitment to the safeguarding of the rights of defendants in criminal cases was deeply rooted in the COM-MON LAW system which the earliest settlers brought with them from England. In ancient Anglo-Saxon and Norman times, questions of guilt or innocence were determined by such ritualistic devices as trial by battle or ordeal, or by compurgation (oath-taking), which were largely appeals to God to work a miracle establishing the defendant's innocence. Actually, private vengeance, taking the form of private war or blood feuds, was the principal check on criminal conduct. But by the time the first colonies were established in America, the basic procedures characteristic of modern jurisprudence had taken form. The essence of modern adjudication is the discovery of innocence or guilt through the presentation of proofs and reasoned argument.

Furthermore, it is important that under common law a person accused of crime carries with him the presumption of innocence, which means that the defendant is not obliged to prove his innocence, but rather that the BURDEN OF PROOF is on the prosecution to prove guilt. In addition, jurors must be instructed by the presiding judge that they may convict only if they find that guilt has been established "beyond a REASONABLE DOUBT," which is the greatest quantum of proof known to the law. In most civil litigation a preponderance of evidence suffices to support a verdict. Thus, in a landmark English case, *Woolmington v. D.P.P.* (1935), the House of Lords ruled clearly wrong an instruction of the trial judge to the effect that since the accused had shot his wife, the law presumed him to be guilty of murder unless he could satisfy the jury that death was due to an accident. "No matter what the charge or where the trial," Lord Sankey declared, "the principle that the prosecution must prove the guilt of the prisoner is part of the common law of England and no attempt to whittle it down can be entertained."

The common law rules relating to the presumption of innocence and the burden of proof are part of the law prevailing in every American state. For example, following the completion of a modern, revised criminal code in Wisconsin, the legislature adopted a statute that declared: "No provision of the criminal code shall be construed as changing the existing law with respect to presumption of innocence or burden of proof." These principles are also firmly rooted in federal jurisprudence. As Justice FELIX FRANK-FURTER, dissenting in *Leland v. Oregon* (1952), wrote, "From the time that the law which we have inherited has emerged from dark and barbaric times, the conception of justice which has dominated our criminal law has refused to put an accused at the hazard of punishment if he fails to remove every reasonable doubt of his innocence in the minds of jurors. It is the duty of the Government to establish his guilt beyond a reasonable doubt." Similarly, the Supreme Court has ruled that the standard of proof beyond a reasonable doubt in criminal cases is a due process requirement binding upon the state courts. It is, Justice WILLIAM J. BRENNAN asserted in IN RE WINSHIP (1970), "a prime instrument for reducing the risk of convictions resting on factual error. The standard provides concrete substance for the presumption of innocence. . . ." According to the Supreme Court, the states are required to prove beyond a reasonable doubt all elements of the crime with which the defendant was charged, and the jury must be so instructed. An instruction is improper if it has the effect of reducing substantially the prosecution's burden of proof or of requiring the defendant to establish his innocence beyond a reasonable doubt.

The solicitude of American constitutional law for the rights of the accused is so great that the American system has been described as a defendant's law, in contrast with inquisitorial systems of other countries which give the prosecution many advantages not available in the United States. American public law on this important subject rests upon the recognition of several important considerations that are not the product of abstract theorizing or mere sentimentalism but rather the result of historical experience over centuries of time. For one thing, it is an unquestionably legitimate, indeed essential, function of government to apprehend, try, and punish convicted criminals. But it is also the duty of those public officials who operate the criminal justice system to avoid violating the law themselves in their zeal to combat crime. Of course, our society has a serious crime problem which government cannot and should not ignore, but it has long been recognized that at some point the price of law enforcement may be exorbitant. As Justice Frankfurter observed in *Feldman v. United States Oil Refining Co.* (1944), "The effective enforcement of a well designed penal code is of course indispensable for social security," but he went on to say: "The Bill of Rights was added to the original constitution in the conviction that too high a price may be paid even for the unhampered enforcement of the criminal law and that, in its attainment, other social objects of a free society should not be sacrificed."

Surely, one of the indispensable objectives of a free society is to avoid the disorganizing consequences of lawlessness by public officials. Thus Justice OLIVER WENDELL HOLMES observed in his celebrated dissenting opinion in the Supreme Court's first WIRETAPPING case, OLMSTEAD V. UNITED STATES (1928), that "we must consider two objects of desire, both of which we cannot have, and make up our minds which to choose. It is desirable that criminals should be detected and to that end that all available evidence should be used. It is also desirable that the government should not itself foster and pay for other crimes, when they are the means by which the evidence is to be obtained. . . . We have to choose, and for my part I think is a less evil that some criminals should escape than that the Government should play an ignoble part." In a separate dissenting opinion in the same case, Justice LOUIS D. BRANDEIS warned that government forcefully teaches by example, that crime is contagious, and that "if the Government becomes a lawbreaker, it breeds contempt for law; it invites every man to become a law unto himself; it invites anarchy." To permit the government to commit crimes, he asserted, in order to convict criminals, "would bring terrible retribution."

Without question, if unrestrained by law, the police could apprehend and prosecutors could secure the conviction of far more lawbreakers than they now manage to catch and convict. For example, if the police had a free hand to break into any dwelling or other building and to rummage around as they please, looking for stolen goods or other contraband, such as controlled substances, unquestionably they would solve more crimes and put more thieves, burglars, drug peddlers, and other criminal characters in jail. But the price would be prohibitively high, since it would entail the destruction of a cherished aspect of privacy. Similarly, if the police were completely free to torture suspects, more confessions would be secured, and the conviction rate would rise significantly, but again, other values must be weighed in the balance. These values include avoiding the risk of convicting innocent people who cannot endure the pain and avoiding the danger of encouraging unprofessional, brutal police conduct which employs uncivilized methods shocking to the conscience. Obviously, choices must be made between the desire to catch and punish lawbreakers and our concern for maintaining the legal amenities of a civilized society. The search for a tolerable balance between these competing objectives is what much of our constitutional law is all about. As Justice WILLIAM O. DOUGLAS remarked, in *An Almanac of Liberty* (1954), "a degree of inefficiency is a price we necessarily pay for a civilized, decent society. The free state offers what a police state denies—the privacy of the home, the dignity and peace of mind of the individual." Aside from the fact that one hundred percent law enforcement would make the building of additional jails the highest priority of the country, it simply cannot be achieved without devoting resources far beyond what we can afford, considering all the other important functions for which government is responsible, and without resorting to methods that are almost universally deplored in civilized countries.

The various rights secured for the accused by our constitutional law are not technicalities; due process of law is at the center of our concept of justice. The overall purpose of our legal system is not so much to secure convictions as to render justice. Our rules of constitutional law are not only designed to protect people who are in trouble with the law but also to assure us that those who are engaged in the often exciting business of law enforcement will observe those time-tested rules which in large measure constitute the essence of fair procedure. "Let it not be overlooked," Justice ROBERT H. JACKSON, dissenting in SHAUGHNESSY V. UNITED STATES (1953), wrote, "that due process of law is not for the sole benefit of the accused. It is the best insurance for the Government itself against those blunders which leave lasting stains on a system of justice. . . ."

There are additional compelling reasons that explain and support our legal system's concern for protecting the rights of persons accused of crime. For one thing, a criminal case is essentially a contest between an individual and a government, that is to say, between parties of vastly unequal strength. This disparity in the strength of the parties is especially visible in the modern age of powerful governments. The teaching of experience the world over is that inequality tends to beget injustice, and where the parties are so unequal, a determined effort must be made to redress the imbalance of power. Thus, the accused is entitled to seek a reversal of a conviction in an appellate court, but the prosecution may not get an acquittal reversed, for the double jeopardy principle forbids it. In this respect, the scales of justice are tipped in favor of the weaker party.

In addition, our concern for the defendant's rights rests upon an understanding that for most people it is a very serious matter indeed to be accused by the government of having committed a crime. The possible consequences range from loss of employment to disruption of family life, injury to reputation, and, ultimately, loss of personal liberty. It follows that one accused of crime is likely to be in such deep trouble that he or she must have every opportunity to combat the charges, as fully, as quickly, and as decisively, as possible. Many rights—bail, a public and SPEEDY TRIAL, CONFRONTATION, of accusers, and assistance of counsel—facilitate an early and effective defense, or at the very least, make one possible.

Furthermore, one of the major purposes of assuring a full measure of due process of law is to promote the sense of community by giving all of us the feeling that even guilty persons have been treated fairly. As Justice Douglas observed in *Brady v. Maryland* (1963), "Society wins not only when the guilty are convicted but when criminal trials are fair; our system of the administration of criminal justice suffers when any accused is treated unfairly." As Justice Brennan said in FURMAN V. GEORGIA (1972), "Even the vilest criminal remains a human being possessed of common human dignity."

In a larger sense, our body of procedural law in the criminal field seeks to combat abuse of the POLICE POWER of the state. Police brutality is the hallmark of totalitarian and dictatorial systems of government. The twentieth century has been well schooled in the fearful menace of the midnight knock on the door, the ransacking of private dwellings by the police without legal warrant, the use of torture to break the will, and the ultimate indignity of incarceration in brutal concentration camps. For these compelling reasons our constitutional law was deliberately formulated to prevent the unrestrained exercise of police power.

Indeed, if one looks closely at the elements of the constitutional right to a FAIR TRIAL it becomes clear that for every rule there is a persuasive reason. The basic rights of the accused are responses to our concrete historical experience. Why, for example, does American constitutional law assure defendants representation by counsel? The answer was explained with convincing clarity by Justice GEORGE SUTHERLAND in POWELL V. ALABAMA (1932):

> The right to be heard would be, in many cases, of little avail if it did not comprehend the right to be heard by counsel. Even the intelligent and educated layman has small and sometimes no skill in the science of law. If charged with crime, he is incapable, generally, of determining for himself whether the indictment is good or bad. He is unfamiliar with the rules of evidence. Left without the aid of counsel he may be put on trial without a proper charge, and convicted upon incompetent evidence, or evidence irrelevant to the issue or otherwise inadmissible. He lacks both the skill and knowledge adequately to prepare his defense, even though he has a perfect one. He requires the guiding hand of counsel at every step in the proceedings against him.

In GIDEON V. WAINWRIGHT (1963), the case that extended the RIGHT TO COUNSEL in state courts to all persons charged with felonies, Justice HUGO L. BLACK argued that it was an obvious truth that a person too poor to hire a lawyer cannot be assured a fair trial. He pointed out that government spends vast sums of money to engage the services of lawyers to prosecute, and that few defendants who can afford them fail to hire the best lawyers they can find to present their defenses, from which it follows that "lawyers in criminal courts are necessities, not luxuries."

To cite another example, in all American jurisdictions, state and federal, double jeopardy—which means essentially putting a person on trial twice for the same offense—is forbidden. Once a defendant has been tried and acquitted, he may not be put on trial a second time, even though the prosecution has found fresh relevant evidence not previously available to it or has discovered that serious legal errors were made at the trial. As explained by Justice Black in *Green v. United States* (1957): "The underlying idea, one that is deeply ingrained in at least the Anglo-American system of jurisprudence, is that the State with all its resources and power should not be allowed to make repeated attempts to convict an individual for an alleged offense, thereby subjecting him to embarrassment, expense, and ordeal and compelling him to live in a continuing state of anxiety and insecurity, as well as enhancing the possibility that even though innocent he may be found guilty."

There are equally persuasive reasons for the guarantee of trial by jury. Justice BYRON R. WHITE noted, in the landmark case of DUNCAN V. LOUISIANA (1968), that the right of trial by jury is "an inestimable safeguard against the corrupt or overzealous prosecutor and against the compliant, biased, or eccentric judge." The jury, one of the distinctive features of Anglo-American jurisprudence, is the result of several centuries of concrete experience; it has changed in the past, in many different ways, and it is still a dynamic institution. The authors of the Constitution were thoroughly familiar with the jury system and made careful provision for it in the original document, before the Bill of Rights filled in additional details. Thus, our criminal law procedure has always reflected a reluctance to entrust prosecutors and judges with unchecked powers over life and liberty.

Similarly, there are compelling reasons why American constitutional law protects the individual against UNREASONABLE SEARCHES AND SEIZURES, the main reason being the desire to protect the RIGHT OF PRIVACY. This "right to be left alone," as Justice Brandeis asserted in his notable dissenting opinion in *Olmstead,* is "the most comprehensive of rights and the right most valued by civilized man." Fresh from his Nuremberg experience, Justice Robert Jackson wrote, in a spirited dissent in BRINEGAR V. UNITED STATES (1949), that the Fourth Amendment rights "are not mere second-class rights but belong in the catalog of indispensable freedoms. Among deprivation of rights, none is so effective in cowing a population, crushing the spirit of the individual and putting terror in every heart. Uncontrolled search and seizure is one of the first and most effective weapons in the arsenal of every arbitrary government." Justice Jackson also pointed out that because police officers are themselves the chief invaders of this right, the responsibility for protection against unreasonable searches and seizures has fallen on the courts.

An ancient teaching of English and American law is that to compel a person to convict himself or herself of a crime by being coerced into giving unwilling testimony is inadmissible. Our criminal jurisprudence makes the assumption that everyone is innocent until proved guilty beyond a reasonable doubt on the basis of competent evidence; the prosecution has the duty to prove guilt. Because the accused is not required to establish his innocence, it follows that he cannot be required to supply testimony that would lead to a conviction. The Fifth Amendment's guarantee against compulsory self-incrimination is thus neither an alien nor a novel doctrine but rather, as Justice Douglas wrote in *An Almanac of Liberty,* "one of the great landmarks in man's struggle to be free of tyranny, to be decent and civilized. It is our way of escape from the use of torture. It is part of our respect for the dignity of man."

The rights of the accused in American criminal procedure are not static but respond to changing social values and moral concepts. This dynamism is reflected in the judicial interpretation of the Eighth Amendment's prohibition of cruel and unusual punishment. Thus Chief Justice EARL WARREN wrote in TROP V. DULLES (1958): "The Amendment must draw its meaning from the evolving standards of decency that mark the progress of a maturing society." Similarly, in FURMAN V. GEORGIA, the Supreme Court for

the first time held that the death penalty is unconstitutional under certain circumstances, Justice THURGOOD MARSHALL observing that "a penalty that was permissible at one time in our Nation's history is not necessarily permissible today." The court similarly made new law when it ruled in *Estelle v. Gamble* (1976) that deliberate indifference of a jailer to the medical needs of prisoners constituted an "unnecessary and wanton infliction of pain" proscribed by the Eighth Amendment. Similarly, the right to be free from unreasonable searches or seizures had to be given a progressively broadened scope as we moved into the age of electronic gadgetry. Given the dynamic character of American life, flexibility of interpretation was inevitable if a living Constitution was to retain its vitality, and the broad and generous character of constitutional language contributed to that flexibility.

Many policy questions relating to criminal procedure must be understood in the context of the federal character of the American system of government. Certain important powers are delegated by the Constitution to the national government, and except as the states are limited by that Constitution—which is the supreme law of the land—the TENTH AMENDMENT confirms that the states retain power over all other matters. One of the most important residual powers of the states is the power to define and punish crimes. Although Congress was not expressly empowered to enact a general code of criminal statutes, it was assumed from the beginning that the national government could enforce its laws by imposing criminal sanctions. The doctrine of IMPLIED POWERS provided the necessary doctrinal underpinning. For example, the delegated power to tax includes by implication the power to punish persons who commit tax frauds. The federal criminal code has expanded steadily since 1789 and is today a lengthy document. Even so, most criminal laws are state laws, and a very large majority of persons in jail are incarcerated in state institutions. That the criminal law in all its facets is mainly state law is a well-understood fact of American life. In a special message to Congress in 1968, President LYNDON B. JOHNSON pointed out that crime "is essentially a local matter. Police operations—if they are to be effective and responsible—must likewise remain basically local. This is the fundamental premise of our constitutional structure and of our heritage of liberty." It follows, said the President, that "the Federal Government must never assume the role of the Nation's policeman."

Decisions of state courts are not reviewable by the Supreme Court if they involve only issues of state law, as to which the highest state court speaks the last word. For example, a 1967 case involved an appeal from the Texas courts regarding the state's habitual-criminal statute. Under this statute, the trial jury is fully informed of previous criminal convictions and the state is not obliged to have a two-stage trial, one devoted to the pending charge and a second to a consideration of the previous convictions. On appeal, the Supreme Court ruled in *Spencer v. Texas* that as a matter of national constitutional law the state is not required to provide a two-stage trial. Declining to interfere, the Court held that this matter is controlled by state procedural law; the Court is not "a rule-making organ for the promulgation of state rules of procedure."

There are, in fact, two avenues available to seek federal judicial review of the decisions of state courts in criminal cases. First of all, if a convicted defendant has taken whatever appeals are available to him under state law in the state courts and if he has sought review of a substantial federal (as distinguished from state law) question, then the Supreme Court has JURISDICTION to review the judgment on direct review if it chooses to do so. Second, one who is in custody following conviction in a state court and has exhausted his available postconviction state remedies may, in a proper case, assert his federal legal claim by applying to a federal district court for a writ of habeas corpus. Accordingly, whether through direct review by the Supreme Court or through habeas corpus proceedings, federal courts often correct state courts where federal rights have been denied. But federal courts do not sit merely to correct errors alleged to have occurred in state courts. As the Supreme Court said in *Herb v. Pitcairn* (1945), "Our only power over state judgments is to correct them to the extent that they incorrectly adjudge federal rights."

The key question, then, is: what is a federal right? A short answer is: any right arising under the Constitution of the United States, statutes of Congress, or treaties. But the provisions of the Constitution relating to basic rights are stated in vague and general language that does not in terms apply to the states. Indeed the Court held in a landmark case, BARRON V. BALTIMORE (1833), that the Bill of Rights did not apply to the states. This holding was based on the proposition that the Bill of Rights was intended only to supply additional protection from violations by the new, untested national government, and that wherever the states were limited by the constitution, the language to this effect was always explicit. Prior to the Civil War, federal court review of state criminal convictions under the Bill of Rights was not possible.

A major change in our whole system of government began in 1868 with the adoption of the Fourteenth Amendment, which provides that no state shall "deprive any person of life, liberty, or property, without due process of law." Not until 1923, however, did the Supreme Court undertake to employ this clause as a limit on state criminal procedure. In the leading case of MOORE V. DEMPSEY, the Court held that a conviction in a trial dominated by a mob was a violation of due process and could be remedied by a federal court through issuance of a writ of habeas corpus.

In such a proceeding the federal court must make an independent evaluation of the facts, even though the state's highest appellate court has upheld the correctness of the conviction. The Supreme Court, too, on direct review, began to reverse state convictions as violations of due process. In 1932 the Court ruled that the Sixth Amendment right to representation by counsel, at least in capital cases, is an indispensable element of a fair trial which is guaranteed by the Fourteenth Amendment's due process clause. Later decisions extended the constitutional right to counsel in state courts to include any offense punishable by imprisonment for any period of time. Other decisions, most of which were made after World War II by the WARREN COURT, applied to the states, as due process requirements, most of the other provisions of the Bill of Rights which are designed to protect persons accused of crime. For example, in MAPP V. OHIO (1961) the Court extended to the states the EXCLUSIONARY RULE, long applicable in federal prosecutions by reason of the Fourth Amendment. Henceforth state courts, too, would be required to exclude from criminal trials all evidence secured as a result of unreasonable searches and seizures. Similarly, a state violates due process if it subjects a person to compulsory self-incrimination (MALLOY V. HOGAN, 1964), if it denies trial by jury at least where nonpetty offenses are involved (DUNCAN V. LOUISIANA, 1968), or if it subjects a defendant to the hazards of double jeopardy (BENTON V. MARYLAND, 1969). In fact, by 1970 all of the criminal procedure provisions of the Bill of Rights were made applicable to the states by way of Fourteenth Amendment due process, except the Fifth Amendment guarantee of indictment by grand jury and the Eighth Amendment prohibition of excessive bail. The bail guarantee very likely will be incorporated into the Fourteenth Amendment when the issue comes to the Supreme Court in the proper form. All the other rights of the accused guaranteed by the Bill of Rights are now regarded as elements of Fourteenth Amendment due process, enforceable against the states through federal judicial process. In the words of the Court, they are "fundamental principles of liberty and justice," or are "basic in our system of jurisprudence," or are " FUNDAMENTAL RIGHTS essential to a fair trial," or are "the very essence of a scheme of ordered liberty." (See INCORPORATION DOCTRINE.)

Not only does Fourteenth Amendment due process now incorporate most of the Bill of Rights, it also has an independent force wholly outside of the Bill of Rights. For example, in the famous case of *Mooney v. Holohan* (1935), the Court ruled that a state has denied the accused due process of law if the prosecution has deceived the court and jury by presenting testimony known to be perjured. Similarly, in *Jackson v. Virginia* (1979), the Court ruled that a state court conviction can pass the test of Fourteenth Amendment due process only if a rational trier of fact could find that each essential element of the crime had been established "beyond a reasonable doubt."

The expansion of the list of federally enforceable constitutional rights available to defendants in state courts has come a long way in enlarging both the review powers of the Supreme Court and the habeas corpus jurisdiction of the federal district courts. The federal courts are establishing more and more standards in the area of criminal justice which the states are obliged to observe.

In operating the CRIMINAL JUSTICE SYSTEM, government must make some hard choices, since basic objectives undergirding that system often conflict. On the one hand, there is the due process model, preferred by the courts, which stresses our concern for maintaining the legal amenities of a civilized community. This process, adversarial and judicial in character, seeks to protect the dignity and autonomy of the individual. On the other hand, there is the crime control model, preferred by most law enforcement officials, which emphasizes the need to apprehend, try, and punish lawbreakers. The principal procedural objective is the quick, efficient, and reliable handling of persons accused of crime. The method is essentially administrative and managerial in character, operating, especially in respect to MISDEMEANORS, on assembly-line principles. Accordingly, many law enforcement officials are critical of what they see as the Supreme Court's tenderness on the subject of defendants' rights, arguing that change has been too rapid and too far-reaching. Impatience has even been expressed by a few Justices of the Court itself. An experienced California trial judge, Macklin Fleming, has gone so far as to accuse the Court of pursuing the unattainable objective of "perfect justice." It is difficult, perhaps impossible, to locate the exactly right balance between the due process model and the crime control model. But in seeking to achieve a tolerable balance the Supreme Court has moved with considerable caution, deciding one case at a time, and always within the mainstream of American culture and its dominant legal traditions.

DAVID FELLMAN
(1986)

Bibliography

CASPER, JONATHON D. 1972 *American Criminal Justice: The Defendant's Perspective.* Englewood Cliffs, N.J.: Prentice-Hall.

CORTNER, RICHARD C. 1980 *The Supreme Court and the Second Bill of Rights.* Madison: University of Wisconsin Press.

FELLMAN, DAVID 1976 *The Defendant's Rights Today.* Madison: University of Wisconsin Press.

FLEMING, MACKLIN 1974 *The Price of Perfect Justice.* New York: Basic Books.

FRIENDLY, HENRY J. 1967 The Bill of Rights as a Code of Criminal Procedure, in *Benchmarks.* Chicago: University of Chicago Press.

GOLDSTEIN, ABRAHAM S. 1960 The State and the Accused: Balance of Advantage in Criminal Procedure. *Yale Law Journal* 69:1149–1199.

PACKER, HERBERT L. 1964 Two Models of the Criminal Process. *University of Pennsylvania Law Review* 113:1–68.

CRIMINAL SYNDICALISM LAWS

Criminal syndicalism statutes were but one of several kinds of statutes punishing manifestations of unpopular thought and expression for their probable bad tendency enacted during and just after WORLD WAR I by many midwestern and western states. The laws were a response to the economic unrest of the postwar period, specifically to the doctrines and activities of the Industrial Workers of the World (IWW), and to the antiradical hysteria prompted by the Russian Revolution of 1917. Twenty-two states and territories enacted—and eight other states considered but rejected—criminal syndicalism statutes between 1917 and 1920. Attempts to enact a federal criminal syndicalism law in 1919 and 1920 came to nothing, but the Smith Act of 1940 was patterned after the earlier model.

The Idaho statute, the first of its kind and a model for those adopted by other states, defined criminal syndicalism as "the doctrine which advocates crime, sabotage, violence or other unlawful methods of terrorism as a means of accomplishing industrial or political reform." Offenses punished as FELONIES under such statutes included oral or written advocacy of criminal syndicalism; justifying commission of or attempts to commit criminal syndicalism; printing or displaying written or printed matter advocating or advising criminal syndicalism; organizing or being or becoming a member of any organization organized or assembled to teach or advocate criminal syndicalism, or even presence at such an assembly. Though most citizens and state legislators believed that these statutes were directed solely against the use or advocacy of force and violence, in practice they jeopardized FREEDOM OF SPEECH, because they were used to punish those who expressed or even held opinions offensive to the majority of the community.

Criminal syndicalism statutes almost uniformly survived constitutional challenges in the state courts. In WHITNEY V. CALIFORNIA (1927) the United States Supreme Court upheld the California Criminal Syndicalism Act; Justice LOUIS D. BRANDEIS's eloquent opinion, concurring only in the result, set forth the most sophisticated formulation of the theoretical foundations and practical applications of the CLEAR AND PRESENT DANGER test previously formulated in other FIRST AMENDMENT cases. In *Fiske v. Kansas* (1927), the first decision overturning a conviction under a criminal syndicalism statute, the Supreme Court merely invalidated the statute's application, holding that the state had not shown that the defendant had advocated any but lawful methods to achieve the goals of the IWW. In DE JONGE v. OREGON (1937) a unanimous Court struck down the application of the Oregon Criminal Syndicalism Act to defendants who had merely attended a peaceful meeting of the Communist party; the Oregon legislature later repealed the statute. The labor troubles of the 1930s prompted efforts to strengthen existing criminal syndicalism laws, but these came to nothing, and several states followed Oregon's example in repealing their criminal syndicalism statutes. State criminal syndicalism statutes fell into disuse after the 1930s; in BRANDENBERG v. OHIO (1969) the Supreme Court declared the Ohio Criminal Syndicalism Act unconstitutional on its face, overruling *Whitney*, adopting the principles of Justice Brandeis's concurring opinion, and making successful prosecutions under criminal syndicalism statutes virtually impossible.

RICHARD B. BERNSTEIN
(1986)

Bibliography

CHAFEE, ZECHARIAH, JR. 1941 *Free Speech in the United States.* Cambridge, Mass.: Harvard University Press.

DOWELL, ELDRIDGE FOSTER 1939 *A History of Criminal Syndicalism Legislation in the United States.* Baltimore: Johns Hopkins University Studies in Historical and Political Science, Series 57, No. 1.

CRITICAL LEGAL STUDIES

"Critical legal studies" refers to a development in American jurisprudence in the late 1970s and 1980s. Its originators were self-consciously affiliated with leftist political movements. Their understanding of the law, including constitutional law, was influenced by the experience of the movements for CIVIL RIGHTS and against the VIETNAM WAR, in which, as they saw it, appeals to legality—in the form of saying that RACIAL DISCRIMINATION was unconstitutional and that the war was being conducted illegally—played an important but complex role. Their intellectual position was shaped in large measure by an understanding of American LEGAL REALISM that took realism's implications to be more radical than many of its first proponents may have believed. The radical reading of legal realism was supported, in critical legal studies, by an understanding of what were perceived as the intellectual difficulties of the liberal tradition, which produced the tensions that the realists attempted unsuccessfully to resolve.

The most direct legacy of legal realism to critical legal studies was the idea of indeterminacy. Critical legal studies understood the realist message to be that law, again including constitutional law, was shot through with "contradictions," in the sense that, at least in any socially significant case, legal arguments that were professionally defensible were available for a rather wide range of outcomes and rules, some of which might differ radically from others. According to critical legal studies, this indeterminacy resulted from the fact that the liberal tradition attempted to, but could not, suppress what Duncan Kennedy, an early proponent of critical legal studies, called "the fundamental contradiction" of social life—that people are both fearful of, and dependent upon, other people. In the critical legal studies analysis, the central themes of the liberal tradition, expressing suspicion of government efforts to promote "the good" in societies where there were fundamental differences over what constitutes the good, drew primarily on the fear of other people. Yet, according to critical legal studies, because social life necessarily places people in relations of dependence on each other, law cannot, and does not, simply express the fear of others. Rather, law attempts to express both aspects of the fundamental contradiction, which is what generates the possibility of acceptable legal arguments leading to radically different results.

To deal with the point that the indeterminacy thesis is in tension with the fact that lawyers can predict with some assurance how judges will resolve many contentious legal issues, even if the issues could in some sense be regarded as open to decision either way, critical legal studies relies on claims about law as ideology. In one version, influenced by Marxist social thought, indeterminacy is resolved in fact by the political predispositions of the judges, and predictability occurs because the judges, and lawyers too, are drawn from a relatively narrow range of social classes, whose interests they promote. The conspiratorial overtones of this account are reduced in another version of the argument that law is a form of ideology. This version, influenced by the work of Michel Foucault, argues that indeterminacy is resolved because on a higher level of abstraction some general ideology about reason and the state is embedded in modern culture, so that many of the more radical possibilities are ruled out of contention from the start.

Critical legal studies is a form of general jurisprudence, and the indeterminacy thesis was developed primarily in connection with private law. The critical legal studies analysis of constitutional law has two important strands. The first, drawing on the private law studies, is a critique of the distinction between public and private that pervades law and appears in constitutional law in the form of the STATE ACTION doctrine. According to that doctrine, the Constitution regulates only actions by government, leaving private parties free to shape their relations and to control their property without regard to constitutional norms.

One key element in the legal realist analysis of private law, however, was that the private law of property and contract could fairly be characterized as a form of delegating public authority to private individuals, subject always to public control through, for example, doctrines restricting the enforcement of contracts on the ground that they violate public policy. Given that analysis of private law, the state action doctrine appears incoherent, and for critical legal studies SHELLEY V. KRAEMER (1948), holding unconstitutional judicial enforcement of racially restrictive property covenants, is not an anomaly, as it is in many mainstream accounts of constitutional law, but is instead a necessary implication of the analysis of the public private distinction.

The second important strand in the critical legal studies analysis of constitutional law has been the "critique of rights." The critique of rights applies the indeterminacy thesis to the individual rights provisions of the Constitution. Vacillation by the Supreme Court over the importance of intent versus effect in antidiscrimination law, for example, is taken to reflect not just the political shift from the WARREN COURT to the BURGER COURT and now the REHNQUIST COURT but also the indeterminacy of the idea of nondiscrimination itself. The critique of rights accepts the proposition that there is general agreement on the importance of certain FUNDAMENTAL RIGHTS, so long as the claims are either that there are such rights (without specifying what they are) or that the rights are acknowledged and enforced in abstract terms. But, the critique of rights contends that, as is always the case when socially significant claims are made, when it comes to enforcing these abstract rights in particular contexts, neither the Constitution nor the Court's precedents even weakly determine what the Court does. Rather, what matters are the current political predispositions of the members of the Supreme Court, a fact that is reflected in the general understanding that we can talk about "conservatives" and "liberals" on the Court.

The critique of rights is augmented and given a political twist by an analysis of the Supreme Court as one of the branches of a unitary government. In this analysis, influenced by mainstream political science, the Court is treated as a political body whose central role, symbolized by the political processes by which Justices are appointed, is to act on behalf of those interests who control the political system over the medium to long run. With this political understanding as a background, the critique of rights argues that, as a general matter with some exceptions, the Supreme Court will interpret—and historically has interpreted—the individual rights provisions of the Constitution primarily to protect the interests of established groups, particularly the owners of large aggregations of property. LOCHNER V. NEW YORK (1905), for an earlier period, and the Court's recent CAMPAIGN FINANCE decisions, for the modern period, exemplify the Court's

commitment to an interpretation of the Constitution in the service of established power groups.

Apart from general challenges to the indeterminacy thesis across the board, the main criticism of the critique of rights has been offered by minority scholars and liberal defenders of the legacy of the Warren Court. For them, the Warren Court's decisions show that, at least on occasion, the Supreme Court's articulation of individual rights can both advance the interests of minority groups and express a vision of a way of organizing society in which existing holders of power might be displaced.

Most proponents of the critique of rights accept both of these points. As to the first, though, they make several points. First, if we examine the entire history of the Supreme Court, the Warren era appears almost as an aberration. Second, many of the Warren Court's decisions might be understood in political terms as advancing the political agenda of the NEW DEAL political coalition, which may have retained control of the courts after it shattered in the political branches. BROWN V. BOARD OF EDUCATION (1954, 1955), a key example used against the critique of rights, would be seen as the Court's enforcement of a national view against SEGREGATION—which was, among other things, embarrassing the United States during the period of Cold War ideological competition with the Soviet Union—against the wishes of a recalcitrant region. If the Warren Court was the judicial expression of the New Deal coalition, it is not surprising, according to the critique of rights, that when the New Deal coalition lost power in the political branches, the Supreme Court eventually abandoned the Warren Court's ideology.

The critique of rights also argues, in response to both of the minority challenges, that the appeal to rights may indeed be a way of expressing opposition to the existing social order, but that those appeals may also be politically damaging. The appeal to rights can be politically damaging because it may divert resources into litigation and a focus on the courts. According to this view, successful legal appeals to rights may sometimes be more harmful than unsuccessful ones. Having secured one victory in the courts, a minority movement may rest on its laurels, relying on the courts to continue to protect its interests and overlooking the fact that permanent victories occur, given the role of the courts in the political system, only if the winners in the courts eventually secure the backing of the political branches. In addition, once a movement achieves a major victory in the courts, such as ROE V. WADE (1973) was for the women's movement, it may make the reasonable short-term judgment that it should devote resources to further judicial action—for example, relying on the courts to strike down laws aimed at undermining or whittling away at *Roe*. This would allow its opponents to adopt the strategy (which may be more successful in the long run) of influencing state and local legislatures, Congress, and the President.

In this view, however, the appeal to rights can also be an expression of opposition to the established order, precisely because the indeterminacy of law rests on the fundamental contradiction of social life. That contradiction means that any system of law contains competing views of the good social order. Thus, adherents of utopian visions of an alternative social order can argue that their preferred social order would realize values already acknowledged in the law but imperfectly implemented in the present order. In addition, the general public respect for fundamental human rights—at least when they are stated in the abstract—gives the advocate of some novel right or of the extension of an acknowledged right an initial rhetorical advantage in public discussions of those claims.

According to the critique of rights, then, the utility of appeals to rights will depend on a careful analysis of the particular circumstances and settings in which the appeals are made. If a social movement can rely on the language of rights without diverting its resources into litigation, for example, many of the disadvantages of the appeals to rights disappear. Yet, although the idea of making appeals to rights without relying on the courts is sensible, in the political culture of the United States, people who invoke rights but do not seek to have the courts implement them are likely to be seen as using a form of language that their behavior belies. Similarly, political circumstances sometimes are favorable for the use of the utopian appeals to rights in litigation as a method of securing legal victories or as a method of mobilizing a constituency. Such favorable circumstances appear to have been present for the civil rights movement during the Warren era. Proponents of the critique of rights would caution, however, that careful analysis of the particulars is necessary in order to make a judgment about whether the advantages of an appeal to rights outweigh the disadvantages.

With the apparent dissolution of much of the Warren Court legacy on the Supreme Court in the late 1980s, the critical legal studies perspective on constitutional law may gain some added force, for the Warren era may become understood as the kind of aberration that critical legal studies has always contended it was. On the other hand, to the extent that critical legal studies is a self-consciously leftist political movement, leftists and liberals may find recourse to the language of rights even more essential in a conservative era.

MARK TUSHNET
(1992)

Bibliography

KELMAN, MARK   1987   *A Guide to Critical Legal Studies.* Cambridge, Mass.: Harvard University Press.

TUSHNET, MARK   1988   *Red, White, and Blue: A Critical Analysis of Constitutional Law.* Cambridge, Mass.: Harvard University Press.

UNGER, ROBERTO   1986   *The Critical Legal Studies Movement* Cambridge, Mass.: Harvard University Press.

CRITICAL RACE THEORY

Critical race theory embraces a movement of leftist scholars, most of them scholars of color situated in law schools, whose work challenges the ways in which race and racial power are constructed and represented in American legal culture and more generally in American society. Although critical race theory scholars differ in object, argument, accent, and emphasis, their work is unified by two common interests. The first is to understand how a regime of white supremacy and its subordination of people of color have been maintained in America, and, in particular, to examine the relationship between that social structure and professed ideals such as "the RULE OF LAW" and "EQUAL PROTECTION". The second is a desire not merely to understand the vexed bond between law and racial power but to change it. Critical race theory scholars share an ethical commitment to human liberation—even as they reject conventional notions of what such a conception means, and often disagree among themselves over the specific directions of change.

Critical race theory expresses deep dissatisfaction with traditional mainstream CIVIL RIGHTS discourse, which has been shaped in terms that exclude radical or fundamental challenges to status quo institutional practices in American society by treating the exercise of racial power as rare and aberrational rather than as systemic and ingrained. In this view, liberal race reform, by reinforcing the basic myths of American meritocracy, has served to legitimize the very social practices—in employment offices and admission departments—that were originally targeted for reform. Critical race theory scholars have drawn important insights from the CRITICAL LEGAL STUDIES movement's critique of the role of law in constituting and rationalizing an unjust social order. In particular they agree with critical legal studies scholars in rejecting a traditional view that distinguishes law from politics, holding that politics is open-ended, subjective, discretionary, and ideological, whereas law is determinate, objective, bounded, and neutral. Critical race theory scholars embrace the critical legal studies critique of this view, but they part company with one strand of critical legal studies scholarship that deploys a certain postmodern critique of racial identity to challenge the coherence of any intellectual project centered on race. Critical race theory scholars have framed this particular critique as an attack against color-consciousness that differs from the recent conservative devotion to "colorblindness" only in its rhetorical politics. For critical race theory scholars, even though race is socially constructed—the idea of biological race is "false"—race is nonetheless real in the sense that there is a material dimension and weight to the experience of being "raced" in American society, a materiality that in significant ways has been produced and sustained by law.

Critical race theory scholarship thus offers a theoretical vocabulary for the practice of progressive racial politics in contemporary America, even as it seeks to expose the irreducibly political character of the REHNQUIST COURT majority's hostility toward policies that would take race into account in redressing historical and contemporary patterns of RACIAL DISCRIMINATION. One arena for deployment of critical race theory is the debate over AFFIRMATIVE ACTION, in which civil rights liberals have seemed unwilling to see the hidden racial dimensions of the meritocratic mythology that their conservative opponents have so deftly used to control the terms of current debate. Critical race theory understands that, claims to the contrary notwithstanding, distributions of power and resources that were racially determined before the advent of affirmative action will continue to produce predictable patterns of racial disempowerment if affirmative action be abandoned. The conceptions of merit employed by opponents of affirmative action function not as a rational basis for distributing resources and opportunity, but rather as a repository of hidden, race-specific preferences for those who have the power to determine the meaning and consequences of "merit." Critical race theory scholars have shown that the putatively neutral baseline from which affirmative action is said to represent a deviation is in fact a mechanism for perpetuating the distribution of rights, privileges, and opportunity established under a regime of uncontested white supremacy. A return to that so-called neutral baseline would mean a return to an unjust system of racial power.

Critical race theory can also bring a useful perspective to the debate over the proliferation of economic, political, and social relations across national borders which has come to be known as globalization. In this perspective, generalized references to "north" and "south" or to "rich" and "poor" nations figure as metaphorical substitutes for serious and sustained attention to the racial and ethnic character of the massive distributive transformations that globalization has set in motion. An indifference to questions of racial ideology and power is seen in liberal and leftist efforts to emphasize questions of class structure in explaining the political significance of global economic processes within the United States. These explanations leave out the current dynamics of racial power, ignoring the racial composition of the communities that have been chosen to bear the sharp edge of economic dislocation. Yet, even a cursory review of current national discourses

about issues such as public education, IMMIGRATION, and WELFARE reform demonstrates the degree to which questions of race and racial ideology stand at the very center of today's debates. These developments defy explanations in terms of liberal accounts of poverty and social inequality, or leftist formulations about the historical class relations between labor and capital. An inquiry informed by critical race theory would examine the way a certain brand of racial politics has been mobilized to buffer the massive upward distribution of resources and opportunity in the United States, and would explore the way racial ideologies have been used to justify relatively open border policies toward our northern neighbors, even as we close off our borders to those from the south.

Finally, critical race theory scholars seek to contribute to the discussion within communities of color over the future direction of antiracist politics. Powerful voices of racialism have been raised, particularly within the African American community, in which contemporary racial crisis is frequently represented as a reflection of unmediated white power. What racialists too often fail to note is that the same narrow politics of racial solidarity helped to rally African Americans behind the nomination of CLARENCE THOMAS to the Supreme Court. Justice Thomas has been an active participant in the evisceration of the post– civil rights political coalition. Similarly, the black racialist account proffers a vision of racism that portrays racial power primarily through its impact on African American males. By rendering the particular experiences of black females invisible, this form of racialist politics effectively denies the struggle against racialized gender oppression a place on the antiracist agenda.

Questioning regnant visions of racial meaning and racial power, critical race theorists seek to fashion a set of tools for thinking about race that will avoid the traps of racial thinking. Political interventions that overlook the multiple ways in which people of color are situated and resituated as communities, subcommunities, and individuals will do little to promote effective countermobilization against today's newly empowered right. Critical race theory scholars have sought to prevent this waste of political effort by illuminating the ways in which issues of racial ideology and power continue to matter in American life.

KIMBERLÉ CRENSHAW
NEIL GOTANDA
GARY PELLER
KENDALL THOMAS
(2000)

Bibliography

CRENSHAW, KIMBERLÉ; GOTANDA, NEIL; PELLER, GARY; and THOMAS, KENDALL, eds. 1995 *Critical Race Theory: The Key Writings That Formed the Movement.* New York: New Press.

DELGADO, RICHARD, ed. 1995 *Critical Race Theory: The Cutting Edge.* Philadelphia: Temple Uiversity Press.

CRITTENDEN, JOHN J.
(1787–1863)

A Kentucky lawyer, John Jordan Crittenden was a United States attorney general (1841, 1850–1853) and senator (1817–1819, 1835–1841, 1842–1848, 1855–1861). In late 1828 President JOHN QUINCY ADAMS nominated him to the Supreme Court, but the Senate's Democratic majority killed the appointment. A border state Whig, Crittenden always supported compromise on slavery. Thus, as President Millard Fillmore's attorney general, Crittenden vigorously enforced the 1850 fugitive slave law. But he also opposed ANNEXATION OF TEXAS, the Mexican War, the KANSAS-NEBRASKA ACT, and Kansas statehood, because these issues raised the politically disruptive question of SLAVERY IN THE TERRITORIES. In December 1860 Crittenden proposed four resolutions and six constitutional amendments to settle the SECESSION crisis. The resolutions condemned the northern PERSONAL LIBERTY LAWS and reasserted the constitutionality of the fugitive slave laws. The amendments—one of which declared the others "unrepealable"—would have compensated masters for unrecovered fugitive slaves and given permanent protection to slavery where it already existed and in all existing territories or those "hereafter acquired" which were south of the MISSOURI COMPROMISE line. Crittenden's only concession to northern sentiments was to propose the permanent prohibition of slavery north of the Missouri Compromise line; however, many Northerners read "hereafter acquired" as an invitation for proslavery filibustering in Latin America. Furthermore, Republicans opposed any western extension of slavery. Southern extremists, on the other hand, wanted secession, and not compromise. Thus, only the amendment permanently protecting slavery in the existing states was approved by Congress. From 1861 to 1863 Crittenden worked to prevent Kentucky's secession and limit the war to preserving the Union. Thus, he opposed the EMANCIPATION PROCLAMATION, the CONFISCATION ACTS, the use of black troops, West Virginia statehood, and other administration policies.

PAUL FINKELMAN
(1986)

Bibliography

KIRWAN, ALBERT D. 1962 *John J. Crittenden: The Struggle for the Union.* Lexington: University of Kentucky Press.

CROLY, HERBERT
(1869–1930)

New York journalist and social critic Herbert David Croly was the leading intellectual of the Progressive movement. Croly's *The Promise of American Life* (1909) became the programmatic handbook of the reformers: in it he advocated strengthening the federal government as the special protector of working people and the creation of a "WELFARE STATE." His inspiration was the nationalism of ALEXANDER HAMILTON rather than the individualism of THOMAS JEFFERSON. Croly believed that the process of government should be separated from politics and placed in the hands of experts. Croly advised President WOODROW WILSON, but his greatest influence on public affairs was as editor of *The New Republic.*

DENNIS J. MAHONEY
(1986)

CROSS-EXAMINATION, RIGHT OF

See: Confrontation, Right of

CROSSKEY, WILLIAM W.
(1894–1968)

William Winslow Crosskey's reputation as a constitutional historian rests upon his *Politics and the Constitution in the History of the United States* (1953, 1960), a learned, controversial reinterpretation of the framing of the Constitution. Crosskey, a professor of law at the University of Chicago, argued that the Framers of the Constitution sought to create a unitary system of government with virtually unlimited legislative powers, that Congress would have supreme authority within the constitutional system, and that the power of JUDICIAL REVIEW was intended merely as a means for the judiciary to defend itself against encroachments by the other branches of government. Crosskey began with two premises: first, that the words of the Constitution should be understood according to the meanings they had in common usage in 1787; and, second, that the source relied upon by most historians to determine the intent of the Framers, JAMES MADISON's *Notes of the Debates in the Federal Convention of 1787*, had been deliberately distorted by Madison to support the "limited-powers" interpretation of the Constitution favored by Jeffersonian Republicans. Crosskey's third volume, completed posthumously by William W. Jeffrey, Jr., and published in 1980, asserted that nationalist sentiments and ideas pervaded the political climate in the United States from the Revolution to the opening of the CONSTITUTIONAL CONVENTION OF 1787.

RICHARD B. BERNSTEIN
(1986)

CRUEL AND UNUSUAL PUNISHMENT

The Eighth Amendment provides that "excessive BAIL shall not be required . . . nor cruel and unusual punishment inflicted." Similar provisions now exist in virtually all state constitutions. Even if they did not, the federal constitutional prohibition has been held in *Robinson v. California* (1962) to be binding on the states through the FOURTEENTH AMENDMENT'S DUE PROCESS CLAUSE.

A legal prohibition against cruel and unusual punishment appears to have originated in the English BILL OF RIGHTS in 1688. Its purpose then was to curtail the shockingly barbarous punishments that were so common during that period.

How the prohibition was to be applied to American society, with its different values and legal system, remained unclear a century after the enactment of the American BILL OF RIGHTS. In the late nineteenth and early twentieth centuries, the Supreme Court did occasionally interpret the cruel and unusual punishment language, mostly as it related to the means for executing CAPITAL PUNISHMENT. However, not until the 1970s did the Supreme Court begin to give extensive consideration to the scope and meaning of the prohibition apart from capital punishment. The Court did not decide until 1977, for example, whether the cruel and unusual punishment clause applied to persons who had not been convicted of crime. INGRAHAM V. WRIGHT (1977) raised the question whether the corporal punishment of school children constituted cruel and unusual punishment. The Court held that it did not, stating that the Eighth Amendment provision is applicable only to persons convicted and incarcerated for crimes. In the Court's view, the prohibition was not necessary to protect children in public institutions, as other protections were available. Since *Ingraham,* the Supreme Court has also held that the Eighth Amendment is inapplicable to persons detained for treatment or detention and not punishment, such as persons committed to mental institutions (*Youngblood v. Romero,* 1982) or detained awaiting trial (*Bell v. Wolfish,* 1979). Any protection against improper punishments in such situations derives from due process of law and not the Eighth Amendment prohibition against cruel and unusual punishment.

Since the late 1970s, in a number of cases involving noncapital sentences and the treatment of prison inmates, the Court has generally given a narrow interpretation of the cruel and unusual punishment clause.

Prior to Supreme Court review of the issue, several federal and state courts had held that a sentence could be invalid on cruel and unusual punishment grounds if its length was disproportionate to the offense. Courts used several measures to determine whether a particular sentence violated the Eight Amendment: the nature of the crime, and particularly whether violence was involved; comparison of the individual sentence or statutory sentencing scheme with sentences or schemes for similar crimes in other jurisdictions; and comparison of the individual sentence or statutory sentencing scheme for the particular crime with those for other similar or more serious crimes in the same jurisdiction. Thus a federal court of appeals struck down a life sentence imposed on an offender under a Texas statute authorizing a life sentence for a person convicted of felonies on three separate occasions. In this case, the three felonies included: fraudulently using a credit card to obtain $80.00 worth of services; passing a forged check for $28.36; and obtaining $120.75 by false pretenses. The three convictions occurred over a nine-year period. In RUMMEL V. ESTELLE the Supreme Court reversed; the 5–4 majority refused to apply the comparative measures used by lower courts. Instead, it gave great weight to legislative judgments on criminal sentences and to the deterrence of habitual offenders. The fact that Rummel was eligible for early release on parole apparently eased the majority's decision. After *Rummel,* it was uncertain what circumstances might justify judicial intervention on cruel and unusual punishment grounds in cases not involving habitual offender statutes. In *Hutto v. Davis* (1982), in a PER CURIAM opinion, the Court, over three dissents, held that a forty-year sentence for possession of nine ounces of marijuana did not constitute cruel and unusual punishment. The Court reiterated the *Rummel* majority's view that federal courts should be "reluctan[t] to review legislatively mandated terms of imprisonment" and that "successful challenges to the proportionality of particular sentences" should be "exceedingly rare."

In 1983, in SOLEM V. HELM, however, the Supreme Court invalidated a life sentence without possibility of parole for a person convicted under a recidivist statute. The immediate charge involved passing a check for one hundred dollars written on a nonexistent account; all his prior felony convictions were for nonviolent crimes against property. The Court, in a 5–4 decision, applied a proportionality test in applying the cruel and unusual punishment clause. Even after this decision, it appears that the burden of attacking a sentence of a term of years on disproportionality grounds, at least in the federal courts, will be difficult to carry. Some state supreme courts have been more willing to use state constitutional counterparts to the Eighth Amendment to strike down terms that seem excessive relative to the crime committed.

In earlier cases, the Supreme Court did reverse some sentences involving issues other than their length. In TROP V. DULLES (1958), for example, the Court concluded that depriving a person of nationality for conviction by court-martial of wartime desertion constituted cruel and unusual punishment. Also, in WEEMS V. UNITED STATES (1909), the Court held that the crime of being an accessory to the falsification of a public document could not justify a twelve-to-twenty-year sentence at hard labor with chains and a permanent deprivation of civil rights.

The Supreme Court has also applied the Eighth Amendment to reverse the punishment of a person simply because of his status or condition. In *Robinson v. California* (1962) the Court held that punishing a person for being a drug addict constitutes cruel and unusual punishment. The Court refused, however, to apply this same reasoning six years later when it was asked to invalidate an alcoholic's conviction of public drunkenness in *Powell v. Texas* (1968).

In summary, the Supreme Court has rarely relied on the federal prohibition against cruel and unusual punishment to overturn a criminal sentence. The Court has also applied the prohibition sparingly to challenges by prisoners to prison conditions, even though courts have frequently found these conditions to be shocking.

Without question, most prisons throughout the country are archaic, overcrowded, filthy, and understaffed, and provide few worthwhile vocational or recreational activities for prisoners. Because the prison population is growing dramatically at a time when resources to maintain it are shrinking proportionately, prison conditions are deteriorating. In several cases in the late 1970s and early 1980s, the Supreme Court attempted to articulate standards for applying the prohibition against cruel and unusual punishment to challenges against prison conditions. In *Rhodes v. Chapman* (1981) the Court summarized these standards as follows: "Today the Eighth Amendment prohibits punishments which, although not physically barbarous, involve the unnecessary and wanton infliction of pain, or are grossly disproportionate to the severity of the crime. Among unnecessary and wanton infliction of pain are those that are totally without penological justification." The Court has not yet applied these standards to the intentional physical abuse of prisoners. It has, however, cited with approval a court of appeals decision, *Jackson v. Bishop* (1968), which proscribed the whipping of prisoners.

Holt v. Finney (1978) confronted the Supreme Court with its first Eighth Amendment challenge to prison con-

ditions. The lower courts had declared that the general conditions of the Arkansas state prison system constituted cruel and unusual punishment. Among the conditions challenged were: administration of much of the prisons' activities by inmate trustees; dangerous barracks; overcrowded and filthy conditions in isolation or punishment cells and the poor diet of prisoners in these cells; and lack of any rehabilitation programs. The lower courts entered sweeping orders requiring major improvements in the prisons. Among these improvements were restrictions on the numbers of prisoners placed in isolation cells, a requirement that bunks be placed in these cells, a discontinuation of the "grue" diet, and a limit of thirty days in an isolation cell. The state appealed the thirty-day limitation. In a cautious opinion, the Supreme Court upheld the lower court's conclusion. Although it held that confinement in punitive isolation is not a per se violation of the Eighth Amendment, the Court stated that such confinement may become a violation depending on the conditions of isolation. If violations do occur, the Court said, remedies may include a limit on the time to be spent in isolation; the thirty-day restriction of the lower court seemed supportable in this case.

The Supreme Court reached a different result in a constitutional challenge to overcrowding in an Ohio prison. In *Rhodes v. Chapman* (1981) the issue was "double-bunking" prisoners in cells originally designed for single inmates. The courts below had found this practice to violate the Eighth Amendment because prisoners were serving long sentences; the prison was thirty-eight percent over capacity; decency required more living space; prisoners spent much of their time in their cells; and double-bunking was a regular practice, not a temporary condition.

The Supreme Court reversed, holding that there was no evidence that double-bunking in this case "inflicted unnecessary or wanton pain or [was] grossly disproportionate to the severity of crimes warranting punishment." The Court found that double-bunking did not lead to "deprivation of essential food, medical care, or sanitation" or to increased violence among inmates. In the Court's view, the Constitution "does not mandate comfortable prisons," and judges should be reluctant to intervene in prison condition cases unless the conditions were "deplorable" or "sordid": "In discharging [their] oversight responsibility, however, [federal] courts cannot assume that State legislatures and prison officials are insensitive to the requirements of the Constitution or to the perplexing sociological problems of how best to achieve the penal function in the criminal justice system."

In another opinion, *Estelle v. Gamble* (1976), the Supreme Court established some minimum requirements for the provision of health care in prisons. Stating that the government must provide medical care to those whom it punishes by incarceration, the Court held that "deliberate indifference to the serious medical needs of prisoners constitutes unnecessary and wanton infliction of pain proscribed by the Eighth Amendment." The Court placed several limits on successful claims, however. For example, 'an inadvertent failure to provide adequate medical care would not constitute "unnecessary and wanton infliction of pain." Nor would an accident, simple negligence, or a disagreement as to treatment options.

Thus, although the Supreme Court had indicated that the Eighth Amendment does protect prisoners from deplorable conditions, for the most part the Court has not shared the view of many lower courts or of prison experts as to what conditions are deplorable.

The Supreme Court has yet to consider a number of other important questions, such as the factors that must be weighed in assessing challenges to the conditions of a prison as a whole; the constitutional limits on behavior modification programs, including drug usage programs; and the minimum requirements for providing a secure environment for prisoners. Precedent suggests that the Supreme Court will be as cautious in addressing these and other related prison condition issues as it has been in confronting other asserted impositions of cruel and unusual punishment.

SHELDON KRANTZ
(1986)

(SEE ALSO: *Institutional Litigation.*)

Bibliography

GRANNUCCI, ANTHON F.   1969   Nor Cruel and Unusual Punishment Inflicted. *California Law Review* 57:839–865.

JOINT COMMITTEE ON THE LEGAL STATUS OF PRISONERS   1977   American Bar Association Standards Relating to the Legal Status of Prisoners. *American Criminal Law Review* 14:377–629.

KRANTZ, SHELDON   1983   *Corrections and Prisoners' Rights in a Nutshell,* 2nd ed. St. Paul, Minn.: West Publishing Co.

SHERMAN, MICHAEL and HAWKINS, GORDON   1981   *Imprisonment in America: Choosing the Future.* Chicago: University of Chicago Press.

UNIFORM LAW COMMISSION   1978   *Model Sentencing and Convictions Act.* New York: National Conference of Commissioners on Uniform State Laws.

UNITED NATIONS ECONOMIC AND SOCIAL COUNCIL   1957   *Minimum Rules for the Treatment of Prisoners.* New York: United Nations Publications.

CRUEL AND UNUSUAL PUNISHMENT
(Update 1)

The Eighth Amendment's cruel and unusual punishment clause, derived from COMMON LAW and held to restrain the states as well as the federal government, applies to noncapital as well as capital criminal punishments. The concept of cruel and unusual punishments, while undoubtedly meant to address extremely harsh or painful methods and kinds of PUNISHMENT, also incorporates ideas of excessiveness, proportionality, and appropriateness. It is therefore relative, and whether a particular punishment is cruel and unusual depends on prevailing societal standards, objectively determined, regarding punishments. The Supreme Court has held that the clause outlaws not only punishments that are barbarous, involving torture or the intentional and unjustifiable infliction of unnecessary pain, but also forbids confinements whose length or conditions are disproportionate to the severity of crimes, serious deprivations of prisoners' basic human needs, loss of CITIZENSHIP as a punishment, and punishments for status.

In WEEMS V. UNITED STATES (1910) the Court held the Philippine punishment of *cadena temporal* unconstitutional as applied. The imposed punishment for the crime of making a false entry in a public record—not shown to have injured anyone—was fifteen years' imprisonment at hard and painful labor with chains, loss of CIVIL LIBERTIES, and governmental surveillance for life. The Court, in *Estelle v. Gamble* (1976), also held that deliberate indifference to a prisoner's serious medical needs constitutes cruel and unusual punishment. In *Hutto v. Finney* (1978) it upheld a lower court's conclusion that routine conditions in the Arkansas prison system were so inhumane as to be cruel and unusual. Earlier, the Court had determined in TROP V. DULLES (1968) that imposing loss of citizenship on a native-born citizen for desertion in wartime was cruel and unusual because it destroyed the person's political existence and made him stateless. In implicit recognition that states may define as crimes only acts, conduct, or behavior, the Court, in *Robinson v. California* (1962), held criminal imprisonment for the status of being a drug addict, unaccompanied by any acts, cruel and unusual.

The question to what degree the Eighth Amendment's cruel and unusual punishment clause may limit the power of a state to define the length of a prison sentence has been troublesome. The issue arises most often in challenges to recidivist statutes mandating life sentences on persons having three or more consecutive felony convictions or to sentencing statutes requiring extremely long sentences for those convicted of small drug offenses. Originally, in a number of cases raising disproportionate-length challenges to such statutes, the Court took the view that legislatures had extremely wide latitude in setting felony sentence lengths and that it would rarely, if ever, find such statutes unconstitutional. Thus, in RUMMEL V. ESTELLE (1980) the Court upheld a life sentence imposed on a person who was separately convicted and imprisoned for three nonviolent felonies, involving illegally acquiring money in the amounts of $80, $28.36, and $120.75. The only mitigation in the sentence was a possibility of parole after twelve years. In *Hutto v. Davis* (1982) the defendant received a sentence of forty years in prison and a fine of $20,000 for possession and distribution of nine ounces of marijuana, and the Court upheld this statute as well, although the average sentence for similar offenders was approximately three years.

Although these two cases suggested that the Court, in practice, did not accept any constitutional standard of length proportionality in felony cases, in a subsequent case a different Court majority strongly endorsed and articulated just such a standard. In SOLEM V. HELM (1983) the Court struck down, as uconstitutionally disproportionate in length, a sentence of life imprisonment without possibility of parole for a defendant convicted for a seventh felony, which involved uttering a "no-account" check for $100. The Court held that although no sentence is per se unconstitutional, the cruel and unusual punishment clause requires that criminal sentences must be proportionate to the crime for which the defendant has been convicted. The judgment whether a sentence is proportionate turns on an analysis guided by consideration of the gravity of the offense and harshness of the penalty; sentences imposed on other criminals in the same JURISDICTION; and sentences imposed on commission of the same crime in other jurisdictions. *Solem*, however, overturned no prior case law, and the current Court is strongly disposed to accept legislative judgments. The only reasonable conclusion to draw is that the principle of length proportionality is weak and, except in rare cases, unlikely to stand as a check on disparate and extremely long sentences.

GARY GOODPASTER
(1992)

(SEE ALSO: *Prisoners' Rights*.)

Bibliography

GRANUCCI, ANTHONY F. 1969 "Nor Cruel and Unusual Punishments Inflicted": The Original Meaning. *California Law Review* 57:839–865.

CRUEL AND UNUSUAL PUNISHMENT
(Update 2)

Three major trends in state and federal SENTENCING have dominated the punishment arena during the last two decades: first, the reduction of judicial discretion and the correlative enactment of fixed sentencing guidelines in non-CAPITAL PUNISHMENT cases; second, the adoption of severe prison terms for habitual offenders and for desig-

nated crimes, also known as "three strikes, you're out" (or CAREER CRIMINAL SENTENCING LAWS) and "mandatory minimum" statutes; and third, the implementation of new capital murder statutes after the Supreme Court's decision in *Gregg v. Georgia* (1976), as well as the more recent adoption of the death penalty by the federal government and by several states. These developments have presented a number of challenges to Eighth Amendment jurisprudence and have given rise to three important controversies: first, what proportionality test applies to noncapital sentences; second, whether the twin constitutional goals of consistency and individualized sentencing in capital cases can be reconciled; and third, whether the risk that RACIAL DISCRIMINATION may infect the imposition of the death penalty violates the Eighth Amendment.

The Court has been deeply divided over the proportionality test to apply in noncapital cases. In *Harmelin v. Michigan* (1991), a case involving a mandatory sentence of life imprisonment without the possibility of parole for the possession of 672 grams of cocaine, the Court severely narrowed the proportionality test that it had articulated in SOLEM V. HELM (1983). Justice ANTONIN SCALIA, joined by Chief Justice WILLIAM H. REHNQUIST, invited the Court to eliminate all proportionality review in noncapital cases. Scalia and Rehnquist interpreted the Eighth Amendment to prohibit only certain modes of punishment (like drawing and quartering) and unusual penalties not prescribed by law. In the controlling, CONCURRING OPINION of Justice ANTHONY M. KENNEDY, joined by Justices SANDRA DAY O'CONNOR and DAVID H. SOUTER, Kennedy preserved a narrow proportionality principle that "forbids only extreme sentences that are 'grossly disproportionate' to the crime," but nevertheless concluded that the sentence at issue was not grossly disproportionate. Kennedy relegated the analysis of the other two prongs of the earlier three-prong *Solem* proportionality test, namely intrajurisdictional and interjurisdictional comparative analyses, to cases where gross disproportionality is found.

In the capital context, the Court has articulated an intricate set of constitutional rules in an attempt to fulfill the mandate of *Furman v. Georgia* (1972) and *Gregg* to eliminate arbitrariness and ensure fairness in capital sentencing. The Court's opinions have pursued the twin Eighth Amendment objectives of consistency and individualized sentencing. In pursuit of consistency, the Court has narrowed the definition of permissible aggravating circumstances and required that the discretion of sentencing juries be channeled. In pursuit of individualized sentencing, the Court has required the admission of any mitigating evidence and the jury's consideration of that evidence. The increasing tension in recent years between these twin constitutional commands has led several members of the Court to conclude that they are simply incompatible. Former Justice HARRY A. BLACKMUN, dissenting from the denial of CERTIORARI in *Callins v. Collins* (1994), concluded that the Eighth Amendment's competing constitutional commands could not be reconciled and that the death penalty, as presently administered, violates the Eighth Amendment. Justices Scalia and CLARENCE THOMAS have joined Blackmun in acknowledging the incompatibility of the goals of consistency and individualized sentencing, but have instead decided to discard the principle of individualized sentencing.

Racial discrimination has continued to plague capital sentencing schemes in a number of states. The Baldus study found that, in Georgia during the 1970s, the likelihood of being sentenced to death for killing white victims was 4.3 times greater than the likelihood of being sentenced to death for killing black victims, holding constant 39 other nonracial explanatory variables. The study raised the possibility that considerations of race were injecting arbitrariness in the imposition of the death penalty. The Court assumed the validity of the Baldus study in MCCLESKEY V. KEMP (1986), but nevertheless concluded that the risk that racial bias infected the Georgia capital sentencing system was not significant under the Eighth Amendment.

BERNARD E. HARCOURT
(2000)

Bibliography

KENNEDY, RANDALL 1988 *McCleskey v. Kemp:* Race, Capital Punishment, and the Supreme Court. *Harvard Law Review* 101:1388–1443.

STEIKER, CAROL and STEIKER, JORDAN 1995 Sober Second Thoughts: Reflections on Two Decades of Constitutional Regulation of Capital Punishment. *Harvard Law Review* 109: 355–438.

SUNDBY, SCOTT E. 1991 The Lockett Paradox: Reconciling Guided Discretion and Unguided Mitigation in Capital Sentencing. *UCLA Law Review* 38:1147–1208.

CRUIKSHANK, UNITED STATES v.
92 U.S. 542 (1876)

Cruikshank paralyzed the federal government's attempt to protect black citizens by punishing violators of their CIVIL RIGHTS and, in effect, shaped the Constitution to the advantage of the Ku Klux Klan. The case arose out of a federal prosecution of nightriders responsible for the Colfax Massacre of 1873 in Grant Parish, Louisiana. Several hundred armed whites besieged a courthouse where hundreds of blacks were holding a public assembly; the attackers burned down the building and murdered about 100 people. The United States tried Cruikshank and others involved in the massacre and convicted three for violating

section six of the FORCE ACT OF 1870. That act, which survives as section 241 of Title 18 of the United States Code, is a general conspiracy statute making it a federal crime, then punishable by a $5,000 fine and up to ten years in prison, for two or more persons to conspire to injure or intimidate any citizen with the intent of hindering his free exercise of any right or privilege guaranteed him by the Constitution or laws of the United States.

In a unanimous opinion by Chief Justice MORRISON R. WAITE, the Court ignored the statute and focused on the INDICTMENT to ascertain whether the rights Cruikshank and others interfered with were granted or secured by the United States. Reasserting the theory of dual CITIZENSHIP advanced in the SLAUGHTERHOUSE CASES (1873), Waite concluded that the United States cannot grant or secure rights not under its JURISDICTION. Examining in turn each right named in the indictment as having been deprived, Waite found that they were all "left under the protection of the States." None was a federal right. The right to peaceably assemble predated the Constitution and remained "subject to state jurisdiction." The United States could neither infringe it nor protect it, for it was not an attribute of United States citizenship. So too the right to bear arms. The right to be secure in one's person, life, and liberty was protected by the FOURTEENTH AMENDMENT against state deprivation, but for protection of that right, sovereignty "rests alone with the States." The amendment, said Waite, "adds nothing to the rights of one citizen as against another." Thus the violence here conducted by private persons could not be reached by Congress, which was limited to assuring that the states do not violate the amendment's prohibitions. As for the right to vote, the FIFTEENTH AMENDMENT merely protected against discrimination based on race. The Constitution did not confer the right to vote on anyone; that right was not, Waite said, an attribute of national citizenship.

By such reasoning the Court held that the indictment did not show that the conspirators had hindered or prevented the enjoyment of any right granted or secured by the Constitution. Accordingly, no conviction based on the indictment could be sustained, and the Court ordered the defendants discharged. The conspiracy statute remained impotent until revived in recent times by the Department of Justice, but the Court did not sustain a conviction under the statute until 1966 (*United States v. Price*; *United States v. Guest*), when the Court vitiated *Cruikshank*.

LEONARD W. LEVY
(1986)

Bibliography

MAGRATH, C. PETER 1963 *Morrison R. Waite.* Pages 120–134. New York: Macmillan.

CRUZ v. BETO

See: Religious Liberty

CRUZAN v. DIRECTOR, MISSOURI DEPARTMENT OF HEALTH

See: Right to Die

CULTS AND THE CONSTITUTION

The term "cult," currently used to designate a particular unpopular and feared new religious group often claiming a personal relationship between its leader and the Divinity, is not found explicitly in the original Constitution, the FIRST AMENDMENT's free exercise or establishment clause, or the FOURTEENTH AMENDMENT'S EQUAL PROTECTION clause. Among the most prominent of these groups in recent times have been the Unification Church, the Worldwide Church of God, Inc., the Church of Scientology, and the International Society for Krishna Consciousness.

Cults, which have experienced varying degrees of discrimination and persecution by law enforcement officials, have consistently claimed that the Constitution does not sanction legal distinctions between them on the one hand and long-established and respected faiths on the other. They note, too, that historically most of the now well-established and fully respected faiths, including Baptists, Roman Catholics, Jews, Mormons, Christian Scientists, and Jehovah's Witnesses, have been subjected to governmental discrimination before achieving acceptability and equal treatment.

The claim to equal treatment was upheld in LARSON V. VALENTE (1982) where the Supreme Court held unconstitutional a Minnesota statute, enforced against the Unification Church, that imposed special registration and reporting requirements upon religious groups that received more than half of their income from nonmembers, a provision the Court found to have been aimed at unpopular cults. This provision, the Court said, constituted precisely the sort of official denominational preference and discrimination forbidden by the establishment clause in the absence of a compelling interest not otherwise amenable to protection. Moreover, the statute also violated the clause by authorizing excessive governmental entanglement with and politicizing of religion.

Compelling registration is only one comparatively mild sanction imposed by government upon religious cults. Although that term had not yet become popular in 1944, when *United States v. Ballard* was decided by the Supreme Court, that decision ruled unconstitutional a mail fraud conviction of "I Am" members who obtained donations by representing that their leader was divinely appointed with supernatural powers to heal the incurably ill. To allow a jury to determine the truth or falsity of religious doctrines, the Court said, would render vulnerable representations concerning the miracles of the New Testament, the divinity of Christ, life after death, and the power of prayer. The First Amendment permits only a determination whether the defendants themselves actually believed that what they recounted was true, not whether it was actually true.

Other devices applied against cults include denial of tax exemption, dissolution of the corporate structure and seizure of assets (as in CHURCH OF JESUS CHRIST OF LATTER DAY SAINTS V. UNITED STATES, 1890), and prosecution for disturbance of the peace (as in CANTWELL V. CONNECTICUT, 1940, involving Jehovah's Witnesses).

Whatever may have been the Court's response in earlier times, today it accords cults the same constitutional protection accorded to long-standing and commonly accepted faiths.

LEO PFEFFER
(1986)

Bibliography

New York University Review of Law and Social Change 1979– 1980 Volume 9, #1: *Proceedings of Conference on Alternative Religions, Government Control and the First Amendment.*

CUMBERLAND ROAD BILL

See: Internal Improvements

CUMMINGS, HOMER S.
(1870–1956)

A prominent Connecticut Democrat, Homer S. Cummings served as attorney general under President FRANKLIN D. ROOSEVELT from 1933 to 1939, defending much of the NEW DEAL legislation in the Supreme Court. He broke with recent practice when he personally argued the GOLD CLAUSE CASES (1935), and the Court reiterated much of his argument in its opinions. Cummings strongly supported Roosevelt's COURT-PACKING plan as "clearly constitutional" and privately suggested a constitutional amendment requiring justices to retire at seventy. With Carl McFarland, he wrote *Federal Justice* (1937), a history of the Department of Justice based on previously neglected manuscript materials. Cummings instituted reform of federal criminal

inadequate salary, and the *Dred Scott* imbroglio convinced him that he and his colleagues could no longer work together effectively and harmoniously.

During the Civil War, Curtis emerged as an outspoken critic of Lincoln's unprecedented exercise of PRESIDENTIAL POWERS. In good Whig fashion, he leveled constitutional attacks on Lincoln for suspending the writ of HABEAS CORPUS and for issuing the EMANCIPATION PROCLAMATION. Yet, following the war, he endorsed the sentiments of the National Union Convention in 1866 and advocated exclusive presidential control of reconstruction. Two years later, he joined WILLIAM M. EVARTS and others to represent President ANDREW JOHNSON in his IMPEACHMENT trial. Curtis's defense of the President argued that Johnson was not an "acting President," as some claimed, and that the TENURE OF OFFICE ACT unduly interfered with the President's constitutional prerogative to remove executive officers—an argument the Supreme Court came to accept half a century later. Finally, he offered a ringing affirmation of the FIRST AMENDMENT to defend Johnson against the charge that he had "improperly" spoken of Congress.

In his last years, Curtis had a lucrative law practice and argued more than fifty cases before the Supreme Court. Most noteworthy were his briefs in behalf of federal regulation of the insurance industry in PAUL V. VIRGINIA (1869) and his defense of the legal tender laws in *Hepburn v. Griswold* (1870).

Curtis's all too brief career on the Supreme Court must exclude him from a short list of truly great jurists. But he displayed uncommon skills, especially a talent for closely reasoned and logical arguments. His defense and understanding of the Constitution, on and off the bench, mark contributions that have been affirmed by the passage of time.

STANLEY I. KUTLER
(1986)

Bibliography

CURTIS, GEORGE TICKNOR and CURTIS, BENJAMIN R., eds. 1879 *Life and Writings of Benjamin Robbins Curtis.* Boston: Little, Brown.

FEHRENBACHER, DON E. 1978 *The Dred Scott Case: Its Significance in American Law and Politics.* New York: Oxford University Press.

LEACH, RICHARD H. 1952 Benjamin Robbins Curtis: Judicial Misfit. *New England Quarterly* 25:507–523.

CURTIS, GEORGE T.
(1812–1894)

A leading Boston attorney, George Ticknor Curtis ordered the rendition to SLAVERY of Thomas Sims in 1852 while serving as a Fugitive Slave Law Commissioner. (See SIMS' CASE.) In 1856 he represented Dred Scott before the United States Supreme Court in DRED SCOTT V. SANDFORD. Curtis wrote numerous legal treatises, three political biographies, and a two-volume *History of the Origin, Formation, and Adoption of the Constitution* (1854–1858)—revised as *Constitutional History of the United States* (1889–1896). This work presents a classic Federalist-Whig interpretation of American political and constitutional history. It was begun at the suggestion of DANIEL WEBSTER and reflects the senator's approach to the Constitution and the Union.

PAUL FINKELMAN
(1986)

Bibliography

FISH, CARL RUSSELL 1930 George T. Curtis. *Dictionary of American Biography*, Vol. 4, pp. 613–614.

CURTISS-WRIGHT EXPORT CORPORATION, UNITED STATES v.
299 U.S. 304 (1936)

Nearly two years after Paraguay and Bolivia went to war in 1932, Congress authorized President FRANKLIN D. ROOSEVELT to embargo American arms shipments to the belligerents if he found that the action might contribute to reestablishing peace. Indicted in January 1936 for conspiring to violate the embargo resolution and Roosevelt's implementing proclamation, Curtiss-Wright Export Corporation demurred on grounds of unconstitutional DELEGATION OF POWER. Recent rulings against NEW DEAL legislation in PANAMA REFINING CO. V. RYAN (1935) and SCHECHTER POULTRY CORP. V. UNITED STATES (1935) lent weight to the company's position, and the district court sustained the demurrer. On appeal, however, the Supreme Court approved the embargo resolution and proclamation with a ringing endorsement of independent presidential authority in the area of FOREIGN AFFAIRS.

For a 7–1 majority, Justice GEORGE SUTHERLAND defended the embargo measures by distinguishing between powers of internal and external SOVEREIGNTY, a distinction the government had not employed in arguing *Curtiss-Wright*. For him, the federal government's domestic authority derived from states having delegated power via the Constitution. External sovereignty had passed, however, from the British Crown to the United Colonies and then to the United States in their collective capacities, with the states severally never possessing it nor delegating it. "Rulers come and go; governments end and forms of government change; but sovereignty survives." In the realm of

and administrative procedures, helping secure adoption of the FEDERAL RULES OF CIVIL PROCEDURE in 1938.

DAVID GORDON
(1986)

CUMMINGS v. MISSOURI

See: Test Oath Cases

CURFEW LAWS

See: Juvenile Curfew Laws

CURTILAGE

See: Open Fields Doctrine

CURTIS, BENJAMIN R.
(1809–1874)

Benjamin Robbins Curtis of Massachusetts generally rates high marks for his six-year tenure on the Supreme Court. His bold dissent in DRED SCOTT V. SANDFORD (1857), followed by his dramatic resignation, largely accounts for his reputation. Yet Curtis's contributions to the development of constitutional law transcend that one case.

Curtis's prominence in the *Dred Scott* case is ironic, considering the fact that he received his appointment in 1851 because he was a northern Whig, acceptable to southern slave interests. By that time, he already was a leading figure in Boston legal circles. He had been selected in 1846 to succeed Justice JOSEPH STORY as an overseer (trustee) of Harvard College, and he was highly regarded for his promotion of procedure and litigation reforms. In 1851 he represented the Boston school board against the desegregationists in ROBERTS V. CITY OF BOSTON. But most important, Curtis had also endorsed Senator DANIEL WEBSTER's efforts in the COMPROMISE OF 1850, had advocated strict enforcement of the new Fugitive Slave Act, and had fought abolitionists and free-soilers, even opposing CHARLES SUMNER's successful Senate campaign in 1851. Shortly afterward, President MILLARD FILLMORE, following Webster's recommendation, nominated Curtis to succeed Justice LEVI WOODBURY. The only criticism came from the abolitionist press. Southern politicians, however, were satisfied and the Democratic Senate quickly confirmed the appointment.

Curtis's first major opinion, in COOLEY V. BOARD OF WARDENS (1851), reflected both his legal skills and his willingness to follow the middle ground of his patron, Daniel Webster. The case involved the limiting effects of the COMMERCE CLAUSE on state regulation, a subject that had divided the TANEY COURT since 1837. Southerners fe congressional regulation of interstate traffic in slaves, consequently sought to interpret the commerce po narrowly. In *Cooley* Curtis acknowledged broad cong sional authority over foreign and INTERSTATE COMMEI but the case challenged the validity not of congressio action but of local pilotage regulations for the port Philadelphia. Curtis devised a compromise between EXCLUSIVE POWER and CONCURRENT POWER views. His d trine of SELECTIVE EXCLUSIVENESS recognized exclusi congressional power over subjects demanding uniform r tional regulation, but invited state regulation, in cas where Congress had not acted, of subjects admitting diverse local regulation.

Curtis again demonstrated a shrewd practicality cou pled with an ability to make law responsive to new con ditions when he upheld federal regulations of steamboa operations. In *Steamboat New World v. King* (1854) Curti applied the emerging law of negligence to the rapidly ex panding technology of steamboating. In addition, he con firmed that federal admiralty jurisdiction applied to all inland, navigable waters. A year before the *Dred Scott* controversy over the content of the Fifth Amendment's DUE PROCESS clause, Curtis had discussed the subject in MURRAY'S LESSEE V. HOBOKEN LAND AND IMPROVEMENT COMPANY (1856) and had followed a traditional procedural interpretation of the clause.

The understanding of Curtis's role in *Dred Scott* has shifted with historiographical tides. When it was fashionable to view the CIVIL WAR as a "reconcilable conflict," Curtis was seen as a *provocateur;* but when the *Dred Scott* decision is seen as Chief Justice ROGER TANEY's attempt to make the nation safe for slavery, Curtis's opinion emerges as a calm, reasoned historical and legal brief properly explicating national authority to regulate SLAVERY IN THE TERRITORIES. Curtis's opinion differed from Taney's conclusions in nearly every respect. He demonstrated historically that blacks could be American citizens, and hence could sue in the federal courts. Equally important, he offered constitutional language and long-standing historical precedent to justify congressional regulation of slavery in the territories. Curtis's comments on the need for judicial restraint were pointed: "To engraft on any instrument a substantive exception not found in it must be admitted to be a matter attended with great difficulty. . . . To allow this to be done with the Constitution, upon reasons purely political, renders its judicial interpretation impossible because judicial tribunals . . . cannot decide upon political considerations."

Curtis resigned a few months after the *Dred Scott* decision. He was dissatisfied with his circuit duties and his

foreign relations, the authority of the federal government therefore equaled that of any sovereign nation, and the usual constitutional divisions between the President and Congress were largely irrelevant, as was the normal prohibition on delegation of legislative power. Keenly aware of the need for energy and dispatch in the delicate business of conducting foreign relations, the Framers had endorsed this arrangement, Sutherland claimed, and early statesmen put it into practice. Although dissenting, Justice JAMES C. MCREYNOLDS filed no opinion.

Later characterized as dictum-laden, Sutherland's argument made sense within the constitutional climate of the 1930s and in view of his own commitments. The government, for example, had claimed that the 1934 embargo resolution and proclamation met the straited *Panama-Schechter* requirement that delegatory legislation specify the findings of fact the President must make before taking the anticipated action. Such an approach ignored the plausible objection that findings involving diplomatic and military imponderables were no firmer than those already disallowed as "opinion" in *Schechter*. An alternative was simply to rely on judicial precedent and legislative practice regarding delegation in areas cognate to foreign relations. Sutherland did examine earlier embargo, tariff, and kindred measures in which Congress had given latitude to the President, but he did so primarily as a means of showing that his view of external sovereignty had been accepted from the beginning. Neither judicial nor legislative iterations carried the same weight as the original intent and first principles he valued so highly. Perhaps most important, Sutherland himself had broached the external-internal distinction the previous May, in CARTER V. CARTER COAL COMPANY (1936), and had earlier explicated his full theory of sovereignty in his book *Constitutional Power and World Affairs* (1919).

The real weakness of Sutherland's opinion was its faulty history. Scant evidence exists that the Framers held the extraconstitutional understanding of the foreign relations power he attributed to them. Sutherland also misconstrued many of the earlier episodes and commentaries that, he argued, were informed by his theories of sovereignty and plenary executive authority. *Curtiss-Wright* nevertheless had timing on its side. It soon provided a base for upholding EXECUTIVE AGREEMENTS as domestic law in UNITED STATES V. BELMONT (1937) and UNITED STATES V. PINK (1942). More broadly, Sutherland's opinion appealed to proponents of an expanded presidential role as the United States acquired global responsibilities, engaged in nuclear diplomacy, fought undeclared wars, and debated the requirements of internal security.

CHARLES A. LOFGREN
(1986)

Bibliography

LEVITAN, DAVID M. 1946 The Foreign Relations Power: An Analysis of Mr. Justice Sutherland's Theory. *Yale Law Journal* 55:467–497.
LOFGREN, CHARLES A. 1973 *United States v. Curtiss-Wright Export Corporation:* An Historical Reassessment. *Yale Law Journal* 83:1–32.

CUSHING, WILLIAM
(1732–1810)

William Cushing served on the United States Supreme Court, in an undistinguished manner, for nearly twenty-one years. Born into a politically well-connected, upper middle class Massachusetts family, he graduated from Harvard College, and then studied law; he was admitted to the bar in 1755. He practiced law in Maine, where he represented the interests of large landholders against squatters and debtors. In 1771 he succeeded his father as a judge of the Massachusetts Superior Court. Because many of his family had loyalist leanings and he owed his position to a royal appointment, Cushing expressed his political views cautiously during the 1770s, when colonial resistance to British policies turned into revolution. Although he chose the patriot side in 1776, some ardent radicals doubted his enthusiasm for independence. Nonetheless he was appointed to the newly created superior court and became chief justice for the state in 1777 when JOHN ADAMS resigned the post. He also served as a member of the convention that wrote the MASSACHUSETTS CONSTITUTION of 1780.

While chief justice, Cushing played an important role in bringing about the end of slavery in Massachusetts, beginning with COMMONWEALTH V. JENNISON (1783). In his charge to the jury, Cushing interpreted the clause of the state constitution that declared that "all men are born free and equal" as abolishing slavery in the state. Unsympathetic to the debtors in western Massachusetts who prevented the collection of taxes and closed the courts during SHAYS' REBELLION, Cushing opposed their activities while riding circuit and presided over the TREASON trial of the leaders; some of his sentences included the death penalty. He advocated RATIFICATION OF THE CONSTITUTION in 1788 and served as vice-president of the state ratifying convention.

GEORGE WASHINGTON appointed Cushing the first associate Justice of the United States Supreme Court in 1789. Despite his extensive judicial experience he did not play a very active role on the Court. Although he participated in many of the most important cases of the 1790s—CHISHOLM V. GEORGIA (1973), *Ware v. Hylton* (1796), HYLTON V.

UNITED STATES, (1796), and CALDER V. BULL (1798)—his opinions tended to be brief, and dealt with narrow legal and procedural questions. Ceremonious in his deportment, Cushing was the last member of the Court to wear a wig. His affability and courtesy enabled him to enforce the Sedition Act with minimal rancor. After 1800, illness, age, and the difficulties of riding circuit caused him considerable hardship. He could no longer adequately perform his duties, and he probably would have retired early if a federal pension had been available. He died, while still a member of the Supreme Court, in 1810.

RICHARD E. ELLIS
(1986)

Bibliography

JOHNSON, HERBERT ALAN   1969   William Cushing. Pages 57–70 in Leon Friedman and Fred L. Israel, eds., *Justices of the Supreme Court, 1789–1969*, Vol. I. New York: Chelsea House.

CUSHMAN, ROBERT E.
(1889–1969)

Robert Eugene Cushman taught constitutional law for many years at Cornell University. His landmark anthology, *Leading Constitutional Decisions* (1925; 16th ed. by Robert F. Cushman, 1982), quickly established itself as a standard casebook for constitutional law and history courses. Cushman founded and edited the Cornell Studies on Civil Liberty; the contributors to this series of monographs included Robert K. Carr, Milton R. Convitz, Walter Gellhorn, James Morton Smith, and Cushman himself. Cushman described his monograph, *Civil Liberties in the United States* (1956), as "a guide to current problems and experience." A synoptic description of the state of the law and an attempt to chart its future development, it was well-received, although some critics questioned its formalistic approach and its skeletal coverage of various issues. Cushman's major scholarly work, *The Independent Regulatory Commissions* (1941), a byproduct of his service with the President's Committee on Administrative Management (1937); prophetically proposed the separation in independent regulatory commissions of the prosecutorial and adjudicative functions. For many years he wrote the *American Political Science Review*'s annual survey of the work of the Supreme Court. From 1958 until his death, Cushman was editor-in-chief of the *Documentary History of the Ratification of the Constitution;* he was succeeded by MERRILL JENSEN.

RICHARD B. BERNSTEIN
(1986)

CUSTODIAL INTERROGATION

See: Police Interrogation and Confessions

DAIRY QUEEN, INC. v. WOOD
369 U.S. 469 (1962)

The owners of the "Dairy Queen" trademark sued a licensee alleging breach of contract and trademark infringement and asking for injunctive relief and an "accounting." Since this was a case in EQUITY, U.S. District Judge Wood denied the defendant's motion for a jury trial.

A unanimous Supreme Court, speaking through Justice HUGO L. BLACK, held that Wood's decision deprived Dairy Queen of its SEVENTH AMENDMENT rights: although the complaint asked for an "accounting," it was really a suit for damages or debt. As Black wrote, "the constitutional right of TRIAL BY JURY cannot be made dependent upon the choice of words used in the pleadings."

DENNIS J. MAHONEY
(1986)

DALLAS, ALEXANDER J.
(1759–1817)

Admitted to the bar in 1785, Alexander James Dallas practiced law in Philadelphia. He supplemented his income by reporting the opinions of the courts that sat in that city, including the Supreme Court of the United States (1790–1800). From 1801 to 1814 he was United States attorney for eastern Pennsylvania.

As secretary of the treasury under President JAMES MADISON (1814–1816), Dallas secured enactment of the highest federal taxes to that date, restored confidence in the currency, and dictated terms of the second BANK OF THE UNITED STATES ACT (1816). In 1815 he was also acting secretary of war.

DENNIS J. MAHONEY
(1986)

DAMAGES

From the earliest days of COMMON LAW, courts have ordered the payment of money ("damages") to compensate for legal wrongs. Two related but separable lines of cases shape the availability of damages for violations of constitutional rights. One line of cases involves inyterpretation of SECTION 1983, TITLE 42, UNITED STATES CODE, and its express provision for "an action at law" to redress deprivations of constitutional rights by state officials. Since the revival of section 1983 in MONROE V. PAPE (1961), it has been understood that damages are available to compensate for sonstitutional violations by state officials. CAREY V. PIPHUS (1978) reaffirmed this understanding, but held that substantial damages could not be recovered for PROCEDURAL DUE PROCESS violations without proof of injury. *Smith v. Wade* (1983) clarified the standards governing awards of PUNITIVE DAMAGES under section 1983.

In actions against federal officials, which are not governed by section 1983, the Court, in BIVENS V. SIX UNKNOWN NAMED AGENTS OF THE FEDERAL BUREAU OF NARCOTICS (1971), inferred a damages action based on the FOURTH AMENDMENT. Later cases, such as DAVIS V. PASSMAN (1979), extended the implied constitutional damages action to other constitutional provisions. The *Bivens* line of cases may be viewed as an extension of EX PARTE YOUNG (1908)

739

and other decisions that allowed actions for injunctive relief to be based directly on the Constitution.

THEODORE EISENBERG
(1986)

Bibliography

NEWMAN, JON O. 1978 Suing the Lawbreakers: Proposals to Strngthen the Section 1983 Damages Remedy for Law Enforcers' Misconduct. *Yale Law Journal* 87:447–467.

DAMAGES CLAIMS
(Update to Damages)

At least since MARBURY V. MADISON was decided in 1803, it has been understood that the United States Constitution is law, enforceable by courts and superior in status to LEGISLATION. In some surprising particulars, however, exactly what that means is far from clear. Since the early 1970s a good deal of both judicial and academic attention has been focused on the propriety of recognizing what are called constitutional damages claims. Compensatory and punitive actions based directly on the Constitution raise significant questions concerning the role of the judiciary in the American system of govenment. The Supreme Court's response to the tensions presented by the creation of constitutional damages actions has been a complex and confusing one.

The Constitution has traditionally been enforced through a variety of remedial mechanisms. *Marbury's* embrace of JUDICIAL REVIEW itself adopts a constitutional enforcement measure—a "negative" judicial authority to ignore statutes that conflict with the terms of the Constitution. Since OSBORN V. BANK OF THE UNITED STATES was decided in 1824, INJUNCTIONS have been used to prevent government officials from engaging in future constitutional violations. In this century, the judiciary's equitable enforcement powers have been stretched to include certain nontraditional remedies, such as the exclusion of relevant evidence in criminal trials and the busing of school children in DESEGREGATION cases.

On one level, lawsuits seeking monetary compensation for the violation of constitutional rights are commonplace. SECTION 1983, TITLE 42, U.S. CODE, creates an action at law for constitutional injuries sustained at the hands of persons acting "under color" of state or local authority. Public employees terminated unconstitutionally by state agencies, the victims of unlawful arrests, persons subjected to discrimination prohibited by the FOURTEENTH AMENDMENT, and myriad other plaintiffs have successfully recovered money damages from state and local officials in constitutional causes of action based on section 1983.

There is, however, no counterpart to section 1983 for federal officials. If, for example, an FBI agent or a treasury officer exceeds the strictures of the FOURTH AMENDMENT, any damage claim instigated by the victim must be rooted directly in the Constitution. The general federal-question jurisdictional statute (28 U.S.C. 1331) empowers the UNITED STATES DISTRICT COURTS to entertain cases arising under the Constitution. But no statutory directive explicitly creates a cause of action for money damages. And the power of federal judges to infer such claims from the sparse language of the constitutional charter has proven a matter of considerable complexity.

In BIVENS V. SIX UNKNOWN NAMED AGENTS, decided in 1971, the Supreme Court held for the first time that federal officials can be sued for damages under the Fourth Amendment. Bivens, allegedly without PROBABLE CAUSE, had been "manacled . . . in front of his wife and children" while federal officials threatened to "arrest the entire family." The Court concluded that the "injuries consequent" to an illegal search provide the basis for an "independent claim both necessary and sufficient to make out . . . [a] cause of action." The *Bivens* case thus seemed to open the door to the recognition of a full complement of constitutional damage claims.

To a significant degree, however, *Bivens's* promise has remained unfulfilled. The decision determined that the Fourth Amendment is directly enforceable against federal officials through damage decrees. It was silent, however, about other provisions of the BILL OF RIGHTS. In the decade following the ruling, the Supreme Court held that the implied antidiscrimination component of the Fifth Amendment (DAVIS V. PASSMAN (1979)) and the CRUEL AND UNUSUAL PUNISHMENTS prohibition of the Eighth Amendment (*Carlson v. Green,* 1980) would sustain damages actions. But in *Stanley v. Lucas* (1987), the Justices determined that a former serviceman could not assert a constitutional damage claim against the ARMED FORCES for being involuntarily subjected to LSD testing—in apparent violation of the DUE PROCESS clause of the Fifth Amendment. And other decisions have disapproved free speech (*Bush v. Lucas,* 1983) and PROCEDURAL DUE PROCESS (*Schweiker v. Chilicky,* 1988) claims lodged against federal officials.

The set of principles that guide the Supreme Court's constitutional damages claims cases is, in several aspects, surprising. According to *Carlson v. Green,* victims of individualized constitutional violations by federal officials are said to "have a right to recover damages . . . in federal court despite the absence of any statute conferring such a right." The action may be defeated, however, in two instances. First, relief will be denied if the government official demonstrates the existence of "special factors counselling hesitation in the absence of affirmative action by Congress." Second, the constitutional claim will fail if Congress, by providing an alternative remedy or by clear legislative directive, has indicated that JUDICIAL POWER should not be exercised. "Special factors" have been found to exist in the military and civil service contexts, and more recently, intricate statutory schemes like the SOCIAL SECURITY system have been deemed adequate substitutes for constitutional review.

It is unusual, of course, for exercises in CONSTITUTIONAL INTERPRETATION—like *Bivens* itself—to be effectively overturned or displaced by congressional enactment. *Marbury v. Madison* would seem to argue otherwise. Nor is it commonplace for the Court openly to admit that constitutional violations will be remedied unless "special factors" counsel against enforcement. Chief Justice JOHN MARSHALL argued in COHENS V. VIRGINIA (1821), for example, that "we have no more right to decline the exercise of jurisdiction which is given, than to usurp that which is not given."

Damages actions are typically either created by statute or, if fashioned through the COMMON LAW process, subject to legislative revision or rejection. *Bivens*-type cases occupy a hazy middle ground between traditional constitutional interpretations and common law adjudication. It is perhaps not surprising, therefore, that the decisions are riddled with compromise as well.

GENE R. NICHOL
(1992)

Bibliography

DELLINGER, WALTER E.   1972   Of Rights and Remedies: The Constitution as a Sword. *Harvard Law Review* 85:1532–1564.

HILL, ALFRED   1969   Constitutional Remedies. *Columbia Law Review* 69:1009–1161.

MERRILL, THOMAS W.   1985   The Common Law Powers of Federal Courts. *University of Chicago Law Review* 52:1–72.

MONAGHAN, HENRY P.   1975   Foreword: Constitutional Common Law. *Harvard Law Review* 89:1–45.

NICHOL, GENE R.   1989   *Bivens, Chilicky* and Constitutional Damages Claims. *Virginia Law Review* 75:1117–1154.

DAMES & MOORE v. REGAN
453 U.S. 654 (1981)

The United States hostage crisis was settled by the 1981 Algerian Agreement under which, *inter alia*, the United States undertook to terminate certain litigation by American claimants against Iran and its agencies. Under the agreement, the claims involved were required to be submitted to binding international arbitration. By EXECUTIVE ORDER, President JIMMY CARTER suspended various claims pending in American courts. Certain American claimants challenged this action as exceeding presidential authority. The Supreme Court upheld the President's authority to conclude and implement this part of the agreement on the basis of his constitutional FOREIGN AFFAIRS powers. It relied on congressional acceptance of broad presidential power during crises in foreign affairs, and on Congress's historic acquiescence in the practice of settling American claims by EXECUTIVE AGREEMENT. The Court also held that if the agreement caused a TAKING OF PROPERTY within the scope of the Fifth Amendment, American nationals had a remedy for compensation in the CLAIMS COURT OF THE UNITED STATES.

The decision effectively permitted the President to remove a category of cases from federal court JURISDICTION (although the Court characterized its action as only approving a change in the "applicable substantive law"). And it opened the way to subsequent "takings" litigation over a broad area of foreign economic policy. In both respects the Court went beyond previous decisions involving presidential executive agreement authority, and treated the presidential executive agreement as fully equivalent to a Senate-approved treaty. Accordingly, it seems to be the most sweeping judicial recognition to date of presidential foreign relations power.

PHILLIP R. TRIMBLE
(1986)

Bibliography

MARKS, LEE R. and GRABOW, JOHN C.   1982   The President's Foreign Economic Powers after Dames & Moore v. Regan: Legislation by Acquiescence. *Cornell Law Review* 68:68–103.

TRIMBLE, PHILLIP R.   1984   Foreign Policy Frustrated—Dames & Moore, Claims Court Jurisdiction and a New Raid on the Treasury. *Columbia Law Review* 84:317–385.

DANDRIDGE v. WILLIAMS
397 U.S. 471 (1970)

Dandridge stifled the infant DOCTRINE, born in cases such as GRIFFIN V. ILLINOIS (1956) and DOUGLAS V. CALIFORNIA (1963), that governmental WEALTH DISCRIMINATION, like RACIAL DISCRIMINATION, demanded strict judicial scrutiny of its justifications. Maryland provided welfare aid to dependent children on the basis of need, partly determined by the number of children in a family. However, payment to any one family was limited to $250 per month, irrespective of the family's size. A 6–3 Supreme Court, speaking through Justice POTTER STEWART, characterized the case as one involving "social and economic" regulation, and applied the RATIONAL BASIS standard of review. Here there were legitimate state interests in encouraging employment and avoiding distinctions between welfare recipients and the working poor. Although some welfare beneficiaries were unemployable, the maximum-grant rule was generally reasonable.

Justice THURGOOD MARSHALL, dissenting, rejected the idea of two separate STANDARDS OF REVIEW, rational basis and STRICT SCRUTINY. He argued for a "sliding scale" of judicial supervision that would demand progressively more state justification as the classification in question bore more heavily on the powerless and in proportion to the importance of the interest at stake. Here, where indigent children were being deprived of basic subsistence as defined by the state's own standards of need, the permissive rational basis standard was inappropriate. Marshall also argued that the maximum-grant rule was invalid even under that permissive standard, given the state's aim of aiding children and the unemployability of a large proportion of welfare recipients.

After *Dandridge,* it became futile to argue to the Supreme Court either that welfare subsistence was a FUNDAMENTAL INTEREST or that wealth discrimination implied a SUSPECT CLASSIFICATION. Since 1970 the Court has regularly shied away from decisions that would place the judiciary in the position of allocating state resources.

KENNETH L. KARST
(1986)

DANE, NATHAN
(1752–1835)

A loyal graduate of Harvard College, Nathan Dane of Beverly, Massachusetts, became a lawyer, politician, and scholar. In 1787, while representing his state in Congress, he single-handedly composed the NORTHWEST ORDINANCE. Its provision outlawing slavery derived from Thomas Jefferson's LAND ORDINANCE OF 1785, but Dane deserves credit for writing the various other provisions that amounted to the first national BILL OF RIGHTS. It included, too, a precursor of the CONTRACT CLAUSE.

After serving in various state offices, Dane was forced by deafness to retire to his law practice and to legal scholarship as the century ended. Although he attended the HARTFORD CONVENTION, he spent most of his energies on a compendium of American law, published in eight volumes between 1820 and 1829 and known as "Dane's Abridgment." The work earned him the name of "the American Blackstone" and the money that he gave to develop Harvard Law School. Dane Hall was the first building and Dane himself chose the first Dane Professor, Justice JOSEPH STORY.

LEONARD W. LEVY
(1986)

Bibliography

JOHNSON, ANDREW W.   1986   *The Life and Constitutional Thought of Nathan Dane.* New York: Garland Publishing.

DANIEL, PETER V.
(1784–1860)

Peter Vivian Daniel, a Virginian born in 1784, served as an Associate Justice of the Supreme Court of the United States from 1841 until his death in 1860. His opinions were notable for the extremist positions he adopted on constitutional issues, including the powers of the federal and state governments, the status of CORPORATIONS, and SLAVERY.

Daniel, a Republican and later a Jacksonian Democrat, served in the Virginia General Assembly, as privy councillor, and as lieutenant governor. President ANDREW JACKSON appointed him to the U. S. District Court in 1836 and President MARTIN VAN BUREN to the Supreme Court in 1841. There the bulk of his work involved cases concerning land titles, procedure, and EQUITY. However, he did participate in most of the major constitutional decisions of the TANEY COURT. But in all instances save one, he spoke either in a concurring or in a dissenting opinion.

Viewing the federal Constitution as a compact among sovereign states, Daniel opposed the extension of federal regulatory authority in COMMERCE CLAUSE cases and extolled the states' POLICE POWER (LICENSE CASES, 1847; PASSENGER CASES, 1849). He concurred in COOLEY V. BOARD OF WARDENS (1851) because he denied that the subject matter of that case (pilotage regulation) was within the federal commerce power at all. In the first *Pennsylvania v. Wheeling Bridge* case (1851), Daniel condemned the use of the commerce power to restrict commerce on navigable rivers. Daniel's hostility to federal ADMIRALTY JURISDICTION sprang from the same source and was buttressed by his insistence on preservation of JURY TRIAL. He dissented in PROPELLER GENESEE CHIEF V. FITZHUGH (1851), one of the few times in which he disagreed with Chief Justice ROGER B. TANEY, opposing the extension of federal admiralty jurisdiction to nontidal waters. In his *Searight v. Stokes* dissent (1845), Daniel insisted that the federal government lacked any power at all to finance INTERNAL IMPROVEMENTS, going far beyond the constitutional doctrine of Jackson's MAYSVILLE ROAD BILL veto (1830).

Daniel was an inveterate foe of banks and corporations, seeking unsuccessfully to deny them access to federal courts as the "Citizens" requisite to Article III jurisdiction (*Rundle v. Delaware and Raritan Canal Co.,* 1852, dissent). In his dissent in *Planters Bank v. Sharp* (1848), he sought to limit the CONTRACT CLAUSE's scope as a restraint on state regulatory power over corporations. In the only significant constitutional case where he spoke for the Court, WEST RIVER BRIDGE V. DIX (1848), Daniel upheld the state's use of EMINENT DOMAIN and police power to condemn corporate property.

In his later years, Daniel came to despise the institutions and values of the free states. His concurrence in DRED SCOTT V. SANDFORD (1857) was remarkable for its intemperate condemnation of the MISSOURI COMPROMISE and for his insistence that no free blacks could be citizens.

Daniel himself best evaluated his contribution to the work of the Court in his *Genesee Chief* dissent: "My opinions may be deemed to be contracted and antiquated, unsuited to the day in which we live, but they are founded upon deliberate convictions as to the nature and objects of LIMITED GOVERNMENT."

WILLIAM M. WIECEK
(1986)

Bibliography

FRANK, JOHN P. 1964 *Justice Daniel Dissenting: Peter V. Daniel.* Cambridge, Mass.: Harvard University Press.

DARBY LUMBER COMPANY, UNITED STATES v.
312 U.S. 100 (1941)

This decision held the FAIR LABOR STANDARDS ACT of 1938 to be a valid exercise of federal power under the COMMERCE CLAUSE. That was no surprise after the 1937 decisions upholding the WAGNER (NATIONAL LABOR RELATIONS) ACT and after the retirement of the four Justices who had voted consistently for a narrow interpretation of the commerce clause. The opinion of Justice HARLAN FISKE STONE was nevertheless of great significance. For instead of speaking in terms of such nonconstitutional concepts as "direct" and "indirect," it returned to basic constitutional principles as to the scope of the power of Congress.

The commerce clause itself precluded states with high labor standards from protecting their wage levels by forbidding the entry of goods produced elsewhere at lower wages. This meant that in the absence of federal legislative action, states with the lowest labor standards could drive the standards down throughout the country. In 1916 Congress first sought to meet this problem by barring the interstate transportation of goods produced by children. Although that statute was clearly a regulation of INTERSTATE COMMERCE the Supreme Court held it unconstitutional by a vote of 5–4 in HAMMER V. DAGENHART (1918) because the purpose of the act was to control what occurred during the course of intrastate PRODUCTION. Five years later, in ADKINS V. CHILDREN'S HOSPITAL (1923), the Court ruled, 6–3, that the DUE PROCESS clause forbade the fixing of minimum wages by either federal or state governments.

The downward spiral of prices and wages during the Great Depression of the 1930s forced employers seeking to survive to reduce wages to incredibly low levels. Congress sought to deal with this problem by requiring the codes of fair competition under the NATIONAL INDUSTRIAL RECOVERY ACT to prescribe MAXIMUM HOURS AND MINIMUM WAGES. SCHECHTER POULTRY CORP. V. UNITED STATES (1935), holding the NRA unconstitutional, brought this program to a halt, and CARTER V. CARTER COAL COMPANY (1936), holding that Congress lacked power to regulate labor conditions and relations in the coal industry, seemed to create an insurmountable impediment. Unpredictably, this lasted for only a year, when *Carter* was in substance overruled in the WAGNER ACT CASES (1937) and *Adkins* was overruled in WEST COAST HOTEL CO. V. PARRISH (1937). The result was passage of the Fair Labor Standards Act in June 1938.

That statute prescribed a minimum wage of twenty-five cents per hour for employees engaged in interstate commerce or in producing goods for such commerce. Payment of fifty percent more for overtime was required for all hours over forty-four per week (to be reduced to forty after two years). The act penalized violation of those standards or interstate shipment of goods produced in violation of them.

The lumber industry was typically afflicted with depressed wage rates; wages ranged from ten to twenty-seven and one-half cents per hour. The annual average wage for all lumber industry employees in Georgia in 1937 was $389. Fred Darby was paying his employees twelve and one-half to seventeen cents per hour; he devised a scheme to continue doing so after the Fair Labor Standards Act became effective, and he was indicted.

Although the other federal lower courts had seen the light after the Labor Board cases and sustained the new statute, the Georgia district judge deemed himself bound to follow HAMMER V. DAGENHART and CARTER until the Supreme Court explicitly overruled them. Accordingly, he dismissed the INDICTMENT as an invalid regulation of manufacture, not interstate commerce, and the government appealed directly to the Supreme Court.

In upholding the statute Justice Stone spoke for a unanimous Court—undoubtedly because Justice JAMES C. MCREYNOLDS had retired three days before. The Court first held that the prohibition against the interstate shipment of goods produced under substandard labor conditions was "indubitably a regulation of [interstate] commerce." And this was none the less so because the motive or purpose may have been to control the "wages and hours of persons engaged in manufacture." The commerce power of Congress, as defined in GIBBONS V. OGDEN (1824), "may be exercised to its utmost extent, and acknowledges no limitations other than are prescribed in the Constitution." "The motive and purpose of a regulation of interstate commerce are matters for the legislative judgment upon which the courts are given no control." The contrary decision in

HAMMER V. DAGENHART "by a bare majority of the Court over the powerful and now classic dissent of Mr. Justice [OLIVER WENDELL] HOLMES" was accordingly overruled.

In determining the validity of the regulation of wages and hours for manufacturers, the Court adopted the approach approved in MCCULLOCH V. MARYLAND (1819), the initial pronouncement on the scope of the ENUMERATED POWERS. The test was whether a regulation of intrastate activities was an "appropriate means to the attainment of a legitimate end, the exercise of the granted power of Congress to regulate interstate commerce." The directness or indirectness of the effect on such commerce was not mentioned, although the substantiality of the effect was. (See EFFECTS ON COMMERCE). The Court noted that legislation under other powers had often been sustained "when the means chosen, although not themselves within the granted power, were nevertheless deemed appropriate aids to the accomplishment of some purpose within an admitted power. . . ." The policy of excluding from interstate commerce goods produced under substandard labor conditions could reasonably be effectuated by prohibiting such conditions for manufacturers producing for interstate distribution. That would suppress a method of interstate competition Congress deemed unfair.

The opinion flatly rejected the contention that the TENTH AMENDMENT restricted the enumerated powers. That amendment, which provides that "the powers not delegated to the United States by the Constitution nor prohibited by it to the states are reserved to the states respectively or to the people," did not deprive the federal government of "authority to resort to all means for the exercise of a granted power which are appropriate and plainly adapted to the permitted end." "The amendment states but a truism that all is retained which has not been surrendered."

Darby was followed a year later by WICKARD V. FILBURN in which the Court alluded to the NECESSARY AND PROPER clause, which MCCULLOCH V. MARYLAND had emphasized, as the source of the power of Congress to regulate intrastate transactions. It also identified the cases which *Darby* had disapproved by implication, among others *Hammer, Schechter,* and *Carter. Darby* and *Wickard* together have provided the foundation for commerce clause interpretation thereafter. They firmly establish that the national economic system is subject to the control of the only entity that can possibly control it, the federal government.

ROBERT L. STERN
(1986)

Bibliography

DODD, E. MERRICK 1946 The Supreme Court and Fair Labor Standards, 1941–1945. *Harvard Law Review* 59:321–375.
STERN, ROBERT L. 1946 The Commerce Clause and the National Economy, 1933–1946. *Harvard Law Review* 59:645–693, 883–947.

DARNEL'S CASE

See: Petition of Right

DARTMOUTH COLLEGE v. WOODWARD
4 Wheaton 518 (1819)

The most famous and influential CONTRACT CLAUSE case in our history, *Dartmouth College* was a boon to higher education and to corporate capitalism. The case established the DOCTRINE, never overruled, that a CORPORATION charter or the grant by a state of corporate rights to private interests comes within the protection of the contract clause. Although the case involved a small college in New Hampshire rather than a manufacturing concern, a bank, or a transportation company, the Court seized an opportunity to broaden the contract clause by making all private corporations its beneficiaries. DANIEL WEBSTER, counsel for the college, said that the judgment was a "defense of VESTED RIGHTS against Courts and Sovereignties," and his co-counsel, Joseph Hopkinson, asserted that it would "secure corporations . . . from legislative despotism. . . ." Corporations were still a recent innovation; JAMES KENT, in his *Commentaries on American Law* (1826), remarked that their rapid multiplication and the avidity with which they were sought by charter from the states arose as a result of the power that large, consolidated capital gave them over business of every sort. The Court's decision in the *Dartmouth College* case, Kent said, more than any other act proceeding from the authority of the United States, threw "an impregnable barrier around all rights and franchises derived from the grant of government; and [gave] solidity and inviolability to the literary, charitable, religious, and commercial institutions of our country." Actually, FLETCHER V. PECK (1810) had made the crucial and original extension of the contract clause, construing it to cover public and executed contracts as well as private executory ones. The *Dartmouth College* doctrine was a logical implication.

The college case was a strange vehicle for the doctrine that emerged from it. Dartmouth, having been chartered in 1769 in the name of the crown to christianize and educate Indians, had become a Christian college for whites and a stronghold of the Congregationalist Church, which had benefited most from the laws establishing the Protestant religion in New Hampshire. The college had become embroiled in state politics on the side of the

Federalists, who supported the establishment. When in 1815 the trustees removed the president of the college, they loosed a controversy that drew to the ousted president a coalition of Jeffersonians and religious denominations demanding separation of church and state. The reformers having swept the state elections in 1816, the legislature sought to democratize the college by a series of statutes that converted it into a state university under public control, rather than a private college as provided by the original charter. The state supreme court sustained the state acts, reasoning that the institution had been established with public aid for public purposes of an educational and religious nature. The state court held that the contract clause did not limit the state's power over its own public corporations.

On APPEAL, the Supreme Court held that Dartmouth was a private eleemosynary corporation whose VESTED RIGHTS could not be divested without infringing a continuing obligation to respect inviolably the trustees' control of property given to the corporation for the advancement of its objectives. The Court held unconstitutional the state acts subjecting Dartmouth to state control and ordered Woodward, the treasurer of the institution who had sided with the state, to return to the trustees the records, corporate seal, and other corporate property which he held.

At every step of his opinion Chief Justice JOHN MARSHALL misstated the facts about the history of the original charter in order to prove that it established a purely private corporation. That, perhaps, was a matter primarily of interest to the college, which, contrary to Marshall, had received its charter not from George III but from the governor of the colony; moreover, the private donations, which Marshall said had been given to Dartmouth on condition of receiving the charter, had been given unconditionally to an entirely different institution, Moor's Charity School for Indians, and had been transferred to Dartmouth over the donors' objections. Also, the funds of the college, contrary to Marshall, did not consist "entirely of private donations," because the endowment of the college at the time of the issuance of the chapter derived mainly from grants of public lands. Even if the grant of the charter were a contract, as Marshall said it "plainly" was, Parliament could have repealed it at will. The Chief Justice conceded the fact but added that a repeal would have been morally perfidious. If, however, the charter were subject to revocation at the will of the sovereign authority, or the grantor, the "contract" did not bind that party and created no obligation that could be impaired.

Marshall conceded that at the time of Independence, the state succeeded to the power of Parliament and might have repealed or altered the charter at any time before the adoption of the Constitution. The provision in Article I, section 10, preventing states from impairing the obligation of a contract, altered the situation. That clause, Marshall conceded, was not specifically intended to protect charters of incorporation: "It is," he said boldly, "more than possible that the preservation of rights of this description was not particularly in the view of the framers of the constitution," but the clause admitted no exceptions as far as private rights were concerned. "It is not enough to say that this particular case was not in the mind of the convention when the article was framed, nor of the American people when it was adopted." In the absence of proof that the language of the Constitution would have been altered had charters of incorporation been considered, the case came within its injunction against state acts impairing the OBLIGATION OF CONTRACTS.

Although Marshall can be doubted when he said, "It can require no argument to prove that the circumstances of this case constitute a contract," his general doctrine, that any state charter for a private corporation is a constitutionally protected contract, was not far-fetched. The Court must construe the text, not the minds of its framers, and, as he said, "There is no exception in the constitution, no sentiment delivered by its contemporaneous expounders, which would justify us in making it." If a state granted a charter of incorporation to private interests, the charter has "every ingredient of a complete and legitimate contract," should it be made on a valuable consideration for the security and disposition of the property conveyed to the corporation for management by its trustees in perpetuity. Unless, as Justice JOSEPH STORY stressed in his concurring opinion, the government should reserve, in the grant of the charter, a power to alter, modify, or repeal, the rights vested cannot be divested, except by the consent of the incorporators, assuming they have not defaulted. Whether, however, a modification of the charter, as in this case, impairs an obligation, if the charter be executed and by its terms should not specify a term of years for the corporation's existence, is another question. In *Fletcher v. Peck*, however, the Court had brought executed as well as public contracts within the meaning of the contract clause. Marshall construed contract rights sweepingly, state powers narrowly.

Max Lerner's comment on the case, referring to Webster's peroration, is provocative. "Every schoolboy," he wrote, "knows Webster's eloquent plea and how Marshall, whom the Yazoo land scandals had left cold, found his own eyes suffused with tears, as Webster, overcome by the emotion of his words, wept. But few schoolboys know that the case had ultimately less to do with colleges than with business corporations; that sanctity of contract was invoked to give them immunity against legislative control, and that business enterprise in America never had more useful mercenaries than the tears Daniel Webster and John Marshall are reputed to have shed so devotedly that

March day in Washington. . . ." In fact, the reserved power to alter or repeal, of which Story spoke, limited corporate immunity from legislative control. Moreover, the protection given by the Court to corporate charters came into play after the legislatures, not the Court, issued these charters, often recklessly and corruptly, without consideration of the public good; Marshall's opinion should have put the legislatures and the public on guard. Finally, the case had a great deal to do with higher education as well as business. *Dartmouth College* is the MAGNA CARTA of private colleges and universities, and, by putting them beyond state control, provided a powerful stimulus, not only to business corporations but also to the chartering of state institutions of higher learning. Unable to make private institutions public ones, the states established state universities.

LEONARD W. LEVY
(1986)

Bibliography

BEVERIDGE, ALBERT J. 1916–1919 *The Life of John Marshall*, 4 vols. Vol. IV:220–281. Boston: Little, Brown.

HAINES, CHARLES GROVE 1944 *The Role of the Supreme Court in American Government and Politics, 1789–1835*. Pages 378–419. Berkeley: University of California Press.

SHIRLEY, JOHN M. (1879) 1971 *The Dartmouth College Causes and the Supreme Court*. New York: Da Capo Press.

STITES, FRANCIS N. 1972 *Private Interest and Public Gain: The Dartmouth College Case, 1819*. Amherst: University of Massachusetts Press.

DAVIS, DAVID
(1815–1883)

David Davis's Supreme Court appointment in 1862 stemmed from his longtime legal and political association with ABRAHAM LINCOLN. Throughout the CIVIL WAR, Davis loyally supported the administration in the PRIZE CASES (1863) and EX PARTE VALLANDIGHAM (1864), but he opposed the President regarding emancipation and military trials of civilians. At one point, Davis urged Lincoln to withdraw the EMANCIPATION PROCLAMATION, believing that it would only increase southern resistance and border-state hostility toward the Union. The military trial issue, however, aroused Davis's unrelenting enmity and criticism. Appropriately, Davis delivered the Court's unanimous opinion in EX PARTE MILLIGAN in 1866, holding that civilian trials by presidentially created military commissions were unconstitutional. Davis, joined by the four Democrats on the bench, added that Congress could not authorize such commissions, provoking sharp dissent from Chief Justice SALMON P. CHASE and the other three Republicans.

Democrats and Southerners claimed that the subsequent Republican military reconstruction program was unconstitutional on the basis of *Milligan*. But Davis's opinion really offered little comfort on this point. While he found that the "laws and usages of war" could not apply where civil courts were open, he qualified this conclusion by specifying those "states which have upheld the authority of the government." In his private correspondence, Davis showed that he was disturbed by contemporary interpretations. He noted that there was "not a word said in the opinion about reconstruction, the power is conceded in insurrectionary states."

Disenchanted with the Republicans, and equally wary of the Democrats, Davis castigated the partisan wrangling that characterized the RECONSTRUCTION period. He opposed suffrage for blacks, stating that "the thrusting on them [of] political rights is to their injury." He advocated the preservation of traditional state powers, and he expressed alarm "at the tendency to consolidated Govt manifested by the Republican party." Yet he believed that the military reconstruction program would have been avoided if the Democrats and the South had accepted the FOURTEENTH AMENDMENT. Davis displayed little inclination to have the judiciary thwart the Republican program, however. He was with the majority in TEXAS V. WHITE (1869). He also resisted the attempts of some colleagues to force a decision in EX PARTE MCCARDLE (1868) before Congress repealed the appropriate JURISDICTION legislation, thinking "it was unjudicial to run a race with Congress." Finally, he opposed a motion to challenge the Reconstruction Act on property rights grounds in *Mississippi v. Stanton* (1868).

Davis's sense of restraint characterized his votes in most of the other issues involving the Civil War and Reconstruction. Despite the libertarian concerns he had expressed in *Milligan*, he joined the dissenters who favored upholding both federal and state TEST OATHS. He also joined the dissenters who favored sustaining LEGAL TENDERS in *Hepburn v. Griswold* (1870) and then joined the new majority a year later when the decision was reversed. His political conservatism, combined with his notions of JUDICIAL RESTRAINT, best explains his adherence to the majority view in the SLAUGHTERHOUSE CASES (1873).

Davis's literal reading of the compact clause (Article I, section 10), however, led him to dissent in *Virginia v. West Virginia* (1871) when he denied the legality of West Virginia's annexation of two western Virginia counties during the Civil War. And in *Miller v. United States* (1871), a key case testing the CONFISCATION ACT of 1862, he supported the act's constitutionality but found reversible error. In a number of circuit rulings involving confiscation, his insistence on procedural fairness largely masked his distaste for the law.

In the Court's consideration of emerging economic

questions in the 1870s, Davis again adopted rather traditional views on federalism and state prerogatives. He dissented, for example, in PHILADELPHIA & READING RAILROAD V. PENNSYLVANIA (the *State Freight Tax Case*, 1873), arguing that a state tax imposed on freight tonnage was simply a business tax and not an interference with INTERSTATE COMMERCE. In a long series of municipal bond cases in the 1860s and 1870s, Davis usually supported Justice SAMUEL F. MILLER's vigorous battle against the Court's attempts to provide bondholders protection from state taxation or repudiation. In his most notable statement on the issue, Davis dissented when the Court held that the interest of nonresident bondholders could not be taxed. In *State Tax on Foreign-Held Bonds* (1873), Davis relied on traditional state statutes requiring taxation of "all mortgages [and] money owned by solvent debtors." Such taxation, he said, did not impair any contractual obligations between creditors and those who issued bonds. A quarter-century later, Davis's views were adopted by a new majority.

Despite his prominence and reputation, Davis produced few noteworthy constitutional opinions beyond his contribution in *Milligan*. In truth, he was misplaced as a Supreme Court Justice. He preferred the involvement of political life or trial court work. Davis eagerly sought the presidency and he courted anti-Grant elements within the Republican party in 1872. He finally resigned in 1877 when the Illinois legislature elected him to the Senate. He eventually was elected President *pro tem,* prompting Chief Justice MORRISON R. WAITE, who deplored Davis's political ambitions, to remark that the position was "as near to the Presidency as he can get."

Davis himself offered the most candid and fitting estimate of his judicial career. "[A]s I never did like hard study, the work is not always agreeable," he wrote to his brother-in-law in 1870. "I believe I write the shortest opinions of any one on the bench, & if I had to elaborate opinions & write legal essays as some Judges do, I would quit the concern. I like to hold trial court, but this work on an appellate bench is too much like hard labor."

STANLEY I. KUTLER
(1986)

(SEE ALSO: *Constitutional History, 1861–1865; Constitutional History, 1865–1877.*)

DAVIS, JEFFERSON
(1808–1889)

A Mississippi planter, Jefferson Davis graduated from West Point, served with distinction in the Mexican War, and was a congressman (1845–1846), senator (1847–1851, 1857–1861) and secretary of war (1853–1857). In 1861 he reluctantly resigned from the Senate when Mississippi left the Union. Davis served as Confederate President (1861–1865) and at the end of the CIVIL WAR was indicted for TREASON and jailed but never tried because prosecutors were unsure they could legally convict him. Stripped of his CITIZENSHIP, Davis never returned to politics, but he did write a tedious and defensive two-volume history of SECESSION and his presidency, *The Rise and Fall of the Confederate Government* (1881).

Davis came to national political prominence with his opposition to the COMPROMISE OF 1850. He was one of ten senators who voted against California statehood. Davis supported only the 1850 Fugitive Slave Act, which he thought should be passed and enforced "as a right not to be estimated . . . by the value of the property, but for the principles involved." Unlike JOHN C. CALHOUN, with whom he usually agreed, Davis opposed a constitutional amendment to secure southern rights in all the TERRITORIES. Davis supported extending the MISSOURI COMPROMISE line to California.

After Calhoun's death Davis was the Senate's foremost supporter of southern rights and STATES' RIGHTS. He asserted that secession was constitutional because: the Constitution did not prohibit it nor provide power to coerce a state to remain in the Union; the national government was created by "the states," not "the people," and therefore the states could exist separately from the national government; and the Union "was in the nature of a partnership between individuals without limitation of time" and could be dissolved by the unilateral action of any of the parties.

Davis was ambivalent, however, on whether the theoretical right of secession should be implemented. He opposed secession at the NASHVILLE CONVENTION (1850), arguing that southern rights could be protected within the Union. In 1851 he unsuccessfully sought the Mississippi governorship on a "states' rights" ticket, but later in the decade he opposed states' rights parties because he thought southern interests could best be protected by alliances with sympathetic northern Democrats. In 1860 he attempted to mediate a compromise that would have taken John Bell, JOHN C. BRECKINRIDGE, and STEPHEN A. DOUGLAS out of the presidential contest, in favor of a single Democratic candidate. In 1858 he said publicly that if a Republican were elected "I should deem it your duty to provide for your safety outside the Union." In 1859 he said that the John Brown raid meant that loyalty to the Constitution required secession. Even so, after ABRAHAM LINCOLN's election Davis urged compromise, and served on the Committee of Thirty-Three. Only when this committee failed did he support secession.

Davis was ambivalent in other ways. He believed that blacks were inferior to whites, that congressional prohibition of the African slave trade was unconstitutional, and that the federal government should not interfere with slavery. Yet his plantation was a model, surpassed only by his brother's for treating blacks with compassion and for giving them a great deal of self-government. He opposed reopening the slave trade on moral grounds and in 1865 advocated emancipation to save the Confederacy. He saw secession as a conservative measure to protect the Constitution from tyranny by Lincoln and the national government. But as Confederate president, Davis implemented CONSCRIPTION, suspension of HABEAS CORPUS, and impressment of supplies. A lifelong states' rights man, Davis was vilified by politicians and governors as he sought, unsuccessfully, to create a Confederate national policy.

PAUL FINKELMAN
(1986)

Bibliography

DODD, WILLIAM E.   1907   *Jefferson Davis*. Philadelphia: George Jacobs.

MCCARDELL, JOHN   1979   *The Idea of a Southern Nation*. New York: Norton.

DAVIS, JOHN W.
(1873–1955)

One of the nation's most celebrated lawyers, John William Davis served as SOLICITOR GENERAL under WOODROW WILSON, winning WILSON V. NEW (1917) and the SELECTIVE DRAFT LAW CASES (1918). In 1924 he was the Democratic candidate for President. He remained prominent at the Supreme Court bar, successfully challenging NEW DEAL legislation, and in 1952 Davis attacked HARRY S. TRUMAN's seizure of the steel mills as a "usurpation" of power "without parallel in American history." (See YOUNGSTOWN SHEET AND TUBE COMPANY V. SAWYER.) He won that case but would lose his last one: *Briggs v. Elliott* (1954). Arguing this companion case to BROWN V. BOARD OF EDUCATION (1954), Davis dismissed arguments about SEGREGATION's psychological harm and urged the continued validity of the SEPARATE BUT EQUAL rule.

DAVID GORDON
(1986)

DAVIS v. ALASKA

See: Compulsory Process, Right to

DAVIS v. BEASON
130 U.S. 333 (1890)

Davis involved an Idaho territorial statute directed at POLYGAMY. The law required voters to foreswear membership in any organization that "teaches, advocates, counsels or encourages" its members to undertake polygamous relationships. Davis was convicted of swearing falsely.

Justice STEPHEN J. FIELD, speaking for the Supreme Court, saw the case as identical to REYNOLDS V. UNITED STATES (1879). The free exercise clause of the FIRST AMENDMENT protected religious beliefs not acts that prejudiced the health, safety, or good order of society as defined by the legislature operating under its POLICE POWER. Field concluded that if something is a crime, then to teach, advise, or counsel it cannot be protected by evoking religious tenets.

The decision became one of the principal underpinnings of what later came to be called the "secular regulation" approach to the free exercise clause whereby no religious exemptions are required from otherwise valid secular regulations.

RICHARD E. MORGAN
(1986)

DAVIS v. PASSMAN
442 U.S. 228 (1979)

Congressman Otto Passman fired Davis, a female member of his staff, because "it was essential that the [job] be [held by] a man." Such SEX DISCRIMINATION normally violates Title VII of the CIVIL RIGHTS ACT OF 1964 but Congress had exempted itself from that act's coverage. Davis therefore brought suit directly under the Constitution, alleging that sex discrimination by members of Congress violates the EQUAL PROTECTION guarantees contained in the Fifth Amendment. The Supreme Court, in an opinion by Justice WILLIAM J. BRENNAN and over four dissents, found that Davis had stated a cause of action. The Court extended its holding in BIVENS V. SIX UNKNOWN NAMED AGENTS OF THE FEDERAL BUREAU OF NARCOTICS (1971) to allow direct private damage actions under the Fifth Amendment. The majority did not discuss the SPEECH OR DEBATE CLAUSES' effect, if any, on the action.

THEODORE EISENBERG
(1986)

DAVIS v. SCHNELL

See: Literacy Test

DAY, WILLIAM R.
(1849–1923)

William Rufus Day was named to the Supreme Court by THEODORE ROOSEVELT in 1903, after WILLIAM HOWARD TAFT had declined the nomination to remain at his post in the Philippines. Coincidentally, Day had replaced Taft on the Sixth Circuit Court of Appeals in 1899 when President WILLIAM MCKINLEY dispatched Taft to the Pacific outpost.

Day's tenure spanned the Progressive era. He generally favored the movement's interventionist thrust, particularly state regulatory actions. Day's decisions relating to federal power, however, were more ambivalent, as reflected by his famous opinion in HAMMER V. DAGENHART (1918), which invalidated a congressional attempt to regulate child labor premised on the COMMERCE CLAUSE. Unlike many STATES' RIGHTS advocates, he consistently supported state police regulations.

Justice Day faithfully followed the precedent of UNITED STATES V. E. C. KNIGHT COMPANY (1895), holding that Congress's INTERSTATE COMMERCE power did not extend to PRODUCTION. For example, in *Delaware, Lackawanna and Western Railroad Company v. Yurkonis* (1915) he declined to extend coverage of the federal EMPLOYERS LIABILITY ACT to coal miners even though the coal they produced eventually was used in interstate commerce. Three years later, in the child labor case, Day elaborated his conception of FEDERALISM with an expansive discussion of the TENTH AMENDMENT and its limitations on national power. He found that a congressional law prohibiting the interstate transportation of goods made by child labor unconstitutionally regulated production.

Generally, however, Day supported federal regulation of business. In *Atchison, Topeka and Santa Fe Railway Company v. Robinson* (1914), he wrote an opinion sustaining amendments to the HEPBURN ACT that greatly expanded federal JURISDICTION in railroad regulation, and in *Harriman v. Interstate Commerce Commission* (1908) he vigorously dissented from an opinion by Justice OLIVER WENDELL HOLMES that weakened the commission's SUBPOENA powers. Day also consistently sided with the government in antitrust suits. Soon after his appointment, he provided the decisive vote for the government in NORTHERN SECURITIES COMPANY V. UNITED STATES (1904). Although he acquiesced in the Court's RULE OF REASON doctrine in STANDARD OIL COMPANY V. UNITED STATES and UNITED STATES V. AMERICAN TOBACCO COMPANY(1911), Day expressed reservations toward the doctrine in a number of opinions that strongly supported the SHERMAN ACT. Finally, in *United States v. United States Steel Corporation* (1920), he led the dissenters who hotly disputed the Court's approval of the corporation's control of most of the steel industry. Consistently acting as a principled foe of monopoly, Day advocated governmental intervention to destroy concentrated power and insure competition.

Despite Day's views in the child labor case, he supported the concept of a NATIONAL POLICE POWER based on the commerce clause. In *Pittsburgh Melting Company v.*

Totten (1918) he sustained the Meat Inspection Act of 1906, and in HOKE V. UNITED STATES (1913) he offered a classic defense of the police power to uphold the MANN ACT. Congress's control over commerce, he said, was "complete in itself," and Congress might adopt "not only means necessary but convenient to its exercise, and the means may have the quality of police considerations."

Similarly, Day upheld widespread uses of state police powers. He joined Justice JOHN MARSHALL HARLAN's dissent in LOCHNER V. NEW YORK (1905), and he supported the Court's approval of compulsory VACCINATION in JACOBSON V. MASSACHUSETTS (1905). Day consistently rejected the rigid FREEDOM OF CONTRACT dogma of *Lochner*. In *McLean v. Arkansas* (1909) he wrote to sustain state mining safety regulations and deferred to legislative prerogative: "The [state] legislature being familiar with local conditions is, primarily, the judge of the necessity of such enactments." Although the judiciary might have different views of social policy, Day insisted judges had no warrant to interfere. When the Court invalidated a state law prohibiting YELLOW DOG CONTRACTS in COPPAGE V. KANSAS (1915), Day protested against a literalist view of liberty of contract and, ignoring the *Lochner* precedent, he argued that "liberty of contract may be circumscribed in the interest of the State and the welfare of its people."

Day served on the Court until 1922. His opinions, though not memorable, were relatively free from rigid dogma. He contributed significantly to the Court's general approval of the expanded scope of governmental authority, federal and state. In the latter part of his career, that support extended to the prosecution of dissenters and radicals as he consistently sided with the government in the "Red Scare" cases. His 1918 child labor opinion unfortunately has served to obscure his more enduring contributions to constitutional law, such as his support for national regulatory power and an expanded state police power authority.

STANLEY I. KUTLER
(1986)

Bibliography

MCLEAN, JOSEPH E. 1946 *William Rufus Day: Supreme Court Justice from Ohio*. Baltimore: Johns Hopkins University Press.

DAYTON, JONATHAN
(1760–1824)

Jonathan Dayton, the youngest signer of the Constitution, represented New Jersey at the CONSTITUTIONAL CONVENTION OF 1787. He spoke several times at the Convention in support of small-state positions. He was afterward speaker of the HOUSE OF REPRESENTATIVES and a senator. In 1807 he was arrested for conspiring with AARON BURR but was not tried.

DENNIS J. MAHONEY
(1986)

DAYTON BOARD OF EDUCATION v. BRINKMAN

See: *Columbus Board of Education v. Penick*

DAYTON-GOOSE CREEK RAILWAY COMPANY v. UNITED STATES
263 U.S. 456 (1924)

A unanimous Supreme Court here sustained the constitutionality of the recapture provision of the ESCH-CUMMINGS TRANSPORTATION ACT of 1920. The Dayton-Goose Creek Railway earned a return exceeding six percent of its property value, prompting the Interstate Commerce Commission to ask what arrangements it had made to contribute to the fund for which the act had provided. The railroad then sought an INJUNCTION against enforcement of the act, alleging the provision's unconstitutionality. Sixteen railroads, including some of the most powerful of the day, filed AMICUS CURIAE briefs.

Chief Justice WILLIAM HOWARD TAFT asserted that Congress's power over INTERSTATE COMMERCE was not limited to prescribing reasonable rates and voiding unjust ones. Its regulatory power was "intended . . . to foster, protect, and control the commerce with appropriate regard to the welfare of those who are immediately concerned, as well as the public at large, and to promote its growth and insure its safety." Because private railroads offered a public service, Congress might regulate them in order to assure performance of that function. After considering the necessity and justification for the recapture provisions, Taft concluded that the railroad's obligation to serve the public limits it to only "fair or reasonable profit." Reducing a carrier's income to what the Court deemed a FAIR RETURN did not constitute a TAKING OF PROPERTY without compensation because the act made the carrier only a trustee of any "excess." The government was entitled to appropriate that amount for "public uses because the appropriation takes away nothing which equitably belongs either to the shipper or to the carrier."

DAVID GORDON
(1986)

DEAN MILK COMPANY v. CITY OF MADISON
340 U.S. 349 (1951)

A Madison, Wisconsin, city ordinance that prohibited the sale of milk pasteurized at a plant more than five miles outside city limits provided the basis for clarification of the limits on STATE REGULATION OF COMMERCE. A 6–3 Supreme Court invalidated the law as an "undue burden on INTERSTATE COMMERCE" because it effectively barred the sale of milk from firms in neighboring Illinois. Justice TOM C. CLARK also found a discrimination against outside producers which could not be sustained as an exercise of the state's POLICE POWER when "reasonable nondiscriminatory alternatives" were available, as here.

DAVID GORDON
(1986)

DEATH PENALTY

See: Capital Punishment; Capital Punishment and Race; Capital Punishment Cases of 1972; Capital Punishment Cases of 1976

DEBS, IN RE
158 U.S. 564 (1895)

Eugene V. Debs, head of the American Railway Union, petitioned for a writ of HABEAS CORPUS on the ground that he had been imprisoned illegally, for contempt of court, because of his defiance of an INJUNCTION issued by a United States CIRCUIT COURT. That draconian injunction, which became a model for subsequent injunctions in American LABOR disputes, sought to end the strike by Debs's union against railroads hauling Pullman sleeping cars. The Pullman Company and the managers association of twenty-four railroad CORPORATIONS, according to a later federal investigation, sought to crush the strike and the union rather than accept any peaceable solution. The managers jubilantly described the injunction as a "gatling gun on paper." It prohibited the strikers from attempting to obstruct the movement of mail or INTERSTATE COMMERCE by the struck railroads. It also forbade the use of "persuasion" aimed at preventing workers from doing their jobs.

Justice DAVID J. BREWER, speaking for a unanimous Supreme Court, delivered a breathtakingly broad opinion based not on any statutory authority for the injunction, but on general principles of national supremacy. "The strong arm of the national government," he declared, "may be put forth to brush away all obstructions to the freedom of INTERSTATE COMMERCE or the transportation of the mails.

If the emergency arises, the army of the Nation, and all its militia, are at the service of the Nation to compel obedience to its laws." Similarly, Brewer added, the United States might invoke the power of its courts to remove obstructions by injunctions. Brewer's opinion transcended the particular injunction in this case; he failed to examine its terms, though it outlawed persuasion as well as force and assumed that the refusal to work for a railroad is an obstruction of commerce and the mails.

National supremacy, which the Court rendered nearly impotent to cope with obstructions to commerce caused by giant corporations, triumphed against the militant union. The union never recuperated from its defeat in this case and soon disintegrated. *Debs* taught that injunctions could be effective union-smashing devices. They became common afterward. The case also foreshadowed the use of the SHERMAN ANTITRUST ACT against unions. The circuit court had issued the injunction mainly on the ground that the strike was a combination in restraint of interstate commerce. The Supreme Court said that it did not dissent from that conclusion but preferred to rest its judgment on "broader ground."

LEONARD W. LEVY
(1986)

Bibliography

LINDSEY, ALMONT 1942 *The Pullman Strike*. Chicago: University of Chicago Press.

DEBS v. UNITED STATES
249 U.S. 211 (1919)

During his long and controversial career as a LABOR leader and radical, Eugene V. Debs twice ran afoul of the federal government, which looked upon his activities as a threat to the nation's economic and political orthodoxy. In 1894 he was sentenced to six months' imprisonment for contempt of court as part of the GROVER CLEVELAND administration's efforts to crush the Pullman boycott in Chicago. In IN RE DEBS (1895) the United States Supreme Court affirmed this conviction and upheld the sweeping labor INJUNCTION which Debs and other leaders of the American Railway Union were alleged to have violated. Two decades later, as the leader of the American Socialist Party and one of the most visible critics of the WOODROW WILSON administration's decision to enter WORLD WAR I, Debs again found himself in federal court, this time charged with violating the ESPIONAGE ACT of 1917.

Debs was tried and convicted on the basis of a speech he delivered at a socialist, antiwar rally in Canton, Ohio, for inciting insubordination, disloyalty, and mutiny in the armed forces and for obstructing military recruitment. In his oration, Debs praised other imprisoned leaders of the party who had been convicted for aiding and abetting resistance to the draft. In the course of his speech Debs also accused the government of using false testimony to convict another antiwar activist and he labeled the war as a plot by "the predatory capitalist in the United States" against the working class, "who furnish the corpses, having never yet had a voice in declaring war and . . . never yet had a voice in declaring peace." He told the audience that "you need to know that you are fit for something better than slavery and cannon fodder," and he ended by noting: "Don't worry about the charge of TREASON to your masters; but be concerned about the treason that involves yourselves." Debs was sentenced to ten years in prison.

When the *Debs* case reached the Supreme Court, a postwar "red scare" had descended on the nation. CRIMINAL CONSPIRACY trials of leaders of the Industrial Workers of the World were still underway. The Department of Justice had embarked on a large-scale program that would culminate in the PALMER RAIDS and the deportation of hundreds of ALIEN radicals.

Without even a reference to the CLEAR AND PRESENT DANGER test enunciated a week earlier, a unanimous Supreme Court affirmed Debs's conviction in an opinion written by Justice OLIVER WENDELL HOLMES. Although Holmes conceded that "the main theme" of Debs's speech had concerned socialism, its growth, and its eventual triumph, he argued that "if a part of the manifest intent of the more general utterance was to encourage those present to obstruct recruiting . . . the immunity of the general theme may not be enough to protect the speech." As Harry Kalven has remarked, "It is somewhat as though George McGovern had been sent to prison for his criticism of the [VIETNAM] war." Holmes saw the case as a routine criminal appeal; in a letter to Sir Frederick Pollock, Holmes referred to the *Debs* case, saying, "there was a lot of jaw about free speech."

Debs remained in federal prison long after the armistice. Although a convicted felon, he received the Socialist Party nomination for President in 1920 and nearly a million votes. President Wilson, in failing health and embittered by the war and its critics, refused to pardon Debs before leaving the White House in 1921. His successor, the Republican conservative WARREN G. HARDING, displayed greater compassion by granting the socialist leader a pardon.

MICHAEL E. PARRISH
(1986)

Bibliography

FREUND, ERNST 1919 The Debs Case and Freedom of Speech. *The New Republic*, May 3, 1919, p. 13. Reprinted in *University of Chicago Law Review* 40:239–42 (1973).

DECISION

A decision is the final determination by a competent tribunal of matters of law and fact submitted to it in a CASE OR CONTROVERSY. The decision is ordinarily in writing and comprises the JUDGMENT or decree in the case. The decision is not itself law, but only evidence of the law; and the value of a case as precedent derives less from the decision than from the reasoning behind the decision. The term "decision" is one of popular usage and not a technical legal term.

The Supreme Court reaches its decisions in CONFERENCE following the ORAL ARGUMENT of a case. A vote is taken after each Justice has had a chance to state his or her views. The decision is announced by means of a memorandum order or as part of a formal opinion.

In casual usage, the decision is often confounded with the OPINION OF THE COURT, a usage sanctioned by certain law dictionaries and a number of court opinions. In precise usage, however, the decision is the conclusion reached by the court, while the opinion is a statement of the reasoning by which the decision was reached. In the simplest terms, the decision answers the question: who won the case.

DENNIS J. MAHONEY
(1986)

DECLARATION AND RESOLVES OF FIRST CONTINENTAL CONGRESS

See: First Continental Congress, Declarations and Resolves of

DECLARATION OF INDEPENDENCE
1 Stat. 1 (July 4, 1776)

America's most fundamental constitutional document was adopted by the United States in Congress on July 4, 1776. The Declaration of Independence may carry little weight in the courts; it may, for all its being placed at the head of the *Statutes at Large* and described in the United States Code as part of the "organic law," have no legally binding force. Yet it is the Declaration that constitutes the American nation. John Hancock, president of the Continental Congress, transmitting the Declaration to the several states, described it as "the Ground & Foundation of a future Government." JAMES MADISON, the Father of the Constitution, called it "the fundamental Act of Union of these States."

The Declaration of Independence is the definitive statement for the American policy of the ends of government, of the necessary conditions for the legitimate exercise of political power, and of the SOVEREIGNTY of the people who establish the government and, when circumstances warrant, may alter or abolish it. No mere tract in support of a bygone event, the Declaration was and remains the basic statement of the meaning of the United States as a political entity.

The historical event, the Revolution, provided the occasion for making that statement. RICHARD HENRY LEE, on instructions from the Virginia convention, introduced three resolutions on June 7, 1776: to declare the colonies independent, to establish a confederation, and to seek foreign alliances. Each of the resolutions was referred to a select committee, one of which was charged with preparing "a declaration to the effect of the first resolution." Lee's motion was adopted on July 2, the Declaration two days later.

Although the Congress had appointed for the task a distinguished committee, including JOHN ADAMS of Massachusetts, BENJAMIN FRANKLIN of Pennsylvania, ROGER SHERMAN of Connecticut, and ROBERT LIVINGSTON of New York, THOMAS JEFFERSON of Virginia actually penned the Declaration. So well did Jefferson express the sentiments of the Congress that his committee colleagues made only a few changes in his draft.

Jefferson, by his own account, turned to neither book nor pamphlet for ideas. Nor did he seek to expound a novel political theory. His aim was to set forth the common sense of the American people on the subject of political legitimacy. To be sure, there are ideas, and even phrases, that recall JOHN LOCKE: the Declaration follows Locke in stressing the NATURAL RIGHTS of man as the foundation of the political order. But the concept of man's natural autonomy, modifiable only by his consent to the rule of others in a SOCIAL COMPACT, was long acknowledged in the American colonies; it inhered in congregational church polity, and it was transmitted through such theoretical and legal writers as EMERICH DE VATTEL, Jean-Jacques Burlamaqui, and Samuel Pufendorf, as well as by the authors of CATO'S LETTERS and other popular works.

The Declaration of Independence has a structure that emphasizes its content. It begins with a preamble, by which the document is addressed not to the king of Great Britain or to the English public, but to the world at large, to the "opinion of mankind." Moreover, the purpose of the document is said explicitly to be to "declare the causes" that impelled the Americans to declare their independence from Britain.

There had been other revolutions in British history, but this one was different. From the barons at Runnymede to the Whigs who drove James II from the throne, British insurgents had appealed to the historic rights of Englishmen. The declarations they extracted—from MAGNA CARTA to the BILL OF RIGHTS—were the assurances of their kings that the ancient laws obtaining in their island would be respected. The preamble of the Declaration of Independence makes clear that this is not the case with the American Revolution. The case of Britain's rule in America was to be held up to a universal standard and exposed as tyrannical before a "candid world." Against the selfsame standard all government everywhere could be measured. Everyone who reads the Declaration with his eyes open must be struck by this fact: the Declaration justifies the independence of the American nation by appeal not to an English or an Anglo-American standard, but to the universal standard of human rights.

There follows next a statement of the ends of government and of the conditions under which obedience to government is proper. "All men are created equal . . . endowed by their Creator with certain unalienable rights . . . among [which] are life, liberty, and the pursuit of happiness." Equality is the condition of men prior to government—logically prior, not chronologically. But that equality is not equality of condition, or even equality of opportunity; certainly it is not equality of intelligence, strength, or skill. The equality that men possess by nature is equality of *right*. There is, among human beings, none with a right to rule the others; God may claim to rule human beings by right, human beings may rule the brutes by right, but no human being has a claim to rule another by right.

The rights with which men are endowed are said to be "unalienable." That is, human rights may be neither usurped nor surrendered, neither taken away nor given up. The Declaration rejects the false doctrine of Thomas Hobbes (more gently echoed by WILLIAM BLACKSTONE) that men on entering society and submitting to government yield their natural rights and retain only "civil" rights, dispensed and revoked at the pleasure of the sovereign.

"To secure these rights, governments are instituted among men." The purpose of government is to protect the natural rights which men possess, but which, in the absence of government, they are not secure enough to enjoy. Government in society is not optional, it is a necessary condition for the enjoyment of natural rights. But the institution of government does not create an independent motive or will in society. All just powers of government derive "from the consent of the governed."

The Declaration asserts that the people retain the right of revolution, the right to substitute new constitutions for old. But it also asserts that the exercise of that right is properly governed by prudence—a prudence that the Americans had shown in the face of great provocation.

The next section of the Declaration is a bill of indictment against George III on the charge of attempted tyranny. The specifications are divided almost evenly between procedural and substantive offenses. The fact that the king—by his representatives in America—assembled the provincial legislatures at places far from their capitals or required persons accused of certain crimes to be transported to England for trial, evinced a tyrannical design by disregard of procedural safeguards. But even when the established procedures were followed, as in giving or withholding assent to legislation, the result could be tyrannical; for example, the suppression of trade, the discouragement of population growth, and the keeping of standing armies in peacetime were acts according to the forms of due process that unjustly deprived the Americans of their liberty. Still other acts, such as making the royal assent conditional on surrender of the right of representation and withholding assent from bills to create provincial courts, were tyrannical in both form and substance.

The most critical charge, the thirteenth, was that the king had conspired with others—the British Parliament—to subject the Americans to a JURISDICTION foreign to their constitution. The Americans had come to see that a compact existed between the British king and each of his American provinces by which the king exercised executive power in each even as he did in the home island, and that the common executive was the sole governmental connection between America and Britain. The imperial constitution, as the Americans had come to understand it, no more permitted the British legislature to regulate the internal affairs of Massachusetts or Virginia than it did the provincial legislatures to regulate the internal affairs of England or Scotland. But the British legislature could not breach the compact between the king and the provinces because Parliament was not a party to that compact. The king, however, by conniving at that usurpation, did breach the compact.

The final five accusations deal with the fact that Britain and America were at war. One charge that Jefferson included, but Congress struck out, accused the king of waging "cruel war against human nature itself" by tolerating the introduction of SLAVERY into the colonies and sanctioning the slave trade. Only two states, Georgia and South Carolina, objected to the passage, but the others acquiesced to preserve unanimity. In any case, the condemnation of slavery was implicit in the opening paragraphs of the Declaration.

The conclusion of the document asserts that the Americans had tried peaceably to resolve their differences with the mother country while remaining within the empire, and in a final paragraph contains the actual declaration that the erstwhile colonies were now independent states.

Whether the colonies became independent collectively or individually was a matter of debate for at least a hundred years. At the CONSTITUTIONAL CONVENTION OF 1787,

JAMES WILSON, and ALEXANDER HAMILTON advanced the former position, while LUTHER MARTIN maintained the latter position. At least until the Civil War, different THEORIES OF THE UNION arose based on differing interpretations of the act of declaring independence.

Considered as a tract for the times, as a manifesto for the Revolutionary cause, the Declaration marks an important step in American constitutional development. The resistance to British misrule in America had, at least since the French and Indian Wars, been based on an appeal to the British constitution. The Americans had charged that the imposition of taxes by a body in which they were not represented and the extension to them of domestic LEGISLATION by a Parliament to whose authority they had not consented violated the ancient traditions of British government. The constitution, that is, the arrangement of offices and powers within the government and the privileges of the subjects, had been overridden or altered by the British Parliament. Although the differences between the American provinces and the mother country were great, they were differences about, and capable of resolution within, the British constitutional framework. The liberties that the colonists had claimed were based on prescription.

When independence was declared, the British constitution became irrelevant. The liberties claimed in the Declaration are grounded in natural law; they are justified by reason, not by historical use. The American Revolution was, therefore, the first and most revolutionary of modern revolutions. Not the quantity of carnage but the quality of ideas distinguishes the true revolution. In the Declaration was recognized a HIGHER LAW to which every human law—constitution or statute—is answerable. The British constitution, as it then existed, was tried by the standards of that higher law and found guilty of tyranny. As the British constitution, so every constitution, including the American Constitution, may be tried; and on conviction the sentence is that the bonds of allegiance are dissolved.

Much of American constitutional history has revolved around the attempt to reconcile the nation's political practice with the teachings of the Declaration. The gravest problem in our constitutional history was SLAVERY. Although the Congress struck out Jefferson's condemnation of slavery as "cruel war against human nature," the founders clearly understood that slavery was incompatible with the principles of liberty and equality that they espoused.

Chief Justice ROGER B. TANEY, in DRED SCOTT V. SANDFORD (1857), tried to read the black man out of the Declaration. But this was a distortion of the history and the plain meaning of the document. Even JOHN C. CALHOUN had not stooped to this, choosing rather to denounce the Declaration than to pervert its meaning. The antithesis between the Declaration and the existence of chattel slavery was recognized by the slave power in Congress when, during the gag rule controversy, any petition referring to the Declaration of Independence was automatically treated as a petition against slavery and laid on the table.

The intimate connection between the Declaration of Independence (and therefore of antislavery) and the Constitution became the theme of the political career of ABRAHAM LINCOLN. When the slavery question divided the nation, Lincoln, with the voice of an Old Testament prophet, called for rededication to the principles of the Declaration. During Lincoln's presidency, the Civil War, begun as a challenge to the Union, was won as a struggle to vindicate the Declaration of Independence. It was fought to prove that a nation "dedicated to the proposition that all men are created equal" could endure.

The putative antagonism between America's two basic documents, invented by the slave power in the nineteenth century, was revived as a political theme during the Progressive movement. Authors like J. ALLEN SMITH and CHARLES A. BEARD contended that the Constitution's system of FEDERALISM, SEPARATION OF POWERS, CHECKS AND BALANCES, and bicameralism frustrated the unfettered will of the people allegedly set free by the Declaration. Smith and Beard posited a virtually bloodless coup d'état by wealthy conservatives—a "Thermidorian reaction" to the success of the democratic revolution. Thus constitutional forms were attacked as illegitimate, notwithstanding that they were intended to preserve the Declaration's regime of LIMITED GOVERNMENT.

The Beard-Smith thesis remained popular as long as the Constitution seemed to be a barrier to social reform and redistribution of wealth and income by the government. The later twentieth century, however, witnessed another change in the attitude of intellectuals toward the two documents. President FRANKLIN D. ROOSEVELT appointed a sufficient number of Supreme Court Justices to insure that the Court would ratify his policies as constitutional. Later, the WARREN COURT devised a host of new "constitutional" rights and remedies for criminal defendants, ethnic minorities, and political dissenters. The Constitution was transformed into a "living" document, that is, one almost infinitely malleable in the hands of enlightened judges. History, understood as progress, rather than nature thereafter dictated the ends of government. The Declaration of Independence, with its references to "the laws of nature and of nature's God," although revered as a symbol of American nationality, ceased to be regarded as the source of authoritative guidance for American politics.

The Constitution of the United States is sometimes pronounced, by scholars or politicians, to be neutral with respect to political principles. But the Constitution was not framed in a vacuum. It was devised as the Constitution of the nation founded by the Declaration of Independence. The Declaration prescribes the ends and limits of government, and proclaims the illegitimacy of any government that fails to serve those ends or observe those limits. The Constitution is thus ruled by the Declaration. The Constitution provides for the government of the regime created by the Declaration: the regime of equality and liberty.

DENNIS J. MAHONEY
(1986)

Bibliography

BECKER, CARL L. 1922 *The Declaration of Independence.* Cambridge, Mass.: Harvard University Press.
DIAMOND, MARTIN 1975 The Declaration and the Constitution: Liberty, Democracy and the Founders. *The Public Interest* 42:39–55.
HAWKE, DAVID 1964 *A Transaction of Free Men: The Birth and Course of the Declaration of Independence.* New York: Scribner's.
JAFFA, HARRY V. 1959 The Universal Meaning of the Declaration of Independence. Chap. 14 of *The Crisis of the House Divided.* New York: Doubleday.
WHITE, MORTON 1978 *The Philosophy of the American Revolution.* New York: Oxford University Press.

DECLARATION OF WAR

The Constitution gives Congress the power "to declare War . . ." (Article I, section 8, clause 11). There is no explicit provision for any other exercise by the United States of its sovereign power to make war, although the President is made "COMMANDER IN CHIEF of the Army and Navy of the United States . . ." (Article II, section 2). But the draftsmen were certainly familiar with the concept of undeclared war, usually with limited purposes and theaters of operation, such as the French and Indian War of 1754–1756 and the opening campaign of the Seven Years War between England and France, in which GEORGE WASHINGTON had fought as a lieutenant colonel. Indeed, ALEXANDER HAMILTON observed that "the ceremony of a formal denunciation [i.e., declaration] of war has of late fallen into disuse" (THE FEDERALIST #25). Whether the Framers intended to give Congress the paramount power to wage war against other sovereigns is a question that has ever since been debated but not formally resolved. The problem had not, of course, arisen under the ARTICLES OF CONFEDERATION, when all federal (or confederate) power was vested in the Continental Congress. The records of the CONSTITUTIONAL CONVENTION furnish no clear answer. The draft submitted by the Committee on Detail on August 6, 1787, gave Congress the power "to make war." When it was considered eleven days later, on motion by ELBRIDGE GERRY

and JAMES MADISON, "make" was changed to "declare." The brief debate gives no indication of any effect the change was intended to have on the allocation of war-making power between President and Congress. For what it is worth, some years later Hamilton expressed the view that making war was essentially an executive function, while Madison thought the power belonged primarily to Congress.

Whatever the Framers may have intended, the practice has clearly been in accord with the Hamiltonian view. The United States has fought only five declared wars (the War of 1812, the Mexican War, the Spanish War, WORLD WAR I, and WORLD WAR II), but the President has committed the armed forces to combat on more than 150 other occasions, from JOHN ADAMS's undeclared naval war with France in 1798–1799 to the KOREAN WAR and the VIETNAM WAR. (See also POLICE ACTION; STATE OF WAR.) The CIVIL WAR was, of course, undeclared, since a declaration would have constituted a recognition of Confederate SOVEREIGNTY, but it was treated as war for the purposes of international law. (See PRIZE CASES, 1863.) As a practical matter, whether a formal declaration of war adds much to the power of the President is doubtful, so long as Congress furnishes the necessary men and money. Thus, during the Vietnam War the lower federal courts held that Congress, by supplying troops and arms, made the President's actions constitutional; and the Supreme Court let their decisions stand. (See MASSACHUSETTS V. LAIRD.)

Congress has occasionally attempted to assert its primacy in war, but without much success. In 1896, when a group of congressmen proposed to declare war on Spain, GROVER CLEVELAND scotched the project by informing them that as Commander in Chief he had no intention of using the Army and Navy for any such purpose. The WAR POWERS RESOLUTION of 1973, enacted over President RICHARD M. NIXON's veto, provides in substance that before the President can commit the armed forces to actual or potential combat he must first "consult" with Congress and must withdraw the forces within ninety days unless Congress declares war or provides "specific authorization" for their continued employment.

Scholars disagree on the constitutionality of the War Powers Resolution. In any case, it seems unlikely to have much practical effect, as President GERALD R. FORD demonstrated in 1975 when he immediately, and with a minimum of "consultation," used the armed forces to rescue an American vessel, the *Mayaguez,* and its crew, who had been seized by the communist regime in Cambodia. History suggests that it will be politically very difficult for Congress to deny support when the troops are actually fighting. If there is any historical difference between wars declared by Congress and other wars, it seems to be that the former have usually been larger in scale and have had as their goal not some more or less limited objective, such as rescuing American citizens or defending an ally from attack, but the total defeat of the enemy.

JOSEPH W. BISHOP, JR.
(1986)

Bibliography

CRUDEN, JOHN C. 1975 The War-Making Process. *Military Law Review* 69:35–143.

LOFGREN, CHARLES A. 1972 War-Making Power under the Constitution: The Original Understanding. *Yale Law Journal* 81:672–702.

ROSTOW, EUGENE V. 1972 Great Cases Make Bad Laws: The War Powers Act. *Texas Law Review* 50:833–900.

DECLARATORY JUDGMENT

Until the beginning of the twentieth century, most American courts would entertain lawsuits only when plaintiffs sought redress for harm already suffered or imminently threatened. Except in certain real property actions, the plaintiff was not deemed harmed simply because uncertainty about his or her legal rights made potentially beneficial conduct too risky to undertake. For example, if a manufacturer were uncertain about whether a new product would infringe another's patent, or a would-be demonstrator were uncertain whether the planned demonstration was protected under the FIRST AMENDMENT, the only choices were to refrain from acting or to proceed and wait to be sued or prosecuted.

The declaratory judgment is a judicial remedy that allows the uncertain individual instead to file suit, asking a court to determine the legal rights in question. It reflects the view, long accepted in land title law, that paralysis due to uncertainty is real harm that courts should alleviate.

Over the first decades of the twentieth century, the states and the federal government adopted this remedy by statute. Declaratory judgments came into use not only to eliminate uncertainty but also to provide a similar but less coercive remedy to individuals eligible for injunctive relief.

Under Article III, the life-tenured federal judiciary may not give ADVISORY OPINIONS but may hear only real disputes between adverse, concretely interested parties. Because declaratory judgments are typically sought in advance of liability-causing conduct, there were early doubts that declaratory judgment actions would satisfy this requirement, known as RIPENESS. To allay this concern, the drafters of the federal declaratory judgment statute limited the remedy to "case[s] of actual controversy within [the courts'] JURISDICTION."

The Supreme Court held in *Perez v. Ledesma* (1971) that, for reasons of comity, a person being prosecuted in a state court for violation of a state criminal law may not seek a declaratory judgment in a federal court that the law is unconstitutional. Prior to a state prosecution, however, an individual may obtain a federal declaration of constitutional rights. That individual may have to flirt so dangerously with actual prosecution in order to satisfy the ripeness requirement, however, that the declaratory judgment may not be able to perform its salutary function of encouraging constitutionally protected conduct.

The plaintiff in a declaratory judgment action is frequently the person who would be a defendant in a more traditional lawsuit, and the elements of a complaint for declaratory relief often differ from those of a more traditional complaint. In applying legal doctrines that antedated the declaratory remedy to this new form of litigation, courts sometimes require that the suit be transposed to what it would have been had the declaratory remedy not existed. Thus, in determining whether the right to TRIAL BY JURY exists in a suit for a declaratory judgment, the courts must ascertain whether the claim could have been filed as an action at COMMON LAW had the declaratory judgment not been invented. Similarly, in determining whether a suit arises under federal law within the meaning of the FEDERAL QUESTION statute, the courts must ascertain whether the federal element would have appeared in the plaintiff's *prima facie* case had the suit been brought for a conventional remedy. Unfortunately, there is not always only one conventional alternative to a given declaratory judgment action, and this cumbersome transposition process has been difficult to administer.

CAROLE E. GOLDBERG-AMBROSE
(1986)

Bibliography

NOTE 1949 Developments in the Law: Declaratory Judgments, 1941–1949. *Harvard Law Review* 62:787–885.

DECONSTRUCTION

The topic of deconstruction and the Constitution arises chiefly because of work done since 1978 by the left-oriented scholars of the Conference on CRITICAL LEGAL STUDIES, who have applied modern continental critical theory, including literary theory, to Anglo-American law. The issues involved also descend from the rise of PRAGMATISM in American philosophy in the late nineteenth century and its influence on American JURISPRUDENCE via the skepticism of OLIVER WENDELL HOLMES, JR., and the later adherents of LEGAL REALISM. This dual ancestry is not coincidental. Deconstruction was popularized by the

French critical philosopher Jacques Derrida, especially in his 1974 book *Of Grammatology*. Though most influenced by Friedrich Nietzsche, Derrida also drew on a forebear of American pragmatism, Charles Peirce.

Like many pragmatists, deconstructionists take a radical stance toward the epistemological doubts that have occupied modern philosophy since Descartes. In their view, although the various ways in which human minds represent their experiences to themselves (from organic sensations to oral languages, to conventional writing) may bear some complex relationship to an external physical reality, they never provide a direct, unmediated grasp of it. The visual sensation of seeing the color "red," the sounds of the English adjective "red," and the written word "red" may somehow signify to us something that is really out there, but we cannot claim that our physical sensation or our oral or written terms are full or necessary representations of it. The something might cause different physical sensations in different individuals or sensory apparatuses, and certainly it can be signified by different sounds or written marks. All this is uncontroversial in most modern epistemologies.

What deconstructionists distinctively stress is that our sense of the meaning of our particular representations, our regard of those representations as signs for external somethings, is heavily dependent on the relationship of the representations or signs to some existing system of representations or signs. Obviously, the meaning readers of written English assign to the written marks "red" requires familiarity with the system of signs that is written English. The meaning speakers of English assign to the spoken sounds of "red" requires knowledge of English as a system of sound signs. Even the visual sensation we call "red" has its meaning for us only by reference to other sensations and to a system of terms that classifies and labels those sensations for us, a system that partly constitutes our knowledge of colors. The sensation, too, is for us a sign that gains much of its sense from a system of signs.

Deconstructionists therefore see all human experience as heavily defined and constructed by vast webs of signs that get their meaning more clearly from their relationship to other signs than from reality. We still presume that some such reality exists, that human minds have formed systems of signs to give reality a measure of order and meaning, and that reality can somehow prompt sensations in us that may persuade us to revise the signs we use to depict it. But deconstructionists stress that our choice of particular signs to represent reality is always in some measure arbitrary, influenced more by the preexisting set of signs available to us than any self-evident demands of external reality. Hence, we cannot have much confidence that any set of signs is an accurate representation of reality. All such systems are but partial interpretations, discerni-

bly built out of other partial interpretations that at best show aspects of the world, and those through a glass darkly.

Yet we persist in taking our interpretations, our systems of signs, to be something more. We present them to ourselves (or they present themselves to us) as reliable windows or maps revealing an external reality of matter andor reason that can be rendered present to our minds and senses. Like Nietzsche and the pragmatists, deconstructionists urge us to abandon this old dualistic "metaphysics of presence," in which we try to pierce through our mental limitations to grasp fully an external truth beyond. Instead, we should admit that our world of experience is *always* composed largely of questionable interpretations, partial perspectives, and contingent systems of signs. We should therefore turn inquiry away from the "reality" for which signs allegedly stand, toward a greater understanding of the components, possibilities, and limitations of systems of signs. The world will then be seen as sets of signs or texts, melding philosophy and other modes of inquiry into literary theory.

Deconstruction is one means toward a better understanding of these texts. One deconstructs something—a novel, a treatise, a law, a political institution—by viewing it as a system of signs and unraveling it to reveal its reliance on preexisting systems of signs to make it meaningful; its consequent vulnerability to multiple meanings, depending on which of the systems of signs it incorporates, is stressed, along with its embodiment of those systems' biases and of the contradictions within them and among them, and thus its inevitable incompleteness and incoherencies. To be sure, one may also find insights that seem worth preserving. But ultimately one can always show any text to be another partial, ambiguous system of signs constructed out of other such systems.

Unlike the early scientific resolutive-compositive method of inquiry, moreover, the point of deconstruction is not to give us a fuller understanding of how the object of analysis functions while otherwise leaving it intact after we mentally reconstruct it. Deconstruction always invalidates much of what a text initially appeared to do or say, altering our sense of it. We may then strive to construct new accounts of the text's themes that are more comprehensive because they encompass what we have learned; but those accounts will ultimately remain partial interpretations.

The appeal of all this for critical scholars in Anglo-American law should be clear. National legal systems can plausibly be viewed as systems of signs for which people make strong claims. They are said to have considerable internal coherence and to be largely accurate representations of external social and political worlds and of appropriate moral principles. Those claims seem integral to a legal system's very legitimacy. But, via deconstruction, one can often show that many legal terms derive from preexisting discourses identified with particular ruling groups and that they express those groups' interests more clearly than they express any objective moral principles. Legal language can also be shown to be subject to multiple inconsistent interpretations, depending on which elements are stressed. Thus, the law may seem indeterminate or incoherent, gaining definition only from those who wield enough power to make their interpretations stick.

Critical legal scholars have deconstructed the doctrines of judicial and ADMINISTRATIVE LAW in numerous areas of American law, such as contracts, property, and criminal law, in just these ways. At times, however, they have moved too quickly to two types of conclusions that represent shallow readings of the implications of deconstruction. Some align deconstruction with Marxism, attempting to show that legal doctrines at bottom express capitalist class interests rooted in material relations of production. Such readings have some force, but in deconstructionist terms they do not go far enough unless they concede that the various Marxisms are but further systems of signs and that Marxist claims to have grasped the truth of external material reality are highly vulnerable to deconstructionist debunking. Other critical legal scholars write as if the American legal system is peculiarly guilty of insuperable internal contradictions and ambiguities, implying that a system ordered on different principles would overcome these problems. But again deconstruction suggests that although there are more or less encompassing interpretations, all systems of signs will always be vulnerable to demonstrations of their inadequacy.

These points can be exemplified by showing how we might begin deconstructing the Constitution. Its PREAMBLE says that "We the People of the United States" are ordaining and establishing the document. Those words seem to assume a traditional understanding of flesh-and-blood persons consciously using words as authoritative signs, accurately representing themselves and their thoughts and giving new order to their lives.

But deconstructing interpreters can challenge that picture in all the ways just suggested. "We the People" is, after all, plainly a kind of metaphor: no reader really thinks all the people of the United States directly established the Constitution. Interpreters can easily show, moreover, that the text's terms, derived largely from the discourse of American elites, treat many as virtually invisible nonpeople (e.g., indentured servants, women, African Americans, Native Americans, all of whom the document relegates to lesser categories, explicitly or implicitly). Thus, deconstruction might first suggest that the Constitution is a misleading, biased creation of elites alone, as leftist critics assert.

Next, one can deconstruct the Constitution to display internal dissonances. For instance, in contrast to the Preamble, the last article of the original Constitution (Article VII) indicates that the Constitution must be ratified by nine state conventions. Here the Constitution seems established more by a supermajority of the states, or of these state conventions, than by "We the People." Wrestling with whether the text finally describes itself as a product of the national populace or the states has long led analysts to conclude that it is opaque or inconsistent, incapable of constituting a government without added meaning supplied by its interpreters. If so, it is less a constitution than it purports to be.

Deconstruction of "We the People" can be taken still deeper yet. We might question how much of its meaning derives from reference to *any* flesh-and-blood inhabitants of the United States, then or now, be they a national populace, ruling elites, or state citizens. For some readers, the opening words actually summon up thoughts of Founding Fathers who are plainly not all "the People," but a few, and whose identities are provided much more by enduring national myths than any perceptions of the Founders' physical reality. Insofar as readers do think of "the People," moreover, they are likely to imagine the type of entity portrayed in certain traditions of political writing and novels—a heroic demos of anti-aristocratic republicans, unified by a general will and acting as a collective moral agent capable of political transformations. That may be a stirring image, but it is one expressing knowledge of certain systems of signs, not of the particular persons living in the United States in 1787–1789.

The power of those political traditions in shaping our reading of the Constitution suggests in turn that these systems of signs are actually providing much of the Constitution's meaning that the text purports to derive from "the People." If so, the most fundamental political claim of the Constitution, the claim that it is the creation of responsible human agents who are guiding their own collective destiny, may appear to be a myth. The Constitution now seems much more a set of signs drawn from other systems of signs that constituted the consciousness of "We the People" than a law created by "We the People." In short, deconstruction of "We the People" can lead us to think of political agency in a different way, a subjectless way that is sharply opposed to what the text initially seemed to suggest.

There is something to be learned from each of these three deconstructionist readings of the Constitution, culminating in this challenge to meaningful human agency itself. Yet we should also recall that the partiality of every existing interpretation does not by itself show that they are all simply false. The existence of contradictions in a text or a body of laws does not alone prove that its essential themes are indefensible. And the dependence of our minds on the many systems of signs that order our worlds of experience does not prove that we cannot play a significant role in coming to understand those worlds somewhat better and in reordering them beneficially.

Like the "cynical acid" concerning the determinacy of legal rules and factual judgments that the legal realists earlier provided, deconstruction simply renders certain particular claims of these sorts less credible. It does not prevent us, after encompassing the insights it provides us, from going on to construct systems of ideas and institutions that seem more satisfactory than their predecessors, albeit still imperfect. Nor does it tell us much about how such constructive efforts should proceed. Thus, deconstruction itself represents but a partial contribution to understanding the Constitution and judging what it can and should mean, how and whether it can and should work, today and in the future.

ROGERS M. SMITH
(1992)

(SEE ALSO: *Political Philosophy of the Constitution.*)

Bibliography

DERRIDA, JACQUES 1974 *Of Grammatology,* trans. Gayatri Spivak. Baltimore: Johns Hopkins University Press.

KELMAN, MARK 1987 *A Guide to Critical Legal Studies.* Cambridge, Mass.: Harvard University Press.

NIETZSCHE, FRIEDRICH 1966 *Beyond Good and Evil: Prelude to a Philosophy of the Future,* ed. Walter Kaufmann. New York: Random House.

DE FACTO/DE JURE

De facto and de jure are old COMMON LAW terms meaning, respectively, "in fact" and "in law." In older usage, de facto carried at least a hint of reference to illegitimacy or illegality. Thus, a usurper might be called a de facto king, or a corporation whose formation was irregular might be called a de facto corporation. As these examples suggest, the connotation often was that for some legal purposes the person or institution would be treated *as if* there were no irregularity. De jure, on the other hand, carried a suggestion of lawfulness or rightfulness.

In modern constitutional law, these terms have come to be used almost exclusively in the context of racial SEGREGATION, and particularly segregation in the public schools. In this context the connotations concerning lawfulness are reversed. De jure segregation refers to the separation of pupils by race resulting from deliberate action by state officials, such as the legislature or the school board. De facto segregation refers to the racial separation of pupils by other causes, and particularly through the adoption of the "neighborhood school" policy in a community characterized by residential separation of the races. The Supreme Court has held that only de jure segregation violates the Constitution. (See COLUMBUS BOARD OF EDUCATION V. PENICK; DAYTON BOARD OF EDUCATION V. BRINKMAN.)

There is some artificiality in this distinction. When a school board's members are aware of racial patterns in residential neighborhoods, and they draw school attendance district lines in ways that do not minimize the racial separation of pupils, it would not do violence to the language to call the results of their action de jure segregation. Yet the courts tend not to "find" the "fact" of de jure segregation in this circumstance.

On the other hand, deliberately segregative actions of the school board in the rather distant past may be held to constitute de jure segregation, so that the school board remains under a continuing obligation to dismantle a "dual" (segregated) system by taking affirmative remedial action, such as the busing of children. The *Columbus* and *Dayton* cases that are cited above exemplify this line of reasoning.

KENNETH L. KARST
(1986)

(SEE ALSO: *Keyes v. School District No. 1; School Busing; Swann v. Charlotte-Mechlenburg Board of Education.*)

Bibliography

SEDLER, ROBERT ALAN 1979–1980 The Constitution and School Desegregation: An Inquiry into the Nature of the Substantive Right. *Kentucky Law Journal* 68:879–969.

DEFAMATION

See: Libel and the First Amendment

DEFUNIS v. ODEGAARD
416 U.S. 312 (1974)

DeFunis challenged the constitutionality of the University of Washington law school's use of racial preferences in admitting students. The case was expected to be a decisive test for AFFIRMATIVE ACTION programs in higher education. Instead, by a 5–4 vote, the Supreme Court held that the case was moot, because the law school would graduate DeFunis at the end of the current term, however the case might be decided. Cynics, remembering how the Court had recently dealt with the argument of MOOTNESS in ROE V. WADE (1973), suggested that the majority had been readier to reach the merits of the ABORTION issue in *Roe* than it was to face the problem presented by *DeFunis.*

Justice WILLIAM O. DOUGLAS, who thought the case was not moot, wrote an opinion on the merits. He concluded that the law school had denied DeFunis, a nonminority applicant, the EQUAL PROTECTION OF THE LAWS by awarding a preference solely on the basis of race. Justice Douglas commented that minority applicants should be evaluated specially to avoid cultural bias in admissions, but he did not explain how a school could evaluate minority applicants separately without devising a scale to measure them against other applicants. Such a scale would necessarily involve setting goals for minority representation. *DeFunis* was Justice Douglas's last chance to speak to these issues, which returned to the Court in REGENTS OF UNIVERSITY OF CALIFORNIA V. BAKKE (1978), after his retirement.

KENNETH L. KARST
(1986)

DE JONGE v. OREGON
299 U.S. 353 (1937)

The Oregon Criminal Syndicalism Law was declared unconstitutional as applied to a person who conducted a meeting of the Communist party at which "neither CRIMINAL SYNDICALISM nor any unlawful conduct was taught or advocated." The Supreme Court held that peaceful speech at a peaceful, open meeting could not be punished constitutionally simply because of party sponsorship even if it were assumed that the party advocated violent overthrow of government. "Peaceable assembly for lawful discussion," declared Chief Justice CHARLES EVANS HUGHES for an 8–0 Court, "cannot be made a crime."

This is one of the early cases "incorporating" the FREEDOM OF SPEECH and FREEDOM OF ASSEMBLY provisions of the FIRST AMENDMENT into the DUE PROCESS clause of the Fourteenth Amendment, thus making them binding on the states. Unlike many other speech cases of the 1920s and 1930s, *De Jonge* rests firmly on freedom of speech rather than on collateral due process grounds such as VAGUENESS. It also foreshadows later, not altogether successful, attempts by the Court to distinguish between those Communist party members and activities devoted to constitutionally protected advocacy and those implicated in incitement to revolutionary violence.

MARTIN SHAPIRO
(1986)

DELEGATION OF POWER

Early in American constitutional history the Supreme Court announced a rule that Congress could not delegate its power to the President or others. Yet the practical demands of an increasingly complex governmental environment have forced Congress to delegate, often quite broadly. The Court has rationalized all but a few delegations without abandoning the rule of nondelegation. This has been accomplished through successively more permissive formulations of the rule. Though the rule is in a state of desuetude, some revival is possible in the aftermath of the Court's invalidation of a LEGISLATIVE VETO in IMMIGRATION AND NATURALIZATION SERVICE V. CHADHA (1983).

A few commentators call the rule against delegations a judge-made doctrine lacking genuine constitutional status. This suggests the untenable proposition that genuine rules of constitutional law must be explicit in the constitutional document. Building on a COMMON LAW maxim against redelegation of delegated authority and on JOHN LOCKE's observation that only the sovereign people can determine the legitimate location of legislative authority, most commentators have found nondelegation implicit in the SEPARATION OF POWERS and in concepts of representative government and DUE PROCESS OF LAW. The status of the rule thus secured, debate has concentrated on exactly what it prohibits.

As if the rule prohibited all delegations, nineteenth-century judges tried to reconcile it with the practical needs of government by denying that delegations in fact were delegations in law. In *The Brig Aurora* (1813) the Supreme Court held that Congress had not breached the rule by empowering the President to make factual finding on which the application of a previously declared congressional policy—an embargo—was contingent. In *Wayman v. Southard* (1825) the Court permitted a delegation to federal judges for "filling up the details" of part of the Federal Process Act of 1792. Though the rules announced in these cases were modest when stated in the abstract, the delegations themselves were the objects of acrimonious political conflict. By the early 1900s, power to declare facts and fill up details had become the foundation for the delegation of such discretionary authority to the President and administrative agencies as power to decide which grades of tea to exclude from import, to make rules regulating grazing on lands in national forests, and even to vary tariffs on imported goods.

In J. W. HAMPTON & COMPANY V. UNITED STATES (1928) the Court formulated a more realistic delegation doctrine when it acknowledged that transfers of discretionary authority were essential to the effectiveness of Congress's will in modern conditions. The new rule was that congressional delegation is permissible if governed by adequate "legislative standards," a term that now includes statutory specifications of facts to be declared, preambulatory statements of legislative purpose, and even judicial imputations of legislative purpose inferred from legislative and administrative history.

The Court has rarely taken the standards requirement

seriously. Illustrative of a pattern that prevails to the present, *Federal Radio Commission v. Nelson Brothers* (1933) found adequate guidance for issuing radio station licenses in what Congress called the "public convenience, interest, and necessity." This pattern was interrupted when the Court unexpectedly used the delegation doctrine against the NATIONAL INDUSTRIAL RECOVERY ACT (1933) in PANAMA REFINING COMPANY V. RYAN (1935) and SCHECHTER POULTRY CORPORATION V. UNITED STATES (1935). But the spirit of these decisions was not to survive, and by the middle of World War II the Court had returned to using the delegation doctrine more for rationalizing than for limiting transfers of congressional power.

As if delegations were not broad enough, the Court in *United States v. Mazurie* (1975) suggested an even more permissive approach. UNITED STATES V. CURTISS-WRIGHT EXPORT CORPORATION (1936) had seemed to hold that because the President had independent powers in the field of FOREIGN AFFAIRS, the standards requirement for congressional delegations to the President could be relaxed in that area. At a time when *Panama* and *Schechter* had recently limited the scope of delegated power, *Curtiss-Wright* was a reasonable move toward flexibility in foreign affairs. But *Curtiss-Wright* featured an unorthodox theory of extraconstitutional or inherent governmental power, and the need for a special approach to foreign affairs delegations disappeared as the Court returned to its old permissiveness toward delegations generally. During the VIETNAM WAR, however, the nondelegation doctrine was raised in opposition to American policy, and, although the Court successfully avoided the issue, government lawyers invoked *CurtissWright* before congressional committees. One of these lawyers was WILLIAM H. REHNQUIST, who later led the Court to its first reaffirmation of *Curtiss-Wright's* delegation doctrine in *Mazurie*, a relatively noncontroversial case involving a delegation to the tribal council of an American Indian tribe over liquor sales on a reservation. The tribe's council, said Justice Rehnquist, had "independent authority over tribal life," just as the President had over foreign affairs, and *Curtiss-Wright* was cited for a new rule that the standards requirement is "less stringent in cases where the entity exercising the delegated authority itself possesses independent authority over the subject matter." In light of what "less stringent" can mean today, *Mazurie* has a potential for rationalizing virtual abdications of congressional responsibility, not only to the President but to the states, whose legal claims to "independent authority" are stronger than that of Indian tribal councils.

Since the 1930s and with accelerated frequency after the Vietnam War, Congress used the legislative veto to recapture power lost through broad delegations. To the extent—perhaps modest—that regulatory and political conditions permit, Congress may choose to delegate more

narrowly now that the legislative veto is unavailable. And if the Court really has renewed its commitment to the separation of powers, it may honor the standards requirement with something more than mere lip service.

SOTIRIOS A. BARBER
(1986)

Bibliography

BARBER, SOTIRIOS A. 1975 *The Constitution and the Delegation of Congressional Power.* Chicago: University of Chicago Press.

DAVIS, KENNETH C. 1958 *Administrative Law Treatise.* St. Paul, Minn.: West Publishing Co.

DELEGATION OF POWER
(Update)

The delegation doctrine concerns Congress's power to give or delegate the rulemaking authority it has to the executive or judicial branches. In most of the cases involving the doctrine, litigants have challenged congressional delegation of rulemaking authority to ADMINISTRATIVE AGENCIES.

By the early 1980s the Supreme Court seemed to have a well-established position on the scope of Congress's power to delegate its rulemaking power. The Court held, as a matter of formal doctrine, that Congress could not delegate its power "to legislate," for such a delegation would violate the Constitution's command that "all legislative Powers . . . shall be vested in a Congress." But the Court also held that Congress could seek "assistance" from the other branches in exercising its LEGISLATIVE POWER and therefore could give the other branches authority to enact rules to "fill in" the details of congressional policy. Yet, although the formal doctrine purported to set some judicially enforceable limits on congressional delegations, the Court's application of the doctrine imposed virtually no limits on Congress's power to delegate rulemaking authority.

The Court's decisions held that to be constitutional a delegation must contain a congressionally adopted policy or set of "intelligible principles" to guide and confine the other branch in its rulemaking activity. The Court stated that such intelligible principles were necessary to ensure that the other branch merely implemented or filled in the details of policy that Congress had adopted. It also held that the standards were necessary to give the courts a means of measuring whether the other branch had complied with the scope of Congress's delegation and thus to measure whether the other branch had acted in conformity with the "will of Congress."

This delegation doctrine was virtually without force. With two exceptions in the 1930s, the Court found that all of Congress's delegations contained sufficient intelligible principles. Many of the approved principles—such as "consistent with public convenience, interest and necessity" and "just and reasonable"—were so broad and vague that they gave the other branch seemingly unconfined discretion in exercising its rulemaking authority.

The Court's lenient, accommodating approach in applying the "intelligible principles test" led many commentators to charge that the Court paid mere lip service to the test and, as a result, failed to enforce a meaningful judicial limitation on Congress's delegations. Indeed, the Court's approach seemed to reflect a judicial judgment that congressional delegation of rulemaking authority is inevitable and desirable and that the difficulties of creating more restrictive constitutional rules or principles were greater than the benefits of doing so.

Then, in 1983, the Supreme Court did invalidate a congressional delegation of its decision-making power, and some thought that the Court might be signaling a stricter approach to delegation challenges. In IMMIGRATION AND NATURALIZATION SERVICE V. CHADHA (1983) the Court held that the one-house LEGISLATIVE VETO was unconstitutional. For over fifty years, some legislation delegating congressional authority to the executive branch had provided that specified executive action could be annulled by one house of Congress. In *Chadha*, for example, Congress delegated power to the ATTORNEY GENERAL to allow ALIENS to remain in the country, even though their visas had expired. The legislation delegating this power provided that either house of Congress could, nonetheless, overturn the attorney general's determination in a particular case by adopting a resolution. The attorney general allowed Chadha to stay after his visa expired, but the HOUSE OF REPRESENTATIVES passed a resolution ordering him to leave. Accepting that Congress has the power to set the terms for aliens to remain in the country, the Court ruled that setting or revising those terms was a legislative act and that Congress could exercise its legislative power only through legislation, which requires action by both houses and presentation to the President. Congress could not vest its legislative power in one of its own houses.

The *Chadha* majority did not consider the one-house veto as a delegation issue. But as Justice BYRON R. WHITE pointed out in dissent, *Chadha* in effect imposed a significantly more stringent limitation on Congress's power to delegate its authority than the Court had imposed in the preceding fifty years. Some thought that the Court's more stringent approach would be limited to congressional delegations to parts of Congress. Others speculated that *Chadha* might signal the Court's willingness to scrutinize all the delegations more closely, as some members of the Court, most notably Chief Justice WILLIAM H. REHNQUIST, have sometimes urged.

The Court has recently indicated that speculation about the broader implications of *Chadha* probably is not warranted. In two significant cases during the 1988 term, the Court reaffirmed its use of the intelligible principles test and emphasized its long tradition of upholding delegations in light of the need for flexibility in formulating and enforcing federal policy. In MISTRETTA V. UNITED STATES (1989), the Court upheld Congress's delegation of power to the Sentencing Commission to promulgate a new system of determinate sentences for federal crimes. And in *Skinner v. Mid-America Pipeline* (1989), the Court sustained Congress's delegation of power to the secretary of transportation to establish and collect pipeline-safety user fees. The pipeline case seems particularly significant because in an earlier decision the Court had seemed to suggest that it might employ greater scrutiny in testing the constitutionality of Congress's delegation of its power to tax. *Skinner* belies that suggestion.

The Court's approach in delegation cases can be contrasted with its approach in cases charging that Congress has appropriated the powers of another branch. In those cases, the Court is far less deferential. For example, in BOWSHER V. SYNAR (1986) the Court held that Congress acted beyond its authority in attempting to give "executive" power to the comptroller general, who is responsible to Congress, not the executive branch. The difference in judicial scrutiny may reflect a conclusion that JUDICIAL POWER need not be exercised to prevent one branch from giving away some of its powers but should be exercised to prevent one branch from usurping the powers of another. A branch can protect against relinquishing its own power simply by refusing to delegate; it must rely on the courts to prevent another branch from invading its domain.

Moreover, although the Court rarely invalidates congressional delegation of its rulemaking authority on constitutional grounds, the Court does require that such delegations be clearly made. Such a requirement protects against congressionally unauthorized rulemaking by the other branches. For example, in *National Cable Television Association v. United States* (1974), the Court held that the Federal Communications Commission overstepped its delegated authority in seeking to cover its administrative costs through user fees, noting that such fees could be viewed as taxes and that congressional delegations of its revenue-raising power should be "narrowly construed." As the *Skinner* case shows, Congress can delegate the power to collect revenue when it chooses to do so, but the Court will require a clear statement that such delegation is intended, lest the other branches intrude without permission into the congressional domain.

SCOTT H. BICE
(1992)

Bibliography

ARANSON, PETER H. et al. 1982 A Theory of Legislative Delegation. *Cornell Law Review* 68:1–67.

SYMPOSIUM 1987 The Uneasy Constitutional Status of the Administrative Agencies: Part 1, Delegation of Powers to Administrative Agencies. *American University Law Review* 36: 295–442.

DELIBERATE SPEED

See: All Deliberate Speed

DELIBERATIVE DEMOCRACY

Deliberative democracy aspires to combine two fundamental values in the design of political institutions— political equality and deliberation. The idea is to combine the equal consideration of everyone's views (political equality) with conditions that facilitate those views' being formed on the basis of good information, good faith discussion, and a balanced account of competing arguments (deliberation). Some theorists have held that the American Constitution has, from the beginning, been an attempt to create the social conditions where deliberative democracy might be possible, at least among representatives who speak for, or act for, the people.

JAMES MADISON, most notably, was committed to the "republican principle" (which entailed political equality) as well as to a scheme of government that would "refine the popular appointments by successive filtrations," as he said at the CONSTITUTIONAL CONVENTION OF 1787. The aspiration for deliberative democracy was famously expressed by Madison in FEDERALIST No. 10, where he said representatives "refine and enlarge the public views by passing them through a chosen body of citizens." ALEXANDER HAMILTON added, in *Federalist* No. 71, "The republican principle demands that the deliberate sense of the community should govern . . . but it does not require an unqualified complaisance to every sudden breeze of passion, or to every transient impulse which the people may receive from the arts of men, who flatter their prejudices to betray their interests." It is representatives who must "withstand the temporary delusion" to "give time and opportunity for more cool and sedate reflection." The *Federalist* distinguishes deliberative public opinion, filtered through representatives considering the public interest on the basis of cool and sedate reflection, from the more direct expressions of the public will that can be twisted by vicious arts of campaigning and persuasion. Directly consulting the people can be dangerous because the people may be motivated by passions or interests to form factions adverse to the rights of others or to the general interest. Such factions are not motivated by deliberative public opinion, the Federalists believed. Indeed deliberation might well have prevented the evils of more DIRECT DEMOCRACY as experienced by the ancient Athenians. Madison speculates in *Federalist* No. 63 that a representative and deliberative body like the U.S. SENATE might have protected the Athenians from "decreeing to the same citizens the hemlock on one day and statues on the next." It was, after all, the Athenians who killed Socrates.

The Federalist position was that deliberative democracy could be practiced only in small representative bodies that preserved some independence from the public. No matter what the character of the participants, too large a body would make deliberative democracy impossible. "Had every Athenian citizen been a Socrates, every Athenian Assembly would still have been a mob," Madison asserts in *Federalist* No. 55. Madison also resisted attempts to include a "right of instruction" in the BILL OF RIGHTS, a right that would have stripped legislators of decisionmaking autonomy. Similarly, the Federalists opposed annual or even very frequent ELECTIONS in order to give legislators flexibility to deliberate in the public interest.

The ANTI-FEDERALISTS opposed the "filter" theory of REPRESENTATION because they thought that only the more educated and privileged would get to do the representing or filtering for everyone else. In such elite bodies, ordinary citizens such as simple farmers would not be included. The Anti-Federalists advocated a very different theory of representation, one modeled on a different metaphor, the "mirror." As Melancton Smith argued, in opposing the Constitution at the New York ratification convention, representatives "should be a true picture of the people, possess a knowledge of their circumstances and their wants, sympathize in all their distresses, and be disposed to seek their true interests." Anti-Federalists sought frequent elections, TERM LIMITS, and any measures that would increase the closeness of resemblance between representatives and those they represented. In Rhode Island, the Anti-Federalists even held a REFERENDUM on the Constitution. Tiny Rhode Island was the only state to submit the Constitution to direct vote of the people. The Federalists, thinking such a method inappropriate and sensing probable defeat, boycotted the referendum and the Constitution was voted down. The Federalists argued that the only way to consult "the people in their assembled collective capacity" would be to gather representatives who "could reason, confer and convince each other." Only through a small representative body, such as the state conventions prescribed for approving the Constitution, could a deliberative decision be taken. The Anti-Federalist strategy of consulting the public without a requirement of organized deliberation (although the Anti-Federalists did conduct their referendum through votes of town meetings) represented the first salvo in a long war of competing conceptions of democracy. In the long run, the Federalist emphasis on deliberation and discussion may well have lost out to a form of democracy, embodied in referendums and INITIATIVES, and in other forms of direct consultation that achieve political equality—regardless of whether or not it is also accompanied by deliberation.

In the more than two centuries since the founding of the Republic, many changes, both formal and informal, in the American political system have served to promote political equality through more direct public consultation, but at the cost of deliberation. Consider what has happened to the ELECTORAL COLLEGE, the election of senators, the presidential selection system, the development and transformation of the national POLITICAL PARTY conventions, the rise of referenda (particularly in the Western states), and the development of public opinion polling. People vote directly and their votes are counted equally. Many aspects of Madisonian "filtration" have disappeared in a system that has taken on increasing elements of what might be called "plebescitary" democracy (embodied in referenda, primaries, and the influence of polls).

The Electoral College was originally intended to be a deliberative body, meeting state by state, that would choose the most qualified person. Now if members of the Electoral College exercise independent judgment, they are condemned as "faithless electors" and may be subject to challenge in the courts. Senators are elected directly since the SEVENTEENTH AMENDMENT (which came into effect in 1913). Primaries and referenda bring to the people decisions that were previously made by political elites—party leaders in the case of nominations and legislators in the case of laws. Public opinion polls bring substantive issues directly to the public (in representative samples) without any opportunity for "filtering" or deliberation.

Yet this movement to more direct consultation has come at a cost—a loss in the institutional structures that provide incentives for deliberation. Much SOCIAL SCIENCE RESEARCH has established that ordinary citizens suffer from "rational ignorance" (to use Anthony Downs's famous phrase). Each individual voter or citizen can see that his or her individual vote or opinion will not make much difference to policy outcomes, and so there is little reason to make the effort to become more informed. The result is a consistently low level of knowledge in the American electorate about politics and policy. Hence, the pursuit of political equality through increasingly direct methods of public consultation has produced a loss in political information, informed choice, and deliberation.

Some theorists have held that the Framers of the Constitution foresaw this problem from the beginning and, in the words of Yale Law School Professor Bruce Ackerman, developed a "dualist theory" of democracy. Most of the time the public is inattentive and uninformed, just as social science has established. Ackerman calls the resulting condition "normal politics." However, every once in a while, the Republic is seized by an issue or a crisis and there are sustained periods of "mobilized deliberation,"

which Ackerman calls "constitutional moments." Thus far, there have been at least three: the founding of the Republic, RECONSTRUCTION, and the NEW DEAL. In each case, deliberative democracy is practiced for a period long enough for fundamental principles to be seriously debated and established. The result is the possibility of informal constitutional change—informal because it takes place outside the confines of the formal amendment process specified in Article V.

The "constitutional moment" combines political equality and deliberation—for a "moment" or brief period of time. There are other efforts to realize both principles, at least for informal processes of public consultation that might advise policymakers and improve the public dialogue. "Deliberative Opinion Polling" selects random samples of the public and brings them together for several days of deliberation. The result is an explicit attempt to combine the two forms of representation at odds in the founding of the Republic: the filter and the mirror, the process of deliberation, and a small microcosm that is a picture of the whole. Through scientific random sampling a more representative group can be created than anything envisioned by the Anti-Federalists. And through sustained deliberation, the public's views can, in a sense, be refined and enlarged. All of this is to say that the quest to realize "deliberative democracy" continues in policymaking, the study of public opinion, and CONSTITUTIONAL INTERPRETATION.

JAMES S. FISHKIN
(2000)

(SEE ALSO: *Amending Process; Amendment Process (Outside Article V); Constitutional Dualism.*)

Bibliography

ACKERMAN, BRUCE A. 1991 *We the People: Foundations.* Cambridge, Mass.: Harvard University Press.

—— 1998 *We the People: Transformations.* Cambridge, Mass.: Harvard University Press.

BESSETTE, JOSEPH M. 1994 *The Mild Voice of Reason: Deliberative Democracy and the American National Government.* Chicago: University of Chicago Press.

DOWNS, ANTHONY 1956 *An Economic Theory of Democracy.* New York: Harper and Row.

FISHKIN, JAMES S. 1991 *Democracy and Deliberation: New Directions for Democratic Reform.* New Haven, Conn.: Yale University Press.

—— 1995 *The Voice of the People: Public Opinion and Democracy.* New Haven, Conn.: Yale University Press.

KRAMNICK, ISAAC 1988 The "Great National Discussion": The Discourse of Politics in 1787. *William and Mary Quarterly* 45:3–31.

MADISON, JAMES; HAMILTON, ALEXANDER; and JAY, JOHN 1987 *The Federalist Papers* (originally published 1788). New York: Penguin Books.

RAKOVE, JACK N. 1996 *Original Meanings: Politics and Ideas in the Making of the Constitution.* New York: Random House.

STORING, HERBERT J. 1981 *What the Anti-Federalists Were For.* Chicago: University of Chicago Press.

SUNSTEIN, CASS R. 1993 *Democracy and the Problem of Free Speech.* New York: Free Press.

—— 1993 *The Partial Constitution.* Cambridge, Mass.: Harvard University Press.

DELIMA v. BIDWELL

See: Insular Cases

DEMEANOR EVIDENCE

See: Confrontation, Right of

DE MINIMIS NON CURAT LEX

(Latin: "The law does not concern itself with trifles.") It is a maxim of the COMMON LAW that the courts will not intervene in disputes where the substance of the controversy is insignificant. For example, a court will not hear a case that turns on an amount less than a dollar or a time period shorter than a day.

DAVID GORDON
(1986)

(SEE ALSO: *Cases and Controversies.*)

DEMOCRACY

See: Communications and Democracy; Corporate Power, Free Speech, and Democracy; Deliberative Democracy; Democratic Theory and Constitutional Law; Direct Democracy

DEMOCRATIC THEORY AND CONSTITUTIONAL LAW

Much of American CONSTITUTIONAL THEORY and law is concerned with the existence and significance of conflict between democracy and constitutionalism as implemented in this country. Democracy is often thought to be in conflict both with constitutionalism as a general matter and with the institutional implementation that Americans have largely come to identify with constitutionalism, JUDICIAL REVIEW.

Whether there is any inconsistency depends first on the nature of constitutionalism and the particular features of the constitution in question. At the very least a consti-

tution is a set of rules that describe a structure of government, a way of making official decisions. The U.S. Constitution, like many others, is entrenched, which is to say that the ordinary legislative processes for which it provides are not empowered to change the Constitution itself. Congress, for example, may not provide in LEGISLATION that there shall be three senators from every state. Again like many others, the U.S. Constitution goes beyond prescribing a structure and places substantive limits on the power of the government it creates. The theory of constitutionalism is especially concerned with entrenchment and the hierarchical system of legal rules that produces it.

A constitution can conflict with democratic principles if it sets out a nondemocratic structure of government or if it sets out a democratic structure but limits the power of the government so created. The standard argument that the U.S. Constitution is undemocratic rests on a relatively simple concept of democracy, assuming that it consists of simple majority rule, either directly or through a representative legislature. By this test the constitutional structure itself is undemocratic because the U.S. SENATE and the ELECTORAL COLLEGE give disproportionate weight to the influence of voters in small states. Moreover, the ordinary government, itself only somewhat majoritarian, is subject to limits that can be overridden only through the even less-majoritarian AMENDING PROCESS of Article V. Amendment requires a SUPERMAJORITY of three-fourths of the states, so that even a small minority of the population can block constitutional change.

To the extent that the Constitution still protects state autonomy from national legislation it might be said to be undemocratic in one more way, because reserved state powers can block the decision of a national majority. Yet, clashes between local and national majorities present a problem concerning the definition of the relevant political community.

Whether there is really a conflict between the Constitution and democracy, however, depends on the content of democratic theory. Much of American constitutional commentary concerns the presence or absence of that conflict, and hence turns on the proper understanding of democracy. In particular, those who argue that constitutionalism and the U.S. Constitution do not actually conflict with democracy commonly appeal to a more sophisticated notion of democracy than the absolute rule of a majoritarian assembly. Three strategies of reconciling constitutionalism and democracy are especially important. Of those, two maintain that entrenchment and substantive limitations can provide prodemocratic corrections for the failings of ordinary representative government, while the third rejects an essentially procedural understanding of democracy.

According to the first such argument, representative assemblies are prone to make decisions that reflect the short-term but not the long-term views of their constituents. Seemingly undemocratic structures like BICAMERALISM and substantive limitations like the CONTRACT CLAUSE can respond to those tendencies. On this account such limitations are a form of collective self-binding, the standard example of which is Odysseus's strategy of having himself bound to the mast while he listened to the Sirens' song. Fearful of what they and their representatives may do in perilous economic times, for example, the people in a sober moment of constitution-making may adopt a provision like the contracts clause banning state impairment of contractual obligations, thus limiting the legislature's flexibility in times of crisis.

Whether such arrangements perform as designed is a question for political science. Whether they are consistent with democracy is a question for normative democratic theory. Three questions seem particularly important. First is the basic issue of establishing the power of decision when the people are divided. May a majority, or a supermajority, properly bind a minority? To the extent that democracy entails such binding, as in most conceptions it does, it is in an important sense collectivist, allowing the choices of individuals to be overridden by those of groups. Second are issues associated specifically with self-binding where the model is an action by one individual, for example, someone who puts the alarm clock on the other side of the room before going to bed. Whether such self-management techniques are actually desirable requires a surprisingly intricate investigation. It must be explained, for example, why the choices made by an individual at one time are more authentic than those made at another. Finally, because constitutions generally endure beyond the lives of those who make them, the claim that constitutional self-binding is consistent with democracy requires a theory in which the decisions of one group of citizens count as self-binding with respect to their successors.

Much has been said about the last question, the problem of the "dead hand." It becomes serious when there is a real question whether a self-binding limitation introduced into the constitution in the past would enjoy contemporary democratic support. If not, whether the constitution is consistent with democracy depends on the temporal dimension of democracy. According to some approaches, collective political entities are continuous for purposes of establishing political obligation, with the result that people alive today may legitimately be bound by the choices of their predecessors. The question of intertemporal political obligation was debated with particular vigor around the time of the U.S. Constitution's framing.

The second approach to reconciling constitutionalism and democracy rests on the claim that representative assemblies and other policymakers are apt to reflect the views of their constituents too little, not too much. Where the interests of agents and principals are different, the principals will want to take steps to check the power of their agents. A classic example involves political dissent. Incumbents in office have strong incentives to suppress dissent, for example by limiting the ability of outsiders to report on official misconduct. A strong law of SEDITIOUS LIBEL is one familiar way of accomplishing that end.

If the people are to rule, however, they must have information about the conduct of their agents and in particular must have information about official misconduct. They thus have interests very different from those of incumbents in office. One way of dealing with this divergence of interests is to take basic questions concerning the operation of the political process out of the hands of the ordinary legislature by resolving those questions in a constitution. Protections for FREEDOM OF SPEECH and FREEDOM OF THE PRESS are central examples.

As regulation of the political process moves beyond basic protection for political dissent it raises questions that must be referred to democratic theory. For example, many people believe that political influence will depend on personal wealth when the most effective means of access to public debate are controlled by private hands. Such disparities of influence are thought by some to be inconsistent with democracy. That conclusion has important implications for the rules governing political debate and hence for the constitutional entrenchment of such rules.

Finally, it is possible to reconcile familiar features of the U.S. Constitution with democracy by taking a nonprocedural view of democracy, one that breaks democracy's usual association with majority, or indeed popular, rule. One might think, for example, that the commitment to POPULAR SOVEREIGNTY really rests on a commitment to equality in certain substantive respects, so that what is more substantively egalitarian is more democratic. Whether a constitution is democratic, according to this theory, depends on that constitution's consonance with the deeper theory on which democracy itself rests.

This step is especially attractive if one is seeking to justify the substantive limitations in the U.S. Constitution that are now widely thought predominantly to protect political minorities. For example, constitutional antidiscrimination norms often provide such protection. Reconciling such norms with majoritarian democracy has posed a major problem for constitutional theory. If an important component of democracy is truly substantive, however, and if its substance is egalitarian, that problem of theory becomes much easier to solve. Nonprocedural conceptions of democracy, however, are quite controversial.

As the preceding discussion suggests, the potential inconsistency between democracy and an entrenched constitution is not tied to the particular enforcement mechanisms that any constitution may employ. Judicial review is not a necessary condition for that conflict. Nor is it a sufficient condition. A judiciary that somehow was confined to enforcing clear rules in a constitution that was itself democratic would raise no problems with respect to democracy. That would be true no matter how the judges were chosen and no matter how they could be removed.

Judicial review is potentially undemocratic to the extent that it puts the power of choice in the hands of judges. The supposed clash between democracy and judicial review is so prominent in American constitutional debate because it is so common for the judiciary to apply textually unclear constitutional provisions, or to apply principles that the judges have found to be implicit in the Constitution, in ways that appear closely to track the views of the judges as to desirable outcomes. When that happens constitutional adjudication resembles substantive policymaking whereby the judiciary displaces the decisions made by nonjudicial governmental actors. Because of their indirect selection and life tenure, American federal judges are frequently regarded as less accountable to the people than are elected officers.

As a result, judicial review as practiced in America encounters what ALEXANDER M. BICKEL called the countermajoritarian difficulty. Whether that difficulty is real depends first of all on the extent to which the courts make substantive choices. When they do, the question whether their decisions are likely to be less democratic than those of other governmental decisionmakers is once again one for political science and democratic theory. Leading attempts to solve the countermajoritarian difficulty generally rely on arguments that reconcile the Constitution itself with democracy. Thus Bickel argued that because of the institutional characteristics of the judiciary, substantive judicial choice will in certain important areas reflect the long-term views of the people better than will the output of the more directly electoral process. In a similar vein, John Hart Ely has sought to justify large parts of contemporary constitutional doctrine on the grounds that it enhances democracy by mitigating the agency problems associated with representative legislatures. Implicit in a position like Ely's is a claim concerning the institutional tendencies of courts: that they will in general produce the kinds of doctrines that reinforce, rather than hinder, democracy.

There are commentators who reject all such attempts to reconcile American constitutional practice with democracy and conclude that the conflict is irresolvable. Those who take that position often then say, so much the worse for constitutionalism, or so much the worse for democracy.

JOHN C. HARRISON
(2000)

Bibliography

AMAR, AKHIL R. 1991 The Bill of Rights As a Constitution. *Yale Law Journal* 100:1131–1210.
BICKEL, ALEXANDER M. 1962 *The Least Dangerous Branch*. Indianapolis, Ind.: Bobbs-Merrill.
DWORKIN, RONALD 1996 *Freedom's Law*. Cambridge, Mass.: Harvard University Press.
ELSTER, JON and SLAGSTAD, RUNE, eds. 1988 *Constitutionalism and Democracy*. New York: Cambridge University Press.
GOLDWIN, ROBERT A. and SCHAMBRA, WILLIAM A., eds. 1980 *How Democratic is the Constitution?* Washington, D.C.: American Enterprise Institute for Public Policy Research.
HART ELY, JOHN 1980 *Democracy and Distrust*. Cambridge, Mass.: Harvard University Press.

DEMONSTRATION

The FIRST AMENDMENT guarantees the right of persons to congregate peaceably in large numbers in appropriate public spaces in order to communicate ideas or grievances. In *Edwards v. South Carolina* (1963) the Court described an assemblage of 187 protesters on the grounds of a state capitol as "an exercise of . . . basic constitutional rights in their most pristine and classic form." Mass demonstrations cannot be prohibited simply on account of their size or their need to occupy public land.

Constitutional litigation over demonstrations tends to focus on three issues. First is the question of what public spaces must be made available to demonstrators. By virtue of the number of persons involved, mass demonstrations can be disruptive of other activities even when the demonstrators remain peaceable and orderly. When must those other activities give way to the First Amendment claims of persons who wish to engage in a mass demonstration?

The Supreme Court has never given a definitive and comprehensive answer to that question, and probably never could. The Court has indicated, however, that demonstrations in PUBLIC FORUMS such as streets, sidewalks, and parks cannot be subjected to a blanket prohibition. On the other hand, the Court has upheld regulations that entirely prohibited demonstrations in a jailyard and in areas of a military base otherwise open to the public.

Second, the issue has arisen whether a demonstration can be prohibited or postponed on the ground that audience hostility to the demonstrators threatens to produce a BREACH OF THE PEACE. The Court has inveighed against any such "heckler's veto" in OBITER DICTUM, and has reversed disorderly conduct convictions of speakers who continued their orderly protests in the face of potentially threatening crowds. In language quoted many times in the United States Reports, the Court stated in TERMINIELLO V. CHICAGO (1949):

[A] function of free speech under our system of government is to invite dispute. It may indeed best serve its high purpose when it induces a condition of unrest, creates dissatisfaction with conditions as they are, or even stirs people to anger. Speech is often provocative and challenging. It may strike at prejudices and preconceptions and have profound unsettling effects as it presses for acceptance of an idea. That is why freedom of speech . . . is . . . protected against censorship or punishment, unless shown likely to produce a clear and present danger of a serious substantive evil that rises far above public inconvenience, annoyance, or unrest.

Despite strong dicta and case outcomes favorable to speakers, it cannot be said with assurance that a hostile audience can in no circumstances provide a basis for disallowing a demonstration. The Court has yet to decide a case in which the regulatory authority was confined by a narrowly drawn statute and the police could not contain the HOSTILE AUDIENCE by the exercise of due diligence. There is also the unresolved question of whether demonstrators who wish to proceed in the face of a hostile audience have a First Amendment right to do so on repeated occasions, or whether at some point the mounting costs of police protection for the demonstrators might justify a prohibition on the continuation of their expressive activity.

A third set of issues that arise frequently in disputes over demonstrations concerns the doctrine of prior restraint. Demonstrators who wish to assemble in large numbers can be required to obtain permits in advance, despite the general presumption in First Amendment law against licensing. Officials who administer permit systems for marches and rallies are required to rule upon permit requests expeditiously, and to validate denials in court on a strict timetable. Thus, administrative delay is not permitted to serve as an indirect means of prohibiting mass demonstrations. If a permit request is under administrative or judicial consideration by the time a demonstration is scheduled to take place, the demonstrators may be permitted to proceed without a permit and defend against a prosecution on the ground that they exhausted all channels of prior approval and were entitled under the First Amendment to have their permit request granted. However, demonstrators who do not both apply for a permit and pursue all channels of appeal may be prosecuted for holding a march or rally without a permit, despite the fact that had they applied for a permit they would have been entitled under the Constitution to have it issued.

A fourth issue concerning demonstrations that has not generated a great deal of litigation to date but could do so in the future is whether persons who engage in mass demonstrations can be made to pay the costs of municipal services that attend the event. The Court has indicated in dictum that reasonable costs for such services as clean-up,

police protection, and the provision of toilets can be assessed against the demonstrators. However, such assessments can be quite large for major events and can be used as a means of discouraging demonstrations. This issue of cost assessment was important in the litigations during the 1970s over the proposed march of American Nazis in the predominantly Jewish community of Skokie, Illinois, and could emerge as a focus of controversy in other cases.

VINCENT BLASI
(1986)

Bibliography

BAKER, C. EDWIN 1983 Unreasoned Reasonableness: Mandatory Parade Permits and Time, Place, and Manner Regulations. *Northwestern University Law Review* 78:937–1024.
BOLLINGER, LEE C. 1982 The Skokie Legacy: Reflections on an "Easy Case" and Free Speech Theory. *Michigan Law Review* 80:617–633.

DENATURALIZATION

American CITIZENSHIP can be lost in two ways: denaturalization and EXPATRIATION. Denaturalization is the official cancellation, for cause, of a certificate of naturalization. It can be employed only against a person who has secured his citizenship by NATURALIZATION. Once denaturalized, a person is again an ALIEN in the eyes of the law; unlike the expatriate, he is considered never to have been a citizen. As an alien, the denaturalized former citizen is vulnerable to DEPORTATION and, in the case of a denaturalized criminal, to extradition.

Denaturalization, like naturalization, is governed by statute—currently, the Immigration and Nationality Act of 1952. Congress derives the implied power to denaturalize from its express power set forth in Article I, section 8, to "establish a uniform Rule of Naturalization." Congress has provided for denaturalization when a person's citizenship has been "illegally procured" or "procured by concealment of a material fact or by willful misrepresentation."

Denaturalization has been employed against naturalized citizens because of their membership in communist, Nazi, or other organizations espousing doctrines deemed antithetical to American allegiance. In such cases, the ground for denaturalization is that citizenship has been illegally procured because the applicant failed to comply with the statutory condition that he be attached to the principles of the American Constitution for the five years immediately preceding his naturalization. Also under the act, membership in such an organization within five years of naturalization is "prima facie evidence" of a lack of attachment prior to naturalization.

Denaturalization has also been employed against criminals and racketeers (thereby rendering them subject to deportation), on the ground that they obtained their American citizenship by lying about their criminal past. In such a case, even though the courts have held that denaturalization proceedings are suits in EQUITY and are governed by the FEDERAL RULES OF CIVIL PROCEDURE, the government must prove that the naturalized citizen lied about his criminal past, and thus, in effect, must prove the crime. The Supreme Court has stated, however, that the government need not meet the usual standard of proof for criminal guilt, as the defendant is subject not to penal sanctions but only to denaturalization.

Recently denaturalization suits have also been brought against Nazi war criminals. The central issue in these cases has been falsification or concealment of objective facts about the person's past. Although the courts have been unanimous that the alleged misrepresentations must be material, they have disagreed over whether a misrepresentation is sufficiently material if the truth, which by itself would not have been sufficient to bar the granting of citizenship, would nevertheless have provided leads for uncovering facts of the person's past that would have precluded his naturalization.

Litigants sometimes challenge the constitutionality of denaturalization, arguing either that it reduces naturalized citizens to second class status (in that they can be stripped of citizenship on grounds and by procedures that cannot be applied to native-born citizens), or that Congress's power to naturalize does not carry with it the implied power to denaturalize. To date such arguments have proven unsuccessful.

RALPH A. ROSSUM
(1986)

Bibliography

GORDON, CHARLES and ROSENFIELD, HARRY N. 1984 *Immigration Law and Procedure*, Vol. 3, chap. 20. New York: Matthew Bender.

ROCHE, JOHN P. 1952 Statutory Denaturalization. *University of Pittsburgh Law Review* 13:276–327.

DENNIS v. UNITED STATES
341 U.S. 494 (1951)

Eugene Dennis and other high officials of the Communist party had been convicted of violating the ALIEN REGISTRATION ACT of 1940 (the Smith Act) by conspiring to advocate overthrow of the government by force and violence. LEARNED HAND, writing the Court of Appeals opinion upholding the constitutionality of the act and of the conviction, was caught in a dilemma. He was bound by the Supreme Court's CLEAR AND PRESENT DANGER rule, and the government had presented no evidence that Dennis's activities had created a present danger of communist revolution in the United States. Hand, however, believed that courts had limited authority to enforce the FIRST AMENDMENT. His solution was to restate the danger test as: "whether the gravity of the evil, discounted by its improbability, justifies such invasion of free speech as is necessary to avoid the danger." Because Dennis's conspiracy to advocate was linked to a grave evil, communist revolution, he could be punished despite the remote danger of communist revolution. Hand's restatement allowed a court to pay lip service to the danger rule while upholding nearly any government infringement on speech. If the ultimate threat posed by the speech is great enough, the speaker may be punished even though there is little or no immediate threat.

The Supreme Court upheld Dennis's conviction with only Justices HUGO L. BLACK and WILLIAM O. DOUGLAS dissenting. Chief Justice FRED M. VINSON'S PLURALITY OPINION adopted Hand's restatement of the danger rule. At least where an organized subversive group was involved, speakers might be punished so long as they intended to bring about overthrow "as speedily as circumstances would permit."

Justice FELIX FRANKFURTER's concurrence openly substituted a BALANCING TEST for the danger rule, arguing that the constitutionality of speech limitations ultimately depended on whether the government had a weighty enough interest. Congress, he said, surely was entitled to conclude that the interest in national security outweighed the speech interests of those advocating violent overthrow.

Decided at the height of the Cold War campaign against communists, *Dennis* allied the Court with anticommunist sentiment. No statute would seem more flatly violative on its face of the First Amendment than one that made "advocacy" a crime. Indeed, in YATES V. UNITED STATES (1957) the Court later sought to distinguish between active urging or incitement to revolution, which was constitutionally punishable "advocacy," and abstract teaching of Marxist doctrine, which was constitutionally protected speech.

Defenders of the clear and present danger rule criticize *Dennis* for abandoning that rule's essential feature, the immediacy requirement. Such commentators see the Court as correcting its *Dennis* error in BRANDENBURG V. OHIO (1969) in which the Court returned to something like "clear and present danger" and placed heavy emphasis on the immediacy requirement. Justices Black and Douglas subsequently treated *Dennis* as a case applying the clear and present danger rule and thus as an illustration of the failure of the rule to provide sufficient protection for speech and of the need to replace it with the more "absolute" free speech protections urged by ALEXANDER MEIKLEJOHN. Proponents of balancing applaud Hand's "discounting" formula as one of the roots of the balancing doctrine, although only the most ardent proponents of judicial self-restraint support Frankfurter's conclusion that Congress, not the Court, should do the final balancing.

It is possible to read *Dennis, Yates,* and *Brandenburg* together as supporting the following theory. The clear and present danger rule, including a strong immediacy requirement, applies to street-corner speakers; so long as their speech does not trigger immediate serious harms, others will have the opportunity to respond to it in the marketplace of ideas, and the government will be able to prepare protective measures against violence that may follow. However, where organized, subversive groups engage in covert speech aimed at secret preparations that will suddenly burst forth in revolution, the "as speedily as circumstances will permit" test is substituted for the immediacy requirement. Covert speech cannot easily be rebutted in the marketplace of ideas; by the time underground groups pose a threat of immediate revolution, they may be so strong that a democratic government cannot stop them or can do so only at the cost of many lives.

Whether or not the Communist party of Eugene Dennis constituted such a covert, underground group impervious to the speech of others and posing a real threat of eventual revolution, a theory such as this is probably the reason the Smith Act was never declared unconstitutional and *Dennis* was never overruled although both have been drastically narrowed by subsequent judicial interpretation.

MARTIN SHAPIRO
(1986)

Bibliography

CORWIN, EDWARD S. 1951 Bowing Out Clear and Present Danger. *Notre Dame Lawyer* 27:325–359.
MENDELSON, WALLACE 1952 Clear and Present Danger—From Schenk to Dennis. *Columbia Law Review* 52:313–333.

DEPARTMENT OF AGRICULTURE v. MORENO

See: *Department of Agriculture v. Murry*

DEPARTMENT OF AGRICULTURE v. MURRY
413 U.S. 508 (1973)
DEPARTMENT OF AGRICULTURE v. MORENO
413 U.S. 528 (1973)

Piqued by the activities of protesting students and members of "hippie communes" during the VIETNAM years of agony, Congress in 1971 amended the Food Stamp Act to deny eligibility for food subsidies to two classes of applicants: "unrelated" persons living together and persons claimed by others in the previous year as tax dependents. On the same day the Supreme Court struck down both these amendments. *Moreno,* 7–2, invalidated the "unrelated" limitation on "Fifth Amendment EQUAL PROTECTION" grounds; the amendment was irrelevant to the act's goals of nourishing the needy and aiding agriculture, and harming "hippies" for their unpopularity was not a legitimate legislative purpose. The law thus lacked a RATIONAL BASIS. *Murry,* 5–4, held the "tax dependency" limitation an unconstitutional IRREBUTTABLE PRESUMPTION. A claimant might be needy during the current year although dependent on another during a previous year; yet the law denied any opportunity to qualify for aid by demonstrating need.

KENNETH L. KARST
(1986)

DEPORTATION

Deportation is the removal of an ALIEN out of the country. Congress has plenary power to deport aliens, even of long residence; its power rests upon the same grounds and is as unqualified as its power to exclude aliens from entering the country. Aliens permitted to enter and reside in the United States remain subject to the power of Congress to order them deported. Congress may direct that all aliens leave the country, or that some leave and others stay, distinguishing between the two by such tests as it thinks appropriate. While aliens cannot be deported without DUE PROCESS OF LAW, guaranteed to them by the Fifth Amendment, they are entitled only to PROCEDURAL DUE PROCESS: NOTICE and a HEARING at which they may seek to show that they do not come within the classification of aliens whose deportation Congress has directed. (A resident of the United States who claims to be a citizen cannot be deported without a judicial trial.)

Initially, deportation was conceived of only as a method for expelling aliens who had entered the country illegally. Soon, however, Congress employed it to remove aliens who had entered legally but had violated conditions attached to continued residence. Thus, for example, the Immigration Act of 1917 provided for the deportation of aliens convicted of crimes involving moral turpitude. Other statutory grounds for deportation, now codified in the Immigration and Nationality Act of 1952, include violation of alien registration requirements, drug trafficking, addiction to narcotics, becoming a public charge within five years after entry, or membership in the Communist party or other subversive organizations.

By its express terms, the Immigration and Nationality

Act applies retroactively to any alien belonging to any class enumerated in the statute, notwithstanding that the alien entered the United States prior to the date of the statute or that the facts alleged to justify deportation occurred prior to that date. Because deportation is not considered a punishment, the prohibition of the EX POST FACTO clause of the Constitution does not apply, and retroactive application of provisions specifying grounds for deportation was upheld in *Lehmann v. Carson* (1957).

In *Harisiades v. Shaughnessy* (1952) Justice WILLIAM O. DOUGLAS declared in his dissent that "an alien, who is assimilated in our society, is treated as a citizen so far as his property and his liberty are concerned. . . . If those rights, great as they are, have constitutional protection, I think the more important one—the right to remain here—has a like dignity." To date, this view has not been able to overcome the two basic propositions announced in the Court's seminal deportation case, *Fong Yue Ting v. United States* (1893), that Congress has the INHERENT POWER to order deportation and that deportation is not a criminal punishment.

RALPH A. ROSSUM
(1986)

Bibliography

GORDON, CHARLES and ROSENFIELD, HARRY N. 1984 *Immigration Law and Procedure*, Vol. 1, chaps. 4–5; Vol. 2, chaps. 6–8. New York: Matthew Bender.

NOTE 1962 Deportation and Exclusion. *Yale Law Journal* 71: 760–792.

DESEGREGATION

Freed finally of slavery's shackles, blacks in America began the long quest for racial equality. Desegregation, a generic term used to describe elimination of the SEGREGATION and RACIAL DISCRIMINATION that nonwhites confronted at life's every turn, has been the equivalent of their Holy Grail.

While blacks have attacked barriers based on color across a spectrum that includes VOTING, employment, housing, the administration of justice, access to public facilities, and even sex and marriage, the elimination of discrimination in the public schools has been and remains the most important goal for black Americans in their continuing struggle against racism in this country.

At an early time in the nation's history, blacks hoped an already hostile society might at least share their fear, as a black minister phrased it, "for our rising offspring to see them in ignorance in a land of gospel light." That petition presented in 1787 to the Massachusetts legislature sought a separate school for Boston's black children whose parents had withdrawn them from the harassment and ridi-

cule heaped on them by white teachers and students in some of the new nation's first public schools.

The legislature denied the petition, which reflected fears shared by succeeding generations of black parents who all during the nineteenth century filed dozens of law suits with state courts seeking relief from the racial discrimination they found in the public schools. Depending on the times and the character of the discrimination they faced, black parents have sought equal educational opportunity for their children through the advocacy of either racially separate or integrated schools.

With few exceptions, the courts were no more sympathetic to these petitions than were the school boards whose policies sometimes excluded black children from the public schools entirely and always subjected them to conditions that left little doubt as to which students were deemed members of the superior race. In ROBERTS V. CITY OF BOSTON (1850) a state court rejected a school desegregation petition almost two decades before the adoption of the FOURTEENTH AMENDMENT; three decades after its ratification, the United States Supreme Court concluded in PLESSY V. FERGUSON (1896) that the Fourteenth Amendment did not prohibit state-sanctioned segregation, citing the *Roberts* decision as support for the reasonableness of what it called SEPARATE BUT EQUAL facilities. *Plessy* provided the Constitution's blessing for laws throughout the South that required racial segregation not only in public schools, but in every possible public facility, including cemeteries and houses of prostitution.

The law and much of society enforced the "separate" phase of the *Plessy* standard to the letter, but the promise of "equal" facilities received only the grudging attention of a public whose racial attitudes ranged from apathy to outright hostility. Deep-South states spent far less for the schooling of black children than for whites. Despite a major effort to equalize segregated schools as a means of forestalling the steadily increasing number of CIVIL RIGHTS challenges in the 1950s, the South as a whole expended an average of $165 for every white child, and only $115 for each black in 1954, the year in which segregated schools were ruled unconstitutional.

More than a half century after its *Plessy* decision, the Supreme Court in BROWN V. BOARD OF EDUCATION (1954) reviewed the "separate but equal" DOCTRINE in the light of education's importance for children in a modern society, and concluded that the Fourteenth Amendment's EQUAL PROTECTION clause was violated by segregated schools "even though the physical facilities and other "tangible" factors may be equal. . . ."

Chief Justice EARL WARREN's ringing rhetoric in the *Brown* opinion condemned racially segregated schooling as "inherently unequal." He found that the separation by the state of children in grade and high schools solely on the basis of race "generates a feeling of inferiority as to their status in the community that may affect their hearts and minds in a way unlikely ever to be undone."

This decision was the result of long years of planning and litigation by the NAACP, and the committed work of lawyers including THURGOOD MARSHALL and Robert L. Carter, social scientists like Kenneth Clark, and hundreds of courageous black parents and their children. The decision, most blacks were convinced, required the elimination of segregated school facilities. Black parents knew that state-mandated black schools were a racial insult, and most hoped that if their children attended schools with whites, they would more likely gain access to the same educational resources as white children.

But the determination of civil rights groups representing an ever-increasing number of black parents seeking to join in school desegregation suits was met by the equally determined and, at least initially, far more powerful resistance of southern whites who strongly opposed sending their children to school with blacks and greatly resented the federal coercion involved in school desegregation orders which they equated with the occupation of the region by Union forces following the CIVIL WAR.

Arguably, opposition by southern working class whites could be predicated on the basis that, by invalidating segregation laws, *Brown* betrayed postReconstruction promises of white superior status made to them by policymakers in return for political support given during periods when populist movements sought to challenge the monopoly of economic power held by the upper class.

Although the Supreme Court refused to turn the clock back to 1868 to determine whether the framers of the Fourteenth Amendment had intended to condone segregated schools, an examination of postReconstruction history shows that policies of segregation reflected a series of political compromises through which working class whites settled their demands for social reform and greater political power. C. Vann Woodward and other historians have shown that segregated schools and facilities were established by legislatures at the insistence of the white working classes who saw color barriers as official confirmation that the society's policymakers would maintain even the poorest whites in a permanent status superior to that designated for blacks.

While not willing to acknowledge that its school desegregation decision would deprive whites of long-held rights of superior status based on race, the Court in *Brown v. Board of Education II* (1955), signaled that it was aware of the major social upheaval its ruling would require. Rejecting the black petitioners' requests for immediate relief, the Court chose a procedure that would permit the individual resolution of administrative and academic problems. It mandated only a "prompt and reasonable start toward full compliance," and returned the cases to the district courts with the admonition that orders and decrees be entered to admit plaintiffs to public schools on a racially nondiscriminatory basis "with ALL DELIBERATE SPEED. . . ."

But the Court's conciliatory efforts did not avoid and may have encouraged a period of massive resistance by southern elected officials, a rise in the Ku Klux Klan and other white supremacist groups, and a general upswing in economic intimidation and threats of physical violence against blacks deemed responsible for or participants in the civil rights movement. The Court met open resistance in Little Rock, Arkansas, and elsewhere with firm resolve, as in COOPER V. AARON (1958), but for several years condoned pupil placement laws and other procedural devices clearly designed to frustrate any meaningful compliance with the *Brown* mandate.

Federal courts were far less cautious in applying the *Brown* decision as the controlling precedent in cases challenging racial segregation in other public facilities. Thus, in the first half-dozen years following *Brown*, civil rights groups succeeded in desegregating state-operated places of recreation, government buildings, and transportation facilities.

Finally, in 1964, during the height of the SIT-IN protest movement that was bringing an end to "Jim Crow" policies in many hitherto segregated privately owned facilities not covered by the Fourteenth Amendment, the Court indicated that the time for mere deliberate speed had run out, in GRIFFIN V. SCHOOL BOARD OF PRINCE EDWARD COUNTY (1964). But the success of a decade of white resistance to school desegregation was reflected in the statistics. In the eleven states of the old Confederacy, a mere 1.17 percent of black students were attending school with white students by the 1963–1964 school year. The dirgelike progress of school desegregation finally gained momentum through a series of far-reaching lower court orders combined with the federal government's enforcement of Title VI of the CIVIL RIGHTS ACT OF 1964. This provision required the cut-off of federal financial assistance to entities that followed racially discriminatory policies. The federal government's enforcement of Title VI was seldom vigorous, but even the threat of losing the federal monies made available under a host of new antipoverty and educational assistance programs in the late 1960s persuaded hundreds of southern school districts that some form of compliance was in their best interests.

In 1968, the Supreme Court in GREEN V. NEW KENT COUNTY SCHOOL BOARD virtually eliminated the offer by a school board of "freedom of choice" to all children as a sufficient compliance with desegregation requirements. The decision was hailed by civil rights lawyers who believed that the *Brown* mandate could not be implemented unless public schools were rendered nonidentifiable by race. This goal, articulated in the *Green* case by Justice WILLIAM J. BRENNAN as requiring school boards to formulate plans that promise "realistically to convert promptly to a system without a "white' school and a "Negro' school, but just schools," was furthered when the Court applied the *Green* standard to a large, urban school district in North Carolina in SWANN V. CHARLOTTE-MECKLENBURG BOARD OF EDUCATION (1971). A few years later, the Court held a large northern school district subject to a similar standard in KEYES V. SCHOOL DISTRICT NO. 1 OF DENVER, COLORADO, (1973). (See SCHOOL BUSING.)

But while the percentage of children attending desegregated schools increased impressively, opposition to school desegregation remained. Resistance focused on plans like those approved in both *Swann* and *Keyes* requiring the transportation of children in order to achieve a measure of desegregation in each school roughly equivalent to the percentages of white and nonwhite children in the district as a whole. Opponents had gained national political strength, and their support likely played an important role in the election of RICHARD M. NIXON as President in 1968. The Nixon administration adopted policies that had the effect of slowing the federal government's participation in the school desegregation campaign, but the Supreme Court rejected Administration-sponsored delay requests in ALEXANDER V. HOLMES COUNTY BOARD OF EDUCATION (1969) and *Carter v. West Feliciana Parish School Board* (1970), although not without cracks in the solid front of unanimous opinions the Court had handed down in school desegregation cases since *Brown I*.

By 1974, in MILLIKEN V. BRADLEY, an APPEAL from lower court orders requiring the consolidation with the seventy percent black Detroit school system of fifty-three predominantly white suburban school districts, those cracks had grown into a chasm between divergent viewpoints on the appropriateness of school desegregation remedies. The insistence of civil rights lawyers that courts had unlimited discretion to impose racial-balance oriented plans to remedy proven segregation resulted in a significant change in the standards for proving school district liability for violating the Constitution.

In a 5–4 decision, the Court in *Milliken* held that federal courts could not impose multidistrict remedies to cure a single district's segregation absent findings that the other included school districts had failed to operate unitary school systems within their districts, or were responsible for the segregation in the other districts. Proof of this character could be found in few districts without histories of official, statemandated segregation, and thus plans to desegregate large, urban school districts through metropolitanwide plans were rendered inoperable.

By the late 1970s, roughly half of all nonwhite children in the nation resided in the country's twenty to thirty largest school districts. Minority children averaged sixty percent of the school population in these districts and close to seventy percent in the ten largest districts. Politically if not physically, desegregation in these districts on the *Green-Swann* model became increasingly difficult.

Lower courts, impressed by detailed prescriptions of racial wrongdoing by urban school boards, continued at the urging of civil rights lawyers to grant relief requiring reassignments and busing to change the racial makeup of schools. But the Supreme Court, now quite divided, set increasingly difficult liability standards in cases from Dayton and Columbus, Ohio; Omaha, Nebraska; Austin, Texas; Milwaukee, Wisconsin; and Indianapolis, Indiana. Plans requiring wholesale reassignment of children in these districts were finally approved, mainly because the proof of past discrimination was so clear. There was little judicial enthusiasm for continued reliance on a remedial process about which there was so much controversy as to its effectiveness even among civil rights proponents.

By this time, a great many black communities were questioning the continued validity of the "neither black schools nor white schools" desegregation approach that had stood as an article of faith since the early post-*Brown* years. Disenchantment was prompted by the hundreds of black schools closed and the scores of black teachers and principals dismissed in the course of the school desegregation process. In addition, black parents were discovering that the sacrifice involved in busing children across town to mainly white schools did not always eliminate racial discrimination. More litigation had to be prosecuted to challenge resegregation tactics as varied as the use of standardized tests to track black students into virtually all-black classrooms, to the exclusion of blacks from extracurricular programs. In most desegregated school systems, black students were far more likely to be suspended and expelled for disciplinary violations than white students. Black parents able to enroll their children in desegregated schools all too often found themselves protesting policies of in-school discrimination quite similar to those that had led their late eighteenth-century predecessors to petition for separate schools.

The NAACP and the few other groups who sponsored most school desegregation litigation remained firm in their belief that identifiably black schools would always be inferior and must be eliminated. But local black groups in several cities including Atlanta, St. Louis, Detroit, Dallas, Boston, and Portland, Oregon, decided that mainly black schools in black neighborhoods might provide effective schooling for their children if black parents could be involved more closely in faculty hiring, curriculum selection, and other policymaking aspects of these schools.

In 1975, a court of appeals approved in *Calhoun v.*

Cook, over the vigorous objection of the national NAACP office, a settlement of a twenty-year-old Atlanta school case providing full faculty and employee desegregation but only limited pupil desegregation in exchange for a school board promise to hire a number of blacks in top administrative positions, including a black superintendent of schools.

A few years later, in *Milliken v. Bradley II* (1977), the Supreme Court approved without dissent a Detroit desegregation plan that gave priority to a range of "educational components" while limiting pupil desegregation in the district that was by now more than eighty percent black to a provision that no school be less than thirty percent black. The Court though was unable to decide and left standing a lower court ruling that an almost all-black subdistrict created by the Dallas school desegregation plan met school desegregation standards. The record showed both that housing patterns and geographical conditions would have made desegregation difficult and that much of the black community in the subdistrict supported its retention.

Public resistance to school desegregation continued into the 1980s even though the likelihood of new court orders was lessened by the Supreme Court's application of higher standards of proof even in litigation where metropolitan relief was not sought. For example, California voters approved an amendment to their state constitution barring state courts from ordering racial balance remedies in cases where, absent a finding that the school board was guilty of a specific intent to discriminate, the Fourteenth Amendment would not require racial balance relief. The Supreme Court upheld this provision in *Crawford v. Los Angeles Unified School District* (1982).

Civil rights organizations mobilized to meet such challenges, but local black groups increasingly opted for programs that promised to provide equal educational opportunity in neighborhood schools. At the same time, many black parents either moved to suburban areas or sent their children out of their neighborhoods to enable them to attend predominantly white schools.

The quest for effective schooling in the 1980s mirrors those made by black parents in the 1780s and during all the periods between. They and their children have recognized that neither separate schools nor integrated schools will automatically eliminate racist policies intended to provide priority to white children for scarce educational resources. School desegregation programs mandated by the *Brown* decision, and earnestly sought in hundreds of court cases, have served to slow but have not otherwise much discouraged those policies.

Beyond the real gains made by blacks during the *Brown* years, there remain millions of black and other minority children whose schooling remains both segregated and inferior. For them, there is ample basis for parental fears as they watch their rising offspring grow "in ignorance in a land of gospel light."

DERRICK A. BELL
(1986)

Bibliography

BELL, DERRICK A.   (1973) 1980   *Race, Racism and American Law.* Boston: Little, Brown.
KALODNER, HOWARD I. and FISHMAN, JAMES J., eds.   1978   *Limits of Justice: The Courts' Role in School Desegregation.* Cambridge, Mass.: Ballinger.
KLUGER, RICHARD   1976   *Simple Justice: The History of Brown v. Board of Education and Black America's Struggle for Equality.* New York: Knopf.
WOODWARD, C. VANN   (1955) 1974   *The Strange Career of Jim Crow.* New York: Oxford University Press.

DESHANEY v. WINNEBAGO COUNTY DEPARTMENT OF SOCIAL SERVICES
488 U.S. 189 (1989)

When Joshua DeShaney was one year old, his parents were divorced; the court awarded custody of Joshua to his father, who moved to Wisconsin and remarried. When Joshua was three, his father's second wife complained to the county department of social services (DSS) that the father was abusing the child, hitting him and leaving marks on him. DSS officials interviewed the father, who denied the charges; DSS did not pursue the matter. A year later Joshua was admitted to a hospital with multiple bruises and abrasions; the examining doctor notified DSS; DSS immediately obtained a court order taking custody over Joshua, but the DSS investigating team decided there was insufficient evidence of child abuse to retain Joshua in the court's custody. The father promised DSS that he would enroll Joshua in a preschool program and undertake counseling for himself. A month later the hospital emergency room notified DSS that Joshua had been treated again for suspicious injuries; the caseworker concluded there was no basis for action. Over the next six months the caseworker visited the home, repeatedly saw injuries on Joshua's head, and noted that he had not been enrolled in the preschool program. She recorded all this in her files and did nothing more. About a month later, the emergency room notified DSS that Joshua had been admitted with injuries they believed caused by child abuse. On the caseworker's next two home visits, she was told Joshua was too ill to see her. DSS took no action. Four months later, the father beat four-year-old Joshua, who lapsed into a coma; Joshua suffered severe brain damage, but lived. He is expected to spend the rest of his life in an institution for the profoundly retarded.

The father was tried and convicted of child abuse, but the case that reached the Supreme Court was a civil action, brought by Joshua's mother against DSS and some DSS employees, seeking damages on the ground that DSS had deprived Joshua of SUBSTANTIVE DUE PROCESS OF LAW in violation of the FOURTEENTH AMENDMENT. The lower courts denied relief and the Supreme Court affirmed, 6–3. For the majority, Chief Justice WILLIAM H. REHNQUIST concluded that the due process clause imposed no affirmative duty on the state or its officers to protect a citizen's life or liberty against private persons' invasions. Furthermore, no such constitutional duty arose merely because DSS had known of Joshua's situation and indicated its intention to protect him. The case differed from those in which the Court had recognized a state duty to assure minimal safety and medical treatment for prisoners and institutionalized mental patients, for here the state had done nothing to restrain Joshua or otherwise prevent him from protecting himself or receiving protection from other persons. The harm, in other words, "was inflicted not by the State of Wisconsin, but by Joshua's father."

For the dissenters, Justice WILLIAM J. BRENNAN castigated the majority for so limited a view of the prison- and mental-hospital cases. Here the state had set up DSS to protect children in precisely Joshua's situation, thus encouraging citizens generally to rely on DSS to prevent child abuse. One had to ignore this context to conclude, as the majority did, that the state had simply failed to act. Justice HARRY A. BLACKMUN, in a separate dissent, objected to the majority's formalistic distinction between STATE ACTION and state inaction; the state had assumed responsibility for protecting Joshua from the very abuse that deprived him of much of what it means to have a life.

In a great many ways the Supreme Court has imposed affirmative duties on the states to compensate for inequalities or other harms not directly of the states' making. (See ACCESS TO THE COURTS; RIGHT TO COUNSEL; MENTAL RETARDATION AND THE CONSTITUTION; PROCEDURAL DUE PROCESS OF LAW, CIVIL.) Its decisions in these areas recognize, if only partially, the artificiality of insisting that constitutional guarantees be rigidly confined to action that is formally governmental, ignoring the interlacing of public and private action that characterizes much behavior in America's complex society. As *DeShaney* sadly illustrates, a mechanical application of the judge-made state-action limitation on the Fourteenth Amendment can permit the systematic evasion of public responsibility.

KENNETH L. KARST
(1992)

Bibliography

TRIBE, LAURENCE H. 1989 The Curvature of Constitutional Space: What Lawyers Can Learn from Modern Physics. *Harvard Law Review* 103:1–39.

DEVELOPMENTALLY DISABLED ASSISTANCE AND BILL OF RIGHTS ACT
89 Stat. 486 (1975)

This statute established a grant program under which participating states receive federal financial assistance to aid them in creating programs for the developmentally disabled, a term that refers mainly to the mentally retarded. To qualify for federal funds states must take AFFIRMATIVE ACTION to hire qualified handicapped individuals, submit a plan to evaluate the services provided under the act, have a habitation plan for each person receiving services under a program funded under the act, and have in effect a system to protect and advocate the rights of persons with developmental disabilities. The act's "bill of rights" for the developmentally disabled includes the rights to appropriate treatment in a setting least restrictive of the patient's liberty, to a well-balanced diet, to sufficient medical and dental services, to be free of restraint as punishment, to be free of excessive use of chemical restraints, to be visited by relatives, and to a safe environment. In PENNHURST STATE SCHOOL AND HOSPITAL V. HALDERMAN (1981) the Supreme Court, in an opinion by Justice WILLIAM H. REHNQUIST and over three dissents, held that the "bill of rights" portion of the act does not confer on the developmentally disabled any substantive rights to appropriate treatment in the least restrictive setting. The act "does no more than express a congressional preference for certain kinds of treatment."

THEODORE EISENBERG
(1986)

(SEE ALSO: *Disabilities, Rights of Persons With.*)

Bibliography

EISENBERG, THEODORE 1981 *Civil Rights Legislation.* Pages 886–887. Charlottesville, Va.: Michie Co.

DEVOLUTION AND FEDERALISM IN HISTORICAL PERSPECTIVE

The word "devolution" became a staple in political discourse with the capture by the REPUBLICAN PARTY of decisive majorities in both houses of Congress in the 1994 election. Under the banner of a "Contract with America," and directed by Speaker Newt Gingrich, who outspokenly demanded absolute acceptance of party leadership, the new majority in the U.S. HOUSE OF REPRESENTATIVES undertook to implement a broadly based neoconservative agenda. One main instrument for achievement of that agenda's specific goals was a carefully crafted shift in policymaking authority and administrative responsibility, away from the national government and into the hands of the states.

Many of the key portions of the 1994 conservative agenda were a restatement of main themes in the policies pursued by the White House and the Republican Party during the administrations of RONALD REAGAN and GEORGE H.W. BUSH. One of these themes was embodied in an attack on the powers of federal regulatory agencies in general, with emphasis particularly on the Environmental Protection Agency, the National Labor Relations Board, and the Occupational Safety and Health Administration. Also prominent were demands for reduction of federal capital gains taxes and for tempering the progressivity of federal taxation. Conservatives also condemned what they termed an unwarranted "activism" by so-called liberal judges in the federal courts—a reflection of the conservatives' dissatisfaction (dating from the time of the WARREN COURT DESEGREGATION and criminal justice decisions) with the Supreme Court's interpretations of minority rights, with judicial broadening of the criteria for STANDING to litigate environmental and consumer causes, and with the emerging concept of the entitlement rights of welfare clients and others against bureaucratic decisions. Withal, as Herman Belz indicated in his "CONSTITUTIONAL HISTORY, 1980–1989" entry in this encyclopedia, the 1980s witnessed the consolidation of a conservative program of deregulation and reestablishment of "market values"; pursuit of a social agenda; and the paradoxical attack on taxes and the bugaboo of "big government" that went forward with a steady burgeoning of federal deficits in the annual budgets of the Reagan years. And, as Belz emphasized, polarization of political differences and the dynamics of conflict were heightened by the persistence of divided government, with one party controlling one or both houses of Congress while the other held the presidency—a situation that would continue to pertain throughout most of the presidency of WILLIAM J. CLINTON as well.

Other elements of the 1994 "Contract with America" platform, however, reflected a significant extension of the earlier programs and a distinct hardening of ideological lines. These developments involved opposition to ABORTION rights; AFFIRMATIVE ACTION in the schools and the workplace; and federal welfare and health programs, especially those designed to reach the poorest (and hence politically the most vulnerable) elements of the nation's citizenry. (The only plank in the 1994 platform that was not pursued zealously was CAMPAIGN FINANCE reform, which proved to be of less interest as a concrete legislative goal to the newly elected senators and representatives than it had been as a campaign pledge.)

A notable feature of the 1994 agenda was the extent to which conservatives pursued their goals through a shifting of policymaking responsibility and administrative authority out of the federal government's control and into that of the states. So insistent and so broad in scope was this effort that some analysts applied the term "devolution revolution" to what was being attempted, especially with regard to the attack on the inherited policies and institutions of the post-1935 welfare state and its social security, health care, and welfare programs. An increasing number of state legislatures and governorships won by the Republicans enhanced the attractiveness of such devolution ideas as they were advanced by the congressional leadership. And, indeed, the 1994 Republican Governors' Conference welcomed the election as "a historic moment of opportunity—an occasion when the political climate makes possible fundamental change in the federal–state relationship."

Whatever the differences between 1980s conservatism and the heightened ideological character of the new Republican strategies that crystallized in 1994, a vital element of continuity was the extent to which the conservative appeal was articulated in explicitly constitutional terms, and not merely in the language of policy or the imperatives of specific versions of morality. Devolution, in this sense, appeared as a constitutional imperative, a return to "ORIGINAL INTENT" and "correct" principles. The champions of devolution thus appealed to a version of the Framers' principles in 1787, downplaying the intent or historical development of the post–CIVIL WAR "nationalizing" amendments (the THIRTEENTH, FOURTEENTH, and FIFTEENTH), to argue for a federal constitutional order in which state sovereignty was central to governmental legitimacy. Also mobilized was a new emphasis on the need to rebuild safeguards of state autonomy that conservatives regarded as assured by the TENTH AMENDMENT, which they interpreted anew in terms akin to the Supreme Court's view in the 1850s and again in the 1920s and early 1930s, at the height of conservative STATES' RIGHTS jurisprudence.

Reinforcing this political campaign to devolve powers and programs was the movement of the conservative bloc on the REHNQUIST COURT to revitalize Tenth Amendment restraints on the reach of congressional regulatory powers, to reassert ELEVENTH AMENDMENT–based barriers to suits against the state governments, and to retrench in the important realm of federal procedure with regard to welfare clients' rights and standing for litigants in public interest suits. Now the 1980s strategy of appointing federal judges at all levels who would be likely to advance the conservative agenda was reinforced by a strategy of withholding consent for Clinton judicial appointments seen as "too liberal." By the end of the 1990s, the results of this strategy were evident in, for example, the decisions in *Seminole Tribe of Florida v. Florida* (1996) and UNITED STATES V. LÓPEZ (1995) that dramatically revealed the cramped and hostile view of modern federal government powers that was held generally by a five-Justice majority on the Court. Then, in June 1999, the Court handed down three decisions (*Alden v. Maine* and related cases) that heavy-handedly reversed long-held DOCTRINES so that the states and their agencies (including state research universities) would be immunized from damages in PATENT and trademark suits, and so that millions of state employees would be denied the right to sue in state courts for damages for violation of national labor-law entitlements and (presumably) other federally guaranteed rights.

Viewed in a longer historical perspective, the political and constitutional confrontations of the 1990s over devolution policy and law are new variants of a persistent dynamic—the debate over "sorting out" which realms of law and policy should be governed from Washington, and which from the states and local governments. The issue had been joined in the earliest years of the Republic, when the Federalists and the emerging Jeffersonian parties had debated in constitutional terms such questions as the powers appropriate to a national bank (questions that ultimately reached the Supreme Court in formal constitutional terms in the 1819 case of MCCULLOCH V. MARYLAND). Throughout the pre–Civil War years, too, every aspect of the anti-SLAVERY debate had been embedded in a constitutional framework of doctrine regarding FEDERALISM. The new and explicitly nationalized constitutional order that emerged after the Civil War fundamentally changed the framework of those debates, but the terms of argument had remarkable continuities. Thus, even after the foundations of a federal administrative law in the 1880s, and significant expansion of centralized power in banking, ANTITRUST, and LABOR relations, much of the Progressive era's politics was dominated by the question of how much power the national government ought to excercise and to what extent states' rights—a cause always kept at the forefront, partly because Southern segregationists were determined to retain state control of race relations—should be respected. Similarly, the constitutional issues of the interwar years, climaxing in the responses to the Great Depression in the NEW DEAL period, were constantly framed in terms of the legitimate reach and limitations of state versus federal power.

Those who would recite the mantra of states' rights and "state sovereignty" in recent times have had to carry the burden of its historic association with racism and Jim Crow. Still, a determination to take seriously the constitutional requirements of federalism has never been the exclusive preoccupation of extremists. A federal "creed" commonly has been given respect, or at least lip service, by politicians and lawyers across the political spectrum. Progressive intellectuals and judges, too, have recognized the imperatives of federalism as a consideration in policy.

Thus FELIX FRANKFURTER, writing in 1922 of the Court's invalidation of a federal anti-child labor law, said "We must pay a price for federalism," even when that price must be "the [constitutional] impotence of the federal government to correct glaring evils unheeded by some of the states." Even the New Deal administration fashioned some of its major departures in policy, such as the Social Security system, in the style of "cooperative federalism" that gave the states a major policy role and extensive fiscal support through grants-in-aid, rather than going full-bore toward nationalization of policy and administration. And during the administration of LYNDON B. JOHNSON—the high point of post-war expansion of the national government's role in social legislation, regulation, and welfare programs—the President's principal advisers contended that by adopting a cooperative state–federal approach for many of his initiatives Johnson was honoring "our whole national history as a federal system." Similarly, few in the Democratic Party's leadership in the post-Johnson years have taken an ideological position against devolution in areas of law they have seen as susceptible of assignment to the states or as requiring for efficiency's sake a shift of authority away from the center. It has been intended and anticipated consequences, not the issue of devolution in raw ideological or constitutional form, that have divided the liberal and centrist elements in both major POLITICAL PARTIES on questions of major policy change. Despite the conservative opposition to Clinton's posture on major policy questions—concededly not a posture of wholesale antigovernmentalism—he too has been willing to make important concessions to the states, as for example in accepting the compromise of a sweeping WELFARE RIGHTS reform bill in 1996 that diminished federal authority and transferred vital discretionary powers to the states.

At the end of the twentieth century, it would appear likely that one reform successfully supported by conservatives and more generally by state officials has been set in place for a long time. This is the policy against "unfunded mandates," by which Congress had extended rights as entitlements to individuals and groups without providing state and local governments with funding that would permit them to fulfill those mandates. This change is a two-faceted victory for its proponents. On the one hand, it constrains the national government with respect to instituting new programs; on the other, it is linked with the larger, and legally distinct, policy of devolution insofar as it effectively curbs the power of federal courts to play a major role in defining benefits and entitlements in terms of constitutional rights, or to extend the terms of specific LEGISLATION through STATUTORY INTERPRETATION. Moreover, many of the same political leaders who call for devolution and for enhancement of state authority have led a successful campaign since the late 1970s to curtail, often radically, the fiscal competence of the states by dint of extreme constraints on their taxing powers.

Still, the ongoing controversy over federalism and devolution can take unexpected turns in the hands of judges. Thus, the REHNQUIST COURT, in a decision that startled nearly all commentators but was welcomed on its substantive terms by opponents of the new welfare cutbacks, in SAENZ V. ROE (1999) eviscerated one of the strongest devolutionist features of the 1996 welfare law. The Court held invalid Congress's devolution to state governments of the power to establish a two-tier system of benefits that would disadvantage newly arrived residents by limiting them to the level of benefits that the states of their previous residency allowed. In respect to devolution, then, not only evolving Tenth Amendment law and the enhanced political power of neoconservatives, but also as a countervailing force in the courts, the PRIVILEGES AND IMMUNITIES clause of the Fourteenth Amendment might well operate in a complex judicial role in the continuing evolution of state–federal relations.

The latest moves by the Justices seem to confirm the wisdom of the late Carl Friedrich when he contended that as a working system, American federalism cannot be understood unless it is analyzed in dynamic terms—as a process, and not only a concept to be interpreted in formalistic doctrinal terms.

HARRY N. SCHEIBER
(2000)

Bibliography

MASHAW, JERRY L. and CALSYN, DYLAN S. 1996 Block Grants, Entitlements, and Federalism: A Conceptual Map of Contested Terrain. *Yale Law & Policy Review/Yale Journal on Regulation* 14:297–323.
MELNICK, R. SHEP 1994 *Between the Lines: Interpreting Welfare Rights.* Washington, D.C.: Brookings Institution.
SCHEIBER, HARRY N. 1996 Redesigning the Architecture of Federalism—An American Tradition: Modern Devolution Policies in Perspective. *Yale Law & Policy Review/Yale Journal on Regulation* 14:227–296.

DIAL-A-PORN

With the development of new telephone technologies, the transmission of sexually explicit messages over the phone lines has become a multimillion dollar business. Telephone pornography raises special difficulties because many children call telephone sex lines unbeknown to parents. Some companies engaged in telephone pornography actually solicit business from minors, distributing advertisements for their services on school playgrounds. In one highly publicized case in California, a twelve-year-old boy who had been exposed to a pornographic phone message sexually assaulted a four-year-old girl.

In response to concerns about the effects of telephone pornography on children, Congress in 1983 banned all "obscene or indecent" commercial phone messages transmitted to persons under the age of eighteen. Pursuant to provisions of the law, the Federal Communications Commission (FCC) developed procedures by which telephone pornography companies could restrict their services to adults, including message scrambling, mandatory payment by credit card, and special access codes for users. Use of these procedures provided a defense against prosecution under the law. In 1988, however, an appellate court held the FCC regulations unconstitutional; and a few months later, Congress decided that its previous law was not sufficient to remedy the problem and subsequently banned "obscene or indecent" telephone messages directed to all persons, regardless of age.

In *Sable Communications of California, Inc. v. FCC* (1989), the Supreme Court upheld Congress's ban on "obscene" phone messages by a vote of 6–3, but it unanimously struck down the prohibition against "indecent" messages. Writing for the majority, Justice BYRON R. WHITE noted that the Court had already decided that OBSCENITY is not protected by the FIRST AMENDMENT; hence the ban on obscene phone messages was clearly constitutional under the Court's previous decisions. The indecency restriction was a different matter. Applying the COMPELLING STATE INTEREST test the Court regularly uses in free speech cases, White argued that the government undoubtedly has a compelling interest in eliminating indecent messages directed at children. However, the wholesale ban on indecent phone messages was not narrowly tailored to further that interest. According to White, nothing indicated that the regulations promulgated under the previous law would not have protected children sufficiently. White hinted, but did not decide, that those previous regulations were constitutional.

Concurring, Justice ANTONIN SCALIA pointed out that while the Court forbade the government from prohibiting all indecent phone messages, it did not hold that public utilities have an obligation to carry such messages. In other words, regardless of the provisions of federal law, a utility could make a business decision not to carry sexually explicit message services.

Justice WILLIAM J. BRENNAN agreed with the Court's invalidation of the ban on indecent phone messages, but he objected to its approval of the obscenity provisions, noting: "I have long been convinced that the exaction of criminal penalties for the distribution of obscene materials to consenting adults is constitutionally intolerable."

JOHN G. WEST, JR.
(1992)

DIAMOND v. CHAKRABARTY

See: Patent

DICEY, ARTHUR V.

See: Rule of Law

DICKINSON, JOHN
(1732–1808)

The conservative patriot leader John Dickinson, scion of a wealthy Quaker family, was called to the bar at the Middle Temple in London in 1757 and soon after returning to America became one of the most prosperous lawyers in Philadelphia. He served in the colonial legislatures of both Delaware and Pennsylvania, and in 1765 he rose to continental prominence with his pamphlets opposing the Sugar Act and the Stamp Act.

A delegate to the STAMP ACT CONGRESS (1765), Dickinson was the author of that body's Declaration of Rights and Grievances, ostensibly a loyal, even humble, petition to the king. Dickinson's resolutions condemned as unconstitutional the levying of internal taxes upon the colonists by the British Parliament and denounced as subversive of liberty the trial of offenses against tax laws by admiralty courts without juries. Dickinson himself later referred to the Declaration of Rights and Grievances as the first American BILL OF RIGHTS.

After the passage of the TOWNSHEND ACTS in 1767 Dickinson established himself as the preeminent American interpreter of the constitutional relationship between the colonies and Britain. His "Letters from a Farmer in Pennsylvania" (1767–1768), published in all but four American newspapers, advanced an understanding of the British constitution that made Parliament supreme in imperial matters but proscribed all TAXATION WITHOUT REPRESENTATION. Moreover, he abandoned the distinction between external and internal taxes in favor of a distinction based on purpose: if a duty was laid for the purpose of raising revenue, rather than regulating commerce, then it was taxation and fell under the constitutional proscription. The Farmer's Letters counseled petition for repeal of, rather than resistance to, unconstitutional legislation.

By the time he wrote his long essay on "The Constitutional Power of Great Britain" in 1774, Dickinson had come to think of the British Empire as federal—comparable to the Swiss Confederation or the United Netherlands. The British king was king of the American colonies, but "a parliamentary power of internal legislation over these colonies appears ... equally contradictory to humanity and to the Constitution, and illegal."

In 1774 Dickinson represented Pennsylvania in the First Continental Congress. The petition to the king and the address to the inhabitants of Canada, adopted pursuant to the DECLARATION AND RESOLVES, were products of Dickinson's pen. In 1775, at the Second Continental Congress, he worked with THOMAS JEFFERSON drafting the Declaration of the Causes and Necessity of Taking Up Arms. But Dickinson was still committed to the idea of a resolution of the crisis within the constitutional system of the British Empire. He opposed immediate separation from Britain and refused to sign the DECLARATION OF INDEPENDENCE.

On June 12, 1776, the Congress, anticipating independence, appointed a committee to draft a plan of union. Dickinson was the dominant member of that committee and the principal author of the draft ARTICLES OF CONFEDERATION reported to Congress on July 12. Dickinson's draft called for no mere alliance or league of sovereign states but for a permanent union with a national government. The "United States assembled" was to be heir to those powers of regulation and general legislation legitimately exercised before independence by the British Parliament, while each "colony" retained "sole and exclusive Regulation and Government of its internal police, in all matters that shall not interfere with the Articles of this Confederation." True to the "Farmer's" principles, Dickinson inserted a provision that "the United States assembled shall never impose or levy any Taxes or Duties, except in managing the Post-Office." Dickinson's draft Articles were regarded by many in Congress, especially Southerners, as too centralizing, and even some who favored Dickinson's position despaired of securing ratification. Only after considerably weakening the government to be established by the Articles did Congress finally propose them to the states.

When his stand on independence cost Dickinson his seat in Congress and his colonelcy in the militia, he enlisted in the army as a private soldier. But in November 1776 he was elected to Congress by Delaware, and he was later made a brigadier general in the Delaware militia. In 1779 he signed the Articles of Confederation to signify Delaware's ratification.

Dickinson served as president of Delaware in 1781–1782 and as president of Pennsylvania in 1782–1785. In both states he was recognized as a leader of the conservative party. Although a slaveholder, he favored abolition of SLAVERY, and he opposed its extension into the Northwest Territory.

In 1785 he retired to his estate in Delaware, but he was recalled to public service in 1786 and elected a delegate from Delaware to the ANNAPOLIS CONVENTION. Dickinson was chosen president of the convention, which discussed commercial problems under the Confederation and which issued the first call for a federal constitutional convention.

Notwithstanding his poor health, Dickinson accepted appointment to represent Delaware at the CONSTITUTIONAL CONVENTION OF 1787. Although he was an active and conscientious delegate, his contribution to the work of the convention was not among the most important. A nationalist of long standing, he represented a small state and often had to balance competing interests. He was the first to propose a bicameral congress with equal REPRESENTATION of the states in one house and representation apportioned by population or financial contribution in the other—a proposal that later became the basis of the GREAT COMPROMISE. He favored abolition of the slave trade but acquiesced in the compromise that imposed a twenty-year moratorium on congressional power to accomplish it. He wanted Congress to be the dominant branch of government, with full authority to remove Presidents and judges; and he wanted to limit executive power and to create a council to share the President's appointing power. Forced by illness to leave the convention early, Dickinson authorized a colleague to sign his name to the finished Constitution.

Dickinson wrote a series of nine newspaper essays (signed "Fabius") in support of RATIFICATION OF THE CONSTITUTION; they were influential, especially in Pennsylvania. He declined appointment as a United States senator from Delaware and never held public office under the new Constitution.

DENNIS J. MAHONEY
(1986)

Bibliography

FORD, PAUL LEICESTER, ed. 1970 *Political Writings of John Dickinson.* New York: DaCapo.

JACOBSON, D. L. 1965 *John Dickinson and the Revolution in Pennsylvania.* Berkeley: University of California Press.

STILLE, CHARLES J. 1891 *Life and Times of John Dickinson.* Philadelphia: Historical Society of Philadelphia.

DICTA

See: Obiter Dictum

DIES, MARTIN
(1900–1972)

Martin Dies, an anti-NEW DEAL Democrat from Texas, served in the HOUSE OF REPRESENTATIVES from 1931 to 1945 and from 1953 to 1961. In 1938 he became chairman of the special Committee to Investigate Un-American Activities, forerunner of the HOUSE COMMITTEE ON UN-AMERICAN ACTIVITIES. Dies and his committee attained national prominence through sensational exposés of supposed Fascist, Nazi, and communist activity in government, labor unions, and industry. His published lists of government employees who were "Communists or Communist dupes," the publicity he gave to unsubstantiated accusations, and his disregard of normal CIVIL LIBERTIES foreshadowed the activities of Senator Joseph McCarthy.

DENNIS J. MAHONEY
(1986)

DIFFERENCE AND CONSTITUTIONAL EQUALITY

Central to our liberal tradition is the conviction that we share a universal human nature, from which follows our common entitlement, or right, to be treated with respect and dignity. Central to our commitment to the RULE OF LAW, and to our constitutional scheme of governance, is the conviction that we are all entitled to legal equality, or equal treatment under the law. And yet our individual identity is clearly formed, in part, by traits that we share with some but not others. Women and men have different biological roles and capacities in reproduction, for example, and African Americans and whites have profoundly different political and cultural histories. Furthermore, all LEGISLATION, from the simplest criminal statute to the highest constitutional norm, virtually by definition, categorizes citizens, treating some quite differently from others. Thus, we claim and aspire to a universality belied by our differentiating traits, and we are committed to legal equality in the face of the brute inequalities that law itself creates. How, then, to justify law, and the differences it creates and mirrors among us?

In the mid- and late-twentieth century, the Supreme Court, under the sweeping language of the FOURTEENTH AMENDMENT guarantee of EQUAL PROTECTION OF THE LAWS, developed a rich body of law and principle in response to these central paradoxes. Basically, the Court now reads the mandate of "equal protection of the laws" as imposing upon state and federal legislation a requirement of rationality. If the lines drawn by a law between different groups of people reflect a real difference between them, then the law is rational and upheld; if not, it constitutes a failure of equal protection and might be struck. A law imposing a minimum age on drivers, for example, is not a denial of equal protection because the line it draws is basically rational: the legally created difference between sixteen and seventeen year-olds does reflect, albeit only crudely, a real relation between the driving abilities and maturity of older and younger teenagers. Some legislative categories, however, are based on inherently SUSPECT CLASSIFICATIONS, some so suspect as to create a virtually insurmountable presumption against their constitutionality. Racial categories are of this sort. Racially segregatory laws simply do not reflect any real difference between citizens. They are presumptively irrational, and consequently unconstitutional.

This deceptively simple formula—equality requires rationality—has the virtue of underscoring the coherence of our basic liberal and legalistic ideals. The prohibition on irrational legal categories and the insistence that racial categories are presumptively irrational not only restate our commitment to universality while permitting the categorization of citizens necessary to sensible legislation, but also remind us of the deeply divisive consequences of the historically disastrous belief, held by most whites through most of this country's history, in black difference and inferiority. The "folding" of the liberal commitment to universalism, the legalistic ideal of equal treatment, and the clear understanding that legislation premised on a belief in black difference and inferiority violates the equal protection clause of the Fourteenth Amendment protects us against the danger of repeating the most horrific chapter of our history. In spite of its strengths, however, and its breathtakingly elegant restatement of liberal ideals, this deceptively simple understanding of the meaning of equal protection has produced tremendous dissension and division within the Supreme Court, and has triggered the production of a vast and exceedingly complex body of DOCTRINE. The core problems with the Court's formulaic solution—that equality requires rationality, that rationality requires that legislative distinctions track real differences, and that racial differences are simply not real, but rather a product of bigoted perception—are threefold.

First, not all racial differences are a problem of or created by bigoted perception, and not all legislation that tracks or targets those differences is necessarily malign. That the belief in black inferiority necessarily rests on a belief in black difference certainly does not imply that all claims of racial difference rest on a racist and false commitment to black inferiority or white superiority. Rather, some differences are real and in need of redress: differences in average income levels, educational achievement, and infant mortality rates between otherwise comparable black and white communities are examples. Noting these differences, and legislating in a way meant to redress them, may be good or bad policy, but it is clearly not the same thing, and not the same evil, as legislatively segregating the races because of the presumed inferiority of African Americans. Nevertheless, and in spite of the clear difference between "benign" discrimination, or AFFIRMATIVE ACTION (meant to eradicate the patterns of subordination from which perceptible differences stem) and "malign" discrimination (meant to create, tolerate, or perpetuate that very subordination), the Court's commitment to the ideal of a "colorblind" constitution, which would neither see nor tolerate legislated racial difference, has cast the constitutionality of affirmative legislation designed to ameliorate the consequences of our racist past into considerable doubt.

The second problem with the Court's understanding of equality and difference is simply that even if it be true that claims of racial difference are so often coupled with beliefs in racial inferiority that it is morally sensible to view with suspicion all legislation that racially delineates, it is not at all clear that a recognition of other deep or inherent differences between groups of people—between men and women, or ALIENS and citizens, or mentally competent and incompetent adults—is similarly badly motivated, or that legislation that presumes or respects those differences courts social disaster. Sometimes, of course, such delineations are indeed badly motivated, and in a way that does echo our racial histories. The turn of the century "paternalistic" laws prohibiting women's participation in professional life, or denying women VOTING RIGHTS, or excusing them from JURY SERVICE, for example, did seem to be premised in part on a claim of women's intrinsic differences, and that claim was in turn wedded to a belief in female inferiority and vulnerability. But some "paternalistic" laws are not so clearly harmful, or so unambiguously motivated. Laws granting widows but not widowers a presumption of dependency in determining various benefits, for example, might be based on a wrongful and harmful "stereotype" of female dependency, or it might be an attempt, akin to an affirmative action program, to protect women who have spent their adult lives in nonremunerative domestic realms, against the harmful effects of a market economy that fails to recognize or compensate household and domestic labor. Laws that permit or require employers to protect female workers' job security against the risk of a pregnancy-related disability, even when they do not similarly protect all disabled workers, might be based on the paternalistic and pernicious notion that because women but not men have babies they must be protected against the harsh reality of the workaday world, or it might be based on a commendable attempt to equalize the abilities of men and women to combine parenthood and work.

The third problem with the Court's equation of equality with rationality, and of rationality with a tracking of difference, is that it is blind to the harms law can effect by ignoring, rather than fetishizing, differences. Just as a flat tax will disproportionately hurt the poor and help the rich, so a flat rule requiring, for example, that all firefighters or police officers have a minimum height or weight, will disproportionately exclude women from the ranks, and, to whatever extent height and weight fail to correlate with job performance, they effect this exclusion for no good reason. Similarly, a language proficiency requirement, evenhandedly applied, will disproportionately exclude those for whom English is a second language, and test score requirements will disproportionately exclude those who do not test well. If laws permitting or requiring either private or public employers to use such criteria are constitutionally permissible even where their relevance to the performance legitimately expected of employees is weak or nonexistent, then these laws will themselves be complicit in the perpetuation of societal subordination of already disadvantaged groups. And, their complicity lies in their failure to take real differences into account, not in their counterfactual and demeaning insistence on difference in the face of a deeper, more real, or truer universality.

These problems have prompted constitutional commentators to suggest alternative approaches to the problems of equality and difference. One approach, originating in some forms of radical FEMINIST THEORY and CRITICAL RACE THEORY, suggests that societal differentiations between groups such as women and men and blacks and whites are themselves invariably a function of, or caused by, political subordination, and that it is precisely that political subordination that is forbidden by our constitutional commitment to equality. It is subordination that creates the perception of difference, and it is subordination that is, basically, unconstitutional. Hence, all perceived "differences" are windows to subordination, which the law should be required to address. This is sometimes called the "antisubordination" approach: the law should concern itself with the eradication of the subordination that causes differentiation, rather than with a rational mirroring of difference. Where a law aggravates or furthers, rather than ameliorates or addresses, such subordination, it should be invalidated as unconstitutional and violative of our commitment to equality, and it should be struck down regardless of whether it echoes or challenges perceived differences.

A second approach, sometimes called an "acceptance" approach and which stems from some forms of difference feminism or cultural feminism, reads in the equal protection clause a mandate that states take whatever steps are necessary, not to track differences nor to eradicate them, but rather to render the differences harmless or inconsequential. This approach has enormous appeal, particularly for its common-sense acknowledgment that some differences are properly cherished rather than viewed with suspicion, and should only cause concern to the degree they may cause unnecessary suffering. That women generally undergo pregnancy, childbirth, and lactation in order to reproduce, while men simply ejaculate, for example, is surely one such difference: it is a difference that is impossible to deny, and one that many men and women take

great pleasure in. But it is also one that, presently, does have harmful consequences for women. Those consequences, however, are not necessarily consequences of the difference, or put differently, the difference itself need not have harmful consequences. Laws, such as those requiring employers to protect the job security of pregnant workers, can be used to prevent harm. Similarly, that women presently earn less than men at least in part because women engage in more childcare, is a difference that also has enormous consequences, many of them harmful to women. Those harms as well could be at least in part ameliorated through legal intervention: laws could, for example, require that the paycheck of a wage earner married to a spouse working in the home be issued jointly to both spouses, or even be divided equally between them, with the stay-at-home spouse receiving a full half. On this approach, it would be the failure to take action to render difference harmless—rather than the recognition of difference itself—that constituted the constitutional violation.

Both of these alternative approaches, however, arguably founder on the slippery slope to socialism. Surely the differences that are most subordinating are the differences caused by our unequal distribution of wealth in this society, and surely those wealth differences are the precise differences that most cry out to be rendered "harmless." Under either an antisubordination or an acceptance approach to difference and equality, the wealth difference would raise a constitutional problem, it would be something to be eradicated or something to be "made harmless." These two alternative approaches would suggest that at least vast differences in wealth should be viewed as constitutionally suspect. This result seems counterintuitive, and counterexperiential, particularly given the undeniable historical role of the Constitution in the protection of private PROPERTY against public redistribution.

What should we make of this conclusion? If we hold fast to our commitment to private property, and to our view of the Constitution as its guardian, then that commitment and that view should indeed weigh against either of these alternative conceptions of equality and difference. Perhaps, though, the difficulty lies not so much with these alternative conceptions of equality, as with our assurance that vast wealth differences are constitutionally unobjectionable, and even constitutionally protected. Such assurance might not be warranted. Minimally, the emergence of these alternative conceptions of constitutional equality might prompt us to reexamine our conviction that our constitutional ideals of equality, equal protection, and liberty all buttress, rather than undermine our conviction that unchecked differences of wealth produced by an unchecked market are constitutionally protected against redistribution. Rather than discard conceptions of constitutional equality on the grounds that they throw the constitutionality of unchecked capital into question, perhaps we should reexamine, openly and without precommitment, whether or not it is truly the case that our constitutional commitment to an ideal of equality can co-exist with our tolerance of massive wealth differences, and the extraordinary inequalities to which it leads. Perhaps our tolerance of great wealth disparities and our espousal of ideals of equality can co-exist. But perhaps they cannot. If not, then this simultaneous constitutional tolerance of the institutions of wealth and capital, and constitutional celebration of equality, is surely a contradiction as central, and as momentous, and as disabling, as our country's contradictory embrace, in the first century of its existence, of the peculiar institution of SLAVERY, and our simultaneous espousal of the moral and constitutional ideal of liberty.

ROBIN WEST
(2000)

Bibliography

BECKER, MARY 1987 Prince Charming: Abstract Equality. *Supreme Court Review* 1987:201–247.

FISS, OWEN 1976 Groups and the Equal Protection Clause. *Philosophy and Public Affairs* 5:107–177.

GILLIGAN, CAROL 1982 *In a Different Voice: Psychological Theory and Women's Development.* Cambridge, Mass.: Harvard University Press.

LAWRENCE, CHARLES and MATSUDA, MARI 1996 *We Will Not Go Back: Making the Case for Affirmative Action.* Boston, Mass.: Houghton-Mifflin.

LITTLETON, CHRISTINE 1987 Reconstructing Sexual Equality. *California Law Review* 75:1279–1337.

MACKINNON, CATHERINE 1987 *Feminism Unmodified: Discourses on Life and Law.* Cambridge, Mass.: Harvard University Press.

—— 1991 Reflections on Sex Equality Under Law. *Yale Law Journal* 100:1281–1328.

MINOW, MARTHA 1990 *Making All the Difference: Inclusion, Exclusion and American Law.* Ithaca, N.Y.: Cornell University Press.

WEST, ROBIN 1997 *Caring for Justice.* New York: New York University Press.

DIFRANCESCO, UNITED STATES v.
449 U.S. 117 (1980)

In this case on the DOUBLE JEOPARDY clause of the Fifth Amendment a 5–4 Supreme Court sustained the constitutionality of the ORGANIZED CRIME CONTROL ACT OF 1970, which in special instances granted to the United States the right to APPEAL a criminal sentence. Justice HARRY A. BLACKMUN for the majority, rejecting the dissenters' contention that review of a sentence is comparable to the review of a verdict of acquittal, held that a government appeal that succeeded in increasing a sentence did not constitute double jeopardy.

LEONARD W. LEVY
(1986)

DILLON, JOHN F.
(1831–1914)

Elected a member of the Iowa Supreme Court at thirty-one, John Forrest Dillon was a leading advocate of the PUBLIC PURPOSE doctrine. In 1869 President ULYSSES S. GRANT appointed Dillon to the Eighth Circuit Court, but after ten years' service Dillon resigned to accept a professorship at Columbia University Law School. Within three years he left that post to enter private practice, and he soon represented major business interests including Jay Gould and the Union Pacific Railroad.

Although Dillon was not an original thinker, his writings and speeches helped establish his tremendous reputation. He served as president of the American Bar Association in 1892 and delivered the prestigious Storrs Lectures at Yale University shortly thereafter. These were published in 1895 as *The Laws and Jurisprudence in England and America,* and in them Dillon claimed that the DUE PROCESS CLAUSE of the FOURTEENTH AMENDMENT "in the most impressive and solemn form places life, liberty, contracts, and property . . . among the fundamental and indestructible rights of all the people of the United States." He endorsed SUBSTANTIVE DUE PROCESS and rhapsodized on the distinction of America's written CONSTITUTIONS: their limitations on government. Restraints such as SEPARATION OF POWERS and CHECKS AND BALANCES were just two of the many means available to prevent "despotism of the many,—of the majority." Dillon also wrote an influential treatise on *Municipal Corporations* (1872).

As a judge, Dillon narrowly construed the public purpose DOCTRINE. He believed that a municipal corporation had the authority to tax to support a public purpose, but incidental public benefits did not justify such taxation. Moreover, he believed that the judiciary could inquire into the legislative purpose and that private enterprises (with the sole exception of railroads) did not qualify under the doctrine. He thus wrote laissez-faire ideas into the law as limitations on legislative power (*Loan Association v. Topeka, Commercial National Bank of Cleveland v. Iola,* both 1873). Dillon appeared frequently before the Supreme Court where, in UNITED STATES V. TRANS-MISSOURI FREIGHT ASSOCIATION (1897) he urged the Court to adopt the RULE OF REASON whereby the SHERMAN ANTITRUST ACT would be read to prohibit only unreasonable restraints of trade, a position finally adopted in STANDARD OIL COMPANY V. UNITED STATES (1911).

DAVID GORDON
(1986)

Bibliography

JACOBS, CLYDE E. (1954)1973 *Law Writers and the Courts.* New York: Da Capo Press.

DIONISIO, UNITED STATES v.
410 U.S. 1 (1973)

A gambling suspect refused a federal court's order to provide a voice sample to a GRAND JURY, and was adjudged in civil contempt and committed to custody. The Supreme Court affirmed. The Court rejected, 7–2, a claim that the order violated the suspect's RIGHT AGAINST SELF-INCRIMI-NATION, saying that the voice sample was to be used only for identification, not for the content of the statements. A 6–3 majority also rejected a claim that the order violated the FOURTH AMENDMENT. Because there was no "seizure" here, there was no need to demonstrate the reasonableness of the grand jury's request.

DAVID GORDON
(1986)

DIRECT AND INDIRECT TAXES

The Constitution imposes two major limitations on the federal power to tax. Direct taxes can be levied only if allocated among the states according to population. All other taxes (indirect taxes) must be uniform among the United States.

The requirement of apportioning direct taxes apparently was included because the southern states feared that they would bear excessive burdens on land and slaves—a fear demonstrated by the fact that (until the FOURTEENTH AMENDMENT) only three-fifths of slaves were counted in the population. Nobody in the Convention appeared to be very clear, however, on just what was a direct tax that had to be allocated.

The issue first came to the Supreme Court in HYLTON V. UNITED STATES (1796). A duty laid on carriages was challenged as being a direct tax. The Court pointed out the difficulties with direct taxes, particularly the fact that while the total amount allocated to each state related to the population of that state, the individual taxpayers (in this case the owners of carriages) would pay quite different amounts depending not only on population but also on the relative numbers of the taxable subjects within the

state. The Court expressed doubt that any taxes other than a capitation tax or a tax on the value of land could be called direct taxes. Over the next century the issue seldom arose, for Congress levied very few taxes beyond customs duties until the CIVIL WAR. However, the Court did hold that a tax of ten percent on state-issued currency (VEAZIE BANK V. FENNO, 1869), a tax on the succession to a decedent's property (*Scholey v. Rew*, 1875), and income taxes (*Springer v. United States*, (1881) were all indirect, not direct taxes.

The income tax involved in *Springer* had remained in effect only until 1872. By the 1890s, however, many groups called for a reduction in federal dependence on tariffs for revenue and for an income tax on wealthier persons. In 1894 a statute was passed imposing a tax on all incomes over $4,000. Facing a challenge to this tax, the Supreme Court reversed its earlier stand and in POLLOCK V. FARMERS' LOANTRUST CO. (1895) held the tax a direct tax and so invalid because not apportioned. The Court's new position was that taxes on the rents or income of real estate and taxes on personal property or the income from personal property were direct taxes and must be apportioned, though taxes on income from other sources would not be direct taxes.

A few years later there was another attempt to enact an income tax law. More conservative members of Congress countered by presenting a proposal to amend the Constitution to provide that income taxes need not be apportioned. Perhaps to their surprise, the SIXTEENTH AMENDMENT was proposed by Congress in 1909 and secured ratification by three-fourths of the states in 1913. The result, of course, was to open the door to the major federal revenue producer.

During the twentieth century there have been occasional attempts to litigate various taxes as being direct—but never with success. Congress does not impose capitation taxes nor property taxes—and all other kinds of taxes apparently are indirect.

The requirement that indirect taxes be uniform has given little difficulty. In upholding a federal tax on legacies in *Knowlton v. Moore* (1900), the Court said that what is required is geographical uniformity. A tax is uniform when it operates with the same force and effect in every place where the subject of it is found. It does not matter that the subject may exist in some states and not in others so long as the tax is the same. Thus, the Court in *Fernandez v. Wiener* (1945) upheld a federal statute imposing death taxes on community property—even though such property existed in only the few states that had adopted the community property system. In *United States v. Ptasynski* (1983) the Court cast some doubt on the geographical limitation by upholding a provision exempting Alaskan oil from a crude oil windfall profit tax. (See TAXING AND SPEND-ING POWER.)

EDWARD L. BARRETT, JR.
(1986)

Bibliography
PAUL, RANDOLPH E. 1954 *Taxation in the United States*. Pages 46–58. Boston: Little, Brown.

DIRECT DEMOCRACY

Those who framed the Constitution opted for a system of representative government rather than direct democracy. The true distinction between the "pure democracies of Greece" and the American government, explained JAMES MADISON in THE FEDERALIST #63, lay "in the total exclusion of the people in their collective capacity from any share in the latter." It was this distinction that the Federalists believed might permit American government to succeed where other democracies had failed. Placing the exclusive power of ordinary lawmaking in governors distinct from the governed, said Madison, would refine and enlarge public views "by passing them through the medium of a chosen body of citizens" whose wisdom, patriotism, and love of justice would make them unlikely to sacrifice the interest of the country "to temporal or partial considerations." Representative bodies afforded greater opportunities for deliberation and debate. Popular masses were perceived as too quick to form preferences, frequently failing to consider adequately the interests of others, and overly susceptible to contagious passions.

Part of the Framers' distrust of popular rule was the threat it posed to creditor rights and individual property interests. And the well-heeled delegates had plenty to fear from the masses of have-nots. Indeed, some historians contend that the central problem that prompted the convening of the delegates at Philadelphia was not the weaknesses of the ARTICLES OF CONFEDERATION but concern over an excess of POPULISM in the states. In any case, Madison and his fellow Federalists labored mightily—and successfully—to block an attempt to include in the FIRST AMENDMENT a right of the people to "instruct their representatives."

In the early part of the twentieth century the Progressives successfully introduced two forms of direct democracy at the state level—the INITIATIVE and the REFERENDUM. These innovative reforms, now a part of the lawmaking process in more than half the states, were a response to the widely perceived corruption and control of legislators by wealthy interest groups. The Progressives sought to curb legislatures by placing corrective power in

the citizenry. The initiative allows the voters to propose and enact legislation by simple majority vote. Initiatives are thus designed to rectify corruption that impedes legislation by circumventing the legislative framework. Conversely, referenda are directed against corruption that produces legislation by adding an additional layer to the lawmaking process. The referendum allows the voters to reject laws previously enacted by the legislature. Thus, the two Progressive reforms simultaneously make it both less difficult and more difficult to enact laws.

Not long after many of the western states began to use the initiative device, its constitutionality came under attack. In *Pacific States Telephone & Telegraph Co. v. Oregon* (1912), the Supreme Court was asked to rule whether a state's use of a voter initiative to enact a tax measure was consistent with the REPUBLICAN FORM OF GOVERNMENT guaranteed to the states by Article IV, section 4, of the Constitution. The taxpayer argued that the representative nature of republican government precluded the people from taking legislative functions into their own hands. The Court never reached the merits of this claim, holding instead that whether a state government is "republican" was a POLITICAL QUESTION that courts were not competent to answer. The Court, treating the challenge as an attack on the legitimacy of the Oregon government, relied on LUTHER V. BORDEN (1849) for the proposition that such a matter was properly to be resolved by the political branches of the national government (Congress and the President).

The JUSTICIABILITY bar to the resolution of the constitutional challenge to citizen lawmaking remains securely in place. But although the Supreme Court has never passed on the constitutionality of direct democracy devices in general, the Court has condemned its use in particular applications. In HUNTER V. ERICKSON (1969) the Supreme Court struck down a voter initiative altering a city charter to require that any OPEN HOUSING LAWS passed by the city council be approved by voter referendum before taking effect. The Court's majority held that by making open housing laws more difficult to enact, the charter amendment erected special barriers to legislation favoring ethnic and religious minorities and therefore violated the EQUAL PROTECTION clause of the FOURTEENTH AMENDMENT.

Similar concerns led the Court to invalidate an anti-SCHOOL BUSING initiative passed by the voters of the state of Washington. In *Washington v. Seattle School District No. 1* (1982), a 5–4 majority thwarted the voter reversal of an attempt by Seattle school authorities to achieve racial balance through involuntary busing. The majority's route to its conclusion that the initiative offended the equal protection clause cannot easily be mapped. At times, Justice HARRY A. BLACKMUN, the opinion's author, appears to find impermissible racial motivation. He notes that "there is little doubt that the initiative was effectively drawn for racial purposes," a fact of which he believed the Washington electorate was "surely aware." Elsewhere in the opinion, he seems to rest the decision on the customized alteration of the normal decision-making process for issues of unique interest to minority groups. In such instances, Blackmun suggests, inquiry into motivation is not necessary. This latter reading is reinforced by the 8–1 decision in CRAWFORD V. BOARD OF EDUCATION (1982), handed down the same day.

Over Justice THURGOOD MARSHALL's lone dissenting observation that the case was indistinguishable from *Seattle*, the Court in *Crawford* sustained an amendment to the California Constitution (approved overwhelmingly by both houses of the California legislature and ratified by the voters) stripping state courts of the power to order busing, except in cases of Fourteenth Amendment violations. It is not uncommon for commentators to express amazement that the two cases were decided by the same Court, much less on the same day. The Court's conclusion in *Crawford* that the California amendment was not adopted with a racially discriminatory purpose is difficult to square with its opposite assessment on a similar record in *Seattle*.

What differentiates *Seattle* from *Crawford*, however, is the role of direct democracy. The sponsors of the Washington initiative sought to circumvent the representative process that produced Seattle's pupil reassignment plan. The school board had historically made considerable efforts to alleviate the isolation of the district's sizable minority population. Local attempts to recall the board members responsible for some of these efforts had failed. The initiative process afforded an opportunity for the populace to reverse the minority's gains. In marked contrast to the Washington process, the California amendment in *Crawford* was a joint effort of the legislature and the voters. Here was not a case of the people bypassing a representative body. The Madisonian nightmare, so stark in *Seattle*, was largely absent from the California reaction against a zealous judiciary. None of this is explicit in the two opinions. Indeed, neither opinion makes any serious effort to distinguish its companion case. The Justices were understandably hesitant to announce explicitly a distinction grounded on a distrust of electoral majorities. But it is hard to reconcile the two results on any other ground.

Nowhere is the tension between the Madisonian fears of popular masses and the American democratic ideal more in evidence than in an interchange between Justice HUGO L. BLACK and Thurgood Marshall, then solicitor general, that occurred during the oral argument in REITMAN V. MULKEY (1967). By an overwhelming majority, California voters had adopted an initiative measure amending the state constitution to repeal existing open housing laws and forbid the enactment of new ones. During ORAL ARGUMENT, Marshall stressed that this authorization of RACIAL DISCRIMINATION in the private housing market had been the result of voters bypassing the representative process. "Wouldn't you have exactly the same argument," he was asked, if the provision challenged "had been enacted by the California legislature?" "It's the same argument," Marshall replied, "I just have more force with this." "No," interjected Justice Black, "it seems to me you have less. Because here, it's moving in the direction of letting the people of the States . . . establish their policy, which is as near to a democracy as you can get."

Hugo Black was undoubtedly right in observing that direct voter legislation is quite a bit closer to "democracy" than legislative products. What his vision obscures, however, is the intentional nature of the gap between true democracy and the republican form of government carved out by those who drafted the Constitution. Representative government was designed to capture the virtues of POPULAR SOVEREIGNTY without being tainted by its vices. Accountability to the electorate was to be the touchstone of legitimacy. But the Framers opted for the virtues of agency, favoring a removed deliberation over the impassioned decision making of participatory democracy.

Two-thirds of those questioned in a 1987 nationwide Gallup survey said that citizens ought to be able to vote directly on some state and local laws, and a poll conducted in 1977 found more than half in favor of a constitutional amendment for a national initiative. In the late 1970s, the Senate held extensive hearings on just such a proposed amendment. Despite the sponsorship of more than fifty members of Congress and supportive testimony by a wide range of both conservatives and liberals, the proposal died in committee. Americans are not, it seems, quite ready to abandon their commitment to the Framers' preferences.

JULIAN N. EULE
(1992)

Bibliography

BELL, DERRICK 1978 The Referendum: Democracy's Barrier to Racial Equality. *Washington Law Review* 54:1–29.
CRONIN, THOMAS E. 1989 *Direct Democracy*. Cambridge, Mass.: Harvard University Press.
EULE, JULIAN N. 1990 Judicial Review of Direct Democracy. *Yale Law Journal* 99:1503–1590.

DIRECT DEMOCRACY
(Update)

The 1990s witnessed no abatement in the trend for American voters to employ the direct ballot increasingly in their politics, and vital constitutional questions have continued to surface in the federal courts centering on the legitimacy of various INITIATIVE and REFERENDUM measures. Indeed, the term "government by initiative" has become a commonplace in political commentary. Most of the initiatives and referenda in the states have been designed to achieve legislative reforms. However, many of the most controversial, both as to their policy effects and as to their constitutionality, have been framed not as ordinary LEGISLATION but rather as amendments to the state constitutions. Especially notable in recent years have been direct-ballot measures that may be termed "rights-reducing," that is to say, intended to reduce the rights that may be claimed under state law by individuals and groups. The constitutionality of the plebiscitary process itself, in its several variants, has also been the subject of attention in these debates and in several cases before the Supreme Court.

The Court has sought on the one hand to define the standards by which the constitutionality of specific procedures for the direct ballot can be tested, and, on the other, it has applied EQUAL PROTECTION analysis and other criteria to decide on the constitutional validity of the legislative results of plebiscites in the states. As noted by the late JULIAN N. EULE and other notable commentators, the Court's record has been marked by significant ambiguities, lacunae, and apparent inconsistencies. The impression of inconsistencies in the jurisprudence of direct-ballot constitutionality has left open the door to widely varying results in the lower courts. This uncertainty is evident, for example, in the litigative history of Proposition 209, a California constitutional amendment passed by the state's voters in 1996 with the result of ending state AFFIRMATIVE ACTION programs that employed gender or race classifications. The federal district court issued an INJUNCTION against enforcement, on the ground that in order to reverse this measure, the minorities and women affected adversely could not use ordinary political and legislative process but instead carried the special burdens of action exclusively through constitutional amendment—a more costly and difficult procedure. In this respect, the district court applied the standard regarding "special barriers" to obtaining redress through regular political processes, as formulated in HUNTER V. ERICKSON (1969) and later opinions. The district court also cited several Supreme Court decisions requiring STRICT SCRUTINY of measures that could disadvantage racial minorities, and contended that in light of predictable adverse effects on minorities and women the Proposition 209 amendment was invalid as a violation of equal protection. Shortly afterward, however, a three-judge panel of the U.S. Court of Appeals for the Ninth Circuit overturned the district court's decision, declaring that because women and minorities actually comprised in

total a majority of the citizenry of California, no equal protection issue or procedural flaw stood in the way of its validation. Tellingly, however, the Ninth Circuit judges also complained that they found themselves "caught in the cross-fire of seemingly irreconcilable Supreme Court precedent." In the last analysis, they declared, it was properly "the general rule of our constitutional democracy" that the judgment of federal courts should not be exercised to "trump self-government." The Supreme Court declined to hear arguments in an appeal of the Ninth Circuit decision.

The Ninth Circuit decision reflected a strong strain of historic deference to state direct-ballot measures that had been articulated in the Supreme Court by, for example, Justice HUGO L. BLACK, who believed that, absent a COMPELLING STATE INTEREST or clear indication of discriminatory animus and effects, plebiscitary measures should be regarded as admirable examples of "devotion to democracy, not to bias, discrimination, or prejudice." An example of where such deference can lead, especially in a taxation case, was the decision of the Supreme Court in *Nordlinger v. Hahn* (1992). The Court upheld the constitutionality of a 1978 California ballot measure, Proposition 13, which set up a two-tier tax system that gave vast advantages to existing PROPERTY owners over those who would acquire property after the amendment went into effect; the majority upheld the measure even though explicitly declaring that it was manifestly unjust in its operation.

The same Justices who let stand the Proposition 209 decision when appealed from the Ninth Circuit had decided differently in an earlier direct-ballot case, ROMER V. EVANS (1996), which also concerned minority rights and special barriers in political process. Over protests by the dissenters that the Court was involving itself in "cultural debate[s]" that ought not concern the judiciary, the majority ruled unconstitutional a Colorado state constitutional amendment, adopted by initiative, that would have invalidated all local ordinances barring discrimination based on SEXUAL ORIENTATION. Declaring that this amendment violated the equal protection clause of the FOURTEENTH AMENDMENT "[by making] a class of persons a stranger to its laws," Justice ANTHONY M. KENNEDY wrote for the majority that homosexuals would thereby be denied the "safeguards that others enjoy" and would be rendered "unequal to everyone else." The Court also referred to the extra political barrier placed on homosexual citizens to obtain redress: They would need to resort to state-level constitutional amendment as the only procedure available if the amendment were to be applied.

A different strain in the Court's jurisprudence on the direct ballot has been intertwined with FIRST AMENDMENT DOCTRINE, and to some degree also with FEDERALISM considerations, as the Court has assessed state measures designed to address alleged flaws of direct democracy in actual practice. Criticisms have been directed especially at the influence of money, the use of professional signature gatherers and data banks, manipulation of public opinion through distortive ballot language and printed arguments in voter pamphlets, and the like. These ills are often compounded by low rates of participation by eligible voters in elections that institute fundamental changes of policy and law. Because of these features of actual practice, the critics contend, the initiative and referendum have become the very embodiment of special-interest and single-issue politics that undermine the deliberative virtues (and the checks and balance) of ordinary legislative procedure. There is, in this view, an "excess of democracy."

But how far can the states legitimately regulate the direct-ballot process, and still have their legislation survive challenges under the "exacting scrutiny" standard that pertains in First Amendment matters? This issue came before the Court in *Buckley v. American Constitutional Law Foundation* (1998), commonly referred to as *"Buckley II"* to differentiate it from the landmark case BUCKLEY V. VALEO (1976) in which First Amendment protection of speech was invoked to strike down strict federal restrictions on political campaign contributions. In *Buckley II*, the Court struck down a set of regulations affecting the solicitation of signatures in the petition phase of the direct ballot process in Colorado. The state had required solicitors to wear badges with personal name identification and had prohibited signature gathering by nonresidents and residents who were not registered to vote. No compelling state interest was shown, the majority ruled, because other means were available to control corruption or fraud. But the Justices also reaffirmed a concept of the initiative process—especially the petition phase when measures are qualified for the ballot—as involving "core political speech" protected by the First Amendment. In dissent, however, Chief Justice WILLIAM H. REHNQUIST, consistently with the view of state prerogatives that he has expressed in many federalism opinions, declared flatly that "[s]tate ballot initiatives are a matter of state concern"; he found no merit in the majority's application of First Amendment constraints.

The continuing importance of the direct ballot has been manifested in hundreds of measures in recent years, among them votes to restrict the rights of immigrants; reduce state protection of defendants' rights in CRIMINAL PROCEDURE; enhance "victims' rights"; articulate environmental rights; establish a RIGHT OF PRIVACY; introduce new economic regulations or, alternatively, immunize private property from some of regulation's economic effects; limit the TAXING OR SPENDING POWERS; and reform the structure and powers of state government. In sum, the plebiscitary movement maintains its momentum at the century's close. And it is safe to anticipate a continuing debate over the constitutional dimensions of the great historic question regarding the place of populistic lawmaking process in a republican polity. The core dilemma was expressed by JAMES MADISON when he argued in FEDERALIST No. 49, that "a constitutional road to the decision of the people" must be kept open, as it was the people on which a republic's legitimacy must rest; but that because plebiscitary process carried "the danger of disturbing the public tranquillity by interesting too strongly the public passions," only rarely, and on great issues of public life, should the citizenry want to resort to direct votes. This cautionary view will undoubtedly continue to operate in counterpoint with arguments that the direct ballot is the "most democratic of procedures" (as it was termed in the dissent in *Romer*), requiring special deference from the judiciary. And it will continue to be an urgent question whether the JUDICIAL POWER should be deployed more vigorously so as to assure that fundamental constitutional values are not overwhelmed by the "public passions" that Madison and his colleagues feared so greatly at the nation's founding.

HARRY N. SCHEIBER
(2000)

Bibliography

EULE, JULIAN N.   1990   Judicial Review of Direct Democracy. *Yale Law Journal* 99:1503.

MICHELMAN, FRANK I.   1998   "Protecting the People from Themselves," or How Direct Can Democracy Be? *UCLA Law Review* 45:1717–1734.

SCHACTER, JANE S.   1995   The Pursuit of "Popular Intent": Interpretive Dilemmas in Direct Democracy. *Yale Law Journal* 105:107–176.

SCHEIBER, HARRY N.   1007   The Direct Ballot and State Constitutionalism. *Rutgers Law Journal* 28:787–823.

TARR, G. ALAN, ed.   1996   *Constitutional Politics in the States: Contemporary Controversies and Historical Patterns.* Westport, Conn.: Greenwood Press.

DIRECT ELECTIONS

Whenever there has been dissatisfaction with the performance of appointing officials, whether party, legislative, or electoral college, there has been a demand for direct elections. The Progressive era (1890–1920) marked a heyday for such demands, producing direct election of senators (SEVENTEENTH AMENDMENT), direct nomination of state party candidates (through PRIMARY ELECTIONS), and, in many cities and states, direct legislation through INITIATIVE and REFERENDUM, and direct RECALL of candidates. After most close presidential elections, there has also been talk of direct election of the President in place of the ELECTORAL COLLEGE.

Direct election of the President and direct party primaries have been criticized on policy (but not constitutional) grounds for weakening the two-party system. Initiative and referendum, besides being criticized as "plebiscitary," have been challenged as violative of the GUARANTEE CLAUSE, but such challenges have uniformly been found nonjusticiable. The leading case is *Pacific States Telephone Company v. Oregon* (1912).

WARD E. Y. ELLIOTT
(1986)

Bibliography

BONFIELD, ARTHUR E. 1962 The Guarantee Clause of Article IV, Section 4: A Study in Constitutional Desuetude. *Minnesota Law Review* 46:513–572.

DIRKSEN, EVERETT M.
(1896–1969)

Everett McKinley Dirksen represented Illinois as a United States congressman (1933–1949) and senator (1951–1969). Despite a previous record as an isolationist in FOREIGN AFFAIRS and a reactionary in domestic affairs, he contributed to the legislative successes of the Democratic Presidents when he was the Republican leader of the SENATE in the 1960s. Dirksen was an eccentric—flamboyant in style, florid in oratory, and organ-voiced; he was also a superb parliamentary tactician and a politician who was exceptionally inconsistent in his policies. On matters of constitutional interest, he supported MCCARTHYISM and opposed the censure of Senator Joseph R. McCarthy, and savagely criticized the Supreme Court for opinions he disliked, especially on REAPPORTIONMENT, SEPARATION OF CHURCH AND STATE, and the rights of the criminally accused. Dirksen favored bills to curb the Court's APPELLATE JURISDICTION, proposed a constitutional amendment to allow prayers in public schools, and led a movement that failed by the vote of one state to convene a constitutional convention. Yet the CIVIL RIGHTS ACT OF 1964 and the VOTING RIGHTS ACTS OF 1965 would not have been passed without his support.

LEONARD W. LEVY
(1986)

Bibliography

SCHAPSMEIER, EDWARD L. 1985 *Dirksen of Illinois: Senatorial Statesman.* Urbana: University of Illinois Press.

DISABILITIES, RIGHTS OF PERSONS WITH

When Justice OLIVER WENDELL HOLMES, JR., declared in BUCK V. BELL (1927) that the state's POLICE POWER authorized involuntary sterilization of individuals thought to be mentally impaired, he asserted, "It is better for all the world, if instead of waiting to execute degenerate offspring for crime, or to let them starve for their imbecility, society can prevent those who are manifestly unfit from continuing their kind. . . . Three generations of imbeciles is enough." His statement embodied three assumptions about people with disabilities that have since provoked repeated and partially successful constitutional challenges. The first assumption was that people with disabilities do not enjoy the same basic rights as anyone else, such as the rights to procreate or to be free from involuntary medical treatment. The second assumption was that people with disabilities have no special rights should their conditions leave them vulnerable to legal, social, or physical jeopardy. The third assumption was that society's interests always outweigh the interests of people who have or who are perceived to have disabilities.

Inspired by the CIVIL RIGHTS MOVEMENTS for blacks and for women, in the 1950s and 1960s, advocates for people with disabilities drew on changing medical knowledge about mental and physical disabilities. During the same years, increased federal funds for research and services reached those with mental disabilities and helped to support a movement for their rights. Advocates attacked the segregation produced by institutional settings. They also challenged the deprivation of VOTING RIGHTS; rights to have sexual relations; rights to marry; rights to have children; rights of access to jobs, housing, and transportation; and rights to treatment and services. The disability rights movement attained periodic success in constitutional adjudication in the lower federal courts, which in turn supported federal legislation backed by congressional findings of constitutional rights and also provided the backdrop for landmark Supreme Court DUE PROCESS, and EQUAL PROTECTION decisions.

Initial lawsuits maintained that people with disabilities retained the same rights held by others. On this theory, confinement of persons on grounds of MENTAL ILLNESS or MENTAL RETARDATION should not deprive them of other liberties, and the confinement itself should be justified by provision of services or treatment. The court of appeals so reasoned in *Donaldson v. O'Connor* (1974) and then built on this judgment with *Wyatt v. Aderholt* (1974), which declared on PROCEDURAL DUE PROCESS grounds a right to treatment for persons civilly committed to state mental institutions. It was this right to treatment that Congress incorporated in the DEVELOPMENTALLY DISABLED ASSISTANCE AND BILL OF RIGHTS ACT (1975).

Although the Supreme Court refrained from endorsing the right to treatment at that time, it reinforced the disability rights movement by unanimously announcing in O'CONNOR V. DONALDSON (1975) that "a State cannot constitutionally confine without more [justification] a nondangerous individual who is capable of surviving safely in freedom by himself or with the help of willing and responsible family members or friends." The Court also reasoned that mere public intolerance could not justify the deprivation of physical liberty.

Elaborating the FOURTEENTH AMENDMENT due process theory of liberty, advocates argued that the right to treatment included a right to be treated in the least restrictive setting possible, which meant the setting least confined and removed from the rest of the community. A series of lawsuits challenging the conditions and absence of treatment at a large institution in Pennsylvania produced the disappointing decision in PENNHURST STATE SCHOOL V. HALDERMAN (1981) that the Developmental Disability Act did not confer any substantive right to appropriate treatment in the least restrictive environment. This Supreme Court conclusion occurred after years of litigation had already propelled the states to move people from institutions to community-based facilities.

Then the Supreme Court took the occasion of one more lawsuit arising from the same Pennsylvania institution to announce a constitutional right to treatment for people with disabilities confined in state institutions. In *Youngberg v. Romeo* (1982) the Court declared that the due-process clause of the Fourteenth Amendment assures (1) safe conditions of confinement; (2) freedom from bodily restraints; and (3) training or "habilitation," meaning a duty to provide at least "such training as an appropriate professional would consider reasonable to ensure the individual's safety and to facilitate his ability to function free from bodily restraints."

The emerging right to treatment also spawned arguments for a right to refuse treatment. Lower federal courts in cases such as *Rennie v. Klein* (1978) recognized a constitutional privacy right of involuntary mental patients to refuse medication. In WASHINGTON V. HARPER (1990) the Supreme Court announced that forced administration of antipsychotic drugs violates a constitutional liberty interest, but that due process can be satisfied by administrative processes less formal than a court hearing. During the same term, the Court acknowledged in *Cruzan v. Missouri Department of Health* (1990) that a constitutionally protected liberty interest in refusing unwanted medical treatment may be inferred from its prior decisions. In *Cruzan,* the first Supreme Court decision addressing the RIGHT TO DIE, the Court acknowledged that incompetent as well as competent persons have a constitutionally protected liberty interest in consenting to or refusing treatment. Yet this interest did not forbid a state from requiring clear and convincing evidence that the patient herself would want to terminate life-sustaining treatment. Having spoken on this issue, the Court, like many state courts, may start to

hear right-to-die and treatment cases affecting severely disabled adults, infants, and children.

Implicit in the due process liberty cases is the theme of equal protection, which has also inspired an independent line of opinions articulating rights of persons with disabilities. Advocates achieved early constitutional success by linking claims about disabilities to arguments against racial SEGREGATION. Thus in *Hobson v. Hansen* (1967), affirmed in *Smuck v. Hobson* (1969), the district court ruled public-school ability-tracking unconstitutional in light of its racially segregative impact. In *Larry P. v. Riles* (1979) the district court found unconstitutional I.Q. tests for placing students in classes for the "educable mentally retarded" because of a foreseeable racial impact.

Charges of RACIAL DISCRIMINATION trigger STRICT SCRUTINY under the equal-protection clause. Yet the Supreme Court has resisted claims that strict scrutiny should also apply to charges of discrimination on the basis of disability. In CLEBURNE V. CLEBURNE LIVING CENTER, INC. (1985) the Court expressly rejected the assertion that persons with disabilities are members of a suspect or semisuspect classification.

Nonetheless, the Court in *Cleburne* did give unusually sharp teeth to its low-level rational-relationship scrutiny. It found that a city requirement of a special-use permit for a proposed group home for persons with mental retardation violated the equal-protection clause. Locating group homes in residential neighborhoods would be essential to the goal of moving disabled people out of remote institutions and into the mainstream community. The city of Cleburne had created a special ZONING permit requirement for the operation of a group home for mentally retarded persons. The majority of the Court found no RATIONAL BASIS for believing that the proposed group home would pose a special threat to the city's interests and rejected fear and negative attitudes by community members as inadequate bases for treating mentally retarded individuals differently from others. Justice THURGOOD MARSHALL, joined by Justices WILLIAM J. BRENNAN and HARRY A. BLACKMUN, maintained that the Court's majority had in effect applied heightened scrutiny and should explicitly accord such scrutiny given the history and continuing legacy of segregation of and discrimination against people with mental retardation.

A combination of equal protection and due process arguments produced the landmark decisions in *Mills v. Board of Education* (1973) and *Pennsylvania Ass'n for Retarded Children v. Pennsylvania* (1971), which decreed that children with disabilities have constitutional rights to equal educational opportunity, and exclusion from public schooling violates these rights. Congress expressly relied on the constitutional dimensions of these district court decisions in promulgating the EDUCATION FOR ALL HANDI-

CAPPED CHILDREN ACT of 1975. Sometimes known as the "special education" statute, this act provides federal moneys to assist states in extending free appropriate public education to children with disabilities.

Drawing from procedural due-process doctrines, the act calls for individualized evaluations of each child's educational and health needs and an administrative process providing opportunities for parents to participate and raise objections to proposed placements. The act also echoes the right to treatment, but locates it within the context of compulsory schooling. The act introduces the desegregation concept of mainstreaming children with disabilities in regular classrooms to the extent possible. For students who still require instruction in separate classrooms or separate facilities, the act calls for selecting the placement that is the least restrictive—the one most approximating the mainsteam classroom. Finally, the statute calls for related medical services to ensure that students with special physical needs are not excluded from instruction due to medical needs.

Disability rights advocates have struggled to combine arguments for extending to people with disabilities the same liberty interests enjoyed by others with the use of arguments for special claims for treatment and even rights to refuse treatment that might not arise for others. The REHABILITATION ACT of 1973 included section 504, a nondiscrimination provision modeled after the CIVIL RIGHTS statutes drafted to guard against both racial discrimination and SEX DISCRIMINATION. A central idea developed in this context is that people entitled to protection against discrimination include those who are perceived to be disabled, whether or not they actually are disabled. On this basis, people who have had a disease or an illness or people who may be perceived to have an illness or a deformity have been extended statutory protections, as in *School Board of Nassau County v. Arline* (1987).

Antidiscrimination principles also animate the Fair Housing Act Amendments of 1988 that protect persons with disability and the AMERICANS WITH DISABILITY ACT (1990), heralded by many as the most important and extensive legislation ever adopted on behalf of persons with disability. Yet enduring questions about the meaning of equality and the degree of requisite accommodation will arise both as statutory questions and as constitutional questions concerning the scope of JUDICIAL POWER to order expenditures to accommodate previously excluded groups. Ending the exclusion of physically handicapped persons requires architectural renovation, new communication technologies, and other potentially costly changes. Ending the exclusion of persons with mental disabilities may require the creation of new kinds of institutions, like group homes, which involve money and trained personnel as well as changed community attitudes. Devis-

ing programs for persons with AIDS or at risk of AIDS would also involve large expenditures.

Federal courts implementing statutory and constitutional rights for persons with disabilities may confront claims of ELEVENTH AMENDMENT immunity asserted by states against court-ordered expenditures. In analogous cases involving court-ordered remedies for school segregation and prison conditions, courts have ruled that inadequate resources can never be an adequate justification for a state to deprive persons of their constitutional rights.

Much has changed since Justice Holmes's 1927 opinion in *Buck v. Bell;* the law recognizes many of the same rights for persons with disabilities as for others. Courts and legislatures have articulated special rights to help disabled persons overcome legal, social, and physical jeopardy. Will the Constitution direct an answer to the question when societal interests outweigh the interests of persons with disabilities? Perhaps the future constitutional challenge is to locate within societal interests the interests of persons with disabilities so the very terms of the questions will change.

MARTHA MINOW
(1992)

Bibliography

BURGDORF, ROBERT L. and BURGDORF, MARCIA PEARCE   1977   The Wicked Witch Is Almost Dead: *Buck v. Bell* and the Sterilization of Handicapped Persons. *Temple Law Quarterly* 50: 955–1034.

MINOW, MARTHA   1990   *Making All the Difference: Inclusion, Exclusion, and American Law.* Ithaca, N.Y.: Cornell University Press.

NOTE   1973   Right to Treatment. *Harvard Law Review* 86: 1282–1306.

STUDENT AUTHORS   1974   Developments in the Law: Civil Commitment of the Mentally Ill. *Harvard Law Review* 87:1190–1406.

TRIBE, LAURENCE   1988   *American Constitutional Law,* 2nd ed. Mineola, N.Y.: Foundation Press.

DISABILITY DISCRIMINATION

The rights of people with disabilities have not received much protection under the Constitution. Statutes such as the Individuals with Disabilities Education Act, section 504 of the REHABILITATION ACT of 1973, and the AMERICANS WITH DISABILITIES ACT of 1990 have created most of the rights that exist in this area.

The most disappointing decision by the Supreme Court involving people with disabilities was the Court's 1927 decision in BUCK V. BELL. At the age of sixteen, Carrie Buck became pregnant and had her baby taken away from her. She was most likely raped in the foster home at which she was working as a caretaker. Because her mother had been found to be "feeble-minded," it was easy for her foster parents to claim that Carrie, too, was "feeble-minded" and have her housed in the "State Colony for Epileptics and Feeble Minded" where the superintendent, empowered by state law to perform a surgical procedure upon her for the purpose of rendering her sterile, began proceedings to do so. She was eighteen at the time of the intended procedure.

In upholding the power of the state to sterilize her, Justice OLIVER WENDELL HOLMES, JR., delivered the OPINION OF THE COURT in which he recited the now- famous passage: "Three generations of imbeciles are enough." "It is better for all the world, if instead of waiting to execute degenerate offspring for crime, or to let them starve for their imbecility, society can prevent those who are manifestly unfit from continuing their kind." Scholars, in fact, have disputed whether Carrie or her daughter were "feeble-minded." Her mother appears to have been an unfortunate victim of poor family circumstances—her husband died at a young age leaving her with three children to raise and no means of support. In *Buck*, the various courts accepted the unchallenged assertion that Carrie was illegitimate whereas public records indicate that her parents were married at the time of her birth. Her school records also reveal that she had performed well in school before being sent to live in a foster home. In her impoverished world, however, it was easy to have the facts distorted with little or no legal challenge.

The Court's decision in *Buck* is often blamed for spurring on other states to enact compulsory sterilization statutes. And as recently as 1973, the Court mentioned the Court's holding in *Buck* without disapproval in ROE V. WADE.

The legal status of people with disabilities improved somewhat with the Court's 1985 decision in CLEBURNE V. CLEBURNE LIVING CENTER, INC. (1985). In that case, a Texas city denied a special use permit for the operation of a group home for the mentally retarded, acting pursuant to a municipal ZONING ordinance requiring permits for such homes. Under city law, a special use permit was required for "hospitals for the insane or feeble-minded." The city council had determined that the proposed group home should be classified as a "hospital for the feebleminded" and voted 3–1 to deny a special use permit. Cleburne Living Center challenged that decision under the FOURTEENTH AMENDMENT.

The Cleburne Living Center urged the Supreme Court to follow the lower court and apply "heightened scrutiny" to their claim, analogous to the intermediate scrutiny used in cases of SEX DISCRIMINATION. The Court rejected this invitation, concluding that such a standard would not give state and local government sufficient latitude to respond to the genuine differences between mentally retarded persons and others. Instead, the Court applied "RATIONAL BASIS; scrutiny under which a state "may not rely on a classification whose relationship to an asserted goal is so attenuated as to render the distinction arbitrary or irrational." Usually, classifications are found to be constitutional under this lower STANDARD OF REVIEW. In *Cleburne*, however, the Court concluded that the city's action could not pass constitutional muster. "The short of it is that requiring the permit in this case appears to rest on an irrational prejudice against the mentally retarded, including those who would occupy the [group home]." It therefore affirmed the holding of the appellate court that the ordinance was unconstitutional.

The *Cleburne* decision was hailed as a victory for the disability rights community, and a possible first step toward recognition of heightened scrutiny. That possibility, however, has not been realized. The appellate courts have steadfastly interpreted *Cleburne* as holding that mere rational basis scrutiny applies to disability-based distinctions. Thus, individuals with disabilities have generally found that statutory rather than constitutional challenges are a more successful avenue for their complaints.

RUTH COLKER
(2000)

Bibliography

SMITH, J. DAVID and NELSON, K. RAY 1989 *The Sterilization of Carrie Buck: Was She Feebleminded or Society's Pawn?* Far Hills, N.J.: New Horizon Press.

DISANTO v. PENNSYLVANIA
273 U.S. 34 (1927)

Protection of the public health and welfare temporarily lost ground to the COMMERCE CLAUSE in this case. A Pennsylvania statute required the licensing of persons selling steamship tickets to or from foreign countries. The Court declared the law a "direct" interference with FOREIGN COMMERCE, over the dissents of Justices Harlan Fiske Stone, Oliver Wendell Holmes, and LOUIS D. BRANDEIS. Stone found the directindirect test of EFFECTS ON COMMERCE "too mechanical, too uncertain . . . and too remote . . . to be of value." He proposed a more pragmatic test: "the actual effect on the flow of commerce," a view which prevailed in 1941 when this decision was overruled by *California v. Thompson.*

DAVID GORDON
(1986)

(SEE ALSO: *Parker v. Brown.*)

DISCOVERY

Discovery is a procedure by which one party obtains information from the adverse party in his case. This disclosure of information in criminal proceedings includes statements, documents, test results, reports, and other similar items. Although there is a very broad power to discover items in the exclusive possession of an adverse party in civil proceedings, the Supreme Court stated in *Weatherford v. Bursey* (1977) that "there is no general constitutional right to discovery in a criminal case."

In civil cases, the predominant means for discovery are depositions and interrogatories. In criminal cases, no jurisdiction expressly permits the defense to discover prosecutorial information through interrogatories. Most juruisdictions allow depositions in criminal cases only for the purpose of preserving testimony. Most jusdictions also have statutes or court rules similar to FEDERAL RULE OF CRIMINAL PROCEDURE 16 governing defense discovery which require the prosecution to disclose items such as: (1) written or recorded statements (including GRAND JURY testimony) of the defendant and, in some states, of any co-defendant; (2) the substance of any oral statment of the defendant (and, in some states of a co-defendant) that the prosecution intends to use at trial; (3) the defendant's prior criminal record; (4) relevant documents and other tangible objects; and (5) results and reports of physical or mental examinations and of scientific tests or experiments.

The prosecutorial duty to disclose exculpatory information is based on the view that the primary task of the prosecutor is to see justice done and DUE PROCESS upheld through the fair treatment of accused persons. If this duty is breached, the defendant is entitled to a new trial.

The leading modern case on this duty is *Brady v. Maryland* (1963). In separate trials, the petitioner and a companion were convicted of murder and sentenced to death. At his trial, the petitioner admitted participating in the crime but claimed that his companion had done the actual killing. Prior to trial the petitioner's attorney requested the prosecution to allow him to examine all the companion's statements to the police. One such statement, in which the companion admitted the actual killing, was withheld by the prosecution and did not come to the petitioner's attention until after his conviction was affirmed on APPEAL. The Supreme Court held that "the suppression by the prosecution of EVIDENCE favorable to an accused upon request violates due process where the evidence is material either to guilt or to punishment, irrespective of the good faith or bad faith of the prosecution."

In order to determine whether particular information should have been disclosed, courts consider whether the defendant made a specific request for the information at issue or a more general request for exculpatory informa-

tion. They also consider to what extent the information was material to the outcome of the trial. When a specific request is made, withholding information is seldom excusable. Even when a general request is made or the defense fails to request exculpatory information, withholding clearly material information, such as the fact that particular testimony is perjured, is not permissible. In determining materiality, the test is whether the withheld information creates a reasonable doubt in the mind of the trial judge as to the defendant's guilt.

There is no clear rule as to when exculpatory information must be disclosed, but it would seem that some circumstances would require pretrial disclosure in order to permit the defense adequate time to prepare its case.

Generally, the prosecutor decides what evidence should be disclosed, although the trial court may occasionally decide *in camera* whether a particular piece of evidence is favorable to the defendant and should therefore be disclosed to him.

Finally the Supreme Court indicated in *United States v. Agurs* (1976) and *Smith v. Phillips* (1982) that the focus should be whether the prosecutor's failure to disclose rendered the trial fundamentally unfair, not the extent of prosecutorial culpability.

CHARLES H. WHITEBREAD
(1986)

Bibliography

SALTZBURG, STEPHEN 1980 *American Criminal Procedure.* St. Paul, Minn.: West Publishing Co.

WHITEBREAD, CHARLES H. 1980 *Criminal Procedure.* Mineola, N.Y.: Foundation Press.

DISCRETE AND INSULAR MINORITIES

The idea of the "discrete and insular minority" originated in the now famous footnote four of the opinion in UNITED STATES V. CAROLENE PRODUCTS COMPANY (1938). Justice HARLAN F. STONE, writing for only a plurality of the Court, queried—without answering the question—"whether prejudice against discrete and insular minorities may be a special condition, which tends seriously to curtail those political processes ordinarily to be relied upon to protect minorities, and which may call for a correspondingly more searching judicial inquiry." In the wake of the Court's about-face in 1937, Justice Stone was serving notice that the Court might not accord the same deference to statutes directed at "discrete and insular minorities" that it would to statutes directed at ECONOMIC REGULATION.

The Court made little use of the concept until the early 1970s, when it began to delineate the class characteristics of such groups. Included were groups that had been "saddled with such disabilities, or subjected to such a history of purposeful unequal treatment, or relegated to such a position of political powerlessness as to command extraordinary protection from the majoritarian political process." Although race, nationality, and alienage seem to have been firmly established as class characteristics of the "discrete and insular minority," the Court has refused to extend such class status to illegitimates, the poor, or conscientious objectors.

REGENTS OF THE UNIVERSITY OF CALIFORNIA V. BAKKE (1978) presented the question of the "discrete and insular minority" in a new light. The question in *Bakke* was whether the same "solicitude" should be applied to test a governmental action designed to benefit rather than injure a "discrete and insular" minority. The university, citing *Carolene Products*, argued that STRICT SCRUTINY was reserved exclusively for "discrete and insular minorities." Four Justices agreed that a white male needed no special protection from the political process that authorized the actions of the university. Justice LEWIS F. POWELL rejected this argument: "the "rights created by the . . . FOURTEENTH AMENDMENT are, by its terms, guaranteed to the individual. The rights established are personal rights. . . .' The guarantee of EQUAL PROTECTION cannot mean one thing when applied to one individual and something else when applied to a person of another color."

In FULLILOVE V. KLUTZNICK (1980) the Court, for the first time since the JAPANESE AMERICAN CASES (1943–1944), upheld a racial classification that was expressed on the face of a law. *Fullilove* involved a challenge to an act of Congress authorizing federal funds for local public works projects and setting aside ten percent of those funds for employment of businesses owned by Negroes, Hispanics, Orientals, AMERICAN INDIANS, and Aleuts. Chief Justice WARREN E. BURGER, writing for a plurality, called for judicial deference to Congress's power under section 5 of the Fourteenth Amendment, as equivalent to "the broad powers expressed in the NECESSARY AND PROPER CLAUSE. . . ." The irony was that the idea of the "discrete and insular minority" in its inception was designed to curtail such deference when racial classifications were involved.

BENIGN RACIAL CLASSIFICATIONS, it is sometimes said, are justified because they do not involve the stigma of INVIDIOUS DISCRIMINATION. The recipients of the benefits that accrue from the "benign" classification are not branded as members of an "inferior race" as they would be if the classification were an invidious one. This theory erects "stigma" as the standard for equal protection rights. Absent any such stigma the implication is that the Constitution is not offended, even if individuals must bear burdens created by a classification that otherwise would be disallowed by the equal protection clause. As Burger stated in *Fullilove*, "a sharing of the burden' by innocent parties is not impermissible." To use the idea of stigma as a racial class concept is, in effect, to translate equal protection rights into class rights.

But the intrusion of class into the Constitution is a dangerous proposition, one that is at odds with the principles of the constitutional regime—principles ultimately derived from the proposition that "all men are created equal." Class considerations explicitly deny this equality because they necessarily abstract from the individual and ascribe to him class characteristics that are different—and necessarily unequal—from those of individuals outside the class. A liberal jurisprudence must disallow all class considerations. When there is a conflict between two different "discrete and insular minorities," which should be accorded preference? No principle can answer this question. And the question is not merely theoretical. The Court has already faced this dilemma in cases such as UNITED JEWISH ORGANIZATIONS V. CAREY (1977) and *Castenada v. Partida* (1977), and in a pluralistic society it is inevitable that many more such cases will arise. Equal protection can be the foundation of a genuine liberal jurisprudence only if it applies to individuals. As Justice JOHN MARSHALL HARLAN remarked in his powerful dissent in PLESSY V. FERGUSON (1896), the case that established the SEPARATE-BUT-EQUAL DOCTRINE, "[o]ur Constitution is color-blind, and neither knows nor tolerates classes among citizens. In respect of CIVIL RIGHTS, all citizens are equal before the law." This is undoubtedly still the essential principle of liberal government.

JAMES MADISON argued, in THE FEDERALIST #10, that in a large, diverse republic with a multiplicity of interests it was unlikely that there would ever be permanent majorities and permanent minorities; thus there would be little probability that "a majority of the whole will have a common motive to invade the rights of other citizens." On this assumption, the majorities that do form will be composed of coalitions of minorities that come together for limited self-interested purposes. The majority will thus never have a sense of its own interest as a majority.

By and large, the solution of the Founders has worked remarkably well. There have been no permanent majorities, and certainly none based exclusively on race. Understanding American politics in terms of monolithic majorities and "discrete and insular minorities"—as the Supreme Court appears to do—precludes the creation of a common interest that transcends racial class considerations. By transforming the Fourteenth Amendment into an instrument of class politics, the Court risks either making a majority faction more likely by heightening the majority's awareness of its class status as a majority, or transforming the liberal constitutional regime into one no longer based on majority rule.

EDWARD J. ERLER
(1986)

Bibliography

ELY, JOHN H. 1980 *Democracy and Distrust: A Theory of Judicial Review.* Pages 75–77 and 135–179. Cambrige, Mass.: Harvard University Press.

ERLER, EDWARD J. 1982 Equal Protection and Personal Rights: The Regime of the "Discrete and Insular Minority." *Georgia Law Review* 16:407–444.

KARST, KENNETH L. and HOROWITZ, HAROLD W. 1974 Affirmative Action and Equal Protection. *Virginia Law Review* 60:955–974.

DISCRIMINATION

See: Age Discrimination; Antidiscrimination Legislation; Disability Discrimination; Race and Sex in Antidiscrimination Law; Racial Discrimination; Sex Discrimination

DISMISSED TIME

See: Released Time

DISORDERLY CONDUCT

See: Breach of the Peace

DISSENTING OPINION

In cases in which the judges of a multijudge court are divided as to the DECISION, it is customary for those in the minority to file a dissenting OPINION. This practice is followed in the Supreme Court of the United States. In recent years, dissenting opinions have been filed in as many as seventy percent of all cases decided by the Court. In a typical TERM over 150 separate dissenting opinions are filed by Justices who find themselves on the losing side.

The author of a dissenting opinion tries to explain why the Court should have decided the case differently. Often a dissenting Justice will attempt to provide the public with an interpretation of the MAJORITY OPINION in order to narrow its scope or to restrict its impact. A strong dissenting opinion may go far to weaken the decision and may point the way for future litigation.

The opinion of the Court is written by a Justice on the prevailing side designated by the Chief Justice (or the se-

nior Justice in the majority), and must reflect a consensus of the majority. Dissenters have a freer hand: they can make their point more sharply because they do not need to accommodate colleagues who might balk at aspects of their argument. Before the decision of a case is announced, the draft opinions circulate among the Justices. A well-argued dissent can induce the author of the majority opinion to modify its content, either to retain majority support, as in EVERSON V. BOARD OF EDUCATION (1947), or to respond in kind to a particularly harsh attack, as in DRED SCOTT V. SANDFORD (1857). In an extraordinary case, the dissent may attract enough support actually to become the majority opinion.

Dissents are most common during change in the ideological composition of the Court. For a time the dissents portend an imminent revolution in the tendency of judicial thought and point to the future course of decisions. Once the revolution is perfected there follows a time when the dissents resist the new orientation and recall the old orthodoxy. Two of the Court's great dissenters were Justices JOHN MARSHALL HARLAN (1833–1911) and OLIVER WENDELL HOLMES, each of whom stood against the majority of his day and took positions that much later were adopted by the Court.

CHARLES EVANS HUGHES once wrote that "a dissent in the court of last resort is an appeal to the brooding spirit of the law, to the intelligence of a future day. . . ." Contemporaneously, HARLAN F. STONE wrote that "dissents seldom aid in the right development of the law. They often do harm."

DENNIS J. MAHONEY
(1986)

DISTRICT OF COLUMBIA

"If any of their officers, or creatures, should attempt to oppress the people, or should actually perpetrate the blackest deed, he has nothing to do but get into the ten miles square. Why was this dangerous power given?" The "dangerous power" to which GEORGE MASON objected so vehemently at the Virginia ratifying convention was that vested in Congress by the seventeenth clause of Article I, section 8, "to exercise exclusive legislation in all cases whatsoever, over such district (not exceeding ten miles square) as may . . . become the seat of the government of the United States." That the power to legislate for the capital district should be controversial was a surprise to JAMES MADISON, who had proposed it in the CONSTITUTIONAL CONVENTION OF 1787. He defended the provision as the means by which the federal government might "be guarded from the influence of particular states, or from insults."

The district was established on the banks of the Potomac River between Maryland and Virginia, at a site chosen by GEORGE WASHINGTON, and Congress assumed JURISDICTION over it on February 27, 1801. The location of the capital was agreed to by northern Federalists in exchange for southern acquiescence in federal assumption of state revolutionary war debts. But that location, south of Mason's and Dixon's line, resulted in the greatest national disgrace before the Civil War, namely, that the federal capital was a bastion of slavery and the home of a flourishing slave market. Not until the COMPROMISE OF 1850 was even abomination of slave trading extinguished.

Originally, the District of Columbia comprised one hundred square miles of land ceded by Virginia and Maryland, and three municipal corporations, Washington, Georgetown, and Alexandria. Alexandria was retroceded to Virginia in 1846, at the request of its inhabitants, and the district has since comprised less than seventy square miles. Since 1871, there has been a single municipal corporation coextensive with the district. The 1980 population of over 600,000 was larger than the populations of each of four states.

During most of its history the district's lawmaking was done directly by Congress. There was a brief period of home rule, under a government like those of the TERRITORIES, from 1871 to 1874, during which the district plunged deeply into debt. From 1878 until 1974 the district was governed by three commissioners appointed by the President. Home rule was restored by passage of the DISTRICT OF COLUMBIA GOVERNMENT REORGANIZATION AND SELF-GOVERNING ACT in 1973 and adoption of a city charter in 1974. Since that time the district has been governed by an elected mayor and council, although Congress must approve the budget and retains a veto over other legislation.

The legal status of residents of the District of Columbia is anomalous. The Framers of the Constitution apparently did not foresee a large permanent population in the district distinct from the population of the surrounding states. Even the CITIZENSHIP of district residents, who were not citizens of any state, was uncertain until adoption of the FOURTEENTH AMENDMENT (1868). At least from *Hepburn v. Ellzey* (1805) until the Supreme Court sustained an amendment to the JUDICIAL CODE in *National Mutual Insurance Company v. Tidewater Transfer Company* (1949), citizens of the district could not sue or be sued in federal court under DIVERSITY JURISDICTION. Moreover, district residents were unable to vote for presidential electors until passage of the TWENTY-THIRD AMENDMENT (1961), and they remain unrepresented in Congress to this day (except, since 1970, by a nonvoting delegate). In 1978, Congress proposed the DISTRICT OF COLUMBIA REPRESENTATION AMENDMENT, which would have given the district a status equivalent to statehood, but the amendment failed of RATIFICATION by the state legislatures.

The district has often been the site of experiments in "model legislation," such as the DISTRICT OF COLUMBIA MINIMUM WAGE ACT (1918) and the District of Columbia Crime Control Act (1970). The district is also the focus of demonstrations, small and great, against government policies, ranging from Coxey's army (1894) and the bonus marchers (1932) to Resurrection City (1968) and the marches against the VIETNAM WAR. The right to carry demands for redress of grievances directly to the seat of government is a unique expression of FREEDOM OF PETITION.

Creation of a capital district outside the jurisdiction of any of the constituent states has been copied by other federal unions, including Australia, Brazil, India, and Mexico. The idea that no one member of the federation should control the conditions under which the central government works has thus become a part of the modern theory of FEDERALISM. The all-too-real practical difficulty is that the conditions come to be controlled instead by those who make up the permanent infrastructure of the government and whose perceived interest is in the perpetual growth of that government. In the United States itself, the District of Columbia remains an anomaly, a city dependent almost entirely upon the public payroll serving as the capital of a republic dedicated to the principle of free private enterprise.

DENNIS J. MAHONEY
(1986)

DISTRICT OF COLUMBIA
(Update)

After nearly two hundred years since assuming exclusive JURISDICTION over the District of Columbia, Congress continues to tinker with the governmental structure of the district and to disfranchise its citizens.

The 1990s witnessed the effective end of a twenty-year experiment with home rule in the district. A series of fiscal and management crises, coupled with remarkably high crime rates, led Congress to pass LEGISLATION creating a "control board" to oversee the district's governance. Its five members appointed by the President, the control board assumed most of the powers of the elected mayor and city council.

The institution of the control board further diluted the limited opportunities for self-government enjoyed by the district's citizens. Although the TWENTY-THIRD AMENDMENT granted the district a voice in the ELECTORAL COLLEGE, district citizens do not have full REPRESENTATION in Congress.

(They have a delegate in the U.S. HOUSE OF REPRESENTATIVES who can vote in committee, but not on the final passage of legislation.) With the end of home rule, the over 500,000 citizens of the district have no formal say in legislation governing their communities.

The disfranchisement of district citizens contravenes the famous rallying principle of the AMERICAN REVOLUTION, "No taxation without representation." Yet, despite scholars' sound constitutional arguments for extending VOTING RIGHTS to district citizens based on the EQUAL PROTECTION clause of the FOURTEENTH AMENDMENT, neither the courts nor the political branches show any inclination to establish a truly REPUBLICAN FORM OF GOVERNMENT in the district.

ADAM WINKLER
(2000)

DISTRICT OF COLUMBIA MINIMUM WAGE LAW
40 Stat. 960 (1918)

Congress, in its capacity as legislature for the DISTRICT OF COLUMBIA, enacted this minimum wage law for women and minors "to maintain them in good health and to protect their morals." Seeking to ground the act on the POLICE POWER, Congress established a Minimum Wage Board with power to compel testimony and other EVIDENCE. The act authorized the board to investigate wage conditions of women and minors in the District of Columbia and to fix their minimum wages on the basis of adequacy "to supply the necessary cost of living." The act required the board to provide PROCEDURAL DUE PROCESS; it also provided for APPEALS to courts of the District and made violations punishable as MISDEMEANORS. The Supreme Court declared the act unconstitutional in *Adkins v. Children's Hospital* (1923) as a violation of SUBSTANTIVE DUE PROCESS OF LAW, but when the Court overruled *Adkins* in WEST COAST HOTEL CO. V. PARRISH (1937), Attorney General HOMER CUMMINGS declared that the law was in effect without any need for congressional reenactment.

DAVID GORDON
(1986)

(SEE ALSO: *Unconstitutionality.*)

DISTRICT OF COLUMBIA REPRESENTATION AMENDMENT
92 Stat. 3795 (1978)

Twenty-three times since 1800, congressional representation for the DISTRICT OF COLUMBIA had been sought, mainly on the grounds that taxation of District residents without REPRESENTATION in Congress was undemocratic. The modern District's predominantly black population is larger than that of each of ten states. In 1978 Congress proposed a constitutional amendment that would treat the district as a state is treated for purposes of congressional and ELECTORAL COLLEGE representation and for participation in presidential elections and RATIFICATION OF CONSTITUTIONAL AMENDMENTS. It would have repealed the TWENTY-THIRD AMENDMENT, which had allowed district residents to vote for President and vice-president, while limiting district representation in the electoral college to that of the least populous state. As with other recent amendments, Congress fixed a seven-year time limit for ratification and provided that it would implement the amendment by legislation at a later date.

Although both houses of Congress passed the proposed amendment enthusiastically, it had slight chance of ratification because it would have added two senators and one representative to Congress, all almost certain to be both black and Democrats. In 1985, the period for ratification expired.

PAUL L. MURPHY
(1986)

Bibliography

BEST, JUDITH 1983 *National Representation of the District of Columbia.* Frederick, Md.: University Publications of America.

DISTRICT OF COLUMBIA SELF-GOVERNING AND GOVERNMENT REORGANIZATION ACT
87 Stat. 774 (1973)

Limited home rule in the DISTRICT OF COLUMBIA had been a long-time desire of its inhabitants. Since 1874, the President had chosen the city's administrators and Congress had acted as the city's governing council. Washingtonians elected only their school board and a nonvoting delegate to the House of Representatives.

This 1973 act granted the District a council, a mayor, and increased self-government. It provided a charter for local government, subject to approval by a majority of the registered voters. Although Congress sought to avoid day-to-day responsibility for District affairs, it retained ultimate legislative authority as provided in Article I, section 8, including the power to legislate generally for the District and to veto local laws. The city government exercised the functions of several quasi-federal agencies: the Redevelopment Land Agency, the National Capital Housing Authority, and the District of Columbia Manpower Administration. The Act reorganized the National Capital

Planning Commission, giving the mayor responsibility for District planning, excepting federal and international projects. Further, it required the President, in appointing judges to the District of Columbia Court of Appeals and the Superior Court, to choose from candidates submitted to him by a newly created District of Columbia Judicial Nomination Commission.

The act, while still denying the District congressional REPRESENTATION, satisfied a number of city residents' demands for local control over city affairs.

PAUL L. MURPHY
(1986)

DIVERSITY JURISDICTION

Under Article III of the Constitution, the JUDICIAL POWER OF THE UNITED STATES extends to "Controversies between Citizens of different States . . . and between . . . the Citizens [of a State] . . . and foreign . . . Citizens or Subjects." This power is called diversity jurisdiction because its basis is the difference in CITIZENSHIP of the parties.

The accepted justification for diversity jurisdiction has been the need to protect out-of-state citizens against discrimination in state courts. However, the extent of such discrimination as of the time the Constitution was written is uncertain, and there is evidence that financial and commercial interests supported diversity jurisdiction in the hope of finding shelter from state laws and judicial systems favorable to debtors.

In fact, the diversity jurisdiction authorized in Article III is not confined to situations in which out-of-state citizens require protection. For example, a plaintiff may file a diversity action in her home state's federal court if she can obtain personal JURISDICTION over the defendant there. Also, it is constitutionally permissible for Congress to confer diversity jurisdiction even when citizens of the same state are on both sides of the litigation, so long as some out-of-state citizens are also parties. Congress has conferred jurisdiction in just such cases in the federal interpleader statute.

Congress has the power to determine how much of the constitutionally authorized diversity jurisdiction the lower federal courts may exercise. It has enacted a general statute that allows the federal courts to hear some but not all types of diversity cases either originally or on REMOVAL. Examples of excluded cases are those in which less than a required amount is in controversy, those in which there is incomplete diversity (that is, at least one plaintiff is from the same state as at least one defendant), and those which the defendant seeks to remove from his or her home state's court.

In 1946 Congress first provided expressly for diversity jurisdiction over suits involving citizens of the DISTRICT OF COLUMBIA and TERRITORIES. In *National Mutual Insurance Co. v. Tidewater Co.* (1949), the Supreme Court upheld the law because two Justices were willing to declare that the District of Columbia was a "state" within the meaning of the diversity clause of Article III, and three Justices concluded that Congress could confer the jurisdiction even if it were not within the Article III judicial power.

The citizenship of parties for purposes of applying the general diversity statute is not always obvious. Some problems have been solved by statute. For example, problems arising from the Court's 1844 decision that a CORPORATION is a citizen of its state of incorporation were resolved by a congressional declaration that a corporation is a citizen of both the state of its incorporation and of the state where its principal place of business is located. Others have been handled by judicial interpretation, which has held, for example, that an individual is a citizen of the state in which he or she is domiciled at the time suit is filed. Difficult interpretive problems remain, however.

Under the Rules of Decision Act, as interpreted in ERIE RAILROAD V. TOMPKINS (1938), a federal court hearing a diversity case must apply the substantive law of the state in which it is located. It must also employ that state's CHOICE OF LAW rules and any of the state's procedural rules that have a predictable effect on the outcome of the case and do not conflict with the FEDERAL RULES OF CIVIL PROCEDURE or some overriding federal policy. In cases in which state law is unclear or has not yet been decided, the federal court must strive to resolve the case as the state's highest court would, drawing direction from trends and policies manifest in state judicial opinions at all levels. The state courts are not bound by the federal court's decisions interpreting state law.

It is doubtful that Congress could constitutionally enact a law giving to the federal courts or assuming for itself the power to develop substantive law for diversity cases. Although the *Erie* opinion avoided this constitutional issue, fundamental notions of state sovereignty and the limited role of the federal government dictated the decision's interpretation of the Rules of Decision Act. Notwithstanding these limitations, Congress may enact and has enacted rules of procedure regulating diversity cases, even though the rules also affect substantive rights. And because of the federal interest in the orderly and fair treatment of individuals engaged in multistate transactions, Congress likely could also constitutionally enact a body of federal choice of law rules applicable to diversity actions.

Declining concern over the need to protect out-of-state citizens against discrimination in state courts, coupled with rising distress over the heavy caseload of the federal courts, has spawned proposals to eliminate the federal courts' general diversity jurisdiction. While some continue to praise diversity jurisdiction for the continued acquaintance it offers federal judges with the common law process and the access it offers litigants (albeit selectively) to the often superior federal procedural system, those who support congressional repeal of diversity jurisdiction seem to be approaching success. Eventually it may come to be used only in complex, multistate cases, such as CLASS ACTIONS and interpleaders, in which the federal courts' power to issue process nationwide offers substantial advantages over state jurisdiction.

CAROLE E. GOLDBERG-AMBROSE
(1986)

Bibliography

ELY, JOHN HART 1974 The Irrepressible Myth of *Erie. Harvard Law Review* 87:693–740.

SHAPIRO, DAVID 1977 Federal Diversity Jurisdiction: A Survey and a Proposal. *Harvard Law Review* 91:317–355.

DIVORCE AND THE CONSTITUTION

The constitutional power of the states to prescribe conditions for marriage and divorce went largely unchallenged until the mid-twentieth century. Once Americans became highly mobile, however, new constitutional questions emerged. Divorce might be difficult under some states' laws, and well-nigh impossible under others', but in some places the courthouse doors were open. Could two North Carolinians go to Nevada, stay there for six weeks of "residence," obtain EX PARTE divorces from their respective North Carolina spouses, marry each other, and return to live in North Carolina without being guilty of bigamous cohabitation? In two cases entitled *Williams v. North Carolina* (1942, 1945), the Supreme Court answered that question conditionally. The Nevada divorces were valid, and must be given FULL FAITH AND CREDIT by North Carolina, if the travelers really were domiciled in Nevada when they received their divorces. However, domicile was a jurisdictional requirement for the Nevada courts; North Carolina might constitutionally retry the issue of the previous Nevada domicile, and, if its courts found that domicile lacking, might punish its straying residents.

The *Williams* "solution" soon crumbled. The Court held in 1948 that if both husband and wife entered appearances in the Nevada proceeding, then neither of them could later challenge the Nevada divorce by way of COLLATERAL ATTACK. Nor could a third party attack such a JUDGMENT. Perhaps the "true" domiciliary state might prosecute for bigamy in a case just like *Williams*, but few states had North Carolina's zeal for such prosecutions.

Since mid-century American law in this area has undergone two distinct but related revolutions. First, almost all the states now permit the dissolution of marriage on at least one "no fault" ground. Second, in a variety of contexts the Supreme Court has recognized not only a constitutional right to marry but a broad FREEDOM OF INTIMATE ASSOCIATION. It is doubtful that a state's interest in preserving a marriage against the will of one spouse would be given the same weight today that the Court gave it in the 1940s. In SOSNA V. IOWA (1975) the majority did remark that domicile was still a jurisdictional requirement for divorce, but the Court might take a different view if a latter-day prosecutor were to bring bigamy charges in circumstances closely resembling the *Williams* facts. (See MARRIAGE AND THE CONSTITUTION.)

Sosna itself upheld Iowa's one-year durational RESIDENCE REQUIREMENT as a condition on access to the state's divorce court, rejecting the argument that this limitation denied the constitutional RIGHT TO TRAVEL with the comment that the state had not denied divorce but only delayed it. Lawyers, including Justices, are experts in rationalizing; each day's delay in getting a divorce is surely a denial of one day's single status and of the right to remarry. The *Sosna* rationalization was aimed at distinguishing the Court's earlier decision in BODDIE V. CONNECTICUT (1971). *Boddie* held, on PROCEDURAL DUE PROCESS grounds, that INDIGENTS could not constitutionally be denied ACCESS TO THE COURTS in divorce cases for inability to pay filing fees. The Court there remarked on the "basic importance" of marriage, and took note that the state had a monopoly over its dissolution—and thus the availability of lawful remarriage.

The Court has not recognized a "right to divorce" analogous to the "right to marry" confirmed in LOVING V. VIRGINIA (1967) and ZABLOCKI V. REDHAIL (1978). However, we are not far from the recognition that the Constitution demands important justification for any significant interference with a spouse's freedom to terminate a marriage. Although the virtual disappearance of highly restrictive divorce laws makes less urgent the recognition of this constitutional liberty, that same change in state law surely alters the climate in which the Justices would evaluate the state's interests urged in opposition to the claim of associational freedom.

The collateral issue of child custody can also raise constitutional issues. Of necessity, a domestic relations court must have wide discretion in awarding custody. Yet because the parent-child relation is itself an intimate association of "fundamental" importance, it is vital that the custody decision not be made arbitrarily. The presumption of custody for the mother over a child of "tender years," for example, raises grave issues concerning SEX DISCRIMINATION. Racial and religious grounds for custody obviously raise constitutional danger signals, as PALMORE V. SIDOTI (1984) shows. And for a court to deny custody to a parent simply because he or she is living with another adult outside marriage, or is involved in a homosexual relationship, would also raise serious problems of associational freedom. Of course, at some level of maturity well below the age of adulthood, the child's preference—his or her own associational freedom—takes on constitutional weight that may dominate the custody decision. The Supreme Court has only begun its exploration of these painful subjects. Surely an early priority for the Court will be the reexamination of its old assumptions about the interests that justify a state's imposing its own preferred family patterns on the individuals who must live in them.

KENNETH L. KARST
(1986)

Bibliography

GARFIELD, HELEN 1980 The Transitory Divorce Action: Jurisdiction in the No-Fault Era. *Texas Law Review* 58:501–547.

KARST, KENNETH L. 1980 The Freedom of Intimate Association. *Yale Law Journal* 89:624–692.

NOTE 1980 Developments in the Law: The Constitution and the Family. *Harvard Law Review* 93:1156, 1308–1350.

DNA TESTING AND GENETIC PRIVACY

Constitutional RIGHT OF PRIVACY issues in the context of genetic testing may arise as federal, state, and local governments engage in the collection of DNA samples for DNA identification testing. These tests produce patterns of DNA banding that are highly specific to each individual. Such DNA banding patterns are useful for determining disputed paternity and for matching suspects to forensic samples in either criminal or military settings, among others. To facilitate such genetic identification, both law enforcement agencies and the military have begun assembling databases of DNA patterns. Additionally, many states have enacted laws requiring compulsory DNA sampling of convicted criminals. In analyzing the privacy implications of such testing, it is important to bear in mind that the patterns themselves contain essentially no information related to genetic disease or other expressed physical or behavioral genetic traits, only a highly individualized pattern of DNA fragments.

The federal Constitution contains no explicit right of privacy, but privacy is implicated in the constitutional restrictions on SEARCH AND SEIZURE under the FOURTH AMENDMENT, and the RIGHT AGAINST SELF-INCRIMINATION under the Fifth Amendment. In SCHMERBER V. CALIFORNIA (1966),

the Supreme Court held that warrantless removal of a blood sample from a suspect for purposes of blood alcohol testing constitutes a search under the Fourth Amendment. However, the Court held that because blood drawing is a safe, routine, and minimally invasive medical procedure, such a search did not intrude on the suspect's privacy, and was permissible with PROBABLE CAUSE. The Court also held that the taking of such evidence did not implicate the Fifth Amendment right against self-incrimination, as this right extends only to compelled oral testimony.

From this PRECEDENT, courts have more recently held that taking forensic DNA samples is not a form of compelled "self-incrimination," and is a permissible government search. Indeed, some forms of DNA identification tests can be done with a hair root or other bodily samples obtained by even less invasive procedures than drawing blood. Additionally, where compulsory testing of convicted criminals is concerned, the required showing of probable cause is much lower because convicts, having forfeited many of their CIVIL RIGHTS, have diminished privacy interests.

An additional important source of constitutional privacy arises from the line of reproductive rights cases including ROE V. WADE (1973). These cases establish a constitutional right against governmental intrusion into aspects of reproductive privacy. Despite the conceptual relationship between genetics and procreation, reproductive privacy does not appear to be implicated by DNA identification tests. The Supreme Court has stressed that these cases deal only with direct governmental intrusion into "protected decisionmaking" related to procreation, childbearing, and related familial choices. DNA identification testing does not impede or directly burden an individual's ability to beget, bear, or rear a child.

An additional aspect of constitutional privacy arises from a right of informational privacy found by the Supreme Court in WHALEN V. ROE (1977). This constitutional right restricts the ability of the government to compile personal information about individuals. However, the courts have held this right to be sharply limited. Government collection of such information is usually permissible when the government can show a legitimate reason for doing so, and takes some steps to restrict access to the information. Because DNA identification patterns contain little personal information, and governmental need for such information is compelling, collection of such patterns is probably permissible under *Whalen*, particularly since Congress has enacted some statutory protections against unauthorized disclosure or use of information in law enforcement DNA collection.

DAN L. BURK
(2000)

DOCTRINE

In constitutional law as in other pursuits of revelation, initiates commonly refer to "doctrines": bodies of rules or principles either authoritatively declared or systematically advocated. Some such doctrines have been simple; the ORIGINAL PACKAGE DOCTRINE is an example. Others, such as the INCORPORATION DOCTRINE, may become shorthand references to larger and more complex creations of the legal mind. More inclusively, one may speak of a doctrine as the body of principles ruling any branch of law, including constitutional law: the doctrine governing PRIOR RESTRAINTS on speech, for example, or the doctrine governing discrimination based on ILLEGITIMACY. In any such use, "doctrine" refers to a body of judicial interpretations of a particular branch of law.

Even more generally, one may speak of constitutional "doctrine" in the abstract, referring to the whole body of rules and principles resulting from the judicial process of CONSTITUTIONAL INTERPRETATION. Our constitutional law, apart from a few rules explicitly stated in the text of the Constitution (such as the requirement that a senator be thirty years old), consists almost entirely of doctrine made by judges in the tradition of the Anglo-American COMMON LAW. Doctrine thus develops as precedents are made by decisions in particular cases. One branch of constitutional doctrine, in fact, is designed in part to assure that the federal courts' lawmaking is informed by the need to apply doctrine to concrete facts. (See CASES AND CONTROVERSIES.) There is therefore a human quality in nearly every constitutional case; a court's opinion normally begins with a recitation of actual facts touching the lives of named individuals. One danger in an era of CLASS ACTIONS and INSTITUTIONAL LITIGATION is that those techniques carry some risk of squeezing the human flavor out of a case, with attendant costs to the process of keeping doctrine attuned to life. Yet implied in the idea of doctrine is the elaboration of principles transcending the concerns of particular individuals, to provide guidance—or comfort—to people in the aggregate.

Doctrinal formulas may outlive their usefulness, as the "original package doctrine" has. When they do, they fall into disuse or are explicitly abandoned. One of the paradoxes of law is that it strives to provide the security of enduring rules and principles yet is compelled to adjust to the demands of an evolving human society. Constitutional doctrine is rarely tidy and nearly always susceptible to manipulation; it is full of ambiguity and vagueness; "absolute" rules either give way to interest-balancing or serve as interest-balancing's disguises. Doctrine was ever history's handmaiden.

Yet constitutional doctrine has had generating force of its own. It is hard to imagine what this country would have been like but for the nation-building doctrinal contributions of the MARSHALL COURT. And the doctrinal development begun by BROWN V. BOARD OF EDUCATION (1954) has been a major influence in our twentieth-century social and political life. If constitutional doctrine sometimes seems no more than a chapter in a given era's political story, it is sometimes a chapter that advances the plot.

KENNETH L. KARST
(1986)

Bibliography

BICKEL, ALEXANDER M. 1962 *The Least Dangerous Branch: The Supreme Court at the Bar of Politics.* Indianapolis: Bobbs-Merrill.

DODGE v. WOOLSEY
18 Howard 331 (1856)

The PIQUA BRANCH BANK V. KNOOP (1854) decision striking down the tax on banks enraged the people of Ohio. They exercised SOVEREIGNTY by amending their state CONSTITUTION to empower and require their legislature to tax all banks, regardless of any tax-immunity or tax-preference clauses in their charters. Woolsey, a stockholder of a bank, sued the bank, as well as the tax collector, in a state court to enjoin the collection of a tax authorized by the state legislature under the new amendment to the state constitution. The Supreme Court, by a vote of 6–3, for the first time sustained its JURISDICTION in a STOCKHOLDER'S SUIT and ruled that the state could no more impair the OBLIGATION OF A CONTRACT, contrary to the CONTRACT CLAUSE, by its constitution than by a statute. Justice JOHN A. CAMPBELL, one of the dissenters, angrily asserted that his brethren had established the DOCTRINE that the final power over public revenues was to be found not in the people "but in the numerical majority of the judges of this court. . . ." Besides his heat, he raised a profound question: "Should it be that a state of this Union had become the victim of vicious legislation, its property alienated, its powers of taxation renounced in favor of chartered associations, and the resources of the body politic cut off, what remedy has the people against the misgovernment?" Chief Justice ROGER B. TANEY answered for the majority by saying that the people govern themselves, wisely or not, and are bound to their contracts by the Constitution. By 1862 the Court handed down five more decisions involving the taxation of Ohio banks. The state finally capitulated, and the Court irrevocably committed itself to the doctrine that a grant of tax privileges could not be repealed for the life of the contract.

LEONARD W. LEVY
(1986)

DOE, CHARLES
(1830–1896)

Charles Cogswell Doe, associate justice of the New Hampshire Supreme Court from 1859 to 1874, and chief justice from 1876 to 1896, is remembered as one of the country's greatest COMMON LAW judges. He is less renowned for his contributions to constitutional law. One reason may have been his bold originality. During his years on the bench, constitutional law was less tolerant of the unorthodox and less receptive to eccentric genius than was the common law. And Doe was original if not eccentric. The perspective from which he viewed the state constitution is an example. The drafters of the document had adopted words indicating they were writing a SOCIAL COMPACT and Doe insisted it had to be interpreted as a social compact. Under the other types of constitutions—those that were organic laws, not compacts—the government, Doe maintained, possesses INHERENT POWERS limited by certain enumerated provisions (for example, the federal BILL OF RIGHTS). When the liberty of a citizen is pitted against the authority of the state, the citizen must find specific wording to restrain government. A constitution that is a compact, by contrast, has no place for inherent power. As a result, Doe held in *Wooster v. Plymouth* (1882), CIVIL RIGHTS are not immunities but "privileges which society has engaged to provide in lieu of the natural liberties so given up by individuals" under the "contract." The proposition that the compact made government an agent, and individual rights absolute except when specifically surrendered, permitted Doe to relieve the citizen of the burden of establishing constitutional limits on state authority. The state had to demonstrate that the power it claimed had, by compact, been delegated to it.

The chief constitutional DOCTRINE resulting from the social compact doctrine was equality. "The bill of rights," Doe ruled in *State v. U.S. & Canada Express Co.* (1880), "is a bill of their equal, private rights, reserved by the grantors of public power." Equality, he added, is "practically the source and sum of all rights, and the substance of the constitution." Doe sought to make equality the most fundamental civil right protecting nineteenth-century Americans.

The national development in constitutional law most troublesome to Judge Doe was the United States Supreme Court's decision in the SINKING FUND CASES (1879). Fearing that the ruling endangered private property rights, he wrote several opinions hoping to diminish those cases' influence. In *Corbin's Case* (1891) Doe even invented the concept of "constitutional estoppel" to bar the state government from taking an action that in a corporate charter it had expressly reserved the right to take. Doe's particular genius even led him to criticize FLETCHER V. PECK (1810) and DARTMOUTH COLLEGE V. WOODWARD (1819), two decisions most contemporaries thought protected property rights. Doe believed they weakened property rights and increased arbitrary legislative power. Better had they been decided on the SEPARATION OF POWERS principle than on the CONTRACT CLAUSE.

In Doe's hands, the separation of powers principle became a means of enlarging his court's JURISDICTION. His distrust of legislative power resulted in support of laissez-faire principles, but his belief that courts should impose common law tests of reasonableness on business supported a measure of regulation. The supremacy of constitutional limitations was his foremost principle.

JOHN PHILLIP REID
(1986)

Bibliography

REID, JOHN PHILLIP   1967   *Chief Justice: The Judicial World of Charles Doe.* Cambridge, Mass.: Harvard University Press.

DOE v. BOLTON

See: *Roe v. Wade*

DOLAN v. CITY OF TIGARD
512 U.S. 374 (1994)

Governments often require landowners to satisfy conditions before issuing building permits. Under the Supreme Court's opinion in *Nollan v. California Coastal Commission* (1987), landowners can challenge such conditions as violating the Fifth Amendment's TAKINGS clause when they lack an "essential nexus" to the harms of development.

Dolan sought permission from the City of Tigard, Oregon to expand her retail hardware business, which was partially situated on a floodplain. The Planning Commission conditioned its approval on Dolan's agreeing to dedicate both her land within the floodplain to improve the city's flood control system and an additional 15-foot strip for a pedestrian/bicycle pathway. The Court held, 5–4, that these conditions constituted a taking of property.

The MAJORITY OPINION, authored by Chief Justice WILLIAM H. REHNQUIST, found that the "essential nexus" test of *Nollan* was met. But this was not enough. An exaction should also bear a "rough proportionality" to the corresponding harm. "No precise mathematical calculation is required, but the city must make some sort of individualized determination that the required dedication is related both in nature and extent to the impact of the proposed development." Finding no such "individualized determination" in the case, the Court found an unconstitutional takings instead.

In dissent, Justice JOHN PAUL STEVENS criticized the Court for resurrecting heightened JUDICIAL REVIEW of regulations similar to *Lochner*-era SUBSTANTIVE DUE PROCESS jurisprudence. He argued that the uncertainty of assessing environmental harms should justify deference to legislative processes where the government can demonstrate rationality and impartiality of its conditions. Justice DAVID H. SOUTER wrote a separate dissent, in which he argued that proportionality ought to be considered part of the "essential nexus" test of *Nollan*.

EDWARD J. MCCAFFERY
(2000)

DOMBROWSKI v. PFISTER
380 U.S. 479 (1965)

Dombrowski marks the high point of the Supreme Court's willingness to authorize federal district court interference with pending state criminal proceedings. When decided, *Dombrowski* seemed to suggest that such interference was warranted when the state statutes forming the basis of the prosecution were alleged to violate the First Amendment overbreadth doctrine. The CHILLING EFFECT—a term first used in *Dombrowski*—on First Amendment rights of prosecutions under such statutes derived from the fact of the prosecution, thereby rendering successful defense of the prosecution an inadequate remedy for the chilling effect. *Dombrowski* was "reinterpreted" in YOUNGER V. HARRIS (1971) and has since been of little precedential or practical importance.

THEODORE EISENBERG
(1986)

DOMESTIC COMMERCE

See: Intrastate Commerce

DOMESTIC VIOLENCE CLAUSE

Article IV, section 4 of the U.S. Constitution provides:

The United States shall guarantee to every State in this Union a Republican Form of Government, and shall protect each of them against Invasion; and on Application of the Legislature, or of the Executive (when the Legislature cannot be convened) against domestic Violence.

The last phrase in this section, known as the domestic violence clause, was added to the Constitution in response to SHAYS' REBELLION in Massachusetts in 1786–1787 in which disgruntled Massachusetts farmers shut down the state courts and threatened the legislature. Congress, acting under the ARTICLES OF CONFEDERATION and concerned that rebellion might affect other states, attempted to raise federal troops from neighboring states, but was ignored. When the CONSTITUTIONAL CONVENTION began, three months after Shays' Rebellion was resolved, the drafters included among the Constitution's purposes the need "to insure domestic tranquility" and added the domestic violence clause.

The domestic violence clause commits the power to protect the states to the "United States" rather than to any particular branch. In 1792 Congress assigned to the President the duty to respond on behalf of the United States, a statutory power the President retains today. Presidents have used their authority sparingly. The first President to use this authority was apparently RUTHERFORD B. HAYES who, in 1877, was asked by the governor of West Virginia (because the state legislature was not in session) to send federal troops to help suppress a railroad LABOR riot. On several occasions Presidents have declined to respond to requests for assistance because the state had not demonstrated the insufficiency of its own resources or because an official, and not the state legislature, had made the request.

The domestic violence clause has long had a secondary meaning. It was frequently cited during two critical periods—the drafting of the Constitution in 1787 and the FOURTEENTH AMENDMENT enforcement debates— as evidence that the states, not the federal government, had the primary responsibility for criminal law enforcement. Some of the Framers, who were concerned that the new federal government would usurp traditional state power over crime, pointed out that the Constitution expressly granted to the United States the power to punish only three crimes: treason, counterfeiting, and piracy on the high seas. They then argued that the domestic violence clause reserved to the states the power to define and punish domestic crime.

These arguments were renewed during the debates over early CIVIL RIGHTS legislation enforcing the Fourteenth Amendment. Those who favored an expansive view of the Fourteenth Amendment made a two-step argument: (1) The clause obligated the federal government to intervene when a state was overwhelmed by domestic disturbances and requested assistance, and (2) crimes committed within a state constituted evidence of the state's inability to deal with domestic disturbances and, accordingly, the guarantee of EQUAL PROTECTION OF THE LAWS justified federal intervention whether or not the state requested it. Those who favored a more limited view of the Fourteenth Amendment argued that the domestic violence clause was itself a limitation on the powers of Congress and that the federal government could not invade the inherent power of states to punish crime, at least not without a proper request from the state.

The arguments over the relationship between the domestic violence clause and the power of Congress to punish crime have never been addressed by the courts. In LUTHER V. BORDEN (1849), the Supreme Court held that the determination of when a state government has properly requested federal assistance under the domestic violence clause belongs to the political branches exclusively. Since that time the courts have declined invitation to construe the duty of the United States under the clause. Accordingly, the constitutional role of the domestic violence clause remains somewhat obscure.

JAY S. BYBEE
(2000)

Bibliography

BYBEE, JAY S. 1997 Insuring Domestic Tranquility, *Lopez,* Federalization of Crime and the Forgotten Role of the Domestic Violence Clause. *George Washington Law Review* 66:1–83.
COMMENT 1966 Federal Intervention in the States for the Suppression of Domestic Violence: Constitutionality, Statutory Power, and Policy. *Duke Law Journal* 1966:415–462.
FERGUSON, CLARENCE C. 1959 The Inherent Justiciability of the Constitutional Guaranty Against Domestic Violence. *Rutgers Law Review* 13:407–425.
RICH, BENNETT M. 1941 *The Presidents and Civil Disorder.* Washington, D.C.: The Brookings Institution.
WIECEK, WILLIAM M. 1972 *The Guarantee Clause of the U.S. Constitution.* Ithaca, N.Y.: Cornell University Press.

DOREMUS, UNITED STATES v.
249 U.S. 86 (1919)

Congress moved to suppress illegal drug trafficking in the HARRISON ACT of 1919 by compelling persons dealing in narcotics to register with the federal government. The act further imposed a $1 annual license tax, an exercise of the NATIONAL POLICE POWER. Justice WILLIAM R. DAY, for a 5–4 Supreme Court, sustained the entire act even though the provision at issue was the one requiring the use of federal forms for recording transactions. "The act may not be declared unconstitutional," Day said, "because its effect may be to accomplish another purpose as well as the raising of revenue." He found the tax section closely related to the rest of the act. By ignoring LEGISLATIVE INTENT—and his own recent opinion in HAMMER V. DAGENHART (1918) where such intent had been dispositive—he chose to follow the line of precedents beginning with CHAMPION V. AMES (1903). A single-sentence dissent found that the act over-

stepped Congress's delegated powers and invaded the states' RESERVED POLICE POWER.

DAVID GORDON
(1986)

(SEE ALSO: *Drug Regulation; Taxing and Spending Powers.*)

DOREMUS v. BOARD OF EDUCATION
342 U.S. (1952)

A New Jersey statute provided for the reading, without comment, of five verses of the Old Testament at the opening of each public school day. This was challenged as an ESTABLISHMENT OF RELIGION by a taxpayer of the town of Hawthorne who had had a child in its school system.

Justice ROBERT H. JACKSON, writing for the Supreme Court, rejected the STANDING of the plaintiff to raise the constitutional question. His child had been graduated from school, so that his claim as a parent suffered from MOOTNESS. Furthermore, because there was no showing that public money was spent on the practice, the plaintiff's taxpayer status gave him no stake in the litigation.

Justice WILLIAM O. DOUGLAS, with whom Justices STANLEY F. REED and HAROLD BURTON agreed, dissented. A taxpayer, Douglas argued, had a general interest in how the schools of the community were managed. The effect of this disposition was to defer for a decade decision on the constitutional merits of religious exercises in public schools.

RICHARD E. MORGAN
(1986)

DORMANT COMMERCE CLAUSE

The Constitution does not explicitly restrict STATE REGULATION OF COMMERCE. While the COMMERCE CLAUSE of Article I authorizes congressional displacement of state commercial regulation, the constitutional text is silent regarding the residuum of power left to the states where Congress has not acted. It has long been accepted, however, that the mere grant of authority to Congress—even if unexercised—implies some restrictions on the states. A panoply of terms is applied to this constitutional implication. Among the most popular are the "negative commerce clause" or the "dormant commerce clause."

Surprisingly there was little discussion at the CONSTITUTIONAL CONVENTION OF 1787 on the subject of free trade. Consequently, the Supreme Court felt obligated to justify the implied limitation on the state by reference to the events that precipitated the call for a convention rather than to what transpired at the gathering. The ARTICLES OF

CONFEDERATION era was marked by commercial warfare between the states. The resulting barriers to national trade, which threatened the vitality and peace of the Union, are often viewed as a primary catalyst for the Convention of 1787.

Judging from the constitutional language alone, one might conclude that the Framers left protection of national trade to congressional supervision rather than judicial enforcement. This expectation, however, does not appear to have been the vision of the principal Framer. JAMES MADISON anticipated that competing economic interests would neutralize each other in Congress and prevent the enactment of national regulation of interstate trade. The commerce clause, explained Madison in a letter written a half-century after the Constitution's drafting, would act "as a negative and preventive provision against injustice among the States themselves, rather than as a power to be used for the positive purposes of the General Government." Under Madison's impasse theory, Congress would be unable to act because of political impediments, and the state would be powerless to act because of limited authority.

Madison's theory did not address the question of who was to bring the states back in line when they transcended their authority. Logic pointed to the courts. If Congress were paralyzed in the face of potent and conflicting local interests, only the courts could protect the national interest in free trade. Few expressed this sentiment better than OLIVER WENDELL HOLMES, JR. Too often, observed Holmes, state action is taken "that embodies what the Commerce Clause is meant to end." The Union "would be imperiled," he warned, if the Court lacked power to void such laws. The Court's active role in scrutinizing state commercial regulation suggests that most of Holmes's successors have shared his concern.

The Court's dormant commerce clause jurisprudence has two distinctive branches. Under the "discrimination" branch, the Court invalidates state legislation discriminating against INTERSTATE COMMERCE. Under the "undue burdens" branch, the Court will strike down even neutral state regulations if the burden imposed on the interstate commerce is clearly excessive in relation to the local benefits.

The discrimination branch has been relatively noncontroversial. Even those who question the propriety of judicial balancing of trade burdens and local benefits generally concede the need for discrimination review. The dormant commerce clause, however, seems an odd vehicle for attacking interstate discrimination. The antidiscrimination provision of Article IV's PRIVILEGE AND IMMUNITIES clause seems far more appropriate.

In its original form, as contained in the Articles of Confederation, the privileges and immunities clause specifically addressed the problem of commercial isolationism, providing that the inhabitants of each state "shall be entitled to all privileges and immunities of free citizens in the several states; and . . . shall have free ingress and regress to and from any other States, and shall enjoy therein all the privileges of trade and commerce, subject to the same duties, impositions and restrictions as the inhabitants thereof." Little evidence exists on why the clause was pared down when carried over to the Constitution. CHARLES PINCKNEY, generally believed to have drafted the shorter version, assured the convention that no change in substance was intended. The term "privileges and immunities" probably was seen as sufficiently comprehensive to obviate the need for explicit references to ingress, regress, trade, and commerce.

If the positive command of the privileges and immunities clause were given the broad scope that was likely intended, resort to the commerce clause's negative inferences would be unnecessary for resolution of the discrimination cases. That the Court has not followed this route is attributable largely to PAUL V. VIRGINIA (1869). *Paul* held that CORPORATIONS were not "citizens" within the privileges and immunities clause. Notwithstanding subsequent construction of the DUE PROCESS and EQUAL PROTECTION clauses to encompass corporations as "persons" and the recognition of corporate CITIZENSHIP for purposes of Article III's diversity provisions, the holding in *Paul* remains a bar to corporate invocation of the antidiscrimination shield of Article IV.

Although some Justices and commentators believe that the Court may be proceeding under the wrong constitutional provision, almost no one questions the validity of the judicial role in voiding state discrimination against interstate commerce. However, the Court's continued willingness to strike down evenhanded state regulation because of "undue" burdens on the nation's free trade is a matter of substantial controversy. The present scope of congressional power dwarfs whatever James Madison may have anticipated. Moreover, the judicial expansion of the national commercial power is punctuated by the frequency with which Congress exercises its authority. Madison's image of a Congress deadlocked by competing geographic economic interests is seldom visible. Naturally, differences of perspective within Congress sometimes prevent consensus. But Congress has mechanisms to circumvent such stalemates. When impasses occur, Congress can shift decision-making responsibility onto the shoulders of REGULATORY AGENCIES by broad and often standardless delegations of power.

The rationale for the Court's zealous oversight of state commercial regulation has thus been substantially undermined. This led Justice ANTONIN SCALIA, in a CONCURRING OPINION in *CTS Corp. v. Dynamics Corp.* (1985) and a dissent in *Tyler Pipe Industries, Inc. v. Washington State Department of Revenue* (1987), to observe that absent rank discrimination—which he suggested is better dealt with under the privileges and immunities clause—the role of invalidating state legislation that unduly burdens free trade properly belongs with Congress. This view parallels another FEDERALISM development.

In GARCIA V. SAN ANTONIO METROPOLITAN TRANSIT AUTHORITY (1985), the Supreme Court abdicated any role in preserving the balance of power between the states and the federal government, deciding that the struggle over the scope of Congress's commercial power was best suited for the political arena. The states that petitioned for judicial assistance were told to fight their battle in Congress. This, said the Court, is how the Framers wished the scales of power to be balanced. Yet when a state regulates commerce in a congressional vacuum, the Court is there to ensure that the national economic interest will be adequately protected. The scales are not, after all, allowed to tip according to the political wind. The Court is keeping its thumb on the congressional side.

JULIAN N. EULE
(1992)

(SEE ALSO: *Dormant Powers.*)

Bibliography

EULE, JULIAN N.   1982   Laying the Dormant Commerce Clause to Rest. *Yale Law Journal* 99:425–485.

REGAN, DONALD H.   1986   The Supreme Court and State Protectionism: Making Sense of the Dormant Commerce Clause. *Michigan Law Review* 84:1091–1287.

DORMANT COMMERCE CLAUSE
(Update)

The "dormant commerce clause" limits state power to obstruct economic nationalism. At the core of this principle is the idea that states may not overtly discriminate against INTERSTATE COMMERCE. For example, when New Jersey blocked importation of solid WASTE from other states, the Supreme Court found a constitutional violation in PHILADELPHIA V. NEW JERSEY (1978). In cases like *West Lynn Creamery, Inc. v. Healy* (1994), the Court has continued to insist that protective tariffs and similar trade barriers offend this antidiscrimination principle.

Courts sometimes invoke the dormant commerce clause to strike down state laws that are not discriminatory on their face. In a leading case, *Hunt v. Washington State Apple Advertising Commission* (1977), the Supreme Court invalidated a North Carolina law that barred the display of apple crates of any grading symbol other than the federal Department of Agriculture grade. The Court reasoned that this law, although superficially neutral, unjustifiably burdened growers from the state of Washington, who had developed their own distinctive grading system. Courts often evaluate evenhanded regulatory laws under the BALANCING TEST set forth in *Pike v. Bruce Church, Inc.* (1970), which provides that such laws "will be upheld unless the burden imposed on [interstate] commerce is clearly excessive in relation to the putative local benefits."

State taxing measures have provided a common source of dormant commerce clause litigation. In *Complete Auto Transit, Inc. v. Brady* (1977), the Court summarized its many holdings in the tax field with a test that focuses on the presence of (1) nondiscrimination; (2) fair apportionment; (3) a reasonable nexus between the taxed activity and the taxing state; and (4) an appropriate relation between the burden imposed by the tax and the services afforded to the taxpayer by the state. In cases like *Oklahoma Tax Commission v. Jefferson Lines, Inc.* (1995), the Court has continued to apply this four-step methodology.

In some situations the dormant commerce clause does not operate even when state laws are facially discriminatory. A quarantine exception permits states to block the importation of articles, such as germ-infested rags, whose very movement creates risks of contagion. The dormant commerce clause also does not apply when a state acts as a market participant rather than a market regulator; for example, courts have upheld "buy local" laws under which a state insists on making its own purchases solely from in-state suppliers. Discriminatory state laws may escape invalidation if there is no less-restrictive alternative for achieving an important state interest; thus the Court, in *Maine v. Taylor* (1986), upheld a state's outright ban on the importation of baitfish where there was no other way to safeguard native fish populations from certain diseases. In *Camps Newfound/Owatonna, Inc. v. Town of Harrison* (1997), the Court suggested that the dormant commerce clause would not invalidate monetary subsidies limited to in-state businesses even if they had the same effect as unlawfully discriminatory tax benefits. Finally, even if a state law otherwise would violate the dormant commerce clause, Congress can validate the law by way of ordinary LEGISLATION enacted pursuant to its commerce power, without the need for a constitutional amendment.

Particularly because the dormant commerce clause lacks a clear textual foundation, it is sometimes decried as illegitimate. But such luminaries as JAMES MADISON endorsed the principle, and many analysts argue that it reflects the central aims of the Framers. In the end, proponents of the principle have won out, for the Court has recognized and applied some form of the dormant commerce clause for more than 140 years.

DAN T. COENEN
(2000)

Bibliography

BITTKER, BORIS I. 1999 *Bittker on the Regulation of Interstate and Foreign Commerce.* Gaithersburg, Maryland: Aspen Law & Business.

COENEN, DAN T. 1989 Untangling the Market Participant Exemption to the Dormant Commerce Clause. *Michigan Law Review* 89:395–488.

—— 1998 Business Subsidies and the Dormant Commerce Clause. *Yale Law Journal* 107:965–1053

COLLINS, RICHARD P. 1988 Economic Union as a Constitutional Value. *New York University Law Review* 63:43–129.

EULE, JULIAN N. 1982 Laying the Dormant Commerce Clause to Rest. *Yale Law Journal* 99:425–485.

HELLERSTEIN, JEROME R. and HELLERSTEIN, WALTER 1993 *State Taxation,* 2nd ed. Boston, Mass.: Warren Gorham Lamont.

REGAN, DONALD H. 1985 The Supreme Court and State Protectionism: Making Sense of the Dormant Commerce Clause. *Michigan Law Review* 84:1091–1287.

DORMANT POWERS

A constitutional power is called dormant if it is granted by the constitution but is not currently being exercised. For a variety of reasons Congress may not see fit to exercise power which it has been granted by the Constitution. These dormant powers may be "awakened" whenever Congress chooses to exercise them.

The federal system of the United States presumes that the states possess the governmental powers not taken away from them by the Constitution. In vesting powers in the federal government, the Constitution grants the national government EXCLUSIVE POWER over some matters of national scope, but CONCURRENT POWERS with the states over other matters. When a power granted to the federal government lies dormant, its effect depends on whether it is an exclusive or concurrent power. When the Supreme Court concludes that the subject matter requires uniform national regulation, then the states are not free to exercise the power even though Congress has not legislated in the area. By its silence Congress is presumed to have decreed that the subject shall remain free of regulation. If, on the other hand, the subject of the power admits of locally diverse regulation, as in COOLEY V. BOARD OF WARDENS (1851), states may legislate until Congress intervenes.

When Congress awakens a dormant power by legislating, its act will preempt inconsistent state laws by force of the SUPREMACY CLAUSE of Article VI. However, the courts do not always hold that Congress has preempted state law simply because it has granted power to a federal administrative agency to regulate an area. If the agency has not exercised the power given to it, then the states may yet be free to regulate the subject just as if the power were still dormant.

GLEN E. THUROW
(1986)

Bibliography

PRITCHETT, C. HERMAN 1977 *The American Constitution,* 3d ed. Pages 150–216. New York: McGraw-Hill.

DORR v. UNITED STATES

See: Insular Cases

DOUBLE JEOPARDY

Double jeopardy is the most ancient procedural guarantee provided by the American BILL OF RIGHTS. Rooted in Greek, Roman, and canon law, the right not to be put twice in jeopardy may be regarded as essential to a right to TRIAL BY JURY, and is well established in the law of other nations.

The Fifth Amendment of the Constitution includes the simple phrase: "nor shall any person be subject for the same offense to be twice put in jeopardy of life or limb." Yet this phrase, which has been copied in most American state constitutions, conceals a number of complex policy issues, many of which are still unsettled in American law in spite of numerous judicial interpretations since its birth in 1791.

In the course of time American courts abandoned any insistence that the jeopardy required involve a risk of life or limb, even though that had been an important consideration under the harsh criminal law of eighteenth-century England. Thus, the policy underlying the double jeopardy protection does not depend upon the hazard of severe physical punishment or death.

The English COMMON LAW recognizes the pleas of *autrefois acquit* (former acquittal) and *autrefois convict* (former conviction) to preclude retrial of an accused person, but American law has taken a more expansive view of the right. In America a prior accusation without a verdict could result in a successful plea of double jeopardy. The American version of the right is more generous to accused persons in many other respects, making double jeopardy an important potential source of protection.

In *Green v. United States* (1957) Justice HUGO L. BLACK provided a persuasive explanation of the American concept of double jeopardy. He suggested that the guarantee against double jeopardy is aimed primarily at three potential abuses of governmental power: "The underlying idea, one that is deeply ingrained in at least the Anglo-American system of jurisprudence, is that the state with all its resources and power should not be allowed to make repeated attempts to convict an individual for an alleged offense, thereby (1) subjecting him to embarrassment, expense and ordeal and (2) compelling him to live in a continuing state of anxiety and insecurity, as well as (3) enhancing the possibility that even though innocent he may be found guilty."

Double jeopardy policy embodies a conflict between a defendant's interest in "being able once and for all, to conclude his confrontation with society," as the Court said in *United States v. Jorn* (1970), and the public interest in a full and accurate prosecution. To preclude retrial of an accused person on some technical defect in the presentation of the prosecution's case is not in the public interest. Conversely, individuals must be protected against repeated risks of criminal punishment so that they may conclude their confrontation with society in a just manner and resume their normal lives as free citizens.

Surprisingly, it was not until 1969 that the Supreme Court extended the Fifth Amendment's double jeopardy prohibition to state criminal prosecutions. In BENTON V. MARYLAND (1969) the Court finally held "that the double jeopardy prohibition of the Fifth Amendment represents a fundamental ideal in our constitutional heritage." Since then the Court has been deeply involved in reviewing double jeopardy questions, refining and reconsidering many of its earlier interpretations of the clause. Now the Supreme Court is the chief source of policymaking in double jeopardy matters, although some state legislatures have begun to reexamine the DOCTRINE in the process of revising state criminal codes to eliminate overlapping criminal offenses.

Double jeopardy law involves at least four distinct policy questions. The first concerns the time when jeopardy begins or "attaches." Clearly, pretrial proceedings are not covered by double jeopardy, but at some point after a trial opens jeopardy is said to "attach." The second double jeopardy question is the legal significance to be accorded political boundaries such as statefederal, statemunicipal, nationalinternational. Third is the problem arising from the numerous definitions of crime which sometimes carve up criminal deeds into small parcels of criminalized behavior. These multiple offense categories could give rise to multiple prosecutions unless bounded by the double jeopardy protection. Finally, there is the issue raised by a criminal appeal (by the defendant or the state) with its potential of a new trial reviving the same risks to the liberty of the defendant.

All these issues are embraced within the American doctrine of double jeopardy and none has been definitively resolved. American double jeopardy law has become one of the most complex areas of JUDICIAL POLICYMAKING. English law on the subject lacks the complexity of American law because it is confined largely to the issue of the effect of a prior final judgment. American law is distinctive in its subtle interplay among the interests of the accused person, the prosecution, and the society at large. However, American double jeopardy law is confused by the judicial failure to separate the strands of double jeopardy and to pursue the essential purposes served by double jeopardy. Indeed, close reading of Supreme Court decisions reveals some conflict among the Justices concerning the goals of double jeopardy policy.

In *Crist v. Betz* (1978) the issue of attachment of double jeopardy was called "the lynchpin for all double jeopardy jurisprudence," but it still is not clearly settled. The federal rule is that jeopardy attaches at the time when the jury is sworn, and this federal rule now extends to state proceedings as well. The rule takes effect when the first witness is sworn in a case tried before a judge. After this point, in the absence of exceptional circumstances, the defendant's jeopardy begins, and it cannot be begun again merely because the prosecution wishes to retry a stronger case at a later time.

However, it is possible for the prosecution to retry a case that has been aborted short of FINAL JUDGMENT if it can bear the heavy burden of showing "manifest necessity" for repetitious proceedings. Courts have wrestled vainly in an effort to define the nature of the "manifest necessity" that justifies reprosecution. Recently the Supreme Court has developed a balancing test to weigh the interests of the prosecution and the defendant. Now, if a mistrial is based upon an error by the state that could be manipulated to strengthen the prosecution's case, a defendant is entitled to immunity from reprosecution if he chooses to oppose the mistrial, but not if he requests it. But the Supreme Court has wavered in its mistrial decisions, even overruling itself at times.

Attachment doctrines apply to JUVENILE PROCEEDINGS as well as to adult criminal trials, so that jeopardy attaches to an adjudicatory finding in juvenile court, preventing a subsequent trial in the criminal court for the same conduct. However, a closed master's hearing for a juvenile has been treated as a pretrial event, not an attachment of jeopardy.

The clearest interpretation of double jeopardy policy appears in the area of separate prosecutions for the same offense by federal and state governments. According to BARTKUS V. ILLINOIS (1959), double jeopardy is inapplicable when a defendant is charged with having violated the laws of two or more different "sovereigns." Yet, after a barrage of criticism of the Supreme Court ruling, the attorney general adopted a policy of avoiding federal reprosecution of a matter already tried by a state where the state prosecution rested upon the same act or acts. This discretionary policy remains an administrative restraint upon federal prosecution. In 1970 the Supreme Court held in *Waller v. Florida* that a state and its municipalities were not "separate sovereigns" in this sense; successive prosecutions thus were barred by the double jeopardy clause.

The most complex and least settled area of double jeopardy involves the meaning of "same offense" in the Fifth Amendment clause. The basic federal rule does not prohibit imposition of two or more punishments for the same activity. Instead, the Supreme Court has largely left it to the Congress and the state legislatures to carve up a single act or series of acts into an appropriate set of criminal offenses. The possibility of fragmentation of a single act into a number of criminal offenses with separate trials for each generally is not an occasion for judges to invoke the double jeopardy protection, although the Supreme Court has made some limited attempts to do so.

The double jeopardy clause is not a barrier to an APPEAL by the prosecution in a criminal case. The government may appeal decisions in a criminal case only if authorized by statute. Since the ORGANIZED CRIME CONTROL ACT OF 1970, which grants the right to appeal a sentence imposed upon a "dangerous special offender," reviews of sentences are available to the federal government. The Supreme Court has held in *United States v. DiFrancesco* (1980) that the increase of a sentence on review under this statute does not constitute multiple punishment in violation of the double jeopardy clause. Whenever a defendant appeals from his own conviction he is usually said to have "waived" his right to plead double jeopardy.

Taken together, double jeopardy doctrines appear still to be somewhat unsettled in the United States. The general contours of double jeopardy have been described since 1969 in increasing detail. Yet inconsistencies and uncertainties continue. This most ancient of American rights is subject to judicial balancing. Increasingly, the balance has been more favorable to the prosecution, contracting the generous scope of double jeopardy evident in earlier years. Since the Supreme Court has been deeply divided on double jeopardy issues we may expect continued developments of policy with changes in judicial personnel. States may have more stringent views of double jeopardy policy under their own double jeopardy provisions. Therefore some states may set higher standards than the Supreme Court for the protection of defendants.

JAY A. SIGLER
(1986)

Bibliography

FRIEDLAND, MARTIN 1969 *Double Jeopardy.* Oxford: Clarendon Press.

SIGLER, JAY A. 1969 *Double Jeopardy: The Development of a Legal and Social Policy.* Ithaca, N.Y.: Cornell University Press.

WESTIN, PETER and DRUBEL, RICHARD 1979 Toward a General Theory of Double Jeopardy. *Supreme Court Review* 1978:81–169.

DOUBLE JEOPARDY
(Update 1)

Over the past few years, the Supreme Court has decided a substantial number of cases involving double jeopardy issues. For the most part, these decisions continued a trend noted in the *Encyclopedia* of giving additional flexibility to the doctrine, although several notable exceptions expanded the protection provided by the clause. The most significant developments concerned two topics: multiple crimes arising from the same conduct and sentencing. The most disturbing development occurred under the dual-sovereignty doctrine.

In the area of multiple offenses, the Supreme Court continues to adhere to the position that the legilslative branch has virtually unlimited power to define as seperate crimes and to punish cumulatively individual steps within a criminal trasaction and the completed transaction as well. The well-worn test set out in *Blockburger v. United States* (1932) determined whether the offenses are seperate by asking if each "requires proof of a fact which the other does not," This has been constructed as a rule of statutory construction, which is not controlling within a single prosecution if the LEGISLATIVE INTENT is clear and that multiple punishments are intended.

However, where individual crimes arising from the same events are adjudicated separately, a sharply divided Court expanded the protection of the double jeopardy clause beyond the confines of the *Blockberger* test. In *Grady v. Corbin* (1990), the Court concluded that a prosecution for vehicular manslaughter was barred where the defendant had been convicted previously of driving while intoxicated based on the same automobile accident. The Court reasoned that successive prosecutions present dangers that require protection under the double jeopardy doctrine even in circumstances where the two crimes do not constitute the "same offense" under the *Blockberger* test. It formulated a new and certainly more complicated test: The guarantee against double jeopardy is violated by subsequent criminal prosecution when the government establishes an essential element of that crime by proving conduct that constituted an offense for which the defendant has been previously prosecuted.

The decision in *Grady v. Corbin* unsettled the law with regard to the important concept of what constitutes the "same offense." Its immediate practical effect will be to encourage, if not require, the government to prosecute in a single case all charges arising from the same transaction because some of those that share a common element will be barred by the double jeopardy clause if they are prosecuted later. How this decision will be reconciled with the body of related doctrine—and even whether it will stand the test of time given the Court's history of dramatically changing course on double jeopardy issues—remains to be seen. Indeed, the conflicting nature of the Court's double jeopardy jurisprudence was apparent from cases decided during the same term. In *Dowling v. United States* (1990), the Supreme Court determined that EVIDENCE of criminal conduct was not barred by the collateral estoppel concept of double jeopardy, even though the defendant had been found not guilty in an earlier trial of that criminal conduct. *Dowling* and *Grady v. Corbin* can be reconciled because the crimes in *Dowling* were not part of the same transaction, but the two cases demonstrate that there is no broad consensus within the Court on basic principles, particularly the application of this "same transaction" concept.

In the area of SENTENCING, the Court decided a number of significant cases. Although the clause does not apply to civil penalties, the Court concluded that in a very rare case a penalty traditionally considered remedial can be so overwhelmingly disproportionate to the damage caused that it must be considered punishment with a purpose of deterrence or retribution. In this circumstance, presented by a series of penalties in *United States v. Halper* (1989), the double jeopardy clause bars imposition of civil penalties subsequent to criminal conviction and punishment.

The Court has determined that the double jeopardy clause does not in general prohibit the government, pursuant to statutory authorization, from appealing a sentence or prohibit a court from increasing that sentence after review. In contrast, the double jeopardy clause does impose some limits on resentencing in CAPITAL PUNISHMENT litigation. In *Bullington v. Missouri* (1981), the Court concluded that the clause prohibits imposing a death sentence on resentencing where a jury initially imposed a life sentence. The trial-type proceedings involved in such a determination render a decision not to impose a death penalty the equivalent of an acquittal at trial. The double jeopardy clause does not, however, bar the trial judge, under statutory authorization, from overriding a jury recommendation of life imprisonment and imposing a death sentence.

The Court concluded that the double jeopardy doctrine permits either resentencing or judicial modification of a sentence in two other areas. First, it held in *Morris v. Mathews* (1986) that where the defendant is convicted of both a jeopardy-barred greater offense and a lesser offense that is not so barred the error may be corrected without resentencing by simply substituting the lesser-included conviction, unless the defendant can demonstrate a reasonable probability that he or she would not have been convicted of the lesser offense absent the joint trial with the jeopardy-barred offense. Second, the decision in *Jones v. Thomas* (1989) held that as long as the resentencing remains within legislatively intended limits an appellate court could modify an initially invalid consecutive sentence by vacating the shorter sentence and crediting the defendant for the time served even after the defendant had fully satisfied the shorter sentence. In reaching this conclusion, the Court dismissed longstanding PRECEDENT apparently prohibiting resentencing after the defendant had satisfied one of two alternative sentences.

In a disturbing, although not doctrinally surprising, opinion, the Court extended to prosecutions by separate states its very broad HOLDING that double jeopardy is inapplicable where the same conduct is prosecuted by state and federal governments. Reasoning that this dual-sovereignty doctrine rests on the critical determination that two entities draw authority to punish from separate sources of power, the Court concluded in HEATH V. ALABAMA (1985) that the doctrine operates between states as it does between state and federal governments.

On first examination, applying the doctrine to two states appears to present no major issues. However, an examination of the facts of the case and the underlying policies presents a different picture. *Heath* involved a kidnapping that began in Alabama and ended in a murder across the nearby state line in Georgia. Pursuant to a plea bargain in Georgia, the defendant avoided the death penalty in exchange for a life sentence. He was then prosecuted in Alabama for the same murder and sentenced to death. The Supreme Court's decision resulted in affirming that death sentence.

At a practical level, the operation of the dual-sovereignty doctrine permitted two states to enjoy all the advantages of multiple prosecutions that the double jeopardy clause was intended to prevent. Admittedly, however, these advantages can accrue to the prosecution whenever the dual-sovereignty doctrine is applied. The major difference in this case is that the two sovereigns were protecting the same policy interest—punishing the taking of human life. When the state and federal government are involved, there has historically been not only a separate source of political power, but also a separate interest protected.

Heath demonstrates that the Supreme Court is steadfast in its commitment to a monolithic and absolute dual-sovereignty doctrine in the context of double jeopardy. Given the expansion of federal JURISDICTION to almost every area of state criminal law, this position is understandable, if not defensible. Currently, the different policy interest protected by the federal prosecution is often imaginary, and the decision in *Heath* makes recognition of this fact unnecessary.

ROBERT P. MOSTELLER
(1992)

Bibliography

LAFAVE, WAYNE R. and ISRAEL, JEROLD H. 1985 *Criminal Procedure.* St. Paul, Minn.: West Publishing Co.

THOMAS, GEORGE C. 1988 An Elegant Theory of Double Jeopardy. *University of Illinois Law Review* 1988:827–885.

DOUBLE JEOPARDY
(Update 2)

In the 1990s, the Supreme Court decided a number of cases dramatically revising the prevailing interpretation of the Fifth Amendment's double jeopardy clause. These decisions have generally continued the Court's trend of leaving more leeway for state and federal legislatures, as well as prosecutors, to decide how many prosecutions and civil proceedings they will bring to punish a defendant for an act or course of conduct.

On the subject of what constitutes the "same offense" for double jeopardy purposes, a sharply divided Court, only three terms after deciding *Grady v. Corbin* (1990) on a 5–4 vote, overruled that decision by a similarly split vote in *United States v. Dixon* (1993) and returned to the older *Blockburger* definition of "same offense." Instead of defining "offenses" by determining whether two prosecutions are based on the same conduct (as in *Grady*), courts will now ask only whether each of the two statutes defining the offenses charged contains an element the other does not. Under this test, the Court allowed a defendant to be prosecuted for an assault even though he had already been punished, in a CONTEMPT proceeding, for violating a protective order by committing the same assault, as long as the statutes defining the two offenses each required proof of a different additional fact.

Defining when the double jeopardy clause prohibits successive proceedings for the same offense also caused the Court considerable trouble and second thoughts. A person who is convicted of an offense may be subjected to more than one kind of punishment for that offense—both a fine and a prison sentence, for example. But the double jeopardy clause prohibits the government from taking two bites of the apple by bringing multiple proceedings seeking different "punishments" for the same offense, even if one of those proceedings is labeled "civil." *United States v. Halper* (1989) ruled that the government

could not criminally prosecute a person who had already been punished in a "civil" proceeding by a fine so disproportionate to the harm done that it could not be considered "solely remedial." Applying a similar test, a bitterly divided Court in *Montana Department of Revenue v. Kurth Ranch* (1994) found that a Montana tax for possession and storage of dangerous drugs was "punishment," and that the state was therefore not allowed to impose that fine in a civil proceeding and also bring a separate criminal prosecution (although both penalties could have been leveled in the same proceeding). But applying this same subjective test and distinguishing *Halper* rather tortuously, the Court two years later concluded that CIVIL FORFEITURE is not "punishment" for double jeopardy purposes, partly because of its historical pedigree. Because of this conclusion, the defendant in *United States v. Ursery* (1996) was allowed to be criminally prosecuted for a marijuana offense even though, in an earlier proceeding, the government had forfeited his home and PROPERTY due to the presence of the same marijuana; and another defendant, in *United States v. $405,089.23* (1996), faced a forfeiture proceeding after a separate criminal prosecution even though the government could have sought forfeiture as a penalty originally. Finally, in *Hudson v. United States* (1998), the Court, split 5–4, disavowed *Halper's* mode of analysis. Even though a "civil" fine is intended in part as a deterrent, it may still be considered a remedial measure that therefore does not constitute "punishment" within the meaning of the double jeopardy clause, especially if it can be shown that the legislature intended the measure to be a civil penalty. Like the newly restricted definition of "same offense," which frees legislatures from judicial supervision of their decisions about how many offenses may be based on the same conduct, this new, narrowed test allows the government freedom to decide how many proceedings to bring, even when based on the "same offense."

The same split on the Court over the issue of how much leeway legislatures should be allowed reappeared in the area of SENTENCING. The Court had previously held that double jeopardy protections do not generally attach at sentencing. Applying this maxim expansively, the Court in *Witte v. United States* (1995) ruled that a defendant may be prosecuted for an offense on the basis of conduct that has already been used as "relevant conduct" at a sentencing proceeding in an earlier prosecution, leading to a substantial increase in that sentence. Taking the theory that sentencing is not governed by the same rules as trial one step further, the Court in *United States v. Watts* (1996) held that a defendant's sentence may even be enhanced by an allegation on which the jury at his trial had actually acquitted him (because the standard of proof at sentencing is lower).

In the past, the Court had applied double jeopardy

principles to capital sentencing in *Bullington v. Missouri* (1981), holding that the prosecution may not seek the death penalty in a retrial of a defendant who had been given a life sentence on the same charge and then successfully appealed the conviction. But in *Schiro v. Farley* (1994), the Court allowed a state to proceed to the penalty phase of a capital proceeding even though the jury had implicitly acquitted the defendant of facts the state would be required to prove at the penalty phase in order to sustain a capital sentence. The Court also distinguished *Bullington* in the noncapital case of *Monge v. California* (1998), a case brought under a state "three strikes" law where the state had not proven all the facts required by the statute to show that the defendant should have his sentence doubled because he had an eligible earlier conviction. After the enhanced sentence was reversed on appeal for insufficient evidence about the previous conviction, the state was allowed to try again, and to submit proof of the required factors. The Court, split 5–4 once again, held that this relitigation was permissible because it only concerned a sentencing factor in a noncapital case.

One of the few areas of double jeopardy law that has caused no dissension on the Court has been one of the most controversial in other arenas. Although the Court has never overruled or even questioned the dual sovereignty DOCTRINE, the successive state and federal prosecutions of the Los Angeles police officers who were videotaped beating Rodney King provoked a new flurry of academic and public debate about whether the Court's interpretation of the double jeopardy clause is more formalistic than fair. Scholarly opposition to the doctrine, from academics writing from a wide range of perspectives (from civil libertarians to adherents of ORIGINALISM), continued to be overwhelming. The officers' conviction in federal court, following their acquittal in state court, convinced many observers of the truth of one of the double jeopardy clause's central tenets—prosecutorial practice makes perfect.

SUSAN N. HERMAN
(2000)

Bibliography

AMAR, AKHIL REED and MARCUS, JONATHAN 1995 Double Jeopardy Law After Rodney King. *Columbia Law Review* 95:1–59.

HERMAN, SUSAN N. 1995 Reconstructing the Bill of Rights: A Reply to Amar and Marcus's Triple Play on Double Jeopardy. *Columbia Law Review* 95:1090–1111.

SYMPOSIUM 1994 The Rodney King Trials: Civil Rights Prosecutions and Double Jeopardy. *UCLA Law Review* 41:509–720.

THOMAS, GEORGE C., III 1998 *Double Jeopardy: The History, the Law.* New York: New York University Press.

DOUGLAS, STEPHEN A.
(1813–1861)

An Illinois lawyer and judge, Stephen Arnold Douglas served in the HOUSE OF REPRESENTATIVES (1843–1847) and the SENATE (1847–1861), where he chaired the powerful committee on the TERRITORIES from 1847 until 1859. Throughout his career Douglas was a strong Democratic partisan who advocated western expansion, railroad development, and compromise on slavery. A major political figure throughout the 1850s, Douglas closed his career with his losing presidential campaign in 1860. When the CIVIL WAR began Douglas rallied to the cause of the Union despite his hostility toward Lincoln and his familial and residual political ties to the South.

Throughout his career Douglas attempted to finesse the issue of SLAVERY IN THE TERRITORIES while supporting territorial acquisition and western settlement. Douglas hoped such a policy would lead to a presidential nomination from a united Democratic party. Practical politics dovetailed with Douglas's personal beliefs that blacks were inferior to whites, that slavery was a legitimate institution deserving of constitutional and political protection, and that ABOLITIONISTS were troublemakers or worse.

The key to Douglas's program was POPULAR SOVEREIGNTY, which would allow settlers to decide the slavery issue for themselves, and thus not require Congress, and the national Democratic party, to take a position on slavery in any particular territory. Ultimately, Douglas's position proved costly. Proslavery Democrats eventually demanded federal protection for slavery in the territories and opposed any Democrat who would not support them. On the other hand, Northerners, in Illinois and elsewhere, came to oppose the spread of slavery into the western territories. By 1858 Douglas discovered he could not satisfy the voters at home and remain a viable presidential candidate in the South.

As early as 1844–1845 Douglas had advocated that settlers in the West be allowed to decide for themselves the status of slavery. In Congress he urged the organization of the Oregon Territory without slavery because settlers there did not want slavery. In the House and Senate Douglas enthusiastically supported all American claims in Oregon and the Mexican War, and he opposed the WILMOT PROVISO. As chairman of the Committee on the Territories, Douglas secured the organization of the Oregon and Minnesota territories without slavery. In August 1850, Douglas resurrected the compromise measures of HENRY CLAY's "Omnibus Bill" and adroitly guided them through the Senate, one bill at a time, as the COMPROMISE OF 1850. The Compromise included the infamous Fugitive Slave Law of

1850, the admission of California without slavery, and organization of the rest of the Mexican Cession with slavery. The compromise satisfied few, but it halted a SECESSION movement then building in the South and probably delayed the Civil War by ten years.

In 1854 Douglas supported the KANSAS-NEBRASKA ACT in the expectation that it would stimulate western expansion and set the stage for a transcontinental railroad, which he hoped would begin in Chicago. The act repealed the MISSOURI COMPROMISE, refused "to legislate slavery into any Territory of State, nor to exclude it therefrom," and left the settlers "perfectly free to form and regulate their domestic institutions in their own way." Northern resentment of this sellout to slavery resulted in Democratic electoral defeats and formation of the Republican party, while popular sovereignty in the territories quickly degenerated into "bleeding Kansas." Douglas lost political support throughout the North, but he explained to hostile constituents that popular sovereignty would lead to a free Kansas. In 1858, however, Kansas petitioned for statehood under the proslavery LECOMPTON CONSTITUTION. Douglas opposed the Lecompton Constitution because it was ratified by fraud, did not represent the majority in Kansas, and thus was not a fair expression of popular sovereignty. For this opposition Douglas was virtually read out of his party. Later that year, in debate with ABRAHAM LINCOLN during the Senate race, Douglas defended the Supreme Court's decision in DRED SCOTT V. SANDFORD (1857) and the Kansas-Nebraska Act by asserting in the FREEPORT DOCTRINE that territorial governments could prevent slavery by denying it police protection or supportive legislation. Despite opposition from the Buchanan wing of his own party, as well as Lincoln, Douglas was reelected to the Senate. In 1859 his party, dominated by Southerners, stripped him of his Territorial Committee chairmanship because of his apostasy on the Lecompton Constitution and his Freeport Doctrine. Openly a presidential candidate since 1852, Douglas led a divided party in 1860. He ran second in popular votes and a distant fourth in electoral votes. Douglas opposed SECESSION and before his death in 1861 urged Lincoln to call out enough troops to defend the Union.

PAUL FINKELMAN
(1986)

Bibliography

JAFFA, HARRY V. 1959 *Crisis of the House Divided: An Interpretation of the Lincoln-Douglas Debates.* Garden City, N.Y.: Doubleday.

JOHANNSEN, ROBERT W. 1973 *Stephen A. Douglas.* New York: Oxford University Press.

DOUGLAS, WILLIAM O.
(1898–1980)

William Orville Douglas was appointed to the Supreme Court by President FRANKLIN D. ROOSEVELT on April 15, 1939, the youngest appointee since JOSEPH STORY, 128 years earlier. Illness forced his retirement on November 12, 1975, but he had surpassed by nearly two years the record for longevity of service previously held by STEPHEN J. FIELD.

As a child, Douglas contracted polio and overcame the residual weakness in his legs through long solitary hikes. When his father died before Douglas's sixth birthday, his mother was left nearly penniless with three children. Douglas knew grinding poverty and from his childhood, through all of his education, he worked to support himself and his family. Three views that colored his outlook on life emerged from this period and strongly influenced his legal views. Above all an individualist, he believed that, if given enough room by society, one could achieve full potential through self-reliance and hard work. At the same time, he formed a deep sympathetic bond with the outcasts and disadvantaged of society, particularly the poor, racial minorities, and political radicals. Finally, he harbored a lingering resentment of "the establishment," a view that later matured into a distrust of concentrations of power, whether of the private sector, the police, or government generally. A number of Douglas's legal positions trace their origin to these three linked premises, from his populist view of the antitrust laws to his repeated insistence that the function of the BILL OF RIGHTS was to take government off the backs of the people.

Douglas's career prior to his appointment to the Court also explains the hallmarks of his judicial style. (Over the years, even admirers of the Justice's substantive conclusions criticized his opinions for insufficiently explaining the origins of novel legal DOCTRINES, for carelessness in setting out the limits and definitions of the principles announced, and for unnecessary inconsistency in arguments made from one case to another.) Douglas was always a superior student, with an intellect in the genius range, yet from high school through law school, as he explained in his autobiography, "I had been trotting while I learned." His work obligations and his other activities left little time for reflection. Douglas was a quick study.

Douglas described both his initial appointment as a law teacher and his appointment to the Supreme Court as furnishing new leisure for intellectual contemplation. Intellectual habits, however, are not so easily set aside. Douglas was never contemplative. His habit was to analyze swiftly mountains of data, get to the heart of a controversy, and decide. He was impatient with extended discussion as an aid to decision, with long indecision prior to decision, and with excessive concern for peripheral issues. He remained a loner who spent little time trying to proselytize other members of the Court to his own views. In the Court's conferences and in his separate opinions, he was content to state his positions without adapting them to gain greater acceptance from either his brethren or the scholarly community.

Douglas's impatience with traditional legal style in opinions is also easily explained. As a law professor at Columbia and Yale, Douglas was at the center of the realist movement in jurisprudence. (See LEGAL REALISM.) The realists shared the view that traditional judicial opinions obscured rather than explained the reasons for decision. Douglas's own approach to his fields of business organization, securities regulation, and bankruptcy was to study the political, economic, and social institutions with which the law dealt and to shape the law to cope with contemporary problems presented by those institutions. And so it was with his approach to constitutional law. Douglas viewed much of the elaborate argument in standard Court opinions as so much "Harvard fly paper." Indeed, he delighted in sharp criticism of his opinion-writing style, which he viewed as the carping of the conservative legal establishment. He remained a pragmatist who did not try to develop a general theory of constitutional adjudication. Often he was content to let Justices with whom he agreed develop the overarching theories. He was indifferent to scholarly debates about the abstract limits of JUDICIAL ACTIVISM, and he did not have a consistent theory explaining his own pattern of judicial restraint and active judicial intervention.

The substance of Douglas's constitutional jurisprudence can best be explained by contrast with the views of the two other major figures among Roosevelt's appointees to the Court—FELIX FRANKFURTER and HUGO L. BLACK. Between 1937 and 1939, when these three joined the Court, the chief constitutional controversies were still perceived as those of the previous decade—the Court's "economic due process" theory had restrained state ECONOMIC REGULATION, and its "dual federalism" theory had limited federal power to regulate the national economy. The mainstream of constitutional law thought was still preoccupied by the mistakes of the "old Court" in writing its own notions of laissez-faire economics into constitutional limits on state and federal power. All of Roosevelt's appointees shared the opinion that these decisions of the old Court had been erroneous. The major battles surrounding economic due process, and the legitimate scope of federal economic regulatory authority, however, were over before Roosevelt appointed a single Justice to the Court. (See WAGNER ACT CASES; WEST COAST HOTEL V. PARRISH.)

The early 1940s brought new problems, with personal liberty claims asserted under the FIRST AMENDMENT, and attacks on criminal convictions for procedural irregularities of constitutional dimension. For Frankfurter, the lessons of the Court's previous excesses in second-guessing state and federal economic regulation applied here. It was inappropriate for judges to block decisions of political majorities simply because judges held deep personal views that those decisions were wrong. Issues of personal liberty involved a balance between legitimate interests of government and claims of constitutionally protected liberty. Judges must defer to reasonable governmental accommodations of these competing interests. Moreover, in the case of challenged state laws, interests of FEDERALISM imposed additional constraints.

For a brief initial period, Black and Douglas accepted the Frankfurter position. In *Minersville School District v. Gobitis* (1940), the first of the FLAG SALUTE CASES, Justice Frankfurter wrote for the Court, sustaining a law compelling salute to the flag against a challenge by children of Jehovah's Witnesses, whose religious beliefs forbade their participation. (Only Justice HARLAN FISKE STONE dissented.)

The break with Frankfurter came soon. Black and Douglas shared similar concerns about the rights of minorities and about fair procedures in state and federal criminal trials. In 1942, dissenting in *Jones v. Opelika,* a case sustaining a state license tax applied to the sale of religious literature, they announced that they had recanted their position in *Gobitis. Jones* was overruled a year later in MURDOCK V. PENNSYLVANIA (1943), with Douglas writing for the Court. The same year, *West Virginia State Board of Education v. Barnette* overruled *Gobitis,* with Black and Douglas joining Justice ROBERT H. JACKSON's opinion.

Even though Black and Douglas often wrote jointly in constitutional cases involving claims of constitutionally protected liberty, it was Black who was the theoretician. Black gradually evolved the views that protection of liberty required the Court to give liberal—and even literal—construction to the Bill of Rights, and that the Bill of Rights restricted not only the national government but also state governments, because, historically, it had been "incorporated" into section one of the FOURTEENTH AMENDMENT. (See INCORPORATION DOCTRINE.) Douglas and Black often clashed with Frankfurter on both issues throughout the 1940s and 1950s.

In *Adamson v. California* (1947) the Court decided, 5–4, that the RIGHT AGAINST SELF-INCRIMINATION of the Fifth Amendment was inapplicable to the states. Justice Frankfurter, concurring, defended the Court's position that the historic and practical meaning of due process was not contained in the specific provisions of the Bill of Rights, but he also insisted that working out the limits of DUE PROCESS OF LAW required more than personal judgments according to a judge's idiosyncratic sense of justice. Black, joined by Douglas, wrote a lengthy dissent arguing that the Fourteenth Amendment incorporated the "specific" standards of the Bill of Rights.

As time passed, Black, again joined by Douglas, further insisted that the guarantees of the Bill of Rights were specific indeed. Characteristic was their position concerning the First Amendment—that it literally forbade all government restrictions upon the content of "speech," leaving to the government power only to regulate "conduct" (for example, YATES V. UNITED STATES, 1957, separate opinion). Justice Frankfurter predictably insisted that free speech claims involved a balance between competing interests and required deference to legislative choices (BEAUHARNAIS V. ILLINOIS, 1952). During the 1950s, the Frankfurter position usually prevailed. Black and Douglas were often in lonely dissent as the Court sustained a series of state and federal antisubversion measures. With the appointment of Chief Justice EARL WARREN and Justice WILLIAM J. BRENNAN in the mid-1950s, the dissenting group grew to four.

After Frankfurter's retirement in 1962, the substance, if not the rhetoric, of many of the Black and Douglas dissenting opinions prevailed. Although the Court rejected total "incorporation" of the Bill of Rights, a process of "selective incorporation" of "fundamental" provisions applied nearly all of its provisions to state governments (for example, GRIFFIN V. CALIFORNIA, 1965, overruling *Adamson v. California*). The provisions of the Bill of Rights governing procedure in criminal trials were expansively construed in cases such as MIRANDA V. ARIZONA (1966). And while no other Justice accepted the Black-Douglas theory that the First Amendment literally protected all speech, the Court's cases of the 1960s rejected the Frankfurter position that the First Amendment tolerated all reasonable governmental restriction on speech. (See NEW YORK TIMES V. SULLIVAN; BRANDENBURG V. OHIO.)

The 1960s, however, brought new constitutional problems and a noticeable split between Justices Black and Douglas. There was a negative side to Black's theory pinning activist protection of liberty to the literal meaning of the Bill of Rights. For Black, the Bill of Rights defined not only the minimum guarantees of constitutionally protected liberty but also the maximum. As with Frankfurter's approach, the restrictive branch of Black's theory could be traced to the judicial excesses of the past. The "old Court" had used a natural law approach to write into the Constitution laissez-faire economic policies not fairly reflected in the document's history or text. For Black it was equally wrong for judges to import subjective notions of personal liberty into the Constitution. If judges balanced competing interests in interpreting the Constitution, there was danger beyond the certainty that judges would "balance away" constitutional restrictions with which they were unsympathetic. Judges might also use an open-ended balancing process to create rights according to their subjective predilections.

In *Adamson v. California*, two other dissenting Justices—FRANK MURPHY AND WILEY B. RUTLEDGE—had agreed with Black and Douglas that the Fourteenth Amendment incorporated the Bill of Rights as restrictions on state government. They had disagreed, however, with the contention that the Bill of Rights was the outer limit of constitutionally protected liberty. In their view, the Fourteenth Amendment's conception of due process required "fundamental standards of procedure . . . despite the absence of a specific provision of the Bill of Rights." Black and Douglas, on the other hand, had condemned the "natural law-due process formula" which allowed courts "to roam at large in the broad expanse of policy and morals and to trespass, all too freely, on the legislative domain. . . ."

In the late 1940s and the 1950s Douglas continued to support Black's literalist position. Occasional votes can be identified during this period, however, to suggest that his agreement with Black was only skin deep. In *Francis v. Resweber* (1947), decided only months before *Adamson*, the Court permitted a state to electrocute a man after a first attempt at his execution had failed. The vote was again 5–4. This time Black concurred in the result, without opinion. Douglas, along with Murphy and Rutledge, joined Justice HAROLD BURTON's dissent. The same year, another 5–4 vote, in *Kotch v. Board of River Pilot Commissioners* (1947), sustained a Louisiana law that limited the occupation of river pilots to friends and relatives of incumbents. Black wrote for the Court, but Douglas and Murphy joined Rutledge's dissent.

In the late 1960s, more cases arose testing the negative side of Black's constitutional literalism and the break with Black had become apparent. (Interestingly, Douglas never openly conceded that he had recanted his agreement with Black in the *Adamson* case. Only in the posthumously published second volume of his autobiography does he admit that the Murphy and Rutledge position was one with which he "in the years to come, was inclined to agree.") The pattern of voting disagreements with Black in the 1960s was no longer episodic but dramatic. Their differences can be seen on a wide range of issues, all centering on Black's consistent rejection of what he called the "natural law" approach to constitutional adjudication and Douglas's growing willingness to go beyond the literal text of the document.

Douglas wrote the Court's opinion in HARPER V. VIRGINIA STATE BOARD OF ELECTIONS (1966), striking down poll taxes in state elections under the EQUAL PROTECTION clause. Black dissented. Douglas also wrote for the Court in LEVY V. LOUISIANA (1968), striking down a state law discriminating against children born out of wedlock. Again, he relied on an expansive interpretation of the equal protection clause. Justice Black was in dissent and, three years later (*Labine v. Vincent*, 1971), wrote an opinion for the Court that seemed at the time to overrule *Levy*. Here, Black emphasized the absence of any "specific constitutional guarantee." Douglas, of course, was in dissent. Douglas endorsed open-ended theories extending the Fourteenth Amendment's restrictions on STATE ACTION to actions by private business. Black disagreed, insisting that in the absence of federal legislation, the Fourteenth Amendment was inapplicable to private conduct. (See BELL V. MARYLAND.) With reference to limitations on the time, place, or manner of speech activities on public property, Douglas was prepared to balance the need for available avenues of dissent against competing state interests, if the balance favored freedom of expression. Black disagreed. In ADDERLEY V. FLORIDA (1966), a 5–4 decision sustaining a sheriff's order that protesters leave a jail driveway, Black wrote for the Court and Douglas for the dissent. Finally, Douglas was prepared to interpret the Constitution to require government to follow fair criminal, civil, and administrative procedures even where those requirements could not be tied to specific guarantees of the Bill of Rights. Black, of course, disagreed. (See IN RE WINSHIP; GOLDBERG V. KELLY.)

The most dramatic clash between the two former judicial allies occurred in GRISWOLD V. CONNECTICUT (1965). Douglas wrote for the Court, striking down a state law forbidding the use of contraceptive devices. In that case, Black's dissent was predictable, since no provision of the Bill of Rights dealt with the issue. Douglas made a valiant attempt in his opinion to maintain the façade of his agreement with Black eighteen years earlier in *Adamson*. The opinion explained that the right of marital privacy was within "penumbras, formed by emanations" of specific guarantees of the Bill of Rights. (See PENUMBRA THEORY.) The façade was thin, particularly as Douglas relied on the NINTH AMENDMENT for the proposition that constitutionally protected liberty was not limited to the specific guarantees of the Bill of Rights. Just how far removed from even the "penumbras" of the Bill of Rights was Douglas's own conception of the constitutional guarantee of privacy became apparent years later in his concurrence in the abortion cases (*Doe v. Bolton* and ROE V. WADE, 1973; see also RIGHT OF PRIVACY.) Here, he explained that the term "liberty" in the Fourteenth Amendment, as he read it, was broader than the Court's conception of a right to freedom of choice in the areas of marriage, divorce, procreation, contraception, and the education and upbringing of children. It included "the freedom to care for one's health and person, freedom from bodily restraint or compulsion, freedom to walk, stroll or loaf." These, too, were rights that he insisted could not be abridged by government absent a COMPELLING STATE INTEREST.

Douglas had come to believe that the excesses of the old Court in the economic due process cases had not been that the judges read personal values into the fabric of the Constitution. The problem was, rather, that the Court's laissez-faire economic values were the wrong values. For Douglas, the "right" values had been clear all along. They required protecting the individual's right to self-fulfillment, protecting the politically powerless from unsympathetic legislative majorities, insulating the individual from excess concentrations of governmental and private power, and insisting that government procedures be fundamentally fair.

These values best explain Douglas's decisions, up until the end. In his own written instructions for his funeral service, conducted in Washington, D.C., in January 1980, Douglas requested that Woody Guthrie's song "This Land is Your Land" be sung. He patiently explained that some had falsely assumed the song to be a hymn to socialism. Quite to the contrary, he said, the song was in praise of the freedom to wander from place to place which had received constitutional protection in his opinion for the Court in *Papachristou v. City of Jacksonville* (1972).

The *Papachristou* decision was a fitting epitaph. Douglas had written for a unanimous Court striking down a local VAGRANCY ordinance under the due process clause of the Fourteenth Amendment. The technical basis for the decision was that the ordinance was unconstitutionally vague. Insofar as activities that were "normally innocent" were made crimes, an unfettered discretion was placed in the hands of the police. But, quoting Walt Whitman, Henry David Thoreau, and Vachel Lindsay, he went on to argue that wandering and strolling were more than merely "innocent" activities. They were "historically part of the amenities of life as we have known them. They are not mentioned in the Constitution or in the Bill of Rights. These unwritten amenities have been in part responsible for giving our people the feeling of independence and self-confidence, the feeling of creativity. These amenities have dignified the right of dissent and have honored the right to be nonconformists and the right to defy submissiveness. They have encouraged lives of high spirits rather than hushed, suffocating silence." The *Papachristou* opinion, in its results, its style, and the values it enshrined, was vintage Douglas.

WILLIAM COHEN
(1986)

Bibliography

COUNTRYMAN, VERN   1977   *The Douglas Opinions*. New York: Random House.

DOUGLAS, WILLIAM O. 1974 *Go East, Young Man: The Early Years.* New York: Random House.

—— 1980 *The Court Years: 1939–1975.* New York: Random House.

KARST, KENNETH L. 1969 Invidious Discrimination: Justice Douglas and the Return of the "Natural-Law-Due-Process Formula." *UCLA Law Review* 16:716–750.

POWE, L. A., JR. 1974 Evolution to Absolutism: Justice Douglas and the First Amendment. *Columbia Law Review* 74:371–411.

SIMON, JAMES F. 1980 *Independent Journey: The Life of William O. Douglas.* New York: Harper & Row.

DOUGLAS v. CALIFORNIA
372 U.S. 353 (1963)

Douglas, decided the same day as GIDEON V. WAINWRIGHT (1963), established an EQUAL PROTECTION right for INDIGENTS to be supplied counsel by the state, free of charge, to represent them in direct APPEALS from their criminal convictions. Justice WILLIAM O. DOUGLAS, for a 6–3 majority, followed the lead of GRIFFIN V. ILLINOIS (1956): DUE PROCESS might not require the state to offer appellate review of convictions, but once appeals were granted as of right, they must be made *effectively* available for all. The state's procedure, which provided appellate counsel only when the appeals court found such an appointment appropriate, denied "that equality demanded by the FOURTEENTH AMENDMENT."

Justice JOHN MARSHALL HARLAN, dissenting, elaborated on his *Griffin* dissent. The Fourteenth Amendment had enacted no "philosophy of leveling"; the state had no affirmative duty to relieve the poor from the handicaps of poverty. Due process was satisfied by the reasonableness of the state's procedure for appointing counsel.

Douglas appeared to be a major precedent pointing toward strict judicial scrutiny of WEALTH DISCRIMINATION. However, the BURGER COURT ended such speculations, even in the field of criminal justice. (See ROSS V. MOFFITT; STRICT SCRUTINY.)

KENNETH L. KARST
(1986)

DOWDELL v. UNITED STATES

See: Insular Cases

DOWLING, NOEL T.
(1885–1969)

Constitutional problems of FEDERALISM were the chief interest of Noel Thomas Dowling, Columbia University's principal teacher of constitutional law for three decades (1926–1956). Joining the Columbia faculty in 1922, Dowling, a gentle Alabamian, moved into constitutional law when the more corrosive THOMAS REED POWELL departed for Harvard. The main sources of Dowling's influence were his casebook, his articles, and his consulting activities.

Dowling's widely used book, *Cases on Constitutional Law,* was first published in 1937, at the height of the New Deal crisis. Its major theme reflected his lifelong concern: "the regulatory power of government, national and state." His teaching stressed the lawyer's role in constitutional litigation. His emphasis on statutes and LEGISLATIVE FACTS reflected his long participation in the work of Columbia's Legislative Drafting Research Fund.

Dowling advised on the drafting of a number of federal and state statutes. PRUDENTIAL INSURANCE CO. V. BENJAMIN (1946), upholding the MCCARRAN ACT of 1945 granting congressional permission for continued state regulation of insurance, was a special vindication for Dowling's emphasis on the broad scope of the congressional "consent" power. Similarly, Chief Justice HARLAN F. STONE's "balancing" opinion in SOUTHERN PACIFIC CO. V. ARIZONA (1945) vindicated Dowling's advocacy of a significant judicial role in curbing state intrusions on free trade in the absence of congressional action.

GERALD GUNTHER
(1986)

Bibliography

SYNPOSIUM 1958 A Tribute to Noel Thomas Dowling. *Columbia Law Review* 58:589–613.

DOWNES v. BIDWELL

See: Insular Cases

DRAFT CARD BURNING

The burning of Selective Service registration certificates—or "draft cards"—was a brief and dramatic episode that punctuated the early opposition to the VIETNAM WAR. Many draft registrants, often before television cameras, publicly burned their cards to demonstrate their refusal to participate in the draft. These events attracted wide attention and often served as a rallying point for war protesters.

Congress responded in 1965 by amending the Universal Military Training and Service Act to make it a FELONY when any person "knowingly destroys [or] knowingly mutilates" his registration certificate. This law was challenged by David O'Brien with the aid of the AMERICAN CIVIL LIB-

ERTIES UNION. O'Brien had burned his registration certificate before a sizable Boston crowd, including several FBI agents. He was indicted, tried, convicted, and sentenced to prison in the Massachusetts District Court, but the United States Court of Appeals held that the 1965 law unconstitutionally abridged FREEDOM OF SPEECH because it interfered with O'Brien's "symbolic" protest against the war.

In *United States v. O'Brien* (1968), the Supreme Court in an opinion by Chief Justice EARL WARREN reversed the Court of Appeals and upheld the challenged law and O'Brien's conviction. The Court first ruled that the Government has a "substantial interest in assuring the continued availability" of draft cards—for example, so that the individual can prove he has registered and so communication between registrants and local boards can be facilitated, particularly in an emergency. Second, in a more far-reaching holding, the Court rejected O'Brien's claim that the 1965 amendment was unconstitutional because Congress sought to suppress freedom of speech. The Court did not determine whether that in fact was Congress's purpose. Instead it ruled that such a purpose would not invalidate the law in light of the principle that courts may not "restrain the exercise of lawful [congressional] power on the assumption that a wrongful purpose or motive has caused the power to be exercised." (See MCCRAY V. UNITED STATES.)

Only Justice WILLIAM O. DOUGLAS dissented from the Court's decision, in an opinion that dwelt less on draft card burning than on the power of Congress to initiate a peacetime draft. The *O'Brien* case led to a sharp curtailment of draft card burning and opponents of the Vietnam War turned to other forms of protest.

NORMAN DORSEN
(1986)

Bibliography

ALFANGE, DEAN, JR. 1968 Free Speech and Symbolic Conduct: The Draft Card Burning Case. *Supreme Court Review* 1968: 1–52.

DRAPER v. UNITED STATES
358 U.S. 307 (1959)

In *Draper* the Supreme Court held that information provided by a previously reliable informer, even though hearsay and not within the personal knowledge of the police, is sufficient to establish PROBABLE CAUSE for an arrest, at least when there is substantial corroboration for the information.

JACOB W. LANDYNSKI
(1986)

DR. BONHAM'S CASE

See: Bonham's Case

DRED SCOTT v. SANDFORD
19 Howard 393 (1857)

Closely associated with the coming of the CIVIL WAR, DRED SCOTT V. SANDFORD remains one of the most famous decisions of the United States Supreme Court. It is certainly the prime historical example of judicial power exercised in the interest of racial subordination, and, as such, it stands in sharp contrast with BROWN V. BOARD OF EDUCATION (1954), handed down almost a century later.

Scott was a Missouri slave owned by an army medical officer named John Emerson, who took him to live at military posts in Illinois and in federal territory north of 3630 where SLAVERY had been prohibited by the MISSOURI COMPROMISE. In 1846, Scott brought suit against Emerson's widow in St. Louis, claiming that he had been emancipated by his residence on free soil. Missouri precedent was on his side, and after two trials he won his freedom. In 1852, however, the state supreme court reversed that judgment. By a 2–1 vote and in bitterly sectional language, it declared that the state would no longer enforce the antislavery law of other jurisdictions against Missouri's own citizens. Scott's residence elsewhere, it held, did not change his status as a slave in Missouri.

Normally, the next step should have been an APPEAL to the United States Supreme Court, but a recent decision in the somewhat similar case of STRADER V. GRAHAM (1851) may have persuaded Scott's legal advisers that the Court would refuse to accept JURISDICTION. They decided instead to initiate a brand new suit for freedom in the federal CIRCUIT COURT for Missouri against Mrs. Emerson's brother, John F. A. Sanford of New York, who had been acting as her agent in the Scott litigation and may even have become the slave's owner. Sanford's New York CITIZENSHIP provided the foundation for DIVERSITY JURISDICTION. So began the case of *Dred Scott v. Sandford* (with Sanford's name misspelled in the official record).

Up to this point, the principal issue in Scott's suit had been how residence on free soil affected the legal status of a slave. It was a familiar issue that dated back to the noted British case of *Somerset v. Stewart* (1772) and had been dealt with in a number of state court decisions. (See SOMERSET'S CASE.) During the early decades of American independence, a tacit sectional accommodation had prevailed. Southerners accompanied by slaves were generally able to travel and sojourn in free states without interference. At the same time, southern courts joined in upholding the rule that a slave domiciled in a free state became forever free. Beginning in the 1830s, however, this arrangement broke down under antislavery pressure. State after state in the North withdrew the privilege of maintaining slaves while sojourning, and there was growing judicial acceptance of the view that any slave other than a fugitive became free the moment he set foot on free soil. (See COMMONWEALTH V. AVES.) To Southerners the change meant not only inconvenience but also insult, and by the 1850s they were retaliating in various ways.

Dred Scott v. Sandford raised an additional issue. In order to maintain a suit in federal court, Scott had to aver that he was a citizen of Missouri. Sanford's counsel challenged this assertion with a plea in abatement arguing that Negroes were not citizens and that the Court therefore lacked jurisdiction. The trial judge ruled that any person residing in a state and legally capable of owning property was qualified to bring suit under the diverse-citizenship clauses of the Constitution and the JUDICIARY ACT. On the merits of the case, however, he instructed the jury in favor of the defendant. Like the Missouri Supreme Court in *Scott v. Emerson,* he declared that Scott's status, after returning to Missouri, depended entirely upon the law of that state, without regard to his residence in Illinois and free federal territory. The jury accordingly brought in a verdict for Sanford.

The case then proceeded on WRIT OF ERROR to the United States Supreme Court, whose membership at the time consisted of five southern Democrats, two northern Democrats, one northern Whig, and one Republican. Argument before the Court in February 1856 introduced another new issue. For the first time, Sanford's lawyers maintained that Scott had not become free in federal territory because the law forbidding slavery there was unconstitutional. This, of course, was the issue that had inflamed national politics for the past decade and would continue to do so in the final years of the sectional crisis. With a presidential contest about to begin, the Justices prudently ordered the case to be reargued at the next session. On March 6, 1857, two days after the inauguration of James Buchanan, Chief Justice ROGER B. TANEY finally read the decision of the Court.

Although Taney spoke officially for the Court, every other member had something to say, and only one concurred with him in every particular. The effect of the decision was therefore unclear, except that Dred Scott had certainly lost. Seven Justices concluded that at law he remained a slave. Taney, in reasoning his way to that judgment, also ruled that free blacks were not citizens and that Congress had no power to prohibit SLAVERY IN THE TERRITORIES. But were these declarations authoritative parts of the decision?

According to some contemporary critics and later historians, Taney did not speak for a majority of the Court in excluding Negroes from citizenship. Their conclusion rests upon the assumption that only those Justices expressly agreeing with him can be counted on his side. Yet, since Taney's opinion was the authorized opinion of the Court, it seems more reasonable to regard only those Justices expressly disagreeing with him as constituting the opposition. By this measure, the opinion never encountered dissent from more than two Justices at any major point. Furthermore, five Justices in their opinions spoke of the citizenship question as having been decided by the Court. In other words, the authoritativeness of that part of Taney's opinion was attested to by a majority of the Court itself.

More familiar is the charge that Taney indulged in OBITER DICTUM when he ruled against the constitutionality of the Missouri Compromise restriction after having decided that Scott was not a citizen and so had no right to bring suit in a federal court. "Obiter dictum" was the principal battle cry of the Republicans in their attacks on the decision. By dismissing Taney's ruling against territorial power as illegitimate, they were able to salvage the main plank of their party platform without assuming the role of open rebels against judicial authority. What the argument ignored was Taney's not unreasonable contention that throughout his opinion he was canvassing the question of jurisdiction. Having concluded that Scott could not be a citizen because he was a *Negro,* the Chief Justice elected to fortify the conclusion by demonstrating also that Scott could not be a citizen because he was a *slave.* Such reinforcement was especially appropriate because some of the Justices were convinced that the Court could not properly review the citizenship question.

It therefore appears that none of Taney's major rulings can be pushed aside as unauthoritative. In any case, the long-standing argument over what the Court "really decided" has been largely beside the point; for Taney's opinion was accepted as the opinion of the Court by its critics as well as its defenders. As a matter of historical reality, the *Dred Scott* decision is what he declared it to be.

Taney devoted about forty-four percent of his opinion to the question of Negro citizenship, thirty-eight percent to the territorial question, sixteen percent to various technical issues, and only two percent to the original question of whether residence on free soil had the legal effect of emancipating a slave. Throughout the entire document, he made not a single concession to antislavery feeling but instead committed the JUDICIAL POWER OF THE UNITED STATES totally to the defense of slavery. Behind his mask of judicial propriety, the Chief Justice had become privately a fierce southern sectionalist, seething with anger at "Northern insult and Northern aggression." His flat legal prose does not entirely conceal the intensity of emotion that animated his *Dred Scott* opinion.

The citizenship issue concerned the status of free Negroes only; for everyone agreed that slaves were not citizens. Yet Taney persistently lumped free Negroes and slaves together as one degraded class of beings who "had been subjugated by the dominant race, and, whether emancipated or not, yet remained subject to their authority." Thus all blacks, in his view, stood on the same ground. Emancipation made no difference. Negroes could not have been regarded as citizens by the Framers of the Constitution, he declared, because at the time they "had no rights which the white man was bound to respect." These notorious words were not mere historical commentary as defenders of the Chief Justice have often insisted. Taney also held that the constitutional status of Negroes had not changed at all since 1787, which meant that in 1857 they still had no federal rights that white men were bound to respect. His reasoning excluded blacks not only from citizenship but also from every protection given to *persons* by the Constitution.

Much more forceful in its political impact was Taney's ruling against the constitutionality of the antislavery provision in the Missouri Compromise. He began by dismissing as irrelevant the one clause of the Constitution in which the word "territory" appears, preferring instead to derive the territorial power of Congress by implication from the power to admit new states. No less remarkable is the fact that he never said precisely why the antislavery provision was unconstitutional. Historians have inferred from one brief passage that he based his holding on the DUE PROCESS clause of the Fifth Amendment. Yet there is no explicit statement to that effect, and in the end he did not declare that congressional prohibition of slavery in the territories *violated* any part of the Constitution; he said only that it was "not warranted" by the Constitution, a phrasing that suggests reliance on the principle of strict construction.

Not satisfied with ruling in effect that the Republican party was organized for an illegal purpose, the Chief Justice also struck a hard blow at northern Democrats and the doctrine of POPULAR SOVEREIGNTY. If Congress could not prohibit slavery in a territory, he said, neither could it authorize a territorial legislature to do so. This statement, being on a subject that did not arise in the case, was *dictum*. It exemplified Taney's determination to cover all ground in providing judicial protection for slavery. The dissenting Justices, JOHN MCLEAN and BENJAMIN R. CURTIS, rejected Taney's blanket exclusion of Negroes from citizenship. Having thus affirmed Scott's capacity to bring suit in a federal court, they proceeded to the merits of the case while denying the right of the Court majority to do so. Both men upheld the constitutionality of the Missouri Compromise restriction by interpreting the territory clause, in Republican style, as an express and plenary del-

egation of power to Congress. They went on to maintain that antislavery law, state or federal, dissolved the legal relationship between any master and slave coming within its purview, thereby working irrevocable emancipation.

Antislavery critics made good use of the dissenting opinions in launching an angry, abusive attack upon the Court majority and its judgment. The influence of the decision on the sectional conflict is difficult to assess. No doubt it contributed significantly to the general accumulation of sectional animosity that made some kind of national crisis increasingly unavoidable. It also aggravated the split in the Democratic party by eliciting STEPHEN A. DOUGLAS'S FREEPORT DOCTRINE and inspiring southern demands for a territorial slave code. At the same time, there is reason to doubt that the decision enhanced Republican recruiting or had a critical effect on the election of ABRAHAM LINCOLN.

For the two principals in the case, the verdict of the Court made little difference. John Sanford died in an insane asylum two months after the reading of the decision. Dred Scott was soon manumitted, but he lived only sixteen months as a free man before succumbing to tuberculosis. The constitutional effect of the decision likewise proved to be slight, especially after the outbreak of the Civil War. The wartime Union government treated *Dred Scott v. Sandford* as though it had never been rendered. In June 1862, Congress abolished slavery in all the federal territories. Later the same year, Lincoln's ATTORNEY GENERAL issued an official opinion holding that free men of color born in the United States were citizens of the United States. The THIRTEENTH AMENDMENT (1865) and the FOURTEENTH AMENDMENT (1868) completed the work of overthrowing Taney's decision.

The *Dred Scott* case damaged Taney's reputation but did not seriously weaken the Supreme Court as an institution. Aside from its immediate political effects, the case is significant as the first instance in which a major federal law was ruled unconstitutional. It is accordingly a landmark in the growth of JUDICIAL REVIEW and an early assertion of the policymaking authority that the Court would come to exercise more and more.

DON E. FEHRENBACHER
(1986)

Bibliography

EHRLICH, WALTER 1979 *They Have No Rights: Dred Scott's Struggle for Freedom.* Westport, Conn.: Greenwood Press.

FEHRENBACHER, DON E. 1978 *The Dred Scott Case: Its Significance in American Law and Politics.* New York: Oxford University Press.

SWISHER, CARL B. 1974 *The Taney Period, 1836–1864,* Volume V of the Oliver Wendell Holmes Devise *History of the Supreme Court of the United States.* New York: Macmillan.

DRUG ABUSE

See: Controlled-Substance Abuse; Drug Regulation

DRUG REGULATION

Congress's power to regulate the manufacture, distribution, and use of narcotic drugs, formerly limited by a considerable body of constitutional DOCTRINE based on the TENTH AMENDMENT, today is regarded as plenary, limited only by the guarantees of the BILL OF RIGHTS.

The Constitution nowhere expressly grants to Congress power to regulate narcotics. Congress's efforts to regulate the area have thus relied on its powers to tax and regulate foreign and interstate commerce, and on its implied power to make laws enforcing treaty obligations. In the early part of this century, though, the Supreme Court viewed these powers as being constrained by the Tenth Amendment, which, the Court repeatedly held, reserved the POLICE POWER exclusively to the states; federal laws attempting to usurp the police power were void.

Thus, for example, tax statutes were void unless they indicated on their face a revenue purpose rather than an intent to exercise reserved police power. As the Court stated in *United States v. Jin Fuey Moy* (1916), a tax statute would be upheld where it was clearly designed to raise revenue, even though it had "a moral end as well as revenue in view," provided that moral ends were reached "within the limits of a revenue measure." In practice, purported taxes would seldom be voided, but ambiguities in statutory language would be resolved by reference to the purported revenue purpose.

The requirement of a revenue purpose has become less important over time. Congress quickly became adept at structuring tax measures to pass the facial scrutiny of the courts. At the same time, the Court's review of purpose became more cursory. Indeed, at least one lower court expressed the view that a tax purpose is no longer required. In any case, the expansion of the COMMERCE CLAUSE power has made the use of the TAXING POWER unnecessary, and the Comprehensive Drug Abuse Prevention and Control Act of 1970 repealed most prior federal statutes based on the taxing power.

The development of the commerce power largely paralleled that of the taxing power. The Court for many years distinguished sharply between the commerce power granted to the federal government and the police power reserved to the states. The Court's decision in CHAMPION V. AMES (1903), though, established that Congress had the power to ban goods dangerous in themselves from interstate and FOREIGN COMMERCE. Under this power, Congress was free to ban trade in narcotics with foreign countries and between states, but had no power to regulate the intrastate manufacture or sale of narcotics. Thus, prosecution of narcotics violators under federal law required a case-by-case showing that the drugs in question were involved in foreign or interstate commerce, although Congress could create a statutory presumption that drugs of a type normally imported from foreign countries had been so imported.

Now that the courts have sweepingly interpreted the commerce clause, Congress may impose sanctions without showing in each prosecution that the narcotics transaction affected interstate commerce. Challenges to recent federal narcotics regulations have been routinely brushed aside by the courts.

Congress has also occasionally regulated drugs through the TREATY POWER. Thus, a law requiring narcotics addicts to register with customs upon leaving the United States was valid as a measure to carry out the nation's obligations under the Hague Convention of 1912, a treaty ratified by the Senate. With the rise of the commerce power, however, Congress has had little need for the treaty power in regulating narcotics.

Congress's power to regulate narcotics is, of course, limited by the Bill of Rights. In general, these limits are the same in narcotics cases as in other criminal cases; for example, Congress may not authorize unreasonable SEARCHES AND SEIZURES or CRUEL AND UNUSUAL PUNISHMENT of narcotics violators. Nonetheless, the BURGER COURT's contraction of the reach of the Fourth Amendment has led some commentators to speak ironically of a "narcotics exception" to that guarantee.

One issue unique to the narcotics laws, however, has arisen from the FIRST AMENDMENT's guarantee of RELIGIOUS LIBERTY. Several religious groups in the United States use drugs in their observance. The question thus arises whether the federal and state governments may constitutionally forbid the possession and use of drugs for religious purposes. The Supreme Court has held that only a COMPELLING STATE INTEREST can justify substantial infringement of the right to free exercise of religion. This compelling interest must, under the holding in SHERBERT V. VERNER (1963), be "some substantial threat to public safety, peace or order."

Two state courts have found that this standard bars legislative prohibition of the use of peyote by members of the Native American Church in their religious ceremonies. California, indeed, has found that the same ban applies to any person who uses peyote in connection with a bona fide religious practice, even if the person is not a member of any recognized religious group. In a 1964 case involving a "self-styled peyote preacher" the California Supreme Court granted a new trial to determine whether the defendant's professed religious belief was bona fide. Most courts, however, have rejected this view. As of 1983, courts in at least five states have held that the interest of defendants in free exercise of religion is outweighed by the compelling governmental interest in controlling the distribution and use of dangerous drugs.

Whether or not Congress is constitutionally compelled to do so, it has occasionally granted exemptions for the sacramental use of otherwise controlled substances. Just as sacramental wine was exempted from the provisions of the National Prohibition Act (1919), the Controlled Substances Act of 1970 exempted from its prohibitions the sacramental use of peyote. Although the Drug Enforcement Agency has consistently interpreted this exemption as being available only to members of the Native American Church, at least one lower court has held that Congress intended to exempt all bona fide religious groups using peyote for sacramental purposes and regarding the drug as a deity.

Other than this single exemption for peyote, however, the federal narcotics laws have not authorized sacramental use of otherwise forbidden drugs. Nor have the courts yet recognized any religious claims other than those made for peyote. The Supreme Court has not yet spoken on the matter, and constitutional claims for religious exemptions to the narcotics laws cannot be regarded as wholly frivolous. Still, neither the Supreme Court nor the lower courts seem currently to view these claims with favor.

JOHN KAPLAN
(1986)

Bibliography

BONNIE, RICHARD J. 1980 *Marijuana Use and Criminal Sanctions.* Charlottesville, Va. Michie Co.

KAPLAN, JOHN 1970 *Marijuana: The New Prohibition.* New York: World Publishing Co.

———— 1983 *The Hardest Drug: Heroin and Public Policy.* Chicago: University of Chicago Press.

MOORE, MARK H. and GERSTEIN, DEAN R., eds. 1981 *Alcohol and Public Policy: Beyond the Shadow of Prohibition.* Washington, D.C.: National Academy Press.

NATIONAL COMMISSION ON MARIHUANA AND DRUG ABUSE 1973 *Drug Use in America: Problem in Perspective.* Washington, D.C.: Government Printing Office.

DRUG REGULATION
(Update 1)

The breadth of congressional power under the COMMERCE CLAUSE to regulate the manufacture, distribution, and possession of psychoactive drugs remains unquestioned. In recent years, however, strong measures taken by the federal and state governments to prevent and punish drug offenses have raised constitutional objections grounded in the BILL OF RIGHTS. The most controversial of these measures has been the use of chemical testing to detect the presence of illicit drugs in a person's urine or other body fluids.

Beginning in the mid-1980s, many public and private employers began to require urine testing as a condition of employment. The FOURTH AMENDMENT ban against UNREASONABLE SEARCHES is implicated when a governmental agency requires its employees or applicants for employment to submit to urine testing or when the government requires private employers (such as railroads) to test their employees. The collection and subsequent analysis of a person's urine is clearly a "search" for Fourth Amendment purposes, so the constitutional controversy has focused on when such testing is "reasonable" in light of the government's objectives and the employees' interests in personal privacy. It is generally agreed that urine testing is "reasonable," even in the absence of a SEARCH WARRANT, if it is based on PROBABLE CAUSE, or "individualized suspicion," that a particular employee has used illicit drugs. The controversial question is whether, and under what circumstances, employees can be required to submit to urine testing as part of a random or universal screening program.

In 1989 the Supreme Court upheld two screening programs, rejecting the argument that urine testing is per se unreasonable in the absence of individualized suspicion. However, in upholding testing programs for U.S. Customs agents and for railroad employees, the Court closely scrutinized the governmental objectives and the testing protocols. For example, in NATIONAL TREASURY EMPLOYEES UNION V. VON RAAB (1989), the Court held that the Customs Service's interests in the integrity and safety of its work force and in the protection of sensitive information justified the urine testing of all employees applying for or holding positions involving interdiction of illicit drugs or requiring the carrying of firearms. Taking its cue from *Von Raab*, the District of Columbia Court of Appeals subsequently held in *Harmon v. Thornburgh* (1989) that these same interests did not justify the random testing of attorneys in the Justice Department's antitrust division.

Measures taken to suppress drug use have also been challenged under the Eighth Amendment's prohibition against CRUEL AND UNUSUAL PUNISHMENT. Trafficking in illicit drugs is typically punishable by lengthy periods of imprisonment, and under many statutes, severe sentences are mandatory. However, in *Hutto v. Davis* (1982), the Supreme Court rejected a proportionality challenge to two consecutive twenty-year sentences for possessing and distributing nine ounces of marijuana, and the Sixth Circuit Court in *Young v. Miller* (1989) refused to set aside a mandatory nonparolable life sentence imposed by Michigan on a female first offender who had been convicted of possessing at least 650 grams of heroin. Acknowledging that the sentence "borders on overkill," that Michigan permits parolable life sentences for armed robbery or second-degree murder, and that only one other state authorized a sentence of such severity for drug offenses, the Sixth Circuit Court nonetheless found no constitutional impediment to "Michigan's efforts to punish major drug traffickers to the fullest extent of the law, even those who are first offenders."

In 1990 the Supreme Court resolved a question discussed at length in the main volumes of the *Encyclopedia*—whether bona fide sacramental use of peyote is protected by the FIRST AMENDMENT guarantee of RELIGIOUS LIBERTY. In EMPLOYMENT DIVISION, DEPARTMENT OF HUMAN RESOURCES OF OREGON V. SMITH (1990) the Court held that Oregon's criminal prohibition against possession of peyote could constitutionally be applied to sacramental use of the drug and that a state employee could therefore be fired and denied unemployment compensation for having used peyote at a religious ceremony of the Native American Church. The Court's opinion is less noteworthy for the result it reached than for its reformulation of the governing constitutional rule. As noted in the *Encyclopedia*, under the BALANCING TEST articulated in SHERBERT V. VERNER (1963), the issue is whether the state's interest in suppressing use of illicit drugs is sufficiently compelling to override the individual's interest in religious liberty. However, in the peyote case, the Court held that the government is not required to exempt religiously motivated actors from generally applicable and otherwise valid criminal prohibitions.

RICHARD J. BONNIE
(1992)

Bibliography

ROTHSTEIN, MARK   1987   Drug Testing in the Workplace: The Challenge to Employment Relations and Employment Law. *Chicago-Kent Law Review* 63:683–743.

DRUG REGULATION
(Update 2)

Congress and the states have broad authority to regulate the sale, possession, and manufacture of narcotic drugs. The states regulate under their inherent POLICE POWER to act for the health, safety, and welfare of the public. Congress's power arises from its constitutional grants of power to tax and to regulate FOREIGN COMMERCE and INTERSTATE COMMERCE. To date, the expansive powers of Congress have been unaffected by a recent Supreme Court decision resurrecting a FEDERALISM-based limitation on the reach of the COMMERCE CLAUSE. In UNITED STATES V. LÓPEZ (1995), the Court held that a federal statute prohibiting gun possession near schools exceeded the authority of Congress. Such activity, the Court said, was not economic in nature and, even if engaged in on a large scale, did not substantially affect interstate commerce. This ruling produced a flurry of challenges to federal statues, including major drug regulation statutes such as the Comprehensive Drug Abuse Prevention and Control Act of 1970. Although none of these cases has yet reached the Court, lower courts have uniformly accepted Congress's detailed findings that intrastate manufacture, distribution, and possession of controlled substances, as a class of activities, have a substantial and direct effect on interstate drug trafficking and that effective control of interstate trafficking requires regulation of both intrastate and interstate activities. Congress may regulate all such activities and may impose sanctions without showing in each prosecution that a particular narcotics transaction affected interstate commerce.

Despite the broad scope of their powers, federal and state governments must still comply with the individual liberty protections of the BILL OF RIGHTS. Over the past decade strong, even harsh, antidrug laws have provoked numerous constitutional challenges. But successful challenges have been few. Courts have, for example, rejected claims that lengthy, mandatory sentences for drug offenses constitutes CRUEL AND UNUSUAL PUNISHMENT. Courts have also given federal and state governments a relatively free hand to employ two of their most controversial antidrug strategies: suspicionless DRUG TESTING and forfeitures of PROPERTY connected to drug activity.

When the government conducts drug testing of employees, students, or persons under government supervision or when it requires private industry such as railroads or airlines to conduct such testing, the chief constitutional check is the FOURTH AMENDMENT prohibition on UNREASONABLE SEARCH and seizures. Courts agree that the collection and analysis of a person's blood, urine, or hair intrudes on recognized expectations of privacy and amounts to a search. The essential question is whether such testing is reasonable.

If the government conducts a SEARCH OR SEIZURE as part of a criminal investigation, reasonableness requires PROBABLE CAUSE or reasonable suspicion that the individual has engaged in wrongdoing. But drug testing programs subject persons such as police officers, airline pilots, or job applicants to testing solely because they are within the targeted group. To evaluate these suspicionless drug testing programs, the Court has developed the "special needs" DOCTRINE. The Court permits abandonment of individualized suspicion if a search or seizure is prompted by a purpose, or special need, other than criminal law enforcement. To determine whether such suspicionless schemes are reasonable, the Court asks whether, on balance, the need to search outweighs the intrusion the search entails. This free-form, case-by-case BALANCING TEST has resulted in Court approval of most drug testing programs.

First, the courts almost always characterize the intrusion of drug testing as "minimal." In the absence of strip searches or other similarly intrusive methods, they view the taking of blood or the collection of urine or hair as a common occurrence, usually no more intrusive than a physical exam in a doctor's office or the loss of privacy associated with using a public restroom. And, usually, testing data are disclosed only to a limited number of persons and reveal only illicit drug use and not other information, such as pregnancy or diabetes.

Second, the government's need to conduct drug tests is routinely found to outweigh the minimal intrusion that they involve. The Court has upheld mass, suspicionless drug testing of high school athletes to respond to the "crisis" of drug use and insubordination in the schools. It has permitted suspicionless testing of U.S. Customs Service employees to deter drug use among agents whose job was drug interdiction, or who carried guns, or handled classified information. But the government's justification for drug testing can sometimes be too flimsy. In CHANDLER V. MILLER (1997), the Court struck down a Georgia law that required all candidates for public office to undergo drug testing. Georgia failed to show there was any drug use problem among candidates or any danger to public safety. It also failed to show why ordinary public scrutiny of such officials was inadequate to deter or detect drug use. After *Chandler*, government drug testing remains relatively easy to justify, but some actual drug use problem or concern for public safety must be demonstrated.

One of the government's most popular (and most profitable) antidrug devices is CIVIL FORFEITURE of assets. Typical civil forfeiture laws permit the government, on a bare bones showing of probable cause, to seize any property thought to be proceeds of a crime or suspected of being used or intended for use in criminal activity. The prime targets for forfeiture are assets connected to drug trafficking and possession. The government has seized cars, boats, planes, farms, houses, cash, and even livestock connected to drug manufacture and possession.

In civil forfeitures, the property is thought to be the guilty or offending party and seizure is permitted whether or not the owner is charged with or convicted of a crime. The government does not have to honor rights associated with criminal proceedings, such as proof beyond a REASONABLE DOUBT or TRIAL BY JURY. Indeed, the owner must prove the property's innocence or lose it entirely. Civil forfeitures are subject to some constitutional boundaries. PROCEDURAL DUE PROCESS requires that property owners have prior NOTICE and a hearing before the government

seizes land or other immovable property. Seizure of property only incidentally or haphazardly associated with criminal activity can be equivalent to a fine and limited by the excessive fines clause. However, although individual Justices have acknowledged the harshness of the civil forfeiture remedy, the Court has taken refuge in the long historical acceptance of civil forfeitures and has rejected any fundamental assault on its scope. Thus it declined to view forfeiture as a punishment subject to the DOUBLE JEOPARDY clause. It also rejected the idea that DUE PROCESS prevents the seizure of property from innocent owners; that is, owners who were unaware that others used their property, such as a car, to engage in drug trafficking.

MARY M. CHEH
(2000)

Bibliography

CHEH, MARY M. 1994 Can Something This Easy, Quick, and Profitable Also Be Fair? Runaway Civil Forfeiture Stumbles On the Constitution. *New York Law School Law Review* 39: 1–48.

LAFAVE, WAYNE 1996 *Search and Seizure: A Treatise on the Fourth Amendment* (with 1998 Supplement). St. Paul, Minn.: West Publishing Co.

LEADING CASE 1997 Suspicionless Drug Testing. *Harvard Law Review* 111:289–299.

NOTE 1997 Drug Testing and the Fourth Amendment: What Happened to Individualized Suspicion? *Drake Law Review* 46:149–172.

DRUG TESTING

Increasingly through the 1980s, federal and state governments required testing of a person's blood, urine, breath, and hair to try to determine recent drug or alcohol use. President Ronald Reagan's Executive Order No. 12564 hastened this trend by ordering federal executive agencies to develop and implement such programs for their employees. Other tested groups have included military personnel, defendants subject to pretrial release, probationers, PRISONERS and parolees, state employees (especially those involved in law enforcement and transportation), high school and college athletes and other students, women seeking obstetrical care and their neonates, and parents in child abuse and neglect cases.

When required or encouraged by the government, drug-testing programs raise fundamental issues for FOURTH AMENDMENT jurisprudence. Judicial legitimation of such programs may over time lead to substantial alteration of the predominant paradigms of privacy. Such programs present very different issues from the blood test in SCHMERBER V. CALIFORNIA (1966), which the Supreme Court permitted on the grounds that medical personnel administered it based on PROBABLE CAUSE of intoxication and that EXIGENT CIRCUMSTANCES excused the lack of a SEARCH WARRANT.

In its 1988 term the Supreme Court upheld in large part two federal testing programs. In SKINNER V. RAILWAY LABOR EXECUTIVES' ASS'N. (1989), the Court upheld regulations of the Federal Railroad Administration that required railroads to test the urine and blood of employees in major train accidents. NATIONAL TREASURY EMPLOYEES UNION V. VON RAAB (1989) upheld urine testing of Customs Service employees as a condition of promotion to positions that involve direct drug interdiction or the carrying of guns. The Court remanded for further consideration the issue of employee testing for promotion to positions allowing access to "sensitive" information.

All Justices agreed that a compelled production and subsequent chemical analysis of urine, blood, and breath are invasions of a person's REASONABLE EXPECTATION OF PRIVACY and therefore a search and possibly a seizure. For the first time outside of a prison context, the Court's majority concluded that a search of a person's body may be analyzed as an ADMINISTRATIVE SEARCH and thus may be upheld without individualized suspicion. Applying a test derived from a 1985 school search case, NEW JERSEY V. T.L.O., and developed in the 1986 term in cases involving searches of a junkyard, a probationer's home, and an employee's desk, the Court concluded that a government's "special needs," apart from those of normal law enforcement, can justify dispensing with the presumption that compliance with the warrant clause determines the reasonableness of the search. Such justification occurs at least when a warrant or probable clause requirement (or some lesser standard of individualized suspicion) would interfere with the state's satisfying its special needs.

Finding that such requirements were not practical because they would frustrate the government's achievement of its goals, the Court concluded that the drug-testing programs were reasonable in view of the importance of the state's interest, as weighed against individual privacy interests. It treated the latter as limited because of the reduced privacy expectation of employees, especially those in such highly regulated and scrutinized jobs as railroaders and Customs Service officers. The Court also noted the programs' efforts to employ accurate tests and to obtain employee medical data that could improve test interpretation, recognizing that the accuracy of a test affects a search's reasonableness (as well as the due process validity of any decision, such as dismissal, predicated on the test). To the extent the testing procedure is not particularly reliable, as can easily be the case, the government's interest is reduced.

Although these decisions approve widespread testing without individualized suspicion, they involve only testing that is triggered by a special event such as an accident or an application for promotion. Some lower court decisions have more deferentially reviewed the facts of challenged programs and upheld testing that lacked some of the restrictions crafted into the Customs Service program. Such programs involve more sustained and less predictable invasions of privacy and increase the discretionary power of superiors over subordinates that Fourth Amendment jurisprudence can limit. For example, courts have upheld repeated random or systematic drug tests of employees, such as flight controllers, police officers, and prison guards, without a triggering event. With respect to large classes of employees among whom the interest in deterring drug use is less substantial, lower courts have also approved testing based on an individualized suspicion that is less than probable cause.

As the Court gives more scope to administrative search doctrine, officials may rely increasingly on such searches rather than on a police officer's discretionary decision to search based on an individual suspicion of crime. Any such development will increasingly pose the question of the appropriate standard of JUDICIAL REVIEW in assessing the reasonableness not of an individual officer's acts but of a general legislative or executive program. The evidence justifying the program and the rules limiting discretion will be relevant to such an assessment. While in *Von Raab* the government plausibly hypothesized risks that might arise from a Customs officer's drug use, no evidence of drug abuse within the Customs Service was available. In accepting such hypothetical justifications, the Court's scrutiny was far from searching. This deference is consistent with the Court's explicit refusal to consider the availability of less intrusive means in determining reasonableness. Yet, in remanding some of the regulations for further consideration, the Court showed that its scrutiny was not of the lowest order.

The Court could confine the reach of these two cases largely to governmental employment by attributing them to the special scrutiny to which public employees may be subjected in hiring, retention, and promotion and thus treat these cases as variants of an UNCONSTITUTIONAL CONDITIONS problem. Yet, the numbers of persons covered by such testing and the intensity of these searches raise the question whether these decisions may signal a basic paradigm shift in Fourth Amendment law away from the presumption that reasonableness is defined by the warrant clause. The BURGER COURT and the REHNQUIST COURT have for years been edging in this direction rhetorically and in a series of ad hoc judgments; whether in retrospect *Von Raab* will be a watershed case cannot yet be determined.

The "special needs" rule risks a doctrinal unraveling of the warrant clause presumption in two ways. If the range and number of administrative searches increase, distinguishing administrative searches with a civil enforcement rationale from criminal enforcement searches will become ever more difficult. Second, a burgeoning of administrative searches will have the doctrinally unjustified and politically unattractive result of affording the criminal suspect more privacy protection than the populace at large.

These decisions are also noteworthy for the extent to which they permit intrusions on the body as a routine matter. They legitimate the role that intruding on bodily privacy can play in disciplining the civilian adult population. No appreciation is found in the Court's opinions that the body is the home of the self. The only noticeable concern is with the shame of scrutinized urination, a matter that testing programs sometimes address by providing only for aural supervision.

Also of note is their impact on the Fourth Amendment values of particularity and informational privacy. Depending on the kind of chemical analyses permitted, drug tests can provide a recent history—whether accurate or not, extending back many weeks—of legal and illegal drug use, which may have occurred solely in the home's privacy. They can also provide information about bodily and psychosomatic conditions such as pregnancy, HIV antibodies, diabetes, epilepsy, and depression.

In other, often more public situations that do not involve the employment relationship, the need to identify and seize a person may present a preliminary practical impediment to drug testing. In MICHIGAN DEPARTMENT OF STATE POLICE V. SITZ (1990), the Supreme Court upheld the constitutionality of temporary seizures at sobriety checkpoints. Officers briefly stopped all cars, examined the driver for signs of intoxication, and presumably observed what was in plain view. Upon finding signs of intoxication, the officer would direct the driver to a side location to examine his license and registration and to test sobriety. The state police established these checkpoints for short periods of time without prior notice to the public and without providing reasons for their location and timing.

The court reviewed these seizures by appling a reasonableness BALANCING TEST derived from *Brown v. Texas* (1979), but without first making a finding of "special needs" as in *Von Raab*. Presumably, the distinction between these two tests is that the Court treats brief seizures of persons in cars upon the highway, even for the routine law enforcement purposes, as less intrusive than searches. Subjecting the program's justification to a more lenient scrutiny than was used in *Von Raab*, the Court easily concluded that the state's interest in a program that outweighs the individual's liberty interests in avoiding brief detention. As in *Von Raab*, the Court refused to base its reasonableness judgement on the availability of other effective means of achieving state objectives that less seriously burden Fourth Amendment values. Accordingly, it refused to consider substantial evidence that checkpoints are far less effective in identifying and apprehending drunk drivers than are seizures based on articulable suspicion. It is too early to tell whether and how the power to seize without individualized suspicion will be combined with a *Von Raab* drug search.

ROBERT D. GOLDSTEIN
(1992)

(SEE ALSO: *Search and Seizure.*)

Bibliography

LAFAVE, WAYNE   1987   *Search and Seizure: A Treatise on the Fourth Amendment.* St. Paul, Minn.: West Publishing Co.

SCHULHOFER, STEPHEN   1989   On the Fourth Amendment Right of the Law-Abiding Public. *Supreme Court Review* 1989:87–163.

ZEESE, KEVIN   1989   *Drug Testing: Legal Manual.* New York: Clark Boardman.

DRUG TESTING
(Update)

Government drug testing of employees, students, and others such as persons on probation, is now a widespread and entrenched phenomenon. The chief constitutional limit on such testing is the FOURTH AMENDMENT prohibition on UNREASONABLE SEARCH and seizures. Because courts agree that the collection and analysis of a person's blood, urine, or hair is a search, the key question is whether such testing is reasonable.

When the government conducts a SEARCH OR SEIZURE as part of a criminal investigation, reasonableness requires PROBABLE CAUSE or reasonable suspicion that the individual has engaged in wrongdoing. But the requirement of individualized suspicion would doom modern drug testing programs because they are blanket, suspicionless searches of mostly innocent people. In a series of cases the Supreme Court excused the need for individualized suspicion when a search was conducted for a "special need" other than ordinary law enforcement. But it was unclear whether a special need was a standard for judging testing programs or simply an invitation to balance the "minimal" intrusion of drug testing against the important social problem the government was addressing.

In *Vernonia School District 47J v. Acton* (1995) the Court upheld random urinalysis of public school student athletes, saying that students in school had a reduced expectation of privacy; that being monitored while providing a urine specimen was no more intrusive than using a public restroom; and that testing was needed to combat a proven drug use problem in the schools. In dissent, Justice SANDRA DAY O'CONNOR insisted that suspicionless testing was contrary to bedrock Fourth Amendment requirements and could only be justified if the government had a specific and substantial need to test and proved that a suspicion-based approach was unworkable.

The Court moved toward O'Connor's position in CHANDLER V. MILLER (1997). Although the Court did not reverse any prior rulings, it said that suspicionless testing, even if only minimally intrusive, is permissible only if the government shows actual evidence of a drug use problem or real hazards flowing from possible drug use. The government must also explain why ordinary suspicion-based law enforcement methods are inadequate and show that its testing program actually responds to the problem it identified. In *Chandler*, the Court struck down a Georgia law that required all candidates for public office to undergo drug testing. Georgia failed to show there was any drug use problem among candidates or any danger to public safety. It also failed to show why ordinary public scrutiny of such officials was inadequate to deter or detect drug use.

MARY M. CHEH
(2000)

(SEE ALSO: *Drug Regulation.*)

Bibliography

RECENT DEVELOPMENT 1998 Reining in the National Drug Testing Epidemic: *Chandler v. Miller. Harvard Civil Rights–Civil Liberties Law Review* 33:253–272.

ZEESE, KEVIN 1996 *Drug Testing: Legal Manual.* Deerfield, Ill.: Clark Boardman Callaghan.

DUAL FEDERALISM

EDWARD S. CORWIN devised the term "dual federalism" to describe a constitutional theory enunciated by the Supreme Court and by many COMMENTATORS ON THE CONSTITUTION at various times (and to various purposes) in the nation's history—a theory concerning the proper relationships between the national government and the states. This theory, Corwin wrote, embodied four postulates of constitutional interpretation: "1. The national government is one of ENUMERATED POWERS only; 2. Also, the purposes which it may constitutionally promote are few; 3. Within their respective spheres the two centers of government are 'sovereign' and hence 'equal'; 4. The relation of the two centers with each other is one of tension rather than collaboration."

This theory gives enormous importance to the TENTH AMENDMENT, with its declaration that powers not delegated to the national government and not prohibited to the states by the Constitution "are reserved to the States respectively, or the people." (The ARTICLES OF CONFEDERATION had reserved to the states powers that were not "expressly delegated" to Congress.) Confronted with the competing concept of national authority in the Constitution's SUPREMACY CLAUSE, proponents of dual federalism have insisted that the Tenth Amendment holds a superior position. The TANEY COURT, especially in the LICENSE CASES, often portrayed the states' reserved powers as a constitutional limitation on the legitimate authority of Congress. In the post-CIVIL WAR period, the Court built another constitutional monument to dual federalism theory in its doctrine of INTERGOVERNMENTAL IMMUNITIES. In the hands of a conservative, property-minded judiciary in the late nineteenth century, dual federalism became a potent instrument for invalidation of federal regulatory measures. In HAMMER V. DAGENHART (1918) the Court's majority took an extreme view of the Tenth Amendment, declaring that it forbade even a federal regulation of interstate commerce when the regulation's purpose was to invade the province of the states' reserved powers.

A series of decisions in the late 1930s, however, put to rest the formal constitutional theory of dual federalism. The Court's revised interpretations of the COMMERCE POWER, the CONTRACT CLAUSE, and the TAXING AND SPENDING POWER all rejected Tenth Amendment limitations on national authority. Meanwhile, the Court also validated the administrative innovations of COOPERATIVE FEDERALISM, in the form of extensive programs of FEDERAL GRANTS-IN-AID to the states.

The only serious reappearance of dual federalism theory in post-NEW DEAL constitutional law has been in NATIONAL LEAGUE OF CITIES V. USERY (1976), in which a concept of inviolable powers and functions of the "states as states" became a limitation on congressional regulatory power, in this instance the power to establish wages and hours for municipal workers.

HARRY N. SCHEIBER
(1986)

Bibliography

CORWIN, EDWARD S. 1950 The Passing of Dual Federalism. *Virginia Law Review* 36:1–24.

MASON, ALPHEUS THOMAS 1968 Federalism: Historic Questions and Contemporary Meanings. The Role of the Court. In Valerie, Earl, ed., *Federalism: Infinite Variety in Theory and Practice.* Itasca, Ill.: F. E. Peacock Publishers.

SCHEIBER, HARRY N. 1978 American Federalism and the Diffusion of Power. *University of Toledo Law Review* 9:619–680.

DUANE, JAMES
(1733–1797)

James Duane, a wealthy New York lawyer and conservative political leader of the Revolutionary period, served in the Continental Congress (1774–1784) and helped write and secure ratification of the ARTICLES OF CONFEDERATION. As mayor of New York City (1784–1789) he presided over the Mayor's Court case of RUTGERS V. WADDINGTON (1784), a disputed precedent for JUDICIAL REVIEW. Not named, because of his nationalist views, as a delegate to the CONSTITUTIONAL CONVENTION OF 1787, he attended the New York convention and worked for RATIFICATION OF THE CONSTITUTION. He was later the first UNITED STATES DISTRICT COURT judge in New York (1789–1794).

DENNIS J. MAHONEY
(1986)

DUE PROCESS OF LAW

A 1354 act of Parliament reconfirming MAGNA CARTA paraphrased its chapter 29 as follows: "That no man . . . shall be put out of Land or Tenement, nor taken, nor imprisoned, nor disinherited, nor put to death, without being brought in Answer by due Process of Law." This was the first reference to due process in English legal history. Chapter 29 of the 1225 issue of Magna Carta originally concluded with the phrase "by the LAW OF THE LAND." Very probably the 1354 reconfirmation did not equate "the law of the land" with "due process of law"; the two were not synonymous. Due process in the 1354 enactment, and until the seventeenth century, meant an appropriate COMMON LAW writ.

In the Five Knights Case (see PETITION OF RIGHT), JOHN SELDEN, the great parliamentarian, said in defense of the accused that "No freeman shall be imprisoned without due process of law," meaning that the "law of the land" was an equivalent for "either INDICTMENT or PRESENTMENT." Sir EDWARD COKE, in his commentary on Magna Carta, also equated due process with the law of the land, meaning regularized courses of proceeding in common law prosecutions for crime. Coke's primary claim was that the law of the land was the common law, one of several rival systems of law then prevalent in England. When abolishing the courts of High Commission and Star Chamber, Parliament in 1641 quoted the due process phraseology of the act of 1354 and added that trials by "ordinary Courts of Justice and by the ordinary course of law" protected property right against arbitrary proceedings. JOHN LILBURNE and his Levellers agreed, but they also asserted that due process signified a cluster of procedural protections of the criminally accused, including TRIAL BY JURY, the RIGHT TO COUNSEL, and the RIGHT AGAINST SELF-INCRIMINATION. By the mid-seventeenth century due process and the law of the land referred to PROCEDURAL DUE PROCESS in both civil and criminal cases. The "law of the land" usage, however, was the dominant one, and "due process" continued to be used in the very limited sense of a writ appropriate to a legal proceeding. A century later WILLIAM BLACKSTONE discussed various processes—original, mesne, and final—without discoursing on due process of law per se. After referring to indictment in capital cases and the principle that "no man can be put to death without being brought to answer by due process of law," Blackstone referred to the different writs that summoned an accused to trial in MISDEMEANOR and FELONY cases.

In the American colonies the usage was similar. In deference to Magna Carta, the "law of the land" formulation was by far the most common, although a variety of paraphrases existed. The MASSACHUSETTS BODY OF LIBERTIES (1641) guaranteed that one's life, liberty, and property could not be deprived except by "some expresse law of the Country warranting the same, established by a generall Court and sufficiently published"—that is, by known, standing law. West New Jersey protected the same substantive rights by a clause guaranteeing "due trial and judgment passed by twelve good and lawful men." New York in 1683 sought a charter that incorporated the famous chapter of Magna Carta with a clause requiring "by due course of law." Probably the first American reference to "due process of law" was in a Massachusetts act of 1692 endorsing chapter 29 of Magna Carta.

During the controversy with Great Britain leading to the American Revolution, Americans frequently spoke of trial by jury, FUNDAMENTAL LAW, the law of the land, no TAXATION WITHOUT REPRESENTATION, and a gamut of CIVIL LIBERTIES, but rarely referred to due process of law. Their references to the "law of the land" had no fixed or single meaning. They meant by it a variety of safeguards against injustice and abuses of CRIMINAL PROCEDURE; they equated it with NOTICE, hearing, indictment, trial by jury, and, more generally, with regular forms of common law procedure and even the fundamental law itself or constitutional limitations on government. The "law of the land" was an omnibus phrase whose content ranged from specific writs to the concept of CONSTITUTIONALISM, and the phrase connoted protection of substantive rights—life, liberty, and property—as well as various precedural rights. Later, due process inherited all the content and connotations of law of the land.

All the first state constitutions used the "law of the land" phraseology, as did the NORTHWEST ORDINANCE OF 1787. No state constitution included a due process clause until New York's of 1821, although Mississippi's constitution of 1817 referred to "due course of law." Before the

Civil War, only five state constitutions referred to "due process of law." All others had the older "law of the land" equivalent.

The first American constitution to include a due process clause was the Constitution of the United States in its Fifth Amendment, ratified in 1791. The clause reflected JAMES MADISON's preference. For reasons unknown, he recommended that no person should be "deprived of life, liberty, or property without due process of law." The four states which had ratified the Constitution with recommendations for a comprehensive BILL OF RIGHTS urged versions of chapter 29 of Magna Carta, although only one, New York, referred to "due process of law" rather than "law of the land." The due process clause of the Fifth Amendment was ratified without any discussions that illumine its meaning. Although every clause of the Constitution is supposed to have its own independent meaning, rendering no clause tautological, the due process clause was an exception. It pacified public apprehensions, bowed toward Magna Carta, and reinforced specific rights such as trial by jury.

When the Supreme Court construed the due process clause of the Fifth Amendment for the first time in MURRAY V. HOBOKEN LAND COMPANY (1856), it declared that although due process limited all branches of the government, it had only the procedural connotations that derived from the settled usages and modes of proceeding which characterized old English law suited to American conditions. Chief Justice ROGER B. TANEY's opinion in DRED SCOTT V. SANDFORD (1857) passingly employed SUBSTANTIVE DUE PROCESS OF LAW, which had cropped up in some state decisions and in ABOLITIONIST CONSTITUTIONAL THEORY as well as proslavery theory. The FOURTEENTH AMENDMENT's due process clause, taken verbatim from the Fifth's, proved to be the turning point in the national acceptance of "due process of law" as the common usage rather than the "law of the land" usage. In the last third of the nineteenth century, state constitutions finally substituted "due process" for "law of the land," and judicial decisions, state and federal, as well as legal treatises, expounded "due process of law," making it the most important and influential term in American constitutional law.

LEONARD W. LEVY
(1986)

Bibliography

HOWARD, A. E. DICK 1968 *The Road from Runnymede: Magna Carta and Constitutionalism in America.* Charlottesville: University Press of Virginia.

JUROW, KEITH 1975 Untimely Thoughts: A Reconsideration of the Origins of Due Process of Law. *American Journal of Legal History* 19:265–279.

MOTT, RODNEY 1926 *Due Process of Law.* Indianapolis: Bobbs-Merrill.

DUE PROCESS OF LAW, PROCEDURAL

See: Procedural Due Process of Law, Civil; Procedural Due Process of Law, Criminal

DUE PROCESS OF LAW, SUBSTANTIVE

See: Substantive Due Process

DULANY, DANIEL
(1722–1797)

Daniel Dulany was a member of the Delaware governor's council (1757–1774) and one of the most prominent lawyers in America. In 1765 he published a pamphlet opposing the Stamp Act and arguing that "there is a clear distinction between an Act imposing a Tax for the single Purpose of raising a Revenue, and those Acts which have been made for Regulation of Trade." He denounced the doctrine of virtual representation as a "cobweb, spread to catch the unwary, and intangle the weak."

Dulany was a delegate to the STAMP ACT CONGRESS but later opposed the AMERICAN REVOLUTION.

DENNIS J. MAHONEY
(1986)

DUN & BRADSTREET, INC. v. GREENMOSS BUILDERS, INC.
472 U.S. 749 (1985)

The PLURALITY OPINION in this case may portend significant changes in the constitutional DOCTRINE governing LIBEL AND THE FIRST AMENDMENT. Dun & Bradstreet, a credit reporting business, falsely and negligently reported to five subscribers that Greenmoss had filed a petition in bankruptcy, and also negligently misrepresented Greenmoss's assets and liabilities. In an action for defamation, Greenmoss recovered substantial compensatory and punitive damages. Vermont's highest court held that the principle of GERTZ V. ROBERT WELCH, INC. (1974) did not apply in actions against defendants who were not part of the press or broadcast media. A fragmented Supreme Court avoided this question but affirmed, 5–4.

Justice LEWIS F. POWELL, for a three-Justice plurality, concluded that *Gertz*—which had held, among other things, that punitive damages could not be awarded against a magazine without proof of knowing or reckless disregard of the falsity of the statement—was applicable only to "expression on a matter of public concern." Justice Powell spoke only generally about the content of the "matter of public concern" standard, but hinted that "media" speech might qualify automatically for protection under *Gertz*. Dun & Bradstreet's report, however, involved "matters of purely private concern." Although such speech is "not wholly unprotected" by the FIRST AMENDMENT, he concluded, it can be the basis of a punitive damages award even absent a showing of reckless disregard of the truth. Chief Justice WARREN E. BURGER and Justice BYRON R. WHITE, in separate CONCURRING OPINIONS, expressed willingness to abandon *Gertz* altogether, but meanwhile agreed with this radical surgery on *Gertz*.

In a footnote pregnant with meaning, Justice Powell remarked that some kinds of constitutionally protected speech are entitled only to "reduced protection"—COMMERCIAL SPEECH, for example. But he did not place Dun & Bradstreet's report in the latter category, and thus raised speculation that the majority may be prepared to adopt a "sliding scale" for the FREEDOM OF SPEECH, with varying (and, as yet, unspecified) degrees of constitutional protection for each kind of speech, depending on the Justices' determinations about the value of the speech and the context in which it is uttered.

Justice WILLIAM J. BRENNAN, for the four dissenters, agreed that credit reports were not central to First Amendment values, but argued nonetheless that the *Gertz* requirements should apply to this case: credit and bankruptcy information was "of public concern." Justice Brennan noted with satisfaction that six Justices (the dissenters and authors of the concurring opinions) had rejected a distinction between the First Amendment rights of "media defendants" and of others sued for defamation.

KENNETH L. KARST
(1986)

DUNCAN v. KAHANAMOKU
327 U.S. 304 (1946)

Interpreting the scope of MARTIAL LAW established in Hawaii after the bombing of Pearl Harbor, Justice HUGO L. BLACK, for the Supreme Court, concluded that the Hawaiian Organic Act of 1900 extended constitutional guarantees to that TERRITORY. The creation of military courts empowered to try civilians violated the SIXTH AMENDMENT right to a FAIR TRIAL, thus contravening the intent of Congress. Chief Justice HARLAN FISKE STONE and Justice FRANK MURPHY wrote separate CONCURRING OPINIONS. Stone would have given greater scope to martial law but found the

claim of EMERGENCY POWER unjustified here. Murphy joined the Court's opinion but preferred to rest on constitutional grounds, citing EX PARTE MILLIGAN (1866). Justices HAROLD BURTON and FELIX FRANKFURTER, in dissent, argued that the military situation and the conduct of the war, as an executive function, justified the emergency steps taken here.

DAVID GORDON
(1986)

DUNCAN v. LOUISIANA
391 U.S. 145 (1968)

A 7–2 Supreme Court here overruled several earlier decisions and held that the FOURTEENTH AMENDMENT incorporated the Sixth Amendment right to TRIAL BY JURY. Louisiana tried Duncan for battery, a MISDEMEANOR charge punishable by up to two years' imprisonment. The court denied his request for a jury trial and sentenced him, upon conviction, to sixty days and a $150 fine. On appeal to the Supreme Court, the Justices abandoned the approach used in PALKO V. CONNECTICUT (1937) and *Adamson v. California* (1947), where the Court had examined the circumstances to determine whether they preserved the implicit DUE PROCESS requirement of "fundamental fairness." In his opinion in *Duncan*, Justice BYRON R. WHITE asked instead whether trial by jury was "fundamental to the American scheme of justice" and concluded that history supported an affirmative response. Conceding a court's duty to distinguish between petty and serious offenses to determine which cases warranted this protection, White declined to do so as a general rule. He declared that an offense punishable by more than two years' imprisonment was sufficiently serious to apply the Sixth Amendment guarantee. Penalties involving less than six months' time were not accorded that right. As usual, Justices HUGO L. BLACK and WILLIAM O. DOUGLAS, concurring separately, advocated the total INCORPORATION DOCTRINE. Justices JOHN MARSHALL HARLAN and POTTER STEWART, dissenting, asserted that "the Court's approach and its reading of history are altogether topsy-turvy." Later decisions in WILLIAMS V. FLORIDA (1970) and *Apodaca v. Oregon* (1972) have limited the extent of the right incorporated.

DAVID GORDON
(1986)

DUNN v. BLUMSTEIN
405 U.S. 330 (1972)

Tennessee restricted voting to persons with one year of residence in the state and three months in the county. The

Supreme Court, 6–1, speaking through Justice THURGOOD MARSHALL, held this limitation a denial of the EQUAL PROTECTION OF THE LAWS. The durational RESIDENCE REQUIREMENTS had to pass the test of STRICT SCRUTINY, both because they penalized exercise of the RIGHT TO TRAVEL interstate and because they restricted the FUNDAMENTAL INTEREST in voting. The state's asserted justifications for the requirements were not necessary for achieving COMPELLING STATE INTERESTS. Fraud could be prevented by the LESS RESTRICTIVE MEANS of requiring registration thirty days before an election. The objective of an informed electorate bore only a tenuous relation to length of residence. Chief Justice WARREN E. BURGER dissented. The recently appointed Justices LEWIS F. POWELL and WILLIAM H. REHNQUIST did not participate.

The following year, the Court approved fifty-day residency requirements in *Marston v. Lewis* (1973) and *Burns v. Fortson* (1973).

KENNETH L. KARST
(1986)

DUPLEX PRINTING PRESS COMPANY v. DEERING
254 U.S. 443 (1921)

In a case that brought the apparently prolabor provisions of the CLAYTON ACT before the Supreme Court, a 6–3 majority held that the act had placed no substantial bar to issuing INJUNCTIONS against labor unions. Section 6 of the act allowed unions to "lawfully [carry] out . . . legitimate objects," and section 20 denied the issuance of injunctions in a labor dispute unless essential to protect property. Duplex sought an injunction against a SECONDARY BOYCOTT which had been brought to force unionization of their open shop, claiming injury to and destruction of INTERSTATE COMMERCE. The Court declared that the boycott, even though peaceful, was not a "lawful method" of achieving the union's ends and thus violated the antitrust laws. According to the Court, section 6 only approved methods not expressly forbidden. Moreover, the majority redefined section 20: "labor dispute" was not meant generically but applied only "to parties standing in proximate relation to a controversy," an unwarranted gloss. They thus confined the section to a mere reflection of precedent, undoing congressional action.

Justice LOUIS D. BRANDEIS, joined by Justices OLIVER WENDELL HOLMES and JOHN H. CLARKE, dissented. Brandeis argued that the defendants shared a "common interest" with the employees, and the majority's denial of the existence of a dispute, within the act's meaning, simply ignored reality. Section 20, said the dissenters, attempted to render both sides equal. Although the Court refused to acknowledge that the Clayton Act had legalized any new methods for labor's use, a similar decision in BEDFORD CUT STONE V. JOURNEYMEN STONECUTTERS (1927) prompted enactment of the NORRIS-LAGUARDIA ACT in 1932, reversing the doctrinal direction.

DAVID GORDON
(1986)

(SEE ALSO: *Labor and the Antitrust Laws.*)

DU PONCEAU, PETER S.
(1760–1844)

Peter S. Du Ponceau arrived in America from France as Baron von Steuben's interpreter. Following service in the Revolution, he became a citizen of Pennsylvania where he was admitted to the bar in 1785. He defended the radical state CONSTITUTION of 1776 and was an ANTI-FEDERALIST, but as time passed he became a Jeffersonian Republican. He declined THOMAS JEFFERSON's offer of the chief justiceship of Louisiana. Du Ponceau was a founder and provost of the Law Academy of Pennsylvania. Among his books were *A Dissertation on the Nature and Extent of the Jurisdiction of the Courts of the United States* (1824), in which he advocated a FEDERAL COMMON LAW, and *A Brief View of the Constitution of the United States* (1834), in which he sought a middle course between a consolidated government and STATES' RIGHTS. In general he taught moderate nationalism and the supremacy of the union.

LEONARD W. LEVY
(1986)

Bibliography

BAUER, ELIZABETH K. 1952 *Commentaries on the Constitution.* Pages 65–78. New York: Columbia University Press.

DUVALL, GABRIEL
(1752–1844)

Although he served as a Justice of the United States Supreme Court for nearly a quarter of a century, Gabriel Duvall had a relatively small impact on the development of American constitutional law. Born into a prominent Maryland Huguenot family, he studied law and was admitted to the bar in 1788. He supported the movement for independence during the 1770s, and held a number of minor posts under the revolutionary government. Following the adoption of the Maryland Constitution of 1777 he served as clerk of the State House of Delegates. In 1782 he was elected to the Maryland State Council and in 1787 to the House of Delegates as a representative from Annapolis. He was selected to be a delegate to the CONSTITUTIONAL CONVENTION, but, for reasons that are unclear, he declined to serve. He supported THOMAS JEFFERSON during the political battles of the 1790s, and was elected as a Democratic-Republican to Congress in 1794. He resigned the position less than two years later to become a judge of the Maryland Supreme Court. He helped to organize Maryland successfully for the Republicans in 1800 and often advised Jefferson and JAMES MADISON on appointments there. In December 1802 Jefferson appointed him to be the first comptroller of the United States Treasury.

In 1811 President Madison appointed Duvall to the United States Supreme Court. On the most important and controversial cases of the period—*Martin v. Hunter's Lessee* (1816), *Gibbons v. Ogden* (1824), and BROWN V. MARYLAND (1827)—Duvall followed the lead of JOSEPH STORY and JOHN MARSHALL, and he even supported the Chief Justice when he dissented in *Ogden v. Saunders* (1827). *Dartmouth College v. Woodward* was the only major case in which he failed to support Marshall, but since he dissented without opinion, it is not possible to determine his reasons. It is clear that Duvall knew and understood the law, and he did write straightforward and creditable opinions for the Court in several minor commercial law and maritime cases: *Archibald Freeland v. Heron, Lenox and Company* (1812); *United States v. January and Patterson* (1813), *Prince v. Bartlett* (1814); and *The Frances and Eliza v. Coates* (1823).

Although no abolitionist, Duvall had definite antislavery leanings. Dissenting from a Supreme Court ruling in *Mina Queen and Child v. Hepburn* (1812), in which HEARSAY evidence had been excluded "from a trial in which two black persons attempted to establish their freedom," he argued, with some force, "It appears to me that the reason for admitting hearsay evidence upon a question of freedom is much stronger than in cases of pedigree or in controversies relative to the boundaries of land. It will be universally admitted that the right to freedom is more important than the right of property." In another case, *LeGrand v. Darnall* (1829), speaking on behalf of the Court, Duvall ruled that a slaveholder's deeding of property to his ten-year-old son by a slave woman implied an intention to free the boy, despite a Maryland law that denied manumission to any slave under forty-five years of age.

As he grew older, Duvall's increasing infirmities and deafness caused numerous problems and considerable embarrassment for the Court. For almost a decade his resignation was expected, but he did not step down until January 1835, when he received assurances that ANDREW JACKSON planned to appoint fellow Marylander ROGER B. TANEY to the bench. Duvall died nine years later at the age of ninety-two.

RICHARD E. ELLIS
(1986)

Bibliography

DILLARD, IRVING 1969 Gabriel Duvall. Pages 419–429 in Leon Friedman and Fred L. Israel, eds., *Justices of the Supreme Court 1789–1969*. New York: Chelsea House.

EAKIN v. RAUB
12 Sargeant & Rawle 330 (Pa. 1825)

In this otherwise insignificant Pennsylvania case, JOHN BANNISTER GIBSON offered the classic rationale for JUDICIAL RESTRAINT. His opinion is an explicit refutation of JOHN MARSHALL's arguments for JUDICIAL REVIEW in MARBURY V. MADISON (1803), a position which Gibson confessed he had once accepted, but more as "a matter of faith than of reason."

Gibson's major premise was that the judiciary had no right or power to void legislation without express constitutional warrant. Like Marshall, Gibson agreed that under a written CONSTITUTION, no branch of government could claim more than its granted powers. But as the legislature was supreme within the limits of its grant, Gibson argued, the judiciary could not annul those powers without "direct authority" from the constitution, "either in terms or by irresistible implication." While the judiciary might interpret legislation, it had no power to "scan the authority of the lawgiver." The legislature was superior, Gibson concluded, because "the power to will and to command is essentially superior to the power to act and obey."

Legislative indiscretions and abuses severely tested Gibson's fidelity to his principles. In *Norris v. Clymer* (1845) Gibson acknowledged that he had altered his views on judicial review because the Pennsylvania constitutional convention of 1837, by its silence, apparently sanctioned the power, and also "from experience of the necessity of the case." While Gibson undoubtedly moderated his views for some circumstances, he remained generally faithful to the notion of legislative superiority and the wisdom of judicial restraint. The "experience of the necessity of the case" involved legislative private acts that granted equity.

The legislature had given substantially complete EQUITY jurisdiction to the courts in 1836, yet continued to act on its own, inevitably provoking clashes with the judiciary. In *Greenough v. Greenough* (1849) Gibson strongly defended an exclusive sphere for judicial power: "[T]he judicial power . . . is . . . so distributed . . . that the legislature cannot exercise any part of it." The next year, in *De Chastellux v. Fairchild,* he struck down an act ordering a new trial in an action of TRESPASS." The power to order new trials is judicial," he said; "but the power of the legislature is not judicial."

In the *Eakin* opinion Gibson emphasized judicial independence, and he acknowledged legislative sovereignty, but only "within the limit of its powers." Further, he anticipated cases such as *De Chastellux* when he said that a legislative act directing a reversal of a court judgment would be "a usurpation of judicial power." Finally, he declared that when the judiciary was the prescribed organ to execute the constitution, such as in the conduct of trials, the judges were bound to follow the constitution, a legislative act notwithstanding.

Throughout the remainder of his long career, Gibson adhered to the spirit of *Eakin.* He insisted that the legislature's apprehension of public sentiment, not the fear of judicial interposition, offered the most effective barrier to unconstitutional action. With language similar to later opinions by MORRISON R. WAITE and OLIVER WENDELL HOLMES, Gibson declared that the responsibility for overcoming abusive acts rested not with the courts, but with the people, who were "wise, virtuous, and competent to manage their own affairs."

STANLEY I. KUTLER
(1986)

E. C. KNIGHT COMPANY, UNITED STATES v.

See: *Knight Company, E. C., United States v.*

ECONOMIC ANALYSIS AND THE CONSTITUTION

To what extent do "economic" ideas and concepts better enable us to understand the American Constitution?

One persisting characterization of the Constitution is that it succeeded both in arresting a decline in the American economy occurring under (and because of) the ARTICLES OF CONFEDERATION and in initiating an epoch of great prosperity. In reality, the shape of the economy during the 1780s was not particularly unsatisfactory. Indeed, in 1786 BENJAMIN FRANKLIN was willing to declare that "America was never in higher prosperity." But deflation injured creditors such as farmers, thereby provoking SHAYS' REBELLION in Massachusetts as well as inducing the enactment by the states of debtors' relief legislation.

The 1789 Constitution authorized the federal government to tax and to regulate commerce and centralized in the national government the power to print money. The long-range economic implications of these particular grants of power have been profound; their short-range consequences, however, may well have been modest. The federal power to tax was lightly exercised for many decades, and the federal power to print money was of limited importance in an era when "monetary policy" had not yet been recognized as a major instrument of national economic policy. The burst of prosperity in the decades following adoption of the Constitution owed largely to a surge in foreign trade, promoted by America's neutrality during the Napoleonic Wars—a neutrality that had been facilitated, to be sure, by the Constitution's recognition of centralized authority over foreign policy.

The first comprehensive "Economic Interpretation of the Constitution" to attract great attention was that of CHARLES A. BEARD in his celebrated 1913 study. Rejecting the popular view of the Constitution as the noble product of patriotic impulses, Beard assessed the Constitution as an "economic document" designed to advance certain economic interests to the detriment of others. In particular, he believed that "personalty" interests—"money, public security, manufacturers, and trade and shipping"— prevailed at the expense of "landed" interests of farmers and others, as well as at the expense of the unpropertied general public. Beard further asserted that the entire constitutional process had been initiated by a small group of men "immediately interested through their personal possessions in the outcome of their labors." In the preface to his 1935 edition, however, Beard denied that he had meant to suggest that the Framers were merely seeking to enrich themselves personally; rather, Beard explained, the Framers' own economic holdings merely made them receptive to the claims of more general economic groups.

The empirical ambitions that Beard displayed in his research remain commendable. But his particular empirical conclusions have been disputed by more recent scholarship. For example, those attending the CONSTITUTIONAL CONVENTION owned more in realty than they owned in securities; and it is not clearly true that creditors as a class supported the Constitution's RATIFICATION. Those portions of the Constitution that Beard singled out as establishing its economic preferences were the Constitution's general system of CHECKS AND BALANCES, which supposedly served to inhibit the unpropertied majorities; Congress's powers over taxation, war, commerce, and public lands; and the prohibitions on state coinage of money and on state impairment of contractual obligations. The DUE PROCESS clause of the FIFTH AMENDMENT Beard barely mentioned— even though the due process clause of the FOURTEENTH AMENDMENT had served as the basis for the Supreme Court's notorious decision in LOCHNER V. NEW YORK (1905) just eight years previously. Much of Beard's analysis of the Constitution now seems badly forced. In particular, his treatment of checks and balances is extraordinarily reductionistic in its failure to acknowledge that they were designed to serve any purpose other than the protection of certain property interests. In all, Beard's economic interpretation—though a major event in constitutional historiography—no longer commands adherents.

Economists have long been concerned with the objective of economic efficiency, and modern economists have developed an elaborate analysis in support of this objective. Might it be that the goal of efficiency has constitutional status? Insofar as original intent is relevant, information is needed on the economic views of the Framers. One philosophy common in eighteenth-century America was classical republicanism, which, in commending community, equality, and public virtue, was capable of disparaging commercial activity. The Framers, however, were also exposed to the newer tradition of Lockean liberalism, which strongly endorsed individualism and commercial activity. Propitiously, Adam Smith's *The Wealth of Nations* was published in 1776, the year of the DECLARATION OF INDEPENDENCE. Consistent with Smith's free market approach, ALEXANDER HAMILTON in THE FEDERALIST #11 espoused the idea of an open national economy: "The veins of commerce in every part will be replenished and will acquire additional motion and vigor from a free circulation of the commodities of every part." Hamilton began that paper with the observation that "the prosperity of commerce" is "a primary object of [enlightened statesmen's] political cares"—an observation that evidently contemplated mercantilist, rather than laissez-faire, policies. In *The Federalist* #10, JAMES MADISON made clear that he was hardly an economic egalitarian. "The first object of government" is to protect "the diversity of faculties of man, from which the rights of property originate." Elsewhere, however, *The Federalist* set forth theories that were imbued with republicanism; and in a 1792 essay Madison recommended policies that would "raise extreme indigence towards a state of comfort." In all, the free market interests of the Framers should neither be ignored nor exaggerated.

From the early nineteenth century on, free-market norms have exerted their most continuing influence upon constitutional doctrine through the negative underside of the COMMERCE CLAUSE. According to Justice ROBERT JACKSON in *H. P. Hood & Sons v. DuMond* (1949), "Our system . . . is that every farmer and every craftsman shall be encouraged to produce by the certainty that he will have free access to every market in the nation, that no home embargoes will withhold his exports, and that no foreign state will by custom duties or regulation exclude them. Likewise, every consumer may look to the free competition from every producing area in the Nation to protect him from exploitation by any." The Supreme Court has frequently endeavored to protect out-of-state sellers, out-of-state buyers, and multistate transportation concerns from discriminatory or excessive burdens imposed by self-interested state governments. In SOUTHERN PACIFIC COMPANY V. ARIZONA (1945), for example, the Court invalidated an Arizona statute limiting the lengths of trains operating in Arizona: the Court found that the statute's burdens on INTERSTATE COMMERCE were substantial, its safety benefits probably trivial. At times, however, the Court has been reluctant to intervene even when the prospect of Justice Jackson's "exploitation" has seemed keen. If a state enjoys a monopoly on an important natural resource, then the state, by imposing a substantial tax on the extraction of that resource, can "export" its tax burden, enriching its local treasury at the expense of consumers throughout the nation. Yet in *Commonwealth Edison Company v. Montana* (1981) a divided Supreme Court declined to hold that Montana's thirty percent severance tax on coal violated the commerce clause. The Court majority did not clearly disagree with the proposition that an "exported" state tax violates commerce clause ideals if it is not "fairly related to the services provided by the state." But the majority seemed to regard it as beyond the judicial function to assess the incidence of such a tax and to compute the value of those state-provided "services." (See STATE REGULATION OF COMMERCE.)

Though the commerce clause imposes some limits on the states, its primary and explicit purpose is to confer powers on the federal Congress. In GIBBONS V. OGDEN (1824) the Court, in expansively interpreting what counts as interstate commerce, upheld a congressional enactment that implicitly abrogated a New York rule creating a steamboat monopoly between certain New York and New Jersey ports. Because this monopoly plainly offended free-market norms, the federal statute in *Gibbons* vindicated what Justice Jackson in *Hood* regarded as the "vision of the Founders." But what would the result have been in *Gibbons* had it been Congress, rather than the state, that had insisted on a monopoly? In exercising its commerce clause powers in the twentieth century, Congress has frequently chosen to restrict rather than enhance the competitive process. What is noteworthy is that the Supreme Court has found this in no way problematic. Justice Jackson's opinion in WICKARD V. FILBURN (1942) was shrewd in its perception of how intra-farm (and hence intrastate) events could have an aggregate impact on interstate economic arrangements. But the opinion was strikingly uninterested in the extent to which the federal statute it was approving brought about the cartelization of the otherwise highly competitive agricultural economy, thereby curtailing production and elevating consumer prices. Perhaps the point is that the "vision of the Founders," as understood by the Court, is not a competitive economy as such, but merely an economy free of anti-competitive restrictions imposed by the states. Besides accounting for the assumed irrelevance of free-market norms to congressional action under the commerce clause, this attribution of purpose can also explain the fact that the negative underside of the commerce clause has never been thought directly applicable to private monopolies that might severely restrict competition. Consider, however, Paul Freund's view that the spirit—though not the letter—of the commerce clause anticipates a "free national market," and that the commerce clause therefore needs to be supplemented by a strong federal antitrust program.

In the first third of the Twentieth Century, the Court did engage in a rather broad-ranging implementation of free-market values. The Court proceeded primarily in the name of the due process clauses of the Fourteenth and Fifth Amendments, clauses which enabled it to review all state and federal legislation, without regard to interstate impacts. During these years, the quite sophisticated approach of an Adam Smith was frequently replaced by the insensitive dogmatism of the Social Darwinist movement, thereby provoking Justice OLIVER WENDELL HOLMES's *Lochner* quip that "the Fourteenth Amendment does not enact Mr. Herbert Spencer's Social Statics." Since 1937, by contrast, the Court has consistently declined to invalidate "economic" legislation on substantive due process grounds and has stubbornly refused to subject that legislation to even minimal review. In WILLIAMSON V. LEE OPTI-

CAL CO. (1955), for example, the Court unanimously and unhesitatingly upheld an Oklahoma statute requiring consumers to employ a licensed doctor merely in order to fit old eyeglass lenses into new frames.

Judicial tolerance of inefficient economic enactments is probably for the best. Economic analysis is an acquired taste; courts should not insist that legislators be educated in basic economic concepts, let alone that they keep abreast of the current literature on externalities and public goods. Moreover, most economists would acknowledge that a legislature might properly choose to sacrifice economic efficiency in order to achieve some desired distribution of wealth among societal groups. Also, even if certain private conduct is economically acceptable, a legislature could properly conclude that the conduct is interpersonally unfair in the particular way it enables A to cause harm to B.

Nevertheless, the argument favoring somewhat greater judicial scrutiny of inefficient legislation is not altogether without merit. In *Lynch v. Household Finance Corp.* (1972), a PROCEDURAL DUE PROCESS case, the Court—drawing on John Locke, John Adams, and WILLIAM BLACKSTONE—recognized an important connection between property and liberty. In addition, recent "commercial speech" cases such as VIRGINIA STATE BOARD OF PHARMACY V. VIRGINIA CITIZENS CONSUMER COUNCIL, INC. (1976) have attached considerable constitutional significance to marketplace norms. Moreover, aggressive JUDICIAL REVIEW is often defended on the ground of its ability to correct predictable breakdowns in the legislative process. *Southern Pacific* itself relied, for commerce clause purposes, on the Court's idea that out-of-state railroads are likely to be unrepresented in the state's legislative processes. For due process purposes, "consumers" as such are anything but a DISCRETE AND INSULAR MINORITY. But—as an economic analysis of the legislative process lucidly suggests—the very diffusion of consumers throughout society signifies that consumers may fare poorly in the legislature when challenged by producer groups, which are far better able to mobilize themselves in seeking protective legislation.

In any event, given the Supreme Court's position that neither the commerce clause (as a grant of power) nor the due process clause (as a restriction of power) includes any significant free-market content, it appears likely that Congress, if it chooses, could enact socialism (the ultimate rejection of market values) as this country's form of economic organization. It seems hard to deny that Congress could offer a RATIONAL BASIS on behalf of a socialist program that would satisfy the trivial demands of the commerce and due process clauses. To be sure, the takings clause would require that the nationalization of industry achieve a PUBLIC USE. But recent interpretations of the public use doctrine make it doubtful that the doctrine places any limits on Congress's choice of economic philosophy.

It is true that the takings clause would require Congress to afford JUST COMPENSATION to the shareholders of any companies nationalized. As a general matter, the just compensation requirement serves to rule out at least certain legislative efforts to redistribute wealth, whether by socialism or by more modest measures. It should not be forgotten that the progressive federal income tax—a central feature of federal policy during the last forty years—required for its legality a constitutional amendment. Still, the Supreme Court's invalidation of a pre-amendment federal income tax in POLLOCK V. FARMERS' LOAN & TRUST COMPANY (1895) rested on a dubious interpretation of the DIRECT TAXES clause. Consider, moreover, a general tax on wealth or property, the proceeds of which are dedicated to financing welfare programs: it seems entirely clear that such a tax would not constitute a prohibited "taking." It appears, then, that wealth redistribution is constitutionally quite acceptable so long as it is both candid and evenhanded.

When a "taking" does occur, the "just compensation" that the takings clause requires has long been defined in terms of "fair market value." This "fair market value" gloss introduces, almost by hypothesis, certain capitalist values into constitutional doctrine. Yet that gloss can also be critiqued precisely from a free-market perspective. Assume a neighborhood of homes which, if individually available for sale, would each yield a price of $100,000. At any one time, however, only a limited number of houses are in fact offered for sale. To state that a homeowner is not interested in selling for $100,000 is to acknowledge that he presently values his ownership of the house at some figure in excess of $100,000. That excess is what economists call "consumer surplus." "Fair market value" provides less than full compensation in that it deprives the homeowner of this consumer surplus. From an ethical perspective, compensation that is less than full is arguably less than "just." Moreover, economic analysis can make clear that a "fair market value" standard for compensation has the practical effects of subsidizing government in its land acquisitions (by negating consumer surplus) and distorting government EMINENT DOMAIN choices (by encouraging government to ignore variations in consumer surplus among property owners).

Yet an economic analysis also verifies that the problem of measuring full compensation resists easy solution. Rendering consumer surplus compensable would not be satisfactory: consumer surplus would be notably difficult to quantify on an individual basis, and compensability would invite owners to dissemble in representing their surpluses' magnitude. Reminded of the difficulties involved in establishing the proper price for an eminent-domain forced sale, an economist might question the very practice of forced sales: he might suggest that the government be deprived of the eminent domain power altogether, thereby remitting the government to the opportunities afforded by the ordinary real estate market for purposes of acquiring land. Yet it is precisely the economist who can explain why this solution, too, would not always be satisfactory. Without the government's power of eminent domain, the owner of the final parcel within a tract of land that the government has otherwise succeeded in acquiring would be in a position—knowing of the government's situation—to extract an excessive monopoly price from the government-buyer. Because governments engage in tract acquisition more frequently than private parties do (only governments build superhighways, for example), it may make sense to limit the eminent domain power to governmental bodies. Obversely, the fact that the eminent domain power *is* generally limited to governments helps explain why private parties often are not in a good position to initiate large-tract projects.

As suggested above, an economic analysis is at least able to deepen understanding of the implications of constitutional doctrine. Correspondingly, such an analysis can correct what would otherwise be misunderstandings. In SHAPIRO V. THOMPSON (1969), for example, the Supreme Court considered the states' argument that WELFARE BENEFITS can be properly be denied to indigents who move into a state in order to collect higher benefits. Such an argument, the Court suggested, rested on the implicit premise that such welfare applicants are not "deserving"—a premise that the Court then rejected as unsound. But from the economist's useful perspective, the problem is not the grantee's desert but rather the grantor's incentives. States, anticipating an influx of indigents if welfare benefits are increased, may be dissuaded from raising those benefits, a dissuasion that might ill serve whatever the public's preference may be for compassionate welfare programs. Given an economic point of view, *Shapiro* unwittingly reduces the feasibility of state-administered welfare programs, thereby strengthening the argument in favor of the nationalization of welfare.

At the minimum, economic analysis can assist in identifying the costs or inefficiences of any proposed constitutional ruling. It is, of course, for the courts then to determine what weight to accord these costs in interpreting constitutional doctrine. The economist would be disturbed, however, by any disparagement of these costs that seems naive or inadequately considered. In *Shapiro*, for example, there is language stating that administrative inefficiencies, no matter what their magnitude, are automatically "uncompelling" for purposes of STRICT SCRUTINY review. But it is far from clear that the Court really adheres to such a position. In recent procedural due process

opinions such as MATHEWS V. ELDRIDGE (1976), the Court has taken the efficiency criterion significantly into account.

In a number of important ways, then, an economic analysis can be clearly beneficial in the process of constitutional analysis. Nevertheless, economics will probably never achieve, in constitutional studies, the influence that it has secured in certain other fields of law. There are too many constitutional doctrines that endorse ideas or values that are largely beyond the economist's jurisdiction. To employ an extreme example, the economist's recognition of people's "taste for discrimination" is of little help in understanding the Constitution's moral assessment that racial discriminations are inherently invidious.

GARY T. SCHWARTZ
(1986)

Bibliography

BEARD, CHARLES A. (1913) 1935 *An Economic Interpretation of the Constitution.* New York: Macmillan.

ELLIOT, B. W. (1941) 1979 *Dynamics of Ascent.* New York: Knopf.

EPSTEIN, DAVID F. 1984 *The Political Theory of the Federalist.* Chicago: University of Chicago Press.

EPSTEIN, RICHARD A. 1985 *Takings.* Cambridge, Mass.: Harvard University Press.

FREUND, PAUL A. 1961 *The Supreme Court of the United States.* Cleveland, Ohio: World Publishing Co.

GOLDWIN, ROBERT A. and SCHAMBRA, WILLIAM A., eds. 1982 *How Capitalist Is the American Constitution?* Washington, D.C.: American Enterprise Institute.

LEE, SUSAN P. and PASSELL, PETER 1979 *A New Economic View of American History.* New York: Norton.

MCDONALD, FORREST 1979 *We the People: The Economic Origins of the Constitution.* New York: Samuel Insull.

POSNER, RICHARD A. 1977 *Economic Analysis of Law.* Boston: Little, Brown.

WOOD, GORDON S. 1969 *The Creation of the American Republic, 1776–1787.* Chapel Hill: University of North Carolina Press.

WRIGHT, ESMOND 1978 *Fabric of Freedom 1763–1800.* New York: Hill & Wang.

ECONOMIC DUE PROCESS

"Economic due process" is the name given to the doctrine that the Supreme Court used to strike down a variety of economic regulations in the first third of the twentieth century. The core of the doctrine is the conception that the central interest protected by the DUE PROCESS clauses is "liberty of contract." Given that assumption, the Court could not justify ECONOMIC REGULATION as a means to redress inequality of bargaining power between contracting parties, such as workers and employers. Moreover, economic legislation that purported to be based on other objectives—such as protecting public health, morals, or safety—was examined by the Court to ensure that the challenged legislation reasonably advanced those objectives.

The doctrine reached its full form in LOCHNER V. NEW YORK (1905), where a bare majority of the Court struck down a state law limiting bakery workers' maximum hours to sixty per week. Because the Constitution protected liberty of contract, economic regulation for its own sake was invalid, and thus, a state legislature could not regulate the hours of bakery workers to protect them from exploitation. A "labor law, pure and simple" would be unconstitutional. The hours of workers could be regulated only to protect the interests within the POLICE POWER—health, safety, welfare, or morality. Even if the legislature passed the law with the stated purpose of protecting workers' health, the Court would still ask whether the law was necessary for that purpose. This inquiry was designed to ensure that the law was not in fact a pretext for forbidden economic regulation.

There were two distinct criticisms of the *Lochner* decision. One was that the Court did not give sufficient weight to the judgment of the New York legislature that excessive hours of work jeopardized the health of bakery workers. Three of the four dissenting Justices in *Lochner* conceded that New York could not limit bakers' hours to prevent their economic exploitation. They would, however, have accepted New York's judgment that the measure was necessary to protect health. A more fundamental objection was that the Constitution permitted economic regulation for economic motives. A prophetic solo dissent by Justice OLIVER WENDELL HOLMES, JR., disagreed with the Court's major premise that the Constitution protected liberty of contract. He said, "A Constitution is not intended to embody a particular economic theory. . . . It is made for people of fundamentally differing views."

In the three decades that followed, the Court upheld most challenged economic regulations on the ground that they protected public health, safety, or morals. Indeed, in BUNTING V. OREGON (1971) it upheld a law fixing maximum hours for factory workers. However, the Court struck down a significant number of laws that it considered to be interferences with a free market. In ADAIR V. UNITED STATES (1908) and COPPAGE V. KANSAS (1915), the Court invalidated laws that outlawed labor contracts forbidding employees to join labor unions. The Court overturned a minimum wage law in ADKINS V. CHILDREN'S HOSPITAL (1923) and a law that fixed prices in TYSON BROTHER V. BANTON (1927). And in NEW STATE ICE COMPANY V. LIEBMANN (1932), the Court invalidated a law that limited business entry for businesses that were not public utilities.

The Court abandoned its free-market approach to the due process clause in NEBBIA V. NEW YORK (1934), where it sustained a Depression-era law fixing minimum prices for milk. A bare majority of the Court concluded that a "state may regulate a business in any of its aspects, including the prices to be charged for the products or commodities it sells." Two years later, in MOREHEAD V. NEW YORK EX REL. TIPALDO (1936), the Court unexpectedly invalidated a law setting minimum wages for women workers. That decision was, however, overruled the following year in WEST COAST HOTEL CO. V. PARRISH (1937). Since 1937, no decision of the Supreme Court has held an economic regulatory measure invalid under the due process clause.

The decision in *Nebbia* abandoned the idea that business regulation for economic motives was forbidden. During the *Lochner* era, the Court had decided whether laws were reasonably necessary to promote police-power objectives only because it sought to ensure that the police power was not a subterfuge for economic regulation. Once the Court decided that economic regulation need not be justified by the police power, it might have been concluded that economic regulations are valid whether or not they are reasonable, and occasionally, the Supreme Court has said this. In FERGUSON V. SKRUPA (1963), Justice HUGO L. BLACK, writing for the Court, said that in rejecting *Lochner* the Court had abandoned the doctrine "that due process authorizes courts to hold laws unconstitutional when they believe the legislature has acted unwisely."

Conventional due process doctrine seems to say, however, that economic regulatory legislation might be invalid if sufficiently unreasonable. In *Nebbia* the Court stated that laws violated due process if they did not have "a reasonable relation to a proper legislative purpose" or if they were "arbitrary." In UNITED STATES V. CAROLENE PRODUCTS CO. (1938), the Court upheld the Filled Milk Act of 1923, which prohibited the shipment of skimmed milk compounded with vegetable oil in interstate commerce. A lower federal court decided that the law lacked RATIONAL BASIS because filled milk was not deleterious to health. The opinion of Justice HARLAN F. STONE said that in the application of the rational basis test, "the existence of facts supporting the legislative judgment is to be presumed, for regulatory legislation affecting ordinary commercial transactions is not to be pronounced unconstitutional unless in the light of the facts made known or generally assumed it is of such a character as to preclude the assumption that it rests upon some rational basis within the knowledge and experience of legislators."

Although the Court, in the *Carolene Products* case, concluded that the Filled Milk Act did rest on a permissible congressional finding that filled milk was injurious to health, its OBITER DICTA suggested that the law could be challenged if the facts presented to the lower court proved that the law's lack of wisdom was not debatable: "Where the existence of a rational basis for legislation whose constitutionality is attacked depends upon facts . . . such facts may properly be made the subject of judicial inquiry, . . . and the constitutionality of a statute predicated upon the existence of a particular state of facts may be challenged by showing to the court that those facts have ceased to exist."

In one sense, there is no difference between the dictum in *Ferguson v. Skrupa*—that the due process clause does not permit an inquiry into legislative reasonableness—and the dictum of *Carolene Products* that suggests the possibility of a trial to show that a law lacks a rational basis. For more than fifty years, Supreme Court decisions, without exception, have upheld all economic regulations challenged under the due process clause.

In another sense, however, the *Carolene Products* approach has produced a different outcome than would have occurred if the Court had adhered consistently to the *Ferguson* dictum. Lower courts frequently conduct trials to determine whether laws challenged as a violation of due process are reasonable. Occasionally, lower federal courts decide that state or federal laws lack a rational basis. Although the Supreme Court has uniformly reversed those decisions when appealed, the laws may be effectively invalidated when there is no appeal. For example, in *Milnot Co. v. Richardson* a lower federal court decided that the Filled Milk Act—the same law sustained in *Carolene Products*—was unconstitutional because it lacked a rational basis. The federal government, not sympathetic to the objectives of the statute, did not appeal.

A few academic commentators have argued that the Court's withdrawal from judgment in the economic due process area has gone too far. Some have argued that the Court should use the rational basis formula to invalidate laws that have no real purpose except to favor one economic interest at the expense of a competing interest or the public. Indeed, some state courts use the due process clause, or some other provision, in state constitutions in exactly this manner. The Supreme Court, however, has neither acknowledged nor followed that advice. In WILLIAMSON V. LEE OPTICAL COMPANY (1955), for example, the Court sustained a state law forbidding a dispensing optician to duplicate eyeglasses without a prescription from an optometrist or ophthalmologist. Opticians argued, with some merit, that the law was unnecessary to protect public health and that the legislature's real purpose was to give optometrists and ophthalmologists a monopoly on the sale of eyeglasses. The Court answered that the law might encourage people to have their eyes examined more often, although a more candid answer might have been that it did not matter whether the law was unabashed economic favoritism.

All the Justices appointed in the last fifty years have agreed that the *Lochner* line of decisions represented an abuse of JUDICIAL POWER. The consensus about economic due process is the starting point of current debate about constitutional law. The point of Justice Holmes's *Lochner* dissent was that it was irresponsible for Justices to read their own subjective economic preferences into the due process clause. Is it equally an abuse of power to read the due process clause to overturn state legislation that restricts noneconomic liberties? Justice WILLIAM O. DOUGLAS, writing for the Court when it struck down a state ban on BIRTH CONTROL devices in GRISWOLD V. CONNECTICUT (1965), insisted that there was a difference between judging the propriety of laws that "touch economic problems, business affairs or social conditions" and those that involve such personal liberties as "an intimate relation of husband and wife." Justice HARRY A. BLACKMUN, writing for the Court in ROE V. WADE (1973), which struck down laws restricting ABORTION, acknowledged and quoted Holmes's admonition in his *Lochner* dissent that the Constitution "is made for people of fundamentally differing views, and the accident of our finding certain opinions natural and even familiar, or novel, and even shocking, ought not to conclude our judgment upon the question whether statutes embodying them conflict with the Constitution of the United States." The opinion went on, however, to conclude that the due process clause protects "personal rights that can be deemed "fundamental."

Lochner is a discredited and overruled decision, but its ghost continues to haunt contemporary constitutional law debate.

WILLIAM COHEN
(1992)

(SEE ALSO: *Labor Movement; State Police Power.*)

Bibliography

COX, ARCHIBALD 1987 *The Court and the Constitution.* Boston: Houghton Mifflin.
HETHERINGTON, JOHN A. C. 1958 State Economic Regulation and Substantive Due Process of Law. *Northwestern University Law Review* 53:13–32.
LINDE, HANS A. 1970 Without "Due Process": Unconstitutional Law in Oregon. *Oregon Law Review* 49:125–187.
MCCLOSKY, ROBERT G. 1962 Economic Due Process and the Supreme Court: An Exhumation and Reburial. *Supreme Court Review* 1962: 34–62.
WONNELL, CHRISTOPHER T. 1983 Economic Due Process and the Preservation of Competition. *Hastings Constitutional Law Quarterly* 11:91–134.

ECONOMIC EQUAL PROTECTION

During the heyday of the doctrine of ECONOMIC DUE PROCESS, the EQUAL PROTECTION clause took a backseat to the

DUE PROCESS clause. In BUCK V. BELL (1927), Justice OLIVER WENDELL HOLMES, JR., called an argument that a law was invalid because its application was confined to an unreasonably small number of people "the usual last resort of constitutional arguments." Still, the "last resort" succeeded, and laws were invalidated under the equal protection clause when burdensome business regulations unreasonably (in the Court's view) exempted some businesses from the burden. In *Smith v. Cahoon* (1931), for example, the Supreme Court invalidated a law requiring compulsory insurance for trucks because it exempted those carrying agricultural products. The next-to-last decision of this kind was *Hartford Steam Boiler Inspection & Insurance Co. v. Harrison* (1937). The Court held that a law forbidding stock insurance companies from acting through salaried agents violated equal protection because the restriction did not apply to mutual insurance companies.

Since 1937, the Court has invalidated an economic regulatory law on the basis of similar reasoning only once: *Morey v. Doud* (1957) struck down an Illinois law regulating the sale of money orders because American Express money orders were exempted by name. In NEW ORLEANS V. DUKES (1976) the Court characterized *Morey* as "the only case in the last half century to invalidate a wholly economic regulation solely on equal protection grounds" and overruled it.

Since 1976, two cases have applied the equal protection clause to "wholly economic regulations," but each case was unique. In METROPOLITAN LIFE INSURANCE COMPANY V. WARD (1985), a bare majority of the Court invalidated a tax on insurance companies because local companies were exempted. This discriminatory tax statute would have been invalid under the COMMERCE CLAUSE, except that Congress had authorized states to impose taxes that burdened out-of-state insurance companies. The Court concluded that discrimination against out-of-state business was nonetheless prohibited by the equal protection clause. *Allegheny Pittsburgh Coal Co. v. County Commission of Webster County* (1989) invalidated a tax assessor's practice of valuing recently sold property at its sale price for property tax purposes, while valuing property that had not changed hands at a level far below its present market value. In a footnote, the Court commented that its decision was only applicable to an "aberrational" administrative practice that was illegal under state law. The Court did not decide whether the assessor could justify an identical but legally authorized practice on the ground that it was unfair to tax "unrealized paper gains in the value of property."

In a much-cited CONCURRING OPINION in an earlier case, Justice ROBERT H. JACKSON argued that there was a substantial difference between economic due process, which the Court had appropriately rejected, and economic equal protection. In RAILWAY EXPRESS AGENCY V. NEW YORK (1949), the Court upheld a law that prohibited advertising signs on vehicles, but exempted a sign advertising the business of the vehicle owner. The Court lamely concluded that the distinction between signs advertising the vehicle owner's own business and those advertising some other business was reasonable, because New York could reasonably conclude that the latter signs were more distracting. Concurring, Justice Jackson concluded that signs of both classes were equally distracting, but argued that a better reason to uphold the distinction was that New York could decide that it was fair to exempt those who advertised their own businesses. In a much-quoted OBITER DICTUM he argued that a requirement of equality should be given more than lip service in cases of ECONOMIC REGULATION: "There is no more effective practical guaranty against arbitrary and unreasonable government than to require that the principle of law which officials would impose upon a minority must be imposed generally. . . . Courts can take no better measure to assure that laws will be just than to require that laws be equal in operation."

Justice Jackson's dictum has had only a minor influence on Supreme Court decisions. Government lawyers rarely respond to equal protection challenges with the bald reply that the difference in treatment between groups is simply the outcome of INTEREST GROUP politics. Most often, there is an attempt to justify a particular group's exemption from a burden with the argument that exemption promotes a praiseworthy public purpose. The Court has uniformly credited those arguments, no matter how farfetched, in economic regulation cases. In WILLIAMSON V. LEE OPTICAL COMPANY (1955), for example, the Court sustained a law prohibiting opticians from duplicating eyeglasses without a prescription from an ophthalmologist or optometrist. The Court said that a legislature might conclude that although the optician had the ability to duplicate the lenses without a prescription, the prohibition would encourage people to have their eyes examined more often. It is easy enough to show that the public health justification in *Williamson* was an afterthought to uphold a law that the legislature passed to protect the business of two groups of eye-care professionals from competition of a third.

Much contemporary legislation is, in fact, based on interest-group politics. But because the Court has rejected the free-market constitutional command of economic due process, it is doubtful that the Court would accept the argument of a few legal commentators that it should seriously ask whether the outcomes of interest-group pressures further the public good. Questions about whether it is fair to promote the interests of one economic group at the expense of another will likely be left to the political processes for the foreseeable future.

One prominent argument in this area begins by conceding the point that laws can be justified as the outcomes of interest-group politics. So long as government lawyers seek to uphold a law's exemptions and classifications on good-government grounds, however, courts should limit themselves to those arguments and insist that there be a "real and substantial" relationship to those good-government grounds. Critics of this approach argue, among other things, that its adoption would only promote more elaborate legislative "boilerplate," to supply stronger less-than-candid good-government justifications to explain the outcomes of interest-group politics.

Be that as it may, in cases involving economic regulation, economic equal protection has met the same fate as economic due process.

WILLIAM COHEN
(1992)

(SEE ALSO: *Economic Freedom; Economy.*)

Bibliography

GUNTHER, GERALD 1972 Forward: In Search of Evolving Doctrine on a Changing Court: A Model for a Newer Equal Protection. *Harvard Law Review* 86:1–48.

LINDE, HANS A. 1975 Due Process of Lawmaking. *Nebraska Law Review* 55:197–255.

SUSTEIN, CASS R. 1985 Interest Groups in American Public Law. *Stanford Law Review* 38:29–87.

ECONOMIC LIBERTIES AND THE CONSTITUTION

Contrary to its existing practice, the United States Supreme Court was once a strong guarantor of economic liberties. This was the period (1897–1937) of "economic due process." The Fifth Amendment and FOURTEENTH AMENDMENT provide that neither the federal nor state governments shall deprive any person "of life, liberty, or PROPERTY, without DUE PROCESS OF LAW." The Court interpreted these prohibitions to mean that government could not, except in specified or extraordinary circumstances, prevent individuals or corporations from freely engaging in the production and distribution of goods and services.

However, since 1936 the Supreme Court has abandoned this interpretation; economic regulations now are subject to a very low level of review pursuant to which they are upheld whenever rationally related to the achievement of legitimate state purposes. Supporters of the more recent policy conclude that as a result, the Court has wisely steered a neutral role in the nation's economic affairs. Another interpretation of this policy, however, is that it has denied many people a fundamental liberty in a society dedicated to liberty—the opportunity to engage in

economic activity. Our Constitution, it is argued, was not intended to be neutral in the conflict between liberty and authority, especially in the economic area.

There is little question that the Framers of the Constitution sought to limit greatly the commercial powers of the states. The tariffs and other economic barriers erected by the states against each other were a major source of discontent with the existing confederation. The regulatory abuses of the state legislatures are not so well detailed, but probably were no less responsible for such sentiments. According to ALEXANDER HAMILTON, writing in 1801, "creditors had been ruined or in a very extensive degree, much injured, confidence in pecuniary transactions had been destroyed, and the springs of industry have been proportionately relaxed" because of the failure of the states to safeguard commercial freedoms.

The deterioration of the economy that followed the revolutionary period led the states to what CHARLES EVANS HUGHES once described as "an ignoble array of legislative schemes for the defeat of creditors and invasion of contractual relations." Among other things, the states passed stay laws extending the due dates of notes and installment laws allowing debtors to pay their obligations in installments after they had fallen due. (See Debtors' Relief Legislation.)

JOHN MARSHALL, later Chief Justice, said in Virginia's ratification convention that economy and industry were essential to happiness, but the ARTICLES OF CONFEDERATION took away "the incitement to industry by rendering property insecure and unprotected." The Constitution, on the contrary, would "promote and encourage industry." JAMES MADISON stated that the passage of laws infringing contractual obligations "contributed more to that uneasiness which produced the convention . . . than those which accrued . . . from the inadequacy of the Confederation to its immediate objectives." During the CONSTITUTIONAL CONVENTION OF 1787 Madison said that an important object of the Union was "the necessity of providing more effectively for the security of private rights, and the steady dispensation of justice. . . . Was it to be supposed that Republican liberty could long exist under the abuses of it, practiced in [some of the] states?" ALBERT J. BEVERIDGE, Marshall's biographer, understandably concluded that the "determination of commercial and financial interests to get some plan adopted under which business could be transacted, was the most effective force that brought about [the Philadelphia convention]."

Several provisions of the Constitution appear to have been intended to curtail the economic regulatory authority of government. These are the prohibitions on the passage of EX POST FACTO laws which affect both the state and federal governments, and the ban on state laws impairing the OBLIGATION OF CONTRACTS. At the time the Constitution was framed and ratified, the term "ex post facto law" was applied to both penal and civil retroactive laws. In the criminal law, it was accepted that an ex post facto law was one that rendered an act punishable that was not punishable when it was committed. The term also described civil laws that operated retroactively to the detriment of a private owner of an iterest acquired or existing under prior law. Justice JOSEPH STORY of the MARSHALL COURT asserted that "every statute, which takes away or impairs VESTED RIGHTS acquired under existing laws, or creates a new obligation, imposes a new duty, or attaches a new disability, in respect to the transactions or considerations already passed, must be deemed retrospective."

Newspapers and judges of that period considered that stay and installment laws operated ex post facto. Members of Congress used the term in the broad sense. Some leading constitutional scholars held similar views on the meaning of the clauses. Although accounts of the CONSTITUTIONAL CONVENTION do not disclose precisely how the Framers defined the term, they are consistent with the view that ex post facto included retroactive civil laws. Nevertheless, a 1798 Supreme Court decision, CALDER V. BULL, interpreted the ex post facto clauses as applying solely to penal laws, thereby removing them as an important restraint on the regulatory powers of the federal and state legislatures.

In Chief Justice Marshall's opinion, the CONTRACT CLAUSE was intended to safeguard FREEDOM OF CONTRACT— which made it, under this view, a severe curb on state economic regulation. According to the Chief Justice, if a law limited the written understanding of the parties, it impaired their contractual obligation whether it was enacted before or after execution of the agreement.

However, the Supreme Court, in a 4–3 decision in OGDEN V. SAUNDERS (1827), ruled that the clause did not cover contracts executed subsequent to the adoption of a law: that is, it applied only to retroactive and not to prospective laws. The case involved a New York bankruptcy law, adopted prior to the execution of the promissory obligation in issue. In his only dissent on a constitutional issue in his thirty-four years as Chief Justice, Marshall vigorously contended that the New York law, although passed before the execution of the note, changed the understanding of the parties, and therefore impaired the obligation of their contract. The majority decision in the case followed a quarter of a century of failure to obtain a national bankruptcy law. Marshall's interpretation would have greatly limited the operation of state bankruptcy laws, and the majority rejected this outcome.

The BILL OF RIGHTS also evidences constitutional concern for material rights. The TAKINGS clause of the Fifth Amendment states that private property shall not be taken for PUBLIC USE without JUST COMPENSATION. The Fifth Amendment also states that no person shall be deprived of life, liberty, or property without due process of law. The SECOND AMENDMENT prohibits the confiscation of arms. The THIRD AMENDMENT restricts the quartering of troops. The FOURTH AMENDMENT prohibits unreasonable SEARCHES AND SEIZURES, and the Eighth Amendment prohibits excessive BAIL and fines.

Those who doubt that the Constitution protects the material rights from infringement by the states should consider section 1 of the Fourteenth Amendment, the second sentence of which reads: "No state shall make or enforce any law which shall abridge the privileges or immunities of citizens of the United States: nor shall any State deprive any person of life, liberty, or property, without due process of law; nor deny to any person within its jurisdiction the equal protection of the law." The framers of this amendment, the Congress of 1866, were concerned about protecting property and economic liberties as well as other personal rights.

While opinion is divergent as to the full meaning of the quoted language, commentators generally agree that it was primarily intended to make constitutional the CIVIL RIGHTS ACT OF 1866, placing it beyond the power of any subsequent Congress to repeal. The chief purpose of this act was to provide federal protection for the freed blacks in the exercise of certain described liberties.

The 1866 law was not confined to the protection of blacks. It was also intended to secure equality of rights for most other citizens. Thus Senator Lyman Trumbull, who wrote the original bill, viewed it as affecting state legislation generally, quoting in his introductory statement from a note to WILLIAM BLACKSTONE's commentaries: "In this definition of civil liberty it ought to be understood, or rather expressed, that the restraints introduced by the law should be equal to all, or as much as the nature of things will admit." The statute emphasized material, and not political or intellectual, considerations. It protected against discriminatory treatment the rights of most native-born citizens "to make and enforce contracts . . . and to inherit, purchase, lease, sell, hold and convey real and personal property."

The debates on section 1 of the Fourteenth Amendment further spell out Congress's commitment to preserving the material rights. Frequently quoted in the debates was Justice BUSHROD WASHINGTON's definition in CORFIELD V. CORYELL (1823), stating that privileges and immunities included "the right to acquire and possess property of every kind." For the thirty-ninth Congress, Sir William Blackstone and Chancellor JAMES KENT were highly authoritative on the powers and purposes of government. Both strongly emphasized the importance of economic and property rights in a free society.

There should be little doubt that the values of foremost

importance to the Framers of many provisions of the Constitution encompassed the protection of economic and property rights.

BERNARD H. SIEGAN
(1986)

Bibliography

CORWIN, EDWARD S. 1948 *Liberty Against Government.* Baton Rouge: Louisiana State University Press.

MCCLOSKEY, ROBERT G. 1962 Economic Due Process and the Supreme Court. *Supreme Court Review* 1962:34–62.

SIEGAN, BERNARD H. 1981 *Economic Liberties and the Constitution.* Chicago: University of Chicago Press.

——— 1984 The Economic Constitution in Historical Perspective. In Richard M. McKenzie, ed., *Constitutional Economics.* Pages 39–53. Lexington, Mass.: D.C. Heath.

ECONOMIC OPPORTUNITY ACT
78 Stat. 580 (1964)

Moving rapidly to consolidate his control over the administration he inherited from JOHN F. KENNEDY, President LYNDON B. JOHNSON in January 1964 declared "war on poverty" and announced his aim of building a "Great Society." The Economic Opportunity Act of 1964 was the centerpiece of the Johnson program.

Building on a BROAD CONSTRUCTION of the TAXING AND SPENDING POWER, the architects of the act erected a new conception of the role of the federal government. The government was to eliminate the "culture of poverty" that kept some people in economic distress. The act established several new agencies, the most important of which was the Office of Economic Opportunity (later the Community Services Administration) within the Executive Office of the President. It also created a plethora of new programs: Job Corps, Neighborhood Youth Corps, Head Start, etcetera.

From the beginning the war on poverty faced problems, and no poor person ever benefited from it as much as the bureaucrats who ran it. Funds were targeted on the basis less of economic need than of political patronage. And simultaneous expenditure for the war on poverty and the war in Vietnam depleted the treasury and fueled runaway inflation.

DENNIS J. MAHONEY
(1986)

ECONOMIC REGULATION

In the field of economic policy, the composite constitutional powers of American governments—federal, state, and local—are extremely broad. Granted that governments may not implement economic policies that would violate the guarantees of the BILL OF RIGHTS or a few other constitutional limitations, within these spacious constraints there is little that governments may not do. But what they must or should do is more complex. As to macroeconomic policy, whose main instruments are monetary and fiscal, powers amount virtually to duties, for government could not function without taxing and borrowing, nor could the economy run at all smoothly if government declined to issue any money or take any steps to control its value. (See BORROWING POWER; MONETARY POWER; TAXING AND SPENDING POWER.) Just how these essential functions should be carried out is a matter of art and of debate, but few contend that the functions need not be carried out at all. However, as to microeconomic policies—those identified by usage as the substance of "economic regulation"—constitutional powers have not been regarded as inescapable duties. Although governments may intervene directly to regulate prices, wages, quality of products, and various other aspects of markets, they need not do so. Wages, for instance, have been regulated at some times but not others, in some occupations but not all, and so as to set minima but not maxima. In short, economic regulation is constitutionally optional.

Nonetheless, American governments have always practiced economic regulation, albeit in varying forms and degrees. Moreover, they have always been considered to possess broad authority to regulate, even if during a relatively short interval at the beginning of this century the federal courts invalidated a few particular forms of economic regulation without, however, casting doubt on the legitimacy of most other forms. This historically continuous practice of economic regulation shows that American governments were never dogmatically addicted to laissez-faire, notwithstanding a broad though sometimes faltering preference for private enterprise, and that the Constitution, as intended, written, and interpreted, is not a manifesto in favor of laissez-faire.

Before the CIVIL WAR, the constitutional authority of the states to carry on any and every form of economic regulation was seldom questioned. And this acceptance was not for want of regulations to question. On the contrary, state and local governments set the prices to be charged by wagoners, wood sawyers, chimneysweeps, pawnbrokers, hackney carriages, ferries, wharfs, bridges, and bakers; required licensing of auctioneers, retailers, restaurants, taverns, vendors of lottery tickets, and slaughterhouses; and inspected the quality of timber, shingles, onions, butter, nails, tobacco, salted meat and fish, and bread. This very incomplete list attests to an intention to exercise detailed control over the operation of markets, especially (though not only) those that have since been characterized as providing "public services" and those thought to be morally dubious because of association with usury, betting, intoxication, or excessive jubilation.

In the few instances before the Civil War when such regulations came before its eyes, the Supreme Court roundly affirmed their constitutional propriety, always provided (for so the issues arose) that the state's legislation did not collide with the federal commerce power. So in GIBBONS V. OGDEN (1824) JOHN MARSHALL referred to "the acknowledged power of a state to regulate . . . its domestic trade" and to adopt "inspection laws, quarantine laws, health laws . . . , and those which respect turnpike roads, ferries, etc." In the LICENSE CASES (1847), ROGER B. TANEY defined the STATE POLICE POWER as "nothing more or less than the powers of . . . every sovereignty . . . to govern men and things," including commerce within its domain, powers absolute except as restrained by the Constitution. Again, in COOLEY V. BOARD OF WARDENS (1851) the Court upheld the constitutionality of a state law requiring ships in the port of Philadelphia to employ local pilots, and further regulating the qualifications of pilots and their fees. Only one notable judgment of the time, by the highest court of New York, seems on casual reading to cast doubt on a state's regulatory power. In WYNEHAMER V. PEOPLE (1856) that court invalidated a law prohibiting the sale, and even the possession, of hard liquor on the ground that the statute acted retroactively and thus fell afoul of the DUE PROCESS clause in the state's constitution. The Justices agreed that a PROHIBITION law framed to operate prospectively would lie entirely within the legislature's power, and the only Justice who expressed reservations about outright prohibition went on to say: "It is . . . certain that the legislature can regulate trade in property of all kinds." Long and widespread practice throughout the country confirmed that state legislatures can indeed regulate the terms and conditions not only of trade but also of PRODUCTION, as well as entry into various occupations—though courts repeatedly insisted that the states' police powers, broad though they were, must be limited by profound constitutional antipathy to arbitrary action, such as that instanced by Justice SAMUEL CHASE in CALDER V. BULL (1798): "a law that takes property from A. and gives it to B."

Nor was this broad scope of the police power curtailed by decisions following shortly after the ratification of the FOURTEENTH AMENDMENT in 1868. In the SLAUGHTERHOUSE CASES (1873) the majority of the Supreme Court upheld a Louisiana law that closed down all slaughtering inside New Orleans, confined it to a designated area outside the city, and gave a single private company the right to operate a slaughterhouse there, despite the complaint by butchers that the statute, by depriving them of part of their usual trade, violated the PRIVILEGES AND IMMUNITIES and due process clauses of the Fourteenth Amendment. The Court concluded that the police power undoubtedly authorized regulation of slaughtering, and that the prohibitions imposed on the states by the amendment should not be interpreted as a limitation on reasonable exercises of the police power.

A broadly similar view prevailed in *Munn v. Illinois* (1877), which concerned the validity of a statute fixing the maximum charge to be levied by grain elevators in Chicago. Against the defendants' plea that the ceiling thus set on their earnings effectively deprived them of property without due process, Chief Justice MORRISON R. WAITE marshaled the long history of adjudication prior to 1868: "It was not supposed that statutes regulating the use, or even the price of the use, of private property necessarily deprived an owner of his property without due process of law." The word "necessarily" signaled a departure from the majority's blunt assertion in *Slaughterhouse* that due process should not box in the police power. Instead, the Court adopted in *Munn* the pared-down principle that states could, without offending against due process, regulate the prices of some kinds of business, "those AFFECTED WITH A PUBLIC INTEREST" or, as later usage had it, public service businesses. The tempting inference, that ordinary, "private" businesses are immune to economic regulation, though lent plausibility by some hints in the text, is not confirmed by any forthright judicial statement. (See GRANGER CASES.)

The "affectation with a public interest" DOCTRINE, though frequently invoked by courts in support of state regulation of railroads and public utilities, did not always carry the day. The first notable deviation, not only from *Munn* but from the longer previous tradition, took place in ALLGEYER V. LOUISIANA (1897). In question was Allgeyer's right to buy marine insurance from a New York company despite a Louisiana statute prohibiting out of state insurance companies from doing business there without a license. While conceding the state's power to regulate or even to exclude insurance companies domiciled in other states, the Court concentrated on every American citizen's privilege to pursue an "ordinary calling or trade" and, in the course of it, to make such contracts as might be useful and proper. By interfering with a person's exercise of that privilege, the Court unanimously held, Louisiana had abridged the Fourteenth Amendment's guarantee of liberty and property. To believe, however, as the decision's admirers and detractors alike have believed, that the Court thus read a sweeping FREEDOM OF CONTRACT into the Fourteenth Amendment, so as to equate all economic regulation with denial of due process, is to ignore a vital passage in the opinion, where RUFUS PECKHAM declared that the police power of a state "cannot extend to prohibiting a citizen from making contracts . . . outside the limits and JURISDICTION of the State, and which are also to be performed outside of such jurisdiction." Cavalier disregard of that essential qualification has made the *Allgeyer* opinion seem what it was not. If further evidence were needed, it was supplied by the Court's decision one year later in HOLDEN V. HARDY (1898), where the majority of seven upheld an act of Utah regulating the hours of labor in mines and smelters, without any suggestion that mines and smelters are businesses affected with a public interest, and notwithstanding considerable interference with freedom of contract.

Supposedly initiated by *Allgeyer,* the triumph of "economic due process" or SUBSTANTIVE DUE PROCESS—a triumph never fully consummated—was supposedly completed by LOCHNER V. NEW YORK (1905). Inasmuch as the Supreme Court there struck down a statute that limited the work of bakers to sixty hours a week, the decision could be so represented. But a close reading of the opinions, including the dissents, leads to the sounder conclusion that the statute was invalidated because, while purporting to be a measure for the public health, it adopted means that (in the majority's view) had no reasonable relation to that end, or alternatively because it was really an effort to interfere in the bargaining between master and employee, an effort lying outside the proper scope of the police power as constrained by the due process clause.

That the *Lochner* decision did not undermine economic regulation was demonstrated three years later in MULLER V. OREGON (1908), when the Supreme Court (with only one new member) upheld a restriction on hours of work of women as a reasonable means of achieving the proper end of public health, and was demonstrated again in BUNTING V. OREGON (1917), where the statute applied to men as well as women and to overtime wage rates as well as to hours. In ADKINS V. CHILDREN'S HOSPITAL (1923), however, the Court once again sailed closer to the *Lochner* tack, when it disallowed a minimum wage law. Nevertheless, despite the *Lochner-Adkins* line and reliance on decisions before, during, and after the brief era of laissez-faire activism, many states continued to pass and enforce laws regulating the conditions of labor as well as other economic relations, especially after the onset of the Great Depression.

The older line of interpretation, temporarily obscured but not reversed, was restored to predominance by the Supreme Court's decision in NEBBIA V. NEW YORK (1934). Here, while apparently relying on *Munn v. Illinois* (1877), the Court effectively reversed it by holding "that the private character of a business does not necessarily remove it from the realm of regulation of charges or prices." Indeed, the Court went on to say that it had upheld an extensive variety of economic regulations, a statement the accuracy of which it vindicated by citing some hundred PRECEDENTS that it had laid down during the three or four

decades earlier. A further step toward closing the *Lochner* episode was taken in WEST COAST HOTEL V. PARRISH (1937); and the final (at least until the present) bit of punctuation was supplied in UNITED STATES V. CAROLENE PRODUCTS COMPANY (1938) when the Court committed itself not to invalidate regulatory legislation unless the law's irrationality offended against due process or it otherwise contravened specific constitutional guarantees such as those in the Bill of Rights.

Meanwhile, economic regulation by the federal government had been undergoing a roughly parallel development. Substantively it was less extensive, because until about the Civil War economic activity within the several states far outweighed that which crossed the boundaries of any state, because the federal government spent less and did less than state and local governments, and not at all because the federal government was more attached than were state and local governments to laissez-faire. Ample evidence to the contrary is afforded by the protective tariffs so vigorously advocated by ALEXANDER HAMILTON and HENRY CLAY and so widely supported, by the subsidies granted to transportation facilities in the name of INTERNAL IMPROVEMENTS, and by close regulation of ships and sailors involved in interstate and foreign navigation. If nevertheless the federal government did little to implement the COMMERCE CLAUSE during its first century, Congress's latent constitutional power was recognized and approved. When Marshall wrote in GIBBONS V. OGDEN (1824) that the commerce power "is complete in itself, may be exercised to its utmost extent, and acknowledges no limitations, other than are prescribed in the constitution," he prefigured later judicial pronouncements that the commerce power is effectively the NATIONAL POLICE POWER.

As might have been expected, the coexistence of two tiers of police power occasioned increasing collisions when, after the Civil War, the federal government expanded the exercise of its own power. Such collisions might have been resolved by simple-minded recourse to the SUPREMACY CLAUSE, but that solution would not have appealed strongly to judges who remembered that the professed objective of the Civil War had been, on the one side, to protect the autonomy of the states and, on the other side, to preserve a Union (rather than replace it by a unitary state). Recollections of the crisis reinforced the traditional effort to delineate clear boundaries between the domains of the states and that of the federal government.

A striking specimen of this issue arose from the increasing efforts of state governments after the Civil War to regulate railroad rates, and in particular to prohibit what many shippers regarded as iniquitous discrimination. In this instance a railroad had charged a shipper a certain amount for sending goods from one place in Illinois to

New York City while charging another shipper less for sending the same sort of goods from another place in Illinois to New York City, though the latter distance was greater than the former. This habitual practice, known as LONG-HAUL-SHORT-HAUL DISCRIMINATION, violated an Illinois statute. In WABASH, ST. LOUIS, PACIFIC RAILWAY V. ILLINOIS (1886) the Supreme Court decided that, although the Illinois courts had confined application of the statute to transportation within the state, the statute was nevertheless invalid as applied to contracts for continous transportation through several states, so "interfering with and seriously embarrassing" interstate commerce. The counterargument, that state statutes of this sort might be permitted to stand until the federal government might occupy the field, became moot when in the following year Congress passed the INTERSTATE COMMERCE ACT, which among other things established the first federal REGULATORY AGENCY, the Interstate Commerce Commission. For twenty-seven years thereafter, until announcement of the SHREVEPORT DOCTRINE, a relatively comfortable equilibrium recognized the exclusive power of states to regulate purely intrastate transportation and of the federal government to regulate purely interstate transportation, though controversy occasionally erupted as to whether some particular regulation by one tier of government materially spilled over into the other's domain.

Concerning enterprises other than transportation, it was harder to draw a neat line between what is a fixture within a state and what though within a state is visiting it as a bird of passage or, according to a habitual metaphor, "flowing" through it. This difficulty was manifested in UNITED STATES V. E. C. KNIGHT CO. (1894), the Supreme Court's first ruling on the SHERMAN ANTITRUST ACT. It arose from a suit asking that the courts invalidate contracts by which the "Sugar Trust" had purchased four independent refineries, so achieving an almost complete monopoly of refining. Considering that the government had attacked the contracts rather than the trust itself, that the contracts concerned factories necessarily installed within a state, and that no proof had been offered to connect the contracts with a scheme to restrain interstate commerce, the Court held that the contracts were not reached by the Sherman Act; as so construed, the act was valid. In dissent, Justice JOHN MARSHALL HARLAN objected that the nub of the case was not the sugar trust's acquisition of the four refineries but its monopolization of interstate commerce. One may suppose that, contrary to Chief Justice MELVILLE W. FULLER's pronouncement that "commerce succeeds to manufacture," Harlan would have preferred to say that manufacture, when ancillary to interstate commerce, falls within federal legislative power.

Similar partitioning of state and federal domains persisted in most such decisions down to 1936, accompanied by judicial reminders that if the reach of the commerce power were excessively widened, the states would be rendered economically otiose. So in HAMMER V. DAGENHART (1918) the Supreme Court, while agreeing that the working hours of children in mines and factories should be regulated (and in fact was regulated by every state), invalidated a federal child labor law on the ground that it would disturb the desirably "harmonious" balance between the police power and the commerce power. Similarly, when ruling in *Schechter Poultry Corporation v. United States* (1935) that poultry slaughterers in New York City could not be reached by federal regulation, Chief Justice CHARLES EVANS HUGHES wrote: "If the commerce clause were construed to reach all enterprises and transactions which could be said to have an indirect effect upon interstate commerce, the Federal authority would embrace practically all the activities of the people and all the authority of the State over its domestic concerns would exist only by sufferance of the Federal Government."

That traditional view was substantially revised by *National Labor Relations Board v. Jones & Laughlin Steel Corporation* (1937), decided while President Franklin D. Roosevelt's Court reorganization plan was being vigorously debated. Technically the turn hinged on the Court's finding that the defendant company, besides owning steel mills and mines, owned and operated interstate railroads and water carriers and sales offices throughout the country; as the company was "a completely integrated enterprise," one in which manufacture and commerce might be said to have been completely unified, its relations with labor unions in its steelworks and mines as well as in its railroads and water carriers were properly subject to federal regulation. On a narrow view, the Court continued to adhere to the principle that state and federal regulation must coexist—as the Court took trouble to emphasize in UNITED STATES V. DARBY LUMBER COMPANY (1941)—and merely found federal power applicable to "national" firms; on a broader view the Court had considerably shifted the dividing line. The virtual obliteration of the line was confirmed by WICKARD V. FILBURN (1942), where the Court upheld federal regulation of wheat farming, by reinterpreting production as well as consumption on the farm, previously understood to be inherently local, as ingredients of an "economic market" which, being national and indeed international, was properly subject to federal regulation.

Rash though it may be to suppose that one can identify historical patterns, it might nevertheless be ventured that economic regulation by the states was never impeded by laissez-faire nor, except briefly and partially, by the doctrine of substantive due process, and that economic regulation by the federal government has expanded, generally though unsteadily, as a proportion of the whole. This summary, assuming it to be accurate, does not of course endorse the logical rigor of CONSTITUTIONAL INTERPRETATION that underlay those tendencies, nor does it prejudge their political desirability. Those who see private enterprise as self-serving and chaotic conclude that extensive economic regulation is a condition of social welfare; whereas minimalists maintain that economic regulation is desirable only in the event of market failure, that is, only in relation to enterprises that give rise to oppressive externalities or to industries that are natural monopolies. The Constitution provides ample scope for the former view but imposes no restrictions corresponding to the latter view. Despite some indications of "deregulation" in legislation and adjudication since 1960, it would be foolhardy to predict whether economic regulation will diminish or increase during the future.

WILLIAM LETWIN
(1986)

Bibliography

HALE, ROBERT L.   1952   *Freedom Through Law: Public Control of Private Governing Power.* New York: Columbia University Press.

HAMMOND, BRAY   1957   *Banks and Politics in America from the Revolution to the Civil War.* Princeton, N.J.: Princeton University Press.

HANDLIN, OSCAR   1947   *Commonwealth: A Study of the Role of Government in the American Economy.* New York: Oxford University Press.

KOONTZ, HAROLD and GABLE, RICHARD W.   1956   *Public Control of Economic Enterprise.* New York: McGraw-Hill.

LETWIN, WILLIAM   1965   *Law and Economic Policy in America: The Evolution of the Sherman Antitrust Act.* Chicago: University of Chicago Press.

LIEBHOFSKY, H. H.   1971   *American Government and Business.* New York: Wiley.

MORRIS, RICHARD B.   1946   *Government and Labor in Early America.* New York: Columbia University Press.

WILSON, JAMES Q., ed.   1980   *The Politics of Regulation.* New York: Basic Books.

ECONOMIC REGULATION
(Update)

The term "economic regulation" has no clearly defined meaning. In its narrowest sense, it is probably limited to government control of prices, outputs, and market entry. At one time, such regulation was widespread, covering major industries such as transportation, energy, telecommunications, and agriculture. Beginning in the mid-1970s, however, such traditional forms of government regulation have been in retreat, and "deregulation" has been the watchword. Since the 1930s, constitutional law has been

thought to place little restriction on these traditional forms of economic regulation. Even less constitutional guidance has been found relating to deregulation.

In the meantime, business activities have been subjected to new federal forms of regulation governing EMPLOYMENT DISCRIMINATION, worker safety, pollution, and other "social" issues. We might more broadly define economic regulation, then, as government regulation of activities relating to market transactions, actual or potential. Given this very broad subject matter, it is obvious that in specific cases economic regulations might happen to implicate all manner of constitutional DOCTRINES. Thus, in some sense, the constitutional topic of "economic regulation" is indeed a broad one.

Yet, the fact that some constitutional rule may happen to apply to an economic activity as well as to noneconomic activities is of no particular interest. Rather, the interesting question is the distinctive constitutional status of economic regulation. In other words, we need to ask when the government's power is either increased or decreased by virtue of the fact that the regulated activity is connected with the marketplace.

Although this distinction does not play a central role in current doctrine, the Supreme Court does sometimes give distinctive treatment to regulation of economic activities. A familiar example is the COMMERCIAL SPEECH doctrine, which provides a lower protection for speech that is integrally related to market transactions. Two recent cases from other areas of constitutional law also provide illustrations that the marketplace nexus retains significance in constitutional analysis.

The first example is UNITED STATES V. LÓPEZ (1995). *López* involved a federal statute that criminalized possession of firearms in school zones. The Court held, for the first time since the NEW DEAL, that a federal regulation of private activity exceeded congressional power under the COMMERCE CLAUSE. What is most notable for present purposes, however, is the Court's care to distinguish the case from PRECEDENTS involving economic regulation. For instance, the Court observed that even WICKARD V. FILBURN (1942) (which the Court called "perhaps the most far reaching example of commerce clause authority over intrastate activity"), "involved economic activity in a way that the possession of a gun in a school zone does not." In contrast, the statute before the Court had "nothing to do with 'commerce' or any sort of economic enterprise, however broadly one might define those terms." Nor was it "an essential part of a larger regulation of economic activity, in which the regulatory scheme could be undercut unless the intrastate activity were regulated." Hence, the firearms statute could not be sustained "under our cases upholding regulations of activities that arise out of or are connected with a commercial transaction, which viewed in the aggregate, substantially affects interstate commerce."

Justice ANTHONY M. KENNEDY'S CONCURRING OPINION (joined by Justice SANDRA DAY O'CONNOR), also stressed the distinction between congressional power over economic and noneconomic activity. He felt bound by precedent to recognize "congressional power to regulate transactions of a commercial nature." Hence, he argued, the Court was foreclosed "from reverting to an understanding of commerce that would serve only an eighteenth-century economy"; precedent also precluded "returning to the time when congressional activity was limited by a judicial determination that those matters had an insufficient connection to an interstate system." In short, he said, "Congress can regulate in the commercial sphere on the assumption that we have a single market and a unified purpose to build a stable national economy."

Although governmental authority to restrict economic activity is broad, it is not unlimited. That is the teaching of LUCAS V. SOUTH CAROLINA COASTAL COUNCIL (1992). *Lucas* involved a state regulation that, as construed by the lower courts, completely eliminated the economic value of certain beachfront land. With narrow exceptions, the Court held, a regulation must be considered a TAKING OF PROPERTY if it "denies all economically beneficial or productive use of land." Note that it is only economically beneficial uses that are protected; that is, only the ways in which the land or its product might enter into some market transaction. The Court found "the notion . . . that title is somehow held subject to the 'implied limitation' that the State may subsequently eliminate all economically valuable use is inconsistent with the historical compact recorded in the Takings Clause that has become part of our constitutional culture." But *Lucas*, assuming it would continue to receive the support of a majority today, is a narrow holding, applying only to direct regulations of land (as opposed to personal PROPERTY) that destroy 100 percent of its economic value. The holdings in other recent takings cases are also quite narrow. Land is protected from economic regulation, but apparently only in extreme cases.

In short, the commercial sphere continues to be subject to nearly plenary regulation. (Contrast the much broader protection given to the "noneconomic" spheres of politics, media, religion, and family.) FEDERALISM plays little role in restraining national LEGISLATION of commercial activities, and the right to enter into such activities receives special protection only in the case of extreme restrictions on land use. Thus, despite its critics, the post– New Deal distinction between personal and economic rights seems largely intact.

DANIEL A. FARBER
(2000)

(SEE ALSO: *Economic Due Process; Economic Liberties; Interstate Commerce; Property Rights; State Regulation of Commerce.*)

Bibliography

FARBER, DANIEL A.; ESKDRIGE, WILLIAM N., JR.; and FRICKEY, PHILIP P. 1998 *Constitutional Law: Themes for the Constitution's Third Century,* 2nd ed. St. Paul, Minn.: West Group.

LAZARUS, RICHARD 1997 Counting Votes and Discounting Holdings in the Supreme Court's Taking Cases. *William and Mary Law Review* 38:1099.

LESSIG, LAWRENCE 1995 Translating Federalism: *United States v. López. Supreme Court Review* 1995:125–215.

ECONOMICS OF AFFIRMATIVE ACTION

The Supreme Court has mandated that government AFFIRMATIVE ACTION plans must serve some COMPELLING STATE INTEREST and must be narrowly tailored to further this interest. Economics doesn't have much to say about whether, say, remedying RACIAL DISCRIMINATION is a compelling interest, but the tools of economics can shed light on what types of affirmative action programs satisfy the narrow tailoring requirement (or LEAST RESTRICTIVE MEANS TEST). Economic analysis suggests that the most narrowly tailored affirmative action program (1) will be racially explicit (rather than the Court's current preference for "race neutral means to increase minority participation"); (2) will use a sliding scale of credits in which the size of the racial preferences declines with minority participation; and (3) may at times create "quasi-quotas" that effectively ensure a participation floor for minorities.

The idea that a remedy needs to be tailored to further the government's legitimate interest is captured in part by the unexceptional idea that remedial classifications should not be too overinclusive or underinclusive. The Court, for example, in RICHMOND (CITY OF) V. J.A. CROSON CO. (1989) was particularly concerned about the problem of overinclusion; that is, giving affirmative action preferences to people (such as Aleuts) who were not injured by past discrimination in a particular jurisdiction. However, the same opinion also expressed a strong preference for the "the use of race-neutral means to increase minority business participation." This preference for "race-neutral means"—such as general subsidies for small entrepreneurs—necessarily conflicts with the Court's aversion to overly inclusive programs. If preferring the minuscule number of Aleuts in Richmond is "grossly overinclusive," then extending preferences to a much larger class of whites—as would race-neutral subsidies—*a fortiori* would fail the narrow tailoring requirement. Narrowly tailoring the beneficiary class for remedial subsidies so that it will not be overinclusive necessitates explicit racial classifications.

Clearly, the Court has something more in mind by narrow tailoring than a mere insistence on not too much over- or underinclusion. Indeed, the Court's decisions suggest that narrow tailoring may also require that racial preferences not unduly burden nonminorities. Government decisionmakers are constitutionally required to remedy discrimination using the least restrictive alternative. Here, too, economic analysis can be of help—especially in evaluating the relative costs (burdens to minorities) and benefits (remedying racial discrimination) of different affirmative action programs. Narrow tailoring implies a sensitivity to the contours and scope of racial preferences and economic analysis is especially attuned to analyzing effects on the margin.

Simple economics suggests that the Court's antipathy for quotas is overstated. Quotas may be more narrowly tailored to achieve the government's remedial interest than many other types of racial preferences. While quotas are imperfectly tailored because they mandate an inflexible level of minority participation, bidding credits (and other preferences) may be poorly tailored because they induce too much uncertainty and volatility in minority participation.

The question of whether affirmative action racial preferences should be implemented with quotas or credits is similar to the more general question of whether laws should take the form of quantity or price regulation. Economists such as Martin Weitzman and Robert Cooter have suggested circumstances where either type of regulation might be the most efficient. Applied to the question of affirmative action, these models suggest that more narrowly tailored programs will exhibit a "sliding scale" of racial preferences in which the size of the preference will vary inversely with the degree of successful minority participation in the program. Under a narrowly tailored program, the farther minority participation falls below what it would be in the absence of discrimination, the larger the racial preference government might legitimately confer.

Sliding-scale preferences may come close to setting aside a minimum quota of contracts for minority bidders, but such quasi-quotas (for fractions of the legitimate remedial goal) are consistent with narrow tailoring when dramatic shortfalls in minority participation would undermine the government's remedial effort. For example, in an industry where the government has a legitimate interest in increasing minority participation to 30 percent (the fair estimate of what it would have been absent discrimination), the government might find that allowing minority participation to fall below 5 percent would affect the long-term viability of all minority business. Under such circumstances, the government might be justified under the narrow tailoring principle in granting substantial bidding credits for 5 percent of government contracts, effectively guaranteeing that at least 5 percent will go to minorities.

Quasi-quotas can be defended as narrowly tailored remedies because they cause decisionmakers to internalize the true social costs of dramatic shortfalls in minority participation. The problem with simple (invariant) bidding credits is that the participation of minorities may fluctuate in ways that are inconsistent with narrow tailoring of the preferences to the government's underlying remedial interest. Quasi-quotas for a fraction of the overall remedial goal dampen this potential damaging fluctuation. And because the quasi-quota would only set aside a fraction of the government's legitimate remedial goal, it would impose a smaller burden on the interests of nonbeneficiaries. Finally, granting minority enterprises guarantees of minimum participation can increase the quality of minority participants—so as to reduce the long-term disparity between minority and nonminority recipients.

Economics also suggests that sometimes government can remedy private discrimination without unduly burdening nonminorities. Government racial preferences in procurement, for example, can counteract private underutilization in the same market without unduly burdening nonminority firms who are by hypothesis overutilized in the overall market because of their race.

IAN AYRES
(2000)

Bibliography

AYRES, IAN 1996 Narrow Tailoring. *UCLA Law Review* 43: 1781–1838.
AYRES, IAN and VARS, FREDERICK E. 1998 When Does Private Discrimination Justify Public Affirmative Action? *Columbia Law Review* 1998:1577–1641.
COOTER, ROBERT 1984 Prices and Sanctions. *Columbia Law Review* 84:1523–1560.

ECONOMIC STABILIZATION ACT
84 Stat. 799 (1970)

This measure authorized the most comprehensive peacetime ECONOMIC REGULATION in American history. The act extended a temporary sweeping DELEGATION OF POWER which authorized the President "to issue such orders and regulations as he may deem appropriate to stabilize prices, rents, wages, and salaries at levels not less than those prevailing on May 25, 1970." It authorized federal courts to issue INJUNCTIONS to enforce the presidential orders and mandated a $5,000 penalty for violation. A Democratic Congress passed the act at a time of persistent inflation; Republicans charged it was an election-year ploy attacking President RICHARD M. NIXON for failure to curtail rising unemployment, high interest rates, and a balance of payments deficit.

Nixon signed the measure but indicated he would have preferred to veto it and had no intention of using its authority. He opposed committing vast regulatory power to presidential discretion; if Congress favored controls, he said, it should "face up to its responsibilities and make such controls mandatory." One year later, amid growing disapproval of his economic policies, Nixon used the act to impose a ninety-day freeze on wages, prices, and rents. The President twice requested and received congressional extension as "in the public interest." The act was allowed to expire in 1974.

PAUL L. MURPHY
(1986)

Bibliography

SILK, LEONARD   1973   *Nixonomics.* New York: Praeger.

ECONOMY

The United States Constitution is much more than the formal document ratified in 1789. It is the preeminent symbol of the American preference for continuity over radical change, a collection of myths that provides a common faith, and a complicated dialogue between written and unwritten rules of law. As such it reflects and embodies many of the conflicting values at the core of American culture. The law itself, as an extended commentary on the Constitution, has perpetuated many of those conflicts by seeking to balance essentially irreconcilable objectives. It has always attempted, with mixed success, to reconcile elitism and democracy, individual opportunity and community, enterprise and equity, growth and stability, competition and cooperation, and freedom and responsibility. Moreover, it has both liberated and encouraged economic growth even as it has tried to make economic institutions responsible and accountable.

The Constitution's Framers could not anticipate the dramatic changes that occurred in the United States during the first half of the nineteenth century. After all, they drafted the document to serve an economy in which most farmers practiced subsistence agriculture and in which factories were rare, transportation limited, banking and credit primitive, and business transactions simple and direct. Nevertheless, the Constitution provided a congenial legal environment during the first phase of industrialization. The rapid expansion of the nation in size and population was an inherently decentralizing force, as the Supreme Court recognized when it began to interpret the COMMERCE CLAUSE and the CONTRACT CLAUSE. The Court might have defined constitutional power over the economy in several ways. For example, in explaining the meaning of the commerce clause, it might have prohibited the states from enacting any statutes regarding interstate trade. It might also have ruled that state laws could coexist with federal laws in the absence of direct conflict between the two or that the states could legislate only until Congress decided to address the same subject. But in an age when the fear of centralized power was all-pervasive, particularly in the South, the Court's decisions were inevitably compromises. Although the Court prohibited states from taxing the federal government, blocked them from limiting or excusing debts, denied their right to violate corporate charters, banned them from directly interfering with INTERSTATE COMMERCE, confirmed the sanctity of contracts between individuals in two or more states, and granted CORPORATIONS perpetual existence—all important prerequisites to the establishment of national markets— it left the states plenty of responsibilities. They could charter, license, and regulate businesses, and they could regulate working conditions. And because the Constitution provided for a government of ENUMERATED POWERS, leaving a broad economic arena to the states under the TENTH AMENDMENT, the relationship between federal and state law hinged on the assumption that state statutes were constitutional unless prohibited by the Constitution or preempted by Congress.

In short, even JOHN MARSHALL's most nationalistic decisions reinforced the idea of separate realms of power with separate responsibilities. The Supreme Court's commentary on economic powers did not end with its early decisions regarding the commerce and the contract clauses. Following the depression of 1837, the Court formally recognized a general federal commercial law and a national credit system protected by "impartial" federal courts. That business law provided national rules for the marketplace, but did not entirely displace state rules. Hence, corporations could "forum shop" for the laws, state or federal, best suited to their needs. Then, at the end of the century, the I. M. Singer Company and the Big Four meat-packing firms persuaded the Court to strike down state licensing and tax laws designed to exclude the products of out-of-state corporations. By doing so, the Court may have played an even more important part in creating a continental market than did the railroads.

During the nineteenth century the Constitution was defined as much by the inaction of Congress as by the actions of the Supreme Court. Preoccupied as it was with a host of thorny sectional issues, Congress refused to intervene in new questions concerning the relative powers of the states and the federal government. For example, although the Constitution granted the power to coin money to the national government, Congress did not authorize the issuance of national bank notes until the CIVIL WAR. In the meantime, state-chartered commercial banks issued debt instruments that doubled as the nation's currency. Equally significant, Congress used the central government's power to issue corporate charters, which Marshall had read into the Constitution in 1819, only to create national banks and to encourage a few land-grant railroads. Congress might have used the commerce power to license bridges and highways—a logical extension of the power over interstate trade—but transportation decisions were left almost entirely to the states and to private enterprise. Moreover, although the Constitution permitted Congress to enact uniform BANKRUPTCY laws, Congress used that power seldom and reluctantly, leaving the states to pass extensive debtor legislation.

By failing to limit the states' powers in most economic spheres, the Constitution indirectly encouraged legal experimentation and innovation. So did the structure of government mandated by the Constitution. The tendency of FEDERALISM to disperse power to the local level reinforced the dependence of Americans on quasi-governmental associations, such as commercial federations, civic organizations, and booster clubs—organizations that often served as better forums for collective action than did formal institutions of government. Given the decentralized nature of the pre-Civil War political system and the lack of major ideological differences between the POLITICAL PARTIES, the controversies over tariffs, banks, and internal improvements reflected localism and particularism more than STATES' RIGHTS. Not only did federalism institutionalize the nation's centrifugal, localistic impulses; it also reinforced the American tendency to view economic conflicts in constitutional and legal terms, and it reduced tension among competing economic groups by providing a variety of jurisdictions in which to fight for their objectives.

By barring certain acts, the Constitution encouraged the states to expand powers indisputably their own, especially their POLICE POWERS over private property. For example, had the EMINENT DOMAIN power not been granted to private companies, the construction of bridges, turnpikes, canals, and railroads—and industrial development in general—would have been impeded. Individual property owners could be recalcitrant. Railroads needed to acquire broad ribbons of land; without the state's power of condemnation, the property had to be purchased at great expense on the open market. In 1807 the Schuylkill and Susquehanna Navigation Company failed to complete its canal because of the high prices it had to pay for land and water rights.

But under the new eminent domain statutes, which spread throughout the nation after the 1830s, indirect damages were not subject to compensation, and benefits to property not taken—such as any appreciation in property values—could be deducted from required compensation. Those were important subsidies to public works. The courts also limited the liability of transportation companies for injuries to workers, and the legislatures enacted new laws relaxing penalties for usury and debt.

The transformation of law was linked to the emergence of the business corporation, which tapped a vast pool of small investors, permitted them to transfer and withdraw their funds quickly, spread the risk of investment, and limited their liability. But the railroads grew so fast and became so powerful that by the 1870s and 1880s the promotion of capital investment had given way to demands for regulation in many parts of the nation.

Regulation has served many purposes, including the disclosure of illicit activities, the restraint of monopolies and oligopolies, fact gathering, the protection of industries from harmful competition, publicizing the problems of various businesses, and coordinating business activities. It has also served more ritualistic, almost mythic, purposes consistent with the dictates of CONSTITUTIONALISM. For example, it has maintained the illusion of accountability, the notion that the economy works in rational ways subject to public control. It has also perpetuated the idea that there is a "public interest," not just a multitude of special interests competing for preference in an open market. And it has formally acknowledged free competition, one of the most cherished American values. The classical model of free competition was valued not only because it promoted economic efficiency or even provided maximum individual opportunity but also because it built character and mollified some of the antisocial elements in unrestrained individualism.

The promotion of businesses by the state—such as providing exclusive charters, tax exemptions, land, or capital—had always implied a right to regulate those businesses. That right had been freely admitted, at least by businesses that served the public, such as canals and railroads. But by the end of the nineteenth century, corporations tried to free themselves from restrictions—except when restrictions served their interests. State and federal courts aided them in many ways, such as by limiting the state police powers, exalting freedom of the courts, and devising SUBSTANTIVE DUE PROCESS to limit the power of Congress and the state legislatures. Because many congressional leaders shared the assumptions of the Supreme Court's conservative majority, Congress failed to provide the basic ground rules needed for effective antitrust actions. It did not, and probably could not, define what size business should be. Those who supported antitrust actions were not well armed with evidence concerning the potential impact of that policy on income distribution, on the concentration of wealth, on the efficiency of production, and on a host of related matters.

The American respect for private property and the RULE OF LAW, as well as the inability of Congress and the legislatures to decide how big was too big and what constituted "unfair" business practices, made regulation all the more difficult. The SHERMAN ANTITRUST ACT (1890) failed more for this reason than because of opposition from the courts or the power of special interests. Not surprisingly, the regulatory commission became the favored alternative not just to antitrust prosecutions but also to using taxation, federal incorporation, or NATIONAL POLICE POWER to discipline the economy. The Interstate Commerce Commission, created in 1887, set the legalistic precedent of case-by-case regulation, and that approach blended well with the faith of many Progressive politicians in panels of experts working through a process relatively immune from political influence. Many reformers favored regulatory commissions because they considered the political process clumsy and easily corrupted. They also assumed that men of good will could compromise or reconcile their differences if they could find reliable facts and that fact-finding was a job for experts.

At the federal level, the regulatory commission was a child of the Progressive Era, but the number of commissions proliferated during the 1930s with the establishment of the Civil Aeronautics Board, the Tennessee Valley Authority, the Bonneville Power Authority, the Securities and Exchange Commission (SEC), and the multitude of National Recovery Administration code boards. The SEC brought credibility and order to the securities industry largely because the agency's first chairman, James M. Landis, recognized the value of close relations with the stock industry. For example, the SEC provided "advance opinions" in response to specific regulatory questions, a dramatic departure from the formal adjudicatory procedures followed by both the ICC and the Federal Trade Commission (FTC). Yet, despite the number and influence of the NEW DEAL commissions, they did little to change the shape of industrial America. Instead, they showed the limits of commission-style regulation. The reform movement of the 1930s included many competing visions: a cartelized industrial order regulated by business leaders through trade associations; a sink-or-swim free market economy; a corporate state in which government provided both centralized planning and a forum where different interest groups could resolve their differences; and the older Progressive ideal of government as a referee, intervening only to insure that participants followed the rules. The regulatory commission had become a cheap alternative to structural reform.

After WORLD WAR II, regulatory commissions faced increasing criticism. Some critics charged that the commissions were elitist and undemocratic: by combining executive, legislative, and judicial functions in appointive bodies, the agencies constituted a "fourth branch of government" that was clandestine, remote, and capricious. Other critics insisted that over time regulatory boards became narcissistic and bureaucratized as the reform impulse suffocated under crushing caseloads and the staggering range of trivial detail encountered in day-to-day deliberations. Others complained that commissions were not independent enough, that they were too subject to political interference, such as being staffed by political hacks and cronies unsympathetic to regulation. Still another criticism was that commissions were easily "captured" by those they regulated, either through direct means or through the subtle process by which the regulator gradually came to speak the same language and to hold the same economic philosophy as the regulated. Finally, many politicians and academics charged that commissions were grossly inefficient, a judgment hard to dispute when cases brought before the Civil Aeronautics Board and the FTC often took years to settle.

Two things happened in the postwar period. First, the old constitutional goal of balancing public and private, individual acquisitiveness and the common welfare, and stability and growth seemed anachronistic—perhaps even faintly absurd—to many Americans who had come of age in the RONALD REAGAN era. And second, to most Americans the size of a business became far less important than its sense of social responsibility. During the 1960s and 1970s, Americans discovered the dangers of DDT, phosphates in laundry detergents, propellants in aerosol cans, lead-based paints, nuclear power, radioactive wastes, chemical dumps, oil spills, saccharin, Pintos, Corvairs, Volkswagens, and dozens of other staples of modern industrial society. Economic regulation gave way to social and environmental regulation as the Environmental Protection Agency (1970), the Occupational Safety and Health Review Commission (1970), the Consumer Product Safety Commission (1972), the Mining Enforcement and Safety Administration (1973), the Office of Strip Mining Regulation and Enforcement (1977), and a host of other agencies demonstrated their popularity. In 1981 the EPA alone had more employees than the ICC, FTC, SEC, and Federal Power Commission, even though the youngest of those four had been around for nearly fifty years and the oldest for almost a hundred. Moreover, while "con sumers" had little affect on New Deal regulatory policies, the Sierra Club, the National Audubon Society, Common Cause, and many other citizen groups gave the public far greater influence over the new regulation.

Over time, the law has been far more successful in its

quest to encourage economic growth than in its representation of interests outside the marketplace. The Framers faced many difficult problems, none more vexing than how to elevate basic principles of law above the push and pull of day-to-day politics without rendering those principles blind to new economic needs. Of necessity, the Constitution transcended time and place. To ensure that the law would be responsive yet responsible, two choices were made: vast economic power was granted to state and local governments to decide their economic futures, and the courts and stand-in regulatory commissions were left to resolve most conflicts. Promotion and regulation were clearly complementary, and they often pulled in the same direction, but the balance inherent in the nineteenth-century law was impossible to maintain.

DONALD J. PISANI
(1992)

(SEE ALSO: *Environmental Regulation and the Constitution; Federal Trade Commission Act; Interstate Commerce Act; Preemption; Progressive Constitutional Thought; Progressivism; Property Rights; Regulatory Agencies; Securities Law.*)

Bibliography

FRIEDMAN, LAWRENCE M. 1985 *A History of American Law.* New York: Simon and Schuster.
——— and SCHEIBER, HARRY N., eds. 1988 *American Law and the Constitutional Order: Historical Perspectives.* Cambridge, Mass.: Harvard University Press.
HALL, KERMIT L. 1989 *The Magic Mirror: Law in American History.* New York: Oxford University Press.
PISANI, DONALD J. 1987 Promotion and Regulation: Constitutionalism and the American Economy. *Journal of American History* 74:740–768.

EDELMAN v. JORDAN
415 U.S. 651 (1974)

This decision defines states' ELEVENTH AMENDMENT immunity from suit in federal court. Plaintiffs, alleging that Illinois welfare officials were unconstitutionally administering a welfare program financed by state and federal funds, sought the payments wrongfully withheld. The Supreme Court, in an opinion by Justice WILLIAM H. REHNQUIST, held the Eleventh Amendment to bar the request for retroactive relief but suggested that, as in EX PARTE YOUNG (1908), the Eleventh Amendment would not bar relief requiring the state to pay the costs of future constitutional compliance. In MILLIKEN V. BRADLEY (1977), the Court reconfirmed *Edelman* by requiring a state to pay the costs of future constitutional compliance.

Edelman also developed the principles regulating Congress's power to modify the states' Eleventh Amendment

immunity. First, limiting earlier holdings such as *Parden v. Terminal Railway* (1964), *Edelman* held that mere participation by a state in a federal welfare program does not constitute a waiver of the state's Eleventh Amendment protection. It thus confirmed the narrow approach to waiver signaled by *Employees v. Department of Public Health and Welfare* (1973). Second, despite Congress's power to abrogate states' Eleventh Amendment immunity, *Edelman* stated that actions brought under SECTION 1983, TITLE 42, UNITED STATES CODE, are limited by the Eleventh Amendment. At the time, the state's protection from section 1983 actions seemed to stem from the Court's holding in MONROE V. PAPE (1961) that Congress had not meant to render cities liable under section 1983. With the overruling of that portion of *Monroe* in MONELL V. DEPARTMENT OF SOCIAL SERVICES (1978), the question whether section 1983 abrogated the states' Eleventh Amendment immunities reemerged. In QUERN V. JORDAN (1979), a sequel to *Edelman,* the Court held that section 1983 was not meant to abrogate the states' Eleventh Amendment protection.

THEODORE EISENBERG
(1986)

EDUCATION AMENDMENTS OF 1972 (TITLE IX)
86 Stat. 373

Title VI of the CIVIL RIGHTS ACT OF 1964 prohibits discrimination on the ground of race, color, or national origin in programs receiving federal financial assistance. Title IX of the Education Amendments of 1972 extends Title VI's ban to discrimination on the basis of sex in federally assisted education programs. Title IX excludes from its coverage fraternities, sororities, Girl Scouts, Boy Scouts, and similar organizations, and scholarships awarded to beauty contest winners; the act does not require sexually integrated living facilities. Title IX instructs federal departments to implement its provisions through rules or regulations and authorizes termination of funding in cases of noncompliance.

Title IX has played a major role in increasing female athletic opportunities at educational institutions, and *North Haven Board of Education v. Bell* (1982) held that Title IX could reach sexually discriminatory employment practices. In *Cannon v. University of Chicago* (1979) the Supreme Court held that Title IX may be enforced through private civil actions. (See SEX DISCRIMINATION.)

THEODORE EISENBERG
(1986)

Bibliography

DORSEN, NORMAN et al. 1979 *Emerson, Haber and Dorsen's Political and Civil Rights in the United States,* 4th ed. Vol. II: 771–774, 883–893. Boston: Little, Brown.

EDUCATION AND THE CONSTITUTION

Basic to any discussion of the role of courts in educational decision making is the primacy of education in American ideology. Americans believe that education is central to the realization of a truly democratic and egalitarian society. It is through education that the skills necessary to exercise the responsibilities of citizenship and to benefit from the opportunities of a free economy will be imparted, no matter how recently arrived or previously disadvantaged the individual. Thus courts are concerned with protecting access to education. Moreover, since decision making by those charged with the administration of public education is seen as one of the most significant areas of law in terms of its effects on the lives of individuals and groups in our society, courts are inevitably drawn into reviewing the legitimacy of those decisions.

Education is primarily a state function in large part delegated to local school districts; the federal government has no direct constitutional responsibility for education. Nevertheless, Congress has enacted laws providing FEDERAL GRANTS-IN-AID to state and local educational agencies, as well as laws protecting the CIVIL RIGHTS of various categories of students. The constitutional authority for these statutes and their implementing regulations comes from Article I, section 8, clause 1, of the Constitution—the TAXING AND SPENDING POWER—which has been interpreted to permit Congress to attach conditions to the receipt of federal funds. Constitutional authority for congressional civil rights mandates governing educational institutions may also lie in section 5 of the FOURTEENTH AMENDMENT.

In the absence of federal legislation, are there constitutional constraints on the extent to which school authorities can control education and regulate the lives of students and teachers? Conversely, do students and teachers have the same constitutional rights as all citizens in our society, or are these rights limited within the school environment? The courts have acknowledged the importance of education to our democratic society and the importance of schools in preserving and transmitting the values—social, moral, or political—on which our society rests. The challenge is to inculcate those values without stifling the exercise of the freedom of expression, the freedom of religion, and other constitutional rights.

Until the middle of the twentieth century, education was almost the sole prerogative of school administrators and local boards of education. There were few legal constraints on school authorities and even fewer legal entitlements for teachers and students. Today various competing groups and individuals seek to control educational decision making—school boards, school administrators, teachers, parents, students, community leaders, minority groups, and federal and state agencies. Their struggles for control have often ended up in the courts. Since BROWN V. BOARD OF EDUCATION (1954), the Supreme Court has decided cases involving nearly every major area of educational policy.

Whether states may constitutionally compel all children to be educated in state-run schools was resolved by the Supreme Court in PIERCE V. SOCIETY OF SISTERS (1925), which held that while the state may compel all children to obtain schooling, parents have a constitutional right to choose between public and private schools. Nearly fifty years after *Pierce*, however, the Court held that there are certain constitutional interests of parents and children that may outweigh the state's interest in compelling children to attend school. The Court, in WISCONSIN V. YODER (1972), emphasized that parental direction of the religious upbringing of their children is an important interest to be protected. Although education is important to our democratic society, the interest of the state in compelling two more years of education beyond the eighth grade was outweighed by the burden on the RELIGIOUS LIBERTY of Amish parents. Only the dissent discussed the possibility that the child's interest might differ from that of the parent. In this perspective, *Yoder* seems not so much a case about the rights of children as a contest between parents and state over the power to inculcate values.

The state has a much greater role to play in selecting the curriculum and regulating what is taught in its own schools than it does in private schools. Education necessarily involves the process of selection; it also requires some degree of order to carry out the educational mission. However, as the Supreme Court noted in TINKER V. DES MOINES INDEPENDENT SCHOOL DISTRICT (1909), students (and teachers) do not "shed their constitutional rights . . . at the schoolhouse gate." Nevertheless, these rights may be circumscribed because of the "special characteristics of the school environment." The constitutional claims made on the courts with regard to schooling have been directed principally toward the protection of individual freedom and the attainment of equality. In the first instance, the countervailing factors are the stability and order of the educational enterprise; in the second instance, they center on differing conceptions of equality and the extent to which the educational enterprise is constitutionally obligated to respond to the equity-based claims of various groups absent a showing of intentional discrimination.

There has been much litigation regarding constitutional limitations on the inculcation of religious, political, and moral values in the public schools. The principal cases resolving the question of the proper place of RELIGION IN THE PUBLIC SCHOOLS were decided in the early 1960s. In

ENGEL V. VITALE (1962) the Supreme Court held that a nondenominational prayer written by the New York Board of Regents for use in the public schools violated the FIRST AMENDMENT's prohibition of an ESTABLISHMENT OF RELIGION. A year later, in ABINGTON SCHOOL DISTRICT V. SCHEMPP (1963), the Court struck down the practice of reading verses from the Bible and the recitation of the Lord's Prayer in public schools, holding that the state's obligation to be neutral with regard to religion forbids it to conduct a religious service even with the consent of the majority of those affected. Justice TOM C. CLARK was careful, however, to distinguish between the study of religion or of the Bible "when presented objectively as part of a secular program of education" and religious exercises. In *Stone v. Graham* (1980), the Court held unconstitutional a Kentucky law that required that the Ten Commandments be posted on the walls of public school classrooms. The Court indicated, however, that the case would be different if the Ten Commandments were integrated into the school's curriculum, where the Bible could be studied as history, ethics, or comparative religion.

Although the extent to which religious socialization can be undertaken by school authorities has been sharply limited by the courts, the constitutional limits on political and moral socialization are less clear. *West Virginia State Board of Education v. Barnette* acknowledged the right of school authorities to attempt to foster patriotism in the schools, but held that the Constitution protects the right of nonparticipation in a patriotic ritual that, in effect, coerces an expression of belief. So too, the First Amendment appears to prevent the editing out of particular ideas with a view to prescribing orthodoxy in politics, religion, or other matters of opinion, but the removal of books and curricular materials from the school library may be permitted when it is done for educational reasons. In so holding, the PLURALITY OPINION in BOARD OF EDUCATION V. PICO (1982) recognized a limited right of students to receive information, at least in the context of removal of books from a school library, that was protected by the First Amendment.

The reverse side of the coin involves the extent to which parents have a constitutional right to exempt their children from being socialized by public schools to values to which they object. Absent a clear establishment clause claim, it is unlikely that parents can demand, on moral or philosophical grounds, that certain books or courses be excluded from the public school curriculum approved by school authorities. And absent a clear free exercise claim, it is also unlikely that parents can exempt their children from courses to which they may object, particularly as *Pierce* protects the option of sending their children to private schools if they disagree with the values being taught in the public school.

To what extent does the Constitution protect the right of free expression of students and teachers in the school environment? Complete freedom of expression is inconsistent with the schooling enterprise, which requires order and control. In *Tinker v. Des Moines Independent Community School District* (1969) the Court said that although an "undifferentiated fear or apprehension of disturbance is not enough to overcome the right to freedom of expression," school officials could limit expression if they showed that "the forbidden conduct would "materially and substantially interfere with the requirements of appropriate discipline in the operation of the school."

With regard to First Amendment protection for student organizations, the Supreme Court, in *Healy v. James* (1972), held that "associational activities need not be tolerated where they infringe reasonable campus rules, interrupt classes, or substantially interfere with the opportunity of other students to obtain an education." Nevertheless, because the denial of recognition of a student organization is a form of prior restraint, school authorities have a heavy burden of proving the likelihood of disruption. Although the college in the *Healy* case had denied Students for a Democratic Society access to campus facilities, various other student organizations were permitted such access. Thus, *Healy* might be read as concerned with equal treatment—that is, if a college generally permits student organizations access to its facilities, although it could exclude all such organizations, it may not exclude an organization based on the political or social views it espouses. (See also WIDMAR V. VINCENT, 1981.)

May a teacher's right of expression be restricted in light of the special demands of the school environment? This question arises in a variety of contexts. Is the right of the teacher as citizen to free expression circumscribed by being an employee of the school system? Does the teacher as a professional have the right to determine course content, the selection of books, and the ideas and values to be presented in the classroom? Another question, not yet clearly resolved, is whether there is an independent right of ACADEMIC FREEDOM protected by the Constitution or whether that freedom is merely a corollary of the students' RIGHT TO KNOW.

The Supreme Court has never decided a case that squarely dealt with academic freedom in the classroom. Although KEYISHIAN V. BOARD OF REGENTS (1967) noted that academic freedom is "a special concern of the First Amendment" and that "the classroom is peculiarly the " MARKETPLACE OF IDEAS'," the case involved neither the classroom nor the teacher's right to choose the curriculum or to teach in any particular way. Justice HUGO L. BLACK, in his concurring opinion in EPPERSON V. ARKANSAS (1968), expressed a narrow view of the "academic freedom" protected by the First Amendment: "I am . . . not ready to hold that a person hired to teach school children takes with him into the classroom a constitutional right to teach sociological, economic, political, or religious subjects that the school's managers do not want discussed. . . . I question whether . . . "academic freedom' permits a teacher to breach his contractual agreement to teach only the subjects designated by the school authorities that hired him."

Although lower court decisions vary significantly as to whether "academic freedom" in the classroom is constitutionally protected, OBITER DICTUM in the PLURALITY OPINION in *Pico* suggested that school authorities have unfettered discretion to inculcate community values through the curriculum. If this view prevails, the teacher would appear to have no unilateral right to dictate the lessons (especially value lessons) to which the student will be exposed. If the classroom is the vehicle for imparting values, it cannot also be an open "marketplace of ideas."

Other issues of "academic freedom" actually involve the extent to which the freedom of expression of teachers as citizens, outside the classroom, must be balanced against the interest of the state as employer. For example, the Supreme Court held in *Pickering v. Board of Education* (1968) that, "absent proof of false statements knowingly or recklessly made by him, a teacher's exercise of his right to speak on issues of public importance may not furnish the basis for his dismissal from public employment." However, if the teacher's statements had been shown to have impeded his or her performance in the classroom or otherwise interfered with the regular operation of the schools, the speech might not be protected. And it is not clear whether protection would extend to teachers who voice their criticisms in the classroom.

The extent to which the Constitution constrains school authorities in the manner in which institutional rules and regulations are applied to students and teachers has been extensively litigated. Must certain procedures be followed before a student can be searched for EVIDENCE of the commission of a crime or a violation of a school rule, or before disciplinary action can be taken for failure to comply with institutional rules and norms?

A search made of private property is ordinarily held to be "unreasonable" under the FOURTH AMENDMENT if made without a valid SEARCH WARRANT. Even when the circumstances are such that courts have permitted warrantless searches, however (such as when necessary to prevent concealment or destruction of evidence), such searches usually require a showing of a PROBABLE CAUSE. However, the Supreme Court, in balancing school authorities' "substantial" interest in maintaining discipline against students' legitimate expectations of privacy, has fashioned a less protective standard. In NEW JERSEY V. T.L.O. (1985) the Court held that a search by school authorities is constitutional when there are reasonable grounds for suspecting

that the search will turn up evidence, and when "the measures adopted are reasonably related to the objectives of the search and not excessively intrusive in light of the age and sex of the student and the nature of the infraction." Moreover, there is no warrant requirement for school searches.

Important constitutional values are incorporated in our notions of procedural fairness. GOSS V. LOPEZ (1975) held that state-created entitlements to a public education are protected by the due process clause of the Fourteenth Amendment; thus, the right to attend school may not be withdrawn on the ground of misconduct, absent fair procedures for determining whether the misconduct has occurred. However, having decided that some process is due, the procedural requirements in the school environment are minimal. In the case of a ten-day suspension of a student for disciplinary reasons, *Goss* required only that the student be given notice of the charges and an opportunity to explain his or her version of the story. Immediate removal from school may be justified in some cases even before the hearing. The hearing itself may simply be a brief meeting between the student and the administrator minutes after the alleged transgression. More stringent safeguards, however, may be required for deprivations of education significantly longer than the ten-day period involved in *Goss*. Just two years after *Goss*, the Court held, in INGRAHAM V. WRIGHT (1977), that although the administration of corporal punishment for violating school rules implicated a constitutionally protected liberty interest, "the traditional COMMON LAW remedies were fully adequate to afford due process." Thus, no advance procedural safeguards were constitutionally required. Because, according to the Supreme Court in BOARD OF CURATORS V. HOROWITZ (1978), academic grades and evaluations typically involve more subjective and evaluative judgments than do disciplinary decisions, the determination of "what process is due" turns on whether the disputed action is deemed to be academic or disciplinary in nature.

Yet another constitutional constraint on the public schools is embodied in the Fourteenth Amendment's EQUAL PROTECTION clause. The assertion of an entitlement to a minimum educational opportunity, to equal access to the schooling process, or to a specified educational outcome seeks to impose an affirmative obligation upon public schools. The most fully matured and litigated definition of equal educational opportunity is the right of minority students to be free of RACIAL DISCRIMINATION. The principal issues have concerned the requirements for finding that the Constitution has been violated, and the scope of the remedy once a constitutional violation has been established. The courts have held that intentional actions of school authorities constitute de jure SEGREGATION and, in some cases, that intent to segregate can be inferred from actions that have the foreseeable effect of fostering segregation. The courts have also held that the lapse of time between past acts and present segregation does not alone eliminate the presumption of causation and intent. Courts have also coped with the question whether RACIAL QUOTAS or AFFIRMATIVE ACTION to assist minorities who have been handicapped by past discrimination are unconstitutional, what are permissible remedial techniques (such as zoning, pairing of schools, or SCHOOL BUSING), when a systemwide remedy is permissible and what proof is required before a systemwide remedy can be ordered, and whether a court may require that school district boundaries be reorganized in order to devise an effective remedy.

Some students seeking equal educational opportunity are asserting a right to be free of dicrimination on the basis of gender. However, most of the case law has developed under Title IX of the EDUCATION AMENDMENTS OF 1972 and its implementing regulations, and few of these cases have been decided on constitutional grounds.

In CRAIG V. BOREN (1976) the Supreme Court indicated that gender would not be treated as a SUSPECT CLASSIFICATION as is race, but as a category requiring an intermediate level of judicial scrutiny. Thus, a gender classification must serve important governmental objectives and must be substantially related to the achievement of those objectives before it can be upheld. MISSISSIPPI UNIVERSITY FOR WOMEN V. HOGAN (1982), involving the exclusion of males from MUW's School of Nursing, held that the state had failed to meet this standard. The state had argued that its single-sex admissions policy was designed to compensate for discrimination against women, but was unable to show that women had suffered discrimination in the field of nursing. For the majority, not only was the policy excluding males from the School of Nursing not compensatory, it tended "to perpetuate the stereotyped view of nursing as an exclusively women's job." The state also failed to show that the gender-based classification was substantially related to its purported compensatory objective. SEPARATE BUT EQUAL educational offerings, if truly equal, and policies that are truly compensatory may still be constitutionally permitted in the case of gender.

Equal educational opportunity has sometimes been defined in terms of financial resources. The school finance reform movement of the early 1970s concerned inequalities in educational resources among school districts within a state. The issue in those cases was whether such inequalities were constitutionally impermissible. In SAN ANTONIO INDEPENDENT SCHOOL DISTRICT V. RODRIGUEZ (1973) the Supreme Court held that because Texas's school finance system neither employed a SUSPECT CLASSIFICATION nor touched on a fundamental interest, the financing scheme must be assessed in terms of the RATIONAL BASIS standard of review. The Supreme Court's opinion distinguished differences among school districts from a state "financing system that occasioned an absolute denial of educational opportunities to any of its children." Those statements raise two related questions: First, under what circumstances, if any, is exclusion of a class of children from public schools constitutionally justifiable? Second, if absolute deprivation of an education is unconstitutional, can this principle be extended to certain children who, although attending public schools, are "functionally excluded?" PLYLER V. DOE (1982) raised the first question and LAU V. NICHOLS (1974) the second.

In *Plyler v. Doe* the Court held invalid a state statute that permitted school districts to bar illegal alien children from public schooling. *Lau v. Nichols* involved non-English-speaking children who, even though they had the same access as other children to teachers and books, were "functionally excluded" because they could not understand what went on in the classroom where only English was spoken. The Court struck down this "functional exclusion" of students on statutory grounds.

Although students with limited English proficiency and handicapped students, like minorities or women generally, have sought equal treatment with respect to educational offerings, in some circumstances they have sought to impose affirmative duties on government to remove barriers to their opportunity to obtain an equal education—barriers that were not of the government's making. If they do not receive special treatment, the argument goes, they do not have an opportunity equal to that of others to take advantage of the education the government offers to all. The Supreme Court has not yet held that this latter approach to equal educational opportunity, focusing on an affirmative duty to provide special, additional services for certain groups, is constitutionally dictated; the only cases to come before the Court have been decided on statutory grounds.

CLEBURNE V. CLEBURNE LIVING CENTER, INC. (1985) suggested in OBITER DICTUM that the handicapped are entitled only to application of the rational relationship standard to their equal protection claims. However, now that *Plyler v. Doe* has recognized the importance of education, perhaps the handicapped will receive some special solicitude for their claims to education. On the other hand, *Plyler v. Doe* involved the total exclusion of undocumented alien children from public schooling. Even in *Rodriguez*, the Court suggested that the total deprivation of education might be constitutionally impermissible. Thus, arguably, the total exclusion—or perhaps even the functional exclusion—of handicapped children from education would be unconstitutional, but there would be no constitutional violation in a state's failure to provide the special treatment and additional educational resources needed to bring them to the same starting line as other children.

Since Americans view education as of utmost importance to the maintenance of both their political and their economic systems, as well as to the well-being of the individual and his or her family, schooling is compulsory. The school is, on the one hand, the agency of government closest to the day-to-day lives of people and, on the other hand, the most inherently coercive. Thus courts have been concerned with the appropriate balance between individual liberties and societal interests as well as equal access to an education.

BETSY LEVIN
(1986)

Bibliography

GOLDSTEIN, STEPHEN R. 1976 The Asserted Constitutional Right of Public School Teachers to Determine What They Teach. *University of Pennsylvania Law Review* 124:1293–1357.

HIRSCHOFF, JON 1977 Parents and the Public School Curriculum: Is There a Right to Have One's Child Excused from Objectionable Instruction? *Southern California Law Review* 50:871–959.

LEVIN, BETSY 1977 Current Trends in School Finance Reform Litigation. *Duke Law Journal* 1977:1099–1137.

VAN ALSTYNE, WILLIAM W. 1970 The Constitutional Rights of Teachers and Professors. *Duke Law Journal* 1970:841–879.

YUDOF, MARK G.; KIRP, DAVID L.; VAN GEEL, TYLL; and LEVIN, BETSY 1982 *Educational Policy and the Law*. Berkeley, Calif.: McCutchan.

EDUCATION AND THE CONSTITUTION
(Update)

Although the first compulsory attendance law was enacted in Massachusetts in 1852, public and private education were almost exclusively governed by state constitutional provisions and statutes until the 1920s. In three landmark constitutional decisions from 1923 to 1927—MEYER V. NEBRASKA (1923), PIERCE V. SOCIETY OF SISTERS (1925), and *Farrington v. Tokushige* (1927)—the Supreme Court affirmed the authority of the states to compel attendance at public or private schools. In so doing, however, it declared that the states may neither abolish private education nor regulate it so severely that private schools are effectively turned into public schools.

The "Pierce compromise," which recognized the role of the state in compelling school attendance, but preserved private alternatives, was premised on the economic rights of private schools, the recognition that there are constitutional limits on the states' legitimate authority to inculcate particular values and attitudes in children, and on natural law theories of the rights of parents to direct the upbringing of their children. Put somewhat differently, parents may choose to supplement the basic education provided by the state by relying on private schools, but governments have no constitutional obligation to pay for private education. Parents may choose a private school that reflects their religious, educational, and other values, but the state has the authority to regulate those schools reasonably to accomplish its legitimate socialization and citizenship objectives.

Meyer and its progeny have never been overruled by the Supreme Court, despite their reliance on now repudiated notions of SUBSTANTIVE DUE PROCESS in the economic sphere, and they provide the foundation for all subsequent constitutional decisions in the education field. Only one narrow constitutional exception to compulsory attendance has been fashioned, in WISCONSIN V. YODER (1972), and this exception was for Amish students claiming that modern public high schools undermined their religious faith and practices. Furthermore, state courts, under federal and state constitutional provisions, have restrained state authorities from too closely constraining the operation of private religious schools.

Some modern commentators, however, believe that the "Pierce compromise" would rest more comfortably on FIRST AMENDMENT grounds. The idea is that a state monopoly over elementary and secondary education would imperil democratic values as government agencies sought to establish an ideological conformity that would jeopardize the rights of adult citizens to formulate and express their own points of view, particularly with respect to matters of public policy. The underlying assumption is that indoctrination by the state may be as dangerous to freedom of expression as direct government censorship of what speakers may say.

The theme of *Meyer* and *Pierce* was carried forward in *West Virginia Board of Education v. Barnette*, decided by the Court in 1943. A majority of the Justices held that West Virginia could not constitutionally require its students to salute the American flag in violation of their personal beliefs. Justice ROBERT H. JACKSON did not challenge the notion that public schools may seek to inculcate patriotic values, but he held that the compelled expression of belief was an unconstitutional means of achieving that end. Although the case involved Jehovah's Witnesses, the decision rested on the students' freedom of expression, not their right of free exercise of religion. AMBACH V. NORWICK (1979) reinforces the view that the key factual element in *Barnette* was the coerced declaration of belief. In *Ambach*, the Court held that a state may prefer American citizens to resident aliens in selecting teachers on the theory that citizens are more knowledgeable and effective in communicating American cultural and political values.

Two decades after *Barnette*, the Court, acting under the

ESTABLISHMENT CLAUSE of the First Amendment, declared in ENGEL V. VITALE (1962) and ABINGTON TOWNSHIP SCHOOL DISTRICT V. SCHEMPP (1963) that the states and school districts may not require or sponsor SCHOOL PRAYER. The Court, evidencing some skepticism as to whether such prayers ever might be genuinely voluntary, completely abolished sponsored prayer in public schools, even for students wishing to engage in such prayer. In effect, the Court treated the ban on establishing religion as a substantive limit on governmental expression in public schools. In reaching this result, the Court was at pains to distinguish between ritual indoctrination of religion and the study of religion as an academic subject.

But in the years after WORLD WAR II, the major concern of the federal courts was less the need to cabin state indoctrination than it was to vindicate the rights of African Americans and other groups to an equal educational opportunity. The landmark decision, of course, was BROWN V. BOARD OF EDUCATION OF TOPEKA, a 1954 decision in which a unanimous Supreme Court declared that segregation of students by race in public schools violated the EQUAL PROTECTION clause of the FOURTEENTH AMENDMENT. *Brown* was elaborated on in a series of decisions—including GREEN V. COUNTY SCHOOL BOARD OF NEW KENT (1969), SWANN V. CHARLOTTE-MECKLENBURG BOARD OF EDUCATION (1971), KEYES V. SCHOOL DISTRICT NO. 1 OF DENVER (1973), MILLIKEN V. BRADLEY (1974), and *Board of Education of Oklahoma City Public Schools v. Dowell* (1991)—seeking to define unlawful SEGREGATION, to establish the legal framework for remedying past RACIAL DISCRIMINATION (including the constitutionality of continuing to rely on neighborhood assignment of pupils), to pass on the appropriateness of interdistrict remedies, and to define when a "unitary" or nondiscriminatory school system had been established. Much of the debate centered on what affirmative steps a school district must take, including the busing of children to more remote schools to achieve a racial balance, once a constitutional violation has been proven.

In the 1960s and early 1970s, a number of groups sought to be included under the umbrella of *Brown*, urging that they had been victims of discrimination in the public schools. For example, handicapped students argued that they could not constitutionally be excluded from public schooling, students from poor families urged that the District of Columbia allocated less money to schools in the poorer neighborhoods, and Asian American students, in LAU V. NICHOLS (1974), alleged that the absence of special instruction in English for students with limited proficiency in English functionally excluded them from a public education in violation of the equal protection clause. These lawsuits met with varying degrees of success.

The era of equal educational opportunity in constitutional litigation largely came to an end in 1973 with the Supreme Court's ruling in SAN ANTONIO INDEPENDENT SCHOOL DISTRICT V. RODRIGUEZ (1973). Texas relied extensively on local property taxes to support public education, and students from poor districts, with low property values, alleged that the resultant distribution of funds discriminated against them in violation of the equal protection clause. In this context, the Court held that education is not a fundamental interest under the Fourteenth Amendment. Unless a particular group was the object of a SUSPECT CLASSIFICATION (that is, historically disadvantaged groups such as African Americans), the Court would not apply a rigorous standard of review to relative denials of educational opportunity, but would uphold educational policies that "bear some rational relationship to legitimate state purposes." The Court concluded that the state's interest in local control of education constituted such a legitimate purpose and that local financing was a rational means of achieving it. After *Rodriquez*, and with few exceptions outside the realms of race and alienage (e.g., PLYLER V. DOE, 1982), equal educational opportunity claims were litigated under federal statutes enacted to protect particular classes of students (for example, the handicapped, students with limited English proficiency, and women) and under state constitutional provisions.

The modern era in constitutional litigation in the education field is dominated by the struggle for the hearts and minds of coming generations of citizens. The public schools have become the battlegrounds for essentially ideological wars. Under a variety of constitutional provisions, most notably the speech and religion clauses of the First Amendment, the Supreme Court has been asked to intervene to resolve disputes over Darwinism and creationism, fundamentalist Christianity and secularism, CONSERVATISM and LIBERALISM, and feminism and advocacy of traditional roles for women. In addressing these divisive and controversial issues, the Court has tended to focus on the motivation of school authorities. If they make curricular and other choices in good faith and if they seek to advance educational objectives, then the decision is virtually insulated from JUDICIAL REVIEW. If, in contrast, they act to suppress a political ideology or to indoctrinate religious values in children, then their actions may violate the First Amendment.

By way of example, under WALLACE V. JAFFREE (1985), moments of silence are permissible only if their purpose, in context, is not to advance religion. Similarly, according to *Edwards v. Aguillard* (1987), a state may not require that theories of the origin of Homo sapiens contrary to Darwinism be taught if the decision is motivated by religious concerns. And federal appellate courts have held in *Smith v. Board of School Commissioners* (1987) and *Mozert v. Hawkins County Board of Education* (1987) that an emphasis on secular values in textbooks and courses is permissible so long as the impetus is not hostility toward religion.

The socialization perspective also yields insights into constitutional decisions involving students and teachers. In TINKER V. DES MOINES INDEPENDENT COMMUNITY SCHOOL DISTRICT (1969) the Supreme Court held that students may engage in expressive activity in public schools (wearing black armbands to protest the VIETNAM WAR) as long as their speech does not threaten a substantial disruption of or material interference with the schools' educational activities. In other words, students may not thwart the schools' ability to communicate, but subject to that caveat, they may express their personal points of view—even if they are inconsistent with those taken by school authorities, thereby reducing the schools' ability to indoctrinate students.

Under BETHEL SCHOOL DISTRICT V. FRASER (1986), *Tinker* is inapplicable to vulgar student expression because limits on such expression are appropriate to schools' educational mission. Furthermore, according to the Court's decision in HAZELWOOD SCHOOL DISTRICT V. KUHLMEIER (1988), *Tinker* protects only the personal speech of students. When they participate in curricular activities—for example, as staff members for a school newspaper organized as part of a journalism course—they must conform to reasonable school policies on the content of the publication. Finally, 0a majority of the Justices have stated in BOARD OF EDUCATION V. PICO (1982) that library books may be removed from a school library if the books are pedagogically unsuitable or vulgar; they may not be removed because the school board wishes to suppress an ideology with which it disagrees.

A similar analysis may be applied to the academic freedom of elementary and secondary school teachers. If a school district insists on educational grounds that teachers assign particular books, then their academic freedom in the classroom has not been violated, according to a Tenth Circuit decision in *Carey v. Board of Education* (598 F.2nd 535, 1979). If, however, there is a systematic effort to suppress a type of book in order to exclude particular ideas or ideologies, then the school authorities have invaded the academic freedom of the teachers. Thus, for example, it is one thing to exclude books on Russian history because no courses on Russian history are offered or resources are limited; it is quite another thing to do so because the books discuss Marxist ideas.

The current constitutional standard seeks to distinguish between indoctrination and education. It is questionable whether such a distinction can be applied by federal courts in a principled and predictable manner. Schools stress many values: students are told that racial discrimination, drug abuse, and murder are wrong; they are told

that democratic participation, civility, and honesty are right. Thus, the source of the distinction between indoctrination and education may lie more in the nature of the values being promulgated than in the process of communication.

MARK G. YUDOF
(1992)

Bibliography

VAN GEEL, TYLL 1987 *The Court and American Education Law.* Buffalo, N.Y.: Prometheus Books.
YUDOF, MARK G. 1983 *When Government Speaks.* Berkeley: University of California Press.
——— 1984 The Quest for the Archimedean Point. *Indiana Law Journal* 59:527–564.
YUDOF, MARK G. et al. 1991 *Educational Policy and the Law*, 3rd ed. St. Paul, Minn.: West Publishing Co.

EDUCATION OF HANDICAPPED CHILDREN ACTS
84 Stat. 175, 88 Stat. 579, 89 Stat. 773, 91 Stat. 230

Title VI of the Elementary and Secondary Education Amendments of 1970, the Education for All Handicapped Children Act of 1975 (EAHCA), and the Education of the Handicapped Amendments of 1974 and 1977 provide funds and a variety of federal programs to assist states in educating and training handicapped individuals. In states receiving federal educational assistance for handicapped children, the acts require a state policy assuring all handicapped children the right to a free appropriate public education, assuring private school education at no cost to parents if children are placed in private schools as the means of fulfilling state responsibilities under the acts, offering an individual educational plan for every handicapped child, and providing education with nonhandicapped children to the "maximum extent appropriate." The acts require substantial procedural safeguards to assure receipt of a free appropriate public education. EAHCA provides a private right of action, after exhaustion of administrative remedies, to compel compliance.

Board of Education v. Rowley (1982), the Supreme Court's first interpretation of EAHCA, held that the statutorily mandated "free appropriate public education" need not provide each child an opportunity to achieve her full potential. The statute mandates only an "adequate" education, one reasonably calculated to enable the child to achieve passing marks and advance from grade to grade.

THEODORE EISENBERG
(1986)

(SEE ALSO: *Disabilities, Rights of Persons With.*)

Bibliography
BURGDORF, ROBERT L., JR. 1980 ` *The Legal Rights of Handicapped Persons.* Pages 213–245. Baltimore: Paul H. Brookes.

EDWARDS v. AGUILLARD

See: Creationism

EDWARDS v. ARIZONA
451 U.S. 477 (1981)
OREGON v. BRADSHAW
462 U.S. 1039 (1983)

In *Edwards*, involving application of the MIRANDA RULES, the Court held that when an accused has invoked his right to have counsel present during interrogation, he has not waived that right simply by responding to further POLICE INTERROGATION unless he himself initiated additional communication. In *Bradshaw* the defendant, who had been advised of his rights and had asked for an attorney, later initiated a conversation with an officer who reminded him that he had no obligation to speak to the police. The prisoner said he understood, continued talking, and confessed. A plurality of the Court decided that the conviction in *Bradshaw* involved no breach of the rule of *Edwards*, which was meant to prevent badgering by the police.

LEONARD W. LEVY
(1986)

EDWARDS v. CALIFORNIA
314 U.S. 160 (1941)

The years of the Great Depression were especially harsh for residents of the Dust Bowl. Many migrated to the West, and particularly California, in conditions of poverty graphically detailed in John Steinbeck's novel, *The Grapes of Wrath* (1939). California's hospitality to this "huge influx of migrants" was reflected in its "Okie law," making it a MISDEMEANOR knowingly to assist an indigent person in entering the state. Edwards, a Californian, went to Texas and drove his indigent brother-in-law back to California. For his troubles, he was given a six-month suspended jail sentence for violating the Okie law.

The Supreme Court unanimously reversed the conviction. Justice JAMES F. BYRNES, for the Court, concluded that the law violated the COMMERCE CLAUSE. The state's concerns with health and the integrity of its welfare funds were insufficient to justify so severe a burden on INTER-STATE COMMERCE. Justice WILLIAM O. DOUGLAS, concurring, would have rested decision on the PRIVILEGES AND IMMUNITIES clause of the FOURTEENTH AMENDMENT. Interstate travel was a privilege of national CITIZENSHIP, and to deny that privilege to indigents would create an inferior class of citizens. Justices HUGO L. BLACK and FRANK MURPHY joined this opinion.

Justice ROBERT H. JACKSON, concurring, agreed with Justice Douglas but also remarked that indigence was "a neutral fact—constitutionally an irrelevance, like race, creed, or color."

KENNETH L. KARST
(1986)

(SEE ALSO: *Equal Protection of the Laws; Wealth Discrimination.*)

EFFECTS ON COMMERCE

"At the beginning Chief Justice [JOHN] MARSHALL described the federal commerce power with a breadth never yet exceeded." So said Justice ROBERT H. JACKSON for a unanimous Supreme Court in WICKARD V. FILBURN (1946), in the course of an opinion recognizing the broad sweep of Congress's modern power to regulate the national economy under the COMMERCE CLAUSE. Marshall's opinion in GIBBONS V. OGDEN (1824) read that clause's reference to commerce "among the several States" to mean "that commerce which concerns more States than one."

For the Constitution's first century, however, Congress did little to regulate INTERSTATE COMMERCE. The first major national regulatory laws were the INTERSTATE COMMERCE ACT of 1887, regulating railroads, and the SHERMAN ANTITRUST ACT of 1890. It fell to another Supreme Court to define the scope of congressional power, and at first the Court's definition was narrow. In UNITED STATES V. E. C. KNIGHT CO. (1895) the Court interpreted the Sherman Act, which prohibited monopolizing "any part of the trade or commerce among the several States," to exclude from its coverage a monopoly of sugar refining. Manufacturing was not commerce, said the Court; that "commerce might be indirectly affected" by a manufacturing combination producing ninety-eight percent of the nation's refined sugar was insufficient to bring the combination under the act's terms.

"Direct" effects on commerce, however, were found in a series of Sherman Act cases culminating in SWIFT & CO. V. UNITED STATES (1905). (See also STAFFORD V. WALLACE.) Yet the Court persisted in its assertion that manufacturing was not commerce, even to the extent of holding in HAMMER V. DAGENHART (1918) that a congressional regulation of the interstate transportation of goods made by child labor was invalid because its purpose was to regulate manufacturing.

Meanwhile, the Court was developing quite another view of congressional power to regulate railroads. In *Houston, East and West Texas Railway Co. v. United States,* the "Shreveport case" (1914), the Court upheld an Interstate Commerce Commission order requiring a railroad to equalize certain interstate and intrastate rates. Such railroads were "common instrumentalities" of interstate and local commerce; the ICC was regulating only the relation between local and interstate rates. Taken seriously, the SHREVEPORT DOCTRINE implies congressional power to regulate intrastate activity because of its effect on interstate commerce.

After two decades of resisting the implications of the Shreveport case, the Court returned to its logic in *National Labor Relations Board v. Jones & Laughlin Steel Corporation* (1937), the most important judicial victory for FRANKLIN ROOSEVELT'S NEW DEAL. There the Court upheld the WAGNER ACT's regulation of collective bargaining in application to a large steel manufacturer that obtained its raw materials in interstate commerce, manufactured steel in Pennsylvania, and shipped finished products to many other states. The opinion was written by Chief Justice CHARLES EVANS HUGHES, who had written the Shreveport case's opinion. A strike by manufacturing employees, said Hughes, would "directly" obstruct interstate commerce. "It is the effect upon commerce, not the source of the injury, which is the criterion."

In every succeeding case, the Supreme Court has applied this "effects on commerce" rationale to sustain congressional power. WICKARD V. FILBURN was the culminating case of ECONOMIC REGULATION, upholding congressional control of a small farmer's on-the-farm consumption of wheat, on the theory that Congress had a RATIONAL BASIS for believing that the aggregate of all such farmers' consumption would have "a substantial economic effect" on commerce. More recently the Court has employed similar reasoning to sustain congressional regulations aimed at distinctly noneconomic purposes. (See PEREZ V. UNITED STATES, extortion through "loan sharking"; HEART OF ATLANTA MOTEL V. UNITED STATES, racial segregation). Today, the "effects on commerce" rationale effectively allows Congress to be the judge of its own commerce clause powers.

KENNETH L. KARST
(1986)

Bibliography

STERN, ROBERT L. 1946 The Commerce Clause and the National Economy, 1933–1946. *Harvard Law Review* 59:645–693, 883–947.

EICHMAN, UNITED STATES v.

See: Flag Desecration

EIGHTEENTH AMENDMENT

The Eighteenth Amendment was framed and adopted to give a peacetime constitutional basis to the national PROHIBITION of alcoholic beverages, originally imposed as a war measure. Congress proposed the amendment in December 1917, and ratification was completed thirteen months later. Congress adopted the National Prohibition Act (VOLSTEAD ACT) to provide a mechanism for enforcement and penalties for violation of the prohibition.

The prohibition amendment provided the occasion for several controversies about the character and extent of the amending power. In Ohio, for example, the voters, by REFERENDUM, attempted to rescind their legislature's ratification of the amendment; but the Supreme Court held that procedure unconstitutional in *Hawke v. Smith* (1920). The Court, in the *National Prohibition Cases* (1920), rejected a number of arguments that the amendment was itself unconstitutional because of purported inherent limitations on the AMENDING POWER, including the contention that ordinary legislation cannot be made part of the Constitution and the assertion that the Constitution cannot be amended so as to diminish the residual SOVEREIGNTY of the states. In the same case the Court held that the requirement of a two-thirds vote in each house to propose amendments was met by the vote of two-thirds of the members present and voting and that amendments automatically become part of the Constitution when ratified by three-fourths of the states, whether or not promulgated by Congress or the secretary of state. In *United States v. Sprague* (1931) the Court rejected the argument that the amendment should have been ratified by state conventions rather than by state legislatures, holding that the mode of RATIFICATION OF CONSTITUTIONAL AMENDMENTS was a matter of congressional discretion.

Prohibition, a product of the reforming impulse that characterized PROGRESSIVE CONSTITUTIONAL THOUGHT, proved very difficult to enforce; and the widespread disregard of federal law scarcely tended toward that moral improvement that the authors intended. In 1933, the Eighteenth Amendment became the only constitutional amendment ever to be wholly rescinded when it was repealed by passage of the TWENTY-FIRST AMENDMENT.

DENNIS J. MAHONEY
(1986)

EIGHTH AMENDMENT

See: Bail; Capital Punishment; Cruel and Unusual
Punishment; Punitive Damages

EISENHOWER, DWIGHT D.
(1890–1969)

The nation has often rewarded its military heroes by electing them to the presidency. General of the Army Dwight David Eisenhower, who had commanded the Allied forces in Europe during WORLD WAR II, was President from 1953 to 1961. A 1915 graduate of West Point, Eisenhower held no public office—except his military command—before being elected President.

Eisenhower was a "moderate" Republican: conservative on economic matters but often liberal on social issues. Although he privately expressed to Chief Justice EARL WARREN his disapproval of BROWN V. BOARD OF EDUCATION (1954), he proposed, and successfully pressed for passage of, the CIVIL RIGHTS ACTS OF 1957 and 1960, the first such acts since Reconstruction. They expanded VOTING RIGHTS and created the CIVIL RIGHTS COMMISSION. In 1957, when the governor of Arkansas resisted a federal court's SCHOOL DESEGREGATION order (see COOPER V. AARON), the Eisenhower administration obtained an INJUNCTION forbidding the use of the National Guard to prevent INTEGRATION. When anti-integration rioting broke out in Little Rock, and the local authorities proved unable or unwilling to suppress it, Eisenhower ordered regular federal troops to the city.

Perhaps because of his military background Eisenhower was more cautious than some Presidents in exercising his power as COMMANDER-IN-CHIEF. He brought the KOREAN WAR to an end and, thereafter, no American troops were actively engaged in combat during his administration. When Chinese communists bombarded the Nationalist-held islands of Quemoy and Matsu, Eisenhower sought, and obtained, a JOINT RESOLUTION of Congress authorizing American military action, if necessary. In 1958, again authorized by congressional resolution, he ordered Marines to Lebanon to maintain order, but they did no actual fighting.

In foreign affairs, Eisenhower's was an activist administration. During the Eisenhower presidency the mutual defense treaty with Nationalist China and the Southeast Asia (SEATO) Treaty were signed, each committing the United States to the defense of distant—and not necessarily democratic—countries. Under the SEATO pact Eisenhower in 1954 began the American policy of assistance to South Vietnam that continued through the VIETNAM WAR (1965–1973). Eisenhower supported the United Nations campaign of "anticolonialism," opposing America's European allies in Suez and Africa.

Domestically, Eisenhower was criticized for not speaking out forcefully against Senator Joseph R. McCarthy of Wisconsin, whose inquiries into communist influence in government threatened CIVIL LIBERTIES and often involved GUILT BY ASSOCIATION. Eisenhower promulgated EXECUTIVE ORDER 10450, which revamped the existing LOYALTY-SECURITY PROGRAM for federal employees.

During his two terms in the White House Eisenhower suffered three serious illnesses and was, for a time, virtually incapacitated. During those periods, Vice-President RICHARD M. NIXON presided over the cabinet and the National Security Council while routine matters were handled by a powerful White House staff. Eisenhower's illnesses raised questions about PRESIDENTIAL SUCCESSION in case of disability that were not resolved until passage of the TWENTY-FIFTH AMENDMENT.

Eisenhower made four APPOINTMENTS OF SUPREME COURT JUSTICES: Chief Justice EARL WARREN (1953) and Associate Justices JOHN MARSHALL HARLAN (1955), WILLIAM J. BRENNAN (1956), and CHARLES E. WHITTAKER (1957). Ironically, the moderate conservative Eisenhower made his most lasting mark on American constitutional history by appointing Justices who turned the Court toward liberal activism.

DENNIS J. MAHONEY
(1986)

Bibliography

GREENSTEIN, FRED I.   1982   *The Hidden Hand Presidency: Eisenhower as Leader.* New York: Basic Books.

EISENSTADT v. BAIRD
405 U.S. 438 (1972)

At a BIRTH CONTROL lecture, Baird gave contraceptive foam to a woman presumed to be unmarried. Convicted in a Massachusetts court for distributing a contraceptive device, Baird sought federal HABEAS CORPUS. On appeal the Supreme Court, 6–1, held the conviction unconstitutional. Four Justices, concluding that GRISWOLD V. CONNECTICUT (1965) would bar prosecution for distribution of contraceptives to married persons, held that the EQUAL PROTECTION clause forbade the state to outlaw their distribution to the unmarried. Two Justices relied on *Griswold* alone, saying the record had not shown the recipient to be unmarried. Chief Justice WARREN BURGER dissented.

KENNETH L. KARST
(1986)

(SEE ALSO: *Freedom of Intimate Association; Right of Privacy.*)

EISNER v. MACOMBER
252 U.S. 189 (1920)

A 5–4 Supreme Court declared that stock dividends did not constitute income subject to taxation under the SIX-

TEENTH AMENDMENT. Justice MAHLON PITNEY agreed that dividends were a "mere readjustment of the evidence of a capital interest already owned." Justices OLIVER WENDELL HOLMES, WILLIAM R. DAY, and JOHN H. CLARKE joined the DISSENTING OPINION of LOUIS D. BRANDEIS, who argued that the dividends represented profit (and thus income) and that the power conferred by the amendment ought to be measured by "the substance of the transaction, not its form." The Court subsequently narrowed the DOCTRINE of *Eisner* through a series of exquisite distinctions.

DAVID GORDON
(1986)

ELASTIC CLAUSE

See: Necessary and Proper Clause

ELECTED JUDICIARY

Federal judges are appointed by the President, with the advice and consent of the Senate. Appointment is for life. Although there was substantial disagreement among the delegates to the CONSTITUTIONAL CONVENTION OF 1787 about how to select judges, ALEXANDER HAMILTON's proposal for lifetime presidential appointments ultimately prevailed and has remained intact for two centuries.

This system was not without its critics, however. Chief among them was THOMAS JEFFERSON, who argued that the independence of the judiciary should be subject to the people's will. While President, Jefferson urged that federal judges should be removed from office upon the recommendation of Congress to the President. In his old age, Jefferson expressed regret that the Constitution did not provide for the removal of judges on a simple majority vote of the legislature, the branch most responsive to the public will. Many historians have attributed Jefferson's antipathy toward the judiciary to his personal animosity toward his distant cousin, Chief Justice JOHN MARSHALL.

Initially, the states also established appointive systems for the selection of judges. Five states entrusted the appointive power to the governor, and eight vested the appointive power in one or both houses of the legislature. To this day, the legislature selects most judges in Connecticut, South Carolina, and Virginia, and state supreme court justices are elected by the legislature in Rhode Island.

Gradually, however, states began adopting systems by which judges were popularly elected. Public perception that property owners controlled the judiciary led to reform, initially at the lower trial court levels. In 1832, Mississippi became the first state in which all judges were popularly elected. An electoral system was adopted in New York at the New York Constitutional Convention of 1846. By the time the CIVIL WAR began, twenty-four of the thirty-four states had established elected judiciaries. Newly admitted states all adopted popular election for most judges.

Disenchantment with the popular election of judges grew during the latter half of the nineteenth century. Judicial candidates were invariably selected by political machines, which typically controlled them after their election. Judicial corruption and incompetence became commonplace. In 1906, in his classic address on the "Causes of Popular Dissatisfaction with the Administration of Justice," ROSCOE POUND claimed that "putting courts into politics, and compelling judges to become politicians in many JURISDICTIONS . . . has almost destroyed the traditional respect for the bench." By the turn of the century, several states converted their judicial elections into nonpartisan races. Today, nonpartisan elections are used to select most or all judges in seventeen states. Only thirteen states still utilize partisan elections to select most or all judges.

A return to the appointive system, utilizing a commission to make nominations, was endorsed by the American Bar Association in 1937. Three years later, Missouri became the first state to adopt this scheme, since known as the Missouri Plan. Thirty-one states now use some variation of the plan for selection of at least some of their judges. In many of these states, the appointment is not for life, however. The judge serves a limited term and must face the voters in a retention election. Normally, retention elections are uncontested. In 1986, however, a well-financed campaign against the retention of three justices of the state supreme court in California succeeded in removing them from the court.

The rising cost of election campaigns for judicial offices has led to increasing concerns about the propriety of campaign fund-raising by judges. In many states, million-dollar campaigns for state supreme court seats represent the largest share of judicial campaign expenditures and large corporations are major contributors to the campaigns. In 1986, for example, five justices of the Texas Supreme Court received $387,700 in campaign contributions from Texaco and Pennzoil while a lawsuit between them was pending before the court.

Unfortunately, the debate between proponents of judicial independence and those who exalt judicial accountability frequently masks a hidden agenda. Thus, in one era, those with a liberal agenda decry the entrenched power of a conservative judiciary; in another era, liberal judges are defended with fervent loyalty to the concept of judicial independence.

At a time when political campaigns have been reduced to raising large campaign chests to finance blizzards of fifteen-second television commercials, however, the wisdom of subjecting judges to election contests must be seriously questioned. In political campaigns the complex issues being decided by judges tend to be oversimplified. Frequently, an emotional issue such as CAPITAL PUNISHMENT or ABORTION becomes the campaign's focal point. The risk becomes substantial that judicial outcomes will become simple reflections of the prevailing political winds. The death penalty offers a startling example. The three justices removed from the California Supreme Court in 1986 were subjected to a bitter campaign that characterized voting for their removal as "three votes for the death penalty." After they were replaced, the affirmance rate in review of death penalty judgments jumped from 7.8 percent to 71.8 percent, with very few precedents being overtly overruled. Nationally, there is a close correlation between the method of selection of justices of a state supreme court and that court's affirmance rate in death penalty appeals. For the period 1977–1987, death penalty affirmance rates varied among state supreme courts according to manner of judicial selection as follows:

Executive appointment:	26.3%
Uncontested retention elections:	55.3%
Nonpartisan contested elections:	62.9%
Partisan contested elections:	62.5%
Legislative appointments:	63.7%

The dependence of judges upon traditional sources of campaign funds also raises serious questions about their ability to remain impartial when their campaign supporters appear as litigants or lawyers in cases before them. The Code of Judicial Conduct, adopted by the American Bar Association in 1972, does not require a judge to disqualify himself or herself if a campaign contributor is a party to a case.

Often when lawyers have a choice of filing a case in state or federal court, they opt for federal court because they have greater confidence the case will be decided by an impartial tribunal, unaffected by the vagaries of local politics. Even the most conscientious state judges have expressed discomfort with the prospect of campaigning for reelection and with that prospect's subliminal impact upon their decision-making process. As California Supreme Court Justice Otto Kaus put it, "It's hard to ignore a crocodile in your bathtub."

Although many of those appointed to the state and federal benches are politicians before they get there, the goal should be to permit them to cease political activity once they put on their robes. At the federal level, that goal has been largely achieved. At the state level, however, it does not appear that an elected judiciary can be insulated from the corrupting influence of campaign fund-raising. A 1971 report of the American Bar Association concluded, "There

is no harm in turning a politician into a judge. He may become a good judge. The curse of the elective system is that it turns every elected judge into a politician."

GERALD F. UELMEN
(1992)

Bibliography

BERKSON, LARRY et al. 1981 *Judicial Selection in the United States: A Compendium of Provisions.* Chicago: American Judicature Society.

DuBois, PHILLIP L. 1980 *From Ballot to Bench: Judicial Elections and the Quest for Accountability.* Austin: University of Texas Press.

ELECTION FINANCE

See: Campaign Finance

ELECTIONS, REGULATION OF

Defining "democracy," Henry B. Mayo has argued that the "one institutional embodiment . . . universally regarded as indispensable in modern democracies is that of choosing the policy-makers [representatives] at elections held at more or less regular intervals." In addition to their central democratic function of providing a mechanism for popular choice of officials, parties, and policies, elections have also been credited with two other important democratic functions: offering a forum for public participation and education in politics; and legitimizing the state's coercive authority and peacefully resolving social conflicts, because the public will generally accept officials and policies selected through fair, participative processes.

The Constitution, by its terms, mandates elections only for members of the House of Representatives and of the Senate. Article I, section 2, provides that members of the House shall be elected by the people of the respective states, and the SEVENTEENTH AMENDMENT provides similarly for senators. Persons meeting the qualifications necessary to vote for members of the larger house of the legislature in each state are constitutionally eligible to vote for representatives and senators. The Supreme Court, in WESBERRY V. SANDERS (1964), held also that "as nearly as practicable one man's vote in a congressional election is to be worth as much as another's." Subsequently, the Court has reaffirmed, in *Kirkpatrick v. Preisler* (1969), that in drawing congressional district boundaries states must "make a good-faith effort to achieve precise mathematical equality."

Characterizing its previous decisions, the Supreme Court, in *Rivera-Rodriguez v. Popular Democratic Party* (1982), said that it has "rejected claims that the Constitution compels a fixed method of choosing state or local officers or representatives." The guarantee clause of Article IV, section 4, has been construed to raise only POLITICAL QUESTIONS within the exclusive jurisdiction of Congress and does not, therefore, make state methods for selecting officials subject to constitutional adjudication in the federal courts. Nonetheless, every state employs popular elections to select presidential electors and its governor and legislature. Other state executive, administrative, and judicial officials, and all manner of local officials are also elected. In all, about 540,000 federal, state, and local offices are filled by election. In addition, the prevailing method of selecting political party nominees and of choosing final contenders in nonpartisan elections is the primary election.

Thirty-seven states provide for popular review of policymaking by the use of referenda, and twenty-one states allow popular instigation of policy through initiative elections. Referendum elections are also widely used in local governments throughout the nation, especially to review tax levies and charter revisions; and initiative elections are available in some local jurisdictions.

Although the Constitution prescribes elections only for Congress, virtually all elections have gradually been constitutionalized and therefore in some degree nationalized. The FIFTEENTH AMENDMENT prohibits the states from impairing the franchise on the basis of race, color, or previous condition of servitude. The NINETEENTH AMENDMENT forbids discrimination in electoral qualification based on sex; and the TWENTY-FOURTH AMENDMENT prevents the states from imposing "any poll tax or other tax" as a condition of voting for a candidate for federal office. The TWENTY-SIXTH AMENDMENT effectively grants the right to vote to all eligible citizens at eighteen years of age.

In the modern era, the right to vote has been declared a "fundamental right" under the FOURTEENTH AMENDMENT, in REYNOLDS V. SIMS (1964), because it is "preservative of other basic civil and political rights." The Supreme Court has therefore declared, in KRAMER V. UNION FREE SCHOOL DISTRICT (1969) and HARPER V. VIRGINIA BOARD OF ELECTIONS (1966), that every classification defining the right to vote in elections must be subject to strict judicial scrutiny and can be sustained only by independent judicial examination which finds "important," "compelling," or "overriding" state interests justifying restrictions on voting rights.

Mayo has argued that elections effectively promote democracy only if two conditions obtain. First, there must be "political equality in which [each] person should have one vote . . . and each vote should count equally." Second, citizens must have the "freedom to oppose," consisting of "formal rules . . . of effective choice—secret ballot, freedom to run for office, and freedom to speak, assemble, and organize for political purposes." It is these conditions

for effective elections that the Supreme Court has generally promoted by declaring the vote a fundamental right and by rejecting poll taxes, residence requirements of extended duration, race and sex qualifications, limits on campaign spending, wide deviations from the ONE PERSON, ONE VOTE principle, and impediments to candidacy that significantly narrow voters' choices.

DAVID ADAMANY
(1986)

(SEE ALSO: *Brown v. Socialist Workers '74 Campaign Committee.*)

Bibliography

MAYO, HENRY B.   1960   *An Introduction to Democratic Theory.* New York: Oxford University Press.

NOTE   1975   Developments in the Law—Elections. *Harvard Law Review* 88:1111–1339.

ELECTORAL COLLEGE

The Electoral College was hurriedly improvised by the Framers to placate all factions, provide a mechanism for electing GEORGE WASHINGTON, and leave hard questions for the states to resolve after Washington's retirement. Yet it turned out, unexpectedly, to be the forming and sustaining mold of the American party system.

At conception, the College was partly democratic and responsive to the large states, partly aristocratic and answerable to small states. It was apportioned mostly by population, with a delegate for each congressman and senator, and a state could select its delegates in any way it pleased. The Framers seem to have expected that, after Washington, the delegates—acting deliberatively or as agents of state legislatures—would normally fail to muster a majority for one candidate, and that most elections would be settled in the House of Representatives, with one vote per state.

This happened only in 1824, when the House chose JOHN QUINCY ADAMS over ANDREW JACKSON, the frontrunner in popular and electoral votes. In 1800 the House also elected THOMAS JEFFERSON, who tied with his running mate AARON BURR in the Electoral College. This deadlock led to the adoption of the TWELFTH AMENDMENT, which separated the votes for President and vice-president and gave the College its essential modern written constitutional constraints.

In the same decades, the College acquired two powerful unwritten constraints: party control and unit vote. Party control originated in congressional nominating caucuses in 1796 and shifted to state and national nominating conventions during the 1830s. It ended the notion of unbound, deliberative delegates seeking "continental" leadership. POLITICAL PARTIES, not delegates, did the deliberation.

The unit vote, chosen by all but one state by 1836, delivered each state's delegation as a unit to the winner of its popular vote. Unit voting already prevailed in the House and in most state elections, but the Electoral College gave it its widest leverage. It is kind to winners, hard on second parties, and almost prohibitive of third parties. It forces competition for shiftable votes, and it rewards inclusive, center-seeking, accommodational parties (and groups) while discouraging narrow, ideological, exclusive ones. Many scholars believe that the American two-party system has its roots in the unit vote and its taproot in the Electoral College.

The College has prompted two complaints, both largely, but not wholly, theoretical. It might elect as President an "unrepresentative" candidate who had won a minority of the popular vote or had been chosen deliberatively by "unfaithful" delegates, or who was chosen by a House manipulated by splinter groups. Or it might favor some voters against others: urban against rural, liberal against conservative, North against South, or large state against small. Yet we have had only two clear minority Presidents (RUTHERFORD B. HAYES and BENJAMIN HARRISON), one House-chosen President (John Quincy Adams), no Presidents chosen by the rare, unfaithful delegate, and no constitutional crisis over any of these contretemps.

The College was once thought to favor "pivotal" large-state over small-state voters, and hence urban, liberal over rural, conservative interests, but political change and closer analysis have qualified this impression. Liberals who defended the College in the 1950s fought unsuccessfully to abolish it in favor of direct election, in the 1960s and 1970s.

Any of the major reform proposals—direct election, proportional representation by state, and election by congressional district—arguably would change outcomes of close elections. JOHN F. KENNEDY would have lost the 1960 election, with the same votes cast, under the proportional or district systems. But surely the same vote would not have been cast, for any alternative system would have changed voting and campaign strategies. The district system might have given more weight to rural voters, the direct or proportional systems to third parties. Changes in the party system in either case could have been profound.

These complexities may explain why Congress, which considers proposing an amendment to abolish the Electoral College after most close elections, has never actually done so. The Supreme Court has been likewise acquiescent, upholding state delegate allocations against all challenges and refusing, in *Delaware v. New York* (1966), to hear Delaware's complaint that New York voters had 2.3 times better odds of affecting the outcome of a presidential election.

WARD E. Y. ELLIOTT
(1986)

Bibliography

CEASER, JAMES W.   1979   *Presidential Selection: Theory and Development.* Princeton, N.J.: Princeton University Press.

ELLIOTT, WARD E. Y.   1975   *The Rise of Guardian Democracy: The Supreme Court's Role in Voting Rights Disputes, 1845–1969.* Cambridge, Mass.: Harvard University Press.

PIERCE, NEAL R.   1968   *The People's President: The Electoral College in American History and the Direct-Vote Alternative.* New York: Simon & Schuster.

ELECTORAL DISTRICTING, I

The number of members to be elected to a given legislative body and the voting rule by which that body will be chosen are commonly laid down in statute. The United States, like most democratic nations of the world, elects representatives from geographically defined election districts. At issue are the election method, the criteria for drawing district lines (or GERRYMANDERING), specifying who will actually do the redistricting, and the nature of legal and/or administrative review of redistricting choices.

In the United States most elections are conducted under the rule that the candidate receiving the greatest number of votes will be chosen. Congressional elections now take place in single-member districts, but this practice has not always been uniform. Prior to 1842, the smaller states commonly elected members to Congress in at-large elections with entire states as the electorate. At both the state and local level, at-large and multimember district elections in areas of high minority concentration have come under increasing challenge as dilutive of minority voting rights as a result of litigation brought under the VOTING RIGHTS ACT OF 1965 (as Amended in 1982) or directly under the EQUAL PROTECTION clause of the FOURTEENTH AMENDMENT to the Constitution. Both the proportion of states using multimember districts for state legislative elections and the proportion of cities using at-large elections have declined over the past several decades.

In the overwhelming majority of states the legislative body itself is responsible for drawing new plans (usually after the decennial CENSUS). In most states the governor has VETO POWER over state and congressional plans. In some states, legislative or congressional districting is entrusted to nonpartisan or bipartisan commissions.

Many criteria have been proposed to guide districting in the United States and multiple and potentially conflicting "reasonable" goals can be advocated for redistricting decisionmaking. The exercise of state redistricting authority is subject to JUDICIAL REVIEW under federal standards involving Article I, section 2; the equal protection clause of the Fourteenth Amendment; the FIFTEENTH AMENDMENT; and the Voting Rights Act of 1965 (as amended); as well as by state courts acting exclusively in terms of state law issues. Until 1993, redistricting case law appeared to be a largely settled area, with no real changes from the 1980s to the 1990s apparent in terms of "ONE PERSON, ONE VOTE" or vote dilution standards. That situation changed dramatically when the Supreme Court decided SHAW V. RENO (1993) and its progeny and brought turmoil into the area of race-related districting.

It is convenient to divide proposed districting criteria into three categories: (1) formal (e.g., one person, one vote; compactness; contiguity), (2) racial, and (3) political. In the racial and political categories, we can usefully further distinguish between criteria that focus on intent and those that focus on the outcomes (or anticipated outcomes) of the redistricting process. It is also useful to differentiate different criteria for districting according to their legal derivations and legal force. In this analysis, "primary" criteria are mandated by the Constitution. "Secondary" criteria are those that derive explicitly from state constitutional provisions or from federal statutes. "Tertiary" criteria are those that, in a particular instance, derive their force from being implicitly embedded in state or local statute. "Supplementary" criteria, finally, are those that have no legal sanction in constitution or statute, whatever may be their moral force or the normative arguments in their favor.

Primary criteria must be satisfied by any redistricting plan. Lower-order criteria cannot, of course, override the primary criteria of the federal Constitution. It is important, however, to recognize that the status of any particular criterion as secondary, tertiary, or supplemental will vary with the particular legal context (e.g., from state to state, locality to locality). Moreover, the binding force of any particular criterion will vary with the nature of the constitutional or statutory language concerning its use. Some criteria may be lexicographically ordered. Some may be specified to apply only to the extent that they do not come into conflict with other criteria of higher or coordinate status.

The most important of the primary districting criteria is the one person, one vote standard derived from the Fourteenth Amendment (for state and local legislative bodies) and from Article I (for the U.S. HOUSE OF REPRESENTATIVES). The Court has taken a two-pronged approach to operationalizing the one person, one vote standard. For state and local bodies, plans where the maximum deviation from strict population equality is less than 10 percent are generally considered to be prima facie valid and some plans with even higher deviations have been approved. In

contrast, for the U.S. House, one person, one vote has been interpreted to require that deviations be reduced to the greatest extent feasible, and this has led the Court to reject congressional plans with even minuscule population deviations.

Almost all academic commentators on the one person, one vote cases have expressed the view that a zero-deviation-tolerance standard for congressional districting makes no sense, given measurement errors in the underlying census data and the reality that the decennial U.S. census provides only a snapshot of a constantly changing population. Moreover, an undue insistence on numerical equality substantially interferes with the implementation of other districting criteria.

The next most important primary districting criterion is the equal protection standard for the REPRESENTATION of various types of minority groupings. This standard has been instantiated in different ways for different types of groups.

For POLITICAL PARTY supporters, the test laid down in *Davis v. Bandemer* (1986) seems to invalidate only virtual exclusion of a group from the political process and/or electoral success. However, there is considerable dispute as to how to interpret the *Bandemer* test. What can be said is that only one of the post-*Bandemer* challenges to plans as being unconstitutional partisan gerrymanders has proved successful, and the facts of that successful challenge are so unusual that it is hard to extrapolate from that case to others. Thus, for all intents and purposes, *Bandemer* appears not to be influential.

For racial groups (and certain other ethnic groups designated for special protection by the Voting Rights Act), at minimum, the equal protection standard requires that there be no "retrogression" in racial representation other than what would occur on the basis of demographic shifts in underlying populations.

In 1993, in *Shaw*, with further clarifications in subsequent cases such as MILLER V. JOHNSON (1995), the Court laid down a new constitutional test: plans may not use race as their predominant or exclusive criterion. We will need to wait until the post-2000 districting cases to see how the *Shaw* test is to be reconciled with the nonretrogression test and with the most important of the secondary redistricting criteria—the need to avoid "minimizing or canceling out the vote" of the racial and ethnic groups protected under the Voting Rights Act.

In states covered in whole or in part by section 5 of the Voting Rights Act, the Voting Rights Section of the Civil Rights Division of the U.S. Department of Justice (DOJ) must verify that proposed plans "do not have the purpose and will not have the effect of denying or abridging the right to vote." If DOJ is not convinced, it can deny preclearance, which voids the plan unless the DOJ decision be reversed by the U.S. District Court for the District of Columbia—something that in the 1980s and 1990s almost never happened. In any districting situation, litigation can also be brought to challenge a plan as a "dilution" under the standards laid down in the 1982 amendments to section 2 of the Voting Rights Act as interpreted in *Thornburg v. Gingles* (1986).

Other secondary criteria may be embedded in state constitutions, such as language about contiguity and/or compactness of districts. Tertiary criteria may be found in a bill enacting a districting plan and stating the criteria that the proposed plan is supposed to have followed, such as respecting political subunit boundaries to the extent feasible or nonfragmentation of "communities of interest." Even when such criteria are not explicitly mentioned they may serve as a test for whether a plan is one in which race was not the sole or preponderant criterion. Other criteria, such as minimizing change from previous district lines, although not in any way mandated, have been held to be permissible by courts.

BERNARD GROFMAN
(2000)

(SEE ALSO: *Voting Rights.*)

Bibliography

DAVIDSON, CHANDLER and GROFMAN, BERNARD 1994 *The Quiet Revolution in the South: The Impact of the Voting Right Act, 1965–1990.* Princeton, N.J.: Princeton University Press.

GROFMAN, BERNARD 1983 "Criteria for Districting: A Social Science Perspective." *UCLA Law Review* 33:77–184.

GROFMAN, BERNARD, ed. 1990 *Political Gerrymandering and the Courts.* New York: Agathon Press.

GROFMAN, BERNARD; HANDLEY, LISA; and NIEMI, RICHARD 1992 *Minority Representation and the Quest for Voting Equality.* New York and London: Cambridge University Press.

ELECTORAL DISTRICTING, II

The constitutional guidelines governing federal electoral districting require that federal representatives be apportioned among the states "according to their respective Numbers," that representatives not exceed one for every thirty thousand persons, that every state have at least one representative, and that federal district boundaries not cross state lines.

Originally, the Constitution made few demands on states in the conduct of their electoral districting practices and for good reason. As JAMES MADISON and ALEXANDER HAMILTON highlighted in THE FEDERALIST Nos. 52 and 59, electoral practices and procedures were highly political in nature, subject to a variety of considerations in every state, and would not lend themselves to a uniform rule of res-

olution. It made little sense to provide more than the minimum required in the constitutional text, because additional restrictions were impractical and arguably unnecessary. Hamilton added that had the Constitution introduced an authority in the federal government to regulate state elections, this would have been immediately denounced as an unwarranted transposition of power and a premeditated attempt to destroy state governments.

In the early 1960s, the Supreme Court ignored Hamilton's and Madison's admonitions—and perhaps the Constitution itself—imposing new and unparalleled restrictions on state and federal districting. The circumstances—disproportionate legislative districts that frequently imposed a rural stranglehold on state and congressional elections—may have justified judicial intervention. In BAKER V. CARR (1962), the Court ruled that REAPPORTIONMENT issues were no longer POLITICAL QUESTIONS best left to the political departments of government to resolve but could be reviewed by the judiciary for potential constitutional violations. One year later the Court established the ONE PERSON, ONE VOTE rule, and two years later the Court mandated equipopulous districts for congressional elections and for both houses of state legislatures.

The one person, one vote decisions raised a host of problems for electoral districting. First, how precise was the numerical equality required by the equipopulous districts requirement? In 1983 the ineluctable logic of one person, one vote was used by the Court to strike down a New Jersey congressional districting scheme in which the difference between the largest and smallest districts was less than 0.7 percent. Justice BYRON R. WHITE, dissenting, proclaimed that it suspended credulity to believe that such a trifling deviation from absolute population equality somehow detracted from "fair and effective" REPRESENTATION, the touchstone in reapportionment and redistricting cases. Yet the New Jersey ruling was consistent with the assumption throughout the reapportionment cases: that equal representation meant equally populated districts. Once this identification had been made, such exacting demands on population equality were the natural, if perhaps austere, consummation of the earlier reapportionment case law.

The one person, one vote rule formalized the reapportionment process, employing a standard that was easy to quantify but that failed to account for other factors that might create voting inequalities: the influence of POLITICAL PARTIES, money, and INTEREST GROUPS, in addition to GERRYMANDERING, multimember districts, and bloc voting. If voters had a right to effective representation, as the Court had declared in the reapportionment cases, was the Court not obliged to account for these electoral inequalities as well? This second problem evades resolution because it is impossible to distribute political power in such a way as not to advantage or disadvantage one group while attempting to accommodate another.

In the context of racial and ethnic minorities, the courts and federal government have attempted to provide effective representation by generally mandating that jurisdictions dismantle multimember or at-large districts and create some majority-minority single-member districts. Again, the intractable nature of the politics of representation arises here, for it is by no means clear that minorities are more effectively represented when packed into districts in which minority-preferred candidates may be elected than when they are spread out through a number of districts in which their influence may be broader, even if their preferred candidates are not elected.

In the 1990s, the constitutional requirement of equipopulous districts, the sophisticated districting technology available, and the demand by the U.S. Department of Justice that states covered by the VOTING RIGHTS ACT OF 1965 create majority-minority districts in proportion to the minority populations in the jurisdictions covered, combined to create bizarrely shaped racially gerrymandered districts in a number of states. These districts were successfully challenged on EQUAL PROTECTION grounds in SHAW V. RENO (1993) AND ITS PROGENY, where the Court held that districts in which race was the predominant factor motivating the creation of their boundaries were unconstitutional.

Ironically, the equal protection clause from which the right to effective representation derived, a right incorporated into the Voting Rights Act, has now been used successfully to attack the very race-conscious districting that was intended to promote effective representation. The difficult question that courts and the other branches of government will have to resolve in the future is how to reconcile the now reasserted individual rights protected by the equal protection clause with the group or interest-based rights underlying effective representation.

ANTHONY A. PEACOCK
(2000)

Bibliography

CORTNER, RICHARD C. 1970 *The Apportionment Cases.* Knoxville:University of Tennessee Press.

ELLIOTT, WARD E. Y. 1974 *The Rise of Guardian Democracy: The Supreme Court's Role in Voting Rights Disputes, 1845–1969.* Cambridge, Mass.: Harvard University Press.

GROFMAN, BERNARD N. and DAVIDSON, CHANDLER, eds. 1992 *Controversies in Minority Voting: The Voting Rights Act in Perspective.* Washington, D.C.: The Brooking Institution.

PEACOCK, ANTHONY A., ed. 1997 *Affirmative Action and Representation:* Shaw v. Reno *and the Future of Voting Rights.* Durham, N.C.: Carolina Academic Press.

RUSH, MARK E. 1993 *Does Redistricting Make a Difference? Partisan Representation and Electoral Behavior.* Baltimore, Maryland: Johns Hopkins University Press.

SCHER, RICHARD K.; MILLS, JON L.; and HOTALING, JOHN J. 1996 *Voting Rights and Democracy: The Law and Politics of Districting.* Chicago: Nelson-Hall Publishers.

SWAIN, CAROL M. 1993 *Black Faces, Black Interests: The Representation of African Americans in Congress.* Cambridge, Mass.: Harvard University Press.

THERNSTROM, ABIGAIL M. 1987 *Whose Votes Count? Affirmative Action and Minority Voting Rights.* Cambridge, Mass.: Harvard University Press.

ELECTORAL DISTRICTING, FAIRNESS, AND JUDICIAL REVIEW

Democratic governance requires that governors be accountable to the voters. As political thinkers from Condorcet to Kenneth Arrow have noted, however, the will of the voters can only be determined through institutional channels that imperfectly reflect the electorate's preferences. Those institutional channels are controlled by incumbent officials who, unfortunately, have every incentive to resist change that may threaten their sinecure. The Constitution responds to this problem only partially by requiring a population-based apportionment of the Congress every ten years, but saying little else about the mechanisms for selecting governors.

Even the limited apportionment constraint is not self-executing. For example, the 1920 CENSUS revealed that, for the first time, a majority of the population was found in urban areas and was concentrated in the manufacturing centers of the North and Midwest. The incumbent Congress simply refused to reapportion itself out of office and the constitutional command of REAPPORTIONMENT was disregarded for an entire decade. The same pattern was repeated in most states, despite comparable state constitutional commands for apportioning legislative seats. By the time of the reapportionment cases of the 1960s, disparities in the population base of state legislative districts exceeded 40 to 1.

In COLEGROVE V. GREEN (1946), Justice FELIX FRANKFURTER, writing for a plurality of the Supreme Court, forbade any judicial intervention lest the courts be dragged into the "political thicket" of apportionment. Despite the Court's invocation of institutional limitations, no other actor could address the maldistribution of political opportunity. The election of federal and state legislatures was contaminated by malapportionment and officials so elected saw no gain in disrupting a beneficial status quo. State courts proved as unresponsive as the Supreme Court, leaving underrepresented voters no channel through which to wrest back political power.

The stalemate ended abruptly with the landmark cases

of BAKER V. CARR (1962) and REYNOLDS V. SIMS (1964) which, in turn, rejected the POLITICAL QUESTION doctrine and announced the ONE PERSON, ONE VOTE rule of apportionment. Together with their companion cases of the early 1960s, *Baker* and *Reynolds* quickly undid the most visible and egregious affront to fair distribution of political opportunity. The sweep of these cases cannot be underestimated: the reapportionment cases were arguably the most far-reaching pronouncement of JUDICIAL REVIEW since the first enunciation of that power in MARBURY V. MADISON (1803). Within only a few years, the system of REPRESENTATION in virtually every state in the country had been radically overhauled under an exercise of judicial power that was as popularly accepted as it was effective.

While malapportionment was the visible target, the reapportionment cases introduced a more substantive concern with what *Reynolds* termed "the achieving of fair and effective representation for all citizens." The early reapportionment cases reveal a fundamental concern that control over the redistricting process could distort the outcomes of a legitimate electoral process. In the first blush of its reapportionment revolution, the Court entertained the idea that numerical equality could guarantee fundamental political fairness. Over the next two decades, that illusion fell victim to computer-driven GERRYMANDERING through which partisan aims could be achieved consistent with the equipopulation principle. The legacy of *Baker* and *Reynolds* was a readily JUSTICIABLE one person, one vote principle that served as a mild constraint on partisan distortions of the political process. The promise to deliver a broader conception of "political fairness" was largely unrealized.

The limits of that legacy were apparent in *Karcher v. Daggett* (1983), a clear partisan gerrymander of New Jersey that was, at bottom, faithful to the equipopulation principle. The Court refused to undertake a more searching inquiry into political fairness, and instead struck down the plan under an absolutist requirement of numerical exactness among districts—even though the population deviations involved were less than the margin of error of the underlying census numbers.

In *Davis v. Bandemer* (1986), the Court finally unmoored the issue of political fairness from numerical malapportionment by creating an independent constitutional cause of action for partisan gerrymandering. However, the Court's evidentiary standard of proving "consistent degradation" of political opportunity has proven impossible to meet in light of the limited number of elections available within the decennial redistricting cycle. Unlike *Baker*, whose Delphic musings were quickly followed by the easily applied one person, one vote standard of *Reynolds*, *Bandemer* has yielded no progeny capable of operationalizing its efforts to constrain excesses of partisan manip-

ulation of the political process. The unenforceability of *Bandemer* stands in marked contrast to the more aggressive enforcement of the prohibition on racial gerrymandering under equally uncertain constitutional standards, as evidenced by SHAW V. RENO (1993) and its progeny.

The Court's elusive search for appropriate judicial review of political fairness hesitates between the need to police abuses in the political order and uncertainty over how to avoid unseemly judicial immersion in pure politics. So far, the Court has resisted the appeal of Justice JOHN PAUL STEVENS to a uniform albeit complex test for self-serving dealing that focuses on procedural irregularities and outward appearances of improper consideration. Perhaps inspired by the ready application of the equipopulation principle, the Court appears stuck awaiting the next appearance of an easily applied justiciable standard.

SAMUEL ISSACHAROFF
(2000)

Bibliography

ISSACHAROFF, SAMUEL 1993 Judging Politics: The Elusive Quest for Judicial Review of Political Fairness. *Texas Law Review* 71:1643–1703.

ISSACHAROFF, SAMUEL; KARLAN, PAMELA S.; and PILDES, RICHARD H. 1998 *The Law of Democracy.* New York: Foundation Press.

KARLAN, PAMELA S. 1996 Cousins' Kin: Justice Stevens and Voting Rights. *Rutgers Law Journal* 27:521–541.

KLARMAN, MICHAEL J. 1997 Majoritarian Judicial Review: The Entrenchment Problem. *Georgetown Law Review* 85:491–553.

ELECTORAL PROCESS AND THE FIRST AMENDMENT

Prior to 1890, political activity in the United States was generally unregulated. By 1990, however, government regulation of the electoral process extended to CAMPAIGN FINANCE, BALLOT ACCESS, candidate speech, and regulation of POLITICAL PARTY affairs. This regulation is motivated by a variety of perceived problems, including negative campaigning and the influence of large campaign donors, and by the need for orderly elections.

Although the extent to which the FIRST AMENDMENT covers COMMERCIAL SPEECH or PORNOGRAPHY has long been a topic of debate, there has been virtually unanimous agreement that political speech and association is at the core of the First Amendment, and so entitled to the highest level of protection. Regulation of the electoral process, almost by definition, implicates this speech and association.

First Amendment problems are obvious when the state seeks to prohibit candidates who express certain views from running for office, as in *Communist Party v. Whitcomb* (1974), striking down a requirement that candidates take a LOYALTY OATH, or when LEGISLATION directly limits political speech, as in *Mills v. Alabama* (1966), striking down a ban on election-day newspaper editorials. For similar reasons, proposals to ban negative campaign ads have been constitutional nonstarters.

However, electoral regulation can also raise less obvious First Amendment concerns. For example, the FREEDOM OF ASSOCIATION means little if the state refuses to grant a party a place on the ballot. Such regulation can be necessary to provide for orderly elections, but there is evidence, such as *Williams v. Rhodes* (1968), that these laws have also been used to reduce political competition and to prevent unpopular views from gaining a public hearing.

Rights of association can also be infringed by regulation of political parties' internal affairs. Parties are intimately woven into the electoral law of many states, yet remain voluntary, private associations, not state agencies. The Supreme Court has found it difficult to balance these roles, but in the 1980s and 1990s issued several decisions striking down, on freedom of association grounds, state efforts to regulate party affairs.

The clash between free speech and the regulatory impulse is most troublesome in the field of campaign finance. Large contributions to candidates raise concerns of both political equality and corruption. But, as the Court recognized in BUCKLEY V. VALEO (1976), limits on political contributions and spending have the effect of limiting political speech, and so can be justified only by the most COMPELLING STATE INTEREST.

Ultimately, efforts to curtail the influence of private spending on political campaigns may be futile. By the 1990s many politically active groups were bypassing candidates' campaigns completely, choosing instead to run advertisements that discussed candidates' positions on issues, often in harsh or glowing terms, but which stopped short of specifically endorsing or opposing a candidate. Because these "issue ads" can influence election results, numerous proposals have been made to restrict them. But the Court struck down such limits in *Buckley*, noting that the discussion of issues is perhaps the most vital part of the First Amendment, and that the distinction between discussion of candidates and discussion of issues often dissolves in practice. Candidates both campaign on, and are identified with, issues.

By 1997, some had become so frustrated with the constitutional restraints on campaign finance regulation that the U.S. SENATE considered a constitutional amendment to allow greater restrictions on issues ads and private campaign donations. But such restrictions would have the odd result, in many situations, of leaving overtly political speech with less protection than commercial speech, NUDE DANCING, or FLAG DESECRATION. Absent such an amendment, the Court has shown little inclination to move in that direction.

BRADLEY A. SMITH
(2000)

Bibliography

LOWENSTEIN, DANIEL H. 1993 Associational Rights of Major Political Parties: A Skeptical Inquiry. *Texas Law Review* 71: 1741–1792.
POLSBY, DANIEL D. 1976 *Buckley v. Valeo:* The Special Nature of Political Speech. *Supreme Court Review* 1976:1–47.
SMITH, BRADLEY A. 1991 Judicial Protection of Ballot Access Rights. *Harvard Journal of Legislation* 28:167–217.
—— 1997 Money Talks: Speech, Corruption, Equality, and Campaign Finance. *Georgetown Law Journal* 86:45–99.
SUNSTEIN, CASS R. 1992 Free Speech Now. Pages 255–316 in Cass R. Sunstein and Richard A. Epstein, eds., *The Bill of Rights in the Modern State*. Chicago: University of Chicago Press.

ELECTRONIC EAVESDROPPING

A Constitution written in the eighteenth century does not easily accommodate events and developments two centuries later. This has been especially true of the FOURTH AMENDMENT guarantee against unreasonable SEARCHES AND SEIZURES. Originally designed to deal with British soldiers breaking into buildings to search for smuggled goods under overly broad GENERAL WARRANTS, in this century it has had to deal with electronic eavesdropping. In 1928 Justice LOUIS D. BRANDEIS, dissenting in OLMSTEAD V. UNITED STATES, observed that " WRITS OF ASSISTANCE and GENERAL WARRANTS are but puny instruments of tyranny and oppression when compared with wiretapping." Today, there are surveillance devices far more penetrating and efficient than wiretapping, such as tiny microphones that catch the softest utterance hundreds of feet away; pen registers that record telephone numbers; "beepers" that trace movements over miles and for days; and electronic intensifiers that permit photography in almost complete darkness. Continuing advances in miniaturization and surveillance technology will produce even more intrusive and undetectable devices.

At first, the Supreme Court refused to apply any of the BILL OF RIGHTS to these technologies. The FIRST AMENDMENT ramifications were emphasized by Justice Brandeis in his *Olmstead* dissent when he pointed out the link between freedom of expression and invasions of personal security, a link established as early as the WILKES CASES (1763–1770), the first great English cases establishing the right of personal security against governmental intrusion. The *Olmstead* majority did not even mention the First

Amendment, however, and that silence continues—the First Amendment has played an insignificant role in constitutional analyses of electronic surveillance, although in UNITED STATES V. UNITED STATES DISTRICT COURT (1972) the Supreme Court did address First Amendment considerations relevant to domestic NATIONAL SECURITY intelligence surveillance. In *Olmstead* the Fifth Amendment was explicitly ruled inapplicable, and electronic surveillance was held not to be a form of compelled self-incrimination. That ruling has been reaffirmed in cases such as HOFFA V. UNITED STATES (1966).

It is the Fourth Amendment that has become the primary constitutional instrument for control of electronic surveillance, and even that development was delayed some forty years. In 1928, the Supreme Court ruled in *Olmstead*, over dissents by Justices Brandeis and OLIVER WENDELL HOLMES, that the Fourth Amendment was limited to physical intrusions on property (TRESPASSES) that "seized" material objects, not intangible conversations. *Olmstead* was gradually eroded in the 1950s and 1960s, particularly with respect to conversations. The trespass aspect of *Olmstead* remained applicable, however, until 1967, when KATZ V. UNITED STATES extended Fourth Amendment protection to conversations and other things that people reasonably expect to keep private.

During the forty years between *Olmstead* and *Katz*, electronic surveillance was not left completely uncontrolled, however. Although the trespass requirement produced the ruling in *Goldman v. United States* (1942) that a room microphone placed against the outside of a wall did not violate the Fourth Amendment, telephone wiretapping itself was held to be prohibited by section 605 of the COMMUNICATIONS ACT of 1934, and this prohibition was applied to both federal and state law enforcement officers in NARDONE V. UNITED STATES (1937) and *Benanti v. United States* (1955). New York State also established statutory procedures for regulating electronic surveillance.

Empirical studies of wiretapping prior to 1968 showed that the controls established by these laws were ineffective. The Justice Department construed section 605 so narrowly that it was rarely invoked; judicial supervision of state wiretapping was virtually nonexistent. In addition, two forms of wiretapping and bugging remained completely uncontrolled: national security wiretapping, done pursuant to presidential directives; and surveillance with the consent of one of the parties to the conversation.

As to national security surveillances, the FEDERAL BUREAU OF INVESTIGATION (FBI) installed over 7,000 wiretaps and room microphones during 1940–1960, and one treasury agent additionally admitted to having installed over 10,000 wiretaps and microphones between 1934 and 1948; other federal agencies also did electronic eavesdropping.

Although all of these intrusions were purportedly for national security purposes, many were revealed to be for crime control or political purposes, the most notorious of which was the massive electronic surveillance of MARTIN LUTHER KING, JR., between 1963 and 1968 ordered by FBI Director J. EDGAR HOOVER.

Consent surveillance, either on a telephone extension or with informers equipped with secret radio transmitters or recorders, is probably the most widely practiced type of electronic surveillance, although so much of electronic surveillance remains secret that one cannot be certain. The Supreme Court had consistently held, before and after the *Katz* decision, that under both the Constitution and the Communications Act, consent surveillance is free from virtually all constitutional or statutory controls. Leading cases on this point include ON LEE V. UNITED STATES (1952) and UNITED STATES V. WHITE (1971). The only federal restriction prior to 1968 was a very limited rule of the Federal Communications Commission barring secret recordings.

Ever since the 1937 *Nardone* decision, the Justice Department had sought authority for electronic surveillance. This effort gained impetus from Attorney General ROBERT F. KENNEDY's campaign against organized crime in 1961–1963 and the revelation that FBI Director Hoover had illegally installed hundreds of taps and bugs on alleged organized crime figures under the "national security" authority, many of which stayed in place for many years; the disclosure of these surveillances placed scores of convictions in jeopardy. With the Court's decisions in BERGER V. NEW YORK (1967) and *Katz*, the stage was set for congressional action. In these two decisions the Court discarded the "trespass" requirement imposed by *Olmstead*, ruled that electronic surveillance was subject to Fourth Amendment requirements, and set out relatively detailed requirements for a valid statute, including: (1) a specification and detailed description of the place to be searched, the conversations to be overheard, and the crime under investigation; (2) a limit on the period of intrusion; and (3) adequate NOTICE of the eavesdropping to the people overheard.

Six months after *Katz*, Congress passed the OMNIBUS CRIME CONTROL AND SAFE STREETS ACT (1968), Title III of which legitimated electronic surveillance for law enforcement purposes. The statute provides that electronic surveillance of conversations is prohibited, upon pain of a substantial jail sentence and fine, except for: (1) law enforcement surveillance under a court order; (2) certain telephone company monitoring to ensure adequate service or to protect company property; (3) surveillance of a conversation where one participant consents to the surveillance; and (4) national security surveillance insofar as it is within the President's inherent constitutional powers, whatever those may be. Law enforcement surveillance must meet certain procedural requirements, which include: (1) an application by a high ranking prosecutor; (2) surveillance for one of the crimes specified in Title III; (3) PROBABLE CAUSE to believe that a crime has occurred, that the target of the surveillance is involved, and that EVIDENCE of that crime will be obtained by the surveillance; (4) a statement indicating that other investigative procedures are ineffective; and (5) an effort to minimize the interception.

A judge must pass on the application and may issue the order and any extensions if the application meets the statutory requirements. Shortly after the surveillance ends, notice must be given of the surveillance to some or all of the persons affected, as the judge decides, unless he agrees to postpone the notice. Illegally obtained evidence may not be used in any official proceedings, and a suit for damages may be brought for illegal surveillance, though a very strong good faith defense is allowed. In addition, the manufacture, distribution, possession, and advertising of devices for electronic surveillance for private use are prohibited.

The legislation is written in terms of federal officials but it also authorizes state surveillance if a state passes a law modeled on the federal statute, though the state may (as have some states, like Connecticut) impose more stringent requirements. More than half the states plus the DISTRICT OF COLUMBIA have passed such statutes, though many rarely use the authority. State surveillance is concentrated in New York, New Jersey, and Florida, mostly for narcotics and gambling offenses.

Title III raised many constitutional issues but almost all have been resolved in its favor. For example, a common contention is that electronic eavesdropping is inherently uncontrollable and necessarily intrudes on vast numbers of innocent people who use phones or rooms under surveillance, thus violating the particularization requirements of the Fourth Amendment. In order to meet this objection, and to avoid turning the surveillance authorization into a general warrant, Title III requires that interceptions be minimized. The Supreme Court, however, made this requirement very easy to meet by its decision in *Scott v. United States* (1978). The lower courts do not impose sanctions for the failure to minimize interception, partly because minimization is often very difficult to achieve or supervise. One federal judge in a major drug case excused the interception of seventy-three calls between a suspect's babysitter and her friends and classmates with the comment that although these conversations were indeed "teenage trivia . . . the eavesdropper, unless possessed of the prescience of a clairvoyant, could hardly predict when they might become

relevant, or when they might be interrupted by an adult with more pressing problems." There are also many cases where police do not minimize interceptions even though they could. For example, some police listen to every conversation, including privileged conversations between lawyers and their clients, but record only those they think appropriate. In one case, it was accidentally revealed that police had recorded all conversations but had prepared a minimized set for use in court. Where room microphones are used, minimizing the interceptions is virtually impossible, especially if the microphones are placed in areas to which the public has access.

The *Berger* case also seemed to require that the interception be limited to specific and quite short time periods. Title III, however, permits thirty-day authorizations on a twenty-four-hour per day basis, with an unlimited number of extensions, and many interceptions remain in continuous operation for many months. The Report on Applications for Orders Authorizing or Approving the Interception of Wire or Oral Communications for 1981, issued by the Administrative Office of the United States Court, indicates that almost half the 106 federal interceptions reported for 1981 lasted thirty or more days.

One of the most significant ways of enforcing Fourth Amendment requirements is by imposing sanctions for their violation. Imposing these sanctions, of course, requires an awareness by the victim that a search has taken place, and of how it was conducted. With a conventional search, such conditions are easy to meet, but electronic surveillance is surreptitious and may never be discovered. The Supreme Court has therefore insisted that notice of the interception be given to the persons named in the application as targets of the surveillance. The statute, however, permits indefinite postponement of this notice, and this provision, too, has been upheld.

Critics have charged that judicial supervision has been minimal and ineffective, particularly on the state level. At hearings before the National Commission for the Review of Federal and State Laws Relating to Electronic Surveillance, many witnesses lamented the inability or unwillingness of state judges to supervise the process closely.

Passage of the statute, while effectively ending the constitutional debate, has not ended the dispute over the value of electronic eavesdropping. Critics have charged that the device is used almost exclusively for minor crimes involving gambling and drugs; is quite useless for major crimes and especially those involving organized crime, the avowed target of the statute; is very expensive; is largely unsupervised by the judiciary; and has invaded the privacy of millions. For support, they rely on the staff studies of the National Commission. Proponents reply that the technique has produced some very useful results, that many of the problems are those attending any new technique, and that more sophisticated use will produce better results. The opposing views were set out in detail in the Report of the National Commission; over a vigorous minority dissent the majority of the commission supported the use of electronic surveillance under the statute, with some modification.

Two types of surveillance remain uncontrolled by Title III: consent intrusions and national security surveillance. Title III totally exempts interceptions by government officials if an official is a party to the conversation of if there is consent by one of the parties; a private interception that is consented to is also exempt, unless the interception is for the purpose of committing a tortious, criminal, or "other injurious act," the meaning of which is not clear. Several states, however, have imposed more stringent requirements on consent surveillance than the federal statute, such as a warrant, either by statute (California, Georgia) or under their own state constitutions (Alaska, Montana). The Supreme Court, however, continues to rule in cases like *United States v. White* (1971) that consent surveillance does not implicate the Fourth Amendment.

National security surveillance continues to pose difficult constitutional questions. Presidents since FRANKLIN D. ROOSEVELT have claimed inherent executive power to use electronic surveillance to obtain intelligence for national security purposes, and have authorized such intrusions on their own, without prior judicial approval. Most courts have upheld such a power, where national security surveillance involving foreign powers and agents is concerned. But where American citizens or groups are targeted for domestic security purposes, the Supreme Court, in *United States v. United States District Court*, ruled unanimously that the President has no INHERENT POWER to use warrantless electronic surveillance. The Court did suggest that Congress could authorize procedures for domestic intelligence gathering that are less stringent than those of Title III for law enforcement, but so far Congress has not done so.

Intelligence gathering for foreign security purposes is now governed by statute. The 1976 Report of the Senate Select Committee to Study Governmental Operations with Respect to the Intelligence Agencies disclosed massive abuses of executive power to tap telephones and bug rooms for national security purposes, often with the approval of the incumbent President. These abuses included taps on the telephones of National Security Agency advisers authorized by President RICHARD M. NIXON in 1969; on the Los Angeles Chamber of Commerce in 1941; on congressmen in the early 1960s in connection with the "sugar lobby"; and FBI taps and bugs on Martin Luther King, Jr., to find "communist" influence. From 1940 to 1975, the FBI alone installed some 10,000 taps and bugs; the National Security Agency, the Central Intelligence Agency, local police, and many other governmental agencies have also engaged in national security surveillance.

These disclosures resulted in the passage in 1978 of the Foreign Intelligence Surveillance Act, which requires approval from a court for national security surveillances of foreign powers or agents. The President is denied extrastatutory inherent or other power to use electronic surveillance for foreign intelligence within the United States—though not outside—and no Americans may be eavesdropped upon unless their activities have some element of criminality about them. The court operates secretly, and there have been very few published rulings and very little public information about it. The constitutionality of this act and its procedures—which are much less demanding than those under Title III for law enforcement purposes—has been sustained.

The courts have also tried to grapple with other forms of electronic surveillance. In *Smith v. Maryland* (1979) pen registers, which record the telephone numbers called, were held outside Title III and not in conflict with the Fourth Amendment; the Supreme Court concluded that the user has no reasonable expectation of privacy in the numbers called. Electronic signaling devices ("beepers") attached to cars to enable their movements to be traced have also been held to be without Fourth Amendment protection because cars are generally traced while on public streets and highways (*United States v. Knotts, 1983*); if the device is attached to a container or other item that is taken into a private area, however, a warrant and probable cause are required (*United States v. Karo*, 1984).

In 1928, after describing the dangers that the emerging modern technology presented to individual liberty, Justice Brandeis asked, "Can it be that the Constitution affords no protection against such invasions of individual security?" Almost a half century later, it is clear that such protection is available—if the nation wants it.

HERMAN SCHWARTZ
(1986)

(SEE ALSO: *Criminal Justice and Technology*.)

Bibliography

ADMINISTRATIVE OFFICE OF THE UNITED STATES COURTS 1968–1982 *Reports on Applications for Orders Authorizing or Approving the Interception of Wire or Oral Communications.* Washington, D.C.: Administrative Office.

AMERICAN BAR ASSOCIATION PROJECT ON STANDARDS FOR CRIMINAL JUSTICE 1974 *Standards Relating to the Administration of Criminal Justice; Electronic Surveillance.* Pages 33–52. New York: Institute of Judicial Administration.

CARR, JAMES G. 1977 (with 1983 supp.) *The Law of Electronic Surveillance.* New York: Clark Boardman.

NATIONAL COMMISSION FOR THE REVIEW OF FEDERAL AND STATE LAW RELATING TO ELECTRONIC SURVEILLANCE 1976 *Report* and *Staff Studies.* Washington, D.C.: Government Printing Office.

SCHWARTZ, HERMAN 1968 The Legitimation of Electronic Eavesdropping: The Politics of "Law and Order." *Michigan Law Review* 67:455–510.

———— 1977 *Taps, Bugs, and Fooling the People.* New York: Field Foundation.

UNITED STATES CONGRESS, SENATE SELECT COMMITTEE TO STUDY GOVERNMENTAL OPERATIONS WITH RESPECT TO INTELLIGENCE ACTIVITIES 1976 *III Final Report.* 94th Congress, 2d session.

ELEMENTARY AND SECONDARY EDUCATION ACT
79 Stat. 27 (1965)

This first general school aid bill in American history broke an impasse that had long stymied legislation to provide federal moneys to elementary and secondary schools. Previous efforts toward such action had foundered on the question whether EDUCATION was a state, not federal, function; whether segregated school systems should receive federal aid; and whether aid to private as well as public schools would violate the FIRST AMENDMENT's establishment clause. The segregation issue had been settled by the CIVIL RIGHTS ACT OF 1964. The 1964 elections had filled Congress with federal aid advocates untroubled by STATES' RIGHTS issues. The church-state controversy over federal assistance to parochial schools continued but was generally resolved here for the first time.

As passed, the measure, which appealed to the CHILD BENEFIT THEORY, authorized specialized aid to districts with children from low-income families. Private schools would share in aid to some specialized services such as shared-time projects and educational television. The act gave school districts wide discretion in using the federal funds; it required, however, that the funds be used to meet the special needs of educationally deprived children and that private schools be included in any benefit sharing. The act also authorized for five years grants to states for purchase of textbooks and library material, and for funding supplementary community educational services that schools could not provide. It expanded the 1954 Cooperative Research Act, authorizing a five-year program of grants for new research and training in teacher methods, and it provided for grants to strengthen state departments of education.

Despite overwhelming congressional support for the act, critics continued to express constitutional doubts. The use of public funds for books in parochial schools and special educational centers could not be justified, it was argued, because funds would be channeled directly to religious schools. The AMERICAN CIVIL LIBERTIES UNION contended that providing instructional materials and supplementary services to church schools was an unconstitutional subversion of the principle of SEPARATION OF CHURCH AND STATE. In FLAST V. COHEN (1968) the measure was challenged on First Amendment grounds, but the Court did not rule on the constitutional issues in the case.

PAUL L. MURPHY
(1986)

ELEVENTH AMENDMENT

The Eleventh Amendment of the Constitution provides that "the JUDICIAL POWER OF THE UNITED STATES shall not be construed to extend to any suit in law or EQUITY, commenced or prosecuted against one of the United States by citizens of another State, or by citizens or subjects of a foreign State." Congress submitted this amendment, on votes of twenty-three to two in the Senate and eighty-one to nine in the House of Representatives, for ratification in March 1794. By February 1795, the legislatures of three-fourths of the states had ratified, but, because of delays in certification of this action, adoption of the amendment was not proclaimed until 1798.

According to traditional theory the purpose of the amendment was to correct an erroneous interpretation of the Constitution by the Supreme Court. Impetus for the amendment undoubtedly was the unpopular decision in CHISHOLM V. GEORGIA (1793)—one of seven early suits instituted against a state by citizens of other states or by ALIENS. In *Chisholm* the Court, voting 4–1, held that the judicial power of the United States and the JURISDICTION of the Court reached such suits under the provision in Article III extending the federal judicial power to "Controversies between a State and Citizens of another State . . . and between a State . . . and foreign States, Citizens or Subjects."

Although the language of Article III is broad enough to support the *Chisholm* holding, proponents of the theory that the amendment was adopted to correct an error in constitutional interpretation have argued that (1) the doctrine of SOVEREIGN IMMUNITY, exempting the sovereign from unconsented suits, was part of the COMMON LAW heritage at the time the Constitution was adopted, and hence implicitly qualified some delegations of judicial power in Article III; and (2) an understanding to that effect emerged during the ratification debates.

Existence of an implicit common law qualification upon the various delegations of federal judicial power is doubtful, however. While the supposition that the immunity doctrine was already incorporated into American law appears sound, at least some state immunity surely was surrendered under the Constitution. The purpose behind the various delegations of judicial power to the United States was to create a judiciary competent to decide all cases "involving the National peace and harmony." Surrender—rather than retention—of state immunity is consonant with that objective. Nor is the argument that the ratification debates evidenced an understanding that the states would be immune from suit persuasive. While ALEXANDER HAMILTON, JAMES MADISON, and JOHN MARSHALL offered assurances to that effect in reply to Anti-Federalist objections, these objections were not quieted; and other leading Federalists, including EDMUND RANDOLPH and JAMES WILSON—members of the Committee of Detail where most provisions of Article III were drafted—took the contrary view.

While some proponents of the Eleventh Amendment probably understood it to be corrective, the broad support enlisted for its adoption can be better explained in terms of diverse perceptions and objectives. These ranged from the desire of STATES' RIGHTS advocates to repudiate the extravagant nationalism manifested by Federalist justices in their *Chisholm* opinions, to Federalist perceptions that the amendment effected only a relatively insignificant restriction upon part of the DIVERSITY JURISDICTION of the federal judiciary. Experience was accumulating that suit against a state in the Supreme Court was cumbersome and unnecessary for the maintenance of federal supremacy. Moreover, assumption of a major portion of state indebtedness and rapid liquidation of the remainder had allayed a Federalist concern that partially accounted for the original grant of federal judicial power.

Judicial construction of the amendment has been shaped by the view that as a corrective measure, it restored common law sovereign immunity as an implicit qualification upon some grants of judicial power in Article III. As interpreted, the amendment bars any suit against a state, including those raising federal questions, instituted by private plaintiffs, regardless of CITIZENSHIP (*Hans v. Louisiana*, 1890), as well as by foreign states (*Monaco v. Mississippi*, 1934) in federal court. In general, only where another state or the United States is plaintiff, is a state subject to unconsented suit in federal court (*Virginia v. West Virginia*, 1907; *United States v. Mississippi*, 1965). The amendment does not affect Article III rights of a state to institute suits in federal courts, nor does it preclude appeals by private plaintiffs in actions commenced by a state. (See COHENS V. VIRGINIA.)

Although the amendment literally limits the federal judicial power—which, by general rule, may not be modified by consent of the parties—as shorthand for the doctrine of sovereign immunity, it has always been interpreted to permit exercises of Article III powers upon a

state's waiver of immunity from suit in federal court. Such waivers ordinarily must be explicit (EDELMAN V. JORDAN, 1974); however, implied and imputed waivers, although exceptional, are not unknown (*Parden v. Terminal Railway*, 1964).

The amendment imposes an absolute bar against unconsented suits commenced in federal court by private plaintiffs against state governments and their agencies. To this generalization, there is a single but increasingly important exception. Congress, pursuant to its enforcement powers under the FOURTEENTH AMENDMENT, may create federal causes of action against the states and thereby deprive them of immunity (FITZPATRICK V. BITZER, 1976). Whether such authority can be inferred from other powers delegated to the national government has not been settled.

The exemption from suit enjoyed by the states under the amendment does not extend to their political subdivisions nor, in general, to governmental corporations (*Lincoln County v. Luning*, 1890). Of paramount importance in restricting the impact of the amendment is the availability of relief in suits instituted against state officers for acts performed or threatened under color of unconstitutional state legislation. The issues whether and to what extent the amendment bars suits against state officers for official acts have occasioned more litigation under the amendment than any others, and the course traversed by the Court from OSBORN V. BANK OF THE UNITED STATES (1824) through *In re Ayers* (1887) to EX PARTE YOUNG (1908) was tortuous. In some early cases the amendment was held applicable only to suits in which a state was a defendant of record, but this rule was never firmly established. Later cases turned on whether a suit against a state officer was substantially a suit against the state itself. In *Ayers* the Court held that a suit against a state officer is a suit against the state unless the officer's act, if stripped of its official character, constitutes a private wrong; but this rigorous test was abandoned in *Ex parte Young*, a landmark case which, despite its unpopularity at the time, fixed the law for the future. While adhering to the general rule that a suit against a state officer is barred by the amendment if it is substantially against the state itself, the Court adopted the fiction that mere institution of state judicial proceedings by a state officer pursuant to an allegedly unconstitutional statute is a wrong for which federal equitable relief is available. The theoretical difficulties posed by this formulation are grave and many, but in facilitating direct access to the federal courts to test the validity of state legislation, *Young* is of transcendent importance in maintaining federal supremacy and the RULE OF LAW. Adopted as the instrument of judicial protection of the rights of property and enterprise, the *Young* principle today does the same essential service in the protection of personal rights and liberties. Even so, not every act of a state may be reached through suit against its officers. Where such suits are adjudged to be against the state itself—actions affecting the public treasury for past wrongs and those seeking to dispossess the state of property—the Eleventh Amendment remains a bar (*Edelman v. Jordan*, 1974).

CLYDE E. JACOBS
(1986)

(SEE ALSO: *Atascadero State Hospital v. Scanlon; Pennhurst State School & Hospital v. Halderman.*)

Bibliography

JACOBS, CLYDE E.   1972   *The Eleventh Amendment and Sovereign Immunity.* Westport, Conn.: Greenwood Press.
NOWAK, JOHN E.   1975   The Scope of Congressional Power to Create Causes of Action Against State Governments and the History of the Eleventh and Fourteenth Amendments. *Columbia Law Review* 75:1413–1469.

ELEVENTH AMENDMENT
(Update 1)

The Eleventh Amendment is at the center of an important debate about state accountability under federal law. Part of the debate is historical: What was the amendment originally intended to do? Part of the debate concerns modern doctrine: What should the amendment mean today?

Everyone agrees that the Eleventh Amendment was adopted to overturn the result reached by the Supreme Court in CHISHOLM V. GEORGIA (1793). In *Chisholm*, the Court heard a case brought by a citizen of South Carolina against the state of Georgia on a contract. The suit involved no question of federal law. It was brought under a provision of Article III conferring jurisdiction over "Controversies between a State and Citizens of another State." Despite Georgia's claim of SOVEREIGN IMMUNITY from suit, the Court held that Georgia could be compelled to appear.

The amendment provides: "The Judicial power of the United States shall not be construed to extend to any suit in law or equity, commenced or prosecuted against one of the United States by Citizens of another State, or by Citizens or Subjects of any foreign state." The historical debate concerns not whether but how the amendment was intended to overrule *Chisholm*. There are two ways to understand what the adopters of the amendment intended.

The first is to read the amendment as *forbidding* suits brought against states by out-of-state citizens or by foreign citizens or subjects. Under this reading, federal courts cannot take jurisdiction over such suits, even if a federal question is involved. The second is to read the amendment as *repealing* a jurisdiction that had previously been authorized. Under this reading, suits cannot be brought against states by out-of-state citizens or by foreign citizens or subjects merely because of the character of the parties. But if there is any other basis for jurisdiction, such as the existence of a federal question, suits are permitted. Under either reading of the amendment, ADMIRALTY AND MARITIME JURISDICTION is not affected, for the amendment refers only to suits "in law or equity."

The Supreme Court was not forcEd to choose between the two readings of the amendment until after the CIVIL WAR. Eventually, the Court chose to read the amendment as *forbidding* jurisdiction whenever an out-of-stater or a foreigner sued a state, as a way of protecting southern states from suit under the federal CONTRACT CLAUSE after they defaulted on state-issued revenue bonds. The Court then filled in the "missing" term of the amendment by holding in *Hans v. Louisiana* (1890) that the underlying principle of the amendment required that suits by in-staters be forbidden as well. In this century, the Court has further expanded the prohibition of the amendment by reading it to prohibit suits by foreign countries (*Principality of Monaco v. Mississippi*, 1934) and in admiralty (*Ex parte New York, No. 1*, 1921).

In recent years, a number of legal scholars have argued that reading the amendment as only *repealing* the party-based jurisdiction of Article III is historically more accurate. Four Justices of the Supreme Court, led by Justice WILLIAM J. BRENNAN, have shared this view and have argued that modern doctrine should be brought into line with this understanding. In *Pennsylvania v. Union Gas Co.* (1989), however, a majority of the Court refused to incorporate this historical view into modern doctrine.

Although the Court reads the Eleventh Amendment to forbid federal court jurisdiction even when federal law provides the basis for private parties' suits against the states, the prohibition may be avoided or overcome in a number of ways. First, a state may waive its sovereign immunity by a voluntary appearance. As *Edelman v. Jordan* (1974) illustrates, however, a state may raise a sovereign immunity defense for the first time on appeal after having made a voluntary appearance at trial and having lost on the merits of the dispute. Second, the Supreme Court held in *Cohens v. Virginia* (1821) that the Eleventh Amendment does not apply to appeals to the Supreme Court from the state courts. Third, a state's subdivisions are not protected by the amendment. Under the principle enunciated in *Lincoln County v. Luning* (1890) a municipality, county, or school board may be sued in federal court under federal law without regard to the Eleventh Amendment.

Fourth, suit may be brought against a state officer for prospective relief. The foundation case is *Ex parte Young*

(1908), in which the Court permitted an INJUNCTION prohibiting a state officer from acting unconstitutionally. The principle was expanded to permit injunctions ordering affirmative actions by state officials in *Edelman v. Jordan* (1974). But the same decision held that a federal court is forbidden to award monetary relief that will necessarily come out of the state treasury.

Finally, Congress may abrogate the states' sovereign immunity by statutes explicitly so providing. Under an abrogating statute, a state may be sued directly for the retroactive monetary relief otherwise unavailable under *Edelman*. The first case to allow congressional abrogation was *Fitzpatrick v. Bitzer* (1976), which sustained a statute enacted under the FOURTEENTH AMENDMENT. The Court suggested in *City of Rome v. United States* (1980) that statutes passed under the FIFTEENTH AMENDMENT could also abrogate state sovereign immunity. Most recently, the Court sustained an abrogating statute passed under the COMMERCE CLAUSE in *Pennsylvania v. Union Gas* (1989). The combined reach of the Fourteenth Amendment and the commerce clause is such that Congress has considerable freedom to abrogate state sovereign immunity so long as it employs language making its intention clear.

After the Court's decision in *Union Gas*, the debate among the Justices over the original meaning of the amendment may have lost most of its practical significance. Under current doctrine there appears to be no significant constraint on the power of Congress to authorize suit against the states, beyond the limitations inherent in the ENUMERATED POWERS under which Congress has acted. This position is not greatly different from that which would be achieved if the Eleventh Amendment were read as merely repealing party-based jurisdiction, leaving intact FEDERAL QUESTION JURISDICTION for private suits brought under valid federal law. The most important difference is that the present doctrine requires Congress to speak clearly in lifting the states' Eleventh Amendment immunity from suit in federal court.

WILLIAM A. FLETCHER
(1992)

Bibliography

FLETCHER, WILLIAM A.   1983   A Historical Interpretation of the Eleventh Amendment: A Narrow Construction of an Affirmative Grant of Jurisdiction Rather than a Prohibition Against Jurisdiction. *Stanford Law Review* 35:1033–1131.

GIBBONS, JOHN J.   1983   The Eleventh Amendment and State Sovereign Immunity: A Reinterpretation. *Columbia Law Review* 83:1889–2005.

ORTH, JOHN V.   1987   *The Judicial Power of the United States: The Eleventh Amendment in American History*. New York: Oxford University Press.

ELEVENTH AMENDMENT
(Update 2)

The Eleventh Amendment was the first change in the Constitution in response to a Supreme Court decision. In 1793, CHISHOLM V. GEORGIA upheld the Court's ORIGINAL JURISDICTION over an action on a contract by a citizen of South Carolina against the state of Georgia. The Eleventh Amendment, adopted in 1798, responded to that decision. It provides: "The Judicial power of the United States shall not be construed to extend to any suit in law or equity, commenced or prosecuted against one of the United States by Citizens of another State, or by Citizens or Subjects of any Foreign State."

There is substantial disagreement over what this amendment means. The current view of the Court is that *Chisholm* created a "shock of surprise," because it had never been thought that a state could be sued by private persons, and that the amendment was intended to protect states from such suits. This view reads the amendment, though in terms a limitation on federal JURISDICTION, as embodying a doctrine of state SOVEREIGN IMMUNITY. To understand why this reading is controversial, more history is in order.

Pre–CIVIL WAR decisions raised alternative and at times narrow interpretations of the amendment, for example, suggesting a "party of record" rule to avoid a bar when a state as such was not named as defendant, or hinting that the amendment did not apply when jurisdiction was based, not on who the parties were, but on the "arising under federal law" grant of power. By 1890, however, *Hans v. Louisiana* laid the basis for the current view, holding that a federal court could not hear a suit by a Louisiana bondholder against his state on a federal claim of unconstitutional impairment of contract. Even though the Eleventh Amendment by terms prohibited only a limited class of plaintiffs from suing, *Hans* reasoned that the amendment would never have been passed had it been understood to permit claims by in-staters, and that it should be read to provide immunity to a state from a suit by any private person. Later decisions expanded this immunity to include, for example, suits brought by foreign states or suits in ADMIRALTY.

As the activities of modern governments grew and came to overlap, state and local governments increasingly became subject to the substantive reach of federal statutes. Under *Lincoln Co. v. Luning* (1890), local governments are not regarded as "the state" for purposes of the Eleventh Amendment and accordingly can be sued in federal court. In *Parden v. Terminal Railway of Alabama* (1964), the Court, in a 5–4 decision, permitted a federal statutory claim against a state in federal court, arguing that states "surrendered a portion of their sovereignty" in agreeing to Congress's ENUMERATED POWERS and that by participating in the regulated activity (running a railroad) states waived their immunity. Soon the Court modulated its approach, insisting on more explicit "clear statements" to find congressional intent to authorize federal court suits against states or to find state waiver of immunity.

In a significant advance for state accountability under law, *Fitzpatrick v. Bitzer* (1974) upheld Congress's power, when acting to enforce the FOURTEENTH AMENDMENT, to subject states to suit in federal courts. New scholarship began to reexamine the amendment's text and history, arguing that the amendment did not restrain Congress from specifically authorizing suits, based on federal laws, against states. Many concluded that the amendment did not embody a broad principle of state immunity from federal court suit, but rather was a carefully limited repeal of a party-based head of jurisdiction over states, that left intact both FEDERAL QUESTION and admiralty heads of power. This "diversity repeal" view made sense of the limited text of the amendment, of the support for its enactment from both FEDERALISTS and ANTI-FEDERALISTS, and of the Court's subsequent appellate practice in federal question cases coming from the state courts.

In 1989, *Union Gas v. Pennsylvania*, by a 5–4 vote, upheld Congress's power to authorize suits against states under Article I. The PLURALITY OPINION extended the reasoning of *Fitzpatrick* to the COMMERCE CLAUSE, holding that if Congress spoke clearly enough, it could abrogate states' immunity when acting under the commerce clause, a plenary power that also limits state powers. In some tension with other DOCTRINES, the plurality treated the amendment as a limit on the Court's power to construe jurisdictional provisions to abrogate sovereign immunity, but not as a limit on Congress's power to abrogate state sovereign immunity pursuant to its plenary powers. The plurality's rationale would permit congressional abrogation of immunity, if in clear terms, under other Article I provisions. But its reign was short. *Union Gas* was OVERRULED by *Seminole Tribe v. Florida* (1996).

Endorsing *Hans*, *Seminole Tribe*, 5–4, concluded that Congress lacks power under Article I to abrogate states' constitutional immunity from suit. This immunity, merely exemplified by the amendment, protects state treasuries from federal judgments and state sovereignty from the "indignity" of being sued by individuals for any kind of relief. Thus, "[e]ven when the Constitution vests in Congress complete lawmaking authority over a particular area," Congress cannot authorize "suits by private parties against unconsenting states," and a law extending federal jurisdiction to disagreements between tribes and states over gambling on AMERICAN INDIAN reservations was thus

unconstitutional. *Seminole Tribe* distinguished, and thus apparently preserved, Congress's power to abrogate immunity from suit under the Fourteenth Amendment, added to the Constitution after the Eleventh Amendment and designed as an explicit limit on state power.

Under *Seminole Tribe*, it is thus important to determine whether a particular federal statute that subjects states to suits in federal court has been properly enacted under Congress's powers under the FOURTEENTH AMENDMENT, SECTION 5, or instead has been validly enacted only under an Article I power, for example, over INTERSTATE COMMERCE. For it is only under the Fourteenth Amendment (or possibly other post–Civil War amendments) that Congress may have power to create causes of action enforceable against states, as such, without their consent. Since *Seminole Tribe*, lower court decisions have considered whether Congress validly abrogated state immunity in enacting laws concerning, for example, BANKRUPTCY, COPYRIGHT PATENT, minimum wage, AGE DISCRIMINATION, and DISABILITY DISCRIMINATION under the Fourteenth Amendment. In two 1999 decisions, the Court gave a narrow reading to Congress's power under section 5 of the Fourteenth Amendment, holding unconstitutional two different federal remedial statutes authorizing suits against states. In *Florida Prepaid Postsecondary Education Expense Board v. College Savings Bank* (1999), the Court held that, although patents were a form of property protected by the Fourteenth Amendment from state "deprivations" without DUE PROCESS OF LAW, Congress's abrogation of states' immunity from suit for patent infringement was unconstitutional because of the possibility that state remedies would sufficiently compensate the patentholder and thereby provide due process. In *College Savings Bank v. Florida Prepaid Postsecondary Education Expense Board* (1999), the Court held that injuries to a business from unfair competition in violation of the federal Lanham Act were not deprivations of "property interests" for due process purposes and thus Congress had no basis under the Fourteenth Amendment for abrogating states' immunity to such claims. As of this writing, the Court has granted CERTIORARI in a case challenging the constitutionality of the Age Discrimination in Employment Act's abrogation of state immunity.

Eleventh Amendment doctrine does permit mechanisms for affirmative enforcement of federal law other than suits against states in federal courts. The most important of these are EX PARTE YOUNG (1908) actions against state officers for prospective injunctive relief against violations of federal (though not state) law. But while state officers may be sued for damages in their individual capacities, suits against state officers for such "retroactive" relief as accrued monetary liabilities payable from the state treasury are prohibited, as are some suits against state officers involving state interests in property. *Seminole Tribe* preserves the rule that prospective relief against state officers to prevent continuing violations of federal law is generally permitted, though the Court there refused to permit such an action on the somewhat implausible ground that it was impliedly precluded by the federal statute's authorization (held unconstitutional) of suit against the state directly. Whether the *Ex parte Young* doctrine will be substantially narrowed remains to be seen.

Other mechanisms for enforcing federal law against states include suits by the federal government, consented-to suits in state or federal courts, and suits by other states. The Eleventh Amendment does not bar the United States from suing a state. Some federal statutes, for example, the Fair Labor Standards Act, include provisions authorizing suit by the United States with recoveries ultimately payable over to individual beneficiaries. (The constitutionality of "qui tam" actions against states—that is, actions brought by private parties in the name of the United States to recover damages for fraud against the federal government, a portion of which recovery goes to the private party—is before the Court as of this writing.) States are not immune from suits by sister states, so long as the plaintiff state is not suing merely as parens patriae for a small number of private interests. Although the amendment does not apply to a suit against one state in the courts of another under *Nevada v. Hall* (1979), *Alden v. Maine* (1999) holds that states can constitutionally refuse to consent to suits against themselves in their own courts under federal law, thereby substantially limiting the practical availability of relief in state courts.

Finally, unlike other constitutional limits on federal JUDICIAL POWER that cannot be disregarded on the parties' consent, a state can waive its constitutional immunity, consenting to jurisdiction in either federal or state court. However, in *College Savings Bank* the Court overruled *Parden* and held that Congress may not require states to consent to suit as a condition of being permitted to engage in activity subject to regulation under the commerce clause. Such a constructive waiver theory, the Court said, was indistinguishable from abrogation, and the "voluntariness of the waiver [is] destroyed when what is attached to the refusal to waive is the exclusion of the State from otherwise lawful activity." The Court, however, preserved Congress's authority to insist on a consent-to-suit clause in approving bi-state compacts, or as a condition for receiving federal funds.

The recent expansion of states' immunity from federal jurisdiction is in tension with RULE OF LAW ideas spreading elsewhere in the world. While this entry describes the current state of the law, the closely split decisions of the decade beginning in 1989 may foreshadow further uncertainties on the amenability of states to federal court process for enforcement of federal law, particularly considering *Seminole Tribe*'s interaction with other developments in FEDERALISM. For now, the Eleventh Amendment bars Congress from subjecting states to suits in federal court for violations of federal laws enacted under Article I of the Constitution, and limits the relief that may be sought against state officers, and a comparable doctrine of constitutional sovereign immunity protects states from suit on federal claims in their own courts.

Postscript. In *Kimel v. Florida Board of Regents* (2000), the Court held that Congress's attempted abrogation of states' Eleventh Amendment immunity for claims under the Age Discrimination in Employment Act (ADEA) was not constitutional. Application of the ADEA to the states had been upheld as an exercise of commerce clause power in EQUAL EMPLOYMENT OPPORTUNITY COMMISSION (EEOC) V. WYOMING (1983), but *Seminole Tribe* held that Congress lacks power to abrogate sovereign immunity from suit under that clause. The basic question in *Kimel* was whether the ADEA was a valid exercise of Congress's power under the Fourteenth Amendment, section 5, so as to authorize Congress to abrogate the states' immunity from suit. The Court, finding that the ADEA was clearly intended to abrogate the states' immunity, nonetheless held that Congress lacked power to act under the Fourteenth Amendment. The Court reasoned that age is not a "suspect" basis for classification, and that states accordingly had latitude to make rational age classifications; yet the ADEA generally prohibits state employers from relying on "age as a proxy for other qualities." Because rational age classifications by states are permissible under the Constitution, the Court held that the act could not be justified as "proportional" to violations of section 1 that Congress has power to remedy. And because the ADEA could not be upheld as an exercise of Fourteenth Amendment power, it could not constitutionally abrogate the states' immunity from suit.

VICKI C. JACKSON
(2000)

Bibliography

AMAR, AKHIL REED 1987 Of Sovereignty and Federalism. *Yale Law Journal* 96:1425–1520.

FLETCHER, WILLIAM A. 1983 A Historical Interpretation of the Eleventh Amendment: A Narrow Construction of an Affirmative Grant of Jurisdiction Rather Than A Prohibition Against Jurisdiction. *Stanford Law Review* 35:1033–1131.

GIBBONS, JOHN 1983 The Eleventh Amendment and State Sovereign Immunity: A Reinterpretation. *Columbia Law Review* 83:1889–2129.

JACKSON, VICKI C. 1988 The Supreme Court, The Eleventh Amendment, and State Sovereign Immunity. *Yale Law Journal* 88:1–126.

—— 1997 Seminole Tribe, the Eleventh Amendment and

the Potential Evisceration of Ex Parte Young. *New York University Law Review* 72:495–546.

MARSHALL, WILLIAM P.   1989   The Diversity Theory of the Eleventh Amendment: A Critical Evaluation. *Harvard Law Review* 102:1372–1396.

MELTZER, DANIEL J.   1996   The Seminole Decision and State Sovereign Immunity. *Supreme Court Review* 1996:1–65.

ORTH, JOHN V.   1987   *The Judicial Power of the United States: The Eleventh Amendment in American History.* New York: Oxford University Press.

VAZQUEZ, CARLOS   1997   What Is Eleventh Amendment Immunity? *Yale Law Journal* 106:1683–1806.

ELFBRANDT v. RUSSELL
384 U.S. 11 (1966)

By a 5–4 vote, the WARREN COURT struck down a section of Arizona's Communist Control Act of 1961, which subjected state employees to perjury prosecutions if they subscribed to a state LOYALTY OATH while members of the Communist party, later joined the party, or joined "any other organization" having for "one of its purposes" the overthrow of the government. For the majority, Justice WILLIAM O. DOUGLAS argued that even knowing membership in the Communist party could not expose one to criminal punishment without proof of specific intent to further the organization's illegal goals of violent revolution. Such a law "infringes unnecessarily on protected freedoms. It rests on the doctrine of ' GUILT BY ASSOCIATION' which has no place here. . . ."

The dissenters were led by Justice BYRON R. WHITE. "If a government may remove from office . . . and . . . criminally punish . . . its employees who engage in certain political activities," White wrote, "it is unsound to hold that it may not, on pain of criminal penalties, prevent its employees from affiliating with the Communist Party or other organizations prepared to employ violent means to overthrow constitutional government."

MICHAEL E. PARRISH
(1986)

ELKINS v. UNITED STATES
364 U.S. 206 (1960)

In Elkins the Supreme Court overthrew the SILVER PLATTER DOCTRINE, an exception to the EXCLUSIONARY RULE allowing use in federal prosecutions of evidence seized by state officers in illegal searches. Two changes had undermined the authority of the doctrine since it was formulated in WEEKS V. UNITED STATES (1914). First, the extension of the constitutional prohibition of unreasonable searches

to the states in WOLF V. COLORADO (1949) meant that the doctrine now permitted federal courts to admit evidence unconstitutionally seized. Second, the doctrine vitiated the policies of about half the states, which had in the meantime independently adopted an exclusionary rule.

The *Elkins* opinion, in addition, contains the most thorough and convincing analysis in favor of the exclusionary rule to be found in any opinion of the Court; it thus laid the groundwork for imposition of the rule on the states the following year in MAPP V. OHIO (1961).

JACOB W. LANDYNSKI
(1986)

ELKINS ACT
32 Stat. 847 (1903)

The decisions in INTERSTATE COMMERCE COMMISSION V. CINCINNATI, NEW ORLEANS & TEXAS PACIFIC RAILWAY (1897) and its companion case, *ICC v. Alabama Midland Railway Company*, had stripped the Interstate Commerce Commission of much of its regulatory power. As a result, many of the evils the INTERSTATE COMMERCE ACT had been designed to remedy had revived. One of the most pernicious abuses was the practice of rebating. Federal legislation forbidding the practice would not only save the railroads money but also protect them against demands imposed by the trusts. Sponsored by the railroads, the Elkins Act made any deviation from the published rate schedule (whether a rebate or a general rate reduction) a criminal offense. Although Congress repealed the imprisonment penalty, it quadrupled the fine and directly subjected the corporations to the penalty; no longer could the principal escape punishment for its agents' acts. Anyone who sought or received a rebate (or other rate concession) was equally liable to criminal penalties. Despite the act's significance, further legislation would prove necessary. Charges were now enforced, but the ICC was still powerless to replace discriminatory rates. Congress would expand ICC powers and extend regulatory control over the rails in the HEPBURN and MANN-ELKINS ACTS.

DAVID GORDON
(1986)

Bibliography

SHARFMAN, ISAIAH L.   1931–1937   *The Interstate Commerce Commission.* Vol. 1. New York: Commonwealth Fund.

ELLSWORTH, OLIVER
(1745–1807)

Oliver Ellsworth played a key role in the creation of the United States Constitution in 1787 and the establishment of a national judiciary during the Constitution's first decade.

Born into a well-established Connecticut family, he entered Yale in 1762, but left after two years to attend the College of New Jersey (Princeton) where he was graduated with a B.A. in 1766. Ellsworth returned to Connecticut and studied theology for about a year, but abandoned it for the law and was admitted to the bar in 1771. One of the ablest lawyers of his day, he built up an extremely lucrative practice. He also entered politics and was elected to the state's General Assembly in 1773. A warm supporter of the patriot cause against Great Britain, he helped supervise the state's military expenditures during the war for independence, was appointed state attorney for Hartford in 1777, a member of the Governor's Council in 1780, and a judge of the Connecticut Supreme Court in 1785. He also served as one of the state's representatives to the Continental Congress for six terms (1777–1783). While in Congress he became a member of the Committee of Appeals which heard appeals from state admiralty courts, and in this capacity he ruled on the important case of Gideon Olmstead and the British sloop *Active* which eventually culminated in UNITED STATES V. PETERS (1809).

In 1787 Connecticut selected him to be one of its three delegates to the federal CONSTITUTIONAL CONVENTION in Philadelphia. He played an active role at the convention and won respect for his orderly mind and his effectiveness as a debater. Ellsworth favored the movement to establish a strong and active federal government with the power to act directly on individuals and to levy taxes, as a substitute for the weak central government created by the ARTICLES OF CONFEDERATION. But he also thought that the VIRGINIA PLAN went too far in a nationalist direction. "The only chance of supporting a general government lies in grafting it on those of the original states," he argued. In particular, he opposed the idea of apportioning representation in both houses of Congress according to population, to the clear advantage of larger states. To resolve the differences between the large and the small states he helped forge the successful GREAT COMPROMISE which apportioned representation in the lower house according to population and in the Senate by a rule of equality, with each state having two senators. Ellsworth also played an active role on the Committee on Detail which produced the basic draft of the United States Constitution.

Following adoption of the Constitution, Connecticut elected Ellsworth to the United States Senate. He recognized that the Constitution as written and ratified was only a basic outline; an actual government had to be created and its powers implemented. He supported ALEXANDER HAMILTON's financial program and was opposed to attempts to ally the United States too closely with France, but his most important contribution was the drafting of the JUDICIARY ACT OF 1789. This law was in many ways an extension of the Constitution itself, for it fleshed out the terse third article of that document which dealt with the nature and powers of the federal judiciary. The Judiciary Act of 1789 specified that the Supreme Court should consist of six Justices, that each state should have a district court, and that there should be three circuit courts consisting of two Supreme Court Justices sitting with a district judge. Under this law the fedral courts were given exclusive JURISDICTION in a number of important areas and CONCURRENT JURISDICTION with the state courts in other matters. The act also provided that decisions of the state courts involving the Constitution or laws or treaties of the United States could be appealed to the Supreme Court.

In 1796 President GEORGE WASHINGTON appointed Ellsworth Chief Justice of the United States. He held the post for three years but had little impact. The cases he heard were not very significant, illness limited his participation in the duties of the Court, and a diplomatic mission took him out of the country. Perhaps his most important decision came in *Wiscart v. Dauchy* (1796) in which he examined the relationship of the Supreme Court to the district and circuit courts, established a series of important rules dealing with WRITS OF ERROR, and extended COMMON LAW procedures in APPEALS to EQUITY and ADMIRALTY jurisdiction as well. His opinions tended to be brief, to the point, and nationalist in orientation. In *United States v. La Vengeance* (1796) he expanded the admiralty jurisdiction of the federal courts to inland navigable rivers, the Great Lakes, and other water routes away from the high seas; and while riding circuit in *United States v. Isaac Williams* (1799) he upheld the English common law DOCTRINE that citizens of a country did not have a right to expatriate themselves without their native country's consent.

As Chief Justice, Ellsworth encouraged the practice of the Supreme Court's handing down PER CURIAM opinions, with a single decision representing the will of the entire court, as opposed to having separate SERIATIM opinions by the individual Justices. JOHN MARSHALL, who succeeded Ellsworth as Chief Justice, considered the continuation and further development of this practice all-important in maintaining respect for the authority of the Court when it handed down controversial decisions.

In 1799 Ellsworth, over the protest of some of his closest associates, agreed to a request from President JOHN ADAMS to be part of a special diplomatic mission to resolve the undeclared naval war with France. The mission was a success, but Ellsworth became ill while abroad, resigned the chief justiceship in October 1800, and stayed in England to recuperate. By the time he returned to America the Jeffersonians had triumphed and he retired from public life.

RICHARD E. ELLIS
(1986)

Bibliography

BROWN, WILLIAM GARROTT 1905 *The Life of Oliver Ellsworth.* New York: Macmillan.
GOEBEL, JULIUS, JR. 1971 *History of the Supreme Court of the United States, Vol. 1: Antecedents and Beginnings to 1801.* New York: Macmillan.

ELLSWORTH COURT

See: Supreme Court, 1789–1801

EMANCIPATION PROCLAMATION
12 Stat. 68 (1863)

ABRAHAM LINCOLN, employing the Constitution's WAR POWERS, announced the Emancipation Proclamation on September 22, 1862. It had its roots in ABOLITIONIST CONSTITUTIONAL THEORY. Although Lincoln's swift rise in the Republican party was due in part to his outspoken opposition to the extension of SLAVERY, on the outset of the war he was bound by the Constitution (Article IV, section 2) and federal laws on FUGITIVE SLAVES that required federal officials to return runaways, even to disloyal owners. Politically ambitious Union general George B. McClellan, a conservative would-be Democratic presidential candidate, sternly enforced the 1850 law; generals BENJAMIN F. BUTLER and John Charles Frémont, by contrast, refused to return runaways in their commands and armed some against rebel guerrillas. Lincoln countermanded the latter's orders to dim the issue of arming Negroes and to keep policy in civilians' hands.

Negroes continued to flee to Union lines no matter what orders civilians or generals issued. Awareness grew in the Union army and among bluecoats' families and other correspondents that almost the only trustworthy southerners were blacks. Gradually, sentiment increased that to return runaways was indecent and illogical, for slaves were the South's labor force. In Congress, with few exceptions, Democrats remained uneducable on the runaway issue and damned as unconstitutional any mass emancipation whether by EXECUTIVE ORDER or statute and whether or not involving colonization of freedmen abroad or compensation to loyal owners. Republicans, from Lincoln down, altered their opinions on race matters. Some northern states softened racist BLACK CODE clauses in constitutions and civil and criminal laws; some made laws color-blind. Congress, in addition to the CONFISCATION ACTS

and with Lincoln's assent, enacted laws in March, April, and June 1862, respectively, that prohibited military returns of disloyal owners' runaways without requiring a judicial verdict of disloyalty, ended slavery in the DISTRICT OF COLUMBIA with compensation to owners, and forbade slavery in the federal TERRITORIES, thus challenging part of DRED SCOTT V. SANDFORD (1857). In effect, Republicans, retaining their basic view of the Constitution as an adaptable instrument, were adopting aspirations that abolitionist constitutionalists had long advanced.

Fearing conservative gains in the 1862 congressional and state elections, congressional Republicans then marked time. Lincoln did not have this option. He determined to reverse two centuries of race history *if* continued Confederate intransigence forced further changes and *if* the Union won the war.

Therefore, following the Antietam "victory," Lincoln proclaimed that unless slaveowners in still-unoccupied states of the Confederacy (he excluded unseceded slaveholding states) publicly renounced the rebellion by January 1, 1863, their slaves "shall be then, thenceforward, and forever free." All Union military personnel must positively assist, not merely not impede, runaways from slavery. With respect to unseceded slaveholding states, Lincoln encouraged "immediate or gradual" emancipation by state initiative, with compensation to loyal owners and colonization of freedmen abroad.

The Proclamation was not an immediate success. It diminished opinion abroad favoring recognition of the Confederacy. Few southern whites abjured the rebellion before the deadline. Lincoln, on New Year's Day 1863, announced the Proclamation to be in effect. But he had enlarged his horizons, adding an announcement that he would recruit blacks for the Union's armies. Relatively few blacks lived in northern states. Lincoln's new policy, if successful—which meant if Union voters persevered, if enough slaves kept coming into Union lines, and if Union forces occupied enough Confederate areas—could drain the South of its basic labor force and augment the Union's military power.

The policy eventually succeeded. Almost 200,000 black bluecoats, overwhelmingly southern in origin, helped to crush the rebellion. *Dred Scott* was made irrelevant. Though black Union soldiers and sailors suffered inequities in rank, pay, and dignity compared to whites, their military record made it impossible for the nation to consider them again as submen in law, though racists advocated the retrograde view. Compared to their prewar status even in the free states, blacks' legal and constitutional conditions improved as a result of the Proclamation. It initiated also an irreversible revolution in race relationships leading to the WADE-DAVIS BILL, the THIRTEENTH AMENDMENT, and the CIVIL RIGHTS ACT OF 1866. But the eventual consequence of the Emancipation Proclamation was Appomattox; thereby, alternatives forbidden by *Dred Scott*, by the 1861 Crittenden Compromise, and by the aborted Thirteenth Amendment of 1861, became options. This society could be slaveless, biracial, and more decently equal in the constitutions, laws, and customs of the nation and the states.

HAROLD M. HYMAN
(1986)

(SEE ALSO: *Civil War.*)

Bibliography

BELZ, HERMAN 1978 *Emancipation and Equal Rights: Politics and Constitutionalism in the Civil War Era.* New York: Norton.

HYMAN, HAROLD M. and WIECEK, WILLIAM M. 1982 *Equal Justice under Law: Constitutional Development 1835–1875.* Pages 252–255. New York: Harper & Row.

OATES, STEPHEN B. 1977 *With Malice Toward None: The Life of Abraham Lincoln.* New York: Harper & Row.

VOEGELI, V. JACQUES 1967 *Free But Not Equal: The Midwest and the Negro During the Civil War.* Chicago: University of Chicago Press.

EMBARGO ACTS
(1807–1809)

For fifteen months the United States under President THOMAS JEFFERSON pursued a policy of economic coercion against foreign powers as an alternative to war. In retaliation for attacks on American commerce during the Napoleonic wars, a compliant Congress gave Jefferson everything he requested, including five embargo acts which sought to compel England and France to respect American maritime rights in return for a restoration of American trade. The first three acts, which interdicted that trade, could be constitutionally defended by a doctrine of IMPLIED POWERS that Jefferson once thought inimical to American liberty. In *United States v. The William* (1808) a federal district court invoked a BROAD CONSTRUCTION of the COMMERCE CLAUSE, reinforced by the NECESSARY AND PROPER CLAUSE, to justify a ruling that the power to regulate commerce included the power to prohibit it. Justice WILLIAM JOHNSON of the Supreme Court, a Jefferson appointee, rebuked the President in a circuit case, *Gilchrist v. Collector* (1808), for having exceeded his statutory authority in enforcing the embargo acts, and another Jefferson appointee, Justice BROCKHOLST LIVINGSTON, in *United States v. Hoxie* (1808), scathed the President for insinuating the doctrine of constructive treason into a prosecution for violation of the acts. The draconian fourth embargo act carried the administration to the precipice of

unlimited enforcement powers and mocked Republican principles by its concentration of authority in the President, its employment of the navy for enforcement, and its disregard of the FOURTH AMENDMENT's protection against UNREASONABLE SEARCHES and seizures. Unconstitutional military enforcement characterized the fifth embargo act, which rivaled any legislation in American history for its suppressiveness. The embargo acts, having failed their purpose, lapsed when Jefferson left office.

LEONARD W. LEVY
(1986)

EMERGENCY BANK ACT
48 Stat. 1 (1933)

When FRANKLIN D. ROOSEVELT took office on March 4, 1933, banks had closed in thirty-eight states. The next day Roosevelt declared a national bank holiday, suspended all gold transactions, and called a special session of Congress for March 9. On that day Congress rushed through, and that same evening Roosevelt signed, a bill submitted by the White House aimed at ending the panic that had begun earlier that year. The bill ratified Roosevelt's actions, which he had based on the questionable authority of the 1917 Trading With the Enemy Act. The act gained constitutional significance by thus expanding executive authority. Congress also gave the President discretionary authority over national and Federal Reserve banks. The act provided for calling in all gold and gold certificates in circulation and assessed criminal penalties for hoarding. The government could appoint conservators for the assets of insolvent banks, and the Treasury could license the reopening of sound ones and reorganize the remainder. The act further authorized the emergency issuance of paper notes up to a limit of one hundred percent of the value of government bonds in its member banks.

DAVID GORDON
(1986)

EMERGENCY COURT OF APPEALS

In the Emergency Price Control Act of 1942, Congress established a comprehensive system of administrative control over prices, as a means of checking the inflation that accompanied this country's entry into WORLD WAR II. The Act created a temporary Emergency Court of Appeals, staffed by federal judges from the district courts and courts of appeals, with exclusive JURISDICTION to determine the validity of price control regulations. Regulated persons thus could not challenge the administrative regulations' constitutionality or statutory authorization in the ordinary state or federal courts—either in injunctive proceedings or by way of defense to criminal prosecutions for their violation. The only course open was to obey the regulations and challenge their validity in the newly created court.

In a series of decisions, the most important of which was YAKUS V. UNITED STATES (1944), the Supreme Court upheld the validity of this scheme (*Lockerty v. Phillips*, 1943; *Bowles v. Willingham*, 1944; see also JUDICIAL SYSTEM).

A Temporary Emergency Court of Appeals, established in 1971, is similarly staffed by judges from other federal courts. It hears appeals from the district courts in cases arising under various congressional statutes regulating allocation and pricing of certain commodities.

KENNETH L. KARST
(1986)

Bibliography

BATOR, PAUL M.; MISHKIN, PAUL J.; SHAPIRO, DAVID L.; and WECHSLER, HERBERT, eds. 1973 *Hart and Wechsler's The Federal Courts and the Federal System,* 2nd ed. Pages 317–322. Mineola, N.Y.: Foundation Press.

EMERGENCY POWERS

As justifications for taking emergency action without first receiving legislative authority, chief executives from different countries have relied on "reason of state" (*raison d'état*) and "prerogative." JOHN LOCKE, in the *Second Treatise on Civil Government* (1690), defined prerogative as the power to act "according to discretion for the common good, without the prescription of the law and sometimes even against it. . . ." More concise is the maxim *salus populi suprema lex:* the safety of the people is the supreme law.

The United States Constitution contains few provisions for emergency power. Congress has the power to meet emergencies by passing LEGISLATION. Under Article I, section 8, Congress may declare war and call forth the militia to suppress insurrections and to repel invasions. Article II authorizes the President to convene Congress "on extraordinary Occasions" for the purpose of enacting emergency legislation.

An exception to this statutory process is implied in the debates at the CONSTITUTIONAL CONVENTION. The Framers recognized that the President might have to begin military operations for defensive purposes before Congress could act. When one of the delegates proposed that Congress be empowered to "make war," it was objected that legislative proceedings might at times be too slow for the safety of the country. "Declare" was substituted for "make," giving Congress the power to declare war but allowing the President discretionary authority "to repel sudden attacks."

For twentieth-century America, the concept of "defensive war" has expanded to include military actions far beyond the nation's borders. The long drawn-out war in Southeast Asia led to the WAR POWERS RESOLUTION of 1973, an effort to reconcile the war-making power of the President with the war-declaring power of Congress. The statute attempts to insure the "collective judgment" of both branches by requiring the President to consult with Congress "in every possible instance," to report to Congress within forty-eight hours after introducing forces into hostilities, and to withdraw those forces unless he receives congressional support within sixty or ninety days. Congress may at any time during this period pass a CONCURRENT RESOLUTION (which is not subject to veto) directing the President to remove forces engaged in hostilities. The consultation and reporting provisions have had mixed results. The LEGISLATIVE VETO mechanism in the War Powers Resolution was declared invalid in IMMIGRATION AND NATURALIZATION SERVICE V. CHADHA (1983).

Article I, section 9, permits the suspension of the writ of HABEAS CORPUS "in Cases of Rebellion or Invasion [when] the public Safety may require it." It has never been determined conclusively whether this power resides solely in Congress or is shared with the President. History supports the latter interpretation. In April 1861, while Congress was in recess, President ABRAHAM LINCOLN issued proclamations ordering a number of emergency actions, including the suspension of the writ of habeas corpus. Congress supported his initiatives, as did a sharply divided Supreme Court in the PRIZE CASES (1863).

Although Chief Justice ROGER B. TANEY had earlier placed the power of suspension exclusively with Congress, in *Ex parte Merryman* (1861), Lincoln ignored the court order and continued to exercise emergency powers. His attorney general, EDWARD BATES, argued that the President shared with Congress the power to suspend the writ of habeas corpus. In such cases as EX PARTE MILLIGAN (1866) and DUNCAN V. KAHANAMOKU (1946), the Supreme Court has held illegal the establishment of military tribunals to try civilians in areas where the civil courts are open. In these decisions, however, the Court took care to assert judicial control at the close of, rather than during, hostilities.

The President's emergency power has also grown because of authority delegated to him by Congress. These authorities would sometimes come to life whenever the President issued a proclamation declaring the nation to be in a state of emergency. A report issued by a Senate special committee in 1973 disclosed that four proclamations (issued by FRANKLIN D. ROOSEVELT in 1933, HARRY S. TRUMAN in 1950, and RICHARD M. NIXON in 1970 and 1971) brought to life 470 provisions of federal law. Each statute conferred upon the President some facet of control over the lives and property of American citizens.

The NATIONAL EMERGENCIES ACT of 1976 restricted the use of presidential emergency powers. The statute terminated emergency authorities two years from the date of the bill's enactment (September 14, 1976). For future national emergencies the President must publish a declaration in the *Federal Register.* Congress could terminate the national emergency by passing a concurrent resolution. After the *Chadha* decision, Congress substituted a joint resolution for the concurrent resolution. To prevent "emergencies" from lingering for decades without congressional attention or action, the 1976 statute contained an action-forcing mechanism. No later than six months after the President declares a national emergency, and at least every six months thereafter while the emergency continues, each House of Congress must meet to consider a vote to terminate the emergency.

The 1976 statute exempted certain provisions of law, including section 5(b) of the Trading With the Enemy Act, first enacted in 1917. This section had become a source of presidential authority in peacetime as well as wartime. President Roosevelt, for example, used section 5(b) in 1933 to declare a national emergency. Legislation in 1977 attempted to strengthen congressional control, allowing Congress to terminate an emergency by passing a concurrent resolution (a joint resolution would now be required). It was under the 1977 legislation that President Jimmy Carter seized Iranian assets in 1979, an action upheld by the Supreme Court two years later in DAMES & MOORE V. REGAN (1981).

LOUIS FISHER
(1986)

Bibliography

ROSSITER, CLINTON 1963 *Constitutional Dictatorship: Crisis Government in the Modern Democracies.* New York: Harcourt, Brace & world.

U.S. CONGRESS 1976 *The National Emergencies Act (Public Law 94–412). Source Book: Legislative History, Texts, and Other Documents.* Senate Committee on Government Operations and Senate Special Committee on National Emergencies and Delegated Emergency Powers. 94th Congress, 2d session.

EMERGENCY PRICE CONTROL ACT
56 Stat. 23 (1942)

The most important independent administrative agency set up during WORLD WAR II was the Office of Price Ad-

ministration (OPA). The agency began studying plans for rationing and price fixing in April 1941 without benefit of statutory authority. The Emergency Price Control Act of 1942 gave the OPA official status, with broad powers for price regulation and a price administrator to make the act effective. The administrator was given broad discretion to supervise and fix prices and rent ceilings, combat profiteering and speculation, expedite defense purchases without excessive waste, and place limits on wages and other income from PRODUCTION. From 1942 to 1945, the OPA approached complete regulation of prices and rents. To prevent sellers and landlords from seeking INJUNCTIONS in state or federal courts against enforcement of particular price orders, the statute directed all determinations of the legality of price orders, including their constitutionality, to an EMERGENCY COURT OF APPEALS, established in Washington, D.C.

Unlike most wartime agencies, the OPA was challenged in the courts. The Supreme Court was supportive, upholding in YAKUS V. UNITED STATES (1944) those portions of the EPCA delegating to the OPA power to fix prices; in *Bowles v. Willingham* (1944) the Court upheld an OPA rent-fixing directive. *Yakus* also upheld the channeling of issues of legality to the Emergency Court of Appeals, which had the effect of requiring other courts to enforce price orders irrespective of the question of their lawfulness. In *Steuart and Bros. v. Bowles* (1944), the system of "indirect sanctions," whereby the OPA imposed its controls on the economy without formal resort to the judicial process, was sustained; the Court refused to interfere with the principal coercive device whereby various executive agencies gave practical force to their directives.

PAUL L. MURPHY
(1986)

Bibliography

UNITED STATES OFFICE OF TEMPORARY CONTROLS 1947 *The Beginnings of OPA.* Washington, D.C.: Office of Temporary Controls.

EMINENT DOMAIN

In his argument as counsel in WEST RIVER BRIDGE COMPANY V. DIX (1848), the first case in which the Supreme Court ruled directly on the constitutionality of the states' power of eminent domain, DANIEL WEBSTER thundered against the whole concept of state discretion in "takings." Only in the past few years, he contended, had this power of eminent domain been recognized in American law. Claims for its legitimacy, moreover, were "adopted from writers on other and arbitrary [civil law] governments," he declared; and eminent domain could easily become an instrument for establishment by the states of "unlimited despotisms over the private citizens." Webster tried, in effect, to get the court to impose Fifth Amendment standards on the states.

Webster was engaged in a failing cause. Besides, his history was inaccurate and his predictions of disaster were simplistic. He was certainly right, however, in seeing the eminent domain power as a formidable threat to VESTED RIGHTS, corporate or individual. He understood that eminent domain condemnations might become a proxy for regulation under the POLICE POWER, undermining the CONTRACT CLAUSE as a bulwark of PROPERTY RIGHTS. He was right in raising the alarm when he did; when *West River Bridge* was argued there had been a vast increase in activity by government and private CORPORATIONS in exercise of eminent domain. The transportation revolution in America was in an expansionary phase; extensive new railroad construction reinforced the effects on PROPERTY law already felt from canal, turnpike, and bridge enterprises. All these ventures required use of the "taking" power in order to accomplish their purposes.

Contrary to Webster's version of legal history, government's power to expropriate privately owned property for a variety of public purposes had long been an element of Anglo-American law. The power of eminent domain was the power to compel transfers to government or government's assignees. In its constitutional version, even in the 1840s, it was understood as a power that could be exercised legitimately only for a PUBLIC USE or PUBLIC PURPOSE, and that required the payment of JUST COMPENSATION. In English decisions and statutes going back several centuries, in American colonial law, and in the state law of the early republic, this power of taking by governmental authority had been exercised for such purposes as roadbuilding, fortifications, drainage (including the great Fens projects of England in the seventeenth century), navigational improvement on rivers, and construction of bridges and canals. In colonial Massachusetts, statute had extended a variant of the power into the manufacturing sector by authorizing builders of mills to dam up streams, flooding neighboring lands; these "milldam laws" provided for assessment of damages and payment of compensation in cash.

The Fifth Amendment—which the Supreme Court would rule in BARRON V. BALTIMORE (1833) was not applicable to the states—expressed the views and used language already embodied in several of the state constitutions adopted during the Revolutionary era. Thus the amendment's requirement that property could be taken "for public use" and on payment of "just compensation" had been foreshadowed by such documents as the 1780 Massachusetts Declaration of Rights, which declared that "whenever the public exigencies require that the property of any individual should be appropriated to public uses, he shall receive reasonable compensation therefor."

Although several early state constitutions lacked such language, uniformly the state courts, in reviewing takings cases, ruled that general principles of justice, the writings of the natural-law jurists, or the constitutional values reflected in the Fifth Amendment justified imposition by judges of both a "public use" and a "just compensation" limitation upon their legislatures' uses of the eminent domain power. It was a singular feature of legal development in the states, however, that despite the widespread formal adoption of such limitations, in fact only slight constraints were placed on the legislatures. In practice, compensation paid to persons suffering from takings was far below market value (and, because of offsetting benefits commonly calculated against damages, often they were paid nothing in cash); hence, eminent domain became an instrument for the subsidization, through cost reduction, of both governmental enterprises and favored private undertakings. "Public convenience" became, in most states, a legitimate reading of the "public use" requirement; and in practice, the legislatures enjoyed wide discretion in deciding what types of enterprise might be vested with the power to expropriate private property. Ironically, the very bridge and railroad corporations that Webster represented so often were among the greatest beneficiaries of eminent domain devolution in that era.

The Court in *West River Bridge* wholly rejected Webster's contentions, ruling that state eminent domain powers were "paramount to all private rights vested under the government." It left the state courts to decide for themselves whether compensation payments were just in particular cases, or whether DUE PROCESS requirements of state constitutions had been met.

So stood constitutional doctrine until the adoption of the FOURTEENTH AMENDMENT. Under its due process clause, the door was opened to challenges in federal courts of state eminent domain actions. Increasingly, too, in the late nineteenth century, the Supreme Court was called upon to rule upon the constitutionality of regulatory measures that activist state legislatures were enacting. The issue tended to take the form of defining a "taking," with the constitutional requirement it connoted, as opposed to bona fide use of the police power, which did not require compensation. The Court ruled in a succession of cases that the Fourteenth Amendment embodied the requirements of "public use" and "just compensation." It took a broad view, however, of what types of enterprise the states might aid with devolutions of the eminent domain power; in a series of cases on irrigation districts, drainage companies, individual enterprises and corporation activities in other areas such as logging and mining, and the more traditional areas of state activity, the Court upheld legislative discretion under a permissive "public use" standard.

In MUGLER V. KANSAS (1887), the Court attempted to distinguish between a taking, which required compensation, and uses of the police power, which it defined as laws abating nuisances or limiting uses of property that were harmful to "health, morals, or safety of the community," not compensable. But drawing the police power—eminent domain line proved difficult; indeed, it perplexes the Court to the present day. In *Pennsylvania Coal Company v. Mahon* (1922), Justice OLIVER WENDELL HOLMES argued that the police power and eminent domain power are on a single continuum; differences are a matter of degree, not qualitative. The Court has continued to struggle with the issue, and in modern land-use ZONING cases from EUCLID V. AMBLER REALTY (1926) to *Agins v. Tiburon* (1980) it has sought a firmer ground to replace the distinction Holmes found so appropriate.

The Court has upheld congressional discretion in deciding what purposes of federal eminent domain met the Fifth Amendment's "public use" requirement. In *United States v. Gettysburg Electric Railway Company* (1896), the Court declared acceptable any use "which is legitimate and lies within the scope of the Constitution." In *United States ex rel. Tennessee Valley Authority v. Welch* (1946) the Court carried the doctrine to an extreme, concluding that a congressional decision to authorize expropriation of property "is entitled to deference until it is shown to involve an impossibility." A few years later, *Berman v. Parker* (1954) upheld federal eminent domain takings to conduct an urban redevelopment project in the District of Columbia. Here the end was the public welfare, a "broad and inclusive" concept, the Court declared, that certainly embraced slum clearance and an urban development designed to be "beautiful as well as sanitary." Given the validity of this purpose, it was legitimate to invoke eminent domain, which was only a means. Congress must decide as to the need for the project and its design.

In its quest to develop standards to distinguish takings from legitimate exercise of the police power, the Court has probed to the heart of property concepts. What rights are "vested," how "reasonable expectations" should be defined, what obligations inhere in the ownership of private property—all are questions that come to the surface repeatedly in continuing litigation. Nearly 150 years ago, Chief Justice LEMUEL SHAW of Massachusetts admonished, in *Boston Water Power Company v. Railroad* (1839), that the eminent domain power "must be large and liberal, so as to meet the public exigencies, and it must be so limited and constrained, as to secure effectually the rights of the citizen; and it must depend, in some instances, upon the

nature of the exigencies as they arise, and the circumstances of individual cases." Shaw's view may have lacked prescriptive potential, but it has proved remarkably accurate in predicting the direction that the law would take—and the perplexities that would beset the best efforts of lawmakers and judges to produce definitive formulae.

HARRY N. SCHEIBER
(1986)

(SEE ALSO: *Hawaii Housing Authority v. Midkiff*.)

Bibliography

DUNHAM, ALLISON 1962 *Griggs v. Allegheny County* in Perspective: Thirty Years of Supreme Court Expropriation Law. *Supreme Court Review* 1962:63–106.
GRANT, J. A. C. 1931 The "Higher Law" Background of the Law of Eminent Domain. *Wisconsin Law Review* 6:67–85.
HURST, JAMES WILLARD 1964 *Law and Economic Growth: The Legal History of the Lumber Industry in Wisconsin, 1836–1915.* Cambridge, Mass.: Harvard University Press.
SCHEIBER, HARRY N. 1971 The Road to *Munn:* Eminent Domain and the Concept of Public Purpose in the State Courts. *Perspectives in American History* 5:327–402.
STOEBUCK, WILLIAM B. 1972 A General Theory of Eminent Domain. *Washington Law Review* 47:553–608.
——— 1980 Police Power, Takings, and Due Process. *Washington and Lee Law Review* 37:1057–1099.

EMINENT DOMAIN
(Update)

One of the most challenging and enduring puzzles in American constitutional law is how one distinguishes a compensable TAKING OF PROPERTY from a legitimate and noncompensable exercise of the POLICE POWER. To suggest the Supreme Court's approach to the question, Harry N. Scheiber, author of the *Encyclopedia's* principal article on eminent domain, looked back and away from the Court to Chief Justice LEMUEL SHAW of Massachusetts. Shaw had observed in 1839 that much depends "upon the nature of the exigencies as they arise, and the circumstances of individual cases." As of 1985, Scheiber concluded, Shaw's view "lacked prescriptive potential, but it has proved remarkably accurate in predicting the direction that the law would take—and the perplexities that would beset the best efforts of lawmakers and judges to produce definitive formulae."

Even in 1985, however, there were at least some "definitive formulae" by which to identify regulatory takings. First, it had long been thought that government regulatory action resulting in physical invasion of private PROPERTY should always be regarded as a taking, no matter how trivial the intrusion, and this per se rule was firmly endorsed by the Court in LORETTO V. TELEPROMPTER, INC. (1982), at least if the government invasion was "permanent." A second per se rule—that government regulation of nuisance-like activity was never to be regarded as a taking, no matter how substantial the burden of the regulation—was also clear enough.

Neither of these per se rules could be of much importance in the modern regulatory state, for modern regulation seldom results in physical invasions and commonly reaches beyond the mere control of nuisances. Yet, in this broad and important middle ground, the Court in 1985 was self-consciously drawing the line between takings and the police power in just the ad hoc fashion that Shaw had long ago foreseen. The two per se rules aside, the Court's approach was one of balancing a number of considerations, including the mix and breadth of benefits and burdens worked by a regulation, its economic impact, and the extent of its interference with concrete investment-backed expectations. The ad hoc approach played into the two per se rules as well, because temporary physical invasions were to be examined in terms of balancing and because the characterization of something as a nuisance is itself a matter of more or less.

Have matters changed since 1985? The answer depends in large part on three cases decided by the Court in 1987: *Nollan v. California Coastal Commission, Keystone Bituminous Coal Association v. DeBenedictis,* and *First English Evangelical Lutheran Church v. County of Los Angeles.* Unfortunately, the meaning of these cases is hardly clear. Some analysts see in them an unwelcome move away from ad hoc balancing. In their view, the Court has now confirmed the two per se rules mentioned above and added more, such that the law of regulatory takings is being resolved into a series of categorical "either-ors." Either a regulation (controlling other than nuisances) is categorically a taking because it results in a permanent physical invasion, specifically undermines a distinct investment-backed expectation, or totally eliminates the property's economic value, or it is categorically not a taking at all. But other commentators see in the 1987 decisions yet more evidence that the Court remains unable to develop what Scheiber called "definitive formulae."

The foregoing disagreement aside, there are other puzzles in the takings cases of 1987. *Nollan* found a taking where the regulatory authority had conditioned a development permit on the property owners' dedication of a lateral easement of public passage across their land. This decision suggests that some regulatory programs will be subjected to heightened judicial scrutiny in the course of determining takings questions, but it is far from clear how broadly this suggestion should be read. *Keystone Bitumi-*

nous, in the course of upholding Pennsylvania's Subsidence Act against a takings claim, seems to overrule the opinion of Justice OLIVER WENDELL HOLMES, JR., in *Pennsylvania Coal Company v. Mahon* (1922), the centerpiece of regulatory takings law; yet the Court never says as much. And Justice JOHN PAUL STEVENS, in his dissent in *First English Evangelical Lutheran Church,* poses a nice problem for the Court's endorsement in that case of IN-VERSE CONDEMNATION as a remedy for regulatory takings.

First English finally announced what had been anticipated ever since the dissenting opinion of Justice WILLIAM J. BRENNAN in *San Diego Gas and Electric Company v. City of San Diego* (1981). *First English* holds that in the event of regulatory takings, property owners are entitled to the JUST COMPENSATION required by the Fifth Amendment, including interim DAMAGES for the period the offending regulation remains in effect. "Once a court determines that a taking has occurred, the government retains the whole range of options already available—amendment of the regulation, withdrawal of the invalidated regulation, or exercise of eminent domain." But amendment or withdrawal no longer permits the government to escape liability, as it did before. Once the taking has occurred, "no subsequent action by the government can relieve it of the duty to provide compensation for the period during which the taking was effective."

Of all that the Court has decided about takings since 1985, only the remedy of inverse condemnation appears to be clear, yet even it is cloudy. The cloud looms because of the Court's admonition that it is not dealing "with the quite different questions that would arise in the case of normal delays in obtaining building permits, changes in zoning ordinances, and the like which are not before us." Here a temporary loss of use might not be a taking at all. But how, Justice Stevens wonders, is one to draw the line between such "everyday regulatory inconveniences" and compensable temporary takings? In any event, if a regulation can affect a significant percentage of some property's *value* without being held a taking—and this is clearly the law—then why should a regulation not be allowed to affect as well a significant percentage of the property's useful *life?*

The law of takings seems little clearer today than it did in 1985, inverse condemnation *in principle* aside.

JAMES E. KRIER
(1992)

(SEE ALSO: *Environmental Regulation and the Constitution; Property Rights; Regulatory Agencies.*)

Bibliography

SYMPOSIUM   1988   The Jurisprudence of Takings. *Columbia Law Review* 88:1581–1794.

EMPLOYEE SPEECH RIGHTS
(Private)

Employees in the private sector enjoy FIRST AMENDMENT rights like any other citizens. But those constitutional rights run only against the government—against STATE ACTION—and not against the private employer, who poses the chief threat to employees' FREEDOM OF SPEECH at and about the workplace. So the speech of private sector employees implicates the First Amendment only in those rare instances when the government acts to suppress that speech.

The paucity of First Amendment issues in the private sector workplace has contributed to an impoverished conception of the significance of employee speech and of the workplace as a forum for expression. The workplace is often seen as simply a component of the market, a domain of purely instrumental relations. Yet workplace issues, and related issues of class and wealth, are central to individuals' lives and to public debate. The workplace is where people discuss these issues, as well as other social and political issues, current events, popular culture, and personal concerns. It is thus an important arena for deliberation among citizens and for the formation of personal ties that transcend family, neighborhood, and racial and ethnic boundaries. But there is little recognition of the unique importance of workplace speech in those relatively rare cases in which private sector employee speech is threatened by state action.

Until recently, government suppression of private employee speech was largely confined to the arena of LABOR law—the law governing unions and collective bargaining. First Amendment challenges to restrictions on labor speech have a mixed record. Although peaceful labor picketing is a recognized form of protected expression, the Supreme Court has upheld numerous laws that prohibit picketing based on its purpose or effect. The Court has treated the constitutional implications of these prohibitions rather casually, failing to explain, for example, why labor picketing is less protected than CIVIL RIGHTS picketing. On the other hand, the Court has cited First Amendment concerns as the basis for narrowly construing a National Labor Relations Act provision to avoid banning consumer handbilling.

The law of discriminatory WORKPLACE HARASSMENT has recently called attention to the constitutional speech rights of private sector employees. Title VII of the CIVIL RIGHTS ACT OF 1964 prohibits employers from discriminating against employees, and from subjecting them to a "hostile work environment," on the basis of sex, race, ethnicity, and religion. Other laws, state and federal, extend the hostile environment theory to harassment on the basis of age, disability, and veteran status. Employers can be held liable for a hostile environment based partly or entirely on the speech of subordinate employees. As a result, harassment DOCTRINE induces employers to prohibit employee speech that could contribute to harassment liability, whether or not it constitutes harassment. Because Title VII operates indirectly, by inducing private actors to censor speech, the constitutional issue is obscured and seldom litigated. But it is serious nonetheless. Citing fear of liability, some employers have sought to purge the workplace of comments, jokes, or cartoons that might offend some employee on the basis of race, sex, religion, ethnicity, or other protected status.

Employers who read harassment law as a reason to ban any "suggestive" or conceivably offensive speech may be overreacting to the law; but in the absence of clear limitations on the sort of expression that may count toward liability, the reaction is foreseeable. The vague contours of hostile environment law are thus responsible for a serious constriction of the freedom of working people to communicate at work. Some pruning is in order.

The Court suggested a drastic solution in R.A.V. V. CITY OF ST. PAUL (1992). While condemning most attempts to suppress racist and sexist speech, the majority suggested in dicta that Title VII may be defensible: It is "directed not against speech but against conduct"—that is, EMPLOYMENT DISCRIMINATION—and it only "incidentally" restricts "a particular content-based subcategory of a proscribable class of speech," such as "sexually derogatory 'fighting words.'" This defense of harassment law is strikingly narrow: Hostile environment law would be drastically pruned if only FIGHTING WORDS, OBSCENITY, and other traditionally unprotected speech could be actionable. This standard takes too little account of the peculiar vulnerability of the workplace audience. It would render discrimination law powerless to prevent hostile coworkers from using obnoxious and bigoted speech to make the workplace intolerable for minority and female coworkers.

The solution to this dilemma may lie in a workplace-specific standard focusing on the time, place, and manner of alleged harassing speech. For example, speech that is personally directed at an unwilling listener, or that is not reasonably avoidable by unwilling listeners, exploits the workplace setting and the economic constraints on employees, and deserves lesser constitutional protection. Employers and employees alike need a definitive resolution of the problem of verbal workplace harassment, a resolution that recognizes both the free speech interests of employees and the special vulnerability of the workplace audience.

CYNTHIA L. ESTLUND
(2000)

Bibliography

BECKER, MARY 1996 How Free Is Speech at Work? *UC Davis Law Review* 29:815–873.

ESTLUND, CYNTHIA L. 1997 Freedom of Expression in the Workplace and the Problem of Discriminatory Harassment. *Texas Law Review* 75:687–777.

GREENAWALT, KENT 1995 *Fighting Words: Individuals, Communities, and Liberties of Speech.* Princeton, N.J.: Princeton University Press.

VOLOKH, EUGENE 1992 Freedom of Speech and Workplace Harassment. *UCLA Law Review* 39:1791–1872.

EMPLOYEE SPEECH RIGHTS
(Public)

The FREEDOM OF SPEECH rights of PUBLIC EMPLOYEES have evolved from simplicity to complexity. Late nineteenth and early twentieth century judges thought public officials could require citizens to surrender their constitutional rights in order to obtain or continue receiving government benefits or government jobs. "The petitioner may have a constitutional right to talk politics," Justice OLIVER WENDELL HOLMES, JR., famously declared in *McAuliffe v. Mayor of New Bedford* (1892), "but he has no constitutional right to be a policeman." *McAuliffe* and other cases allowed public employees to be fired for criticizing their departments, because "[t]he servant . . . takes the employment on the terms which are offered him."

This rule did not survive the coming of the welfare state, where most Americans depended on some government benefit and many held government jobs. The Supreme Court during the second half of the century sensibly rejected both *McAuliffe* and the hard distinction between constitutional rights and mere state privileges that had enabled public officials to trade state benefits for constitutional liberty. Public employees first gained a measure of freedom when in WIEMAN V. UPDEGRAFF (1952) the Justices unanimously agreed that persons who belonged to "innocent" political organizations could not be banned from state jobs. Sixteen years later, the Justices extended this ruling and laid down vague guidelines for determining when public employees could speak without fear of losing their jobs. Justice THURGOOD MARSHALL in *Pickering v. Board of Education of Will County, Illinois* (1968) declared that the official constitutional standard required "a balance between the interests of the [public employee], as a citizen, in commenting upon matters of public concern and the interest of the State, as an employer, in promoting the efficiency of the public services it performs through its employees."

The general rules governing the free-speech rights of public employees seem fairly libertarian at first glance. Judicial opinions celebrate the contribution such public employees as Nathaniel Hawthorne and Herman Melville have made to public discourse, and constitutional protection has been extended, in *Board of Commissioners v. Wabaunsee County v. Umbehr* (1996), to private contractors who do business with the state. The BURGER COURT struck a blow at traditional PATRONAGE practices, ruling in *Elrod v. Burns* (1976) and *Branti v. Fishel* (1980) that public employees could not be hired or fired simply on the basis of their political affiliations, unless "party affiliation is an appropriate requirement for the effective performance of the public office involved." Although the Justices have sustained measures forbidding political campaigning by public employees, the Court in UNITED STATES V. NATIONAL TREASURY EMPLOYEES UNION (1995) declared unconstitutional as applied to civil servants below the level of GS-16 a 1989 statute barring all federal employees from accepting any compensation for outside speeches or articles.

When actually applied on a case-by-case basis, however, the *Pickering* guidelines have strongly favored public employers. The Justices in *Connick v. Myers* (1983) narrowly defined matters of public concern when ruling that an assistant district attorney could be fired for complaining about working conditions in her department. Several years later, in WATERS V. CHURCHILL (1994), the Justices held that public employees could be constitutionally fired on the basis of what their supervisors erroneously thought they said, even though their actual statements may have been constitutionally protected. The opinion of Justice SANDRA DAY O'CONNOR in that case emphasized that courts should generally defer to government claims concerning what restrictions on speech were necessary to the efficient operation of public services.

Waters and other recent cases may indicate that public employees have free-speech rights only when a government attorney foolishly asserts that the Constitution does not give that employee any rights. Whenever public employers give more particularized reasons as to why a particular speech warrants termination, the FIRST AMENDMENT as construed by the REHNQUIST COURT is not likely to be very protective of the free-speech rights of public employees. In the latter half of the 1990s, the Justices may begin their opinions by highlighting the value of speech by public employees; however, maintaining the efficiency of the public workplace as defined by public employers remains the more important value.

MARK A. GRABER
(2000)

EMPLOYERS' LIABILITY ACTS
34 Stat. 232 (1906)
35 Stat. 65 (1908)

In the first Employers' Liability Act of June 1906, Congress extended nationwide protection to railroad workers against the arsenal of COMMON LAW defenses which employers had so effectively used to defeat personal injury suits. This act rendered every common carrier engaged in INTERSTATE COMMERCE liable to its employees for all damages resulting from negligence. Congress thus discarded the "fellow-servant" rule which had exculpated employers in accidents caused by another workman's negligence. Moreover, contributory negligence would not bar recovery and the law directed juries, not judges, to determine questions of negligence and assess damages proportionally. The act also prohibited the use of insurance or other benefits as a defense against damage suits. When a 5–4 Supreme Court declared this act unconstitutional because it extended to railroad employees not engaged in interstate commerce, Congress passed a second version of the act in April 1908. Although substantially the same, the new act covered only employees actually working in interstate commerce. Congress also added several sections further protecting employees and extended the period of limitation on actions from one to two years. As it had implied in its first decision, the Court unanimously sustained the act in the second set of EMPLOYERS' LIABILITY CASES (1912).

DAVID GORDON
(1986)

EMPLOYERS' LIABILITY CASES
207 U.S. 463 (1908)
223 U.S. 1 (1912)

The first EMPLOYERS' LIABILITY ACT, passed in 1906, made a common carrier liable for the on-the-job injury or death of any employee and eliminated the "fellow-servant" rule by which an employer had been relieved of liability for an injury to one worker caused by another's negligence. In the first *Employers' Liability Cases*, a 5–4 Supreme Court held that Congress had exceeded its INTERSTATE COMMERCE power.

Justice EDWARD D. WHITE's opinion for the Court (only Justice WILLIAM R. DAY concurred completely in his opinion) addressed two objections to the act: that Congress had no power to regulate the subject, and that the act regulated things outside the scope of the commerce power. He dismissed the first objection. The COMMERCE CLAUSE set no limits on subjects regulated. Indeed, the Court decided only the extent of Congress's power, not the wisdom of its action. "We fail to perceive any just reason for holding that Congress is without power to regulate the relation of master and servant . . . [as a subject of] interstate commerce." The argument that the act had unconstitutionally regulated INTERSTATE COMMERCE proved more troublesome. Because the act imposed liability on employers "without qualification or restriction as to the business in which the carriers or their employees may be engaged at the time of injury, of necessity [it] includes subjects wholly outside the power of Congress to regulate commerce." White refused to accept the contention that the Court ought to interpret the act as applying solely to interstate commerce even though it did not explicitly say so.

Chief Justice MELVILLE W. FULLER and Justice DAVID J. BREWER concurred in Justice RUFUS PECKHAM's opinion endorsing White's result but retreating from White's statement about Congress's power over master-servant relations. In a lengthy dissent, Justice WILLIAM MOODY argued that the Court was obliged to read the statute so as to preserve its constitutionality. "We think that the act, reasonably and properly interpreted, applies . . . only to cases of interstate commerce . . . and not to domestic commerce."

After Congress enacted another version of the law accommodating the majority's objections, a unanimous Court upheld its constitutionality. Justice WILLIS VAN DEVANTER's opinion broadly asserted the reach of Congress's power over the subject. He disposed of the objection that the act, by discarding COMMON LAW doctrines, had exceeded Congress's power: "A person has no property, no vested interest, in any rule of common law." The act also promoted safety and advanced commerce, and Van Devanter dismissed the contention that it violated the DUE PROCESS CLAUSE's guarantee of FREEDOM OF CONTRACT.

DAVID GORDON
(1986)

EMPLOYMENT DISCRIMINATION

Employment discrimination on grounds of race, sex, nationality, or religion may be challenged under two acts of Congress. One of the statutes, now codified as Title 42 of the United States Code, section 1981, is a survivor of the CIVIL RIGHTS ACT OF 1866, enacted for the protection of former slaves. As originally enacted, the statute was not seen as an employment discrimination statute. It conferred upon blacks the right to make and enforce contracts, to sue and to enjoy on a par with whites the protection of laws. The act was passed pursuant to Congress's authority under section 2 of the THIRTEENTH AMENDMENT, and Congress proposed the FOURTEENTH AMENDMENT in order to assure the act's validity. After the Reconstruction era, however, it and other Reconstruction-era civil rights legislation fell into disuse until the 1960s. Not until *Johnson v. Railway Express Agency, Inc.* (1975) did the United States Supreme Court confirm the application of section 1981 to RACIAL DISCRIMINATION in private-sector employment. This statute's use in employment discrimination cases has become secondary to reliance on Title VII of the CIVIL RIGHTS ACT OF 1964, which was enacted by Congress as part of a comprehensive statute prohibiting discrimination on grounds of race, sex, religion, or national origin in employment, PUBLIC ACCOMMODATIONS, and federally funded programs.

Enactment of the 1964 Act followed a long period of civil rights DEMONSTRATIONS against the kinds of discrimination the act prohibited. For twenty years preceding the enactment of Title VII, more than 200 fair employment practice bills had been proposed in the Congress, but none had passed. Allegations of a Title VII violation often are accompanied by additional allegations of a section 1981 violation.

Another survivor of Reconstruction-era legislation now codified as 42 United States Code 1985(c), was originally designed to protect blacks from Ku Klux Klan violence. The Supreme Court, in *Great American Federal Savings and Loan Association v. Novotny* (1979), rejected the view that section 1985(c) provides an independent remedy for the adjudication of rights protected by Title VII.

The constitutionality of Title VII of the 1964 act was never seriously questioned. The power of Congress to enact Title VII, either under the COMMERCE CLAUSE or to enforce the FOURTEENTH AMENDMENT, seems to have been assumed. In 1972 Congress extended the coverage of Title VII to include employment discrimination by state and local governments. Subsequently, it was argued that back-pay awards and attorneys' fees levied by a federal court against a state under the amended Title VII violated the jurisdictional limitations of the ELEVENTH AMENDMENT. However, in FITZPATRICK V. BITZER (1976) the Supreme Court rejected that argument, holding that the 1972 amendment was a valid exercise of Congress's enforcement power under section 5 of the FOURTEENTH AMENDMENT.

REGINALD ALLEYNE
(1986)

Bibliography

COMMENT   1980   Developments in the Law—Section 1981. *Harvard Civil Rights-Civil Liberties Law Review* 15:29–277.
DEAN, JOHN P.   1978   Title VII and Public Employers: Did Congress Exceed Its Powers? *Columbia Law Review* 78:372–408.
HILL, HERBERT   1977   The Equal Employment Opportunity Acts of 1964 and 1972: A Critical Analysis of the Legislative History and Administration of the Law. *Industrial Relations Law Journal* 2:1–96.

EMPLOYMENT DIVISION, DEPARTMENT OF HUMAN RESOURCES OF OREGON *v.* SMITH
484 U.S. 872 (1990)

Two drug and alcohol abuse counselors were fired from their jobs after ingesting the hallucinogenic drug peyote during a religious ceremony of the Native American Church. They were subsequently denied unemployment compensation by the state of Oregon because the state determined they had been discharged for work-related "misconduct." The workers filed suit, alleging that the denial of compensation violated the free exercise clause of the FIRST AMENDMENT. The Supreme Court disagreed by a vote of 6–3.

If the Court had handled *Smith* as it had handled most of its previous cases in the field of RELIGIOUS LIBERTY, it would have first asked whether Oregon had a COMPELLING STATE INTEREST to deny unemployment compensation to the fired workers. If Oregon could demonstrate such an interest, and the denial of compensation was narrowly tailored to further that end, the denial would have been upheld. But the Court did not treat *Smith* as it had previous cases. Instead, it used *Smith* to abolish the compelling-interest standard for challenges brought under the free exercise clause.

Writing for five members of the Court, Justice ANTONIN SCALIA made the astonishing claim that the Court had never really applied the compelling-interest standard to free exercise claims. According to Scalia, the Court had "never held that an individual's religious beliefs excuse him from compliance with an otherwise valid law prohibiting conduct that the State is free to regulate." Of course, the Court had held precisely that in several cases, most notably CANTWELL V. CONNECTICUT (1943) and WISCONSIN V. YODER (1972). But Scalia noted that these cases implicated other constitutional rights besides free exercise, and he suggested that those other rights were the decisive factor in the Court's decisions to hold unconstitutional particular applications of certain general laws. In *Cantwell*, the invalidated licensing law impinged on the FREEDOM OF SPEECH; in *Yoder*, the compulsory education law infringed on the "right of parents . . . to direct the education of their children." Scalia concluded from this that only when the free-exercise clause is joined with other constitutional protections may it invalidate particular applications of general laws. As a practical matter, this means that the free exercise clause alone means very little. Generally applicable laws that do not implicate other constitutional rights are constitutional, no matter how difficult they make it for certain persons to practice their religion; indeed, it is conceivable that a generally applicable law could destroy certain religious groups entirely and yet survive a free exercise challenge under Scalia's approach. Only laws that expressly seek to regulate religious beliefs or to proscribe certain actions only when they are engaged in for religious reasons violate the free exercise clause according to the Court's new standard.

Concurring in the judgment, but disavowing the Court's reasoning, Justice SANDRA DAY O'CONNOR attacked the majority opinion as "incompatible with our Nation's fundamental commitment to individual religious liberty." Carefully recalling prior precedents, O'Connor showed that the compelling-interest test had been applied much more consistently by the Court in free exercise cases than Scalia had suggested. O'Connor further defended the test as an appropriate method by which to enforce "the First Amendment's command that religious liberty is an independent liberty. . . ." Applied to the case at hand, O'Connor believed that the free exercise claim could not prevail, however, because exempting the two workers from drug laws would significantly impair the government's "overriding interest in preventing the physical harm caused by the use of a Schedule I controlled substance."

Justices THURGOOD MARSHALL, WILLIAM J. BRENNAN, and HARRY A. BLACKMUN joined most of Justice O'Connor's concurring opinion, but they disagreed with her ultimate conclusion, arguing that enforcement of drug laws against the religious ingestion of peyote was in no way necessary to fulfill the state's legitimate interest in circumscribing drug use. The state had argued that an exemption of the claimants in *Smith* would invite a flood of other claims for exemption to drug laws based on religious beliefs; but Blackmun pointed out that many states already have statutory exemptions for religious peyote use and have suffered no such difficulty.

The debate on the Court that erupted in *Smith* over what standard to apply to free exercise claims was dramatic; and yet it was not entirely unexpected, having been foreshadowed in several previous cases, including GOLDMAN V. WEINBERGER (1986) and O'LONE V. ESTATE OF SHABAZZ (1987). It also had been preceded for some years by a vigorous debate among scholars such as Walter Berns and Michael McConnell. Berns had long characterized the Court's decision in *Yoder* as contrary to American republicanism. His view clearly triumphed in *Smith*. Whether or not the Court's new approach is any better than its old one, however, is open to question.

One can certainly understand why the Court might want to restrict challenges under the free exercise clause. When only the members of a particular religious group may use an illegal drug or ignore compulsory education laws, the free exercise clause appears to undermine the equality before the law established by the rest of the Constitution. Scalia's approach seeks to avoid this contradiction by defining free exercise in terms of other constitutional rights, such as freedom of speech, FREEDOM OF ASSOCIATION, and EQUAL PROTECTION. Scalia has a keen theoretical mind, and one can readily see the analytical power of his approach. Under his scheme, religious liberty will be protected by general rights applicable to all, rather than by specific exemptions granted only to those who

hold peculiar religious beliefs. The principle of equality before the law will be maintained. That this approach may indeed afford protection to religious liberty is demonstrated by the recent development of the doctrine of EQUAL ACCESS, which is premised on free-speech and free-association protections rather than the free-exercise clause.

Yet one can legitimately wonder—as Justice O'Connor did in *Smith*—whether Scalia's approach will actually protect the free exercise of religion to its fullest extent. One suspects that it could only do so if the Court were willing to give an expansive reading to other constitutional rights in order to make up for its restricted interpretation of free exercise. Indeed, Scalia himself had to resort to an UNENUMERATED RIGHT of parental control over a child's education to explain the Court's previous ruling in *Wisconsin v. Yoder* within his framework. But the REHNQUIST COURT appears to be in no mood to give a broad reading to any rights just now, which makes its evisceration of the free exercise clause all the more troubling.

Government today wields a wide array of regulatory powers that the Court no longer even presumes to question; the "compelling state interest" test may be the only practical way to insulate religious groups from the destructive effects of such regulatory powers. The Court's failure to appreciate this fact raises troubling questions about its commitment to religious freedom for all.

JOHN G. WEST, JR.
(1992)

Bibliography

BERNS, WALTER. 1976 *The First Amendment and the Future of American Democracy*, Chapter 2. New York: Basic Books.

MCCONNELL, MICHAEL W. 1990 The Origins and Historical Understanding of Free Exercise of Religion. *Harvard Law Review* 103:1409–1517.

EN BANC

(French: "As a bench.") The term often applies to appellate courts, and in particular to the UNITED STATES COURTS OF APPEALS. Commonly only a three-member panel of a federal court of appeals hears a case. When the full membership is sitting—whether by its own choice or at a litigant's request—the case is heard before them *en banc*. In the federal courts of appeals, the decision of a panel is reconsidered *en banc* if a majority of the full court's members agree on such a hearing.

DAVID GORDON
(1986)

ENDO, EX PARTE

See: Japanese American Cases

ENFORCEMENT ACTS

See: Force Acts

ENGEL v. VITALE
370 U.S. 421 (1962)

The Board of Regents of the State of New York authorized a short prayer for recitation in schools. The Regents were seeking to defuse the emotional issue of religious exercises in the classroom. The matter was taken out of the hands of school boards and teachers, and the blandest sort of invocation of the Deity was provided: "Almighty God, we acknowledge our dependence upon Thee, and beg Thy blessings upon us, our teachers, and our country." School districts in New York did not have to use the prayer, and if they did, no child was required to repeat it. But if there were any prayer in a New York classroom it would have to be this one. The Board of Education of New Hyde Park, New York, chose to use the Regents' Prayer and directed its principals to cause it to be said aloud at the beginning of each school day in every classroom.

Use of the prayer was challenged as an ESTABLISHMENT OF RELIGION. Justice HUGO L. BLACK, writing for the Court, concluded that neither the nondenominational nature of the prayer nor the fact that it was voluntary could save it from unconstitutionality under the establishment clause. By providing the prayer, New York officially approved theistic religion. With his usual generous quotations from JAMES MADISON and THOMAS JEFFERSON, Black found such state support impermissible.

Justice WILLIAM O. DOUGLAS concurred separately. He had more trouble than Black concluding that the prayer established religion "in the strictly historic meaning of these words." What Douglas feared was the divisiveness engendered in a community when government sponsored a religious exercise.

Only Justice POTTER STEWART dissented, concluding that "the Court has misapplied a great constitutional principle." Stewart could not see how a purely voluntary prayer could be held to constitute state adoption of an official religion. For Stewart, an official religion was the only meaning of "establishment of religion." He noted that invocations of the Deity in public ceremonies of all sorts had been a feature of our national life from its outset. Without quite saying so, Stewart asked his brethren how the Regents' Prayer could be anathematized on establish-ment clause grounds without scraping "In God We Trust" off the pennies.

Engel v. Vitale was the first of a series of cases in which the Court used the establishment clause to extirpate from the public schools the least-commondenominator religious invocations which had been a traditional part of public ceremonies—especially school ceremonies—in America.

The decision proved extremely controversial. It has been widely circumvented and there have been repeated attempts to amend the Constitution to undo the effect of *Engel*.

RICHARD E. MORGAN
(1986)

Bibliography

BERNS, WALTER 1976 *The First Amendment and the Future of American Democracy*. Pages 33–76. New York: Basic Books.
MUIR, WILLIAM K., JR. 1967 *Prayer in the Public Schools*. Chicago: University of Chicago Press.

ENGLISH BILL OF RIGHTS

See: Bill of Rights (English)

ENGLISH CONSTITUTION

See: British Constitution

"ENGLISH ONLY" LAWS

See: "Official English" Laws

ENMUND v. FLORIDA
458 U.S. 782 (1982)

Before this decision, nine states permitted infliction of the death penalty on one who participated in a FELONY resulting in a murder, even if committed by confederates. Earl Enmund drove the getaway car in a robbery at which co-defendants killed the victims when he was not present and had not premeditated murder. A 5–4 Court held that the CRUEL AND UNUSUAL PUNISHMENT clause of the EIGHTH AMENDMENT, which the FOURTEENTH AMENDMENT extended to the states, prevented imposition of the death penalty. Capital punishment was disproportionate to the crime when Enmund had not himself killed, attempted to kill, intended to kill, or even intended the use of lethal force.

LEONARD W. LEVY
(1986)

ENTANGLEMENT TEST

See: Government Aid to Religious Institutions

ENTITLEMENT

Both the Fifth Amendment and the FOURTEENTH AMENDMENT protect "life, liberty or property" against deprivation "without due process of law." At least according to the constitutional text, when citizens seek to challenge a government's action as a violation of the due process clause, they must adduce some interest in "life, liberty or property" of which they have been deprived.

In the field of PROCEDURAL DUE PROCESS OF LAW, the Supreme Court traditionally read the phrase "life, liberty or property" as an undifferentiated whole, giving individuals the right to appropriate NOTICE and hearing whenever the government subjected them to "grievous loss." This broad interpretation, however, was often limited by the RIGHT-PRIVILEGE DISTINCTION, according to which benefits that the government was not legally obligated to grant could be denied or terminated without constitutional constraint. Thus, a "grievous loss" occasioned by a denial of "largess" would not trigger constitutional requirements of fair procedure under the due process clause.

In the years following WORLD WAR II, as the involvement of government in social welfare programs and the domestic economy continued to increase, it became clear that government allocation of largess constituted a powerful mechanism for government oppression if left unconstrained. In GOLDBERG V. KELLY (1970), in the course of an opinion imposing constitutionally mandated procedural requirements on the termination of WELFARE BENEFITS, the Court announced in obiter dictum the elimination of the largess or privilege exception to the demands of due process. The claim that "public assistance benefits are a privilege and not a right" was unavailing, according to Justice WILLIAM J. BRENNAN, because "welfare benefits are a matter of statutory entitlement for persons qualified to receive them," functioning more like "property" than "gratuity." The loss of benefits imposed a "grievous loss" and thus called forth the demands of due process.

Two years later, in BOARD OF REGENTS V. ROTH (1972) and *Perry v. Sinderman* (1972), the Court moved the concept of "entitlement" from the margins of due process doctrine to its core. In passing on the claims of untenured professors employed by state colleges to hearings before being dismissed from their posts, the majority opinions of Justice POTTER STEWART took the position that it was not the "weight" of interests affected by public action that invoked the protection of due process but their "nature." Rather than evaluating the "grievousness" of injuries in-flicted by discharge, the Court required the instructors to demonstrate that their discharge amounted to a deprivation of technically defined "liberty" or "property."

The liberty protected by due process was delineated in *Roth* as a matter of federal constitutional law. The Court referred to historically rooted concepts of liberty: beyond freedom from bodily restraint and assault, it included the "privileges long recognized as essential to the orderly pursuit of happiness by free men." Property interests, on the other hand, were said to find their source outside the Constitution in "rules or understandings that secure certain benefits and that support claims of entitlement to those benefits." Beyond the areas protected as liberty, therefore, an entitlement grounded in "some independent source such as state law" was a necessary condition for a claim to procedural due process protection. Because under state law Roth's employment was terminable at will, he had no property entitlement upon which to base his demands for due process. The Court left it open for Perry to show some "binding understanding" not embodied in the written terms of his contract that could support a "legitimate claim of entitlement."

In subsequent cases, the Court clarified the proposition that legislative alteration of the terms of the entitlement does not trigger a requirement of notice and hearing, but only administrative action predicated upon alleged failures to meet the terms of the entitlement. Decisions involving prison release and good-time credit programs, like *Wolff v. McDonnell* (1974) and *Greenholtz v. Inmates of Nebraska Penal and Correctional Complex* (1979) have extended the entitlement concept to conditions of liberty conferred by state laws or regulations. A hearing before deprivation of credit toward release or other prison perquisites granted to a duly sentenced prisoner is required only when the law granting the liberty is sufficient to vest an entitlement.

The reliance on positive law entitlements outside of the Constitution to define the applicability of constitutional protection forces the Supreme Court to spend considerable effort defining what constitutes a sufficiently clear and binding entitlement to invoke the protection of procedural due process. In *Roth* the Court differentiated between an unprotected "unilateral expectation" and a "legitimate claim of entitlement" that could support a property interest. Subsequent opinions have looked primarily to statutes, regulations, and contractual provisions to draw the line of demarcation, but have not required great specificity of entitlement to generate protection. Positive law that leaves official decision makers entirely unconstrained in dispensing benefits or employment has been held to create no protected interests; when criteria in positive law provide substantive limitations on official discretion binding on the decision-makers, even standards as vague as "good cause" or "probable ability to fulfill the obligations of a law abiding life" have enabled citizens to claim the protection of due process.

A great deal has been held to turn on the particular official choice of language, as well as state court glosses on it. The difference between benefits that "shall be granted if" and that "shall not be granted unless" particular criteria are met can lead to outcomes that vary considerably among cases that seem otherwise quite similar. Under current doctrine, policymakers who seek to control the decisions of street-level bureaucrats with written criteria for actions must pay the price of providing due process to the citizens whom those decisions affect. Given the rule-governed nature of most modern bureaucracies, this doctrine means hearings are widely available. It also means, however, that policymakers who seek to escape federal due process constraints have an incentive to leave their subordinates entirely without formal guidance.

The reliance on positive law in defining entitlements has led to a doctrinal conundrum. It is not uncommon for the very statute or regulation that defines the property or liberty entitlement to provide procedures to terminate that interest. In these cases, it has been argued that the entitlement protected is simply the entitlement to retain the benefit until it has been terminated in accordance with statutory procedures. If those procedures have been followed, the argument goes, termination deprives the citizen of no property and federal due process can require nothing more.

Whatever its logical appeal, this argument, originally articulated by Justice WILLIAM H. REHNQUIST in his PLURALITY OPINION in ARNETT V. KENNEDY (1974), is an invitation for government to eliminate the constraints of due process in the administration of statutorily created interests by attaching nugatory procedural protections to their statutory definition of interests. The Court, in *Cleveland Board of Education v. Loudermill* (1985), acknowledged this danger in forcefully rejecting the Rehnquist argument. Justice BYRON R. WHITE wrote for eight members of the Court that once the positive law of a state lays the groundwork for an entitlement, the constitutionally mandated procedures for terminating that interest were unaffected by the procedures that a state might attach. Although state law determines whether an individual is entitled to the protections of due process by defining their entitlements, the Constitution defines what due process requires. "The categories of substance and procedure are distinct," the Court held. "Were the rule otherwise, the due process clause would be reduced to a mere tautology."

SETH F. KREIMER
(1992)

Bibliography

MONAGHAN, HENRY P.   1977   Of Liberty and Property. *Cornell Law Review* 62:401–444.

SMOLLA, RODNEY   1982   The Reemergence of the Right-Privilege Distinction in Constitutional Law: The Price of Protesting Too Much. *Stanford Law Review* 35:69–120.
TRIBE, LAURENCE H.   1987   *American Constitutional Law*, 2nd. ed. pp. 663–714. Westbury, N.Y.: Foundation Press.

ENTRAPMENT DEFENSE

The entrapment defense is not constitutionally safeguarded and raises no constitutional issue unless a guilty defendant claims that law enforcement conduct violates the fundamental fairness mandated by DUE PROCESS OF LAW; if such a constitutional defense were to be recognized by the Supreme Court the effect would, like an EXCLUSIONARY RULE, be aimed at deterring unlawful police conduct.

Entrapment is a means of securing evidence to convict by luring a person into the commission of a crime of which he is suspected. Ordinarily the duty of an officer of the law is to deter crime and apprehend those who commit it, not to incite or instigate it. Certain offenses of a clandestine or consensual character, however, are difficult to expose and punish except by some degree of covert government participation. Official deceit is not necessarily illegal or unconstitutional. Undercover police work is particularly effective in uncovering crimes that involve gambling, drugs, prostitution, and official corruption. Nevertheless the government should not fight crime with crime.

When an undercover officer has gained the confidence of a radical organization and encouraged its members to engage in terrorist activities and provided them with the weapons and explosives to do so, he has become an *agent provocateur* who has conceived and procured the commission of a crime that would not have occurred but for him. If an officer posing as an imposter approaches a law-abiding person with no criminal record and induces him to smuggle contraband, the officer has passed the law's tolerance and the smuggler's guilty conduct may be legally excusable. When entrapment goes too far, it creates a legal defense which, like insanity or killing to save one's own life, merits a verdict of not guilty. The question in any case is whether the evidence shows that entrapment is a sufficient defense by a person who has in fact committed the crime charged against him. The mere fact that a government agent provides a favorable opportunity to one willing and ready to break the law is not entrapment for the purpose of making good a defense; if, however, the defendant had no previous intent to commit the offense and did so only because the police induced him, the verdict should be an acquittal.

Entrapment comes before the Supreme Court as a nonconstitutional defense in cases involving federal crimes. The Justices have always divided into two wings: one focuses on the criminal intent or predisposition of the defendant to commit the crime; the other focuses on the conduct of law enforcement officers. The view that has always prevailed, from the first case, *Sorrells v. United States* (1932), to *Hampton v. United States* (1976), is that it is no entrapment for the police merely to instigate the crime; they must also instigate its commission by luring an innocent person with no previous disposition to commit it. The criminal design, as Chief Justice CHARLES EVANS HUGHES said in 1932, must originate with the authorities who implant the predisposition in the mind of an otherwise innocent person and incite him to commit it so that they may prosecute. Thus, in *United States v. Russell* (1973), the Court sustained the conviction of the manufacturer of an illegal drug, who claimed that the government had violated due process when an undercover agent supplied him with an essential chemical ingredient. But the ingredient was harmless, its possession was not illegal, and, above all, the defendant was already engaged in the criminal enterprise. In *Hampton*, however, a government informant supplied an illegal drug and arranged its sale by the defendant to undercover agents. Although the government deliberately set him up, the Court stressed that his previous propensity to commit the crime negated his entrapment defense. He was, in a phrase of Chief Justice EARL WARREN, "an unwary criminal" rather than an "unwary innocent."

Justice WILLIAM H. REHNQUIST wrote the entrapment opinions of the BURGER COURT, from which Justices POTTER STEWART, WILLIAM J. BRENNAN, and THURGOOD MARSHALL dissented. The dissenters insisted that the majority's focus on the criminal's predisposition is "subjective," and they preferred an "objective" test, whether, despite predisposition, police conduct instigated the offense. The objectivity of that view, however, can be deceptive, and it ignores criminal intent. Doubtless, though, the trend of decision has made the entrapment defense nearly useless if a jury does not accept it. If the "outrageousness" of police conduct should pass the threshold of judicial tolerance in some future case, the Court may find a due process basis for the entrapment defense.

LEONARD W. LEVY
(1986)

Bibliography

DUNHAM, DAN S. 1977 Hampton v. United States: Last Rites for the "Objective" Theory of Entrapment? *Columbia Human Rights Law Review* 9:223–262.
O'CONNER, PETER J. 1978 Entrapment versus Due Process: A Solution to the Problem of the Criminal Conviction Obtained by Law Enforcement Misconduct. *Fordham Urban Law Journal* 7:32–53.
ROSSUM, RALPH A. 1978 The Entrapment Defense and the Teaching of Political Responsibility. *American Journal of Criminal Law* 6:287–306.

ENUMERATED POWERS

Instead of establishing a national government with a general power to do whatever it might deem in the public interest, the Constitution lists the authorized powers of Congress. The chief source of these "enumerated powers" is Article I, section 8, which authorizes Congress to regulate commerce among the several states, tax and spend, raise and support military forces, and so on. This enumeration has been supplemented by other grants, including authority to enforce the CIVIL WAR amendments.

The enumeration of powers has both a negative and a positive implication. Enumerating or specifying powers implies that some of government's ordinary concerns are beyond the constitutional competence of the national government. This implication is made explicit by the TENTH AMENDMENT. Nevertheless, the founding generation wanted to solve such specific problems as commercial hostility among the states and an unpaid war debt. When THE FEDERALIST defended the proposed national powers it cited the desiderata that might be achieved through their successful exercise. The enumeration of powers thus implies affirmative responsibilities as well as limited concerns. These competing implications are associated with competing approaches to constitutional interpretation and different conceptions of the normative character of the Constitution as a whole. As a reminder of a line between national and state powers, the enumeration of powers suggests THOMAS JEFFERSON's view of the Constitution as a contract between sovereign states to be construed with an eye to preserving state prerogatives. As a reminder of affirmative responsibilities the enumeration suggests JOHN MARSHALL's view of the Constitution as a charter of government to be construed in ways that permit achievement of the social objectives it envisions. History has not favored the Jeffersonian view.

ALEXANDER HAMILTON, in *The Federalist* #84, cited the enumeration of powers as one reason for opposing a BILL OF RIGHTS. Not only were bills of rights unnecessary in countries whose governments possessed only those powers that their people had expressly granted, specifying rights could undermine the enumeration of powers by suggesting "to men disposed to usurp" that the Constitution authorized all that the bill of rights did not prohibit. The result Hamilton ostensibly feared was achieved through constitutional doctrines that accompanied the nation's progress toward the economically integrated industrial society Hamilton favored. These doctrines included Hamilton's own theories of the SUPREMACY CLAUSE and the NECESSARY AND PROPER CLAUSE, theories that influenced

John Marshall's doctrine of IMPLIED POWERS in MCCULLOCH V. MARYLAND (1819).

Marshall's original theory of implied powers was consistent with the idea of enumerated powers because it removed STATES' RIGHTS burdens on national power while insisting that national concerns were limited. In the twentieth century, however, the Supreme Court changed the meaning of implied powers and gave nationalist readings to the general welfare clause and other powers. The aggregate and practical effect of these interpretations was to empower the national government to deal with anything that Congress may perceive as a national problem. This development has all but eliminated the restrictive implication of the enumeration of powers, leaving the Bill of Rights and the Constitution's institutional norms as the principal limitations on national power.

SOTIRIOS A. BARBER
(1986)

(SEE ALSO: *General Welfare Clause; Tenth Amendment.*)

Bibliography
ALFANGE, DEAN, JR. 1969 Congressional Power and Constitutional Limitations. *Journal of Public Law* 18:103–134.
BARBER, SOTIRIOS A. 1984 *On What the Constitution Means.* Chap. 4. Baltimore: Johns Hopkins University Press.

ENVIRONMENTAL QUALITY IMPROVEMENT ACT

See: Environmental Regulation and the Constitution

ENVIRONMENTAL REGULATION AND THE CONSTITUTION

Indirectly, at least, the Constitution provides the federal government with power to regulate on behalf of environmental quality, but it also sets limits on the power. It sets limits, likewise, on the regulatory power of the states. What it does not do, at present, is grant the "constitutional right to a clean environment" so avidly sought in the heyday of environmental concern, the decade of the 1970s. Thus, the one unique aspect of the general topic considered here has no doctrinal standing; the remaining aspects are matters of doctrine, but they are not unique to environmental regulation. It is quite sufficient, then, merely to illustrate the wide range of constitutional issues that arise in the context of environmental regulation, and to suggest the nature of the debate on the question of a constitutional right to an environment of good quality.

Environmental lawmaking at the national level of government—whether by Congress, the executive, or indeed the federal courts—became important only in the 1970s, but the beginnings reach back well into the nineteenth century, if not farther. This history, especially the strong federal presence of recent years, makes apparent the significant constitutional authority of the central government in regard to the environment. Granting that it is a government of LIMITED POWERS, and mindful of occasional suggestions "that these powers fall short of encompassing the breadth of concerns potentially subject to environmental regulation," one can still conclude, with Philip Soper, "that no conceivable measure reasonably intended to protect the environment is beyond the reach" of federal authority.

The most important source of federal power to regulate in the environmental field is found in the COMMERCE CLAUSE. The clause, especially as it pertains to congressional authority to regulate activities *affecting* commerce, has been so expansively applied by the federal courts as to justify federal control of virtually any problem of environmental pollution. Some pollution sources, such as automobiles and ships, move in INTERSTATE COMMERCE; other sources manufacture products that do so; pollution affects such mainstays of interstate commerce as agricultural commodities, livestock, and many raw materials; pollutants themselves can be seen as products, or at least byproducts, moving "in commerce" across state lines. An imaginative federal district court relied upon this last theory to sustain the Clean Air Act in *United States v. Bishop Processing Company* (D.Md. 1968).

These views lend support not only to the federal air pollution control program but also to programs concerning noise, pesticides, solid waste, toxic substances, and water pollution. Regarding the last especially, Congress can draw on its unquestioned authority over navigable waters, and on the willingness of the federal courts to regard as navigable any waters of a depth sufficient, as someone once said, to float a Supreme Court opinion.

The federal government can draw on other sources of power, at least on a selective basis, to support programs of environmental regulation. The property clause of Article IV, section 3, for example, gives Congress the power to "make all needful Rules and Regulations respecting" the property of the United States. In *Kleppe v. New Mexico* (1976) the clause was relied upon to sustain the Wild Free-Roaming Horses and Burros Act of 1971 as a "needful regulation" "respecting" public lands, against New Mexico's claim that the federal government lacked authority to control the animals unless they were moving in interstate commerce or damaging public lands. It seems clear that under the property clause Congress may regulate the use of its own lands, and perhaps adjacent lands as well, to protect environmental conditions and promote ecological balance on government property.

Other powers relevant to environmental regulation include the TAXING POWER, which presumably would authorize effluent and emission fees to control pollution; perhaps the ADMIRALTY power, as a basis for controlling pollution from ships; and the power to approve INTERSTATE COMPACTS, as an indirect means by which to impose federal environmental standards on compacting states, as the Court suggested in *West Virginia ex rel. Dyer v. Sims* (1951), involving a compact among eight states to control pollution in the Ohio River system. And the Supreme Court may draw on its ORIGINAL JURISDICTION to shape a FEDERAL COMMON LAW of pollution in suits between states or between a state and the citizens of another state.

The TREATY POWER provides yet another basis for federal environmental quality and conservation measures. The leading case here is MISSOURI V. HOLLAND (1920), sustaining the Migratory Bird Act of 1918. Congress enacted the legislation in question in order to give effect to a treaty between the United States and Great Britain. Missouri, claiming "title" to birds within its borders, sought to prevent a federal game warden from enforcing the Act. The Court, through Justice OLIVER WENDELL HOLMES, rejected the state's contention. Treaties, under the SUPREMACY CLAUSE, are the "supreme Law of the Land"; so too are acts of Congress " NECESSARY AND PROPER for carrying into Execution" the treaty power vested in the president and the Senate. *Missouri v. Holland* is of particular interest because the Court upheld the Migratory Bird Act notwithstanding the fact that a similar act, not based on a treaty, had earlier been invalidated as beyond the scope of congressional power. As Soper remarks, the case "accordingly seems to stand for the proposition that Congress may do by statute and treaty what it has no power to do by statute alone."

The specific basis for the state's claim in *Missouri v. Holland* was the TENTH AMENDMENT, which reserves to the states powers not delegated to the United States by the Constitution. The provision introduces the subject of constitutional limitations (as opposed to powers) that may apply to programs of environmental regulation, and illustrates a limitation applicable only to the federal government, and not to the states.

The Tenth Amendment figured prominently in a series of cases involving the federal Clean Air Act and decided by several courts of appeals in the 1970s. A central question in the cases was whether the amendment foreclosed the federal Environmental Protection Agency from promulgating regulations compelling various implementation and enforcement measures by the states, under threat of fines and imprisonment for recalcitrant state and local officials. The courts of appeals divided on the question, at least one of them intimating a constitutional violation, one explicitly finding no violation, and one interpreting the

Clean Air Act in such a way as to sidestep the issue. The Supreme Court granted certiorari and heard argument in several of the cases, but it ultimately declined to reach the merits because counsel for the United States conceded that the regulations in question would have to be rewritten to eliminate requirements that states adopt implementation and enforcement measures. The Court's later decisions in HODEL V. VIRGINIA SURFACE MINING AND RECLAMATION ASSOCIATION (1981) and *Federal Energy Regulatory Commission v. Mississippi* (1982) show that Congress can constitutionally place great pressures on the states to regulate, so long as it uses indirect means for doing so.

Another constitutional limitation operating upon state but not federal environmental protection programs arises from the supremacy clause. The limitation may come into play in two common respects. One of these involves PREEMPTION and is illustrated by BURBANK V. LOCKHEED AIR TERMINAL, INC. (1973), where the Court concluded that federal legislation, including the Noise Control Act of 1972, reflected a congressional intention to "occupy the field" of aircraft noise regulation; hence, Burbank's noise ordinance was held invalid under the supremacy clause. The second application of the clause is illustrated in *Hancock v. Train* (1976) and *Environmental Protection Agency v. State Water Resources Control Board* (1976), in which the Court held that the supremacy clause sheltered federal facilities from permit requirements imposed by state governments pursuant to the Clean Air Act and the Federal Water Pollution Control Act, respectively, absent a clear congressional indication to the contrary.

The remaining constitutional limitations on environmental regulation apply more or less equally to state and federal government alike. We can put aside the general question of state *authority* to regulate on behalf of the environment. States, unlike the federal government, are not creatures of limited powers. It has long been acknowledged that the STATE POLICE POWER justifies the widest range of health and safety measures insofar as the federal Constitution is concerned, absent some conflict with supreme federal law. This generalization stood fairly firm even during the most active period of SUBSTANTIVE DUE PROCESS review by the federal judiciary. And it bears mention, regarding health and safety measures, as the Court said in *Northwestern Laundry v. Des Moines* (1916), that "the harshness of such legislation, or its effect upon business interests, short of a merely arbitrary enactment, are not valid constitutional objections. Nor is there any valid Federal constitutional objection in the fact that the regulation may require the discontinuance of the use of property or subject the occupant to large expense in complying with the terms of the law or ordinance."

The BILL OF RIGHTS may bear on state and federal environmental regulation just as it may bear on regulation generally. Recent cases illustrate the point. Thus the FIRST AMENDMENT came into play in *Metromedia, Inc. v. San Diego* (1981), where a local ordinance controlling billboards and the like for the sake of safety and aesthetics was invalidated insofar as it pertained to noncommercial advertising. In *Air Pollution Variance Board of Colorado v. Western Alfalfa Corporation* (1974), the issue was whether the FOURTH AMENDMENT prohibition of unreasonable searches and seizures was violated when a health inspector entered the grounds of a pollution source to make an opacity check of smoke coming from a chimney. The Court held the entry lawful under a line of cases sustaining "open field" searches. In *United States v. Ward* (1980), the Court held that civil penalties imposed for violating certain provisions of the Federal Water Pollution Control Act pertaining to oil spills were not "quasi-criminal" so as to implicate the Fifth Amendment RIGHT AGAINST SELF-INCRIMINATION (or, presumably, the Sixth Amendment's procedural restrictions applicable to criminal prosecutions). Similarly, *Atlas Roofing Co. v. Occupational Safety and Health Review Commission* (1976) held that administrative civil penalty provisions of the Occupational Safety and Health Act did not contravene the SEVENTH AMENDMENT right to TRIAL BY JURY.

In principle, the takings clause of the Fifth Amendment might be thought to contain the most significant restriction on state and federal environmental regulation. The clause, which applies to the states through the FOURTEENTH AMENDMENT, provides: "nor shall private property be taken for PUBLIC USE, without JUST COMPENSATION." It is clearly recognized that a government regulation can work a taking, but it is seldom held that it actually does. Most environmental regulations challenged on taking grounds are alleged to reach too far, to reduce value too much, and thus to transgress the bounds drawn by Justice Holmes in one of his most famous—and least informative—generalizations, uttered in *Pennsylvania Coal Co. v. Mahon* (1922): "that while property may be regulated to a certain extent, if regulation goes too far it will be recognized as a taking." The statement suggests that if a regulation reduces property value by a great deal, a taking will be found. In practice, however, the courts tend to look not at value lost but value left. If the regulation leaves significant value intact, then usually it will be upheld. The central case in point is PENN CENTRAL TRANSPORTATION COMPANY V. NEW YORK CITY (1978), upholding New York's historic landmark preservation law as applied to Grand Central Terminal, notwithstanding very large losses to the terminal's owners. In any event, the takings clause has little bite in the context of conventional environmental regulation because control of nuisance-like activities has long escaped takings challenges even if the value of the regulated property is reduced to zero. Because virtually any environmental regulation can be characterized as a nuisance control measure, virtually none is likely to be regarded as a taking.

The state and federal governments, then, may regulate rather freely on behalf of environmental quality, but are they constitutionally obliged to do so? Nothing in the federal Constitution says as much. There are arguments that diligent and imaginative searching would find the right between the lines of text, chiefly in the "penumbra" of the Bill of Rights, or as a fundamental personal right protected by the NINTH AMENDMENT, or as a right "implicit in the concept of ORDERED LIBERTY" and guaranteed by the DUE PROCESS clause. The Supreme Court and all but a few federal district courts have been unmoved by these arguments. Courts generally have displayed an unwillingness to make the difficult business of environmental policy a matter of constitutional principle, a point reflected in state court decisions holding that state constitutional amendments setting out environmental rights are not self-executing but require, rather, legislative implementation. The courts, quite obviously, feel ill-equipped to play a role thought better suited to legislatures. It is not that the environment is somehow less important than other recognized constitutional values, but rather that it is less amenable to adjudication.

Richard B. Stewart summarizes the arguments in this regard: a constitutional right to environmental quality would give courts ultimate responsibilities for making resource allocation decisions beyond their analytic capabilities; for trading off allocative efficiency and distributional equity without any principled means by which to do so; and for engineering and implementing dynamic policies through the clumsy and apolitical means of litigation. Stewart adds:

> A familiar justification for constitutional protection of given interests is that they are held by a "discrete and insular" minority or are otherwise chronically undervalued because of basic structural defects in the political process. This rationale has been utilized by advocates of a constitutional right to environmental quality, buttressing it by claims that environmental degradation violates "fundamental" interests in health and human survival and implicates the fate of future generations that are unrepresented in the political process. But the spate of environmental legislation enacted by federal and state governments over the past ten years flatly contradicts the general claim that the political process suffers from structural defects that necessitate a constitutional right to environmental quality [*Development*, 1977: 714–715].

Whether future generations will agree is an open question.

JAMES E. KRIER
(1986)

Bibliography

SOPER, PHILIP   1974   The Constitutional Framework of Environmental Law. Pages 20–125 in E. Dolgin and T. Guilbert, eds., *Federal Environmental Law*. St. Paul, Minn.: West Publishing Co.

STEWART, RICHARD B.   1977   The Development of Administrative and Quasi-Constitutional Law in Judicial Review of Environmental Decisionmaking: Lessons from the Clean Air Act. *Iowa Law Review* 62:713–769.

——— 1977   Pyramids of Sacrifice? Problems of Federalism in Mandating State Implementation of National Environmental Policy. *Yale Law Journal* 86:1196–1272.

ENVIRONMENTAL REGULATION AND THE CONSTITUTION
(Update 1)

In recent years, three issues have dominated the constitutional side of environmental law. The first issue involves the ability of administrative agencies to obtain access to private property and business records for purposes of inspection. These FOURTH AMENDMENT problems are not, however, distinctive to the environmental area, but are typical of those involving ADMINISTRATIVE SEARCH in general.

The second issue involves FEDERALISM. Since the doctrine of NATIONAL LEAGUE OF CITIES V. USERY (1976) met its demise in GARCIA V. SAN ANTONIO METROPOLITAN TRANSIT AUTHORITY (1985), Congress has faced no constitutional obstacles to environmental regulation. Where state regulation is concerned, however, COMMERCE CLAUSE and PREEMPTION problems remain recurring sources of litigation. State environmental regulations often burden interstate businesses and may sometimes be a pretext for protectionism. Although some state regulatory measures have fallen afoul of the dormant commerce clause, courts on the whole have been sympathetic to environmental measures and willing to give them the benefit of the doubt in commerce clause cases. The results in preemption cases are much less predictable. As the federal regulatory presence has grown, the difficulties of coordinating local regulations with federal rules have become more widespread. As a result, state regulations are not infrequently held to be preempted by federal law.

The third major constitutional issue involves government regulation of private lands. Under some circumstances, a regulation that "goes too far" can be an unconstitutional TAKING OF PROPERTY. Efforts at environmental preservation can severely restrict the use of property, therby raising taking problems.

One of the best-known cases is a Wisconsin Supreme Court decision, *Just v. Marinette County* (1972). *Just* involved a Wisconsin statute that allowed only limited uses of wetlands, such as harvesting of wild crops, forestry, hunting, and fishing. Other uses required a special permit. Essentially, this law required special permission before any commercial or residential use could be made of the property. The Wisconsin Supreme Court upheld the statute, despite the severe restriction on land use, because of the strong public interest in preserving wetlands. Other state courts have split on the constitutionality of similar statutes.

The Supreme Court has considered several environmental takings cases. In *Keystone Bituminous Coal Association v. DeBenedictus* (1987) the Court upheld a Pennsylvania statute that required underground coal miners to provide support for surface structures. A similar Pennsylvania statute had been held unconstitutional in a wellknown opinion by Justice OLIVER WENDELL HOLMES, JR.,, but the current statute was found to be unobjectionable because it required only a small fraction of the total coal deposits to be left in the ground. On the other hand, in *Nollan v. California Coastal Commission* (1987) the Court took a much different approach. *Nollan* involved a couple who wanted to build a larger beach house. As a condition for receiving a permit, the California Coastal Commission required them to allow the public to walk along the beach. Justice ANTONIN SCALIA found a taking because there was an insufficient nexus between the state's goal of preserving the public's right to view the ocean and the requirement that the public be allowed to walk along the beach.

As these two decisions indicate, the outcomes in taking cases are often unpredictable. This uncertainty is a particular problem for environmental regulators and land use planners, for a mistake can result in an award of damages as well as an injunction against the taking.

With these exceptions, constitutional issues have not loomed large in federal environmental law. By and large, like most regulations of economic activities, environmental statutes have received only minimal judicial scrutiny. As a result, the major issues in environmental law have involved statutory interpretation rather than constitutional disputes.

DANIEL A. FARBER
(1992)

Bibliography

MICHELMAN, FRANK   1988   Takings, 1987. *Columbia Law Review* 88:1600–1629.

ROSE, CAROL   1984   *Mahon* Reconsidered: Why the Takings Issue Is Still a Muddle. *Southern California Law Review* 57:561–599.

ENVIRONMENTAL REGULATION AND THE CONSTITUTION
(Update 2)

While disputes over STATUTORY INTERPRETATION and other subconstitutional issues continue to dominate environmental law, in recent years the field of environmental law has been significantly influenced by the Supreme Court's constitutional jurisprudence on FEDERALISM, the TAKINGS clause of the Fifth Amendment, and Article III STANDING. Taken together, these constitutional developments may signal a period of retrenchment and decentralization in environmental regulation. The Court's renewed concern for state SOVEREIGNTY and PROPERTY RIGHTS, and its resistance to liberal standing principles for "private attorneys general" are noticeable departures from past trends. At a minimum, it is clear that constitutional issues now loom larger than ever in environmental law.

In a series of split decisions, the REHNQUIST COURT has tightened the constraints on Congress's authority to direct state institutions or impose upon state resources. In NEW YORK V. UNITED STATES (1992), the Court invalidated the "take title" provision of the Low-Level Radioactive Waste Act Amendments of 1985 as violative of the TENTH AMENDMENT prohibition on "commandeering" state legislatures. The offending section specified that a state or regional compact that fails to provide for the disposal of all internally generated WASTE by a particular date must, upon the request of the waste's generator or owner, take title to, and possession of, the waste. In *New York*, the Court clarified the relationship between the COMMERCE CLAUSE and the Tenth Amendment, holding that even where Congress exercises its legitimate commerce clause authority, the method it chooses must not run afoul of the Tenth Amendment. Relying on *New York*, the Court in *Printz v. United States* (1997) held unconstitutional provisions that imposed on state law enforcement officers a duty to investigate the eligibility of would-be gun purchasers. The Court held that the Tenth Amendment forbids the commandeering of state executive officers just as it does the conscription of state legislatures in the service of federal regulatory objectives.

In UNITED STATES V. LÓPEZ (1995), the Court invalidated as insufficiently related to INTERSTATE COMMERCE a federal statute criminalizing handgun possession near schools. For the first time in over fifty years, the Court explicitly limited Congress's commerce clause authority, raising potential questions about the extent of federal environmental power. In still another important case for state sovereignty, *Seminole Tribe v. Florida* (1996), the Court held that Congress cannot abrogate states' ELEVENTH AMENDMENT immunity from suit in federal court pursuant to its Article I powers.

After *Seminole*, claims for damages against states or state agencies for liability pursuant to federal environmental statutes were to be adjudicated in state courts unless a state waived its immunity from suit in federal court. However, in the 1998–1999 term, the Supreme Court further curbed federal authority over states in three controversial 5–4 rulings. Most significantly for environmental law, the Court held in *Alden v. Maine* (1999) that Congress lacks the power under Article I to subject non-consenting states to private suits for damages in state courts for violations of federal law. Still available post-*Alden* are private suits in both state and federal court seeking injunctive relief against state officers for ongoing violations of law under the EX PARTE YOUNG (1908) exception to SOVEREIGN IMMUNITY. The effect of *Alden* on environmental law remains an open question. Injunctive relief rather than penalties tends to be the most important feature of private actions against states for violations of federal environmental law, making the continued availability of injunctive relief in such private actions important. *Alden* may significantly impair private cost–recovery suits against states for remediation of hazardous waste sites under the federal superfund law, however. Of course, the federal government itself may still seek damages in both state and federal courts for state violations of federal law.

The revival of a states' rights vision of federalism and the imposition of constraints on federal power has significant implications for environmental law. Most federal environmental statutes passed since 1970 extend Congress's reach into historically local matters and rely heavily on the states for implementation and administration, an approach to regulation known as "cooperative federalism." These statutes contain a range of measures designed to induce state cooperation—measures that invite closer constitutional scrutiny in the wake of the Court's federalism jurisprudence. Following *López*, several federal courts have entertained commerce clause challenges to major environmental statutes such as the Endangered Species Act, the Clean Water Act, and the Comprehensive Environmental Response, Compensation and Recovery Act. To date, however, these challenges have been mostly unsuccessful. Following *New York*, federal courts have struck down a number of statutory provisions for conscripting state governments to administer federal programs in violation of the Tenth Amendment.

Still, although federal courts have repudiated the most obvious examples of federal commandeering, nonetheless they seem prepared to tolerate the liberal use of Congress's TAXING AND SPENDING POWER in "inducing" state cooperation. For example, in *Virginia v. Browner* (1996), the

U.S. Court of Appeals for the Fourth Circuit rejected a challenge to the Clean Air Act's sanction provisions, which allow the Environmental Protection Agency (EPA) to withhold federal highway funds and impose other measures on noncomplying states. The Court upheld the provisions as "inducements," as opposed to "outright coercion." The question remains whether imposing conditions on a state's receipt of federal funds can ever rise to the level of coercion. While the revival of federalism symbolically undermines the strong federal role in environmental regulation, perhaps the federalism cases portend less a judicial brake on federal environmental regulation than a warning to the federal government to be careful in crafting state inducements.

Over the last decade, the Court has also ventured further into land use regulation. Building upon its holding in *Nollan v. California Coastal Commission* (1987), the Court in DOLAN V. TIGARD (1994) invalidated an exaction requiring a landowner to provide a public greenway in exchange for a permit to build a parking lot adjacent to her plumbing and electrical supply store. The Court held that in addition to a "sufficient nexus" between the regulated use and the proposed exaction, there must be a "rough proportionality" between the two. The exaction in *Dolan* failed to meet the latter criterion, thus violating the takings clause of the FOURTEENTH AMENDMENT. Taken together, *Nollan* and *Dolan* threaten to chill local land use regulation.

In LUCAS V. SOUTH CAROLINA COASTAL COUNCIL (1992), the Court invalidated South Carolina's Beachfront Management Act as an unconstitutional taking of private property, as applied to a particular landowner. The impugned legislation forbade development of beachfront property on the barrier island beach where Lucas had, prior to the act's passage, purchased an empty lot. The trial court had held that the act's prohibition on development reduced the value of Lucas's land to nothing, a finding left undisturbed on appeal. The Court held that state regulatory statutes that reduce land value to nothing are unconstitutional takings unless the proposed restrictions are part of the landowner's title to begin with, consonant with background COMMON LAW nuisance or property principles. Of particular interest is the Court's decision in *Eastern Enterprises v. Apfel* (1998), in which a plurality opined that severe, disproportionate, and extremely retroactive liability in the form of economic regulation may amount to an unconstitutional taking. The trend in takings law may constrict the ability of federal and state governments to impose environmentally protective regulation on private property without paying substantial costs.

The Rehnquist Court has also retreated from the liberal standing principles that helped to open the administrative process to citizen participation over the last several de-

cades. In LUJAN V. DEFENDERS OF WILDLIFE (1992), the Court denied standing to a national environmental organization suing under the citizen suit provision of the Endangered Species Act. The plaintiffs challenged the exemption of overseas projects from a rule requiring that federal agencies consult with the U.S. Department of the Interior to minimize the effect of their projects on endangered species. The plaintiffs alleged that their own personal and professional interests in endangered species would be harmed by federally funded development projects. In denying standing, the Court held that the plaintiffs' injuries were not sufficiently "imminent" to establish the Article III standing requirement of injury in fact, nor, according to a plurality, would those injuries be redressable by a favorable court decision. While in many cases the more stringent "imminence" requirement will merely require plaintiffs to be more precise in alleging injury, the redressability requirement, which forces plaintiffs to demonstrate that a favorable decision would in fact alleviate the harm, is less easily rectified and may result in the dismissal of some cases if adopted by a majority of the Court in the future. The Court acknowledged in *Lujan* that its holding made standing "substantially more difficult" to achieve when the plaintiff is not herself the object of government action. At this writing, the Court has granted CERTIORARI on a case—*Friends of the Earth, Inc. v. Laidlaw Environmental Services*—that will clarify the stringency of the redressability requirement.

In coming years, the DUE PROCESS clause may be a fertile source of constitutional jurisprudence relevant to environmental law. Due process issues to watch include the imposition of caps on PUNITIVE DAMAGE awards in toxic contamination suits; the definition of knowledge and fault requirements for environmental crimes; environmental justice challenges to federal and state environmental laws that disproportionately burden minorities with environmental risk; and the retrospective imposition of strict liability on defendants in toxic tort suits.

JODY FREEMAN
(2000)

EPPERSON v. ARKANSAS
393 U.S. 97 (1968)

Arkansas prohibited the teaching in its public schools "that mankind ascended or descended from a lower order of animals." In dealing with a challenge to the law based on establishment clause and FREEDOM OF SPEECH grounds, Justice ABE FORTAS, speaking for the Supreme Court, concluded that the Arkansas law violated the establishment clause. "There can be no doubt," he said, "that Arkansas sought to prevent its teachers from discussing the theory of evolution because it is contrary to the beliefs of some that the book of Genesis must be the exclusive source of the doctrine of the origin of man."

Justice HUGO L. BLACK and Justice POTTER STEWART concurred in brief opinions resting on VAGUENESS grounds. The Black opinion raised important GOVERNMENT SPEECH issues that are still unresolved.

RICHARD E. MORGAN
(1986)

(SEE ALSO: *Creationism.*)

EQUAL ACCESS

For over two decades litigation involving religion and the public schools focused on state-sponsored religious exercises. This pattern changed during the 1980s, as student-led religious groups sought access to school facilities on the same basis as other student groups. These groups claimed that once a public school opened its premises to extracurricular student groups, it created a limited PUBLIC FORUM and could not discriminate against some groups on the basis of the content of their speech; hence, the school was obliged to grant "equal access" to religious student groups that wanted to use school facilities. Equal access found a legal footing in WIDMAR V. VINCENT (1981), where the Supreme Court held that a public university could not close its facilities to religious student groups once it had opened them for use by other groups because to do so would violate the religious students' FREEDOM OF SPEECH guaranteed by the FIRST AMENDMENT.

Despite *Widmar,* most secondary schools continued to reject requests by religious students to meet on school premises, as did most federal courts; indeed, until 1989 every federal appellate court to rule on the issue held that it would violate the ESTABLISHMENT CLAUSE for secondary schools to allow religious student groups to meet on the same basis as other student groups. The basic rationale for these lower-court holdings came from a federal appellate opinion by Judge Irving Kaufman in *Brandon v. Guilderland* (1980). In *Brandon,* a group of high school students sought permission to meet before school in an empty classroom to pray and read the Bible. The school district denied the request. Judge Kaufman argued that the district could not accede to the students' petition because to do so would impermissibly advance religion and excessively entangle church and state in violation of the second and third prongs of the LEMON TEST.

Kaufman's main argument was psychological: "To an impressionable student even the mere appearance of secular involvement in religious activities might indicate that the state has placed its imprimatur on a particular creed.

This symbolic inference is too dangerous to permit." Critics of the decision disagreed. Chief Justice WARREN BURGER, dissenting in BENDER V. WILLIAMSPORT (1986), argued that one must objectively distinguish between state advancement of religion and individual advocacy of religion; whereas the former activity is prohibited by the First Amendment, the latter is "affirmatively protected." The fact that "some hypothetical students" might mistake individual religious expression for state religion was irrelevant according to Burger, who added: "No one would contend that the State would be authorized to dismantle a church erected by private persons on private property because overwhelming evidence showed that other members of the community thought the church was owned and operated by the state."

When the Supreme Court declined to resolve the constitutionality of equal access, Congress intervened by passing the Equal Access Act in 1984. The act applies to all public secondary schools receiving federal money that also maintain a "limited open forum," which exists whenever a school allows "one or more noncurriculum related student groups to meet on school premises during noninstructional time." The act forbids schools with a limited open forum from discriminating against student groups because of the content of their speech.

In BOARD OF EDUCATION OF THE WESTSIDE COMMUNITY SCHOOLS V. MERGENS (1990) the Supreme Court held that the act does not violate the establishment clause as applied to religious student groups, but declined to rule whether the equal-access rights guaranteed by statute are also required by the First Amendment. The Court will likely have another opportunity to deal with this First Amendment issue. As equal-access theory is based primarily on the freedom of speech, it lends itself to a broader range of activities than just the student meetings protected by the Equal Access Act. More recent cases have focused, for example, on the right of students to distribute religious publications to classmates on school premises. These cases have yet to reach the Supreme Court.

JOHN G. WEST, JR.
(1992)

(SEE ALSO: *Religion in Public Schools; Religious Fundamentalism; Religious Liberty; Separation of Church and State.*)

Bibliography

WEST, JOHN G., JR. 1991 The Changing Battle over Religion in the Public Schools. *Wake Forest Law Review* 26:361–401.

WHITEHEAD, JOHN W. 1989 Avoiding Religious Apartheid: Affording Equal Treatment for Student-Initiated Religious Expression in Public Schools. *Pepperdine Law Review* 16:229–258.

EQUAL EMPLOYMENT OPPORTUNITY COMMISSION (EEOC) v. WYOMING
460 U.S. 226 (1983)

The EEOC sought to enforce the AGE DISCRIMINATION IN EMPLOYMENT ACT (ADEA) against the state of Wyoming in a case involving the involuntary retirement of a fifty-five-year-old game warden. The Supreme Court, 5–4, upheld the ADEA as so applied. Justice WILLIAM J. BRENNAN, for the Court, found congressional power in the COMMERCE CLAUSE, and rejected the state's claim, based on NATIONAL LEAGUE OF CITIES V. USERY (1976), that it was immune to this form of congressional regulation. The majority was composed of the four dissenters in *Usery* plus Justice HARRY A. BLACKMUN.

Wyoming, Brennan said, failed the third part of the formula of *Hodel v. Virginia Surface Mining and Reclamation Association* (1981): the ADEA did not "directly impair" Wyoming's ability to "structure integral operations in areas of traditional governmental functions." Wyoming could use other means to test the fitness of game wardens—or, as the ADEA allowed, justify the necessity of the age limit. The ADEA would affect state finances and state policies only marginally. Chief Justice WARREN E. BURGER, for the four dissenters, employed the same *Hodel* formula and concluded that the ADEA was unconstitutional as applied to a state.

This decision helped set the stage for *Usery*'s overruling in GARCIA V. SAN ANTONIO METROPOLITAN TRANSIT AUTHORITY (1984).

KENNETH L. KARST
(1986)

(SEE ALSO: *Intergovernmental Immunity.*)

EQUALITY

See: Difference and Constitutional Equality;
Equal Protection of the Laws

EQUAL PROTECTION OF THE LAWS

The ancient political ideal of equality did not find explicit recognition in the text of the Constitution until the FOURTEENTH AMENDMENT was ratified in 1868. Yet equality was an American ideal from the earliest colonial times. There was irony in the expression of the ideal in the DECLARATION OF INDEPENDENCE; the newly independent states generally limited voting to white male property owners, and THOMAS JEFFERSON, the Declaration's author, was the troubled owner of slaves. Even so, one feature of white American society that set it apart from Europe was an egalitarian climate for social relations. The Constitution's ban on TITLES OF NOBILITY symbolized the nation's determination to leave behind the old world's privileges of monarchy and aristocracy.

Jefferson, who believed in an aristocracy of "virtue and talents," understood that equality of opportunity was consistent with wide disparities among individuals' wealth and power. The equality he envisioned was, above all, equality before the law. The principle of universal laws, equally applicable to all citizens, itself provided a foundation for a market economy whose competitive struggles would lead to further inequalities. An equality that was formal, or legal, thus would undermine the "equality of condition" that attracted some of Jefferson's contemporaries. Yet formal equality was something that mattered greatly in the nation's first decades, and it matters greatly today. When Europeans remark, as they still do, on America's relatively high degree of equality, they are referring not to equality of wealth or political power but to equality of social status. With pardonable literary exaggeration, Simone de Beauvoir said it this way: "the rich American has no grandeur; the poor man no servility; human relations in daily life are on a footing of equality. . . ."

The Fourteenth Amendment's wording emphasizes legal equality. A state is forbidden to "deny to any person within its jurisdiction the equal protection of the laws." On its face this language seems to demand no more than even-handed enforcement of laws as they are written. Such a reading, however, would drain all life from the guarantee of equal protection. On this view even a law barring blue-eyed persons from state employment would pass constitutional muster if the state applied it equally, without discrimination, to all applicants, refusing jobs only to those who were blue-eyed. No one has ever seriously argued for so restricted a scope for the equal protection clause. The Supreme Court casually dismissed the idea with a passing comment in YICK WO V. HOPKINS (1886): "the equal protection of the laws is a pledge of the protection of equal laws."

At the other extreme of silliness, the *Yick Wo* statement might be taken literally, interpreting the equal protection clause to forbid the enforcement of any law that imposed any inequality. As Joseph Tussman and JACOBUS TEN BROEK showed nearly forty years ago, so sweeping a reading would convert the clause into a constitutional prohibition on legislation itself. All laws draw lines of classification, applying their rules only to some people (or some transactions or phenomena) and not to others. Furthermore, the very existence of law—that is, of governmental regulation of human behavior—implies inequality, for some individuals must evaluate the behavior of others and enforce the state's norms by imposing sanctions on the recalcitrant. In Ralf Dahrendorf's biting formulation, "all men are equal *before* the law but they are no longer equal *after* it." Given the diverse characteristics of humans, the achievement of equality as to one aspect of life necessarily implies inequalities as to other aspects. And if it were possible to construct a society characterized by total, uncompromising equality, no one would want to live in that society.

Then what kinds of inequality are prohibited by the equal protection clause? The abstraction, equality, cannot resolve cases; the question always remains, equality as to what? To give meaning to the equal protection clause requires identification of the substantive values that are its central concern. The inquiry begins in the history leading to the adoption of the Fourteenth Amendment, but it does not end there. To understand the substantive content of the equal protection clause, we must consider not only what it meant to its framers, but also what it has come to mean to succeeding generations of judges and other citizens.

Just what role the framers had in mind for the equal protection clause remains unclear; the amendment's sketchy "legislative history" has been given widely divergent interpretations. All the interpreters agree, however, that the framers' immediate objective was to provide an unshakable constitutional foundation for the CIVIL RIGHTS ACT OF 1866. That act had been passed over the veto of President ANDREW JOHNSON, who had asserted that it exceeded the powers of Congress.

The 1866 act had declared the CITIZENSHIP of all persons born in the United States and subject to its JURISDICTION. This declaration, later echoed in the text of the Fourteenth Amendment, had been designed to "overrule" the assertion by Chief Justice ROGER B. TANEY in his opinion for the Supreme Court in DRED SCOTT V. SANDFORD (1857) that black persons were incapable of being citizens. Taney had said that blacks—not just slaves but any blacks—were incapable of citizenship, because blacks had not been members of "the People of the United States" identified in the Constitution's PREAMBLE as the body who adopted that document. Blacks has been excluded from membership in the national community, according to Taney, because they were "considered as a subordinate and inferior class of beings, who had been subjugated by the dominant race, and, whether emancipated or not, yet remained subject to their authority. . . ." Discriminatory state legislation in force when the Constitution was adopted, Taney said, negated the conclusion that the states "regarded at that time, as fellow-citizens and members of the sovereignty, a class of beings whom they had thus stigmatized; . . . and

upon whom they had impressed such deep and enduring marks of inferiority and degradation. . . ."

This dubious reading of history is beside the point; *Dred Scott's* relevance to our inquiry is that Taney's assumptions about racial inferiority and restricted citizenship were just what the drafters of the 1866 act sought to destroy. There was to be no "dominant race" and no "subordinate and inferior class of beings," but only citizens. Indeed the act's conferral of various CIVIL RIGHTS was aimed at abolishing a new system of serfdom designed to replace SLAVERY in the southern states. That system rested on the BLACK CODES, laws methodically imposing legal disabilities on blacks for the purpose of maintaining them in a state of dependency and inferiority.

The 1866 act, after its declaration of citizenship, provided that "such citizens, of every race and color [including former slaves], shall have the same right [to contract and sue in court and deal with property, etc.] as is enjoyed by white citizens. . . ." The "civil rights" thus guaranteed were seen as the equal rights of citizens. When President Johnson vetoed the bill, he similarly linked the ideas of citizenship and equality, and argued that the THIRTEENTH AMENDMENT was an insufficient basis for congressional power. Congress overrode Johnson's veto, but from the time of the veto forward, a major purpose of the promoters of the Fourteenth Amendment, then under consideration in Congress, was to secure the constitutional foundations of the 1866 act.

The amendment, like the act, begins with a declaration of citizenship. In the same first section, the amendment goes on to forbid a state to "abridge the PRIVILEGES OR IMMUNITIES of citizens of the United States," to "deprive any person of life, liberty, or property, without DUE PROCESS OF LAW," or to deny a person "the equal protection of the laws." No serious effort was made during the debates on the amendment to identify separate functions for the three clauses that followed the declaration of citizenship. The section as a whole was taken to guarantee the equal enjoyment of the rights of citizens.

Beyond those specific goals, nothing in the consensus of the Fourteenth Amendment's framers would have caused anyone to anticipate what the Supreme Court made of the amendment in the latter half of the twentieth century. Yet the Fourteenth Amendment was not written in the language of specific rights, such as the right to contract or buy or sell property, but was deliberately cast in the most general terms. The broad language of the amendment strongly suggests that its framers were proposing to write into the Constitution not a "laundry list" of specific civil rights but a principle of equal citizenship.

To be a citizen is to enjoy the dignity of membership in the society, to be respected as a person who "belongs."

The principle of equal citizenship presumptively forbids the organized society to treat an individual either as a member of an inferior or dependent caste or as a nonparticipant. As Taney recognized in his *Dred Scott* opinion, the stigma of caste is inconsistent with equal citizenship, which demands respect for each individual's humanity. Further, a citizen is a participant in society, a member of a moral community who must be taken into account when community decisions are made. Citizenship also implies obligations to one's fellow citizens. The values of participation and responsibility contribute to the primary citizenship value of respect, but they are also independently significant as aspects of citizenship.

For the first eight decades of the Fourteenth Amendment's existence, its interpretation by the Supreme Court was largely a betrayal of the constitutional ideal of equal citizenship. First by inventing the STATE ACTION limitation on the Fourteenth Amendment in the CIVIL RIGHTS CASES (1883), and then by giving racial SEGREGATION the stamp of constitutional validity in the SEPARATE BUT EQUAL decision of PLESSY V. FERGUSON (1896), the Supreme Court delivered virtually the entire subject of race relations back into the hands of the white South. The equal citizenship principle was left to be articulated in dissenting opinions. Notable among those dissents were the opinions of Justice JOSEPH P. BRADLEY in the SLAUGHTERHOUSE CASES (1873) and of Justice JOHN MARSHALL HARLAN in the *Civil Rights Cases* and *Plessy v. Ferguson.* The latter dissent included a passage that is now famous: "In view of the Constitution, in the eye of the law, there is in this country no superior, dominant, ruling class of citizens. There is no caste here. Our Constitution is color-blind, and neither knows nor tolerates classes among citizens." For half a century, those words expressed not a reality but a hope.

Outside the field of RACIAL DISCRIMINATION, the equal protection clause had little force even during the period when the due process clause of the Fourteenth Amendment was in active use as a defense against various forms of ECONOMIC REGULATION. By the 1920s, Justice OLIVER WENDELL HOLMES could say in BUCK V. BELL (1927), with accuracy if not with compassion, that the equal protection clause was the "usual last resort of constitutional arguments."

Even during the years when Holmes's "last resort" epithet summarized equal protection jurisprudence, the NAACP was pinning its hopes for racial justice on the federal judiciary, and was winning some victories. The Supreme Court had struck down LITERACY TESTS for voting that contained GRANDFATHER CLAUSES exempting most white voters, in GUINN V. UNITED STATES (1915) and *Lane v. Wilson* (1939); the Court had begun the process of holding "white primaries" unconstitutional; and it had invalidated racial zoning in BUCHANAN V. WARLEY (1917). And after the nation had emerged from the Great Depression and World War II, the judicial climate was distinctly more hospitable to equal protection claims.

The Depression had brought to dominance a new political majority, committed to active governmental intervention in economic affairs for the purpose of achieving full employment and major improvements in wages and the conditions of labor. The judiciary's main contribution to those egalitarian goals was to free the legislative process from the close judicial supervision of economic regulation that had attended the flowering of SUBSTANTIVE DUE PROCESS doctrines in the recent past. The war not only ended the Depression; it was a watershed in race relations. The migration of blacks from the rural South to northern and western cities, which had slowed during the Depression, dramatically accelerated, as wartime industry offered jobs that black workers had previously filled only rarely. Urban blacks were soon seen as a potent national political force. By the end of the war, the Army had begun the process of racial integration. Wartime ideology, with its scorn for Nazi racism, had lasting effects on the public mind. Even as the Supreme Court was upholding severe—and racist—wartime restrictions in the JAPANESE AMERICAN CASES (1943–1944), it reflected a new national state of mind in its celebrated OBITER DICTUM in KOREMATSU V. UNITED STATES (1944): "All legal restrictions which curtail the civil rights of a single racial group are immediately suspect.... [C]ourts must subject them to the most rigid scrutiny."

In the immediate postwar years the Supreme Court held unconstitutional the judicial enforcement of RESTRICTIVE COVENANTS in SHELLEY V. KRAEMER (1948), and it even ruled that the equal protection clause forbade some forms of segregation in state universities. (See SWEATT V. PAINTER, 1950.) The expected return to economic depression did not materialize. Instead, the country entered a period of unprecedented economic expansion. Good times are the most propitious for egalitarian public policies; it is relatively easy for "haves" to share with "have-nots" when they see their own conditions as steadily improving. The time was ripe, in the 1950s, for important successes in the movement for racial equality.

On the national scene, however, the political branches of government remained disinclined to act. One-party politics in the South had given disproportionate influence in the Congress to Southerners whose seniority gave them chairs of major committees. With President DWIGHT D. EISENHOWER reluctant to intervene, the prospects for effective civil rights legislation seemed dim. Thus was the stage furnished when Eisenhower appointed EARL WARREN to the Chief Justiceship in 1953.

In Warren's first term the Court decided BROWN V.

BOARD OF EDUCATION (1954)—still the leading authoritative affirmation that the Constitution forbids a system of caste—and in so doing began what PHILIP KURLAND has called an "egalitarian revolution" in constitutional law. *Brown* was a major event in modern American history. Race relations in America would never again be what they were on the eve of the decision. The political movement for racial equality took on new vitality, and other egalitarian movements drew encouragement from that example. The constitutional law of equal protection gained powerful momentum, and the doctrinal effects went well beyond the subject of racial equality. If *Brown* itself represented JUDICIAL ACTIVISM, it was no more than a shadow of what was to come. The equal protection clause became the cutting edge of the WARREN COURT's active intervention into realms that previously had been left to legislative choice.

Two doctrinal techniques served these egalitarian ends. First, the Court heightened the STANDARD OF REVIEW used to test the constitutionality of certain laws, insisting on STRICT SCRUTINY by the courts of legislation that employed a SUSPECT CLASSIFICATION or discriminated against the exercise of a FUNDAMENTAL INTEREST. Second, the Court relaxed the "state action" limitation on the Fourteenth Amendment, bringing new forms of private conduct under the amendment's reach. Although the BURGER COURT later revitalized the "state action" limitation and slowed the advance of equal protection into new doctrinal territory, it made its own contributions to the development of the principle of equal citizenship.

Once the Court had firmly fastened the "suspect classification" label to racial discrimination, other forms of discrimination were attacked in the same terms. Some Justices have refused to find any legislative classification other than race to be constitutionally disfavored, but most of them have been receptive to arguments that at least some nonracial discriminations deserve heightened scrutiny. Thus, while only discrimination against ALIENS has been assimilated to the "suspect classifications" category—and even that assimilation is a sometime thing—the Court has announced clearly that judicial scrutiny should be heightened in some significant degree for SEX DISCRIMINATION or legislative classifications based on ILLEGITIMACY. Not only in these opinions but also in opinions refusing to apply similar reasoning to other forms of discrimination, the Court has developed a consensus on two sets of factors that are relevant in determining a classification's degree of "suspectness" or disfavor, and thus the level of justification which courts should demand for it.

The first set of factors emphasizes the equal citizenship value of respect; these factors reflect the judiciary's solicitude for the victims of stigma. A classification on the basis of a trait that is immutable and highly visible—such as race or sex—promotes stereotyping, the automatic assignment of an individual to a general category, often implying inferiority. The second set of factors, emphasizing the equal citizenship value of participation, focuses on the historic disadvantages (especially political disadvantages) of DISCRETE AND INSULAR MINORITIES. Both the phrase and the idea antedate Warren Court activism; they come from Justice HARLAN FISKE STONE's opinion for the Court in UNITED STATES V. CAROLENE PRODUCTS CO. (1938). Legislation that burdens a group likely to be neglected by the legislature is a natural candidate for special judicial scrutiny.

The equal citizenship themes of respect, participation, and responsibility also informed the Warren Court's decisions demanding close examination of the justifications for legislative discrimination against the exercise of "fundamental interests." Those decisions, in theory, might have been rested on grounds of substantive due process rather than equal protection. In fact, the Burger Court, which refused to recognize any new "fundamental" interests in equal protection doctrine, employed similar reasoning under the heading of due process, with corresponding attention to the values of equal citizenship. (See ABORTION AND THE CONSTITUTION; FAMILY AND THE CONSTITUTION; RIGHT OF PRIVACY.) The equal protection cases, however, identify only three clusters of interests as "fundamental": VOTING RIGHTS and related interests in equal access to the electoral process; certain rights of ACCESS TO THE COURTS (which have come to be explained more recently on due process grounds); and rights concerning marriage, procreation, and family relations. (See FREEDOM OF INTIMATE ASSOCIATION.)

Voting, of course, is one of the core responsibilities of citizenship. Perhaps more important, it is the citizen's preeminent symbol of participation as a valued member of the community. Access to the courts, like voting, is instrumentally valuable as a way to protect other interests. But—also like voting—the chance to be heard is an important citizenship symbol. To be listened to, to be treated as a person and not an object of administration, is to be afforded the dignity owed to a citizen. Finally, the marriage and family cases similarly implicate the citizenship values of respect, responsibility, and participation. Marriage and parenthood do not merely define one's legal obligations; they define one's status and social role and self-concept. For the state to deny a person the right and responsibility of choice about such matters is to take away the presumptive right to be treated as a person, one of equal worth among citizens. None of these "fundamental" interests is entirely immune from state interference; what the principle of equal citizenship requires is that government offer weighty justification before denying their equal enjoyment.

In retrospect the whole apparatus of differential standards of review can be seen as judicial interest-balancing, thinly disguised: the more important the interest in equality, the more justification was required for its invasion by the government. Perhaps the Warren Court's majority chose to clothe its decisions in a "judicial"-sounding system of categories because the Justices were sensitive to the charge that they were writing their own policy preferences into the equal protection clause, and not just "interpreting" it. As a consequence, the Court extended the reach of equal protection without ever explicitly articulating the substantive content of the equal protection clause.

The Warren Court, in its final years, was well on the way to effective abandonment of the "state action" limitation on the Fourteenth Amendment, finding "significant state involvement" in all manner of private racial discriminations that denied their victims full participation in the public life of the community. Once Congress passed the CIVIL RIGHTS ACT OF 1964, however, it became unnecessary for the Court to complete its dismantling job; now there was a federal statutory right of access to PUBLIC ACCOMMODATIONS such as hotels, restaurants, and theaters. When the Court in JONES V. ALFRED H. MAYER CO. (1968) discovered the Thirteenth Amendment as a source of congressional power to forbid most other private racial discrimination, the chief practical motivation for doing away with the "state action" doctrine was removed. In later years, a different majority of Justices has gone far to restore the "state action" limitation to its former status but at the same time it has both reaffirmed the power of Congress to stamp out private racial discrimination and promoted that purpose with an expansive interpretation of existing civil rights acts.

The right to participate in the community's public life—even those portions of public life that are owned and managed by private persons—is an essential ingredient of effective citizenship, part of what it means to be a respected member of society. The "state action" limitation, when the Supreme Court invented it, insulated the "private" choices of the owners of public accommodations and other commercial businesses not only from the direct reach of the Fourteenth Amendment's guarantee of equal protection but also from congressional vindication of the rights of equal citizenship. Although "state action" remains an impediment to the application of the equal protection clause to some private conduct, Congress can protect, and has protected, the most important claims to participation by all citizens in society's public life.

To say that the principle of equal citizenship is the substantive core of the equal protection clause, and that the Supreme Court's recent equal protection jurisprudence has centered on the values of equal citizenship, is not to decide particular cases. Equal citizenship is not a decisional machine but a principle that informs judgment by

reference to certain substantive values. Like other constitutional principles, it is inescapably open-ended. The Warren Court's expansion of the content of equal protection doctrine was regularly greeted with the criticism that the Court had not specified exactly how far its egalitarian principles would reach. The critics did no more than echo what Jeremy Bentham had said more than a century earlier: the abstraction, equality, is insatiable; where would it all end?

This "stopping-place" problem is implicit in any constitutional guarantee of equality. Most obviously, it lies at the center of the question of affirmative governmental obligations to reduce inequality. In a few decisions over the past three decades the Supreme Court has imposed on government the duty to compensate for the inability of INDIGENTS to pay various costs or fees required for effective access to the courts. The Burger Court's consciousness of the stopping-place problem produced two types of response. Some claims of access, although accepted, were explained as resting on rights to procedural fairness, and thus on due process rather than equal protection grounds. (See BODDIE V. CONNECTICUT.) Other access claims were rejected, halting further extension of the demands of equal protection. (See ROSS V. MOFFITT.) Yet the Court has not been willing to put an end to the notion that some inequalities, although not caused directly by the state, are constitutionally intolerable, requiring governmental action to relieve their victims from some of their consequences.

Similarly, consciousness of the stopping-place problem has influenced the Court's definition of what constitutes a legislative discrimination based on race, or gender, or, presumably, any other disfavored classification. After flirting in some school segregation cases with a view that would equate de facto with de jure segregation, the Court declared in the employment discrimination case of WASHINGTON V. DAVIS (1976) that it was not enough, in making a claim of racial discrimination, to show that legislation had a racially discriminatory impact. To succeed, such a claim must be based on a showing of official discriminatory purpose. (See LEGISLATION.) The "impact" principle, said the Court, "would be far reaching and would raise serious questions about, and perhaps invalidate, a whole range of tax, welfare, public service, regulatory, and licensing statutes that may be more burdensome to the poor and to the average black than to the more affluent white." In other words, where would it all end?

What is needed, in dealing with the stopping-place problem as with any other aspect of equal protection interest-balancing, is the guidance that can be found in the Fourteenth Amendment's substantive values. Some inequalities will invade the core values of equal citizenship, and others will touch them hardly at all. The level of justification required for governmental action—or failure to act—will vary according to the magnitude of that invasion. Some economic inequalities may be so severe as to impose a stigma of caste, but most do not. Part of our tradition of responsible citizenship, after all, is to provide for oneself and one's family. The principle of equal citizenship is not a charter for economic leveling but a presumptive guarantee against those inequalities that dehumanize or seriously impair one's ability to participate as a member of society. To say that such determinations turn on questions of degree is merely to acknowledge that no constitutional principle is a substitute for judicial judgment.

Since the late 1960s a number of governmental and private bodies have voluntarily taken steps to compensate for inequalities that are the legacy of past societal discrimination, and generally to integrate various institutions by race and by gender. These AFFIRMATIVE ACTION programs, sometimes in the form of racial or gender-based quotas for employment or housing or admission to higher education, do not merely equalize. Every equality begets another inequality. Even absent a quota, when a person's race becomes a relevant qualification for a job, all other relevant factors are diminished in weight. To put the matter more concretely, an individual can lose the competition for the job on the basis of his or her race. If affirmative action is constitutionally justified—and the Supreme Court has largely validated it—the reasons lie not in any lack of sympathy for such arguments, but in the weight of countervailing considerations supporting the programs. The Justices' various opinions upholding affirmative action have mainly sounded the theme of remedying past discrimination, but other arguments emphasize the urgency of integrating American institutions in the present generation.

The debate over affirmative action has touched a more general issue: the appropriate role of groups in equal protection analysis. In one view, group membership is simply irrelevant. The text of the equal protection clause provides its guarantees to "any person," and much of our constitutional tradition is individualistic. Yet, inescapably, a claim to equality is a claim made on behalf of a group. If every law draws some line of classification, then it is also true that every individual is potentially classifiable according to an enormous variety of characteristics. Legislative classification implies a selection of certain attributes as the relevant ones—the "merits" that justify conferring a benefit (or "demerits" that justify a burden). Once such a classification is written into law, any individual is classified either with the group of persons who possess the "merits" (or "demerits") or with the group of those who do not. To complain against a classification scheme is not merely to say "I am wronged," but to say "We—the whole group of individuals disadvantaged—are wronged." Indeed, any claim based on a rule of law is intelligible only as a demand

to be treated the same as other members of a group, that is, all others who share the relevant "individual" attributes specified by the rule.

The origins of the Fourteenth Amendment strongly suggest that a group, defined by race just as the *Dred Scott* opinion had defined it, was intended to be the amendment's chief beneficiary. If today the equal protection clause prohibits other forms of inequality, there is nothing incongruous about viewing that development in one perspective as the recognition of the claims of groups of people: women, aliens, illegitimate children, homosexuals, the handicapped. When equal citizenship is denied, the denial typically takes a form that affects not merely isolated individuals but classes of people.

The equal protection clause limits only the states; nothing in the constitutional text expressly imposes an analogous limit on the federal government. Yet since BOLLING V. SHARPE (1954) the Supreme Court has consistently interpreted the Fifth Amendment's due process clause to guarantee equal protection against federal denial. This interpretation has roots in the original Constitution's assumption that the new national government would have a direct relationship with individuals. The idea of national citizenship was current long before the Civil Rights Act of 1866. And that citizenship, as Justice Bradley argued in his dissent in the *Slaughterhouse Cases*, implies some measure of equality before the law. *Bolling*, a companion case to *Brown v. Board of Education*, presented a challenge to school segregation in the District of Columbia. *Brown* held the segregation of state schools unconstitutional, and Chief Justice Warren said it would be "unthinkable" if a similar principle were not applied to the national government. After the Fourteenth Amendment's reaffirmation of national citizenship, such a result would, indeed, have been unthinkable.

The Warren Court's expansion of constitutional guarantees of equality necessarily implied an expansion of the powers of the national government. The Civil War amendments were reinterpreted to give Congress sweeping powers to reach virtually all racial discriminations, public and private. The Fourteenth Amendment's equal protection clause became the basis for intensified intervention by the federal courts into areas previously governed by local law and custom, as a new body of uniform national law replaced local autonomy. As the "state action" limitation was relaxed, the Constitution brought the commands of law to areas previously regulated by private institutional decision. In ALEXANDER BICKEL's phrase, the Warren Court's main themes were "egalitarian, legalitarian, and centralizing."

The desegregation of places of public accommodations in the South is an instructive example. The Supreme Court first held unconstitutional all forms of state-sponsored segregation, including segregation of public beaches, parks, golf courses, and restaurants. Then, cautiously, it began to apply the same reasoning to some privately owned public accommodations, finding "state action" in the most tenuous connections between public policy and the private decision to segregate. Finally, in HEART OF ATLANTA MOTEL CO. V. UNITED STATES (1964) the Court moved swiftly to validate the Civil Rights Act of 1964, which forbade segregation in most public accommodations that mattered. In all these actions the Court promoted the extension of a body of uniform national law to replace the local laws and customs that had long governed southern communities, with an earlier Supreme Court's blessing.

These changes in the law governing racial discrimination in public accommodations were, in one perspective, a repetition of a course of events that had been common in the Western world since the seventeenth century. An older system, basing a person's legal rights on his or her status in a hierarchical structure, came to be replaced by a newer law that applied impersonally to everyone. The abolition of slavery, the 1866 Civil Rights Act, the Civil War amendments—all had been earlier episodes in this same historical line. And the law that liberated individuals from domination based on race, like the law that previously had broken feudal hierarchies and the power of the guilds, was the law of the centralized state. If one were asked to compress three centuries of Western political history into three words, the words might be: "egalitarian, legalitarian, and centralizing."

Justice ROBERT H. JACKSON, concurring in EDWARDS V. CALIFORNIA (1941), remarked that the Fourteenth Amendment's privileges and immunities clause was aimed at making United States citizenship "the dominant and paramount allegiance among us." Whatever the historical warrant for that assertion, it reflects today's social fact. We think of ourselves primarily as citizens of the nation, and only secondarily as citizens of the several states. The Constitution itself has become our pre-eminent symbol of national community, and the judiciary's modern contributions to our sense of community have centered on the principle of equal citizenship.

It is hard to overstate the importance of the ideal of equality as a legitimizing force in American history. For the SOCIAL COMPACT theorists of the eighteenth century whose thinking was well-known to the Framers of the original Constitution, some measure of equality before the law was implicit in the idea of citizenship. DANIEL WEBSTER, speaking of "the LAW OF THE LAND," agreed: "The meaning is, that every citizen shall hold his life, liberty, property, and immunities, under the protection of the general rules which govern society." By Webster's time, support for the principle of equality of opportunity could be found even among the most comfortable Americans, who saw in that

principle a way to justify their advantages. More generally, the egalitarian spirit that has promoted a national consciousness has also lent legitimacy to government. There has been just enough truth in the belief that "anyone can grow up to be President" to provide a critical measure of the diffuse loyalty that is an essential ingredient of nationhood.

Never in our history has it been true that *anyone* might aspire to the presidency. Slavery and racial discrimination are only the most obvious and uglier counterexamples; not until our own time have women's aspirations to such high position become realistic. Yet the guarantee of equal protection of the laws, even during the long decades when lawyers deemed it a constitutional trifle, stood as a statement of an important American ideal. Much of the growth in our constitutional law has resulted when the downtrodden have called the rest of us to account, asking whether we intend to live up to the principles we profess. Vindication of the constitutional promise of equal citizenship did not take its rightful place on our judicial agenda for an unconscionably long time, and it remains far from complete. What is most remarkable, however, is the nourishment that the promise—the promise alone—has provided for a national community.

KANNETH L. KARST
(1986)

Bibliography

BELL, DERRICK A., JR. 1980 *Race, Racism, and American Law,* 2nd ed. Boston: Little, Brown.
BICKEL, ALEXANDER M. 1970 *The Supreme Court and the Idea of Progress.* New York: Harper & Row.
BLACK, CHARLES L., JR. 1969 *Structure and Relationship in Constitutional Law.* Pages 51–66. Baton Rouge: Louisiana State University Press.
ELY, JOHN HART 1980 *Democracy and Distrust: A Theory of Judicial Review.* Cambridge, Mass.: Harvard University Press.
FISS, OWEN M. 1976 Groups and the Equal Protection Clause. *Philosophy and Public Affairs* 5:107–177.
KARST, KENNETH L. 1977 The Supreme Court, 1976 Term—Foreword: Equal Citizenship under the Fourteenth Amendment. *Harvard Law Review* 91:1–68.
KINOY, ARTHUR 1967 The Constitutional Right of Negro Freedom. *Rutgers Law Review* 21:387–441.
MICHELMAN, FRANK I. 1969 The Supreme Court, 1968 Term—Foreword: On Protecting the Poor Through the Fourteenth Amendment. *Harvard Law Review* 83:7–59.
POLE, J. R. 1978 *The Pursuit of Equality in American History.* Berkeley: University of California Press.
RAE, DOUGLAS 1981 *Equalities.* Cambridge, Mass.: Harvard University Press.
TOCQUEVILLE, ALEXIS DE 1945 *Democracy in America,* P. Bradley, ed., 2 vols. New York: Vintage Books.
TUSSMAN, JOSEPH and TEN BROEK, JACOBUS 1949 The Equal Protection of the Laws. *California Law Review* 37:341–381.

WESTEN, PETER 1982 The Empty Idea of Equality. *Harvard Law Review* 95:537–596.

EQUAL PROTECTION OF THE LAWS
(Update 1)

Two questions have dominated the Supreme Court's equal protection opinions since 1985. The first, largely a matter of rhetoric, is the question of the appropriate STANDARD OF REVIEW. The second and more important question is the relevance of racial groups in determining the existence of discrimination and in providing legislative or judicial remedies for the harms of discrimination.

The uninitiated reader of the Court's opinions surely would think the process of decision in an equal protection case begins with a selection of the appropriate standard of judicial review from among three well-worn formulas: (1) STRICT SCRUTINY, which requires the government to offer compelling justification for an inequality it has imposed, and so generally results in the invalidation of governmental action; (2) RATIONAL BASIS, in which the Court pays strong deference to the government's assertions of justification and generally upholds the governmental action; or (3) the "intermediate," "heightened" scrutiny that falls between these two polar extremes, requiring "important" justification. Then, the same reader might imagine, the Court measures the government's asserted justifications against the proper standard of review, and on that basis reaches judgment.

More skeptical readers know that the order of the decisional process is often quite the reverse, with a judgment on the merits of the case preceding—even dictating—the selection of a standard of review as an opinion's rhetorical structure. The skeptics know, too, how misleading it is to speak of "the" standard of review, given the Court's occasional willingness to require significant justification in the name of "rational basis" review. Justice THURGOOD MARSHALL has long (and accurately) insisted that the Court's decisions add up to a sliding scale in which the standard of review varies according to the importance of the interests at stake. Justice JOHN PAUL STEVENS made a similar point when he said, "There is only one equal protection clause." In equal protection cases, as in other cases, the Court decides by weighing interests.

The Court's post-1985 equal protection decisions are illustrative. A 6–3 majority of the Justices used the traditional, highly deferential, "rational basis" standard to uphold two acts of Congress governing eligibility for welfare benefits and food stamps in *Lyng v. Castillo* (1986) and *Lyng v. Automobile, Aerospace and Agricultural Imple-*ment Workers* (1988). Similarly, in *Kadrmas v. Dickinson Public Schools* (1988), the Court upheld, 5–4, a state law authorizing some school districts to impose on unwilling parents user fees for school-bus transportation. The majority specifically rejected the argument of two dissenting Justices that PLYLER V. DOE (1982) demanded heightened judicial scrutiny for wealth classifications governing access to public education. *Plyler's* opinion had been written in the language of "rational basis" review, but no one among the Justices or the Court's commentators had been deceived into believing that the Court was being deferential to the legislature's judgment. In fact, the Court in *Kadrmas* explicitly called *Plyler* a case of heightened scrutiny. The post-1985 decisions may be less than satisfying, but they are conventional applications of existing doctrine.

The dissenters' invocation of *Plyler v. Doe* reminds one, however, that Justices can make "rational basis" into the equivalent of heightened scrutiny when they are so inclined. Two recent cases evoked such responses. ATTORNEY GENERAL OF NEW YORK V. SOTO-LOPEZ (1986) was a challenge to a state law that gave veterans of the armed forces a preference in civil-service hiring, but only if the veterans were New York residents when they entered the forces. A four-Justice plurality concluded that the law failed to pass the heightened scrutiny demanded by the RIGHT TO TRAVEL. Two other Justices rejected both the "right to travel" argument and the conclusion that heightened scrutiny was appropriate; nonetheless, they concluded that the law lacked a rational basis and so violated the equal protection clause. Plainly, this is not a classical "rational basis" decision, any more than was *Plyler v. Doe.*

In CLEBURNE V. CLEBURNE LIVING CENTER (1985) the Justices were unanimous in holding unconstitutional a Texas town's refusal to grant a ZONING variance to allow the operation of a group home for mentally retarded persons. The court of appeals had concluded that an official classification based on MENTAL RETARDATION required justification at the level of "intermediate" scrutiny, but a majority of the Supreme Court disagreed. Vigorously arguing that the proper standard was "rational basis," the majority proceeded to a meticulous examination of the justifications offered by the town, rejecting each one as insufficient. As Justice Marshall, concurring, pointed out, *Cleburne* has taken its place alongside *Plyler* as a leading modern example of the sliding scale of standards of review in action.

In at least two kinds of cases, the "rational basis" standard, initially given "bite" in the fashion of *Plyler* and *Cleburne*, has been transformed into candid recognition of a more rigorous judicial scrutiny of governmental justifications. The law of SEX DISCRIMINATION moved from the "rational basis" explanation of *Reed v. Reed* (1971) to the explicit "intermediate" scrutiny of CRAIG V. BOREN (1976). A similar rhetorical change is visible in the law governing classifications based on the legal status of ILLEGITIMACY. First came the "rational basis" language of LEVY V. LOUISIANA (1968); eventually, the open adoption of "intermediate" scrutiny in *Clark v. Jeter* (1988). These progressions exemplify the normative power of the factual: the practice of heightened scrutiny eventually leads to its formal recognition as doctrine. It is not extravagant to expect a similar treatment of the claims of the mentally retarded in some future opinion. In the end, the standard of JUDICIAL REVIEW seems not so much to govern decisions as to provide a rhetorical framework on which lawyers and judges can fasten the substantive considerations that are the heart of argument and decision: the harms of governmental actions to constitutionally protected interests and the government's justifications for those actions.

In contrast, arguments about the relevance of group harms and the validity of group remedies are of major importance in deciding cases—and, indeed, in deciding whether the nation will seriously address the continuing harms of RACIAL DISCRIMINATION. Certainly racial discrimination happens to people one by one, but it happens because they are members of a racial group. The harms of group subordination have multiple causes; actions are harmful because of their contexts. Yet our current constitutional law pays little attention to context and, instead, centers on a principle demanding no more of government than formal racial neutrality. To establish a claim of racial discrimination that violates the equal protection clause, normally one must show that identifiable officers of the government have purposefully acted on a racial ground to produce the harm in question—a proposition typically hard to prove.

A rare case in which the requisite purpose was found was *Hunter v. Underwood* (1985). The Supreme Court concluded that a clause in Alabama's 1901 state constitution disenfranchising persons convicted of crimes of "moral turpitude" had been adopted for the purpose of preventing black citizens from voting and continued in the present to have racially disparate effects. Accordingly, the Court held that it was unconstitutional for the state to deny the vote on the basis of a conviction for the MISDEMEANOR of passing a worthless check. The Court based its conclusion about the law's continuing racially disparate effects on statistics showing that blacks in two Alabama counties had been disenfranchised under the law at a rate at least 1.7 times the rate for whites.

Two years later, however, in rejecting an equal protection attack on the constitutionality of the death penalty, a majority of the Justices refused to give similar weight to a statistical demonstration of racial discrimination. A study

of some 2,000 Georgia murder cases in the 1970s showed dramatic racial disparities in the likelihood that CAPITAL PUNISHMENT would be imposed. In MCCLESKEY V. KEMP (1987) the Court decided, 5–4, that those statistics were irrelevant; to prevail on a claim of racial discrimination, a defendant must show some specific acts of purposeful discrimination by the prosecutor, jury, or judge in his or her own case. Surely the majority Justices understood that a contrary decision would have threatened wholesale reversals of death sentences—a course they were unwilling to take.

Both the *Hunter* and *McCleskey* cases raised questions concerning the relevance of group subordination in equal protection analysis. *McCleskey* illustrates the present majority's devotion to the principle of formal racial neutrality and its reluctance to accept a showing of disparity among racial groups as proof of the discrimination that violates the equal protection clause. In interpreting a number of federal CIVIL RIGHTS statutes, however, the Court has accepted this sort of statistical proof of discrimination.

The issue of the constitutionality of AFFIRMATIVE ACTION brings together the rhetorical question of the standard of judicial review and the more substantive question of group remedies. Although, since 1985, the Supreme Court has remained fragmented on both these aspects of affirmative action, the practical effects of the decisions show a remarkable stability.

Given the acceptability of statistical proof of violation of a number of major antidiscrimination laws, many an affirmative-action program amounts to the substitution of one group remedy for another. Accordingly, there is broad agreement among the Justices on the validity of affirmative-action programs that are seen to be genuinely remedial. Yet the dominant principle for the Court's current majority is one of formal racial neutrality, and there is some awkwardness in squaring affirmative action with this principle. In two recent affirmative-action cases—WYGANT V. JACKSON BOARD OF EDUCATION (1986), on public hiring, and RICHMOND (CITY OF) V. J. A. CROSON CO. (1989), on public contracting—the key opinions were written by Justices LEWIS F. POWELL and SANDRA DAY O'CONNOR. On the surface, these opinions minimize group concerns, but together they make clear how a public institution can constitutionally adopt an affirmative action program. The approved method, explained as a form of remedy for past discrimination, makes judicious use of statistics showing racial disparities. In short, Justices Powell and O'Connor have found a way to use the language of individual justice in the cause of ending group subordination.

The prevailing opinions in *Wygant* and *Croson* emphasize the "strict scrutiny" standard of review, employing this standard both in evaluating the justifications for affirmative action as a remedy for past discrimination and in requiring "narrow tailoring" of a racially based remedy. In METRO BROADCASTING, INC. V. FCC (1990), however, a different 5–4 majority announced that the less demanding "intermediate" scrutiny was appropriate in evaluating an affirmative-action program approved by Congress. In an opinion by Justice WILLIAM J. BRENNAN, the majority upheld a congressionally approved program of the Federal Communications Commission (FCC) for a limited number of racial preferences in the distribution of broadcast licenses. Here the majority said that Congress was not limited to providing remedies for past discrimination; rather, the affirmative-action program was aimed at achieving a greater diversity in broadcast programming. The four dissenters, in opinions by Justice O'Connor and Justice ANTHONY M. KENNEDY, insisted on "strict scrutiny" for congressional affirmative action as well as for state or local governmental programs and argued that the nonremedial purpose of broadcasting diversity was not a sufficiently compelling governmental purpose to pass the test.

Even after the retirement of Justice Brennan, there remains a majority of Justices who agree that Congress has the power, in enforcing the FOURTEENTH AMENDMENT, to remedy societal discrimination, both private and governmental, through affirmative-action programs. Presumably, in future cases, that result will be described, as it was in *Croson*, as consistent with "strict scrutiny." Indeed, in *Metro Broadcasting* itself one might have imagined an opinion upholding the FCC's diversity program as broadly "remedial." In the affirmative-action context, as elsewhere in equal protection doctrine, discussions of the standard of review serve purposes that are mainly rhetorical.

KENNETH L. KARST
(1992)

(SEE ALSO: *Capital Punishment and Race; Discrete and Insular Minorities; Race and Criminal Justice; Race-Consciousness; Racial Preference.*)

Bibliography

BELL, DERRICK A. 1987 *And We Are Not Saved: The Elusive Quest for Racial Justice.* New York: Basic Books.

KARST, KENNETH L. 1989 *Belonging to America: Equal Citizenship and the Constitution.* New Haven, Conn.: Yale University Press.

KENNEDY, RANDALL L. 1988 McCleskey v. Kamp: Race, Capital Punishment, and the Supreme Court. *Harvard Law Review* 101:1388–1433.

LAWRENCE, CHARLES R., III 1987 The Id, the Ego, and Equal Protection: Reckoning with Unconscious Racism. *Stanford Law Review* 39:317–388.

MINOW, MARTHA 1987 The Supreme Court, 1986 Term— Foreword: Justice Engendered. *Harvard Law Review* 101: 10–95.

EQUAL PROTECTION OF THE LAWS
(Update 2)

The equality value of the equal protection clause is implicated most strongly when the government discriminates against groups. Discrimination on the basis of identifiable group membership, such as race, gender, alienage, birth out of wedlock, or SEXUAL ORIENTATION means that all members of the disfavored group are disadvantaged by governmental action because of their group membership. The constitutional permissibility of discrimination on the basis of group membership depends on whether the government can provide an adequate justification for the specific act of discrimination. The matter of adequate justification is influenced in part by the degree of scrutiny called for under the articulated STANDARD OF REVIEW applicable to discrimination against the particular group. But it is also influenced by the Supreme Court's value judgments about the premises underlying the discrimination.

The paradigmatic form of discrimination on the basis of identifiable group membership in American society has been RACIAL DISCRIMINATION. The Court has long held that all racial discrimination is suspect and so is subject to the STRICT SCRUTINY standard of review. The specific act of racial discrimination must be shown to be "precisely tailored to advance a compelling governmental interest." Applying this exacting standard of review, the Court has held unconstitutional virtually all governmental action discriminating against African Americans and other racial or ethnic minorities in the last half of the twentieth century. However, the Court has also held that the equal protection clause prohibits only intentional racial discrimination. Facially neutral laws that have the demonstrable effect of disadvantaging racial minorities as a group are not subject to constitutional challenge absent evidence of an invidious purpose to discriminate on a racial basis.

The most controverted constitutional issue of racial equality today is the permissibility of race-based AFFIRMATIVE ACTION designed to overcome the inequality that exists between African Americans (and other racial- ethnic minorities) and whites, inequality that has resulted from a long history of official and unofficial racial discrimination. On the one hand, the preference for racial minorities as a group embodied in affirmative action programs causes individual whites to suffer discrimination because of their race, and so is inconsistent with the principle of formal racial neutrality. On the other hand, this racial preference advances the objective of substantive racial equality. The tension between the principle of formal racial neutrality and the objective of substantive racial equality is reflected in the difficult and often divided Court decisions as to the constitutional permissibility of race-based affirmative action.

The one point on which the Court is agreed is that racial preference is constitutionally permissible when it is precisely tailored to overcome the present consequences of identified past discrimination for which the governmental entity employing racial preference is itself responsible. Since 1990, however, the Court has limited the use of race-based affirmative action for this purpose, emphasizing that there must be a substantial basis in evidence for finding the existence of identified past discrimination. In ADARAND CONSTRUCTORS, INC. V. PEÑA (1995), the Court held that racial preference programs adopted by Congress are subject to the same "strict scrutiny" standard of review as racial preference programs adopted by state and local governments, effectively overruling METRO BROADCASTING, INC. V. FCC (1990).

The Court, in SHAW V. RENO (1993) AND ITS PROGENY, has also held that when a state seeks to remedy the dilution of minority political power caused by past discrimination in voting, it is not justified in using race as the predominant factor in ELECTORAL DISTRICTING. The state may not draw electoral districts in an irregular form in disregard of "traditional districting criteria" in order to create a legislative district in which racial minority voters are in the majority. There is also a question as to whether the Court will continue to follow its earlier decision in REGENTS OF UNIVERSITY OF CALIFORNIA V. BAKKE (1978), where it held that a public university may use race-conscious admissions criteria in order to achieve a racially diverse student body.

The clear trend in equal protection jurisprudence today is toward a requirement of formal racial neutrality. For the most part, governmental efforts to overcome substantive racial inequality will have to be accomplished by racially neutral means, which are likely to be less effective than race-based affirmative action. This result, interacting with the conclusion that the equal protection clause prohibits only intentional racial discrimination, seriously limits governmental efforts to achieve substantive racial equality in American society.

In times past, classifications on the basis of gender were pervasive in American law, and were based on stereotyped assumptions about men and women and their respective societal roles. These gender-based classifications reinforced male domination and female subordination, but in many of their specific applications they disadvantaged men as well as women. The Court held in CRAIG V. BOREN (1976) that SEX DISCRIMINATION is subject to "intermediate" scrutiny, and that in order to be upheld, it must be "substantially related to advancing an important governmental interest."

In applying this standard of review, the Court has insisted on an "exceedingly persuasive justification" for any gender-based classification. The Court has found such a justification to exist only where the particular gender-based classification had the purpose and effect of remedying the present consequences of past societal discrimination suffered by women as a group or was related to biological and physical differences between men and women and their different roles in the reproductive process. Because gender-based classifications are constitutionally disfavored, they have generally been eliminated in federal and state laws and replaced with gender-neutral criteria, such as "surviving spouse," "dependent spouse," "custodial parent," and the like. In UNITED STATES V. VIRGINIA (1996), one of the very few cases involving gender-based classifications to come before the Court in recent years, the Court held that Virginia could not constitutionally exclude women from the citizen-soldier training afforded by the Virginia Military Institute, a state-supported military college.

The Court's interpretation of the equal protection clause necessarily influences the political decisions of Congress and the state legislatures with respect to discrimination on the basis of identifiable group membership. Although the Court, applying strict scrutiny, has held that the equal protection clause precludes the states from discriminating against resident ALIENS with respect to entitlement to governmental benefits, such as WELFARE, it has also held that Congress's plenary power over IMMIGRATION and NATURALIZATION requires extreme judicial deference to Congress's treatment of resident aliens. When Congress discriminates against resident aliens, for example, by denying them WELFARE BENEFITS, the deferential RATIONAL BASIS standard of review applies, and such discriminations are routinely held to be constitutionally permissible. This broad constitutional power has played a role in the political process in recent years. In the Welfare Reform Act of 1996, Congress denied many welfare benefits to resident aliens.

The Court's approach to discrimination against NON-MARITAL CHILDREN highlights how the matter of adequate justification is influenced by the Court's value judgments about the premises underlying the discrimination. Saying that it is "illogical and unjust" to penalize out-of-wedlock children for the circumstances of their birth, the Court, applying an articulated "important and substantial relationship" standard of review, has held unconstitutional all of the traditional forms of discrimination against children born out of wedlock, such as denying welfare benefits to a family that includes nonmarital children.

The Court held that discrimination against gay and lesbian persons solely on the basis of their sexual orientation was "arbitrary and irrational" and so was unconstitutional even under the lower scrutiny of the rational basis standard of review. In ROMER V. EVANS (1996), the Court, applying this standard of review, held violative of equal protection a Colorado state constitutional provision that excluded discrimination on the basis of sexual orientation from the protection of state and local antidiscrimination laws. Writing for the Court, Justice ANTHONY M. KENNEDY, said that the law "imposed a disadvantage born of animosity toward the class of persons affected," and that, "[a] law declaring that in general it shall be more difficult for one group of citizens than for others to seek aid from the government itself is a denial of equal protection of the laws in the most literal sense." Justice ANTONIN SCALIA, in dissent, accused the majority of taking sides in a "culture war," and said that Colorado was entitled to enact a law expressing the view that homosexuality was "morally wrong and socially harmful."

The Court's opinion in *Romer* reflects a strong commitment to the value of equality and makes clear that the constitutional guarantee of equal protection forbids government to discriminate against gay and lesbian persons solely because of their status as members of a disfavored group. Any laws that disadvantage persons because of their sexual orientation thus must be justified on grounds that are independent of majority hostility. In this connection, Congress has excluded openly homosexual persons from serving in the Armed Forces. The government has generally succeeded in persuading lower courts that this exclusion is rationally related to legitimate military concerns. The constitutionality of this exclusion has not yet been decided by the Court.

ROBERT A. SEDLER
(2000)

(SEE ALSO: *Adoption, Race, and the Constitution; Antidiscrimination Legislation; Asian Americans and the Constitution; Race, Reproduction, and Constitutional Law; Sexual Orientation and the Armed Forces.*)

Bibliography

ALEINIKOFF, ALEXANDER T.   1991   A Case for Race-Consciousness. *Columbia Law Review* 91:1060–1125.

BRADLEY, CRAIG M.   1994   The Right Not to Endorse Gay Rights: A Reply to Sunstein. *Indiana Law Journal* 70:29–38.

CARTER, STEPHEN L.   1991   *Reflections of an Affirmative Action Baby.* New York: Basic Books.

CULP, JEROME M., JR.   1994   Colorblind Remedies and the Intersectionality of Oppression: Policy Arguments Masquerading as Moral Claims. *New York University Law Review* 69:162–196.

FARBER, DANIEL A. and SHERRY, SUZANNA   1996   The Pariah Principle. *Constitutional Commentary* 13:257–284.

FLAGG, BARBARA J.   1994   Enduring Principles: On Race, Process and Constitutional Law. *California Law Review* 82:935–980.

FOSTER, SHEILA   1993   Difference and Equality: A Critical Assessment of the Concept of "Diversity." *Wisconsin Law Review* 1993:105–161.

FRANKE, KATHERINE M.   1995   The Central Mistake of Sex Discrimination Law: The Disaggregation of Sex from Gender. *University of Pennsylvania Law Review* 144:1–99.

GINSBURG, RUTH BADER   1992   Speaking in a Judicial Voice. *New York University Law Review* 67:1185–1209.

GRAGLIA, LINO A.   1996   "Affirmative Action," Past, Present, and Future. *Ohio Northern Law Journal* 23:1207–1225.

MACKINNON, CATHERINE A.   1991   Reflections on Sex Equality Under Law. *Yale Law Journal* 100:1281–1328.

SUNSTEIN, CASS R.   1994   Homosexuality and the Constitution. *Indiana Law Journal* 70:1–28.

SYMPOSIUM   1993   Sexual Orientation and the Law. *Virginia Law Review* 79:1419–1902.

———   1995   Voting Rights After *Shaw v. Reno. Rutgers Law Review* 26:517–773.

EQUAL RIGHTS AMENDMENT

In March 1972, Congress proposed an Equal Rights Amendment (ERA) to the United States Constitution. The amendment provided:

Section 1. Equality of rights under the law shall not be denied or abridged by the United States or by any State on account of sex.
Section 2. The Congress shall have the power to enforce, by appropriate legislation, the provisions of this article.
Section 3. The Amendment shall take effect two years after the date of ratification.

In May 1982, the extended deadline for ratification expired without the necessary approval from three-fourths of the states; fifteen had never ratified and five had voted to rescind their ratification. Challenges to the legality of those rescissions and to Congress's extension of the ratification deadline became moot.

Proponents subsequently reintroduced the amendment in Congress, thus continuing a campaign that began a half-century earlier. Some version of an equal rights amendment had surfaced in every congressional term between 1923 and 1972. In the view of most proponents, the text adopted in 1972 was designed to prohibit gender classifications except those concerning personal privacy, physical characteristics, or past discrimination. The rationale was that a constitutional prohibition would avoid piecemeal remedies for various forms of discrimination. Such a mandate would also subject sex-based classifications to a more rigorous standard of review than that prevailing under FOURTEENTH AMENDMENT doctrine, which allows discrimination substantially related to an important state purpose.

Although conceived as a measure to unite women, the amendment has often divided them. Throughout its history, the ERA campaign has triggered fundamental controversies about the meaning of equality and the means to attain it in a society marked by significant disparities in sexual roles. Much debate has centered not on legal entitlements but on cultural aspirations. Dispute has focused on the amendment's effect concerning laws purportedly advantaging women, such as protective labor legislation, marital support requirements, and military service exemptions. Particularly during the earlier part of the century, opponents contended that equality in formal mandates could never secure equality in fact. So long as female wage earners and homemakers were more economically vulnerable than men, a demand for equal rights appeared out of touch with social realities. By contrast, ERA proponents contended that protective legislation had often "protected" women from opportunities for higher paid vocations, and had legitimated stereotypes on which invidious discrimination rested. Supporters also noted that by the time Congress proposed the amendment in 1972, much sex-based regulation had been either invalidated or extended to men, and that which remained could be cast in sex-neutral terms.

So too, much of the discrimination that the amendment was originally designed to redress was, by the 1970s, illegal under various judicial, executive, and legislative mandates. Accordingly, the ERA ratification campaign frequently focused on symbolic rather than legal implications. To proponents, a constitutional mandate would serve as an important affirmation of women's equal status and as a catalyst for change in social practices beyond the scope of legal regulation. For opponents, however, the amendment's symbolic subtext represented an assault less on gender discrimination than on gender differences, and an invitation for further encroachments on states' rights.

In the ratification struggle of the 1970s, ERA supporters lacked the leverage to make their interests felt. But if the equal rights campaign helps inspire and empower women to expand their political influence, then the struggle itself may prove more important than its constitutional consequences.

DEBORAH L. RHODE
(1986)

(SEE ALSO: *Feminist Theory*.)

Bibliography

BOLES, JANET   1979   *The Politics of the Equal Rights Amendment.* New York: Longmans.

BROWN, BARBARA A.; EMERSON, THOMAS I.; FALK, GAIL; and FREEDMAN, ANN E.   1971   The Equal Rights Amendment: A Constitutional Basis for Equal Rights for Women. *Yale Law Journal* 80:872–985.

RHODE, DEBORAH L.   1983   Equal Rights in Retrospect. *Journal of Law and Inequality* 1:1–72.

EQUITABLE RESTRAINT

See: Abstention Doctrine

EQUITY

First named (in Article III) among the subjects to which the judicial power "shall extend" are "all Cases, in Law and Equity, arising under this Constitution, the Laws of the United States, and Treaties made, or which shall be made, under their authority." The word "equity" has here a technical meaning well comprehended by American lawyers of the eighteenth century, and today still generally familiar to lawyers in all legal systems derived from that of England. The explanation is necessarily historical.

In a development more than well begun in the Middle Ages, and pretty much completed by Stuart times, England developed a unique double system of courts at the national level—the courts of "law," or COMMON LAW courts, and the "court of equity"—or, as it was often called, the "court of chancery."

The common law courts administered a system of law that was radically deficient, first as to remedies available, and, second, as to the breadth of considerations that could be taken into account in the formation of decisions. These courts could in most cases award only damages in money, in many cases a step inadequate to the doing of full justice. The common law courts were also excessively formalistic. If, for example, an error occurred in the transcription of a written contract, the common law courts had no conceptual apparatus for dealing with the mistake. Similarly, they had little capacity for taking into account the problems created by fraud. And the "trust," an institution of great importance, was utterly unknown to the "common law."

During the Middle Ages, suitors who could not get full justice out of the common law courts began to appeal to the Lord Chancellor, a high royal official, for supplementary or corrective help. By Tudor times, this practice had become firmly institutionalized, so that the Lord Chancellor became in some sense a judicial officer, hearing and dealing with such pleas. Little by little, the "chancery" came to be a court. This court had at its disposal a remedy enormously more versatile and efficient than the award of damages—the remedy of the order, or command, that the defendant do or refrain from doing something. The chancery court, in contrast to the courts of common law, knew nothing of the jury; the Chancellor decided all issues of fact and law.

This "court of chancery" opened its eyes, moreover, to many things the common law courts were institutionally disabled from seeing. While a suitor in the common law courts might, for example, get a JUDGMENT in his favor on a written contract procured by fraud on his part, the chancery court might order him to give up the fraudulently procured instrument, or to refrain from suing on it, or even to refrain from collecting on a "law" judgment he had already procured by using it.

Because this chancery court so often intervened in the name of a higher justice or of "conscience," it came to be thought of as (and called) a "court of equity." By the time of the drafting of the Constitution, the doctrines and practices of this kind of "equity" had become well systematized. And most of the new states had borrowed from English practice the two-part system of "law" courts and "chancery" courts, with the doctrines and remedial apparatus of equity available in the latter. It is against this background that the constitutional phrase, "cases in law and equity," is to be understood. "Cases in law" were such cases as would be heard by the common law courts; "cases in equity" were such as would be heard by the Court of Chancery, in England or in a state mirroring the English division.

At the very beginning, the new national government rejected (in the JUDICIARY ACT OF 1789) the idea of totally separate courts of "law" and of "equity." The lower federal courts combined "legal" and "equitable" JURISDICTION in the same judges. But the ancient division was in some sense continued. Down to 1938, the federal district court had the two separate sides of "law" and "equity," respectively—in addition to such special jurisdictions as admiralty and bankruptcy. Even today, after the formal merger of "law" and "equity" cases under the single name of "civil action," lawyers still refer, for example, to the INJUNCTION (an order to do or not to do something) as "equitable relief."

"Equity" cases, in the language of Article III, are of great importance. The injunction is enormously more flexible and powerful than the remedies—mostly the award of damages—available to the court in a "case at law." Dramatic examples abound. It would have been impossible even to begin thinking about the lower federal courts' desegregating the schools if those courts had not had jurisdiction over "cases in equity" seeking orders to state officials. On this jurisdictional grant, indeed, rests the whole elaborate development of efficacious relief against official action thought to be unconstitutional—ranging from injunctions against the enforcement of unconstitutional laws (as in PIERCE V. SOCIETY OF SISTERS, 1925, enjoining state enforcement of a law requiring all pupils to go to public schools) to the running of state prisons by an Alabama district judge. (See INSTITUTIONAL LITIGATION.) The modern history of practical constitutional safeguards is a history of the use of the "equitable" remedy of in-

junction, together with the remedy of the DECLARATORY JUDGMENT—a remedy that would probably have been judged outside the "judicial power" were it not for its close analogy to "cases in equity."

Another characteristic of "cases in equity," overpoweringly important in the use of the national judicial power to protect constitutional rights against action of the states, is that the "court of equity" does not use the jury. This, as far as we can tell, is a gift of history; there appears to be no intrinsic reason why a local jury should not find "the facts" in, say, school desegregation cases. Experience shows that local juries will not often convict, for example, in prosecutions for CIVIL RIGHTS crimes, where the jury is constitutionally required. The whole course of development of national protection of human rights against local oppression might have been quite different if it were not for the fact that the "court of equity," the Lord Chancellor's court, sat without a jury—so that the federal judge, wielding the vital weapons in the "equity" remedial armory, does the same.

CHARLES L. BLACK, JR.
(1986)

Bibliography

FISS, OWEN M.   1972   *Injunctions*. Mineola, N.Y.: Foundation Press.

MCCLINTOCK, HENRY LACY   1948   *Handbook of the Principles of Equity*. St. Paul, Minn.: West Publishing Co.

ERDMAN ACT
30 Stat. 424 (1898)

The report of a commission appointed by President GROVER CLEVELAND to investigate the Pullman strike of 1894 (see IN RE DEBS) prompted this act, one of the earliest federal acts providing for the arbitration of railway labor disputes. The act applied to all railroads and their employees engaged in INTERSTATE COMMERCE and provided mediation of any labor dispute "seriously interrupting or threatening to interrupt" interstate commerce. If mediation failed to resolve the dispute, the parties could turn to an arbitration board whose award would be binding and enforceable through EQUITY proceedings. Neither strikes nor lockouts were permitted during arbitration or ninety days after an award. Section 10 made it a MISDEMEANOR for any employer to require, as a condition of employment, any discriminatory agreements, particularly with regard to union membership. Clearly aimed at outlawing YELLOW DOG CONTRACTS, section 10 fell in *Adair v. United States* (1906) as a violation of FREEDOM OF CONTRACT. The act otherwise operated quite successfully, and Congress fortified its mediation provisions in 1913. A bitter nationwide strike in which both sides refused to invoke mediation, however, forced replacement of the act three years later with the ADAMSON EIGHT-HOUR ACT.

DAVID GORDON
(1986)

Bibliography

TAYLOR, BENJAMIN J. and WITNEY, FRED 1971 *Labor Relations Law*, 2nd ed. Englewood Cliffs, N.J.: Prentice-Hall.

ERIE RAILROAD CO. v. TOMPKINS
304 U.S. 64 (1938)

The Supreme Court in *Erie* posed the question whether the "oft-challenged doctrine of SWIFT V. TYSON (1842) shall now be disapproved," and answered that it should. The Court rejected its earlier construction of the Rules of Decision Act, originally section 34 of the JUDICIARY ACT OF 1789, and held that the "laws of the several states"—which, except as otherwise required by federal law, are to be "regarded as rules of decision" in civil actions in the federal courts "in cases where they apply"—included all of the decisional or COMMON LAW of the states.

Erie, like *Swift*, involved an exercise of the DIVERSITY JURISDICTION of the federal courts. In *Erie*, plaintiff Tompkins brought a federal court suit against the railroad for personal injuries, and the court of appeals upheld a substantial jury verdict in the face of the railroad's claim that it had not violated the limited duty owned to plaintiff under the decisional law of the state where the injury occurred. That court concluded that, in the absence of a state statute, the question of the scope of the railroad's duty was one not of "local" but of "general" law, and under the general law the railroad had a duty of care that the jury could properly find to have been broken.

The Supreme Court, in an opinion by Justice LOUIS D. BRANDEIS, reversed and remanded for application of state law with respect to the scope of the railroad's duty. The Court concluded that (1) the refusal in *Swift* to read the mandate of the Rules of Decision Act as embracing all of the decisional law of the states was based on an incorrect construction of the purpose of that act; (2) the construction in *Swift* had prevented uniformity in the administration of state law and had permitted "grave discrimination by noncitizens [of a state] against citizens"; and (3) the doctrine of *Swift* represented "an unconstitutional assumption of powers by the Courts of the United States." Justices PIERCE BUTLER and JAMES C. MCREYNOLDS dissented; Justice STANLEY F. REED concurred in part, believing it unnecessary to reach the constitutional issue addressed by the Court.

Although the parties in *Erie* had not briefed the question whether *Swift* should be overruled, there had been intimations of the Court's intentions in earlier majority and dissenting opinions. And while the *Erie* result itself still finds general acceptance, the years since the decision have seen much debate about its rationale, scope, and application.

DAVID L. SHAPIRO
(1986)

(SEE ALSO: *Federal Common Law, Civil.*)

ERNST, MORRIS
(1888–1976)

With his colleague ARTHUR GARFIELD HAYS, Morris Ernst served as general counsel to the AMERICAN CIVIL LIBERTIES UNION from 1929 to 1954. Together with Hays and ROGER BALDWIN, Ernst fought to protect individual rights against government action. Although he excoriated both the Ku Klux Klan and the Communist party, he defended members of both organizations. He was a staunch opponent of government censorship and defended James Joyce's novel against OBSCENITY charges in the Ulysses trial (1934). Ernst participated in a number of well-known cases, including COMMONWEALTH OF MASSACHUSETTS V. SACCO AND VANZETTI (1921), HAGUE V. CIO (1939), and the *Associated Press v. NLRB* (1937), one of the WAGNER ACT CASES. He wrote several popular books championing civil liberties.

DAVID GORDON
(1986)

ERROR, WRIT OF

A writ of error is an order of an appellate court, directing a lower court to transmit the record of a case that it has decided, for review by the appellate court. The JUDICIARY ACT OF 1789 established the writ of error as the means of invoking the APPELLATE JURISDICTION of both the CIRCUIT COURTS and the Supreme Court. For a century, the writ of error was, in practice, virtually the exclusive method of invoking review by the Supreme Court. In the cases specified by law for issuance of the writ, review by the Supreme Court was obligatory. In 1891 Congress reorganized the federal judiciary, establishing the circuit courts of appeals. (See CIRCUIT COURTS OF APPEALS ACT.) In some cases, these courts' decisions were final, unless the courts certified questions for review by the Supreme Court, or the Supreme Court in its discretion granted WRITS OF CERTIORARI to review their decisions. In 1925, in the course of reducing the Supreme Court's obligatory JURISDICTION and expanding the Court's discretionary control of its docket,

Congress changed the name of the writ of error; since that time the Supreme Court's theoretically obligatory appellate jurisdiction has been invoked by APPEAL.

KENNETH L. KARST
(1986)

Bibliography

ROBERTSON, REYNOLDS and KIRKHAM, FRANCIS R. 1951 *Jurisdiction of the Supreme Court of the United States,* ed. Richard F. Wolfson and Philip B. Kurland. Pages 191–196, 756, 806–807. Albany, N.Y.: Matthew Bender.

ERVIN, SAMUEL J.
(1896–1985)

A conservative Democrat who graduated from Harvard Law School in 1922, Samuel J. Ervin described himself as an "ol' country lawyer" from North Carolina, his native state. In 1954 he left that state's supreme court to enter the United States SENATE. During his two decades as a senator, he supported business against labor and opposed CIVIL RIGHTS legislation, equal rights for women, voting by eighteen-year-olds, and federal encroachments on STATES' RIGHTS. He also became a strict separationist on church–state issues, and he opposed intrusive searches, computer invasions of privacy, preventive detention, and any other measures he deemed subversive of the Constitution. By 1973 he was respected as the Senate's expert on the Constitution. Central casting destined him to be chairman that year of the Senate's Select Committee on Presidential Campaign Activities—the WATERGATE committee. As chairman, he was a relentless but fair interrogator who expressed outrage when witnesses equivocated or lied. The televised hearings made him a national celebrity as the watchdog of the Constitution who preached the constitutional responsibilities of those entrusted with public office. Ervin projected a grandfatherly image of a judicious moralist, the very model of integrity when models were in short supply. The public adored "Senator Sam," and he adored the Constitution.

LEONARD W. LEVY
(1986)

Bibliography

ERVIN, SAMUEL J., JR. 1980 *The Whole Truth: The Watergate Conspiracy.* New York: Random House.

ERZNOZNIK v. CITY OF JACKSONVILLE
422 U.S. 205 (1975)

An ordinance prohibited drive-in movie theaters from showing films containing nudity on screens visible from public streets or places. Conceding that the films were constitutionally protected speech, the city asserted an authority to protect its citizens, particularly minors, against unwilling exposure to offensive materials. The Supreme Court declared the ordinance unconstitutional, holding that people on public streets, unlike people in their homes or people on buses who are a captive audience, have only a limited interest in privacy which does not justify the city's discrimination among movies based solely on content.

KIM MCLANE WARDLAW
(1986)

(SEE ALSO: *Obscenity.*)

ESCH-CUMMINGS TRANSPORTATION ACT
41 Stat. 456 (1920)

Congress favored the return of the railroads to private ownership and operation after government control during WORLD WAR I. This act accomplished that objective and altered Congress's regulatory approach. It did not seek to prevent abuses so much as to strengthen the industry and foster the public interest. The act granted the Interstate Commerce Commission extensive new powers including the authority to set minimum rates, oversee fiscal operation of the roads, regulate acquisitions and consolidations, and supervise services. One provision prescribed a rate-making rule to assure "a FAIR RETURN upon the aggregate value of the railroad property," allowing the ICC to determine what constituted such a return. A recapture clause, inserted to protect weaker lines, required that roads earning a return over six percent divide that profit between a reserve fund for their own stability and a general fund (administered by the ICC) to compensate those railroads earning under four and one-half percent. The Supreme Court sustained this clause in DAYTON-GOOSE CREEK RAILWAY V. UNITED STATES (1924). The act also established labor boards with JURISDICTION over a variety of disputes.

DAVID GORDON
(1986)

Bibliography

SHARFMAN, ISAIAH L. 1931–1937 *The Interstate Commerce Commission.* Vol. 1. New York: Commonwealth Fund.

ESCOBEDO v. ILLINOIS
378 U.S. 478 (1964)

Daniel Escobedo was arrested and taken to the police station for questioning. Over the course of several hours, his repeated requests to see his lawyer were refused and his lawyer sought unsuccessfully to consult with him. The Supreme Court held that Escobedo's subsequent confession was obtained in violation of his Sixth Amendment RIGHT TO COUNSEL. For the first time, the Court spoke of "an absolute constitutional right to remain silent," which the presence of a lawyer would facilitate. *Escobedo* is important also because it presaged MIRANDA V. ARIZONA (1966) in discussing the possibility that warnings about the right to counsel might serve to cure the infirmity of in-custody interrogation.

Although *Escobedo* retains historical significance, the arguments in POLICE INTERROGATION AND CONFESSION cases have largely shifted from the Sixth to the Fifth Amendment with an emphasis on whether warnings were given, and given correctly, and whether the right to remain silent was waived.

The case has lost authority as precedent in another respect. It seemed to establish a practical flexible standard for the time when Sixth Amendment rights would come into play: when "the investigation is no longer a general inquiry into an unresolved crime but has begun to focus on a particular suspect." This approach was specifically abandoned in *Kirby v. Illinois* (1972), when the court limited *Escobedo* to its facts and ruled that the right to counsel does not attach until adversary judicial proceedings have been initiated.

BARBARA ALLEN BABCOCK
(1986)

ESPIONAGE ACT
40 Stat. 451 (1917)

When on April 2, 1917, President WOODROW WILSON asked Congress to recognize a STATE OF WAR, he included in his indictment of Germany the activities of German agents in the United States. Such activity, he said, should be treated with "a firm hand of stern repression." Nine weeks later, a much discussed and much amended Espionage Act was signed into law.

The initial measure, an amalgamation of seventeen bills prepared in the attorney general's office, was intended to "outlaw spies and subversive activities by foreign agents." Critics, particularly in the American press, quickly complained that the measure was far too restrictive and imposed a type of PRIOR RESTRAINT AND CENSORSHIP potentially destructive to basic American liberties. Thus, despite Wilson's contention that the administration must have authority to censor the press since this was "absolutely necessary to the public safety," the most overt censorship provisions were removed. The belief of a majority of national lawmakers that now the bill could not be used

to suppress critical opinion overlooked the fact that two of the twelve titles of the act as passed still bore directly on freedom of expression. One provided punishment for (1) making or conveying false reports for the benefit of the enemy; (2) seeking to cause disobedience in the armed forces; and (3) willfully obstructing the recruiting or enlistment service. Another section closed the mails to any item violating any of the act's provisions.

The constitutional basis of these two provisions rested on a broad interpretation of the federal WAR POWERS and upon the argument that a denial of use of the mails did not constitute censorship, since the federal courts had ruled that the mails constituted an optional federal service. Thus, it was argued, refusal to extend the facility did not deprive anyone of a constitutional right. Further, the measure's supporters argued that FREEDOM OF SPEECH was not absolute and could not protect a person who deliberately sought to obstruct the national war effort.

The difficulty of applying the law, however, was clear from the outset, since the statute sought to punish questionable intent, a difficult factor to measure. With punishment set at a $10,000 fine, imprisonment for up to twenty years, or both, and with its interpretation largely in the hands of patriotic enforcers, many suffered under the measure and its subsequent amendments. The Justice Department prosecuted more than 2,000 cases. At least 1,050 citizens were convicted under its terms, including Industrial Workers of the World leaders, Socialists (especially Eugene V. Debs), and a number of suspect hyphenates, particularly German Americans, whose verbal criticism of aspects of the war were often brutally repressed. The Supreme Court upheld the constitutionality of the act's prohibitions on causing disobedience in the armed forces and obstructing enlistment in a series of postwar decisions: SCHENCK V. UNITED STATES (1919), *Frohwerk v. United States* (1919), DEBS V. UNITED STATES (1919).

Under the mails provisions, the postmaster general exercised virtually dictatorial authority over the effective circulation of the American press, a power which he used capriciously and subjectively for punitive reasons. In an effort to preserve FIRST AMENDMENT values through the process of statutory construction, Judge LEARNED HAND construed the mails provision narrowly to exclude its application to ordinary criticism of government policies, including war policy. Hand's decision, however, was reversed by the court of appeals. (See MASSES PUBLISHING CO. V. PATTEN.)

The measure remained on the books through the 1920s and 1930s and was reenacted in March 1940, Congress increasing its penalties for peacetime violation. The Supreme Court narrowed its application in *Hartzel v. United States* (1944) by interpreting its provisions through a literal application of Holmes's clear and present danger test.

The government again turned to it in 1971, seeking unsuccessfully to prevent the publication by the *New York Times* of the "Pentagon papers," which the government called harmful to the security of the United States. (See NEW YORK TIMES CO. V. UNITED STATES.)

PAUL L. MURPHY
(1986)

(SEE ALSO: *World War I.*)

Bibliography

CHAFEE, ZECHARIAH   1941   *Free Speech in the United States.* Cambridge, Mass.: Harvard University Press.
MURPHY, PAUL   1979   *World War I and the Origin of Civil Liberties in the United States.* New York: Norton.

ESTABLISHMENT CLAUSE

Three themes dominate recent Supreme Court decision making under the First Amendment's ESTABLISHMENT OF RELIGION clause. First, the Court has continued to follow the doctrinal framework of EVERSON V. BOARD OF EDUCATION (1947) and LEMON V. KURTZMAN (1971), but with increasing emphasis on the "endorsement or disapproval" inquiry advocated by Justice SANDRA DAY O'CONNOR. Second, the Court has steered a selective course in applying this framework, upholding certain governmental practices but invalidating others. Third, and potentially most significant, the Justices stand at the brink of a radical change in doctrine. Although a majority of the Court continues to follow *Everson* and *Lemon*, there is growing support for an alternative interpretation that would dramatically weaken the principle of SEPARATION OF CHURCH AND STATE.

In *Everson*, the Supreme Court adopted a broad interpretation of the establishment clause, one that forbids governmental favoritism for religion over irreligion as well as for one religion over another. Since 1971, this broad interpretation has been implemented through the three-part LEMON TEST. Under *Lemon*, a statute (or other governmental action) can be upheld only if it satisfies three requirements: "First, the statute must have a secular legislative purpose; second, its principal or primary effect must be one that neither advances nor inhibitsreligion...; finally, the statute must not foster "an excessive governmental entanglement with religion."

Despite persistent criticism, the Court continues to embrace the *Everson* interpretation and the *Lemon* test. The Court has reformulated the first two parts of *Lemon*, however, by emphasizing the "endorsement or disapproval" inquiry that Justice O'Connor initially proposed in her concurring opinion in LYNCH V. DONNELLY (1984). In WALLACE V. JAFFREE (1985) and *Edwards v. Aguillard*

(1987), the Court adopted O'Connor's formulation of the "purpose" inquiry: "The purpose prong of the *Lemon* test asks whether government's actual purpose is to endorse or disapprove of religion." In COUNTY OF ALLEGHENY V. ACLU (1989) the Justices likewise relied on O'Connor's formulation to modify *Lemon*'s "primary effect" requirement. Thus, the Court held that regardless of purpose, governmental action has a constitutionally impermissible effect if it *appears* to endorse or disapprove religion. "The Establishment Clause, at the very least," wrote the Court, "prohibits government from appearing to take a position on questions of religious belief."

Justice O'Connor's approach does not eliminate difficult questions of application. As suggested by *Corporation of Presiding Bishop v. Amos* (1987), for example, there is no "endorsement" when government merely "accommodates" religion by removing burdens that government itself has created. More generally, the line between partisan "endorsement" and neutral "acknowledgment" may be exceedingly difficult to draw.

With or without the O'Connor reformulation, the *Lemon* test provides no more than a framework for analysis. Its application requires an exercise of judgment, an exercise of judgment that depends on the context of specific cases and on the individual philosophies of the Justices. In its recent cases, the Court's applications of *Lemon* have suggested a relaxation of establishment clause restraints on GOVERNMENT AID TO RELIGIOUS INSTITUTIONS and activities. At the same time, the Court has applied the clause forcefully to prohibit government from advancing religion through the public school curriculum, and it has adopted a fact-specific approach for cases involving religious symbols.

If government singles out religion for special economic benefits, the Supreme Court continues to find an establishment clause violation. Thus, in TEXAS MONTHLY, INC. V. BULLOCK (1989) the Court invalidated a Texas sales tax exemption that was limited to religious periodicals. For governmental programs that include secular as well as religious beneficiaries, however, the Court's decisions in WITTERS V. WASHINGTON DEPARTMENT OF SERVICES FOR THE BLIND (1986) and BOWEN V. KENDRICK (1988) suggest a relaxation of the Court's prior doctrine. In *Witters*, the question was whether the establishment clause required the state of Washington to deny vocational rehabilitation funds to an individual attending a Christian college in preparation for a religious career. The Washington State Supreme Court had held that the denial was mandated by *Lemon*'s second prong, but the United States Supreme Court unanimously disagreed. Although the opinion of the Court was narrowly drawn, separate concurring opinions, joined by a majority of the Justices, gave a broad reading to MUELLER V. ALLEN (1983), one that apparently would support the constitutionality of any neutrally drawn educational assistance program, even if most of the individual beneficiaries used the funds for religious training.

In *Bowen* the Court rejected a facial challenge to a federal statute designed to combat teenage sexual relations and pregnancy. In addressing these religiously sensitive topics, the statute not only permitted but expressly encouraged the involvement of religious organizations. Nonetheless, the Court refused to invalidate the statute either in its entirety or with respect to religiously affiliated grantees. Although the Court remanded for a determination of whether particular grants might render the statute unconstitutional as applied, it refused to presume that religiously affiliated grantees would use their grants "in a way that would have the primary effect of advancing religion."

The Court's permissive treatment of governmental funding programs has not been duplicated in the public school context. In *Edwards v. Aguillard* the Court considered a challenge to Louisiana's Balanced Treatment Act, which provided that evolution could not be taught in the public schools unless accompanied by the teaching of CREATIONISM. With only two Justices dissenting, the Court concluded that the act violated the first prong of *Lemon* and therefore was unconstitutional. Citing mandatory attendance policies and the impressionability of young students, the Court noted that it was "particularly vigilant in monitoring compliance with the Establishment Clause in elementary and secondary schools." Unpersuaded by the legislature's articulation of a secular purpose, the Court concluded that the act was designed "to alter the science curriculum to reflect endorsement of a religious view that is antagonistic to the theory of evolution." The Court found that this "preeminent religious purpose" was at least the "primary purpose" of the act and that the act therefore "endorses religion in violation of the First Amendment."

The Supreme Court's treatment of governmental displays of religious symbols shows neither the permissiveness of the funding cases nor the "particular vigilance" the Court has exercised in policing the public school curriculum. Instead, the Court has adopted a fact-specific approach that requires case-by-case determinations of whether particular religious displays have the purpose or effect of endorsing religion. In *County of Allegheny v. ACLU* the Court considered challenges to two separate holiday displays in downtown Pittsburgh, one of a crèche, the other of a menorah. A sharply divided Court found that the crèche violated the establishment clause but that the menorah did not. The Court emphasized that the crèche stood essentially alone in the Allegheny County Courthouse and included a banner that read "Gloria in

Excelsis Deo." By contrast, the menorah was placed beside a large Christmas tree and was accompanied by a sign proclaiming the City of Pittsburgh's "salute to liberty." Focusing on the second prong of *Lemon*, as modified by Justice O'Connor, the Court concluded that the crèche sent an impermissible message of religious endorsement, whereas the menorah, in context, sent a permissible message of cultural diversity and freedom of belief.

The Court's recent applications of its establishment clause doctrine are significant and controversial in their own right. A far more important development, however, may be just around the corner. For years, critics have attacked *Everson* and *Lemon* for their alleged hostility to religion. To date, the Court has resisted these attacks, affirming the basic wisdom of its doctrinal framework and continuing to enforce a meaningful separation of church and state. The Court is changing, however, and it may be within one vote of a dramatic shift in doctrine. Speaking for four Justices in *County of Allegheny*, Justice ANTHONY M. KENNEDY wrote that "substantial revision of our Establishment Clause doctrine may be in order." Suggesting the direction such revision might take, he argued that governmental "support" for religion should be permitted unless it involves coercion, "proselytizing" for a particular religion, or "direct benefits" so substantial as to in fact establish or tend to establish a state religion. It seems clear that the four Justices joining this opinion would support a fundamental retreat from the Court's existing doctrine.

Justice Kennedy's suggested course would seriously threaten the political-moral principles and policies that are furthered by the Court's prevailing approach. Governmental "support" for religion causes harm to the religious and irreligious individuals who are not within the government's favor. This harm creates feelings of resentment and alienation, which in turn cause injury to the political community itself. At the same time, the purported support for religion is often illusory; it may demean religion and work to its long-term detriment. The Supreme Court's establishment clause doctrine works to ensure a proper respect for the religious and irreligious beliefs of individuals, supports the maintenance of a religiously inclusive political community, and does no disservice to the important role of religion in our society. Whatever its weaknesses, this doctrine should not be abandoned.

DANIEL O. CONKLE
(1992)

Bibliography

CONKLE, DANIEL O.   1988   Toward a General Theory of the Establishment Clause. *Northwestern University Law Review* 82: 1113–1194.

NOTE   1987   Developments in the Law: Religion and the State. *Harvard Law Review* 100:1606–1781.

SMITH, STEVEN D. 1987 Symbols, Perceptions, and Doctrinal Illusions: Establishment Neutrality and the "No Endorsement" Test. *Michigan Law Review* 86:266–332.

ESTABLISHMENT CLAUSE
(Update)

At the close of the twentieth century, the Supreme Court's jurisprudence of the establishment clause appears to be in radical transition. Between WORLD WAR II and the 1980s, the Court adhered to a largely separationist understanding of the establishment clause, under which public institutions and programs—and especially public schools—were understood to be exclusively secular, and religious institutions were barred from participation in many government-funded programs. That understanding was reflected in the controversial three-part test of LEMON V. KURTZMAN (1971), which required that government action have a secular purpose; have a primary effect that neither advances nor inhibits religion; and refrain from excessive entanglement between religion and government.

Each of these parts of the LEMON TEST received criticism, mostly on the ground that they had the effect of requiring discrimination against, or hostility toward, religion. As the years wore on, the *Lemon* test became encrusted with multiple conflicting interpretations, rendering it largely indeterminate.

Beginning with WIDMAR V. VINCENT (1981), the Supreme Court began a shift toward an interpretation based on the idea of neutrality: that the FIRST AMENDMENT prohibition on the ESTABLISHMENT OF RELIGION permits the government to allow religious institutions and religiously motivated individuals to share in the benefits of public life without discrimination. *Widmar* involved a public university that allowed student groups to use empty facilities for meetings. In order to preserve a strict SEPARATION OF CHURCH AND STATE, the university refused to permit the use of facilities for religious activities. That meant that a student group could meet on campus to discuss sex, drugs, rock and roll, politics, or Shakespeare, but could not meet to pray or study the Bible. Reversing the appellate court, the Supreme Court held that the establishment clause is not offended by the neutral provision of facilities to religious and secular student groups on an evenhanded basis, and that the FREEDOM OF SPEECH guarantee forbids the exclusion of any group on the basis of the content of its speech.

The *Widmar* paradigm of "equal access" soon began to spread to other constitutional issues. First, the Court approved tax credits that could be used for expenses at public or private schools. Then, Congress extended the principle of "equal access" to high school student groups. In 1986, the principle was extended by a unanimous Supreme Court to an issue of funding, which had previously been the area of the most rigid strict separationism. In that case, WITTERS V. WASHINGTON DEPARTMENT OF SERVICES FOR THE BLIND (1986), the Court held that aid that is "made available generally without regard to the sectarian-nonsectarian, or public-nonpublic nature of the institutions benefited" does not generally violate the establishment clause.

In subsequent cases, the Court held that a government-provided sign language interpreter could be used by a student at a Roman Catholic high school; that religious symbols may be displayed in a public square; and that a public university may (indeed must) fund a student publication with a religious viewpoint. In all of these cases, the dispositive consideration was that the aid was provided on a neutral basis, without favoring or disfavoring religion.

It is a sign of the shift in DOCTRINE that every one of these decisions required reversing the lower court. It takes a certain period of time before a new legal principle works its way into the ordinary law of the lower courts. In this context, the process has been prolonged by the Court's reluctance to OVERRULE its earlier decisions. In particular, the Court has declined to overrule *Lemon* even though it has not relied on that case to strike down a government policy in almost fifteen years. As a result, inconsistent decisions have piled up, and lower courts are uncertain about the state of the law.

Indeed, the Supreme Court has not been prepared to adopt the neutrality approach unreservedly. In ROSENBERGER V. RECTOR & VISITORS OF THE UNIVERSITY OF VIRGINIA (1995), where the Court approved the funding of a religious student magazine on a neutral basis, the MAJORITY OPINION, authored by Justice ANTHONY M. KENNEDY, cabined the holding with three distinctions that are difficult to square with any coherent theory of the First Amendment: that the aid came in the form of a payment of the printer's bill rather than a subsidy to the group; that the student group was not organized as a "religious organization"; and that student mandatory activity fees are not the same as taxes. One suspects that the purpose of these distinctions is to allow the Court to retreat from the neutrality principle in the future, if it wishes, without overruling this decision.

In other important areas of establishment clause jurisprudence, doctrine is also in flux. Since the mid-1980s, the Court has generally approved the idea that legislatures and executive officials may accommodate the exercise of religion, even when not compelled to do so under the free exercise clause, subject to certain limitations. However, in practice, the Court has been reluctant to approve of AC-

COMMODATION OF RELIGION in many cases. The standard for legitimacy of religious accommodations therefore remains unsettled.

The closest to a "test" for legitimate accommodations is found in the PLURALITY OPINION written by Justice WILLIAM J. BRENNAN, JR., in TEXAS MONTHLY, INC. V. BULLOCK (1989). The plurality stated that the government may single out religious organizations for a special accommodation when it is designed to relieve a substantial government-imposed burden on the exercise of religion, or where the accommodation does not impose a substantial burden on third parties. (It is unclear whether both of these criteria need to be satisfied, or just either one.) As a result of the vagueness of these standards, as well as the lack of a majority opinion, this area remains very much in doubt.

In BOARD OF EDUCATION OF KIRYAS JOEL VILLAGE SCHOOL DISTRICT V. GRUMET (1994), the Court implied that it is generally unconstitutional for the government to accommodate a particular religious group, where there is no satisfactory legal guarantee that similarly situated religious groups would receive comparable accommodations. As a practical matter, that makes it difficult for legislatures to make accommodations except in broad terms, and makes it difficult for executive officers to do so at all. It is not clear whether that principle was intended to be so sweeping.

MICHAEL W. MCCONNELL
(2000)

(SEE ALSO: *Government Aid to Religious Institutions; Religion in Public Schools; Religious Liberty.*)

Bibliography

LUPU, IRA C. 1993 The Lingering Death of Separationism. *Geroge Washington Law Review* 62:230–279.

MCCONNELL, MICHAEL 1992 Religious Freedom at a Crossroads. *University of Chicago Law Review* 59:115–194.

MONSMA, STEPHEN V. and SOPER, J. CHRISTOPHER, eds. 1998 *Equal Treatment of Religion in a Pluralistic Society.* Grand Rapids, Mich.: W. B. Eerdmans.

SYMPOSIUM 1992 Religion in Public Life: Access, Accommodation, and Accountability. *George Washington Law Review* 60:599–856.

ESTABLISHMENT OF RELIGION

The FIRST AMENDMENT begins with the clause, "Congress shall make no law respecting an establishment of religion. . . ." There are two basic interpretations of what the framers meant by this clause. In EVERSON V. BOARD OF EDUCATION (1947), the first decision on the clause, the Supreme Court unanimously adopted the broad interpretation, although the Justices then and thereafter disagreed on its application. (See SEPARATION OF CHURCH AND STATE.) Justice HUGO L. BLACK declared that the clause means not only that government cannot set up a church but also that government cannot aid all religions impartially or levy a tax for the support of any religious activities, institutions, or practices. "In the words of [THOMAS] JEFFERSON," Black said, "the clause against establishment of religion by laws was intended to erect "a wall of separation between Church and State."

EDWARD S. CORWIN, a distinguished constitutional scholar who espoused the narrow view of the clause, asserted that the Court's interpretation was "untrue historically." What the clause does, he wrote, "and all that it does, is to forbid Congress to give any religious faith, sect, or denomination preferred status. . . . The historical record shows beyond peradventure that the core idea of "an establishment of religion' comprises the idea of preference; and that any act of public authority favorable to religion in general cannot, without manifest falsification of history, be brought under the ban of that phase" (Corwin, "Supreme Court as National School Board," pp. 10, 20). Justice POTTER STEWART, dissenting in ENGEL V. VITALE (1962), endorsed the narrow view when he noted that a nondenominational school prayer did not confront the Court with "the establishment of a state church" or an "official religion."

The debate in the First Congress, which proposed the First Amendment, provides support for neither the broad nor the narrow interpretation. The history of the drafting of the clause, however, is revealing. Congress carefully considered and rejected various phrasings that embraced the narrow interpretation. At bottom the amendment was an expression of the intention of the Framers of the Constitution to prevent Congress from acting in the field of religion. The "great object" of the BILL OF RIGHTS, JAMES MADISON, had said, when introducing his draft of amendments to the House, was to "limit and qualify the powers of Government" for the purpose of making certain that none of the powers granted could be exercised in forbidden fields, including religion. The history of the drafting of the establishment clause does not provide a clear understanding of what was meant by the phrase "an establishment of religion." But the narrow interpretation, which permits government aid to religion in general or on a nonpreferential basis, leads to the impossible conclusion that the First Amendment *added* to Congress's powers. The amendment meant to restrict Congress to the powers that it possessed, and since it had no power to legislate on matters concerning religion, and therefore could not support religion on any basis, Congress would have had no such power even in the absence of the First Amendment. To suppose that an express prohibition on power vests or creates power is capriciously unreasonable. The Bill of Rights, as Madison said, was not framed "to imply powers not meant to be included in the enumeration."

Congress did not define "an establishment of religion" because its members knew from common experience what they meant. At the time of the framing of the amendment, six states maintained or authorized establishments of religion. That amendment denied to Congress the power to do what those states were doing, and since *Everson* the states come under the same ban. An establishment meant to the framers of the amendment what it meant in those states. Thus, reference to the American experience with establishments at the time of the framing of the Bill of Rights is essential to any understanding of what the clause in question meant.

The narrow interpretation is based on European precedents but the European form of an establishment was not the American form, except in the Southern colonies before the AMERICAN REVOLUTION, and the European meaning of establishment was not the American meaning. The revolution triggered a pent-up movement for separation of church and state in the nine states that had establishments. Of these nine, North Carolina (1776), New York (1777), and Virginia (1786) separated church and state. Each of the remaining six states made concessions to anti-establishment sentiment by broadening their old establishments. After the Revolution, none maintained a single or exclusive establishment. In all six an establishment of religion was not restricted to a state church or a system of public support of one denomination; in all an establishment meant public support of all denominations and sects on a nonpreferential basis.

Three of these six states were in New England. The MASSACHUSETTS CONSTITUTION (1780) authorized its towns and parishes to levy taxes for the support of Protestant churches, provided that each taxpayer's money go to the support "of his own religious sect or denomination" and added that "no subordination of any one sect or denomination to the other shall ever be established by law." An establishment in Massachusetts meant government support of religion. Congregationalists, for a few decades, benefited the most, because they were the most numerous and resorted to various tricks to fleece non-Congregationalists out of their share of religious taxes. But the fact remains that Massachusetts had a multiple, not a single, establishment under which Baptist, Episcopalian, Methodist, and Unitarian churches were publicly supported until the establishment ended in 1833. In 1784 Connecticut and New Hampshire modeled their multiple establishments after that of Massachusetts, ending them in 1818 and 1819, respectively.

In the South, where the Episcopal Church was the sole established church before the revolution, three states either maintained or permitted establishments of religion, and in each the multiple form was the only legal one. Maryland (1776) permitted its legislature to tax for the support of "the Christian religion," with the proviso that every person had the right to designate the church of his choice, making every Christian church an established church on a nonpreferential basis. The legislature sought to pass an enabling act in 1785, but the nonpreferential system was denounced as an establishment and defeated. The situation in Georgia was the same as in Maryland, and a revised constitution (1789), which was in effect when the First Amendment was adopted, continued the multiple establishment system, allowing each person to support only his own church. South Carolina restricted its multiple nonpreferential establishment to Protestant churches. The last Southern establishment died in 1810. Virginia sought to emulate the Maryland system, but a general assessment bill benefiting all Christian churches failed, thanks to the opposition of most non-Episcopal denominations and to MADISON'S MEMORIAL AND REMONSTRANCE; the VIRGINIA STATUTE OF RELIGIOUS FREEDOM (1786) then separated church and state.

In none of the six states maintaining or allowing establishments at the time of the framing of the First Amendment was any church but a Christian one established. The multiple establishments of that time comprehended the churches of every denomination and sect with a sufficient number of adherents to form a church. Where Protestantism was established it was synonymous with religion; there were either no Jews or no Roman Catholics or too few of them to make a difference. Where Christianity was established, as in Maryland, which had a significant Roman Catholic minority, Jews were scarcely known. To contend that exclusive establishments of one religion existed in each of the six states ignores the novel American experiment with multiple establishments on an impartial basis. Europe knew only single-church establishments. An establishment of religion in the United States at the time of the First Amendment included nonpreferential government recognition, aid, or sponsorship of religion. The framers of the amendment looked to their own experience, not Europe's.

LEONARD W. LEVY
(1986)

(SEE ALSO: *Creationism; Larkin v. Grendel's Den, Incorporated; Lynch v. Donnelly; Marsh v. Chambers; Mueller v. Allen; Thornton v. Caldor, Inc.; Valley Forge Christian College v. Americans United for Separation of Church and State; Wallace v. Jaffree; Widmar v. Vincent.*)

Bibliography

ANTIEAU, CHESTER JAMES et al. 1964 *Freedom from Federal Establishment: Formation and Early History of the First Amendment Religion Clauses.* Milwaukee, Wisc.: Bruce Publishing Co.

COBB, SANFORD H. 1902 *The Rise of Religious Liberty in America.* New York: Macmillan.

CORWIN, EDWARD S. 1949 The Supreme Court as National School Board. *Law and Contemporary Problems* 14:3–22.

LEVY, LEONARD W. 1986 *The Establishment Clause: Religion and the First Amendment.* New York: Macmillan.

ESTELLE v. SMITH
451 U.S. 454 (1981)

A unanimous Supreme Court held that the protection of the MIRANDA RULES applied to every phase of an in-custody prosecution, and that a psychiatrist's testimony introduced at the penalty phase of a capital trial violated the RIGHT AGAINST SELF-INCRIMINATION. At the pretrial interview on which the testimony was based, the defendant had not received the appropriate warnings about his right to silence.

LEONARD W. LEVY
(1986)

ESTES v. TEXAS
381 U.S. 532 (1965)

The trial of Billy Sol Estes for swindling involved a FREE PRESS/FAIR TRIAL confrontation in which the Supreme Court held that televising trials was inherently prejudicial to a FAIR TRIAL. Circuslike live television and radio broadcasts of Estes's pretrial hearings involved such extensive disruption of the courtroom that many changes were ordered for coverage of the trial. Although live broadcasts of the actual trial were forbidden, excerpts from the proceedings were broadcast regularly.

The Court split 5–4 on the constitutionality of televising the proceedings. Justices HUGO L. BLACK, WILLIAM J. BRENNAN, POTTER STEWART, and BYRON R. WHITE called the practice unwise and dangerous, but not constitutionally objectionable. Chief Justice EARL WARREN and Justices ARTHUR J. GOLDBERG and WILLIAM O. DOUGLAS joined an opinion by Justice TOM C. CLARK seeking to ban television completely from the courts—subject to future developments (see CHANDLER V. FLORIDA)—as a violation of the right to a fair trial. Both the jury and the witnesses, Clark declared, would be under great pressure and be more self-conscious, aware of a large public audience; prospective witnesses might be influenced by the proceedings. The judge would have additional responsibilities (and temptations), and the defendant would be subject to "a form of mental—if not physical—harassment." Clark said, "A defendant on trial for a specific crime is entitled to his day in court, not in a stadium, or a city or nationwide arena." Justice JOHN MARSHALL HARLAN approved the ban here, but indicated he would do so only in cases of "great notoriety."

DAVID GORDON
(1986)

EUCLID v. AMBLER REALTY COMPANY
272 U.S. 365 (1926)

This case established the constitutionality of ZONING laws to regulate land use. In *Euclid* a Cleveland suburb sought to preserve an area of single-family dwellings by excluding even two-family dwellings and apartment houses, as well as commercial properties and public buildings. Against claims drawn from supposed deprivations of liberty and property without DUE PROCESS OF LAW and a supposed denial of the EQUAL PROTECTION OF THE LAWS, a 6–3 Supreme Court, speaking through Justice GEORGE SUTHERLAND, sustained the comprehensive zoning ordinance. It was, the Court ruled, a legitimate STATE POLICE POWER measure intended to maintain the residential area and thus protect the community's health, peace, and safety. As a result of this leading decision on comprehensive zoning laws, no argument drawn from the FOURTEENTH AMENDMENT or from the takings clause is likely to survive judicial scrutiny in the absence of an ordinance that is demonstrably unrelated to the improvement of a community.

LEONARD W. LEVY
(1986)

EULE, JULIAN N.
(1949–1997)

Julian N. Eule was an exceptionally successful classroom teacher in the law schools at Temple University (1977–1984) and the University of California, Los Angeles (1984–1997). His enthusiasm and ebullience stimulated and challenged his colleagues and students and enlivened his constitutional law scholarship. Those writings centered on three concerns vital to representative government: keeping the channels open for the people's communications, keeping government actors accountable to the people, and seeking institutional strategies to protect against the subordination of groups. Eule's scholarship was not just an academic exercise; it was a quest for usable principles to make American democracy work. In striving for that high purpose he insisted on testing his arguments against the facts of American political life. Even during his last illness, he gave energy and hope to everyone around him. His gallantry in the face of adversity is a lesson for democracy's advocates throughout the legal profession.

KENNETH L. KARST
(2000)

Bibliography

SIDEBAR 1997 Julian Eule, 1949–1997. *UCLA Law* 20:2–7.
SYMPOSIUM 1998 Voices of the People: Essays on Constitutional Democracy in Memory of Professor Julian N. Eule. *UCLA Law Review* 45:1523–1776.

EUTHANASIA

Euthanasia, or mercy killing, has long engaged the attention of philosophers and others concerned with the morality of offering the incurably ill the dignity of a choice whether to end their lives. Only recently, however, has euthanasia become a subject of constitutional debate. Active assistance to suicide remains a crime throughout the country, and the sort of euthanasia actively practiced on the defective newborn and on some very old persons who are ill beyond hope is also murder. Neither of these forms of euthanasia raises any serious constitutional issue. It is "passive euthanasia"—the withholding of aids to the preservation of life—that has been discussed in constitutional terms. Unfortunately, "the RIGHT TO DIE," perhaps because it is so effective a slogan, has beclouded discussion of genuine issues of personal choice.

The Supreme Court has not yet confronted these matters. Undoubtedly, however, there is some constitutional right to refuse medical treatment. Compulsory VACCINATION has been upheld against the claim that it deprived its reluctant beneficiary of liberty without DUE PROCESS OF LAW. A strong governmental interest in protecting public health justified that invasion of an unwilling person's body, however, and no such interest is present in the ordinary case of a person who refuses medical treatment. Even absent any claim to RELIGIOUS LIBERTY, the idea of a right to refuse treatment follows easily from the Supreme Court's modern recognition of constitutional rights to personal autonomy, offered in the name of "privacy." The Court's decisions affirming the right of a woman to have an abortion are cases in point.

In the context of euthanasia, however, the constitutional right to refuse treatment fits awkwardly into the typical dilemma a patient's doctors and relatives face. Even if a person has previously directed her doctors not to use artificial means to prolong life, she will ordinarily be unconscious for a time before dying and thus incapable of forming any present intention to refuse aid. Usually, of course, the problem of passive euthanasia arises in connection with patients in a persistent vegetative state who have given no directions whatever to their doctors. To invoke the concept of a constitutional right to die in such a case, as New Jersey's supreme court did in *Matter of Quinlan* (1976), is to beg the critical question whether someone in such a state can have any rights at all. The decision of the *Quinlan* court authorizing the termination of artificial life supports seems justified, but surely its justification appropriately responds to interests of the patient's relatives, not the patient's constitutional RIGHT OF PRIVACY.

KENNETH L. KARST
(1986)

Bibliography

SYMPOSIUM 1977 In Re Quinlan. *Rutgers Law Review* 30:243–328.

EVANGELICALS AND THE CONSTITUTION

See: Religious Fundamentalism

EVANS v. ABNEY
396 U.S. 435 (1970)

The 1911 will of U.S. Senator Augustus O. Bacon gave land to the city of Macon, Georgia, in trust for use as a park for white persons only. The city's operation of the park on these terms could not survive the Supreme Court's decisions invalidating state-sponsored SEGREGATION, and the city was replaced by private trustees. When the Supreme Court held, in *Evans v. Newton* (1966), that the park must still be open to all races, Bacon's residuary heirs claimed the land, arguing that the trust had failed. The Georgia courts agreed, and the Supreme Court held, 5–2, that this judicial enforcement of Bacon's racially discriminatory disposition of property did not constitute STATE ACTION in violation of the FOURTEENTH AMENDMENT. Justice HUGO L. BLACK, for the majority, distinguished SHELLEY V. KRAEMER (1948), saying that *Abney* involved no RACIAL DISCRIMINATION: the terminated park was unavailable for blacks and whites alike. Justices WILLIAM O. DOUGLAS and WILLIAM J. BRENNAN dissented.

Abney's importance lay in showing that *Shelley* did not stand for a broad principle forbidding judicial enforcement of any and all private racial discrimination. It also began the BURGER COURT's revitalization of the state action limitation as a barrier to enforcement of the Fourteenth Amendment.

KENNETH L. KARST
(1986)

EVARTS, WILLIAM MAXWELL
(1818–1901)

William Maxwell Evarts, called "the Prince of the American Bar," was probably the most famous, successful, and influential lawyer of his time. He defended ANDREW JOHNSON in the President's IMPEACHMENT trial, and he served as attorney general, secretary of state, and United States senator (Republican, New York). Twice Evarts almost became CHIEF JUSTICE of the United States. His lasting impact on American constitutional law derived from his pathbreaking arguments as counsel and his authorship of the CIRCUIT COURTS OF APPEALS ACT (1891). In the GRANGER CASES (1877) he argued that rate regulation interfered with the management and beneficial use of private property, reducing profits and thereby taking private property without JUST COMPENSATION or DUE PROCESS OF LAW. He lost that case, but his argument was destined for eventual acceptance. IN RE JACOBS (1885) was his greatest constitutional triumph. His argument, which the New York Court of Appeals adopted, advanced SUBSTANTIVE DUE PROCESS OF LAW and the doctrine of FREEDOM OF CONTRACT. Evarts was a stalwart champion of VESTED RIGHTS and an opponent of government regulation. The Circuit Courts of Appeals Act (Evarts Act) created the modern three-tier structure of the federal courts and the discretionary WRIT OF CERTIORARI by which the Supreme Court manages its APPELLATE JURISDICTION.

LEONARD W. LEVY
(1986)

Bibliography
TWISS, BENJAMIN 1942 *Lawyers and the Constitution.* Pages 93–109. Princeton, N.J.: Princeton University Press.

EVARTS ACT

See: Circuit Courts of Appeals Act

EVERSON v. BOARD OF EDUCATION
330 U.S. 1 (1947)

A New Jersey statute authorized local school boards to reimburse parents for the cost of public transportation of students to both public and private schools. Such reimbursement for the cost of transportation to church-related schools was challenged as an unconstitutional ESTABLISHMENT OF RELIGION.

Justice HUGO L. BLACK delivered the opinion of a 5–4 Supreme Court. He began with a consideration of the background of the establishment clause, which relied heavily on the writings of JAMES MADISON and THOMAS JEFFERSON, but he had little to say about the actual legislative history of the FIRST AMENDMENT's language in the First Congress. Black concluded that the establishment clause "means at least this":

> Neither a state nor the federal government can set up a church. Neither can pass laws which aid one religion, aid all religions or prefer one religion over another. . . . No tax in any amount, large or small, can be levied to support any religious activities or institutions, whatever they may be called, or whatever form they may adopt to teach and practice religion. . . . In the words of Jefferson, the clause against the establishment of religion by law was intended to erect "a wall of separation between church and State."

But after this sweeping separationist pronouncement, Justice Black pirouetted neatly and upheld the New Jersey program on the grounds that the state aid in that case was a public safety measure designed to protect students and could in no way be construed as aid to church-related schools.

Four dissenters were convinced that Justice Black had missed the point. Justice ROBERT H. JACKSON likened Black's MAJORITY OPINION to Byron's Julia who, "whispering I will ne'er consent, consented." What could be more helpful to a school, Jackson asked, than depositing the students at its door? Justice WILEY B. RUTLEDGE, with whom Justices Jackson, FELIX FRANKFURTER, and HAROLD BURTON joined, also filed a lengthy dissent. Justice Rutledge also made lavish use of the writings of Madison and Jefferson, and argued that the New Jersey program could not be justified as a public safety expenditure.

Everson stands at the entrance to the maze of law and litigation concerning participation by church-related schools in public programs. It was the first major utterance by the Supreme Court on the meaning of the establishment clause. Those favoring strict separation between religious institutions and government were pleased by Black's rhetoric and dismayed by his conclusion; those favoring a policy of flexibility or accommodation in church-state relations reacted the opposite way. That *Everson* satisfied no one and enraged many was portentous.

RICHARD E. MORGAN
(1986)

Bibliography
JOHNSON, RICHARD M. 1967 *The Dynamics of Compliance.* Evanston, Ill.: Northwestern University Press.

MORGAN, RICHARD E. 1972 *The Supreme Court and Religion.* Pages 76–122. New York: Free Press.

EVIDENCE

Excepting cases that may be decided by applying legal rules to undisputed facts, the determination of disputed factual propositions must be central to adjudicating the rights and liabilities of litigants. As an initial matter, a society might adopt an "inquisitorial" system, under which a public official investigates and decides the facts. In the Anglo-American legal tradition, however, we structure the litigation process so that every dispute has at least two parties, each charged with the primary responsibility for proving its factual propositions and therefore discovering and presenting the evidence to support its version of the facts before an impartial arbiter.

In criminal cases, this adversary system is reinforced by rules that place the BURDEN OF PROOF on the prosecution, presuming that the defendant is innocent, and that grant the defendant a RIGHT AGAINST SELF-INCRIMINATION—thus shielding him from being forced to be a witness against himself, and depriving the prosecution of an obvious source of evidence. The structuring of criminal litigation as a contest between the state as prosecutor and the defendant—with the judge as arbiter—has two major consequences. First, this procedure gives greater weight to the autonomy of the individual litigant. Second, placing responsibility on each party to advance its own cause will, in general, result in the production of more evidence for the finder of fact than would be produced by disinterested—and perhaps bored and overworked—public officials. Though our prototypical case is the criminal case, we use similar procedures and rules in civil cases.

In both civil and criminal cases, TRIAL BY JURY means that a group of laymen decides issues of disputed fact. A great many of the intricacies of our laws of evidence result from two specific worries about the jury. The first is that the jury may systematically overvalue or undervalue some kinds of evidence, such as HEARSAY. The second is that the ad hoc nature of the jury, which is empaneled to decide a particular case, will produce a verdict at odds with the values of a legal system handling many cases over a long period of time. Often a rule of evidence will keep out testimony not so much because a jury might overweigh it but simply because other policies of the law are entitled to equal weight along with the proper resolution of factual issues. In this category fall the exclusion of reliable evidence because it has been unconstitutionally seized; because it has been obtained in violation of the MIRANDA RULES; because it is a coerced confession (which, though typically unreliable, may in a particular case be thoroughly corroborated); or because its exclusion is necessary to enforce a privilege, such as that protecting confidential communications between the attorney and the client.

Nor is the exclusion of evidence confined to cases where we choose this means of vindicating the rights of the individual. Though it is by no means clear that the rule is of constitutional dimension, every Anglo-American JURISDICTION in civil and (until the passage of California's "Victims' Bill of Rights" initiative) in criminal cases kept from the jury certain evidence of the prior character of the accused—not so much because the jury might overvalue it as out of fear that the jury might succumb to the temptation to be lawless and decide that the defendant was either so bad a person that he should be punished regardless of his fault in the particular case at issue. That kind of jury behavior might appeal to common sense, but it would be at odds with our principles requiring a particular act as a precondition of guilt and requiring fair NOTICE of the charge made against a defendant.

Despite the huge body of statutory and COMMON LAW evidence law, the Constitution nowhere states flatly a rule as to admissibility of evidence and refers to evidence in only one place—the requirement of two witnesses to the same overt act before a conviction of TREASON may be returned. Moreover, apart from the rules as to SEARCH AND SEIZURE and selfincrimination, the rules of evidence have largely escaped the Supreme Court's constitutional supervision. In criminal cases, however, two lines of cases have partially constitutionalized the law of evidence. The first involves the defendant's right to exclude inculpatory hearsay evidence that otherwise would be admitted under one or another of the exceptions to the general rule excluding hearsay; the second involves the defendant's rights to introduce exculpatory evidence notwithstanding common or statutory law purporting to exclude such evidence. Both these lines grow out of the Sixth Amendment. The first grows out of the CONFRONTATION clause, which guarantees that "[i]n all criminal prosecutions, the accused shall enjoy the right . . . to be confronted with the witnesses against him." The second line also stems in part from the Sixth Amendment right of the accused to " COMPULSORY PROCESS for obtaining witnesses in his favor," and in part from the DUE PROCESS clause.

Historically, courts read the confrontation clause as guaranteeing only the right of the accused to be present at his trial and to cross-examine any witnesses testifying there. In the 1960s, however, the Supreme Court began to view the clause as forbidding use in a criminal trial of certain inculpatory hearsay declarations. Thus, the Court held in POINTER V. TEXAS (1965) that the clause rendered inadmissible at a criminal trial a transcript of inculpatory testimony elicited during a preliminary hearing at which the defendant was not represented by counsel from a prosecution witness who was no longer available to testify. Likewise, a codefendant's out-of-court confession that also implicated the accused was held inadmissible in *Bruton v. United States* (1968) when the codefendant invoked his right against self-incrimination and refused to take the stand at the trial. Similarly, in *Barber v. Page* (1968) the Court held that preliminary hearing testimony of an absent witness was inadmissible when the prosecutor had failed to make a good-faith effort to obtain the presence of the witness at the trial. These rulings by the Court threw the validity of inculpatory hearsay evidence into doubt. The Court seemed to be drifting toward a rule that would in effect preclude the use of all such hearsay.

California v. Green (1970) arrested this drift. In *Green,* a prosecution witness testified adversely to the defendant during a preliminary hearing at which the defendant's attorney subjected him to a rigorous cross-examination. At the later trial, however, the witness claimed to have suffered a memory lapse and refused to repeat his testimony. The prosecutor then read into evidence portions of the preliminary hearing testimony. The Court held that, under these circumstances, admission of the hearsay did not violate the confrontation clause. The Court stated that its previous confrontation clause decisions had all rested on the inability of the defendant effectively to cross-examine witnesses, and that where, as here, defendant had once had a full and fair opportunity to cross-examine, there was no constitutional impediment to the hearsay.

Green made it clear that when the declarant was unavailable at the trial, his declaration would be admissible if he had been subject to meaningful cross-examination by defendant's counsel at the time he made the declaration. The meaning of "unavailability" and the nature of "meaningful cross-examination" were left open to interpretation, but clearly where these criteria were met, the evidence was admissible. By the same token, *Green* left little doubt that when the declarant was available at the trial for meaningful cross-examination, evidence of his out-of-court declaration would be admissible even if he had not been subject to cross-examination at the time he made the statement.

Since *Green,* the Court's decisions have withdrawn even further from the constitutionalization of hearsay law. The Court made apparent in *Ohio v. Roberts* (1980) that hearsay evidence of a declarant's out-of-court statements will be admissible, even when the defendant has never had an opportunity to cross-examine the declarant, provided that the declarant is truly unavailable and that the statements bear adequate "indicia of reliability." "Reliability can be inferred without more in a case where the evidence fails within a firmly footed hearsay exception," that is, an exception "rest[ing] upon such solid foundations" that "virtually any evidence within them" will in fact be reli-

able. Thus, dying declarations are admissible, as are properly administered business and public records. Hearsay evidence is admissible even under less "firmly rooted" exceptions when there is a particularized showing of its trustworthiness under the circumstances. Thus, under some circumstances, at least, declarations against penal interest and party admissions by coconspirators (such as a spontaneous admission by a coconspirator to his prison cellmate) are admissible.

The Court's decisions since *Green* thus have confined the pre-*Green* decisions narrowly to their facts. Apparently, the Court is unlikely to find that evidence admitted under an established hearsay exception offends the confrontation clause, unless, as in *Barber v. Page,* a prosecutor falsely alleges for purposes of the exception that a declarant is unavailable, or, as in *Bruton v. United States,* the hearsay consists of a codefendant's confession which ostensibly is read into evidence against him alone but in fact contains statements inculpating other defendants in the same trial, and the codefendant refuses to take the stand. Moreover, even when a defendant alleges a *Barber* or *Bruton* violation, the Court is unlikely to find that the facts of the case at hand justify reversal. Twice since *Green* the Court has refused to sustain arguments that a prosecutor had failed to make a good-faith effort to find absent declarants, and repeatedly the Court has found even clear and admitted violations of the *Bruton* rule to result in merely HARMLESS ERROR not justifying reversal.

It would seem, then, that the Court has substantially withdrawn from the field of writing hearsay law. While it has not explicitly reverted to the traditional view of the confrontation clause in this area, the manner in which it has analyzed hearsay exceptions in recent cases leaves little doubt of its reluctance significantly to reduce the prosecutor's ability to introduce evidence falling within ancient, recognized exceptions.

The rules of evidence traditionally have been held to bind defendants as well as the state. The first significant developments in the line of cases recognizing defendants' rights to introduce exculpatory evidence despite rules of evidence excluding it grew out of the compulsory process clause. In *Washington v. Texas* (1967) the Court overturned a Texas statute that rendered accomplices incompetent to testify for each other. The Court held that the compulsory process clause forbade the state "arbitrarily [to] den[y defendants] the right to put on the stand a witness who was physically and mentally capable of testifying to events that he had personally observed and whose testimony would have been relevant and material to the defense."

In *Chambers v. Mississippi* (1973) the Court faced a case in which it might have used compulsory process reasoning but used the due process clause instead. In *Cham-*

bers the defendant was charged with murder for shooting a police officer during a crowd incident. Another man, McDonald, who had been in the crowd, had confessed to the shooting, and substantial evidence pointed to the truth of this confession, but McDonald had repudiated the confession and had not been charged in the case. The trial judge allowed Chambers to present two witnesses who claimed actually to have seen McDonald fire the shots, but the judge barred the testimony of witnesses who had not seen the incident but to whom McDonald had made damaging admissions, ruling that this testimony did not fall within any applicable state hearsay exception. In addition, the judge permitted Chambers to call McDonald to the stand and to read his prior confession into evidence, but when McDonald repudiated the confession on the stand and offered an alibi, the judge refused to allow Chambers to examine McDonald as an "adverse witness," ruling that because McDonald had not actually alleged the defendant's guilt, his testimony was not "adverse" within the meaning of Mississippi's exception to the rule that a party may not impeach his own witness.

The Supreme Court reversed, holding that the trial judge's exclusion of this exculpatory evidence had violated the due process clause of the FOURTEENTH AMENDMENT. The trial judge's refusal to allow Chambers to examine McDonald, who was a "witness against him" even if not an "adverse" witness under Mississippi law, constituted prejudicial error. In addition, the Court held that the trial judge's refusal to allow the exculpatory hearsay testimony of the three witnesses to whom McDonald had confessed violated Chambers's right "to present witnesses in his own defense." Although the language used by the Court in discussing these issues is reminiscent of the confrontation and compulsory process clauses of the Sixth Amendment, the Court did not explicitly rest its decision on these clauses. Rather, the Court announced only that "[t]he right of an accused in a criminal trial to due process is, in essence, the right to a fair opportunity to defend against the State's accusations," and that "under the facts and circumstances of this case the rulings of the trial court deprived Chambers of a fair trial."

The Court has applied *Chambers* in only one other case. In *Green v. Georgia* (1979) the defendant was convicted of rape and murder, and a second trial was then held to decide whether CAPITAL PUNISHMENT would be imposed. At this trial, the defendant sought to introduce a witness who had previously testified for the prosecution at the trial of Moore, the defendant's coconspirator. The witness intended to testify, as he had testified at Moore's trial, that Moore had admitted to him that Moore alone had fired the shots that killed the victim, and that the defendant had not been present when the shots were fired. The trial judge, however, ruled this testimony inadmissible

as hearsay. At Moore's trial the witness's repetition of Moore's declaration had fallen within the admission exception to the hearsay rule, but its repetition at Green's trial did not fall within the exception. In a brief opinion, the Supreme Court reversed. It noted that the excluded evidence was highly relevant to a critical issue in the trial and that substantial reasons existed to assume its reliability: it was a statement against Moore's penal interest made spontaneously by him to a close friend and for which there was ample corroborating evidence. Most important, the prosecution had considered the evidence reliable enough to use against Moore at his trial. Under these circumstances, the Court ruled, "the hearsay rule may not be applied mechanistically to defeat the ends of justice."

The future of this line of cases is not easy to foresee. The cases may stand for no more than the proposition that the Court will reverse a conviction when it is convinced that a gross injustice has been done. But they seem to stand for more. They seem to suggest that the Court has begun to read into the Constitution the ethical rule that the state's proper goal is not merely to get a conviction but to get a conviction only if justice demands it. Thus, the cases suggest, the prosecutor may not object to evidence that the defense seeks to introduce on any ground other than that it is wasteful of time, or likely to distract the jury's attention from the real issues of the case. This consideration, always important ethically, rises to constitutional significance when failure to abide by it leads to the exclusion of strongly credible exculpatory evidence that is highly relevant to critical issues in the trial.

JOHN KAPLAN
(1986)

Bibliography

MAGUIRE, JOHN M. 1947 *Evidence, Common Sense, and Common Law.* Mineola, N.Y.: Foundation Press.

MCCORMICK, CHARLES T. 1954 *Handbook of the Law of Evidence.* St. Paul, Minn.: West Publishing Co.

MORGAN, EDMUND M. 1961 *Basic Problems of Evidence.* Philadelphia: American Bar Association.

THAYER, JAMES BRADLEY 1898 *Preliminary Treatise on Evidence at Common Law.* Boston: Little, Brown.

WIGMORE, JOHN HENRY 1961 *Evidence in Trials at Common Law,* rev. by John T. Naughton. Boston: Little, Brown.

EVIDENTIARY PRIVILEGE

To say that a person possesses an evidentiary privilege means that he or she cannot be compelled, as a witness, to disclose certain ("privileged") information. The possessor of the privilege (the privilege "holder") may also be entitled to prevent others who share the privileged information from disclosing it. The holder may waive the privilege by failing to assert it in timely fashion, by explicitly consenting to the disclosure of privileged information, or by engaging in conduct interpreted as consent (for example, voluntarily testifying to a portion of the privileged matter). In state courts, the contours of evidentiary privileges are determined by state law. In federal courts, they are determined by federal law, though at times the federal approach has been to defer to state rules of privilege, as specified, for example, in Federal Rule of Evidence 501.

Unlike most of the evidentiary rules of exclusion (such as those excluding HEARSAY or irrelevant evidence), the testimonial privileges do not exclude EVIDENCE because it is unreliable, prejudicial, or lacking in fact-finding utility. Rather, they exclude it *despite* its potential value; the privileges promote goals other than rational fact-finding. To be aware of these goals is to understand why traditional evidentiary privileges can readily take on constitutional dimensions. The interests served by the privileges are commonly phrased in terms that are uncompromisingly utilitarian. For example, privileges concerned with the protection of confidential communications—such as those between husband and wife, attorney and client, doctor and patient, priest and penitant, parent and child (a developing privilege)—are commonly justified on such reasoning: first, that the free flow of communication is indispensable to these important relationships; second, that confidentiality is essential to their free flow. An alternative perspective would support the claims of confidentiality not for such narrowly instrumental reasons but because confidentiality serves the participants' interest in privacy, whether or not the possibility of compulsory disclosure would hinder free communication.

Similar justifications, both instrumental and noninstrumental, could be generated in support of another kind of privilege, protecting interests other than confidentiality. An example is the phase of the husband-wife privilege permitting one spouse to refuse to testify against another, whether or not the testimony may concern intraspousal communications.

Although these privileges were not in their original conception constitutionally based, today they are often seen as implicating constitutional values. The justifications for many of the privileges could be reformulated in terms of constitutional principles. The attorney-client privilege, invoked by a criminal defendant, could draw support from the RIGHT TO COUNSEL, the RIGHT AGAINST SELF-INCRIMINATION, and the DUE PROCESS clauses of the Constitution. Indeed, if the attorney-client privilege were not a common law privilege, some version of it probably would have to be invented to satisfy constitutional requirements. FIRST AMENDMENT arguments could likewise be mustered in support of the priest-penitent privilege and the REPORTER'S PRIVILEGE (which in some states protects against compelled disclosure of a newsperson's sources of information). And, efforts to pierce the confidentiality of certain communications—such as those between husband and wife, priest and penitent, or psychiatrist and patient—could be challenged as infringements of a constitutionally protected RIGHT OF PRIVACY.

On the other hand, just as evidentiary privileges sometimes draw support from constitutional principles, sometimes their enforcement may prove incompatible with other constitutional requirements. Thus to deny a criminal defendant the use of testimony important to his or her defense, out of respect for a privilege invoked by a witness, might run afoul of the defendant's right of CONFRONTATION, to COMPULSORY PROCESS, or to due process of law; the conflicting constitutional claims of the defendant and the witness would then have to be resolved.

LEON LETWIN
(1986)

Bibliography

CLEARY, E.   1984   *McCormick on Evidence*, 3rd ed. Pages 170–187. St. Paul, Minn.: West Publishing Co.
NOTE   1985   Developments in the Law—Privileged Communications. *Harvard Law Review* 98:1450–1666.

EVITTS v. LUCEY
469 U.S. 387 (1985)

Interpreting DOUGLAS V. CALIFORNIA (1963), the Supreme Court held, 7–2, in an opinion by Justice WILLIAM J. BRENNAN, that the DUE PROCESS clause of the FOURTEENTH AMENDMENT requires the effective assistance of counsel during a defendant's first appeal, as of right, from a criminal conviction. (The Court had previously held that the RIGHT TO COUNSEL at the trial level comprehended effective assistance.) The procedural posture of this case made it unnecessary to spell out standards for judging the effectiveness of counsel on appeal; the Court thus left those standards for another day. Justice WILLIAM H. REHNQUIST and Chief Justice WARREN E. BURGER dissented, arguing that the trial and appellate levels presented different degrees of need for counsel's assistance, and predicting that the decision would allow convicted defendants to "tie up the courts" with petitions for HABEAS CORPUS based on claims of ineffectiveness of appellate counsel.

KENNETH L. KARST
(1986)

EXCESSIVE FINES

See: Punitive Damages

EXCISE TAX

In its original meaning an excise was a tax on goods manufactured or produced within the taxing country, as opposed to a duty or IMPOST on imports. Undoubtedly, this was the sense in which it was used in the constitutional grant of power to Congress to collect "taxes, duties, imposts and excises." In modern times an excise tax is any tax imposed on the manufacture or sale of a commodity, engaging in an occupation, or enjoying any other privilege. It is distinguished from a direct tax, such as a POLL TAX or an *ad valorem* property tax.

EDWARD L. BARRETT, JR.
(1986)

(SEE ALSO: *Direct and Indirect Taxes; State Taxation of Commerce.*)

EXCLUSIONARY RULE

When the police obtain evidence by violating the BILL OF RIGHTS, the victim of their misconduct may lack any effective legal remedy. Yet some enforcement mechanism is necessary if several important constitutional guarantees are to be a reality and not merely expressions of hope. The Supreme Court responded to this concern by developing a series of rules that have come to be known in the aggregate as the exclusionary rule. In typical application, the rule is that evidence obtained in violation of a person's constitutional rights cannot be used against that person in his or her trial for a criminal offense. The rule is most frequently applied to exclude evidence produced by SEARCHES OR SEIZURES made in violation of the FOURTH AMENDMENT. However, a coerced confession obtained in violation of the defendant's Fifth Amendment RIGHT AGAINST SELF-INCRIMINATION, or a statement taken from the defendant in violation of his Sixth Amendment's guarantee of the RIGHT TO COUNSEL, would also be inadmissible at his trial.

The term "exclusionary rule" is of modern origin, but even at COMMON LAW a coerced confession was excluded or inadmissible as evidence, because its involuntariness cast serious doubt on its reliability. No one today seriously argues that this long-standing rule of evidence should be abandoned. Other aspects of the exclusionary rule, however, have been the source of major controversy among members of the judiciary, professional commentators, law enforcement officials, and the public.

The controversy did not become intense until the era of the WARREN COURT. But as far back as WEEKS V. UNITED STATES (1914) the Supreme Court had unanimously held that evidence seized in violation of the Fourth Amendment was inadmissible in a *federal* criminal prosecution. However, even after the Court had held in WOLF V. COLORADO (1949) that the Fourth Amendment's guarantee against unreasonable searches and seizures was applicable to the states, the Court had continued until 1961 to resist the argument that the exclusionary rule should also be extended to *state* prosecutions. In that year, in MAPP V. OHIO, the Warren Court held that the Fourteenth Amendment did, indeed, impose on the states the exclusionary rule derived from the Fourth Amendment. Subsequent decisions broadened the Sixth Amendment guarantee of the right to counsel to govern the procedures for police interrogation and for the use of LINEUPS; each of these developments was accompanied by an extension of the exclusionary rule to state-court proceedings. Since the "FRUIT OF THE POISONOUS TREE" DOCTRINE requires the exclusion not only of evidence immediately obtained by these various forms of constitutional violation but also of other evidence derived from the initial violations, the exclusionary rule in its modern form results in the suppression of many items of evidence of unquestioned reliability and the acquittal of many persons who are guilty.

The primary purpose of the exclusionary rule, as the Supreme Court said in *Elkins v. United States* (1960), "is to deter—to compel respect for the constitutional guaranty in the only effectively available way—by removing the incentive to disregard it." Yet this deterrent function is only part of the exclusionary rule's justification. A court that allows the government to profit from unconstitutional police action sullies the judicial process itself, by becoming an accomplice in an unlawful course of conduct. When the Court first applied the rule in *Mapp* to state-court prosecutions, it said:

> There are those who say, as did Justice (then Judge) [BEN-JAMIN N.] CARDOZO, that under our constitutional exclusionary doctrine "the criminal is to go free because the constable has blundered." . . . In some cases this will undoubtedly be the result. But, . . . "there is another consideration—the imperative of judicial integrity." . . . The criminal goes free, if he must, but it is the law that sets him free. Nothing can destroy a government more quickly than its failure to observe its own laws, or worse, its disregard of the charter of its own existence. As Mr. Justice LOUIS D. BRANDEIS, dissenting, said: . . . "Our government is the potent, the omnipresent teacher. For good or for ill, it teaches the whole people by its example. . . . If the government becomes a lawbreaker, it breeds contempt for law."

The evidence seized in an illegal search—a knife, a packet of heroin, counterfeit plates—is as trustworthy and material as if the search had been lawful. The rule's critics argue that to protect the privacy of the search victim by letting a guilty person escape responsibility for his crime is illogical. It would make more sense, they say, to use the evidence (as do the courts in Great Britain, for example) and provide civil or criminal remedies against the errant police officers. If the rule's purpose is to deter police lawlessness, the critics argue, the rule misses the point: prosecutors, not police officers, feel the immediate effects of the rule. If the rule is designed to maintain respect for the courts, they ask how the public can be expected to respect a system that frees criminals by suppressing trustworthy evidence of their guilt.

How many criminals do go free when the constable blunders? Inadequate studies provide no clear-cut answer, except that opponents of the exclusionary rule grossly exaggerate the number of felons it sets loose, and they tend to dramatize the worst cases. In California, whose supreme court has created the most stringent exclusionary rule in the nation, a study by the National Institute of Justice showed that .78 percent of all accused felons are not prosecuted because of search and seizure problems, and of those released, nearly three-fourths were involved in drug-related cases. The effect of the exclusionary rule is slight in cases involving violent crimes. When the charge is murder, rape, assault, or robbery, prosecutors decide not to proceed in one out of every 2,500 cases. Studies of felony court records in other states reach similar conclusions. Only 0.4 percent of all cases that federal prosecutors decide not to prosecute are rejected because of search problems. At the trial level, motions to suppress illegally seized evidence are rarely granted in cases of violent crime. If the exclusionary rule were abolished, the conviction rate in all felony cases would increase by less than half of one percent. Translated into absolute figures, however, thousands of accused felons are released nationally as a result of the exclusionary rule, most of them in drug and weapons possession cases. Street crime does not flourish, though, because of the exclusionary rule, even though it does protect criminals, as do all constitutional rights. They also protect society and help keep us free.

The rule's effectiveness in deterring illegal searches is hotly debated. The critics point out that some ninety percent of criminal prosecutions do not go to trial but are disposed of by pleas of "guilty." (The figure varies from state to state, and according to the nature of the crime.) Without a trial, there is no evidence for the rule to exclude. In the huge number of cases in which the police make arrests but the persons arrested are not prosecuted, the exclusionary rule has, of course, no immediate application. The rule's proponents reply that the decision whether to prosecute or accept a defendant's "guilty" pleas on a lesser offense may itself be influenced by the prosecutor's estimate of the potential operation of the exclusionary rule if the case should go to trial. (In jurisdictions where separate procedures are established to rule on

motions to suppress evidence, the rule normally will have operated in advance of the trial.)

Undeniably, however, the exclusionary rule has no application at all to the cases that cry out most for a remedy: cases of police misconduct against innocent persons, who are never even brought to the prosecutors' attention, and cases of illegal searches and seizures made for purposes other than collecting evidence to support prosecutions. In TERRY V. OHIO (1968) Chief Justice EARL WARREN admitted: "Regardless how effective the rule may be where obtaining conviction is an important objective of the police, it is powerless to deter invasions of constitutionally guaranteed rights where the police either have no interest in prosecuting or are willing to forego successful prosecution in the interest of serving some other goal." The police may deliberately engage in illegal searches and seizures for a number of reasons: to control crimes such as gambling or prostitution; to confiscate weapons or contraband or stolen property; or to maintain high visibility either to deter crime or to satisfy a public clamoring for aggressive police action. In none of these cases will the exclusionary rule inhibit police violations of the Bill of Rights.

The rule does not in fact significantly impede the police, despite contentions from the rule's opponents that it handcuffs the police. A 1984 report prepared for the National Center for State Courts concluded that a properly administered search warrant process can protect constitutional rights without hampering effective law enforcement. Nevertheless, police try when possible to conduct search and seizure under some exception to the warrant requirement. The overwhelming number of searches and seizures are warrantless. In 1980, for example, only about 1,000 warrants were issued in Los Angeles in about 300,000 cases. Police usually try to make CONSENT SEARCHES or searches under what they claim to be EXIGENT CIRCUMSTANCES, or they conduct a search to confiscate contraband or harass criminals, without attempting a prosecution. In the few cases in which they seek warrants, they get them almost as if magistrates rubber-stamp their applications, and almost all warrants survive in court despite motions to suppress. Motions to suppress are made in about five percent of all cases but are successful in only less than one percent of all cases. Still more important is the fact that only slightly over half of one percent of all cases result in acquittals because of the exclusion of evidence.

Even when the rule does operate to exclude evidence in a criminal trial, it has no direct, personal effect on the police officer whose misconduct caused the rule to be invoked. The rule does not require discipline to be imposed by the officer's superiors, nor does either civil or criminal responsibility follow as a matter of course. Police officers are prosecuted only extremely rarely for their official misdeeds. Suits for damages by victims are inhibited not only by the defense of "good faith" and PROBABLE CAUSE but also by the realization that most officers are neither wealthy nor insured against liability for their official acts. Unsurprisingly, most victims conclude that a lawsuit is not worth its trouble and expense. In the typical case of an illegal search, neither the judge who excludes the fruits of the search from evidence nor the prosecutor whose case is thereby undermined will explain to the officer the error of his ways. The intended educational effect of judicial decisions is also diminished by the time-lag between the police action and its final evaluation by the courts. Even if an officer should hear that a court has excluded the evidence he found in an illegal search some months ago, he will probably have forgotten the details of the event. Incentives and sanctions that might influence the officer's future behavior are not within the exclusionary rule's contemplation. On the other hand, advocates of the rule emphasize that it is meant to have an institutional or systemic effect on law enforcement agencies generally, not necessarily on particular officers.

The officer is apt to respond not to judicial decisions (which he may regard as unrealistic if they impede his work) but to departmental policies and the approval of his colleagues and superiors. One whose main job is the apprehension of criminals and the deterrence of crime will have a low tolerance for what he sees as procedural niceties. He may even shade the truth in making out a report on a search or when testifying in court. It is not unheard of for the police to arrange to make a valid arrest at a place where they can conduct a warrantless SEARCH INCIDENT TO THE ARREST, and thus evade the requirement of a SEARCH WARRANT based on probable cause to believe that evidence of crime is in that place. To the extent that the courts have used the exclusionary rule to educate the police, then, the main things learned seem to have been the techniques for evading the rule.

Summarizing the criticisms of the exclusionary rule, Dallin H. Oaks has said:

> The harshest criticism of the rule is that it is ineffective. It is the sole means of enforcing the essential guarantees of freedom from unreasonable arrests and searches and seizures by law enforcement officers, and it is a failure in that vital task.
>
> The use of the exclusionary rule imposes excessive costs on the criminal justice system. It provides no recompense for the innocent and it frees the guilty. It creates the occasion and incentive for large-scale lying by law enforcement officers. It diverts the focus on the criminal prosecution from the guilt or innocence of the defendant to a trial of the police. Only a system with limitless patience with irrationality could tolerate the fact that where there has been one wrong, the defendant's, he will be pun-

ished, but where there have been two wrongs, the defendant's and the officer's, both will go free. This would not be an excessive cost for an effective remedy against police misconduct, but it is a prohibitive price to pay for an illusory one.

Despite the severity of criticisms, the exclusionary rule's chief critics have not proposed its total abolition. However, the Supreme Court has limited the rule's application in significant ways. Thus, for the most part, only the victim of an illegal search has standing to claim the benefits of the exclusionary rule; if A's house is searched in violation of the Fourth Amendment, and evidence is found incriminating B, the evidence can be used in B's trial. (State courts are free to extend the exclusionary rule to such cases; some state courts have done so, concluding that the point of the rule is not to protect people against being convicted but to deter the police.) Similarly, in UNITED STATES V. CALANDRA (1974) the Court held that illegally obtained evidence is admissible in grand jury proceedings, and it ruled in HARRIS V. NEW YORK (1971) that it can be used for the purpose of impeaching the testimony of the accused at his trial. Some uses of illegally obtained evidence have been tolerated as HARMLESS ERROR. More important, the GOOD FAITH EXCEPTION to the exclusionary rule allows the use of evidence obtained with a search warrant if the police reasonably believed the warrant to be valid, even though it later proves to be illegal. The rule has also been held inapplicable to collateral proceedings for postconviction relief such as HABEAS CORPUS. The Court's opinions in these cases have repeated the familiar criticisms of the exclusionary rule; their logic would seem to suggest abandonment of the rule altogether.

Yet the exclusionary rule remains, largely because no one has yet suggested an effective alternative means for enforcing the Bill of Rights against police misconduct. A federal statute dating from Reconstruction authorizes the award of damages against state or local officials (including police officers) who violate individuals' constitutional rights. In 1971, the Supreme Court found that the Fourth Amendment itself implicitly authorized similar damages awards against federal officers who violated the Amendment. The future effectiveness of such remedies will depend in part on the Supreme Court itself, as it spells out the victim's BURDEN OF PROOF in these cases and the measure of damages. Partly, however, the civil-damages alternative depends for its effectiveness on legislation to provide for real compensation to victims when the police officers are judgment-proof, and for real punishment of officers for constitutional violations when the payment of damages is unrealistic.

Meanwhile, the Supreme Court has only the exclusionary rule, which everyone agrees is an imperfect deterrent to police misbehavior. The rule survives, then, for want of better alternatives. But it also stands as a symbol that government itself is not above the law.

LEONARD W. LEVY
(1986)

(SEE ALSO: *Electronic Eavesdropping; New York v. Quarles; Police Interrogation and Confessions; Warrantless Searches; Wiretapping.*)

Bibliography

LaFAVE, WAYNE R. 1978 *Search and Seizure: A Treatise on the Fourth Amendment*, 3 vols. St. Paul: West Publishing Co.

OAKS, DALLIN H. 1970 Studying the Exclusionary Rule. *University of Chicago Law Review* 37:665–757.

SCHROEDER, WILLIAM 1981 Deterring Fourth Amendment Violations: Alternatives to the Exclusionary Rule. *Georgetown Law Review* 68:1361–1426.

STEWART, POTTER 1983 The Road to *Mapp v. Ohio* and Beyond: The Origins, Development and Future of the Exclusionary Rule in Search-and-Seizure Cases. *Columbia Law Review* 83:1365–1404.

EXCLUSIVE POWERS

The Constitution divides governmental power in two ways: between the states and the federal government, and among the three branches of the federal government. Some powers are vested exclusively in one authority, and may not be exercised by any other authority.

The exclusive powers of the federal government include not only all power over FOREIGN AFFAIRS but also certain domestic powers that affect the whole country. Not all of the powers granted to the federal government by the Constitution are exclusive in character; some may be exercised concurrently and independently by both state and federal governments, or may be exercised by the states until Congress acts.

The Constitution makes clear the exclusive character of some powers by explicitly prohibiting the states from exercising them (such as the treaty power). In some other cases, the courts have held the grant to be exclusive when the subject of the power is national in character or requires one uniform system or plan. In some cases the states, with the express permission of Congress, may exercise an exclusive power of the national government.

The states also possess exclusive powers. Because the Constitution establishes a government of limited powers, any domestic governmental power not granted to the federal government by the Constitution and not prohibited by it to the states remains an exclusive power of the state government.

Within the federal government a power may be possessed exclusively by one of the three branches of government. The separation of powers implies that each branch of government has its exclusive sphere of power, which it can independently exercise and from which the other branches are excluded. In theory the legislative power, executive power, and judicial power each belong exclusively to one branch of government. This exclusive power is compatible with the influence of other branches over some part of its exercise. Only Congress may legislate, but legislation may be affected by the President's veto power and the power of the courts to declare statutes unconstitutional. Powers not explicitly granted to one branch have been found by the courts to belong exclusively to Congress, the President, or the courts when they are in their nature exclusively legislative, executive, or judicial.

Although the complexities of modern government require much sharing of power among governmental authorities, the constitutional principles of federalism and the separation of powers require also the maintenance of the proper exclusive spheres of power.

GLEN E. THUROW
(1986)

Bibliography

PRITCHETT, C. HERMAN 1977 *The American Constitution*, 3d ed. Pages 150–216. New York: McGraw-Hill.

EXECUTIVE AGREEMENTS

Executive agreements—that is, international agreements concluded between heads of state or their representatives, commonly without the necessity of parliamentary approval—are nowhere explicitly authorized in the Constitution. The Constitution is silent about international agreement-making except as it vests in the President, in cooperation with the Senate, the power to make and enter into treaties. Nevertheless the principle has long been established that the capacity of the United States to negotiate and enter into international agreements is not exhausted by the TREATY POWER. This principle has been repeatedly recognized in the actual conduct of United States FOREIGN AFFAIRS since the early days of the Republic. Since the mid-nineteenth century, but especially since WORLD WAR II, the use of executive agreements in United States practice has exceeded the use of treaties by an increasingly wide margin.

The expression "executive agreement," which is not widely used outside the United States but which has its equivalents abroad, is understood by the Department of State to refer, in general, to any international agreement brought into force relative to the United States without the ADVICE AND CONSENT of the Senate that is constitutionally required for treaties. In particular, it is understood to refer to three kinds of agreements: those made pursuant to, or in accordance with, an existing treaty; those made subject to congressional approval or implementation ("congressional-executive agreements"); and those made under, and in accordance with, the President's constitutional powers ("sole executive agreements"). None of these executive agreements is subject to the formal treaty-making process specified in Article II, section 2, clause 2, of the Constitution.

A treaty-based executive agreement, provided that it is within the intent, scope, and subject matter of the parent treaty, has the same validity and effect as the treaty itself and is subject to the same constitutional limitations. Deriving from one of the elements of "the supreme law of the land," it takes precedence over all inconsistent state laws and follows the customary rule favoring the instrument later in time in case of inconsistency with a federal statute. A conspicuous example of a treaty-based executive agreement is the traditional *compromis* defining the terms of submission to adjudication or arbitration under a basic convention. Another is found in the hundreds of STATUS OF FORCES AGREEMENTS and other agreements required to carry out the NORTH ATLANTIC TREATY, the linchpin of United States policy in Europe since WORLD WAR II.

A congressional-executive agreement is based on either a prior or a subsequent act of Congress authorizing the making of the agreement or providing general authority for the executive action needed internationally to implement the legislation in question. The scope or subject matter of the agreement is the same whether the congressional act comes before or after the negotiation of the agreement; the act of Congress often takes the form of an authorization to enter into or effectuate an agreement already negotiated. In principle, however, the agreement must reside within the joint powers of Congress and the President in order to have constitutional validity. An agreement outside the legal competence of Congress or the President, authorities generally agree, would be unconstitutional. On the other hand, as the American Law Institute has commented, "the source of authority to make a congressional-executive agreement may be broader even than the sum of the respective powers of Congress and the President," and "in international matters the President and Congress together have all the powers of the United States inherent in its SOVEREIGNTY and nationhood and can therefore make any international agreement on any subject." In any event, partly out of a concern to CHECK AND BALANCE the President in the conduct of foreign affairs, the vast majority of executive agreements entered into by the United States—for example, the Lend-Lease Agreements of World War II and the Trade Expansion Acts of 1934 and 1962—are of this type. Like its treaty-based

counterpart, deriving from one of the elements of "the supreme law of the land," the congressional-executive agreement supersedes all inconsistent state law and follows the customary rule favoring the instrument later in time in case of inconsistency with a federal statute.

Sole executive agreements are international agreements entered into by the President without reference to treaty or statutory authority, that is, exclusively on the basis of the President's constitutional powers as chief executive and COMMANDER-IN-CHIEF, responsible for United States foreign relations and military affairs. Department of State records indicate that only a small percentage of executive agreements are of this type and that the great majority have dealt with essentially routine diplomatic and military matters. Accordingly, with relatively minor exception (such as agreements settling pecuniary and personal injury claims of citizens against foreign governments), they have had little direct impact on private interests and therefore have given rise to little domestic litigation. However, in part out of fear that the President might undertake by international agreement what would be unconstitutional by statute, as in fact occurred in MISSOURI V. HOLLAND (1920), such agreements have not been free of controversy. Two issues in particular continue to stand out.

First there is the question, not yet conclusively settled, of whether Congress may legislate to prohibit or otherwise limit sole executive agreements. Although comprehensive limitations on such agreements, including the proposed BRICKER AMENDMENT of 1953–1954, have so far failed to be adopted, Congress has nonetheless occasionally restricted presidential authority in ways that appear to preclude some executive agreements. For example, the War Powers Resolution of 1973, requiring congressional authorization to introduce combat troops into hostile situations, arguably restrains the President from making agreements that would commit United States armed forces to undeclared foreign wars. Similarly, the Arms Control and Disarmament Act of 1961 forbids the limitation or reduction of armaments "except pursuant to the treaty making power . . . or unless authorized by further legislation of the Congress of the United States." The validity of such restrictions upon presidential authority has been challenged by Presidents and has yet to be determined by the Supreme Court.

Second, while it is widely accepted that the President, under the "executive power" clause, has the authority to conclude sole executive agreements that are not inconsistent with legislation in areas where Congress has primary responsibility, there is a question as to whether the President alone may make an agreement inconsistent with an act of Congress or, alternatively, whether a sole executive agreement may supersede earlier inconsistent congressional legislation. The prevailing view, rooted in the belief that it would be unconscionable for an act of a single person—the President—to repeal an act of Congress, is that sole executive agreements are inoperative as law in the United States to the extent that they conflict with a prior act of Congress in an area of congressional competence. This is the position taken by a federal appeals court in *United States v. Guy W. Capps, Inc.* (4th Circuit, 1953) and by the American Law Institute. The Supreme Court has not yet rendered a definitive decision in these respects, however.

The foregoing two issues aside, there is broad agreement about the scope and effect of sole executive agreements as a matter of constitutional law. Like the other two kinds of executive agreements, they are subject to the same limitations applicable to treaties, they are not limited by the TENTH AMENDMENT, and they supersede all inconsistent state law.

In sum, all three categories of executive agreements bespeak a historic trend toward strong executive leadership in foreign affairs. Only three final points need be added. First, the judgment to resort to these agreements in lieu of the treaty alternative is essentially a political one, affected more by surrounding circumstances than by abstract theories of law. Second, once in force, executive agreements are presumptively binding upon the United States and the other parties to them under international law, to the same extent and in the same way as treaties. Third, the international obligations assumed under such agreements survive all subsequent limitations or restrictions in domestic law.

BURNS H. WESTON
(1986)

Bibliography

AMERICAN LAW INSTITUTE 1965 *Restatement of the Law, Second: Foreign Relations Law of the United States.* Pages 361–448. St. Paul, Minn.: American Law Institute.

——— 1980 *Restatement of the Law: Foreign Relations Law of the United States (Revised), Tentative Draft No. 1.* Pages 71–144. Philadelphia: American Law Institute.

BERGER, RAOUL 1972 The Presidential Monopoly of Foreign Relations. *Michigan Law Review* 71:1–58.

BORCHARD, EDWIN 1944 Shall the Executive Agreement Replace the Treaty? *Yale Law Journal* 53:664–683.

HENKIN, LOUIS 1972 *Foreign Affairs and the Constitution.* Pages 173–188. Mineola, N.Y.: Foundation Press.

McDOUGAL, MYRES and LANS, ASHER 1945 Treaties and Congressional-Executive Agreements: Interchangeable Instruments of National Policy. *Yale Law Journal* 54:181–351, 534–615.

EXECUTIVE AGREEMENTS
(Update)

Article II of the Constitution empowers the President to make treaties with the ADVICE AND CONSENT of two-thirds of the U.S. SENATE. An "executive agreement" is an agreement with a foreign government signed by a member of the executive branch without the advice and consent of the Senate. When the executive acts unilaterally the agreement is known as a "sole executive agreement"; when the executive acts with the approval of a simple majority of both houses of Congress the agreement is known as a "congressional–executive agreement." The President has discretion to decide whether to sign an international agreement in the form of an Article II treaty, a sole executive agreement, or a congressional–executive agreement. In deciding which form of agreement is appropriate, the President will consider the relative importance of the agreement, the likelihood of obtaining a SUPERMAJORITY of the Senate or a simple majority of both houses, and the domestic legal effect of the agreement.

The Constitution does not expressly authorize executive agreements. Article I prohibits states from entering into "an Agreement or Compact with another State, or with a foreign Power," without congressional authorization. Some commentators have suggested that this reference indicates that the Framers understood that there were forms of international agreements other than Article II treaties. There is strong evidence that the Framers were referring to international agreements that do not bind the nation in the future. The term "Agreement or Compact" probably derived from the eighteenth-century treatise *The Law of Nations* by EMERICH DE VATTEL. In this treatise, Vattel defined an agreement or compact as a contemporaneous exchange that imposes no future obligation. For example, a state might use a compact to settle disputed borders with another state or foreign government. By contrast, Vattel defined a treaty as binding the state in perpetuity. One could infer that the Framers intended that an Article II treaty would bind future administrations, unlike other forms of agreements, including executive agreements.

No executive agreements were concluded until 1817, when President JAMES MONROE signed the Rush–Bagot Agreement with Britain to limit military forces along the Great Lakes. Monroe subsequently doubted the constitutionality of this executive agreement and sought the Senate's advice and consent. By 1900, only 124 executive agreements had been concluded over 111 years, and none of them operated to bind the United States prospectively. Presidents understood that an executive agreement, unlike an Article II treaty, could not bind a President's successors. For example, President THEODORE ROOSEVELT concluded an executive agreement to assume responsibility for Santo Domingo's customs house, but subsequently he decided that, because the agreement might operate prospectively, he needed the Senate's advice and consent.

By the 1930s Presidents increasingly relied on executive agreements. President FRANKLIN D. ROOSEVELT signed more than 600 agreements in his four terms in office. Still, Roosevelt respected the traditional distinction between treaties and executive agreements. Then–Attorney General ROBERT H. JACKSON advised Roosevelt that when "negotiations involve commitments as to the future," they "are customarily submitted for the ratification by a two-thirds vote of the Senate before the future legislative power of the country is committed."

President HARRY S. TRUMAN used executive agreements for the first time in lieu of treaties to bind the nation prospectively when he signed the Bretton Woods Agreements in 1945 establishing the International Monetary Fund and the World Bank, and a protocol in 1947 binding the United States to the General Agreement on Tariffs and Trade (GATT). Congress approved the Bretton Woods Agreements as congressional–executive agreements, but neither the Senate nor Congress ever approved the 1947 GATT.

Since 1947, Presidents have employed Article II treaties and executive agreements interchangeably. The vast majority of all international agreements has been in the form of executive agreements. These include important trade agreements such as the NORTH AMERICAN FREE TRADE AGREEMENT (NAFTA), the Canadian Free Trade Agreement, and the World Trade Organization (WTO).

One critical issue is whether an executive agreement should have the same effect on domestic law as an Article II treaty. Article VI of the Constitution provides that treaties "shall be the Supreme Law of the Land." The Supreme Court has interpreted that provision to mean that a treaty supersedes any contrary state law or state constitutional provision and any prior inconsistent federal law. Some commentators have argued that an executive agreement can have the same effect as an Article II treaty in displacing state and federal law. In *United States v. Belmont* (1937) and *United States v. Pink* (1942), the Court enforced a sole executive agreement settling outstanding claims by U.S. nationals against the Soviet Union as a condition to reestablishing diplomatic relations. In DAMES & MOORE V. REGAN (1981), the Court upheld a claims settlement agreement negotiated unilaterally by President JIMMY CARTER with Iran for the release of U.S. hostages. The agreement effectively nullified a default judgment obtained by Dames & Moore for a breach of contract by Iran. Other scholars dispute the implication that a President could legislate federal law without any congressional authorization simply by making an agreement with a foreign leader. The domestic legal status of executive agreements remains contestable.

JOEL R. PAUL
(2000)

(SEE ALSO: *Treaty Power.*)

Bibliography

ACKERMAN, BRUCE and GOLOVE, DAVID 1995 Is NAFTA Constitutional? *Harvard Law Review* 108:799–928.

BORCHARD, EDWIN 1944 Shall the Executive Agreement Replace the Treaty? *Yale Law Journal* 53:616–683.

JACKSON, JOHN H. 1967 The General Agreement on Tariffs and Trade in United States Domestic Law. *Michigan Law Review* 66:249–313.

McDOUGAL, MYERS and LANS, ASHER 1945 Treaties and Congressional-Executive or Presidential Agreements: Interchangeable Instruments of National Policy: I. *Yale Law Journal* 54:181–351.

McLURE, WALLACE 1941 *International Executive Agreements.* New York: Columbia University Press.

PAUL, JOEL R. 1998 The Geopolitical Constitution: Executive Expediency and Executive Agreements. *California Law Review* 86:671–773.

TRIBE, LAURENCE H. 1995 Taking Text and Structure Seriously: Reflections on Free-Form Method in Constitutional Interpretation. *Harvard Law Review* 108:1221–1303.

EXECUTIVE DEFIANCE OF "UNCONSTITUTIONAL" LAWS

Presidents in recent years have asserted that they may refuse to comply with any provision of law that they believe is unconstitutional. This weapon is far more versatile and more potent than the VETO POWER, for it may be applied surgically to selected portions of a law and cannot be overridden by Congress. Defenders of this claimed executive authority urge that since each branch takes an oath to support the Constitution, each therefore has an equal right to interpret that document for itself. Just as JUDICIAL REVIEW permits judges to reject unconstitutional laws, "presidential review" gives the President the same option. Yet even accepting the "departmentalist" view that each branch enjoys autonomy in construing the Constitution, it does not follow that the President may refuse to execute an allegedly unconstitutional law. Despite its appeal in terms of symmetry and logic, "presidential review" is contrary to the ORIGINAL INTENT. Unlike judicial review, which was frequently endorsed at the Federal Convention and in the state ratification debates, the Founders rejected the notion that the executive may refuse to execute laws that it deems to be unconstitutional.

The President's failure to honor a statute because of its alleged unconstitutionality is equivalent to the "suspending power" that English kings employed for 400 years before it was abolished by the BILL OF RIGHTS (ENGLISH) of 1689. Through this royal prerogative, the Crown was able to nullify all or portions of a law—sometimes on the ground that it was unconstitutional.

The Founders were careful not to confer this prerogative on the American President. Article II thus enjoins the President to "take Care that the Laws be faithfully executed." In marked contrast to the duty placed on judges by the SUPREMACY CLAUSE, the President's obligation extends to all laws, not just those "made in pursuance" of the Constitution. The Framers also insisted on giving the President only a qualified rather than an absolute veto, even though the primary purpose of the veto was to shield the executive against unconstitutional laws. By rejecting an absolute veto, the Convention necessarily anticipated that laws might be enacted over a President's constitutional objection. Should this occur it would be up to the judiciary—not the executive—to check the statute's enforcement. Had the Founders envisioned that Presidents could refuse to execute "unconstitutional" laws, the veto would have been superfluous in the very setting for which it was principally designed. Finally, if there had been any hint that the President would have authority to suspend allegedly unconstitutional laws, the ANTIFEDERALISTS would have been quick to object, for one of their chief objections to the Constitution was that the President would be "as much a King as the King of Great-Britain." Yet nowhere in the Antifederalist literature is there any mention of a presidential suspending power.

Throughout most of our history, the executive has honored this original understanding by implementing even those statutes to which the President has constitutional objections. The first known instance of presidential defiance of an "unconstitutional" law occurred in 1860, almost three-quarters of a century after the Constitution was ratified. Between 1789 and 1973 there were only ten occasions when a President refused to comply with an allegedly unconstitutional law. Since the mid-1970s, however, such defiance has become more common. Rather than using the veto against laws it believes to be unconstitutional, the White House now often issues a "signing statement" charging that parts of a bill the President has just signed into law are invalid. Though the executive does not always follow through on these objections, refusals to comply with allegedly unconstitutional laws are no longer a rarity. From 1974 through 1980, there were as many instances of presidential defiance as had occurred during the previous 185 years. The Supreme Court has not yet been presented with a case challenging this growing presidential practice. If the Court respects the intent of the Founders it will declare the practice to be unconstitutional.

CHRISTOPHER N. MAY
(2000)

(SEE ALSO: *Impoundment of Funds; Judicial Supremacy; Line-Item Veto; Nonjudicial Interpretation of the Constitution.*)

Bibliography

CALABRESI, STEVEN G. and PRAKASH, SAIKRISHNA B. 1994 The President's Power to Execute the Laws. *Yale Law Journal* 104: 541–665.
EASTERBROOK, FRANK H. 1989–1990 Presidential Review. *Case Western Reserve Law Review* 40:905–929.
MAY, CHRISTOPHER N. 1998 *Presidential Defiance of "Unconstitutional" Laws: Reviving the Royal Prerogative.* Westport, Conn.: Greenwood Press.
PAULSEN, MICHAEL S. 1994 The Most Dangerous Branch: Executive Power to Say What the Law Is. *Georgetown Law Journal* 83:217–345.
RECENT LEGAL OPINIONS CONCERNING PRESIDENTIAL POWERS 1994 *Arkansas Law Review* 48:311–346.
SCIGLIANO, ROBERT 1989 The President's "Prerogative Power." Pages 236–256 in Thomas E. Cronin, ed., *Inventing the American Presidency.* Lawrence: University Press of Kansas.

EXECUTIVE IMMUNITY

In tracing the development of executive immunity in the United States, one should separate immunity for constitutional violations from immunity for nonconstitutional violations and immunity of federal officials from immunity of state officials. State officials' immunity for nonconstitutional violations is a matter left to each state's laws. At least since enactment in 1871 of SECTION 1983, TITLE 42, UNITED STATES CODE, state officials have been liable for some federal constitutional violations. Until well into the twentieth century, however, their immunity in constitutional cases had not been fully explored because there were relatively few federal constitutional restrictions on state officials' behavior. By the middle of the twentieth century, federal officials, who are not covered by section 1983, seemed immune from actions for both constitutional and nonconstitutional misbehavior. Within a few decades, however, with the exception of the President, no executive official, state or federal, was fully immune from damage actions for constitutional violations.

In the Massachusetts case of *Miller v. Horton* (1891) Justice OLIVER WENDELL HOLMES, writing for the majority, narrowly restricted state officials' state-law immunity from suit. Even reasonable, good-faith behavior might trigger liability if found to violate the Constitution or some other legal limit. But in *Spaulding v. Vilas* (1896) and other cases, the Supreme Court was more protective of federal executives. And in subsequent years, many states provided their executives with more generous protection from suits in state courts, particularly when their acts were viewed as discretionary rather than ministerial.

Gregoire v. Biddle (1949) highlighted the movement away from *Miller v. Horton*. In an influential opinion by Judge LEARNED HAND for the United States Court of Appeals, *Gregoire* suggested that a federal executive officer's malice would not render him liable for an otherwise lawful act. *Gregoire* was read as conferring broad immunity upon federal officials. *Barr v. Matteo* (1959) accentuated this trend when, in a case generating no majority opinion, the

Supreme Court seemed to hold federal officials absolutely immune from defamation suits.

After *Barr*, the Supreme Court paused in its treatment of federal executive immunity to explore the liability, under section 1983, of state officers charged with constitutional violations. In a series of cases, including PIERSON V. RAY (1967), SCHEUER V. RHODES (1974), and WOOD V. STRICKLAND (1975), the Court held that unconstitutional acts by state executive officials would not trigger liability under section 1983 if the officials acted under a reasonable, good-faith belief that their behavior was constitutional. But they enjoyed no absolute immunity. *Scheuer v. Rhodes*, in which a governor was found not to have absolute immunity, dispelled illusions some had entertained about special status for high officials.

This experience with state officials undoubtedly influenced the Court's subsequent treatment of federal officials. In BUTZ V. ECONOMOU (1978), over four dissents, the Supreme Court held that the good-faith defense, and not the rule of *Barr*, applied to damage actions against federal officials for constitutional violations. Prior statements about absolute immunity, and the importance of the ministerialdiscretionary dichotomy, in effect were limited to cases involving common law torts. *Harlow v. Fitzgerald* (1982) reaffirmed and modified the limited immunity of high federal executive officials and NIXON V. FITZGERALD (1982) found the federal chief executive, the President, to enjoy the absolute immunity that *Scheuer* had denied to state chief executives.

THEODORE EISENBERG
(1986)

Bibliography

JAFFE, LOUIS L.   1963   Suits against Governments and Officers: Damage Actions. *Harvard Law Review* 77:209–239.
SCHUCK, PETER H.   1981   Suing Our Servants: The Court, Congress, and the Liability of Public Officials for Damages. *Supreme Court Review* 1980:281–368.

EXECUTIVE ORDER

Executive orders, a class of presidential documents, primarily regulate actions of government officials and agencies. Although most executive orders are issued under specific statutory authorization, some, including President HARRY S. TRUMAN'S STEEL SEIZURE order and executive orders affecting CIVIL RIGHTS, are issued on the President's own authority under Article II. Executive orders were not numbered until 1907 and were not required to be published until 1935.

Executive orders have taken on particular importance in times of war and in the field of civil rights. President FRANKLIN D. ROOSEVELT's executive orders played a key role in the WORLD WAR II Japanese relocation program, sustained in the JAPANESE AMERICAN CASES (1943–1944). Most executive orders concerning civil rights relate to employment by government contractors. Executive Order 8802 (1941), generated by a wartime need for labor, established a Committee on Fair Employment Practices to carry out a policy of nondiscrimination in defense industries. EXECUTIVE ORDERS 9980 AND 9981 (1948) declared a national policy of nondiscrimination in federal employment and sought to foster equality of treatment in the armed services. Executive Order 11603 (1962) attempted to promote nondiscrimination in federally assisted housing. On the more mundane level, executive orders also have been a vehicle through which Presidents promulgate the never-ending plans for reorganizing the executive branch of government.

With the enactment of ANTIDISCRIMINATION LEGISLATION in the 1960s and the expansion of constitutional prohibitions on government discrimination, executive orders prohibiting discrimination became less important. They continue, however, to provide internal authority regulating the federal government's employment and contracting policies. And in requiring employers to take AFFIRMATIVE ACTION to hire minorities and women, EXECUTIVE ORDER 11246 (1965) goes further than fair employment statutes. It has been a significant factor in pressuring government contractors to hire minority and female workers.

THEODORE EISENBERG
(1986)

(SEE ALSO: *Presidential Ordinance-Making Power.*)

Bibliography

MORGAN, RUTH P.   1970   *The President and Civil Rights: Policy-Making by Executive Order.* New York: St. Martin's Press.

EXECUTIVE ORDER 9066 AND PUBLIC LAW 503
(1942)

On February 19, 1942, citing the necessity for "every possible protection against espionage and against sabotage," President FRANKLIN D. ROOSEVELT issued an EXECUTIVE ORDER authorizing various military commanders to designate any area in the United States from which "any or all persons may be excluded" at their discretion. Although based on a 1918 WAR POWERS act, the order resulted from vigorous anti-Japanese sentiment on the West Coast. Despite its broad wording, the order was enforced almost exclusively against persons of Japanese ancestry. The order conveyed a remarkably broad DELEGATION OF POWER but failed to distinguish between American citizens and ALIENS or even between loyal and disloyal citizens. To provide for enforcement, the War Department drafted a bill making it a federal crime for a civilian to disobey a military relocation order. The bill passed Congress without dissent and Roosevelt signed it into law on March 21. Few spoke out against the use of these two measures to deprive some 110,000 people (an entire community was relocated in ten "camps") of their CIVIL RIGHTS. The Supreme Court sustained the evacuation and relocation in three JAPANESE AMERICAN CASES (1943–1944), despite a vigorous dissent by Justice FRANK MURPHY objecting to the "legalization of racism."

DAVID GORDON
(1986)

EXECUTIVE ORDER 10340
(1952)

On April 8, 1952, on the eve of a nationwide strike of steelworkers, President HARRY S. TRUMAN issued Executive Order 10340, directing the secretary of commerce to take possession of and operate the plants and facilities of eighty-seven major steel companies. The order anticipated that the plants would continue to be run by company managers, preserving the rights and obligations of the companies until corporation officials and union leaders settled their dispute. As justification for averting a work stoppage, the order referred to Truman's proclamation of December 16, 1950, declaring the existence of a national emergency and the dispatch of American fighting men to Korea. The order called steel "indispensable" for producing weapons and war materials, for carrying out the programs of the Atomic Energy Commission, and for maintaining the health and vitality of the American economy.

Although Truman based the order on authority under "the Constitution and laws of the United States, and as President of the United States and COMMANDER-IN-CHIEF of the armed forces of the United States," the Justice Department later argued in court that Truman had acted solely on inherent executive power without any statutory support. On June 2, 1952, the Supreme Court declared the Executive Order invalid.

LOUIS FISHER
(1986)

(SEE ALSO: *Steel Seizure Controversy; Youngstown Sheet and Tube Co. v. Sawyer.*)

Bibliography
MARCUS, MAEVA 1977 *Truman and the Steel Seizure Case: The Limits of Presidential Power.* New York: Columbia University Press.

EXECUTIVE ORDER 11246
(1965)

Executive Order 11246 required government contractors to take AFFIRMATIVE ACTION to ensure nondiscriminatory employment practices. Employers complying with the order may encounter employees or potential employees who claim that affirmative action violates Title VII of the CIVIL RIGHTS ACT OF 1964 or the Constitution. UNITED STEELWORKERS OF AMERICA V. WEBER (1979), which sustained some affirmative action by private employers, does not foreclose all such claims. Efforts to undermine the order by amending the 1964 act have failed. Part I of the order, which banned discrimination and required affirmative action by the federal government, was superseded by Executive Order 11478 (1969) and by the 1972 extension of the 1964 act to government employees.

THEODORE EISENBERG
(1986)

EXECUTIVE ORDERS 9835 AND 10450
(1947, 1953)

As a result of domestic political and security pressures after 1945, Presidents HARRY S. TRUMAN and DWIGHT D. EISENHOWER instituted sweeping loyalty investigations of federal workers. Truman's Executive Order 9835, affecting over two million employees, established loyalty review boards in executive departments to evaluate information provided by Federal Bureau of Investigation or Civil Service Commission investigations and informants. The basic standards for dismissal required "reasonable grounds for belief in disloyalty," which included evidence of affiliation with groups on the ATTORNEY GENERAL'S LIST of subversive organizations. Critics who alleged widespread subversion nevertheless demanded more stringent measures, and Truman's Executive Order 10241 (April 28, 1951) altered the criterion to one of "reasonable doubt" of loyalty. The change effectively shifted the burden of proof to the accused or suspected employee. Eisenhower, however, later complained that the Truman program reflected "a complacency . . . toward security risks," such as homosexuals and alcoholics, and in April 1953, he issued Executive Order 10450 that made security, not loyalty, the primary concern.

The loyalty probes produced new bureaucracies, with agendas of their own and standards and practices that varied widely in different departments. Between 1947 and 1956, approximately 2,700 employees were dismissed and another 12,000 resigned because of the inquiries. After 1953, the security program provided for immediate suspension without pay, and many employees undoubtedly resigned to avoid the stigma of combating the charges, however flimsy. Then, too, the program's shroud of secrecy, including the use of unknown informants, made challenges difficult.

The Supreme Court responded cautiously to the program. In *Bailey v. Richardson* (1951) an evenly divided bench sustained Bailey's dismissal even though she had been denied an opportunity to confront her accusers. The same day, in JOINT ANTI-FASCIST REFUGEE COMMITTEE V. MCGRATH, the Court questioned the procedures for compiling the attorney general's list of subversive organizations, yet did not prevent its continued use. Some individuals successfully challenged their dismissals, but courts carefully avoided broader constitutional issues. In *Peters v. Hobby* (1955) the Supreme Court overturned a medical professor's dismissal because his position was nonsensitive, yet the Justices ignored Peters's challenge against secret informers. Similar reasoning was employed in *Cole v. Young* (1956) to reverse the discharge of an employee who had challenged the use of the attorney general's list as a violation of rights of association. The real turning point came in *Service v. Dulles* (1957) when the Court reversed the dismissal of one of the "China Hands" who had been purged from the State Department. Finally, in *Greene v. McElroy* (1959), Chief Justice EARL WARREN condemned the use of "faceless informers," unknown to the accused. Without determining constitutional issues, the Court held that the government's evidence must be disclosed to the individual to give him an opportunity to refute it.

Although the Court's decisions undoubtedly demonstrated that abusive, illegal governmental actions could be brought to account, such challenges required extraordinary individual persistence and courage as well as financial and emotional cost. For all the government's efforts, the results were dubious. Judith Coplon, convicted of passing Justice Department documents to a Soviet agent, had escaped the program's net. And in 1954, the Civil Service Commission acknowledged that no communist or fellow traveler had been uncovered in its probes.

STANLEY I. KUTLER
(1986)

Bibliography

HARPER, ALAN D. 1969 *The Politics of Loyalty.* Greenwich, Conn.: Greenwood Press.

EXECUTIVE ORDERS 9980 AND 9981
(1948)

When issued by President HARRY S. TRUMAN, Executive Orders 9980 and 9981 were among the most far-reaching federal antidiscrimination measures adopted since Reconstruction. Executive Order 9980 authorized the establishment of review boards within federal executive departments and agencies to which employees claiming racially discriminatory treatment could appeal. It also established a Fair Employment Board to coordinate and supervise executive antidiscrimination policy and to hear appeals from agency and department review boards.

Executive Order 9981 declared it "to be the policy of the President that there shall be equality of treatment and opportunity for all persons in the armed services without regard to race, color, religion or national origin." To this end, the order established the President's Committee on Equality of Treatment and Opportunity in the Armed Services to study and resolve the problem of SEGREGATION in the armed forces. Issued under pressure from black leaders, and in the midst of a reelection campaign, the order and the committee's recommendations were crucial first steps to desegregating the armed services.

THEODORE EISENBERG
(1986)

Bibliography

BERMAN, WILLIAM C. 1970 *The Politics of Civil Rights in the Truman Administration.* Pages 116–120. Columbus: Ohio State University Press.

EXECUTIVE POWER

Article II of the Constitution vests "the executive power" of the United States in the President, whereas Article I vests in Congress those legislative powers "herein granted," and Article III says that the JURISDICTION of the federal courts extends only to the subjects enumerated in the article. The common reader would normally construe these provisions to confer the entire executive power on the President, while granting Congress and the courts only parts of the legislative and judicial authority of the United States. As so often happens, however, the common reader has had a difficult time. From the first term of President GEORGE WASHINGTON, there has been a considerable debate over the scope of the President's executive power.

One party, labeled "Super-Whigs" by EDWARD S. CORWIN, views all the powers of the national government with grudging suspicion as necessary but distasteful restraints on the powers of the states or the people. For members of this party, the first principle of constitutional exegesis is that the Constitution provides limited and ENUMERATED POWERS that should be narrowly construed. They read the first sentence of Article II as a "mere designation" of the President's office and would confine the President's authority strictly to those examples of the executive power mentioned in the constitutional text: the VETO POWER, the power to receive ambassadors, the duty to execute faithfully the laws, and the others.

The other participant in the debate, the party of those who interpret law in the manner of JOHN MARSHALL, read the vesting clause of Article II as a grant to the President of a broad and independent range of authority to be defined historically and by the necessities of circumstance, and not limited to the powers and duties mentioned in the text. For this party, "the executive power" includes not only IMPLIED POWERS, but also the prerogative and emergency powers of the British Crown unless limited or denied to the President by the Constitution.

The issue has long since been settled by usage and by decisions of the Supreme Court in cases such as EX PARTE MILLIGAN, *In re Neagle* (1890), and IN RE DEBS (1895), but it continues to enjoy a half-life in the literature of the Constitution.

In his perceptive study, *The Creation of the Presidency, 1775–1789*, C. C. Thach, Jr. concludes that Article II admits "an interpretation of executive power which would give to the President a field of action much wider than that outlined by the enumerated powers." Thach has no doubt that this consequence of the text was contemplated and intended because the dominant force governing the CONSTITUTIONAL CONVENTION OF 1787 was not the theories of MONTESQUIEU and WILLIAM BLACKSTONE, popular as they were, but the experience of the state and the national governments between 1776 and 1787. To the majority of the founding fathers, led by JAMES WILSON, JOHN JAY, JAMES MADISON, and GOUVERNEUR MORRIS, the lesson of this experience was the danger of unbridled legislative power and the necessity for a strong and accountable national executive "to counterbalance legislative predominance. Neither theorist nor foreign model was needed to demonstrate that fact. The state legislatures' excesses and the incompetency of Congress as an administrative body produced the presidency." This is why Article I, section 6, forbids any member of Congress from holding an executive office during his or her term and why the Convention rejected several proposals that would have diluted the unity of the presidency or subordinated the office to a congressional committee.

Thach's judgment has been vindicated by the ebb and flow of history, despite the survival of a minority view favoring congressional supremacy. Upheavals of public opinion like those of the later stages of the VIETNAM WAR and the WATERGATE scandal caused the pendulum to swing more violently than usual in the direction of congressional power, but—thus far, at any rate—James Wilson's conception of the presidency has recovered from the vehemence of periodic congressional attacks and prevails in public opinion, governmental practice, and constitutional law.

The reasons for this pattern are simple, but fundamental: they correspond to functional necessity. Congress cannot conduct the day-to-day business of a vast government, the central task of the executive power. The size, history, and habits of Congress make it an admirable legislative body, but for these reasons also make it impossible for Congress, even through committees and committee staff, to constitute the operational arm of a government capable of "energy, secrecy, and dispatch."

It is equally apparent that no American President can preempt the legislative power and rule by decree, at least not for long. It is not always easy to discover at what point in the process of government a statute is constitutionally necessary. But as a matter of principle, there is a boundary between the legislative and executive functions, no matter how difficult it sometimes is to draw. As a matter not only of legal obligation, but of institutional resistance, every President is forced sooner or later to respect the limits of the tripartite system of government, sanctioned as it is by the conviction that "there can be no liberty" in a society where the executive and legislative functions are combined and where the judiciary is not separated from both the other branches.

Congress had to consider the indispensable elasticity of these concepts when it met for the first time in 1789. In considering a statute to establish the first three departments of the government, Congress faced the question as to whether it was constitutionally required to give the President the power to remove heads of the departments or whether the President had that power under Article II, with or without a statute. The Constitution made it clear that only the President could nominate these officers, but could not appoint them without the ADVICE AND CONSENT of the SENATE. Congress could provide other procedures for "inferior" officers or officers to be appointed by the courts. Were the new cabinet ministers to serve at the President's pleasure or was IMPEACHMENT required to remove them? Could the President remove them only with the advice and consent of the Senate? Could the Senate or Congress as a whole remove them on its own motion, whatever the President thought?

Madison led the extended debate on the bill in the HOUSE OF REPRESENTATIVES, and in the end, Congress decided to say nothing on the subject, but to leave the outcome to practice and to the courts. Madison contended that the officers should be deemed to serve at the President's pleasure. The principal reason he offered for discovering an "implied" power of removal in Article II was that the President could not be expected faithfully to execute the laws if he were not given a free hand to dismiss his chief subordinates; neither the Senate nor Congress as a whole should have a binding vote in the conduct of the administrative business of the government, save through legislation. It followed, Madison concluded, that the President alone was responsible and accountable for the removal of officials.

Madison's position on the constitutional basis of the President's removal power was tested in a famous episode. During the passionate battles between President ANDREW JOHNSON and Congress over policy in the military occupation of the South, Congress passed the TENURE OF OFFICE ACT, providing that certain heads of departments could serve until their successors were qualified. The provision was designed by Congress to prevent Johnson from dismissing Secretary of War EDWIN M. STANTON, who was in charge of the military occupation of the South. Stanton was removed by Johnson, however, and the House of Representatives proceeded to impeach the President, largely for violating the statute. The President, of course, was acquitted by the Senate. Some sixty years later, the Supreme Court declared the Tenure of Office Act unconstitutional in MYERS V. UNITED STATES (1926).

To confirm that the authority of a President to remove a member of his CABINET is an integral part of "the" executive power was hardly the end of the story. The *Myers* case did not concern the removal of a cabinet member, but of a postmaster. At the present stage in the evolution of the law on the subject, it can be said that the President's "absolute" power to remove federal officials is clear only for those of senior political responsibility whose appointments have been confirmed by the Senate. In contrast, military officers and foreign-service officers receive their commissions from the President after a senatorial vote of consent, but can only be discharged after compliance with statutory procedures for assuring them justice. For officials below the political level, Congress can qualify or abolish the President's removal power by passing civil-service legislation or by other means and direct the appointment of members of boards, commissions, and independent agencies for fixed terms. However, the Supreme Court has held in RUTAN V. REPUBLICAN PARTY OF ILLINOIS (1990) that the FIRST AMENDMENT prevents state governors from discriminating among lower-level state officials on political grounds with regard to promotions, dismissals, and other aspects of employment. This line of cases surely applies also to the national government.

The same pattern of adjustment and accommodation between President and Congress is manifest in other lines of decisions that distinguish between the executive and the legislative functions—those on pardons, for example. This *Encyclopedia* considers the relations of Congress and the President in the field of FOREIGN AFFAIRS in a number of articles, so this phase of the problem will not be addressed here. This article will, however, recall the ways in which the President and Congress share powers with respect to the important subject of appropriations.

It is often said that Congress has exclusive authority over the national purse because of the provisions in Article I, section 9, that "no money shall be drawn from the Treasury but in Consequence of appropriations made by law," and in Article I, section 7, that all money bills must originate in the House of Representatives. From the beginning, however, questions have arisen about the import of these words. The questions were raised with new intensity by the controversy over President RONALD REAGAN's handling of the IRAN-CONTRA AFFAIR.

Does the word "law" in the phrase "appropriations made by law" mean only statutory law, or does it include the President's actions pursuant to his prerogative and EMERGENCY POWERS under the Constitution as well? President Washington spent unappropriated funds to put down the WHISKEY REBELLION, and ABRAHAM LINCOLN spent two million dollars in unappropriated funds for war material during the early months of the CIVIL WAR, while Congress was not in session. President WOODROW WILSON and a number of other Presidents have taken comparable actions.

Article I, section 9, prohibits the spending of unappropriated funds. Does it therefore by implication allow the President not to spend funds, even when they have been appropriated? When the Armistice in Europe was signed in 1945, could President HARRY S. TRUMAN cancel military procurement contracts? The practice of presidential IMPOUNDMENT OF FUNDS already appropriated goes back at least to President THOMAS JEFFERSON. On rare occasion, Presidents have relied on their inherent constitutional powers both to spend funds without benefit of statutory authority and not to make expenditures that had been authorized by statute.

Such acts have been treated as presenting a special constitutional problem fraught with overtones of tyranny. In situations of this kind, it has been normal practice for Presidents to report such expenditures or decisions not to spend to Congress, often with a request that Congress join its authority to that of the President by approving the action already taken. While some conclude that President Lincoln acted unconstitutionally in spending two million dollars of unappropriated funds in 1861 for the purpose of resisting the Confederacy, this author is of the opinion that Lincoln was legally correct in characterizing his action as constitutional.

The existence of an emergency does not suspend the Constitution; it merely changes the state of facts to which the law must be applied. As a matter of international law and constitutional law alike, the government of the United

States possesses all the powers it requires to function in the society of nations. Like every other constitution, the Constitution of the United States contemplates the possibility of emergencies and makes provision for dealing with them. When Presidents invoke their emergency powers, they are acting under the Constitution, not beyond its limits, regardless of whether they are right or wrong in judging the scope of their powers. There is no other way for them to act. The general constitutional norms of reasonableness apply to the field of emergency actions as they do to other exercises of executive (and legislative) authority. In scrutinizing actions taken by the executive in the name of emergency, however, Congress, the courts, and the people may conclude that what the President did was justifiable as going no further than was reasonably necessary to carry out the President's constitutional responsibility under the circumstances.

Even if Lincoln could have assembled Congress in emergency session in the spring of 1861, his political judgment that such a session would have been impolitic, to say the least, was an important part of this constitutional responsibility. In defending Washington's unorthodox method of financing the suppression of the Whiskey Rebellion, ALEXANDER HAMILTON spoke of a presidential prerogative to make temporary "advances" against future congressional appropriations. This is a possible approach to the constitutional problem; it is analytically more precise, however, to treat such presidential actions as exercises of an autonomous presidential power. Congress may approve after the event, as frequently happens when Presidents use the national force on their own authority. The PRIZE CASES (1863). But the President's action meets the standard of Article I, section 9, whether Congress approves or not.

Involving the claim of emergency, however, by no means justifies every decision the President (or Congress) takes to resolve it, as shown in *Ex Parte Milligan* (1866). In the context of the Constitution as a whole and considering the possibilities of abuse, the President's power to spend unappropriated funds should be confined to the minimum necessary for the purpose.

During the administration of RICHARD M. NIXON, a major controversy between Congress and the presidency developed about the existence and the extent of the President's power not to spend appropriated funds. The controversy resulted in the CONGRESSIONAL BUDGET AND IMPOUNDMENT ACT of 1974. This statute distinguishes between appropriations that authorize expenditures and those that mandate them. In the first category, the Act acknowledges a power in the President to sequester appropriated funds for a limited period, giving Congress time to reconsider its prior decision. Where an appropriation is mandatory, however, the President is required to carry it out.

These problems in determining the respective role of the legislature and the executive in spending public funds, important as they are, do not address the principal constitutional issues raised by the growing tendency of Congress to use riders on appropriation bills, LEGISLATIVE VETOES, standing congressional oversight committees, and other legislative methods as devices for taking executive powers unto itself. The pracitce of "tacking foreign matter to money bills" was familiar to the Constitutional Convention and has been familiar ever since, both in money bills and more generally. No constitutional way to protect the President's veto by requiring Congress to enforce a rule of "germaneness"—that is, a rule that would confine each act to one subject—has yet been developed. Two approaches to the problem are currently being discussed: the LINE ITEM VETO and a more vigorous judicial development of the Supreme Court's analysis and conclusions in cases like *Springer v. Government of the Philippine Islands* (1928), IMMIGRATION AND NATURALIZATION SERVICE V. CHADHA (1983), BOWSHER V. SYNAR (1986), and *Commodity Future Trading Commission v. Schor* (1986), all of which recognize the importance of enforcing the constitutional distinction between legislative and executive power, whatever form the encroachment may take. There has been some support for the novel argument that a constitutional basis for the item veto already exists and should be declared by the Supreme Court rather than by constitutional amendment. Whether or not so radical a step is taken, however, it is to be expected that the Court will pursue the initiative it took in *Chadha* and *Bowsher*.

EUGENE V. ROSTOW
(1992)

(SEE ALSO: *Congress and Foreign Policy; Congressional War Powers; Executive Prerogative; Pardoning Power; Senate and Foreign Policy.*)

Bibliography

CORWIN, EDWIN S.   1940 and 1957   *The President: Office and Powers.* New York: New York University Press.

FISHER, LOUIS   1975   *Presidential Spending Power.* Princeton, N.J.: Princeton University Press.

THACH, CHARLES C., JR.   1922   *The Creation of the Presidency, 1775–1789.* Baltimore Md.: The Johns Hopkins Press

EXECUTIVE PREROGATIVE

Executive prerogative refers to the President's constitutionally based authority to declare policy, take action, and make law without congressional support or in the face of inconsistent congressional LEGISLATION. This authority may be seen as a corollary of the SEPARATION OF POWERS under which the President has exclusive EXECUTIVE POWER that Congress may not invade because Congress's authority is limited to LEGISLATIVE POWERS. Executive prerogative may also refer to certain EMERGENCY POWERS under which the President may act contrary to the Constitution, such as spending funds without an appropriation or contrary to an act of Congress that would properly be classified as a legislative act. In the view of some eighteenth-century political theorists, the President could act extraconstitutionally or illegally if circumstances required, but he would have to seek subsequent ratification of the act. More recently, the President has justified such action on the basis of an inherent or implied authority conferred by the Constitution.

Executive prerogative mostly relates to FOREIGN AFFAIRS but may also include domestic acts, such as actions during war or national emergency, dismissal of CABINET officers appointed with Senate participation, and assertion of EXECUTIVE PRIVILEGE to protect communications of executive branch officials from congressional or judicial inquiry.

The Constitution does not expressly delegate a "foreign affairs" power to the President or to any single branch of the government. Indeed, the Constitution delegates most specific foreign relations powers to the Congress. These powers include the powers to declare war, to regulate FOREIGN COMMERCE, and to define and punish offenses against the law of nations, piracy, and FELONIES committed on the high seas, as well as the powers to authorize an army, navy, and MILITIA and to make rules for the regulation of land and naval forces. Congress therefore has concurrent authority and substantial practical influence over all aspects of foreign affairs. Notwithstanding this authority, the President dominates foreign affairs. Yet the Constitution delegates relatively few foreign relations powers to the President, and several of these powers are shared with the Senate or Congress. The President has the power to make treaties and appoint ambassadors, but only with the participation of the Senate. His power as COMMANDER-IN-CHIEF is subject to limitation by the congressional war, legislative, and appropriations powers. The President has the power to receive ambassadors, the duty (and implicitly the power) to take care that laws (including treaties and customary international law) be faithfully executed, and a general executive power. But executive prerogative rests more on historical practice and functional necessity than on constitutional text.

Much of the President's dominance of foreign affairs is based on extralegal factors, such as access to the media and political party status. Most presidential foreign affairs authority derives from congressional support. For example, Congress has delegated to the President plenary authority over foreign commerce. It has also authorized and funded a standing armed force, a vast intelligence bureaucracy, and dozens of agencies with thousands of officials participating in all facets of international organization and activities. Having created the bureaucracies, Congress has generally been content to let the executive run them. Executive prerogative has historically sanctioned the President's right to recognize foreign states and governments, establish diplomatic relations, initiate negotiations, determine the content of communications with foreign governments, conduct intelligence operations, conclude presidential EXECUTIVE AGREEMENTS, and initiate military action.

Executive prerogative has been controversial since the first administration of GEORGE WASHINGTON. After Washington declared neutrality in 1793 in the war between France and Great Britain, ALEXANDER HAMILTON and JAMES MADISON debated his authority under the pseudonyms Pacificus and Helvidius. The structure of the debate, and even the arguments advanced, have been used repeatedly in foreign policy clashes between the President and Congress, most recently in the IRAN-CONTRA AFFAIR. The Washington declaration amounted to a decision not to declare war and implicitly interpreted a treaty with France not to require U.S. entry into the war.

Madison rejected Washington's authority to issue the declaration because in his view neutrality pertained to declaration of war, a congressional power, and to the application of a treaty, a power shared with the Senate. Madison viewed constitutional powers as strictly separated so that any activity within the scope of a legislative power was precluded to the President. He also advocated a narrow construction of the executive power and other presidential authorities specified in the constitutional text. In Madison's view, the President could only execute laws and policies established by Congress.

Hamilton took a broad view of the executive power, arguing that its scope was limited only by explicit exceptions such as Senate participation in treaty making and congressional power to declare war. Thus, the President could preserve peace until Congress declared war. As the "organ of intercourse" between the United States and foreign nations, the President could make, interpret, suspend, and terminate treaties; recognize foreign governments; and execute the laws of nations (including the law of neutrality). In Hamilton's view, the President shared power with the legislature in war and treaty making.

Washington established other important precedents supporting presidential foreign affairs power. He authorized military actions against AMERICAN INDIANS without congressional authorization and dispatched an envoy without Senate approval. He also asserted executive privilege against both the Senate and Congress to protect treaty-negotiating instructions, and he effectively eliminated the Senate's "advice" function in treaty making. Other early Presidents also established major precedents justifying presidential foreign affairs power. JOHN ADAMS initiated presidential executive agreements. THOMAS JEFFERSON committed funds to purchase military supplies without an appropriation and dispatched the navy to protect U.S. vessels against pirates off Africa.

Since then, presidential authority has fluctuated with the strength of particular Presidents and the exigencies of the moment, depending on what the President has claimed and what the Congress has tolerated. The courts generally have declined to adjudicate these controversies. On the few occasions when the Supreme Court has addressed questions of presidential power, it has almost always sided with the President.

In a much-quoted passage, Justice GEORGE SUTHERLAND, in UNITED STATES V. CURTISS-WRIGHT EXPORT CORP. (1936), referred to "the very delicate, plenary and exclusive power of the President as the sole organ of the federal government in the field of international relations." Sutherland explained that "[t]he President alone has the power to speak or listen as a representative of the nation. He *makes* treaties with the advice and consent of the Senate; but he alone negotiates. Into the field of negotiation the Senate cannot intrude; and Congress itself is powerless to invade it." Sutherland offered a functional explanation: "if, in the maintenance of our international relations, embarrassment ... is to be avoided and success for our aims achieved, congressional legislation ... must often accord to the President a degree of discretion and freedom. ... [H]e, not Congress, has the better opportunity of knowing the conditions which prevail in foreign countries. ... He has his confidential sources of information. He has his agents in the form of diplomatic, consular and other officials. Secrecy in respect of information gathered by them may be highly necessary, and the premature disclosure of it productive of harmful results. ...."

In *Chicago and Southern Air Lines v. Waterman S. S. Corp.* (1948) Justice ROBERT H. JACKSON, after noting the importance of secret intelligence in executive decision making, added: "[T]he very nature of executive decisions as to foreign policy is political, not judicial. Such decisions are wholly confided by our Constitution to the political department of the government. ... They are delicate, complex and involve large elements of prophecy. They are and should be undertaken only by those directly responsible to the people whose welfare they advance or imperil. They are decisions of a kind for which the Judiciary has neither aptitude, facilities nor responsibility and have long been held to belong in the domain of political power not subject to judicial intrusion or inquiry."

In YOUNGSTOWN SHEET TUBE CO. V. SAWYER (1952), however, the Court denied an executive emergency power to seize steel mills during the KOREAN WAR. The determinative factor was that Congress had earlier declined to give the President such authority. Jackson's concurring opinion, which is now the standard framework for analysis, held that the President's authority is maximum when exercised pursuant to express or implied congressional authorization, but is "at its lowest ebb" when exercised contrary to the express or implied will of Congress. Jackson recognized a "zone of twilight" where there is neither a grant nor a denial of presidential authority. The branches then have concurrent authority, and "Congressional inertia, indifference or quiescence may sometimes, at least as a practical matter, enable if not invite, measure on independent presidential responsibility." In DAMES & MOORE V. REGAN (1981) the Court upheld a presidential executive agreement eliminating causes of action in federal courts for claims against foreign governments, contrary to a statute conferring jurisdiction over such cases, on the basis of congressional acquiescence to earlier executive agreements dealing with such claims. Presidents have also negotiated export restraint measures covering steel and automobiles at odds with the antitrust laws, and Congress has acquiesced.

In the absence of much judicial guidance, presidential foreign affairs power has been shaped by political compromises between Congress and the President. Almost all exercises of presidential power, including politically controversial ones, have the sanction of congressional acquiescence.

Executive prerogative builds on the negotiation function. Everyone agrees that the President has exclusive authority to recognize foreign states and governments, establish diplomatic relations, and control official communications with foreign governments. The President declares foreign policy, although important declarations like the MONROE DOCTRINE or support for the African National Congress typically require congressional action to be effective. Executive branch officials, with congressional acquiescence, have also construed executive prerogative to include the right to preserve confidentiality of diplomatic communications and related executive deliberations.

The President may negotiate an international agreement on any subject matter. He decides whether to conclude it on the basis of Article II or the constitutionally equivalent procedure of authorization by Congress. He may conclude some international agreements without any congressional participation. These agreements have sometimes been controversial, but the Supreme Court has approved. In UNITED STATES V. BELMONT (1937) and UNITED STATES V. PINK (1942), the Court upheld an executive agreement that superseded state law. In *Dames & Moore v. Regan* (1981) the Court upheld an executive agreement inconsistent with a federal statute. After the VIETNAM WAR and WATERGATE, the President fended off congressional attempts to regulate executive agreements. The President may also interpret, suspend, and terminate Article II treaties without Senate participation.

The most controversial aspect of executive prerogative concerns the presidential war power. This authority rests in part on the commander-in-chief clause and in part on congressional authorization of military forces and acquiescence in their use. Since WORLD WAR II, the President has frequently initiated military activities without a congressional DECLARATION OF WAR. Examples include military actions in Korea, the Dominican Republic, Lebanon, Grenada, the Persian Gulf, and Panama. During the Vietnam War, Congress challenged the President, passing the War Powers Resolution over the President's veto. Subsequent presidents disregarded its major limitation, sending troops to the Middle East, Asia, Africa, and Latin America. Some members of Congress complained, but Congress acquiesced to presidential military action, at least for limited purposes. Executive branch officials have also claimed constitutionally based authority to initiate covert intelligence operations.

Only rarely has a President acted contrary to congressional prohibition. In some contexts, however, functional theory and historical practice constitutionally justify such action, whether as an emergency power or, under contemporary theory, as a synergistic product of the textual powers of the President. One cannot anticipate the contexts in which such action may be required, and it is therefore difficult to define rules in principled terms. The prospect for congressional acquiescence seems crucial. The President does not have a general power to override acts of Congress for foreign-policy purposes. Nevertheless, the foreign relations power may justify action inconsistent with acts of Congress when foreign policy urgency requires and Congress seems likely to acquiesce. Presidential exercise of power is subject to congressional review to weigh the genuineness of the urgency and wisdom of the action. If Congress disagrees, it can repudiate the President formally. Congressional action in response to assertions of presidential prerogative should in turn prevail and constitutional lawmaking continue.

PHILLIP R. TRIMBLE
(1992)

(SEE ALSO: *Congress and Foreign Policy; Congressional War Powers; Presidential War Powers; Senate and Foreign Policy; War, Foreign Affairs, and the Constitution; War Powers.*)

Bibliography

BALDWIN, GORDON　1976　The Foreign Affairs Advice Privilege. *Wisconsin Law Review* 1976:16–46.

CORWIN, EDWARD　1917　*The President's Control of Foreign Relations.* Princeton, N.J.: Princeton University Press.

FISHER, LOUIS　1985　*Constitutional Conflicts Between Congress and the President.* Princeton, N.J.: Princeton University Press.

GLENNON, MICHAEL J.　1990　*Constitutional Diplomacy.* Princeton, N.J.: Princeton University Press.

HENKIN, LOUIS　1972　*Foreign Affairs and the Constitution.* Mineola, N.Y.: Foundation Press.

KOH, HAROLD HONJU　1990　*The National Security Constitution.* New Haven, Conn.: Yale University Press.

LOBEL, JULES　1989　Emergency Power and the Decline of Liberalism. *Yale Law Journal* 98:1385–1433.

NOTE　1968　Congress, the President, and the Power to Commit Forces to Combat. *Harvard Law Review* 81:1771–1805.

——　1984　The Extent of Independent Presidential Authority to Conduct Foreign Intelligence Activities. *Georgetown Law Journal* 72:1855–1883.

WRIGHT, QUINCY　1922　*The Control of American Foreign Relations.* New York: Macmillan.

EXECUTIVE PRIVILEGE

Executive privilege refers to a right of the chief executive to refuse to produce documents within his control in response to a demand from either the legislative or judicial departments of the national government. There would seem to be no question that the chief magistrate need not respond to such demands from departments of state governments. Raoul Berger has asserted that "executive privilege is a myth," a creature of the Presidents who have asserted this claim to immunity without foundation in the Constitution. Although the Constitution does provide for legislative privilege, there are no words in the Constitution on which to base any such executive privilege. Nevertheless, the Supreme Court, in UNITED STATES V. NIXON (1974), wrote executive privilege into the Constitution on the grounds that it inheres in the notion of SEPARATION OF POWERS that is immanent in our basic document:

> The expectation of a President to the confidentiality of his conversations and correspondence, like the claim of confidentiality of judicial deliberations, for example, has all the values to which we accord deference for the privacy of all citizens and, added to these values, is the necessity for protection of the public interest in candid, objective, and even blunt or harsh opinions in presidential decision-making. A President and those who assist him must be free to explore alternatives in the process of shaping policies and making decisions and to do so in a way many would be unwilling to express except privately. These are the considerations justifying a presumptive privilege for Presidential communications. The privilege is fundamental to the operation of Government and inextricably rooted in the separation of powers under the Constitution.

The privilege as created by the Court in *Nixon* is not, however, an absolute one. Interests of the other branches of government may override the presidential interest in the privilege. And in *Nixon* the executive privilege was held subordinate to the claim of a GRAND JURY for EVIDENCE "that is demonstrably relevant in a criminal trial." Thus, the weight of the privilege to withhold information differs according to its function. It is at its lowest force when it "is based only on the generalized interest in confidentiality." It is at its strongest when the claim is based on the ground of "military or diplomatic secrets."

The Supreme Court's constitutional DOCTRINE of executive privilege is still in its nascency. The Court, in *Nixon*, particularly eschewed passing on "the balance between the President's generalized interest in confidentiality and the need for relevant evidence in civil litigation, [or] with that between the confidentiality interest and congressional demands for information, [or] with the President's interest in preserving state secrets." In the absence of constitutional language, the constitutional meaning of executive privilege depends totally on judicial creation, for "it is the province and duty of this Court "to say what the law is."

Prior to the *Nixon* decision, the question of executive privilege, especially as it related to demands of Congress on the executive branch, was resolved in the political rather than the judicial arena. It was a contest of wills, with each side exerting its own powers and its own claims on public opinion, which was frequently dispositive of the issue. The strongest power of the Congress lies in its control over the purse and its threat to cut off funding from programs as to which Congress makes inquiry and as to which the executive branch declines to produce the documents sought. The greatest force on the side of the executive branch lies in its capacity to delay acquiescence, since most executive privilege questions become moot or stale through the passage of time.

The problem has a long history in this country, going back to the time that President GEORGE WASHINGTON declined to deliver to the House of Representatives documents relating to JAY'S TREATY, on the grounds that it was none of the business of the House to participate in the treaty process and that all relevant information had, indeed, been delivered to the Senate, whose job it was to advise and consent on the content of treaties. When in the *Burr* case JOHN MARSHALL subpoenaed communications in the hands of President THOMAS JEFFERSON, Jefferson decided which he would and which he would not provide. In *Burr* the judiciary proved helpless against the adamancy of the President to withhold documents, although the Court might have tried to invoke the CONTEMPT POWER.

Since the investigatory or oversight power of Congress is itself an implied rather than a granted power, its claim to access to presidential papers generally rests on as weak a reed as does the President's claim to immunity from producing the information. Both are implicit rather than express constitutional rights. But the case differs where

Congress, particularly the House, is investigating the question of misbehavior of executive branch officials. The Congress is particularly charged by the IMPEACHMENT provisions of the Constitution with the duty of "throwing the rascals out." And surely they must have access to relevant information to determine whether an executive official, be it the President himself, has committed "high crimes and misdemeanors" for which he might be impeached and convicted. But the problem of executive privilege has not arisen in the impeachment context. Rather the impeachment power is used to justify a general congressional power of investigation.

It is with regard to Congress's legislative duty to secure knowledge on which to base its laws or to assure itself that the President is, indeed, engaged in the faithful execution of the laws which Congress has enacted that "executive privilege" problems tend to arise. History provides us with no doctrinal answer to the correct meaning of executive privilege here. Most are agreed that the privilege can be claimed only by the President himself or by a government official at the command of the President. It is not to be invoked even by the vice-president or the secretary of state except through the President. There is little other consensus. Impeachable offenses aside, the privilege is strong where, as the Court noted, it is concerned with military or state secrets. Beyond this, history shows only that the balance between the two constitutional claims, Congress's to be able to perform its duties and the President's to perform his own, has been resolved on an ad hoc basis, with the President having the greater ability to manipulate public opinion, and Congress being able to invoke only the time-consuming processes of contempt and fiscal restraints.

Now that the Supreme Court seems to have made the question of executive privilege a judicial rather than a political one, some further elucidation may be forthcoming. But, except in times of crisis such as the Watergate affair, the mills of the courts, like the mills of the gods, grind so very slowly that they may prove inadequate to provide greater definition to the amorphous concept of executive privilege. This is especially the case since the Court recognized the privilege as a conditional one and not an absolute one, requiring balancing by a judicial arbiter without any special competence to perform the task. It may be predicted, however, that where the conflict is between the judicial and executive branches, as it was in the *Nixon* case, the judicial branch is more likely to prevail, at least in a criminal case or one in which the government itself is seeking the information. But, as between Congress and the President, the Court is likely to be found where it is usually found, aligned with the executive branch.

Executive privilege could cover immunities other than the right to reject a demand for information from another branch. In the Nixon period, the question arose, speculatively, whether a President of the United States could be arrested, indicted, and tried for crime while still in office. That a successful impeachment would leave the person charged with no immunity to arrest, INDICTMENT, and trial is made clear by the words of the Constitution itself. On the other hand, it says nothing about executive immunity while in office. Without judicial precedent or judgment, there appeared to be agreement that the President of the United States and only the President must be immune from interruption of his duties while he holds office, subject only to the necessity for responding to impeachment charges. There is no moment when the President is not on duty, even while on vacation. This immunity, whether termed executive privilege or not, derives from the implications of the Constitution much more readily than his right to refuse to produce documents, which need not interrupt his presidential obligations.

One must assume, too, that the President, like everyone in the nation, can claim the RIGHT AGAINST SELF-INCRIMINATION both in Congress and in the courts. The practical effects on the electorate of such a claim make it highly unlikely that it will ever be invoked. And again, the privilege not to incriminate himself is not the executive privilege as that term is generally used.

The contours of executive privilege remain hard to define, and certainty is not likely to come soon, if ever.

PHILIP B. KURLAND
(1986)

Bibliography

BERGER, RAOUL   1974   *Executive Privilege: A Constitutional Myth.* Cambridge, Mass.: Harvard University Press.

KURLAND, PHILIP B.   1978   *Watergate and the Constitution.* Chicago: University of Chicago Press.

UNITED STATES SENATE, JUDICIARY COMMITTEE, SUBCOMMITTEE ON SEPARATION OF POWERS   1971   *Executive Privilege: The Withholding of Information by the Executive.* 92nd Congress, 1st session. Washington, D.C.: Government Printing Office.

———, SUBCOMMITTEE ON ADMINISTRATIVE PRACTICE AND PROCEDURE AND SEPARATION OF POWERS, AND COMMITTEE ON GOVERNMENT OPERATIONS, SUBCOMMITTEE ON INTERGOVERNMENTAL RELATIONS   1973   *Freedom of Information: Executive Privilege; Secrecy in Government.* 3 Vols. 93rd Congress, 1st session. Washington, D.C.: Government Printing Office.

EXECUTIVE PRIVILEGE
(Update)

The term "executive privilege" has been applied to explain and define a variety of immunities claimed by the President to resist inquiries or impositions by other branches of government.

In the broadest sense, the term covers claims by the President that he is not subject to any type of judicial process while serving in his office. However, whether or not the President can be indicted and tried for a criminal offense while in office (an issue that has yet to be resolved), the Supreme Court held in CLINTON V. JONES (1997) that he can be required to appear and answer as a defendant and to testify in a civil case for acts committed before he became President. A President can also be ordered to respond to a subpoena for tapes (and documentary materials) in a criminal case, as the Court held in UNITED STATES V. NIXON (1974). Presumably he could also be obliged to give testimony in such cases, so long as one of the narrower testimonial privileges described below does not specifically apply. When President WILLIAM J. CLINTON was asked to give testimony before the Monica Lewinsky GRAND JURY convened by INDEPENDENT COUNSEL Kenneth Starr, he chose to appear voluntarily rather than test the extent of his testimonial immunity.

On the other hand, in NIXON V. FITZGERALD (1982), the Court held that Presidents cannot be sued for damages for acts taken while in office.

In the narrowest sense, executive privilege covers only specific testimonial privileges under which the President may refuse to produce documents or permit testimony by members of the executive department to either Congress or the courts on matters relating to the operation of that branch.

With respect to resisting inquiries by Congress, Presidents going back to GEORGE WASHINGTON have refused to disclose materials relating to the interior workings of the presidential office. Presidents JOHN ADAMS, THOMAS JEFFERSON, and ANDREW JACKSON similarly asserted the privilege in the nineteenth century and every President since FRANKLIN D. ROOSEVELT did so in our time.

When privilege is asserted before Congress, the only weapon available to the legislative branch is to vote a CONTEMPT citation and seek to obtain penalties or a compliance order before the courts. Generally, a compromise is then worked out between the two branches. In the rare instances that an assertion of executive privilege before Congress was presented to the courts, generally the executive department's claim has been upheld or the case has been held to lack JUSTICIABILITY.

Executive privilege has also been asserted by the President or executive department members in judicial proceedings, generally in criminal cases. Commentators and the courts have noted that the term has been applied in at least five separate situations. Included in this category are the "state secrets" privilege covering NATIONAL SECU-

RITY matters, and the privilege to withhold the names of informers or information relating to pending criminal investigations.

Another recognized privilege is the "presidential communications" privilege established by the Court in *United States v. Nixon.* Under that DOCTRINE, communications to and from the President before and after a presidential decision has been made are ordinarily immune from process, based on SEPARATION OF POWERS concerns. Breach of that privilege is possible only after a compelling showing of need by the person seeking the information.

The most frequently invoked form of executive privilege is the "deliberative process" privilege. Under that doctrine, the President, on behalf of any executive branch officer, may refuse to disclose recommendations and deliberations comprising part of the process by which governmental decisions and policies are formulated. To invoke this privilege, the President must show that the material sought to be discovered related to communications made before a governmental decision was made (it was "predecisional") and that it related to the method chosen or advice given to arrive at the decision.

Even if such a showing is made, the privilege can be overcome by a showing of need, less than that required to breach the "presidential communications" privilege. Among the considerations that must be balanced by the courts are the importance of the evidence, the availability of alternate sources of information, the significance of the litigation and the extent of government misconduct sought to be examined.

New assertions of executive privilege were made during the Monica Lewinsky investigation involving President Clinton. But the courts rejected any claim of privilege by U.S. Secret Service agents or by government lawyers asserting an attorney–client privilege not to respond to questions involving possible criminal activity within their knowledge.

LEON FRIEDMAN
(2000)

Bibliography

BERGER, RAOUL 1974 *Executive Privilege: A Constitutional Myth.* Cambridge, Mass.: Harvard University Press.

ROZELL, MARK J. 1994 *Executive Privilege: The Dilemma of Secrecy and Democratic Accountability.* Baltimore, Md.: Johns Hopkins University Press.

EXHAUSTION OF REMEDIES

Exhaustion-of-remedies questions arise in at least two areas of constitutional adjudication. Since *Ex parte Royall*

(1886), state prisoners have been required to exhaust available, effective state court remedies before seeking federal HABEAS CORPUS relief from allegedly unconstitutional state convictions. Congress codified this result more than half a century later. The exhaustion requirement, which is not constitutionally mandated, is said to reflect the Court's sensitivity to relations between federal and state courts; a federal court is prevented from reviewing a state conviction until state courts have had a chance to correct constitutional errors.

In another class of cases seeking to vindicate constitutional rights, the Supreme Court does not require exhaustion of state judicial remedies. In MONROE V. PAPE (1961) and a series of later cases, the Court has stated that there is no requirement of exhaustion of state judicial remedies before bringing an action against state officials under SECTION 1983, TITLE 42, UNITED STATES CODE. *Patsy v. Board of Regents* (1982) held that litigants bringing section 1983 cases also need not exhaust state administrative remedies and thereby resolved a long-standing conflict among the courts of appeal. In the Civil Rights of Institutionalized Persons Act (1980),Congress imposed an exhaustion-of-administrative-remedies requirement upon certain prisoners bringing actions under section 1983.,

The exhaustion requirement in habeas corpus cases, and its absence in section 1983 cases, generates difficulty in deciding whether to require exhaustion in constitutional actions brought by prisoners, many of which may be brought either as habeas actions or as section 1983 cases. In *Preiser v. Rodriguez* (1973) the Court held that exhaustion was required in a case close to "the core of habeas corpus," that is, one attacking the validity of a prisoner's conviction or otherwise challenging the fact or duration of confinement. When the prisoner challenges the conditions of confinement, the Court said, the nonexhaustion rule applicable to section 1983 cases governs. Perhaps inspired in part by the long-standing exhaustion requirement in habeas corpus cases, much modern CIVIL RIGHTS legislation reflects sensitivity to state prerogatives by requiring complainants initially to present claims to state authorities. Title VII of the CIVIL RIGHTS ACT OF 1964 requires resort to state antidiscrimination agencies before the Equal Employment Opportunity Commission may act on a complaint. Title VIII of the CIVIL RIGHTS ACT OF 1968 requires federal administrators to allow state and local housing agencies the first chance at a housing discrimination complaint. But post-Civil War ANTIDISCRIMINATION LEGISLATION, such as the CIVIL RIGHTS ACT OF 1866 and 1870, reflected no such sensitivity. And the practice is not uniform in modern statutes. The VOTING RIGHTS ACT OF 1965 expressly rejects any requirement of exhaustion of administrative or other remedies before initiation of actions in federal court. Other civil rights statutes simply do not address the issue.

THEODORE EISENBERG
(1986)

Bibliography

COMMENT   1974   Exhaustion of State Administrative Remedies in Section 1983 Cases. *University of Chicago Law Review* 41: 537–556.

NAHMOD, SHELDON H.   1979   *Civil Rights & Civil Liberties Litigation.* Pages 143–148. Colorado Springs, Colo.: Shepard's.

EXIGENT CIRCUMSTANCES SEARCH

Although the Supreme Court has denounced WARRANTLESS SEARCHES as *"per se* unreasonable under the FOURTH AMENDMENT," it has recognized "a few specifically established and well-delineated exceptions" to this rule based on exigent circumstances. A SEARCH WARRANT, which in ordinary circumstances provides constitutional reasonableness for a search, may be dispensed with if the delay involved in obtaining the warrant might defeat the purpose of the search. In fact, far more searches are made without warrants than with them. The warrantless search is "exceptional" only in the sense that exceptional (that is, exigent) circumstances are needed to justify it.

Five types of warrantless searches have thus far received the Court's sanction. In WEEKS V. UNITED STATES (1914) the Court upheld SEARCH INCIDENT TO ARREST of a person—and, in later cases, of the area under the arrestee's control—in order to disarm him and prevent the destruction of EVIDENCE. The search of an automobile on the road is constitutional when there is PROBABLE CAUSE to believe the automobile is transporting contraband. As the Court said in CARROLL V. UNITED STATES (1925), to delay the AUTOMOBILE SEARCH is to risk the escape of driver and vehicle. "Hot pursuit" of a suspected felon into a building was held reasonable in WARDEN V. HAYDEN (1967). Delaying to obtain a warrant might endanger the lives of the pursuing officers and others. Such a search may continue until the suspect is apprehended and his weapons are seized. In SCHMERBER V. CALIFORNIA (1966) the Court permitted the compulsory taking of blood from an individual to determine whether he was intoxicated while driving when there was probable cause to believe that he was. The exigency in such cases is furnished by the fact that the level of alcohol in the blood diminishes after its intake ceases. In TERRY V. OHIO (1968) the Court upheld the practice of stopping a suspect and frisking his outer clothing to discover concealed weapons, even when probable cause for an arrest is lacking, provided that circumstances entitle an officer to believe that a criminal venture is about to be launched and that his safety or that of others is endangered.

The concept of exigent circumstances is an open one. Indeed, in *Mincey v. Arizona* (1978) the Court indicated that officers may enter and search without a warrant upon reasonable belief that there is a "need to protect or preserve life or avoid serious injury. . . ."

JACOB W. LANDYNSKI
(1986)

Bibliography

LANDYNSKI, JACOB W.   1971   The Supreme Court's Search for Fourth Amendment Standards: The Warrantless Search. *Connecticut Bar Journal* 45:2–39.

EX PARTE

(Latin: "From the part [of]. . . .") A legal proceeding is said to be *ex parte* if it occurs on the application or for the benefit of one party without NOTICE to or contest by an adverse party. In the reports such a case is entitled *"Ex parte. . ."* followed by the name of the party at whose instance the case is heard. A proceeding of which an adverse party has notice, but at which he declines to appear, is not considered *ex parte.* Writs, INJUNCTIONS, etcetera, are said to be *ex parte* when they are issued without prior notice to an affected party.

DENNIS J. MAHONEY
(1986)

EX PARTE . . .

See under name of party

EXPATRIATION

Expatriation was defined by the Supreme Court in *Perkins v. Elg* (1939) as "the voluntary renunciation or abandonment of nationality and allegiance." It refers to the loss of CITIZENSHIP as a result of voluntary action taken by a citizen, either native-born or naturalized. By expatriation, a citizen becomes an ALIEN; he divests himself of the obligations of citizenship and loses the rights connected with those obligations. In general, he can regain citizenship only by the process of NATURALIZATION.

At COMMON LAW, a person owed perpetual allegiance to the country of his birth and could not expatriate himself without the consent of that country. Initially, there was an inclination in the United States to follow this rule. In 1868, however, Congress explicitly broke with that tradition and declared by statute that "the right of expatriation is a natural and inherent right of all people, indispensable to the enjoyment of the rights of life, liberty, and the pursuit of happiness." Congress did so in order to establish that persons naturalized in the United States did not continue to owe allegiance to foreign governments. Congress seemed to rely on the simple mechanism of formal renunciation to determine whether a citizen actually wished to expatriate himself. Because the statute made expatriation dependent upon the voluntary action of the individual, it raised no constitutional questions about Congress's power over expatriation.

Determination of volition, however, has never been limited to formal renunciation, and through a series of nationality statutes, culminating in the Immigration and Nationality Act of 1952, Congress has identified various actions that indicate a citizen's desire voluntarily to expatriate himself. These actions include obtaining naturalization in a foreign state, taking an oath of allegiance to a foreign state, serving in a foreign army, voting in a foreign election, desertion from the armed forces, TREASON against the United States, assuming public office under the government of a foreign state for which only nationals of that state are eligible, formal renunciation of citizenship either in the United States or abroad, and leaving or remaining outside the United States during either a war or a national emergency for the purpose of evading military service.

Congress's power to declare that such actions constitute voluntary renunciation, even when the individual who so acts claims not to have intended to renounce his citizenship, was rarely challenged by the courts until the 1960s. Nationality laws were shielded from judicial scrutiny because the courts believed it was beyond their competence to examine matters so intimately related to foreign affairs. However, in the landmark decision of AFROYIM V. RUSK (1967), the Supreme Court restored citizenship to a naturalized citizen who was considered by the government to have expatriated himself by voting in an Israeli parliamentary election. The Court held that although Congress can provide a mechanism by which an individual can voluntarily expatriate himself, volition is a judicially ascertainable quality and the government bears the BURDEN OF PROOF that the citizen's renunciation was truly voluntary. Put simply, *Afroyim* made the statutory presumption of volition rebuttable rather than conclusive.

While the BURGER COURT seemed to retreat from these principles in *Rogers v. Bellei* (1971), in *Vance v. Terrazas* (1980) it reaffirmed *Afroyim* and held that the government must prove specific intent to surrender citizenship and not simply the voluntary commission of an expatriating act. At the same time, the Court upheld the rebuttable presumption that an act of expatriation is performed with the specific intention of relinquishing citizenship and held that

Congress is free to prescribe as the evidentiary standard for proving this intention the "preponderance-of-the-evidence" standard of proof.

RALPH A. ROSSUM
(1986)

Bibliography

GORDON, CHARLES and ROSENFIELD, HARRY N. 1984 *Immigration Law and Procedure*, Vol. 3, chap. 20. New York: Matthew Bender.

SCHWARTZ, DAVID F. 1975 American Citizenship after *Afroyim* and *Bellei:* Continuing Controversy. *Hastings Constitutional Law Quarterly* 2:1003–1028.

EXPOSITION AND PROTEST
(1828–1829)

JOHN C. CALHOUN drafted the *Exposition* in 1828. The next year, the legislature of South Carolina published the *Exposition* in amended form along with its own resolution of protest against the TARIFF ACT OF 1828. Like most of the great controversial documents in American politics it took the form of a discourse on the meaning of the Constitution. It argued the case for STRICT CONSTRUCTION of the powers of the federal government and spelled out the doctrine of NULLIFICATION.

Rejecting the argument that a protective tariff was justified by custom and precedent, the *Exposition* declared: "Ours is not a government of precedent. . . . The only safe rule is the Constitution itself." But even the Constitution was not a safe rule if its interpretation were left to Congress and the Supreme Court, which were its creatures. The only authoritative interpreter was the constituent body itself, the people of the states in convention.

According to the *Exposition,* if a convention in any state declared a federal law unconstitutional, the law was null and void in that state until the Constitution was amended to authorize the disputed act. Should an amendment pass the state would have no recourse but SECESSION.

DENNIS J. MAHONEY
(1986)

Bibliography

FREEHLING, WILLIAM W. 1965 *Prelude to Civil War: The Nullification Controversy in South Carolina, 1816–1865.* New York: Harper & Row.

EX POST FACTO

In THE FEDERALIST #84 ALEXANDER HAMILTON argued that "the creation of crimes after the commission of the fact, or, in other words, the subjecting of men to punishment for things which, when they were done, were breaches of no law" has been "in all ages" one of "the favorite and most formidable instruments of tyranny." Indeed, ex post facto legislation has generally been regarded as a violation of the fundamental DUE PROCESS requirement that there must be fair warning of the conduct which gives rise to criminal penalties. The Framers of the Constitution believed so strongly that ex post facto laws were contrary to the principles of republican government that they proscribed their use in two different provisions of the Constitution: Article I, section 9, as a specific exception to the powers of the United States Congress, and Article I, section 10, as a specific prohibition on the powers of state legislatures.

Justice SAMUEL CHASE in CALDER V. BULL (1798) provided what has since come to be regarded as the authoritative delineation of the kinds of LEGISLATION that fall within the Constitution's prohibition against ex post facto enactments:

> 1st. Every law that makes an action done before the passing of the law, and which was *innocent* when done, criminal; and punishes such action. 2d. Every law that *aggravates a crime*, or makes it *greater* than it was, when committed. 3d. Every law that *changes the punishment*, and inflicts a *greater punishment*, than the law annexed to the crime, when committed. 4th. Every law that alters the *legal* rules of *evidence*, and received less, or different, testimony, than the law required at the time of the commission of the offence, *in order to convict the offender.*

Although there is some question about the Framers' intent, the Supreme Court has consistently followed Chase's lead in restricting the ex post facto rule to criminal laws. Thus the Court has held that the deportation of ALIENS, the loss of a passport, and the denial of certain benefits do not fall within the ex post facto exception because they are not punishments in a criminal sense even though they may be "burdensome and severe." In the TEST OATH CASES (1867), however, the Court held that oaths that disqualified people from holding certain offices or practicing certain professions constituted ex post facto laws.

The essential ingredient of an ex post facto law is its retrospective character; but not all retrospective laws are ex post facto in the technical meaning of the term. An ex post facto law not only is retrospective but also injures those to whom it is directed by imposing or increasing criminal penalties. For example, *Weaver v. Graham* (1981) invalidated retroactive application to a prisoner of a law reducing "good time" credits against a sentence. Retrospective laws that ameliorate penalties, however, are not ex post facto.

The rights affected by retrospective legislation must be substantial. As the Court held in *Beazell v. Ohio* (1925), statutory changes in trial procedures or rules of EVIDENCE "which do not deprive the accused of a defense and which operate only in a limited and unsubstantial manner to his disadvantage, are not prohibited." Thus, the ex post facto prohibition secures "substantial personal rights against arbitrary and oppressive legislation without limiting legislative control of remedies and procedures that do not affect matters of substance." Of its own weight, the ex post facto prohibition applies only to legislative acts, and not to changes in the law effected by judicial decisions. But where an unforeseeable statutory construction by a court is applied retrospectively in a manner that is tantamount to ex post facto legislation, that construction is barred by the due process clause. Although the particular application of the ex post facto clause has generated much controversy and debate, and involves, on occasion, the most intricate and detailed considerations, there seems to be almost universal agreement that the Constitution's prohibition against ex post facto legislation remains one of the mainstays of constitutional government.

EDWARD J. ERLER
(1986)

Bibliography

FIELD, OLIVER P. 1922 Ex Post Facto in the Constitution. *Michigan Law Review* 20:315–331.
NOTE 1975 Ex Post Facto Limitations on Legislative Power. *Michigan Law Review* 73:1491–1516.

EXTRADITION

See: Fugitive from Justice

EXTRATERRITORIALITY

Around the turn of the century, the Supreme Court placed strict territorial limits on the application of United States constitutional and statutory law. In the case of *In re Ross* (1891) the Court held that a citizen could be tried by an American consular court, without INDICTMENT by GRAND JURY and without TRIAL BY JURY, for crimes aboard an American ship in Japan. The Court flatly declared that "[t]he Constitution can have no operation in another country." And in *American Banana Co. v. United Fruit Co.* (1909) Justice OLIVER WENDELL HOLMES asserted that "[a]ll legislation is prima facie territorial." Although he acknowledged that exceptions could be found in the case of laws applying on the high seas or in "uncivilized" countries, Holmes said "the general and almost universal rule is that the character of an act as lawful or unlawful must be determined wholly by the law of the country where the act is done." No doubt these sweeping statements, even then, were not literally followed. In any event, today DOCTRINES

limiting the extraterritorial application of both the Constitution and statutory law have been abandoned.

In REID V. COVERT (1956) the Court effectively overruled *Ross* and held that Congress could not deprive a citizen of the right to a jury trial in a court-martial abroad where CAPITAL PUNISHMENT was potentially involved. Justice HUGO L. BLACK said: "When the Government reaches out to punish a citizen who is abroad, the shield which the Bill of Rights and other parts of the Constitution provide to protect his life and liberty should not be stripped away just because he happens to be in another land." This decision signaled the end of territorial limitations on the Constitution.

In *United States v. Toscanino* (2d Cir. 1974) a lower court applied the FOURTH and Fifth AMENDMENTS where American officials instigated enforcement activity by foreign officials that included torture and violated United States treaty obligations. Although other courts have declined to apply CONSTITUTIONAL REMEDIES in the circumstances of particular cases before them, they agree that the Bill of Rights may apply where the United States government instigates conduct that "shocks the conscience." The JUST COMPENSATION clause of the Fifth Amendment has also been held applicable to TAKINGS OF PROPERTY abroad in several lower court cases. As a general rule, therefore, the Constitution now unquestionably applies to acts of government abroad.

At the same time the special circumstances that are invariably present in these cases influence the scope of constitutional protection afforded. Although the court only occasionally confronts these questions, it seems clear that protection against government action abroad is more difficult to obtain than in similar cases without a foreign element. This is especially true when foreign policy or national security interests are at issue, as was the case in UNITED STATES V. CURTISS-WRIGHT EXPORT CORP. (1936). Indeed, in HAIG V. AGEE (1981) the Supreme Court questioned whether the FIRST AMENDMENT would apply at all to government suppression of speech abroad, where the speech threatened American intelligence activity.

Perhaps the most accurate description of the modern approach to extraterritorial application of constitutional law was made by Justice JOHN MARSHALL HARLAN in *Reid v. Covert.* He took exception to the broad suggestion that "every provision of the Constitution must be deemed automatically applicable to American citizens in every part of the world." He believed that "the question is *which* guarantees of the Constitution *should* apply in view of the particular circumstances, the practical necessities, and the possible alternatives which Congress had before it." The Harlan view seems more likely to prevail in a world of increased American involvement and interdependence than the absolutist approach of Justice Black.

A related issue of historical interest was whether the Constitution applied to TERRITORIES acquired by the United States. Constitutional guarantees limiting legislative and executive power were applicable only when Congress, expressly or by clear implication, "incorporated" the acquired territory into the United States. In unincorporated territories only undefined "fundamental" liberties were guaranteed.

Finally, the courts have repeatedly applied federal statutes to conduct abroad, assuming other jurisdictional prerequisites were met. Occasionally limitations on the application of a particular statute have been imposed, but those limitations have normally been based on the presumed intent of Congress or on international comity, not the Constitution.

PHILLIP R. TRIMBLE
(1986)

Bibliography

COUDERT, FREDERICK R.   1926   The Evolution of the Doctrine of Territorial Incorporation. *Columbia Law Review* 26:823–850; *Iowa State Bar Association Report* 1926:180–228.

HENKIN, LOUIS   1972   *Foreign Affairs and the Constitution.* Pages 266–269. Mineola, N.Y.: Foundation Press.

KAPLAN, STEVEN M.   1977   The Applicability of the Exclusionary Rule in Federal Court to Evidence Seized and Confessions Obtained in Foreign Countries. *Columbia Journal of Transnational Law* 16:495–520.

NOTE   1985   Predictability and Comity: Toward Common Principles of Extraterritorial Jurisdiction. *Harvard Law Review* 98:1310–1330.

EXTRATERRITORIALITY
(Update)

At the start of the twentieth century, both federal LEGISLATION and the U.S. Constitution were presumed to apply only within the territory of the United States. In the case of *In re Ross* (1891), the Supreme Court stated that "[t]he Constitution can have no operation in another country." And in *American Banana Company v. United Fruit Company* (1909), the Court refused to apply the SHERMAN ANTITRUST ACT extraterritorially, declaring that "the general and almost universal rule is that the character of an act as lawful or unlawful must be determined wholly by the law of the country where the act is done." At the end of the twentieth century, however, federal statutes are frequently applied to both U.S. and foreign nationals outside the United States, although the protections of the BILL OF RIGHTS are not always afforded to foreign nationals abroad.

It is clear that Congress has constitutional authority to legislate extraterritorially, even if doing so violates INTERNATIONAL LAW (which it generally does not). The territorial

reach of a statute is therefore a question of congressional intent. The Supreme Court sometimes assumes that Congress does not intend to regulate conduct outside the United States, applying the so-called presumption against extraterritoriality. For example, in *Equal Employment Opportunity Commission v. Arabian American Oil Company* (1991), the Court held that Title VII did not prohibit EMPLOYMENT DISCRIMINATION by an American company against an American citizen abroad. Because the presumption's principal modern justification is the notion that Congress is primarily concerned with domestic conditions, it should not be applied when foreign conduct affects domestic conditions. And in *Hartford Fire Insurance v. California* (1993), the Court ignored the presumption and held that the Sherman Antitrust Act applied to anticompetitive conduct by foreign companies that caused substantial, intended effects in the United States, OVERRULING the specific holding of *American Banana*.

It is also clear that the Bill of Rights applies extraterritorially, but whether it applies to foreign nationals or only to U.S. nationals abroad depends on the theory one adopts. Under an "organic" theory, the Bill of Rights constrains the government wherever it acts. In REID V. COVERT (1957), a case involving a U.S. citizen overseas, Justice HUGO L. BLACK observed, "the United States is entirely a creature of the Constitution. Its power and authority have no other source. It can only act in accordance with all the limitations imposed by the Constitution." Under a "compact" theory, by contrast, the Constitution is viewed as a compact between the American people and their government that does not limit the government's treatment of foreign nationals.

In *United States v. Verdugo-Urquídez* (1990), the Court adopted a compact theory for the FOURTH AMENDMENT prohibition against unreasonable SEARCHES AND SEIZURES. The Court held that the Fourth Amendment did not apply to U.S. Drug Enforcement Administration agents searching the residences of a Mexican national in Mexico. *Verdugo-Urquídez* reasoned that because the text of the Fourth Amendment referred to the right of "the people" to be free from UNREASONABLE SEARCHES and seizures, it applied only to U.S. citizens and to others who had established substantial, voluntary connections with the United States. Such reasoning implies, however, that other provisions of the Bill of Rights, like the FIRST AMENDMENT guarantee of FREEDOM OF SPEECH, the DUE PROCESS clause, and even the TAKINGS clause, which are not limited to "the people," may apply extraterritorially to U.S. and foreign nationals alike.

The due process clause may have particular relevance for the extraterritorial application of federal statutes. One interesting question is whether the extraterritorial application of U.S. law requires "significant contacts" such that its application is "neither arbitrary nor fundamentally unfair," as *Allstate Insurance v. Hague* (1981) required in the domestic, conflict-of-laws context. Another is whether Congress may constitutionally impose liability for conduct that is compelled by foreign law. The Court noted in *Société Internationale v. Rogers* (1958) that dismissing the complaint of a party who could not comply with DISCOVERY orders because of Swiss bank secrecy laws would raise "serious constitutional questions" under the due process clause.

WILLIAM S. DODGE
(2000)

Bibliography

BORN, GARY B. 1992 A Reappraisal of the Extraterritorial Reach of U.S. Law. *Law and Policy in International Business* 24:1–100.

BRILMAYER, LEA and NORCHI, CHARLES 1992 Federal Extraterritoriality and Fifth Amendment Due Process. *Harvard Law Review* 105:1217–1263.

DODGE, WILLIAM S. 1998 Understanding the Presumption Against Extraterritoriality. *Berkeley Journal of International Law* 16:85–125.

KRAMER, LARRY 1991 Vestiges of Beale: Extraterritorial Application of American Law. *Supreme Court Review* 1991:179–224.

NEUMAN, GERALD L. 1991 Whose Constitution? *Yale Law Journal* 100:909–991.

EXTREMIST SPEECH

Extremist speech is generously protected under the FIRST AMENDMENT to the Constitution as interpreted by the Supreme Court in this century. What speech should be classified as "extremist" is, of course, a difficult matter, one that will vary from culture to culture. In some countries advocating FREEDOM OF SPEECH may itself be "extremist." But in the United States the label of extremist speech is reserved for speech that advocates violent overthrow of the government, the commission of serious crimes (such as assassination), racism, and anti-Semitism or discrimination against other minorities or groups. And, in this country, it has been decided that this speech will receive constitutional protection.

Probably the most widely known contemporary instance of the protection of extremist speech arose in the late 1970s when a small group of neo-Nazis from Chicago announced their intention of conducting a march in the Chicago suburb of Skokie, home to some 40,000 Jews and several thousand survivors of WORLD WAR II German concentration camps. The city resisted, enacting a number of ordinances prohibiting, among other things, speech known as group libel, that is, speech that would "portray criminality, depravity or lack of virtue in, or incite vio-

lence, hatred, abuse or hostility toward a person or a group of persons by reason of reference to religious, racial, ethnic, national or regional affiliation." The AMERICAN CIVIL LIBERTIES UNION, on behalf of the neo-Nazi group, challenged the city's interference with the proposed march as unconstitutional under the First Amendment. The Courts sustained the challenge. Both the Illinois Supreme Court and the U.S. Court of Appeals for the Seventh Circuit, in two separate cases, held that under modern Supreme Court precedents it was beyond doubt that even this most offensive speech was constitutionally protected, absent a showing that the speech was about to turn into illegal conduct.

In fact, cases involving extremist speech constitute the backbone of the First Amendment jurisprudence. This is true, in part, because the very first cases involving free speech issues to come before the Supreme Court (which did not occur until 1919) involved extremist speech. The Supreme Court, therefore, began the process of developing modern First Amendment jurisprudence in contexts where the issue at hand was to define the outer boundaries of the principle of free speech. Many cases followed over the next seventy years, of which the Skokie case was one.

As a result of these cases, much judicial and academic ink has been spent on deciding what should be the test for establishing the limits of the First Amendment. Various formulations have been devised. It has been said that First Amendment protection ends when there is a CLEAR AND PRESENT DANGER to the society (the test OLIVER WENDELL HOLMES initially proposed in 1919); when speech explicitly advocates illegal action (the test proposed by Judge LEARNED HAND in 1918); when speech will in the due course of events threaten the overthrow of government (which was approximately the test the Court followed during the nadir of First Amendment protection in the era of MCCARTHYISM); or when speech threatens imminent serious illegal behavior and is directly intended to incite such action (the prevailing test today).

Cases involving extremist speech have been so important to the development of First Amendment jurisprudence because they have raised independent, or separate, theoretical issues about the role and meaning of the modern idea of freedom of speech. Two major issues should be noted.

First, drawing the boundaries of freedom of speech involves more than just knowing what the basic purposes of the First Amendment are. Because we live in an imperfect world, rules of law, including constitutional law, must prepare for tears and snags of a practical world. Language is rarely precise enough to foreclose mistaken applications of the rules we devise. Institutions must be relied upon to apply the rules, and the quality of institutional decisions will be dependent on the quality of the people who com-

pose them. Thus, the extremist speech cases have posed a second issue: To what extent must *unworthy* speech be protected in order to insure that truly *worthy* speech— speech that advances the purposes of the First Amendment—will in fact be preserved? The difficulties of drawing that line, to achieve in a practical world the right level of free speech, are immense. One must consider to what extent legislative institutions will themselves be sensitive to freedom of speech, the degree to which citizens will be deterred from speaking by the perceived possibility of hostile government action, and the courage of judges to stand up to improper legislative attempts to interfere with valuable speech. Therefore, drawing the outer line at which constitutional protection stops generates its own important and fascinating issues, beyond the issue of deciding what purposes or values underlie the First Amendment. As a general proposition it may be said that modern First Amendment protection uses extremist speech to give "breathing space" to the right of freedom of speech.

But there is an even more important reason why extremist speech cases have commanded such attention over the past seventy years. It may well be the case that extremist speech protection furthers a *distinctive* First Amendment value, separate from its function of affording ample leeway to valuable speech. The classic rationales for free speech see the relationship between free speech and the discovery of truth and a democratic system of government. These have been forcefully articulated in cases involving extremist speech. But there is another potential First Amendment meaning, or value, at stake in these cases involving speech deeply threatening to basic values of American society. Extremist speech is often bad, as socially harmful as other bad acts that are regularly subject to social regulation. That means that free speech may be a special context in which the society chooses to let bad acts go unregulated as a symbolic act of self-recognition of the difficulties of dealing appropriately with bad acts— as, for example, by being too intolerant in the ordinary political process or by reacting with excessive harshness when bad acts are punished. This rationale of free speech focuses on the relationship between that principle and the general virtue of tolerance. It may well be, in other words, that the centrality of the extremist speech cases in the First Amendment jurisprudence arises out of the fact that they have added a new and significant, and distinctively American, role to the idea of freedom of speech.

LEE C. BOLLINGER
(1992)

Bibliography

BAKER, C. EDWIN 1989 *Human Liberty and Freedom of Speech.* New York: Oxford University Press.
BOLLINGER, LEE C. 1986 *The Tolerant Society: Freedom of*

Speech and Extremist Speech in America. New York: Oxford University Press.

EYEWITNESS IDENTIFICATION

Eyewitness identification can be powerful EVIDENCE in a criminal prosecution. Yet an identification can easily be wrong, whether made soon after the crime or in court. Because identifications can have a potentially devastating impact and are of questionable reliability, courts are especially concerned with them. Triers of fact typically assume that an eyewitness to a crime can accurately discern and remember the physical characteristics of the perpetrator. However, extensive research proves that powers of observation and recall are quite deficient.

The legal system cannot fully rectify problems with identification; it cannot affect a witness's perceptual and recall capabilities. However, the law can try to control any conscious or unconscious attempt by the police or prosecution to supply what perception and memory cannot.

Although the courts have never directly supervised the use of identification techniques, the Supreme Court has tried to minimize mistaken identification by requiring that procedures most likely to produce inaccurate results comport with certain constitutional requirements. Both the Sixth Amendment RIGHT TO COUNSEL and the DUE PROCESS clauses of the Fifth Amendment and FOURTEENTH AMENDMENT provide defendants with substantive bases for questioning identifications.

In UNITED STATES V. WADE (1967) the defendant participated in a postindictment LINEUP conducted without notice and in the absence of his counsel. The Supreme Court held that the Sixth Amendment required invalidation of the defendant's subsequent conviction because a postindictment lineup was a "critical stage," when substantial prejudice to defendant's rights could result and counsel could help to avoid the prejudice.

However, the Supreme Court held in KIRBY V. ILLINOIS (1972) that the right to counsel does not extend to pretrial identification procedures employed before adversarial judicial proceedings are initiated. In *Kirby* the defendant was arrested and later identified in a police station confrontation at which the defendant was not advised of his right to counsel and his attorney was not present. The Court clarified the "initiation of adversarial proceedings" in *Moore v. Illinois* (1977), where the defendant was identified by a victim during a preliminary hearing where his counsel was not present. In *Moore* the Court held that adversarial proceedings had begun at the preliminary hearing, rather than only after the indictment.

In UNITED STATES V. ASH (1973) a witness observed a photographic array prior to trial, and defendant's counsel was not present. The Court held that there is no right to counsel at such displays and that right to counsel is limited to "trial-like confrontations." In a photographic display, the defendant is not present and does not confront the prosecutor or the adversarial system.

The Supreme Court held in *Stovall v. Denno* (1967) that the guarantee of due process of law protects an accused from identification procedures that are "so unnecessarily suggestive and conducive to irreparable mistaken identification" as to deny a defendant due process of law. In *Stovall* the Court held that a one-to-one emergency confrontation between the accused and an injured witness in a hospital room did not violate due process because it was not unnecessarily suggestive and was not substantially likely to lead to misidentification.

The due process questions of suggestibility returned to the Court in the following years. In *Simmons v. United States* (1968) the felons who had robbed a bank were still at large. The police showed six snapshots to witnesses, who identified the defendants from the photos. Guidelines of the International Association of Chiefs of Police require a photographic array to include eight photographs. However, in this case, the Court found that the compelling need for identification of the robbers justified the suggestive procedure as long as there was little danger of misidentification and rejected the defendants' due process claim. Then in *Neil v. Biggers* (1972) the Court emphasized reliability over suggestibility in analyzing a due process claim. In *Neil* the Court accepted the reliability of a station-house show-up at which the defendant was identified in an accidental encounter at a water fountain seven months after the crime. The Court denied the defendant's due process claim.

In *Manson v. Brathwaite* (1977) the Court reaffirmed that the reliability of an identification is the "linchpin" of due process analysis. In *Manson* an undercover police officer purchased heroin from a seller while standing near him in a well-lit hallway for two or three minutes. A few minutes later the undercover officer described the seller to another officer, who gave the undercover officer a picture of the defendant. Two days later, the undercover officer identified the picture as a photograph of the person from whom he had bought heroin. The *Manson* Court held that a single photographic display of an accused did not create a substantial likelihood of irreparable misidentification, for it was done by a trained police officer. To prevail on a due process claim, then, a defendant must prove both unnecessary suggestiveness and substantial likelihood of misidentification.

The remedy for violation of either the Sixth Amendment right to counsel or the due process standards is exclusion of the pretrial evidence and of any in-court identification derived from the tainted pretrial identification. To limit the application of this severe remedy, the Supreme Court has developed the "independent source" test, by which an in-court identification is admissible if it derives from a source independent of the tainted identification. A source is independent if there has been prior opportunity to observe the criminal act, an easy identification, and no past misidentification. However, in *Moore* the Court held that criminal prosecution may begin as early as the initial appearance, at least for the purpose of determining the right to counsel.

At a suppression hearing, usually held prior to trial, the court determines admissibility of pretrial identification evidence. Generally, the prosecution bears the burden of establishing the presence of counsel or intelligent waiver by the accused or of showing that an in-court identification derives from a source independent of tainted pretrial identification. The burden of proving a violation of due process, however, is on the defendant. In some jurisdictions, if the defendant can show that an identification process was unnecessarily suggestive, then the burden shifts to the government to show the justification of exigent circumstances.

Admissibility and credibility are separate questions. Identification evidence found admissible, usually by the judge, is not necessarily credible. The jury decides whether it believes that the witness has made an accurate identification.

Properly conducted lineups are least likely to result in misidentification. A court has the authority to order an accused to participate in a lineup. A court may, in its discretion, order a lineup at the request of the defendant, but the defendant has no constitutional right to a lineup either before trial or in the courtroom during trial. A court may also allow the defendant to sit in the audience. Sound litigation tactics require counsel for the defendant to observe the lineup procedure for reliability but not participate or use the lineup for DISCOVERY.

CHARLES H. WHITEBREAD
(1992)

(SEE ALSO: *Procedural Due Process of Law, Criminal.*)

Bibliography

BUCKOUT, ROBERT 1980 Nearly 2,000 Witnesses Can Be Wrong. *Bulletin of the Psychonomic Society* 16:307–310.

WHITEBREAD, CHARLES H. 1986 *Criminal Procedure.* Mineola, N.Y.: Foundation Press.